New Acronyms, Initialisms & Abbreviations

ISSN 0270-4404

New Acronyms, Initialisms & Abbreviations

VOLUME 2 of
*Acronyms, Initialisms & Abbreviations
Dictionary*, Nineteenth Edition

*A Guide to Acronyms, Initialisms, Abbreviations, Contractions,
Alphabetic Symbols, and Similar Condensed Appellations*

Covering: Aerospace, Associations, Banking, Biochemistry, Business, Data Processing,
Domestic and International Affairs, Economics, Education, Electronics, Genetics,
Government, Information Technology, Investment, Labor, Law, Medicine,
Military Affairs, Periodicals, Pharmacy, Physiology, Politics, Religion, Science,
Societies, Sports, Technical Drawings and Specifications, Telecommunications,
Transportation, and Other Fields

Jennifer Mossman,
Editor

Pamela Dear
Erin E. Holmberg
Jacqueline L. Longe
Matt Merta
Gerda-Ann Raffaelle
Associate Editors

 **Gale Research Inc.**

An International Thomson Publishing Company

 I⊤P

NEW YORK • LONDON • BONN • BOSTON • DETROIT • MADRID
MELBOURNE • MEXICO CITY • PARIS • SINGAPORE • TOKYO
TORONTO • WASHINGTON • ALBANY NY • BELMONT CA • CINCINNATI OH

Senior Editor: Donna Wood
Editor: Jennifer Mossman

Associate Editors: Thomas Carson, Pamela Dear,
Erin E. Holmberg, Jacqueline L. Longe,
Matt Merta, Gerda-Ann Raffaelle

Contributing Editors: Leland G. Alkire, Jr., Mary Rose Bonk,
Mildred Hunt, Miriam M. Steinert

Manager, Data Entry Services: Benita L. Spight
Data Entry Supervisor: Gwendolyn Tucker
Data Entry Associates: Johnny Carson, LySandra Davis,
James Dundas

Production Manager: Mary Beth Trimper
Production Assistant: Deborah Milliken
Art Director: Cynthia Baldwin
Keyliners: C.J. Jonik, Yolanda Y. Latham

Manager, Technical Support Services: Theresa A. Rocklin
Programmer: Charles Beaumont

∞ This book is printed on acid-free paper that meets the minimum requirements of American National Standard for Information Sciences—Permanence Paper for Printed Library Materials, ANSI Z39.48-1984.

Library of Congress Catalog Card Number 84-643188
ISBN 0-8103-5570-1
ISSN 0270-4404

Printed in the United States of America

Published simultaneously in the United Kingdom
by Gale Research International Limited
(An affiliated company of Gale Research Inc.)

I(T)P™ Gale Research Inc., an International Thomson Publishing Company.
ITP logo is a trademark under license.

Contents

Gale's publications in the acronyms and abbreviations field include:

Acronyms, Initialisms & Abbreviations Dictionary series:

Acronyms, Initialisms & Abbreviations Dictionary (Volume 1). A guide to acronyms, initialisms, abbreviations, and similar contractions, arranged alphabetically by abbreviation.

New Acronyms, Initialisms & Abbreviations (Volume 2). An interedition supplement in which terms are arranged alphabetically both by abbreviation and by meaning.

Reverse Acronyms, Initialisms & Abbreviations Dictionary (Volume 3). A companion to Volume 1 in which terms are arranged alphabetically by meaning of the acronym, initialism, or abbreviation.

Acronyms, Initialisms & Abbreviations Dictionary Subject Guide series:

Computer & Telecommunications Acronyms (Volume 1). A guide to acronyms, initialisms, abbreviations, and similar contractions used in the field of computers and telecommunications in which terms are arranged alphabetically both by abbreviation and by meaning.

Business Acronyms (Volume 2). A guide to business-oriented acronyms, initialisms, abbreviations, and similar contractions in which terms are arranged alphabetically both by abbreviation and by meaning.

International Acronyms, Initialisms & Abbreviations Dictionary series:

International Acronyms, Initialisms & Abbreviations Dictionary (Volume 1). A guide to foreign and international acronyms, initialisms, abbreviations, and similar contractions, arranged alphabetically by abbreviation.

Reverse International Acronyms, Initialisms & Abbreviations Dictionary (Volume 2). A companion to Volume 1, in which terms are arranged alphabetically by meaning of the acronym, initialism, or abbreviation.

Periodical Title Abbreviations series:

Periodical Title Abbreviations: By Abbreviation (Volume 1). A guide to abbreviations commonly used for periodical titles, arranged alphabetically by abbreviation.

Periodical Title Abbreviations: By Title (Volume 2). A guide to abbreviations commonly used for periodical titles, arranged alphabetically by title.

New Periodical Title Abbreviations (Volume 3). An interedition supplement in which terms are arranged alphabetically both by abbreviation and by title.

A Word about
New Acronyms, Initialisms & Abbreviations

Contains over 15,000 newly coined or newly found terms

As acronyms continue to simplify and accelerate modern communication, the need for timely access remains essential. Publication of this supplement to the nineteenth edition of *Acronyms, Initialisms, and Abbreviations Dictionary (AIAD)* makes terms available while their currency is at a peak, keeping you informed and up to date in a constantly expanding field.

Timely Coverage

The more dynamic fields of endeavor tend to generate the largest number of acronyms. *New Acronyms, Initialisms, and Abbreviations (NAIA)* reflects this trend by providing increased coverage in:

- Architecture

- Aviation

- Computer Science

- Engineering

- Mass Media

- Military Affairs

Current events and new technology often produce abbreviated designations intended as time and space savers. Colorful examples in this supplement include:

- BANANA (Build Absolutely Nothing Anywhere Near Anything)

- DGSI (Don't Get Sucked In)

- DWIS (Do What I Say)

- GTFT (Generous Tit for Tat)

- PLOTKA (Press Lots of Keys to Abort)

- WYSBYGI (What You See before You Get It)

Timely and significant international terms continue to be added to the *AIAD* database. Examples include: EDA (European Democratic Alliance), EMCOF (European Monetary Cooperation Fund), and PECDAR (Palestine Economic Council for Development and Reconstruction). Broader coverage of international and foreign terms can be found in the *International Acronyms, Initialisms, and Abbreviations Dictionary (IAIAD)* series.

Major Sources Cited

NAIA, like *AIAD*, contains entries from a wide variety of sources. Although many terms are from published sources, the majority of entries are sent by outside contributors, are uncovered through independent research by the editorial staff, or surface as miscellaneous broadcast or print media references. Therefore, it is impossible to cite a source on every entry in *NAIA*. It was felt, however, that the citation of selected sources would assist the user in his or her research.

A code for the source of the entry (represented in small capital letters within parentheses) is given only for those print sources that provided at least 50 items. Complete bibliographical information about the publications cited can be found in the List of Selected Sources following the User's Guide. The editors will provide further information upon request.

Acknowledgments

Several persons have contributed significantly to the compilation of this supplement. Mildred Hunt and Miriam M. Steinert, editorial consultants, continue to furnish many timely entries along with checking and expanding our collection of science terms. Valuable additions were also provided by John Fobian; Jack Gordon; Hoyt Hammer, Jr; David Jones; and Thomas R. Wood.

Available in Electronic Format

AIAD and *NAIA* are available for licensing on magnetic tape or diskette in a fielded format. Either the complete database or a custom selection of entries may be ordered. The database is available for internal data processing and nonpublishing purposes only. For more information, call 800-877-GALE.

Comments and Suggestions Are Welcome

Users can make unique and important contributions to future supplements and new editions by notifying the editor of subject fields that are not adequately covered, by suggesting sources for covering such fields, and even by sending individual terms they feel should be included.

User's Guide

New Acronyms, Initialisms, and Abbreviations comprises two sections, providing access to entries either by acronym or by meaning.

By Acronym Section

Acronyms are arranged alphabetically in letter-by-letter sequence, regardless of spacing, punctuation, or capitalization. If the same abbreviation has more than one meaning, the various meanings are then subarranged alphabetically in word-by-word sequence. Entries may contain some of the elements noted in the example below:

Abbreviation or Acronym →
Location →
English translation →
Sponsoring organization →

AP.........Absolute Pardon
A/P........Account-Purchase
A & P....Agricultural and Pastoral
ap..........Antiperiplanar [*Chemistry*]
AP.........Appendectomy
APA......Automobile Protection Association [*Canada*]
APB.......All Points Bulletin
APC......Anno post Christum Natum [*Latin*]
APC.......Archives Publiques du Canada [*Public Archives of Canada*]
APC......Area Planning Council [*Department of Education*]
APCA....Aft Power Controller Assembly (MCD)

← Meaning or Phrase
← Subject area
← Language
← Source code (Decoded in the List of Selected Sources)

By Meaning Section

Terms are arranged in word-by-word sequence according to the explanation of the acronym. Minor parts of speech (articles, conjunctions, prepositions) are generally not considered in the alphabetizing. If a particular explanation of the acronym has more than one initialism representing it, the various choices are then subarranged alphabetically, letter-by-letter, as they are in the *By Acronym* section.

Meaning or phrase →

Second Audio Program...............................SAP
Second Audio Program...............................SAPRO
Second Audio Program...............................SECAP
Second Base [*Baseball*]..............................2B
Secondary School Admission Test Board
      [*Princeton, NJ*]......................................SSATB
Secretariat for Catholic-Jewish Relations.................CJR
Secretariat Europeen des Fabricants d'Emballages
      Metalliques Legers [*European Secretariat of*
      Manufacturers of Light Metal Packages]...............SEFEL
Secretariat for Hispanic Affairs [*National*
      Conference of Catholic Bishops]........................SHA
Secundum [*Latin*]...SEC
Secure Acoustic Data Relay (NVT)............................SADR

← Abbreviation or Acronym

List of Selected Sources

Each of the print sources included in the following list contributed at least 50 terms. It would be impossible to cite a source for every entry because the majority of terms are sent by outside contributors, are uncovered through independent research by the editorial staff, or surface as miscellaneous broadcast or print media references.

Unless further described in an annotation, the publications listed here contain no additional information about the acronym, initialism, or abbreviation. The editor will provide further information about these sources upon request.

(ABBR) *Abbreviations: The Comprehensive Dictionary of Abbreviations and Letter Symbols for the Computer Era.* Vol. 1. C. Edward Wall. Ann Arbor, MI: The Pierian Press, 1984.

(ADDR) *Army Dictionary and Desk Reference.* Tim Zurick. Harrisburg, PA: Stackpole Books, 1992.

(AEE) *American Educators' Encyclopedia.* 2nd ed. Edward L. Dejnozka and David E. Kapel. Westport, CT: Greenwood Press, 1991.

(ANA) *"Abbreviations" - U.S. Navy Dictionary.* 3rd revision. Washington, DC: DCP, 1989.

(BI) *British Initials and Abbreviations.* 3rd ed. Ian H. Wilkes. London: Leonard Hill Books, 1971.

(DA) *Dictionary of Aviation.* R. J. Hall and R. D. Campbell. Detroit: St. James Press, 1991.

(DAC) *Dictionary of Architecture and Construction.* 2nd ed. Edited by Cyril M. Harris. New York: McGraw-Hill, Inc., 1993.

(EA) *Encyclopedia of Associations.* 28th ed. Vol. 3, Supplement. Carol A. Schwartz. Detroit: Gale Research Inc., 1993.
> A guide to trade, professional, and other nonprofit associations that are national and international in scope and membership and that are headquartered in the United States. Entries include name and address; telephone and telex number; chief official; and a description of the purposes, activities, and structure of the organization.

(ECON) *The Economist.* London: The Economist Newspaper Ltd., 1994.

(ERG) *Environmental Regulatory Glossary.* 5th ed. Edited by G. William Frick and Thomas F. P. Sullivan. Rockville, MD: Government Institutes, Inc., 1990.

(FAAC) *Contractions Handbook.* Changes. U.S. Department of Transportation. Federal Aviation Administration, 1993. [Use of source began in 1969]

(IAA) *Index of Acronyms and Abbreviations in Electrical and Electronic Engineering.* Compiled by Buro Scientia. New York: VCH Publishers, 1989.

(INF) *Infantry.* Fort Benning, GA: U.S. Army Infantry Training School, 1994.

(MAH)   *Medical Abbreviations Handbook.* 2nd ed. Oradell, NJ: Medical Economics Co., Inc., 1983.

(NFPA)   *Standard for Fire Safety Symbols/NFPA170.*   Quincy, MA: National Fire Protection
           Association, 1994.

(NHD)   *The New Hacker's Dictionary.* Edited by Eric S. Raymond. Cambridge, MA: MIT Press,
           1991.

(NTCM)   *NTC's Mass Media Dictionary.* R. Terry Ellmore. Lincolnwood, IL: National Textbook Co.,
           1991.

(PCM)   *PC Magazine.* New York: Ziff-Davis Publishing Co., 1994.

(PDAA)   *Pugh's Dictionary of Acronyms and Abbreviations: Abbreviations in Management, Technology
           and Information Science.* 5th ed. Eric Pugh. Chicago: American Library Association, 1987.

(PS)   *Popular Science.* New York: Times-Mirror Magazines, Inc., 1994.

(RDA)   *Army RD and A Magazine.* Alexandria, VA: Development, Engineering, and Acquisition
           Directorate, Army Materiel Command, 1994.

New Acronyms, Initialisms & Abbreviations

By Acronym

A

A................. Accent (NTCM)
A................. Advance [*Wire service code*] (NTCM)
A................. Agricultural Program (NTCM)
A................. Airplane (ABBR)
A................. Alcove (ABBR)
A................. Angled (NTCM)
A................. Annealing (ABBR)
A................. Annunciator (NFPA)
A................. Anthracite (ABBR)
A................. Approach Lighting [*Aviation*] (DA)
A................. Arc (ABBR)
A................. Assignment [*FCC*] (NTCM)
A................. Atlantic [*Ocean*] (ABBR)
A................. Atmosphere (ABBR)
A................. Auditory (ABBR)
A................. Aviation [*FCC*] (NTCM)
A................. Axis (ABBR)
A................. Azure (ABBR)
A2................ Botswana [*Aircraft nationality and registration mark*] (FAAC)
A3................ Tonga [*Aircraft nationality and registration mark*] (FAAC)
A5................ Bhutan [*Aircraft nationality and registration mark*] (FAAC)
A6................ United Arab Emirates [*Aircraft nationality and registration mark*] (FAAC)
A40.............. Oman [*Aircraft nationality and registration mark*] (FAAC)
AA.............. Adhesive Active [*Tire manufacturing*]
AA.............. Advertising Agency (NTCM)
AA.............. All After [*Aviation*] (DA)
AA.............. Australian Airlines
AAA........... Androgenic Anabolic Agent [*Biochemistry*] (MAH)
AAA........... Ansett Airlines of Australia [*ICAO designator*] (FAAC)
AAA........... Architectural Aluminum Association (DAC)
AAAS......... Applicable Approved Accounting Standard
AAB........... Abelag Aviation [*Belgium*] [*ICAO designator*] (FAAC)
AABI........... Amateur All-Star Baseball [*An association*] (EA)
AAC........... Agricultural Advisory Council for England and Wales (BI)
AAC........... Angola Air Charter Ltd. [*ICAO designator*] (FAAC)
AAC........... Antique Automobile Coalition [*Legislative lobbying group*]
AAC........... Army Air Corps [*British*] [*ICAO designator*] (FAAC)
AAC........... Aviation Administrative Communication (DA)
AACA........ Aircraft Airworthiness Certification Authority (DA)
AAD........... Aero Aviation Centre Ltd. [*Canada*] [*ICAO designator*] (FAAC)
AAD........... Assigned Altitude Deviation [*Aviation*] (DA)
AADA........ American Academy of Dramatic Arts (NTCM)
AAE........... Arizona Air [*Aviation Services West, Inc.*] [*ICAO designator*] (FAAC)
AAE........... Automatic Assemble Editing (NTCM)
AAF........... Aigle Azur [*France*] [*ICAO designator*] (FAAC)
AAF........... Aircraft and Adventure Factory [*Mallard*]
AAF........... Anti-Icing Fluid [*Aviation*] (DA)
AAFA......... Anglo-American Families Association [*British*] (BI)
AAFR......... Australian Armed Forces Radio
AAG........... Aeronautical Information Service Automation Group [*ICAO*] (DA)
AAG........... Air Atlantique [*British*] [*ICAO designator*] (FAAC)
AAG........... Airports Authority Group [*Transport Canada*] (DA)
AAH........... Aloha Airlines [*ICAO designator*] (FAAC)
AAI............ Air Aurora, Inc. [*ICAO designator*] (FAAC)
AAI............ Australian Air International
AAIP......... American Association of Independent Publishers (NTCM)
AAIP......... Association for Armenian Information Professionals (EA)
AAIS......... Aircraft Accident Investigation System
AAITVL..... Arrival Aircraft Interval [*Aviation*] (FAAC)
AAJ........... Air Alma, Inc. [*Canada*] [*ICAO designator*] (FAAC)
AAK........... Alaska Island Air, Inc. [*ICAO designator*] (FAAC)
AAL........... American Airlines, Inc. [*ICAO designator*] (FAAC)
AALIPS...... Arthur Adaptation of the Leiter International Performance Scale [*Education*]
AAM........... Airline Administrative Message (DA)
AAM........... Association of Assistant Mistresses in Secondary Schools [*British*] (BI)
AAM........... Aviation Management Corp. [*ICAO designator*] (FAAC)
AAN........... Oasis International Airlines [*Spain*] [*ICAO designator*] (FAAC)
AAO........... Atlantis Airlines [*ICAO designator*] (FAAC)

AAOE......... Arrival and Assembly Operations Element [*Navy*] (ANA)
AAOG........ Arrival and Assembly Operations Group [*Navy*] (ANA)
AAP............ Advance Australia Party [*Political party*]
AAP............ Aging Aircraft Program [*FAA*] (DA)
AAP............ Astro Air International, Inc. [*Philippines*] [*ICAO designator*] (FAAC)
AAPM........ American Academy of Pain Medicine (EA)
AAPR......... Average Annual Performance Rate
AAPT......... American Association of Psychiatric Technicians
AAQ........... Air Alliance, Inc. [*Canada*] [*ICAO designator*] (FAAC)
AAQS........ Ambient Air Quality Standard (ERG)
AAR........... Asiana Airlines [*South Korea*] [*ICAO designator*] (FAAC)
AAR........... Atlas of Australian Resources [*A publication*]
AARA........ Air-to-Air Refuelling Area (DA)
AARTE...... Airport Acceptance Rate [*Aviation*] (FAAC)
AAS........... Agnostics' Adoption Society [*British*] (BI)
AAS........... Austrian Air Services [*ICAO designator*] (FAAC)
AASP......... Arrival and Assembly Support Party [*Navy*] (ANA)
AAT........... Austrian Airtransport [*ICAO designator*] (FAAC)
AATF......... Air Assault Task Force [*Army*] (ADDR)
AAU........... Australia Asia Airlines Ltd. [*ICAO designator*] (FAAC)
AAV........... Aly Aviation [*British*] [*ICAO designator*] (FAAC)
AAvnC...... Army Aviation Centre [*British*] (BI)
AAW........... Aberdeen Airways [*British*] [*ICAO designator*] (FAAC)
AAWTA ..... Advise at What Time Able [*Aviation*] (FAAC)
AAY........... Air Antares Ltd. [*Romania*] [*ICAO designator*] (FAAC)
AAZ........... Angus Aviation Ltd. [*Canada*] [*ICAO designator*] (FAAC)
AB.............. Abscess (ABBR)
AB.............. Airborne [*ICAO designator*] (FAAC)
AB.............. Announce Booth [*Soundproof room*] [*Television studio*] (NTCM)
AB.............. Architecture Bulletin [*A publication*]
AB.............. Automatic Weather Broadcast (DA)
AB.............. Bachelor of Arts (AEE)
ABA........... Abbas Air Ltd. [*British*] [*ICAO designator*] (FAAC)
ABAC .... Association of British Aero Clubs (BI)
ABAC .... Association of British Aviation Consultants (DA)
ABANDMT ... Abandonment (ABBR)
ABAS.......... Amateur Basketball Association of Scotland (BI)
ABASG..... Abasing (ABBR)
ABASNT .... Abasement (ABBR)
ABAST ...... Abasement (ABBR)
ABATB...... Abatable (ABBR)
ABATG...... Abating (ABBR)
ABATMT... Abatement (ABBR)
ABATNT.... Abatement (ABBR)
ABB .... Air Belgium [*ICAO designator*] (FAAC)
ABB .... Asea Brown Boveri [*Swedish-Swiss manufacturing company*] (ECON)
ABBA.......... Amateur Basketball Association [*British*] (BI)
ABBF .... Association of Bronze and Brass Founders [*British*] (BI)
ABBRD...... Abbreviated (ABBR)
ABBREVIO ... Abbreviomania (ABBR)
ABBRG...... Abbreviating (ABBR)
ABBRN...... Abbreviation (ABBR)
ABBRR...... Abbreviator (ABBR)
ABC .... ABC World Airways Guide [*ICAO designator*] (FAAC)
ABC .... Adoptee-Birthparent Center [*An association*] (EA)
ABC .... Aggregate Base Course (DAC)
ABC .... Air Business Contact [*France*] [*ICAO designator*] (FAAC)
ABC .... Already Been Chewed [*Gum*]
ABC .... American Board of Criminalistics (EA)
ABC .... Asian Broadcasting Conference (NTCM)
ABC .... Association of Building Centres [*British*] (BI)
A-BCAS..... Active Beacon Collision Avoidance System [*Aviation*] (DA)
ABCO........ Association of British Conference Organisers (BI)
ABCS.......... Abscess (ABBR)
ABCSD....... Abscessed (ABBR)
ABCSG....... Abscessing (ABBR)
ABD .... Atlanta [*Iceland*] [*ICAO designator*] (FAAC)
ABDC .... Adduct (ABBR)
ABDCD ...... Abducted (ABBR)
ABDCG ...... Abducting (ABBR)

ABDCN ...... Abduction (ABBR)
ABDCR....... Abductor (ABBR)
ABDI .... Abdicate (ABBR)
ABDID .... Abdicated (ABBR)
ABDIN .... Abdication (ABBR)
ABDM .... Abdomen (ABBR)
ABDML...... Abdominal (ABBR)
ABDMLY.. Abdominally (ABBR)
ABDMT ..... Abandonment (ABBR)
ABDMY ..... Abdominally (ABBR)
ABDND...... Abandoned (ABBR)
ABDNNT .. Abandonment (ABBR)
ABDNR ...... Abandoner (ABBR)
ABE .... Abbotsford Air Services [Canada] [ICAO designator] (FAAC)
ABE .... Aerodrome Beacon (DA)
ABER........ Abberrant (ABBR)
ABERN...... Aberration (ABBR)
ABERNL..... Aberrational (ABBR)
ABETD....... Abetted (ABBR)
ABETG...... Abetting (ABBR)
ABETMT ... Abetment (ABBR)
ABETNT.... Abetment (ABBR)
ABETR...... Abettor (ABBR)
ABF........... Anchor Block Foundation (EA)
ABF........... Belgian Flight Centre [ICAO designator] (FAAC)
ABFL......... Association of British Foam Laminators (BI)
ABH........... Societe Air Bretagne Service [France] [ICAO designator] (FAAC)
ABHRD....... Abhorred (ABBR)
ABHRG...... Abhorring (ABBR)
ABHRNC ... Abhorrence (ABBR)
ABHRNT... Abhorrent (ABBR)
ABHRNTY ... Abhorrently (ABBR)
ABHRR ..... Abhorrer (ABBR)
ABHRT ..... Abhorrent (ABBR)
ABHRTY.... Abhorrently (ABBR)
ABI .... Advance Boundary Information (DA)
ABI .... Antigua and Barbuda Airways International Ltd. [ICAO designator] (FAAC)
ABI .... Auditory Brainstem Implant [Hearing technology]
ABIDG .... Abiding (ABBR)
ABIDGY.... Abidingly (ABBR)
ABIDNC.... Abidance (ABBR)
ABIL.......... Ability (ABBR)
ABJR......... Abjure (ABBR)
ABJRD....... Abjured (ABBR)
ABJRG...... Abjuring (ABBR)
ABJRN...... Abjuration (ABBR)
ABJRR ...... Abjurer (ABBR)
ABJT .... Abject (ABBR)
ABJTN...... Abjection (ABBR)
ABJTNS.... Abjectness (ABBR)
ABJTY ...... Abjectly (ABBR)
ABK .... Albatros Airline, Inc. [Turkey] [ICAO designator] (FAAC)
ABKA .... Antique Bowie Knife Association (EA)
ABL .... A-Beta-Lipoproteinemia [Medicine] (MAH)
ABL .... Able (ABBR)
ABL .... Air BC Ltd. [Canada] [ICAO designator] (FAAC)
ABLH .... Abolish (ABBR)
ABLHB....... Abolishable (ABBR)
ABLHNT ... Abolishment (ABBR)
ABLHR ..... Abolisher (ABBR)
ABLM........ Abloom (ABBR)
ABLR........ Abler (ABBR)
ABLT......... Ability (ABBR)
ABLT......... Ablest (ABBR)
ABLTV...... Ablative (ABBR)
ABLUN ...... Ablution (ABBR)
ABLUNRY ... Ablutionary (ABBR)
ABLUNY.... Ablutionary (ABBR)
ABLZ......... Ablaze (ABBR)
ABM .... Amber Airways Ltd. [British] [ICAO designator] (FAAC)
ABMAC ..... Association of British Manufacturers of Agricultural Chemicals (BI)
ABMNA ..... Abominate (ABBR)
ABMNAD ... Abonminated (ABBR)
ABMNAG ... Abominating (ABBR)
ABMNAN .. Abomination (ABBR)
ABMNB .... Abominable (ABBR)
ABMNBY... Abominably (ABBR)
ABND........ Abound (ABBR)
ABNDMNT ... Abandonment (ABBR)
ABNDNC... Abundance (ABBR)
ABNDNT... Abundant (ABBR)
ABNDNTY ... Abundantly (ABBR)
ABNG........ Abnegate (ABBR)
ABNGA ...... Abnegate (ABBR)
ABNGAD... Abnegated (ABBR)
ABNGAG... Abnegating (ABBR)
ABNGD...... Abnegated (ABBR)
ABNGG...... Abnegating (ABBR)
ABNGN...... Abnegation (ABBR)
ABNGR ..... Abnegator (ABBR)
ABNGS....... Abnegates (ABBR)

ABNMT ..... Abnormality (ABBR)
ABNMY ..... Abnormally (ABBR)
ABO........... Aboriginal (ABBR)
ABO........... Aborigine (ABBR)
ABO........... Aeroexpreso Bogota [Colombia] [ICAO designator] (FAAC)
ABOCF...... Association of British Organic and Compound Fertilisers Ltd. (BI)
ABOD........ Abode (ABBR)
ABOLD ...... Abolished (ABBR)
ABOLG ..... Abolishing (ABBR)
ABOLN ..... Abolition (ABBR)
ABOLNM .. Abolitionism (ABBR)
ABOLNST ... Abolitionist (ABBR)
ABOLNT.... Abolitionist (ABBR)
ABOLT...... Abolishment (ABBR)
ABOM....... Abominate (ABBR)
ABOMD.... Abominated (ABBR)
ABOMG.... Abominating (ABBR)
ABOML .... Abominable (ABBR)
ABOMN.... Abomination (ABBR)
ABORL...... Aboriginal (ABBR)
ABORLY... Aboriginally (ABBR)
ABP .... Associated Business Papers (NTCM)
ABPC......... Association of British Packing Contractors (BI)
AB-PT........ American Broadcasting-Paramount Theatres, Inc. (NTCM)
ABPT......... Association of Blind Piano Tuners [British] (BI)
ABPVM..... Association of British Plywood and Veneer Manufacturers (BI)
ABR .... Abraham (ABBR)
ABR .... Abrasive (ABBR)
ABR .... Hunting Cargo Airlines Ltd. [British] [ICAO designator] (FAAC)
ABRA .... Abraham (ABBR)
ABRAD ..... Abrade (ABBR)
ABRADD ... Abraded (ABBR)
ABRADG ... Abrading (ABBR)
ABRAM .... Abraham (ABBR)
ABRAN ..... Aberration (ABBR)
ABRAN ..... Abrasion (ABBR)
ABRANL.... Aberrational (ABBR)
ABRAS ..... Abrasion (ABBR)
ABRAV...... Abrasive (ABBR)
ABRD .... Aboard (ABBR)
ABRD .... Abrade (ABBR)
ABRD .... Abroad (ABBR)
ABRDD ..... Abraded (ABBR)
ABRDG ..... Abrading (ABBR)
ABRFM..... Association of British Roofing Felt Manufacturers Ltd. (BI)
ABRG .... Abridge (ABBR)
ABRGA ..... Abrogate (ABBR)
ABRGAD ... Abrogated (ABBR)
ABRGAN .. Abrogation (ABBR)
ABRGB...... Abridgeable (ABBR)
ABRGD...... Abridged (ABBR)
ABRGG...... Abridging (ABBR)
ABRGN...... Aborigine (ABBR)
ABRGNL.... Aboriginal (ABBR)
ABRGNT... Abridgment (ABBR)
ABRGR...... Abridger (ABBR)
ABRGT...... Abridgment (ABBR)
ABRID ...... Abridged (ABBR)
ABRN .... Aberrance (ABBR)
ABRNC ...... Aberrancy (ABBR)
ABRNT...... Aberrant (ABBR)
ABRNTY... Aberrantly (ABBR)
ABROD...... Abroad (ABBR)
ABROG ...... Abrogate (ABBR)
ABROGAG ... Abrogating (ABBR)
ABROGD .. Abrogated (ABBR)
ABROGG ... Abrogating (ABBR)
ABROGN .. Abrogation (ABBR)
ABRP........ Abrupt (ABBR)
ABRPNS ... Abruptness (ABBR)
ABRRM..... Association of British Reclaimed Rubber Manufacturers (BI)
ABRS......... Association of British Riding Schools (BI)
ABRSM...... Associated Board of the Royal Schools of Music [British] (BI)
ABRSN...... Abrasion (ABBR)
ABRST....... Abreast (ABBR)
ABRTD....... Aborted (ABBR)
ABRTG....... Aborting (ABBR)
ABRTN...... Abortion (ABBR)
ABRTNST .. Abortionist (ABBR)
ABRTNT.... Abortionist (ABBR)
ABRTV...... Abortive (ABBR)
ABRTVNS .. Abortiveness (ABBR)
ABRTVY... Abortively (ABBR)
ABS........... Abscesses (ABBR)
ABS........... Absonant (ABBR)
ABS........... Abstrene (ABBR)
ABS........... Abuse (ABBR)
ABS........... Architects' Benevolent Society [British] (BI)
ABS........... Athabaska Airways Ltd. [Canada] [ICAO designator] (FAAC)
ABSAT...... American Broadcasting Co. Television Satellite (NTCM)
ABSB......... Absorb (ABBR)
ABSBB .... Absorbable (ABBR)

ABSBBT..... Absorbability (ABBR)
ABSBCY..... Absorbency (ABBR)
ABSBD....... Absorbed (ABBR)
ABSBG....... Absorbing (ABBR)
ABSBN....... Absorption (ABBR)
ABSBNC.... Absorbance (ABBR)
ABSBNC.... Absorbency (ABBR)
ABSBR....... Absorber (ABBR)
ABSBT....... Absorbent (ABBR)
ABSC......... Abscond (ABBR)
ABSC......... Absence (ABBR)
ABSC......... Association of Boiler Setters, Chimney and Furnace Constructors [*British*] (BI)
ABSCD....... Abscond (ABBR)
ABSD......... Absented (ABBR)
ABSD......... Abused (ABBR)
ABSDT....... Absurdity (ABBR)
ABSG......... Absenting (ABBR)
ABSG......... Abusing (ABBR)
ABSLT....... Absolute (ABBR)
ABSLTM.... Absolutism (ABBR)
ABSLTN.... Absolution (ABBR)
ABSLTST ... Absolutist (ABBR)
ABSLTY..... Absolutely (ABBR)
ABSLV....... Absolve (ABBR)
ABSLVB..... Absolvable (ABBR)
ABSLVD .... Absolved (ABBR)
ABSLVG .... Absolving (ABBR)
ABSLVR..... Absolver (ABBR)
ABSML...... Abysmal (ABBR)
ABSNC....... Absence (ABBR)
ABSNT....... Absent (ABBR)
ABSNTE .... Absentee (ABBR)
ABSNTEM ... Absenteeism (ABBR)
ABSOLN.... Absolution (ABBR)
ABSOLNS ... Absoluteness (ABBR)
ABSOLY .... Absolutely (ABBR)
ABSPN....... Absorption (ABBR)
ABSPT....... Absorptivity (ABBR)
ABSPV .... Absorptive (ABBR)
ABSR......... Abuser (ABBR)
ABSRD....... Absurd (ABBR)
ABSRDNS ... Absurdness (ABBR)
ABSRDT .... Absurdity (ABBR)
ABSRDY .... Absurdly (ABBR)
ABS/SAN... Acrylonitrile-Butadiene-Styrene and Styrene-Acrylonitrile [*Organic chemistry*] (ERG)
ABST......... Absentee (ABBR)
ABSTA....... Abstain (ABBR)
ABSTAD .... Abstained (ABBR)
ABSTAG .... Abstaining (ABBR)
ABSTM...... Absenteeism (ABBR)
ABSTMS.... Abstemious (ABBR)
ABSTMSNS ... Abstemiousness (ABBR)
ABSTMSY ... Abstemiously (ABBR)
ABSTN....... Abstention (ABBR)
ABSTNC .... Abstinence (ABBR)
ABSTNT .... Abstinent (ABBR)
ABSTRD .... Abstracted (ABBR)
ABSTRN .... Abstraction (ABBR)
ABSTRNS ... Abstractness (ABBR)
ABSTRR..... Abstracter (ABBR)
ABSTRS..... Abstruse (ABBR)
ABSTRU .... Abstruse (ABBR)
ABSTRUNS ... Abstruseness (ABBR)
ABSTRUY ... Abstrusely (ABBR)
ABSTRY..... Abstractly (ABBR)
ABSV......... Abusive (ABBR)
ABSVNS .... Abusiveness (ABBR)
ABSVY....... Abusively (ABBR)
ABSY......... Absently (ABBR)
ABT........... Abundant (ABBR)
ABT........... Air Brousse, Inc. [*Canada*] [*ICAO designator*] (FAAC)
ABTD .... Abutted (ABBR)
ABT-FC..... About-Face (ABBR)
ABTG .... Abutting (ABBR)
ABTNT....... Abutment (ABBR)
ABU........... Aerovias Bueno Ltd. [*Colombia*] [*ICAO designator*] (FAAC)
ABUL .... Abulia (ABBR)
ABUL .... Abuliomania (ABBR)
ABUNDNC ... Abundance (ABBR)
ABUNDT ... Abundant (ABBR)
ABUNDTY ... Abundantly (ABBR)
ABUS......... Abuse (ABBR)
ABUSD...... Abused (ABBR)
ABUSG...... Abusing (ABBR)
ABUSR....... Abuser (ABBR)
ABUSV....... Abusive (ABBR)
ABUSVNS ... Abusiveness (ABBR)
ABUSVY .... Abusively (ABBR)
ABUT .... Abutment (ABBR)
ABUTD ...... Abutted (ABBR)
ABUTG ...... Abutting (ABBR)

ABUTMT... Abutment (ABBR)
ABV .... Air Bypass Valve [*Automotive engineering*]
ABV-BRD... Above-Board (ABBR)
ABW .... Albanian Airways [*ICAO designator*] (FAAC)
ABX .... Airborne Express, Inc. [*ICAO designator*] (FAAC)
ABYA .... Association of British Yacht Agents (BI)
ABYNC....... Abeyance (ABBR)
ABYNT....... Abeyant (ABBR)
ABYS......... Abyss (ABBR)
ABYSM....... Abysmal (ABBR)
ABZ .... Association of British Zoologists (BI)
AC.............. Air Conditioning Equipment Room [*NFPA pre-fire planning symbol*] (NFPA)
AC.............. Aircarrier (DA)
AC.............. Airworthiness Circular (DA)
A9C............ Bahrain [*Aircraft nationality and registration mark*] (FAAC)
A2C2.......... Army Airspace Command and Control (ADDR)
ACA .... Advertisement Contractors' Association [*British*] (BI)
ACA .... Advertising Council of America, Inc. (NTCM)
ACA .... Air Canada [*ICAO designator*] (FAAC)
ACA .... Amusement Caterers' Association [*British*] (BI)
ACA .... Arctic Control Area [*Aviation*] (FAAC)
ACAD........ Academic (ABBR)
ACAD........ Acadia (ABBR)
ACADC....... Academic (ABBR)
ACADCLY ... Academically (ABBR)
ACADCN ... Academician (ABBR)
ACADL....... Academical (ABBR)
ACAP........ Acapulco [*Mexico*] (ABBR)
ACAP........ Aeronautical Chart Automation Project [*Military*] (DA)
ACATS ...... Advisory Committee on Advanced Television Service [*FCC high-definition television*] (NTCM)
ACB .... ABC [*Air Business Contact*] [*France*] [*ICAO designator*] (FAAC)
ACB .... Australian Casemix Bulletin [*A publication*]
ACBM .... Asbestos-Containing Building Material (ERG)
ACC .... Access Control Committee
ACC .... Aerocharter Midlands Ltd. [*British*] [*ICAO designator*] (FAAC)
ACC .... Agricultural Credit Corp. Ltd. [*British*] (BI)
ACC .... Annual Course Contribution
ACC .... Area Control Center (DA)
ACC .... Auto Camping Club Ltd. [*British*] (BI)
ACC .... Automotive Climate Control
ACCA .... Agricultural Central Cooperative Association Ltd. [*British*] (BI)
ACCPT ...... Accept (ABBR)
ACCR .... Accrete (ABBR)
ACC-R....... Area Control-RADAR (DA)
ACCRD ...... Accreted (ABBR)
ACCRG...... Accreting (ABBR)
ACCRN ...... Accretion (ABBR)
ACCRV....... Accretive (ABBR)
ACCT........ Accountant (ABBR)
ACCTB ...... Accountable (ABBR)
ACCTBNS ... Accountableness (ABBR)
ACCTBT .... Accountability (ABBR)
ACCTBY .... Accountably (ABBR)
ACCTD ...... Accounted (ABBR)
ACCTNT.... Accountant (ABBR)
ACCTY ...... Accountancy (ABBR)
ACD.......... Accede (ABBR)
ACD.......... Accord (ABBR)
ACD........... Airline Aviation Academy, Inc. [*ICAO designator*] (FAAC)
ACD........... Automatic Closing Device (DAC)
ACDD........ Acceded (ABBR)
ACDG........ Acceding (ABBR)
ACDM....... Academe (ABBR)
ACDMK....... Academic (ABBR)
ACDMKL.... Academical (ABBR)
ACDMKY ... Academically (ABBR)
ACDMN..... Academician (ABBR)
ACDMY .... Academy (ABBR)
ACDNC...... Accedence (ABBR)
ACDNTL.... Accidental (ABBR)
ACDNTLY ... Accidentally (ABBR)
ACDR........ Acceder (ABBR)
ACDTL....... Accidental (ABBR)
ACE.......... Acetic (ABBR)
ACE .... Advanced Combustion Engineering
ACE .... Amplification Controlling Element [*Genetics*]
ACE .... Anode Current Efficiency [*Environmental science*]
ACE .... Architects Council of Europe (DAC)
ACE .... Attendant Care Evaluation
ACE .... Race Cargo Airlines [*Ghana*] [*ICAO designator*] (FAAC)
ACED........ Accede (ABBR)
ACED-I ...... Association of Conference and Events Directors-International (EA)
ACEL........ Accelerate (ABBR)
ACELD....... Accelerated (ABBR)
ACELG....... Accelerating (ABBR)
ACELN....... Acceleration (ABBR)
ACELR....... Accelerator (ABBR)
ACELS ...... Accelerates (ABBR)
ACELV .... Accelerative (ABBR)
ACEO........ Association of Chief Education Officers [*British*] (BI)

ACET......... Advisory Council for the Elimination of Tuberculosis
ACET......... Association for Educational Communications and Technology (NTCM)
ACETL...... Acetylene (ABBR)
ACF............ African Cultural Foundation (EA)
ACF........... Air Charter [*France*] [*ICAO designator*] (FAAC)
ACFF......... Air Cargo Fast Flow (DA)
AC FT........ Acre Foot (ABBR)
ACFTC...... Aircraft Carrier (ABBR)
ACG........... Air London [*British*] [*ICAO designator*] (FAAC)
ACH........... Barcklay Flying Service [*ICAO designator*] (FAAC)
ACHD........ Ached (ABBR)
ACHG........ Aching (ABBR)
ACHIEV..... Achievement (ABBR)
ACHR........ Achromatic (ABBR)
ACHRM..... Achromatism (ABBR)
ACHRMTK ... Achromatic (ABBR)
ACHROM ... Achromatism (ABBR)
ACHRT...... Achromaticity (ABBR)
ACHRY...... Achromatically (ABBR)
ACHS......... Aches (ABBR)
ACHV......... Achieve (ABBR)
ACHVB...... Achievable (ABBR)
ACHVD...... Achieved (ABBR)
ACHVE...... Achieve (ABBR)
ACHVG...... Achieving (ABBR)
ACHVNT ... Achievement (ABBR)
ACHVR...... Achiever (ABBR)
ACHVT...... Achievement (ABBR)
ACI .... Advancing the Consumer Interest [*A publication*]
ACI .... [*The*] Advertising Council, Inc. (NTCM)
ACI .... Air Caledonie International [*France*] [*ICAO designator*] (FAAC)
ACI .... Aspiryl Chloride [*Organic chemistry*] (MAH)
ACIC......... Acicular (ABBR)
ACIF.......... Artillery Counterfire Information [*Army*] (ADDR)
ACJ........... American Citizens for Justice [*An association*] (EA)
ACK .... Air Cape [*ICAO designator*] (FAAC)
ACKB......... Acknowledgeable (ABBR)
ACKG......... Acknowledging (ABBR)
ACKT......... Acknowledgment (ABBR)
ACL .... Air Capitol [*Italy*] [*ICAO designator*] (FAAC)
ACLD .... Accolade (ABBR)
ACLIM....... Acclimate (ABBR)
ACLIMD.... Acclimated (ABBR)
ACLIMG.... Acclimating (ABBR)
ACLIMN.... Acclimation (ABBR)
ACLIMZ.... Acclimatize (ABBR)
ACLIMZD ... Acclimatized (ABBR)
ACLIMZG ... Acclimatizing (ABBR)
ACLIMZN ... Acclimatization (ABBR)
ACLM .... Acclaim (ABBR)
ACLMA...... Acclimate (ABBR)
ACLMAD... Acclimated (ABBR)
ACLMAG... Acclimating (ABBR)
ACLMAN ... Acclamation (ABBR)
ACLMATZ ... Acclimatize (ABBR)
ACLMATZD ... Acclimatized (ABBR)
ACLMATZG ... Acclimatizing (ABBR)
ACLMATZN ... Acclimatization (ABBR)
ACLMN ..... Acclamation (ABBR)
ACLMRS ... Advisory Committee for Land-Mobile Radio Services (NTCM)
ACLMY...... Acclamatory (ABBR)
ACLP......... Association of Contact Lens Practitioners [*British*] (BI)
ACLRA....... Accelerate (ABBR)
ACLRAD.... Accelerated (ABBR)
ACLRAG.... Accelerating (ABBR)
ACLRAN.... Acceleration (ABBR)
ACLRAV .... Accelerative (ABBR)
ACLRTR .... Accelerator (ABBR)
ACLYT...... Acolyte (ABBR)
ACM .... Accelerated Claimant Match
ACM .... Air Caledonia, Inc. [*Canada*] [*ICAO designator*] (FAAC)
ACM .... Association of Crane Makers [*British*] (BI)
ACMA .... Asbestos Cement Manufacturers Association [*British*] (BI)
ACMA .... Athletic Clothing Manufacturers' Association [*British*] (BI)
ACMAPS .. Advanced Computer Program Multiple Array Processor System
ACMD........ Accommodate (ABBR)
ACMDD..... Accommodated (ABBR)
ACMDG..... Accommodating (ABBR)
ACMDN..... Accommodation (ABBR)
ACMDV..... Accommodative (ABBR)
ACML .... Anti-Common Market League [*British*] (BI)
ACMLA...... Accumulate (ABBR)
ACMLAD... Accumulated (ABBR)
ACMLAG... Accumulating (ABBR)
ACMLAN ... Accumulation (ABBR)
ACMLATR ... Accumulator (ABBR)
ACMLAV... Accumulative (ABBR)
ACMN....... Acumen (ABBR)
ACMPD...... Accompanied (ABBR)
ACMPG ..... Accompanying (ABBR)
ACMPL...... Accomplice (ABBR)
ACMPLH... Accomplish (ABBR)

ACMPLHB ... Accomplishable (ABBR)
ACMPLHD ... Accomplished (ABBR)
ACMPLHNT ... Accomplishment (ABBR)
ACMPLS.... Accomplice (ABBR)
ACMPNT... Accompaniment (ABBR)
ACMPST ... Accompanist (ABBR)
ACMPT...... Accompaniment (ABBR)
ACMPY...... Accompany (ABBR)
ACMPYD... Accompanied (ABBR)
ACN........... Aerolineas Centroamericanas SA [*Central American Airlines*] [*Nicaragua*] [*ICAO designator*] (FAAC)
ACN........... Aircraft Classification Number [*Aviation*] (FAAC)
ACN........... American Cable Network, Inc. (NTCM)
ACN........... [*A. C.*] Nielsen Co. (NTCM)
ACNO........ Advisory Council of National Organizations [*Corporation for Public Broadcasting*] (NTCM)
ACN/PCN ... Aircraft Classification Number/Pavement Classification Number (DA)
ACNT .... Accent (ABBR)
ACNTD ...... Accented (ABBR)
ACNTG ...... Accenting (ABBR)
ACNTL ...... Accentual (ABBR)
ACNTU ...... Accentuate (ABBR)
ACNTUD ... Accentuated (ABBR)
ACNTUG ... Accentuating (ABBR)
ACNTUN... Accentuation (ABBR)
ACNWLG ... Acknowledge (ABBR)
ACNWLGB .... Acknowledgeable (ABBR)
ACNWLGD ... Acknowledged (ABBR)
ACNWLGG ... Acknowledging (ABBR)
ACNWLGNT ... Acknowledgment (ABBR)
ACNWLGR ... Acknowledger (ABBR)
ACO........... Aero Sierra Eco SA de CV [*Mexico*] [*ICAO designator*] (FAAC)
ACO........... Air Colombia [*ICAO designator*] (FAAC)
ACO........... Assistant Customs Officer
ACOMP ..... Accompaniment (ABBR)
ACOMP ..... Accompany (ABBR)
ACOMP ..... Accomplish (ABBR)
ACOMPB... Accomplishable (ABBR)
ACOMPD ... Accomplished (ABBR)
ACOMPG ... Accomplishing (ABBR)
ACOMPR... Accomplisher (ABBR)
ACOMPT... Accomplishment (ABBR)
ACONT ...... Account (ABBR)
ACONTB ... Accountable (ABBR)
ACONTBLY ... Accountably (ABBR)
ACONTBT ... Accountability (ABBR)
ACONTG ... Accounting (ABBR)
ACONTNC ... Accountancy (ABBR)
ACORD...... Automotive Consortium on Recycling and Disposal [*Industry research group*]
ACOS .... Accost (ABBR)
ACOSD ...... Accosted (ABBR)
ACOSG ...... Accosting (ABBR)
ACOUST.... Acoustic (ABBR)
ACP .... Air Cape [*South Africa*] [*ICAO designator*] (FAAC)
ACP .... Associate Computer Professional
ACP .... Association of Circus Proprietors of Great Britain (BI)
ACPD .... Alternating Current Plasma Detector [*Spectrometry*]
ACPHOB ... Acrophobia (ABBR)
ACPM .... Association of Corrugated Papermakers [*British*] (BI)
ACPTB ...... Acceptable (ABBR)
ACPTBT..... Acceptability (ABBR)
ACPTBY .... Acceptability (ABBR)
ACPTD ...... Accepted (ABBR)
ACPTG ...... Accepting (ABBR)
ACPTNC ... Acceptance (ABBR)
ACPTNS ... Acceptableness (ABBR)
ACPTY ...... Acceptably (ABBR)
ACQ........... Aero Continente [*Peru*] [*ICAO designator*] (FAAC)
ACQIS....... Acquisition (ABBR)
ACQNT ...... Acquaint (ABBR)
ACQNTD ... Acquainted (ABBR)
ACQNTG ... Acquainting (ABBR)
ACQNTNC ... Acquaintance (ABBR)
ACQNTNCSP ... Acquaintanceship (ABBR)
ACQR........ Acquire (ABBR)
ACQRB ...... Acquirable (ABBR)
ACQRD ...... Acquired (ABBR)
ACQRG ...... Acquiring (ABBR)
ACQRNT ... Acquirement (ABBR)
ACQRR ...... Acquirer (ABBR)
ACQRT ...... Acquirement (ABBR)
ACQS .... Acquiesce (ABBR)
ACQSD ...... Acquiesced (ABBR)
ACQSG .... Acquiescing (ABBR)
ACQSN ...... Acquisition (ABBR)
ACQSNC..... Acquiescence (ABBR)
ACQSNT.... Acquiescent (ABBR)
ACQSNTY ... Acquiescently (ABBR)
ACQT .... Acquit (ABBR)
ACQTD ...... Acquitted (ABBR)
ACQTG ...... Acquitting (ABBR)

ACQTL....... Acquittal (ABBR)
ACQTNC ... Acquittance (ABBR)
ACR .... Ancient Conserved Region [*Genetics*]
ACR .... Anomalous Cosmic Ray
ACR .... ASA, Air Starline, AG [*Switzerland*] [*ICAO designator*]   (FAAC)
ACRA .... Accurate (ABBR)
ACRANS.... Accurateness (ABBR)
ACRAY...... Accurately (ABBR)
ACRBT...... Acerbity (ABBR)
ACRBTC .... Acrobatic (ABBR)
ACRBTCY ... Acrobatically (ABBR)
ACRCY....... Accuracy (ABBR)
ACRD........ Accord (ABBR)
ACRD .... Accredit (ABBR)
ACRD .... Accrued (ABBR)
ACRDD ...... Accorded (ABBR)
ACRDG ...... According (ABBR)
ACRDGY ... Accordingly (ABBR)
ACRDNC ... Accordance (ABBR)
ACRDT...... Accordant (ABBR)
ACRDT...... Acridity (ABBR)
acred........... Accreditation
ACRES ...... American Council on Rural Special Eduction
ACRG .... Acreage (ABBR)
ACRI.......... Acrid (ABBR)
ACRIT....... Acridity (ABBR)
ACRM .... Acrimony (ABBR)
ACRMNIS ... Acrimonious (ABBR)
ACRMNY ... Acrimony (ABBR)
ACRMS...... Acrimonious (ABBR)
ACRN .... Accretion (ABBR)
ACRNM ..... Acronym (ABBR)
ACRO .... Acrophobe [*or Acrophobia*]   (ABBR)
ACROL....... Acrolect (ABBR)
ACROS...... Acrostic (ABBR)
ACRSD....... Accursed (ABBR)
ACRSDNS ... Accursedness (ABBR)
ACRSDY .... Accursedly (ABBR)
ACRST ...... Accurst (ABBR)
ACRT......... Accredit (ABBR)
ACRTD...... Accredited (ABBR)
ACRTG...... Accrediting (ABBR)
ACRU .... Accrue (ABBR)
ACRUD ...... Accrued (ABBR)
ACRUG ...... Accruing (ABBR)
ACRUT ...... Accruement (ABBR)
ACRV .... Accretive (ABBR)
ACS............ Air Commerce [*Yugoslavia*] [*ICAO designator*]   (FAAC)
ACS............ Airbag Central Sensor [*Automotive safety*]
ACS............ Association of Commonwealth Students [*British*]   (BI)
ACS............ Automatic Clutch System [*Powertrain*] [*Automotive engineering*]
ACSB......... Accessible (ABBR)
ACSBNS...... Accessibleness (ABBR)
ACSBT .... Accessibility (ABBR)
ACSBY .... Accessibly (ABBR)
ACSN .... Accession (ABBR)
ACSND ...... Accessioned (ABBR)
ACSNG ...... Accessioning (ABBR)
ACSNL....... Accessional (ABBR)
ACSRY .... Accessory (ABBR)
ACSSB....... Amplitude-Companded Single Sideband   (DA)
ACST .... Accost (ABBR)
ACSTL .... Acoustical (ABBR)
ACSTLY..... Acoustically (ABBR)
ACSTM...... Accustom (ABBR)
ACSTMD... Accustomed (ABBR)
ACSTMG... Accustoming (ABBR)
ACSTV .... Accusative (ABBR)
ACT .... Alternative Control Technology [*Environmental science*]
ACT .... Flight Line, Inc. [*ICAO designator*]   (FAAC)
ACTA .... Acetate (ABBR)
ACTAD ...... Actuated (ABBR)
ACTAG ...... Actuating (ABBR)
ACTAN ...... Actuation (ABBR)
ACTAR...... Actuator (ABBR)
ACTD .... Acted (ABBR)
ACTIV .... Activity (ABBR)
ACTLT ...... Actuality (ABBR)
ACTLY....... Actually (ABBR)
ACTLZ....... Actualize (ABBR)
ACTLZAN ... Actualization (ABBR)
ACTLZD.... Actualized (ABBR)
ACTLZG .... Actualizing (ABBR)
ACTLZN.... Actualization (ABBR)
ACTNB...... Actionable (ABBR)
ACTNE...... Acetone (ABBR)
ACTNS...... Acuteness (ABBR)
ACTRE...... Actress (ABBR)
ACTRS...... Actress (ABBR)
ACTRY...... Actuary (ABBR)
ACTS .... Advisory Committee on Toxic Substances [*British*]
ACTS.......... All-Channel Television Society [*UHF interest group*]   (NTCM)

ACTS......... Asbestos Contractor Tracking System [*Environmental Protection Agency*]   (ERG)
ACTS......... Automatic Clutch and Throttle System [*Automotive powertrain*]
ACTT......... Accountant (ABBR)
ACTT......... Advanced Communication and Timekeeping Technology [*Seiko Telecommunications Systems*] [*FM data receiver chip set*]   (PCM)
ACTU .... Actuate (ABBR)
ACTUD ...... Actuated (ABBR)
ACTUG ...... Actuating (ABBR)
ACTUN ...... Actuation (ABBR)
ACTUR ...... Actuary (ABBR)
ACTV......... Active   (FAAC)
ACTVA...... Activate (ABBR)
ACTVAD.... Activated (ABBR)
ACTVAG.... Activating (ABBR)
ACTVAN.... Activation (ABBR)
ACTVNS.... Activeness (ABBR)
ACTVOR.... Activator (ABBR)
ACTVTD.... Activated (ABBR)
ACTVTG.... Activating (ABBR)
ACTVTN.... Activation (ABBR)
ACTVY...... Actively (ABBR)
ACTY......... Acutely (ABBR)
ACTYLN.... Acetylene (ABBR)
ACU........... Aerocancun [*Mexico*] [*ICAO designator*]   (FAAC)
ACUBS...... Association of College and University Broadcasting Stations   (NTCM)
ACUM....... Accumulate (ABBR)
ACUMB .... Accumulable (ABBR)
ACUMD..... Accumulated (ABBR)
ACUMG..... Accumulating (ABBR)
ACUMN..... Accumulation (ABBR)
ACUMR..... Accumulator (ABBR)
ACUMV..... Accumulative (ABBR)
ACUP........ Acupuncture (ABBR)
ACUR .... Accurate (ABBR)
ACURC ...... Accuracy (ABBR)
ACURNS.... Accurateness (ABBR)
ACURY...... Accurately (ABBR)
ACUS .... Accuse (ABBR)
ACUSD ...... Accused (ABBR)
ACUSG...... Accusing (ABBR)
ACUSGY.... Accusingly (ABBR)
ACUSN...... Accusation (ABBR)
ACUSR...... Accuser (ABBR)
ACUSTL .... Accusatorial (ABBR)
ACUSTRY ... Accusatory (ABBR)
ACUSTY.... Accusatory (ABBR)
ACUSV...... Accusative (ABBR)
ACUTNS.... Acuteness (ABBR)
ACV........... Acellular Vaccine [*Medicine*]
ACW.......... Air Cadets School [*RAF*] [*British*] [*ICAO designator*]   (FAAC)
ACX........... Air Charters, Inc. [*Canada*] [*ICAO designator*]   (FAAC)
ACY .... Air City SA [*Switzerland*] [*ICAO designator*]   (FAAC)
A/D........... Audimeter/Diary System [*A. C. Nielson Co.*]   (NTCM)
ADA........... Americans with Disabilities Act [*An association*]   (EA)
ADA........... Australian Civil Aviation Authority, Flying Unit [*ICAO designator*]   (FAAC)
ADABP...... Adenosine Deceminase Binding Protein [*Biochemistry*]
ADAM....... Adamantine (ABBR)
ADAMT..... Adamant (ABBR)
ADAMTY ... Adamantly (ABBR)
ADAPB...... Adaptable (ABBR)
ADAPD...... Adapted (ABBR)
ADAPG...... Adapting (ABBR)
ADAPN...... Adaptation (ABBR)
ADAPN...... Adaption (ABBR)
ADAPR...... Adapter (ABBR)
ADAPTTN ... Adaptation (ABBR)
ADAPTV.... Adaptive (ABBR)
ADAPV...... Adaptive (ABBR)
ADAPY...... Adaptably (ABBR)
ADAS .... Alzheimer's Disease Assessment Scale
ADB........... Antonov Design Bureau [*Former USSR*] [*ICAO designator*]   (FAAC)
ADC........... Adduce (ABBR)
ADC........... Airline of Adriatic [*Croatia*] [*ICAO designator*]   (FAAC)
ADC........... Automatic Damping Control [*Automotive suspensions*]
ADCF......... Air Defense Control Facility   (FAAC)
ADCN........ Aeronautical Data Communication Network   (DA)
ADCPM ..... Adaptive Differential Pulse Code Modulation [*Computer science*]
ADCT .... Adduct (ABBR)
ADCTN...... Adduction (ABBR)
ADCTV....... Adductive (ABBR)
ADD........... Adastra Aviation Ltd. [*Canada*] [*ICAO designator*]   (FAAC)
ADDA........ Air Defense Operations Area [*Army*]   (ADDR)
ADDC........ Addict (ABBR)
ADDCD...... Addicted (ABBR)
ADDCG...... Addicting (ABBR)
ADDCN...... Addiction (ABBR)
ADDG........ Adding (ABBR)
ADDNDM ... Addendum (ABBR)

ADDNLY ... Additionally (ABBR)
ADDRD...... Addressed (ABBR)
ADDRE ...... Addressee (ABBR)
ADDRG...... Addressing (ABBR)
ADDS .... Area Data Distribution System [*Army*] (ADDR)
ADDSD ...... Addressed (ABBR)
ADDV......... Additive (ABBR)
ADELT....... Automatically Deployable Emergency Locator Transmitter [*Aviation*] (DA)
ADEPNS .... Adeptness (ABBR)
ADG............ Adage (ABBR)
ADG............ Aviones y Servicios del Golfo SA de CV [*Mexico*] [*ICAO designator*] (FAAC)
ADH .... Association of Dental Hospitals of Great Britain and Northern Ireland (BI)
ADH .... Societa' Adriatica [*Italy*] [*ICAO designator*] (FAAC)
ADHN .... Adhesion (ABBR)
ADHR......... Adhere (ABBR)
ADHRD..... Adhered (ABBR)
ADHRG...... Adhering (ABBR)
ADHRNC... Adherence (ABBR)
ADHRNT... Adherent (ABBR)
ADHRT...... Adherent (ABBR)
ADHRTY ... Adherently (ABBR)
ADHSV ..... Adhesive (ABBR)
ADHSVNS ... Adhesiveness (ABBR)
ADHSVY ... Adhesively (ABBR)
ADHVNS... Adhesiveness (ABBR)
ADI .... Audeli Air Express [*Spain*] [*ICAO designator*] (FAAC)
ADIDS........ Aeronautical Digital Information Display System (DA)
ADIOC ...... Archdiocese (ABBR)
ADIOCN.... Archdiocesan (ABBR)
ADIRS........ Air Data Inertial Reference System (DA)
ADIS........... Airport Data Information System (DA)
ADJ .... Adjoint (ABBR)
ADJA.......... Adjacent (ABBR)
ADJAY....... Adjacently (ABBR)
ADJC.......... Adjacency (ABBR)
ADJCNC.... Adjacency (ABBR)
ADJCNT.... Adjacent (ABBR)
ADJCNTY ... Adjacently (ABBR)
ADJDCA.... Adjudicate (ABBR)
ADJDCAD ... Adjudicated (ABBR)
ADJDCAG ... Adjudicating (ABBR)
ADJDCAN ... Adjudication (ABBR)
ADJDCR.... Adjudicator (ABBR)
ADJDG ...... Adjudge (ABBR)
ADJDGD ... Adjudged (ABBR)
ADJDGG.... Adjudging (ABBR)
ADJN .... Adjoin (ABBR)
ADJNC....... Adjunct (ABBR)
ADJNCV.... Adjunctive (ABBR)
ADJNG ...... Adjoining (ABBR)
ADJR .... Adjure (ABBR)
ADJRAN.... Adjuration (ABBR)
ADJRAY ... Adjuratory (ABBR)
ADJRD...... Adjured (ABBR)
ADJRG....... Adjuring (ABBR)
ADJRN....... Adjourn (ABBR)
ADJRND.... Adjourned (ABBR)
ADJRNG.... Adjourning (ABBR)
ADJRNNT ... Adjournment (ABBR)
ADJRNT.... Adjournment (ABBR)
ADJRR ...... Adjurer (ABBR)
ADJS.......... Adjust (ABBR)
ADJSB ...... Adjustable (ABBR)
ADJSBY.... Adjustably (ABBR)
ADJSD....... Adjusted (ABBR)
ADJSG .... Adjusting (ABBR)
ADJSNT..... Adjustment (ABBR)
ADJSR ...... Adjuster (ABBR)
ADJST .... Adjustment (ABBR)
ADJSTB..... Ajustable (ABBR)
ADJSTR.... Adjuster (ABBR)
ADJT......... Adjutant (ABBR)
ADJTNC.... Adjutancy (ABBR)
ADJTS ...... Adjutants (ABBR)
ADJUD ...... Adjudicate (ABBR)
ADJUDD ... Adjudicated (ABBR)
ADJUDG ... Adjudicating (ABBR)
ADJUDN ... Adjudication (ABBR)
ADJUDR.... Adjudicator (ABBR)
ADJUDRY ... Adjudicatory (ABBR)
ADJV......... Adjective (ABBR)
ADJVL....... Adjectival (ABBR)
ADK............ Aviation Development Co. Nigeria Ltd. [*ICAO designator*] (FAAC)
ADL............ Air-Dale Ltd. [*Canada*] [*ICAO designator*] (FAAC)
ADL............ Amateur Drama League [*Republic of Ireland*] (BI)
ADLA .... Adulate (ABBR)
ADLAD...... Adulated (ABBR)
ADLAG ...... Adulating (ABBR)
ADLAN ...... Adulation (ABBR)

ADLAR...... Adulator (ABBR)
ADLARY... Adulatory (ABBR)
ADLRI....... [*Arthur D.*] Little Research Institute [*British*] (BI)
ADLSNC.... Adolescence (ABBR)
ADLSNT.... Adolescent (ABBR)
ADLST ...... Adolescent (ABBR)
ADLT .... Adult (ABBR)
ADLTA...... Adulterate (ABBR)
ADLTAD.... Adulterated (ABBR)
ADLTAG.... Adulterating (ABBR)
ADLTHD ... Adulthood (ABBR)
ADLTNT.... Adulterant (ABBR)
ADLTR...... Adulterer (ABBR)
ADLTRA.... Adulterate (ABBR)
ADLTRAD ... Adulterated (ABBR)
ADLTRAG ... Adulterating (ABBR)
ADLTRAN ... Adulteration (ABBR)
ADLTRES... Adulteress (ABBR)
ADLTRNT ... Adulterant (ABBR)
ADLTRR.... Adulterer (ABBR)
ADLTRS.... Adulteress (ABBR)
ADLTRU... Adulterous (ABBR)
ADLTRY... Adultery (ABBR)
ADLTUS.... Adulterous (ABBR)
ADLTUSY ... Adulterously (ABBR)
ADLY .... Arrival Delay [*Air Traffic Control*] (FAAC)
ADM.......... Aerolineas Dominicanas SA [*Dominican Republic*] [*ICAO designator*] (FAAC)
ADM.......... Automatic Drivetrain Management [*Automotive engineering*]
ADMB........ Adumbrate (ABBR)
ADMBD..... Adumbrated (ABBR)
ADMBG..... Adumbrating (ABBR)
ADMBRA ... Adumbrate (ABBR)
ADMBRAD ... Adumbrated (ABBR)
ADMBRAG ... Adumbrating (ABBR)
ADMLT...... Admiralty (ABBR)
ADMN....... Administer (ABBR)
ADMND..... Administered (ABBR)
ADMNG..... Administering (ABBR)
ADMNH .... Admonish (ABBR)
ADMNHR ... Admonisher (ABBR)
ADMNN .... Admonition (ABBR)
ADMNT..... Adamant (ABBR)
ADMNT..... Administrate (ABBR)
ADMNTD ... Administrated (ABBR)
ADMNTG ... Administrating (ABBR)
ADMNTN ... Administration (ABBR)
ADMNTNS ... Admonitions (ABBR)
ADMNTR ... Administrator (ABBR)
ADMNTS ... Administrates (ABBR)
ADMNTV ... Administrative (ABBR)
ADMNTVY ... Administratively (ABBR)
ADMNTX ... Administratrix (ABBR)
ADMNTY ... Adamantly (ABBR)
ADMON .... Admonish (ABBR)
ADMOND ... Admonished (ABBR)
ADMONG ... Admonishing (ABBR)
ADMONGY ... Admonishingly (ABBR)
ADMONR ... Admonisher (ABBR)
ADMONT ... Admonishment (ABBR)
ADMONTN ... Admonition (ABBR)
ADMR........ Admire (ABBR)
ADMRAN ... Admiration (ABBR)
ADMRB..... Admirable (ABBR)
ADMRD..... Admired (ABBR)
ADMRG..... Admiring (ABBR)
ADMRGY ... Admiringly (ABBR)
ADMRLT... Admiralty (ABBR)
ADMRN..... Admiration (ABBR)
ADMRR..... Admirer (ABBR)
ADMRX..... Administratrix (ABBR)
ADMRY..... Admirably (ABBR)
ADMSB...... Admissible (ABBR)
ADMSBLT ... Admissibility (ABBR)
ADMSBT... Admissibility (ABBR)
ADMSTR... Administer (ABBR)
ADMSTRA ... Administrate (ABBR)
ADMSTRAN ... Administration (ABBR)
ADMSTRATR ... Administrator (ABBR)
ADMSTRAV ... Administrative (ABBR)
ADMSV...... Admissive (ABBR)
ADMT........ Admit (ABBR)
ADMTD..... Admitted (ABBR)
ADMTDY ... Admittedly (ABBR)
ADMTG..... Admitting (ABBR)
ADMTNC ... Admittance (ABBR)
ADMTY..... Admiralty (ABBR)
ADMXR..... Admixture (ABBR)
ADN........... Aerodienst GmbH [*Germany*] [*ICAO designator*] (FAAC)
ADN........... Ammonium Dinitramide [*Potential rocket fuel component*] [*Inorganic chemistry*]
ADND......... Addend (ABBR)
ADNDA...... Addenda (ABBR)

ADNDM..... Addendum (ABBR)
ADNI......... Additional (DA)
ADNL TFC ... Additional Traffic [Air Traffic Control] (FAAC)
ADNV........ Adhesive (ABBR)
ADOCo....... After Dinner Opera Co.
ADOP........ Adoption (ABBR)
ADOPB ...... Adoptable (ABBR)
ADOPD...... Adopted (ABBR)
ADOPG...... Adopting (ABBR)
ADOPN...... Adoption (ABBR)
ADOPR ...... Adopter (ABBR)
ADOPV ...... Adoptive (ABBR)
ADORAN.... Adoration (ABBR)
ADORB ...... Adorable (ABBR)
ADORBL.... Adorably (ABBR)
ADORBNS ... Adorableness (ABBR)
ADORBT ... Adorability (ABBR)
ADORBY .. Adorably (ABBR)
ADORD...... Adored (ABBR)
ADORG...... Adoring (ABBR)
ADORGY ... Adoringly (ABBR)
ADORNT... Adornment (ABBR)
ADORTN... Adoration (ABBR)
ADP........... Acme Aviation Ltd. [British] [ICAO designator] (FAAC)
ADP........... Adaptive Learn Processor [Fuel systems] [Automotive engineering]
ADPB .... Adaptable (ABBR)
ADPBT....... Adaptability (ABBR)
ADPNS....... Adeptness (ABBR)
ADPT .... Adept (ABBR)
ADPY .... Adeptly (ABBR)
ADQ........... Avion Taxi Canada, Inc. [ICAO designator] (FAAC)
ADQA........ Adequate (ABBR)
ADQAY...... Adequately (ABBR)
ADQC........ Adequacy (ABBR)
ADQCY...... Adequacy (ABBR)
ADQTNS ... Adequateness (ABBR)
ADQTY ...... Adequately (ABBR)
ADR........... Adria Airways [Yugoslavia] [ICAO designator] (FAAC)
ADR........... Adriatic (ABBR)
ADR........... Advisory Rule (DA)
ADR........... Aerodrome Damage Repair [NATO]
ADR........... Australian Disabilities Review [A publication]
ADREN ...... Adrenal [Gland] (ABBR)
ADRN......... Adrenaline (ABBR)
ADRNT ...... Adornment (ABBR)
ADRSE....... Addressee (ABBR)
ADRT .... Adroit (ABBR)
ADRT .... Alternate Departure Route [Air Traffic Control] (FAAC)
ADRTNS.... Adroitness (ABBR)
ADRTY....... Adroitly (ABBR)
ADS .... Accident Documentation System [Safety research] [Automotive engineering]
ADS .... Alpha Delta Sigma [Fraternity] (NTCM)
ADS .... Aviones de Sonora SA [Mexico] [ICAO designator] (FAAC)
ADSB......... Adsorb (ABBR)
ADSBNT.... Adsorbent (ABBR)
ADSBT....... Adsorbent (ABBR)
ADSPN....... Adsorption (ABBR)
ADSQ .... Audio Data Sequence [Telecommunications] (NTCM)
ADSS......... Air Data Screening System [Environmental Protection Agency] (ERG)
ADSU .... Automatic Dependent Surveillance Unit [ICAO designator] (FAAC)
ADSYS .... Air Device Systems [Honda Motor Co.] [Automotive air conditioning]
ADT .... Air Dorval Ltd. [Canada] [ICAO designator] (FAAC)
ADT .... Australian Dance Theatre [Adelaide]
ADTN........ Addition (ABBR)
ADTNL ...... Additional (ABBR)
ADTNLY.... Additionally (ABBR)
ADTV .... Additive (ABBR)
ADUC........ Adduce (ABBR)
ADUCB...... Adducable (ABBR)
ADUCD...... Adduced (ABBR)
ADUCG...... Adducing (ABBR)
ADUCTD ... Adducted (ABBR)
ADUCTG ... Adducting (ABBR)
ADUCTN... Adduction (ABBR)
ADUCTV ... Adductive (ABBR)
ADUL........ Adulate (ABBR)
ADULD...... Adulated (ABBR)
ADULG...... Adulating (ABBR)
ADULN...... Adulation (ABBR)
ADULR...... Adulator (ABBR)
ADULT...... Adulterant (ABBR)
ADULT ...... Adulterate (ABBR)
ADULT ...... Adulteration (ABBR)
ADULY...... Adulatory (ABBR)
ADUY........ Arduously (ABBR)
ADV........... Advance Air Charters [Canada] [ICAO designator] (FAAC)
ADVATG ... Advantage (ABBR)
ADVATGUS ... Advantageous (ABBR)

ADVATGUSY ... Advantageously (ABBR)
ADVBL....... Adverbial (ABBR)
ADVCA ...... Advocate (ABBR)
ADVCAD ... Advocated (ABBR)
ADVCAG ... Advocating (ABBR)
ADVCAN ... Advocation (ABBR)
ADVCY ...... Advocacy (ABBR)
ADVEC...... Advection (ABBR)
ADVECT.... Advection (ABBR)
ADVERSAT ... Adversative (ABBR)
ADVERTNC ... Advertence (ABBR)
ADVL .... Adverbial (ABBR)
ADVNC...... Advance (ABBR)
ADVNCD... Advanced (ABBR)
ADVNCG ... Advancing (ABBR)
ADVNCNT ... Advancement (ABBR)
ADVNCT ... Advancement (ABBR)
ADVNT ...... Advent (ABBR)
ADVNTG ... Advantage (ABBR)
ADVNTGD ... Advantaged (ABBR)
ADVNTGG ... Advantaging (ABBR)
ADVNTGU ... Advantageous (ABBR)
ADVNTGUY ... Advantageously (ABBR)
ADVNTR ... Adventure (ABBR)
ADVNTRD ... Adventured (ABBR)
ADVNTRES ... Adventuress (ABBR)
ADVNTRG ... Adventuring (ABBR)
ADVNTRR ... Adventurer (ABBR)
ADVNTRSM ... Adventuresome (ABBR)
ADVNTRU ... Adventurous (ABBR)
ADVNTRUS ... Adventurous (ABBR)
ADVNTRUSY ... Adventurously (ABBR)
ADVO........ Advocate (ABBR)
ADVOD...... Advocated (ABBR)
ADVOG...... Advocating (ABBR)
ADVON..... Advocation (ABBR)
ADVOR...... Advocator (ABBR)
ADVOS ...... Advocates (ABBR)
advp oz ...... Avoirdupois Ounce
ADVRS....... Adverse (ABBR)
ADVRSNS ... Adverseness (ABBR)
ADVRSRY ... Adversary (ABBR)
ADVRST .... Adversity (ABBR)
ADVRSY.... Adversely (ABBR)
ADVRTNT ... Advertent (ABBR)
ADVRTZG ... Advertising (ABBR)
ADVRTZNT ... Advertisement (ABBR)
ADVRTZR ... Advertiser (ABBR)
ADVSB .... Advisable (ABBR)
ADVSBT .... Advisability (ABBR)
ADVSBY.... Advisably (ABBR)
ADVSD ...... Advised (ABBR)
ADVSDY.... Advisedly (ABBR)
ADVSG....... Advising (ABBR)
ADVSNT.... Advisement (ABBR)
ADVSRY.... Advisory (ABBR)
ADVST...... Advisement (ABBR)
ADVSY....... Adversary (ABBR)
ADVTD ...... Advertised (ABBR)
ADVTG ...... Advantage (ABBR)
ADVTG ...... Advertising (ABBR)
ADVTMT... Advertisement (ABBR)
ADVTR ...... Advertiser (ABBR)
ADY........... Aerodyne Executive Aviation Services [ICAO designator] (FAAC)
AE............. Acceleration Enrichment [Automotive fuel systems]
Ae............... Aerodrome Report [Aviation] (DA)
AE.............. Aeronautical (ABBR)
AE.............. Angled End [Outdoor advertising] (NTCM)
AEA .... Air Europa [Spain] [ICAO designator] (FAAC)
AEA .... Aluminum Extruders Association (DAC)
AEB .... Arctic [Iceland] [ICAO designator] (FAAC)
AEC .... Aerocesar, Aerovias del Cesar [Colombia] [ICAO designator] (FAAC)
AEC .... Army Environmental Center [Aberdeen Proving Ground, MD] (RDA)
AEC .... Associate Enforcement Counsel (ERG)
AECD .... Auxiliary Emission Control Device (ERG)
AED........... Advance Electronic Diagnostics [Automotive industry supplier]
AED........... Advanced Engine Development [Automotive industry supplier]
AED........... Air Experienc Flight [British] [ICAO designator] (FAAC)
AED........... Association of Engineering Distributors [British] (BI)
AEE .... Aegean Aviation [Greece] [ICAO designator] (FAAC)
AEE .... Ancillary Education Establishment
AEEC......... Association of European Express Carriers (DA)
AEF........... Aero Lloyd Flugreisen GmbH [Germany] [ICAO designator] (FAAC)
AEF........... Asia Education Foundation
AEG .... Aerial Enterprises Ltd. [British] [ICAO designator] (FAAC)
AEH .... Avia Express Ltd. [Hungary] [ICAO designator] (FAAC)
AEHC......... Aminoethylhomocysteine [Biochemistry]
AEI .... Advanced Education Institution

AEI .... Aeroexpreso Interamerican [Colombia] [ICAO designator] (FAAC)
AEIS .... Aeronautical Enroute Information Service (DA)
AEJ .... Air Affaires EJA France [ICAO designator] (FAAC)
AEK .... Aero Costa Rica [ICAO designator] (FAAC)
AEL .... Air Europe SpA [Italy] [ICAO designator] (FAAC)
AELP .... Allied Electrical Publication [Military]
AEM .... Aero Madrid [Spain] [ICAO designator] (FAAC)
AEME .... American Executives for Management Excellence [An association] (EA)
AEMN .... Australian Energy Management News [A publication]
AEN .... Air Enterprise [France] [ICAO designator] (FAAC)
AENM .... Archenemy (ABBR)
AENPR ...... Aggregate Estimated Net Pool Return [Business term]
AEO .... Aeroservicios Ejecutivos del Occidente SA de CV [Mexico] [ICAO designator] (FAAC)
AEP .... Airports Economic Panel [ICAO] (DA)
AEP .... Association of Embroiderers and Pleaters [British] (BI)
AEP .... Compania Aero Transportes Panamenos SA [Panama] [ICAO designator] (FAAC)
AER .... Ace Air Cargo Express, Inc. [ICAO designator] (FAAC)
AER .... Alpha Epsilon Rho [Also, AERho] [Fraternity] (NTCM)
AERA .... Aeration (ABBR)
AERDYN .. Aerodynamic (ABBR)
AERLT ...... Aerialist (ABBR)
AERN .... Aeronaut (ABBR)
AERNC ...... Aeronautics (ABBR)
AERNL ...... Aeronautical (ABBR)
AERNLY.... Aeronautically (ABBR)
AERO .... Air Education Recreation Organization [British] (DA)
AEROCOR ... Aerolineas Cordillera Ltda. [Chile] [ICAO designator] (FAAC)
AEROSAT ... Aeronautical Satellite (DA)
AEROVENCA ... Aeronautica Venezolana CA [Venezuela] [ICAO designator] (FAAC)
AERSL ...... Aerosol (ABBR)
AERSPC.... Aerospace (ABBR)
AES .... Active Employment Strategy
AES .... Aerodrome Emergency Service (DA)
AES .... Aerolineas Centrales de Colombia [ICAO designator] (FAAC)
AES .... Aeronautical Earth Station (DA)
AES .... Aircraft Earth Station [ICAO designator] (FAAC)
AESD .... AIDS Education/Services for the Deaf [An association]
AESTH ...... Aesthete (ABBR)
AESTHY .... Aesthetically (ABBR)
AET .... Aero-Palma SA [Spain] [ICAO designator] (FAAC)
AET .... Alliance for Environmental Technology
AET .... Association of Autoelectrical Technicians Ltd. [British] (BI)
AETO .... Active Employment Training Organization
AEV .... Aeroventas SA [Mexico] [ICAO designator] (FAAC)
AEZ .... Aerial Transit Co. [ICAO designator] (FAAC)
AF .... Anti-Friction [Lubricants]
AF .... Audio Fidelity (NTCM)
AF .... Australia First [Political party]
AFA .... Alfa Air [Czechoslovakia] [ICAO designator] (FAAC)
AFA .... Amateur Football Alliance [British] (BI)
AFAD .... Association of Fatty Acid Distillers [British] (BI)
AFB .... Affable (ABBR)
AFB .... Force Aerienne Belge [Belgium] [ICAO designator] (FAAC)
AFBT .... Affability (ABBR)
AFBY .... Affably (ABBR)
AFC .... African West Air [Senegal] [ICAO designator] (FAAC)
AFC .... Association of Flooring Contractors [British] (BI)
AFC .... Australian Film Corp.
AFCA .... Area Fuel Consumption Allocation [Environmental Protection Agency] (ERG)
AFCAPS.... Air Force Coronary Atherosclerosis Prevention Study
AFCAS ...... Automatic Flight Control and Augmentation System (DA)
AFCTAN.... Affectation (ABBR)
AFCTD...... Affected (ABBR)
AFCTDY .... Affectedly (ABBR)
AFCTG...... Affecting (ABBR)
AFCTGY .... Affectingly (ABBR)
AFCTN...... Affection (ABBR)
AFCTNA.... Affectionate (ABBR)
AFCTNAY ... Affectionately (ABBR)
AFCTNT .... Affectionate (ABBR)
AFCTNTY ... Affectionately (ABBR)
AFCW........ Association of Family Case-Workers [British] (BI)
AFD .... Panorama Flight Service [ICAO designator] (FAAC)
AFDA .... American Fish Decoy Association (EA)
AFE .... Airfast Service Indonesia PT [ICAO designator] (FAAC)
AFE .... Alternative Fuel Electronics [Fuel systems] [Automotive engineering]
AFF .... Advanced Firefighter [Military]
AFFC .... Australian Film Finance Corp.
AFFM .... Association of Folding Furniture Manufacturers [British] (BI)
AFG .... Ariana Afghan Airlines [Afganistan] [ICAO designator] (FAAC)
AFH .... Air Fecteau Ltd. [Canada] [ICAO designator] (FAAC)
AFH .... Away from Home
AFI .... Aero Filipanas Ltd. [Philippines] [ICAO designator] (FAAC)
AFI .... Assistant Flying Instructor (DA)
AFIA.......... Apparel and Fashion Industry's Association [British] (BI)
AFIC .... Approved Force Inventory Objective [Military]

AFIS .... Automatic Flight Inspection (DA)
AFIS(O)..... Aerodrome Flight Information Service (Officer) (DA)
AFK .... Africa Air Links [Sierra Leone] [ICAO designator] (FAAC)
AFK .... Away from Keyboard [Computer hacker terminology] (NHD)
AFL............ Aeroflot - Russian International Airlines [Russian Federation] [ICAO designator] (FAAC)
AFM .... Abrasive Flow Machining [Mechanical engineering]
AFM .... Affirmative [ICAO designator] (FAAC)
AFM .... Affretair [Zimbabwe] [ICAO designator] (FAAC)
AFMA .... Artificial Flower Manufacturers' Association of Great Britain (BI)
AFMLC...... Aeronautical Frequency Management Committee [British] (DA)
AFMS........ Advanced Flight Management System (DA)
AFN............ African International Airlines [Lesotho] [ICAO designator] (FAAC)
AFO .... Aero Empresa Mexicana SA [Mexico] [ICAO designator] (FAAC)
AFO .... Airport Fire Officer (DA)
AFP............ Portugese Air Force [ICAO designator] (FAAC)
AFPA.......... Advertising Film Producers Association [British] (BI)
AFPL .... Alianza Federal des Pueblos Libres [An association] (NTCM)
AFR .... Air Force Route
AFR .... Air France [ICAO designator] (FAAC)
A-FR .... Algerian-Franc (ABBR)
AFREXIMBANK ... African Export Import Bank
Afr Rpt........ Africa Report [A publication]
AFTEX .... Australia-France Technological Exchange Scheme
AFTS .... Armed Forces Television Service (NTCM)
AFU .... Afro Unity Airways [Benin] [ICAO designator] (FAAC)
AFV .... Alternative Fuel Vehicle
AFV .... Audio Follow Video [Tape editing] (NTCM)
AFWE........ Average Female Weekly Earnings
AFX .... Air Freight Express, Inc. [ICAO designator] (FAAC)
AFY .... Air Foyle (Executive) Ltd. [British] [ICAO designator] (FAAC)
AG............... Above Grade (DAC)
AGA .... Aerodromes, Air Routes, and Ground Aid (DA)
AGA .... Aeronaves del Centro [Venezuela] [ICAO designator] (FAAC)
AGA .... Association of Gaugers and Appraisers Ltd. [British] (BI)
AGB............ Air-Service-Gabon [ICAO designator] (FAAC)
AGC............ Arab Agricultural Aviation [Egypt] [ICAO designator] (FAAC)
AGCD........ Association of Green Crop Driers [British] (BI)
AGCM........ Army Good Conduct Medal
AGD............ Agderfly AS [Norway] [ICAO designator] (FAAC)
AGE............ Servicios Aereos de Los Angeles SA de CV [Mexico] [ICAO designator] (FAAC)
AGF............ Atlantic Gulf Airlines, Inc. [ICAO designator] (FAAC)
AGG............ Algoma Airways, Inc. [Canada] [ICAO designator] (FAAC)
AGI............. Agrar-Aviacion SA [Spain] [ICAO designator] (FAAC)
AGL............ Air Angouleme [France] [ICAO designator] (FAAC)
AGM.......... Air Guam [ICAO designator] (FAAC)
AGM.......... Association of Good Motorists [British] (BI)
AGN............ Compagnie Nationale Air Gabon [ICAO designator] (FAAC)
AGO............ Angola Air Charter Ltd. [ICAO designator] (FAAC)
AGP............ Air Tara Ltd. [Republic of Ireland] [ICAO designator] (FAAC)
AGP............ Association of Gut Processors [British] (BI)
AGR............ Agricultural Research Services, Animal Health Division [Department of Agriculture] [ICAO designator] (FAAC)
AGS .... Air Gambia [ICAO designator] (FAAC)
AGT............ Amadeus Global Travel Distrution SA [Spain] [ICAO designator] (FAAC)
AGU............ Societe Anonyme de Transports Aeriens Air-Guadeloupe [France] [ICAO designator] (FAAC)
AGV............ Air Glaciers SA [Switzerland] [ICAO designator] (FAAC)
AGX............ Aviogenex [Yugoslavia] [ICAO designator] (FAAC)
AGY............ Aeroguayacan [Chile] [ICAO designator] (FAAC)
AH .... At Home
AHA .... Air Alpha, AS [Denmark] [ICAO designator] (FAAC)
AHA .... Alpha-Hydroxy Acid [Organic chemistry]
AHB............ Alpha-Hydroxybutyric Dehydrogenase [An enzyme] (MAH)
AHBA .... Association of Hotel Booking Agents [British] (BI)
AHC............ Auto Headway Control [Mitsubishi] [Automotive engineering]
AHD .... Czech Air Handling [Czechoslovakia] [ICAO designator] (FAAC)
AHES .... American Humane Education Society (EA)
AHG .... Aerochago [Dominican Republic] [ICAO designator] (FAAC)
AHI .... Servicios Aeros de Chihuahua Aerochisa SA de CV [Mexico] [ICAO designator] (FAAC)
AHK .... Air Hong Kong Ltd. [ICAO designator] (FAAC)
AHK............ Aktiv Hinten Kinematik [Active Rear-Axle Movement] [German]
AHL............ Air Hanson Ltd. [British] [ICAO designator] (FAAC)
AHM .... Association of Headmistresses [British] (BI)
AHM .... Garrison Aviation Ltd. [Canada] [ICAO designator] (FAAC)
AHN............ Air Hainaut [France] [ICAO designator] (FAAC)
AHP............ Aerochiapas SA de CV [Mexico] [ICAO designator] (FAAC)
AHPS.......... Association of Headmistresses of Preparatory Schools [British] (BI)
AHR............ Air Holland Regional (AHR) [ICAO designator] (FAAC)
AHS............ Berry Aviation, Inc. [ICAO designator] (FAAC)
AHSP .... Association for High Speed Photography [British] (BI)
AHT............ Animal Health Trust [British] (BI)
AHWA....... Association of Hospital and Welfare Administrators [British] (BI)
AHY............ Azalavia-Azerbaijan Hava Yollari [ICAO designator] (FAAC)

AI .... Altitude Indicator [*Aviation*]   (DA)
AIA .... Anglo-Israel Association [*British*]   (BI)
AIAA .... Area of Intense Air Activity   (DA)
AIAC........... American Indian Arts Council   (EA)
AIB .... Airbus Industrie [*France*] [*ICAO designator*]   (FAAC)
AIB .... Association of Insurance Brokers Ltd. [*British*]   (BI)
AIBCM....... Association of Industrialized Building Component Manufacturers Ltd. [*British*]   (BI)
AIC .... Accretion-Induced Collapse [*Astronomy*]
AIC .... Air India [*ICAO designator*]   (FAAC)
AICC........... Autonomous Intelligent Cruise Control [*Automotive engineering*]
AICE .... Association of Independent Commercial Editors   (NTCM)
AICS.......... Australian Inventory of Chemical Substances
AICV.......... Amphibious Infantry Combat Vehicle [*Army*]   (ADDR)
AID .... Aircraft Installation Delay
AID .... Arbitron's Information on Demand [*Arbitron Co.*] [*Information service or system*]   (NTCM)
AIDS.......... Apple [*Computer*] Infected Disk Syndrome   (NHD)
AIE .... Air Inuit Ltd. [*Canada*] [*ICAO designator*]   (FAAC)
AIEA.......... Association of International Education Administrators   (EA)
AIEEE .... American Institute of Electrical and Electronics Engineers [*Also, IEEE*]   (NTCM)
AIF .... Additional Information Form
AIF .... Air Ile de France [*ICAO designator*]   (FAAC)
AIF .... Altitude Instrument Flying   (DA)
AIG .... Air Inter Gabon [*ICAO designator*]   (FAAC)
AIG .... Alliance of Individual Grocers [*British*]   (BI)
AIH .... Airtours International Airways Ltd. [*British*] [*ICAO designator*]   (FAAC)
AIH .... Association of Independent Hospitals and Kindred Organisations [*British*]   (BI)
AII .... Air Integra, Inc. [*Canada*] [*ICAO designator*]   (FAAC)
AII .... American Indian Institute   (EA)
AIJ .... Air Jet [*ICAO designator*]   (FAAC)
AIK .... African Airlines International Ltd. [*Kenya*] [*ICAO designator*]   (FAAC)
AIL .... Air Illinois, Inc. [*ICAO designator*]   (FAAC)
AIM .... Agile Intelligent Manufacturing [*Computer-assisted manufacturing*]
AIM .... Ambulancias Insulares SA [*Spain*] [*ICAO designator*]   (FAAC)
AIM .... Architectural and Industrial Maintenance [*Coatings*]
AIMC .... Association of Insurance Managers in Industry and Commerce [*British*]   (BI)
AIMG .... Amnesty International Medical Group
AIMO .... Association of Industrial Medical Officers [*British*]   (BI)
AIMS.......... All-India Institute of Medial Sciences
AIMS.......... Association for Improving Moral Standards [*British*]   (BI)
AIMS.......... Association of Independent Metropolitan Stations   (NTCM)
AIN .... African International Airways [*Swaziland*] [*ICAO designator*]   (FAAC)
AIN .... Anterior Interpositus Nucleus [*Anatomy*]
AINS.......... Automotive Information Network Service
AIOA .... Aviation Insurance Officers Association   (DA)
AIP .... Alpine Aviation Inc. [*ICAO designator*]   (FAAC)
AIP .... Australia's Indigenous Peoples Party [*Political party*]
AIPCS .... Aspen Institute Program on Communications and Society   (NTCM)
AIPG .... Amnesty International Parliamentary Group
AIPO .... American Institute of Public Opinion [*Also, ARI*]   (NTCM)
AIPS .... Astronomical Information Processing System [*Computer program*]
AIR .... Airlift International, Inc. [*ICAO designator*]   (FAAC)
AIR COND ... Air Condition [*Technical drawings*]   (DAC)
AIREP .... Air Report [*Aviation*] [*ICAO designator*]   (FAAC)
AIRMLC .... All-Industry Radio Music Licensing Committee   (NTCM)
AIRS.......... Artificial Intelligence Research Support [*Program*] [*Computer science*]
AIRSAR ..... Airborne Synthetic Aperture RADAR [*Instrumentation*]
AIS............. Air Tranport School [*Former USSR*] [*ICAO designator*]   (FAAC)
AIS............. Airport in Sight   (FAAC)
AIS............. Audio Integrating System   (DA)
AISAG .... Aeronautical Information Service Automation Group [*ICAO*]   (DA)
AISAP .... Aeronautical Information Service Automation Specialist Panel [*ICAO*]   (DA)
AIT .... Advanced Instruction Technique   (DA)
AIT .... Agency for Instructional Television   (NTCM)
AIT .... American International Airways, Inc. [*ICAO designator*]   (FAAC)
AIT .... Association of Investment Trusts [*British*]   (BI)
AITS .... Association of Independent Television Stations, Inc.   (NTCM)
AIX .... Air International [*British*] [*ICAO designator*]   (FAAC)
AIYEP .... Australia-Indonesia Youth Exchange Program
AIZ .... Arkia Israel Inland Airlines [*ICAO designator*]   (FAAC)
AJ .... Adherens Junction [*Cytology*]
AJA .... AJ Services Ltd. [*British*] [*ICAO designator*]   (FAAC)
AJC............ Bar Harbor Airlines [*ICAO designator*]   (FAAC)
AJCH .... American Journal of Clinical Hypnosis [*A publication*]
AJE............ Alfa Jet [*Spain*] [*ICAO designator*]   (FAAC)
AJEA .... Australian Journal of Experimental Agriculture [*A publication*]
AJL............ Aero Jalisco SA de CV [*Mexico*] [*ICAO designator*]   (FAAC)
AJM........... Air Jamaica [*ICAO designator*]   (FAAC)
AJO .... Aero Ejecutivo SA de CV [*Mexico*] [*ICAO designator*]   (FAAC)

AJS............ Aeroejecutivos, Aeroservicios Ejecutivos [*Colombia*] [*ICAO designator*]   (FAAC)
AJT............ Amerijet International [*ICAO designator*]   (FAAC)
AKA .... Air Korea Co. Ltd. [*South Korea*] [*ICAO designator*]   (FAAC)
AKA .... Alkyl Ketene Dimer [*Organic chemistry*]
AKC .... Arca Aerovias Colombians Ltda. [*Colombia*] [*ICAO designator*]   (FAAC)
AKH........... Akhal [*Turkmenistan*] [*ICAO designator*]   (FAAC)
AKK .... Aklak Air Ltd. [*Canada*] [*ICAO designator*]   (FAAC)
AKL .... Air Kilroe Ltd. [*British*] [*ICAO designator*]   (FAAC)
AKM .... Acme [*Spain*] [*ICAO designator*]   (FAAC)
AKN .... Alkan Air Ltd. [*Canada*] [*ICAO designator*]   (FAAC)
AL .... Assignment of License [*FCC*]   (NTCM)
ALA .... International Association of Latin American Air Carriers [*ICAO designator*]   (FAAC)
ALAF .... Australian Literary Awards and Fellowships [*A publication*]
ALAPO...... Association of Local Air Pollution Control Officers [*Environmental Protection Agency*]   (ERG)
ALAR......... Association of Light Alloy Refiners and Smelters Ltd. [*British*]   (BI)
ALARP....... As Low as Reasonably Practicable [*Radiation exposure*] [*Nuclear Regulatory Commission*]
ALB .... Aero Albatros [*Mexico*] [*ICAO designator*]   (FAAC)
ALBES .... Association of London Borough Engineers and Surveyors [*British*]   (BI)
ALB/GLOB ... Albumin-Globulin Ratio [*Physiology*]   (MAH)
ALC .... Active Lane Control [*Image control and lane positioning*] [*Automotive engineering*]
ALC .... Agricultural Land Commission [*British*]   (BI)
ALC .... Southern Jersey Airways, Inc. [*ICAO designator*]   (FAAC)
ALD .... Aeronavs La Dprada SA [*Spain*] [*ICAO designator*]   (FAAC)
ALE .... Aerolineas Especiales de Colombia [*ICAO designator*]   (FAAC)
ALF .... Allied Command Europe [*ICAO designator*]   (FAAC)
ALF .... Annual License Fee [*FCC*]   (NTCM)
ALG .... Annapolis Lymphoblast Globulin [*Biochemistry*]   (MAH)
ALG .... Offshore Logistics, Inc. [*ICAO designator*]   (FAAC)
ALH .... Alpha Aviation, Inc. [*ICAO designator*]   (FAAC)
ALI............ Air Liberia [*ICAO designator*]   (FAAC)
ALJ .... Aero Leasing Italiana SpA [*Italy*] [*ICAO designator*]   (FAAC)
ALK .... Air Lanka [*Sri Lanka*] [*ICAO designator*]   (FAAC)
ALL............ Aliserio [*Italy*] [*ICAO designator*]   (FAAC)
ALM .... Antilliaanse Luchtvaart Maatschappij [*Netherlands*] [*ICAO designator*]   (FAAC)
ALMA .... Allyl Methacrylate [*Organic chemistry*]
ALN .... Air Lincoln, Inc. [*ICAO designator*]   (FAAC)
ALO .... Pennsylvania Commuter Airlines, Inc. [*ICAO designator*]   (FAAC)
ALP........... Alpliner AG [*Switzerland*] [*ICAO designator*]   (FAAC)
ALPANSA ... Alas Panamenas SA [*Panama*] [*ICAO designator*]   (FAAC)
ALQ .... Altair Aviation Ltd. [*Canada*] [*ICAO designator*]   (FAAC)
ALR .... Algarvilara Transportes Aereos Algarvios SA [*Portugal*] [*ICAO designator*]   (FAAC)
ALRM .... Alarm System [*Automotive advertising*]
ALS............ Air Alsie, AS [*Denmark*] [*ICAO designator*]   (FAAC)
ALS............ American Lithotripsy Society   (EA)
ALS............ Automatic Leveling Seat [*Automotive engineering*]
ALSB .... Advanced Logistics Support Base [*Navy*]
ALT .... Albatrosz Ltd. [*Hungary*] [*ICAO designator*]   (FAAC)
ALTN .... Alteration [*Technical drawings*]   (DAC)
ALU .... Alpine Luft-Transport AB [*Switzerland*] [*ICAO designator*]   (FAAC)
ALV .... Alarm Valve   (DAC)
ALV .... Alsavia, Societe [*France*] [*ICAO designator*]   (FAAC)
ALW .... Alas Nacionales SA [*Dominican Republic*] [*ICAO designator*]   (FAAC)
ALX .... Alitaxi SRL [*Italy*] [*ICAO designator*]   (FAAC)
ALY .... Alyeska Air Service [*ICAO designator*]   (FAAC)
ALZ .... Alta Flights Ltd. [*Canada*] [*ICAO designator*]   (FAAC)
A & M .... Art and Mechanical [*Graphics*]   (NTCM)
AMA.......... Accumulator Makers' Association [*British*]   (BI)
AMA.......... Area Minimum Altitude [*Aviation*]   (FAAC)
AMA.......... [*Alfred*] McAlpine Aviation Ltd. [*British*] [*ICAO designator*]   (FAAC)
AMB.......... Deutsche Rettungsflugwacht EV [*Germany*] [*ICAO designator*]   (FAAC)
AMC.......... Acceptable Means of Compliance   (DA)
AMC.......... Aerodynamic Mean Chord   (DA)
AMC.......... Air Malta Co. Ltd. [*ICAO designator*]   (FAAC)
AMC.......... Air Mobility Command [*Aviation*]   (FAAC)
AMCA........ Architectural Metal Craftsmen's Association [*British*]   (BI)
AMCITS .... American Citizens [*Military*]   (ADDR)
AMD.......... Acid Mine Drainage [*Mining technology*]
AMD.......... Aerolineas Medellin [*Colombia*] [*ICAO designator*]   (FAAC)
AMD.......... Air-Moving Device [*Technical drawings*]   (DAC)
AME .... Authorized Medical Examiner   (DA)
AME .... Fuerzas Aereas Espanolas [*Spain*] [*ICAO designator*]   (FAAC)
AMECUSD ... Association of Manufacturers and Exporters of Concentrated and Unconcentrated Soft Drinks [*British*]   (BI)
AMEE .... Association of Managerial Electrical Executives [*British*]   (BI)
AMEND.... Association for Relatives of the Mentally, Emotionally, and Nervously Disturbed [*British*]   (BI)
AMEU .... Automotive, Metal, and Engineering Union
AMF .... Ameriflight, Inc. [*ICAO designator*]   (FAAC)

AMFH....... Association of Memoirists and Family Historians (EA)
AMFM .... Automated Mapping/Facility Management [*Computer science*]
AMG.......... Air Material AG [*Switzerland*] [*ICAO designator*] (FAAC)
AMG.......... Ausfrech-Melcher-Grossapach [*Mercedes-Benz cars*] [*High-performance parts supplier*]
AMH .... [*Alan*] Mann Helicopters Ltd. [*British*] [*ICAO designator*] (FAAC)
AMI .... Air Maldives [*ICAO designator*] (FAAC)
AMI .... Air Mercury International [*Belgium*] [*ICAO designator*] (FAAC)
AMI .... American Methanol Institute
AMIDS....... Airport Management and Information Display System (DA)
AMII.......... Association of Musical Instrument Industries [*British*] (BI)
AMJ .... Aviation Amos [*M et J*], Inc. [*Canada*] [*ICAO designator*] (FAAC)
AMK.......... Aeromak [*Yugoslavia*] [*ICAU designator*] (FAAC)
AML.......... Air Malawi [*ICAO designator*] (FAAC)
AML.......... Association of Master Lightermen and Barge Owners [*British*] (BI)
AMM.......... Air 2000, Ltd, [*British*] [*ICAO designator*] (FAAC)
Am M......... American Music [*A publication*]
AMM.......... Association of Manipulative Medicine [*British*] (BI)
AMMO....... Audience Measurement by Market for Outdoor   (NTCM)
AMN.......... Air Montenegro [*Yugoslavia*] [*ICAO designator*] (FAAC)
AMO.......... Air Montreal, Inc. [*Canada*] [*ICAO designator*] (FAAC)
AMP .... Aero Transporte SA [*Peru*] [*ICAO designator*] (FAAC)
AMP .... Associated Music Publishers   (NTCM)
Am Phil...... Americam Philatelist [*A publication*]
AMPM .... Association of Malt Products Manufacturers [*British*] (BI)
AMPS........ Automatic Mapping and Planning System [*Environmental Protection Agency*] (ERG)
AMQ.......... Aeromedicare Ltd. [*British*] [*ICAO designator*] (FAAC)
AMR.......... Air Specialties Corp. [*ICAO designator*] (FAAC)
AMR.......... Airport Movement RADAR   (DA)
AMR.......... Anisotropic Magnetoresistance
AMRA........ Accessory Manufacturers Racing Association [*British*] (BI)
AMRO........ Association of Medical Record Officers [*British*] (BI)
AMS .... Air Muskoka [*Canada*] [*ICAO designator*] (FAAC)
AMS .... Association of Medical Secretaries [*British*] (BI)
AMS .... Automated Manifest System   (DA)
AMS .... Automated Multiphasic Screening [*Medicine*]   (MAH)
AMSE........ Association of Media Sales Executives [*British*] (BI)
AMSH........ Association for Moral and Social Hygiene [*British*] (BI)
AMSS........ Aeronautical Mobile Satellite Service [*ICAO designator*] (FAAC)
AMSSP ...... Aeronautical Mobile Satellite Service Panel [*ICAO*]   (DA)
AMT.......... American Trans Air, Inc. [*ICAO designator*] (FAAC)
AMT.......... Association of Marine Traders [*British*] (BI)
AMU.......... Amadeusair GmbH [*Austria*] [*ICAO designator*] (FAAC)
AMU.......... Association of Master Upholsterers [*British*] (BI)
AMV.......... Aircraft Maintenance Co. [*Egypt*] [*ICAO designator*] (FAAC)
Am Vis ...... American Visions [*A publication*]
AMW......... Air Midwest, Inc. [*ICAO designator*] (FAAC)
AMWE....... Average Male Weekly Earnings
AMX .... Aerovias de Mexico SA de CV [*ICAO designator*] (FAAC)
AMY .... Ambassador Airways Ltd. [*British*] [*ICAO designator*] (FAAC)
AMZ.......... Air Meuse - Dat Wallonie [*Belgium*] [*ICAO designator*] (FAAC)
An............... Anaesthetic
ANA.......... All Nippon Airways Co. Ltd. [*Japan*] [*ICAO designator*] (FAAC)
ANB........... Air Navigation & Trading Co. Ltd. [*British*] [*ICAO designator*] (FAAC)
ANC........... Anglo Cargo Ltd. [*British*] [*ICAO designator*] (FAAC)
ANC........... Asahi New Cast [*Metal fabrication*]
ANCA........ Antineutrophil Cytoplasmic Antibody [*Immunology*]
AND.......... Antenatal Diagnosis
AND........... National Jet Service, Inc. [*ICAO designator*] (FAAC)
ANE.......... Nora-2000 [*Bulgaria*] [*ICAO designator*] (FAAC)
ANF.......... Aero North Icelandic, Inc. [*ICAO designator*] (FAAC)
ANG.......... Air Niugini [*Papua New Guinea*] [*ICAO designator*] (FAAC)
ANGR........ Air Navigation (General) Regulation [*British*] (DA)
ANH .... Anair - Anich Airways [*Croatia*] [*ICAO designator*] (FAAC)
ANI........... Autism Network International   (EA)
ANJ .... Aero-Alentejo, Servicos Aereos Lda. [*Portugal*] [*ICAO designator*] (FAAC)
ANK.......... Air Nippon Co. Ltd. [*Japan*] [*ICAO designator*] (FAAC)
ANN .... Announcer   (NTCM)
ANO .... Air North Ltd. [*Australia*] [*ICAO designator*] (FAAC)
ANP .... Air Navigation Plan   (DA)
ANR .... Aeronorte SA [*Colombia*] [*ICAO designator*] (FAAC)
ANS .... Transportes Aereos Norte-Sur Ltda. [*Chile*] [*ICAO designator*] (FAAC)
ANT .... Air North Charter [*Canada*] [*ICAO designator*] (FAAC)
AntM .... Antarctic Medal
ANU .... Avionair, Inc. [*Canada*] [*ICAO designator*] (FAAC)
ANV.......... Air Nevada Airlines, Inc. [*ICAO designator*] (FAAC)
AnV........... Anisidine Value [*Food science*]
ANW.......... Aviacion del Noroeste SA de CV [*Mexico*] [*ICAO designator*] (FAAC)
ANX.......... Anax Aviation [*France*] [*ICAO designator*] (FAAC)
ANY.......... Architecture New York [*A publication*]
ANZ.......... Air New Zealand Ltd. [*ICAO designator*] (FAAC)
AO .... Aircraft Operator
AO .... Audio Operator   (NTCM)
AOA.......... Accident Offices Association [*British*] (BI)
AOA.......... Aerodrome Owners Association [*British*] (BI)

AOA........... Airport Operation Area   (DA)
AOC........... Administrative Order on Consent [*Environmental Protection Agency*] (ERG)
AOC........... American Oceans Campaign [*An association*] (EA)
AOC........... JV Avcom [*Russian Federation*] [*ICAO designator*] (FAAC)
AOCE......... Apple Open Collaboration Environment [*Computer science*] (PCM)
AOD .... Above Ordnance Datum [*Military*] (DA)
AOE........... Airport of Entry (DA)
AOH.......... North Coast Aviation, Inc. [*ICAO designator*] (FAAC)
AOJ .... Aero-Jet SA [*Switzerland*] [*ICAO designator*] (FAAC)
AOK.......... Aerovias del Atlantico Ltd. [*Colombia*] [*ICAO designator*] (FAAC)
AOL........... Air Exel Executive [*France*] [*ICAO designator*] (FAAC)
AON .... Aero Trade International [*Romania*] [*ICAO designator*] (FAAC)
AOP .... Advanced Oxidation Process [*Chemistry*]
AOP .... Aerodrome Operation (DA)
AOP .... Aeropiloto-Sociedade Exploradora de Servicos Aereos Lda. [*Portugal*] [*ICAO designator*] (FAAC)
AOP .... Association of Optical Practitioners [*British*] (BI)
AOS .... Servicios Aereos del Sol SA de CV [*Mexico*] [*ICAO designator*] (FAAC)
AOT .... Association of Occupational Therapists [*British*] (BI)
AOT .... Deutsche Forschungs-and Versuchsanstalt fur Luft EV [*Germany*] [*ICAO designator*] (FAAC)
AOTF .... Acousto-Optic Tunable Filter [*Instrumentation*]
AOTS .... Acousto-Optic Tunable Scanning [*Instrumentation*]
AOX .... Aerotaxi del Valle [*Colombia*] [*ICAO designator*] (FAAC)
AP .... [*Fire Alarm*] Annunciator Panel [*NFPA pre-fire planning symbol*]   (NFPA)
AP .... Answer Print   (NTCM)
AP .... Assignment of (Construction) Permit [*FCC*]   (NTCM)
APA .... Air Park Aviation Ltd. [*Canada*] [*ICAO designator*] (FAAC)
APA .... Amorphous Polyamide [*Organic chemistry*]
APA .... Association for Parents of Addicts [*British*] (BI)
APACHE.... Acute Physiology and Chronic Health Evaluation
APAE........ Association of Public Address Engineers [*British*] (BI)
APAP........ Approach Path Alignment Panel [*Aviation*] (FAAC)
APAPI .... Abbreviated Precision Approach Path Indicator [*Aviation*] (DA)
APB .... Air Atlantique Air Publicite [*France*] [*ICAO designator*] (FAAC)
APC .... Advertising-Press Club [*Republic of Ireland*] (BI)
APC .... Aeronautical Public Correspondence   (DA)
APC .... Airpac Airlines, Inc. [*ICAO designator*] (FAAC)
APC .... Automatic Power Control   (NTCM)
APCM........ Association of Plastic Cable Makers [*British*] (BI)
APCO........ Association of Pleasure Craft Operators [*British*] (BI)
APCP........ Advance Prediction Computer Program
APCT........ Association of Piano Class Teachers [*British*] (BI)
APD .... Alloy Phase Diagram
APD .... Asia Pacific Distribution [*Australia*] [*ICAO designator*] (FAAC)
APD .... Automated Percutaneous Discectomy [*Spinal surgery*]
APE .... Air Parcel Express [*ICAO designator*] (FAAC)
APEG........ Asia Pacific Economic Group
APEX........ Advance Purchase Excursion Fare [*Aviation*]   (DA)
APF........... Asia-Pacific Fellowship
APF........... Transporte de Carga Aeropacifico SA de CV [*Mexico*] [*ICAO designator*] (FAAC)
APFO......... Association of Playing Fields' Officers [*British*] (BI)
APFT .... Army Physical Fitness Training   (ADDR)
APG .... Aerotaxis Pegaso SA de CV [*Mexico*] [*ICAO designator*] (FAAC)
APH.......... Air Power History [*A publication*]
APH.......... Alpha Aviation, Inc. [*ICAO designator*] (FAAC)
APHAZ....... Aircraft Proximity Hazard   (DA)
APHI......... Animal and Plant Health Inspection Service
API........... Air Panama Internacional [*ICAO designator*] (FAAC)
APICM....... Antipersonnel Improved Conventional Munitions [*Army*]   (ADDR)
APK .... Asia Pacific Air Cargo PTE Ltd. [*Singapore*] [*ICAO designator*] (FAAC)
APL........... Annular Pressure Loss [*Well drilling technology*]
APL........... Appalachian Flying Service, Inc. [*ICAO designator*] (FAAC)
APL........... Assignment of (Construction) Permit and License [*FCC*]   (NTCM)
APLE........ Association of Public Lighting Engineers [*British*] (BI)
APM .... Absolute Plate Motion [*Geophysics*]
APM .... Air Pacific Airlines [*ICAO designator*] (FAAC)
APM .... Alliance for a Paving Moratorium   (EA)
APM .... Attached Pressurized Module [*European Space Agency*]
APN .... Aerovia del Altiplano SA de CV [*Mexico*] [*ICAO designator*] (FAAC)
APO .... Aeropro [*Canada*] [*ICAO designator*] (FAAC)
APOC .... Anglia and Prefect Owners' Club [*British*] (BI)
APP........... Aerolineas Pacifico Atlantico SA [*Spain*] [*ICAO designator*] (FAAC)
APPCS....... Association of Parents Paying Child Support   (EA)
APPL......... Aircraft Precision Position Location Equipment   (DA)
APP-R........ Approach Control RADAR   (DA)
APQ.......... Air Philippines Corporation, Inc. [*ICAO designator*] (FAAC)
APR .... Association for Promoting Retreats [*British*] (BI)
APR .... Societe Nouvelle d'Exploitation Air Provence [*France*] [*ICAO designator*] (FAAC)
APRA......... Air Public Relations Association [*British*] (BI)
APRF......... Acute-Phase Response Factor [*Biochemistry*]

APRL......... Association for the Preservation of Rural Life [*British*]   (BI)
APRN .... Associated Press Radio Network   (NTCM)
APRS......... Association for the Preservation of Rural Scotland   (BI)
APRS......... Association of Professional Recording Studios Ltd. [*British*]   (BI)
APS............ Aerotransporte Peruanos Internacionales SA [*Peru*] [*ICAO designator*]   (FAAC)
APSW........ Association of Psychiatric Social Workers [*British*]   (BI)
APT .... Association of Private Traders [*British*]   (BI)
APT .... Lineas Aereas Petroleras [*Colombia*] [*ICAO designator*]   (FAAC)
APTS......... Advanced Public Transportation Systems
APU .... Aeropuma SA [*El Salvador*] [*ICAO designator*]   (FAAC)
APW .... Arrow Airways, Inc. [*ICAO designator*]   (FAAC)
APWI........ Airborne Proximity Warning Indicator   (DA)
APX .... Ad-Page Exposure   (NTCM)
APX .... Apex Air Cargo [*ICAO designator*]   (FAAC)
APY .... APA Internacional [*Dominican Republic*] [*ICAO designator*]   (FAAC)
AQ............. As Quoted [*Business term*]
AQA........... Accredited Quality Assurance
AQA........... Approved Quality Assurance
AQE .... Air Aquitaine [*France*] [*ICAO designator*]   (FAAC)
AQF .... Advanced Quickfix [*Military*]
AQIRP....... Air Quality Improvement Research Program [*Automotive industry, research consortium*]
AQL .... Aquila Air Ltd. [*Canada*] [*ICAO designator*]   (FAAC)
AQN .... Air Queensland [*Australia*] [*ICAO designator*]   (FAAC)
AQU .... Aquair Luftfahrt GmbH [*Germany*] [*ICAO designator*]   (FAAC)
AQU .... Aquarius [*Constellation*]
AQZ .... Aerodyne Charter [*ICAO designator*]   (FAAC)
A/R........... Altitude Reporting   (DA)
AR.............. As Rolled [*Technical drawings*]   (DAC)
AR.............. Assisted Resonance   (NTCM)
AR.............. Atlantic Route [*Aviation*]   (FAAC)
AR.............. Audience Research   (NTCM)
ARA .... Aerial Ropeways Association [*British*]   (BI)
ARA .... Aerobeira, Sociedade de Transportes Aeros [*Portugal*] [*ICAO designator*]   (FAAC)
ARA .... Asphalt Roads Association [*British*]   (BI)
ARA .... Association of River Authorities [*British*]   (BI)
ARA .... Automotive Recyclers Association [*Salvage yards*]
ARB .... Arubair [*Aruba*] [*ICAO designator*]   (FAAC)
ARC .... Air Routing International Corp. [*ICAO designator*]   (FAAC)
ARCH........ Automatic Remote Cassette Handler   (NTCM)
ARCP........ Aerodrome Reference Code Panel [*ICAO*]   (DA)
ARCS....... Airline Request Communication System   (DA)
ARCUS...... Arctic Research Consortium of the United States
ARD .... Acid Rock Draining [*Mining technology*]
ARD .... Ata-Aerocondor Transportes Aereos Ltda. [*Portugal*] [*ICAO designator*]   (FAAC)
ARDCS...... Association of Rural District Council Surveyors [*British*]   (BI)
ARDI .... Association of Registered Driving Instructors [*British*]   (BI)
ARE .... Aires, Aerovias de Integracion Regional SA [*Colombia*] [*ICAO designator*]   (FAAC)
ARE .... Airline Revenue   (DA)
AResA........ Army Reserve Association
ARF .... Aerofer, SL [*Spain*] [*ICAO designator*]   (FAAC)
ARFF .... Aircraft Rescue and Fire Fighting [*Air Traffic Control*]   (FAAC)
ARFOR...... Area Forecast   (DA)
ARG .... Aerolineas Argentinas [*Argentina*] [*ICAO designator*]   (FAAC)
ARH.......... Antigenreceptor Homology [*Immunochemistry*]
ARH.......... Arrowhead Airways [*ICAO designator*]   (FAAC)
ARI .... Aero Vics SA de CV [*Mexico*] [*ICAO designator*]   (FAAC)
ARI .... Approved Research Institute
ARI .... Audience Research Institute [*Also, AIPO*]   (NTCM)
ARJ.......... Aerojet de Costa Rica SA [*ICAO designator*]   (FAAC)
ARK.......... Air Corse [*France*] [*ICAO designator*]   (FAAC)
ARL .... Airlec [*France*] [*ICAO designator*]   (FAAC)
ARLIS ...... Art Libraries Society [*British*]   (BI)
ARM.......... Advanced RISC [*Reduced Instruction-Set Computerizing*] Machine   (ECON)
ARM.......... Aeromarket Express [*Spain*] [*ICAO designator*]   (FAAC)
ARMS........ All-Radio Methodology Study [*Audience ratings*]   (NTCM)
ARMS........ Army Master Data File Retrieval Microform System
ARN .... Air Nova, Inc. [*Canada*] [*ICAO designator*]   (FAAC)
ARO.......... Arrow Aviation Ltd. [*Canada*] [*ICAO designator*]   (FAAC)
ARO.......... Audio Receive Only   (NTCM)
ARO.......... Authorized Review Officer
AROP .... Association pour le Rayonnement de l'Opera de Paris [*France*]
AROTC...... Army Reserve Officers Training Corps   (AEE)
ARP .... Adjustable Rear Plate [*Air conditioning systems*] [*Automotive engineering*]
ARP .... Societe d'Exploitation Aeropostale [*France*] [*ICAO designator*]   (FAAC)
ARPMV...... Advanced Road Profile Measurement Vehicle [*Suspension design and testing*] [*Automotive engineering*]
ARPO .... Association of Resort Publicity Officers [*British*]   (BI)
ARQ.......... Armstrong Air, Inc. [*Canada*] [*ICAO designator*]   (FAAC)
ARQ.......... Automatic Retransmission Request for Correction [*Computer science*]   (NTCM)
ARR .... Advanced Robotics Research
ARR .... Aerora SA [*Mexico*] [*ICAO designator*]   (FAAC)
ARRE........ Auto Read Reallocation [*Computer science*]
ARRS......... Adverse Reactions Reporting System [*FDA*]

ARS............ Active Roll Stabilization [*Automotive suspension*]
ARS............ Air Sardinia International [*ICAO designator*]   (FAAC)
ARSD......... Association of Road Surface Dressing Contractors [*British*]   (BI)
ARST......... Arrest   (FAAC)
ART .... Achilles Tendon Reflex Test [*Medicine*]   (MAH)
ART .... Aerotal Aerolineas Territoriales de Colombia Ltd. [*ICAO designator*]   (FAAC)
Art Asiae... Artibus Asiae [*A publication*]
ARTYMET ... Artillery Meteorological Team [*Army*]   (ADDR)
ARU........... Administrative Reform Unit
ARU........... Air Aruba [*ICAO designator*]   (FAAC)
ARU........... Airborne RADAR Unit [*Aviation*]   (FAAC)
ARU........... Airspace Reservation Unit [*Canada*]   (FAAC)
ARV........... Aravco Ltd. [*British*] [*ICAO designator*]   (FAAC)
ARW.......... Arrows Ltd. [*British*] [*ICAO designator*]   (FAAC)
ARX........... Air Express, Inc. [*ICAO designator*]   (FAAC)
ARY .... Argosy Airways [*Canada*] [*ICAO designator*]   (FAAC)
ARZ .... Air Resorts [*ICAO designator*]   (FAAC)
AS .... Angle Shot [*Cinematography*]   (NTCM)
AS .... Angled Single [*Outdoor advertising*]   (NTCM)
AS .... Association of Surgeons of Great Britain and Ireland   (BI)
ASA........... Acrylonitrile Styrene Acrylate [*Plastics*] [*Organic chemistry*]
ASA........... Air Services Agreement   (DA)
ASA........... Air Starline AG [*Switzerland*] [*ICAO designator*]   (FAAC)
ASA........... Alaska Airlines, Inc. [*ICAO designator*]   (FAAC)
ASA........... Alkenyl Succinic Anhydride [*Organic chemistry*]
ASAP......... American Society of Advertising and Promotion, Inc.   (NTCM)
ASB............ Air-Spray 1967 Ltd. [*Canada*] [*ICAO designator*]   (FAAC)
ASB............ Artists' Service Bureau   (NTCM)
ASC............ Air Star Corp. [*Canada*] [*ICAO designator*]   (FAAC)
ASC............ Asphalt Surface Course   (DAC)
ASC............ Assistant Sector Controller [*Aviation*]   (DA)
ASC............ Axial Summit Caldera [*Volcanology*]
ASCA......... Advanced Satellite for Cosmology and Astrophysics [*Japanese spacecraft*]
ASCAP ...... Aeronautical Satellite Communications Processor   (DA)
ASCB......... Avionics Standard Communications Bus   (DA)
ASCC......... Association of Scottish Climbing Clubs   (BI)
ASCF......... Application Specific Coding Flag   (NTCM)
ASCIM...... Association of Casing Importers Ltd. [*British*]   (BI)
ASCM........ Association of Ships' Compositions Manufacturers [*British*]   (BI)
ASCT......... Association of String Class Teachers [*British*]   (BI)
ASD .... Air Sinai [*Egypt*] [*ICAO designator*]   (FAAC)
ASDM .... Association of Steel Drum Manufacturers [*British*]   (BI)
ASE........... Altimetry System Error [*Aviation*]   (DA)
ASE........... Association for Special Education [*British*]   (BI)
ASE........... Atlantic Southeast Airlines, Inc. [*ICAO designator*]   (FAAC)
ASEA......... Agricultural Show Exhibitors' Association [*British*]   (BI)
ASED......... Army School of Education and Depot [*British*]   (BI)
ASEE......... American Society of Electrical Engineers   (NTCM)
ASERCA .... Aeroservicios Carabobo CA [*Venezuela*] [*ICAO designator*]   (FAAC)
ASF........... Air Schefferville, Inc. [*Canada*] [*ICAO designator*]   (FAAC)
ASF........... Audi Space Frame [*Concept car*] [*Automotive engineering*]
ASFAP ...... AIDS Society for Asia and the Pacific
ASFP......... Association of Specialised Film Producers [*British*]   (BI)
ASGB........ Adlerian Society of Great Britain   (BI)
ASGB........ Aeronautical Society of Great Britain   (BI)
ASGPR...... Asialoglycoprotein Receptor [*Biochemistry*]
ASH .... Mesa Airlines, Inc. [*ICAO designator*]   (FAAC)
ASI........... AeroSun International, Inc. [*ICAO designator*]   (FAAC)
ASI........... Amperes per Square Inch [*Electrochemistry*]
ASJ........... Air Satellite, Inc. [*Canada*] [*ICAO designator*]   (FAAC)
ASK .... Sudania Aviation Co. [*Sudan*] [*ICAO designator*]   (FAAC)
ASKNG ...... Asking [*Automotive advertising*]
ASL........... Spurling Aviation [*ICAO designator*]   (FAAC)
ASLEC ...... Association of Street Lighting Erection Contractors [*British*]   (BI)
ASM .... Ad Hoc Schedule Message   (DA)
ASM .... Airspace Management   (DA)
ASM .... SCTA Air St. Martin [*ICAO designator*]   (FAAC)
ASMT........ Airspace Management   (DA)
ASN .... Advanced Shipment Notification [*Inventory control*] [*Automotive manufacturing*]
ASN .... Air Services Nantes [*France*] [*ICAO designator*]   (FAAC)
ASO .... Air Sarthe Organisation - Societe [*France*] [*ICAO designator*]   (FAAC)
ASOC .... Administrative Service Officer Class
AsOCOA .... Asia-Oceania Clinical Oncology Association
AsOFNM ... Asia-Oceania Federation of Nuclear Medicine
ASOS......... Administrative Service Officer Structure
ASOS......... Automated Surface Observing System [*Meteorology*]   (FAAC)
AS-OUR..... Anti-Saccade Oculomotor Delayed Response [*Neurobiology*]
ASP........... Aircraft Servicing Platform   (DA)
ASP........... All-Source Production [*Army*]   (ADDR)
AsPALMS ... Asian-Pacific Association of LASER Medical Surgery
AsPASL..... Asian-Pacific Association for the Study of the Liver
AsPAvMA ... Asia-Pacific Aviation Medicine Association
ASPC......... Association of Swimming Pool Contractors [*British*]   (BI)
AsPCDE..... Asian-Pacific Society for Digestive Endoscopy
ASPH .... Asphalt   (DA)
ASPP .... Aeronautical Fixed Systems Planning for Data Interchange Panel [*ICAO*]   (DA)
ASPS .... All-Source Production Section [*Army*]   (ADDR)

AsPSC .... Asian-Pacific Society of Cardiology
AsPSIR .... Asia-Pacific Society for Impotence Research
AsPSN .... Asian-Pacific Society of Nephrology
AsPSPGN ... Asian-Pacific Society of Paediatric Gastroenterology and Nutrition
ASQ .... Air Service [*Poland*] [*ICAO designator*]   (FAAC)
ASR .... All Star Airlines, Inc. [*ICAO designator*]   (FAAC)
ASR .... Automatic Sequence Register   (NTCM)
ASSM .... Association of Shopfront Section Manufacturers [*British*]   (BI)
ASSR .... Airport Surface Surveillance RADAR   (DA)
AST .... Administrative Service Test
AST .... Aerolineas del Oeste SA de CV [*Mexico*] [*ICAO designator*]   (FAAC)
AST .... Automated Screen Trading [*Business term*]
AST .... Automatic Scan Tracking [*Videotape head*]   (NTCM)
ASTA .... Advertiser Syndicated Television Association   (NTCM)
ASTA .... American Scouting Traders Association   (EA)
ASTA .... Association of Short-Circuit Testing Authorities, Inc. [*British*]   (BI)
ASTERIX ... All Purpose Structure Eurocontrol RADAR Information Exchange   (DA)
ASTEX .... Atlantic Stratocumulus Transition Experiment [*Meteorology*]
ASTI .... Association of Secondary Teachers, Ireland   (BI)
ASTRA .... Applications of Space Technology Panel to Requirements of Civil Aviation [*ICAO*]   (DA)
ASTRO .... Amalgamated Slaters, Tilers and Roofing Operatives Society [*British*]   (BI)
ASU .... Compania Aerea del Sur SA [*Uruguay*] [*ICAO designator*]   (FAAC)
ASV .... Advanced Safety Vehicle [*Automotive engineering*]
ASV .... Air Savoie [*France*] [*ICAO designator*]   (FAAC)
ASW .... Air Southwest [*Canada*] [*ICAO designator*]   (FAAC)
ASW .... Amalgamated Society of Woodworkers [*British*]   (BI)
ASW .... Association of Social Workers [*British*]   (BI)
ASWA .... Antiskywave Antenna   (NTCM)
ASWB .... Association of Solid Woven Belting Manufacturers [*British*]   (BI)
ASWM .... Amalgamated Society of Woodcutting Machinists [*British*]   (BI)
ASWP .... American Society of Wedding Professionals   (EA)
ASX .... Air Special [*Czechoslovakia*] [*ICAO designator*]   (FAAC)
ASY .... Royal Australian Air Force [*ICAO designator*]   (FAAC)
ASZ .... Air Sardinia SpA [*Italy*] [*ICAO designator*]   (FAAC)
AT .... Activity Test
AT .... Antiterrorism [*Measure*] [*DoD*]
AT .... Attention [*Electronics*]
ATA .... Air Training Association [*British*]   (DA)
ATA .... Airline Tariff Analysis   (DA)
ATA .... Alternate Training Assemby [*Army*]   (ADDR)
ATA .... Amusement Trades Association [*British*]   (BI)
ATA .... Auction Transfer Authority
ATAA .... Air Transport Auxiliary Association   (DA)
ATAFG .... African Region Traffic Analysis Forecasting Group [*ICAO*]   (DA)
ATAM .... At and Maintain [*Aviation*]   (FAAC)
ATAWT ...... Aerodynamics-Thermodynamics-Acoustic Wind Tunnel [*Automotive research*]
ATB .... Atlantair Ltd. [*Canada*] [*ICAO designator*]   (FAAC)
ATBI .... All Taxa Biodiversity Inventory [*Proposed*] [*National Science Foundation*]
ATC .... Air Tanzania [*ICAO designator*]   (FAAC)
ATC .... Architectural Terra-Cotta [*Technical drawings*]   (DAC)
ATCA .... Air Traffic Control Advises   (FAAC)
ATCA .... Air Traffic Control Assistant   (DA)
ATCALS ..... Air Traffic Control and Landing System [*DoD*]
ATCC .... Air Traffic Control Clears   (FAAC)
ATCPROSAT ... Air Traffic Control Project for Satellite   (DA)
ATCR .... Air Traffic Control Request   (FAAC)
ATD .... Aerotours Dominican, C por A [*Dominican Republic*] [*ICAO designator*]   (FAAC)
ATD .... Air Traffic Division [*Air Traffic Control*]   (FAAC)
ATD .... Anthropometric Test Device [*Automotive safety*]
ATD .... Arrival Time Distribution [*Instrumentation*]
ATD .... Automatic Threat Detection System [*Aviation*]   (DA)
ATD .... Automatic Timing Device [*Diesel engines*]
ATDS .... Association of Teachers of Domestic Science [*British*]   (BI)
ATE .... Air Traffic Engineer [*British*]   (DA)
ATE .... Atlantis Transportation Services Ltd. [*Canada*] [*ICAO designator*]   (FAAC)
ATEM .... Air Traffic Flow Management [*ICAO designator*]   (FAAC)
ATES .... Association for Technical Education in Schools [*British*]   (BI)
ATF .... Compania Aerotecnicas Fotograficas [*Spain*] [*ICAO designator*]   (FAAC)
ATFC .... American-Turkish Friendship Council   (EA)
ATFGF .... Association of Toy and Fancy Goods Factors [*British*]   (BI)
ATFM .... Air Traffic Flow Management   (DA)
ATFMU ...... Air Traffic Flow Management Unit   (DA)
ATH .... Air Travel Corp. [*ICAO designator*]   (FAAC)
ATI .... Aero Transporti Italiani SpA [*Italy*] [*ICAO designator*]   (FAAC)
ATIS .... Advanced Travel Information Systems [*Formerly, ADI*] [*Highway safety research*]
ATIS .... Air Traffic Information Service   (DA)
ATISS .... Advanced Traffic Information Supply System [*Highway traffic management*]
ATITA .... Air Transport Industry Training Association   (DA)
ATJ .... Air Traffic GmbH [*Germany*] [*ICAO designator*]   (FAAC)
ATK .... Aerotaxi Casanare Ltda. [*Colombia*] [*ICAO designator*]   (FAAC)

ATKHB ...... Attack Helicopter Battalion [*Army*]   (ADDR)
ATL .... Air Atlantic [*Canada*] [*ICAO designator*]   (FAAC)
ATM .... Airlines of Tasmania [*Australia*] [*ICAO designator*]   (FAAC)
ATM .... Airspace and Traffic Management [*ICAO*]   (DA)
ATMC .... Airspace and Traffic Management Center   (DA)
ATN .... Air Transport International [*ICAO designator*]   (FAAC)
ATO .... Air Tonga [*ICAO designator*]   (FAAC)
ATO .... Approved Test Officer
ATOC .... Acoustic Thermometry of Ocean Climate [*International oceanographic project*]
ATP .... Advanced Technology Park
ATP .... Aerotransportes Especiales Ltda. [*Colombia*] [*ICAO designator*]   (FAAC)
ATPM .... Association of Toilet Paper Manufacturers [*British*]   (BI)
ATPM .... Association of Touring and Production Managers [*British*]   (BI)
ATQ .... Air Transport Schiphol [*Netherlands*] [*ICAO designator*]   (FAAC)
ATR .... Atlas Airlines [*ICAO designator*]   (FAAC)
ATRP .... Air Transport Regulation Panel [*ICAO*]   (DA)
ATS .... Advanced Television Services [*FCC*]   (NTCM)
ATS .... Advanced Turbo Systems [*Automotive industry supplier*]
ATS .... Air Transport Service [*Zaire*] [*ICAO designator*]   (FAAC)
ATS .... American Television Society   (NTCM)
ATS .... Authorized Terminal Strength
ATS .... Automated Telecommunications System [*Army*]   (ADDR)
ATS .... Automatic Transmission System [*Telecommunications*]   (NTCM)
ATS .... Aviation Transport Services [*Italy*] [*ICAO designator*]   (FAAC)
ATSC .... Advanced Television Systems Committee [*FCC*]   (NTCM)
ATSORA ..... Air Traffic Services Outside Regulated Airspace [*British*]   (DA)
ATSPM .... Air Traffic Services Planning Manual   (DA)
ATT .... Aer Turas Teoranta [*Republic of Ireland*] [*ICAO designator*]   (FAAC)
ATTU .... Air Transportable Telecommunications Unit
ATU .... Air Toulon [*France*] [*ICAO designator*]   (FAAC)
ATUA .... Air Transport Users' Association [*British*]   (DA)
ATV .... Avanti Air [*Austria*] [*ICAO designator*]   (FAAC)
ATVI .... Australia Television International
ATW .... Aero Trades (Western) Ltd. [*Canada*] [*ICAO designator*]   (FAAC)
ATX .... Birmingham Aviation Ltd. [*British*] [*ICAO designator*]   (FAAC)
ATY .... International Airports Authority of India [*ICAO designator*]   (FAAC)
ATZ .... Air Service Training Ltd. [*British*] [*ICAO designator*]   (FAAC)
AUA .... Austrian Airlines [*ICAO designator*]   (FAAC)
AUC .... Ab Urbe Condite [*From the Year of the Founding*] [*Latin*]
AUC .... ADT Aviation Ltd. [*British*] [*ICAO designator*]   (FAAC)
AUD .... Audi Air, Inc. [*ICAO designator*]   (FAAC)
AUD .... Auditorium   (DAC)
AUG .... CPA Cesar Augusto de la Cruze Lepe [*Mexico*] [*ICAO designator*]   (FAAC)
AUGB .... Association of Ukrainians in Great Britain Ltd.   (BI)
AUI .... Air Ukraine International [*ICAO designator*]   (FAAC)
Au(l) .... Australia Antigen [*Medicine*]   (MAH)
AUM .... Air Atlantic Uruguay [*ICAO designator*]   (FAAC)
AUN .... Aviones Unidos SA de CV [*Mexico*] [*ICAO designator*]   (FAAC)
AUO .... Empresa Aero Uruguay SA [*ICAO designator*]   (FAAC)
AUP .... Acceptable Use Policy
AUR .... Aurigny Air Services Ltd. [*British*] [*ICAO designator*]   (FAAC)
AURP .... Apple-Talk Update-Based Routing Protocol [*Computer science*]
AUS .... Australian Airlines [*ICAO designator*]   (FAAC)
AUT .... Austral Lineas Aereas [*Argentina*] [*ICAO designator*]   (FAAC)
AUT-ATFM ... Automation on Air Traffic Flow Management   (DA)
AUTM .... Association of Unit Trust Managers [*British*]   (BI)
AUTM .... Association of Used Tyre Merchants [*British*]   (BI)
AUTOPROC ... Automatic Procurement Capability System
AUY .... Aerolinas Uruguayas SA [*Uruguay*] [*ICAO designator*]   (FAAC)
AUZ .... Aus-Air [*Australia*] [*ICAO designator*]   (FAAC)
AV .... Abbreviated Visual Approach Slope Indicator System [*Aviation*]   (DA)
AVA .... Amateur Volleyball Association [*British*]   (BI)
AVA .... Avianca, Aerovias Nacionales de Colombia SA [*ICAO designator*]   (FAAC)
AVAD .... Automatic Voice Alerting Device   (DA)
AVB .... Aviation Beauport Ltd. [*British*] [*ICAO designator*]   (FAAC)
AVC .... Aeronautica Venezolana, CA [*Venezuela*] [*ICAO designator*]   (FAAC)
AVD .... Air Vendee [*France*] [*ICAO designator*]   (FAAC)
AVE .... Association of Vermiculite Exfoliators Ltd. [*British*]   (BI)
AVE .... Avensa Aerovias Venezolanas SA [*Venezuela*] [*ICAO designator*]   (FAAC)
AVESCA ..... Aerovias Especiales de Carga Ltda. [*Colombia*] [*ICAO designator*]   (FAAC)
AVF .... Aviair Aviation Ltd. [*Canada*] [*ICAO designator*]   (FAAC)
AVG .... Association of Voluntary Groups [*Republic of Ireland*]   (BI)
AVG .... Avialgarve, Taxis Aereos do Algarve Ltd. [*Portugal*] [*ICAO designator*]   (FAAC)
AVH .... Aviser SA [*Spain*] [*ICAO designator*]   (FAAC)
AVI .... Advanced Vehicle Identification
AVI .... Aviorrenta SA [*Mexico*] [*ICAO designator*]   (FAAC)
AVIC .... Aviation Industries of China   (ECON)
AVJ .... Aeroviajes Ejecutvos SA de CV [*Mexico*] [*ICAO designator*]   (FAAC)
AVL .... Aerovial [*Chile*] [*ICAO designator*]   (FAAC)
AVLS .... Automatic Vehicle Location System   (DA)

AVM........... Aviacion Ejecutiva Mexicana SA [*Mexico*] [*ICAO designator*]
     (FAAC)
AVMA........ Automatic Vending Machine Association [*British*] (BI)
AVN............ Air Vanuatu [*ICAO designator*] (FAAC)
AVO........... Aerovias Oaxaquenas SA [*Mexico*] [*ICAO designator*] (FAAC)
AVP .... Aviation Enterprises [*Denmark*] [*ICAO designator*] (FAAC)
AVQ........... Aviation Services, Inc. [*ICAO designator*] (FAAC)
AVR............ Avior Pty Ltd. [*Australia*] [*ICAO designator*] (FAAC)
AVS .... Association of Veterinary Students of Great Britain and Ireland
     (BI)
AVS .... Aviation Seychelles Ltd. [*ICAO designator*] (FAAC)
AVSEC .... Aviation Security Panel [*ICAO*] (DA)
AVT .... Active Valve Train [*Automotive engineering*]
AVT .... Allen Vision Test (MAH)
AVT .... ATS Aircharter Ltd. [*British*] [*ICAO designator*] (FAAC)
AVU........... Avia Sud [*France*] [*ICAO designator*] (FAAC)
AVV........... AirVantage, Inc. [*ICAO designator*] (FAAC)
AVW.......... Aviator SA [*Greece*] [*ICAO designator*] (FAAC)
AVX........... Avcon AG [*Switzerland*] [*ICAO designator*] (FAAC)
AW............. Aerodrome Warning (DA)
AWA.......... African West Air [*Senegal*] [*ICAO designator*] (FAAC)
AWAG....... American Woman above Ground [*Lifestyle classification*]
AWB.......... Airways International, Inc. [*ICAO designator*] (FAAC)
AWC.......... All-Wheel Control [*Mitsubishi*] [*Transmisssion systems*]
AWC........... Titan Airways Ltd. [*British*] [*ICAO designator*] (FAAC)
AWE.......... America West Airlines [*ICAO designator*] (FAAC)
AWF .... Arab Air Cargo [*Jordan*] [*ICAO designator*] (FAAC)
AWG.......... Airtaxi Wings AG [*Switzerland*] [*ICAO designator*] (FAAC)
AWI........... Air Wisconsin [*ICAO designator*] (FAAC)
AWK.......... Airwork Service Training [*British*] [*ICAO designator*] (FAAC)
AWL.......... Association of Women Launderers [*British*] (BI)
AWLLA...... All Wales Ladies Lacrosse Association (BI)
AWLTNI.... Association of the Wholesale Licensed Trade of Northern
     Ireland (BI)
AWN........... Air Niger [*ICAO designator*] (FAAC)
AWO.......... All Weather Operations (DA)
AWO.......... Association of Waterworks Officers [*British*] (BI)
AWO.......... Awood Air Ltd. [*Canada*] [*ICAO designator*] (FAAC)
AWP .... Aviation Weather Processor [*ICAO designator*] (FAAC)
AWR.......... Adventist World Radio (NTCM)
AWS .... All Wood Screw (DAC)
AWS .... Annual Work Schedule
AWS .... Arab Wings Co. [*Jordan*] [*ICAO designator*] (FAAC)
AWS .... Association of Women Surgeons (EA)
AWT .... Air West [*Canada*] [*ICAO designator*] (FAAC)
AWV.......... Airwave Transport, Inc. [*Canada*] [*ICAO designator*] (FAAC)
AWW.......... Alert Weather Watch [*Meteorology*] (DA)
AWWI .... American Wood Window Institute (DAC)
AWWM...... Association of Wholesale Woollen Merchants Ltd. [*British*] (BI)
A/X .... Armani Exchange (ECON)
AXE .... Executive Air [*Zimbabwe*] [*ICAO designator*] (FAAC)
AXI .... Aeron International Airlines, Inc. [*ICAO designator*] (FAAC)
AXL .... Air Exel Netherlands BV [*ICAO designator*] (FAAC)
AXP .... Air Express AS [*Norway*] [*ICAO designator*] (FAAC)
AXQ........... JIB, Inc. [*ICAO designator*] (FAAC)
AXR .... Axel Rent SA [*Mexico*] [*ICAO designator*] (FAAC)
AXS............ Altus Airlines [*ICAO designator*] (FAAC)
AXV-V .... Advanced Experimental Vehicle - 5th Generation [*Toyota*]
AXX........... Avioimpex [*Yugoslavia*] [*ICAO designator*] (FAAC)
AYA........... Federal Aviation Administration [*ICAO designator*] (FAAC)
AYC........... Aviacion y Comercio SA [*Spain*] [*ICAO designator*] (FAAC)
AYR........... British Aerospace Flying College Ltd. [*ICAO designator*] (FAAC)
AZA .... Alitalia-Linee Aeree Italiane SpA [*Italy*] [*ICAO designator*]
     (FAAC)
AZB .... Azamat [*Kazakhstan*] [*ICAO designator*] (FAAC)
AZE .... Arcus-Air-Logistic GmbH [*Germany*] [*ICAO designator*]
     (FAAC)
AZL .... Air Zanzibar [*Tanzania*] [*ICAO designator*] (FAAC)
AZM........... Aerocozumel SA [*Mexico*] [*ICAO designator*] (FAAC)
AZP .... Arizona Pacific Airways [*Arizona Flight School, Inc.*] [*ICAO
     designator*] (FAAC)
AZR .... Air Zaire, Societe [*ICAO designator*] (FAAC)
AZT .... Azimut SA [*Spain*] [*ICAO designator*] (FAAC)
AZU........... Air Star Zanzibar [*Tanzania*] [*ICAO designator*] (FAAC)
AZUR........ Azauridine [*Organic chemistry*] (MAH)
AZV .... Zodiac Air [*Bulgaria*] [*ICAO designator*] (FAAC)
AZW.......... Air Zimbabwe [*ICAO designator*] (FAAC)
AZY .... Arizona Airways, Inc. [*ICAO designator*] (FAAC)

B

B .... Bell (NFPA)
B .... Broadcast [*FCC*] (NTCM)
3B .... Mauritius [*Aircraft nationality and registration mark*] (FAAC)
BA .... Bathroom [*Classified advertising*]
BA .... Berkeley Association (EA)
BA .... Billiards Association [*British*] (BI)
BA .... Bolshoi Ballet Academy [*Former USSR*]
BA .... Bright Annealed (DAC)
BA .... British Association for the Advancement of Science (BI)
B of A .... Bureau of Advertising [*American Newspaper Publishers Association*] (NTCM)
BAA .... Booking Agents Association of Great Britain Ltd. (BI)
BAA .... Bordeaux Agents Association [*British*] (BI)
BAA .... Bosnaair [*Yugoslavia*] [*ICAO designator*] (FAAC)
BAA .... British Acetylene Association (BI)
BAA .... British Alsatian Association (BI)
BAA .... British Association of Accountants and Auditors (BI)
BAACMIR ... British Aerospace Air Combat Maneuvering Instrumentation Range (DA)
BAAEMS ... British Association of Airport Equipment Manufacturers and Services (DA)
BABS .... British Aluminium Building Service (BI)
BAC .... Bateria Artifical Chromosome [*Genetics*]
BACAH ...... British Association of Consultants in Agriculture and Horticulture (BI)
BACMA ..... British Aromatic Compounds Manufacturers' Association (BI)
BACMA ..... British Artists' Colour Manufacturers' Association (BI)
BACS......... Beacon Collision Avoidance System [*Aviation*] (DA)
BAD........... Broken as Designed [*Computer hacker terminology*] (NHD)
BAE .... Board of Architectural Education [*British*] (BI)
BAE .... British Aerospace PLC [*ICAO designator*] (FAAC)
BAF........... British Air Ferries Ltd. [*ICAO designator*] (FAAC)
BAFRA ...... British Aluminium Foil Rollers Association (BI)
BAG .... Broad Audit Guidelines
BAG .... Deutsche Ba Luftfahrtgesellschaft MBH [*Germany*] [*ICAO designator*] (FAAC)
BAH.......... Amiri Flight-Bahrain [*ICAO designator*] (FAAC)
BAI .... Barair SA [*Spain*] [*ICAO designator*] (FAAC)
BAI .... Basic Area of Interest [*Army*] (ADDR)
BAICO....... Bendix Atlantic Inflator Co. [*Automotive industry supplier*]
BAJ........... Baker Aviation, Inc. [*ICAO designator*] (FAAC)
BAK .... Blackhawk Airways, Inc. [*ICAO designator*] (FAAC)
BAK .... Bundesaufsichtsamt fuer das Kreditwesen [*Federal Supervisory Office for Credit*] [*Germany*]
BAL .... Benzaldehyde [*Organic chemistry*]
BAL .... Britannia Airways Ltd. [*British*] [*ICAO designator*] (FAAC)
BALF......... Bronchoalveolar Lavage Fluid [*Medicine*]
BAM.......... Basic and Applied Myology [*A publication*]
BAM.......... Business Air Services (Toronto) Ltd. [*Canada*] [*ICAO designator*] (FAAC)
BAMF........ Bundesamt fuer Militarflugplatze [*Switzerland*] [*ICAO designator*] (FAAC)
BAMS........ British Air Mail Society (BI)
BAMTM .... British Association of Machine Tool Merchants, Inc. (BI)
BAMW .... British Association of Meat Wholesalers Ltd. (BI)
BAN........... Black Audio Network, Inc. (NTCM)
BANANA ... Build Absolutely Nothing Anywhere Near Anything [*Facetious successor to NIMBY*]
BAOFR...... British Association of Overseas Furniture Removers (BI)
Baol........... British Association for Open Learning
BAP .... Bacillary Angiomatosis-Bacillary Peliosis
BAPA......... British Aeromedical Practitioners Association (DA)
BAPA......... British Amateur Press Association (BI)
BAPIP....... British Association of Palestine-Israel Philatelists (BI)
BAPM........ British Association of Physical Medicine (BI)
BAPP......... British Association of Pig Producers (BI)
BAPSA ...... Broadcast Advertising Producers Society of America (NTCM)
BAR .... Bradley Air (Charter) Services Ltd. [*Canada*] [*ICAO designator*] (FAAC)
BARS........ British Association of Residential Settlements (BI)
BARTG....... British Amateur Radio Teleprinter Group (BI)
BAS........... Aero Services [*Barbados*] [*ICAO designator*] (FAAC)

BAS............. Binaural Analysis System [*Noise testing*] [*Automotive engineering*]
BAS............. Building Advisory Service [*British*] (BI)
BASA......... British Architectural Students' Association (BI)
BASIC .... Body Armor System Individual Countermine Armor [*Army*] (INF)
BASLC .... British Association of Sports Ground and Landscape Contractors Ltd. (BI)
BASMA...... Boot and Shoe Manufacturers' Association and Leather Trades Protection Society [*British*] (BI)
BASMON ... British Association Sovereign and Military Order of Malta (BI)
BAT .... Beta, Atla, and Themis [*Regions on planet Venus*]
BATA......... Bakery and Allied Trades Association Ltd. [*British*] (BI)
BATA......... British Air Transport Association (DA)
BAT-D........ Deception Battalion [*Army*] (ADDR)
BATS......... Bakers' and Allied Traders' Golfing Society [*British*] (BI)
BAV .... Air Varna Co. [*Bulgaria*] [*ICAO designator*] (FAAC)
BAW .... British Airways [*ICAO designator*] (FAAC)
BAWA .... British Amateur Wrestling Association (BI)
BAY .... Bay Air Aviation [*New Zealand*] [*ICAO designator*] (FAAC)
BAYS......... British Association of Young Scientists (BI)
BB .... Bayonet Base [*Lens mount*] (NTCM)
BBB............ Back to the Bible Broadcast (NTCM)
BBB............ Balair AG [*Switzerland*] [*ICAO designator*] (FAAC)
BBBA......... British Bird Breeders' Association (BI)
BBC............ Bangladesh Biman [*ICAO designator*] (FAAC)
BBCF......... British Bacon Curers' Federation (BI)
BBCMA..... British Baby Carriage Manufacturers' Association (BI)
BBF........... Brilliant Buff Finishing [*Metal finishing*]
BBFC......... British Board of Film Censors (BI)
BBFO......... Bardsey Bird and Field Observatory [*British*] (BI)
BBGA......... British Broiler Growers' Association (BI)
BBH .... Brown Brothers Harriman (ECON)
BBI............. Builders' Benevolent Institution [*British*] (BI)
BBJ............. Aircorp Airlines, Inc. [*Canada*] [*ICAO designator*] (FAAC)
BBKA......... British Bee Keepers Association (BI)
BBL............ Be Back Later [*Computer hacker terminology*] (NHD)
BBL............ IBM, Euroflight-Operations [*Switzerland*] [*ICAO designator*] (FAAC)
BBM .... Broadcast Bureau of Measurement [*FCC*] (NTCM)
BBM .... Bureau of Broadcast Measurement [*Canada*] (NTCM)
BBMA .... British Bath Manufacturers' Association Ltd. (BI)
BBMA .... British Button Manufacturers Association (BI)
BBMS........ British Battery Makers' Society (BI)
BBN .... Scampton BAE [*British*] [*ICAO designator*] (FAAC)
BBSATRA ... British Boot, Shoe and Allied Trades Research Association (BI)
BBUGVACT ... Black Box Under Glass Variable Angle Controllled Temperature [*Automotive paint duability testing*]
BBusHA ..... Bachelor of Business - Health Administration
BC.............. Become (DA)
BC .... Building Code (DAC)
BCA .... British Carton Association (BI)
BCA .... British Chicken Association Ltd. (BI)
BCA .... British Confectioners' Association (BI)
BCA .... Broadcasting Co. of America (NTCM)
BCA .... Bulgarian Air Cargo [*ICAO designator*] (FAAC)
BCAB......... Birth Control Advisory Bureau [*British*] (BI)
BCCA......... British Correspondence Chess Association (BI)
BCD........... Base-Catalyzed Destination [*Environmental science*]
BCDTA...... British Chemical and Dyestuffs Traders' Association (BI)
BCF........... British Chess Federation (BI)
BCFA......... Britain-China Friendship Association (BI)
BCFG........ British Camp Fire Girls (BI)
BCG........... British Columbia Government [*Canada*] [*ICAO designator*] (FAAC)
BCGA .... British Cotton Growing Association (BI)
BCH........... Basic Decision Height [*Aviation*] (DA)
BCH........... British Columbia Power and Hydro Authority [*Canada*] [*ICAO designator*] (FAAC)
BCHFA...... British-Canadian Holstein-Friesian Association (BI)
BCIA......... British Cooking Industry Association (BI)
BCID......... Battlefield Combat Identification [*Army*] (RDA)
BCK .... Priority Aviation Co., Inc. [*ICAO designator*] (FAAC)

BCL............ British Caribbean Airways Ltd. [*ICAO designator*] (FAAC)
BCLMA...... British Columbia Lumber Manufacturers' Association [*Canada*] (BI)
BCM .... Broken Cubic Meter (DAC)
BCM .... Courier-Mail (Brisbane) [*A publication*]
BCMA........ British Chip Board Manufacturers' Association (BI)
BCOM....... Balance of Commitments
BCOP .... Broken Clouds or Better [*Meteorology*] (DA)
BCPIT .... British Council for the Promotion of International Trade (BI)
BCPMA...... British Chemical Plant Manufacturers' Association (BI)
BCR .... British Charter [*ICAO designator*] (FAAC)
BCR .... British Circus Ring (BI)
BCRA........ British Car Rental Association (BI)
BCRD .... British Council for Rehabilitation of the Disabled (BI)
BCS .... Benefits Control System [*Insurance*]
BCS........... Binary Compatibility Specification [*Computer science*] (PCM)
BCS........... European Air Transport [*ICAO designator*] (FAAC)
BCT........... Best Control Technology [*Environmental Protection Agency*] (ERG)
BCT........... British Columbia Telephone Ltd. [*Canada*] [*ICAO designator*] (FAAC)
BCTA........ British Canadian Trade Association (BI)
BCTC........ British Ceramic Tile Council Ltd. (BI)
BCY .... Broken Cubic Yard (DAC)
BDA .... Belt Driven Type A [*Cosworth racing engines*] [*Automotive engineering*]
BDA .... Border Airways [*South Africa*] [*ICAO designator*] (FAAC)
BDAT .... Beacon Data [*Aviation*] (FAAC)
BDDA .... British Deaf and Dumb Association (BI)
BDG........... Business Development Group
BDMA .... British Disinfectant Manufacturers' Association (BI)
BDN........... Banco di Napoli [*Italy*]
BDN........... Boscombe Down MOD/PE [*British*] [*ICAO designator*] (FAAC)
BDR .... Belt Driven Retrofit [*Cosworth racing engines*] [*Automotive engineering*]
BDRA .... British Drag Racing Association (BI)
BDS .... British Display Society (BI)
BDS .... British Driving Society (BI)
BDSA......... British Dental Students' Association (BI)
BDT .... Belt Driven Turbocharged [*Cosworth racing engines*] [*Automotive engineering*]
B3E .... Beveled on Three Edges [*Lumber*] (DAC)
B4E .... Beveled on Four Edges [*Lumber*] (DAC)
BEA .... British Egg Association (BI)
BEA .... British Esperanto Association, Inc. (BI)
BEA .... British Exhibitors' Association (BI)
BEAMS..... British Emergency Air Medical Service (DA)
BEC........... Beech Aircraft Corp. [*ICAO designator*] (FAAC)
BEC........... Broad Economic Category
BECMA...... British Electro-Ceramic Manufacturers' Association (BI)
BEE........... Busy Bee of Norway AS [*ICAO designator*] (FAAC)
BEFOURRA ... Belgian Fourragere [*Military decoration*]
BEI............ Benair [*Italy*] [*ICAO designator*] (FAAC)
BEJ .... Best Expert Judgment [*Environmental Protection Agency*] (ERG)
BEK .... Bleached Eucalypt Kraft
BEL........... Bell-Air Executive Air Travel Ltd. [*New Zealand*] [*ICAO designator*] (FAAC)
BEL........... Broad Emission Line [*Spectra*]
BEM .... Biological Effect Monitoring [*Toxicology*]
BEMA .... British Essence Manufacturers' Association (BI)
BEMSA ...... British Eastern Merchant Shippers' Association (BI)
BEN .... Bennington Aviation, Inc. [*ICAO designator*] (FAAC)
BER .... Air Berlin, USA [*Germany*] [*ICAO designator*] (FAAC)
BERD .... Business Expenditure Research and Development
BES .... Aero Services Executive [*France*] [*ICAO designator*] (FAAC)
BES .... Bank Education Service [*British*] (BI)
BETS .... Black Elderly Twin Study [*National Institute on Aging*]
BEV .... Barrier-Equivalent Velocity [*Automotive safety*]
BEX .... Benin Air Express [*ICAO designator*] (FAAC)
BFA........... Budget-Funded Agency
BFA........... Business Flights Ltd. [*Canada*] [*ICAO designator*] (FAAC)
BFAC......... British Federation of Aesthetics and Cosmetology (BI)
BFC........... Basler Flight Service, Inc. [*ICAO designator*] (FAAC)
BFC/NCC... Broadcasting and Film Commission/National Council of the Churches of Christ in the USA (NTCM)
BFI............ Broadcaster's Foundation, Inc. (NTCM)
BFISS .... British Federation of Iron and Steel Stockholders (BI)
BFL........... Buffalo Airways Ltd. [*Canada*] [*ICAO designator*] (FAAC)
BFM .... British Furniture Manufacturers' Federated Associations (BI)
BFMC........ British Friction Materials Council (BI)
BFN .... Compagnie Nationale Naganagani [*Burkina Faso*] [*ICAO designator*] (FAAC)
BFPC .... British Farm Produce Council (BI)
BFR........... Biennial Flight Review [*Aviation*] (DA)
BFS........... Benelux Falcon Service [*Belgium*] [*ICAO designator*] (FAAC)
BFS........... Branded Furniture Society [*British*] (BI)
BFS........... British Fuchsia Society (BI)
BGA .... Block Grant Authority
BGGA .... British Golf Greenkeepers' Association (BI)
BGR........... Sigi Air [*Bulgaria*] [*ICAO designator*] (FAAC)
BGS........... British Gladiolus Society (BI)
BGS........... Bundesgrenzschutz [*Germany*] [*ICAO designator*] (FAAC)

BHA........... Bottom Hole Assembly [*Well drilling technology*]
BHB........... Bachelor of Human Biology
BHC........... British Herdsmen's Club (BI)
BHE........... Biggin Executive Aviation Ltd. [*British*] [*ICAO designator*] (FAAC)
BHF........... British Holiday Fellowship Ltd. (BI)
BHL........... Bristow Helicopters Group Ltd. [*British*] [*ICAO designator*] (FAAC)
BHO........... Bhoja Airlines [*Pakistan*] [*ICAO designator*] (FAAC)
BHPC......... British Hardware Promotion Council Ltd. (BI)
BHR........... Bighorn Airways, Inc. [*ICAO designator*] (FAAC)
BHRA........ British Hotels and Restaurants Association (BI)
BHRN........ Black Human Resources Network [*An association*] (EA)
BHS........... Bahamasair Holdings Ltd. [*Bahamas*] [*ICAO designator*] (FAAC)
BHSA........ British Heavy Steel Association (BI)
BHT........... Bogazici Hava Tasimacilik AS [*Turkey*] [*ICAO designator*] (FAAC)
BHY........... Birgenair [*Turkey*] [*ICAO designator*] (FAAC)
BIA .... Baltic International Airlines [*Latvia*] [*ICAO designator*] (FAAC)
BIA .... British Ironfounders Association (BI)
BIC........... Belgian International Air Carriers [*ICAO designator*] (FAAC)
BIDS......... British Institute of Dealers in Securities [*Defunct*]
BIG........... Big Island Air, Inc. [*ICAO designator*] (FAAC)
BIGI......... Bond Investors Guaranty Insurance
BIH........... British International Helicopters Ltd. [*ICAO designator*] (FAAC)
BIHFS .... British Institute of Hardwood Flooring Specialists (BI)
BII............ Bilingual Information Instructor
BIJS......... British Institute of Jazz Studies (BI)
BIM .... Binter-Mediterraneo [*Spain*] [*ICAO designator*] (FAAC)
BIM .... Blade Integrity Monitor [*Aviation*] (DA)
BINA .... Broadcast Institute of North America (NTCM)
BIO........... Bilingual Information Officer
BIPP .... British Institute of Practical Psychology Ltd. (BI)
BIR........... Bird Leasing, Inc. [*ICAO designator*] (FAAC)
BIS........... Beet Invert Syrup [*Food sweetener*]
BISAKTA... British Iron, Steel and Kindred Trades Association (BI)
Bit .... Borrowed Light (DAC)
Bit .... Built (DAC)
BIW .... Body in White [*Automotive manufacturing*]
BJ.............. Bar Journal [*A publication*]
BJA........... Unifly [*Italy*] [*ICAO designator*] (FAAC)
BJCC .... British Junior Chambers of Commerce (BI)
BJK........... Atlantic World Airways, Inc. [*ICAO designator*] (FAAC)
BKA........... Bankair, Inc. [*ICAO designator*] (FAAC)
BKG .... Background (NTCM)
BKJ........... Barken International, Inc. [*ICAO designator*] (FAAC)
BKL........... Baikal [*Russian Federation*] [*ICAO designator*] (FAAC)
BKLKTNG ... Break-Lock ECM [*Electronic Countermeasures*] Training [*Navy*] (ANA)
BKP........... Bangkok Airways [*Thailand*] [*ICAO designator*] (FAAC)
BKR........... Circuit Breaker (NTCM)
BK SH........ Book Shelf [*Technical drawings*] (DAC)
BKWA........ Branded Knitting-Wool Association Ltd. [*British*] (BI)
BLA .... All Charter Ltd. [*British*] [*ICAO designator*] (FAAC)
BLB........... Atlantic Air BVI Ltd. [*British*] [*ICAO designator*] (FAAC)
BLC........... Brasil-Central Linhas Areas Regional SA [*Brazil*] [*ICAO designator*] (FAAC)
BLCO .... Boundary Layer Control Outlet [*Mitsubishi*] [*Aerodynamics*] [*Automotive engineering*]
BLE........... Collingwood Air Services Ltd. [*Canada*] [*ICAO designator*] (FAAC)
BLF........... British Leather Federation (BI)
BLF........... Bulgarian Lucky Flight [*ICAO designator*] (FAAC)
BLG .... Belgavia (Societe de Handling) [*Belgium*] [*ICAO designator*] (FAAC)
BLH........... Blue Horizon Travel Club [*ICAO designator*] (FAAC)
BLI........... Belair [*Belarus*] [*ICAO designator*] (FAAC)
BLM .... Background Luminance Monitor [*Aviation*] (DA)
BLM .... Black Magic Project Ltd. [*British*] [*ICAO designator*] (FAAC)
BLMAS...... Bible Lands' Missions Aid Society [*British*] (BI)
BLN........... Bali International Air Service [*Indonesia*] [*ICAO designator*] (FAAC)
BLO........... Aerotransportes Barlovento SA de CV [*Mexico*] [*ICAO designator*] (FAAC)
BLOX .... Block Order Exposure System [*Business term*]
BLPS .... British Landrace Pig Society (BI)
BLR........... Atlantic Coast Airlines [*Westair Airlines, Inc.*] [*ICAO designator*] (FAAC)
BLR........... Broad-Line Region [*Spectra*]
BLRA......... British Leprosy Relief Association (BI)
BLRG......... Broad-Line Radio Galaxy [*Astrophysics*]
BLS........... Bearskin Lake Air Service Ltd. [*Canada*] [*ICAO designator*] (FAAC)
BLSGMA ... British Lamp Blown Scientific Glassware Manufacturers' Association Ltd. (BI)
BLSN......... Blowing Snow [*Meteorology*] (DA)
BLT........... Baltic Aviation, Inc. [*ICAO designator*] (FAAC)
BLT........... Blit [*Computer science*] (NHD)
BLT........... Branch if Less Than [*Computer science*] (NHD)
BLU........... IMP Aviation Services Ltd. [*Canada*] [*ICAO designator*] (FAAC)
BLV........... Bell-View Airlines Ltd. [*Nigeria*] [*ICAO designator*] (FAAC)
BLWA........ British Laboratory Ware Association Ltd. (BI)
BLZ........... Aero Barloz SA de CV [*Mexico*] [*ICAO designator*] (FAAC)

BM	Beautiful Music (NTCM)
BMA	British Manufacturers' Association Ltd. (BI)
BMA	British Midland Airways Ltd. [*ICAO designator*] (FAAC)
BMAX	Maximum Beam [*IOR*]
BMB	Broadcast Measurement Bureau (NTCM)
BMBA	British Moth Boat Association (BI)
BMBCh	Bachelor of Medicine, Bachelor of Surgery
BMD	British Medical Charter [*ICAO designator*] (FAAC)
BMD	Broadcasting Maintenance District
BMDH	Basic Minimum Descent Height [*Aviation*] (DA)
BMDO	Ballistic Missile Defense Organization
BMFF	British Man-Made Fibres Federation (BI)
BMG	British Menswear Guild Ltd. (BI)
BMH	Bristow Masayu Helicopter PT [*Indonesia*] [*ICAO designator*] (FAAC)
BMHA	Black Mental Health Alliance (EA)
BMHS	British Music Hall Society (BI)
BMIS	Beet Medium Invert Syrup [*Food sweetener*]
BMJ	Bemidji Aviation Services, Inc. [*ICAO designator*] (FAAC)
BMMA	British Mantle Manufacturers' Association (BI)
BMMMA	British Mat and Matting Manufacturers Association (BI)
BMN	Bowman Aviation, Inc. [*ICAO designator*] (FAAC)
BMPS	British Musicians' Pensions Society (BI)
BMRA	British Medical Representatives Association (BI)
BMS	Budget Management System
BMSA	British Medical Students Association (BI)
BMSC	Bone Marrow Stem Cell [*Hematology*]
BMSGMA	British Maize Starch and Glucose Manufacturers Association (BI)
BMTA	British Motor Trade Association (BI)
BMTFA	British Malleable Tube Fittings Association (BI)
BMusPerf	Bachelor of Music (Performance)
BMW	Boilermaker/Welder
BMX	Banco de Mexico [*ICAO designator*] (FAAC)
BNA	British Nursing Association (BI)
BNC	Bayonet Naval Connector [*Electronics*] (NTCM)
BNC	Blimped Noiseless Reflex Camera (NTCM)
BNCS	British National Carnation Society
BNCSAA	British National Committee on Surface Active Agents (BI)
BND	Bond Helicopters Ltd. [*British*] [*ICAO designator*] (FAAC)
BNFMF	British Non-Ferrous Metals Federation (BI)
BNFMS	British Bureau of Non-Ferrous Metal Statistics (BI)
BNGA	British Nursery Goods Association (BI)
BNI	Alberni Airway [*Canada*] [*ICAO designator*] (FAAC)
BNL	Broadcast News Ltd. (NTCM)
BNOM	Background Natural Organic Matter [*Environmental chemistry*]
BNR	Bonair Aviation Ltd. [*Canada*] [*ICAO designator*] (FAAC)
BNS	Broadcast News Service (NTCM)
BNX	Brenair Ltd. [*British*] [*ICAO designator*] (FAAC)
BO	Boundary Lights [*Aviation*] (DA)
BOB	Beginning of Business
BOBMA	British Oil Burner Manufacturers' Association (BI)
Bob W	Best of Both Worlds [*Apple Computer's Macintosh Due System's nickname*] [*Pronounced as a proper name: Bob W.*]
BOD	Bond Air Services Ltd. [*Uganda*] [*ICAO designator*] (FAAC)
BOE	Boeing Commericial Airplane Group [*ICAO designator*] (FAAC)
BOF	Bordaire Ltd. [*Canada*] [*ICAO designator*] (FAAC)
BOGA	British Onion Growers' Association (BI)
BOI	Aboitiz Air Transport Corp. [*Philippines*] [*ICAO designator*] (FAAC)
Bol	Bollard [*Shipping*] [*British*]
BOL	Transportes Aeros Bolivianos [*Bolivia*] [*ICAO designator*] (FAAC)
BOM	Billings Ovulation Method Association of the United States (EA)
BOM	Service Aerien Gouvernemental Ministere des Transports Gouvernement du Quebec [*Canada*] [*ICAO designator*] (FAAC)
BOMA	British Overseas Mining Association (BI)
BON	Bon Accord Airways [*British*] [*ICAO designator*] (FAAC)
BONUS	Borrower's Option for Notes and Underwritten Standby [*Finance*]
BOP	Bop Air (Pty) Ltd. [*South Africa*] [*ICAO designator*] (FAAC)
BOR	Broadcast Officer
BOR	Orion Air [*Bulgaria*] [*ICAO designator*] (FAAC)
BORG	Basic Operational Requirements and Planning Criteria Group [*ICAO*] (DA)
BORIS	Bankruptcy Official Receivers' Information System
BORIS	Broadcasting Operations Recording and Information System
BOS	Bosal International Management NV [*Belgium*] [*ICAO designator*] (FAAC)
BOT	Air Botswana (Pty) Ltd. [*ICAO designator*] (FAAC)
BOU	Bouraq Indonesia Airlines PT [*ICAO designator*] (FAAC)
BOX	Tiphook PCL [*British*] [*ICAO designator*] (FAAC)
BOYSNC	Beginning of Year Significant Non-Complier [*Environmental Protection Agency*] (ERG)
BP	Background Paper
BP	Bearing Pile [*Technical drawings*] (DAC)
Bp	Bipost [*Lamp base*] (NTCM)
BPA	Book Publisher's Association (NTCM)
BPA	Bookmakers' Protection Association Ltd. (BI)
BPA	British Philatelic Association Ltd. (BI)
BPA	British Ploughing Association (BI)
BPA	British Pyrotechnists' Association (BI)
BPAD	Bipolar Affective Disorder [*Genetics*]

BPC	British Pharmaceutical Code
BPCF	British Postal Chess Federation (BI)
BPEF	Broadcast Pioneers Educational Fund, Inc. (NTCM)
BPG	Beveled Plate Glass (DAC)
BPGMA	British Pressure Gauge Manufacturers Association (BI)
BPHS	British Percheron Horse Society (BI)
BPHS	British Polled Hereford Society Ltd. (BI)
BPhysEd	Bachelor of Physical Education
BPL	Broadcast Pioneer's Library (NTCM)
BPO	BP Flight Operations Ltd. [*British*] [*ICAO designator*] (FAAC)
BPO	Branch Processing Unit [*Computer science*]
BPO	Broadcast Production Officer
BPPA	British Precision Pilots Association (DA)
BPPS	Bulleid Pacific Preservation Society [*British*] (BI)
BPR	Business Process Re-Engineering (ECON)
BPRA	Book Publishers Representatives' Association [*British*] (BI)
BPS	Business Plan System
BPSA	British Pharmaceutical Students' Association (BI)
BPT	Black Panel Temperature [*Automotive paint durability testing*]
BPTCA	Best Practicable Control Technology Currently Available [*Clean Water Act*] (ERG)
BQA	Bilateral Quarantine Agreement
BR	Bahama Route [*Aviation*] (FAAC)
BRA	Beef Recording Association [*British*] (BI)
BRA	Braathens South American & Far East Airtransport AS [*Norway*] [*ICAO designator*] (FAAC)
BRA	British Radiesthesia Association (BI)
BRA	British Rheumatism and Arthritis Association (BI)
BRB	Be Right Back [*Computer hacker terminology*] (NHD)
BRC	BCA Charter [*British*] [*ICAO designator*] (FAAC)
BRC	British Rabbit Council (BI)
BRCA	British Roller Canary Association (BI)
BRCC	British Roller Canary Club (BI)
Brcg	Bracing (DAC)
BRD	Brock Air Services Ltd. [*Canada*] [*ICAO designator*] (FAAC)
BRE	Brencham Air Charter Ltd. [*British*] [*ICAO designator*] (FAAC)
BREED	Project Breed Rescue Efforts and Education [*An association*] (EA)
BREG	British Rivet Export Group (BI)
BRESS	Behavioral Risk Factor Surveillance System
BRF	Air Bravo [*Uganda*] [*ICAO designator*] (FAAC)
BRF	British Road Federation Ltd. (BI)
BRG	Bering Air, Inc. [*ICAO designator*] (FAAC)
BRH	Braathens Helicopter AS [*Norway*] [*ICAO designator*] (FAAC)
Bris	Brisbane [*Australia*]
BritGFO	British Guild of Flight Operations Officers (DA)
BRKG	Braking [*Aviation*] (FAAC)
BRL	Air Bras d'Or [*Canada*] [*ICAO designator*] (FAAC)
BRM	Air 500 Ltd. [*Canada*] [*ICAO designator*] (FAAC)
BRMCA	British Ready Mixed Concrete Association (BI)
BRMF	British Rainwear Manufacturers Federation (BI)
BRN	Eclipse Airlines, Inc. [*ICAO designator*] (FAAC)
bRNA	Branched Ribonucleic Acid [*Genetics*]
BROADCAP	Broadcast Capital Fund, Inc. (NTCM)
BRR	Mountain Air Service, Inc. [*ICAO designator*] (FAAC)
BRRAMA	British Rubber and Resin Adhesive Manufacturers' Association (BI)
BRS	Big Red Switch [*Computer science*] (NHD)
BRS	Brazilian Air Force [*ICAO designator*] (FAAC)
BRSKT	Brisket (ABBR)
BRSKY	Briskly (ABBR)
BRSL	Bristle (ABBR)
BRSLD	Bristled (ABBR)
BRSLG	Bristling (ABBR)
BRSNLW	Brothers-in-Law (ABBR)
BRSNS	Brassiness (ABBR)
BRSQ	Brusque (ABBR)
BRSQNS	Brusqueness (ABBR)
BRSQY	Brusquely (ABBR)
BRSR	Bursar (ABBR)
BRSRY	Bursary (ABBR)
BRSSIR	Brassiere (ABBR)
BRSSY	Brassy (ABBR)
BRST	Breast (ABBR)
BRSTBN	Breastbone (ABBR)
BRSTG	Bursting (ABBR)
BRSTPLT	Breastplate (ABBR)
BRSTR	Barrister (ABBR)
BRSTRM	Brainstorm (ABBR)
BRSTRMG	Brainstorming (ABBR)
BRSTS	Bursitis (ABBR)
BRSY	Brassy (ABBR)
BRT	Brute (ABBR)
BRTA	British Racing Tobaggan Association (BI)
BRTA	British Regional Television Association (BI)
BRTA	British Road Tar Association (BI)
BRTC	British Railwaymen's Touring Club (BI)
BRTDY	Birthday (ABBR)
BRTH	Breathe (ABBR)
BRTHD	Breathed (ABBR)
BRTHDY	Birthday (ABBR)
BRTHE	Breathe (ABBR)
BRTHG	Breathing (ABBR)

BRTHL...... Brothel (ABBR)
BRTHMK ... Birthmark (ABBR)
BRTHPL.... Birthplace (ABBR)
BRTHRGT ... Birthright (ABBR)
BRTHRN ... Brethren (ABBR)
BRTHSTN ... Birthstone (ABBR)
BRTHTKG ... Breathtaking (ABBR)
BRTL......... Brittle (ABBR)
BRTL......... Brutal (ABBR)
BRTLT ...... Brutality (ABBR)
BRTLY ...... Brutally (ABBR)
BRTLZ ...... Brutalize (ABBR)
BRTLZD ... Brutalized (ABBR)
BRTLZG ... Brutalizing (ABBR)
BRTMK...... Birthmark (ABBR)
BRTNDR.... Bartender (ABBR)
BRTPLC.... Birthplace (ABBR)
BRTR......... Barter (ABBR)
BRTRT ...... Birthright (ABBR)
BRTSH....... Brutish (ABBR)
BRTSHNS ... Brutishness (ABBR)
BRTSHY .... Brutishly (ABBR)
BRTST ...... Birthstone (ABBR)
BRU .... Belavia [*Belarus*] [*ICAO designator*] (FAAC)
BRUS......... Bruise (ABBR)
BRUSD....... Bruised (ABBR)
BRUSG....... Bruising (ABBR)
BRUSR....... Bruiser (ABBR)
BRUT .... Brunet (ABBR)
BRUTH ...... Brutish (ABBR)
BRV .... Brave (ABBR)
BRVD .... Braved (ABBR)
BRVDO ...... Bravado (ABBR)
BRVE......... Bereave (ABBR)
BRVED....... Bereaved (ABBR)
BRVG .... Braving (ABBR)
BRVNS ...... Braveness (ABBR)
BRVT......... Brevity (ABBR)
BRVY .... Bravely (ABBR)
BRWBT...... Browbeat (ABBR)
BRWBTG ... Browbeating (ABBR)
BRWBTN... Browbeaten (ABBR)
BRWLD...... Brawled (ABBR)
BRWLG...... Brawling (ABBR)
BRWR .... Brewer (ABBR)
BRWS........ Browse (ABBR)
BRWSD...... Browsed (ABBR)
BRWSG...... Browsing (ABBR)
BRX .... Buffalo Express Airlines, Inc. [*ICAO designator*] (FAAC)
BRY .... Berry (ABBR)
BRY .... Brotherly (ABBR)
BRY .... Brymon European Airway [*British*] [*ICAO designator*] (FAAC)
BRYG .... Berrying (ABBR)
BRYG .... Burying (ABBR)
BRZ .... Breeze (ABBR)
BRZD .... Brazed (ABBR)
BRZG .... Brazing (ABBR)
BRZIR .... Brazier (ABBR)
BRZIR .... Breezier (ABBR)
BRZN .... Brazen (ABBR)
BRZND ..... Brazened (ABBR)
BRZNG ..... Brazening (ABBR)
BRZNS ...... Breeziness (ABBR)
BRZST ...... Breeziest (ABBR)
BRZWY..... Breezeway (ABBR)
BRZY .... Breezy (ABBR)
BS .... Beam Spacer (DAC)
BS .... Bismuth Sulfite [*Agar*] [*Bacteriology*]
BS .... Bluestone (ABBR)
B2S .... Bright Two Sides [*Lumber*] (DAC)
BSA............ British Shipbreakers' Association (BI)
BSA............ British Speleological Association (BI)
BSA............ Ecole d'Aviation Civile [*Belgium*] [*ICAO designator*] (FAAC)
BSAC......... British Sub-Aqua Club (BI)
BSAF .... British Sulphate of Ammonia Federation Ltd. (BI)
BSAS .... Bakery Students Association of Scotland (BI)
BSBD......... Baseboard (ABBR)
BSBL .... Baseball (ABBR)
BSBY .... Busboy (ABBR)
BSC............ Bird Sweep Completed [*Aviation*] (FAAC)
BSC............ Blue Sky Carrier Co. Ltd. [*Poland*] [*ICAO designator*] (FAAC)
BSC............ British Samoyed Club (BI)
BSC............ British Society of Commerce (BI)
BSCA......... British Sulphate of Copper Association (Export) Ltd. (BI)
BSCH .... Beseech (ABBR)
BSCHD ...... Beseeched (ABBR)
BSCHG....... Beseeching (ABBR)
BSc(MechEng) ... Bachelor of Science (Mechanical Engineering)
BSc(Oen) .... Bachelor of Science (Oenology)
BSc(Surg) ... Bachelor of Science (Surgery)
BSCUT .... Biscuit (ABBR)
BSCY .... Basically (ABBR)
BSD .... Based (ABBR)

BSD .... Beside (ABBR)
BSDLB .... Block in the Anterosuperior Division of the Left Branch [*Medicine*] (MAH)
BSE............ British Shipbuilding Exports (BI)
B2S1E......... Banded Two Sides and One End [*Lumber*] (DAC)
BSEA......... British Steel Export Association (BI)
BSECH .... Beseech (ABBR)
BSECHD... Beseeched (ABBR)
BSEG.......... Besiege (ABBR)
BSEGD...... Besieged (ABBR)
BSEGG........ Besieging (ABBR)
BSF .... British Stone Federation (BI)
BSF .... Business Flight Service [*Denmark*] [*ICAO designator*] (FAAC)
BSFA .... British Sanitary Fireclay Association (BI)
BSFS .... British Soviet Friendship Society (BI)
BSG............ Basing (ABBR)
BSG............ Besiege (ABBR)
BSGD .... Besieged (ABBR)
BSGG .... Besieging (ABBR)
BSHD .... Bushed (ABBR)
BSHFL .... Bashful (ABBR)
BSHFLNS ... Bashfulness (ABBR)
BSHFLY.... Bashfully (ABBR)
BSHL .... Bushel (ABBR)
BSHNS....... Bushiness (ABBR)
BSHR .... Bushier (ABBR)
BSHST ...... Bushiest (ABBR)
BSHWHK ... Bushwhack (ABBR)
BSHWHKR ... Bushwhacker (ABBR)
BSI............. British Societies Institute (BI)
B & SI .... Building and Service Industry
BSID.......... Beside (ABBR)
BSIU.......... British Society for International Understanding (BI)
BSK............ Miami Air International, Inc. [*ICAO designator*] (FAAC)
BSKBL........ Basketball (ABBR)
BSKD .... Basked (ABBR)
BSKG .... Basking (ABBR)
BSKN .... Buskin (ABBR)
BSKTY ...... Basketry (ABBR)
BSLS.......... Baseless (ABBR)
BSLY .... Busily (ABBR)
BSMA .... British Skate Makers' Association (BI)
BSMER ...... Besmear (ABBR)
BSMGP...... British Society of Master Glass Painters (BI)
BSMR......... Besmear (ABBR)
BSMRCH... Besmirch (ABBR)
BSMRD...... Besmeared (ABBR)
BSMRG....... Besmearing (ABBR)
BSN .... Bison (ABBR)
BSN .... Connectair Charters Ltd. [*Canada*] [*ICAO designator*] (FAAC)
BSNO .... Brake Specific Oxides of Nitrogen [*Exhaust emissions*] [*Automotive engineering*]
BSNS.......... Business (ABBR)
BSNSLK.... Businesslike (ABBR)
BSNSMN ... Businessman (ABBR)
BSNSWMEN ... Businesswomen (ABBR)
BSNSWMN ... Businesswoman (ABBR)
BSOEA....... British Stationery and Office Equipment Association (BI)
BSP............ Bosphorus Hava Yollari Turizm Ve Ticaret AS [*Turkey*] [*ICAO designator*] (FAAC)
BSPA .... British Speedway Promoters Association (BI)
BSQ .... Basque (ABBR)
BSR............ Bacterial Sulfate Reduction
BSR............ Basair AB [*Sweden*] [*ICAO designator*] (FAAC)
BSR............ Building Space Requirement (DAC)
BSRA......... British Sound Recording Association (BI)
BSRAE .... British Society for Research in Agricultural Engineering (BI)
BSRK.......... Berserk (ABBR)
BSS............ British Sailors Society (BI)
BSS............ Business Start-Up Scheme [*British*]
BSSJ........... British Society of Stamp Journalists (BI)
BSSO......... British Society for the Study of Orthodontics (BI)
BSSSA .... British Surgical Support Suppliers Association (BI)
BST............. Ballets de San Juan [*Puerto Rico*]
BST............. Baste (ABBR)
BSTA .... British Surgical Trades Association (BI)
BSTD......... Basted (ABBR)
BSTF .... British Student Tuberculosis Foundation (BI)
BSTG......... Basting (ABBR)
BSTL .... Bestial (ABBR)
BSTL .... Bustle (ABBR)
BSTLD ...... Bustled (ABBR)
BSTLG ...... Bustling (ABBR)
BSTLT .... Bestiality (ABBR)
BSTLY........ Bestially (ABBR)
BSTO......... Bestow (ABBR)
BSTRD....... Bastard (ABBR)
BSTRDY ... Bastardly (ABBR)
BSTRDZ ... Bastardize (ABBR)
BSTRDZD ... Bastardized (ABBR)
BSTRDZG ... Bastardizing (ABBR)
BSTRU....... Boisterous (ABBR)
BSTRUS..... Boisterous (ABBR)

BSTRUSNS ... Boisterousness   (ABBR)
BSTRUSY ... Boisterously   (ABBR)
BSTW .... Bestow   (ABBR)
BSTWB ...... Bestowable   (ABBR)
BSTWD ..... Bestowed   (ABBR)
BSTWG ..... Bestowing   (ABBR)
BSTWL ...... Bestowal   (ABBR)
BSTWT ...... Bestowment   (ABBR)
BSU .... Beam Steering Unit   (DA)
BSWX........ Beeswax   (ABBR)
BSY .... Big Sky Airline [*ICAO designator*]   (FAAC)
BSYBDY .... Busybody   (ABBR)
BSYG......... Busying   (ABBR)
BT .... Back Taxiing [*Aviation*]   (FAAC)
BT .... Bathtub   (ABBR)
BT .... Bolt   (ABBR)
BTA .... Billiards Trade Association [*British*]   (BI)
BTA .... British Travel Association   (BI)
BTA .... British Tugowners Association   (BI)
BTA .... Britt Airways, Inc. [*ICAO designator*]   (FAAC)
BTB............ Bituminous Treated Base   (DAC)
BTB............ Blind Transmission Broadcast [*Army*]   (ADDR)
BTBA........ British Twinning and Bilingual Association   (BI)
BTCHD....... Batched   (ABBR)
BTCHG ...... Batching   (ABBR)
BTCHR ...... Butcher   (ABBR)
BTCHRY.... Butchery   (ABBR)
BTCN .... Beautician   (ABBR)
BTechSc...... Bachelor of Technical Science
BTEMA...... British Tanning Extract Manufacturers' Association   (BI)
BTEX.......... Bezene, Toluene, Ethylbenzene, and Xylene [*Organic mixture*]
BTF............ British Tarpaviors Federation Ltd.   (BI)
BTF............ British Turkey Federation Ltd.   (BI)
BTFCN ...... Beautification   (ABBR)
BTFL.......... Beautiful   (ABBR)
BTFLNS..... Beautifulness   (ABBR)
BTFLY....... Beautifully   (ABBR)
BTFY .... Beautify   (ABBR)
BTFYG ...... Beautifying   (ABBR)
BTG .... Biting   (ABBR)
BTG .... British Toymakers' Guild   (BI)
BTH .... Barth's Aviation [*France*] [*ICAO designator*]   (FAAC)
BTHR .... Bother   (ABBR)
BTHRD ..... Bothered   (ABBR)
BTHRG ...... Bothering   (ABBR)
BTHRSM... Bothersome   (ABBR)
BTK .... Batik   (ABBR)
Btk .... Bruton's Tyrosine Kinase [*An enzyme*]
BTKN .... Betoken   (ABBR)
BTL............ Baltia Air Lines, Inc. [*ICAO designator*]   (FAAC)
BTL............ Battle   (ABBR)
BTL............ Behind the Lens   (NTCM)
BTLD......... Battled   (ABBR)
BTLD......... Bottled   (ABBR)
BTLFLD..... Battlefield   (ABBR)
BTLG......... Battling   (ABBR)
BTLG......... Bottling   (ABBR)
BTLM........ Botulism [*Medicine*]   (ABBR)
BTLMT ...... Battlement   (ABBR)
BTLN......... Battalion   (ABBR)
BTLR......... Butler   (ABBR)
BTLSP........ Battleship   (ABBR)
BTM .... Bantam   (ABBR)
BTM .... British Theatre Museum   (BI)
BTMD .... Bottomed   (ABBR)
BTMG .... Bottoming   (ABBR)
BTMLS ..... Bottomless   (ABBR)
BTMWT..... Bantamweight   (ABBR)
BTPI .... Benzothiopyranoindazole [*Organic chemistry*]
BTR .... Belize Transair [*ICAO designator*]   (FAAC)
BTR .... British Tire & Rubber Co.
BTRE......... Broadcast-Television Recording Engineers [*An association*]   (NTCM)
BTS............ Betsy-Tacy Society   (EA)
BTS............ British Temperance Society   (BI)
BTSC .... British Transport Staff College   (BI)
BTSC .... Broadcast Television Systems Committee Recommendation [*FCC*]   (NTCM)
BTU .... Rolls Royce Ltd. (Bristol Engine Division) [*British*] [*ICAO designator*]   (FAAC)
BUA........... Business Aviation AS [*Denmark*] [*ICAO designator*]   (FAAC)
BUBL......... Bulletin Board for Libraries [*British*]
BUC........... MK Burundi Air Cargo [*ICAO designator*]   (FAAC)
BUD........... Air Budapest Club Ltd. [*Hungary*] [*ICAO designator*]   (FAAC)
BUL .... Blue Airlines [*Zaire*] [*ICAO designator*]   (FAAC)
BUN........... Bulletin   (NTCM)
BUR .... Business Air AG [*Switzerland*] [*ICAO designator*]   (FAAC)
BUSY......... Budget System
BUT .... Business Air Taxi [*Switzerland*] [*ICAO designator*]   (FAAC)
Buzz E J ...... Buzzworm's Earth Journal [*A publication*]
BV .... Butterfly Valve   (DAC)
BVA .... British Vigilance Association   (BI)
BVA .... Buffalo Airways [*ICAO designator*]   (FAAC)

BVC .... British Veterinary Code
BVN .... Baron Aviation Services, Inc. [*ICAO designator*]   (FAAC)
BWA .... British Waterfowl Association   (BI)
BWA .... Trinidad and Tobago Airways Corp. [*ICAO designator*]   (FAAC)
BWC .... [*Barry*] Williams Ltd. [*British*] [*ICAO designator*]   (FAAC)
BWCC........ British Weed Control Council   (BI)
BWF........... British Whiting Federation   (BI)
BWHBC .... Boston Women's Health Book Collective
BWI .... British Workmen's Institute   (BI)
BWMA ...... Baptist Women's Missionary Auxilliary [*British*]   (BI)
BWMA ...... British Woodwork Manufacturers' Association   (BI)
BWO........... BW Air Services Ltd. [*British*] [*ICAO designator*]   (FAAC)
BWPUC..... British Waste Paper Utilisation Council   (BI)
BWQ........... Buzz Word Quotient [*Computer science*]   (NHD)
BWRRA..... British Wire Rod Rollers' Association   (BI)
BWS........... British Water Colour Society   (BI)
BWTA .... British Women's Temperance Association   (BI)
BWY .... Fleet Requirement Air Direction Unit [*British*] [*ICAO designator*]   (FAAC)
BXH........... British Independent Airways [*ICAO designator*]   (FAAC)
BXL........... Air Exel Belgique [*Belgium*] [*ICAO designator*]   (FAAC)
BXS........... Compania Spantax [*Spain*] [*ICAO designator*]   (FAAC)
BYNA .... British Young Naturalists Association   (BI)
BYU .... Bayu Indonesia Air PT [*ICAO designator*]   (FAAC)
BZH........... Britair SA [*France*] [*ICAO designator*]   (FAAC)
BZZ............ Butane Buzzard Aviation Corp. [*British*] [*ICAO designator*]   (FAAC)

C

C .... Cabinet [*Technical drawings*]   (NFPA)
C .... Chemical   (NFPA)
C .... Cimex [*Genus of microorganisms*]   (MAH)
C .... Commercial [*FCC*]   (NTCM)
C .... Common Carrier [*FCC*]   (NTCM)
C .... Connection   (NFPA)
C .... Corynebacterium [*Genus of microorganisms*]   (MAH)
C .... Culex [*Genus of microorganisms*]   (MAH)
C2 .... Nauru [*Aircraft nationality and registration mark*]   (FAAC)
3C .... Equatorial Guinea [*Aircraft nationality and registration mark*]
                  (FAAC)
C5 .... Gambia [*Aircraft nationality and registration mark*]   (FAAC)
C6 .... Bahamas [*Aircraft nationality and registration mark*]   (FAAC)
C9 .... Mozambique [*Aircraft nationality and registration mark*]   (FAAC)
CA .... Commercial Announcement   (NTCM)
CA .... Conditional Authorization [*Environmental science*]
CA .... Cooperating Administrator [*Education*]   (AEE)
CA .... Courtesy Announcement   (NTCM)
CA .... Cranking Amperes [*Battery*] [*Automotive engineering*]
CA .... Cruisermen's Association   (EA)
CAA .... Carbon Adsorption/Absorption [*for vapor recovery*]
CAA .... Carnival Air [*ICAO designator*]   (FAAC)
CAA .... Concert Artists Association [*British*]   (BI)
CAAA .... Canadian Association of Advertising Agencies   (NTCM)
CAAC .... Chinese American Arts Council   (EA)
CAARC........ Commonwealth Advisory Aeronautical Research Council   (BI)
CAAS .... Class A Airspace [*Aviation*]   (FAAC)
CAB .... Cement-Asbestos Board   (DAC)
CAB .... Chesapeake Air Services [*ICAO designator*]   (FAAC)
CAB .... Consortium on Advanced Biosensors   (EA)
CAC .... Chlorinated Aromatic Compound [*Organic chemistry*]
CAC .... Compagnie des Agents de Change
CAC .... Conquest Airlines Corp. [*ICAO designator*]   (FAAC)
CACREP .... Council for Accreditation of Counseling and Related Educational
                  Programs   (AEE)
CAD .... Chilliwack Aviation Ltd. [*Canada*] [*ICAO designator*]   (FAAC)
CADEX....... Combination and Dissemination of Experiment Data System
                  [*Army*]   (RDA)
CADPR....... Cyclic Adenosine Diphosphoribose [*Biochemistry*]
CAE .... Criterion Action Element [*Army*]   (ADDR)
CAEAI .... Chartered Auctioneers' and Estate Agents' Institute [*British*]   (BI)
CAEE......... Committee on Aircraft Engine Emissions [*ICAO*]   (DA)
CAF........... Cable Arts Foundation, Inc.   (NTCM)
CAF........... Colloidal Array Filters [*for LASER applications*]
CAFM........ Cable FM [*Radio*]   (NTCM)
CAFMS ...... Continental Association of Funeral and Memorial Societies
CAFSMNA ... Compound Animal Feeding Stuffs Manufacturers National
                  Association [*British*]   (BI)
CAGE .... Cut Down, Annoyed, Guilty, Eye-Opener [*Clinical questions
                  asked to detect alcoholism*]
CAGR .... Compound Annual Growth Rate [*Business term*]
CAH........... Command Airways [*South Africa*] [*ICAO designator*]   (FAAC)
CAHR........ Center for Advanced Heart Research
CAI .... Carboxyamidoimidazole [*Organic chemistry*]
CAI .... Compagnia Aeronautica Italiana SPA [*Italy*] [*ICAO designator*]
                  (FAAC)
CAI .... Corporacion Aereo Internacional SA de CV [*Mexico*] [*ICAO
                  designator*]   (FAAC)
CAIP........... Civil Aircraft Inspection Procedure   (DA)
CAISM .... Central Association of Irish Schoolmistresses   (BI)
CAJ .... Cougar Air, Inc. [*Canada*] [*ICAO designator*]   (FAAC)
CAK .... County Air Services Ltd. [*British*] [*ICAO designator*]   (FAAC)
CAL .... China Airlines [*Taiwan*] [*ICAO designator*]   (FAAC)
CAL .... Computer-Aided Lighting [*Automotive engineering*]
CALF......... Calfskin [*Book cover material*]   (NTCM)
CALLEV .... California Low-Emission Vehicle [*Automotive industry*]
CALS......... Christadelphian Auxiliary Lecturing Society [*British*]   (BI)
CALULEV ... California Ultra-Low-Emission Vehicle [*Automotive industry*]
CAM .... Composition and Make-Up
CAM .... Village Aviation, Inc. [*ICAO designator*]   (FAAC)
CAMA .... Coated Abrasive Manufacturers' Association [*British*]   (BI)
CAMC .... Carlsberg Automated Meridian Circle [*Astronomy*]
CAMDA ..... Car and Motorcycle Drivers Association Ltd. [*British*]   (BI)

CAMF........ Canadian Association of Metal Finishers
CAMM....... Computer-Assisted Molecular Modeling [*Chemistry*]
CAMU....... Corrective Action Management Unit [*Environmental science*]
CAN........... Air Canarias S. Coop Ltd. [*Spain*] [*ICAO designator*]   (FAAC)
CAN........... Cancer [*Constellation*]
Can............ Canvas   (DAC)
CAN........... Committee on Aircraft Noise [*ICAO*]   (DA)
CAN........... Customer Access Network
CANEX ...... Canadian Flight Experiment [*NASA*]
CANR........ Canadian NORAD Region [*Aviation*]   (FAAC)
CAO........... Casualty Assistance Officer [*Army*]   (ADDR)
CAO........... Civil Aviation Order
CAO........... Complex Assessment Officer
CAO........... Corrective Action Order [*Environmental Protection Agency*]
                  (ERG)
CAP .... Capital Airlines, Inc. [*ICAO designator*]   (FAAC)
CAP .... Chloraromatic Compound [*Organic chemistry*]
CAP .... Contact Approach [*Aviation*]   (DA)
CAP .... Continuing Airworthiness Panel [*ICAO*]   (DA)
CAP .... Contract Amendment Proposal
CAP .... Cultural Awareness Program
CAPCC ...... Canadian Association of Poison Control Centres
CAPCOM... Capture/Compare [*Electronics*] [*Automotive engineering*]
CAPD .... Climb at Pilot's Discretion [*Aviation*]   (FAAC)
CAPE........ Children's Alliance for Protection of the Environment   (EA)
Caplet........ Capsule/Tablet [*Medicine*]
CAPP .... Computer-Aided Pulse Plating [*Electrochemistry*]
CAPS .... Civil Aviation Purchasing Service [*ICAO*]   (DA)
CAPS .... Corporate Affairs Processing System
CAPSIN .... Civil Aviation Packet Switching Integrated Network   (DA)
CAR .... Cable Television Relay   (NTCM)
CAR .... Cost Allocation Review
CAR .... Inter RCA [*Central African Republic*] [*ICAO designator*]
                  (FAAC)
CARAT....... Cargo Agents Reservation Airwaybill Insurance and Tracking
                  System   (DA)
CARAT....... Coating Ageing-Resistant Aluminum Technology [*Materials
                  science*]
Car Dis Ab ... Careers and the Disabled [*A publication*]
CARE......... Coalition for Auto Repair Equality [*Automotive aftermarket parts
                  lobbying group*]
CARH........ Citizens Against Rationing Health [*An association*]
CARI......... Committee for Action for Rural Indians   (EA)
CARP......... Computer-Aided Rapid Prototyping
CARS........ Community Aerodrome Radio Station   (DA)
CART......... Custom Asynchronous Receiver/Transmitter [*Automotive
                  engineering*]
CARTA....... Catholic Apostolate of Radio, Television, and Advertising
                  (NTCM)
CARU .... Canadian Airspace Reservation Unit [*Aviation*]   (FAAC)
Car Wom..... Career Woman [*A publication*]
CAS........... Christman Air System [*ICAO designator*]   (FAAC)
CAS........... County Architects Society [*British*]   (BI)
CASA......... Contemporary Acapella Society of America   (EA)
CASCD...... Cascade [*Meteorology*]   (FAAC)
CASOR...... Civil Mediator Organisation [*British*]   (DA)
CAT .... Commercial Air Transport   (DA)
CAT .... Computer-Assisted Training
CAT .... Copenhagen Airtaxi [*Denmark*] [*ICAO designator*]   (FAAC)
CATC........ Commonwealth Air Transport Council   (BI)
CATS......... Center for Advanced Television Studies [*British*]   (NTCM)
CATSA....... Confectionery and Allied Trades Sports Association [*British*]
                  (BI)
CATTT ...... Curriculum Assessment and Teacher/Trainer Training
CATW .... Catwalk [*Technical drawings*]   (DAC)
CAU........... Cancun Avioturismo SA [*Mexico*] [*ICAO designator*]   (FAAC)
CAV .... Calm Air [*Canada*] [*ICAO designator*]   (FAAC)
CAV .... Component Analog Video   (NTCM)
CAVE........ Company Average VOC [*Volatile Organic Compound*] Emission
                  [*Environmental Protection Agency*]
CAW.......... Commericial Air Services (Pty) Ltd. [*South Africa*] [*ICAO
                  designator*]   (FAAC)
CAWG .... Christian Alliance of Women and Girls [*British*]   (BI)

CAX	Canpax-Air AG [*Switzerland*] [*ICAO designator*] (FAAC)
CAY	Cayman Airways Ltd. [*British*] [*ICAO designator*] (FAAC)
CAZ	Cat Aviation, AG [*Switzerland*] [*ICAO designator*] (FAAC)
CBA	Civil Aviation Inspectorate of the Czech Republic [*ICAO designator*] (FAAC)
CBAP	(Carboxyphenyl)benzoyl-Aminopenicillanic Acid [*Biochemistry*]
CBAS	Class B Airspace [*Aviation*] (FAAC)
CBC	Congressional Border Caucus [*An association*] (EA)
CBC	Country Bound Connection [*An association*] (EA)
CBD	Christian Book Distributors [*An association*] (EA)
CBDA	Chemical Biological Defense Agency [*Army*]
CBE	Aerovias Caribe SA [*Mexico*] [*ICAO designator*] (FAAC)
CBEC	Concentration-Based Exemption Criteria [*Environmental science*]
CBF	Centreboard Factor [*IOR*]
CBF	Confectioners Benevolent Fund [*British*] (BI)
CBF	Shenyang Regional Administration of CAA of China [*ICAO designator*] (FAAC)
CBH	CB Exective Helicopters [*British*] [*ICAO designator*] (FAAC)
CBH	Commonwealth Bureau of Helminthology (BI)
CBJ	Caribjet, Inc. [*Antigua and Barbuda*] [*ICAO designator*] (FAAC)
CBL	Nichols Air Service, Inc. [*ICAO designator*] (FAAC)
CBM	Cherokee Leasing, Inc. [*ICAO designator*] (FAAC)
CBM	Confidence-Building Measure
CBN	Commonwealth Broadcasting Network [*British*] (NTCM)
CBO	Control Board Operator [*Lighting*] (NTCM)
CBRI	Comic Book Retailers International [*An association*] (EA)
CB1S	Center Beam One Side [*Lumber*] (DAC)
CB2S	Center Beam Two Sides [*Lumber*] (DAC)
CBSA	Class B Surface Area [*Aviation*] (FAAC)
C & Btr	Grade C and Better (DAC)
CBY	Coningsby FTU [*British*] [*ICAO designator*] (FAAC)
CC	Commercial Continuity [*Broadcasting*] (NTCM)
CC	Controlled Circulation [*Newspaper and magazine distribution*] (NTCM)
CCA	Air China [*ICAO designator*] (FAAC)
CCA	Canonical Correlation Analysis [*Mathematics*]
CCA	Child Care Assistance
CCA	Citizens for Cable Awareness (NTCM)
CCA	Civic Catering Association [*British*] (BI)
CCA	Commonwealth Correspondents' Association (BI)
CCA	Contamination Control Area [*Army*] (ADDR)
CCA	County Councils Association [*British*] (BI)
CCA	Covered Conductors Association [*British*] (BI)
CCAS	Class C Airspace [*Aviation*] (FAAC)
CCATTD	Common Chassis Advanced Technology Transition Demonstrator
CCBM	Copper Cylinder and Boiler Manufacturers' Association [*British*] (BI)
CCBN	Central Council for British Naturism (BI)
CCC	Canoe-Camping Club [*British*] (BI)
CCC	Citizens Communication Center (NTCM)
CCC	Club Cricket Conference [*British*] (BI)
CCC	European Aviation Services Ltd. [*British*] [*ICAO designator*] (FAAC)
CCD	Carlos Cervantes del Rio [*Mexico*] [*ICAO designator*] (FAAC)
CCD	Countercurrent Decantation [*Engineering*]
CCE	Cairo Air Transport Co. [*Egypt*] [*ICAO designator*] (FAAC)
CCE	Cathode Current Efficiency [*Electrochemistry*]
CCEW	Congregational Church in England and Wales (BI)
CCF	Catholic Communications Foundation (NTCM)
CCF	Central Control Function [*Aviation*] (DA)
CCH	Chilchota Taxi Aereo SA de CV [*Mexico*] [*ICAO designator*] (FAAC)
CCHS	Coalition for Consumer Health and Safety (EA)
CCI	Climate Control International [*Auto industry supplier*]
CCI	Co-Channel Interference (NTCM)
CCIFP	Chambre de Compensation des Instruments Financiers de Paris
CCIR	Commander's Critical Information Requirement [*Army*] (INF)
CCIS	Coaxial Cable Information System (NTCM)
CCL	Continental Aviation Ltd. [*Ghana*] [*ICAO designator*] (FAAC)
CCLO	Classification and Classified List of Occupations
CCLP	National Coalition of Concerned Legal Professionals (EA)
CCM	Corse-Mediterranee Compagnie [*France*] [*ICAO designator*] (FAAC)
CCM	Cross Cultural Medicine
CCMA	Cotton Canvas Manufacturers Association [*British*] (BI)
CCMM	Council on Children, Media, and Merchandising (NTCM)
CCMTS	Crown Cork Manufacturers' Technical Council [*British*] (BI)
CCO	Aerolineas Coco Club Hoteles de Mexico SA de CV [*ICAO designator*] (FAAC)
CCOI	Committee for Crescent Observation International (EA)
CCP	Cushion Control Point [*Navy*] (ANA)
CCR	Carga Aerea Venezolana Caraven SA [*Venezuela*] [*ICAO designator*] (FAAC)
CCRT	Closed Circuit Radio Transmitter (NTCM)
CC/RTS	Chemical Collection/Request Tracking System [*Environmental Protection Agency*] (ERG)
C/CS	County/Coverage Service [*ISI audience data*] (NTCM)
CCSA	Class C Surface Area [*Aviation*] (FAAC)
CCSM	Corporate Customer Satisfaction Monitor
CCT	Citty Taxi Aereo Nacional SA de CV [*Mexico*] [*ICAO designator*] (FAAC)
CCT	Committee for Competitive Television (NTCM)
CCTI	Committee on Children's Television, Inc. (NTCM)

CCV	Computer-Controlled Vehicle [*Public transit systems*]
CCVS	Combustion Control by Vortex Stratification [*Automotive engine design*]
CCX	Indian Ocean Airlines [*Australia*] [*ICAO designator*] (FAAC)
CCZ	Coastal Confluence Zone [*Aviation*] (DA)
CD	Christian Democrats [*European political movement*] (ECON)
CD	Civil Disobedience
CD	Complete Drawing [*Animation*] (NTCM)
CD	Condition [*Automotive advertising*]
C2D	Chrysler Collision Detection [*Automotive safety and electronics*]
CDA	Chemists' Defence Association [*British*] (BI)
CDAS	Class D Airspace [*Aviation*] (FAAC)
CDB	Community Development Bank
CDB	Composite Double-Base [*Propellant*]
CDBS	Central Database System (DA)
CDC	Cancer Detection Centre [*British*]
CDC	Citizens Democracy Corps [*An association*] (EA)
CDCRAFT	Compact Disc and Cathode Ray Tube Applied Format [*Automotive navigation systems*]
CDE	Coal Development Establishment [*British*] (BI)
CDF	Celiac Disease Foundation (EA)
CD-FM	Compact Disc File Manager [*Computer science*] (NTCM)
CDG	Council for Democratic Government [*Japan*] (ECON)
C!Di	Coefficient of Induced Drag [*Aviation*] (DA)
CDK	Cyclin-Dependent Kinase [*Biochemistry*]
CDL	CCAir, Inc. [*ICAO designator*] (FAAC)
CDLG	Championship Drivers Licensing Group [*Automobile racing*]
CDM	Carga Aerea Dominicana [*Dominican Republic*] [*ICAO designator*] (FAAC)
CDN	Canadian Airlines International Ltd. [*ICAO designator*] (FAAC)
CDN	Coordination [*ICAO designator*] (FAAC)
CDO	Cargo Dor Ltd. [*Ghana*] [*ICAO designator*] (FAAC)
C!Dp	Coefficient of Profile Drag [*Aviation*] (DA)
CDPA	Canadian Defense Preparedness Association
CDR	Contents of Decrement Part of Register [*Computer science*] (NHD)
CDRH	Center for Devices and Radiological Health [*FDA*]
CDRTx	Cadaveric Donor Renal Transplantation [*Medicine*]
CDRV	Crankcase Depression Regulator Valve [*Emissions*] [*Automotive engineering*]
CDS	Career Development Scheme
CDS	Cutting Disposal System [*Oil well drilling*]
CDSA	Class D Surface Area [*Aviation*] (FAAC)
CDU	Central Development Unit
CE	Center of Effort [*Sailing*]
C of E	Certificate of Exemption
C of E	Certificate of Experience (DA)
CE	Conditional Exemption [*Environmental science*]
CEA	Certified Environmental Auditor [*Environmental science*]
CEA	Colt Car Co. [*British*] [*ICAO designator*] (FAAC)
CEAS	Class E Airspace [*Aviation*] (FAAC)
CEAT	Contractor Evidence Audit Team [*Environmental Protection Agency*] (ERG)
CEDAR	Construction of Embedded Dedicated Real-Time System [*Computer science*]
CEDEL	Centrale de Livraison de Valeurs Mobilieres
CEDIA	Custom Electronic Design Installation Association (EA)
CEE	Central and Eastern Europe
CEEM	Council for Education on Electronic Media (NTCM)
CEF	Czech Air Force [*ICAO designator*] (FAAC)
CEG	Cega Aviation Ltd. [*British*] [*ICAO designator*] (FAAC)
CEG	Certified Engineering Geologist [*Environmental science*]
CEG	Computer Education Group [*British*] (BI)
CEG	Consumer Electronics Group [*Education Industries Association*] (NTCM)
CEI	Conference of the Electronics Industry [*British*] (BI)
CEJ	Corporacion Area Ejecutiva SA de CV [*Mexico*] [*ICAO designator*] (FAAC)
CEK	Societe Seca [*France*] [*ICAO designator*] (FAAC)
CEL	Ceneast Airlines Ltd. [*Kenya*] [*ICAO designator*] (FAAC)
CELIS	Conservation and Environment Library Information System
CEM	College of Estate Management [*British*] (BI)
CEMA	Catering Equipment Manufacturers' Association [*British*] (BI)
Cem Ab	Cement-Asbestos Board (DAC)
Cem Fin	Cement Finish (DAC)
Cem Fl	Cement Floor [*Technical drawings*] (DAC)
CEML	Committee to End the Marion Lockdown (EA)
Cem Mort	Cement Mortar [*Technical drawings*] (DAC)
Cem Plas	Cement Plaster [*Technical drawings*] (DAC)
CEN	Central Airways Corp. [*Canada*] [*ICAO designator*] (FAAC)
CENPAC	Central North Pacific [*Aviation*] (FAAC)
CEOA	Civic Entertainment Officers' Association [*British*] (BI)
CEP	Catalytic Extraction Processing [*Recycling*]
CEP	Cathode Electrodeposited Paint [*Environmental science*]
CEP	Certified Environmental Professional [*Environmental science*]
CEP	Company Export Planning
CEPH	Centre d'Etude du Polymorphisme Humain [*Medicine*] (ECON)
CER	Celmar Servicios Aereos SA de CV [*Mexico*] [*ICAO designator*] (FAAC)
CERT	Centers for Education and Research in Therapeutics [*FDA*]
CES	China Eastern Airlines [*ICAO designator*] (FAAC)
CESA	Class E Surface Area [*Aviation*] (FAAC)

CESW......... Conditionally Exempt Specified Wastestream [*Environmental science*]
CET............ Ceeta-Kel Air [*France*] [*ICAO designator*]   (FAAC)
CET............ Certified Engineering Technologist [*Environmental science*]
CET............ Certified Environmental Trainer
CETD........ Calculated Estimated Time of Departure [*Aviation*]   (DA)
CETO .... Calculated Estimated Time of Overflight [*Aviation*]   (DA)
CEU .... Central Executive Unit   (DA)
CEV .... Centre d'Essais en Vol [*France*] [*ICAO designator*]   (FAAC)
CEVA........ Centre d'Essaies Vehicule Automobile [*Motor Vehicle Test Center*] [*French*]
CEX .... Capitol Air Express [*ICAO designator*]   (FAAC)
CEYC......... Church of England Youth Council   (BI)
CEZ .... Central Economic Zone
CF .... Condensation Figure [*Surface physical chemistry*]
CF .... Conjugation Factor [*Plant genetics*]
CFA............ Call for Action [*An association*]   (NTCM)
CFA............ Cancer Fund of America
CFA............ Controlled Firing Area [*Aviation*]   (FAAC)
CFA............ Cookery and Food Association [*British*]   (BI)
CFADC....... Canadian Forces Air Defense Command [*ICAO designator*]   (FAAC)
CFBA........ Chinchilla Fur Breeders' Association [*British*]   (BI)
CFC............ Canadian Armed Forces [*ICAO designator*]   (FAAC)
CFD .... Computational Fluid Dynamics [*Chemical engineering*]
CFD .... Crainfield Institute of Technology [*British*] [*ICAO designator*]   (FAAC)
CFDA........ Christian Film Distributors Association   (NTCM)
CFE........... Carbide-Forming Element [*Metal treating*]
CFE........... Cityflyer Express [*British*] [*ICAO designator*]   (FAAC)
CFEWB ..... Colonial, Fish-Eating Water Bird
CFF .... Children's Film Foundation Ltd. [*British*]   (BI)
CFG .... Childrens Fashion Group [*British*]   (BI)
CFG .... Condor Flugdienst GmbH [*Germany*] [*ICAO designator*]   (FAAC)
CFI............. Camp Fire, Inc.   (AEE)
CFI............. Christian Friends of Israel [*British*]   (BI)
CFL............ Compact Fluorescent Light
CFL............ Consort Aviation [*British*] [*ICAO designator*]   (FAAC)
CFM .... Carbon-Free Medium [*Cytology*]
CFM .... Code Fragment Manager [*Computer science*]
CFMA......... Chair Frame Manufacturers' Association [*British*]   (BI)
CFMU .... Centralized Flow Management Unit   (DA)
CFO .... Central Forecast Office   (DA)
CFP .... CompanIa de Aviacion Faucett SA [*Peru*] [*ICAO designator*]   (FAAC)
CFPL .... Carryover from Previous Log [*Aviation*]   (FAAC)
CFR........... Chauffair Ltd. [*British*] [*ICAO designator*]   (FAAC)
CFROI .... Cash Flow Return on Investment
CFS........... Empire Airlines, Inc. [*ICAO designator*]   (FAAC)
CFT............ Jet Freighters, Inc. [*ICAO designator*]   (FAAC)
CFU .... CAA Flying Unit [*British*] [*ICAO designator*]   (FAAC)
CFV-CVS ... Critical Flow Venture-Constant Volume Sampler   (ERG)
CFX........... Flexair Ltd. [*British*] [*ICAO designator*]   (FAAC)
CFZ........... Critical Friendly Zone [*Army*]   (ADDR)
CG .... Ceiling Grille [*Technical drawings*]   (DAC)
CG .... Coarse Grain   (DAC)
CG .... Completion Guarantor [*Motion picture financing*]   (NTCM)
CGA .... Congressional Air Ltd. [*ICAO designator*]   (FAAC)
CGAC........ China General Aviation Corp. [*ICAO designator*]   (FAAC)
CGAS........ Class G Airspace [*Aviation*]   (FAAC)
CGAT .... Chromaffin Granule Amine Transporter [*Biochemistry*]
CGCVA ...... Coast Guard Combat Veterans Association   (EA)
CGE .... Certificate of General Education
CGE .... Nelson Aviation College [*New Zealand*] [*ICAO designator*]   (FAAC)
CG2E .... Center Groove Two Edges [*Lumber*]   (DAC)
CGF .... Czech Government Flying Service [*ICAO designator*]   (FAAC)
CGI .... Capital Guaranty Insurance
CGIC .... Clinical Global Impression of Change
CGL .... Centro Gerontologico Latino [*An association*]   (EA)
CGL .... Circling Guidance Light [*Aviation*]   (FAAC)
CGM......... Cargoman [*Oman*] [*ICAO designator*]   (FAAC)
CGMA ...... Casein Glue Manufacturers Association [*British*]   (BI)
CGMT .... Census of Graduate Medical Trainees
CGO........... Chicago Air, Inc. [*ICAO designator*]   (FAAC)
CGOAP ...... Conjugate Gradient Optimization Algorithm Program [*Lighting system design*]
CGP .... College of General Practitioners [*British*]   (BI)
CGTB........ Clinical Gene Therapy Branch
CGW......... Great Wall Airlines [*China*] [*ICAO designator*]   (FAAC)
CGY .... Centigray   (ADDR)
CH .... Charcoal [*Automotive advertising*]
CH .... Critical Height   (DA)
CHA.......... Chest and Heart Association [*British*]   (BI)
CHA.......... Chiltern Airways [*British*] [*ICAO designator*]   (FAAC)
CHAP .... Challenge Handshake Authentication Protocol [*Telecommunications*]   (PCM)
CHAP .... Child Health Assessment Program
CHAP .... Commission for Historical Architectural Preservation
CHAPI....... Compact Helicopter Approach Path Indicator   (DA)
CHB........... Cyanohydroxybutene [*Organic chemistry*]
CHC........... China Ocean Helicopter Corp. [*ICAO designator*]   (FAAC)

CHE........... Top Flight Air Service, Inc. [*ICAO designator*]   (FAAC)
CHEMNET ... Chemical Network [*Chemical Transportation Emergency Center*]   (ERG)
CHEMS...... Chemical Education Material Study [*American Chemical Society*]   (AEE)
Chess L....... Chess Life [*A publication*]
CHF .... Children's Heart Fund   (EA)
CHH .... Airlines of Hainan Province [*China*] [*ICAO designator*]   (FAAC)
CHI............ Cougar Helicopter, Inc. [*Canada*] [*ICAO designator*]   (FAAC)
Chim .... Chimney [*Technical drawings*]   (DAC)
China T....... China Today [*A publication*]
CHIP .... Classification, Hazard Information and Packaging [*British*]
CHIP .... Customized Health Information Project [*Computer science*]
CHK.......... Flying Boat, Inc. [*ICAO designator*]   (FAAC)
CHL.......... Cohlmia Aviation [*ICAO designator*]   (FAAC)
CHM......... Aero Chombo SA [*Mexico*] [*ICAO designator*]   (FAAC)
CHMM...... Certified Hazardous Materials Manager [*Environmental science*]
CHN.......... Channel Island Aviation [*ICAO designator*]   (FAAC)
CHO .... Ciga Hotels Aviation SpA [*Italy*] [*ICAO designator*]   (FAAC)
CHOL E ..... Cholesterol Esters [*Organic chemistry*]   (MAH)
CHORUS ... Coalition for Harmony of Races in the US   (EA)
CHOV........ Changeover [*Aviation*]   (FAAC)
CHP........... Aviacion de Chiapas [*Mexico*] [*ICAO designator*]   (FAAC)
CHQ .... Chautauqua Airlines [*ICAO designator*]   (FAAC)
CHR........... Air Charter Services [*Zaire*] [*ICAO designator*]   (FAAC)
CHR........... Convent of the Holy Rood [*British*]   (BI)
Ch Rev Int... China Review International
CHRIS/HACS ... Chemical Hazards Response Information System/Hazard Assessment Computer System [*Coast Guard*]   (ERG)
CHS........... Challenge Aviation Pty Ltd. [*Australia*] [*ICAO designator*]   (FAAC)
CHS........... Channel Handicap System [*Yacht racing*]
CHS........... Cripples' Help Society [*British*]   (BI)
CHU .... Church Aircraft Ltd. [*ICAO designator*]   (FAAC)
CHUT........ Cable Households Using Television [*Cable television ratings*]   (NTCM)
CHV.......... Chivenor FTU [*British*] [*ICAO designator*]   (FAAC)
CHX.......... Air Charter Express [*France*] [*ICAO designator*]   (FAAC)
CHY.......... China Air Cargo [*ICAO designator*]   (FAAC)
CHZ........... Cheshire Air Training School [*British*] [*ICAO designator*]   (FAAC)
CIA .... Capital Investment Analysis [*Business term*]
CIA .... Collagen-Induced Arthritis [*Medicine*]
C3IAC........ Command, Control, Communications and Intelligence Acquisition Center [*Army*]   (RDA)
CIAS.......... Crash Impact Absorbing Structure [*Automotive safety*]
CIC............ Celtic Inernational Ltd. [*British*] [*ICAO designator*]   (FAAC)
CIC............ Corn Items Collectors Association   (EA)
CIEIA .... Competitive Inhibition Enzyme Immunoassay [*Analytical biochemistry*]
CIESJ .... Centre International d'Enseignement Superieur de Journalisme [*UNESCO*]   (NTCM)
CIF............. Calcium Influx Factor [*Neurobiology*]
CIFOR........ Center for International Forestry Research
CIG .... Ceiling   (DA)
CII.............. Cook Islands International [*New Zealand*] [*ICAO designator*]   (FAAC)
CIL............. Cecil Aviation Ltd. [*ICAO designator*]   (FAAC)
CIL............. Component Intergation Laboratories
CILA .... Chartered Institute of Loss Adjusters [*British*]   (BI)
CINAA ...... Cyclic Instrumental Neutron Activation Analysis
CINE .... Cinema   (NTCM)
CINP .... Collegium International Neuro-Psychopharmacologicum
CIP............. Command Inspection Program [*Army*]   (INF)
CIP............. Council of Iron Producers [*British*]   (BI)
CIPA.......... Chartered Institute of Patent Agents [*British*]   (BI)
CIR .... Arctic Circle Service, Inc. [*ICAO designator*]   (FAAC)
CIR .... Circulation   (NTCM)
CIR BKR.... Circuit Breaker [*Technical drawings*]   (DAC)
CIS .... Cane Invert Syrup [*Food sweetener*]
CIS .... Card Information Structure [*Computer science*]
CIS .... Cargo Information System [*Aviation*]   (DA)
CIS .... Chaillotine Air Service [*France*] [*ICAO designator*]   (FAAC)
CIS .... Chartered Institute of Secretaries [*British*]   (BI)
CIS .... Coal Industry Society [*British*]   (BI)
CIS .... Cooperative Independent Surveillance   (DA)
CIS .... Cross Industry Standard
CISAC .... Changchu International Symposium on Analytical Chemistry [*1990*]
CISC .... Christmas Island Services Corp.
CIS-COMMS ... Communications and Information Services - Communications
CISTR .... Continuous Ideally Stirred Tank Reactor [*Chemical engineering*]
CIT............. City-Jet Luftverklehrsges, GmbH [*Austria*] [*ICAO designator*]   (FAAC)
CIT............. Corporate Information Technology
CITP .... Corporate Information Technology Plan
CITS .... Corporate Information Technology Strategy
CIU .... Club & Institute Union Ltd. [*British*]   (BI)
CIV .... Civil Aviation Authority of New Zealand [*ICAO designator*]   (FAAC)
CIWS......... Central Instrument Warning System [*Aviation*]   (DA)
CJC............ [*Charles J.*] Colgan & Associates, Inc. [*ICAO designator*]   (FAAC)
CJG............ Zhejiang Airlines [*China*] [*ICAO designator*]   (FAAC)

CJS .... Commonwealth Jet Services, Inc. [*ICAO designator*]   (FAAC)
CKA .... Cook Inlet Aviation, Inc. [*ICAO designator*]   (FAAC)
CKE .... Corporate Aviation Services, Inc. [*ICAO designator*]   (FAAC)
CKR .... Crown Air Systems [*ICAO designator*]   (FAAC)
CKS............. [*Connie*] Kalitta Services, Inc. [*ICAO designator*]   (FAAC)
CKT .... Caledonian Airways Ltd. [*British*] [*ICAO designator*]   (FAAC)
C/L.............. Center Light [*Aviation*]   (DA)
CL .... Centerline Light [*Aviation*]   (DA)
CL .... Centralized Lubrication [*Automotive engineering*]
CLA .... Certified Legal Assistant
CLA .... Church Literature Association [*British*]   (BI)
CLA .... Clear Ice [*Aviation*]   (DA)
CLA .... Columbia [*Italy*] [*ICAO designator*]   (FAAC)
CLA .... Community Legal Aid
CLAD .... Clerical Administration
CLAM .... Coalition for Life for All Mollusks
CLAO .... Council of Lebanese American Organizations   (EA)
CLB .... CAA Calibration Flight [*British*] [*ICAO designator*]   (FAAC)
CLBN.......... Credit Lyonnais Bank Nederland [*Credit Lyonnais' Dutch
                       subsidiary*]   (ECON)
CLC............. Classic Air AG [*Switzerland*] [*ICAO designator*]   (FAAC)
CLD .... Center for Living Democracy   (EA)
CLeaR-TV ... Christian Leaders for Responsible Television   (NTCM)
CLEVITE... Cleveland Graphite [*American Cleveland Graphite Corp.*]
                       [*Automotive parts supplier*]
CLF .... Bristol Flying Centre Ltd. [*British*] [*ICAO designator*]   (FAAC)
CLG .... Societe Chaleng Air [*France*] [*ICAO designator*]   (FAAC)
CLH .... Christian League for the Handicapped   (EA)
CLH .... Lufthansa Cityline [*Germany*] [*ICAO designator*]   (FAAC)
CLIPS......... Chemical List Index and Processing System [*Environmental
                       Protection Agency*]   (ERG)
CLK .... Clark Aviation Corp. [*ICAO designator*]   (FAAC)
CLL............. Aerovias Castillo SA [*Mexico*] [*ICAO designator*]   (FAAC)
CLL............. Centerline Lighting Will be Provided [*Aviation*]   (DA)
CLN .... Barns Olson Aeroleasing Ltd. [*British*] [*ICAO designator*]
                       (FAAC)
CLO .... Client Liaison Officer
CLO .... Complex Layered Oxide [*Physical chemistry*]
CLR............. Trans American Airways, Inc. [*ICAO designator*]   (FAAC)
CLS............. Canadian Lumber Size   (DAC)
CLS............. Centralized Lighting System [*Automotive engineering*]
CLT............. Caribbean Air Transport Co., Inc. [*Netherlands*] [*ICAO
                       designator*]   (FAAC)
CLTE......... Coefficient of Linear Thermal Expansion
CLU .... Club Air Europe Ltd. [*British*] [*ICAO designator*]   (FAAC)
CLU .... Corporate Library Update [*A publication*]
CLV .... Cal Aviation SA [*Greece*] [*ICAO designator*]   (FAAC)
CLX............. Cargolux Airline International [*Luxembourg*] [*ICAO
                       designator*]   (FAAC)
CLY............. Clyde Surveys Ltd. [*British*] [*ICAO designator*]   (FAAC)
CLZ............. Aerotaxis Calzada SA de CV [*Mexico*] [*ICAO designator*]
                       (FAAC)
CLZ............. Cushion Landing Zone [*Navy*]   (ANA)
CM.............. Circular Mail
CMA .... Cable Makers' Association [*British*]   (BI)
CMA .... Catering Managers Association of Great Britain and Northern
                       Ireland   (BI)
CMA .... Central European Airlines [*Czechoslovakia*] [*ICAO designator*]
                       (FAAC)
C-MAC....... Champagne-Mumm Admiral's Cup [*Yacht racing*]
CMB .... Climb [*or Climbing*] [*Aviation*]   (FAAC)
C & MB...... Dressed and Matched Beaded [*Lumber*]   (DAC)
CMBR .... Cosmic Microwave Background Radiation
CMC .... Ceramic Matrix Composite [*Materials science*]
CMC .... Collins Motor Corp. [*Alternative engine technology*]
CMC .... Computer Mediated Communication
CMDB .... Composite-Modified Double-Base [*Propellant*]
CMDC........ Christian-Muslim Dialogue Committee   (EA)
CME .... Comprehensive (Ground Water) Monitoring Evaluation
                       [*Environmental Protection Agency*]   (ERG)
CME .... Prince Edward Air Ltd. [*Canada*] [*ICAO designator*]   (FAAC)
CMEL........ Comprehensive (Ground Water) Monitoring Evaluation Log
                       [*Environmental Protection Agency*]   (ERG)
CMG.......... Camargue Air Transport [*France*] [*ICAO designator*]   (FAAC)
CMI .... Continental Micronesia, Inc. [*Guam*] [*ICAO designator*]   (FAAC)
CMIDR....... Compressed Mosiacked Image Data Record [*Geology*]
CMIS .... Cane Medium Invert Syrup [*Food sweetener*]
CML .... Commander Air Carter Ltd. [*Canada*] [*ICAO designator*]
                       (FAAC)
CML .... Complement Mediated Cell Lysis [*Immunology*]
CMM.......... Air 2000 Airlines Ltd. [*Canada*] [*ICAO designator*]   (FAAC)
CMMA ...... Concrete Mixer Manufacturers' Association [*British*]   (BI)
CMN.......... Children's Miracle Network [*Medicine*]
CMNT........ Children's Miracle Network Television
CMOT........ Caterpillar Micro Oxidation Test [*Automotive lubricant*]
CMP .... Camp   (ABBR)
CMP .... Common-Midpoint
CMP .... Compania Panamena de Aviacion SA [*Panama*] [*ICAO
                       designator*]   (FAAC)
CMPE......... Contractors' Mechanical Plant Engineers [*British*]   (BI)
CMPF........ Commander, Maritime Prepositioned Force [*Navy*]   (ANA)
CMPRS ...... Compress   (ABBR)
CMPRSB.... Compressible   (ABBR)

CMPRSBNS ... Compressibleness   (ABBR)
CMPRSBT ... Compressibility   (ABBR)
CMPRSD ... Compressed   (ABBR)
CMPRSG ... Compressing   (ABBR)
CMPRSN ... Compression   (ABBR)
CMPRSR ... Compressor   (ABBR)
CMPRSV ... Compressive   (ABBR)
CMPRSVY ... Compressively   (ABBR)
CMPRTL ... Compartmental   (ABBR)
CMPRTLZ ... Compartmentalize   (ABBR)
CMPRTLZD ... Compartmentalized   (ABBR)
CMPRTLZG ... Compartmentalizing   (ABBR)
CMPS........ Campus   (ABBR)
CMPS........ Compost   (ABBR)
CMPSIT ... Composite   (ABBR)
CMPSR ..... Compressor   (ABBR)
CMPST ..... Compost   (ABBR)
CMPSTD ... Composted   (ABBR)
CMPSTG ... Composting   (ABBR)
CMPSU...... Composure   (ABBR)
CMPTR...... Comptroller   (ABBR)
CMPU .... Compute   (ABBR)
CMPUG .... Computing   (ABBR)
CMPUL..... Compulsion   (ABBR)
CMPULR... Compulsory   (ABBR)
CMPULRY ... Compulsorily   (ABBR)
CMPULV... Compulsive   (ABBR)
CMPUN..... Compunction   (ABBR)
CMPUNSY ... Compunctiously   (ABBR)
CMPUR ..... Compurgation   (ABBR)
CMPUTAN ... Computation   (ABBR)
CMPUTD... Computed   (ABBR)
CMPUTG... Computing   (ABBR)
CMPUTN ... Computation   (ABBR)
CMPUTR... Computer   (ABBR)
CMPUTRZ ... Computerize   (ABBR)
CMPUTRZD ... Computerized   (ABBR)
CMPUTRZG ... Computerizing   (ABBR)
CMR .... Cam Air Management Ltd. [*British*] [*ICAO designator*]   (FAAC)
CMR .... Children's Medical Research
CMRA .... Camera   (ABBR)
CMRC .... Commerce   (ABBR)
CMRCL...... Commercial   (ABBR)
CMRCLSM ... Commercialism   (ABBR)
CMRCLST ... Commercialist   (ABBR)
CMRCLSTC ... Commercialistic   (ABBR)
CMRCLZ ... Commercialize   (ABBR)
CMRCLZD ... Commercialized   (ABBR)
CMRCLZG ... Commercializing   (ABBR)
CMRD........ Comrade   (ABBR)
CMRDSP... Comradeship   (ABBR)
CMS .... Carbon Molecular Sieve [*Adsorption technology*]
CMS .... Corrective Measure Study [*Environmental science*]
CMSAR...... Commissar   (ABBR)
CMSARY ... Commissary   (ABBR)
CMSNG ..... Commissioning   (ABBR)
CMSNL...... Commissional   (ABBR)
CMSNY...... Commissionary   (ABBR)
CMSR........ Commissar   (ABBR)
CMSRA...... Commiserate   (ABBR)
CMSRAD... Commiserated   (ABBR)
CMSRAG... Commiserating   (ABBR)
CMSRAN... Commiseration   (ABBR)
CMSRAR... Commiserator   (ABBR)
CMSRAV... Commiserative   (ABBR)
CMSRAVY ... Commiseratively   (ABBR)
CMSRY...... Commissary   (ABBR)
CMSSN...... Commission   (ABBR)
CMSSNR ... Commissioner   (ABBR)
CMT .... Casement Aviation [*ICAO designator*]   (FAAC)
CMT .... Church Music Trust [*British*]   (BI)
CMTD .... Commited   (ABBR)
CMTG .... Commiting   (ABBR)
CMTMT...... Commitment   (ABBR)
CMTRLR... Comptroller   (ABBR)
CMTRY...... Cemetery   (ABBR)
CMUL .... Cumulus   (ABBR)
CMULA .... Cumulate   (ABBR)
CMULAD... Cumulated   (ABBR)
CMULAG... Cumulating   (ABBR)
CMULAN... Cumulation   (ABBR)
CMULAV... Cumulative   (ABBR)
CMULAVY ... Cumulatively   (ABBR)
CMULNBMS ... Cumulonimbus   (ABBR)
CMULS...... Cumulus   (ABBR)
CMULU..... Cumulus   (ABBR)
CMUN....... Commune   (ABBR)
CMUNC.... Communicate   (ABBR)
CMUNCB... Communicable   (ABBR)
CMUNCBNS ... Communicableness   (ABBR)
CMUNCBT ... Communicability   (ABBR)
CMUNCBY ... Communicably   (ABBR)
CMUNCD ... Communicated   (ABBR)

CMUNCG ... Communicating (ABBR)
CMUNCN ... Communication (ABBR)
CMUNCNT ... Communicant (ABBR)
CMUNCV ... Communicative (ABBR)
CMUNCVY ... Communicatively (ABBR)
CMUNCY ... Communicatory (ABBR)
CMUND..... Communed (ABBR)
CMUNG..... Communing (ABBR)
CMUNG..... Communique (ABBR)
CMUNN..... Communion (ABBR)
CMUNSM ... Communism (ABBR)
CMUNST... Communist (ABBR)
CMUNSTC ... Communistic (ABBR)
CMUNT..... Community (ABBR)
CMUNZ..... Communize (ABBR)
CMUNZD ... Communized (ABBR)
CMUNZG ... Communizing (ABBR)
CMUNZN ... Communization (ABBR)
CMUT....... Commute (ABBR)
CMUTA ..... Commutate (ABBR)
CMUTAB... Commutable (ABBR)
CMUTABT ... Commutability (ABBR)
CMUTAD ... Commutated (ABBR)
CMUTAG ... Commutating (ABBR)
CMUTAR... Commutator (ABBR)
CMUTAV ... Commutative (ABBR)
CMUTD ..... Commuted (ABBR)
CMUTG ..... Commuting (ABBR)
CMUTR ..... Commuter (ABBR)
CMX .... Compania Mexicana de Taxis Aereos SA [Mexico] [ICAO designator] (FAAC)
CMY .... Cape Smyth Air [ICAO designator] (FAAC)
CN.............. Cneius (ABBR)
CNA........... Centennial [Spain] [ICAO designator] (FAAC)
CNAA......... Chemical Neutron Activation Analysis
CNB........... Air Columbus SA [Portugal] [ICAO designator] (FAAC)
CNC........... Confederate National Congress (EA)
CNC........... Corporacion Aereo Cencor SA de CV [Mexico] [ICAO designator] (FAAC)
CNCDG ...... Concluding (ABBR)
CNCED ...... Concede (ABBR)
CNCED ...... Concentrated (ABBR)
CNCEDD ... Conceded (ABBR)
CNCEDDY ... Concededly (ABBR)
CNCEDG ... Conceding (ABBR)
CNCEDR.... Conceder (ABBR)
CNCEG ...... Concentrating (ABBR)
CNCEL....... Conceal (ABBR)
CNCELB.... Concealable (ABBR)
CNCELD... Concealed (ABBR)
CNCELG.... Concealing (ABBR)
CNCELR... Concealer (ABBR)
CNCELT .... Concealment (ABBR)
CNCEN ...... Concentrate (ABBR)
CNCENC.... Concentric (ABBR)
CNCENCT ... Concentricity (ABBR)
CNCENCY ... Concentrically (ABBR)
CNCENN ... Concentration (ABBR)
CNCENR ... Concentrator (ABBR)
CNCENV ... Concentrative (ABBR)
CNCENVY ... Concentratively (ABBR)
CNCET...... Conceit (ABBR)
CNCETD.... Conceited (ABBR)
CNCETDY ... Conceitedly (ABBR)
CNCETG.... Conceiting (ABBR)
CNCEV....... Conceive (ABBR)
CNCEVB.... Conceivable (ABBR)
CNCEVBT ... Conceivability (ABBR)
CNCEVBY ... Conceivably (ABBR)
CNCEVD.... Conceived (ABBR)
CNCEVG.... Conceiving (ABBR)
CNCEVR.... Conceiver (ABBR)
CNCIS........ Concise (ABBR)
CNCISN..... Concision (ABBR)
CNCISY ..... Concisely (ABBR)
CNCLA....... Conciliate (ABBR)
CNCLAB.... Conciliable (ABBR)
CNCLAD.... Conciliated (ABBR)
CNCLAG.... Conciliating (ABBR)
CNCLAN ... Cancellation (ABBR)
CNCLAN .. Conciliation (ABBR)
CNCLAR.... Conciliator (ABBR)
CNCLARTRY ... Conciliatory (ABBR)
CNCLARY ... Conciliatory (ABBR)
CNCLAV.... Conclave (ABBR)
CNCLB...... Cancelable (ABBR)
CNCLD ...... Canceled (ABBR)
CNCLD ...... Conclude (ABBR)
CNCLG ...... Canceling (ABBR)
CNCLN ...... Cancellation (ABBR)
CNCLR...... Canceler (ABBR)
CNCLR...... Councilor (ABBR)
CNCLSN .... Conclusion (ABBR)

CNCLSV .... Conclusive (ABBR)
CNCLU ...... Conclude (ABBR)
CNCLUD ... Concluded (ABBR)
CNCLUG ... Concluding (ABBR)
CNCLUN ... Conclusion (ABBR)
CNCLUR.... Concluder (ABBR)
CNCLUV ... Conclusive (ABBR)
CNCLUVY ... Conclusively (ABBR)
CNCLV....... Conclave (ABBR)
CNCMTNT ... Concomitant (ABBR)
CNCNTRA ... Concentrate (ABBR)
CNCNTRAG ... Concentrating (ABBR)
CNCNTRC ... Concentric (ABBR)
CNCNTRN ... Concentration (ABBR)
CNCOC...... Concoct (ABBR)
CNCOCD... Concocted (ABBR)
CNCOCG ... Concocting (ABBR)
CNCOCN ... Concoction (ABBR)
CNCOCR ... Concoctor (ABBR)
CNCOCV ... Concoctive (ABBR)
CNCOM..... Concomitance (ABBR)
CNCOMT ... Concomitant (ABBR)
CNCOR...... Concourse (ABBR)
CNCPN ...... Conception (ABBR)
CNCPT...... Concept (ABBR)
CNCPTL .... Conceptual (ABBR)
CNCPTLY ... Conceptually (ABBR)
CNCPTLZ ... Conceptualize (ABBR)
CNCPTLZD ... Conceptualized (ABBR)
CNCPTLZG ... Conceptualizing (ABBR)
CNCPTSM ... Conceptualism (ABBR)
CNCPTST ... Conceptualist (ABBR)
CNCPTV.... Conceptive (ABBR)
CNCR........ Cancer (ABBR)
CNCR........ Concern (ABBR)
CNCRD ...... Concord (ABBR)
CNCRDNC ... Concordance (ABBR)
CNCRDT.... Concordant (ABBR)
CNCRDTY ... Concordantly (ABBR)
CNCRG ...... Concerning (ABBR)
CNCRG ...... Concurring (ABBR)
CNCRN ...... Concern (ABBR)
CNCRND ... Concerned (ABBR)
CNCRNG ... Concerning (ABBR)
CND........... Concord Airlines Nigeria Ltd. [ICAO designator] (FAAC)
CNDA........ Clapham Notre Dame Association [British] (BI)
CNE........... Air Toronto, Inc. [Canada] [ICAO designator] (FAAC)
CNET .... Centre National d'Etudes des Telecommunications [France] [ICAO designator] (FAAC)
CNF........... Canifair Aviation, Inc. [Canada] [ICAO designator] (FAAC)
CNG........... Coastal Airways [ICAO designator] (FAAC)
CNG........... Cyclic Nucelotide-Gated [Neurobiology]
CNI............ Communication Navigation (NFPA)
CNI............ Coordination Number Invariance [Chemistry]
CNIE .... Committee for the National Institute for the Environment [Lobby group]
CNL........... Centennial Airlines, Inc. [ICAO designator] (FAAC)
CNL........... Chemonucleolysis [Surgery]
CNR........... Condor Acro Scrvices, Inc. [ICAO designator] (FAAC)
CNS .... Centennial Flight Centre [Canada] [ICAO designator] (FAAC)
CNT........... Centre National d'Etudes des Telecommunications [France] [ICAO designator] (FAAC)
CNTRL...... Control Key [Electronics]
CNW.......... China Northwest Airlines [ICAO designator] (FAAC)
CNX.......... Allcanada Express Ltd. [Canada] [ICAO designator] (FAAC)
CO............. Certificate of Occupancy (DAC)
C-O .... Company Owned (NTCM)
COA......... Committee for an Open Archives (EA)
COA......... Continental Airlines, Inc. [ICAO designator] (FAAC)
COA......... Council on Aging
COB.......... Commission des Operations de Bourse
COBE .... Council on Broadcast Education [Later, CEEM] (NTCM)
COC.......... Certificate of Compliance [FCC] (NTCM)
COC.......... Chain of Custody
COC.......... Cocesna [ICAO designator] (FAAC)
COC.......... Committee on Carcinogenicity [British]
COCHL AMP ... Cochleare Amplum [Heaping spoonful] [Pharmacy] (MAH)
COCOM..... Combatant Command [Military]
COD.......... Cadkey Object Developer [Computer science]
CODES...... Critical Outcome Data Evaluation System [Auto safety research]
CODIAC.... Centralized or Distributed Integrated Access Control [Computer science]
COF .... Coefficient of Friction
COF .... Confortair, Inc. [Canada] [ICAO designator] (FAAC)
COFACE..... Compagnie Francaise pour l'Assurance du Commerce Exterieur
COG.......... Cleansing Officers' Guild [British] (BI)
COGAID .... Coast Guard Assistance Instruction Data
COGME ..... Council on Graduate Medical Education [Department of Health and Human Services]
COHC........ China Ocean Helicopter Corp. [ICAO designator] (FAAC)
COI............ Cytochrome Oxidase I [An enzyme]
Coin W .... Coin World [A publication]

COK........... Ciskei International Airways Corp. [*South Africa*] [*ICAO designator*]   (FAAC)
COL........... Columbia Airlines Ltd. [*Canada*] [*ICAO designator*]   (FAAC)
Co-Lat........ Complement of Latitude
COLD........ Computer Output to LASER Disk   (PCM)
COLRAM... Committee on Local Radio Audience Measurement [*National Association of Broadcasters*]   (NTCM)
COLRIC..... Council for Learning Resources in Colleges [*British*]
COLTAM... Committee on Local Television Audience Measurement [*National Association of Broadcasters*]   (NTCM)
COM.......... Comair, Inc. [*ICAO designator*]   (FAAC)
COM.......... Committee on Mutagenicity [*British*]
COM.......... Common Object Model [*Microsoft*]
COM.......... Communications Port [*Computer science*]
COMA....... Coke Oven Managers' Association [*British*]   (BI)
COMDEX ... Communications and Data Processing Exposition
COMET ..... Careers on the Move for Engineers of Tomorrow [*An association*]
COMO....... Compass Locator [*Aviation*]   (DA)
COMPAS... Computer-Oriented Metering Planning and Advisory System [*Aviation*]   (DA)
CoMPP....... Coalition of Minority Policy Professionals   (EA)
COMSND ... Commissioned   (DA)
COMSOCCENT ... Commander, Special Operating Forces Central Command [*Navy*]   (ANA)
COMSONOR ... Commander, Allied Forces Southern Norway [*Navy*]   (ANA)
COMTRAIN ... Commodore Training [*Computer science*]
COMUSNAVCENT ... Commander, US Naval Forces Central Command   (ANA)
CON........... Continental Oil Co. [*ICAO designator*]   (FAAC)
CONR........ Continental NORAD Region [*Aviation*]   (FAAC)
Cons .... Conscience [*A publication*]
CONSOB .. Commissione Nazionale per le Societa e la Borsa
Con Spec ..... Construction Specification   (DAC)
CONTAM ... Committee on Nationwide Television Audience Measurement   (NTCM)
Conv .... Convector   (DAC)
CONVWEPS LOADEX ... Conventional Weapons Loading Exercise [*Navy*]   (ANA)
COOL........ Chorus Object-Oriented Layer [*Computer science*]
COP........... Certificate of Participation
COPR......... Control of Pesticides Regulations [*British*]
COPS......... Concerns of Police Survivors [*An association*]
COR........... Committee of the Regions [*Belgium*]   (ECON)
COR BD ..... Corner Bead [*Technical drawings*]   (DAC)
Corn .... Cornice   (DAC)
CORR......... Corridor   (DA)
COS .... Constant Optimum Separation Lane [*Aviation*]   (DA)
COSAC....... Computing System for Air Cargo   (DA)
COSE......... Cooperative Operating System Environment [*Computer science*]
COT........... Cottesmore TTTE [*British*] [*ICAO designator*]   (FAAC)
COW.......... Cow Observers Worldwide [*An association*]   (EA)
COX.......... Cyclooxygenase [*An enzyme*]
COY........... Transportes Aereos Coyhaique [*Chile*] [*ICAO designator*]   (FAAC)
COZ........... Corair [*France*] [*ICAO designator*]   (FAAC)
CP .... Cloud Point [*Petroleum characteristic*]
CP .... [*Fire Alarm Voice*] Communication Panel [*NFPA pre-fire planning symbol*]   (NFPA)
CP .... Constant Power   (DA)
CP .... Custodial Parent
CPA .... Caribbean Press Association   (NTCM)
CPA .... Cathay Pacific Airways Ltd. [*British*] [*ICAO designator*]   (FAAC)
CPA .... Children's Play Activities Ltd. [*British*]   (BI)
CPAE........ Calf Pulmonary Artery Endthelial [*Cell line*]
CPAG .... Child Poverty Action Group [*British*]   (BI)
CPC........... Aero Campeche SA de CV [*Mexico*] [*ICAO designator*]   (FAAC)
CPC........... Capsular Polysaccharide Complex [*Biochemistry*]
CPCC......... Command Power Cruise Control [*Diesel engines*] [*Automotive engineering*]
CPCRA...... Community Program for Clinical Research on AIDS [*FDA*]
CPF........... Central Provident Fund [*Singapore*]   (ECON)
CPG .... Certified Professional Geologist
CPGRP....... Cost per Gross Rating Point [*Advertising*]   (NTCM)
CPI............ Center for Public Integrity
CPI............ Continuous Process Improvement [*Chemical engineering*]
CPKO .... Crude Palm Kernel Oil
CPL........... Chaparral Airlines [*ICAO designator*]   (FAAC)
CPL........... Classification, Packaging and Labelling [*Toxicology*]
CPM .... Collector of Public Moneys
CPMA .... Chinchilla Pelt Marketing Association Ltd. [*British*]   (BI)
CPMA .... Color Pigments Manufacturing Association
CPO .... Central Purchasing Organization
CPO .... Corporate Aircraft Co. [*ICAO designator*]   (FAAC)
CPQ .... Center for Produce Quality
CPR........... Computerized Patient Record
CPR........... Corporate Air, Inc. [*ICAO designator*]   (FAAC)
CPR........... Correct, Pause, Recovery [*Automobile driving*]
CPS........... Cam Profile Switching [*Automotive engine design*]
CPS........... Cargo & Passenger Air Services Ltd. [*Switzerland*] [*ICAO designator*]   (FAAC)
CPS........... Compass Aviation [*British*] [*ICAO designator*]   (FAAC)
CPSB .... Compulsorily Preserved Superannuation Benefit
CPSS........... Certified Professional Soil Scientist [*Environmental science*]

CPT........... Corporate Air [*ICAO designator*]   (FAAC)
CPT........... Cyclopentyltheophylline [*Organic chemistry*]
CPW .... Chippewa Air Commuter, Inc. [*ICAO designator*]   (FAAC)
CPX........... Capital Air Service, Inc. [*ICAO designator*]   (FAAC)
CPZ........... Cargo & Passenger Air Services Ltd. [*Switzerland*] [*ICAO designator*]   (FAAC)
CQA........... Chalk Quarrying Association [*British*]   (BI)
CQA........... Coast Air Ltd. [*Kenya*] [*ICAO designator*]   (FAAC)
CQA........... Construction Quality Assurance [*Environmental science*]
CQC........... Construction Quality Control [*Environmental science*]
CR .... Consolidated Revenue
Cr .... Cross   (DAC)
CRA .... Commercial Rabbit Association [*British*]   (BI)
CRA .... Coronado Aerolineas Ltda. [*Colombia*] [*ICAO designator*]   (FAAC)
CRAA .... Critical Reflection Activation Analysis
CRABI....... Child Restraint and Air Bag Information [*Automotive safety*]
CRAM .... Cumulative Radio Audience Method   (NTCM)
CRASH...... Cornell Reconstruction of Accident Speeds on the Highway
CRB .... Community Research Bureau
CrB........... Coronae Borealis [*Astronomy*]
CRC........... Conair Aviation Ltd. [*Canada*] [*ICAO designator*]   (FAAC)
CRD .... Aerolineas Cordillera Ltda. [*Chile*] [*ICAO designator*]   (FAAC)
CRD .... Criminal Records Directorate [*Army*]   (ADDR)
CRE .... Cree Airways Corp. [*Canada*] [*ICAO designator*]   (FAAC)
CREA .... Conversion for Reclaiming Earth in the Americas [*An association*]
CREM .... Cyclic-Adenosine Monophosphate-Responsive Element Modulator [*Genetics*]
CRG .... Cave Research Group of Great Britain   (BI)
CRG .... City-Link Airlines Ltd. [*Nigeria*] [*ICAO designator*]   (FAAC)
CRI .... Canari Airlines [*Israel*] [*ICAO designator*]   (FAAC)
CRI .... Children's Relief International [*British*]   (BI)
CRI .... Color Reversal Intermediate [*Photography*]   (NTCM)
CRIMS ...... Chemical Reaction Interface Mass Spectrometry
CRK .... Air Pacific Crake [*Philippines*] [*ICAO designator*]   (FAAC)
CRL........... Corse Air International [*France*] [*ICAO designator*]   (FAAC)
CRM .... Collision Risk Model [*Aviation*]   (DA)
CRM .... Commander Mexicana SA de CV [*Mexico*] [*ICAO designator*]   (FAAC)
CRMA .... Cotton and Rayon Merchants Association [*British*]   (BI)
CRMC .... Certified Radio Marketing Consultant   (NTCM)
CRN .... Children's Radio Network   (NTCM)
CRN .... Empresa Aerocaribbean SA [*Cuba*] [*ICAO designator*]   (FAAC)
CRNI .... Certified Registered Nurse of Infusion
CRO.......... Crown Airways, Inc. [*ICAO designator*]   (FAAC)
CRP........... Aerotaxis Corporativo SA de CV [*Mexico*] [*ICAO designator*]   (FAAC)
CRQ .... Air Creebec [*Canada*] [*ICAO designator*]   (FAAC)
CRRS .... CHAMPUS [*Civilian Health and Medical of the Uniformed Services*] Regional Review System
CRS........... Comercial Aerea SA de CV [*Mexico*] [*ICAO designator*]   (FAAC)
CRS........... Computer Readable System
CRS........... Coreceptor Skewed [*Immunology*]
CRSL......... Christian Road Safety League [*British*]   (BI)
CRSS .... Colo-Rectal Surgical Society
CRT .... Caribintair SA [*Haiti*] [*ICAO designator*]   (FAAC)
CRT .... Court Reporting Typist
CRTPB .... Canadian Radio Technical Planning Board   (NTCM)
CRUZ........ Cruise [*Automotive advertising*]
CRW .... Crownair [*Canada*] [*ICAO designator*]   (FAAC)
CRX .... Cross Air AG [*Switzerland*] [*ICAO designator*]   (FAAC)
CRZ .... Servicios Aereos Cruzeiro do Sul SA [*Brazil*] [*ICAO designator*]   (FAAC)
CS .... Caulking Seam   (DAC)
CS .... Culture Supernatant [*Microbiology*]
CSA........... Canavaninosuccinic Acid [*Organic chemistry*]   (MAH)
CSA........... Ceskoslovenske Aerolinie [*Czechoslovakia*] [*ICAO designator*]   (FAAC)
CSA........... Clean Shelter Area [*Army*]   (ADDR)
CSA........... Consumer Savings Alliance   (EA)
CSAC........ Council on Superconductivity for American Competitiveness
CSB........... Carrier and Sideband   (DA)
CSB........... Center for the Study of Beadwork [*An association*]   (EA)
CSC........... Cable/Show Cause [*FCC*]   (NTCM)
CSC........... Church Schools Company Ltd. [*British*]   (BI)
CSC........... Sichuan Airlines [*China*] [*ICAO designator*]   (FAAC)
CSD........... Cold-Shock Domain [*Genetics*]
C & SD....... Corporate and Staff Development
CSD........... Courier Services, Inc. [*ICAO designator*]   (FAAC)
CSDC........ Child Service Demonstration Center [*Department of Education*]
CSF........... Contrast Spatial Frequency [*Vision research*]
CSFV .... Classical Swine Fever Virus
CSGWPP ... Comprehensive State Ground Water Protection Program [*Environmental science*]
CSH .... Shanghai Airlines [*China*] [*ICAO designator*]   (FAAC)
CSI .... Central Skyport, Inc. [*ICAO designator*]   (FAAC)
CSI .... Compressive Safety Index [*Engineering design*]
CSJ .... Castle Aviation, Inc. [*ICAO designator*]   (FAAC)
CSK........... Cytoskeleton [*Cytology*]
CSL........... Minson Aviation, Inc. [*ICAO designator*]   (FAAC)
CSMA........ Civil Service Motoring Association [*British*]   (BI)
CSMTT ...... Combat Systems Mobile Training Team [*Navy*]   (ANA)

CSN .... Guangzhou Regional Administration of CAA of China [*ICAO designator*] (FAAC)
CSNav........ CompuServe Navigator [*CompuServe, Inc.*] [*Telecommunications*] (PCM)
CSNP........ Causeway Section, Nonpowered [*Navy*] (ANA)
CSO .... Community Service Obligation
CSP............. Casper Air Service, Inc. [*ICAO designator*] (FAAC)
CSP............. Control System Program [*Manufacturing engineering*] [*Computer science*]
CSPOE....... Combat Systems Post-Overhaul Examination [*Navy*] (ANA)
CSR............. Cable/Special Relief [*FCC*] (NTCM)
CSR............. Cis-Air [*Czechoslovakia*] [*ICAO designator*] (FAAC)
CSR............. Combat Stress Reaction [*Army*] (ADDR)
CSS .... Complete Service Supplier [*Vendor operations*]
CSS .... Controlled Swirl Scavenging [*Automotive engine design*]
CSS .... Corse Aero Service [*France*] [*ICAO designator*] (FAAC)
CSSO........ Chief State School Officer (AEE)
CSSP........ Certified Security and Safety Professional [*Environmental science*]
CSSQ........ Child Safety Seat Questionnaire [*Auto safety research*]
CSSTR....... Continuous Segregated Stirred Tank Reactor [*Chemical engineering*]
CST............. Certification Short Test [*Exhaust emissions testing*] [*Automotive engineering*]
CST............. Coast Air KS [*Norway*] [*ICAO designator*] (FAAC)
CST............. Crude Sulfate Turpentine
CSTA......... Cable/Special Temporary Authority [*FCC*] (NTCM)
CSTVRP..... Computer Security Technical Vulnerability Reporting Program [*Army*] (ADDR)
CSW .... Commercial Sex Worker [*Social science terminology for a prostitute*]
CSW .... Worldwide Air Charter Systems [*Canada*] [*ICAO designator*] (FAAC)
CSX............. Coastair [*Denmark*] [*ICAO designator*] (FAAC)
CT .... Cartridge Tape (NTCM)
CT .... Color Temperature (NTCM)
CT .... Commercial Television [*FCC*] (NTCM)
CT .... Computerized Tomography (ECON)
CT .... Continental Tropical Air [*Meteorology*] (DA)
CTA .... Calculated Time of Arrival (DA)
CTA .... Camping Trade Association of Great Britain Ltd. (BI)
CTA .... Chain Testers Association of Great Britain (BI)
CTA .... Compagnie de Transport Aerien [*Switzerland*] [*ICAO designator*] (FAAC)
CTAC......... Cable Television Technical Advisory Committee [*FCC*] (NTCM)
CTAC......... Creative Tourist Agents' Conference [*British*] (BI)
CTAS......... Controlled Airspace [*ICAO designator*] (FAAC)
CTC .... Commanders' Target Criteria [*Army*] (ADDR)
CTCM .... Chroma Time Compressed Multiplex (NTCM)
CTCOTP .... Cold Temperature Carbon Monoxide Test Procedure [*Exhaust emissions testing*] [*Automotive engineering*]
CTE............. Air Tenglong [*China*] [*ICAO designator*] (FAAC)
CTEM........ Cryogenic Transmission Electron Microscopy
CTF............. Cetfa SA [*Spain*] [*ICAO designator*] (FAAC)
CTG .... Canadian Coast Guard [*ICAO designator*] (FAAC)
CTG .... Copy to Go (NTCM)
CTH............. China General Aviation Corp. [*ICAO designator*] (FAAC)
CTL............. Central Airlines, Inc. [*ICAO designator*] (FAAC)
CTM .... Commandement du Transport Aerien Militaire Francais [*France*] [*ICAO designator*] (FAAC)
CTMA .... Collapsible Tube Manufacturers' Association [*British*] (BI)
CTMB........ Canal Transport Marketing Board [*British*] (BI)
CTMS........ Computer-Controlled Test Management System [*Environmental science*]
CTN .... Croatia Airlines [*ICAO designator*] (FAAC)
CTO .... Aerotaxis del Centro SA [*Mexico*] [*ICAO designator*] (FAAC)
CTOD........ Character-to-Date [*Microsoft Corp. FoxPro function*] (PCM)
CTR .... Civil Tilt Rotor [*Aviation*] (DA)
CTR .... Transport Air Centre [*France*] [*ICAO designator*] (FAAC)
CTRA........ Coal Tar Research Association [*British*] (BI)
CTS............. Catholic Truth Society [*British*] (BI)
CTS............. China Travel Service (ECON)
CTSA......... Crucible and Tool Steel Association [*British*] (BI)
CTT............. Common Task Training [*Military*] (ADDR)
CTX .... Carolina Air Transit, Inc. [*ICAO designator*] (FAAC)
CTX .... Ciguatoxin [*Agent in fish poisoning*]
CTX .... Combined Training Exercise [*Military*] (ADDR)
CTY .... Cryderman Air Service [*ICAO designator*] (FAAC)
CTZ .... Cata SACIFI [*Argentina*] [*ICAO designator*] (FAAC)
CUA........... China United Airlines [*ICAO designator*] (FAAC)
CUA........... Colour Users' Association [*British*] (BI)
CUB .... Empresa Cubana de Aviacion [*Cuba*] [*ICAO designator*] (FAAC)
CUO........... [*C.C. Enrique*] Cuahonte Delgado [*Mexico*] [*ICAO designator*] (FAAC)
CUPUOS.... Committee on the Peaceful Uses of Outer Space [*United Nations*] (NTCM)
CUS .... Customs Available [*Aviation*] (DA)
CUSD .... Credit Union Share Draft
CV .... Carbonyl Value [*Food science*]
CV .... Conventional Vehicle [*Environmental science*]
CVA .... Air Transport (Chatham Island) Ltd. [*New Zealand*] [*ICAO designator*] (FAAC)
CVCC........ Continuously Varying Cell Constant [*Electrochemical instrumentation*]

CVI .... Cassovia Air [*Slovakia*] [*ICAO designator*] (FAAC)
CVINO ...... Clearance Void if Not Off [*Aviation*] (FAAC)
CVISC .... Combat Visual Information Support Center [*DoD*]
CVJB .... Cryptologic Van Junction Box [*Navy*] (ANA)
CVL .... Coval Air Ltd. [*Canada*] [*ICAO designator*] (FAAC)
CVN .... Bromma Flygskola/Cabair [*Sweden*] [*ICAO designator*] (FAAC)
Cvnr .... Convenor
CVO .... Commercial Vehicle Operations [*Highway safety*]
CVP .... Conservative Party of Australia [*Political party*]
CVRTC....... Commercial Vehicle and Road Transport Club [*British*] (BI)
CVS........... Cyclic Voltametric Stripping [*Electrochemistry*]
CV1S.......... Center Vee One Side [*Lumber*] (DAC)
CV2S.......... Center Vee Two Sides [*Lumber*] (DAC)
C/W........... Clerk of the Works (DAC)
CW............. Cool White (DAC)
CWA........... Canada West Air Ltd. [*ICAO designator*] (FAAC)
CWB .... Commonwealth Writers of Britain (BI)
CWC .... Challenge Air Cargo, Inc. [*ICAO designator*] (FAAC)
CWD.......... Consecutive Weeks Discount (NTCM)
CWD.......... Cotswold Executive Aviation [*British*] [*ICAO designator*] (FAAC)
CWH.......... Canadian Warplane Heritage Museum [*ICAO designator*] (FAAC)
CWIE......... Container, Weapon, Individual Equipment [*Army*] (ADDR)
CWIS......... Campus-Wide Information Systems [*Internet*]
CWL .... Cranwell FTU [*British*] [*ICAO designator*] (FAAC)
CWLM .... Cumulative Working Level Months [*Radon exposure measure*] (ERG)
CWMA ...... Country Wool Merchants Association [*British*] (BI)
CWPR........ Committee on Women in Public Relations (NTCM)
CWR .... Checkwriting Redemptions [*Business term*]
CWS .... Air Swazi Cargo (Pty) Ltd. [*Swaziland*] [*ICAO designator*] (FAAC)
CWU.......... Wuhan Airlines [*China*] [*ICAO designator*] (FAAC)
CWWA ...... Coloured Workers' Welfare Association [*British*] (BI)
CWX .... Cool White Deluxe (DAC)
CXA .... Xiamen Airlines [*China*] [*ICAO designator*] (FAAC)
CXN .... China Southwest Airlines [*ICAO designator*] (FAAC)
CXO .... Conroe Aviation Services, Inc. [*ICAO designator*] (FAAC)
CXP........... TEM Enterprises [*ICAO designator*] (FAAC)
CXT .... Coastal Air Transport [*St. Croix*] [*ICAO designator*] (FAAC)
CYA .... Cheyenne Airways, Inc. [*ICAO designator*] (FAAC)
Cybm.......... Cubic Yard Bank Measurement (DAC)
CYC .... Cypair Tours Ltd. [*Cyprus*] [*ICAO designator*] (FAAC)
CYCM .... Cubic Yard Compacted Measurement (DAC)
CYH........... Yunnan Airlines [*China*] [*ICAO designator*] (FAAC)
CYM........... Compass Airlines of Australia [*ICAO designator*] (FAAC)
CYMS........ Catholic Young Men's Society [*Ireland*] (BI)
CYN........... Zhongyuan Aviation Co. [*China*] [*ICAO designator*] (FAAC)
CYP........... Cyprus Airways Ltd. [*ICAO designator*] (FAAC)
CYT .... Crystal Shamrock [*ICAO designator*] (FAAC)
CZ.............. Coefficient Z-Axis [*Downforce on a racing car*] [*Aerodynamics*]

D

D	Daytime (NTCM)
D	Defendant
D	Detector (NFPA)
D	Digest
D	Dissolve (NTCM)
D	District
D	Dry (NFPA)
D	Duct (NFPA)
D2	Angola [*Aircraft nationality and registration mark*] (FAAC)
3D	Swaziland [*Aircraft nationality and registration mark*] (FAAC)
D4	Cape Verde [*Aircraft nationality and registration mark*] (FAAC)
DA	Danger Area (DA)
DA	Decision Altitude [*Aviation*] (DA)
DA	Distributed Application [*Automotive engineering*]
DAA	Decatur Aviation, Inc. [*ICAO designator*] (FAAC)
DAAC	Distributed Active Archive Center [*NASA*]
DAAR	Deviation Approved as Requested [*Aviation*] (FAAC)
DAC	McDonnell Douglas Corp. [*ICAO designator*] (FAAC)
DACO	Departure Airfield Group [*Army*] (ADDR)
DAD	Dorado Air [*Dominican Republic*] [*ICAO designator*] (FAAC)
DADA	Designers and Art Directors Association [*British*] (BI)
DAE	Danish Air Force [*ICAO designator*] (FAAC)
DAF	Demographic Adjustment Factor (NTCM)
DAF	Dilutin Attenuation Factor [*Metallurgy*]
DAG	Aquadag [*Graphite coating*] (NTCM)
DAH	Air Algerie [*Algeria*] [*ICAO designator*] (FAAC)
DAJ	Direct Air [*British*] [*ICAO designator*] (FAAC)
DAK	Dakair [*France*] [*ICAO designator*] (FAAC)
DAL	Delta Air Lines, Inc. [*ICAO designator*] (FAAC)
DALTA	Dramatic and Lyric Theatres Association [*British*] (BI)
DAMDA	Dairy Appliance Manufacturers' and Distributors' Association Ltd. (BI)
DAN	Danair AS [*Denmark*] [*ICAO designator*] (FAAC)
DAOB	Daily Average Occupied Beds [*Medicine*]
DAP	Aerovias Dap [*Chile*] [*ICAO designator*] (FAAC)
DAP	Direct Aid Program
DAP	Dystrophin-Associated Protein [*Biochemistry*]
DAPD	Descend at Pilot's Discretion [*Aviation*] (FAAC)
DAR	Danish Army [*ICAO designator*] (FAAC)
DAS	Diallyl Sulfide
DAS	Dollar Air Services Ltd. [*British*] [*ICAO designator*] (FAAC)
DASCO	Discriminant Analysis with Shrunken Coveriances [*Mathematics*]
DASH	Digital Audio Stationary Head [*Recording*] (NTCM)
DASHO	Designed Agency Safety and Health Official (ERG)
DAT	Delta Air Transport [*Belgium*] [*ICAO designator*] (FAAC)
DAT	Dental Aptitude Test [*Education*] (AEE)
DATAS	Data Link and Transponder Analysis System (DA)
DATCO	Duty Air Traffic Control Officer (DA)
DAV	Dirac Aviation [*France*] [*ICAO designator*] (FAAC)
DAVSS	Doppler Acoustic Vortex Sensing Equipment [*Meteorology*] (DA)
DAX	Aalborg Airtaxi [*Denmark*] [*ICAO designator*] (FAAC)
DAY	Benday [*Engraving*] (NTCM)
DAY	Daylight (NTCM)
D/B	Digital-to-Binary (NTCM)
DBA	Air Alpha, Inc. [*ICAO designator*] (FAAC)
DBA	Disabled Businesspersons Association (EA)
DBA/M	Data Base Administrator/Manager [*Army*]
DBBL	Dismounted Battlespace Battle Lab [*Army*] (INF)
DB Clg	Double-Headed Ceiling (DAC)
DBD	Air Niagara Express, Inc. [*Canada*] [*ICAO designator*] (FAAC)
DBE	Danube-Air Ltd. [*Hungary*] [*ICAO designator*] (FAAC)
DBJ	Duchess of Brittany (Jersey) Ltd. [*British*] [*ICAO designator*] (FAAC)
DBK	[*N. B.*] MacDonald Service Ltd. [*New Zealand*] [*ICAO designator*] (FAAC)
DBMA	Dibutylmalonic Acid [*Organic chemistry*]
DBO	Royal Phoenix Airlines [*Nigeria*] [*ICAO designator*] (FAAC)
DBT	Dibutyltin [*Organic chemistry*]
DC	Design Change
DC	Developing Country
DC	Direct Operating Cost (DA)
DC	Disconnect (NTCM)

DC	Double Column [*Publishing*] (NTCM)
DC	Double Contact [*Lamp base type*] (NTCM)
D & C	Drill and Ceremony [*Military*] (ADDR)
DC	Dry Chemical System [*NFPA pre-fire planning symbol*] (NFPA)
DCA	Defensive Counterair [*Army*] (ADDR)
DCA	Desoxycorticosterone Acetate [*Endocrinology*] (MAH)
DCC	Caribbean Air Cargo [*Barbados*] [*ICAO designator*] (FAAC)
DCD	Dynamically-Correlated Domain [*Physics*]
DCF	Dry Cubic Feet (ERG)
DCHD	Di(N-carbazoly)hexadiyne [*Organic chemistry*]
DCI	Daily Call-In
DCI	Direct Cylinder Injection [*Engine design*]
D & CM	Dressed and Center Matched [*Lumber*] (DAC)
DCM	Dry Cell Mass
DCN	Federal Armed Forces of Germany [*ICAO designator*] (FAAC)
DCP	Display Control Program (NTCM)
DCRA	Dyers' and Cleaners' Research Association (BI)
DCS	Differential Cross Section [*Chemistry*]
DCSOT	Deputy Chief of Staff for Operations and Intelligence [*Army*]
DCT	Direct Flight Ltd. [*British*] [*ICAO designator*] (FAAC)
DCTS	Data Communication Terminal System [*Computer science*] (DA)
DCU	Data-Cache Unit [*Computer science*]
DCU	Desert Camouflage Uniform [*Military*]
DD	Duct Detector [*NFPA pre-fire planning symbol*] (NFPA)
DDB	Diagnostic Development Branch [*National Institutes of Health*]
DDB	Distribution Disk Builder [*Computer science*]
DDC	Detroit Diesel Corp. [*Automotive industry supplier*]
DDDU	Drug Detector Dog Unit
DDP	Dependents' Dental Plan [*DoD*]
DDT	Double Dual Tandem [*Aviation*] (DA)
DE	Deceleration Enleanment [*Automotive fuel systems*]
DE	Detector (NFPA)
DEA	Dairy Engineers' Association [*British*] (BI)
DEA	Delta Aerotaxi [*Italy*] [*ICAO designator*] (FAAC)
DEBS	Deoxyerythronolide B Synthase [*An enzyme*]
DEB SPIS...	Debita Spissitudo [*Proper Consistency*] [*Pharmacy*] (MAH)
DEC	Daily Effective Circulation (NTCM)
DEE	Transportation America Corp. [*ICAO designator*] (FAAC)
DEESC	Deescalate (ABBR)
DEESCD	Deescalated (ABBR)
DEESCG	Deescalating (ABBR)
DEESCN	Deescalation (ABBR)
DEF	Defection [*or Defector*] (ABBR)
DEF	Deflagrate (ABBR)
DEF	Deflect (ABBR)
DEFI	Deficiency (ABBR)
DEFL	Deflate (ABBR)
DEFLOR	Defloration (ABBR)
DEFMT	Deafmute (ABBR)
DEFN	Deafen (ABBR)
DEFND	Deafened (ABBR)
DEFNG	Deafening (ABBR)
DEFNGY...	Deafeningly (ABBR)
DEFNS	Deafness (ABBR)
DEFR	Deafer (ABBR)
DEFST	Deafest (ABBR)
DEFTNS ...	Deftness (ABBR)
DEFY	Deafly (ABBR)
DEGRAD ...	Degradable (ABBR)
DEIFCN	Deification (ABBR)
DEIFD	Deified (ABBR)
DEIFG	Deifying (ABBR)
DEIFR	Deifier (ABBR)
DEJ	Delta Jet SA [*Spain*] [*ICAO designator*] (FAAC)
DEL	Deliberate (ABBR)
DELCY	Delinquency (ABBR)
DELE	Delete (ABBR)
DELG	Dealing (ABBR)
DELIN........	Delinquency (ABBR)
DELR	Dealer (ABBR)
DELU	Delusion (ABBR)
DEL V	Deluge Valve (DAC)

DEM.........	Demand (ABBR)
DEM.........	Demur (ABBR)
DEMOBED ...	Demobilized (ABBR)
DEMOC....	Democracy (ABBR)
DEMON.....	Demonology (ABBR)
DEMONOL ...	Demonologic (ABBR)
DEND.........	Dendrology (ABBR)
DENDRO...	Dendrometer (ABBR)
DENDROL ...	Dendrology (ABBR)
DENOT.....	Denotation (ABBR)
DENSP.......	Deanship (ABBR)
DENT.........	Denture (ABBR)
DEO...........	Diesel Engine Oil
DEOB........	Dental Explanation of Benefits [Army]
DEOD........	Deodorant (ABBR)
DEODZ.....	Deodorize (ABBR)
DEODZD..	Deodorized (ABBR)
DEODZG..	Deodorizing (ABBR)
DEODZN...	Deodorization (ABBR)
DEODZR ...	Deodorizer (ABBR)
DEP...........	Defence and Ex-Services Party of Australia [Political party]
DEP...........	Depilate (ABBR)
DEP...........	Depilatory (ABBR)
DEPD........	Departed (ABBR)
DEPEND....	Dependency (ABBR)
DEPERM...	Deperming [Navy] (ANA)
DEPEX.......	Deployment Exercise [Military] (ADDR)
DEPG........	Departing (ABBR)
DEPL........	Depilation (ABBR)
DEPON.....	Deponent (ABBR)
DEPT........	Departure (ABBR)
DEPTL.......	Departmental (ABBR)
DEPU.......	Departure (ABBR)
DEPUTN...	Deputation (ABBR)
DER..........	Departure End of Runway [Aviation] (DA)
DERD........	Display of Extracted RADAR Data (DA)
DERIVB.....	Derivable (ABBR)
DERIVD....	Derived (ABBR)
DERIVG....	Deriving (ABBR)
DERIVN....	Derivation (ABBR)
DERIVV....	Derivative (ABBR)
DERM.......	Dermatophyte (ABBR)
DERM.......	Diagnostic Energy Reserve Module [Airbags and safety systems]
DERMAT...	Dermatology (ABBR)
DERNS.......	Dearness (ABBR)
DES..........	Chilcotin Caribou Aviation [Canada] [ICAO designator] (FAAC)
DESAL.......	Desalinization (ABBR)
DESCRPN ...	Description (ABBR)
DESID........	Desiderata (ABBR)
DESID........	Desired (ABBR)
DESIDER...	Desiderative (ABBR)
DESIG........	Designer (ABBR)
DESL........	Diesel (ABBR)
DET..........	Delta Aviation SA [Spain] [ICAO designator] (FAAC)
DET..........	Double End Trimmed (DAC)
DETF........	Data Exchange Test Facility (DA)
DEV..........	Red Devils Parachute Display Team [British] [ICAO designator] (FAAC)
DEVCOM ...	Device Communications [Computer science]
DEX..........	Interflight, Inc. [ICAO designator] (FAAC)
DF............	Daylight Factor (DAC)
DF............	Deere Funk [Automotive industry supplier]
DF............	Deposition Form [Army] (ADDR)
DFA..........	Aero Coach Aviation International, Inc. [ICAO designator] (FAAC)
DFA..........	Dimensional Fund Advisors [Fund-management firm] (ECON)
DFIST.......	Duty-Free Into-Store Cost
DFL...........	Donauflug Bedarfsfluggesellschaft GmbH [Austria] [ICAO designator] (FAAC)
DFL...........	Double Four-Valve Long Distance [Cosworth racing engines]
Dflct..........	Deflection (DAC)
DFMEA.....	Design Failure-Mode Effects Analysis [Automotive engineering]
DFS..........	Detailed Functional Specification (DA)
DFS..........	Dwyer Aircraft Sales, Inc. [ICAO designator] (FAAC)
DFT..........	Air Direct Ltd. [British] [ICAO designator] (FAAC)
DFT..........	Downdraft (DA)
DFTI.........	Distance from Touchdown Indicator [Aviation] (DA)
DFV..........	Double Four Valve [Cosworth racing engines]
DFVR........	Defense Visual Flight Rule [Military] (DA)
DFWMAC ...	Distributed Foundation Wireless Media Access Control [Computer science]
DFX..........	Dylan Flight Service SA [Switzerland] [ICAO designator] (FAAC)
DGD.........	Dialkylglycine Decarboxylase [An enzyme]
DGI...........	Direccion General de la Inteligencia [Intelligence agency] [Cuba]
DGP.........	Dangerous Goods Panel [ICAO] (DA)
DGSI........	Don't Get Sucked In
DGT.........	Digital Equipment Corp. [ICAO designator] (FAAC)
DHA.........	Docosahexaenoic Acid [Organic chemistry]
DHC.........	Boeing Dehavilland Canada [ICAO designator] (FAAC)
DHC.........	Dihydrocodeine [An analgesic] [Pharmacology]
DHHEC.....	Deaf and Hard of Hearing Entrepreneurs Council (EA)
DI............	Detergent Inhibitor [Lubricants]
DI............	Difficulty Index (AEE)
DIA..........	Denver International Airport [Facetious translation: Delay It Again] (ECON)
DIA..........	Dialogue (NTCM)
DIA..........	Diaphragm (NTCM)
DIA..........	Direct Air, Inc. [Germany] [ICAO designator] (FAAC)
DIB..........	Decency in Broadcasting (NTCM)
DIB..........	Defence Information Bulletin [A publication]
DIDMCA...	Depository Institutions Deregulation and Monetary Decontrol Act [1980]
DIN..........	Aerodin SA de CV [Mexico] [ICAO designator] (FAAC)
DIN..........	Do It Now Foundation [An association]
DipAgE......	Diploma in Agricultural Economics
DipAK.......	Diploma in Applied Kinesiology
DipAnat....	Diploma in Anatomy
DipAppSt....	Diploma in Applied Statistics
DipCEpi.....	Diploma in Clinical Epidemiology
DipChD....	Diploma in Chest Diseases
DipClinHyp ...	Diploma in Clinical Hypnosis
DipClinNut ...	Diploma in Clinical Nutrition
DipClinPharm ...	Diploma in Clinical Pharmacology
DipCM......	Diploma in Community Medicine
DipComm(Acc) ...	Diploma in Commerce (Accounting)
DipCPsy....	Diploma in Child Psychiatry
DipCVD....	Diploma in Cardiovascular Disease
DipDDCP...	Diploma in Drug Development and Clinical Pharmacology
DipDermat ...	Diploma in Dermatology
DipEnvHlth ...	Diploma in Environmental Health
DipEpid....	Diploma in Epidemiology
DipFamMed ...	Diploma in Family Medicine
DipFamT ...	Diploma in Family Therapy
DipFinMan ...	Diploma in Financial Management
DipFP.......	Diploma in Family Planning
DipGUM	Diploma in Genito-Urinary Medicine
DipHlthE....	Diploma in Health Education
DipHumBiol ...	Diploma in Human Biology
DipHumNut ...	Diploma in Human Nutrition
DipHyp.......	Diploma in Hypnosis
DipIntMed ...	Diploma in Internal Medicine
DipLLIRel ...	Diploma in Labor Law and Industrial Relations
DipMed......	Diploma in Medicine
DipMedAc..	Diploma in Medical Acupuncture
DipMedHyp ...	Diploma in Medical Hypnosis
DipMEE.....	Diploma in Mechanical and Electrical Engineering
DipMic......	Diploma in Microbiology
DipMid.....	Diploma in Midwifery
DipMJ(Clin) ...	Diploma in Medical Jurisprudence (Clinical)
DipMLT	Diploma in Medical Laboratory Technology
DipMS.......	Diploma in Museum Studies
DipNA	Diploma in Nursing Administration
DipNE........	Diploma in Nursing Education
DipOccHazMan ...	Diploma in Occupational Hazard Management
DipOccHlth ...	Diploma in Occupational Health
DipOccMed ...	Diploma in Occupational Medicine
DipOHS	Diploma in Occupational Health and Safety
DipOS........	Diploma in Oral Surgery
DipPall.......	Diploma in Palliative Care
DipPhilMed ...	Diploma in Philosophy of Medicine
DipPhysAnth ...	Diploma in Physical Anthropology
DipPM.....	Diploma in Professional Management
DipPrDerm ...	Diploma in Practical Dermatology
DipPsy.......	Diploma in Psychiatry
DipPsy.......	Diploma in Psychotherapy
DipSM.......	Diploma in Sports Medicine
DipSObC ...	Diploma in Shared Obstetric Care
DipSpSci.....	Diploma in Sports Science
DipTCD.....	Diploma in Tuberculosis and Chest Diseases
DipTChM...	Diploma in Traditional Chinese Medicine
DIR...........	Departmentally-Initiated Review
DIR...........	Dirgantara Air Service PT [Indonesia] [ICAO designator] (FAAC)
DirLt........	Direction Light [Navigation]
DIS............	Disease Intervention Specialist [Medicine]
DIZ...........	Dissolve (NTCM)
DJA	Disc Jockey Association (NTCM)
DJB...........	Air Djibouti [ICAO designator] (FAAC)
DJT............	Denver Jet, Inc. [ICAO designator] (FAAC)
DKA	Daka [Kazakhstan] [ICAO designator] (FAAC)
DKE..........	Jubilee Airways Ltd. [British] [ICAO designator] (FAAC)
Dkg..........	Decking (DAC)
DKM..........	Dakomat [Poland] [ICAO designator] (FAAC)
DL............	Diffuse Leiomyomatosis [Medicine]
DL............	Draft Legislation
DLA	Air Dolomiti [Italy] [ICAO designator] (FAAC)
DLAT	Delay Time [Aviation] (FAAC)
DLCP........	Data Link Controller-Processor [Automotive engineering] [Electronics]
DLH..........	Deutsche Lufthansa, AG [Germany] [ICAO designator] (FAAC)
DLI	Delay Indefinite (DA)
DLPU........	Data Link Processor Unit (DA)
DLS..........	Data Link Splitter (DA)
DM............	Daily Mirror [A publication]
DM............	Doctor Martens [Footwear]

DMA........... Data-Matching Agency
DMA........... Maersk Air IS [*Denmark*] [*ICAO designator*]   (FAAC)
DMD........... Deputy Managing Director
DMD........... RST Aviation, NV [*Belgium*] [*ICAO designator*]   (FAAC)
DMF........... Dyers of Man-Made Fibre Fabrics Federation [*British*]   (BI)
DMG........... Directed Metalation Group [*Organic chemistry*]
DMR........... Diploma in Medical Rehabilitation
DMRC........ Dynamic Mid-Ride Controls [*Truck seating*]
DMSO........ Defense Modeling and Simulation Office [*Military*]
DMSOG..... Diploma in Medicine, Surgery, Obstetrics and Gynecology
DMVS........ Deutz Magnetic Valve System [*Diesel engines*]
DMWV....... Descendants of Mexican War Veterans [*An association*]   (EA)
DMZ........... Declared Management Zone
Dn .... Dolphin [*Mooring post*] [*British*]
DNA........... Aerodespachos de El Salvador [*ICAO designator*]   (FAAC)
DNCCC ...... Directorate of Naval Command, Control and Communications
DNCE........ Directorate of Naval Communications Engineering
DNCSS ...... Director, Navy Configuration Survival and Safety
DND........... Eldinder Aviation [*Sudan*] [*ICAO designator*]   (FAAC)
DNO........... Alinord [*Italy*] [*ICAO designator*]   (FAAC)
DNR........... Did Not Respond
DNR........... Dynamair Aviation, Inc. [*Canada*] [*ICAO designator*]   (FAAC)
DNS........... Development Needs Analysis
DNS........... Domain Name System [*Computer science*]
DNTM........ Disseminated Nontuberculous Mycobacterial Infection
DNWND .... Downwind [*Aviation*]   (FAAC)
DNY........... Danish Navy [*ICAO designator*]   (FAAC)
DO .... Disability Officer
DO .... Dolly Out [*Cinematography*]   (NTCM)
DOA .... Compania Dominicana de Aviacion SA [*Dominican Republic*] [*ICAO designator*]   (FAAC)
DOB........... Dobrolet Airlines [*Russian Federation*] [*ICAO designator*]   (FAAC)
DOC........... Date of Commencement
DOC........... Designated Operational Coverage   (DA)
DOC........... Distributed Operator Console [*Environmental science*]
DOC........... Dropout Compensator   (NTCM)
DOC .... Norsk Luftambulanse AS [*Norway*] [*ICAO designator*]   (FAAC)
DOD .... Degree of Disorder [*Coatings*]
DODCLIPMI ... Department of Defense Consolidated List of Principal Military Items
DOET .... Dimethoxyethyl Amphetamine [*A hallucinogenic drug, more commonly known as STP*]   (MAH)
DOGIT .... Deed of Grant in Trust
DOI .... Date of Introduction   (ADDR)
DOL .... Ebsco, Inc. [*ICAO designator*]   (FAAC)
DOM .... Dos Mundos [*Dominican Republic*] [*ICAO designator*]   (FAAC)
DOMMDA ... Drawing Office Material Manufacturers' and Dealers' Association [*British*]   (BI)
DOMO .... Dispensing Opticians Manufacturing Organisation [*British*]   (BI)
DON .... Donair Flying Club Ltd. [*British*] [*ICAO designator*]   (FAAC)
DONSS ...... Directorate of Naval Survival and Safety
DOPRT ...... Date of Departure [*Army*]
DOR........... Dornier Reparaturwerft GmbH [*Germany*] [*ICAO designator*]   (FAAC)
DORDEC ... Domestic Refrigeration Development Committee [*British*]   (BI)
DORL .... Diploma in Otorhinolaryngology
DOrth .... Diploma in Orthopedics
DOSS-AF ... Directorate of Operational Support Services - Air Force
DOT........... Dioctyltin [*Organic chemistry*]
DOT........... Directly-Observed Therapy
DOTp......... Department of Transport [*British*]   (DA)
DOTS .... Dynamic Ocean Track System   (DA)
DOW .... Direct Overwrite [*Computer science*]
DP .... Depart   (DA)
DP .... Diaphosgene [*A choking agent*]   (ADDR)
DP .... Diploma in Pediatrics
DP .... Disadvantaged Person
DPA .... Diary Publishers' Association [*British*]   (BI)
DPB .... Deposit Byte [*Computer science*]   (NHD)
DPC .... Departure Control   (DA)
DPE .... Delta Pi Epsilon [*Fraternity*]   (AEE)
DPEC........ Diploma in Parent Education and Counselling
DPF........... Diesel Particulate Filter [*Automotive emissions*]
DPhysiol..... Diploma in Physiology
DPI .... Departmental Personnel Instruction
DPL .... Dome Petroleum Ltd. [*Canada*] [*ICAO designator*]   (FAAC)
Dpm .... Dampproof Membrane   (DAC)
DPMB-AF ... Directorate of Project Management B - Air Force
DPP .... Dual Progress Plan [*Education*]   (AEE)
DPR .... Day Press Rate [*Telegraph rate*]   (NTCM)
DPS........... Dales Pony Society [*British*]   (BI)
DPS........... Diversified Pharmaceutical Services   (ECON)
DpSM........ Diploma in Surgery Medicine
DPsyMedNeuro ... Diploma in Psychiatric Medicine and Neurology
DPT .... Drive Parameter Tracking [*Computer science*]   (PCM)
DQ .... Fiji [*Aircraft nationality and registration mark*]   (FAAC)
DQI .... Cimber Air, Sonderjyllands Flyveselskab [*Denmark*] [*ICAO designator*]   (FAAC)
DR............. Dealer [*Automotive sales*]
DR............. Deposition Rate [*Electrochemistry*]
DR............. Deviation Report
DR............. Dining Room   (DAC)

DR............. Disaster Recovery   (DA)
DR............. Dressing Room   (DAC)
Dr .... Dries [*Maps and charts*] [*British*]
DR............. Drug Rehabilitation
DRA .... Dravidian Air Services Ltd. [*British*] [*ICAO designator*]   (FAAC)
DRAS......... Defense Retiree and Annuitant Pay System [*DoD*]
DRC .... Triton Airlines, Inc. [*Canada*] [*ICAO designator*]   (FAAC)
DRE .... Michigan Airways, Inc. [*ICAO designator*]   (FAAC)
DRK .... Druk Air [*Bhutan*] [*ICAO designator*]   (FAAC)
DRP........... Dystrophin-Related Protein [*Biochemistry*]
DRPLA .... Dentatorubral Pallidoluysian Atrophy [*Medicine*]
DRR .... Deployment Readiness Review [*Aviation*]   (FAAC)
DRS .... Drenair [*Spain*] [*ICAO designator*]   (FAAC)
DRT .... Darta [*France*] [*ICAO designator*]   (FAAC)
DRT .... Domain-Referenced Test [*Education*]   (AEE)
DRTA .... Direct Reading Thinking Activity [*Education*]   (AEE)
Drwl.......... Dry Wall   (DAC)
DRY .... Deraya Air Taxi PT [*Indonesia*] [*ICAO designator*]   (FAAC)
DS .... Differentiated Staffing [*Education*]   (AEE)
DS .... Discriminating Stimulus [*Psychology*]   (AEE)
DS .... Dolly Shot [*Cinematography*]   (NTCM)
DS .... Drafting Site [*NFPA pre-fire planning symbol*]   (NFPA)
D1S........... Dressed One Side [*Lumber*]   (DAC)
D2S........... Dressed Two Sides [*Lumber*]   (DAC)
D4S........... Dressed Four Sides [*Lumber*]   (DAC)
DSA .... Danbury Airways, Inc. [*ICAO designator*]   (FAAC)
DSA .... Deadly Serious Party of Australia [*Political party*]
DSA .... Digital Signature Algorithm [*Telecommunications*]
DSAM .... Defense Systems Acquisition Management [*DoD*]
DSAP......... Designated Security-Assessed Position
DSB .... Air Senegal, Societe Nationale de Transport Aerien [*ICAO designator*]   (FAAC)
DSB .... Direct Support Battery [*Army*]   (ADDR)
DSCEMS ... Depth-Selective Conversion Electron Mossbauer Spectroscopy
D2S & CM ... Dressed Two Sides and Center Matched [*Lumber*]   (DAC)
DSH .... Northeast Management, Inc. [*ICAO designator*]   (FAAC)
DSI........... Defense Simulation Internet [*Army*]   (RDA)
DSL........... Domestic Substances List [*Canada*]
DSL........... Dynamic Simulation Language [*Computer science*]
DSLC......... Digital Synchronizing Load Sensing Control [*Electronic controls*] [*Diesel engines*]
DSLO .... Disaster Services Liaison Officer
D & SM...... Dressed and Standard Matched [*Lumber*]   (DAC)
D2S & M ... Dressed Two Sides and Matched [*Lumber*]   (DAC)
DSMPW..... Director, Submarine Policy and Warfare [*Military*]
DSO .... Defense Security Officer [*Military*]
DSP........... Dimensionally-Stable Polyester [*Tire manufacturing*]
DSR .... Dairo Air Services Ltd. [*Uganda*] [*ICAO designator*]   (FAAC)
DSS........... Digital Satellite System
D2S & SM ... Dressed Two Sides and Standard Matched [*Lumber*]   (DAC)
DST .... Differential Survey Treatment   (NTCM)
DSVP......... Downstream Venous Pressure [*Physiology*]   (MAH)
DT............. Doctor of Technology
DT............. Drum Trap   (DAC)
DT............. Dual Tandem [*Aviation*]   (DA)
DTA .... Distributive Trades' Alliance [*British*]   (BI)
DTA .... TAAG, Linhas Aereas de Angola [*ICAO designator*]   (FAAC)
DTBB......... Di-Tertiary-Butylbiphenyl [*Organic chemistry*]
DTC .... DeskTop Conferencing [*Fujitsu Networks Industry, Inc.*] [*Computer science*]   (PCM)
DTE .... Tamas Darida Enterprise [*Hungary*] [*ICAO designator*]   (FAAC)
DTF........... Domestic Textiles Federation [*British*]   (BI)
DTF .... Dried Tree Fruit
DTG........... Development Training Group
DT & G ...... Double Tongue and Groove   (DAC)
DTH........... Diploma in Tropical Health
DTM.......... Deutsche Tourenwagen Meisterschaft [*German Touring Car Championship*]
DTMS........ Desktop Marketing System [*CD-ROM*] [*Computer science*]
DTR .... Danish Air Transport [*ICAO designator*]   (FAAC)
DTRE .... Diploma in Therapeutic Radiology and Electrology
DTS .... Diametral Tensile Strength [*Material science*]
DTS .... Diploma in Theological Studies
DTTW .... Doctors to the World [*An association*]   (EA)
DTV .... Centre Airlines, Inc. [*ICAO designator*]   (FAAC)
DTX .... Deltex [*Slovakia*] [*ICAO designator*]   (FAAC)
DU............. Disposal Unit   (DAC)
DUAT........ Direct User Access Terminal   (DA)
DUATS...... Direct User Access Terminal System [*Aviation*]   (FAAC)
DUB........... Dubai Airwing [*United Arab Emirates*] [*ICAO designator*]   (FAAC)
DUE........... DNA [*Deoxyribonucleic Acid*] Unwinding Element [*Genetics*]
DUN........... Dunford BAE [*British*] [*ICAO designator*]   (FAAC)
DURC........ During Climb [*Aviation*]   (FAAC)
DURD........ During Descent [*Aviation*]   (FAAC)
DV............. Direct Voice   (NTCM)
DV............. Double Valve [*Stutz car model designation*]
DVA .... Discovery Airways [*ICAO designator*]   (FAAC)
DVC........... Digital Video Compression
DVF........... Dried Vine Fruit
DVI .... Direct Voice Input   (DA)
DVM.......... Distributed Virtual Memory [*Computer science*]
DVP........... Distinguished Visitor Program [*Army*]

DVR............ Digital Video Recording   (NTCM)
DVU............ Orbi [*Former USSR*] [*ICAO designator*]   (FAAC)
DWG.......... Designated Work Group
DWH .... Diploma in Women's Health
DWIMC ..... Do What I Mean, Correctly [*Computer hacker terminology*]
                  (NHD)
DWIS.......... Do What I Say [*Computer science*]
DWM.......... Dead White Male
DWN .... Dawn Air, Inc. [*ICAO designator*]   (FAAC)
DWN .... Downdraft   (DA)
DWVP-A .... Directorate of Weapons and Vehicle Procurement - Army
DWVP-A-VEH ... Directorate of Weapons and Vehicle Procurement - Army -
                  Vehicles
DWW.......... Wright International Express, Inc. [*ICAO designator*]   (FAAC)
DYA............ Alyemda-Democratic Yemen Airlines [*ICAO designator*]
                  (FAAC)
DYE............ Dynamic Air [*Netherlands*] [*ICAO designator*]   (FAAC)
DYN............ Dynamic Ventures, Inc. [*ICAO designator*]   (FAAC)

E

E................ Elbow (DAC)
E................ Electric Shutoff [*NFPA pre-fire planning symbol*] (NFPA)
E................ Electricity (NTCM)
E................ Elevator [*Technical drawings*] (NFPA)
E................ Entertainment [*Wire service code*] (NTCM)
E................ Equipment (NFPA)
E/A .... Engineer/Architect (DAC)
EA .... Evangelical Alliance [*British*] (BI)
EAA .... Elastic Active Aerodynamics [*Mitsubishi*] [*Automotive engineering*]
EAA .... Transporte Aereo Andino SA [*Venezuela*] [*ICAO designator*] (FAAC)
EAB .... Eagle Air Ltd. [*Switzerland*] [*ICAO designator*] (FAAC)
EAC .... Estate Agents' Council [*British*] (BI)
EAC .... Executive Air Charter [*ICAO designator*] (FAAC)
EADSIM .... Extended Air Defense Simulation [*Army*] (RDA)
EAE .... Aerosevicios Ecuatorianos CA [*Ecuador*] [*ICAO designator*] (FAAC)
EAF............. Employment Agents' Federation of Great Britain (BI)
EAG .... Eagle Flying Services Ltd. [*British*] [*ICAO designator*] (FAAC)
EAHTMA ... Engineers' and Allied Hand Tool Makers' Association [*British*] (BI)
EAL .... Ethanolamine Ammonia Lyase [*An enzyme*]
EAM .... [*The*] Evangelical Alliance Mission [*An association*] (NTCM)
EAN .... Express Airways Nigeria Ltd. [*ICAO designator*] (FAAC)
EAOT .... End of Arm Tooling [*Robotics*]
EAP .... Environmental Action Plan [*Environmental Protection Agency*] (ERG)
EAS............. Electronic Air Suspension [*Automotive engineering*]
EAS............. Engineering Analysis Services [*Auto industry supplier*]
EAS............. Excutive Aerospace (Pty) Ltd. [*South Africa*] [*ICAO designator*] (FAAC)
EASA.......... External Architectural Students Association [*British*] (BI)
EASI .... Electronic Acquisition Systems Instrumentation [*Vehicle testing*] [*Automotive engineering*]
EAST .... European Academy of Science and Technology
EASV......... Engine Angular Speed Variation [*Automotive engineering*]
EAT .... Air Transport Ltd. [*Slovakia*] [*ICAO designator*] (FAAC)
EATCHIP ... European Air Traffic Control Harmonization and Integration Program [*Eurocontrol*]
EATX.......... Electronic Automatic Transaxle [*Automotive engineering*]
EAU........... Early Assistance Unit
EAU........... Enabled Artists United [*An association*] (EA)
EAX .... Eastern Air Executive Ltd. [*British*] [*ICAO designator*] (FAAC)
EBC............ Aero Ejecutivo de Baja California SA de CV [*Mexico*] [*ICAO designator*] (FAAC)
EBC............ Environmental Business Council
EBD .... Electronic Brake-Force Distribution [*Anti-lock brake systems*] [*Automotive engineering*]
EBI............. [*The*] Educational Broadcasting Institute [*National Association of Educational Broadcasters*] (NTCM)
EBI............. European Bioinformatics Institute
EBITDA ..... Earnings Before Interest, Taxes, Depreciation and Amortization [*Business term*]
EBNI.......... Electricity Board for Northern Ireland (BI)
EBPAD...... Ethoxylated Bisphenol A Dimethacrylate [*Organic chemistry*]
EBS............ Eli-Fly SpA [*Italy*] [*ICAO designator*] (FAAC)
EBS............ Experimental Building Station
EB1S.......... Edge Bead One Side [*Lumber*] (DAC)
EBU........... English Bridge Union (BI)
ECA .... Electrical Contractors' Association [*British*] (BI)
ECA .... Emergency Call Announcer [*Hearing technology*]
ECA .... Emergency Controlling Authority (DA)
ECA .... Eurocypria Airlines Ltd. [*Cyprus*] [*ICAO designator*] (FAAC)
ECAAR...... Economists Allied for Arms Reduction [*An association*] (EA)
ECAR........ Engineering Concern Action Report [*Industrial engineering*]
E-CARS..... Enhanced Airline Communications and Reporting System (DA)
ECAS......... Enter Controlled Airspace [*Air Traffic Control*] (FAAC)
ECATV...... Educational Cable Television (NTCM)
ECC .... Electrochemichromic [*Optoelectronics*]
ECCC........ English Country Cheese Council (BI)
ECCET ...... Engineering Casualty Control Evaluation Team [*Navy*] (ANA)
ECCU .... English Cross Country Union (BI)

ECD .... Electrochemical Deposition [*Metallurgy*]
ECD .... Equivalent Circulating Density [*Well drilling*]
ECF........... Energy of Crush Factor [*Automotive safety*]
ECF........... Eurocopter [*France*] [*ICAO designator*] (FAAC)
ECGC .... Empire Cotton Growing Corp. [*British*] (BI)
ECH .... Early Childhood Health
ECHO........ Expanded Characteristics Option [*Metallurgy*]
ECI............. Eastern Carolina Aviation, Inc. [*ICAO designator*] (FAAC)
ECIS .... Electrical Cell-Substrate Impedance Sensing [*for cell-culture study*]
ECJ............. Berlin European [*ICAO designator*] (FAAC)
ECK .... East Coast Airlines Ltd. [*Kenya*] [*ICAO designator*] (FAAC)
ECKO .... Eddy-Current Killed Oscillator [*Engineering instrumentation*]
ECLM........ Electronic Compass Logic Module [*Automotive navigation systems*]
ECLPS....... Eclipse (ABBR)
ECLPSD..... Eclipsed (ABBR)
ECLPSG..... Eclipsing (ABBR)
ECLSTCL ... Ecclesiastical (ABBR)
ECLTM .... Eclecticism (ABBR)
ECMC .... Electric Cable Makers' Confederation [*British*] (BI)
ECN .... Export Clearance Number
EC-NCI ...... Electron-Capture Negative Chemical Ionization [*Spectrometry*]
ECO .... East Coast Airlines [*Australia*] [*ICAO designator*] (FAAC)
ECO .... Economic (ABBR)
ECOGEO .. Ecogeographer (ABBR)
ECOGEOC .. Ecogeographic (ABBR)
ECOGEOR ... Ecogeographer (ABBR)
ECOLA....... Extending Concepts through Language Activities [*Education*] (AEE)
ECOLC...... Ecologic (ABBR)
ECOLCL..... Ecological (ABBR)
ECOLCLY ... Ecologically (ABBR)
ECOLST .... Ecologist (ABBR)
ECONC .... Economic (ABBR)
ECONCL.... Economical (ABBR)
ECONCLY ... Economically (ABBR)
ECONL ...... Economical (ABBR)
ECONOMET ... Econometric (ABBR)
ECONST.... Economist (ABBR)
ECONY ...... Economy (ABBR)
ECONZ ...... Economize (ABBR)
ECONZD .. Economized (ABBR)
ECONZG ... Economizing (ABBR)
ECONZR ... Economizer (ABBR)
ECOPHYS ... Ecophysiologic (ABBR)
ECOSYS..... Ecosystem (ABBR)
ECR .... Air Charter Express AS [*Norway*] [*ICAO designator*] (FAAC)
ECRA........ Environmental Cleanup and Responsibility Act [*1983*] (ERG)
ECS............ Economics (ABBR)
ECS............ Electronic Counter Services
ECSSS .... Eighteenth Century Scottish Studies Society (EA)
ECST .... Ecstasy (ABBR)
ECSTC ...... Ecstatic (ABBR)
ECSTCLY ...... Ecstatically (ABBR)
ECSYT ...... Ecosystem (ABBR)
ECSZ .... Eastern California Shear Zone [*Geology*]
ECTCT .... Eccentricity (ABBR)
ECTOHORM ... Ectohormone (ABBR)
ECU .... Ecumania (ABBR)
ECUI.......... Extreme Close-Up Indeed [*Photography*] [*British*] (NTCM)
ECUM .... Ecumenic (ABBR)
ECUMEN ... Ecumenical (ABBR)
ECUML...... Ecumenical (ABBR)
ECUMLSM ... Ecumenicalism (ABBR)
ECUMLY ... Ecumenically (ABBR)
ECUMN .... Ecumenic (ABBR)
ECUMNL ... Ecumenical (ABBR)
ECUMNLY ... Ecumenically (ABBR)
ECUMNM ... Ecumenism (ABBR)
ECZM........ Eczema (ABBR)
ED .... Educational [*FCC*] (NTCM)
ED .... Educational Institution Program (NTCM)

ED.............. Emergency Distance [*Aviation*]   (DA)
ED.............. Ethyldichloroarsine [*Medicine*]   (ADDR)
EDA.......... Aerolinas Nacionales del Ecuador SA [*ICAO designator*]   (FAAC)
EDA.......... European Democratic Alliance [*Political movement*]   (ECON)
EDA.......... Extreme Disablement Adjustment
EDB.......... Edible   (ABBR)
EDC.......... Electronic Diesel Control [*Automotive engineering*]
EDC.......... Electronic Document Collection
EDCA........ Educate   (ABBR)
EDCAB...... Educable   (ABBR)
EDCAD...... Educated   (ABBR)
EDCAG...... Educating   (ABBR)
EDCAN...... Education   (ABBR)
EDCANL...... Educational   (ABBR)
EDCATR...... Educator   (ABBR)
EDCAV...... Educative   (ABBR)
EDCBL....... Educable   (ABBR)
EDCG....... Educating   (ABBR)
EDD.......... Eddied   (ABBR)
EDD.......... Enforcement Decision Document [*Environmental Protection
                Agency*]   (ERG)
EDENT...... Edentate   (ABBR)
EDFC......... Edifice   (ABBR)
EDFCN...... Edification   (ABBR)
EDFD........ Edified   (ABBR)
EDFG........ Edifying   (ABBR)
EDFM....... Educational FM Station   (NTCM)
EDFYD....... Edified   (ABBR)
EDFYG...... Edifying   (ABBR)
EDGD........ Edged   (ABBR)
EDGG........ Edging   (ABBR)
EDGNS...... Edginess   (ABBR)
EDGR........ Edgier   (ABBR)
EDGST....... Edgiest   (ABBR)
EDGWS...... Edgewise   (ABBR)
EDGYR...... Edgier   (ABBR)
EDGYST .... Edgiest   (ABBR)
EDI........... Estimated Daily Intake [*Toxicology*]
EDI/EC ...... Electronic Data Interchange/Electronic Commerce [*Computer
                science*] [*Army*]   (RDA)
EDMN....... Edmonton [*Canada*]   (ABBR)
EDOC....... Expected Date of Confinement
EDPT......... Enhanced Drive Parameter Table [*Computer science*]
EDR.......... Lineas Aereas Eldorado Ltd. [*Colombia*] [*ICAO designator*]
                (FAAC)
EDRS......... ERIC [*Educational Resources Information Center*] Document
                Reproduction Service [*Stanford University*]   (NTCM)
EDT .... Edict   (ABBR)
EDT .... Edit   (ABBR)
EDTD........ Edited   (ABBR)
EDTG........ Editing   (ABBR)
EDTL......... Editorial   (ABBR)
EDTLZ....... Editorialize   (ABBR)
EDTLZD .... Editorialized   (ABBR)
EDTLZG .... Editorializing   (ABBR)
EDTN........ Edition   (ABBR)
EDTR .... Editor   (ABBR)
EDTRSP..... Editorship   (ABBR)
EDTSP .... Editorship   (ABBR)
EDU.......... Endue   (ABBR)
EDUCB ..... Educable   (ABBR)
EDUCD ..... Educated   (ABBR)
EDUCG ..... Educating   (ABBR)
EDUCNLST ... Educationalist   (ABBR)
EDUCR ..... Educator   (ABBR)
EDUCV ..... Educative   (ABBR)
EDV.......... Emission Data Vehicle [*Exhaust emissions testing*] [*Automotive
                engineering*]
EDWNT..... Endowment   (ABBR)
EDYG........ Eddying   (ABBR)
EE.............. Eased Edge   (DAC)
EE.............. Elevator Equipment Room [*NFPA pre-fire planning symbol*]
                (NFPA)
EE.............. Energy Expenditure
EEA .... Ecurie Ecosse Association Ltd. [*British*]   (BI)
EEA .... Educational Exhibitors' Association [*British*]   (BI)
EEA .... Electrostatic Energy Analyzer [*Instrumentation*]
EEA .... Empresa Ecuatoriana de Aviacion [*Ecuador*] [*ICAO designator*]
                (FAAC)
EEB........... Euroberlin [*France*] [*ICAO designator*]   (FAAC)
EEC........... Estimated Exposure Concentration [*Toxicology*]
EEC-V .... Electronic Engine Control - 5th Generation [*Automotive
                engineering*]
EED .... Estimated Exposure Dose [*Toxicology*]
EEDO .... Economic and Employment Development Officer
EEG .... Essence Export Group [*British*]   (BI)
EEL.......... Environmental Exposure Level [*Toxicology*]
EER .... Early Emissions Reduction [*Environmental science*]
EER .... Eerie   (ABBR)
EER .... Excess Emission Report [*Environmental Protection Agency*]
                (ERG)
EERNS....... Eeriness   (ABBR)
EERR.......... Eerier   (ABBR)

EERST ...... Eeriest   (ABBR)
EERY.......... Eerily   (ABBR)
EET........... Edge Enhancement Technology [*Tandy*]
EETEP .... Extended Eligibility Temporary Entry Permit
EEU .... Eurofly [*Italy*] [*ICAO designator*]   (FAAC)
EEUA .... Engineering Equipment Users' Association [*British*]   (BI)
EEUR .... Earth Environment University Roundtable [*of America*]
EEZ........... Eurofly SPA [*Italy*] [*ICAO designator*]   (FAAC)
EF .... Effective   (ABBR)
EFA........... Electrical Floor Warming Association [*British*]   (BI)
EFA........... Evolutionary Factor Analysis [*Statistics*]
EFA........... Excess Fare Allowance
EFACB ...... Effaceable   (ABBR)
EFACD....... Effaced   (ABBR)
EFACG ...... Effacing   (ABBR)
EFACR ...... Effacer   (ABBR)
EFACT ...... Effacement   (ABBR)
EFBTE....... Eastern Federation of Building Trades' Employers [*British*]   (BI)
EFC........... Efface   (ABBR)
EFCD......... Effaced   (ABBR)
EFCG......... Effacing   (ABBR)
EFChE....... European Federation of Chemical Engineering
EFCNT...... Effacement   (ABBR)
EFCR........ Effacer   (ABBR)
EFCT........ Effect   (ABBR)
EFCTA ...... Effectuate   (ABBR)
EFCTAD .... Effectuated   (ABBR)
EFCTAG ... Effectuating   (ABBR)
EFCTB ...... Effectible   (ABBR)
EFCTD ...... Effected   (ABBR)
EFCTG ...... Effecting   (ABBR)
EFCTL....... Effectual   (ABBR)
EFCTLNS ... Effectualness   (ABBR)
EFCTLT .... Effectuality   (ABBR)
EFCTLY.... Effectually   (ABBR)
EFCTR ...... Effector   (ABBR)
EFCTV ...... Effective   (ABBR)
EFCTVNS ... Effectiveness   (ABBR)
EFCTVY.... Effectively   (ABBR)
EFD .... Electronic Forms Designer [*Microsoft Corp.*]   (PCM)
EFECS .... Engine Fuel Economy Control System [*Automotive engineering*]
EFEI .... Equivalent Fuel Efficiency Improvement
EFEM .... Effeminate   (ABBR)
EFEMAY .. Effeminately   (ABBR)
EFEMC ...... Effeminacy   (ABBR)
EFEMNS ... Effeminateness   (ABBR)
EFEMY ...... Effeminately   (ABBR)
EFERVS..... Effervesce   (ABBR)
EFERVSD ... Effervesced   (ABBR)
EFERVSG ... Effervescing   (ABBR)
EFERVSNC ... Effervescence   (ABBR)
EFERVST ... Effervescent   (ABBR)
EFF............ Westair Aviation Ltd. [*Ireland*] [*ICAO designator*]   (FAAC)
EFFCTS ..... Effects [*Automotive advertising*]
EFFECT..... Effective   (ABBR)
EFFECT..... Effectivity   (ABBR)
EFFER....... Efferent   (ABBR)
EFFL.......... Efflorescent   (ABBR)
EFFT.......... Effete   (ABBR)
EFGY......... Effigy   (ABBR)
EFIC......... Efficacy   (ABBR)
EFICNC ..... Efficiency   (ABBR)
EFICNT ..... Efficient   (ABBR)
EFICNTY.. Efficiently   (ABBR)
EFICNY .... Efficiency   (ABBR)
EFICU .... Efficacious   (ABBR)
EFICY .... Efficiently   (ABBR)
EFIF .... Export Finance and Insurance Fund
EFISHG ..... Electric-Field-Induced Second-Harmonic Generation
EFLOR ..... Effloresce   (ABBR)
EFLORD ... Effloresced   (ABBR)
EFLORG ... Efflorescing   (ABBR)
EFLORNC ... Efflorescence   (ABBR)
EFLORT ... Efflorescent   (ABBR)
EFLU......... Effluent   (ABBR)
EFLUNC .... Effluence   (ABBR)
EFLUVA ... Effluvia   (ABBR)
EFLUVL..... Effluvial   (ABBR)
EFLUVM .. Effluvium   (ABBR)
EFMS........ Experimental Flight Management System [*Aviation*]   (DA)
EFP........... Explosively-Formed Penetrator [*Army*]   (RDA)
EFR............ Elf Air Ltd. [*Russian Federation*] [*ICAO designator*]   (FAAC)
EFRNT....... Effrontery   (ABBR)
EFRT......... Effort   (ABBR)
EFRTLS .... Effortless   (ABBR)
EFRTLSNS ... Effortlessness   (ABBR)
EFRTLSY ... Effortlessly   (ABBR)
EFRVS....... Effervesce   (ABBR)
EFRVSD..... Effervesced   (ABBR)
EFRVSG..... Effervescing   (ABBR)
EFRVSNC ... Effervescence   (ABBR)
EFRVST..... Effervescent   (ABBR)
EFS............ Europe Falcon Service [*France*] [*ICAO designator*]   (FAAC)

EFTA......... Effectuate (ABBR)
EFTAD....... Effectuated (ABBR)
EFTAG....... Effecting (ABBR)
EFTL......... Effectual (ABBR)
EFTSU .... Equivalent Full-Time Student Unit
EFTVNS.... Effectiveness (ABBR)
EFTVY ...... Effectively (ABBR)
EFULG....... Effulgent (ABBR)
EFULGNC ... Effulgence (ABBR)
EFUS......... Effuse (ABBR)
EFUSD....... Effused (ABBR)
EFUSG....... Effusing (ABBR)
EFUSN....... Effusion (ABBR)
EFUSV .... Effusive (ABBR)
EFUSVNS ... Effusiveness (ABBR)
EFUSVY .... Effusively (ABBR)
EFX............ Special Effects (NTCM)
EG .... Emergency Generator Room [*NFPA pre-fire planning symbol*] (NFPA)
EGA .... Ecuato Guineana de Aviacion [*Equatorial Guinea*] [*ICAO designator*] (FAAC)
EGALSM ... Egalitarianism (ABBR)
EGALTR .... Egalitarian (ABBR)
EGALTRM ... Egalitarianism (ABBR)
EGF .... AMR American Eagle, Inc. [*ICAO designator*] (FAAC)
EGH........... Everton's Genealogical Helper [*A publication*]
EGHTFD.... Eightfold (ABBR)
EGHTH...... Eightieth (ABBR)
EGL .... Capital Trading Aviation Ltd. [*British*] [*ICAO designator*] (FAAC)
EGL .... External Germinal Layer [*Cytology*]
EGMIA...... Educational Group of the Music Industries Association [*British*] (BI)
EGMS........ Education of Girls in Mathematics and Science
EGS........... Electronic Governor System [*Heavy-duty automotive engines*]
EGS........... Excluded Goods Schedule
EGT .... Eagle Airways Ltd. [*British*] [*ICAO designator*] (FAAC)
EGT .... European Geotraverse [*A collaborative lithosphere study*]
EGT .... Extended Glaciological Timescale [*Climatology*]
EGU .... English Golf Union (BI)
EHA........... East Hampton Aire [*ICAO designator*] (FAAC)
EHAP........ Extremely Hazardous Air Pollutant [*Environmental science*]
EHD........... [*E. H.*] Darby Aviation [*ICAO designator*] (FAAC)
EHIC .... Energetic Heavy Ion Composition Experiment [*NASA*]
EHS........... Elitos SpA [*Italy*] [*ICAO designator*] (FAAC)
EI .... Ecoforestry Institute - United States (EA)
EIA .... Evergreen International Airlines [*ICAO designator*] (FAAC)
EIBA......... Electrical Industries Benevolent Association [*British*] (BI)
EIC............ Elevator Code (NFPA)
E & ID........ Education and Information Dissemination
EIFI .... Electrical Industries Federation of Ireland (BI)
EIN .... Aer Lingus Teoranta [*Ireland*] [*ICAO designator*] (FAAC)
EIR............ Endangerment Information Report [*Environmental Protection Agency*] (ERG)
EIRP......... Environmental Impact Research Program [*Army*] (RDA)
EIS............ Employment Incentive Scheme
EIS............ Eurasian Ice Sheet [*Climatology*]
EIX............ El Air Exports Ltd. [*Ireland*] [*ICAO designator*] (FAAC)
EJA........... Executive Jet Aviation, Inc. [*ICAO designator*] (FAAC)
EJM........... American Air Services, Inc. [*ICAO designator*] (FAAC)
EJT............ Aero Ejecutiva SA [*Mexico*] [*ICAO designator*] (FAAC)
EKC .... East Kansas City Aviation, Inc. [*ICAO designator*] (FAAC)
EL .... Eligible Layout
EL .... Eligible Liability [*British*]
ELA .... Eastland Air [*Australia*] [*ICAO designator*] (FAAC)
ELAD .... Extracorporeal Liver-Assist Device [*Medicine*] (ECON)
ELE........... SW Electricity Board [*British*] [*ICAO designator*] (FAAC)
ELECTRO-OPTINT ... Electrooptical Intelligence [*DoD*]
ELFA .... Electric Light Fittings Association [*British*] (BI)
ELG .... Alpi Eagles SpA [*Italy*] [*ICAO designator*] (FAAC)
ELGI .... European Lubricating Grease Institute [*An association*]
ELIA......... European League of Institutes of the Arts [*British*]
ELIC.......... Electric Lamp Industry Council [*British*] (BI)
ELK........... Eesti Lennukompani [*Estonia*] [*ICAO designator*] (FAAC)
ELL........... Estonian Air [*ICAO designator*] (FAAC)
ELM .... Extended Length Message (DA)
ELMA........ Electric Lamp Manufacturers' Association of Great Britain Ltd. (BI)
ELN .... Nordic East International Aircraft, AB [*Sweden*] [*ICAO designator*] (FAAC)
ELP........... Aerolineas Ejecutivas de San Luis Potosi SA de CV [*Mexico*] [*ICAO designator*] (FAAC)
ELR............ Elrom Aviation & Investments [*Israel*] [*ICAO designator*] (FAAC)
ELR............ Environment Lapse Rate (DA)
ELR............ Existing Lapse Rate (DA)
ELR............ Extra Long Range [*ICAO designator*] (FAAC)
ELS........... El Sal Air [*El Salvador*] [*ICAO designator*] (FAAC)
ELSI .... Ethical, Legal and Social Implications [*Genetic research*]
ELT........... Elliott Beechcraft of Omaha, Inc. [*ICAO designator*] (FAAC)
ELTC......... European Lubricant Testing Committee
ELU .... English Lacrosse Union (BI)

ELU .... Environmental Load Unit [*Recycling, emissions*] [*Automotive engineering*]
ELV............ Edit-Level Video (NTCM)
ELY............ El Al-Israel Airlines Ltd. [*ICAO designator*] (FAAC)
EM .... Explanatory Memorandum
EMA .... Egyptian Aviation Co. [*ICAO designator*] (FAAC)
EMACS..... Editing Macros [*Computer science*] (NHD)
EMB .... Empresa Brasileira de Aeronautica SA [*Brazil*] [*ICAO designator*] (FAAC)
EMB .... Ethambutol Hydrochloride [*Pharmacology*]
EMC .... Electrical Metallic Conduit (DAC)
EMCD .... Electro-Magnetically Controlled Differential [*Powertrain*] [*Automotive engineering*]
EMCOF..... European Monetary Co-Operation Fund
EMCP........ Electronic Modular Control Panel [*Motor-generator set design*]
EMDI .... Estimated Maximum Daily Intake [*Toxicology*]
EME .... Metro Express, Inc. [*ICAO designator*] (FAAC)
EMEA .... European Medicines Evaluation Agency (ECON)
EMERGCON ... Emergency Condition [*Navy*] (ANA)
EMI .... Employers Mutual Indemnity Ltd.
EMI .... Environment Management Industry
EMLA........ Eutectic Mixture of Local Anesthetics [*Topical anesthetic cream*]
EMLAT..... Modern Language Aptitude Test-Elementary [*Education*] (AEE)
EMO .... Export Meat Order
EMP .... Electro-Magnetic Pulse
EMP .... Empire Air Service, Inc. [*ICAO designator*] (FAAC)
EMP .... Environmental Management Plan
EMPSKD ... Employment Schedule [*Navy*] (ANA)
EMR .... External Mold Release [*Plastic fabrications*]
EMS........... Preferred Flights, Inc. [*Canada*] [*ICAO designator*] (FAAC)
EMSS .... Experimental Mobile Satellite System (DA)
EMTA........ Electro-Medical Trade Association [*British*] (BI)
EMTS........ Exposure Monitoring Test Site [*Environmental Protection Agency*] (ERG)
EMU.......... Electronic Mock-Up [*Computer-aided design*]
EMU.......... Engine Monitoring Unit [*Automotive electronics*]
EMW .... Equivalent Mud Weight [*Well drilling technology*]
EN............. Edge Number [*Film stock identification number*] (NTCM)
ENA........... Espana, Direccion General de Aviacion Civil [*Spain*] [*ICAO designator*] (FAAC)
encycl .... Encyclopedia
Endl Vac ..... Endless Vacation [*A publication*]
ENEF......... English New Education Fellowship (BI)
ENHNCD... Enhanced [*ICAO designator*] (FAAC)
ENHNCMNT ... Enhancement [*ICAO designator*] (FAAC)
ENJ............ Nort Jet [*Spain*] [*ICAO designator*] (FAAC)
ENR........... Ensor Air [*Czechoslovakia*] [*ICAO designator*] (FAAC)
ENS .... Entergy Services, Inc. [*ICAO designator*] (FAAC)
ENS .... Enterprise Network Services [*Banyan*] [*Computer science*]
ENT .... Holmstrom Flyg AB [*Sweden*] [*ICAO designator*] (FAAC)
ENZ........... New Zealand Air Services Ltd. [*ICAO designator*] (FAAC)
EO............. Employment Officer
EOA........... English Orienteering Association (BI)
EOBT .... Estimated Off-Block Time [*ICAO designator*] (FAAC)
EOFT......... Engine Oil Filterability Test
EOLCS....... Engine Oil Licensing and Certification System [*American Petroleum Institute*]
EOLN .... End of Line [*Computer science*]
EOO........... Extensible Object Orientation
EOU........... End of User [*Computer hacker terminology*] (NHD)
EOWTF ...... Every Other Week Till Forbid (NTCM)
EOYFS ...... End of Year Financial Statement
EP .... Export Propensity
EP .... Exprisoner
EPA .... Educational Puppetry Association [*British*] (BI)
EPA .... Employer-Paid Advertising
EPA .... Essential Pharmacy Allowance
EPA .... Exparc [*Russian Federation*] [*ICAO designator*] (FAAC)
EPB........... Earth Pressure Balance [*Civil engineering*]
EPB............ Eastern Pacific Aviation Ltd. [*Canada*] [*ICAO designator*] (FAAC)
EPC........... Conti-Flug Koln/Bonn [*Germany*] [*ICAO designator*] (FAAC)
EPF .... Engine and Propeller Factor [*IOR*] [*Yacht racing*]
EPIC .... Electronic Price Information Computer
EPMR........ Embarked Personnel Material Report [*Navy*] (ANA)
EPN .... Extended Parliamentary Network
EPP .... Electronic Postproduction (NTCM)
EPP .... Engineered Polypropylene [*Plastics*] [*Automotive engineering*]
EPPMA ...... Expanded Polystyrene Product Manufacturers' Association [*British*] (BI)
EPR........... Expreso Aereo [*Peru*] [*ICAO designator*] (FAAC)
EPRN .... Eastern Public Radio Network (NTCM)
EPS........... Environmental Priorities Strategies [*Volvo*] [*Automotive engineering*]
EPS........... Epps Air Service, Inc. [*ICAO designator*] (FAAC)
EPSRC....... Engineering and Physical Sciences Research Council [*British*]
EQL .... Equatorial Airlines of Sao Tome and Principe [*ICAO designator*] (FAAC)
Equal Opp... Equal Opportunity [*A publication*]
EQUIP....... Engineering Quality Improvement
ER .... Eley-Rideal Mechanism [*Chemistry*]
ER .... Emergency Relief
ER .... Environmental Requirement

ER .... Environmental Restoration [*Metallurgy*]
ER .... European Right [*Political movement*]   (ECON)
ERA .... Electronic Rentals Association [*British*]   (BI)
ERA .... Eurocommander SA [*Spain*] [*ICAO designator*]   (FAAC)
ERA .... Evangelical Radio Alliance [*British*]   (BI)
ERAD .... Enroute RADAR [*Aviation*]   (FAAC)
ERC .... Electonic Remote Control [*Automotive electronic systems*]
ERC .... Esso Rosources Canada Ltd. [*ICAO designator*]   (FAAC)
ERC .... Extended Range Cap [*Navy*]   (ANA)
ERCC........ Enroute Control Center [*Aviation*]   (DA)
ERD .... Electronic Reference Document
ERE .... Erie Airways, Inc. [*ICAO designator*]   (FAAC)
ERH .... ERA Helicopters, Inc. [*ICAO designator*]   (FAAC)
ERIN .... Environmental Resources Information Network [*Australia*]
ERJ .... Eurojet Italia [*Italy*] [*ICAO designator*]   (FAAC)
ERL .... Euralair [*France*] [*ICAO designator*]   (FAAC)
ERL............ Extraneous Residue Limit [*Toxicology*]
ERMD .... Environment and Resource Management Division [*World Wildlife Fund-United States*]
ERMG .... Enroute Metering [*Aviation*]   (FAAC)
ERO .... Employer Relations Officer
ERO .... Sundor International Air Services Ltd. [*Israel*] [*ICAO designator*]   (FAAC)
EROS........ Experience de Recherche d'Objects Sombres [*Astronomy*]
ERP............ Erase, Record, and Playback   (NTCM)
ERPG .... Emergency Response Planning Guideline [*Environmental science*]
ERR .... Economic Rate of Return
ERS .... Elizabethan Railway Society [*British*]   (BI)
ERS .... Ergonomics Research Society [*British*]   (BI)
ERSP .... Enroute Spacing Program [*Aviation*]   (FAAC)
ERTS .... Emergency Remote Tracking Station [*Navy*]   (ANA)
ESA............ Seagreen Air Transport [*Antigua and Barbuda*] [*ICAO designator*]   (FAAC)
ESAA......... English Schools' Athletic Association   (BI)
ESAP .... Environmental Self-Assessment Program
ESAS .... Education Student Assistance System
ESB............ Effective Sample Base   (NTCM)
ESB............ Electricity Supply Board [*Republic of Ireland*]   (BI)
ESC............ English-Speaking Country
ESCA......... English Schools Cricket Association   (BI)
ESCAPE..... European Symposium on Computer Aided Process Engineering
ESE............ Avesen SA de CV [*Mexico*] [*ICAO designator*]   (FAAC)
ESF............ Expanded Sample Frame   (NTCM)
ESG............ Edit Sync Guide   (NTCM)
ESG............ Editorial Support Group
ESL............ Environmental Sustainment Laboratory   (RDA)
ESM........... Earth Systems Model [*Climatology*]
ESMOA..... Electrotypers' and Stereotypers' Managers and Overseers Association [*British*]   (BI)
ESO .... Avitat [*British*] [*ICAO designator*]   (FAAC)
ESR............ Environmental Science Research [*Concept car*] [*Automotive engineering*]
ESR............ Excelsior Airlines Ltd. [*Ghana*] [*ICAO designator*]   (FAAC)
ESRU......... English Schools' Rugby Union   (BI)
ESS .... Enterprise Support Service
ESS .... TAES [*Tecnicas Aereas de Estudios y Servicios SA*] [*Spain*] [*ICAO designator*]   (FAAC)
ESSA .... English Schools' Swimming Association   (BI)
EST............ Flugfelag Austerlands Ltd. Egilsstadir [*Iceland*] [*ICAO designator*]   (FAAC)
ESTCP....... Environmental Security Technology Certification Program [*Army*]   (RDA)
ESTRA ...... English-Speaking Tape Respondents Association [*British*]   (BI)
ESU .... Employee Skills Upgrade
ESU .... Enterprise Support Unit
ESVEM ..... Electrophysiological Study Versus Electrocardiographic Monitoring [*Medical study*]
ESY............ Executive Aviation Services Ltd. [*Nigeria*] [*ICAO designator*]   (FAAC)
ET .... Educational Television [*FCC*]   (NTCM)
ET .... Electrical/Transformer Room [*NFPA pre-fire planning symbol*]   (NFPA)
ET .... Enhanced Telephone
ET .... Environmental Technician
ETA .... Estrellas del Aire SA de CV [*Mexico*] [*ICAO designator*]   (FAAC)
ETA .... Expected Time of Arrival
ETARS .... Enroute Tracking Automatic RADAR Service [*Aviation*]   (FAAC)
ETCTA ...... Electrical Trades' Commercial Travellers' Association [*British*]   (BI)
ETF............ Economic Transactions Framework
ETG .... Electronic Target Generator [*Military*]   (DA)
ETH............ Ethiopian Airlines Corp. [*ICAO designator*]   (FAAC)
ETL............ Patterson Aviation Co. [*ICAO designator*]   (FAAC)
ETM .... Elaborately-Transformed Manufacture
ETM .... Enhanced Thematic Mapper [*Geoscience*]
ETM .... Escrowed to Maturity
ETMA .... English Timber Merchants' Association   (BI)
ETOPS ...... Extended Range Twin Operation [*Aviation*]   (DA)
ETP............ Empire Test Pilots School [*British*] [*ICAO designator*]   (FAAC)
ETP............ Environmental Training Project [*World Wildlife Fund-United States*]
ETPE .... Elevated Temperature Polyethylene

ETSC .... Electronic Technical Support Center [*DiagSoft*]
ETT............ Excess Travelling Time
ETVS......... Educational Television by Satellite   (NTCM)
ETZ........... Electron Transparent Zone [*Biochemistry*]
EU.............. European Union [*Formerly, European Community*]
EUA .... Europe Air [*France*] [*ICAO designator*]   (FAAC)
EUC .... Eurocontrol [*Belgium*] [*ICAO designator*]   (FAAC)
EUDC .... European Urban Driving Cycle [*Automotive emissions*]
EUI .... Euravia [*Spain*] [*ICAO designator*]   (FAAC)
EUL .... Euralair International [*France*] [*ICAO designator*]   (FAAC)
EUR .... Eurojet SA [*Spain*] [*ICAO designator*]   (FAAC)
EUR ANP... European Air Navigation Plan [*ICAO*]   (DA)
EUR FCB ... European Frequency Coordinating Body [*ICAO*]   (DA)
EUW........... Euroflight Sweden, AB [*ICAO designator*]   (FAAC)
EUX........... European Expidite [*Belgium*] [*ICAO designator*]   (FAAC)
EUZ........... Euroair Transport Ltd. [*British*] [*ICAO designator*]   (FAAC)
EVA .... Electric Vehicle Association of Great Britain Ltd.   (BI)
EVCC........ Electric Vehicle Capsulated Contact [*Automotive electrical systems*]
EVD .... Explosive Vapor Detector   (DA)
EVE .... Air Evex GmbH [*Germany*] [*ICAO designator*]   (FAAC)
EVOH........ Ethylene Vinyl Alcohol [*Plastics*]
EVOP........ European Volcanological Project
EVR .... Electronic Video Recording [*or Recorder*]   (NTCM)
EV1S.......... Edge Vee One Side [*Lumber*]   (DAC)
EVT .... Electronic Valve Timing [*Automobile engine design*]
EWA .... East-West Airlines Ltd. [*Australia*] [*ICAO designator*]   (FAAC)
EWE .... East West European [*Bulgaria*] [*ICAO designator*]   (FAAC)
EWF........... Electrical Wholesalers Federation [*British*]   (BI)
EWL .... Enterprise Workshops Ltd.
EWL .... Excess Weight Loss [*Morbid obesity surgical treatment*]
EWS........... European Wings [*Czechoslovakia*] [*ICAO designator*]   (FAAC)
EWW......... Emery Worldwide Airlines, Inc. [*ICAO designator*]   (FAAC)
EX .... Expect   (DA)
EXA .... Execaire Aviation Ltd. [*Canada*] [*ICAO designator*]   (FAAC)
EXC .... Excalibur Aviation [*British*] [*ICAO designator*]   (FAAC)
EXCEL ...... Export Credit Enhanced Leverage
Ex Child..... Exceptional Children [*A publication*]
EXCOM ...... Extended Communications Search [*DoD*]
EXD .... Export Air del Peru SA Cargo Air Lines [*ICAO designator*]   (FAAC)
EXE .... Executive Flight, Inc. [*ICAO designator*]   (FAAC)
EXG .... Air Exchange, Inc. [*ICAO designator*]   (FAAC)
EXHIB........ Exhibitor   (NTCM)
ExI .... Extropy Institute   (EA)
EXIT .... Export Integrated System
EXJ .... Executive Jet Italiana SRL [*Italy*] [*ICAO designator*]   (FAAC)
EXM .... CAA Flight Examiners [*British*] [*ICAO designator*]   (FAAC)
EXN .... Europeaero Service National [*France*] [*ICAO designator*]   (FAAC)
EXN .... Exin [*Poland*] [*ICAO designator*]   (FAAC)
EXOF........ Expanded Quota Flow [*Aviation*]   (FAAC)
EXP............ Business Express Delivery Ltd. [*Canada*] [*ICAO designator*]   (FAAC)
EXP BT...... Expansion Bolt [*Technical drawings*]   (DAC)
EXQ .... Execujet [*British*] [*ICAO designator*]   (FAAC)
EXR .... Flight Express, Inc. [*ICAO designator*]   (FAAC)
EXS............ Channel Express (Air Services) Ltd. [*British*] [*ICAO designator*]   (FAAC)
EXT .... Extra Executive Transport [*Germany*] [*ICAO designator*]   (FAAC)
EXTEN....... Extended [*Automotive advertising*]
EXTENDEX ... Extended Exercise [*Navy*]   (ANA)
extr............. Extremity   (MAH)
EXU .... Executive Transports [*France*] [*ICAO designator*]   (FAAC)
EXV .... Executive Air Transport Ltd. [*Switzerland*] [*ICAO designator*]   (FAAC)
EYOP .... European Year of Older People and Solidarity Between Generations
EYT .... Europe Aero Service [*France*] [*ICAO designator*]   (FAAC)
EZ .... Easy Listening [*Radio*]   (NTCM)
EZ .... Engagement Zone [*Army*]   (ADDR)

F

F .... Ferrule Contact [*Lamp base type*]   (NTCM)
F .... Flow   (NFPA)
FA .... Faculty of Actuaries [*British*]   (BI)
FA .... Full Aperture [*Photography*]   (NTCM)
FAAD C2.... Forward Area Air Defense Command and Control [*Military*]
FAB............ First Air (Bradley Schedules) Ltd. [*Canada*] [*ICAO designator*]
　　　　　　(FAAC)
FABPA .... Furniture and Bedding Publicity Association Ltd. [*British*]   (BI)
FAC............ Final Approach Course [*Aviation*]   (DA)
FAC............ Firearms Acquisition Certificate [*Canada*]
FAC............ First Air Courier, Inc. [*ICAO designator*]   (FAAC)
FACE......... Fatty-Acid Cellulos Esters [*Organic chemistry*]
FACPTNG ... Forward Air Control Party Training [*Navy*]   (ANA)
FACS .... Funds Allocation Control System
FACW....... Facultative Wetland Plant   (ERG)
FAD .... Rog-Air Ltd. [*Canada*] [*ICAO designator*]   (FAAC)
FAE............ Foundation of Automation and Employment Ltd. [*British*]   (BI)
FAE............ Sat-Air, Inc. [*ICAO designator*]   (FAAC)
FAF............ Final Approach Fix [*Aviation*]   (DA)
FAF............ Forces Aeriennes Francaises [*France*] [*ICAO designator*]   (FAAC)
FAFAB ...... FSS [*Flight Service Station*] Assumes Flight-Plan Area
　　　　　　[*Aviation*]   (FAAC)
FAG .... Fuerza Aerea Argentina [*ICAO designator*]   (FAAC)
FAI .... Falcon Air, Inc. [*ICAO designator*]   (FAAC)
FAJ .... Fiji Air Services Ltd. [*ICAO designator*]   (FAAC)
FAK .... Financial AirExpress [*ICAO designator*]   (FAAC)
FAL............ Foodland Associates Ltd.
FAL............ Friendship Air Alaska [*ICAO designator*]   (FAAC)
FAM .... Family of Frequencies [*Aviation*]   (DA)
FAM .... Fumigacion Aerea Andalusa SA [*Spain*] [*ICAO designator*]
　　　　　　(FAAC)
FAME....... Fellowship of Associates of Medical Evangelism   (EA)
FAMHW .... Federation of Associations of Mental Health Workers [*British*]
　　　　　　(BI)
FAN .... Tauern Air Gesellschaft GmbH [*Austria*] [*ICAO designator*]
　　　　　　(FAAC)
FAOFOG.... Fellow of the Asia-Oceania Federation of Obstetricians and
　　　　　　Gynaecologists
FAP............ Parsons Airways Northern Ltd. [*Canada*] [*ICAO designator*]
　　　　　　(FAAC)
FAQL......... Frequent Asked Question List [*Computer science*]   (NHD)
FAS .... Federal Advertising Services
FAS............ Field Aircraft Services Ltd. [*British*] [*ICAO designator*]   (FAAC)
FAS............ Financial Accounting System
FASS .... Federation of Associations of Specialists and Subcontractors
　　　　　　[*British*]   (BI)
FAST .... Focus, Aperture, Shutter, Tachometer [*Cinematography*]
　　　　　　(NTCM)
FAT............ Farner Air Transport AG [*Switzerland*] [*ICAO designator*]
　　　　　　(FAAC)
FAT............ Final Approach Track [*Aviation*]   (DA)
FATUREC ... Federation of Air Transport User Representatives in the
　　　　　　European Community   (DA)
FAU .... Faucher Aviation [*France*] [*ICAO designator*]   (FAAC)
FAV .... Finnaviation OY [*Finland*] [*ICAO designator*]   (FAAC)
FAW .... Falwell Aviation, Inc. [*ICAO designator*]   (FAAC)
FAX .... Midwest Air Freighters, Inc. [*ICAO designator*]   (FAAC)
FBA........... Federation of British Astrologers Ltd.   (BI)
FBBA........ Fishing Boat Builders Association [*British*]   (BI)
FBBM........ Federation of Building Block Manufacturers [*British*]   (BI)
FBCA........ Federation of British Cremation Authorities   (BI)
FBCAEI..... Federation of Builders Contractors and Allied Employers of
　　　　　　Ireland   (BI)
FBD .... Statens Trafikkflygerskole [*Norway*] [*ICAO designator*]   (FAAC)
FBF............ Fine Airlines, Inc. [*ICAO designator*]   (FAAC)
FBF............ Folkestone-Boulogne Ferries [*English Channel ferry-boat service*]
　　　　　　[*British*]   (ECON)
FBL............ Food Brokers Ltd. [*Canada*] [*ICAO designator*]   (FAAC)
FBL............ Foreign Bird League [*British*]   (BI)
FBO .... Carroll Aircraft Corp. PLC [*British*] [*ICAO designator*]   (FAAC)
FBP........... Foreign Bases Project   (EA)
FBR............ Floating Point Register [*Computer science*]
FBTRC .... Federation of British Tape Recording Clubs   (BI)

FC .... Facilitative Communication [*Autism*]
FC .... Flanged Connection [*Piping*]
FC .... Fluorocarbon   (ERG)
FC .... Foolscap   (NTCM)
FC .... Hydrofluorocarbon
FCA........... Footwear Components Association Ltd. [*British*]   (BI)
FCA........... Frequency Change Approved [*Aviation*]   (FAAC)
FCA........... Stratford Airways Ltd. [*Canada*] [*ICAO designator*]   (FAAC)
FCBM........ Federation of Clinker Block Manufacturers [*British*]   (BI)
FCC............ Ferntree Computer Corp.
FCC............ Foreign Correspondents Club of Japan   (NTCM)
FCCA......... Floor Covering Contractors' Association [*British*]   (BI)
FCCC........ Federation of Commonwealth Chambers of Commerce   (BI)
FCDM .... Flow Control Decision Message   (DA)
FCEC......... Federation of Civil Engineering Contractors [*British*]   (BI)
FCEM........ Flow Control Execution Message   (DA)
FCH .... Flight-Chernobyl Association [*Russian Federation*] [*ICAO
　　　　　　designator*]   (FAAC)
FCI............. Family Communications, Inc. [*Public television*]   (NTCM)
FCL............ Flightcrew Licensing   (DA)
FCM .... Flying Cargo Private Ltd. [*Maldives*] [*ICAO designator*]   (FAAC)
FCMA........ Flushing Cistern Makers' Association [*British*]   (BI)
FCMI......... Federation of Coated Macadam Industries [*British*]   (BI)
FCN .... Falcon Aviation AB [*Sweden*] [*ICAO designator*]   (FAAC)
FCO .... Aerofrisco [*Mexico*] [*ICAO designator*]   (FAAC)
FCOS........ Farm Cash Operating Surplus
FCP............ Flight Corp. [*New Zealand*] [*ICAO designator*]   (FAAC)
FCP............ Fraud Control Plan
FCRP .... Field Condition Report [*Aviation*]   (FAAC)
FCRS .... Flightcrew Record System   (DA)
FCV............ Flight Centre Victoria [*Canada*] [*ICAO designator*]   (FAAC)
FCV............ Future Concept Vehicle
FCX............ Fire Coordination Exercise [*Military*]   (ADDR)
FD .... Finite Difference [*Metallurgy*]
FD .... Fire Department Access Point [*NFPA planning symbol*]   (NFPA)
FD .... Flying Dutchman [*Racing dinghy*]
FDC .... Federation of Dredging Contractors [*British*]   (BI)
FD & C....... Food, Drug, and Cosmetic Act
FDC .... Fully Distributed Cost
FDC .... Furniture Development Council [*British*]   (BI)
FDF............ Footwear Distributors Federation [*British*]   (BI)
FDF............ Francis Drake Fellowship [*British*]   (BI)
FDFM........ Flight Data and Flow Management Group [*ICAO*]   (DA)
FDFU......... Federation of Documentary Film Units [*British*]   (BI)
FDIO .... Flight Data Input/Output [*Aviation*]   (FAAC)
FDIOR....... Flight Data Input/Output Repeater [*Aviation*]   (FAAC)
FDM .... Freedom Airlines, Inc. [*ICAO designator*]   (FAAC)
FDP........... Flying Duty Period   (DA)
FDPS .... Flight Data Processing System   (DA)
FDX .... Federal Express Corp. [*ICAO designator*]   (FAAC)
FE .... Fire Escape   (DAC)
FE .... Foreign Editor   (NTCM)
FE .... Fundamentals of Engineering [*Exam*]
FEA........... Far Eastern Air Transport Corp. [*Taiwan*] [*ICAO designator*]
　　　　　　(FAAC)
FEB............ Field Engineering Bureau [*FCC*]   (NTCM)
FEC............ Denver Express, Inc. [*ICAO designator*]   (FAAC)
FEC............ First Edition Club   (NTCM)
FeCr .... Ferrichrome Recording Tape   (NTCM)
fed .... Federal Agent [*Slang*]
FED .... Linea Federal Argentina SEM [*ICAO designator*]   (FAAC)
FEDLEV..... Federal Low-Emission Vehicle [*Automotive engineering*]
FEI............ Field Engineering Instruction [*British*]   (DA)
FEI............ Fish Exports Inspector
FEJ............ France Europe Avia Jet [*ICAO designator*]   (FAAC)
FEL............ First European Airways Ltd. [*British*] [*ICAO designator*]   (FAAC)
FENKN ...... Fuel Supply Unknown [*Aviation*]   (FAAC)
FEOGA ...... Fonds European d'Orientation et de Garantie Agriculturel
　　　　　　[*European Agricultural Guidance and Guarantee Fund*]
FEP............ Fast Evening Persons Report [*Nielsen Television Index*]   (NTCM)
FEPP .... Free Erythrocyte Protoporphyrin [*Hematoloy*]   (MAH)
FER............ Feria Aviacion [*Spain*] [*ICAO designator*]   (FAAC)
FES .... Field Entry Standard [*Military*]   (ADDR)

FETA......... Fire Extinguisher Trades Association [*British*] (BI)
FETO......... Free Estimated Time of Overflight [*Aviation*] (DA)
FEU .... Compagnie Aeronautique Europeene [*France*] [*ICAO designator*] (FAAC)
FEX........... Flightexec Ltd. [*Canada*] [*ICAO designator*] (FAAC)
FF............... Flexible-Fueled [*Automotive engineering*]
FF............... Flight Ferry [*Navy*] (ANA)
FFB........... Africair Service [*Senegal*] [*ICAO designator*] (FAAC)
FFCPsy...... Fellow of the Faculty of Child and Adolescent Psychiatry
FFE........... Flexible-Fuel Engine [*Automotive engineering*]
FFF........... Free-Form Fabrication (ECON)
FFFF......... Fast Free-Form Fabrication [*Engineering design and modeling*]
FFG........... Flugdienst Fehlhaber GmbH [*Germany*] [*ICAO designator*] (FAAC)
FFH .... For Further Headings (DA)
fFIDA .... Fringe Festival of Independent Dance Artists [*Canada*]
FFS .... Fee for Service
FFU........... Ferranti PLC [*British*] [*ICAO designator*] (FAAC)
FFV........... Foreign Fishing Vessel
FG.............. Fracture Gradient
FGA........... Family Grocer Alliance Ltd. [*British*] (BI)
FGBA........ Fireclay Grate Back Association [*British*] (BI)
FGBI......... Federation of Soroptimist Clubs of Great Britain and Ireland (BI)
FGC .... Departamento de Agricultura de la Generalitat de Cataluna [*Spain*] [*ICAO designator*] (FAAC)
FGGM .... Federation of Gelatine and Glue Manufacturers [*British*] (BI)
FGM.......... Functionally Gradient Material [*Materials science*]
FGN........... Gendarmerie Nationale [*France*] [*ICAO designator*] (FAAC)
FGS............ Finished Goods Store
FGSB......... FFS [*Flight Service Station*] Guarding Service B [*Aviation*] (FAAC)
FGT .... Fairflight Ltd. [*British*] [*ICAO designator*] (FAAC)
FGTT......... Flue-Gas-through-the-Tubes [*Incinerator*]
F!H............. Heeling Force [*Sailing terminology*]
FHA........... Filamentous Hemagglutinin [*Medicine*]
FHH .... Familial Hypocalciuric Hypercalcemia [*Medicine*]
FHM.......... Familial Hemiplegic Migraine [*Medicine*]
FHS .... Forces Help Society [*British*] (BI)
FHT........... Federation of Holistic Therapists [*British*]
FIA............ Four Island Air Ltd. [*Antigua and Barbuda*] [*ICAO designator*] (FAAC)
FIAS .... Financial Information and Accounting System
FIB............ Freeway Iberica SA [*Spain*] [*ICAO designator*] (FAAC)
FIBMA ...... National Federation of Ironmongers' and Builders' Merchants' Staff Associations [*British*] (BI)
FIBS.......... Flight Information Billing System (DA)
FIC............ Fluoriodocarbon [*Fire extinguishing compound*]
FIC............ Flying Instructor Course (DA)
FIDAP .... Fluid Dynamics Analysis Package [*Computer-assisted engineering*]
FIDOR....... Fibre Building Board Development Organisation Ltd. [*British*] (BI)
FIE............. Feuerstein's Instrumental Enrichment [*Education*] (AEE)
FIE............. Field Aviation GmbH & Co. [*Germany*] [*ICAO designator*] (FAAC)
FIE............. Fly-In Echelon [*Navy*] (ANA)
FIE............. Friends of International Education [*An association*] (EA)
FIE............. Fuel Injection Equipment [*Diesel engines*]
FIF .... Foreign Investment Fund
FIF .... Frifly SpA [*Italy*] [*ICAO designator*] (FAAC)
FII .... Federation of Irish Industries Ltd. (BI)
FIIC .... Field Impact Insulation Class (DAC)
FIL............. Avia Filipines International, Inc. [*Philippines*] [*ICAO designator*] (FAAC)
FIL............. Foreign Investment Law
FIMA......... Forging Ingot Makers' Association [*British*] (BI)
FIN .... Finnair OY [*Finland*] [*ICAO designator*] (FAAC)
Fine Gard .... Fine Gardening [*A publication*]
FINMIS...... Financial Management and Information System
FINSAP...... Financial Sector Adjustment Program [*West Africa*]
FIP............. Federal Implementation Plan [*Environmental Protection Agency*] (ERG)
FIPG .... Formed-in-Place Plastic Gasket [*Automotive engineering*]
FIPS........... Federal Information Procedures System [*Environmental Protection Agency*] (ERG)
FIR............ Field Information Report [*CIA*]
FIRE .... Flame Infrared Emission
FIS............ FINSAP Implementation Secretariat [*West Africa*]
FIS............ Fuel Injection System [*Automotive engineering*]
FISA .... Automated Flight Information Service [*ICAO designator*] (FAAC)
FISCO .... Fuji International Speedway Co. [*Automobile racing*]
FIST.......... Fleet Imagery Satellite Terminal [*Navy*] (ANA)
FIT............ Field Investigation Team [*Environmental Protection Agency*] (ERG)
FIT............ Flight Technical Tolerance [*Aviation*] (DA)
FIT............ Foundation to Improve Television (EA)
FITC .... Foundry Industry Training Committee [*British*] (BI)
FIV............ Interface Group, Inc. [*ICAO designator*] (FAAC)
FIW........... Flight Input Workstation (DA)
FJ.............. Fuel-Jet (DA)
FJC .... Falcon Jet Centre [*British*] [*ICAO designator*] (FAAC)
FJI .... Air Pacific Ltd. [*Fiji*] [*ICAO designator*] (FAAC)

F-K............ Feynman-Kak Formula [*Particle physics*]
FL.............. Flash Advisory [*Meteorology*] (FAAC)
FL.............. Flashing (DAC)
FLA............ Air Florida [*ICAO designator*] (FAAC)
FLA............ Film Laboratory Association Ltd. [*British*] (BI)
FLC........... Aviation Standards National Field Office [*ICAO designator*] (FAAC)
FLC........... Forming Limit Curve [*Steel sheet fabrication*]
FLD........... Fieldair Freight Ltd. [*New Zealand*] [*ICAO designator*] (FAAC)
FLG........... Express Airlines I, Inc. [*ICAO designator*] (FAAC)
FLH .... Skybus, Inc. [*ICAO designator*] (FAAC)
FLI .... Atlantic Airways, PF [*Faroe Islands*] [*Denmark*] [*ICAO designator*] (FAAC)
FLITT........ Frigate LAMPS [*Light Airborne Multipurpose System*] Integrated Team Training [*Navy*] (ANA)
FLK........... Falcks Redningskorps Beldringe AS [*Denmark*] [*ICAO designator*] (FAAC)
FLMNAG... Fulminating (ABBR)
FLMNAN... Fulmination (ABBR)
FLMNC...... Flamboyance (ABBR)
FLMNGY... Flamingly (ABBR)
FLMNS...... Filminess (ABBR)
FLMNT...... Flamboyant (ABBR)
FLMNTY... Flamboyantly (ABBR)
FLMR........ Filmier (ABBR)
FLMRY...... Flummery (ABBR)
FLMSNS... Flimsiness (ABBR)
FLMSR...... Flimsier (ABBR)
FLMSST..... Flimsiest (ABBR)
FLMST...... Filmiest (ABBR)
FLMSY...... Flimsily (ABBR)
FLMSY...... Flimsy (ABBR)
FLMY........ Filmy (ABBR)
FLN .... Fallen (ABBR)
FLN .... Feline (ABBR)
FLN .... Felon (ABBR)
FLN .... Flanders Airlines [*Belgium*] [*ICAO designator*] (FAAC)
FLNCD...... Flounced (ABBR)
FLNCG...... Flouncing (ABBR)
FLNDR...... Flounder (ABBR)
FLNDRD... Floundered (ABBR)
FLNDRG.... Floundering (ABBR)
FLNGG...... Flinging (ABBR)
FLNH .... Flinch (ABBR)
FLNHGY ... Flinchingly (ABBR)
FLNHR...... Flincher (ABBR)
FLNK........ Flank (ABBR)
FLNKD...... Flanked (ABBR)
FLNKG...... Flanking (ABBR)
FLNKR...... Flanker (ABBR)
FLNKY...... Flunky (ABBR)
FLNS .... Fluidness (ABBR)
FLNS .... Fluorescence Line-Narrowing Spectroscopy
FLNT........ Felinity (ABBR)
FLNT........ Flint (ABBR)
FLNTEST ... Flauntiest (ABBR)
FLNTNS ... Flintiness (ABBR)
FLNTR...... Flintier (ABBR)
FLNTST..... Flintiest (ABBR)
FLNTY...... Flinty (ABBR)
FLNTYNS ... Flintiness (ABBR)
FLNTYY.... Flintily (ABBR)
FLNUS...... Felonious (ABBR)
FLNUSNS ... Feloniousness (ABBR)
FLNUSY.... Feloniously (ABBR)
FLNY........ Felinely (ABBR)
FLNY........ Felony (ABBR)
FLO .... Falcon Airlines [*Yugoslavia*] [*ICAO designator*] (FAAC)
FLO .... Family Liaison Office
Flo .... Floodlight (DA)
FLOC......... Floccule (ABBR)
FLOC......... Flocculent (ABBR)
FLOC......... Floccus (ABBR)
FLOD .... Flood (ABBR)
FLODD ..... Flooded (ABBR)
FLODG ..... Flooding (ABBR)
FLOP......... Floating Point Operation [*Computer science*]
FLOPD ..... Flopped (ABBR)
FLOPG ..... Flopping (ABBR)
FLOPLY ... Floppily (ABBR)
FLOPNS ... Floppiness (ABBR)
FLOPR ..... Flopper (ABBR)
FLOPR ..... Floppier (ABBR)
FLOPST .... Floppiest (ABBR)
FLOPY ..... Floppy (ABBR)
FLOPYR ... Floppier (ABBR)
FLOPYST .. Floppiest (ABBR)
FLORG ..... Flooring (ABBR)
FLORR...... Flourier (ABBR)
FLORST.... Flouriest (ABBR)
FLOR-WKR ... Floorwalker (ABBR)
FLORY...... Floury (ABBR)
FLOT.......... Float (ABBR)

FLOT......... Flotsam (ABBR)
FLOTD....... Floated (ABBR)
FLOTG....... Floating (ABBR)
FLOTGE.... Floatage (ABBR)
FLOTL....... Flotilla (ABBR)
FLOTM..... Flotsam (ABBR)
FLOTN....... Flotation (ABBR)
FLOTR....... Floater (ABBR)
FLP............ Bristol & Wessex Aeroplane Club Ltd. [British] [ICAO designator] (FAAC)
FLP............ Fillip (ABBR)
FLPD......... Flapped (ABBR)
FLPG......... Flapping (ABBR)
FLPNC....... Flippancy (ABBR)
FLPNT....... Flippant (ABBR)
FLPNTY..... Flippantly (ABBR)
FLRA........ Flora (ABBR)
FLRAL ...... Floral (ABBR)
FLRCLTR ... Floriculture (ABBR)
FLRCLTRL ... Floricultural (ABBR)
FLRCLTRST ... Floriculturalist (ABBR)
FLRD......... Floored (ABBR)
FLRD......... Flurried (ABBR)
FLRDA....... Flouridate (ABBR)
FLRDAD.... Flouridated (ABBR)
FLRDAG.... Flouridating (ABBR)
FLRDN....... Flouridation (ABBR)
FLRG......... Flooring (ABBR)
FLRG......... Flurrying (ABBR)
FLRH......... Flourish (ABBR)
FLRHG....... Flourishing (ABBR)
FLRID....... Florid (ABBR)
FLRIDNS... Floridness (ABBR)
FLRIDT..... Floridity (ABBR)
FLRIDY..... Floridly (ABBR)
FLRSNC.... Flourescence (ABBR)
FLRSNT.... Flourescent (ABBR)
FLRST........ Florist (ABBR)
FLRT........ Floret (ABBR)
FLRTN....... Flirtation (ABBR)
FLRTU....... Flirtatious (ABBR)
FLS............ Flushing, NY (ABBR)
FLS............ Forward Logistics Site [Navy]
FLS............ New Air Ltd. [British] [ICAO designator] (FAAC)
FLSCL........ Fullscale (ABBR)
FLSCP....... Flouroscope (ABBR)
FLS-CP...... Foolscap (ABBR)
FLSFCAN ... Falsification (ABBR)
FLSFD....... Falsified (ABBR)
FLSFG........ Falsifying (ABBR)
FLSFN....... Falsification (ABBR)
FLSFR........ Falsifier (ABBR)
FLSFY....... Falsify (ABBR)
FLSH......... Flash (ABBR)
FLSH-BK ... Flash-Back (ABBR)
FLSHD...... Flashed (ABBR)
FLSHD...... Flashehood (ABBR)
FLSHG....... Flashing (ABBR)
FLSHLT.... Flashlight (ABBR)
FLSHLY..... Flashily (ABBR)
FLSHNS ... Flashiness (ABBR)
FLSH-PTS ... Fleshpots (ABBR)
FLSHR...... Flasher (ABBR)
FLSHR...... Flashier (ABBR)
FLSHST..... Fleshiest (ABBR)
FLSHY ...... Flashy (ABBR)
FLSHY ...... Fleshly (ABBR)
FLSHYNS ... Flashiness (ABBR)
FLSHYR .... Flashier (ABBR)
FLSHYST ... Flashiest (ABBR)
FLSHYY .... Flashily (ABBR)
FLSLY....... Falsely (ABBR)
FLSM .... Fulsome (ABBR)
FLSMNS.... Fulsomeness (ABBR)
FLSMY ..... Fulsomely (ABBR)
FLSNS........ Falseness (ABBR)
FLSR .... Falser (ABBR)
FLSR .... Flossier (ABBR)
FLSSST .... Falsest (ABBR)
FLSSST .... Flossiest (ABBR)
FLST........ Falsest (ABBR)
FLST.......... Falsity (ABBR)
FLST.......... Flautist (ABBR)
FLST.......... Flutist (ABBR)
FLSTR........ Fluster (ABBR)
FLSTY....... Falsity (ABBR)
FLSY .... Falsely (ABBR)
FLSY .... Flossy (ABBR)
FLT............ Fermat's Last Theorem [Mathematics]
FLT............ Flightline [British] [ICAO designator] (FAAC)
FLT............ Fluidity (ABBR)
FLTAN...... Flotation (ABBR)
FLTB .... Floatable (ABBR)

FLTCAL..... Flight Calibration Procedure [Aviation] (DA)
FLT-CR ...... Flat-Car (ABBR)
FLTD......... Flatted (ABBR)
FLT-FT...... Flat-Foot (ABBR)
FLTG......... Flatting (ABBR)
FLTG .... Fleeting (ABBR)
FLTGNS .... Fleetingness (ABBR)
FLTGY ...... Fleetingly (ABBR)
FLTHNS .... Filthiness (ABBR)
FLTHR...... Filthier (ABBR)
FLTHST..... Filthiest (ABBR)
FLTHY ...... Filthy (ABBR)
FLTIO .... Fellatio (ABBR)
FLTLA....... Flotilla (ABBR)
FLTN......... Flatten (ABBR)
FLTN......... Floatation (ABBR)
FLTND...... Flattened (ABBR)
FLTNES...... Flatness (ABBR)
FLTNG ...... Flattening (ABBR)
FLTNS ...... Flatness (ABBR)
FLTNS ...... Fleetness (ABBR)
FLTR .... Flatter (ABBR)
FLTR .... Floater (ABBR)
FLTR .... Flutter (ABBR)
FLTRD ...... Flattered (ABBR)
FLTRG .... Flattering (ABBR)
FLTRG .... Fluttering (ABBR)
FLTRGY .... Flatteringly (ABBR)
FLTRGY .... Flutteringly (ABBR)
FLTRIR..... Flutterier (ABBR)
FLTRIST.... Flutteriest (ABBR)
FLTRNR.... Flattener (ABBR)
FLTRR....... Flattered (ABBR)
FLTRY .... Flattery (ABBR)
FLTRY .... Fluttery (ABBR)
FLTSM ...... Flotsam (ABBR)
FLTST....... Flattest (ABBR)
FLTST....... Flautist (ABBR)
FLTSURBAD ... Flight Surgeon Badge [Military decoration] [Army]
FLTWR ..... Flatware (ABBR)
FLTY .... Flatly (ABBR)
FLTY .... Fleetly (ABBR)
FLUCD...... Fluctuated (ABBR)
FLUCG....... Fluctuating (ABBR)
FLUCN...... Fluctuation (ABBR)
FLUCNT.... Fluctuant (ABBR)
FLUFD...... Fluffed (ABBR)
FLUFG....... Fluffing (ABBR)
FLUFY ...... Fluffy (ABBR)
FLUFYNS ... Fluffiness (ABBR)
FLUFYR..... Fluffier (ABBR)
FLUFYST ... Fluffiest (ABBR)
FLUFYY..... Fluffily (ABBR)
FLUK......... Fluke (ABBR)
FLUNC...... Fluency (ABBR)
FLUNT....... Fluent (ABBR)
FLUNTY .... Fluently (ABBR)
FLUORES ... Fluorescent (ABBR)
FLUT......... Flute (ABBR)
FLUTD...... Fluted (ABBR)
FLUTG....... Fluting (ABBR)
FLUTR....... Flouter (ABBR)
FLUTR....... Flutter (ABBR)
FLUTRD ... Fluttered (ABBR)
FLUTRG .... Fluttering (ABBR)
FLUTRR ... Flutterer (ABBR)
FLUTRY ... Fluttery (ABBR)
FLUTST.... Flutist (ABBR)
FLUX......... Flux (ABBR)
FLUXD...... Fluxed (ABBR)
FLUXG....... Fluxing (ABBR)
FLUXN....... Fluxion (ABBR)
FLVR......... Flavor (ABBR)
FLVRD...... Flavored (ABBR)
FLVRFL..... Flavorful (ABBR)
FLVRFLY ... Flavorfully (ABBR)
FLVRG....... Flavoring (ABBR)
FLVRLS..... Flavorless (ABBR)
FLVRR ...... Flavorer (ABBR)
FLVRSM.... Flavorsome (ABBR)
FLVRUS.... Flavorous (ABBR)
FLX............ Florida Express, Inc. [ICAO designator] (FAAC)
FM .... Frequency Management [Aviation] (DA)
FMA .... Food Machinery Association [British] (BI)
FMA .... Foremost Aviation Ltd. [Nigeria] [ICAO designator] (FAAC)
FMC .... Flexible Manufacturing Cell [Industrial engineering]
FMCC........ Force Movement Control Center [Marines] (ANA)
FMCS........ Factory Monitoring and Control System [Computer science]
FMGS........ Flight Management and Guidance System (DA)
FMH.......... Fan Marker Located with Radio Beacon [Aviation] (FAAC)
FMI........... Fellowship of the Motor Industry [British] (BI)
FMN .... France Marine Nationale [ICAO designator] (FAAC)
FMO .... Federation of Manufacturing Opticians [British] (BI)

FMOB .... Federation of Master Organ Builders [*British*]   (BI)
FMP............ Flow Management Position [*ICAO*]   (DA)
FMPCert .... Family Medicine Program Certificate
FMPE......... Federation of Master Process Engravers [*British*]   (BI)
FMPP .... Familial Male Precocious Puberty [*Medicine*]
FMPTE .... Federation of Municipal Passenger Transport Employers
    [*British*]   (BI)
FMR .... Field Maintenance Request
FMR .... Foundation for Moral Restoration   (EA)
FMS........... Hadison Aviation [*Sudan*] [*ICAO designator*]   (FAAC)
FMT .... Federation of Merchant Tailors of Great Britain, Inc.   (BI)
FMU .... Flow Management Unit [*Aviation*]   (FAAC)
FNA .... Flugfelag Nordurlands [*Iceland*] [*ICAO designator*]   (FAAC)
FNC .... Flexible Numerical Control [*Manufacturing engineering*]
    [*Computer science*]
FNF............ Finnish Air Force Headquarters [*ICAO designator*]   (FAAC)
FNFHFTM ... Federation of Needle Fish Hook and Fishing Tackle Makers
    [*British*]   (BI)
FNT .... Aerostar Airlines, Inc. [*ICAO designator*]   (FAAC)
FO.............. Foam System [*NFPA pre-fire planning symbol*]   (NFPA)
FOA .... Filipinas Orient Airways, Inc. [*Philippines*] [*ICAO designator*]
    (FAAC)
FOA .... Foreign-Owned or Affiliated [*Business term*]
FOB .... Field Operations Bureau [*FCC*]   (NTCM)
FOB .... Ford of Britain [*Corporate subsidiary*]
FOB .... Ford Motor Co. Ltd. [*ICAO designator*]   (FAAC)
FOBFO...... Federation of British Fire Organisations   (BI)
FOC .... Furthest-On Circle [*Navy*]   (ANA)
FOC .... Office Federal de l'Aviation Civile [*Sweden*] [*ICAO designator*]
    (FAAC)
FOD........... Finger of Death [*Fantasy gaming*]   (NHD)
FOF............ [*Fred*] Olsen Flyselskap AS [*Norway*] [*ICAO designator*]   (FAAC)
FOG .... Fiber-Optic Gyroscope [*Automotive navigation systems*]
FOH .... Front of House Spot [*Theatrical lighting*]   (NTCM)
FOHC........ Free of Heart Center   (DAC)
FOJ .... Friends of the Jessup [*An association*]   (EA)
FOL .... Forest Airline South Africa [*ICAO designator*]   (FAAC)
FOLP........ Fitting-Out of Leased Premises
FOMP .... Fuel and Oil Metering Pump [*Engine design*]
FOO .... Fairness of Opportunity [*Competitive bidding*]
FOP .... Fokker Flight Operations [*Netherlands*] [*ICAO designator*]
    (FAAC)
FOPS......... Federation of Playgoers Societies [*British*]   (BI)
FOR .... Fellowship of Riders (Motorcyclists) [*British*]   (BI)
FOR .... Fortune SRL [*Italy*] [*ICAO designator*]   (FAAC)
FORMICA ... Foreign Military Intelligence Collection Activities [*Navy*]
    (ANA)
fort.............. Fortified [*Nutrition*]
FORTE....... Fast Orbital Recording of Transient Events Satellite [*Department*
    of Energy]
FOT .... Frequence Optimum de Travail [*Optimum Working*
    Frequency]   (NTCM)
FOTC........ Force Over-the-Horizon Targeting Coordinator [*Navy*]   (ANA)
FOX .... Jetair APS [*Denmark*] [*ICAO designator*]   (FAAC)
FOY .... Fellowship of Youth [*British*]   (BI)
FP............... Fabry-Perot [*Etalon on interferometer*] [*Optics*]
FP............... Fire Pump Room [*NFPA pre-fire planning symbol*]   (NFPA)
FP............... Foreign Program [*FCC*]   (NTCM)
FP............... Front Projection   (NTCM)
Fp............... Frontispiece   (NTCM)
FP............... Fuel (Petroleum)   (DA)
FPA .... Film Production Association of Great Britain   (BI)
FPA .... Flight Plan Area [*Aviation*]   (FAAC)
FPC .... Flowers Publicity Council Ltd. [*British*]   (BI)
FPCEA .... Fibreboard Packing Case Employers' Association [*British*]   (BI)
FPCMA...... Fibreboard Packing Case Manufacturers' Association [*British*]
    (BI)
FPEEPM.... Floor Proximity Emergency Escape Path Marking [*Aviation*]
    (DA)
FPG........... Aeroleasing SA [*Switzerland*] [*ICAO designator*]   (FAAC)
FPL............ Filed Flight Plan   (DA)
FPL............ Full Performance Level [*Aviation*]   (FAAC)
FPLC .... Fast Performance Liquid Chromatography
FPP .... Family Planning Program
FPP .... Flight Preparation Ltd. [*British*] [*ICAO designator*]   (FAAC)
FPPR .... Fluorescence Pattern Photobleaching Recovery [*for study of*
    surfaces]
FPR .... Fuerza Aerea del Peru [*ICAO designator*]   (FAAC)
FPS .... Fell Pony Society [*British*]   (BI)
FPS .... Friction Pendulum System [*for earthquake protection*]
FPT .... Fan-Powered Terminal   (DAC)
FPTO......... Fluid Power Take-Off [*Hydraulic transmissions*]
FR .... For [*Telecommunications*]   (ADDR)
F!r.............. Frictional Force   (DA)
FRA .... FR Aviation Ltd. [*British*] [*ICAO designator*]   (FAAC)
FRAP......... Federal Rules of Appellate Procedure [*A publication*]
FRCAB....... Felt Roofing Contractors' Advisory Board [*British*]   (BI)
FRD .... Ford Motor Co. [*ICAO designator*]   (FAAC)
FRE .... Aviation Services Ltd. [*Guam*] [*ICAO designator*]   (FAAC)
FRET .... Freezing Rain Endurance Test [*Aviation*]   (DA)
FRET-ANON ... Family-Related Emotional Trauma - Anonymous
FRFAB .... FSS [*Flight Service Station*] Returns Flight-Plan Area and Service
    B [*Aviation*]   (FAAC)

FRFID .... Fast Response Flame Ionization Detector [*Automotive emissions*
    testing]
FRFOURRA ... French Fourragere [*Military decoration*]
FRG .... Freight Runners Express, Inc. [*ICAO designator*]   (FAAC)
FRHB .... Federation of Registered House-Builders [*British*]   (BI)
FRI............ Flandre Air International [*France*] [*ICAO designator*]   (FAAC)
FRL............ [*Maria Elisa*] Gonzales Farelas [*Mexico*] [*ICAO designator*]
    (FAAC)
FRM .... Federal Armored Service, Inc. [*ICAO designator*]   (FAAC)
FRMA........ Floor Rug Manufacturers' Association [*British*]   (BI)
FRO .... Frobisher NV (European Airlines) [*Belgium*] [*ICAO designator*]
    (FAAC)
FRP............ F-Air AS [*Denmark*] [*ICAO designator*]   (FAAC)
FRS............ Flandre Air Service [*France*] [*ICAO designator*]   (FAAC)
FRSB .... FSS [*Flight Service Station*] Returns Service B [*Aviation*]
    (FAAC)
FRST .... Frost [*Meteorology*]   (DA)
FRTO......... Flight Radio Telephony Operator   (DA)
FS.............. Fathers of Sion [*British*]   (BI)
FS.............. Femtosecond [*One quadrillionth of a second*]
FS.............. Follow Shot [*Photography*]   (NTCM)
F/S............. Frames per Second   (NTCM)
FS.............. Full Shot [*Photography*]   (NTCM)
FSA .... Financial Security Assurance
FSA .... Foster Aviation [*ICAO designator*]   (FAAC)
FSA .... Full-State Assumption [*Education*]   (AEE)
FSAPO .... Fade Sound and Picture Out [*Cinematography*]   (NTCM)
FSC .... Foolscap   (NTCM)
FSC .... Four Star Aviation, Inc. [*Virgin Islands*] [*ICAO designator*]
    (FAAC)
FSD............ Efs-Flugservice GmbH [*Germany*] [*ICAO designator*]   (FAAC)
FSD............ File-Set Description [*Computer science*]
FSFA .... Federation of Specialised Film Associations [*British*]   (BI)
FSH .... Flash Airline Ltd. [*Nigeria*] [*ICAO designator*]   (FAAC)
FSI .... Fish and Shellfish Immunology [*A publication*]
FSL............ Flight Safety Ltd. [*British*] [*ICAO designator*]   (FAAC)
FSM .... Fabryka Samochodow Malolotia [*Polish affiliate of Fiat Motors*]
FSM .... Fine Scale Modeler [*A publication*]
FSMF .... Furnishing Springmakers Federation [*British*]   (BI)
FSO............ Fabryka Samochodow Osobowych [*Polish automobile*
    manufacturer]
FST .... Fast Air Ltda. [*Chile*] [*ICAO designator*]   (FAAC)
FSTC .... Field Sound Transmission Class   (DAC)
FSVC .... Financial Services Volunteer Corps [*An association*]   (EA)
FSVDR .... File Structure Volume Descriptor Record   (NTCM)
FSX .... Flagship Express Services, Inc. [*ICAO designator*]   (FAAC)
FS-X .... Future Sports-Sedan Experimental [*Concept car*]
FT .... FM Broadcast Translator [*FCC*]   (NTCM)
FTA .... Federation of Trade Associations [*Republic of Ireland*]   (BI)
FTA .... File Trade Association [*British*]   (BI)
FTA .... Frontier Flying Service, Inc. [*ICAO designator*]   (FAAC)
FTA-AB...... Fluorescent Treponemal Antibody-Absorption Syphilis Test
    [*Medicine*]   (MAH)
FTBA .... Furniture Trades Benevolent Association [*British*]   (BI)
FTCS .... Foreign Tax Credit System
FTD .... Flight Training Device [*Aviation*]   (DA)
FTE .... Flight Technical Error [*Aviation*]   (DA)
FTE .... Fotografia F3 SA [*Spain*] [*ICAO designator*]   (FAAC)
FTF .... Fibre Trade Federation [*British*]   (BI)
FT-ICP .... Fourier Transform Inductively-Coupled Plasma [*Spectrometry*]
FT-ICRMS ... Fourier Transform Ion Cyclotron Resonance Mass Spectrometry
FTITB........ Furniture and Timber Industry Training Board [*British*]   (BI)
FTL .... Flight Time Limitation [*Aviation*]   (DA)
FTN .... Aviation Charter & Management [*British*] [*ICAO designator*]
    (FAAC)
ftp.............. File Transfer Protocol
FTPS......... Food Trades Protection Society Ltd. [*British*]   (BI)
FTR .... Finist' Air [*France*] [*ICAO designator*]   (FAAC)
FTS .... Flexible Track System [*Aviation*]   (DA)
FUA .... Compania Hispano Irlandesa de Aviacion [*Spain*] [*ICAO*
    designator]   (FAAC)
FUBAR...... Failed UNI BUS Address Register [*Computer science*]   (NHD)
FUJ .... Fujairah Aviation Centre [*United Arab Emirates*] [*ICAO*
    designator]   (FAAC)
FUN .... Funtshi Aviation Service [*Zaire*] [*ICAO designator*]   (FAAC)
FURS......... Federal Underground Injection Control Reporting System
    [*Environmental Protection Agency*]   (ERG)
Fus .... Fusible   (DAC)
FUW .... Farmers' Union of Wales   (BI)
FV .... Family Viewing Time [*FCC rule*]   (NTCM)
FV .... Finite Volume [*Metallurgy*]
FV .... Fishing Vessel
FVA .... Avair, Inc. [*ICAO designator*]   (FAAC)
FVA .... Four Valve Type A [*Cosworth racing engines*]
FVG .... Frevag Airlines [*Belgium*] [*ICAO designator*]   (FAAC)
FWA .... Far West Airlines, Inc. [*ICAO designator*]   (FAAC)
FWC .... Fault Warning Computer [*Aviation*]   (DA)
FWC .... Freeway Air BV [*Netherlands*] [*ICAO designator*]   (FAAC)
FWCC........ Friends' Work Camp Committee [*British*]   (BI)
FWH.......... Fast Weekly Household Audience Report [*Nielsen Television*
    Index]   (MAH)
FWL........... Florida West Airlines [*ICAO designator*]   (FAAC)
FWMB........ Federation of Wholesale and Multiple Bakers [*British*]   (BI)

FWQ .... Flight West Airlines [*Australia*] [*ICAO designator*]   (FAAC)
FWRMGB ... Federation of Wire Rope Manufacturers of Great Britain   (BI)
FWY .... Fairways Corp. [*ICAO designator*]   (FAAC)
FXA .... Express Air, Inc. [*ICAO designator*]   (FAAC)
FXGL........... Foreign Exchange Gains and Losses
FXR............ Foxair Ltd. [*British*] [*ICAO designator*]   (FAAC)
FXY............. Flexair BV [*Netherlands*] [*ICAO designator*]   (FAAC)
FYA .... For Your Amusement [*Computer hacker terminology*]   (NHD)
FYY............. Finningley FTU [*British*] [*ICAO designator*]   (FAAC)

G

G .... Gas Shutoff [*NFPA pre-fire planning symbol*]   (NFPA)
G .... Ground Control [*Aviation*]   (DA)
9G .... Ghana [*Aircraft nationality and registration mark*]   (FAAC)
GA .... Goal Attack [*Netball*]
GAA .... Business Express [*ICAO designator*]   (FAAC)
GAA .... Glacial Acrylic Acid [*Organic chemistry*]
GAAP .... Generally Accepted Accounting Principles [*Environmental Protection Agency*]   (ERG)
GAB .... Gendall Air Ltd. [*Canada*] [*ICAO designator*]   (FAAC)
GABA .... Gambling and Betting Addiction
GAC .... General Air Cargo [*Venezuela*] [*ICAO designator*]   (FAAC)
GAF .... German Air Force [*ICAO designator*]   (FAAC)
GAGB .... Gemmological Association of Great Britain   (BI)
GAI .... Guild of Architectural Ironmongers [*British*]   (BI)
GAL .... Gemini Airlines Ltd. [*Ghana*] [*ICAO designator*]   (FAAC)
GALH .... General Association of Ladies Hairdressers [*British*]   (BI)
GAM .... Gambia
GAM .... General Audit Manual
GAM .... German Army [*ICAO designator*]   (FAAC)
GAMAST ... Girls and Mathematics and Science Teaching
GAMPS ..... Gander Automated Message Processing System [*ICAO*]   (DA)
GAMTA ..... General Aviation Manufacturers' and Traders' Association [*British*]   (DA)
GAN .... Gander Aviation Ltd. [*Canada*] [*ICAO designator*]   (FAAC)
GAO .... Golden Air Commuter AB [*Sweden*] [*ICAO designator*]   (FAAC)
GAP .... Good Agricultural Practice [*Toxicology*]
GAPD .... Glyceraldehyde Phosphate Dehydrogenase [*Organic chemistry*]   (MAH)
GAQ .... Golfe Air Quebec Ltd. [*Canada*] [*ICAO designator*]   (FAAC)
GAR .... Commodore Aviation [*Australia*] [*ICAO designator*]   (FAAC)
GARGD ..... Garaged [*Automotive advertising*]
GAS .... Galena Air Services, Inc. [*ICAO designator*]   (FAAC)
GAT .... Gulf Air, Inc. [*ICAO designator*]   (FAAC)
GAUK .... Gamekeepers' Association of the United Kingdom   (BI)
GAV .... Granada Aviacion [*Spain*] [*ICAO designator*]   (FAAC)
GAvA .... Guild of Aviation Artists   (DA)
GAW .... Gambia Airways [*ICAO designator*]   (FAAC)
GAWBS ..... Guided Acoustic Wave Brillouin Scattering [*Physics*]
GB .... Girls Brigade [*British*]   (BI)
GB .... Glass Block   (DAC)
GB .... Guild of Bricklayers [*British*]   (BI)
GBA .... Georgian Bay Airways [*Canada*] [*ICAO designator*]   (FAAC)
GBC .... Globe Air Cargo [*Antigua and Barbuda*] [*ICAO designator*]   (FAAC)
GBCS-L/H ... Ground Based Common Sensor-Light/Heavy [*Military*]
GBDO .... Guild of British Dispensing Opticians   (BI)
GBL .... GB Airways Ltd. [*British*] [*ICAO designator*]   (FAAC)
GBMC .... Golf Ball Manufacturers' Conference [*British*]   (BI)
GBNE .... Guild of British Newspapers Editors   (BI)
GBO .... Ogooue Air Cargo [*Gabon*] [*ICAO designator*]   (FAAC)
GBP .... Guanylate Binding Protein [*Biochemistry*]
GBR .... Rader Aviation, Inc. [*ICAO designator*]   (FAAC)
GBT .... Gold Belt Air Transport, Inc. [*Canada*] [*ICAO designator*]   (FAAC)
GBU .... Transports Aeriens de la Guinee-Bissau [*Guinea-Bissau*] [*ICAO designator*]   (FAAC)
GCA .... Great China Airlines [*Taiwan*] [*ICAO designator*]   (FAAC)
GCB .... Lignes Nationales Aeriennes - Linacongo [*Congo*] [*ICAO designator*]   (FAAC)
GCC .... Glove Collector Club   (EA)
GCCF .... Governing Council of the Cat Fancy [*British*]   (BI)
GCI .... General Cognitive Index
GCITING ... Ground-Control Intercept Training [*Navy*]   (ANA)
GCL .... Greenclose Aviation Services Ltd. [*British*] [*ICAO designator*]   (FAAC)
GCMA .... Glazed Cement Manufacturers Association Ltd. [*British*]   (BI)
GCN .... Gulf Central Airlines, Inc. [*ICAO designator*]   (FAAC)
GCOC .... General Conditions of Contract
GCP .... Golden CommPass [*Front-end computer processor*]   (PCM)
GCS .... Gas Cleaning System [*Combustion technology*]
GD .... Goal Defence [*Netball*]
GD .... Graduate Diploma
GDA .... General Disposal Authority

GDA .... Global Directory Agent
GDA .... Glycidyldiisopropylidenearabitol [*Organic chemistry*]
GDA .... Graduate Diploma in Administration
GDBusAd ... Graduate Diploma in Business Administration
GDC .... Guild of Dyers and Cleaners [*British*]   (BI)
GDCH .... Graduate Diploma in Community Health
GDE .... Servicios Aereos Gadel SA de CV [*Mexico*] [*ICAO designator*]   (FAAC)
GDipA(Couns) ... Graduate Diploma in Arts (Counselling)
GDipCD ...... Graduate Diploma in Child Development
GDipCh ...... Graduate Diploma in Chiropractic
GDipClinSc ... Graduate Diploma in Clinical Science
GDipCompSt ... Graduate Diploma in Computer Studies
GDipEc .... Graduate Diploma in Economics
GDipErg ..... Graduate Diploma in Ergonomics
GDipExerSpSc ... Graduate Diploma in Exercise and Sport Science
GDipHA ...... Graduate Diploma in Health Administration
GDipHC ..... Graduate Diploma in Health Counselling
GDipHSM ... Graduate Diploma in Health Services Management
GDipHumNut ... Graduate Diploma in Human Nutrition
GDipLS ...... Graduate Diploma in Legal Studies
GDipM ...... Graduate Diploma in Management
GDipMLS ... Graduate Diploma in Medical Laboratory Science
GDipPEC ... Graduate Diploma in Parent Education and Counselling
GDipPHC ... Graduate Diploma in Primary Health
GDipPrfMgt ... Graduate Diploma in Professional Management
GDipPubL ... Graduate Diploma in Public Law
GDL .... Gas Discharge Lamp
GDManTher ... Graduate Diploma in Manipulative Therapy
GDOccHlth ... Graduate Diploma in Occupational Health
GDS .... Global Directory Service
GDSafH ...... Graduate Diploma in Safety and Health
GDSafS .... Graduate Diploma in Safety Science
GDSSc .... Graduate Diploma in Sport Science
GDX .... Glycidyldiisopropylidenexylitol [*Organic chemistry*]
GEA .... Georgia Air [*Czechoslovakia*] [*ICAO designator*]   (FAAC)
GEC .... German Cargo Services [*ICAO designator*]   (FAAC)
GECOS ...... General Electric Comprehensive Operating System [*Computer science*]   (NHD)
GEE .... Geeseair [*Canada*] [*ICAO designator*]   (FAAC)
GEF .... Air GEFCO [*France*] [*ICAO designator*]   (FAAC)
GEL .... Gambcrest Enterprises Ltd. [*Gambia*] [*ICAO designator*]   (FAAC)
GEM .... Bristol BAE [*British*] [*ICAO designator*]   (FAAC)
GEM .... General Enrollment Manual
GEM .... Graphic Engine Monitor   (DA)
GEMA .... Gymnastic Equipment Manufacturers' Association [*British*]   (BI)
GEMI .... Global Environmental Management Initiative [*Environmental science*]
GEMS .... Gender Equality in Mathematics and Science
GEN .... Genavco Air Ltd. [*British*] [*ICAO designator*]   (FAAC)
GENSYM ... Generated Symbol [*Computer science*]   (NHD)
GEP .... General Entry Permit
GER .... Guernsey Airlines Ltd. [*British*] [*ICAO designator*]   (FAAC)
GES .... Gestair Executive Jet [*Spain*] [*ICAO designator*]   (FAAC)
GET .... Gaming Entertainment Television [*Interactive-gambling TV station*]   (ECON)
GEY .... Geuserland Airways Ltd. [*New Zealand*] [*ICAO designator*]   (FAAC)
GF .... Gasoline-Fueled [*Automotive engineering*]
GFA .... Gulf Air [*United Arab Emirates*] [*ICAO designator*]   (FAAC)
GFCE .... Gross Fixed Capital Expenditure
GFD .... Gesellschaft fur Flugzieldarstellung GmbH [*Germany*] [*ICAO designator*]   (FAAC)
GFE .... Goal-Free Evaluation [*Education*]   (AEE)
GFL .... Green Forest Lumber Ltd. [*Canada*] [*ICAO designator*]   (FAAC)
GFP .... Green Fluorescent Protein [*Biochemistry*]
GFR .... Grim File Reaper [*Computer hacker terminology*]   (NHD)
GFS .... Grandfather-Father-Son [*Computer science*]   (PCM)
GFS .... Gulfstream Airlines, Inc. [*ICAO designator*]   (FAAC)
GFT .... Gulfstream International Airlines, Inc. [*ICAO designator*]   (FAAC)
GGRA .... Gelatine and Glue Research Association [*British*]   (BI)

GHA .... Ghana Airways Corp. [*ICAO designator*]   (FAAC)
GHL........... Gatwick Handling Ltd. [*British*] [*ICAO designator*]   (FAAC)
GHM .... Aero Service Bolivia [*ICAO designator*]   (FAAC)
GHS........... Gatari Hutama Air Services PT [*Indonesia*] [*ICAO designator*]   (FAAC)
GI .... Gross Impression [*Television ratings*]   (NTCM)
GIA .... Garuda Indonesia PT [*ICAO designator*]   (FAAC)
GIB .... Air Guinea [*Guinea*] [*ICAO designator*]   (FAAC)
GIC .... Compagnie de Bauxites de Guinee [*Guinea*] [*ICAO designator*]   (FAAC)
GID .... Channel Aviation Ltd. [*British*] [*ICAO designator*]   (FAAC)
GID .... Sud Air Transport SA [*Guinea*] [*ICAO designator*]   (FAAC)
GIE .... Guinee Inter Air [*Guinea*] [*ICAO designator*]   (FAAC)
GIF .... Guinee Air Lines SA [*Guinea*] [*ICAO designator*]   (FAAC)
GIG .... Glycidylisopropylideneglycerol [*Organic chemistry*]
GIL .... Gill Aviation Ltd. [*British*] [*ICAO designator*]   (FAAC)
GIM .... Gas Injection Molding [*Plastic fabrications*]
GIN .... Association de Recherche et d'Exploitation de Diamant et de l'Or [*Guinea*] [*ICAO designator*]   (FAAC)
GIO .... Generalist Intelligence Officer
GIO .... Guild of Insurance Officials [*British*]   (BI)
GIO .... Regionnair, Inc. [*Canada*] [*ICAO designator*]   (FAAC)
GIPS .... Giga-Instructions per Second [*Computer science*]   (NHD)
GIS........... Gas-Scintillation Imaging Spectrometer
GIS............ Gastrointestinal System [*Medicine*]   (MAH)
GIS............ Guinee Air Service [*Guinea*] [*ICAO designator*]   (FAAC)
GIU .... Union Guineene de Transports [*Guinea*] [*ICAO designator*]   (FAAC)
GJB........... Trans-Air Link Corp. [*ICAO designator*]   (FAAC)
GK.............. Goal Keeper [*Netball*]
GKA........... US Army Aeronautical Services [*ICAO designator*]   (FAAC)
GKT .... General Knowledge Test
GLA .... Great Lakes Aviation Ltd. [*ICAO designator*]   (FAAC)
GLB .... Global Air [*Bulgaria*] [*ICAO designator*]   (FAAC)
GLBA......... Great Lakes Booksellers Association   (EA)
GLD........... Golden Star Air Cargo Co. Ltd. [*Sudan*] [*ICAO designator*]   (FAAC)
GLF............ Gulfstream Aerospace Corp. [*ICAO designator*]   (FAAC)
GLI .... Gallic Aviation [*France*] [*ICAO designator*]   (FAAC)
GLJ .... Global Getra Ltd. [*Bulgaria*] [*ICAO designator*]   (FAAC)
GLN .... Lennox Airways, Gambia Ltd. [*ICAO designator*]   (FAAC)
GLOBE...... Global Learning and Observations to Benefit the Environment [*NASA*]
GLOV .... Gays and Lesbians Opposing Violence [*An association*]
GLR .... Central Mountain Air Ltd. [*Canada*] [*ICAO designator*]   (FAAC)
GLS........... General Lighting System [*Incandescent lighting*]
GLS........... Global International Ltd. [*Bulgaria*] [*ICAO designator*]   (FAAC)
GLT .... General Corporation for Light Air Transport & Technical Sevices [*Libya*] [*ICAO designator*]   (FAAC)
GMA.......... Gama Aviation Ltd. [*British*] [*ICAO designator*]   (FAAC)
GMC.......... General Motors Corp. [*ICAO designator*]   (FAAC)
GMC.......... Guild of Memorial Craftsmen [*British*]   (BI)
GMDSS...... Global Maritime Distress and Safety System   (DA)
GMH .... Hughes Aircraft Co. (Aeronautical Operations) [*ICAO designator*]   (FAAC)
GMI .... Germania Fluggesellschaft Koln [*Germany*] [*ICAO designator*]   (FAAC)
GML.......... Gemial [*Slovakia*] [*ICAO designator*]   (FAAC)
G-MP......... G-Myeloma Protein [*Biochemistry*]   (MAH)
GMP.......... Gap Media Project [*An association*]   (EA)
GMP.......... Groundwater Modeling Program [*US Army Engineer Waterways Experiment Station*]   (RDA)
GMR .... Giant Magnetoresistance [*Materials science*]
GMR .... Grampian Helicopter Charter Ltd. [*British*] [*ICAO designator*]   (FAAC)
GMSC .... General Medical Services Council [*British*]   (BI)
GN.............. Grid North [*Army*]   (ADDR)
GNB........... Global Air Link [*Nigeria*] [*ICAO designator*]   (FAAC)
GNMS....... Ground Network Management System [*Aviation*]   (DA)
GNT.......... Business Air Ltd. [*British*] [*ICAO designator*]   (FAAC)
GNV.......... Grand Airways, Inc. [*ICAO designator*]   (FAAC)
GNY.......... German Navy [*ICAO designator*]   (FAAC)
GOA.......... Alberta Government [*Canada*] [*ICAO designator*]   (FAAC)
GOB.......... Grants Operations Balance [*Environmental Protection Agency*]   (ERG)
GODA........ Guild of Drama Adjudicators [*British*]   (BI)
GOJ .... Eurojet Aviation Ltd. [*British*] [*ICAO designator*]   (FAAC)
GOLD........ Guild of Lady Drivers [*British*]   (BI)
GON .... Gonni Air Services Ltd. [*Suriname*] [*ICAO designator*]   (FAAC)
GOR.......... Grille Opening Reinforcement [*Automotive engineering*]
GORS .... Grant of Resident Status
GOS........... Gate Operating System [*Aviation*]   (DA)
GOS........... Goldfields Air Services [*Australia*] [*ICAO designator*]   (FAAC)
GOS........... Gross Operating Surplus [*Economics*]
GOT........... Air Express in Norrkoping AB [*Sweden*] [*ICAO designator*]   (FAAC)
GOWR....... Grand Order of Water Rats [*British*]   (BI)
GP.............. Good Practice
GPA .... Kingman Aviation, Inc. [*ICAO designator*]   (FAAC)
GPAY .... General Payments System
GPC .... Government Purpose Classification
GPDA .... Gypsum Plasterboard Development Association [*British*]   (BI)
GPE .... GP Express Airlines, Inc. [*ICAO designator*]   (FAAC)

GPL .... General Public License   (NHD)
GPLC......... Guild of Professional Launderers and Cleaners [*British*]   (BI)
GPP .... Guild of Public Pharmacists [*British*]   (BI)
GPS............ Government Procurement Service
GPV........... General Public Virus [*Computer science*]   (NHD)
GRA .... Great American Airways [*ICAO designator*]   (FAAC)
GRANAS.... Global Radio Navigation System [*Aviation*]   (DA)
GRC........... Grafted Rubber Concentrate [*Organic chemistry*]
GRC........... Greenlandair Charter AS [*Denmark*] [*ICAO designator*]   (FAAC)
GRD........... National Grid Co. [*British*] [*ICAO designator*]   (FAAC)
GRE .... [*The*] Greens [*Australia*] [*Political party*]
GRE .... Ground Run-Up Enclosure [*Aviation*]   (DA)
GRE .... SEEA-Southeast European Airlines [*Greece*] [*ICAO designator*]   (FAAC)
G/Rfg .... Grooved Roofing [*Lumber*]   (DAC)
GRG .... General Recurrent Grant
GRI .... Generic Run-Time [*Computer science*]
GRL .... Gronlandsfly Ltd. [*Denmark*] [*ICAO designator*]   (FAAC)
GRN .... Greenair Hava Tasimaciligi AS [*Turkey*] [*ICAO designator*]   (FAAC)
GRO........... Lineas Aereas Allegro SA de CV [*Mexico*] [*ICAO designator*]   (FAAC)
GRP .... Guyana Republican Party [*Political party*]   (EA)
GRR .... Gastric Reservoir Reduction [*Morbid obesity surgical treatment*]
GRRA .... Gramophone Record Retailers Association [*British*]   (BI)
GRT .... Gabon-Air-Transport [*ICAO designator*]   (FAAC)
GRV .... Grosvenor Aviation Services [*British*] [*ICAO designator*]   (FAAC)
GRVL .... Gravel   (DA)
GS .... Goal Shooter [*Netball*]
GSA .... Garden State Airlines, Inc. [*ICAO designator*]   (FAAC)
GSA .... [*The*] Green Party South Australia [*Political party*]
GSC .... Girls' School Company Ltd. [*British*]   (BI)
GSH........... Gambia Air Shuttle Ltd. [*ICAO designator*]   (FAAC)
GSL........... Geographic Air Surveys Ltd. [*Canada*] [*ICAO designator*]   (FAAC)
GSLTA .... Girls' Schools Lawn Tennis Association [*British*]   (BI)
GSLV......... Geostationary Launch Vehicle [*Indian Space Research Organization*]
GSM .... General System Mobile [*Telephone*]
GSM .... Geological Survey of Great Britain and Museum of Practical Geology   (BI)
GSO........... General Stores Officer
GSP............ M & M Aviation, Inc. [*ICAO designator*]   (FAAC)
GSS............ Global Space Station [*Proposed by NASA and ESA*]
GSSAPI...... Generic Security Service Application Program Interface
GTA .... Gitanair [*Italy*] [*ICAO designator*]   (FAAC)
GTA .... Gun Trade Association Ltd. [*British*]   (BI)
GTBC......... Guild of Teachers of Backward Children [*British*]   (BI)
GTC .... Gran Turismo Cabriolet [*Automobile model designation*]
GTC .... Group Training Company
GTF .... General Transcription Factor [*Genetics*]
GTFT .... Generous Tit for Tat [*Game strategy*]
GTHS .... German-Texan Heritage Society   (EA)
GTI .... Atlas Air, Inc. [*ICAO designator*]   (FAAC)
GTIS .... Ground-Based Traffic Information System [*Aviation*]   (DA)
GTK .... Grosser Touren Kombiwagen [*Grand Touring Station Wagon*] [*German*]
GTMA .... Galvanised Tank Manufacturers' Association [*British*]   (BI)
GTP .... General Training Program
GTP .... Government Technology Productivity
GTS............ Green Tobacco Sickness [*Illness resulting from exposure to dissolved nicotine*]
GTST .... Greatest   (ABBR)
GTY .... Greatly   (ABBR)
GTY .... National Aviation Co. [*Egypt*] [*ICAO designator*]   (FAAC)
GUA .... Aerotaxis de Aguascalientes SA de CV [*Mexico*] [*ICAO designator*]   (FAAC)
GUART ..... Guaranty   (ABBR)
GUARTE.... Guarantee   (ABBR)
GUARTED ... Guaranteed   (ABBR)
GUARTEG ... Guaranteeing   (ABBR)
GUARTR ... Guarantor   (ABBR)
GUBER ..... Gubernatorial   (ABBR)
GUD .... Guide   (ABBR)
GUDBK...... Guidebook   (ABBR)
GUDD .... Guided   (ABBR)
GUDG .... Guiding   (ABBR)
GUDNC...... Guidance   (ABBR)
GUDPST.... Guidepost   (ABBR)
GUERL ...... Guerilla   (ABBR)
GUF .... Global University Funding
GUG .... Empresa Guatemalteca de Aviacion [*Guatemala*] [*ICAO designator*]   (FAAC)
GUIB .... Graphical User Interface for Blind People
GUIL .... Guilder   (ABBR)
GUILDHL ... Guildhall   (ABBR)
GUILFL ..... Guileful   (ABBR)
GUILFY ..... Guilefully   (ABBR)
GUILS........ Guileless   (ABBR)
GUILSY ..... Guilelessly   (ABBR)
GUL........... Gull Air [*ICAO designator*]   (FAAC)
GUL........... Gully   (ABBR)

GULB .... Gullible (ABBR)
GULBLY .... Gullibly (ABBR)
GULBT .... Gullibility (ABBR)
GULT .... Gullet (ABBR)
GULTN ...... Guillotine (ABBR)
GULTND ... Guillotined (ABBR)
GULTNG ... Guillotining (ABBR)
GULYG ...... Gullying (ABBR)
GUMNS ..... Gumminess (ABBR)
GUN .... Guncotton (ABBR)
GUN .... Guncrete (ABBR)
GUN .... Gunny (ABBR)
GUN .... Gunpowder (ABBR)
GUNBT ...... Gunboat (ABBR)
GUND .... Gunned (ABBR)
GUNFIT ..... Gunfight (ABBR)
GUNFITR ... Gunfighter (ABBR)
GUNFR ...... Gunfire (ABBR)
GUNG .... Gunning (ABBR)
GUNMA ..... Gunman (ABBR)
GUNPWDR ... Gunpowder (ABBR)
GUNR .... Gunner (ABBR)
GUNRY ...... Gunnery (ABBR)
GUNSH ...... Gunshot (ABBR)
GUNSM ..... Gunsmith (ABBR)
GUNST ...... Gunstock (ABBR)
GUNWHL ... Gunwhale (ABBR)
GUNYBG ... Gunnybag (ABBR)
GUP .... Guppy (ABBR)
GUR .... Gurgu (ABBR)
GURGLD ... Gurgled (ABBR)
GURGLG ... Gurgling (ABBR)
GURNT ...... Guarantee (ABBR)
GURNTD ... Guaranteed (ABBR)
GURNTG ... Guarantying (ABBR)
GURNTR ... Guarantor (ABBR)
GURNTY ... Guaranty (ABBR)
GURTG ...... Guaranteeing (ABBR)
GUSHG ...... Gushing (ABBR)
GUSHNS ... Gushiness (ABBR)
GUSHR ...... Gushier (ABBR)
GUSHST .... Gushiest (ABBR)
GUST .... Gusset (ABBR)
GUSTNS .... Gustiness (ABBR)
GUSTO ...... Global Utilization of Streptokinase and TPA [*Tissue Plasminogen Activator*] for Occluded Arteries [*Comparative study*]
GUSTR .... Gustier (ABBR)
GUSTST .... Gustiest (ABBR)
GUSTY ...... Gustily (ABBR)
GUTD .... Gutted (ABBR)
GUTG .... Gutting (ABBR)
GUTR .... Gutter (ABBR)
GUTRL .... Gutteral (ABBR)
GUTRY ...... Gutterally (ABBR)
GUY .... Air Guyane [*France*] [*ICAO designator*] (FAAC)
GUZL .... Guzzle (ABBR)
GUZLD ...... Guzzled (ABBR)
GUZLG ...... Guzzling (ABBR)
GUZLR ...... Guzzler (ABBR)
GV .... Gate Valve (DAC)
GV .... Give (ABBR)
GVAWY ..... Giveaway (ABBR)
GVC .... Girls' Venture Corps [*British*] (BI)
GVN .... Given (ABBR)
GVP .... Gross Value of Production
GVX .... Geevax Ltd. [*British*] [*ICAO designator*] (FAAC)
GW .... Gastric Wrap [*Morbid obesity surgical treatment*]
GWA .... Great Wall Airlines [*China*] [*ICAO designator*] (FAAC)
GWA .... [*The*] Greens (Western Australia) Inc.
GWIC .... Global Warming International Center [*An association*] (EA)
GWND .... Gowned (ABBR)
GWVSS ...... Ground Wind Vortex Sensing System [*Aviation*] (DA)
GXY .... Galaxy Airways Ltd. [*Nigeria*] [*ICAO designator*] (FAAC)
GY .... Gaily (ABBR)
GY .... Gunnery (ABBR)
GY .... Gyro (ABBR)
GY .... Gyrocar (ABBR)
GY .... Gyrocompass (ABBR)
GY .... Gyrodyne (ABBR)
GYA .... Guyana Airways Corp. [*ICAO designator*] (FAAC)
GYMN .... Gymnasium (ABBR)
GYMNST ... Gymnast (ABBR)
GYMST ...... Gymnast (ABBR)
GYMSTC ... Gymnastic (ABBR)
GYMSTCY ... Gymnastically (ABBR)
GYNC .... Gynecologic (ABBR)
GYNCL ...... Gynecological (ABBR)
GYNST .... Gynecologist (ABBR)
GYP .... Gypsy (ABBR)
GYPD .... Gypped (ABBR)
GYPG .... Gypping (ABBR)
GYPSIOL... Gypsiologic (ABBR)
GYR .... Gyrafrance [*France*] [*ICAO designator*] (FAAC)

GYR .... Gyration (ABBR)
GYR .... Gyrus (ABBR)
GYRA .... Gyrate (ABBR)
GYRAD ...... Gyrated (ABBR)
GYRAG ..... Gyrating (ABBR)
GYRAN ...... Gyration (ABBR)
GYRAR ...... Gyrator (ABBR)
GYRARY .... Gyratory (ABBR)
GYRCMPS ... Gyrocompass (ABBR)
GYRMTR... Gyrometer (ABBR)
GYRO .... Gyrocompass (ABBR)
GYRO .... Gyroplane (ABBR)
GYROCOP ... Gyrocopter (ABBR)
GYRODYN ... Gyrodynamic (ABBR)
GYRPLN ... Gyroplane (ABBR)
GYRSCP .... Gyroscope (ABBR)
GYRSTBR ... Gyrostabilizer (ABBR)
GYRTD ...... Gyrated (ABBR)
GYSR .... Geyser (ABBR)
GZL .... Guzzle (ABBR)
GZLD .... Guzzled (ABBR)
GZLG .... Guzzling (ABBR)
GZLR .... Guzzler (ABBR)

H

H .... HALON [*Halogenated Hydrocarbon*] (NFPA)
H .... Hazy (ABBR)
H .... Header (NFPA)
H .... Headlines (ABBR)
H .... Headquarters (ABBR)
H .... Heater (ABBR)
H .... Hindu (ABBR)
H .... Horizon (ABBR)
H .... Hose (NFPA)
H4 .... Solomon Islands [*Aircraft nationality and registration mark*] (FAAC)
9H .... Malta [*Aircraft nationality and registration mark*] (FAAC)
HA .... Hydraulic Association of Great Britain (BI)
HAA .... Harrison Air [*Canada*] [*ICAO designator*] (FAAC)
HABTA ...... Habituate (ABBR)
HABTAD ... Habituated (ABBR)
HABTAG .... Habituating (ABBR)
HABTAN ... Habitation (ABBR)
HABTAN ... Habituation (ABBR)
HABTB ...... Habitable (ABBR)
HABTL....... Habitual (ABBR)
HABTLNS ... Habitualness (ABBR)
HABTU ...... Habitue (ABBR)
HABTY ...... Habitually (ABBR)
HAC........... Henebury Aviation Co. [*Australia*] [*ICAO designator*] (FAAC)
HAC........... Horticultural Advisory Council for England and Wales (BI)
HACHD ..... Hatched (ABBR)
HACHG ..... Hatching (ABBR)
HACHWY ... Hatchway (ABBR)
HACHY...... Hatchery (ABBR)
HACN........ Hacienda (ABBR)
HAD .... Helicopteros Andes [*Chile*] [*ICAO designator*] (FAAC)
HAF........... Hellenic Air Force [*Greece*] [*ICAO designator*] (FAAC)
HAFRA ..... Hat and Allied Feltmakers' Research Association [*British*] (BI)
HAG .... Harvest Aviation Ltd. [*British*] [*ICAO designator*] (FAAC)
HAGIOL.... Hagiology (ABBR)
HAGL........ Haggle (ABBR)
HAGLD...... Haggled (ABBR)
HAGLG...... Haggling (ABBR)
HAGLR...... Haggler (ABBR)
HAGLST.... Hagiologist (ABBR)
HAGTNS ... Haughtiness (ABBR)
HAGTR...... Haughtier (ABBR)
HAGTST.... Haughtiest (ABBR)
HAGTY...... Haughtily (ABBR)
HAHO........ High Altitude/High Opening [*Army*] (ADDR)
HAI............ Haiti (ABBR)
HAIA .... Honorary Member, American Institute of Architects (DAC)
HAJ .... Hajvairy Airlines [*Pakistan*] [*ICAO designator*] (FAAC)
HAK........... Hawkish (ABBR)
HAL........... Hawaiian Airlines, Inc. [*ICAO designator*] (FAAC)
HALP .... HAWK [*Homing All the Way Killer*] Equipment Logistics Program [*Army*]
HALSOL.... High-Altitude Solar Energy (PS)
HAMSA ..... Hearing Aid Manufacturers' and Suppliers' Association [*British*] (BI)
HAPS .... Historic Aircraft Preservation Society Ltd. [*British*] (BI)
HAR........... Harbor Airlines, Inc. [*ICAO designator*] (FAAC)
HARS........ Hazardous Area Reporting Service [*Aviation*] (FAAC)
HARV and MARV ... Harvey Ratner and Marvin Wolfenson [*Proprietors of Target Centre basketball arena*] (ECON)
HAS........... Hamburg Airlines, GmbH [*Germany*] [*ICAO designator*] (FAAC)
HASL .... Hot-Air Solder Leveling [*Materials science*]
HAT........... Highest Astronomical Tide
HATRA ...... Hosiery and Allied Trades Research Association [*British*] (BI)
HAVREP.... Have Report [*Navy*] (ANA)
HB.............. Halogen Bulb
HB.............. Hatchback [*Automotive advertising*]
HB.............. Hollowback (DAC)
HBA........... Hispanic Bar Association (EA)
HBA........... Trail Lake Flying Service, Inc. [*ICAO designator*] (FAAC)
HBB .... Human Beta-Globin [*Genetics*]

HBC........... Haitian Aviation Line SA [*ICAO designator*] (FAAC)
HBC........... High Blood Cholesterol
HBCC......... Hosted Bus Controller Chip [*Electronics*]
HBCF .... Hydrobromofluorocarbons [*Organic chemistry*]
HBH .... Hydraulic Brake Hose [*Automotive engineering*]
HBK........... Hardback [*Book cover*] (NTCM)
HbM.......... Hemoglobin M [*Biochemistry*] (MAH)
HBM.......... Mali-Tinbouctou Air Service [*ICAO designator*] (FAAC)
HBMA........ Home-Based Maintenance Allowance
HBN .... Health-Based Number [*Environmental science*]
HC .... Critical Height [*Aviation*] (DA)
HC .... Hose Cabinet [*or Connection*] [*NFPA pre-fire planning symbol*] (NFPA)
HC .... Hostel Care
HC .... Housing Corp. [*British*] (BI)
HCA........... Hot Cranking Amperes [*Battery*] [*Automotive engineering*]
HCA........... Lake Havasu Air Service [*ICAO designator*] (FAAC)
HCD .... Hyundai California Design [*Concept car*]
HCE........... Health Care Education
HCF........... Halt and Catch Fire [*Computer hacker terminology*] (NHD)
HCHBK..... Hatchback [*Automotive advertising*]
HCI........... Hotel and Catering Institute [*British*] (BI)
HCIL .... Human-Computer Interaction Laboratory [*University of Maryland*] (PCM)
HCITB........ Hotel and Catering Industry Training Board [*British*] (BI)
HCO .... Harco Air Services [*Nigeria*] [*ICAO designator*] (FAAC)
HCP .... Home Consumption Price
HCPT .... Historic Churches Preservation Trust [*British*] (BI)
HCRP......... Hominid Corridor Research Project [*Palaeontology*]
HCTBA ...... Hotel and Catering Trades Benevolent Association [*British*] (BI)
HD .... Heat Detector [*NFPA pre-fire planning symbol*] (NFPA)
HDA .... Hong Kong Dragon Airlines Ltd. [*ICAO designator*] (FAAC)
HDA .... Housing Developers Association Ltd. [*British*] (BI)
HDA .... Hydrogen Diffusion Anode [*Electrochemistry*]
HDBMS ..... Hierarchical Database Management System
HD-DI .... Heavy-Duty Direct Injection [*Diesel engines*]
HDEP .... High Definition Electronic Production (NTCM)
HDGA .... Hot Dip Galvanizers Association [*British*] (BI)
HDI............ Heavy-Duty Industrial [*Internal combustion engines*]
HDI............ Hoteles Dinamicos SA de CV [*Mexico*] [*ICAO designator*] (FAAC)
HDIT .... Home Drug Infusion Therapy [*Medicine*]
HDP............ Housing Development Program
HDRI.......... Hannah Dairy Research Institute [*British*] (BI)
HDSB .... Heavy Dry Support Bridge [*Army*] (RDA)
HDTCS ...... Hexadecyltrichlorosilane [*Organic chemistry*]
HEA........... Heliavia-Transporte Aereo Lda. [*Portugal*] [*ICAO designator*] (FAAC)
HEAA........ Higher Education Act Amendment [*1992*]
Heaven B .... Heaven Bone
HEC........... Helicopter Element Coordinator [*Navy*] (ANA)
HEC........... Heliservicio Campeche SA de CV [*Mexico*] [*ICAO designator*] (FAAC)
HEC........... Hella Electronics Corp. [*Automotive industry supplier*]
HEC........... Home Equity Conversion
HECA........ Harpoon Environmental Correction Aid [*Navy*] (ANA)
HEDS .... Hydraulic End Design System [*Computer-aided design*]
HEE........... Heli Europe [*Belgium*] [*ICAO designator*] (FAAC)
HEL........... Helicol Helicopteros Nacionales de Colombia [*ICAO designator*] (FAAC)
HELI .... Heliport [*ICAO designator*] (FAAC)
HEM.......... Hemmeter Aviation, Inc. [*ICAO designator*] (FAAC)
HER........... Hex'air [*France*] [*ICAO designator*] (FAAC)
HES........... Heli Services [*France*] [*ICAO designator*] (FAAC)
HET........... TAF Helicopters SA [*Spain*] [*ICAO designator*] (FAAC)
HETMA ..... Heavy Edge Tool Manufacturers' Association [*British*] (BI)
HEUI.......... Hydraulic Electronic Unit Injector [*Fuel system*] [*Automotive engineering*]
HEV........... Hybrid-Electric Vehicle
HEVAC ...... Heating, Ventilating, and Air Conditioning Manufacturers Association Ltd. [*British*] (BI)
HEX........... Hatfield Executive Aviation Ltd. [*British*] [*ICAO designator*] (FAAC)

HEXIT....... Hexadecimal Digit [*Computer science*]   (NHD)
Hf............... Heat of Combustion of Fuel [*Aviation*]   (DA)
HF.............. Hot Finished [*Drawing*]   (DAC)
HFBR .... Hollow-Fiber Bioreactor [*Chemical engineering*]
HFC............ Home Finance Contract
HFCD .... Hino Fuel Economy Clean Air High-Durability [*Hino diesel engines*]
HFD............ Hatfield BAE [*British*] [*ICAO designator*]   (FAAC)
HFEA .... Human Fertilization and Embryology Authority [*British*]
HFL............ Heliflyg AG [*Sweden*] [*ICAO designator*]   (FAAC)
HFR .... Heli France [*ICAO designator*]   (FAAC)
HFT .... Hollyfordair Travel Ltd. [*New Zealand*] [*ICAO designator*]   (FAAC)
HGA .... Hardware Graphics Accelerator [*Computer science*]
HGA .... Hogan Air [*ICAO designator*]   (FAAC)
HGD .... Hangard Aviation Ltd. [*Mongolia*] [*ICAO designator*]   (FAAC)
HGM .... Human Gene-Mapping
HGP........... Hormonal Growth Promotant
HGTMC..... Home Grown Timber Marketing Corp. Ltd. [*British*]   (BI)
HH .... Herbig-Haro [*Astronomy*]
HHE .... Heli-Holland BV [*Netherlands*] [*ICAO designator*]   (FAAC)
HHFS .... Hilar High-Frequency Stimulation [*Neurophysiology*]
HHL .... Helicopter Hire Ltd. [*British*] [*ICAO designator*]   (FAAC)
HHO .... Houston Helicopters, Inc. [*ICAO designator*]   (FAAC)
HHOCC .... Holiday Happenings Ornament Collectors Club   (EA)
HHOJ........ Ha Ha Only Joking [*Computer hacker terminology*]   (NHD)
HHP .... Hydraulic Horse Power
HIA............. Canadian Eagle Aviation Ltd. [*ICAO designator*]   (FAAC)
HIA............. Hold in Abeyance [*Military*]
HIB .... Hibiscus Air Services Ltd. [*New Zealand*] [*ICAO designator*]   (FAAC)
HIG............ Heli-Inter Guyane [*France*] [*ICAO designator*]   (FAAC)
HIIP........... High Impact Incarceration Program [*60-day paramilitary regimen for prisoners*]
HILS.......... Halogen Interchangeable Light Source
HIM........... Hyper Immunoglobulin Syndrome [*Medicine*]
HIMAC ..... Heavy-Ion Medical Accelerator in Chiba [*Japan*]
HIMIC ...... Highly-Indebted Middle-Income Country
HIN............ Heli Inter [*France*] [*ICAO designator*]   (FAAC)
HIR............ Harvard International Review [*A publication*]
HIRCIS ..... High-Resolution Capacitive Imaging Sensor [*Instrumentation*]
HIS .... Hispaniola Airways [*Dominican Republic*] [*ICAO designator*]   (FAAC)
HIS .... Hunters' Improvement Society [*British*]   (BI)
HIU............ High Interest Unit [*Navy*]   (ANA)
HIWAS ...... Hazardous Inflight Weather Advisory Service [*Aviation*]   (FAAC)
HJA .... Air Haiti [*ICAO designator*]   (FAAC)
HJC .... Heathrow Jet Charter Ltd. [*British*] [*ICAO designator*]   (FAAC)
HJL .... Hamlin Jet Ltd. [*British*] [*ICAO designator*]   (FAAC)
HJS............ Helijet [*Spain*] [*ICAO designator*]   (FAAC)
HKA........... Superior Aviation, Inc. [*ICAO designator*]   (FAAC)
HKAB........ Hong Kong Association of Banks   (ECON)
HKN........... [*Jim*] Hankins Air Service, Inc. [*ICAO designator*]   (FAAC)
HKS........... Helikopter Service AS [*Norway*] [*ICAO designator*]   (FAAC)
HKUST ...... Hong Kong University of Science and Technology   (ECON)
HL.............. HALON [*Halogenated Hydrocarbon*] System [*NFPA pre-fire planning symbol*]   (NFPA)
HL.............. Height Loss [*Aviation*]   (DA)
HLA........... Heavylift Cargo Airlines Ltd. [*British*] [*ICAO designator*]   (FAAC)
HLA........... Hydraulic Lash Adjuster [*Automotive engine design*]
HLB........... High-Line Airways, Inc. [*Canada*] [*ICAO designator*]   (FAAC)
HLC........... Helicap [*France*] [*ICAO designator*]   (FAAC)
HLE .... First Air [*British*] [*ICAO designator*]   (FAAC)
HLF .... Hapag Lloyd Fluggesellschaft GmbH [*Germany*] [*ICAO designator*]   (FAAC)
HLK........... Heli-Link [*Switzerland*] [*ICAO designator*]   (FAAC)
HLL .... Havelet Leasing Ltd. [*British*] [*ICAO designator*]   (FAAC)
HLN........... Hellenic Air SA [*Greece*] [*ICAO designator*]   (FAAC)
HLO........... Samaritan Air Service Ltd. [*Canada*] [*ICAO designator*]   (FAAC)
HLR........... Heli Air Services [*Bulgaria*] [*ICAO designator*]   (FAAC)
HLRS......... Homosexual Law Reform Society [*British*]   (BI)
HLS .... Haiti Air Freight [*ICAO designator*]   (FAAC)
HLT .... Heli Transport [*France*] [*ICAO designator*]   (FAAC)
HLU........... Heli Union Heli Prestations [*France*] [*ICAO designator*]   (FAAC)
HLV........... Heliserv SA de CV [*Mexico*] [*ICAO designator*]   (FAAC)
HMA .... Hardware Manufacturers' Association [*British*]   (BI)
HMA .... Hop Merchants Association [*British*]   (BI)
HMC.......... Her Majesty's Customs and Excise [*British*]   (BI)
HMC.......... Horticultural Marketing Council [*British*]   (BI)
HMD .... [*Charlie*] Hammonds Flying Service, Inc. [*ICAO designator*]   (FAAC)
HMD .... Hollow-Metal Door   (DAC)
HMMS....... Hino Micro Mixing System [*Diesel engines*]
HMP.......... Papair Terminal SA [*Haiti*] [*ICAO designator*]   (FAAC)
Hmr........... Homer   (DA)
HMRS........ Historical Model Railway Society [*British*]   (BI)
HMS......... Hemus Air [*Bulgaria*] [*ICAO designator*]   (FAAC)
HMS.......... High Melt Strength [*Plastic moldings*]
HMT.......... Air Nova [*British*] [*ICAO designator*]   (FAAC)
HMWA ..... Hairdressing Manufacturers' and Wholesalers' Association [*British*]   (BI)

HMZ........... Nigerian International Air Services Ltd. [*ICAO designator*]   (FAAC)
HNPP .... Hereditary Neuropathy with Liability to Pressure Palsies
HNR .... Haiti National Airlines [*ICAO designator*]   (FAAC)
HNSA .... Host Nation Support Agreement [*Navy*]   (ANA)
HOC .... Hydraulic Overspeed Control [*Mechanical power transmission*]
HOCA .... High Osmolar Contrast Agent [*Medicine*]
HOL........... Holiday Airlines, Inc. [*ICAO designator*]   (FAAC)
HON.......... Honington FTU [*British*] [*ICAO designator*]   (FAAC)
HOPO .... Holders of Public Office
HOR........... Horizon Air-Taxi Ltd. [*Switzerland*] [*ICAO designator*]   (FAAC)
HOSP........ Hospital Aircraft [*ICAO designator*]   (FAAC)
HOT .... Baltic Airlines Ltd. [*ICAO designator*]   (FAAC)
HOTX........ Hands-On Training Exercise [*Military*]   (ADDR)
HOX .... Homeobox [*Genetics*]
HPA .... Hectopascal [*ICAO designator*]   (FAAC)
HPA .... Pearl Airways Compagne Haitienne [*Haiti*] [*ICAO designator*]   (FAAC)
HPERD ..... Health, Physical Education, Recreation, and Dance   (AEE)
HPF .... [*Horace*] Plunkett Foundation for Co-Operative Studies [*British*]   (BI)
HPL .... Heliportugal-Trabalhos e Transporte Aereo, Representacoes, Importacao e Exportacao Lda. [*Portugal*] [*ICAO designator*]   (FAAC)
HPL .... Hotel Properties Ltd. [*Singapore*]   (ECON)
HPP .... Health Promotion Pilot
HPQ .... Highly Polarized Quasar [*Galactic science*]
HPS .... Hantavirus Pulmonary Syndrome [*Medicine*]
HPS .... Hydroxypropyl Starch [*Organic chemistry*]
HPTA .... Hire Purchase Trade Association [*British*]   (BI)
HPZ........... Helicopter Protected Zone [*Military*]   (DA)
HQ............. Hazard Quotient [*Toxicology*]
HQIADS ... Headquarters, Integrated Air Defense System [*Air Force*]
HR .... High Resilience [*Plastics*]
HRA........... Heli-Iberica [*Spain*] [*ICAO designator*]   (FAAC)
HRAD....... Hunger Relief and Development [*An association*]   (EA)
HRC........... Hairdressers' Registration Council [*British*]   (BI)
HRC........... Human Rights Committee
HRD .... Hard Top [*Automotive advertising*]
HRE .... Aerosucre SA [*Colombia*] [*ICAO designator*]   (FAAC)
HRH .... Royal Tongan Airlines [*Tonga*] [*ICAO designator*]   (FAAC)
HR Mag..... HR Magazine [*A publication*]
HRN .... Airwork Ltd. [*British*] [*ICAO designator*]   (FAAC)
HRR........... Heat Release Rate [*Engineering*]
HRS........... Hyper-Rayleigh Scattering [*Physics*]
HRT........... Human Resources Training
HRT........... Transporte Aereo Rioplatense [*Argentina*] [*ICAO designator*]   (FAAC)
HrtCC .... Heart Cubic Content   (DAC)
HrtFa .... Heart Facial Area   (DAC)
HrtG .... Heart Girth   (DAC)
HSA .... CHS Aviation Ltd. [*Kenya*] [*ICAO designator*]   (FAAC)
HSA .... Heat-Stable Antigen [*Immunochemistry*]
HSA .... Hill Start Assist [*Transmission and braking systems*] [*Automotive engineering*]
HSA .... Hospital Saving Association [*British*]   (BI)
H Sch M .... High School Magazine [*A publication*]
HSD .... High-Sulfur Diesel Fuel [*Petroleum marketing*]
HSD .... Home Satellite Dish   (NTCM)
HSDI .... High-Speed Direct Injection [*Diesel engines*]
HSE .... Compania Helicopteros del Sureste SA [*Spain*] [*ICAO designator*]   (FAAC)
HSET......... Hino Super Flow Turbine [*Diesel engine*]
HSG .... Health and Safety Guide [*Toxicology*]
HSG........... High Speed Generation [*Hybrid vehicles*] [*Automotive engineering*]
HSIP......... Hsinchu Science-Based Industrial Park [*Taiwan*]   (ECON)
HSL .... Hispania Lineas Aereas SL [*Spain*] [*ICAO designator*]   (FAAC)
HSN........... Southern Air Ltd. [*British*] [*ICAO designator*]   (FAAC)
HSO........... Compania Helicopteros de Transporte SA [*Spain*] [*ICAO designator*]   (FAAC)
HSPG .... Heparan Sulfate Proteoglycan [*Biochemistry*]
HSR........... Human Science Research [*Concept car*] [*Automotive engineering*]
HSSA .... High Speed Steel Association [*British*]   (BI)
HST .... Hawaiian-Aleutian Standard Time
HST .... High Speed Taxi-Way Turn Off [*Aviation*]   (DA)
HSV .... Heliservico-Sociedade Portuguesa de Exploracao de Meios Aeros Lda. [*Portugal*] [*ICAO designator*]   (FAAC)
HSV .... High-Speed Video [*Instrumentation*]
HSW.......... Aerocombi SA [*Spain*] [*ICAO designator*]   (FAAC)
HTA........... Horticultural Trades Association [*British*]   (BI)
HTA........... Household Textiles Association [*British*]   (BI)
HTC........... Haiti Trans Air SA [*ICAO designator*]   (FAAC)
HTF .... Societe Helitrans France [*ICAO designator*]   (FAAC)
HTI .... Haiti International Air SA [*ICAO designator*]   (FAAC)
HTI............ Home Testing Institute, Inc.   (NTCM)
HTMAEW ... Home Timber Merchants' Association of England and Wales   (BI)
HTN .... Haiti North Airline [*ICAO designator*]   (FAAC)
HTPB .... Hydroxy-Terminated Polybutadiene [*Organic chemistry*]
HTR........... Holstenair Lubeck, Luftverkehrsservice GmbH [*Germany*] [*ICAO designator*]   (FAAC)
HTR........... Household Tracking Report [*Television ratings*]   (NTCM)

HTS .... Helitrans Air Service, Inc. [*ICAO designator*]   (FAAC)
HTT .... Air Tchad, Societe de Transport Aeriens [*Chad*] [*ICAO designator*]   (FAAC)
HTV .... Hospital Patient Transport Vehicle
HUA .... Humber Aviation Ltd. [*British*] [*ICAO designator*]   (FAAC)
HUAM .... Home Uterine Activity Monitoring
HUK .... Hungarian-Ukranian Heavy Lift Ltd. [*Hungary*] [*ICAO designator*]   (FAAC)
HUM .... Health and Usage Monitoring   (DA)
HUM .... Hummingbird Helicopters Maldives (Pvt) Ltd. [*ICAO designator*]   (FAAC)
HUN .... Hunting Business Aviation [*British*] [*ICAO designator*]   (FAAC)
HUR .... Homes Using Radio [*Ratings*]   (NTCM)
HUR .... Miami Air Charter [*ICAO designator*]   (FAAC)
HUS .... Heussler Air Service Corp. [*ICAO designator*]   (FAAC)
HV .... HomeVideo [*Videocassette tape*]   (NTCM)
HVA .... Newair, Inc. [*ICAO designator*]   (FAAC)
HVN .... Hang Khong Viet Nam [*ICAO designator*]   (FAAC)
HVOSM ..... Highway Vehicle Object Simulation Model [*Computer-aided design*] [*Automotive engineering*]
HVR .... Home Video Recorder   (NTCM)
HVT .... Hydraulic Variable-Valve Train [*Automotive engine design*]
HWA .... Hawa-Air [*Belgium*] [*ICAO designator*]   (FAAC)
HWA .... Hops Warehousing Association [*British*]   (BI)
HWBTA ..... Home Wine and Beer Trade Association   (EA)
HWK .... Swazi Air Charter (Pty) Ltd. [*Swaziland*] [*ICAO designator*]   (FAAC)
HWRC........ Hot-Water Recirculation   (DAC)
HXT .... Hard X-Ray Telescope
HYA .... Hyack Air Ltd. [*Canada*] [*ICAO designator*]   (FAAC)
HYAPP....... Hays Army Ammunition Plant
HYDO .... Hydraulic Oil
HYE .... Hyeres Aero Service [*France*] [*ICAO designator*]   (FAAC)
HZL .... Hazelton Airlines [*Australia*] [*ICAO designator*]   (FAAC)

I

I.................	Informal [*FCC special temporary authorization*] (NTCM)
I.................	Instructional Program (NTCM)
I.................	Interim [*FCC*] (NTCM)
IA	Incentive Award [*Military*]
IA	International Alliance of Theatrical Stage Employees (NTCM)
IAA	Inex Adria Aviopromet [*Yugoslavia*] [*ICAO designator*] (FAAC)
IAA	Institute of Automobile Assessors [*British*] (BI)
IAB	Industrial Advisers to the Blind Ltd. [*British*] (BI)
IAB	International Association of Broadcasting (NTCM)
IAB	Irish Association for the Blind (BI)
IABA..........	Irish Amateur Boxing Association (BI)
IAC	Indian Airlines Corp. [*ICAO designator*] (FAAC)
IAC	Institute of Amateur Cinematographers [*British*] (BI)
IAC	Intergrated Avionics Computer (DA)
IACC..........	International Air Cargo Corp. [*Egypt*] [*ICAO designator*] (FAAC)
IACE..........	Intergovernmental Advisory Council on Education (AEE)
IACP..........	Industrial Arts Curriculum Project [*Education*] (AEE)
IADB-MED ...	Inter-American Defense Board Medal [*Military decoration*]
IAE	Interstate Airlines Ltd. [*Nigeria*] [*ICAO designator*] (FAAC)
IAEA..........	International Advertising Executives' Association (NTCM)
IAF............	EPAG - Group Air France [*ICAO designator*] (FAAC)
IAF............	Israeli Air-Force [*ICAO designator*] (FAAC)
IAFS	Integrated Air/Fuel System [*Automotive engine design*]
IAI.............	Israel Aircraft Industries Ltd. [*ICAO designator*] (FAAC)
IAK	International Air Cargo Corp. [*Egypt*] [*ICAO designator*] (FAAC)
IAL............	Imperial Art League [*British*] (BI)
IAL............	International Aeradio PLC [*British*] [*ICAO designator*] (FAAC)
IAL............	Irish Academy of Letters (BI)
IAM	Ignition Ackowledge Module [*Diesel engine controls*] [*Automotive engineering*]
IAMA	Incorporated Advertising Managers' Association [*British*] (BI)
IAMB	Irish Association of Master Bakers (BI)
IAN	Compania Internadia de Aviacion [*Colombia*] [*ICAO designator*] (FAAC)
IAOO..........	Irish Agricultural Officers Organisation (BI)
IAOS..........	Irish Agricultural Organisation Society Ltd. (BI)
IAP	Integrated Action Plan
IAPI...........	Institute of Advertising Practitioners in Ireland (BI)
IAR	Iliamna Air Taxi, Inc. [*ICAO designator*] (FAAC)
IAS.............	Impact Assessment Study
IAS.............	International Air Service Co. [*ICAO designator*] (FAAC)
IASAC	International Association of Silver Art Collectors (EA)
IAT	International Air Transport Association [*ICAO designator*] (FAAC)
IAV	Airavia [*France*] [*ICAO designator*] (FAAC)
IAV	Issue Authority Voucher
IAW	Iraqi Airways [*ICAO designator*] (FAAC)
IAWRT.......	International Association of Women in Radio and Television (NTCM)
IAWS..........	Irish Agricultural Wholesale Society Ltd. (BI)
IAZ	Industrie Air Charter [*France*] [*ICAO designator*] (FAAC)
IB	I-Beam [*Lumber*] (DAC)
IBA	Industrial Bankers' Association [*British*] (BI)
IBA	Ion Beam Analysis
IBAA..........	International Business Aircraft Association (DA)
IBB.............	Binter Canarais [*Spain*] [*ICAO designator*] (FAAC)
IBB.............	Institute of British Bakers (BI)
IBC.............	Informatica Bulgarien Corp. [*Bulgaria*] [*ICAO designator*] (FAAC)
IBCAM.......	Institute of British Carriage and Automobile Manufacturers (BI)
IBD	Incorporated Institute of British Decorators and Interior Designers (BI)
IBE.............	Iberia-Lineas Aereas de Espana SA [*Spain*] [*ICAO designator*] (FAAC)
IBE.............	Institute of Broadcast Engineers [*Later, SBE*] (NTCM)
IBE.............	Institute of Building Estimators Ltd. [*British*] (BI)
IBE.............	Institution of Body Engineers [*British*] (BI)
IBG.............	Institute of British Geographers (BI)
IBHA	Insulation, Building, and Hard Board Association [*British*] (BI)
IBICC	Incorporated British Institute of Certified Carpenters (BI)
IBM	Institute of Baths Management [*British*] (BI)
IBMTR	International Bone Marrow Transplant Registry
IBS..............	Ibis [*Belgium*] [*ICAO designator*] (FAAC)
IBS..............	Inter-Byte Separation [*Automotive engineering*] [*Electronics*]
IBS..............	Intron Binding Site [*Genetics*]
IBSM	Institute of Building Site Management [*British*] (BI)
IBST	Institute of British Surgical Technicians (BI)
IBTO..........	International Broadcasting and Television Organization (NTCM)
IBU	International Broadcasting Union [*Defunct*] (NTCM)
IBVA..........	Interactive Brain Wave Analyzer [*IBVA Technology*] [*Computer science*] (PCM)
IBZ.............	International Business Air [*Sweden*] [*ICAO designator*] (FAAC)
IC	Icing [*Aviation*] (FAAC)
IC	Imported Content
IC	Incue [*News broadcasting*] (NTCM)
IC	Inhibitory Concentration [*Toxicology*]
ICA	Ice Cream Alliance Ltd. [*British*] (BI)
ICA	Indigenous Communications Association (EA)
ICA	Institute of Chartered Accountants in England and Wales (BI)
ICA	Irish Countrywomen's Association (BI)
ICAA..........	Indian Church Aid [*British*] (BI)
ICAA..........	International Christian Accrediting Association (EA)
ICAD	Intelligent Computer-Aided Design
ICAM	Institute of Corn and Agricultural Merchants Ltd. [*British*] (BI)
ICAME.......	International Conference on the Applications of the Mossbauer Effect
ICAP..........	Institute of Certified Ambulance Personnel [*British*] (BI)
ICAS..........	Interdepartment Council on Radio Propagation and Standards (NTCM)
ICB.............	Icebird Airline Ltd. [*Iceland*] [*ICAO designator*] (FAAC)
ICC.............	Index of Cranial Capacity [*Cladistics*]
ICC.............	Instituto Cartografico de Cataluna [*Spain*] [*ICAO designator*] (FAAC)
ICCD..........	Institute of Chocolate and Confectionery Distributors [*British*] (BI)
ICD	Implantable Cardioverter-Defibrillator [*Medical device for heart patients*]
ICDA	Industrial Civil Defence Association [*British*] (BI)
ICE.............	Icelandair [*ICAO designator*] (FAAC)
ICE.............	Integrated Clinical Encounters
ICE.............	Interleukin-Converting Enzyme [*Biochemistry*]
ICE.............	International Cultural Exchange [*An association*] (EA)
ICEI...........	Institution of Civil Engineers of Ireland (BI)
ICEP..........	Iberoamerican Cultural Exchange Program [*An association*] (EA)
ICF.............	Ice Cream Federation Ltd. [*British*] (BI)
ICG	Icelandic Coast Guard [*ICAO designator*] (FAAC)
ICHFST......	International Council of Health Fitness and Sports Therapists [*British*]
ICHT	International Council of Holistic Therapists [*British*]
ICI..............	Institute of Chemistry of Ireland (BI)
ICL.............	Cavei Avir Lemitanim [*Israel*] [*ICAO designator*] (FAAC)
ICL.............	Irish Central Library for Students (BI)
ICM	Installable Compression, Manager [*Computer science*]
ICM	International Control Mechanism
ICMA	Independent Cable Makers' Association [*British*] (BI)
ICMR.........	Indian Council of Medical Research
ICMSA	Irish Creamery Milk Suppliers' Association (BI)
ICN	Inter-Canadian [*ICAO designator*] (FAAC)
ICO	Independent Conducting Officer
ICO	International Civil Aviation Organization [*ICAO designator*] (FAAC)
ICP.............	Impact Copolymer Polypropylene [*Plastics*] [*Automotive engineering*]
ICPEM	Independent Computer Peripheral Equipment Manufacturers
ICR	Eagle Aero, Inc. [*ICAO designator*] (FAAC)
ICR	Intercity Relay [*Broadcasting*] (NTCM)
ICR	Interest Coverage Ratio
ICRA..........	International Cartridge Recycling Association (EA)
ICRHS........	Illinois Central Railroad Historical Society (EA)
ICS.............	Institute for the Comparative Study of History, Philosophy, and the Sciences Ltd. [*British*] (BI)
ICS.............	Irish Computer Society
ICT.............	Insulin Convulsive Therapy [*Medicine*] (MAH)
ICT.............	Intercontinental de Aviacion Ltd. [*Colombia*] [*ICAO designator*] (FAAC)

ICTAA........ Imperial College of Tropical Agriculture Association [*British*]
     (BI)
ICTR.......... Institute of Commercial and Technical Representatives Ltd.
     [*British*] (BI)
ICU .... Industry Capacity Utilization [*Engineering economics*]
ICU .... Instruction Cache Unit [*Computer science*]
ICUZ .... Integrated Compatible Use Zone [*Army*] (RDA)
ICW .... Institute of Clay Workers [*British*] (BI)
ICWA .... Institute of Cost and Works Accountants [*British*] (BI)
ICX .... International Charter Xpress Limited Liability Co. [*ICAO
     designator*] (FAAC)
ID............... Independent Dealer [*Automobile sales*]
IDA .... Identification Data Accessory (NTCM)
IDA .... Indonesia Air Transport PT [*ICAO designator*] (FAAC)
IDA .... Industry Development Arrangement
IDA .... Irish Dental Association (BI)
IDA .... Irish Drug Association (BI)
IDAA .... International Diabetic Athletes Association (EA)
IDCS.......... Interdepartment Courier Service
IDDAS....... Intelligent Dummy Data Acquisition System [*Crash testing*]
     [*Automotive engineering*]
IDEA .... Integrated Data for Enforcement Analysis System [*Environmental
     science*]
IDEAS .... International Data Exchange for Aviation Safety [*ICAO*] (DA)
IDF............. Iron Dragon-Fly Ltd. [*Russian Federation*] [*ICAO designator*]
     (FAAC)
IDIB.......... Industrial Diamond Information Bureau [*British*] (BI)
IDIM .... Integrated Departmental Instructions Manual
IDL .... Interface Definition Language [*Computer science*]
IDLHC .... Immediately Dangerous to Life or Health Concentration
     [*Toxicology*]
ID & PD...... Industrial Democracy and Personnel Development
IDRA .... Irish Dinghy Racing Association (BI)
IDS............. Inclined Drive Shaft (DA)
IDS............. Industries Development Strategy
IDS............. Ion Dip Spectroscopy
IDT .... Improved Definition Television (NTCM)
IDTIMS .... Isotope Dilution Thermal Ionization Mass Spectrometry
I & E.......... Innovation and Entrepreneurship
I/E............. Introversion/Extroversion [*Psychology*] (AEE)
IEA .... Intereuropean Airways Ltd. [*British*] [*ICAO designator*] (FAAC)
IED .... Initiative Electronic Deception (ADDR)
IED .... Institution of Engineering Designers [*British*] (BI)
IEI.............. Institution of Engineering Inspection [*British*] (BI)
IEIC .... Institution of Engineers-in-Charge [*British*] (BI)
IEIP .... International Education Information Program
IEJ .... Infite Ltd. [*British*] [*ICAO designator*] (FAAC)
IER .... Institute for Education by Radio [*Defunct*] (NTCM)
IERT .... Institute for Education by Radio-Television (NTCM)
IES .... Inter-Island Air Services Ltd. [*Grenada*] [*ICAO designator*]
     (FAAC)
IEWSE .... Intelligence Electronic Warfare Support Element (ADDR)
IF............... Inside Face (DAC)
IF............... Instructional Television, Fixed [*FCC*] (NTCM)
IF............... Interstitial-Free [*Metallurgical engineering*]
IFA .... Irish Football Association (BI)
IFB .... Interrupted Feedback [*Wireless earphone*] (NTCM)
IFC............. Cefi Aviation SRL [*Italy*] [*ICAO designator*] (FAAC)
IFC............. Inside Front Cover [*Publishing*] (NTCM)
IFCDG .... Injection of Fuel Containing Dissolved Gas [*Diesel engines*]
IFD............. Indentation Force Deflection [*Automotive seat testing*]
IFDFA .... International Freeze-Dry Floral Association (EA)
IFF .... Interfreight Forwarding Ltd. [*Sudan*] [*ICAO designator*] (FAAC)
IFHBT .... International Federation of Health and Beauty Therapists
IFI .... Imperial Forestry Institute [*British*] (BI)
IFK............. Interfunk & Co. [*Yugoslavia*] [*ICAO designator*] (FAAC)
IFL .... Intelligent Forms Language [*Delrina Corp.*] [*Computer science*]
     (PCM)
IFLIPS....... Integrated Flight Prediction System [*Aviation*] (DA)
IFMA .... Irish Flour Millers Association (BI)
IFNP.......... International Federation of Newspaper Publishers (NTCM)
IFOCUS ..... Interprofessional Fostering of Ophthalmic Care for Underserved
     Sectors [*An association*] (EA)
IFORO .... Interphone (Service F) Resumed Operation [*Aviation*] (FAAC)
IFPA .... Independent Film Producers of America (NTCM)
IFPS........... Integrated Initial Flight Plan Processing System [*Aviation*] (DA)
IFR............. In-Frame Response [*Automotive engineering*] [*Electronics*]
IFS .... International Flying Services SRL [*Italy*] [*ICAO designator*]
     (FAAC)
IFT .... Inland Fisheries Trust, Inc. [*Republic of Ireland*] (BI)
IFT .... Interflight [*British*] [*ICAO designator*] (FAAC)
IGA .... Irish Gas Association (BI)
IGB .... Intermediate Gearbox (DA)
IGC .... Institute for Global Communications . (EA)
IGL .... Internal Granule Layer [*Cytology*]
IGRS.......... Irish Genealogical Research Society (BI)
IGS............. Instrument Guidance System [*Aviation*] (DA)
IGS............. Irish Graphical Society (BI)
IGS............. Isla Grande Flying School [*Puerto Rico*] [*ICAO designator*]
     (FAAC)
IGSM.......... International Graduate School of Management
IHA .... Institute of Hospital Administrators [*British*] (BI)
IHBC .... International Health and Beauty Council [*British*]

IHM........... Institute of Housing Managers [*British*] (BI)
IHRMA ...... Irish Hotel and Restaurant Managers' Association (BI)
II .... Institute of Inventors [*British*] (BI)
IIA.............. Interamericana de Aviacion Ltda. [*Colombia*] [*ICAO
     designator*] (FAAC)
IIAC........... Inter-Image Amplifying Chemistry [*Color film technology*]
IIASA .... Institute of Islamic and Arabic Sciences in America (EA)
IIASA .... International Institute for Applied Systems Analysis
IIBDID .... Incorporated Institute of British Decorators and Interior
     Designers (BI)
IIC.............. Instructional Improvement Committee [*Individually-guided
     education*] (AEE)
IICS .... Intelligent Image Caching Software [*Courtland Group, Inc.*]
     (PCM)
IIGB .... International Institute of Genetics and Biophysics [*Italy*]
IIHHT .... International Institute of Health and Holistic Therapies [*British*]
IIL............... India International Airways (P) Ltd. [*ICAO designator*] (FAAC)
IINS .... Inelastic Incoherent Neutron Scattering [*Spectrometry*]
IIP .... International Inter-Visitation Program in Educational
     Administration [*UniverstiyCouncil for Educational
     Administration*] (AEE)
IIPA .... Institute of Incorporated Practitioners in Advertising [*British*]
     (BI)
IIS .... Irish Institute of Secretaries Ltd. (BI)
IIST .... International Institute of Sports Therapy [*British*]
IIT.............. Intra-Industry Trade
IJ .... Institute of Journalists [*British*] (NTCM)
IJE .... Avijet SA de CV [*Mexico*] [*ICAO designator*] (FAAC)
IJL .... International Journal of Leprosy [*A publication*]
IJO .... International Journal of Osteoarchaeology [*A publication*]
IJS .... Silvair, Inc. [*ICAO designator*] (FAAC)
IJT .... Interflight (Learjet) Ltd. [*British*] [*ICAO designator*] (FAAC)
IKR .... Ikaros DK [*Denmark*] [*ICAO designator*] (FAAC)
IKT .... Iakutaviatrans [*Russian Federation*] [*ICAO designator*] (FAAC)
IL .... Institute of Linguists [*British*] (BI)
ILD .... I Love Dance [*Competition in US and Canada*]
ILEV .... Inherently Low-Emissions Vehicle
ILF .... Industrial Leathers Federation [*British*] (BI)
ILL............. Illuminated (NTCM)
ILOA .... Industrial Life Offices Association [*British*] (BI)
ILP .... Ilpo Aruba Cargo NV [*ICAO designator*] (FAAC)
ILR .... Air Iliria [*Yugoslavia*] [*ICAO designator*] (FAAC)
ILSAC .... International Legal Services Advisory Committee
ILSAC .... International Lubricant Standardization and Approval Committee
     [*Automotive engine oils*]
I/M .... Inspection and Maintenance (ERG)
IM .... Intermodulation Distortion (NTCM)
IMA .... Inter-Mountain Airways [*ICAO designator*] (FAAC)
IMAO .... In My Arrogant Opinion [*Computer hacker terminology*] (NHD)
IMBL .... Independent Meat Buyers Ltd. [*British*] (BI)
IMC .... Industrial Microcomputer
IMC .... International Morse Code (ADDR)
IMCS .... Individual Microclimate Cooling System [*Army*] (INF)
IMG .... Imperial Cargo Airlines Ltd. [*Ghana*] [*ICAO designator*] (FAAC)
IMH........... Institute of Materials Handling [*British*] (BI)
IMHI .... Institute for Mental Health Initiatives (EA)
IMHOF ...... International Motor Sports Hall of Fame [*Automotive racing
     history*]
IMI .... Institute of the Motor Industry, Inc. [*British*] (BI)
IMIT .... Institute of Musical Instrument Technology [*British*] (BI)
IML .... Island Air Ltd. [*Fiji*] [*ICAO designator*] (FAAC)
IMME .... Institute of Municipal Maintenance Engineers [*British*] (BI)
IMNSHO ... In My Not-So-Humble Opinion [*Computer hacker terminology*]
     (NHD)
IMP .... Imperial Air [*Peru*] [*ICAO designator*] (FAAC)
IMPA .... Ion Microprobe Analysis
IMR .... Impulse-Aero [*Russian Federation*] [*ICAO designator*] (FAAC)
IMS............. Income Matching System
IMS............. Intermembrane Space [*Biochemistry*]
IMSM........ Institute of Marketing and Sales Management [*British*] (BI)
IMSU.......... International Muslim Students Union (EA)
IMSW......... Institute of Medical Social Workers [*British*] (BI)
IMTA .... Intensive Military Training Area (DA)
IMTD .... Institute of Master Tutors of Driving [*British*] (BI)
IMWoodT... Institute of Machine Woodworking Technology [*British*] (BI)
IMX .... Zimex Aviation Ltd. [*Switzerland*] [*ICAO designator*] (FAAC)
I18N........... Internationalization [*The 18 replaces the eighteen letters between I
     and N*] [*Computer hacker terminology*] (NHD)
INA .... Interair Aviation Ltd. [*British*] [*ICAO designator*] (FAAC)
INB .... Instalbud [*Poland*] [*ICAO designator*] (FAAC)
INC .... Ironfounders' National Confederation [*British*] (BI)
INC .... Jet Air Internacional Charters CA [*Venezuela*] [*ICAO
     designator*] (FAAC)
IND............. Iona National Airways Ltd. [*Republic of Ireland*] [*ICAO
     designator*] (FAAC)
INDEPTH ... International Deep Profiling of Tibet and the Himalaya [*Geology*]
     [*China*]
INGAALP ... Indium-Gallium-Aluminum Phosphide [*Light-emitting diode
     construction*]
INIT........... Initial Training [*Aviation*] (FAAC)
INK .... Kentair (International) Ltd. [*British*] [*ICAO designator*] (FAAC)
INN............ ImagiNation Network [*Entertainment*]
INO............. Irish Nurses Organisation (BI)

INP	FA Naval del Peru [*ICAO designator*] (FAAC)
INPC..........	Irish National Productivity Committee (BI)
INPHO......	Information Network for Public Health Officials [*CDC*]
INPUT.......	International Public Television [*An association*] (NTCM)
INR............	Inter Air AB [*Sweden*] [*ICAO designator*] (FAAC)
INS............	Insert Shot [*Film production*] (NTCM)
InstCES	Institution of Civil Engineering Surveyors (DAC)
instr...........	Instrumental [*Grammar*]
INSUF.......	Insufficient Scheduled Time Available [*Aviation*] (FAAC)
INT	Intair, Inc. [*Canada*] [*ICAO designator*] (FAAC)
INTERSEARCH ...	International Productions and Safety Research [*Auto accident reconstruction*]
INUW........	Irish National Union of Woodworkers (BI)
INV............	Inversia [*Latvia*] [*ICAO designator*] (FAAC)
INVECS	Innovative Vehicle Electronic Control System [*Motor vehicles*]
IOA............	Iowa Airways, Inc. [*ICAO designator*] (FAAC)
IOC............	Inorganic Chemical [*Environmental science*]
IOE............	Irregular Outer Edge [*Army*] (ADDR)
IOF............	Institute of Fuel [*British*] (BI)
IOM...........	Institute of Office Management [*British*] (BI)
IOM...........	Island Aviation & Travel Ltd. [*British*] [*ICAO designator*] (FAAC)
IOP............	Caliop [*France*] [*ICAO designator*] (FAAC)
IOP............	Institute of Packaging [*British*] (BI)
IOP............	Institute of Petroleum [*British*] (BI)
IOPI...........	International Organization for Plant Information
IOS	Isles of Scilly Skybus Ltd. [*British*] [*ICAO designator*] (FAAC)
IP	Import Penetration
IP	Information Paper
IP	Innovative Project
IPA............	Ipec Aviation Pty Ltd. [*Australia*] [*ICAO designator*] (FAAC)
IPB............	Intelligence Property Book [*Army*] (ADDR)
IPBA..........	Irish Paper Box Association (BI)
IPCA..........	Industrial Pest Control Association [*British*] (BI)
IPCR..........	Inverse Polymerase Chain Reaction [*Genetics*]
IPCS	Institution of Professional Civil Servants [*British*] (BI)
IPD	Individual Protective Device [*Toxicology*]
IPDS..........	IBM Personal Dication System [*Computer science*]
IPEC	International Pharmaceutical Excipients Council (EA)
IPF	Irish Printing Federation (BI)
IPG	Industrial Painters Group [*British*] (BI)
IPGRI........	International Plant Genetic Resources Institute [*Italy*]
IPL.............	Air Charter Services (Pty) Ltd. South Africa [*ICAO designator*] (FAAC)
IPL.............	Interested Parties List
IPM	Instructional Programming Model [*Individually-guided education*] (AEE)
IPN	Industri Pesawat Terbang Nusantara PT [*Indonesia*] [*ICAO designator*] (FAAC)
IPP............	Information Privacy Principle
IPP.............	Investment Promotion Program
IPPC	Integrated Pollution Prevention and Control [*Environmental science*]
IPR............	Interactive Photorealistic Rendering [*Computer-assisted design*]
IPRA..........	Institute of Park and Recreation Administration [*British*] (BI)
IPRE..........	Incorporated Practitioners in Radio and Electronics Ltd. [*British*] (BI)
IPRP	Institute for Puerto Rican Policy (EA)
IPS............	Incorporated Phonographic Society [*British*] (BI)
IPS............	Inside Pipe Size (DAC)
IPSA	Industrial Police and Security Association [*British*] (BI)
IPT............	Interport Corp. [*ICAO designator*] (FAAC)
IPU	Individual Patient Usage
IPWA.........	Invisible Panel Warming Association [*British*] (BI)
IQMS.........	Industrial Quality Management Science [*Quality control*]
IQPS..........	Institute of Qualified Private Secretaries Ltd. [*British*] (BI)
IQQ............	Caribbean Airways [*Barbados*] [*ICAO designator*] (FAAC)
I/R.............	Inquiry/Response [*Automotive engineering*] [*Electronics*]
I & R..........	Instruction and Research [*Individually-guided education*] (AEE)
IR	Instrument Restricted Controlled Airspace (DA)
IRA	Iran National Airlines Corp. [*ICAO designator*] (FAAC)
IRB............	Iranair Tours Co. [*Iran*] [*ICAO designator*] (FAAC)
IRC............	International Radio Carrier (NTCM)
IRC............	Iran Asseman Airline [*ICAO designator*] (FAAC)
IRE............	Instrument Rating Examiner [*Aviation*] (DA)
IRETP	Innovative Rural Education and Training Program
IRF	Islamic Research Foundation (EA)
IRK	Kish Air [*Iran*] [*ICAO designator*] (FAAC)
IRL............	Institute of Rural Life at Home and Overseas [*British*] (BI)
IRL............	Irish Air Corps [*ICAO designator*] (FAAC)
IRM	Integrated Review Model
IRO	CSA Air, Inc. [*ICAO designator*] (FAAC)
IRS............	Insulin Receptor Substrate [*Biochemistry*]
IRSA	Irish Research Scientists Association
IRT............	Interot Air Service [*Germany*] [*ICAO designator*] (FAAC)
IRTF	International Radio and Television Foundation, Inc. [*International Radio and Television Society*] (NTCM)
IRVR.........	Instrumented Runway Visual Range [*Aviation*] (DA)
IS...............	Island (DA)
ISA	Independent Stores Association Ltd. [*British*] (BI)
ISA	Island Airlines, Inc. [*ICAO designator*] (FAAC)
ISAA	Institute of Shops Acts Administration [*British*] (BI)
ISACS........	Independent Schools Association of the Central States (EA)

ISAE	International Society for AIDS Education (EA)
ISAR.........	Inverse Synthetic Aperture RADAR [*Navy*] (ANA)
ISC............	Island Air Charters, Inc. [*ICAO designator*] (FAAC)
ISCA.........	International Scientific Collectors Association (EA)
ISCF.........	Inter-School Christian Fellowship [*British*] (BI)
ISCSA........	Industrial Sports Clubs Secretaries' Association [*British*] (BI)
ISD............	Innovative Software Design [*South Africa*] [*ICAO designator*] (FAAC)
ISD............	Intermediate School District (AEE)
ISE............	Institution of Sales Engineers [*British*] (BI)
ISECCo.......	International Space Exploration and Colonization Company [*An association*] (EA)
ISH	Information Superhighway [*Telecommunications*] (PCM)
ISHC.........	Indicated Specific Hydrocarbon [*Automotive exhaust emission testing*]
ISIAME......	International Symposium on the Industrial Applications of the Mossbauer Effect
ISIDPP.......	Initial Shut-In Drill Pipe Pressure
ISIH..........	Interspike Interval Histogram [*Neurophysiology*]
ISIS...........	Image-Selected in Vivo Spectroscopy
ISIS...........	International Superconductivity Industry Summit [*Conference*]
ISITB.........	Iron and Steel Industry Training Board [*British*] (BI)
ISL	Eagle Air Ltd. [*Iceland*] [*ICAO designator*] (FAAC)
ISLAR	International Symposium on Laboratory Automation and Robotics
ISM	International Symposium on Microchemistry
ISNE.........	International Scale of Nuclear Events
ISNOX.......	Indicated Specific Oxides of Nitrogen [*Automotive exhaust emission testing*]
ISO	Industrial Safety Office
ISO	Isolated Camera (NTCM)
ISOB.........	Incorporated Society of Organ Builders [*British*] (BI)
ISOPE........	International Society of Offshore and Polar Engineers
ISPE	Institute and Society of Practitioners in Electrolysis Ltd. [*British*] (BI)
ISR............	Istra Air [*Slovakia*] [*ICAO designator*] (FAAC)
ISRO..........	Indian Space Research Organization
ISS............	Imaging Science Subsystem
ISS............	Injury Severity Score [*Auto safety research*]
ISS............	Integrated Structural Seat [*Automotive engineering*]
ISS............	Meridiana SpA [*Italy*] [*ICAO designator*] (FAAC)
ISSCA........	International Swizzle Stick Collectors Association (EA)
ISSS..........	IBM Speech Server Series
ISSS...........	International Seminars Support Scheme
IS & T	Industry, Science, and Technology
IST............	Inside Trim (DAC)
IST............	Instruction-Set Translator [*IBM Corp.*]
IST............	Istanbul Airlines [*Turkey*] [*ICAO designator*] (FAAC)
ISTEA	Iron and Steel Trades Employers' Association [*British*] (BI)
ISV............	Islena de Inversiones SA [*Honduras*] [*ICAO designator*] (FAAC)
ISVS	In Situ Vapro Stripping [*Environmental science*]
ISW...........	Institute of Social Welfare [*British*] (BI)
ISW...........	Serib Wings [*Italy*] [*ICAO designator*] (FAAC)
ISY............	City Air Ltd. [*British*] [*ICAO designator*] (FAAC)
IT	Individual Transportation [*Urban planning*]
ITA	Institute of Travel Agents [*British*] (BI)
ITA	Inter-Air, Inc. [*ICAO designator*] (FAAC)
ITA	Itapemirim Transportes Aereos SA [*Brazil*] [*ICAO designator*] (FAAC)
ITACCS......	International Trauma Anesthesia and Critical Care Society (EA)
ITBC.........	Instructional Television Funding Cooperative (NTCM)
ITC............	International Air Carrier Association [*ICAO designator*] (FAAC)
ITE............	Interestatal de Aviacion SA de CV [*Mexico*] [*ICAO designator*] (FAAC)
I-TEF	International Toxicity Equivalency Factor [*Toxicology*]
ITEP..........	International Trade Enhancement Program
ITF............	Air Inter, Societe [*France*] [*ICAO designator*] (FAAC)
ITF............	International Toll Free [*Telecommunications*]
ITI............	International Training Institute
ITJ............	Societa' Italjet [*Italy*] [*ICAO designator*] (FAAC)
ITM	ITA [*Itapemirim Transportes Aereos SA*] [*Brazil*] [*ICAO designator*] (FAAC)
ITN	Industrias Titan SA [*Spain*] [*ICAO designator*] (FAAC)
ITN	Internegative [*Photography*] (NTCM)
ITNS..........	International Transplant Nurses Society (EA)
ITO............	Independent Television Organization (NTCM)
ITO............	Irish Tourist Office (BI)
ITOY..........	International Truck of the Year
ITP............	Innovative Training Project
ITP............	Intensive Training Program
ITP............	International Test Pilot School [*British*] [*ICAO designator*] (FAAC)
ITP-NSS.....	Innovative Training Projects - National Skills Shortage
ITPP..........	Institute of Technical Publicity and Publications [*British*] (BI)
ITPS..........	Income Tax Payers' Society [*British*] (BI)
ITQ	Individual Transferable Quota
ITR............	Integrated Tourism Resort
ITRI..........	Invitation to Register Interest
ITS............	Aeronautica Interespacial SA de CV [*Mexico*] [*ICAO designator*] (FAAC)
ITS............	Incompatible Time-sharing System (NHD)
ITS............	Industry Training Support
ITV............	Independently Targeted Vehicle [*Military*] (DA)

ITV.............. Intervuelo SA [*Mexico*] [*ICAO designator*]   (FAAC)
ITVA.......... International Industrial Television Association   (NTCM)
ITW .... Inertia Test Weight [*Exhaust emissions*] [*Automotive engineering*]
ITX.............. Iberiotoxin [*Biochemistry*]
IU................ Industrial User   (ERG)
IUDWC ...... Irish Union of Distributive Workers and Clerks   (BI)
IUTOX .... International Union for Toxicology
I/V .... Instrument/Visual Controlled Airspace   (DA)
IVA .... Innotech Aviation Ltd. [*Canada*] [*ICAO designator*]   (FAAC)
IVCD .... In-Vehicle Communications Device [*Highway safety research*]
IVCT.......... Intervalence Charge-Transfer [*Phyical chemistry*]
IVE.............. Interactive Video Enterprises [*US West, Inc.*]   (PCM)
IVF.............. Inter-Varsity Fellowship of Evangelical Unions [*British*]   (BI)
IVS.............. Air Evasion [*France*] [*ICAO designator*]   (FAAC)
IWBNI........ It Would Be Nice If [*Computer hacker terminology*]   (NHD)
IWC .... International Willow Collectors [*An association*]   (EA)
IWE .... Institution of Water Engineers [*British*]   (BI)
IWG .... Industry Working Group
IWRMA ..... Irish Wholesale Ryegrass Machiners Association   (BI)
IWRP.......... Industrial Waste Reduction Program [*Environmental science*]
IWS............. Institute of Wood Science [*British*]   (BI)
IWSI .... Irish Work Study Institute Ltd.   (BI)
IWSP .... Institute of Work Study Practitioners [*British*]   (BI)
IWTT.......... Industrial Wastewater Treatment Plant
IXP............. Information Exchange Protocol [*Telecommunications*]   (NTCM)
IXT............. Lineas Aereas de Ixtlan SA de CV [*Mexico*] [*ICAO designator*]   (FAAC)
I14Y .... Interoperability [*The 14 replaces the fourteen letters between I and Y*] [*Computer hacker terminology*]   (NHD)
IYC .... International Year of the Child [*United Nations*]   (AEE)
IYE............. Yemenia, Yemen Airways [*ICAO designator*]   (FAAC)
IYF............. International Year of the Family

J

J .... Judge
J2 .... Djibouti [*Aircraft nationality and registration mark*]   (FAAC)
J3 .... Grenada [*Aircraft nationality and registration mark*]   (FAAC)
J6 .... St. Lucia [*Aircraft nationality and registration mark*]   (FAAC)
J7 .... Dominica [*Aircraft nationality and registration mark*]   (FAAC)
J8 .... St. Vincent and the Grenadines [*Aircraft nationality and
                    registration mark*]   (FAAC)
9J .... Zambia [*Aircraft nationality and registration mark*]   (FAAC)
JAA............ Japan Asia Airways Co. Ltd. [*ICAO designator*]   (FAAC)
JAB............ Jet Business Airlines [*Belgium*] [*ICAO designator*]   (FAAC)
JAC............ Japan Air Commuter Co. Ltd. [*ICAO designator*]   (FAAC)
JAC............ Junior American Citizens [*An association*]   (EA)
JADE......... Japan Asian Dance Event
JAG .... Jetag AB [*Switzerland*] [*ICAO designator*]   (FAAC)
JAL............ Japan Air Lines Ltd. [*ICAO designator*]   (FAAC)
JAM .... Just a Minute [*Computer hacker terminology*]   (NHD)
JAN .... Janes Aviation 748 Ltd. [*British*] [*ICAO designator*]   (FAAC)
JANTA....... Journal of the Australian Natural Therapists Association [*A
                    publication*]
JAPOS .... Journalists, Authors and Poets on Stamps Study Unit   (EA)
JAR............ Airlink Luftverkehrsgesellschaft GmbH [*Austria*] [*ICAO
                    designator*]   (FAAC)
JAR............ Jewish Autonomous Region [*Siberia*]
JAS............ Japan Air System Co. Ltd. [*ICAO designator*]   (FAAC)
JAS............ Joint Airmiss Section [*Aviation*]   (DA)
JAT............ Joint Agency Training
JAT............ Jugoslovenski Aerotransport [*Yugoslavia*] [*ICAO designator*]
                    (FAAC)
JAV............ Janes Aviation Ltd. [*British*] [*ICAO designator*]   (FAAC)
JAVCF....... Japan Australia Venture Capital Fund
JAW........... Jamahiriya Airways [*Libya*] [*ICAO designator*]   (FAAC)
JAX........... JanAir, Inc. [*ICAO designator*]   (FAAC)
JAY........... J & J Air Charters Ltd. [*British*] [*ICAO designator*]   (FAAC)
JAZ........... Japan Air Charter Co. Ltd. [*ICAO designator*]   (FAAC)
JBA........... Helijet Airways [*Canada*] [*ICAO designator*]   (FAAC)
JBCPS .... Journeyman Bakers' and Confectioners Pension Society
                    [*British*]   (BI)
JBD........... James Brake [*Aviation*]   (DA)
JBL........... Junior Bird League [*British*]   (BI)
JC.............. Job Center
JC.............. Job Club
JCA........... Jetcom SA [*Switzerland*] [*ICAO designator*]   (FAAC)
JCB........... [*J. C.*] Bamford (Excavators) Ltd. [*British*] [*ICAO designator*]
                    (FAAC)
JCF .... Jet Center Flight Training SA [*Spain*] [*ICAO designator*]   (FAAC)
JCK........... Jackson Air Services Ltd. [*Canada*] [*ICAO designator*]   (FAAC)
JCL........... Jet Cargo-Liberia [*ICAO designator*]   (FAAC)
JCP .... Jetcopter [*Denmark*] [*ICAO designator*]   (FAAC)
JD .... Jack Daniels [*A brand name of whiskey*]
JDC........... Deere & Co. [*ICAO designator*]   (FAAC)
JDE........... Air Med Jetoperations [*Austria*] [*ICAO designator*]   (FAAC)
JDP........... Joint Development Program
JDSCS....... Joint Defense Space Communications Station
JDV........... [*J. D.*] Valenciana de Aviacion [*Venezuela*] [*ICAO designator*]
                    (FAAC)
JE.............. Joint Engineers [*Army*]   (RDA)
JEA........... Jersey European Airways [*British*] [*ICAO designator*]   (FAAC)
JED........... Jet East, Inc. [*ICAO designator*]   (FAAC)
JEF........... Jetflite OY [*Finland*] [*ICAO designator*]   (FAAC)
JEJ .... Jets Ejecutivos SA [*Mexico*] [*ICAO designator*]   (FAAC)
JEJUN ...... Jejunectomy   (ABBR)
JEJUN ...... Jejunitis   (ABBR)
JELOS....... Jealous   (ABBR)
JELOSY..... Jealousy   (ABBR)
JEMP .... Joint Engineers Management Panel [*Army*]   (RDA)
JEN........... Jenair Ltd. [*Cyprus*] [*ICAO designator*]   (FAAC)
JEOP........ Jeopardy   (ABBR)
JEOPZ ...... Jeopardize   (ABBR)
JEOPZD .... Jeopardized   (ABBR)
JEOPZG .... Jeopardizing   (ABBR)
JES .... Jes Air [*Bulgaria*] [*ICAO designator*]   (FAAC)
JET............ European Jet Ltd. [*British*] [*ICAO designator*]   (FAAC)
JET .... Jetsam   (ABBR)

JETD.......... Jetted   (ABBR)
JETG .... Jetting   (ABBR)
JETLNR.... Jetliner   (ABBR)
JEX............ Jet Express, Inc. [*ICAO designator*]   (FAAC)
JFC .... LTV Jet Fleet Corp. [*ICAO designator*]   (FAAC)
JFCL.......... Jump if Flag Set and Then Clear the Flag [*Computer science*]
                    (NHD)
JFO............ Just for Openers [*An association*]   (EA)
JFS............ Juanda Flying School [*Indonesia*] [*ICAO designator*]   (FAAC)
JFT .... Jet Fret [*France*] [*ICAO designator*]   (FAAC)
JFY .... Foster Yeoman Ltd. [*British*] [*ICAO designator*]   (FAAC)
JFY .... Jiffy   (ABBR)
JGB .... Japanese Government Bond   (ECON)
JGR .... Belize Trans Air [*ICAO designator*]   (FAAC)
JGSW .... Jigsaw   (ABBR)
JHB .... Johannesburg [*South Africa*]   (ABBR)
JHL .... Jet Heritage Ltd. [*British*] [*ICAO designator*]   (FAAC)
JHN .... Johnson Air, Inc. [*ICAO designator*]   (FAAC)
JHVH........ Jehovah   (ABBR)
JIA............ Jetstream International Airlines [*ICAO designator*]   (FAAC)
JIBG .... Jibing   (ABBR)
JID............. Air Condal SA [*Spain*] [*ICAO designator*]   (FAAC)
JIGL .... Jiggle   (ABBR)
JIGLD .... Jiggled   (ABBR)
JIGLG .... Jiggling   (ABBR)
JIGLY........ Jiggly   (ABBR)
JIGR .... Jigger   (ABBR)
JILL.......... Jobs Illustrated [*CD-ROM*]
JIM............ Sark International Airways Ltd. [*British*] [*ICAO designator*]
                    (FAAC)
JINGLD ..... Jingled   (ABBR)
JINGLG ..... Jingling   (ABBR)
JITR .... Jitter   (ABBR)
JITRBG ..... Jitterbug   (ABBR)
JITRY........ Jittery   (ABBR)
JKA............ Jakarta [*Indonesia*]   (ABBR)
JKAS......... Jackass   (ABBR)
JKBT .... Jackboot   (ABBR)
JKBX .... Jukebox   (ABBR)
JKD............ Jacked   (ABBR)
JKET .... Jacket   (ABBR)
JKETD ...... Jacketted   (ABBR)
JKG............ Jacking   (ABBR)
JKL............ Jackal   (ABBR)
JKMR .... Jackhammer   (ABBR)
JKNIF .... Jackknife   (ABBR)
JKPT .... Jackpot   (ABBR)
JKS............ Jacks   (ABBR)
JKTD......... Jacketed   (ABBR)
JKTG......... Jacketing   (ABBR)
JLBD......... Jailbird   (ABBR)
JLBRK...... Jailbreak   (ABBR)
JLEM .... Jerusalem   (ABBR)
JLEN......... Julienne   (ABBR)
JLEP......... Julep   (ABBR)
JLP............ Jailer   (ABBR)
JLR .... Jeweler   (ABBR)
JLS .... Jet Alsace [*France*] [*ICAO designator*]   (FAAC)
JLTR .... Jilter   (ABBR)
JLUS .... Jealous   (ABBR)
JLUSLY .... Jealously   (ABBR)
JLUSNS..... Jealousness   (ABBR)
JLUSY....... Jealousy   (ABBR)
JLY .... Jelly   (ABBR)
JLYBN...... Jellybean   (ABBR)
JLYD......... Jellied   (ABBR)
JLYFSH.... Jellyfish   (ABBR)
JLYLK...... Jellylike   (ABBR)
JMA........... Joinery Managers' Association [*British*]   (BI)
JMA .... Juvenile Missionary Association [*British*]   (BI)
JMB........... Jamb   (ABBR)
JMBL......... Jumble   (ABBR)
JMBLD ..... Jumbled   (ABBR)

JMBLG ...... Jumbling (ABBR)
JMBRE ...... Jamboree (ABBR)
JMCY .... Joseph Malins Crusade of Youth [British] (BI)
J Mil H ...... Journal of Military History [A publication]
JMJ .... [James M.] Johnson [ICAO designator] (FAAC)
JML .... Taxi Aereo de Jimulco SA de CV [Mexico] [ICAO designator] (FAAC)
JMPD .... Jumped (ABBR)
JMPG .... Jumping (ABBR)
JMPI .... Jumpmaster Personnel Inspection [Army] (ADDR)
JMPNS ...... Jumpiness (ABBR)
JMPOF ..... Jumpoff (ABBR)
JMR .... Alexandair, Inc. [Canada] [ICAO designator] (FAAC)
JMY .... Jimmy (ABBR)
JMYG .... Jimmying (ABBR)
JNA .... [John] Nurminen OY [Finland] [ICAO designator] (FAAC)
JNB .... Joinable (ABBR)
JNCN .... Junction (ABBR)
JNCUR ...... Juncture (ABBR)
JND .... Joined (ABBR)
JNDR .... Joinder (ABBR)
JNE .... June (ABBR)
JNGL .... Jonquil (ABBR)
JNGL .... Jungle (ABBR)
JNKD .... Junked (ABBR)
JNKG .... Junking (ABBR)
JNKI .... Junkie (ABBR)
JNKMA ..... Junkman (ABBR)
JNKT .... Junket (ABBR)
JNKTD ...... Junketed (ABBR)
JNKTG ...... Junketing (ABBR)
JNKTR ...... Junketer (ABBR)
JNPR .... Juniper (ABBR)
JNR .... Joiner (ABBR)
JNT .... Jaunt (ABBR)
JNT .... Junction (ABBR)
JNT .... Juncture (ABBR)
JNTD .... Jointed (ABBR)
JNTINS ..... Jauntiness (ABBR)
JNTIR .... Jauntier (ABBR)
JNTLY ...... Jauntily (ABBR)
JNTLY ...... Jointly (ABBR)
JNTR .... Janitor (ABBR)
JNTR .... Jointer (ABBR)
JNTST .... Jauntiest (ABBR)
JNTUR ...... Jointure (ABBR)
JNTURD.... Jointured (ABBR)
JNTURG.... Jointuring (ABBR)
JNTY .... Jaunty (ABBR)
JNTY .... Jointly (ABBR)
JNY .... January (ABBR)
JNY .... Jenney Beechcraft, Inc. [ICAO designator] (FAAC)
JOB .... Aerojobeni SA de CV [Mexico] [ICAO designator] (FAAC)
JOBD .... Jobbed (ABBR)
JOBG .... Jobbing (ABBR)
JOBHLDR ... Jobholder (ABBR)
JOBR .... Jobber (ABBR)
JOC .... Jocular (ABBR)
JOCK .... Jockey (ABBR)
JOCK .... Jockstrap (ABBR)
JOG .... Junior Offshore Group [Racing] [British]
JOGD .... Jogged (ABBR)
JOGG .... Jogging (ABBR)
JOGL .... Joggle (ABBR)
JOGLD...... Joggled (ABBR)
JOGLG...... Joggling (ABBR)
JOGR .... Jogger (ABBR)
JOK .... Airtaxi Bedarfsluftverkehrsges GmbH [Austria] [ICAO designator] (FAAC)
JOKG .... Joking (ABBR)
JOKGLY ... Jokingly (ABBR)
JOKGY...... Jokingly (ABBR)
JOKSTR.... Jokester (ABBR)
JOLD........ Jollied (ABBR)
JOLTGLY ... Joltingly (ABBR)
JONR .... Joiner (ABBR)
JOR .... Yorkshire European Airways Ltd. [British] [ICAO designator] (FAAC)
JORD .... Jordan (ABBR)
JOTD........ Jotted (ABBR)
JOTG .... Jotting (ABBR)
JOUR .... Journal (ABBR)
JOURN ..... Journey (ABBR)
JOY .... Joy [Poland] [ICAO designator] (FAAC)
JPC .... Polar Air Co. [Russian Federation] [ICAO designator] (FAAC)
JPN........... Memrykord Ltd. [British] [ICAO designator] (FAAC)
JPR .... Air International (Holdings) PLC [British] [ICAO designator] (FAAC)
JPRDY ...... Jeopardy (ABBR)
JPRDZ ...... Jeopardize (ABBR)
JPRDZG ... Jeopardizing (ABBR)
JPS .... Junior Philatelic Society [British] (BI)
JPSA.......... Japanese Plating Supplier's Association [Environmetal science]

JQA .... Trans Jamaican Airlines Ltd. [ICAO designator] (FAAC)
JRD............ Jarred (ABBR)
JRFL.......... Jarful (ABBR)
JRG........... Jarring (ABBR)
JRGN .... Jargon (ABBR)
JRKD .... Jerked (ABBR)
JRKG .... Jerking (ABBR)
JRKIR .... Jerkier (ABBR)
JRKLY ...... Jerkily (ABBR)
JRKN......... Jerkin (ABBR)
JRKNS ...... Jerkiness (ABBR)
JRKR .... Jerker (ABBR)
JRKST....... Jerkiest (ABBR)
JRN .... Jet Rent SA [Mexico] [ICAO designator] (FAAC)
JRNLM ..... Journalism (ABBR)
JRNLSM.... Journalism (ABBR)
JRNLST.... Journalist (ABBR)
JRNLSTC ... Journalistic (ABBR)
JRNLT ...... Journalist (ABBR)
JRNLTC.... Journalistic (ABBR)
JRNLTCY ... Journalistically (ABBR)
JRNLZ ...... Journalize (ABBR)
JRNLZD ... Journalized (ABBR)
JRNLZG ... Journalizing (ABBR)
JRNLZR.... Journalizer (ABBR)
JRNY .... Journey (ABBR)
JRNYD...... Journeyed (ABBR)
JRNYG...... Journeying (ABBR)
JRNYMAN ... Journeyman (ABBR)
JRR............ Juror (ABBR)
JRSDCNL ... Jurisdictional (ABBR)
JRSPDN.... Jurisprudent (ABBR)
JRSPDNC ... Jurisprudence (ABBR)
JRSPDTL.. Jurisprudential (ABBR)
JRST......... Jurist (ABBR)
JRSY .... Jersey (ABBR)
JRWG........ Job Redesign Working Group
JRY .... Jury (ABBR)
JRYBLD.... Jerrybuild (ABBR)
JRYBLDG ... Jerrybuilding (ABBR)
JRYBLDR ... Jerrybuilder (ABBR)
JRYBLT.... Jerrybuilt (ABBR)
JRYMA ...... Juryman (ABBR)
JSA .... Japanese Standards Association (NTCM)
JSC .... Joint Selection Committee
JSH........... Jetstream Ltd. [Hungary] [ICAO designator] (FAAC)
JSMIN ...... Jasmine (ABBR)
JSR .... Joint Staffing Review
JST .... Japan Universal System Transport Co. Ltd. [ICAO designator] (FAAC)
JST .... Job Skills Training
JSTC......... Job Skills Training Course
JSTP......... Job Search Training Program
JTA .... Japan Transocean Air Co. Ltd. [ICAO designator] (FAAC)
JTAGS ...... Joint Target Acquistion Ground Station [Military]
JTC .... Jets Corporativos SA de CV [Mexico] [ICAO designator] (FAAC)
J-TENS ..... Joint Tactical Exploitation of National Systems [Army] (ADDR)
JTF .... Joint Task Force
JTL .... Jetall Holdings, Corp. [Canada] [ICAO designator] (FAAC)
JTR .... Jet-Air Bedarfsflugunternehmen [Austria] [ICAO designator] (FAAC)
JTRL .... Janitorial (ABBR)
JTWS .... Journal of Third World Studies [A publication]
JUD .... US Department of Justice [ICAO designator] (FAAC)
JVA .... Genavia SRL [Italy] [ICAO designator] (FAAC)
JVS .... Joint Venture Scheme
JWA........... Jetworld Airways Ltd. [Antigua and Barbuda] [ICAO designator] (FAAC)
JWAR........ Jehovah's Witnesses for Animal Rights [An association] (EA)
JWD .... Journal of Workforce Diversity [A publication]
JWEF .... Joinery and Woodwork Employers' Federation [British] (BI)
JWG .... Joint Working Group
JWP .... Joint Working Paper
JWY........... Jet Way, Inc. [ICAO designator] (FAAC)

K

K .... [*Fire Department*] Key Box [*NFPA pre-fire planning symbol*] (NFPA)
KAA .... Asia Aero Survey & Consulting Engineers, Inc. [*Korea*] [*ICAO designator*] (FAAC)
KAC .... Kuwait Airways Corp. [*ICAO designator*] (FAAC)
KAF .... Kafue International Air Services Ltd. [*Zambia*] [*ICAO designator*] (FAAC)
KAH .... Kent Aviation Ltd. [*Canada*] [*ICAO designator*] (FAAC)
KAL .... Korean Air Lines Co. Ltd. [*ICAO designator*] (FAAC)
KAP .... Hyannis Air Service, Inc. [*ICAO designator*] (FAAC)
KAR .... Kar-Air OY [*Finland*] [*ICAO designator*] (FAAC)
KAS .... Kingston Air Services [*Canada*] [*ICAO designator*] (FAAC)
KAT .... Kattegat Air, AS [*Denmark*] [*ICAO designator*] (FAAC)
KAWOL ..... Knowledge, Absent Without Leave [*Army*] (ADDR)
KAZAIR ..... Kazakhstan Airlines [*ICAO designator*] (FAAC)
KBA .... Kenn Borek Air Ltd. [*Canada*] [*ICAO designator*] (FAAC)
KBE .... Knowledge-Based Engineering [*Expert systems*] [*Computer-aided design*]
KBS .... Gamair Ltd. [*Gambia*] [*ICAO designator*] (FAAC)
KBV .... Kustbevakningen [*Sweden*] [*ICAO designator*] (FAAC)
KCE .... [*K. C.*] Piper Sales, Inc. [*ICAO designator*] (FAAC)
KDA .... Kendall Airlines [*Australia*] [*ICAO designator*] (FAAC)
KDC .... KD Air Corp. [*ICAO designator*] (FAAC)
KDEP .... Smoke Layer Estimated (Feet) Deep [*Meteorology*] (FAAC)
KDP .... Kappa Delta Pi [*Honor society*] (AEE)
KDS .... K2 Del Aire SA de CV [*Mexico*] [*ICAO designator*] (FAAC)
KDS .... Keyboard Display Station [*Computer science*] (DA)
KEA .... Kent Executive Aviation Ltd. [*British*] [*ICAO designator*] (FAAC)
KEE .... Keystone Air Services Ltd. [*Canada*] [*ICAO designator*] (FAAC)
KF .... Klenow Fragment [*Genetics*]
KFA .... Kelowna Flightcraft Air Charter Ltd. [*Canada*] [*ICAO designator*] (FAAC)
KFL .... Kenya Flamingo Airways Ltd. [*ICAO designator*] (FAAC)
KGA .... Kyrghyzstan Airlines [*ICAO designator*] (FAAC)
kH .... Kilohertz
KHA .... Kitty Hawk Airways, Inc. [*ICAO designator*] (FAAC)
KHR .... Khazar [*Turkmenistan*] [*ICAO designator*] (FAAC)
KhV .... Khranit' Vechno [*To be Kept in Perpetuity*] [*KGB file status*]
KHX .... Hugo Rizzuto [*ICAO designator*] (FAAC)
KIA .... KIWI International Air Lines, Inc. [*ICAO designator*] (FAAC)
KIET .... Korea Institute for Industrial Economics and Trade (ECON)
KIO .... Kraiaero [*Russian Federation*] [*ICAO designator*] (FAAC)
KIS .... Contactair Flugdienst & Co. [*Germany*] [*ICAO designator*] (FAAC)
KITG .... Kiting (ABBR)
KITN .... Kitten (ABBR)
KIZ .... Kanaf-Arkia Airlines Ltd. [*Israel*] [*ICAO designator*] (FAAC)
KJA .... Avistar (Cyprus) Ltd. [*ICAO designator*] (FAAC)
KLA .... Air Lietuva [*Lithuania*] [*ICAO designator*] (FAAC)
KLC .... KLM Cityhopper BV [*Netherlands*] [*ICAO designator*] (FAAC)
KLCCL .... Kilocycle (ABBR)
KLDR .... Killdeer (ABBR)
KLDSOP ... Kaleidoscope (ABBR)
KLDSOPC ... Kaleidoscopic (ABBR)
Kleb .... Klebsiella [*Genus of microorganisms*] (MAH)
KLEPTO ..... Kleptomania (ABBR)
KLG .... Killing (ABBR)
KLGM .... Kilogram (ABBR)
KLH .... KLM Helicopters NV [*Netherlands*] [*ICAO designator*] (FAAC)
KLJY .... Killjoy (ABBR)
KLM .... KLM Royal Dutch Airlines [*Netherlands*] [*ICAO designator*] (FAAC)
KLMTR ...... Kilometer (ABBR)
KLPTMN .... Kleptomania (ABBR)
KLPTMNC ... Kleptomaniac (ABBR)
KLR .... Columbus Air Transport, Inc. [*ICAO designator*] (FAAC)
KLTN .... Kiloton (ABBR)
KLTR .... Kilter (ABBR)
KLWT .... Kilowatt (ABBR)
KLYR .... Smoke Layer Aloft [*Meteorology*] (FAAC)
KMNO .... Kimono (ABBR)
KMQUT ..... Kumquat (ABBR)

KN .... Khan (ABBR)
KN .... Knight (ABBR)
KN .... Krone (ABBR)
KN .... Kronen (ABBR)
KNA .... Knight Air Ltd. [*Canada*] [*ICAO designator*] (FAAC)
KNBR .... Knobbier (ABBR)
KNBST .... Knobbiest (ABBR)
KNBY .... Knobby (ABBR)
KNCKBT .... Knockabout (ABBR)
KNCKDN .. Knockdown (ABBR)
KNCKKN .. Knock-knee (ABBR)
KNCKOT ... Knockout (ABBR)
KNCKR ...... Knocker (ABBR)
KNDGTN.... Kindergarten (ABBR)
KNDHTD... Kindhearted (ABBR)
KNDHTDNS ... Kindheartedness (ABBR)
KNDL .... Kindle (ABBR)
KNDLD ...... Kindled (ABBR)
KNDLES .... Kindless (ABBR)
KNDLG ...... Kindling (ABBR)
KNDLIR ..... Kindlier (ABBR)
KNDLNS.... Kindliness (ABBR)
KNDLST .... Kindliest (ABBR)
KNDLY ...... Kindly (ABBR)
KNDNS ...... Kindness (ABBR)
KNDR .... Kinder (ABBR)
KNDRD ...... Kindred (ABBR)
KNDRG ...... Kindergarten (ABBR)
KNDRGR ... Kindergartener (ABBR)
KNDST .... Kindest (ABBR)
KNDY .... Kindly (ABBR)
KNECP .... Kneecap (ABBR)
KNEDP ...... Kneedeep (ABBR)
KNELG ...... Kneeling (ABBR)
KNELR ...... Kneller (ABBR)
KNF .... Knife (ABBR)
KNFD .... Knifed (ABBR)
KNFG .... Knifing (ABBR)
KNFLK .... Kinfolk (ABBR)
KNFLK .... Knifelike (ABBR)
KNFP .... Kellogg National Fellowship Program
KNG .... King Aviation [*British*] [*ICAO designator*] (FAAC)
KNGDM ..... Kingdom (ABBR)
KNGFSH ... Kingfish (ABBR)
KNGFSHR ... Kingfisher (ABBR)
KNGLNS.... Kingliness (ABBR)
KNGLR ...... Kinglier (ABBR)
KNGLST .... Kingliest (ABBR)
KNGLY ...... Kingly (ABBR)
KNGPN ...... Kingpin (ABBR)
KNGR .... Kangaroo (ABBR)
KNGSZ .... Kingsize (ABBR)
KNGT .... Knight (ABBR)
KNGTHD ... Knighthood (ABBR)
KNGTLY ... Knightly (ABBR)
KNGT-RNT ... Knight-Errant (ABBR)
KNGY .... Kingly (ABBR)
KNHT .... Knight (ABBR)
KNITG .... Knitting (ABBR)
KNITR .... Knitter (ABBR)
KNKL .... Knuckle (ABBR)
KNKLD ..... Knuckled (ABBR)
KNKLG ...... Knuckling (ABBR)
KNKR .... Kinkier (ABBR)
KNKRS ...... Knickers (ABBR)
KNKST .... Kinkiest (ABBR)
KNL .... Kennel (ABBR)
KNL .... Knoll (ABBR)
KNLD .... Kenneled (ABBR)
KNLG .... Kenneling (ABBR)
KNPSK .... Knapsack (ABBR)
KNRL .... Kernel (ABBR)
KNS .... Kenuz Airlines Ltd. [*Nigeria*] [*ICAO designator*] (FAAC)

KNSCP .... Kinescope (ABBR)
KNSHP ...... Kinship (ABBR)
KNSMN ..... Kinsman (ABBR)
KNSWMN ... Kinswoman (ABBR)
KNT .... Knightway Air Charter Ltd. [*British*] [*ICAO designator*] (FAAC)
KNTC .... Kinetic (ABBR)
KNTD .... Knotted (ABBR)
KNTG .... Knotting (ABBR)
KNTHL ...... Knothole (ABBR)
KNTLK ...... Knotlike (ABBR)
KNTLS .... Knotless (ABBR)
KNTY .... Knotty (ABBR)
KNV .... Knave (ABBR)
KNVH .... Knavish (ABBR)
KNVHLY ... Knavishly (ABBR)
KNVRY ...... Knavery (ABBR)
KNWB .... Knowable (ABBR)
KNWG .... Knowing (ABBR)
KNWGNS ... Knowingness (ABBR)
KNWGY ..... Knowingly (ABBR)
KNWHW ... Know-How (ABBR)
KNWL .... Knowledge (ABBR)
KNWLB ...... Knowledgeable (ABBR)
KNWLDG ... Knowledge (ABBR)
KNWLDGB ... Knowledgeable (ABBR)
KNWNTHG ... Know-Nothing (ABBR)
KNWR .... Knower (ABBR)
KNX .... Knighthawk Air Express Ltd. [*Canada*] [*ICAO designator*]
  (FAAC)
KNXV .... Knoxville [*Tennessee*] (ABBR)
KO .... Kilohm (ABBR)
KOA .... Kone Air Ltd. [*Finland*] [*ICAO designator*] (FAAC)
KOALA ...... Keyfile Open Access Layer [*Workflow automation software*]
  (PCM)
KOB .... Kob Air Ltd. [*Uganda*] [*ICAO designator*] (FAAC)
KOE .... Northland Aviation, Inc. [*ICAO designator*] (FAAC)
KOH .... Potassium Hydroxide [*Electric vehicle batteries*]
KOK .... Horizon Cargo Transport, Inc. [*ICAO designator*] (FAAC)
KOOKR ..... Kookier (ABBR)
KOOKST .... Kookiest (ABBR)
KOR .... Air Koryo [*North Korea*] [*ICAO designator*] (FAAC)
KOS .... Kosovaair [*Yugoslavia*] [*ICAO designator*] (FAAC)
KPCK .... Kopeck (ABBR)
KPI .... Kernel Programming Interface [*Computer science*]
KPK .... Kapok (ABBR)
KPM .... Kensington Palace Gardens [*British interrogation center*]
KPR .... Keeper (ABBR)
KPSK .... Keepsake (ABBR)
KPT .... Karpatair [*Hungary*] [*ICAO designator*] (FAAC)
KQA .... Kenya Airways Ltd. [*ICAO designator*] (FAAC)
KR .... Karat (ABBR)
K-R .... Kuder-Richardson Formula [*Education*] (AEE)
KRA .... Key Result Area
KRCHF ...... Kerchief (ABBR)
KRKN .... Kraken (ABBR)
KRM .... Karma (ABBR)
KRMC .... Karmic (ABBR)
KRNL .... Kernel (ABBR)
KRO .... Aliblu Airways SpA [*Italy*] [*ICAO designator*] (FAAC)
KRS .... Korsar [*Russian Federation*] [*ICAO designator*] (FAAC)
KRSEN ...... Kerosene (ABBR)
KRT .... Cretan Airlines SA [*Greece*] [*ICAO designator*] (FAAC)
KRTE .... Karate (ABBR)
KRTN .... Karatin (ABBR)
KRYPN ...... Krypton (ABBR)
KSE .... Kids for Saving Earth [*An association*] (EA)
KSE .... Kisbee Air Ltd. [*New Zealand*] [*ICAO designator*] (FAAC)
KSHR .... Kosher (ABBR)
KSK .... Kiosk (ABBR)
KSMT .... Kismet (ABBR)
KSP .... Servicios Aereos Especializados en Transportes Petroleros
  [*Colombia*] [*ICAO designator*] (FAAC)
KSR .... Kaiser (ABBR)
KSSB .... Kissable (ABBR)
KSSR .... Kisser (ABBR)
KSTRL .... Kestrel (ABBR)
KTCHP ...... Ketchup (ABBR)
KTCN .... Kitchen (ABBR)
KTCNET .... Kitchennette (ABBR)
KTCNWR ... Kitchenware (ABBR)
KTI .... Kano Transport International Ltd. KATI Air [*Nigeria*] [*ICAO
  designator*] (FAAC)
KTL .... Kettle (ABBR)
KTLDR .... Kettledrum (ABBR)
KTN .... Kitten (ABBR)
KTNH .... Kittenish (ABBR)
KTON .... Ketone [*Organic chemistry*] (ABBR)
KTR .... Helikoptertransport AB [*Sweden*] [*ICAO designator*] (FAAC)
KTSC .... Kitsch (ABBR)
KTY .... Kitty (ABBR)
KTYCR ...... Kitty-Corner (ABBR)
KTYD .... Katydid (ABBR)
KU .... Kilourane (ABBR)

KUS .... Kidney, Ureter, and Spleen [*Anatomy*] (MAH)
KUW .... Kuwait (ABBR)
KVY .... CAI [*Compagnia Aeronautica Italiana SpA*] [*Italy*] [*ICAO
  designator*] (FAAC)
KWHR .... Kilowatthour (ABBR)
KYA .... Yana Air Cargo (Kenya) Ltd. [*ICAO designator*] (FAAC)
KYC .... HCL Aviation, Inc. [*ICAO designator*] (FAAC)
KYHL .... Keyhole (ABBR)
KYK .... Kayak (ABBR)
KYMO .... Kymograph (ABBR)
KYN .... Kyrnair [*France*] [*ICAO designator*] (FAAC)
KYNT .... Keynote (ABBR)
KYNTG ...... Keynoting (ABBR)
KYSTN ...... Keystone (ABBR)
KZA .... Kazakhstan Airlines [*ICAO designator*] (FAAC)

L

L .... Land Transportation [*FCC*]   (NTCM)
L .... Lifestyle [*Wire service code*]   (NTCM)
L .... Line (of Print) [*Publishing*]   (NTCM)
L .... Local [*Broadcasting program*]   (NTCM)
L .... Locking [*Lamp base type*]   (NTCM)
9L .... Sierra Leone [*Aircraft nationality and registration mark*]   (FAAC)
LA .... Live Action   (NTCM)
LA .... Living Allowance
LAA .... Jamahiriya Libyan Arab Airlines [*ICAO designator*]   (FAAC)
LAA .... Local Airport Advisory [*Aviation*]   (FAAC)
LAADBN.... Low Altitude Air Defense Battalion [*Navy*]   (ANA)
L A Ant ...... Latin America Antiquity [*A publication*]
LAB .... Labrador Retriever [*Dog breed*]
LAC .... Lockheed Aircraft Corp. [*ICAO designator*]   (FAAC)
LACAS ...... Lineas Aereas Costarricenses SA [*Costa Rica*] [*ICAO designator*]   (FAAC)
LAD .... Lebanon Airport Development Corp. [*ICAO designator*]   (FAAC)
LAE .... Lineas Aereas Colombianas Ltd. [*Colombia*] [*ICAO designator*]   (FAAC)
LAG .... Aerovias de Lagos SA de CV [*Mexico*] [*ICAO designator*]   (FAAC)
LAG .... Line of Arrested Growth [*Biology*]
LAGO .... Light Atomic Gas Oil [*Petroleum product*]
LAH .... LA Helicopter, Inc. [*ICAO designator*]   (FAAC)
LAI .... Lesotho Airways Corp. [*ICAO designator*]   (FAAC)
LAIS .... Labyrinth Air Induction System [*Automotive engineering*]
LAJ .... London Airtours Ltd. [*British*] [*ICAO designator*]   (FAAC)
LAK .... Lennox Airways [*Kenya*] [*ICAO designator*]   (FAAC)
LAL .... Labrador Airways Ltd. [*Canada*] [*ICAO designator*]   (FAAC)
LAM .... Linhas Aereas de Mocambique [*Mozambique*] [*ICAO designator*]   (FAAC)
LAM .... Logical Acknowledgement Message [*Aviation*]   (DA)
LAMA .... Locomotive and Allied Manufacturers' Association [*British*]   (BI)
LAN .... Linea Aerea Nacional de Chile [*ICAO designator*]   (FAAC)
LAO .... Lao Aviaton [*Laos*] [*ICAO designator*]   (FAAC)
LAP........... Learning Activity Packet   (AEE)
LAP........... Lineas Aereas Paraguayas [*Paraguay*] [*ICAO designator*]   (FAAC)
LAPL .... Library Association Publishing Ltd. [*British*]
LAPR .... Life Assurance Premium Relief [*Business term*]
LAPW........ Linearized Augmented Plane Wave [*Physical chemistry*]
LAQ .... Lebanese Air Transport [*ICAO designator*]   (FAAC)
LAR .... Lawrence Aviation, Inc. [*ICAO designator*]   (FAAC)
LAR .... Linhas Aereas Regionais SA [*Portugal*] [*ICAO designator*]   (FAAC)
LARS .... Lower Airspace RADAR Advisory Service [*British*]   (DA)
LAS............ Lignes Aerienne Seychelles [*ICAO designator*]   (FAAC)
LASSA....... Licensed Animal Slaughterers and Salvage Association [*British*]   (BI)
LAT .... Aviation Legere de l'Armee de Terre [*France*] [*ICAO designator*]   (FAAC)
Latr .... Locator [*Compass*]   (DA)
LAU .... Lineas Aereas Suramericanas Ltd. [*Colombia*] [*ICAO designator*]   (FAAC)
LAV .... Lavaliere [*Lapel microphone*]   (NTCM)
LAV .... Linea Aeropostal Venezolana [*Venezuela*] [*ICAO designator*]   (FAAC)
LAVH .... Laparoscopically-Assisted Vaginal Hysterectomy [*Medicine*]
LAW .... Link Airways of Australia [*Australia*] [*ICAO designator*]   (FAAC)
LAZ .... Balkan-Bulgarian Airlines [*ICAO designator*]   (FAAC)
LB .... Left Base [*Aviation*]   (FAAC)
LB .... Lifeboat Station [*Coast Guard*]
LBA .... Limas Bulgarian Airlines [*ICAO designator*]   (FAAC)
LBC........... Albanian Airline Co. [*ICAO designator*]   (FAAC)
LBC........... Lowband Color [*Broadcasting*]   (NTCM)
LBH .... Laker Airways (Bahamas) Ltd. [*ICAO designator*]   (FAAC)
LBM .... Locator Back Marker [*Aviation*]   (DA)
LBM .... Lowband Monochrome [*Broadcasting*]   (NTCM)
LBS........... London Business Aviation [*British*] [*ICAO designator*]   (FAAC)
LBT........... Air Liberte Tunisie [*Tunisia*] [*ICAO designator*]   (FAAC)
LBT........... Large Binocular Telescope
LCA .... LeConte Airlines [*ICAO designator*]   (FAAC)
LCG .... Load Classification Group   (DA)
LCGB.......... Locomotive Club of Great Britain   (BI)

LCH .... Lynch Flying Service, Inc. [*ICAO designator*]   (FAAC)
LCIGB .... Locomotive and Carriage Institution of Great Britain and Eire   (BI)
LCL............. [*Michael A.*] Lenihan & Associates Ltd. [*British*] [*ICAO designator*]   (FAAC)
LCLo........... Lethal Concentration Low   (ERG)
LCM .... Late Change Message [*Aviation*]   (DA)
L & CM....... Lime and Cement Mortar   (DAC)
LCM .... Loose Cubic Meter   (DAC)
LCN .... Lineas Aereas Canarias SA [*Spain*] [*ICAO designator*]   (FAAC)
LCO .... Linea Aerea del Cobre Ltda. [*Chile*] [*ICAO designator*]   (FAAC)
LCP............. Light Compact Performance [*Filtration systems*] [*Automotive engineering*]
LCR........... Libyan Arab Company for Air Cargo [*ICAO designator*]   (FAAC)
LCY............. Loose Cubic Yard   (DAC)
LD .... LASER Discectomy [*Spinal surgery*]
LD .... Lighting Designer   (NTCM)
LD .... Lighting Director   (NTCM)
LDA .... Last Day of Attendance
LDA .... Lauda Air [*Austria*] [*ICAO designator*]   (FAAC)
LDDT .... Light-Duty Diesel Truck [*Automotive emissions*]
LDE .... Lighting Director Engineer   (NTCM)
LDE .... Lineas Aereas del Estado [*Argentina*] [*ICAO designator*]   (FAAC)
LDF........... Landed Duty Free
LDH........... Limiting Dome Height [*Automotive metal stamping*]
LDI .... Lauda Air [*Italy*] [*ICAO designator*]   (FAAC)
LD/LC........ Line of Departure/Line of Contact [*Army*]   (ADDR)
LDLo........... Lethal Dose Low   (ERG)
LDO........... Local Dental Officer
LDOS .... Local Density of States [*Solid state physics*]
LDR .... Aero Lider SA de CV [*Mexico*] [*ICAO designator*]   (FAAC)
LDR .... Liberal, Democratic, and Reformist Group [*European political movement*]   (ECON)
LDRRIM ... Low-Density Reinforced Reaction Injection Molding [*Plastics*]
LDS............ Lead Design Supervisor [*Engineering*]
LD-SRIM ... Low-Density Structural Reaction Injection Molding [*Plastics*]
LEA .... Lead Air Jet Service [*France*] [*ICAO designator*]   (FAAC)
LEAD USA ... Leadership Education and Development USA   (EA)
LEAF .... Legal Environmental Assistance Foundation   (EA)
LEB............ Lebap [*Turkmenistan*] [*ICAO designator*]   (FAAC)
LEB............ Low-Emissions Bus
LEC............ Lec Refrigeration Ltd. [*British*] [*ICAO designator*]   (FAAC)
LECA......... Landed Estate Companies Association [*British*]   (BI)
LECA......... Light-Expanded Clay Aggregate   (DAC)
Lect y V ...... Lectura y Vida [*A publication*]
L Ed US ...... Supreme Court Reports, Lawyer's Edition [*A publication*]   (NTCM)
LEI .... Air UK (Leisure) Ltd. [*British*] [*ICAO designator*]   (FAAC)
LEI .... Libertarian Education Institute   (EA)
LEMA........ Lifting Equipment Manufacturers Association [*British*]   (BI)
LEMA........ Lighting Equipment Manufacturers' Association   (DAC)
LEN .... Lentini Aviation, Inc. [*ICAO designator*]   (FAAC)
LEO .... Leopair SA [*Switzerland*] [*ICAO designator*]   (FAAC)
LEP............ Air West Airlines, Inc. [*ICAO designator*]   (FAAC)
LEP............ Local Enterprise Program
LER............ Light-Emitting Resistor [*Computer hacker terminology*]   (NHD)
LERP......... Linear Interpolation [*Computer science*]   (NHD)
LES .... Automotors Salta SACYF [*Argentina*] [*ICAO designator*]   (FAAC)
LESAP........ Law Enforcement Security Access Position
LET............ Aerolineas Ejecutivas SA [*Mexico*] [*ICAO designator*]   (FAAC)
LET............ Live Environment Training [*Military*]   (ADDR)
LET............ Low-Emissions Truck
LETATA .... Light Edge Tool and Allied Trades Association [*British*]   (BI)
LEX............ Lexicographer   (ABBR)
LEX............ L'Express, Inc. [*ICAO designator*]   (FAAC)
LEXI .... Lexical   (ABBR)
LEXICO .... Lexicographer   (ABBR)
LEXN .... Lexicon   (ABBR)
LEXOG ...... Lexicology   (ABBR)
LEXOGL.... Lexicological   (ABBR)
LEXOGT.... Lexicologist   (ABBR)
LEXPHR .... Lexicographer   (ABBR)

LEXPHY.... Lexicography (ABBR)
LF.............. Life (ABBR)
LFA............ Local Flying Area [*Aviation*] (DA)
LFAG........ Leafage (ABBR)
LFBD........ Lifeblood (ABBR)
LFBT .... Lifeboat (ABBR)
LFC .... Aero Control Air Ltd. [*Canada*] [*ICAO designator*] (FAAC)
LFGRD....... Lifeguard (ABBR)
LFLK......... Lifelike (ABBR)
LFLN......... Lifeline (ABBR)
LFLS......... Leafless (ABBR)
LFLSY .... Lifelessly (ABBR)
LFM........... LASER Feedback Microscope
LFNS......... Leafiness (ABBR)
LFR........... Leafier (ABBR)
LFR............ Lifer (ABBR)
LFS .... Luftfahrzeug Service - Aircraft Service [*Austria*] [*ICAO designator*] (FAAC)
LFSP........... Landing Force Support Party [*Navy*] (ANA)
LFST.......... Lifestyle (ABBR)
LFSTK....... Leafstalk (ABBR)
LFSV .... Lifesaver (ABBR)
LFSZ......... Lifesize (ABBR)
LFT............ Aerolift Philippines Corp. [*ICAO designator*] (FAAC)
LFT............ Leafiest (ABBR)
LFT............ Left (ABBR)
LFTF.......... Liftoff (ABBR)
LFTHDD.... Lefthanded (ABBR)
LFTHDY.... Lefthandedly (ABBR)
LFTINS...... Loftiness (ABBR)
LFTIR........ Loftier (ABBR)
LFTIT......... Loftiest (ABBR)
LFTM......... Lifetime (ABBR)
LFTOV .... Leftover (ABBR)
LFTT .... Leftist (ABBR)
LFTWF....... Luftwaffe (ABBR)
LFTWG ...... Leftwing (ABBR)
LFTWR .... Leftwinger (ABBR)
LFTY .... Lofty (ABBR)
LFU .... Leonhartsberger Flugunternchmen GmbH [*Austria*] [*ICAO designator*] (FAAC)
LFW........... Linear Friction Welding [*Environmental science*]
LFWK........ Lifework (ABBR)
LFY............ Leafy (ABBR)
LGA............ Elgaz [*Poland*] [*ICAO designator*] (FAAC)
LGAG........ Luggage (ABBR)
LGB .... Legible (ABBR)
LGBR........ Loganberry (ABBR)
LGBRU........ Lugubrious (ABBR)
LGBRUY... Lugubriously (ABBR)
LGBT......... Legibility (ABBR)
LGBY......... Legibly (ABBR)
LGCA .... Land-Grant College of Agriculture
LGCL......... Logical (ABBR)
LGCLT ...... Logicality (ABBR)
LGCLY ...... Logically (ABBR)
LGCN........ Logician (ABBR)
LGCY......... Legacy (ABBR)
LGD............ Compagnie Aerienne du Languedoc [*France*] [*ICAO designator*] (FAAC)
LGDMN..... Legerdemain (ABBR)
LGDR .... Labor of Genetic Disease Research [*National Institutes of Health*]
LGG .... Legging (ABBR)
LGGR........ Logger (ABBR)
LGGRHD... Loggerhead (ABBR)
LGH........... Laugh (ABBR)
LGHB........ Laughable (ABBR)
LGHBY ...... Laughably (ABBR)
LGHD........ Laughed (ABBR)
LGHET ...... Larghetto (ABBR)
LGHG........ Laughing (ABBR)
LGHGY ...... Laughingly (ABBR)
LGHN......... Leghorn (ABBR)
LGHR........ Laugher (ABBR)
LGHTR ...... Laughter (ABBR)
LGITIT....... Legitimist (ABBR)
LGITIZ....... Legitimize (ABBR)
LGITIZD.... Legitimized (ABBR)
LGITIZG.... Legitimizing (ABBR)
LGITMA.... Legitimate (ABBR)
LGITMAD ... Legitimated (ABBR)
LGITMAG ... Legitimating (ABBR)
LGITMC..... Legitimacy (ABBR)
LGITMY..... Legitimately (ABBR)
LGL .... Legal (ABBR)
LGL .... Luxair-Societe Luxembourgeoise de Navigation Aerienne SA [*Germany*] [*ICAO designator*] (FAAC)
LGLA........ Legislate (ABBR)
LGLAD...... Legislated (ABBR)
LGLAG...... Legislating (ABBR)
LGLAN...... Legislation (ABBR)
LGLAR...... Legislator (ABBR)
LGLAR...... Legislature (ABBR)

LGLAY....... Legislative (ABBR)
LGLM........ Legalism (ABBR)
LGLST ...... Legalist (ABBR)
LGLSTC...... Legalistic (ABBR)
LGLSTCY ... Legalistically (ABBR)
LGLT........ Legality (ABBR)
LGLTC ...... Legalistic (ABBR)
LGLY........ Legally (ABBR)
LGLZ........ Legalize (ABBR)
LGLZD...... Legalized (ABBR)
LGLZG...... Legalizing (ABBR)
LGLZN...... Legalization (ABBR)
LGMN....... Ligament (ABBR)
LGN........... Legion (ABBR)
LGNAP...... Lagniappe (ABBR)
LGNAR...... Legionaire (ABBR)
LGNBRY.... Loganberry (ABBR)
LGND........ Legend (ABBR)
LGNDY...... Legendary (ABBR)
LGNS......... Largeness (ABBR)
LGNY .... Legionary (ABBR)
LGO........... Largo (ABBR)
LGOFC...... Linda Gray's Official Fan Club (EA)
LGON........ Lagoon (ABBR)
LGOR........ Langor (ABBR)
LGORU..... Langorous (ABBR)
LGORUY ... Langorously (ABBR)
LGR .... Lager (ABBR)
LGRD .... Laggard (ABBR)
LGSC........ Large Scale (ABBR)
LGSL......... Lugsail (ABBR)
LGSTC ...... Logistic (ABBR)
LGSTCL..... Logistical (ABBR)
LGSTCN..... Logistician (ABBR)
LGT........... Largest (ABBR)
LGT .... Legate (ABBR)
LGTE......... Legatee (ABBR)
LGTFGR ... Lightfingered (ABBR)
LGTFTD ... Lightfooted (ABBR)
LGTFTY ... Lightfootedly (ABBR)
LGTG .... Lighting (ABBR)
LGTHD...... Lightheaded (ABBR)
LGTHDY ... Lightheadedly (ABBR)
LGTHIY.... Lengthily (ABBR)
LGTHN...... Lengthen (ABBR)
LGTHND... Lengthened (ABBR)
LGTHNG .. Lengthening (ABBR)
LGTHNS... Lengthiness (ABBR)
LGTHR...... Lengthier (ABBR)
LGTHRTD ... Lighthearted (ABBR)
LGTHRTNS ... Lightheartedness (ABBR)
LGTHRTY ... Lightheartedly (ABBR)
LGTHS....... Lighthouse (ABBR)
LGTHT ...... Lengthiest (ABBR)
LGTHWS... Lengthwise (ABBR)
LGTHY ..... Lengthy (ABBR)
LGTIC ...... Logistic (ABBR)
LGTICL...... Logistical (ABBR)
LGTMDD ... Lightminded (ABBR)
LGTMDY... Lightmindedly (ABBR)
LGTN........ Legation (ABBR)
LGTN........ Lighten (ABBR)
LGTNG...... Lightning (ABBR)
LGTO........ Legato (ABBR)
LGTR........ Ligature (ABBR)
LGTR........ Lightener (ABBR)
LGTRD...... Ligatured (ABBR)
LGTRG...... Ligaturing (ABBR)
LGTUD ..... Longitude (ABBR)
LGTUDL... Longitudinal (ABBR)
LGTUDY... Longitudinally (ABBR)
LGTWT...... Lightweight (ABBR)
LGTY......... Lightly (ABBR)
LGTYR...... Lightyear (ABBR)
LGU........... Land-Grant University
LGU........... League (ABBR)
LGU........... Legume (ABBR)
LGUD........ Leagued (ABBR)
LGUG........ Leaguing (ABBR)
LGUNU..... Leguminous (ABBR)
LGW........... Lufttarhtgesellschaft Walter GmbH [*Germany*] [*ICAO designator*] (FAAC)
LGY .... Largely (ABBR)
LGY .... Leggy (ABBR)
LH.............. Lamphole (ABBR)
LH.............. Lufthansa (ABBR)
LHA........... Lincoln Highway Association [*Motoring history organization*]
LHAL........ Lethal (ABBR)
LHAR........ Lothario (ABBR)
LHMU........ Ladies' Home Mission Union [*British*] (BI)
LHN........... Express One International, Inc. [*ICAO designator*] (FAAC)
LHR........... Low heat Release [*Adiabatic engines*] [*Automotive engineering*]
LHT........... Light (ABBR)

LHTD .... Lighted   (ABBR)
LHTEN ...... Lighten   (ABBR)
LHTEND ... Lightened   (ABBR)
LHTENG ... Lightening   (ABBR)
LHTG .... Lighting   (ABBR)
LHTNG ...... Lightning   (ABBR)
LHTR .... Lighter   (ABBR)
LHTST .... Lightest   (ABBR)
LHTY .... Lightly   (ABBR)
LI .... Liberia   (ABBR)
LIA............ Leeward Islands Air Transport (1974) Ltd. [*Antigua and Barbuda*] [*ICAO designator*]   (FAAC)
LIABT .... Liability   (ABBR)
LIB............. Air Liberte [*France*] [*ICAO designator*]   (FAAC)
LIBERD ..... Liberated   (ABBR)
LIBERG ..... Liberating   (ABBR)
LIBERN ..... Liberation   (ABBR)
LIBERR...... Liberator   (ABBR)
LIBID .... London Interbank Bid Rate [*Finance*] [*British*]
LIBL .... Liable   (ABBR)
LIBLZG...... Liberalizing   (ABBR)
LIBRLZ...... Liberalize   (ABBR)
LIBRY .... Library   (ABBR)
LIBT .... Liability   (ABBR)
LIBT .... Liberty   (ABBR)
LIC............. Lineas Aereas del Caribe [*Colombia*] [*ICAO designator*]   (FAAC)
LIC............. Local Interstellar Cloud [*Astronomy*]
LICG.......... Licensable   (ABBR)
LICG.......... Licensing   (ABBR)
LID............. Alidaunia SRL [*Italy*] [*ICAO designator*]   (FAAC)
LIECH....... Liechtenstein   (ABBR)
LIEUTC .... Lieutenancy   (ABBR)
LIEUTE ..... Lieutenancy   (ABBR)
LIF .... Lief   (ABBR)
LIFR .... Leukemia Inhibitory Factor Receptor [*Biochemistry*]
LIFTG .... Lifting   (ABBR)
LIG .... Last Interglacial Period [*Climatology*]
LIG .... Liege   (ABBR)
LIGHT....... Lighting   (ABBR)
LIGHT....... Lightning   (ABBR)
LIL .... Lilliputian   (ABBR)
LIL .... Lithuanian Airlines [*ICAO designator*]   (FAAC)
LIL .... Little   (ABBR)
LIM .... Locator Inner Marker [*Aviation*]   (DA)
LIPS........... Lanthanide Ion Probe Spectroscopy
LIR............ Lionair SA [*Luxembourg*] [*ICAO designator*]   (FAAC)
LIRA.......... Linen Industry Research Association [*British*]   (BI)
LIS............. Airlis SA [*Spain*] [*ICAO designator*]   (FAAC)
LIS............. Laurentide Ice Sheet [*Climatology*]
LISB .... Lithium Ion Storage Battery   (PCM)
LIT............. Air Littoral [*France*] [*ICAO designator*]   (FAAC)
LITAS........ Low Intensity Two-Color Approach Slope Indicator [*Aviation*]   (DA)
LITES........ LASER Initiated Transfer Energy Subsystem [*Detonator, developed by US Navy*]
LKA .... Alkair Flight Operations APS [*Denmark*] [*ICAO designator*]   (FAAC)
LKA .... Ladies Kennel Association [*British*]   (BI)
LKI............. Lakeland Aviation [*ICAO designator*]   (FAAC)
LKR .... Lake Air Helicopters Ltd. [*British*] [*ICAO designator*]   (FAAC)
LKS .... Lakeside Aviation Ltd. [*British*] [*ICAO designator*]   (FAAC)
LKZ............ Letaba Airways [*South Africa*] [*ICAO designator*]   (FAAC)
L & L......... Latch and Lock   (DAC)
LLA .... Servicio Leo Lopez SA de CV [*Mexico*] [*ICAO designator*]   (FAAC)
LL & B .... Latch, Lock, and Bolt   (DAC)
LLB............ Lloyd Aereo Boliviano SA [*Bolivia*] [*ICAO designator*]   (FAAC)
LLC............ Lightweight Leader Computer [*Army*]   (INF)
LLL............ Low Level Language [*Computer programming*]   (NTCM)
LLO .... Eliadamello SPA [*Italy*] [*ICAO designator*]   (FAAC)
LLP............ Literacy and Learning Program
LLRA .... LapLink Remote Access [*Traveling Software, Inc.*] [*Computer science*]   (PCM)
LM .... Lime Mortar   (DAC)
LMC........... Local Management Committee
LMCA .... Lorry-Mounted Crane Association [*British*]   (BI)
LMCC........ Logistic Movement Coordination Center [*Navy*]   (ANA)
LMD.......... Lamda Airlines [*Greece*] [*ICAO designator*]   (FAAC)
LMIC........ Lower Middle Income Country
LML .... Lean Misfire Limit [*Automotive engine testing*]
LMMS........ Library Materials Management System
LMP.......... Layered Metal Phosphates [*Physical chemistry*]
LMPCR...... Ligation-Mediated Polymerase Chain Reaction [*Genetics*]
LMS........... Land Mobile Service   (DA)
LMS........... Lomas Helicopters Ltd. [*British*] [*ICAO designator*]   (FAAC)
LMT .... Air Limousin TA [*France*] [*ICAO designator*]   (FAAC)
LMT .... Large Millimeter Telescope [*US-Mexico project*] [*Proposed, 1994*]
LMX .... Aerolineas Mexicanas JS SA de CV [*Mexico*] [*ICAO designator*]   (FAAC)
LNA .... Airlen [*Russian Federation*] [*ICAO designator*]   (FAAC)
LNF .... London Flights (Biggin Hill) Ltd. [*British*] [*ICAO designator*]   (FAAC)

LNK .... Airlink Airlines (Pty) Ltd. [*South Africa*] [*ICAO designator*]   (FAAC)
LNP .... Chieftain Aviation PC [*South Africa*] [*ICAO designator*]   (FAAC)
LNR .... Sky Liners Air Services Ltd. [*Suriname*] [*ICAO designator*]   (FAAC)
LNTC......... Lymph Node T Cells [*Immunology*]
LNX .... Lenex [*Poland*] [*ICAO designator*]   (FAAC)
LOAS......... Loyal Order of Ancient Shepherds [*British*]   (BI)
LOC........... Level of Concern [*Environmental Protection Agency*]   (ERG)
LOC........... Locavia 49 [*France*] [*ICAO designator*]   (FAAC)
LOCA .... Low Osmolar Contrast Agent [*Medicine*]
LOE........... Loeser, Luftfahrtgesellschaft GmbH [*Germany*] [*ICAO designator*]   (FAAC)
LOEL........ Lowest Observed Effect Level [*Toxicology*]
LOF .... Trans States Airlines, Inc. [*ICAO designator*]   (FAAC)
LOG........... Loganair Ltd. [*British*] [*ICAO designator*]   (FAAC)
LOI .... Loss of Imprinting [*Genetics*]
LOICZ....... Land-Ocean Interaction in the Costal Zone [*International Geosphere Biosphere Programme*]
LOIS........... Legal Office Information System
LOM.......... SERTEL [*Servicios Telereservacios SA de CV*] [*ICAO designator*]   (FAAC)
LON........... London European Airways PLC [*British*] [*ICAO designator*]   (FAAC)
LOP .... Linton-on-Ouse FTU [*British*] [*ICAO designator*]   (FAAC)
LOP .... Locally-Originated Program [*Broadcasting*]   (NTCM)
LOR .... Likely Operational Range [*Navy*]   (ANA)
LOS .... Lossiemouth FTU [*British*] [*ICAO designator*]   (FAAC)
LOT .... Leak-Off Test
LOT .... Polskie Linie Lotnicze [*Poland*] [*ICAO designator*]   (FAAC)
LOV .... London Flight Centre (Stansted) Ltd. [*British*] [*ICAO designator*]   (FAAC)
L & P .... Latch and Plaster   (DAC)
LP .... Long Play [*VHS recorder mode*]   (NTCM)
LP .... Longest Perpendicular [*IOR*] [*Yacht racing*]
LPA .... Leather Producers' Association for England, Scotland, and Wales   (BI)
LPA .... PAL Aerolineas SA de CV [*Mexico*] [*ICAO designator*]   (FAAC)
LPDT......... Low Power Distress Transmitter [*Aviation*]   (DA)
LPE .... Lead Piping Engineer
LPF .... League for Programming Freedom   (EA)
LPFA .... Laminated Plastics Fabricators Association [*British*]   (BI)
LPG .... Liquid Propane-Gas Shutoff [*NFPA pre-fire planning symbol*]   (NFPA)
LPL .... Lease-A-Plane International [*ICAO designator*]   (FAAC)
LPMC......... Low-Pressure Molding Compound [*Environmental science*]
LPN .... Alpenair GmbH & Co. KG [*Austria*] [*ICAO designator*]   (FAAC)
LPO .... Lattice-Preferred Orientation [*Geophysics*]
LPR .... Linea Aerea Privadas Argentina [*ICAO designator*]   (FAAC)
LPT .... Local Public Transportation
LQR .... Local Qualitative Radio [*Ratings*]   (NTCM)
L + R .... Left plus Right [*Stereo signals*]   (NTCM)
L - R .... Left minus Right [*Stereo signals*]   (NTCM)
LRA .... Little Red Air Service [*Canada*] [*ICAO designator*]   (FAAC)
LRC............ Light Reflective Capacitor [*Electronics*]   (DA)
LRC............ Lineas Aereas Costarricenses SA [*Costa Rica*] [*ICAO designator*]   (FAAC)
LRC............ Long Range Communications   (NTCM)
LRD............ Laredo Air, Inc. [*ICAO designator*]   (FAAC)
LRDCT....... Linear Rotary Differential Capacitance Transducer [*Instrumentation*]
LRE............ Law-Related Education   (AEE)
LRE............ Library Resources Exhibition [*British*]
LRI............. Limited Range Intercept [*Telecommunications*] [*Navy*]   (ANA)
LRP............ Low Rigging Penalty [*IOR*] [*Yacht racing*]
LRR .... Lagged Reserve Requirement [*Finance*]
LRR .... Leucine-Rich Repeat [*Biochemistry*]
LRTx.......... Living Related Renal Transplantation [*Medicine*]
LSA............ Linea Aerea Nacional (Lansa) [*Dominican Republic*] [*ICAO designator*]   (FAAC)
LSALT........ Lowest Safe Altitude [*Aviation*]   (DA)
LSAS .... Longitudinal Stability Augmentation System [*Aviation*]   (DA)
LSB .... Lucas-Sumitomo Brakes [*Auto industry supplier*]
LSD............ League of Safe Drivers [*British*]   (BI)
LSD............ Low-Sulfur Diesel Fuel [*Petroleum marketing*]
LSDG......... Latitudinal Species-Diversity Gradient [*Biodiversity*]
LSE............ Luxembourg Stock Exchange
LSER .... Linear Solvation Energy Relationship [*Physical chemistry*]
LSF .... Load Sheet Fuel [*Aviation*]   (DA)
LSG........... Legal Services Group
LSR .... Alsair Societe [*France*] [*ICAO designator*]   (FAAC)
LSS .... Exec Express II, Inc. [*ICAO designator*]   (FAAC)
LSV .... Alak [*Former USSR*] [*ICAO designator*]   (FAAC)
LSY .... Lindsay Aviation, Inc. [*ICAO designator*]   (FAAC)
LT .... Last Telecast   (NTCM)
LT .... Turn Left after Takeoff [*Aviation*]   (FAAC)
LTA .... Linea Aerea Tama [*Chile*] [*ICAO designator*]   (FAAC)
LTBC.......... Lawn Tennis Ball Convention [*British*]   (BI)
LTC............ Longitudinal Time Code   (NTCM)
LTF .... Landline Telephony [*Aviation*]   (DA)
LTFC.......... Landing Traffic [*Aviation*]   (FAAC)
LTH .... Leather [*Automotive advertising*]

LTI............. Aerotaxis Latinoamericanos SA de CV [*Mexico*] [*ICAO designator*]   (FAAC)
LTIB .... Lead Technical Information Bureau [*British*]   (BI)
LTL............. Latvian Airlines [*ICAO designator*]   (FAAC)
LTMC........ Lymphoid Tissue Mononuclear Cell [*Physiology*]
LTMS........ Lubricant Test Monitoring System [*Automotive engineering*]
LTN .... Aerolineas Latinas CA [*Venezuela*] [*ICAO designator*]   (FAAC)
LTR............. AS Lufttransport [*Norway*] [*ICAO designator*]   (FAAC)
LTRCA .... Lawn Tennis Registered Coaches Association [*British*]   (BI)
LTS .... LTU [*Lufttransport Unternehmen Sud*] GmbH [*Germany*] [*ICAO designator*]   (FAAC)
LTU .... Long-Term Unemployed
LTU .... Lufttransport Unternehmen GmbH [*Germany*] [*ICAO designator*]   (FAAC)
LTV............. Load Threshold Value   (DA)
LTW .... Long-Term Waviness [*Surface finish*]
LTW .... NV Luchtvaartmaatschappij Twente [*Netherlands*] [*ICAO designator*]   (FAAC)
LTX............. Leo Taxi Aereo SA de CV [*Mexico*] [*ICAO designator*]   (FAAC)
LU .... Left Unity Group [*European political movement*]   (ECON)
LUB .... Lusiana [*Czechoslovakia*] [*ICAO designator*]   (FAAC)
LUP .... Lupenga Air Charters [*Zambia*] [*ICAO designator*]   (FAAC)
LUR .... Lineas Aereas Latur SA de CV [*Mexico*] [*ICAO designator*]   (FAAC)
LURTx .... Living Unrelated Renal Transplantation [*Medicine*]
LUS............. Lusitanair-Transportes Aereos Comercials SA [*Portugal*] [*ICAO designator*]   (FAAC)
LUX .... Lincoln Airlines, Inc. [*ICAO designator*]   (FAAC)
LVAD .... Low Velocity Air Drop [*Military vehicle specifications*]
LVAS.......... Light-Vehicle Animation Simulation [*Accident reconstruction*] [*Automotive engineering*]
LVCD .... Liquid Volume Charge Density [*Automotive fuel systems*]
LVDL.......... Licensed Victuallers' Defence League of England and Wales   (BI)
LVDS.......... Light-Vehicle Dynamics Simulation [*Accident reconstruction*] [*Automotive engineering*]
LVLP .... Large Virus-Like Particle
LW .... Low [*Automotive advertising*]
LW .... United States Law Week [*A publication*]   (NTCM)
LWA .... Liberian World Airlines, Inc. [*ICAO designator*]   (FAAC)
LWD........... Worldwide Airline Services, Inc. [*ICAO designator*]   (FAAC)
LWI .... LASER without Inversion
LWL............ Lambair Ltd. [*Canada*] [*ICAO designator*]   (FAAC)
LWS............ Lightweight Sports [*Concept car*] [*Automotive engineering*]
Lx................. Lux [*Unit of Illumination*]   (NTCM)
LXR .... Airluxor Ltda. [*Portugal*] [*ICAO designator*]   (FAAC)
LYA .... Lyon Air [*France*] [*ICAO designator*]   (FAAC)
LYN............ Lynton Aviation [*British*] [*ICAO designator*]   (FAAC)
LYR .... Layer Cloud [*Meteorology*]   (DA)

M

M............... Magnification (NTCM)
M............... Marine [*FCC*] (NTCM)
M............... Modification [*FCC*] (NTCM)
M............... Monograph
9M............. Malaysia [*Aircraft nationality and registration mark*] (FAAC)
M!a............. Mass Flow of Air [*Aviation*] (DA)
MA............. Mathematical Association [*British*] (BI)
MA............. Mountaineering Association [*British*] (BI)
MA............. Mutual Age
MAA........... Aerotransportes Mas de Carga SA de CV [*Mexico*] [*ICAO designator*] (FAAC)
MAA........... Manufacturers' Agents Association of Great Britain and Ireland (BI)
MAAC....... Mastic Asphalt Advisory Council [*British*] (BI)
MAB.......... Millardair Ltd. [*Canada*] [*ICAO designator*] (FAAC)
MAB.......... Monoclonal Antibody (ERG)
MAC.......... Malta Air Charter Co. Ltd. [*ICAO designator*] (FAAC)
MAC.......... Master Acoustical Console [*Army*]
MAC.......... Maximum Allowable Concentration [*Toxicology*]
MAC.......... Message Act Concellation (DA)
MACDAC ... Man Communication and Display for an Automatic Computer (PDAA)
MACH III ... Maintenance Aided Computer-HAWK-[*Homing All The Way Killer*]- Intelligence/Institutional/Instructor [*Military*]
MACHO..... Massive Compact Halo Objects [*Astronomy*]
MACOM.... Maintenance Assembly and Check-Out Model (PDAA)
MACS........ Management Administration Control System
MACS........ Media Account Control System (PDAA)
MACS........ Merchant Airship Cargo Satellite (PDAA)
MACS........ Migrant Advisory Committee
MAD.......... Major Air Disaster (PDAA)
MAD.......... Maple Air Services Ltd. [*Canada*] [*ICAO designator*] (FAAC)
MAD.......... Methylacridone [*Organic chemistry*]
MAD.......... Militarischer Abschirmdienst [*Military counterintelligence*] [*Germany*]
MADALINE ... Multi-Adaptive Linear Neuron (PDAA)
MADN....... Metropolitan Area Digital Network (NTCM)
MAE.......... Maersk Commuter IS [*Netherlands*] [*ICAO designator*] (FAAC)
MAE.......... Modified Anglia Engine [*Cosworth racing engines*]
MAE.......... Movement After-Effect (PDAA)
MAEF........ Mastic Asphalt Employers' Federation [*British*] (BI)
MAER .... Maximum Allowable Emission Rate [*Environmental Protection Agency*] (ERG)
MAER .... Mobile Ammunition and Reconditioning Unit [*Military*]
MAF .... Mission Aviation Fellowship [*Indonesia*] [*ICAO designator*] (FAAC)
MAF .... Movable Appendage Factor [*IOR*] [*Yacht racing*]
MAFIS .... Management Farm Information Service (PDAA)
MAFR........ Modified Anarchy Flood Routing (PDAA)
MAFTEP ... Method for Analysis of Fleet Tactical Effectiveness Performance [*Navy*] (PDAA)
MAG.......... Air Margarita [*Venezuela*] [*ICAO designator*] (FAAC)
Mag Bl........ Magical Blend [*A publication*]
MAGEN..... Matrix Generating and Reporting System [*Computer science*] (PDAA)
MAGFET... Magnetic Metal-Oxide-Semiconductor Field-Effect Transistor (PDAA)
MAGIC ..... Manual Assisted Gaming of Integrated Combat (PDAA)
MAGIC ..... Method for Asynchronous Graphics Integral Control [*Computer science*] (PDAA)
MAGSIM... Magnetic Shield Simulator (PDAA)
MAH .... Malev-Hungarian Airlines [*ICAO designator*] (FAAC)
MAI .... Air Moravia [*Czechoslovakia*] [*ICAO designator*] (FAAC)
MAI .... Mapper Application Interface [*Computer science*]
MAID......... Magnetic Anti-Intrusion Detector (PDAA)
MAID......... Multiple Aircraft Identification Display (PDAA)
MAIL........ MILES [*Multiple Integrated LASER Engagement System*] Action Item Log [*Army*]
MAINS...... Marine-Aided Inertial Navigation System (PDAA)
MAINSITE ... Modular Automated Integrated Systems / Interoperability Test and Evaluation (PDAA)
MAINTN ... Maintenance [*Automotive advertising*]
MAIS.......... Management Audit Information System

MAJ .... Majestic Airlines, Inc. [*ICAO designator*] (FAAC)
MAK......... Maliair Ltd. [*British*] [*ICAO designator*] (FAAC)
MAK......... Manual Abell-Kendall [*Clinical chemistry*]
MAK......... Methyl Amyl Ketone [*Organic chemistry*]
MAL .... Maximal Acceptable Load (PDAA)
MAL .... McAlpine Aviation Ltd. [*British*] [*ICAO designator*] (FAAC)
MALCD ..... Matrix-Addressed Liquid Crystal Display
MALDI...... Matrix-Assisted LASER Desorption/Ionization [*Spectrometry*]
MALN........ Minimum Air Low Noise (PDAA)
MALR........ Mortar/Artillery Locating RADAR (PDAA)
MALU .... Mode Annunciator and Logic Unit (PDAA)
MAM......... Matter-Anti-Matter (PDAA)
MAM......... Meta Aviotransport-Macedonia [*Yugoslavia*] [*ICAO designator*] (FAAC)
MAMA....... Multi-Anode Microchannel Array (PDAA)
MAMIS...... Mandatory Modification and Inspection Summary [*Aviation*] (DA)
MAMTF..... Mobile Automated Microwave Test Facility (PDAA)
MAN.......... Mannion Air Charter, Inc. [*ICAO designator*] (FAAC)
MANMAM ... Manufacturing Management (PDAA)
MANSA ..... Man-Made Soling Association Ltd. [*British*] (BI)
MANUPACS ... Manufacturing Planning and Control System (PDAA)
MAO.......... MAC Aviation SL [*Spain*] [*ICAO designator*] (FAAC)
MAO.......... Matair Ltd. [*British*] [*ICAO designator*] (FAAC)
MAO.......... Mechanization of Algebraic Operations (PDAA)
MAOA....... Monoamine Oxidase A [*An enzyme*]
MAOT........ Medium Aperture Optical Telescope (PDAA)
MAP.......... Machine Analyzer Package (PDAA)
MAP .... Medicare Advocacy Project
MAP .... Multibus Accounting Package (PDAA)
MAP .... National Oceanic and Atmospheric Administration [*ICAO designator*] (FAAC)
MAPAF...... Military Assistance Program Address File
MAPD....... Maximum Allowable Percent Defective (PDAA)
MAPLE...... Marketing and Product Line Evaluation (PDAA)
MAPLE...... Minor Atomic Prolonged Life Equipment (PDAA)
MAPPLE ... Macro-Associative Processor Programming Language [*Computer science*] (PDAA)
MAPS........ Meteorological Applied Problem Solving
MAPS........ Microprogramable Arithmetic Processor System (PDAA)
MAPS........ Migratory Animal Pathological Survey (PDAA)
MAPS........ Million Adds per Second
MAPS........ Multiple Agency Processing System
MAPS/ALPS ... Multiple Aim Point System / Alternate Launch Point System (PDAA)
MAPT........ Missed Approach Point [*Aviation*] (FAAC)
MAR......... Maintenance Action Request
MAR......... March Helicopters Ltd. [*British*] [*ICAO designator*] (FAAC)
MARAS..... Middle Airspace RADAR Advisory Service [*Military*] (DA)
MARC .... Maryland Automotive Reclamation Corp. [*Automotive materials recycling project*]
MARC .... Methodology for Assessing Radiological Consequences (PDAA)
MARC .... Monitoring and Risk Assessment Centre [*British*]
MARC .... Mutliple Access Remote Computing (PDAA)
MARCCO ... Master Real-Time Circulation Controller (PDAA)
MARCS...... Marine Computer System (PDAA)
MARD....... Military Aeronautical Research and Development (PDAA)
MARLAB... Mobile Air Research Laboratory (PDAA)
MARM....... Microprocessor Arithmetic Model
MARPEX... Management of Repair Parts Expenditure [*Army*] (PDAA)
MARRC ..... Multi-Channel Automatic Remote Recording
MARS........ Multiple Aerial Refueling System (PDAA)
MARSAS ... Marine Search and Attack System (PDAA)
Mart.......... Martinique
MAS .... Malaysian Airline System [*ICAO designator*] (FAAC)
MAS .... Medical Audit Statistics (PDAA)
MAS .... Micro-Alloyed Steel [*Metallurgical engineering*]
MAS .... Middle Air Space (PDAA)
MASA....... Multiple Anodic Stripping Analyzer (PDAA)
MASAR...... Microwave Accurate Surface Antenna Reflector (PDAA)
MASAR...... Multimode Airborne Solid-State Array RADAR System [*Military*] (PDAA)
MASB........ Main Array Signal Band

MASC......... Management Systems Concept (PDAA)
MASCO ..... Maintenance Schedule Code (PDAA)
MASCOM ... Master Communications (PDAA)
MASCOT... Management Advisory System using Computerized Optimization
	Techniques (PDAA)
MASEC..... Multi-Access Systems Control Terminal (PDAA)
MASES ..... Microcomputer Advice and Selection Expert System (PDAA)
MASH....... Micro-Analytic Simulation of Households (PDAA)
MASOA ..... Master and Slave Oscillator Array (PDAA)
MASPAC ... Microfilm Advisory Service of the Public Archives of Canada
	(PDAA)
MASR........ Microwave Atmosphere Sounding Radiometer (PDAA)
MASS........ MARC [Machine-Readable Cataloging] Automated Serials
	System (PDAA)
MASSOP ... Multi-Automatic System for Simulation and Operational
	Planning (PDAA)
MAST........ Machine Automated Speech Transcription (PDAA)
MAST........ Multiple-Aircraft Simulation Terminal (DA)
MASTACS ... Maneuverability Augmentation System for Tactical Air Combat
	Simulation (PDAA)
MAStat...... Master of Applied Statistics
MASTIFF ... Modular Automated System to Identify Friend from Foe
	[Military] (PDAA)
MASU .... Multiple Acceleration Sensor Unit (PDAA)
MAT .... Maine Aviation Corp. [ICAO designator] (FAAC)
MAT .... Missile Acquisition and Track
MAT .... Modular Allocation Technique (PDAA)
MAT .... Monoamine Transporter [Biochemistry]
MATA .... Multiple Answering Teaching Aid (PDAA)
MATADOR ... Mobile and Three-Dimensional Air Defense Operations
	RADAR [Military] (PDAA)
MATCH ..... Manned Attack Torpedo Carrying Helicopter (PDAA)
MATE .... Machine-Aided Translation Editing (PDAA)
MATE .... Manual Adaptive TMA [Target Motion Analysis] Estimator
	[Navy] (ANA)
MATE .... Memory-Assisted Terminal Equipment (PDAA)
MATE .... Meteorological Analog Test and Evaluation (PDAA)
MATIF ...... Marche a Terme des Instruments Financiers [French Financial
	Futures Market]
MATS........ Midcourse Airborne Target Signature [Military] (PDAA)
MAU.......... Air Mauritius Ltd. [ICAO designator] (FAAC)
MAV .... Max-Aviation [Canada] [ICAO designator] (FAAC)
MAV .... Mechanical Auxiliary Ventricle (PDAA)
MAVIS...... Master Vision Screener (PDAA)
MAVIS...... Microprocessor-Based Audio Visual Information System (PDAA)
MAVU...... Modular Audio Visual Unit (PDAA)
MAW......... Mustique Airways [Barbados] [ICAO designator] (FAAC)
MAWA...... Missile Attack Warning and Assessment [Military] (PDAA)
MAWP ...... Maximum Allowable Working Pressure (PDAA)
MAX......... Mediterranean Airlines SA [Greece] [ICAO designator] (FAAC)
MAX......... Mobile Automatic X-Ray (PDAA)
MAXNET... Modular Application Executive for Computer Networks (PDAA)
MAY .... Maya Airways Ltd. [Belize] [ICAO designator] (FAAC)
MAYC .... Methodist Association of Youth Clubs [British] (BI)
MAZ.......... Mines Air Service Zambia Ltd. [ICAO designator] (FAAC)
MB............. Memory Bank
MB............. Microbeam [Physics]
MB............. Mushroom Body [Nerve center in insects]
MBA .... Automobilvertriebs Aktiengesellschaft [Austria] [ICAO
	designator] (FAAC)
MBA .... Male Bonding Alert [Screenwriter's lexicon]
MBA .... Mantle Bouguer Anomaly [Geology]
MBA .... Many-Body Alloy [Metallurgy]
MBA ...... Milk Bars Association of Great Britain and Ireland Ltd. (BI)
MBAA .... Methylene Bisacrylamide (PDAA)
MBAV .... Main Battle Air Vehicle [Military] (PDAA)
MBDI .... Major Business Development Initiative
MBE .... Martin-Baker Ltd. [British] [ICAO designator] (FAAC)
MBE .... Metals-Based Engineering
MBEP......... Metals-Based Engineering Program
MBF .... Master Builders Federation [British] (BI)
MBF .... Musicians Benevolent Fund [British] (BI)
MBioEth.... Master of Bioethics
MBiotech.... Master of Biotechnology
MBMS....... Bachelor of Medicine, Master of Surgery
MBN.......... Mutual Black Network (NTCM)
MBO.......... Mobil Oil Ltd. [Canada] [ICAO designator] (FAAC)
MBRDC ..... Medical Bioengineering Research and Development Command
	[Army] (PDAA)
MBS.......... Mobile-Base Simulator (PDAA)
MBS........... Modular Banking System (PDAA)
MBSA........ Model-Based System Analysis (PDAA)
MBSD........ Multi-Barrel Smoke Discharger [Military] (PDAA)
MBT .... Modified Boiling Test (PDAA)
MBUMA .... Mean Time between Unscheduled Maintenance Actions
MBZ.......... Magnesia-Buffered Zinc Oxide (PDAA)
MBZ.......... Mandatory Broadcast Zone [Telecommunications] (DA)
MC............. Mail Chute (DAC)
MC............. Mass Communication (NTCM)
MC............. Materiel Change [Military]
MC............. Medicine Cabinet [Technical drawings] (NFPA)
MCA .... Marine Cranking Amperes [Battery] [Automotive engineering]
MCA .... Midcontinent Airlines, Inc. [ICAO designator] (FAAC)

MCACS...... Marine Centralized Automatic Control System (PDAA)
MCAE .... Mining, Construction, and Agricultural Equipment
MCA/FYP ... Military Construction, Army / Five Year Plan
MCANW.... Medical Campaign against Nuclear Weapons (PDAA)
MCAP .... Medical Commission on Accident Prevention (PDAA)
MCAP .... Microwave Circuit Analysis Package (PDAA)
MCAR .... Multichannel Acoustic Relay [Navy] (ANA)
MCC .... Manipulative Communications Cover [Military] (ADDR)
MCC .... Microclimatic Conditioning
MCC .... Morrison Commemorative Stamp Committee (EA)
MCCTA...... Manufacturing Confectioners' Commercial Travellers Association
	[British] (BI)
MCD.......... Air Medical Ltd. [British] [ICAO designator] (FAAC)
MCD.......... Metaphyseal Chondrodysplasia [Medicine]
MCE .... Marshall of Cambridge (Engineering) Ltd. [British] [ICAO
	designator] (FAAC)
MCF .... Measurement Compensation Factor (PDAA)
MCF .... Mission-Critical Function (PDAA)
MCFD .... Modular Chaff/Flare Dispenser (PDAA)
MCH.......... McAlpine Helicopters Ltd. [British] [ICAO designator] (FAAC)
MCH.......... Methylcyclohexanol [Organic chemistry]
MCHL .... Mayo Clinic Health Letter [A publication]
MCI .... Maya Carga Internacional SA de CV [Mexico] [ICAO
	designator] (FAAC)
MCI .... Multichip Integration [Computer science] (PDAA)
MCL .... Medical Aviation Services Ltd. [British] [ICAO designator]
	(FAAC)
MClBiochem ... Master of Clinical Biochemistry
MCLC........ Mine Clearing Line Charge [Army]
MCM.......... Heli-Air-Monaco [ICAO designator] (FAAC)
MCMA ...... Marine Corps Mustang Association (EA)
MCMH...... Mine Counter-Measures Hovercraft [Military] (PDAA)
MCN.......... Mac Dan Aviation Corp. [ICAO designator] (FAAC)
MCN.......... Master of Clinical Nutrition
MCO.......... Aerolineas Marcos SA de CV [Mexico] [ICAO designator]
	(FAAC)
MCODA..... Motor Cab Owner Drivers' Association [British] (BI)
MCOQ....... Multiple Choice Objective Question (DA)
MCQC....... Musicassette Quality Committee (NTCM)
MCR.......... Monacair-Agusta [Monaco] [ICAO designator] (FAAC)
MCRL........ Marine Corrosion Research Laboratory [Navy] (PDAA)
MCS .... Manpower Consultative Service [Canada] (PDAA)
MCS .... Mast Check System
MCS .... Maximal Compatible Set (PDAA)
MCS .... Mini Conference System (PDAA)
MCS .... Mobile Computer System
MCS/CHS ... Maneuver Control System / Common Hardware System
	[Computer science]
MCSS......... Mine Countermeasure Support Ship [Military] (PDAA)
MCT .... Magnetic Character Typewriter (PDAA)
MCT .... Metric Color Tag [Computer science] (PCM)
MCTAS....... Military/Commercial Transport Aircraft Simulation (PDAA)
MCU.......... Management Control Unit (PDAA)
MCU.......... Modular Concept Unit (DA)
MCV .... Microbial Check Valve (PDAA)
MD............. Mechanical Diode [Mechanical power transmission]
MD............. Migrant with English Language Difficulty
MD............. Music Director (NTCM)
MDA .... Malfunction Detector Analyzer (PDAA)
MDA .... Mandarian Airlines [ICAO designator] (FAAC)
MDA .... Millinery Distributors Association [British] (BI)
MDA .... Modified Diffusion Approximation (PDAA)
MDAC........ Medical Data Acquisition System
MDAP........ Morphological Dictionary Adaptor Program (PDAA)
MDB.......... Maintenance Data Bank
MDC.......... Atlantic Aero, Inc. [ICAO designator] (FAAC)
MDC.......... Military District Commander
MDCC........ Monaural Detection with Contralateral Cue (PDAA)
MDD.......... Maintenance Design Disclosure
MDDT........ Master Digital Data Tape (PDAA)
MDE .... Mission Defendent Experiment
M-DEMO ... Maintenance Demonstration [DoD]
MDF .... Midtfly Aps [Denmark] [ICAO designator] (FAAC)
MDG.......... Air Madagascar, Societe Nationale Malgache de Transports
	Aeriens [ICAO designator] (FAAC)
MDH .... Minimum Descent Height [Aviation] (FAAC)
MDH .... Multidirectional Harassment (PDAA)
MDIC .... Multi-Disciplinary Counter Intelligence
MDJ .... Jaro International SA [Romania] [ICAO designator] (FAAC)
MDL .... Mandala Airlines PT [Indonesia] [ICAO designator] (FAAC)
MDM......... Master of Development Management
MDM......... Michigan-Dartmouth-Massachusetts Institute of Technology
	[Observatory]
MDN .... Universair [Spain] [ICAO designator] (FAAC)
MDO.......... Macedonia AS [Yugoslavia] [ICAO designator] (FAAC)
MDP.......... Menthyldiphenyphosphine [Organic chemistry]
MDR.......... Compania Mexicana de Aeroplanos SA [Mexico] [ICAO
	designator] (FAAC)
MDR.......... Magnetic Disc Recorder (NTCM)
MDR.......... Munition Data Requirement
MDRSF ...... Multi-Dimensional Random Sea Facility [Hydraulics Research
	Station] (PDAA)
MDS .... Materiel Deployment Schedule

MDS .... Metal-Dielectric Semiconductor [*Electronics*] (PDAA)
MDS .... Metropolitan Dairymen's Society [*British*] (BI)
MDS .... Milford Docks Air Services Ltd. [*British*] [*ICAO designator*] (FAAC)
MDS .... Miller-Dieker Lissencephaly Syndrome [*Medicine*]
MDS .... Minuteman Defense Study [*DoD*]
MDS .... Mobile Data Service (DA)
MDSIC .... Metal-Dielectric-Semiconductor Integrated Circuit [*Electronics*] (PDAA)
MDT .... Compagnie Air Mediterrannee [*France*] [*ICAO designator*] (FAAC)
MDTL .... Modified Diode Transistor Logic [*Electronics*] (PDAA)
MDTP .... Materiel Developer's Test Program [*Military*]
MDU .... Medical Defence Union Ltd. [*British*] (BI)
MDW .... Midway Aviation, Inc. [*ICAO designator*] (FAAC)
ME .... Magneto-Electronic (PDAA)
ME .... Materials Evaluation (PDAA)
ME .... Moment Estimator (PDAA)
MEA .... Metropolitan Entertainers' Association [*British*] (BI)
MEA .... Middle East Airlines - Airliban [*Liberia*] [*ICAO designator*] (FAAC)
MEA .... Moisture Evaluation Analysis (PDAA)
MEACE ...... Military Engineering Applications of Commercial Explosives [*Army*] (PDAA)
MEAD .... Microbial Evaluation Analysis Device (PDAA)
MEC .... Materials Engineering Code
MEC .... Mercury Aircourier Service [*ICAO designator*] (FAAC)
MEC .... Microelectronics Center
MECA .... Missile Electronics and Computer Assembly [*Military*] (PDAA)
MECH/HYD ... Mechanical/Hydraulic
MECOM .... Marine Engine Condition Monitor (PDAA)
MED .... Multiformat Electroluminescent Display (PDAA)
MEDA .... Military Emergency Diversion Aerodrome (DA)
MEDAS ..... Microfilm Enhanced Data System (PDAA)
MEDIA ...... Man's Environments - Display Implication and Applications (PDAA)
MEDIA ...... Modular Electronic Digital Instrumentation Assemblies (PDAA)
Med Lat ..... Medieval Latin [*Language*]
Med L Rptr .. Media Law Reporter [*A publication*] (NTCM)
MEES .... Marine-Estuarine-Environmental Sciences (PDAA)
MEF .... Multi-Purpose Electric Furnace (PDAA)
MEG .... Megacycle (NTCM)
MEGAFLOPS ... Millions of Floating Point Operations per Second (PDAA)
MEHT .... Minimum Eye Height over Threshold [*Aviation*] (FAAC)
MEI .... Major End Item
MEIP .... Mean Effective Injection Pressure [*Diesel engines*]
MEJ .... Medjet International, Inc. [*ICAO designator*] (FAAC)
MEK .... Med-Trans of Florida, Inc. [*ICAO designator*] (FAAC)
MEM .... Magnetic Electron Multiplier (PDAA)
MEM .... Mirror Electron Microscope (PDAA)
MEMBERS ... Microprogrammed Experimental Machine with a Basic Executive for Real-Time Systems (PDAA)
MEMIC...... Mobile Eletromagnetic Incompatibility (PDAA)
MEMLZ..... Memorialize (ABBR)
MEMLZD ... Memorialized (ABBR)
MEMLZG ... Memorializing (ABBR)
MEMLZN ... Memorialization (ABBR)
MEMLZR ... Memorializer (ABBR)
MEN.......... Mennonite (ABBR)
MEN.......... Mense [*or Menses*] (ABBR)
MEN.......... Menstruation (ABBR)
MEN.......... Mensuration (ABBR)
MEN.......... [*E. C.*] Menzies Aviation Ltd. [*New Zealand*] [*ICAO designator*] (FAAC)
MENG........ Meaning (ABBR)
MENGF ..... Meaningful (ABBR)
MENGFY... Meaningfully (ABBR)
MENGLS... Meaningless (ABBR)
MENGLSY ... Meaninglessly (ABBR)
MENNON ... Mennonite (ABBR)
MENNS ..... Meanness (ABBR)
MENO....... Menorrhoea (ABBR)
MENP .... Menopause (ABBR)
MENPL..... Menopausal (ABBR)
MENS .... Missile Element Need Statement
MENSTD... Menstruated (ABBR)
MENSTG... Menstruating (ABBR)
MENSTL... Menstrual (ABBR)
MENSTN... Menstruation (ABBR)
MENT........ Mentalis (ABBR)
MENTNB... Mentionable (ABBR)
MENTND... Mentioned (ABBR)
MENTNG... Mentioning (ABBR)
MENTNR... Mentioner (ABBR)
MENTOR ... Mobile Electrical Network Testing, Observation, and Recording (PDAA)
MENTT....... Mentality (ABBR)
MENTY ..... Mentally (ABBR)
MEnvPlan .. Master of Environmental Planning
MEO.......... Scandinavian Aviation Center AS [*Denmark*] [*ICAO designator*] (FAAC)
MEOH .... Methyl Alcohol
MEP .... Maximum Economic Potential

MEP .... Maximum Entropy Principle (PDAA)
MEP .... Midwest Express Airlines, Inc. [*ICAO designator*] (FAAC)
MEP .... Mogul End Prong [*Lamp base*] (NTCM)
MEPA........ Marine and Estuarine Protected Area
MEPP .... Marine Electric Power Plant (PDAA)
MER .... Magneto-Elastic Resonance (PDAA)
MER .... Mechanical Equipment Room (DAC)
MER .... Methow Aviation, Inc. [*ICAO designator*] (FAAC)
MERC .... Mercurial (ABBR)
MERC .... Minimum Electrical Resistance Condition (PDAA)
MERCM ... Mercantilism (ABBR)
MERCT..... Mercantilist (ABBR)
MERI........ Medical Education Research and Information Database
MERID...... Meridian (ABBR)
MERIT...... Multiple RADAR-Integrated Tracking [*Military*] (PDAA)
MERITOC ... Meritocracy (ABBR)
MERITOC ... Meritocrat (ABBR)
MERLIN .... Management of Expenditure and Resident-Linked Information Network [*Computer science*]
MERPS ...... Multiple Event Record and Playback System (NTCM)
MERS........ Mobile Emergency Response Support
MERSAR .. Merchant Ship Search and Rescue (PDAA)
MERT........ Modified Effective-Range Theory (PDAA)
MES.......... Manufacturing Execution System [*Engineering*]
MES.......... Mesaba Aviation [*ICAO designator*] (FAAC)
MES.......... Mobile Earth Station (DA)
MESAB ..... Medical Education for South African Blacks [*An association*] (EA)
MESC........ Miniature Excitatory Synaptic Current [*Neurophysiology*]
MESGE...... Message (ABBR)
MESGER ... Messenger (ABBR)
MESM....... Mission Essential Subsystem Matrix [*Navy*] (ANA)
MEST........ Mestizo (ABBR)
MESTS...... Missile Electric System Test Set [*Military*] (PDAA)
MET .... Metallic [*Automotive advertising*]
MET .... Meteorological Research Flight [*British*] [*ICAO designator*] (FAAC)
META .... Model Engineering Trade Association [*British*] (BI)
METABC... Metabolic (ABBR)
METABZ... Metabolize (ABBR)
METABZD ... Metabolized (ABBR)
METABZG ... Metabolizing (ABBR)
METADS... Meteorological Acquisition and Display System (PDAA)
METAG ..... Meteorological Advisory Group [*ICAO*] (DA)
METAPH... Metaphysician (ABBR)
METAPHYS ... Metaphysic (ABBR)
MET & E .... Medical Equipment Test and Evaluation [*Army Medical Material Agency*] (PDAA)
METE........ Multiple Engagement Test Environment [*Military*] (PDAA)
METEOROLO ... Meteorology (ABBR)
METER...... Machine Examination Teaching, Evaluation, and Re-education (PDAA)
METH .... Methadone (ABBR)
METH .... Methamphetamine (ABBR)
METH .... Methylmeth (ABBR)
METH .... Methyprylon (ABBR)
METHC .... Methodic (ABBR)
METHO.... Methodology (ABBR)
METHOG ... Methodology (ABBR)
METHOGL ... Methodological (ABBR)
METHZ ..... Methodize (ABBR)
METHZD ... Methodized (ABBR)
METIC...... Meticulous (ABBR)
METRA...... Multiple-Event Time Recording Apparatus (PDAA)
METRO ..... Metering and Traffic Recording with Offline Processing (PDAA)
METROPOL ... Metropolis [*or Metropolitan*] (ABBR)
MEUA .... Million European Units of Account (PDAA)
MeVEMsJ ... Mercury, Venus, Earth, Mars, Jupiter (PDAA)
MEW .... Mean Equivalent Wind [*Meteorology*] (DA)
MEX .... Metro Express II, Inc. [*ICAO designator*] (FAAC)
MEZN....... Mezzanine (ABBR)
MEZT........ Mezzotint [*Printing*] (ABBR)
MEZZ........ Mezzotint [*Printing*] (ABBR)
MEZZO ..... Mezzosoprano (ABBR)
MF .... Mandatory Frequency (DA)
M!f .... Mass Flow of Fuel [*Aviation*] (DA)
MF .... Modifying Factor [*Toxicology*]
MFA .... Minimum Flight Altitude [*Aviation*] (DA)
MFA .... Motor Factors Association [*British*] (BI)
MFAD .... Maneuver Force Air Defense
MFB .... Mass Fraction Burn [*Automotive engine combustion analysis*]
MFC .... Membrane Fecal Coliform (PDAA)
MFC .... Moncton Flying Club [*Canada*] [*ICAO designator*] (FAAC)
MFC .... Multi-Frequency Code [*Telecommunications*] (DA)
MFCD .... Modular Flare Chaff Dispenser [*Military*] (PDAA)
MFC/LB..... Multi-Frequency / Local Battery [*Telecommunications*] (DA)
MFCS........ Mathematical Foundation of Computer Science (PDAA)
MFCS........ Medical Function Control System (PDAA)
M²FCS....... Multi-Microprocessor Flight Control System (PDAA)
MFD .... Malfunctioning Display (DA)
MFD .... Multistage Flash Distillation (PDAA)
MFDCC...... Marine Fire Detection Control Center
MFE .... Mean Fibre Extent (PDAA)

MFE .... Moire Fringe Effect   (PDAA)
MFES .... Main Fixed Earth Station [*NASA*]   (PDAA)
MFFLR ...... Muffler [*Automotive advertising*]
MFHA .... Masters of Foxhounds Association [*British*]   (BI)
MFI............ Metal-Finishing Industy
MFI............ Multi-point Fuel Injection
MFIE .... Magnetic Field Integral Equation   (PDAA)
MFL........... Maintenance-Free Lifetime   (PDAA)
MFL........... Master Force List [*DoD*]
MFLIC .... Modified Fluid in Cell [*Automotive engine combustion analysis*]
MFLOP ...... Mega-Floating Point Operation
MFM .... Materials Flow Management [*Manufacturing*]
MFMBARS ... Multi-Function, Multi-Band Airborne Radio System   (PDAA)
MFN .... Metabolic Fecal Nitrogen   (PDAA)
MFN .... Muffin   (ABBR)
MFOT .... Mean Forced Outage Time   (PDAA)
MFPA .... Monolithic Focal Plane Array   (PDAA)
MFPE .... Minimum Final Prediction Error   (PDAA)
MFR .... Master Frequency Record [*FCC list*]   (NTCM)
MFRD .... Manufactured   (ABBR)
MFRR........ Manufacturer   (ABBR)
MFRT .... Modulated Frequency Radio Telephone   (PDAA)
MFRY........ Manufactory   (ABBR)
MFS........... Miller Flying Services, Inc. [*ICAO designator*]   (FAAC)
MFSTB ...... Manifestable   (ABBR)
MFSTD ..... Manifested   (ABBR)
MFSTG ..... Manifesting   (ABBR)
MFSTN ..... Manifestation   (ABBR)
MFSTO ..... Manifesto   (ABBR)
MFT .... Multiprogramming with a Finite Amount of Trouble [*Computer science*]
MFTL........ My Favorite Toy Language [*Computer hacker terminology*]   (NHD)
MFUSYS.... Microfiche File Update System [*Computer science*]   (PDAA)
MFV .... Forward Visibility More than ___ Miles [*Aviation*]   (FAAC)
MFXT........ Meter Fix Time [*Aviation*]   (FAAC)
MFY .... Manufactory   (ABBR)
MG............. Milligauss   (ABBR)
MG............. Mug   (ABBR)
MGA........... Marble and Granite Association [*British*]   (BI)
MGA........ Mother Guardian Allowance
MGAD........ Machine-Gun Artillery Division [*Former USSR*]
MGALS..... Milligals   (ABBR)
MGB.......... Manageable   (ABBR)
MGBT .... Manageability   (ABBR)
MGBY .... Manageably   (ABBR)
MGC.......... Magec Aviation Ltd. [*British*] [*ICAO designator*]   (FAAC)
MGC.......... Magic   (ABBR)
MGCL....... Magical   (ABBR)
MGCLY..... Magically   (ABBR)
MGCN....... Magician   (ABBR)
MGCS .... Meteosat Ground Computer System [*Aviation*]   (DA)
MGCYL..... Megacycle   (ABBR)
MGD.......... Mugged   (ABBR)
MGD.......... North-East Cargo Airlines [*Russian Federation*] [*ICAO designator*]   (FAAC)
MGE.......... Manage   (ABBR)
MGEB .... Manageable   (ABBR)
MGEBT..... Manageability   (ABBR)
MGEBY..... Manageably   (ABBR)
MGED....... Managed   (ABBR)
MGEG....... Managing   (ABBR)
MGENT ..... Management   (ABBR)
MGER....... Manager   (ABBR)
MGERL..... Managerial   (ABBR)
MGF .... Macrophage Growth Factor   (PDAA)
MGG.......... Managing   (ABBR)
MGG.......... Monopropellant Gas Generator   (PDAA)
MGG.......... Mugging   (ABBR)
MGINS...... Mugginess   (ABBR)
MGIR .... Motor Glider Instructor Rating [*Aviation*]   (DA)
MGL.......... Mingle   (ABBR)
MGL.......... Mongolian Airlines [*ICAO designator*]   (FAAC)
MGL.......... Mongrel   (ABBR)
MGLD....... Mingled   (ABBR)
MGLG....... Mingling   (ABBR)
MGLMNA ... Megalomania   (ABBR)
MGLMNAC ... Megalomaniac   (ABBR)
MGLPS...... Megalopolis   (ABBR)
MGM.......... MGM Grand Air, Inc. [*ICAO designator*]   (FAAC)
MGMA....... Magma   (ABBR)
MGMR....... Ministry of Geology and Mineral Resources [*China*]
MGN .... Magazine   (ABBR)
MGN .... Mendial Geniculate Nucleus   (PDAA)
MGN .... Micrograin   (ABBR)
MGN .... Morgan Aviation Services Ltd. [*Nigeria*] [*ICAO designator*]   (FAAC)
MGNAN .... Margination   (ABBR)
MGNETC ... Magnetic   (ABBR)
MGNETCY ... Magnetically   (ABBR)
MGNETMTR ... Magnetometer   (ABBR)
MGNETSM ... Magnetism   (ABBR)
MGNETZ... Magnetization   (ABBR)

MGNETZ... Magnetize [*or Magnetized*]   (ABBR)
MGNFI ...... Magnify   (ABBR)
MGNFIB.... Magnifiable   (ABBR)
MGNFID ... Magnified   (ABBR)
MGNFIG... Magnifying   (ABBR)
MGNFIN ... Magnification   (ABBR)
MGNFIR... Magnifier   (ABBR)
MGNFNC.. Magnificence   (ABBR)
MGNFNT ... Magnificent   (ABBR)
MGNFTY... Magnificently   (ABBR)
MGNIA ..... Marginalia   (ABBR)
MGNLT ..... Marginality   (ABBR)
MGNLY .... Marginally   (ABBR)
MGNMT.... Magnanimity   (ABBR)
MGNMU ... Magnanimous   (ABBR)
MGNT ...... Magnate   (ABBR)
MGNT....... Magnet   (ABBR)
MGNTUD ... Magnitude   (ABBR)
MGOS...... Metal-Glass-Oxide-Silicon   (PDAA)
MGOT....... Maggot   (ABBR)
MGPHN.... Megaphone   (ABBR)
MGR......... Micro-Graphic Reporting   (PDAA)
MGR.......... Mugger   (ABBR)
MGRA ...... Migrate   (ABBR)
MGRAD .... Migrated   (ABBR)
MGRAG ... Migrating   (ABBR)
MGRAN.... Migration   (ABBR)
MGRATR... Migrator   (ABBR)
MGRATRY ... Migratory   (ABBR)
MGRL .... Managerial   (ABBR)
MGRN....... Migration   (ABBR)
MGRNL .... Migrational   (ABBR)
MGRT....... Migrant   (ABBR)
MGRTY .... Migratory   (ABBR)
MGSTL...... Magisterial   (ABBR)
MGSTRA ... Magistrate   (ABBR)
MGT.......... Margate Air Services [*South Africa*] [*ICAO designator*]   (FAAC)
MGTIR...... Mightier   (ABBR)
MGTIST ... Mightiest   (ABBR)
MGTNS ..... Mightiness   (ABBR)
MGTY .... Mighty   (ABBR)
MGY......... Muggy   (ABBR)
MHA .... Mansion House Association on Transport, Inc. [*British*]   (BI)
MHA .... Methodist Homes for the Aged [*British*]   (BI)
MHA .... Mountain High Aviation [*ICAO designator*]   (FAAC)
MHA .... Mutual Households Associations Ltd. [*British*]   (BI)
MHDG....... Magnetohydrodynamic Generator   (PDAA)
MHDL....... Magnetohydrodynamic LASER   (PDAA)
MHE......... Mean Hook Extent   (PDAA)
MHEA....... Mechanical Handling Engineers' Association [*British*]   (BI)
MHG .... Message Header Generator   (PDAA)
M of Hist ... Magazine of History [*A publication*]
MHME....... More Heart More Edge [*Screenwriter's lexicon*]
MHO .... Millhouse Developments Ltd. [*British*] [*ICAO designator*]   (FAAC)
MHO .... Minehunter Ocean [*Navy*]   (ANA)
MHPE....... Methoxy-Hydroxyphenylethanol [*Organic chemistry*]   (MAH)
MHSO....... Minehunter Sweeper Ocean [*Navy*]   (ANA)
MHSS .... Military Health Service System
MHT......... Main Himalayan Thrust [*Geology*]
MHW-RTG ... Multi-Hundred-Watt Radioisotope Thermoelectric Generator   (PDAA)
MI.............. Michelson Interferometer   (PDAA)
MI.............. Missionary Internship [*An association*]   (EA)
MI.............. Motorola Interconnect [*Electronics*]
MI.............. Multi-Industry Interest
MIA .... AMI (Air Mercury International) [*Belgium*] [*ICAO designator*]   (FAAC)
MIALS ...... Medium Intensity Approach Light System [*Aviation*]   (DA)
MIBAR...... Multi-Channel In-Band Airborne Relay   (PDAA)
MIC .... Aerolineas de Michoacan [*Mexico*] [*ICAO designator*]   (FAAC)
MIC .... Magnesium Industry Council [*British*]   (BI)
MIC .... Military Introductory Letter
MICA .... Major Incidents Computer Application   (PDAA)
MICAM .... Mid-Function Integral Control Alarm Module [*Electronics systems*] [*Automotive engineering*]
MICO........ Mankato Industrial Corp. [*Automotive industry supplier*]
MICRA...... Miniature Insulated Contact Range   (PDAA)
MICRADS ... Microwave Radiation System   (PDAA)
MICROSID ... Small Seismic Intrusion Detector   (PDAA)
MICS........ Medical Instrument Calibration System   (PDAA)
MIDAS...... Mechanism Integration Design and Analysis System [*Computer-assisted engineering*]
MIDAS...... Microscopic Image Digital Acquisition System   (PDAA)
MIDB....... Misr Iran Development Bank
MIDF........ Multiple Input Describing Function   (PDAA)
MIDOR..... Miss Distance Optical Recorder [*Military*]   (PDAA)
MIE.......... Management Improvement and Evaluation
MIEM .... Master in International Economics and Management   (ECON)
MIFF .... Management Information Format File [*Computer science*]
MIGB........ Millinery Institute of Great Britain
MIGS......... Music Industries Golfing Society [*British*]   (BI)
MILES .... Magnetic Intrusion Line Sensor   (PDAA)

MILES/AGES ... Multiple-Integrated LASER Engagement Simulation / Air Ground Engagement Simulator
MILIC .... Millimeter Insular Line Integrated Circuit (PDAA)
MILOC ...... Military Oceanography (PDAA)
MILPOD.... Mixed Integer and Linear Programming Open Deck (PDAA)
MIM .... Metal Injection Molding [*Metal fabrication*]
MIM .... Minimum (DA)
MIMIC ...... Microfilm Information Master Image Converter (PDAA)
MIMICS ..... Micromodule Microprogrammed Computer System (PDAA)
MIN .... Mine Identification and Neutralization (PDAA)
MINERVA ... Minimization of Earthworks for Vertical Alignment (PDAA)
MINI .... Method of Implicit Nonstationary Iteration (PDAA)
MINNEMAST ... Minnesota School Mathematics and Science Teaching Project [*University of Minnesota*] (AEE)
MINOS ...... Mine Operating System (PDAA)
MINOS ...... Mixed Integer Operational Scheduling (PDAA)
MINQUE ... Minimum Norm Quadratic Unbiased Estimation [*Statistics*] (PDAA)
MIO .... Midas Commuter Airlines CA [*Venezuela*] [*ICAO designator*] (FAAC)
MIP .... Marche International des Programmes de Television International [*International Marketplace for Buyers and Sellers of Television Programs*] (NTCM)
MIPAS .... Management Information Planning and Accountancy Service (PDAA)
MIPB .... Monoisopropylbiphenyl (PDAA)
MIPVCE .... Multiple-Input Phase-Variable Canonical Form (PDAA)
MIR .... Maximum Incremental Reactivity [*Exhaust emissions*] [*Automotive engineering*]
MIR .... Miramichi Air Services Ltd. [*Canada*] [*ICAO designator*] (FAAC)
MIRAC ...... Microfilmed Reports and Accounts (PDAA)
MIRADS ..... Marshall [*Space Flight Center*] Information Retrieval and Display System [*NASA*] (PDAA)
MIRID .... Monostatic Infrared Intrusion Detector (PDAA)
MIRS .... Micro Interactive Retrieval System (PDAA)
MIRS .... Multi-purpose Infrared Sight (PDAA)
MIRSIM .... Mineral Resource Simulation Model (PDAA)
MIRV .... Multiple Independently-Guided Re-entry Vehicle [*NASA*] (PDAA)
MIS........... Management Information Strategy
MIS........... Merchandise Information System (PDAA)
MIS........... Midstate Airlines, Inc. [*ICAO designator*] (FAAC)
MIS........... Multicultural Information Strategy
MISA......... Municipal and Industry Strategy for Abatement
MISAR .... Miniature Information Storage and Retrieval (PDAA)
MISER .... Management Information System for Expenditure Reporting (PDAA)
MISER .... Mean Integral Square Error (PDAA)
MISER .... Miniature, Indicating and Sampling Electronic Respirometer (PDAA)
MISI .... Multipath Intersymbol Interference (PDAA)
MISR......... Multi-Impact Signature Register (PDAA)
MISS .... Multi-Input-Safety-Shutdown (PDAA)
MIST .... Music Information System for Theorists (PDAA)
MIT .... Miller Air Transporters [*ICAO designator*] (FAAC)
MITLS .... Man-in-the-Loop Simulator [*Military*]
MITS......... Multiplex Information Transfer System (PDAA)
MIV .... Mi-Avia [*Russian Federation*] [*ICAO designator*] (FAAC)
MIW .... Airborne of Sweden AB [*ICAO designator*] (FAAC)
MJA .... Merchant Jewellers' Association Ltd. [*British*] (BI)
MJD .... Management Job Description (PDAA)
MJN .... Royal Air Force of Oman (Air Transport) [*ICAO designator*] (FAAC)
MKA .... MK Aircargo [*British*] [*ICAO designator*] (FAAC)
MKM........ Myopic Keratomileusis (PDAA)
MKO........ Makung Airlines [*Taiwan*] [*ICAO designator*] (FAAC)
MKY......... Monky Aerotaxis SA [*Mexico*] [*ICAO designator*] (FAAC)
ML........... Main Lobe
ML........... Manipulator Language [*Computer science*]
ML........... Missile Lethality [*Military*]
ML........... Modified License [*FCC*] (NTCM)
MLA .... Forty-Mile Air [*ICAO designator*] (FAAC)
MLA .... Master Locksmiths Association [*British*] (BI)
MLAGB..... Muzzle Loaders Association of Great Britain (BI)
MLC .... Missile Logistics Center [*Army*]
MLCS........ Multilayer Ceramic Substrates [*Electronic circuit boards*]
MLD .... Air Moldova [*ICAO designator*] (FAAC)
MLD .... Maximum Lateral Damage (PDAA)
MLDD........ Mooring Leg Deployment Device (PDAA)
MLDLP...... Mailing Label and Directory Lookup Package (PDAA)
MLH.......... Minimum List Heading [*Standard Industrial Classification*] (PDAA)
MLIS .... Metal-Liquid-Insulator Semiconductor [*Electronics*] (PDAA)
MLLFT ...... Modified Lensless Fourier Transform (PDAA)
MLLWL..... Mean Lower Low Water Line [*Tides and currents*] (PDAA)
MLM .... Membrane Light Modulator (PDAA)
MLMA .... Miners' Lamp Manufacturers' Association [*British*] (BI)
MlInd .... Maximum Landing Weight [*Aviation*] (DA)
MLO .... Media Liaison Officer
MLP .... Multi-Layered Packaging (PDAA)
MLPS .... Myxoid Liposarcoma [*Genetics*]

MLRS ER.... Multiple Launch Rocket System Extended Range Rocket [*Military*]
MLRV .... Manned Lunar Roving Vehicle [*NASA*] (PDAA)
MLS........... Mall Airways, Inc. [*ICAO designator*] (FAAC)
MLS........... Mixed Language System (PDAA)
MLS........... Multi-Layer Steel [*Engine gaskets*] [*Automotive engineering*]
MLU .... Montlucon Air Service [*France*] [*ICAO designator*] (FAAC)
MLWA .... Maximum Landing Weight Authorized [*Aviation*] (DA)
M/M.......... Man/Machine
MM............ Metered Market Service [*A. C. Nielsen Co.*] (NTCM)
MM............ Middle Manager
MMA.......... Metro Manila Airways International, Inc. [*Philippines*] [*ICAO designator*] (FAAC)
MMAP ...... Microwave Multi-Application Payload [*NASA*] (PDAA)
MMAS .... Manufacturing Management Accounting System (PDAA)
MMAS .... Mini-Manned Aircraft System (PDAA)
MMBB .... Molecular Marine Biology and Biotechnology [*A publication*]
MMCS .... Mitsubishi Multi-Communication System [*Driver information system*]
MMCTS..... Material Management Center Theater Supply [*Army*]
MMD......... Middle Management Development
MMD......... Mini-Module Drive (PDAA)
MMD......... Multi-Effect Multistage Distillation (PDAA)
MMDP...... Middle Management Development Program
MMDR...... Microcircuit Module, Driver/Receiver
MMedAnaes ... Master of Medicine (Anaesthesia)
MMedCardiol ... Master of Medicine (Cardiology)
MMed(CM) ... Master of Medicine (Community Medicine)
MMedEd .... Master of Medical Education
MMedPaed ... Master of Medicine (Paediatrics)
MMedPath ... Master of Medicine (Pathology)
MMedRadD ... Master of Medicine (Diagnostic Radiology)
MMedVen ... Master of Medicine (Venereology)
MMEL .... Master Minimum Equipment List (DA)
MMFCS..... Multi-Missile Fire Control System [*Military*]
MMFITB ... Man-Made Fibres Producing Industry Training Board [*British*] (BI)
MMH .... Mikromatika Air Cargo Ltd. [*Hungary*] [*ICAO designator*] (FAAC)
MMIPS...... Man-Machine Interactive Processing System (PDAA)
MMIPS...... Multiple Mode Integrated Propulsion System (PDAA)
MMM........ Margaret Morris Movement [*British*] (BI)
MMM........ Marine & Aviation Management International [*British*] [*ICAO designator*] (FAAC)
MMME...... Martin Marietta Missile Electronics Division [*Military*]
MMMS ...... Martin Marietta Missile System [*Military*]
M!mo........ Maximum Operating Mach Number [*Aviation*] (DA)
MMO .... Methane Monooxygenase [*An enzyme*]
MMP......... Modular Midcourse Package [*DoD*]
MMR........ Method of Mixed Ranges (PDAA)
MMRC....... Mental Retardation Research Center
MMS .... Maintenance Management System
MMS .... Minimum Mean Square (PDAA)
MMT......... Military Maintenance Technician
MMT......... Monolithic Mirror Telescope
MMT......... Morse Mission Trainer
MMU .... Million Monetary Units (PDAA)
MMU .... Monolithic Memory Unit
MMUD ...... Monolithic Memory Unit Diagnostic
MNA.......... Merpati Nusantara Airlines PT [*Indonesia*] [*ICAO designator*] (FAAC)
MNAA....... Molecular Neutron Activation Analysis
MNC.......... MIT Airlines Ltd. [*ICAO designator*] (FAAC)
MNC.......... Multinational Company [*Business term*]
MNFP .... Multiple Number of Faults per Pass (PDAA)
MNG .... Modulated Noise Generator (PDAA)
MNH .... Monarch Airlines [*ICAO designator*] (FAAC)
MNL.......... Miniliner SRL [*Italy*] [*ICAO designator*] (FAAC)
MNLS........ Modified New Least Square (PDAA)
MNMIC.... Modernized National Military Intelligence Center
MNP......... Microcone Networking Protocol
MNPS........ Minimum Navigation Performance Specification [*Aviation*] (FAAC)
MNPSA....... Minimum Navigation Performance Specification Airspace [*Aviation*] (FAAC)
MNR.......... Monair SA [*Switzerland*] [*ICAO designator*] (FAAC)
MNRF .... Moonroof [*Automotive advertising*]
MNS .... Ministic Air [*Canada*] [*ICAO designator*] (FAAC)
MNT.......... Maintained [*Automotive advertising*]
MNT.......... Montserrat Airways Ltd. [*Antigua and Barbuda*] [*ICAO designator*] (FAAC)
MNX.......... Manx Airlines Ltd. [*British*] [*ICAO designator*] (FAAC)
MO .... Maize Oil (PDAA)
MO .... March Order [*Military*]
MO .... Microwave Oven (PDAA)
MOABWEPO ... Members of Anything Bill [*Clinton*] Was Ever Part Of [*Pronounced "Mo-ab-wee-po"*]
MOBS .... Mobile Ocean Basing System (PDAA)
MOC.......... Manufacturing Outreach Center
MOC.......... Maximum Operational Capacity [*Chemical engineering*]
MOC.......... Minimum Obstacle Clearance [*Aviation*] (FAAC)
MOC.......... Modular Organization Charting (PDAA)

MODCON ... Man Machine System for the Optimum Design and Construction of Buildings (PDAA)
Model R ...... Model Railroader [*A publication*]
ModGr .... Modern Greek [*Language*]
MODIA .... Method of Designing Instructional Alternatives (PDAA)
MODIL ...... Manufacturing Operations Development and Integration Laboratory
ModL .... Modern Latin [*Language*]
MOD PRAESC ... Modo Praescripto [*In the Manner Prescribed*] [*Latin*] [*Pharmacy*] (MAH)
MODR......... Microwave Optical Double Resonance (PDAA)
MOE........... Margin of Exposure [*Toxicology*]
MOE........... Maximum Output Entropy (PDAA)
MOFA .... Multi-Option Fuze, Artillery
MOG .... Machinery of Government
MOG .... Medical Oncology Group
MOH .... Tigerfly [*British*] [*ICAO designator*] (FAAC)
MOIRA ...... Model of International Relations in Agriculture (PDAA)
MOL........... Maximum Overall Length (DAC)
MOLE .... Market Odd-Lot Execution (PDAA)
MOLEM .... Mobile Lunar Excursion Module [*NASA*] (PDAA)
MOLP .... Multiple Objective Linear Programming [*Computer science*] (PDAA)
MON .... Monarch Airlines Ltd. [*British*] [*ICAO designator*] (FAAC)
MO & O....... Memorandum Opinion and Order (NTCM)
MOP.......... Maintenance of Property
MOP.......... Minute of Program [*Broadcasting*] (NTCM)
MOP.......... Model Office Project
MOPA .... Mail Order Publisher Authority (PDAA)
MOPS .... Minimum Operational Performance Standard [*Aviation*] (DA)
MOPSY...... Multi-Programming Operating System [*Computer science*] (PDAA)
MOPTARS ... Multi-Object Phase-Tracking and Ranging System [*FAA*] (PDAA)
MOR.......... AS Morefly [*Norway*] [*ICAO designator*] (FAAC)
MOR.......... Maximum Ozone Reactivity [*Exhaust emissions*] [*Automotive engineering*]
MOR.......... Meteorological Optical Range (PDAA)
MORA....... Mimimum Off-Route Altitude [*Aviation*] (DA)
MORD....... Magneto-Optic Rotary Dispersion (PDAA)
MORF .... Male or Female (NHD)
MORP .... Mid-Ocean Ridge Peridotite [*Geology*]
MOS.......... Machinery and Occupational Safety Act [*Environmental science*]
MOS.......... MISR Overseas Airways [*Egypt*] [*ICAO designator*] (FAAC)
MOS.......... Multiple Object Spectroscopy (PDAA)
MOSAIC.... Method of Scenic Alternative Impacts by Computer (PDAA)
MOSAICS ... Melcom Optical Software Applications for Integrated Commercial Systems (PDAA)
MOSASR .... Metal Oxide Semiconductor Analogue Shift Register [*Electronics*] (PDAA)
MOSCAP... Modified Service Contract and Procedures [*DoD*]
MOSES...... Molecular Orbital Self-Consistent Energy System (PDAA)
MOSFETS ... Metal Oxide Substrate Field Effect Transistor
MOST .... Mothers of Super Twins [*Military*]
MOT.......... Aeromonterrey SA [*Mexico*] [*ICAO designator*] (FAAC)
MOTAS..... Member of the Appropriate Sex (NHD)
MOTE .... Measure of Training Effectiveness [*Military*]
MOTOS ..... Member of the Opposite Sex (NHD)
MOTSS..... Member of the Same Sex (NHD)
MOW........ Mohawk Airlines [*ICAO designator*] (FAAC)
MOWOS.... Meteorological Office Weather Observing System (PDAA)
MOZ.......... Aerocharter GmbH [*Austria*] [*ICAO designator*] (FAAC)
MP............ Material Professional [*Army*]
MP............ Message Processor
MP............ Modified Construction Permit [*FCC*] (NTCM)
MP............ Motion Picture (NTCM)
MPA .... Magazine Publisher's Association (NTCM)
MPA .... Master Photographers Association of Great Britain (BI)
MPA .... Mid Pacific Air Corp. [*ICAO designator*] (FAAC)
MPA .... Multiple Product Announcement (NTCM)
MPAA .... Musical Performing Arts Association (NTCM)
MPaed .... Master of Paediatrics
MPASK...... Multi-Phase and Amplitude-Shift-Keying [*Computer science*] (PDAA)
MPC .... Marginal Producers Cost [*Engineering economics*]
MPC .... Mother-of-Pearl Clouds [*Meteorology*] (PDAA)
MPC .... Mountain Pacific Air Ltd. [*Canada*] [*ICAO designator*] (FAAC)
MPC .... Multielectron Photoactive Center [*Physical chemistry*]
MPCF........ Millions of Particles per Cubic Foot (PDAA)
MPDE........ Maximum Permissible Dose Equivalent (ERG)
MPDS........ Missile Piercing Discarding Sabot (PDAA)
MPDS........ Multi-Purpose Display System (DA)
MPE/S .... Maritime Prepositioned Equipment and Supplies [*Navy*] (ANA)
MPF .... Major Project Funding
MPGA .... Metropolitan Public Gardens Association [*British*] (BI)
MPH.......... Martinair Holland NV [*Netherlands*] [*ICAO designator*] (FAAC)
MPHC........ Metal-Skinned, Paper-Honeycomb Cored (PDAA)
MPHP .... Multiple-Pass Heuristic Procedure (PDAA)
MPI .... Maximum Precipitation Intensity [*Meteorology*] (PDAA)
mpl .... Maple (DAC)
MPL .... Master Planner, Inc. [*ICAO designator*] (FAAC)
MPL .... Mathematical Programming Language [*Computer science*] (PDAA)

MPL .... Micro Power Light [*Automotive lighting*]
MP/L......... Modified Construction Permit and License [*FCC*] (NTCM)
MPLAW.... Melamine Paper Laminate (PDAA)
MPLAW.... Modified Programmers Language [*Computer science*] (PDAA)
MPLAW.... Moving Part Logic (PDAA)
MPLAW.... Multipulse Scaling-Law Code using Data Base Interpolation (PDAA)
MPLG........ Multi-Purpose Lithium Grease
MPLPC ...... Multipulse Linear Productive Coding (PDAA)
MPLSM .... Multiple Position Letter Sorting Machine (PDAA)
MP/M .... Multiprogramming Control Program for Microcomputers
MPMA ...... Motion Picture Museum Association [*British*] (BI)
MPMG ...... Multi-Purpose Molybdenum Grease
MP/ML..... Modified Construction Permit and Modified License [*FCC*] (NTCM)
MPMO ...... Motion Picture Machine Operator [*A union*] (NTCM)
MPNE .... Manpower Needs [*Military*]
MPP .... Marine Power Plant (PDAA)
MPPM ...... Materials-Process-Product Model (PDAA)
MPQ .... Manpower Planning Quota (PDAA)
MPR .... Military Photo-Reconnaissance (PDAA)
MPR .... Minimum Processing Requirement
MPRST ..... Maximum Probability Ratio Sequential Test (PDAA)
MPS .... Material Planning System [*Manufacturing management*]
MPS .... Minimum Performance Specification (DA)
MPS .... Mixed Potential System (PDAA)
MPSG........ Multi-Band Portable Signal Generator (PDAA)
MPsychTh ... Master of Psychotherapy
MPT .... Ministry of Posts and Telecommunications [*People's Republic of China*] (ECON)
MPTA........ Municipal Passenger Transport Association, Inc. [*British*] (BI)
MPT-SD.... Multipurpose, Tracer, Self-Destruct [*Army*]
MPU .... Mobile Production Unit [*On-site television recording*] (NTCM)
MQB......... Mining Qualifications Board [*British*] (BI)
MR............ Measured Rating [*IOR*] [*Yacht racing*]
MR............ [*The*] Media Report [*A publication*] (NTCM)
MR............ Multi-Reflecton [*Lighting*]
MR............ Mutual Recognition
MRA .... Magnetic Reaction Analyzer (PDAA)
MRA .... Maneuver Right Area [*Army*]
MRA .... Martinaire [*ICAO designator*] (FAAC)
MRA .... Materials Requirement Analysis (PDAA)
MRA .... Matrix Reducibility Algorithm (PDAA)
MRA .... Metro Rating Area [*Arbitron television ratings*] (NTCM)
MRA .... Module Rack Assembly
MRAM....... Multi-Mission Redeye Air-Launched Missile [*Military*] (PDAA)
MRAR....... Manpower Requirements Analysis Report [*Military*]
MRAS....... Model Reference Adaptive System (PDAA)
MR ATOMIC ... Multiple Rapid Automatic Test of Monolithic Integrated Circuits (PDAA)
MRC .... Medical Research Committee
MRC .... Missile Research Corp.
MRCD........ Memory Raster Colour Display (PDAA)
MRCL........ Master Cross-Reference List
MRCS........ Missile Range Calibration Satellite
MRCS........ Multiple RPV [*Remotely Piloted Vehicle*] Control System (PDAA)
MRD.......... Meridian Air Cargo, Inc. [*ICAO designator*] (FAAC)
MRE.......... Mazda Research of Europe [*Automobile manufacturer operations*]
MRE.......... Missile Recertification Equipment
MREC........ Medical Research Ethics Committee
MREF........ Medical Research Endowment Fund
MRF .... Modular Rigid Frame (PDAA)
MRFC........ Malawi Rural Finance Co. Ltd.
MRG.......... Master Reference Gyro (PDAA)
MRHIB ..... Multiantimicrobial Resistant Hemophilus Influenza B
MRIT........ Marine RADAR Interrogator-Transponder (PDAA)
MRK......... Markair, Inc. [*ICAO designator*] (FAAC)
MRL .... Aeromorelos SA de CV [*Mexico*] [*ICAO designator*] (FAAC)
MRL .... Maximized Relative Likelihood (PDAA)
MRL .... Maximum Residue Limit (PDAA)
MRM......... Aerocharter, Inc. [*Canada*] [*ICAO designator*] (FAAC)
MRN.......... Missions Gouvernementales Francaises [*France*] [*ICAO designator*] (FAAC)
MRO.......... Mine Radiographic Outfit [*Military*] (PDAA)
MRO.......... Morrison Flying Service, Inc. [*ICAO designator*] (FAAC)
MRP .... Machine-Readable Passport (DA)
MRPV .... Mini-Remotely Piloted Vehicle (PDAA)
MRR .... Missile Restraint Release
MRR .... Monomer Reactivity Ratio (PDAA)
MRRS........ Multi-Rail Rocket System (PDAA)
MRS .... Airline of the Marshall Islands [*ICAO designator*] (FAAC)
MRS .... Minimum Reporting Standard [*Broadcasting*] (NTCM)
MRS .... Mobile Radio Service (DA)
MRSA....... Medium Range Surveillance Aircraft [*Military*] (PDAA)
MRSM....... Maintenance and Reliability Simulation Model (PDAA)
MRSS........ Missile Response Simulation Software
MRST........ Minimum Remaining Slack Time (PDAA)
MRT .... Air Mauritanie [*Mauritania*] [*ICAO designator*] (FAAC)
MRT .... Maximum Repair Time (PDAA)
MRT .... Measured Rate of Time (PDAA)
MRT .... Medium Range Truck [*Military*]
MRT .... Milk Ring Test (PDAA)

MRTD .... Minimum Resolvable Temperature Difference   (PDAA)
MRTE........ Missile Round Test Equipment
MRTR .... Mortar [*Technical drawings*]   (DAC)
MRTS........ Microwave Repeater Test Set   (DA)
MRTS........ Missile Round Test Set
MRU.......... Military RADAR Unit [*Aviation*]   (FAAC)
MRV .... Mars Roving Vehicle [*NASA*]   (PDAA)
MRX.......... Hermens/Markair Express [*ICAO designator*]   (FAAC)
MS .... Maintenance Schedule   (DA)
MS .... Man Station [*Military*]
MS .... Manufacturing in Space
MS .... Master Scene [*Major script sequence*]   (NTCM)
MS .... Master Shot [*Film production*]   (NTCM)
MS .... Meteor Scatter   (PDAA)
MS .... Miniature Screw [*Lamp base*]   (NTCM)
MSA .... Male Specific Antigen   (PDAA)
MSA .... Matrix Scheme for Algorithms   (PDAA)
MSA .... Mature Students' Association [*British*]   (BI)
MSA .... Mistral Air SRL [*Italy*] [*ICAO designator*]   (FAAC)
MSA .... Motor Schools' Association of Great Britain   (BI)
MSafSc....... Master of Safety Science
MSB........... Maintenance Support Base [*Military*]
MSBLMS... Multi Station Boundary Layer Model System   (PDAA)
MSBV........ Mooring Salvage and Boom Vessel   (PDAA)
MSC .... Magnitude Square of the Complex Coherence   (PDAA)
MSC .... Microwave Stripline-Circuit   (PDAA)
MSC .... Mono-Stereo Compatible   (PDAA)
MSC .... Moscow Airways [*Russian Federation*] [*ICAO designator*]
                   (FAAC)
MSc(AeroMed) ... Master of Science (Aeromedicine)
MSc(Biochem) ... Master of Science (Biochemistry)
MSc(CommMed) ... Master of Science (Community Medicine)
MSCDR...... Mohawk Synchronous Communication Data Recorder
                   [*Military*]   (PDAA)
MSc(Epid) ... Master of Science (Epidemiology)
MSc(NeuChem) ... Master of Science (Neurochemistry)
MSc(Nut).... Master of Science (Nutrition)
MSc(OccMed) ... Master of Science (Occupational Medicine)
MSc(Ophth) ... Master of Science (Ophthalmology)
MSCR........ Multilayer Side-Cladded Ridge Waveguide   (PDAA)
MSc(Rehab) ... Master of Science (Rehabilitation Medicine)
MSCT .... Miniature Synaptic Calcium Transient [*Neurophysiology*]
MSDBP...... Mean Squared Distance Between Pairs [*Statistics*]   (PDAA)
MSDD .... Milli-Second Delay Detonator [*Military*]   (PDAA)
MSEP........ Mean Square Error of Prediction [*Statistics*]   (PDAA)
MSF........... Max Sea Food SA de CV [*El Salvador*] [*ICAO designator*]
                   (FAAC)
MSGCTR ... Message Center [*Aviation*]   (FAAC)
MSH.......... US Marshal Service [*Department of Justice*] [*ICAO designator*]
                   (FAAC)
MSKP........ Management Skills - Knowledge Profile [*Business term*]
MSMAN .... Master Sign Makers' Association [*British*]   (BI)
MSN .... Median Sample Number   (PDAA)
MSND .... Mercury Substitution and Nucleonic Detection   (PDAA)
MSOG .... Molecular Sieve Oxygen Generating   (PDAA)
MS(Orth) ... Master of Surgery (Orthopedic)
MSP........... Matched Sale-Purchase Agreement [*Business term*]
MSP........... Medium Side Prong [*Lamp base type*]   (NTCM)
MSP........... Servicio de Vigilancia Aerea del Ministerio de Seguridad Publica
                   [*Costa Rica*] [*ICAO designator*]   (FAAC)
MSPD........ Matrix Solid-Phase Dispersion [*Analytical chemistry*]
MSR .... Egypt Air [*ICAO designator*]   (FAAC)
MSR .... Multi-Carrier Station Radio [*or Remote*] Control Equipment
                   (PDAA)
MSRA........ Multiple Shoe Retailers' Association [*British*]   (BI)
MSRI........ Mathematical Sciences Research Institute [*University of
                   California, Berkeley*]   (PDAA)
MSRI........ Mathematical Sciences Research Institute [*University of
                   Minnesota*]   (PDAA)
MSS........... Magnetic Spark Spectrometer   (PDAA)
MSS........... Mobile Satellite System   (DA)
MSS........... Morris Air Service [*ICAO designator*]   (FAAC)
MSSA........ Modification of Special Service Authorization [*FCC*]   (NTCM)
MSSC........ Metropolitan School Study Council [*Columbia University*]
                   (AEE)
MSSL .... Mullard Space Science Laboratory [*University of London*]
                   (PDAA)
MSSM....... Mount Sinai School of Medicine [*New York*]   (PDAA)
MSSM....... Multiple-Sine-Slit Microdensitometer   (PDAA)
MSSR........ Monopulse Secondary Surveillance RADAR   (DA)
MSSU....... Mississippi State University   (PDAA)
MST........... Aeroamistad SA de CV [*Mexico*] [*ICAO designator*]   (FAAC)
MSTP........ Maintenance Support Test Package [*Military*]
MSVA........ Magnetic Speed Variable Assist [*General Motors*] [*Power steering*]
MSY .... Massey University School of Aviation [*New Zealand*] [*ICAO
                   designator*]   (FAAC)
MT............. Miniature Tube   (NTCM)
MT............. Mobile Terminal   (DA)
MT............. Mounting Tray
MTA .... Management by Talking Around [*Business term*]
MTA .... Mean Tryptic Activity   (PDAA)
MTA .... Message Transport Agent [*Telecommunications*]   (PCM)
MTA .... Military Training Area   (DA)

MTA .... Mitchell Aero, Inc. [*ICAO designator*]   (FAAC)
MTA .... Multiple Tailors Association [*British*]   (BI)
MTA .... Music Teachers' Association [*British*]   (BI)
MTA .... Music Trades' Association [*British*]   (BI)
MTAC .... Multiple Test Acceptance Code [*Lubricants testing*] [*Automotive
                   engineering*]
MTAC .... Multiple Test Acceptance Criteria
MTAC .... Multiple Time Around Clutter
MTB .... Marcaptan Terminated Polybutadiene   (PDAA)
MTBCD...... Mean Time between Confirmed Defects [*Quality control*]
                   (PDAA)
MTBD....... Mean Time between Defects [*Quality control*]   (PDAA)
MTBDR...... Mean Time between Depot Repair [*Quality control*]   (PDAA)
MTBFC ..... Mean Time between Failures, Critical [*Military*]
MTBUM .... Mean Time between Unscheduled Maintenance [*Quality
                   control*]   (PDAA)
MTC .... Manufacturing Technology Center
MTC .... Maximum Tolerable Concentration [*Toxicology*]
MTC .... Mobile Tactical Computer   (PDAA)
MTD.......... Macknight Airlines [*Australia*] [*ICAO designator*]   (FAAC)
MTEE......... Mean Transverse Emmission Energy   (PDAA)
MTEL........ Maximum Tolerable Exposure Level [*Toxicology*]
MTF .... Moulded Fiber Technology
MTFA........ Medium-Term Financial Assistance
MTGU........ Main Turbine / Gearing Unit   (PDAA)
MTH.......... Massachusetts Institute of Technology [*ICAO designator*]
                   (FAAC)
MTH.......... Master of Tropical Health
MTI .... Marked Temperature Inversion [*Aviation*]   (DA)
MTI .... Multi-Spectral Thermal Imager Spacecraft [*Department of
                   Energy*]
MTIS .... Multiplex Transmitter Input Signals   (PDAA)
MTL .... Magnetic Tape Loader
MTL .... Minimum Triggering Level [*Aviation*]   (DA)
MTL .... Multiple Conductor Transmission Line   (PDAA)
MTL .... Raf-Avia [*Latvia*] [*ICAO designator*]   (FAAC)
MTLC........ Mass Transfer Limiting Current   (PDAA)
MTM .... Masked Terrain Map [*Military*]
MTM .... Master of Tropical Medicine
MTM-GPD ... Methods Time Measurement and General Purpose Data
                   (PDAA)
MTN.......... Mountain Air Cargo, Inc. [*ICAO designator*]   (FAAC)
MTO.......... Manitoulin Air Services Ltd. [*Canada*] [*ICAO designator*]
                   (FAAC)
MTOPS...... Million Theoretical Operations per Second [*Computer science*]
MTP .... Island Helicopters, Inc. [*ICAO designator*]   (FAAC)
MTP .... Master Training Plan [*Navy*]   (ANA)
MTP .... MOS [*Military Occupation Specialty*] Training Plan
MTPA........ Mobile Transponder Performance Analyzer [*Aviation*]   (DA)
MTPE......... Mission to Planet Earth [*Proposed NASA satellite*]
MTQ.......... CAAA Air Martinique [*France*] [*ICAO designator*]   (FAAC)
MTR .... Main Timing Register
MTR .... Metroflight, Inc. [*ICAO designator*]   (FAAC)
MTR .... Mid-Term Review
MTS........... Mantrust Asahi Airways PT [*Indonesia*] [*ICAO designator*]
                   (FAAC)
MTS........... Mass Target Sensor
MTS........... Morale Tendency Score   (AEE)
MTSF .... Mean Time to System Failure [*Quality control*]   (PDAA)
MTSR........ Maximal Temperature of the Synthesis Reaction [*Chemical
                   engineering*]
MTT .... Masked Terrain Trainer [*Military*]
MTT .... Orion SpA [*Italy*] [*ICAO designator*]   (FAAC)
MTTFSF ... Mean Time to First System Failure [*Quality control*]   (PDAA)
MTTFSR... Mean Time to First System Repair [*Quality control*]   (PDAA)
MTTSF ..... Mean Time to System Failure [*Quality control*]   (PDAA)
MTU .... Mobile Treatment Unit   (ERG)
MTUR .... Mean Time to Unscheduled Replacement [*Quality control*]
                   (PDAA)
MTV .... Mountain Valley Air Service, Inc. [*ICAO designator*]   (FAAC)
MUA .... Machinery Users' Association [*British*]   (BI)
MUA.......... Murray Aviation, Inc. [*ICAO designator*]   (FAAC)
MUC.......... Missionary Union of the Clergy [*British*]   (BI)
MUCROMAF ... Multiple Critical Root Maximally Flat   (PDAA)
MUDAID... Multivariate, Univariate, and Discriminant Analysis of Irregular
                   Data   (PDAA)
MUDD .... Multisource Unified Data Distribution   (PDAA)
MUG .... Make-Up Gas [*Chemical engineering*]
MUK.......... Muk Air Taxi [*Denmark*] [*ICAO designator*]   (FAAC)
MULQUAL ... Multiple Goal Water Quality Model   (PDAA)
MULTIPAC ... Multiple Pool Processor and Computer   (PDAA)
MULTIPLE ... Multipurpose Program that Learns [*Computer science*]
MUP .... Metalworking under Pressure   (PDAA)
MUR.......... Aerolinea Muri [*Mexico*] [*ICAO designator*]   (FAAC)
MURATREC ... Multi-RADAR Track Reconstitution [*Aviation*]   (DA)
MURS .... Machine Utilization Reporting System   (PDAA)
MUSAT...... Multiple Station Analytical Triangulation   (PDAA)
MUSE .... Machine User Symbiotic Environment   (PDAA)
MUSE .... Model to Understand Simple English   (PDAA)
MUSTA...... Mock-Up Spallation Target Assembly   (PDAA)
MUT.......... Multiservicios Aeronauticos SA de CV [*Mexico*] [*ICAO
                   designator*]   (FAAC)

MUTA .... Military Upper Traffic Control Area   (DA)
MUTE .... Mobile Universal Test Equipment   (PDAA)
MUTT .... Military Utility Tactical Transport
MVA .... Mississippi Valley Airlines, Inc. [*ICAO designator*]   (FAAC)
MVA .... Motor Vehicle Allowance
MVCS .... Marine Vapor Control System
MVDA .... Motor Vehicles Dismantlers Association [*British*]   (BI)
MVF .... Moisture Volume Fraction   (PDAA)
MVI .... Medium Viscosity Index   (PDAA)
MVIC .... Mitsubishi Variable Intake System [*Automotive engine design*]
MVIN .... Medium Viscosity Index-Naphthenic   (PDAA)
MVIP .... Medium Viscosity Index-Paraffinic   (PDAA)
MVL .... Magadan Airlines [*Russian Federation*] [*ICAO designator*]
               (FAAC)
MVM .... Air Cargo America, Inc. [*ICAO designator*]   (FAAC)
MVN .... Marvin Ltd. [*British*] [*ICAO designator*]   (FAAC)
MVP .... Multimedia Video Processor [*Texas Instruments*]   (PS)
MVPA .... Motor Vehicle Plan Administration
MVPCCS ... Motor Vehicle Post Crash Communications System   (PDAA)
MVRO .... Minimum-Variance Reduced-Order [*Statistics*]   (PDAA)
MVS .... Mine Ventilation System [*Engineering*]
MVX .... Multiplex
MW .... Mud Weight [*Well drilling technology*]
MWA .... Management by Walking Around
MWAE .... Minimum-Weighted-Absolute Error [*Statistics*]   (PDAA)
MWARS ..... Major Command Worldwide Ammunition Reporting System
               [*Army*]
MWCU .... Molecular Weight Cut-Off [*Metallurgy*]
MWE .... Manufacturer's Weight Empty   (DA)
MWIV .... Mean Wildlife Index Value [*Statistics*]   (PDAA)
MWLAE ..... Millimeter Wave Large Antenna Experiment [*NASA*]   (PDAA)
MWMA .... Multiple Wine Merchants Association [*British*]   (BI)
MWM & R ... Metal-Working Machine and Robot
MWMT ...... Metal-Working Machine Tool
MWSS .... Marine Wing Support Squadron [*Navy*]   (ANA)
MWT .... Midwest Aviation [*Southwest Aviation, Inc.*] [*ICAO
               designator*]   (FAAC)
MWV .... Modulated Wavy Vortex [*Fluid mechanics*]
MXA .... Compania Mexicana de Aviacion SA [*Mexico*] [*ICAO
               designator*]   (FAAC)
MXC .... Mexair SA [*Switzerland*] [*ICAO designator*]   (FAAC)
MXE .... Manx Airlines (Europe) Ltd. [*British*] [*ICAO designator*]   (FAAC)
MX/MM .... Missile X/Minuteman Missile
MXP .... May Air Xpress, Inc. [*ICAO designator*]   (FAAC)
MXR .... Merrix Air Ltd. [*British*] [*ICAO designator*]   (FAAC)
MXX .... Merchant Express Aviation [*Nigeria*] [*ICAO designator*]   (FAAC)
MYA .... Myflug HF [*Iceland*] [*ICAO designator*]   (FAAC)
MYDP .... Multi-Year Development Plan [*Environmental Protection
               Agency*]   (ERG)
MYL .... Aeromyl SA de CV [*Mexico*] [*ICAO designator*]   (FAAC)
MYM .... Managing Your Money [*MECA Software, Inc.*]   (PCM)
MYR .... Miriadair [*France*] [*ICAO designator*]   (FAAC)
MZP .... Modulated Zone Plate   (PDAA)

N

N .... Network [*FCC program source designation*]   (NTCM)
N .... News Program   (NTCM)
N .... Nighttime   (NTCM)
N .... Nontactical [*Military*]
9N .... Nepal [*Aircraft nationality and registration mark*]   (FAAC)
NA.............. Non-Attached [*European political movement*]   (ECON)
NA.............. Not Allowed
NAA............ National Oceanic and Atmospheric Administration [*Department of Commerce*] [*ICAO designator*]   (FAAC)
NAA............ Nuclear Activation Analysis   (PDAA)
NAAC......... National Association of Agricultural Contractors [*British*]   (BI)
NAANP...... National Alliance for the Advancement of Nodnarbian Philosophy   (EA)
NAB........... National Association of Bookmakers Ltd. [*British*]   (BI)
NAB........... National Audience Board [*An association*]   (NTCM)
NABA........ Nitro-(amino)butyric Acid
NABBA ...... National Amateur Body Building Association [*British*]   (BI)
NABC .... National Association of Bingo Clubs [*British*]   (BI)
NABSS....... National Alliance of Black School Superintendents   (AEE)
NABTFP .... National Association of Black Television and Film Producers   (NTCM)
NABTS....... North American Broadcast Teletext Standard   (NTCM)
NAC........... National Association of Choirs [*British*]   (BI)
NAC........... National Association of Counselors   (EA)
NAC........... National Audience Composition [*Nielsen Television Index*]   (NTCM)
NAC........... Net Advertising Circulation [*Outdoor advertising*]   (NTCM)
NAC........... Northern Air Cargo, Inc. [*ICAO designator*]   (FAAC)
NACBP....... No-Adjust Car Building Process [*Ford Motor Co.*] [*Automotive engineering*]
NACC........ North Atlantic Cooperation Council
NACCG ...... National Association of Crankshaft and Cylinder Grinders [*British*]   (BI)
NACCSMA ... NATO Command and Control Systems Management Agency   (PDAA)
NACD......... National Association for Cave Diving   (EA)
NACE .... North American Commission on the Environment
NACF .... National Association of Church Furnishers [*British*]   (BI)
NACH........ National Advisory Committee on the Handicapped
NACM .... National Association of Cider Makers [*British*]   (BI)
NACMW.... North American Council for Muslim Women   (EA)
NACP .... National Academy of Cable Programming   (NTCM)
NACT .... National Association of Craftsman Tailors [*British*]   (BI)
NACT .... National Association of Cycle Traders [*British*]   (BI)
NAD........... National Audience Demographics Report [*Nielsen Television Index*]   (NTCM)
NAD........... Nitric Acid Dihydrate [*Inorganic chemistry*]
NAD........... Nobelair [*Turkey*] [*ICAO designator*]   (FAAC)
NADCAP ... National Aerospace and Defense Contractors Accreditation Program [*DoD*]
NADDRG... North American Deep Drawing Research Group [*Automotive metal stampings*]
NADIBO .... North American Defense Industrial Base Organization
NADME..... Noise Amplitude Distribution Measuring Equipment   (PDAA)
NADOT...... North Atlantic Deepwater Oil Terminal   (PDAA)
NAEC .... National Association of Exhibition Contractors [*British*]   (BI)
NAEDS....... National Association of Engravers and Die-Stampers [*British*]   (BI)
NAEFR...... North American English Ford Registry   (EA)
NAEM........ Naval Air Effect Model   (PDAA)
NAEST....... National Archives for Electrical Science and Technology   (PDAA)
NAET .... National Association for Educational Television   (NTCM)
NAF .... Non-urea Adducting Fatty Acid [*Food science*]
NAF .... Royal Netherlands Air Force [*ICAO designator*]   (FAAC)
NAFAS...... National Association of Flower Arrangement Societies of Great Britain   (BI)
NAFD .... National Association of Farm Directors   (NTCM)
NAFD .... National Association of Funeral Directors [*British*]   (BI)
NAFLAC.... Navy Department Fuel and Lubricants Advisory Committee [*Ministry of Defense*] [*British*]   (PDAA)
NAFRC....... North Atlantic Fisheries Research Center   (PDAA)
NAG........... Net Annual Gain [*Business term*]   (PDAA)
NAGS .... National Allotments and Gardens Society Ltd. [*British*]   (BI)

NAH .... Nahanni Air Services Ltd. [*Canada*] [*ICAO designator*]   (FAAC)
NAHSO..... National Association of Hospital Supplies Officers [*British*]   (BI)
NAIAD...... Nerve Agent Immobilised Enzyme Alarm and Detector   (PDAA)
NAIDA ...... National Agricultural and Industrial Development Association [*Republic of Ireland*]   (BI)
NAIEO .... National Association of Inspectors of Schools and Educational Organisers [*British*]   (BI)
NAIM .... Number Allocation and Inspection Module   (PDAA)
NAIR .... National Arrangements for Incidents Involving Radioactivity   (PDAA)
NAIS.......... National Association for Information Services   (EA)
NAIWC ...... National Association of Inland Water Carriers [*British*]   (BI)
NAL........... North American Lighting [*Automotive industry supplier*]
NAL........... Northway Aviation Ltd. [*Canada*] [*ICAO designator*]   (FAAC)
NaLDAP.... National Learning Disabilities Assistance Project
NALM .... National Association of Lift Makers [*British*]   (BI)
NALMC...... National Association of Labor-Management Committees   (EA)
NALO........ National Association of Launderette Owners Ltd. [*British*]   (BI)
NALSO ...... National Association of Labour Student Organisations [*British*]   (BI)
NALW .... Not an A-List Writer [*Screenwriter's lexicon*]
NAM.......... National Association of Manufacturers   (NTCM)
NAM.......... Nortland Air Manitoba [*Canada*] [*ICAO designator*]   (FAAC)
NAME........ National Association of Marine Enginebuilders [*British*]   (BI)
NAME........ National Association for Mediation in Education   (EA)
NAMES...... NAVDAC [*Naval Data Automation Command*] Assembly, Monitor, Executive System   (PDAA)
NAMG....... National Association of Multiple Grocers [*British*]   (BI)
NAMI........ National Association of Malleable Ironfounders [*British*]   (BI)
NAMME.... National Association of Medical Minority Educators   (EA)
NAMMO ... NATO Multi-Role Combat Aircraft Management Organization   (PDAA)
NAMS .... National Air Monitoring Station [*Environmental Protection Agency*]   (ERG)
NAN .... National Airlines, Inc. [*ICAO designator*]   (FAAC)
NAN .... Non-Ammonia-Nitrogen   (PDAA)
NANT........ National Association of Nephrology Technologists   (EA)
NAO .... Her Majesty's Nautical Almanac Office [*British*]   (PDAA)
NAO .... Non-Asbestos Organic [*Friction materials*]
NAO .... North American Airlines, Inc. [*ICAO designator*]   (FAAC)
NAP........... Napier Air Service, Inc. [*ICAO designator*]   (FAAC)
NAP........... Normal Administrative Practice
NAPA .... National Association of Park Administrators [*British*]   (BI)
NAPC .... National Association of Parish Councils [*British*]   (BI)
NAPC .... Non-Adherent Peritoneal Cell   (PDAA)
NAPD........ National Association of Pharmaceutical Distributors [*British*]   (BI)
NAPGC ...... National Association of Public Golf Courses [*British*]   (BI)
NAPL .... National Air Photo Library [*Canada*]   (PDAA)
NAPP .... National Association of Poultry Packers Ltd. [*British*]   (BI)
NAPRS....... National Airspace Performance Reporting System [*Aviation*]   (FAAC)
NAPS......... National Association of Presbyterian Scouters   (EA)
NAPS......... National Association of Private Secretaries [*British*]   (BI)
NAPV .... National Association of Prison Visitors [*British*]   (BI)
NAR........... Air Continental, Inc. [*ICAO designator*]   (FAAC)
NARB .... National Assocation of Radio Broadcasters   (NTCM)
NARC......... Nuclear Age Resource Center   (EA)
NARCINT ... Narcotics Intelligence [*Military*]   (ADDR)
NARCU ...... National Association of Railroad and Utility Commissioners   (NTCM)
NARF .... Natural Axial Resonant Frequency   (PDAA)
NARGOM ... North American Research Group on Management   (PDAA)
NARI .... National AIDS Research Institute [*India*]
NARL .... National Aero Research Laboratory [*Canada*]   (PDAA)
NAS .... National Association of Shopfitters [*British*]   (BI)
NAS........... Northeast Aviation Services Ltd. [*British*] [*ICAO designator*]   (FAAC)
NASBOSA ... National Academy of Sciences Board on Ocean Science Affairs   (PDAA)
NASCMVE ... National Academy of Sciences Committee on Motor Vehicle Emissions   (PDAA)
NASDA ...... National Space Development Agency [*Japan*]

NASDU...... National Amalgamated Stevedores and Dockers Union [British] (BI)
NASEN ...... National Association of State Enrolled Nurses [British] (BI)
NASM .... National Association for School Magazines [British] (BI)
NASMAR... National Association of Sack Merchants and Reclaimers [British] (BI)
NASP......... Navy Advanced SATCOM [Satellite Communications] Program (ANA)
NASPM...... National Association of Seed Potato Merchants [British] (BI)
NASS........ Naval Armaments Stores System (PDAA)
NASS........ Navigation Satellite System (PDAA)
NASSCOM ... National Association of Software and Service Companies
NAST......... Navigation/Attack Systems Trainer (PDAA)
NASWM .... National Association of Scottish Woollen Manufacturers [British] (BI)
NAT........... Nearly Airborne Truck (PDAA)
NAT........... North Atlantic Air, Inc. [ICAO designator] (FAAC)
NATCA ...... North American Trap Collector Association (EA)
NATCG ...... National Association of Training Corps for Girls [British] (BI)
NATD........ National Association of Tool Dealers [British] (BI)
NATGA ...... National Amateur Tobacco Growers' Association [British] (BI)
NATMATMUS ... National Automotive and Truck Model and Toy Museum of the United States
NATN........ National Association of Theatre Nurses [British] (BI)
NATO AEW ... North Atlantic Treaty Organization Airborne Early Warning Program
NATO MC ... North Atlantic Treaty Organization Military Committee
NATPE....... National Association of Television Program Executives (NTCM)
NATR........ National Association of Tenants and Residents [British] (BI)
NATR .... National Association of Toy Retailers [British] (BI)
NATRA ...... National Association of Television and Radio Announcers (NTCM)
NATSU ...... Nominated Air Traffic Service Unit (DA)
NAUTIC..... Naval Autonomous Intelligent Console (PDAA)
NAVBIT..... Naval Basic Instrument Trainer (PDAA)
NAVEAMS ... Navigational Warning East Atlantic and Mediterranean [Navy] (PDAA)
NAVFECO ... Naval Facilities Engineering Command (PDAA)
NAVHARS ... Navigation Heading and Altitude Reference System [Aviation] (PDAA)
NAVL .... National Anti-Vaccination League [British] (BI)
NAVMEDCOM ... Naval Medical Command (ANA)
NAVRESO ... Navy Resale System Office (PDAA)
NAVSUP.... Naval Supplies
NAVSURFWPNCEN ... Naval Surface Weapons Center (PDAA)
NAW......... Newair [Denmark] [ICAO designator] (FAAC)
NAWBM.... National Association of Window Blind Manufacturers [British] (BI)
NAWESA... Naval Weapons Engineering Support Activity (PDAA)
NAWME.... National Average Weekly Male Earning
NAWPM .... National Association of Wholesale Paint Merchants [British] (BI)
NAY.......... Navegacion y Servicios Aereos Canarios SA [Spain] [ICAO designator] (FAAC)
NAZ........... Servicios Aereos del Nazas SA de CV [Mexico] [ICAO designator] (FAAC)
NB............. Notch-Bend (PDAA)
NBA........... National Benzole and Allied Products Association [British] (BI)
NBA........... National Brassfoundry Association [British] (BI)
NBA........... North East Bolivian Airways [ICAO designator] (FAAC)
NBBA .... National Black Business Alliance (EA)
NBBE .... National Board for Bakery Education [British] (BI)
NBC.......... National Broadcasters' Club (NTCM)
NBCCC...... National Bureau for Co-Operation in Child Care [British] (BI)
NBD.......... Nondirectional Beacon
NBFR......... Not Before [ICAO designator] (FAAC)
NBGRN ..... Narrow Band Gaussian Random Noise (PDAA)
NBI .... Nielsen Broadcast Index [A. C. Nielsen Co.] (NTCM)
NBN.......... North British Airlines Ltd. [ICAO designator] (FAAC)
NBPM .... Network-Based Project Management (PDAA)
NBR.......... Net Borrowing Requirement (PDAA)
NBS.......... National Bakery School [British] (BI)
NBS .... National Biological Survey [Department of the Interior]
NBS .... Nimbus Aviation [British] [ICAO designator] (FAAC)
NBSS......... National British Softbill Society (BI)
NBVM....... Narrow-Band Voice Modulation (PDAA)
NBW.......... National Book Week (NTCM)
NC............ Network Channel [Broadcasting] (NTCM)
NC............ Noiseless Camera (NTCM)
NCA.......... Nippon Cargo Airlines Co. Ltd. [Japan] [ICAO designator] (FAAC)
NCA........... Normal Coordinate Analysis
NCABC ...... National Citizens' Advice Bureaux Committee [British] (BI)
NCAC .... National Civil Aviation Council [British] (BI)
NCAIANMHR ... National Center for American Indian and Alaska Native Mental Health Research (EA)
N Cal......... New Caledonia
NCAO........ National Commission on Air Quality [Environmental Protection Agency] (ERG)
NCATA ...... National Cable Antenna Television Association of Canada (NTCM)
NCB .... North Caribou Flying Service Ltd. [Canada] [ICAO designator] (FAAC)

NCC........... National Caravan Council Ltd. [British] (BI)
NCC........... New Chemical Compound [Food science]
NCC........... North Coast Air Services Ltd. [Canada] [ICAO designator] (FAAC)
NCCA .... National Club Cricket Association [British] (BI)
NCCBN ...... National Council of Churches Broadcasting Network (NTCM)
NCCOP ..... National Corporation for the Care of Old People [British] (BI)
NCCPG ...... National Council for the Conservation of Plants and Gardens (PDAA)
NCCT .... National Council for Civic Theatres Ltd. [British] (BI)
NCC/USA ... National Council of Churches of Christ in the USA (NTCM)
NCDAD..... National Council for Diplomats in Art and Design [British] (BI)
NCE.......... Noncommercial Education [FCC] (NTCM)
NCE.......... Northcoast Executive Airlines [ICAO designator] (FAAC)
NCEMT ..... National Center for Excellence in Metalworking Technology [Navy]
NCEOA ...... National Council of Educational Opportunity Associations (EA)
NCFDITFS ... National Committee for the Full Development of Instructional Television Fixed Services [ITFS regulation] (NTCM)
NCG.......... Nicotine Chewing Gum (PDAA)
NCHGR..... National Center for Human Genome Research
NCL .... National Commuter Airways [British] [ICAO designator] (FAAC)
NCO.......... Negotiated Consent Order [Environmental Protection Agency] (ERG)
NCP .... Non-Custodial Parent
NCPT........ Nationally-Certified Psychiatric Technician
NCQR........ National Council for Quality and Reliabiltiy [British] (BI)
NCR.......... Air Sur [Spain] [ICAO designator] (FAAC)
NCR.......... Non-Selective Catalyst Reduction [Diesel engine emissions]
NCRR........ National Center for Research Resources [National Institutes of Health]
NCRT .... National College of Rubber Technology (PDAA)
NCS .... Naval Compass Stabilizer (PDAA)
NCS .... Non-Collimated Source (PDAA)
NCS .... Nuclear-Powered Container Ship (PDAA)
NCS .... Simpson Air Ltd. [Canada] [ICAO designator] (FAAC)
NCSA .... Noncommercial Spot Announcement [Public service announcement] (NTCM)
NCSCC ...... National Championship Stock Car Racing [Later, NASCAR]
NCSS......... National Cactus and Succulent Society [British] (BI)
NCST........ National Certification Skills Test [Psychiatry]
NCSW .... National Council for the Single Woman and Her Dependants Ltd. [British] (BI)
NCT .... National Chamber of Trade [British] (BI)
NCTF........ National Check Traders Federation [British] (BI)
NCTL........ National Commercial Temperance League [British] (BI)
NCTYL...... National College for the Training of Youth Leaders [British] (BI)
NCUF .... National Computer Users Forum [National Computing Center] (PDAA)
NCV.......... Net Calorific Value (PDAA)
NCW......... National Council of Women of Great Britain (BI)
NCWC .... National Catholic Welfare Conference News Service (NTCM)
NCWP .... National Communications Working Party [Australia] [Political party]
NCY.......... Nancy Aviation [France] [ICAO designator] (FAAC)
NCYA .... National Catholic Youth Association [British] (BI)
ND .... New Democracy [European political movement] (ECON)
ND .... News Director (NTCM)
NDA.......... National Dairymen's Association, Inc. [British] (BI)
NDA........... Northern Airways, Inc. [ICAO designator] (FAAC)
NDAT........ Non-Destructive Assay Technique [Military] (PDAA)
NDBI .... National Dairymen's Benevolent Institution, Inc. [British] (BI)
NDC.......... Naphthalene Dicarboxylate [Organic chemistry]
NDCEE ...... National Defense Center for Environmental Excellence [DoD] (RDA)
NDCS .... National Deaf Children's Society [British] (BI)
NDEA .... National Display Equipment Association [British] (BI)
NDFA .... National Drama Festivals Association [British] (BI)
NDI........... KS Nordic Air, Denmark [ICAO designator] (FAAC)
NDI........... No-Dig International [A publication]
NDL........... Neon Discharge Lighting [Automotive lighting]
NDM .... Nadym Airlines [Russian Federation] [ICAO designator] (FAAC)
NDMS....... Non-Directional Mud-and-Snow (PDAA)
NDMTP .... National Defense Manufacturing Technology Plan
NDOA .... National Dog Owners' Association [British] (BI)
NDP.......... Net Domestic Product [Business term] (PDAA)
NDR.......... Andrea Airlines SA [Peru] [ICAO designator] (FAAC)
NDS.......... Needs [Automotive advertising]
NDSL .... Non Domestic Substances List [Canada]
NDTIAC.... Non-Destructive Testing Information Center [Army Materials and Mechanics Research Center] (PDAA)
NDU .... Navigation Display Unit [Military]
NE............. National Estate
NE............. Not Employed
NE............. Not Engaged
N1E........... Nosed One Edge [Lumber] (DAC)
N2E........... Nosed Two Edges [Lumber] (DAC)
NEA.......... New England Airlines, Inc. [ICAO designator] (FAAC)
NEAAN..... Non-Essential Amino Acid N [Biochemistry] (PDAA)
NEAR .... Nielsen Engineering & Research, Inc.

NEARYP....	National Employers Association of Rayon Yarn Producers [*British*] (BI)
NEASIM....	Network Analytical Simulator (PDAA)
NEB...........	North-Eastbound [*Aviation*]
NEBA.........	North East Bolivian Airways [*ICAO designator*] (FAAC)
NEBBY.......	Negative Equity Baby Boomer [*Home buyers in debt*]
NEBOSH ...	National Examination Board in Occupational Safety and Health (PDAA)
NEC...........	Noise-Equivalent Charge (PDAA)
NECAF.......	National Electromagnetic Compatibility Analysis Facility [*Department of Commerce*] (PDAA)
NECAR	National Engineers Commission on Air Resources (PDAA)
NECI	Noise Exposure Computer Integrator (PDAA)
NECOE	New England Center for Organizational Effectiveness (EA)
Necro.........	Necrofile [*A publication*]
NECTAR....	Network of European CNS [*Central Nervous System*] Transplantation and Restoration
NEDCO......	Non-Electronic Part Data Collection (PDAA)
NEDELA....	Network Definition Language [*Computer science*] (PDAA)
NEDSA......	Non-Erasing Deterministic Stack Automation (PDAA)
NEE...........	Net Ecosystem Exchange [*Biology*]
NEE...........	Northeast Express Regional Airlines, Inc. [*ICAO designator*] (FAAC)
NEEC	Not Entailing Excessive Cost [*Environmental technology*]
NEET	Navy Extended Electrode Technique (PDAA)
NEETU	National Engineering and Electrical Trade Union [*Republic of Ireland*] (BI)
NEFBRACS ...	Nearfield Bearing and Range Accuracy Calibration System (PDAA)
NEGI	National Federation of Engineering and General Ironfounders [*British*] (BI)
NEGISTOR ...	Negative Resistor (PDAA)
NEIS...........	Nuclear Energy Information Service [*An association*] (EA)
NEL	Northern Extratropical Land [*Geography*]
NELTS	Number of Elements Loaded [*Army*]
NEM...........	New Electronic Media
NEMO........	Not Emanating Main Office [*Remote broadcast*] (NTCM)
NEMT	Naval Emergency Monitoring Teams (PDAA)
NEOME.....	New Electroactive Organic Materials for Electronics [*Esprit*]
NEP	Net Ecosystem Production [*Biology*]
NEPAL.......	National Egg Packers' Association Ltd. [*British*] (BI)
NEPE.........	Nitrate Ester Plasticized Polyethylene (PDAA)
NER...........	Air Newark, Inc. [*ICAO designator*] (FAAC)
NER...........	Nuclear Electric Resonance (PDAA)
NER...........	Nucleotide-Excision Repair
NERAM	Network Reliability Assessment Model (PDAA)
NERC	National Electronic Reliability Council (NTCM)
NERC	National English Rabbit Club [*British*] (BI)
NERN........	National Educational Radio Network [*Defunct*] (NTCM)
NES	Nordeste, Linhas Aereas Regionais SA [*Brazil*] [*ICAO designator*] (FAAC)
NESB1........	First Generation Non-English-Speaking Background
NESB2........	Second Generation Non-English-Speaking Background
NESC.........	National Electrical Safety Code [*Also, NEC*] (NTCM)
NESC.........	Non-English-Speaking Country
NETANAL ...	Network Analysis (PDAA)
NETD........	Noise-Equivalent Temperature Difference [*Thermography*]
NETE	Naval Engineering Test Establishment [*Canadian Armed Forces*] (PDAA)
NETR	NATO Electronic Technical Recommendation (PDAA)
NETREM...	Net Requirementes Estimation Model (PDAA)
NEU...........	Transportes Aereos Neuquinos Sociedad de Estado [*Argentina*] [*ICAO designator*] (FAAC)
NEW...........	Hawarden BAE [*British*] [*ICAO designator*] (FAAC)
NEW...........	New England Air Express, Inc. [*ICAO designator*] (FAAC)
NEWSCOMP ...	Newspaper Composition (PDAA)
NEX...........	Northern Executive Aviation Ltd. [*British*] [*ICAO designator*] (FAAC)
NEXCOM ...	Navy Exchange Service Command
NF..............	Nanofiltration
NF..............	Nonfiction (NTCM)
NF..............	Normal Frequency [*Telecommunications*] (NTCM)
NFA...........	National Farmers' Association [*Republic of Ireland*] (BI)
NFA...........	National Federation of Anglers [*British*] (BI)
NFA...........	North Flying AS [*Denmark*] [*ICAO designator*] (FAAC)
NFBPM......	National Federation of Builders' and Plumbers' Merchants [*British*] (BI)
NFBSS.......	National Federation of Bakery Students' Societies [*British*] (BI)
NFC	Native Forest Council (EA)
NFCA	Near-Field Calibration Array (PDAA)
NFCDS......	National Federation of Clubs for Divorced and Separated [*British*] (BI)
NFCGA	National Federation of Constructional Glass Associations [*British*] (BI)
NFCI..........	National Federation of Clay Industries [*British*] (BI)
NFCS.........	National Federation of Construction Supervisors [*British*] (BI)
NFCSIT.....	National Federation of Cold Storage and Ice Trades [*British*] (BI)
NFCTA	National Federation of Corn Trade Associations [*British*] (BI)
NFD...........	Eurowings (NFD & RFG Luftverhehrs AG) [*Germany*] [*ICAO designator*] (FAAC)
NFD...........	National Federation of Drapers and Allied Traders Ltd. [*Republic of Ireland*] (BI)
NFDPS.......	National Flight Data Processing System [*ICAO*] (DA)

NFE	Nitride Forming Element [*Metal treating*]
NFF............	National Froebel Foundation [*British*] (BI)
NFF............	No Frills Fund
NFFC.........	National Film Finance Corp. [*British*] (BI)
NFFF	National Federation of Fish Friers [*British*] (BI)
NFFPT	National Federation of Fruit and Potato Trades [*British*] (BI)
NFFQO	National Federation of Freestone Quarry Owners [*British*] (BI)
NFFTU......	National Federation of Furniture Trade Unions [*British*] (BI)
NFGS........	National Fenton Glass Society (EA)
NFISM	National Federation of Iron and Steel Merchants [*British*] (BI)
NFL	No Field Lubrication (PDAA)
NFL	Northaire Freight Lines Ltd. [*ICAO designator*] (FAAC)
NFLDS	National Fire Loss Data System [*Military*] (PDAA)
NFMA	National Fireplace Makers Association [*British*] (BI)
NFMP	National Federation of Master Painters and Decorators of England and Wales (BI)
NFMR	Non-Linear Ferromagnetic Resonance (PDAA)
NFMRAD ...	Null Filter Mobile RADAR (PDAA)
NFMT	National Federation of Meat Traders [*British*] (BI)
NFOAPA...	National Federation of Old Age Pensioners' Associations [*British*] (BI)
NFOHA......	National Federation of Off-Licence Holders Associations of England and Wales (BI)
NFPC.........	National Federation of Plastering Contractors [*British*] (BI)
NFPDHE....	National Federation of Plumbers and Domestic Heating Engineers [*British*] (BI)
NFPHC	National Federation of Permanent Holiday Camps Ltd. [*British*] (BI)
NFPO	National Federation of Property Owners [*British*] (BI)
NFPR.........	National Fund for Research into Poliomyelitis and Other Crippling Diseases [*British*] (BI)
NFR	Net Financing Requirement
NFT	Navigation Flight Test [*Aviation*] (DA)
NFT	Nefteyugansk Aviation Division [*Russian Federation*] [*ICAO designator*] (FAAC)
NFT	Non-Firing Test [*Military*]
NFTMS......	National Federation of Terrazzo-Mosaic Specialists [*British*] (BI)
NFVT........	National Federation of Vehicle Trades [*British*] (BI)
NFWG	National Federation of Wholesale Grocers and Provision Merchants [*British*] (BI)
NG	Natural Gas Shutoff [*NFPA pre-fire planning symbol*] (NFPA)
NGA...........	WAAC (Nigeria) Ltd. Nigeria Airways [*ICAO designator*] (FAAC)
NGNC........	Non-Government Non-Catholic [*School*]
NGP...........	N-Glycidylpyrrolidone [*Organic chemistry*]
NGP...........	Nearest Grid Point (PDAA)
NGPRP.......	Northern Great Plains Resource Program [*Dept. of the Interior, Dept. of Agriculture and Environmental Protection Agency*] (PDAA)
NGS...........	General Air Services Ltd. [*Nigeria*] [*ICAO designator*] (FAAC)
NGT...........	National Guild of Telephonists [*British*] (BI)
NGT...........	Not Greater Than
NH	National Highway
NH	New Head [*Also, NL*] [*News stories*] (NTCM)
NHA	National Hairdressers' Association [*British*] (BI)
NHE	Nuclease-Hypersensitive Element [*Biochemistry*]
NHF...........	National Hairdressers' Federation [*British*] (BI)
NHI............	Nielsen Home Video Index [*A. C. Nielsen Co.*] (NTCM)
NHJA........	National Hunter and Jumper Association (EA)
NHK	Nippon Hoso Kyokai [*Japanese national broadcasting system*] (NTCM)
NHS...........	National Highway System [*Federal transportation planning*]
NI................	National Interest
NI................	Network Identification [*Broadcasting*] (NTCM)
NI................	Neutralization Index (PDAA)
NI................	Neutraminidase Inhibition (PDAA)
NIA	Norfolk Island Airlines [*Australia*] [*ICAO designator*] (FAAC)
NIBL.........	National Industrial Basic Language (PDAA)
NIC	Natural Image Computer (PDAA)
NIC	Noise Isolation Class (PDAA)
NIC	Northern Illinois Commuter [*ICAO designator*] (FAAC)
NICA	Nicaraguense de Aviacion SA [*Nicaragua*] [*ICAO designator*] (FAAC)
NICE	Nonprofit International Consortium for Eiffel (EA)
NICS..........	National Airspace System Interfacility Communications System (FAAC)
NIE	Newly-Industrialized Economy
NIE	Newspaper in Education Program
NIEF..........	National Ironfounding Employers Association [*British*] (BI)
NIETS	National Imagery Exploitation Tasking Study
NIFOB.......	Non-Injurious Free-on-Board
NIFTP	Network Independent File Transfer Protocol (PDAA)
NIG............	Aero Contractors Company of Nigeria Ltd. [*ICAO designator*] (FAAC)
NIH............	National Institute of Hardware [*British*] (BI)
NIH............	National Institute of Housecraft [*British*] (BI)
NII.............	Negative Immittance Inverter (PDAA)
NIIP	National Institute of Industrial Psychology (PDAA)
NIM...........	National Impact Model [*Environmental Protection Agency*] (ERG)
NIMEX	Nomenclature for Imports and Exports [*European Community*] (PDAA)
NiMH	Nickel-Metal Hydride [*Organic chemistry*] (PS)

NIMP .... New and Improved Materials and Processes (PDAA)
NIMROD... National Institute for Medical Research Online Database (PDAA)
NIMROD... Nineteen-Hundred [*Computer*] Management and Recovery of
                    Documentation (PDAA)
NIN .... Nine Inch Nails [*Rock music group*]
NIN .... Ninhydrine [*Chemical agent used in espionage*]
NINA .... National Institute Northern Accelerator (PDAA)
NINA .... Neutron Instruments for Nuclear Analysis (PDAA)
NINST .... Non-Instrument Runway [*Aviation*] (DA)
NIP .... Normal Incidence Pyrheliometer (PDAA)
NIPERA .... Nickel Producers Environmental Research Association
NIPH .... National Institute of Poultry Husbandry [*British*] (BI)
NIPHL .... Noise-Induced Permanent Hearing Loss (PDAA)
NIR .... Network Information Retrieval
NIR .... Norskair [*Norway*] [*ICAO designator*] (FAAC)
NIS .... Negotiation Information System
NIS .... Network Information Service
NIS .... Nicaraguense de Aviacion SA [*Nicaragua*] [*ICAO designator*]
                    (FAAC)
NIS .... Normal Incidence Spectrometer (PDAA)
NISCON .... National Industrial Safety Conference (PDAA)
NI-SIL .... Nickel-Silver
NISM .... Non-Deterministic Incomplete Sequential Machine (PDAA)
NISRA .... National Industrial Salvage and Recovery Association [*British*]
                    (BI)
NISUS .... Neutron Intermediate Standard Uranium Source (PDAA)
NISW .... Naval In-Shore Warfare (PDAA)
NIT .... Midwest Aviation Corp. [*ICAO designator*] (FAAC)
NITA .... National Instructional Television Association (NTCM)
NITC .... National Instructional Television Center (NTCM)
NJA .... National Jewellers' Association [*British*] (BI)
NJA .... Sky Air Cargo Services (UK) Ltd. [*British*] [*ICAO designator*]
                    (FAAC)
NJT .... Societe Novajet [*France*] [*ICAO designator*] (FAAC)
NKA .... Norcanair [*Canada*] [*ICAO designator*] (FAAC)
NL .... New Lead [*Also, NH*] [*News stories*] (NTCM)
NL .... Nonprogrammer Language [*Computer science*] (PDAA)
NLA .... Neiltown Air Ltd. [*Canada*] [*ICAO designator*] (FAAC)
NLC .... Node Location Code (PDAA)
NLCIF .... National Light Castings Ironfounders' Federation [*British*] (BI)
NLCSE .... Non-Linear Charge Storage Element (PDAA)
NLD .... Namakwaland Lugdiens (EDMS) BPK [*South Africa*] [*ICAO
                    designator*] (FAAC)
NLE .... Northern Commuter Airlines [*New Zealand*] [*ICAO designator*]
                    (FAAC)
NLEA .... Nutrition Labeling Education Act
NLF .... Westair Aviation, Inc. [*Canada*] [*ICAO designator*] (FAAC)
NLK .... Norlink Air Ltd. [*British*] [*ICAO designator*] (FAAC)
NLMC .... National Latino Media Coalition [*Citizen's group*] (NTCM)
NLME .... Non-Linear Material Effect (PDAA)
NLP .... Natural Law Party [*Australia*] [*Political party*]
NLP .... Normal Light Perception [*Physiology*] (MAH)
NLPQ .... Natural Language Processing System for Queuing Problems
                    [*Computer science*] (PDAA)
NLQ .... Nonlinear Quantization [*Telecommunications*] (NTCM)
NLR .... Net Liquidity Ratio (PDAA)
NLS .... New Least Square (PDAA)
NLSU .... National League for Social Understanding (EA)
NLT .... Newfoundland Labrador Air Transport Ltd. [*Canada*] [*ICAO
                    designator*] (FAAC)
NLUC .... National Land Use Classification (PDAA)
NMA.......... Needle Makers Association [*British*] (BI)
NMAC........ Nuclear Materials Accounting and Control
NMAS .... National Map Accuracy Standards (PDAA)
NMAX .... Nonwireline Multiple-Access Communications Exchange
                    System (PDAA)
NMB.......... Namib Air (Pty) Ltd. [*Namibia*] [*ICAO designator*] (FAAC)
NMC.......... National Mouse Club [*British*] (BI)
NMCA .... National Marble Club of America (EA)
NMDAR ..... N-Methyl-D-Aspartic Acid Receptor [*Neurochemistry*]
NMDIS ..... National Music and Disability Information Service [*British*]
NMDP....... Neomenthyldiphenylphosphine [*Organic chemistry*]
NMI .... Nuclear Magnetic Imaging
NMIS .... Newspapers Mutual Insurance Society Ltd. [*British*] (BI)
NML.......... Nuclear Magnetism Log (PDAA)
NMLO .... National Media Liaison Officer
NMMSB .... Non-Nuclear Munitions Safety Board
NMPC .... National Milk Publicity Council [*British*] (BI)
NMPC .... Naval Military Personnel Command (ANA)
NMR......... National Milk Record [*British*] (BI)
NMRD....... Nuclear Magnetic Relaxation Dispension [*Physics*]
NMS.......... Navigation Management System (PDAA)
NMS.......... Network Management System (DA)
NMS.......... Non-Metric Multidimensional Scaling (PDAA)
NMS.......... Nuclear-Powered Merchant Ship (PDAA)
NMSC .... Navy Management Systems Center (PDAA)
NMSCA ..... Navy Material Command Support Activity (PDAA)
NMSK .... Namesake (ABBR)
NMSMK ... Numismatic (ABBR)
NMSMTST ... Numismaticist (ABBR)
NMSS .... Nemesis (ABBR)
NMTLK ..... Nonmetallic (ABBR)
NMTN........ National Music Theater Network (EA)

NMTP .... National Means Test Proposal
NN .... Names (ABBR)
NNC.......... Non-Noise Certificated Aircraft (DA)
NNC.......... Nuance (ABBR)
NNE.......... Noise and Number Exposure (PDAA)
NNI........... Noise Nuisance Index (PDAA)
NNIS .... National Nosocomial Infections Surveillance [*Medicine*]
NNL.......... Non-Nuclear Lance Missile (PDAA)
NNR.......... National Nature Reserve (PDAA)
NNRTI ...... Non-Nucleoside Reverse Transcriptase Inhibitor [*Biochemistry*]
NNRY .... Nunnery (ABBR)
NO .... Noah (ABBR)
NO .... Northern (ABBR)
NOA .... Norontair [*Canada*] [*ICAO designator*] (FAAC)
NOAA-TR-NMFS-Circ ... National Oceanic and Atmospheric Administration
                    Technical Report-National Marine Fisheries Service-Circular
                    [*A publication*] (PDAA)
NOAA-TR-NMFS-SSRF ... National Oceanic and Atmospheric
                    Administration-Technical Report-National Marine Fisheries
                    Service-Special Scientific Report Fisheries (PDAA)
NOAH .... Narrow-Band Optimiziation of the Alignment of Highways
                    (PDAA)
NOB.......... Nobility (ABBR)
NOB.......... Noble (ABBR)
NOBMN.... Nobleman (ABBR)
NOBR....... Nobler (ABBR)
NOBST...... Noblest (ABBR)
NOBT....... Nobility (ABBR)
NOBWN..... Noblewomen (ABBR)
NOBY...... Nobly (ABBR)
NOC.......... Ascor Flyservice AS [*Norway*] [*ICAO designator*] (FAAC)
NOC.......... Natural Organic Carbon
NODS........ Near-Object Detection Sensor [*Automotive electronics*]
NOF.......... Fonnafly AS [*Norway*] [*ICAO designator*] (FAAC)
NOHARMM ... National Organization to Halt the Abuse and Routine
                    Mutilation of Males (EA)
NOHSCP ... National Oil and Hazardous Substances Contingency Plan
                    [*Environmental Protection Agency*] (ERG)
NOIE.......... Naval Ordnance Inspection Establishment [*Ministry of Defence*]
                    [*British*] (PDAA)
NOL.......... National Overseas Airline Co. [*Egypt*] [*ICAO designator*]
                    (FAAC)
NOLAP ...... Non-Linear Analysis Program (PDAA)
NOM .... Natural Organic Matter
NOMAD ... National Organization of Miniaturists and Dollers (EA)
NOMD ...... Nominated (ABBR)
NOMEE ..... Nominee (ABBR)
NOMG .... Nominating (ABBR)
NOMLM..... Nominalism (ABBR)
NOMLT ..... Nominalist (ABBR)
NOMLY .... Nominally (ABBR)
NOMR....... Nominator (ABBR)
NOMV ...... Nominative (ABBR)
NON-CM ... Noncumulative (ABBR)
NONP........ Non-Precision Approach Runway [*Aviation*] (DA)
NONPAR... Nonparticipating (ABBR)
NONPERF ... Nonperforated (ABBR)
NONSKED ... Nonscheduled (ABBR)
NONTT...... Nonentity (ABBR)
NOP.......... Novair-Aviacao Geral SA [*Portugal*] [*ICAO designator*] (FAAC)
NOP.......... Numerical Oceanographic Prediction (PDAA)
NOPAC...... North Pacific [*Aviation*] (FAAC)
NOPAR...... Do Not Pass to Air Defense RADAR [*Air Traffic Control*]
                    (FAAC)
NOPF .... Naval Oceanographic Processing Facility (ANA)
NOPMS ..... Network-Oriented Project Management System (PDAA)
NOR .... AS Norving [*Norway*] [*ICAO designator*] (FAAC)
NORFORM ... Not Releasable to Foreign Nationals
NORIV ...... No Arrival Report [*Aviation*] (FAAC)
NORM....... Naturally-Occurring Radioactive Material
NORTH...... Northerly (ABBR)
NORTH..... Northern (ABBR)
NORTHM ... Northumberland (ABBR)
NOS.......... Norway Airlines [*ICAO designator*] (FAAC)
NOS........... Nosing (ABBR)
NOSAP ...... National Ocean Survey Analytical Plotter [*NOAA*] (PDAA)
NOSD........ Nosed (ABBR)
NOSG .... Nosing (ABBR)
NOSINS.... Nosiness (ABBR)
NOSM....... Noise Diotic, Signal Monaural (PDAA)
NOT.......... New Organization Training
NOTN........ Notion (ABBR)
NOTS .... Nuclear Orbit Transfer Stage (PDAA)
NOUR .... Nourish (ABBR)
NOURD ..... Nourished (ABBR)
NOURG ..... Nourishing (ABBR)
NOURT...... Nourishment (ABBR)
NOV .... Avianova SpA [*Italy*] [*ICAO designator*] (FAAC)
NOV .... Novelist (ABBR)
NOVATOR ... Novye Torit [*Newly Flattened*] [*KGB term for newly recruited
                    agent abroad*]
NOVC........ Novice (ABBR)

NOVCAM ... Nonvolatile Charge-Addressed Memory [*Computer science*] (PDAA)
NOVST ...... Novelist (ABBR)
NOVT........ Novelty (ABBR)
NOW .... Nurture-Outreach-Witness [*Religion*]
NOW .... Royal Norwegian Air Force [*ICAO designator*] (FAAC)
NOWD ...... Northward (ABBR)
NOX .... Air Nordic in Vasteras AB [*Sweden*] [*ICAO designator*] (FAAC)
NOX .... Noxious (ABBR)
NOXY........ Noxiously (ABBR)
NOZ........... No Operating Zone (DA)
NP .... New Position
NP.............. No Printer Listed (NTCM)
NP.............. No Publisher Listed (NTCM)
NP.............. Nurse Practitioner
NPA .... Notice of Proposed Amendment (DA)
NPAB .... Nuclear Power Advisory Board (PDAA)
NPAC .... National Project in Agricultural Communication (PDAA)
NPBA .... National Pig Breeders' Association [*British*] (BI)
NPC .... Nonphased Color [*Television signals*] (NTCM)
NPCA .... National Pig Carvers Association (EA)
NPCDN ...... National Private Circuit Digital Network (PDAA)
NPD .... Napped (ABBR)
NPD........... National Program Director
NPD........... No Pay Due [*Military*] (ADDR)
NPDO........ Non-Profit Distributing Organization (PDAA)
NPDS .... National Pollutant Discharge Elimination System [*Environmental Protection Agency*] (ERG)
NPFM .... Neural Pulse Frequency Modulation (PDAA)
NPG........... N-Phenylglycine [*Organic chemistry*]
NPG........... Napping (ABBR)
NPIPF .... Newspaper and Printing Industries Pension Fund [*British*] (BI)
NPL .... National Priorities List
NPLS......... Nonplus (ABBR)
NPLSD....... Nonplused (ABBR)
NPN .... National Prices Network
NPOC........ National Point of Contact (PDAA)
NPO/HS .... Nulla per Os Hora Somni [*Nothing by Mouth at Bedtime*] [*Latin*] [*Pharmacy*] (MAH)
NPP .... National Pretreatment Program [*Metal finishing technology*]
NPPA .... National Pizza and Pasta Association (EA)
NPPAG....... National Program Production and Aquisition Grant [*Corporation for Public Broadcasting*] [*Radio*] (NTCM)
NPPTS .... Nuclear Power Plant Training Simulator (PDAA)
NPR........... Napper (ABBR)
NPR........... National Performance Review [*A publication*]
NPR........... Noise Preferential Route [*Aviation*] (DA)
NPRFT .... Nonprofit (ABBR)
NPRTSN.... Nonpartisan (ABBR)
NPRTSNSP ... Nonpartisanship (ABBR)
NPS .... Noise Power Spectra [*Spectrometry*]
NPSHA ...... Net Positive Suction Head Available [*Pumps*] (PDAA)
NPSM........ Non-Productive Standard Minute (PDAA)
NPTL......... Nuptial (ABBR)
NPTSM...... Nepotism (ABBR)
NPTST .... Nepotist (ABBR)
NPU........... National Pharmaceutical Union (PDAA)
NPVH........ Net Present Value at the Horizon (PDAA)
NPWC....... National Press Women's Club (NTCM)
NQM .... Navy Quality Management
NQN .... Transportes Aereos Neuquen [*Argentina*] [*ICAO designator*] (FAAC)
NR.............. Next to Reading Matter [*Also, NRM*] [*Advertising*] (NTCM)
NRA .... National Rounders Association [*British*] (BI)
NRA .... Negative Resistance Amplifier (PDAA)
NRBP .... Natural Resource-Based Product
NRC .... National Radio Conference [*Broadcast regulations*] (NTCM)
NRCHB...... Naval Reserve Cargo-Handling Battalion
NRCHTB ... Naval Reserve Cargo-Handling Training Battalion
NRCS......... National Roller Canary Society [*British*] (BI)
NRCSM...... Narcisism (ABBR)
NRCST....... Narcisist (ABBR)
NRCTK...... Narcotic (ABBR)
NRD........... Aeronardi SpA [*Italy*] [*ICAO designator*] (FAAC)
NRD........... Natural Resource Damage [*Environmental science*]
NRDB .... National Residue Database
NRDR .... Non-Resetting Data Reconstruction (PDAA)
NRDR-CF ... Non-Resetting Data Reconstruction with Continuous Feedback (PDAA)
NRDR-DF ... Non-Resetting Data Reconstruction with Discrete Feedback (PDAA)
NRE........... New and Renewable Energy (PDAA)
NREP .... National Registry of Environmental Professionals (EA)
NREVSS .... National Respiratory and Enteric Virus Surveillance System
NRG........... Energy (ABBR)
NRG........... Ross Aviation, Inc. [*ICAO designator*] (FAAC)
NRH .... No Reply Heard [*ICAO designator*] (FAAC)
NRHA .... National Roller Hockey Association of Great Britain (BI)
NRI .... National Research Institute [*Audience research organization*] (NTCM)
NRIA .... Narrow Resonance Infinite Absorber (PDAA)
NRIC .... Non-Reciprocal Impedance Converter (PDAA)
NRJ .... Non-Reciprocal Junction (PDAA)

NRK............ Newark (ABBR)
NRMLC ..... Normalcy (ABBR)
NRMLT...... Normality (ABBR)
NRMLY ..... Normally (ABBR)
NRMLZ ..... Normalize (ABBR)
NRMLZD ... Normalized (ABBR)
NRMLZG.. Normalizing (ABBR)
NRMLZN ... Normalization (ABBR)
NRMLZR... Normalizer (ABBR)
NRMV....... Normative (ABBR)
NRMVY..... Normatively (ABBR)
NRN........... Royal Netherlands Navy [*ICAO designator*] (FAAC)
NRNS........ Nearness (ABBR)
NRP........... Net Rating Points [*Media ratings*] (NTCM)
NRPA........ Non-Redundant Pinhole Array (PDAA)
NRPRA...... Natural Rubber Producers' Research Association [*British*] (BI)
NRPS........ Naval Radiological Protection Service (PDAA)
NRRAD ..... Narrated (ABBR)
NRRAG ..... Narrating (ABBR)
NRRAN ..... Narration (ABBR)
NRRAR ..... Narrator (ABBR)
NRRAV ..... Narrative (ABBR)
NRS .... Atlantic Richfield Co. [*ICAO designator*] (FAAC)
NRS .... Nurse (ABBR)
NRSD .... Nursed (ABBR)
NRSDNC... Nonresidence (ABBR)
NRSDNT.... Nonresident (ABBR)
NRSE......... Nurse (ABBR)
NRSED...... Nursed (ABBR)
NRSEG....... Nursing (ABBR)
NRSEMD... Nursemaid (ABBR)
NRSH........ Nourish (ABBR)
NRSHD...... Nourished (ABBR)
NRSHG...... Nourishing (ABBR)
NRSHNT ... Nourishment (ABBR)
NRSITD .... Near-Sighted (ABBR)
NRSITNS.. Near-Sightedness (ABBR)
NRSTCTV ... Nonrestrictive (ABBR)
NRSTK....... Narcisistic (ABBR)
NRT........... Net Registered Tonnage
NRTH........ North (ABBR)
NRTR........ Nurture (ABBR)
NRTRD ...... Nurtured (ABBR)
NRTRG ...... Nurturing (ABBR)
NRV........... Nerve (ABBR)
NRVD........ Nerved (ABBR)
NRVG........ Nerving (ABBR)
NRVI......... Nervy (ABBR)
NRVLS...... Nerveless (ABBR)
NRVU........ Nervous (ABBR)
NRVUNS... Nervousness (ABBR)
NRVUS ...... Nervous (ABBR)
NRVUSNS ... Nervousness (ABBR)
NRVUSY.... Nervously (ABBR)
NRVUY..... Nervously (ABBR)
NRVWRKG ... Nerve-Wracking (ABBR)
NRW......... Norwegian (ABBR)
NRW......... Number of Remaining Words
NRWD....... Narrowed (ABBR)
NRWG....... Narrowing (ABBR)
NRWMDD ... Narrow-Minded (ABBR)
NRWMDDNS ... Narrow-Mindedness (ABBR)
NRY........... Nearly (ABBR)
NS .... No Sound [*Script notation*] (NTCM)
NS.............. Noise Supressor [*Radio*] (NTCM)
NS.............. Nonslip (ABBR)
NS.............. Not Suitable
NSA .... National Sawmilling Association [*British*] (BI)
NSA .... Nile Safaris Aviation [*Sudan*] [*ICAO designator*] (FAAC)
NSA .... Nominal Stress Approach (PDAA)
NSA .... Non-Sterling Area (PDAA)
NSACS...... National Society for the Abolition of Cruel Sports [*British*] (BI)
NSB .... National Savings Bank [*British*]
NSB .... Non-Statutory Body
NSB .... Nord-Sud [*Benin*] [*ICAO designator*] (FAAC)
NSBA......... National Sheep Breeders' Association [*British*] (BI)
NSC .... National Service Center
NSC .... No Significant Cloud [*Meteorology*] (FAAC)
NSCD .... National School Development Council (AEE)
NSCG .... Northeastern Spoon Collectors Guild (EA)
NSCNC ...... Nascence (ABBR)
NSCNT...... Nascent (ABBR)
NSCS .... National Scouting Collectors Society (EA)
NSCTRN.... Nonsectarian (ABBR)
NSD .... Northside Aviation Ltd. [*British*] [*ICAO designator*] (FAAC)
NSDA .... Nissan Safety Device Advisor [*Driver information system*]
NSDM........ Nuclear Sediment Density Meter (PDAA)
NSE .... Noise (ABBR)
NSE .... Number of Simultaneous Engagements [*Military*]
NSE .... Satena Servicios de Aeronavegacion A Territorios Nac [*Colombia*] [*ICAO designator*] (FAAC)
NSEC......... National Society of Environmental Consultants (EA)
NSELS .... Noiseless (ABBR)

NSENS...... Noisiness (ABBR)
NSES......... National Society of Electrotypers and Stereotypers [*British*] (BI)
NSFORT .... Non-Standard FORTRAN [*Computer science*] (PDAA)
NSFS .... Net Section Fracture Strength (PDAA)
NSG .... Nuclear Suppliers' Group [*Australia*] (ECON)
NSI .... Non-Syncytium-Inducing [*Medicine*]
NSIR .... Nosier (ABBR)
NSL .... Nasal (ABBR)
NSLY........ Nasally (ABBR)
NSLY........ Noisily (ABBR)
NSMHC ..... National Society for Mentally Handicapped Children [*British*] (BI)
NSMP....... National Society of Master Patternmakers [*British*] (BI)
NSMRTS ... Nuclear Submarine Maneuvering Room Training Simulator (PDAA)
NSNCE...... Nuisance (ABBR)
NSNCL...... Nonsensical (ABBR)
NSNS........ Nonsense (ABBR)
NSNSCLY ... Nonsensically (ABBR)
NSPR........ Nonstandard Part Approval Request
NSPRT ...... Nonsupport (ABBR)
NSPS .... National Sweet Pea Society [*British*] (BI)
NSR .... National Air Charter PT [*Indonesia*] [*ICAO designator*] (FAAC)
NSRO .... Navy Resale System Office (PDAA)
NSS .... National Sample Survey (PDAA)
NSS .... National Search and Rescue Secretariat [*Canada*] (DA)
NSS .... Neutral Speed Stability (PDAA)
NSS .... Northstar Aviation, Inc. [*ICAO designator*] (FAAC)
NSS........... Nuclear Science Symposium (PDAA)
NSSK......... North-South Station-Keeping (PDAA)
NSSP .... Neutralization Self-Solidification Process (PDAA)
NST .... Aviacion Ejecutiva del Noroeste SA de CV [*Mexico*] [*ICAO designator*] (FAAC)
NST .... Nasty (ABBR)
NST .... Nest (ABBR)
NST .... Noise, Spikes, and Transients (PDAA)
NST .... Numerical Surveying Technique (PDAA)
NSTC........ National Science Technology Council
NSTG .... Nesting (ABBR)
NSTL........ Nestled (ABBR)
NSTLG...... Nestling (ABBR)
NSTLG...... Nostalgia (ABBR)
NSTLGC ... Nostalgic (ABBR)
NSTNS...... Nastiness (ABBR)
NSTP........ National Society of TV Producers (NTCM)
NSTY........ Nastily (ABBR)
NSV .... Noise, Shock, and Vibration (PDAA)
NSW .... Ansett Airlines of New South Wales [*Australia*] [*ICAO designator*] (FAAC)
NSY .... Noisy (ABBR)
NT............ Natty (ABBR)
NT............ Neurotoxin [*Biochemistry*]
NT............. Niton (ABBR)
NTA.......... National Teachers Association (AEE)
NTA.......... National Telefilm Associates, Inc. (NTCM)
NTA.......... National Type Approval (PDAA)
NTA.......... Northern Thunderbird Air Ltd. [*Canada*] [*ICAO designator*] (FAAC)
NTAB .... Notable (ABBR)
NTABY...... Notably (ABBR)
NTAP .... National Track Analysis Program [*Aviation*] (FAAC)
NTAP .... Notices to Airmen Publication [*A publication*] (FAAC)
NTARY ...... Notary (ABBR)
NTATN ..... Notation (ABBR)
NTATNL.... Notational (ABBR)
NTB .... Notable (ABBR)
NTBK .... Notebook (ABBR)
NTBY .... Notably (ABBR)
NTC .... Gibson Aviation [*ICAO designator*] (FAAC)
NTC .... Network Transmission Committee [*Video Transmission Engineering Committee*] (NTCM)
NTC .... No Traffic Reported [*Air Traffic Control*] (FAAC)
NTCB .... Noticeable (ABBR)
NTCBY...... Noticeably (ABBR)
NTCCS....... Naval Tactical Command and Control System (PDAA)
NTCD .... Noticed (ABBR)
NTCG .... Noticing (ABBR)
NTCHA...... National Taxi and Car Hire Association [*British*] (BI)
NTCKR...... Nutcracker (ABBR)
NTCP........ Nightcap (ABBR)
NTE .... Network-Terminating Equipment (PDAA)
NTE .... Nursing the Environment
NTFC........ Nonlinear Transient Fuel Film Compsensation [*Automotive fuel system*]
NTFWTC ... NATO Tactical Fighter Weapons Training Center
NTHV........ Near-Term Hybrid Vehicle (PDAA)
NTK.......... Newton Tool Kit [*Computer science*]
NTL .... Northair Aviation Ltd. [*British*] [*ICAO designator*] (FAAC)
NTLS......... Non-Transposed Loop Sensor (PDAA)
NTM.......... North American Airlines, Inc. [*Canada*] [*ICAO designator*] (FAAC)
NTN.......... National Airways Corp. (Pty) Ltd. [*South Africa*] [*ICAO designator*] (FAAC)

NTPE......... Non-Tactical Peripheral Equipment [*Military*]
NTR........... Net-of-Tax Rate (ECON)
NTS .... Cirrus Air, Inc. [*ICAO designator*] (FAAC)
NTS .... Navigation Technology Satellite (PDAA)
NTSH........ Near-Term Scout Helicopter [*Army*]
NTT.......... Non-Tactical Tape [*Military*]
NTTE........ Non-Tactical Training Equipment [*Military*]
NTTRL...... National Tissue Typing Reference Laboratory (PDAA)
NTTS........ National Technology Transfer Center
NTVA........ Nondeterministic Time-Variant Automation (PDAA)
NTW.......... Non-Pressure Thermit Welding (PDAA)
NTX........... Northern Air Service, Inc. [*ICAO designator*] (FAAC)
NU .... Not Used
NUA .... Not Under the Act
NUA .... Nuna Air AS [*Denmark*] [*ICAO designator*] (FAAC)
NUCOL...... Numerical Control Language [*Computer science*] (PDAA)
NUCWARN ... Nuclear Warning Message [*Military*] (ADDR)
NUFCW .... National Union of Funeral and Cemetery Workers [*British*] (BI)
NUFUCO ... Nuclear Fuel Cost (PDAA)
NUMEPS... Numeric Meta Language Processing System (PDAA)
NUN .... Nunasi-Central Airlines Ltd. [*Canada*] [*ICAO designator*] (FAAC)
NURA........ National Union of Rate-Payers' Associations [*British*] (BI)
NURC........ National Union of Retail Confectioners [*British*] (BI)
NURT........ National Union of Retail Tobacconists [*British*] (BI)
NUSACC.... National United States-Arab Chamber of Commerce (EA)
NUSCOT ... Nuclear Submarine Control Trainer (PDAA)
NUSS........ Nuclear Safety Standard (PDAA)
NUTIS....... Numerical and Textile Information System (PDAA)
NUTTAB.... Nutrient Data Table
NUWEDS ... Nuclear Weapons Emergency Destruct System [*Navy*] (ANA)
NUWMF.... Naval Undersea Warfare Museum Foundation (PDAA)
N/V .... Number of Engine Revolutions per Minute per Vehicle Miles per Hour [*Automotive engineering*]
NVA.......... National Villa Association [*British*] (BI)
NVA.......... Nile Valley Aviation Co. [*Egypt*] [*ICAO designator*] (FAAC)
NVACP...... Neighborhoods, Voluntary Associations and Consumer Protection [*Environmental Protection Agency*] (ERG)
NVAR........ Normalized Variance (PDAA)
NVE.......... Colvin Aviation, Inc. [*ICAO designator*] (FAAC)
NVEBW.... Non-Vacuum Electron Beam Welding (PDAA)
NVL.......... Hunting Aviation Services Ltd. [*British*] [*ICAO designator*] (FAAC)
NVP.......... N-Vinylpyrrolidone [*Organic chemistry*]
NVPS......... Night Vision Pilotage System [*Military*]
NVS.......... Number of Video Samples
NVSDS....... New Vehicle Satisfaction with Dealer Service [*Quality research*]
NVSMD..... Nonvolatile Semiconductor Memory Device (PDAA)
NVY.......... Royal Navy [*British*] [*ICAO designator*] (FAAC)
NWA.......... Northwest Airlines, Inc. [*ICAO designator*] (FAAC)
NWB.......... Northwestbound [*ICAO designator*] (FAAC)
NWC.......... Nuclear Weapons Control
NWCR........ Naval War College Review [*A publication*]
NWD .... Northwest Air Services Ltd. [*Nigeria*] [*ICAO designator*] (FAAC)
NWDC........ Navigation/Weapon Delivery Computer (PDAA)
NWH .... Nawa Air Transport [*Hungary*] [*ICAO designator*] (FAAC)
NWN .... Northwinds Northern Ltd. [*Canada*] [*ICAO designator*] (FAAC)
NwRSA..... Northwest Region Spinners Association (EA)
NWS-CR .... National Weather Service-Central Region (PDAA)
NWS-ER .... National Weather Service-Eastern Region (PDAA)
NWSI........ New World Services, Inc.
NWS-SR.... National Weather Service-Southern Region (PDAA)
NWS-WR .. National Weather Service-Western Region (PDAA)
NWT.......... Northwest Territorial Airways [*Canada*] [*ICAO designator*] (FAAC)
NWTEC ..... National Wool Textile Export Corp. [*British*] (BI)
NWW........ North West Airline [*Australia*] [*ICAO designator*] (FAAC)
NXA........... Nolisair International, Inc. [*Canada*] [*ICAO designator*] (FAAC)
NXSR........ Non-Extraction Steam Rate (PDAA)
NYG .... Nyge Aero AB [*Sweden*] [*ICAO designator*] (FAAC)
NYH .... New York Helicopter Corp. [*ICAO designator*] (FAAC)
NYHA .... National Yacht Harbour Association [*British*] (BI)
NYO .... Not Yet Operating (DA)
NYS .... Not Yet Specified
NZB .... Royal New Zealand Ballet
NZM.......... Mount Cook Airlines [*New Zealand*] [*ICAO designator*] (FAAC)

O

O .... Other Program   (NTCM)
6O .... Somalia [*Aircraft nationality and registration mark*]   (FAAC)
OA .... Orbit Analysis
OA .... Organizational Analysis
OA .... Osteogenesis Imperfecta [*Brittle bone disease*]
OAA........... Oxley Aviation [*Australia*] [*ICAO designator*]   (FAAC)
OAB........... Outer Air Battle [*Navy*]   (ANA)
OAB........... Owners Abroad Aviation Ltd. [*British*] [*ICAO designator*]
                   (FAAC)
OAC........... Oriental Airlines Ltd. [*Nigeria*] [*ICAO designator*]   (FAAC)
OACP .... Operational Analysis Code Package   (PDAA)
OAD .... Optical Activity Detection
OADAP ...... Office of Alcoholism and Drug Abuse Prevention [*Department of
                   Health and Human Services*]
OAE........... Orbiting Astronomical Explorer   (PDAA)
OAE........... Oscillating-Analyzer Ellipsometer   (PDAA)
OAF........... Austrian Air Ambulance [*ICAO designator*]   (FAAC)
OAF........... Orbital Antenna Farm   (PDAA)
OAG........... Official Airline Guide, Inc. [*ICAO designator*]   (FAAC)
OAI............ Ohio Aerospace Institute
OAL........... Olympic Airways SA [*Greece*] [*ICAO designator*]   (FAAC)
OAMA....... Oil Appliance Manufacturers' Association [*British*]   (BI)
OANR........ Office of Air, Noise, and Radiation [*Environmental Protection
                   Agency*]   (ERG)
OAOR........ Oxygen Adsorption, Out-gassing, and Chemical Reduction
                   (PDAA)
OAP........... On-Axis Pointing   (PDAA)
OAPWL..... Overall Power Watt Level   (PDAA)
OAR........... Ordering as Required   (PDAA)
OAR........... Original Action Record
OAS........... Obstacle Assessment Surface [*Aviation*]   (DA)
OAS........... Ohio Academy of Science   (PDAA)
OAS........... Oman Aviation Services Co. [*ICAO designator*]   (FAAC)
OAS........... Orbitor Avionics Simulator [*NASA*]
OASD(PA) ... Office of the Assistant Secretary of Defense (Public Affairs)
                   (NTCM)
OASIS .... Ownership Accountability of Selected Secondary Items Stocked
OASP........ Over-All Sound Pressure   (PDAA)
OAT........... On Air Test   (NTCM)
OAT........... Oxide-Aligned Transistor [*Electronics*]   (PDAA)
OAT........... Sogervair/Transoceanic Aviation [*France*] [*ICAO designator*]
                   (FAAC)
OATS .... Outdoor Advertising Total System   (PDAA)
OAU .... Oriol Avia [*Russian Federation*] [*ICAO designator*]   (FAAC)
OAV........... Omni-Aviacao e Tecnologia Lda. [*Portugal*] [*ICAO designator*]
                   (FAAC)
OAX........... Operational Aviation Services - Australia [*ICAO designator*]
                   (FAAC)
OB.............. Obidiah [*Old Testament*]
O-B .... Oerlikon-Buehrle [*Switzerland*]
OB.............. Official Board of Ballroom Dancing [*British*]   (BI)
OBGS .... On-Board Gunnery Simulator   (PDAA)
OBL........... Oceanic Boundary Layer
OBOE........ Offshore Buoy-Observing Equipment   (PDAA)
OBOS .... Our Bodies Ourselves [*A publication*]
OBP .... Occupational Back Pain
OBP .... On-Line Benefits Processing
OBRAD ..... Oblate Radial   (PDAA)
Obs............. Obscene [*Legal term*]
OBS .... Obscurant
Obs............. Obstacle Light [*Aviation*]   (DA)
OBTW .... Oh, By the Way [*Computer hacker terminology*]   (NHD)
OBV .... Obstacle Breaching Vehicle [*Military*]
OBV .... Octane Blending Value   (PDAA)
OC.............. Obstacle Clearance
OCA........... Aeroservicios Carabobo CA (ASERCA) [*Venzuela*] [*ICAO
                   designator*]   (FAAC)
OCA........... Obstacle Clearance Altitude [*Aviation*]   (DA)
OCA........... Offensive Counterair [*Army*]   (ADDR)
OCAS .... Out of Controlled Airspace [*Aviation*]   (FAAC)
OCC........... Occluded Corrosion Cell   (PDAA)
OCCI .... Optical Coincidence Coordinate Indexing   (PDAA)
OCCR .... Overseas Custody (Child Removal)

OCE........... Helicocean [*France*] [*ICAO designator*]   (FAAC)
OCF .... Open Computing Facility
OCGT........ Open-Cycle Gas Turbine   (PDAA)
OCH .... Obstacle Clearance Height [*Aviation*]   (FAAC)
OCHRE...... Optical Character Recognition Engine   (PDAA)
OCI............ Occlude   (DA)
OCIS........... OSHA [*Occupational Safety and Health Administration*]
                   Computerized Information System [*Environmental science*]
OCL........... Over-Night Cargo Ltd. [*Nigeria*] [*ICAO designator*]   (FAAC)
OCMA....... Oil Companies' Materials Association [*British*]   (BI)
OCN........... Oceanair-Transportes Aeroes Regional SA [*Portugal*] [*ICAO
                   designator*]   (FAAC)
OCO .... Off-Load Control Officer [*Navy*]   (ANA)
OCOAP ...... Oscillating-Compensator Oscillating-Analyzer Polarimeter
                   (PDAA)
OCP........... Open Circuit Potential   (PDAA)
OCP........... Orbital Combustion Process   (PDAA)
OCPSF .... Organic Chemical, Plastic, and Synthetic Fiber
OCR........... Optional Character Reader [*Computer science*]   (DA)
OCRIT........ Office of Combat Indentification Technology [*Army*]
OCS........... Ocean Color Scanner   (PDAA)
OCST......... Office of Cable Signal Theft [*National Cable Television
                   Association*]   (NTCM)
OCT........... Octanol [*Organic chemistry*]
OCTA .... Oceanic Control Area [*Aviation*]   (DA)
OD .... Orbiter (Operational) Downlink [*NASA*]
OD .... Overburden Drill   (PDAA)
ODB........... Air Service [*Mali*] [*ICAO designator*]   (FAAC)
ODC........... Oxyhaemoglobin Dissociation Curve   (PDAA)
ODCS .... Online Data Compression System   (PDAA)
ODD .... Overseas Deployment Data [*Military*]
ODF........... Official Development Finance
ODI............ [*H.*] Jonsson Air Taxi [*Iceland*] [*ICAO designator*]   (FAAC)
ODM .... Odiham FTU [*British*] [*ICAO designator*]   (FAAC)
ODNMR.... Optically-Detected Nuclear Magnetic Resonance [*Spectroscopy*]
ODPEX ...... Offshore Drilling and Production Exhibition   (PDAA)
ODS........... Open Database Server [*Computer science*]
ODT........... Odor Detection Threshold   (PDAA)
ODTACCS ... Office of the Director, Telecommunications, and Command and
                   Control Systems [*DoD*]   (PDAA)
ODTW........ Oppositely-Directed Travelling Wave   (PDAA)
ODUSD(ES) ... Office of the Deputy Under Secretary of Defense
                   (Environmental Security) [*DoD*]   (RDA)
ODY.......... Odyssey International [*Canada*] [*ICAO designator*]   (FAAC)
OEA........... Orchestral Employers' Association [*British*]   (BI)
OEC........... Observed Effect Concentration [*Environmental science*]   (ERG)
OEC........... Office of Emergency Communications [*FCC*]   (NTCM)
OEC........... Oxygen-Evolving Complex [*Photosynthesis*]
OEDRC ...... Optico-Electronic Device for Registering Coincidences   (PDAA)
OEIC .... Overseas Economic Intelligence Committee [*Military*]
OEL........... Ontario Express Ltd. [*Canada*] [*ICAO designator*]   (FAAC)
OEM.......... Optical Electron Microscope   (PDAA)
OEQ........... Order of Engineers of Quebec [*Canada*]   (PDAA)
OER........... Oxygen Evolution Reaction   (PDAA)
OESBR....... Oil Extended Styrene Butadiene Rubber   (PDAA)
OESR......... Oil Extended Synthetic Rubber   (PDAA)
OFC........... Outside Front Cover [*Publishing*]   (NTCM)
OFD........... Optical Gun Fire Director [*Military*]   (PDAA)
OFDS......... Optimal Financial Decision Strategy   (PDAA)
OFF........... Challenge Air Transport, Inc. [*ICAO designator*]   (FAAC)
OFIS......... Operational Flight Information Service [*ICAO*]   (DA)
OFM.......... Out for Maintenance [*Aviation*]   (FAAC)
OFP-MIR ... Ozone-Forming Potential-Maximum Incremental Reactivity
                   [*Exhaust emissions*] [*Automotive engineering*]
OFS........... Operations Fixed Service [*Microwave service*]   (NTCM)
OFV .... Opposing Forces Vehicle [*Military*]
OFXT......... Outer Fix Time [*Aviation*]   (FAAC)
OG .... Olive Green [*Army*]   (ADDR)
OG .... On Grade   (DAC)
OGD .... Open Government Document   (PDAA)
OGLE .... Optical Gravitational Lens Experiment [*Astronomy*]
OGRE........ Optical Grating Reflectance Evaluator   (PDAA)
OH .... Ontario Hydroelectric [*Canada*]

OHA .... OH Aviationa [*France*] [*ICAO designator*]   (FAAC)
OHAS .... Occupational Health and Safety
OHD ...... Optical Heterodyne Detection
OHDMS ..... Operational Hydromet Data Management System   (PDAA)
OHHA .... Occupational Health Hazard Assessment
OHMES ...... Occupational Health Monitoring and Evaluation System   (PDAA)
OHS .... Oval-Headed Screw   (DAC)
OHST .... Occupational Health and Safety Technologist
OHT .... Overheating Temperature   (PDAA)
OHY .... Onur Hava Tasimacilik AWMS [*Turkey*] [*ICAO designator*]
                 (FAAC)
OID .... Object Identifier [*Computer science*]
OIR .... Slov-Air [*Slovakia*] [*ICAO designator*]   (FAAC)
OIS .... Obstacle Identification Surface [*Aviation*]   (DA)
OIT .... Organization Iberoamericaine de Television   (NTCM)
OJA .... Oriental Pearl Airways Ltd. [*British*] [*ICAO designator*]   (FAAC)
OJE .... Orthodox Job Enrichment   (PDAA)
OJOP .... Olympic Job Opportunities Program
OJY .... Florida Air, Inc. [*ICAO designator*]   (FAAC)
OK .... Optical Klystron   (PDAA)
OKE .... Optical Kerr Effect [*Birefringence induced in an electrical field*]
OKJ .... Okada Airlines Ltd. [*Nigeria*] [*ICAO designator*]   (FAAC)
O/L .... Observation/Losing [*Army*]   (ADDR)
OLA .... Official Languages Act [*Canada*]
OLA .... Optical Link in the Atmosphere   (PDAA)
OLAA .... Office of Legal Aid Administration
OLAFS ...... Office of Legal Aid and Family Services
OLCC .... Optimum Life Cycle Costing   (PDAA)
OLD .... Operating Level Days
OLDAP ...... Online Data Processor   (PDAA)
OLDI .... Online Data Interchange   (DA)
OLE .... Online Enquiry [*System*]
OLF .... Online Filing [*Computer science*]   (PDAA)
OLFO .... Open-Loop Feedback Optimal   (PDAA)
OLI .... Online Information
OLIVER ..... Online Instrumentation via Energetic Radioisotopes [*Computer
                 science*]   (PDAA)
OLOC .... Old Lesbians Organizing for Change [*An association*]   (EA)
OL/PBAR ... Online Patient Billing and Accounts Receivable System
                 [*Computer science*]   (PDAA)
OLR .... Off Load Route [*Aviation*]   (DA)
OLS .... Operational Linescan System [*Navy*]   (ANA)
OLSA .... Orbiter Logistics Support Plan [*NASA*]
OLSASS ..... Online System Availability and Service Simulation [*Computer
                 science*]   (PDAA)
OLT .... Ostfriesische Lufttransport GmbH [*Germany*] [*ICAO
                 designator*]   (FAAC)
OLTE .... Online Test Executive Program [*Computer science*]   (PDAA)
OLY .... Olympic Aviation SA [*Greece*] [*ICAO designator*]   (FAAC)
OM .... Officine Meccaniche [*Italian auto manufacturer*]
OMA .... Oilskin Manufacturers' Association of Great Britain Ltd.   (BI)
OMA .... Overall Manufacturers' Association of Great Britain   (BI)
OMACS ..... Online Manufacturing and Control System [*Computer science*]
                 (PDAA)
OMAS .... One-Man Atmospheric Submersible   (PDAA)
OMF .... Omniflys SA de CV [*Mexico*] [*ICAO designator*]   (FAAC)
OMG .... Aeromega Ltd. [*British*] [*ICAO designator*]   (FAAC)
OMMCS ..... Ordnance Missile and Munitions Center and School [*Army*]
OMO .... Singly-Occupied Molecular Orbital [*Physical chemistry*]
OMP .... Ormetoprim [*Potentiator for antibacterials*] [*Veterinary medicine*]
OMPEC ..... Offshore Mechanics and Polar Engineering Council
OMS .... Octahedral Molecular Sieve [*Inorganic chemistry*]
OMS .... Operational Mission Summary [*Army*]
OMS .... Ovonic Memory Switch   (PDAA)
OMSG .... Our Message [*Aviation*]   (FAAC)
OMV .... Overseas Media Visitor
ON .... Omega Navigation   (PDAA)
ONA .... Office of National Assessments [*Australia*]
ONA .... Overseas National Airways [*Belgium*] [*ICAO designator*]
                 (FAAC)
ONAS .... Outpatient Nonavailability Statement [*DoD*]
ONC+ .... Open Network Computing Plus [*Computer science*]   (PCM)
ONER .... Oceanic Navigational Error Report [*Aviation*]   (FAAC)
ONLAS ...... Optical Night Landing Approach System [*Aviation*]   (PDAA)
ONPG .... Operational Nuclear Planning Group [*Military*]
ONRS .... Oceanic Navigation Research Society   (EA)
ONT .... Air Ontario Ltd. [*Canada*] [*ICAO designator*]   (FAAC)
ONVL .... Over-the-Nose Vision Line   (PDAA)
OODR-MPI ... Optical-Optical Double Resonance Multiphonton Ionization
                 [*Spectrocopy*]
OOM .... Organized Organic Monolayer [*Organic chemistry*]
OOM .... Original Online Module [*Computer science*]   (PDAA)
OOP .... Offline Orthophoto Printer [*Computer science*]   (PDAA)
O & OP ...... Organizational and Operational Plan [*Army*]
OOPS .... Online Object Patching System [*Computer science*]   (PDAA)
OOSH .... Out of School Hours
OP .... Occasional Paper
OP .... Occupational Psychologist
OP .... Osterogenic Protein
OPA .... Office of Producer Affairs [*Federal Telecommunications
                 Commission*]
OPA .... Opal Air Pty Ltd. [*Australia*] [*ICAO designator*]   (FAAC)
OPAS .... Operational Assignment   (DA)

OPC .... Open Promoter Complex [*Genetics*]
OPC .... Optical Particle Counter   (PDAA)
OPD .... Optical Phase Distortion   (PDAA)
OPDAG ...... Original Paper Doll Artists Guild   (EA)
OPDIF .... Operational Planning Identification File [*Military*]
OPDOC ...... Operational Documentation [*Military*]
OPE .... Societe 3S Aviation (Aerope) [*France*] [*ICAO designator*]
                 (FAAC)
OPERUN ... Operation Planning and Execution System for Railway Unified
                 Network   (PDAA)
OPHR .... Olympic Project for Human Rights
Op Hrs .... Operation Hours   (DA)
OPINE .... Operations in a Nuclear Environment [*DoD*]
OPL .... Air Cote d'Opale [*France*] [*ICAO designator*]   (FAAC)
OPMAC ..... Operations for Military Assistance to the Community   (PDAA)
OPMC .... One Player Median Competitive   (PDAA)
OPOS .... Optical Property of Orbiting Satellite [*NASA*]   (PDAA)
O-POS .... Oxygen-Dope Polysilicon   (PDAA)
OPOSTOR ... Oppose Sortie [*Navy*]   (ANA)
OPP .... Off-Load Preparation Party [*Navy*]   (ANA)
OPP .... Oxidative Pentose Phosphate   (PDAA)
OPR .... Operational Preference   (DA)
OPRAD ...... Operations Research and Development Management   (PDAA)
OPS .... Omnidirectional Point Source   (PDAA)
OPS .... On-Site Inspection Agency [*DoD*] [*ICAO designator*]   (FAAC)
OPS .... Operational Performance Standard [*Aviation*]   (DA)
OPS .... Operator System Program [*Manufacturing engineering*]
                 [*Computer science*]
OPS .... Optical Power Spectrum   (PDAA)
OPSA .... Optimal Pneumatic Systems Analysis   (PDAA)
OPSAM ...... Optical Storage Access Method [*Computer science*]   (PDAA)
OPSP .... Operations Panel [*ICAO*]   (DA)
OPSTACOM ... Optical Satellite Communications
OPT'D .... Optioned [*Automotive advertising*]
OPTNET ..... Optimum Private Trunk Network Embodying Tandems   (PDAA)
OPTOL ...... Optimized Test-Oriented Language [*Computer science*]   (PDAA)
OPTRAK .... Optical Tracking and Ranging Kit   (PDAA)
OPV .... Bedarfsflugunternehmen Dr. L. Polsterer [*Austria*] [*ICAO
                 designator*]   (FAAC)
OPV .... Optical Path-Length Variation   (PDAA)
OQA .... Optical Quantum Amplifier   (PDAA)
OR .... Operations Request [*Military*]
ORA .... Montauk Caribbean Airways, Inc. [*ICAO designator*]   (FAAC)
ORA .... Organizational Role Analysis   (PDAA)
ORACLE .... Oversight of Resources and Capability for Logistics
                 Effectiveness   (PDAA)
ORASA ...... Operational Research and Systems Analysis   (PDAA)
ORBE .... Open Reciprocating Brayton Engine   (PDAA)
ORBIS CAL ... Orbiting Radio Beacon Ionosphere Satellite for Calibration
                 [*NASA*]   (PDAA)
ORBIT .... Order Billing Inventory Technique   (PDAA)
ORC .... Offshore Racing Council
ORC .... Organic Rankine Cycle [*for power generation*]   (PDAA)
ORCATS .... Oldtime Radio Collectors and Traders Society   (EA)
ORCID .... Optical Readout Cherenkov Imaging Detector [*Computer
                 science*]   (PDAA)
ORD .... CAP PA Gutierrez [*Hernando R.*] Ordonez [*Mexico*] [*ICAO
                 designator*]   (FAAC)
ORD .... Once-Run Distillate   (PDAA)
ORDC .... Orbiter Data Reduction Center [*NASA*]
ORDEAL .... Oak Ridge Data Evaluation and Analysis Language [*Department
                 of Energy*]   (PDAA)
ORE .... Optimum Resource Extraction   (PDAA)
OREPS .... Operational Research in Electrical Power Systems   (PDAA)
ORF .... Oman Royal Flight [*ICAO designator*]   (FAAC)
ORFEUS ..... Orbiting Far and Extreme Ultraviolet Spectrometer [*Telescope*]
ORG .... Oriental Airlines (Gambia) Ltd. [*ICAO designator*]   (FAAC).
ORI .... Ocurrence of Reinforcing Information   (PDAA)
ORI .... Orient Air Ltd. [*British*] [*ICAO designator*]   (FAAC)
ORK .... Air Orkney [*British*] [*ICAO designator*]   (FAAC)
ORL .... On Air Ltd. [*Canada*] [*ICAO designator*]   (FAAC)
ORLA .... Optimum Report Level Analysis [*Military*]
ORN .... Orient Airways [*Pakistan*] [*ICAO designator*]   (FAAC)
OROSS ...... Operational Readiness-Oriented Supply System [*Army*]   (PDAA)
ORP .... Operational Readiness Platform [*Aviation*]   (DA)
ORRTA ...... Office of the Registrar of Restrictive Trading Agreements
                 (PDAA)
ORTAG ...... Operations Research Technical Assistance Group [*Army*]
                 (PDAA)
ORTF......... Office de Radiodiffusion-Television Francaise [*National
                 Broadcasting Organization*] [*France*]   (NTCM)
ORVID .... Online X-ray Evaluation over Video-Display Including
                 Documentation   (PDAA)
ORW.......... Orwex [*Poland*] [*ICAO designator*]   (FAAC)
ORX .... Oryx Aviation [*South Africa*] [*ICAO designator*]   (FAAC)
OS .... Old Style [*Printing*]   (NTCM)
OS .... Out of Stock   (NTCM)
OS .... Over-the-Shoulder Cinematography   (NTCM)
OSA .... Aero Astra [*Mexico*] [*ICAO designator*]   (FAAC)
OSAIS .... Oil Spillage Analytical and Identification Service [*Laboratory of
                 the Government Chemist*]   (PDAA)
OSCAR....... Oscillogram Scan and Recorder System   (PDAA)

OSCER....... Offshore Survival Craft Emergency Radiotelephone [*Telecommunications*] (PDAA)
OSCOT ...... Overall Systems Combat Operability Test [*Navy*] (ANA)
OSCR.......... Operating and Support Cost Reduction [*Army*]
OSDPT....... Optimization of Systems for Data Processing and Transmission (PDAA)
OSE .... Ocean and Science Engineering Inc.
OSE .... Organizational Support Equipment [*Army*]
OSEAS....... Ocean Sampling and Environmental Analysis System (PDAA)
OSF............. Oxidation-Induced Stacking Fault (PDAA)
OSGR .... Oscillator Single Gain Region (PDAA)
OSHC........ Outside School Hours Care
OSHC........ Overseas Student Health Coverage
OSI .... Aerosi SA de CV [*Mexico*] [*ICAO designator*] (FAAC)
OSIRIS....... Online Search Information Retrieval Information Storage [*Computer science*] (PDAA)
OSLB.......... Operational Search Lower Bound [*RADAR*]
OSM........... Oncostatin [*Antibiotic*]
OS-PIF .... Office of the Secretary of Defense Productivity Investment Funding
OSPRDS .... Oblate Spheroid (PDAA)
OSR .... Output Status Register
OSS............. Occupational Superannuation Standard
OSSD......... Off-Site Surveillance Data [*Military*]
OST .... Ordnance Shock Test [*Military*]
OSWV .... Osteryoung Square Wave Voltammogram [*Electrochemistry*]
OT.............. Ortho Tolidine (PDAA)
OTBE .... Overtaken by Events [*Military*]
OTC........... One-Time Carbon [*Paper*] (PDAA)
OTC........... Organotin Compound [*Organic chemistry*]
OTC........... Oshkosh Truck Corp.
OTC........... Ozone Transport Commission [*State environmental agencies*]
OTCIXS ..... Officer in Tactical Command Information Exchange Subsystem [*Navy*] (ANA)
OTD........... Optimal Terminal Descent (PDAA)
OTIS.......... Observer's Thermal Imaging System (PDAA)
OTJT......... On the Job Training
OTM.......... On-Time Marker [*Computer science*]
OTM.......... Organo-Transition-Metal (PDAA)
OTN........... Lastp-Linhas Aereas de Sao Tome e Principe [*ICAO designator*] (FAAC)
OTN........... Own-the-Night [*Technology*] [*Army*] (INF)
OTP .... Overhead Trickle Purification (PDAA)
OTS .... Octadecyltrichlorosilane [*Organic chemistry*]
OTSOG ...... On the Shoulders of Giants [*Literature*]
OTTB .... Optically-Thin Thermal Bremsstrahlung [*Astrophysics*]
OTTW .... Optical Telescope Technology Workshop [*NASA*] (PDAA)
OUBD........ Outbound [*ICAO designator*] (FAAC)
OUHSC...... Oklahoma University Health Sciences Center
OUL........... Air Atonabee Ltd. [*Canada*] [*ICAO designator*] (FAAC)
OUSDA ...... Office of the Under Secretary of Defense for Acquisition
OVAC........ Organisation Value Analysis Chart (PDAA)
OVER .... Optimum Vehicle for Effective Reconnaissance [*Air Force*] (PDAA)
OVF .... Over-Voltage Factor (PDAA)
OVRN........ Overrun Standard Approach Lighting System [*Aviation*] (DA)
OVRNG...... Overrunning (DA)
OVS .... Online Version Storage [*Computer science*] (PDAA)
OVSEA....... Overseas [*Aviation*] (FAAC)
OWE.......... Office of Water Enforcement [*Environmental Protection Agency*] (ERG)
OWL.......... Maui Airlines, Inc. [*ICAO designator*] (FAAC)
OWN .... Owens Group Ltd. [*New Zealand*] [*ICAO designator*] (FAAC)
OWS.......... Cargosur [*Spain*] [*ICAO designator*] (FAAC)
OWWM...... Office of Water and Waste Management (ERG)
OX.............. Oxidant [*Photochemical*] (ERG)
OXO .... Million Air, Inc. [*ICAO designator*] (FAAC)
OYC........... Conair AS [*Denmark*] [*ICAO designator*] (FAAC)
OZRF......... Opposed Zone Reheating Furnace (PDAA)

P

P .... Democratic People's Republic of Korea [*Aircraft nationality and registration mark*] (FAAC)
P .... Mainsail Hoist Lenght [*IOR*]
P .... Panel (NFPA)
P .... Paved Surface [*Aviation*] (DA)
P .... Personal (DA)
P .... Plaintiff
P .... Public Safety [*FCC*] (NTCM)
P .... Pull (NFPA)
P2 .... Papua New Guinea [*Aircraft nationality and registration mark*] (FAAC)
P4 .... Aruba [*Aircraft nationality and registration mark*] (FAAC)
7P .... Lesotho [*Aircraft nationality and registration mark*] (FAAC)
8P .... Barbados [*Aircraft nationality and registration mark*] (FAAC)
PA .... Passenger Address System [*Aviation*] (DA)
PA .... Preliminary Assessment (ERG)
PAA .... Patriot Airlines, Inc. [*ICAO designator*] (FAAC)
PAB .... Pacific Air Boats Ltd. [*Canada*] [*ICAO designator*] (FAAC)
PABLOS .... Program to Analyse the Block System [*Computer science*] (PDAA)
PAC .... Parent Advisory Committee [*Migrant education*] (AEE)
PAC .... Patriot Antimissile Capability [*Army*]
PAC .... Planned Availability Concept (PDAA)
PAC .... Polyaluminum Chloride [*Inorganic chemistry*]
PACAP .... Pituitary Adenylyl Cyclase-Activating Polypeptide [*Endocrinology*]
PACCT .... Political Action Committee for Cable Television (NTCM)
PACE .... Package for Architectural Computer Evaluation (PDAA)
PACE .... People with Arthritis Can Exercise [*Medical program*]
PACE .... Planning and Control Made Easy (PDAA)
PACE .... Professional Association of Christian Educators (EA)
PACES .... Patient as Customer Evaluation Survey
PAC-FACS ... Programmed Appropriation Commitments - Fixed Asset Control System (PDAA)
PACH .... Publishers' Accounts Clearing House [*British*] (BI)
PACMS ..... Psycho-Acoustical Measuring System (PDAA)
PACOS .... Package Operating System (PDAA)
PACRAD.... Practical Absolute Cavity Radiometer (PDAA)
PACS .... Pitch Augmentation Control System (PDAA)
PACT .... Phased Control Technique (PDAA)
PACT .... Predictive Analysis and Crash Testing [*Automotive safety research*]
PACT .... Protective Action for Children's Television (NTCM)
PAD .... Pressure Anomaly Difference (PDAA)
PAD .... Professional Express Courier Service, Inc. [*ICAO designator*] (FAAC)
PADE .... Pad Automatic Data Equipment (PDAA)
PADIL .... Patriot Air Defense Information Language [*Army*]
PADL......... Performing and Captive Animals Defence League [*British*] (BI)
PADS......... Parametric Array Doppler SONAR (PDAA)
PADS......... Point Air Defense System
PADWSS ... Pulsed Acoustic Doppler Wind Shear Sensing System (PDAA)
PAE .... Paisajes Espanoles SA [*Spain*] [*ICAO designator*] (FAAC)
PAE .... Personal Arms and Equipment [*Army*] (ADDR)
PAE .... Photo-Anodic Engraving (PDAA)
PAE .... Polyaspartic Ester [*Organic chemistry*]
PAEW........ Personnel and Equipment Working [*Aviation*] (FAAC)
PAF........... Panaf Airways Ltd. [*Gambia*] [*ICAO designator*] (FAAC)
PAF........... Partitive Analytical Forecasting (PDAA)
PAFU........ Propulsion Arming and Firing Unit [*Military*]
PAG........... Perimeter Aviation Ltd. [*Canada*] [*ICAO designator*] (FAAC)
PAGE........ Page Generation [*or Generator*] (PDAA)
PAH........... Panorama Air Tour, Inc. [*ICAO designator*] (FAAC)
PAI............ Kitty Hawk Aircargo, Inc. [*ICAO designator*] (FAAC)
PAID........ Parked Aircraft Intrusion Detector (PDAA)
PAIR......... Performance Accountability and Improvement Report
PAIRS .... Private Aircraft Inspection Reporting System (PDAA)
PAJES....... Parents of Adult Jewish Singles
PAK .... Pacific Alaska Airlines [*ICAO designator*] (FAAC)
PAL........... Philippine Air Lines, Inc. [*ICAO designator*] (FAAC)
PAL........... Police Attendance Line
PALMES.... Pulsed Appendage Large Mobile Electromagnetic-Pulse Simulator (PDAA)

PALMNET ... Protocol for Automotive Local Area Network
PALMS ...... Propulsion Alarm and Monitoring System (PDAA)
PALS .... Positioning and Locating System [*Aviation*] (PDAA)
PALS .... Precision Approach Lighting System [*Aviation*] (FAAC)
PAM .... Personnel Availability Model (PDAA)
PAM .... Phoenix Air Service GmbH [*Germany*] [*ICAO designator*] (FAAC)
PAMD .... Parallel Access Multiple Distribution (PDAA)
PAMF........ Programmable Analogue Matched Filter (PDAA)
PAMIRASAT ... Passive Microwave Radiometer Satellite (PDAA)
PAMIRASAT ... Primary Afferent Depolarization (PDAA)
PAMPA...... Precision Aerobatics Model Pilots Association (EA)
PANDA ...... Performance and Demand Analyser (PDAA)
PANSY....... Program Analysis System (PDAA)
PANTHEON ... Public Access by New Technology to Highly Elaborate Online Networks [*Computer science*] (PDAA)
PAO .... Polynesian Airline Operations Ltd. [*Western Samoa*] [*ICAO designator*] (FAAC)
PAP .... Public Awareness Program
PAPA......... Parallax Aircraft Parking Aid (PDAA)
PAPM........ Pulse Amplitude and Phase Modulation (PDAA)
PAPR........ Powered Air Purifying Respirator (ERG)
PAPS .... Performance Analysis and Prediction Study (PDAA)
PAR .... Pacific-Antarctic Ridge [*Geology*]
PAR .... Participation-Achievement-Reward (PDAA)
PAR .... Peak Area Ratio [*Chromatographic analysis*]
PAR .... Planed All Round (DAC)
PAR .... Preferential Arrival Route [*Aviation*] (DA)
PAR .... Spair [*Russian Federation*] [*ICAO designator*] (FAAC)
PARADA.... Preparatory Academy for the Royal Academy of Dramatic Art [*British*] (BI)
PARADISE ... Phased Array RADAR and Divers Integrated Semiconductor Elements (PDAA)
PARAN ...... Perimeter Array Antenna (PDAA)
PARC......... Profile Analysis and Recording Control (PDAA)
Par Ch....... Parents' Choice [*A publication*]
PARD .... Project Activities Relationship Diagram (PDAA)
PARDS....... Phased Array RADAR Detection System (PDAA)
PARENS .... Parentheses (NTCM)
PARIS .... Postal Address Reader Indexer System (PDAA)
PARM .... Precision Anti-Radiation Missile [*Military*] (PDAA)
PARS......... Pershing Audio Reproduction System (PDAA)
PARS......... Private Aircraft Reporting System [*FAA*] (FAAC)
PARSAC .... Particle Size Analogue Computer (PDAA)
PARTES..... Piece-Wise Application of Radiation through the Electromagnetic-Pulse Simulator (PDAA)
PARTIAL... Participation in Architectural Layout (PDAA)
PAS............ Pelita Air Service PT [*Indonesia*] [*ICAO designator*] (FAAC)
PAS............ Power-Assist System [*Motorcycle steering*]
PASP .... Price Adjusting Sampling Plan (PDAA)
PASS .... Parked Aircraft Security System (PDAA)
PASS .... Pilot Aerial Survival System (PDAA)
PASS .... Pooled Analytical Stereoplotter System (PDAA)
PASS .... Price Adjusted Single Sampling (PDAA)
PAT .... Palleted Automated Transport (PDAA)
PAT .... Priority Air Transport [*Army*] (FAAC)
PATA......... Proprietary Articles Trade Association [*British*] (BI)
PATS......... Precise Automated Tracking System (PDAA)
PATSY ...... Pulse-Amplitude Transmission System (PDAA)
PATT......... Programmable Automatic Transistor Tester (PDAA)
PATTI .... Precise and Accurate Time and Time Interval [*An experiment aboard the Spacelab*] [*NASA*] (PDAA)
PATTI .... Prompt Action to Telephone Inquiries (PDAA)
PATWA...... Professional and Technical Workers Aliyah [*British*] (BI)
PATX......... Private Automatic Telegraph Exchange (PDAA)
PAVE......... Parents Active for Vision Education [*An association*] (EA)
PAVE......... Preparing for AIDS/HIV Vaccine Evaluation [*National Institutes of Health project*]
PAVM .... Proximity Automatic Vehicle Monitoring (PDAA)
PAWN .... Photon Adjoint with Neutron (PDAA)
PAX .... Pan Air, Inc. [*ICAO designator*] (FAAC)
PAZ .... PM Air, Inc. [*ICAO designator*] (FAAC)
Pb .... Lead

PB .... Pull Back   (NTCM)
PBA .... Polybutyl Acrylate [*Organic chemistry*]
PBD .... Programmer Brain Damage [*Computer hacker terminology*]   (NHD)
PBE .... Polybutene [*Organic chemistry*]
PBG .... Powszechny Bank Gospodarczy [*Poland*]
PBIB .... Partially-Balanced Incomplete Block   (PDAA)
PBJ .... Peanut Butter and Jelly
PBKTOA .... Printing, Bookbinding, and Kindred Trades' Overseers Association [*British*]   (BI)
PBL .... Public Broadcasting Laboratory   (NTCM)
PBMA .... Polybutyl Methacrylate [*Organic chemistry*]
PBMA .... Pressed Brick Makers' Association Ltd. [*British*]   (BI)
PBMS .... Photonburst Mass Spectrometry
PBN .... Pilatus Britten-Norman Ltd. [*British*] [*ICAO designator*]   (FAAC)
PBO .... Poly(p-phenylene Benzobisoxazole)   (RDA)
PBP .... Performance-Based Pay
PBP............. Picnic Basket Porphyrin [*Organic chemistry*]
PBP............. Pulse Burst Period   (PDAA)
PBRS .... Polybromostyrene [*Organic chemistry*]
PBS .... Parti Bersatu Sabah [*Malaysia*] [*Political party*]   (ECON)
PBS............. Press-Button Signalling   (PDAA)
PBU .... Air-Burundi [*ICAO designator*]   (FAAC)
PBY............. Pearl Air Services (U) Ltd. [*Uganda*] [*ICAO designator*]   (FAAC)
PC .... Parallax Second [*Unit of interstellar-space measure*]
PC .... Percutaneous Cholecystostomy [*Medicine*]
PC .... Personal Care
PC .... Phase-Change [*Physics*]
PC .... Pitting Corrosion   (PDAA)
PC .... Polar Component [*Food science*]
PC .... Press Club   (NTCM)
PC .... Privacy Commission
PC .... Provisional Cut [*Television*]   (NTCM)
PC .... Pull Chain [*Technical drawings*]   (DAC)
PCA .... Polarizer-Compensator-Analyzer   (PDAA)
PCA .... Pre-Conditioned Air System [*Aviation*]   (DA)
PCA .... Printers' Costing Association [*British*]   (BI)
PCD .... Proceed [*ICAO designator*]   (FAAC)
PCD .... Programmed Cell Death [*Biology*]
PCD .... Projected Charge Density   (PDAA)
PCDH .... Polychlorinated Diaromatic Hydrocarbon [*Organic chemistry*]
PCF............. Pacific Air Express [*ICAO designator*]   (FAAC)
P/CG........... Pilot Controller Glossary [*Aviation*]   (FAAC)
PCH .... Presbyterian Church House [*British*]   (BI)
PCI .... Pavement Condition Index [*Aviation*]   (DA)
PCI .... Prothrombin Consumption Index   (PDAA)
PCIMS .... Positive Chemical Ionization Mass Spectroscopy
PCK .... [*H. E.*] Peacock & Son (Thorney) Ltd. [*British*] [*ICAO designator*]   (FAAC)
PCL............. Purkinje Cell Layer [*Cytology*]
PCLST......... Polychlorstyrene [*Organic chemistry*]
PCLW .... Platinum Compensating Lead Wire   (PDAA)
PCM .... WestAir Industries, Inc. [*ICAO designator*]   (FAAC)
PCMA .... Plaited Cordage Manufacturers Association [*British*]   (BI)
PCMO .... Passenger Car Motor Oil
PCMS......... Pattern Card Makers' Society [*British*]   (BI)
PCN .... Parent Country National   (PDAA)
PCN .... Pavement Classification Number [*Aviation*]   (DA)
PCN .... Princeton Aviation Corp. [*ICAO designator*]   (FAAC)
PCNSL....... Polymerised Cashew Nut Shell Liquid   (PDAA)
PCO .... Pacific Coastal Airline [*Canada*] [*ICAO designator*]   (FAAC)
PCO .... Peacetime Contingency Operation [*Army*]   (ADDR)
PCOLA....... Pulse-Coded Optical Landing Aid [*Aviation*]
PCOR......... Pressure Compensator Over-Ride   (PDAA)
PCQT......... Paper-Core Quad Trunk   (PDAA)
PCR .... Pearson Aviation Corp. [*ICAO designator*]   (FAAC)
PCR .... Pollution Control Revenue
PCR............. Post-Consumer Resin [*Plastic recycling*]
PCR............. Postconviction Remedy
PCRC........... Poor Clergy Relief Corp. [*British*]   (BI)
PCS .... Pluto-Charon System [*Planetary science*]
PCS .... Prime Compatible Set   (PDAA)
PCT............. Patent Cooperation Treaty [*World Intellectual Property Organization*]
PCT............. Peace Air Togo [*ICAO designator*]   (FAAC)
PCV .... Pump Control Valve [*Hydraulics*]
PCVN .... Precracked Charpy V-Notch   (PDAA)
PCY............. Aquila Air, Inc. [*ICAO designator*]   (FAAC)
P/D .... Penetration Diameter [*Military*]
PD .... Personnel Development
PD .... Production Director   (NTCM)
PD .... Professional Digital [*Recording*]   (NTCM)
PD .... Professional Diploma [*Education*]   (AEE)
PDA .... Photographic Dealers' Association [*British*]   (BI)
PDAR .... Preferential Departure [*Aviation*]   (DA)
PDC .... Polycrystalline Diamond Compact [*Well drilling technology*]
PDC .... Programmable Digital Controller   (PDAA)
PDC .... Public Dividend Capital   (PDAA)
PDD .... Premenstrual Dysphoric Disorder [*Proposed psychiatric diagnosis*]
PDDC .... Proceed Directly on Course [*Aviation*]   (FAAC)
PDDL .... Perpendicular Diffraction Delay Line   (PDAA)
PDEM .... Personal Dust Exposure Monitor   (PDAA)

PDES.......... Product Data Exchange using STEP [*Sequentially Timed Events Plotting*]
PDES.......... Pulse-Doppler Elevation Scan   (PDAA)
PDF............ LAR Transregional, Linhas Aereas Regionais SA [*Portugal*] [*ICAO designator*]   (FAAC)
PDFES........ Pitch-Synchronous Digital Feature Extraction System   (PDAA)
PDFG.......... Planar Distributed Function Generator   (PDAA)
PDG .... Phosphogluconate Dehydrogenase [*Organic chemistry*]   (MAH)
PDHL......... Peak Design Heat Loss   (PDAA)
PDI .... Paradise Island Airlines, Inc. [*ICAO designator*]   (FAAC)
PDL .... Program Device Librarian [*Computer science*]
PDM .... Pilot Decision Making [*Aviation*]   (DA)
PDM .... Polynomial Discriminant Method   (PDAA)
PDMPO ..... Polydimethyl Phenylene Oxide [*Organic chemistry*]
PDMS......... Photodissociation Mass Spectrometry
PDMT .... Predominant [*National Weather Service*]   (FAAC)
PDNES....... Pulse-Doppler Non-Elevation Scan   (PDAA)
PDNF .... Prime Disjunctive Normal Form   (PDAA)
PDO .... Portable Distributed Objects [*Next*]
PDP .... Passive Driving Periscope [*Military*]   (PDAA)
PDP .... Pesticide Data Program [*Environmental Protection Agency*]
PDP .... Phenyl-Dichlorophosphine   (PDAA)
PDP-CVS ... Positive Displacement Pump-Constant Volume Sampler   (ERG)
PDQ .... PDQ Air Service, Inc. [*ICAO designator*]   (FAAC)
PDR .... Pattern Delayed-Response [*Ophthalmology*]
PDR .... Photodissociation [*or Photodominated*] Region [*Galactic science*]
PDR .... Pre-Determined Route [*Aviation*]   (DA)
PDR .... Primary Demographic Report [*A. C. Nielsen Co.*]   (NTCM)
PDSMS ..... Power Diffraction Search and Match System   (PDAA)
PDSOR...... Positive Definitive Successive Over-Relaxation   (PDAA)
PDSS .... Particle Doppler Shift Spectrometer   (PDAA)
PDT .... Picture Description Test   (PDAA)
PDT .... Piedmont Airlines, Inc. [*ICAO designator*]   (FAAC)
PDT .... Product Development Team [*Automotive project management*]
PDUS......... Primary Data User Station [*Computer science*]   (PDAA)
PDV .... Pyrotechnic Development Vehicle   (PDAA)
PDVOR ..... Precision Doppler VHF Omni-Range   (PDAA)
PE .... Plain End [*Lumber*]   (DAC)
P1E .... Planed One Edge [*Technical drawings*]   (DAC)
PEA .... Pan Europeenne Air Service [*France*] [*ICAO designator*]   (FAAC)
PEA .... Poultry Education Association [*British*]   (BI)
PEB........... Phosphate Ester Base   (PDAA)
PEB........... Phototype Environment Buoy   (PDAA)
PEB........... Plasma Electron Beam   (PDAA)
PEC .... Pacific East Asia Cargo Airline, Inc. [*Philippines*] [*ICAO designator*]   (FAAC)
PEC .... Polyestercarbonate [*Organic chemistry*]
PEC........... Position Error Correction   (DA)
PECDAR .... Palestine Economic Council for Development and Reconstruction   (ECON)
PEDC........ Professional Educational Development Corp. [*An association*]   (EA)
PEETPACK ... Process Engineering Evaluation Techniques Package   (PDAA)
PEETSA..... Parents, Educators and Environmentalists to Save Anchoives [*An association*]
PEG .... Professional Emphasis Group [*National Audience Board*]   (NTCM)
PEG .... Public, Educational, Government [*Cable television access channels*]   (NTCM)
PEIS......... Polyethylene Isopthalate [*Organic chemistry*]
PEL............ Aeropelican Air Services Pty Ltd. [*Australia*] [*ICAO designator*]   (FAAC)
PEL........... Picture Element   (NTCM)
PEM .... PEM-AIR Ltd. [*Canada*] [*ICAO designator*]   (FAAC)
PEM .... Personal-E Mailbox [*Computer software*]   (PCM)
PEM .... Privacy-Enhanced Mail [*Software package*]
PEM .... Proton Exchange Membrane
PEMA......... Polyethyl Methacrylate [*Organic chemistry*]
PEN .... Peninsula Airways, Inc. [*ICAO designator*]   (FAAC)
PEPA .... Per Employee per Annum
PEPA .... Pitch Fibre Pipe Association of Great Britain   (BI)
PEPAE ...... Permanent Entry Permit After Entry
PEPPER..... Photo-Electric Portable Probe Reader   (PDAA)
PEPTP ...... (Phenylethyl)Phenyltetrahydropyridine [*Organic chemistry*]
PER........... Performance   (DA)
PERF .... Planetary Entry Radiation Facility [*Langley Research Center*] [*NASA*]   (PDAA)
PERL .... Portable Electronic Runway Lighting   (PDAA)
PERL......... Practice Extraction and Report Language [*Facetious translation: Pathologically Eclectic Rubbish Lister*] [*Computer science*]   (NHD)
PERS CASREP ... Personnel Casualty Report [*Navy*]   (ANA)
PERT......... Project Evaluation and Review Technique   (DAC)
PESIS .... Photo-Electron Spectroscopy of Inner-Shell   (PDAA)
PESOS ...... Photo-Electron Spectroscopy of Outer-Shell   (PDAA)
PET........... Aeropetrel [*Chile*] [*ICAO designator*]   (FAAC)
PET........... Photoelectric Transducer   (PDAA)
PET........... Prediction Error Transform   (PDAA)
PETMA...... Portable Electric Tool Manufacturers' Association [*British*]   (BI)
PEV........... Permanent Entry Visa
PEV........... Propeller-Excited Vibration   (PDAA)
PEV........... Pyroelectric Vidicon   (PDAA)
PEX........... World Aircraft Flight Operation, Inc. [*ICAO designator*]   (FAAC)

PF.............. Prefetch [Computer science]
PFA............ Polymeric Fatty Acid [Food science]
PFA............ Probability of False Alarm [DoD]
PFA............ Production Flow Analysis (PDAA)
PFA............ Professional Footballers' Association [British] (BI)
PFC............ Parallel-Flow Condenser [Air conditioning systems]
PFCU......... Power Flying Control Unit [Aviation] (DA)
PFCWTS.... Pogo Fan Club and Walt Kelly Society (EA)
PFD............ Planned Flight Data [Aviation] (DA)
PFF............ Plaque-Forming Factor (PDAA)
PFL............ Pol-Fly [Poland] [ICAO designator] (FAAC)
PFMA........ Pressed Felt Manufacturers' Association [British] (BI)
PFP............ Proton Flare Project (PDAA)
PFPH......... Pentafluorophenylhydrazine [Organic chemistry]
PFR............ Patriot Field Report [Army]
PFR............ Permitted Flying Route [Aviation] (DA)
PFS............ Personal Financial Specialist
PFS............ Prairie Flying Service (1976) Ltd. [Canada] [ICAO designator] (FAAC)
PFWS........ Predicted Fire Weapon System [Army]
P & G .... Post and Girder [Lumber] (DAC)
PG.............. Professional Geologist
PGA........... Plate Glass Association [British] (BI)
PGA........... Portugalia, Companhia Portuguesa de Transportes Aeros SA [Portugal] [ICAO designator] (FAAC)
PGC........... Programmable Guidance Controller [Military]
PGFR......... Power-Generating Fusion Reaction
PG/GAG..... Proteoglycans/Glyosaminoglyans
PGGO........ Prescribed Goods (General) Order
PGHS......... Prostaglandin Hydrogen Synthase [An enzyme]
PGM.......... Plant Genetic Materials
PGMA........ Private Grocers' Merchandising Association [British] (BI)
PGMA-EA ... Polyglycidal Methacrylate-Ethyl Acrylate [Organic chemistry] (PDAA)
PGMARV... Precision Guided Maneuvering Re-Entry Vehicle (PDAA)
PGMOT ..... Pollution Generation Multiplier from Output Table (PDAA)
PGMP........ Preliminary Guaranteed Minimum Price
PGP .... Phagocyte Glycoprotein [Biochemistry]
PGRO......... Pea Growing Research Organisation Ltd. [British] (BI)
PGS........... Tauranga Aero Club, Inc. [New Zealand] [ICAO designator] (FAAC)
PGT .... Pegasus Hava Tasimaciligi AS [Turkey] [ICAO designator] (FAAC)
PH.............. Phillips Head (DAC)
PH.............. Professional Hydrologist
PH.............. Public Holiday (DA)
PHA........... Process Hazard Analysis [Environmental science]
PHAM....... Phase Amplitude Monopulse (PDAA)
PHAROS... Plan Handling and RADAR Operating System [Aviation] (DA)
PHC .... Petroleum Helicopters de Colombia SA [ICAO designator] (FAAC)
PHD........... Duncan Aviation, Inc. [ICAO designator] (FAAC)
PHE........... Pawan Hans Ltd. [India] [ICAO designator] (FAAC)
PHI .... Philips Aviation Services [Netherlands] [ICAO designator] (FAAC)
Phil Lit R .... Philatelic Literature Review [A publication]
PHIRB........ Public Health Inspectors' Registration Board [British] (BI)
PHL........... Phillips Michigan City Flying Service, Inc. [ICAO designator] (FAAC)
PHM.......... Petroleum Helicopters, Inc. [ICAO designator] (FAAC)
PHMA........ Polyhexyl Methacrylate [Organic chemistry]
PHMP .... Primordial Hot Mantle Plume (PDAA)
PHOCAS... Photo Optical Cable Controlled Submersible (PDAA)
PHOCIS ..... Photogrammetric Circulatory Survey (PDAA)
PHONE...... Telephone (NTCM)
PHPA .... Partially-Hydrolyzed Polyacrylamide [Well drilling technology]
PHR .... Process Hazardous Review [Environmental science]
PHS .... Precision Hover Sensor (PDAA)
PHX........... Phoenix 2000 Airtaxi Ltd. [Hungary] [ICAO designator] (FAAC)
PHYLIS ..... Physics Online Information System [Computer science] (PDAA)
P₃I............ Planned Program Product Improvement [Army]
PIA............ Pakistan International Airlines Corp. [ICAO designator] (FAAC)
PIA............ Photographic Importers Association [British] (BI)
PIAC......... Peak Instantaneous Airborne Count (DA)
PIAT .... Public Information Assist Team [Environmental Protection Agency] (ERG)
PIB............ Pre-Flight Information Bulletin [Aviation] (DA)
PIC............ Pacific Airlines Holding Co. [Vietnam] [ICAO designator] (FAAC)
PIC............ Positive Immittance Converter (PDAA)
PIC............ Potential Icing Category [Meteorology] (DA)
PIC............ Preinitiation Complex [Genetics]
PIC............ Product of Incomplete Combustion [Environmental Protection Agency] (ERG)
PICA......... Press Independence and Critical Ability (NTCM)
PICASSO... Pen Input to Computer and Scanned Screen Output [Computer science] (PDAA)
PiCO .... Portable Interactive Computing Object
PICOS .... Purchased Input Concept Optimization with Suppliers [Auto industry quality and cost management program]
PID .... Product Innovation and Design
PIDA.......... Pig Industry Development Authority [British] (BI)
PIE............. Primary Industry and Energy

PIER......... Product Inventory Electronically Recorded (PDAA)
PIES .... Pollution Prevention Information Exchange System [Environmental science]
PIESA....... Parasite-Induced Erythrocyte Surface Antigen [Immunology]
PI-FET ...... Piezoelectric Field-Effect Transistor (PDAA)
PIFL .... Pipe Flow (PDAA)
PIGME....... Programmed Inert Gas Multi-Electrode (PDAA)
PIH........... Passive Immune Hemolysis (PDAA)
PIIC.......... Public Interest Immunity Certificate [British] (ECON)
PIL............ Pest Infestation Laboratory [Agricultural Research Council] (PDAA)
PILAR .... Petroleum Industry Local Authority Reporting (PDAA)
PILE .... Product Inventory Level Estimator (PDAA)
PILLS .... Particulate Instrumentation by LASER Light Scattering (PDAA)
PILOT .... Programmed Inquiry, Learning or Teaching [Computer science]
PIM .... Powder Injection Molding [Metallurgy]
PIMP........ Program for Interactive Multiple Process Simulation (PDAA)
PIN .... Procurement Information Notice [Environmental Protection Agency] (ERG)
PIO .... Pioneer Airlines, Inc. [ICAO designator] (FAAC)
PIOFA....... Petroleum Ether Insoluble Oxidized Fatty Acid [Food science]
PIPIT .... Peripheral Interface and Program Interrupt Translator (PDAA)
PIPRS....... Ping Intercept Passive Ranging SONAR [Military]
PIQ .... Program Idea Quotient [Home testing measurement] (NTCM)
PIR............ Prim-Air Aps [Denmark] [ICAO designator] (FAAC)
PIR............ Prisoner-Initiated Review
PIRATE...... Public Information in Rural Areas Technology Experiment [British Library] (PDAA)
PIRC.......... Protocol Implementation Review Committee [National Institutes of Health]
PIRL.......... PRISM [Personnel Record Information System for Management] Information Retrieval Language [Computer science] (PDAA)
PIS............ Penning Ionization Spectroscopy (PDAA)
PISB .... People's Institute for Survival and Beyond (EA)
PISO.......... No Pilot Balloon Observation Due to Snow [Meteorology] (FAAC)
PIT........... Panair International SRL [Italy] [ICAO designator] (FAAC)
PITP .... Phosphatidylinositol Transfer Protein [Biochemistry]
PITS .... Patriot Integration and Test System [Army]
Pixel........... Picture Element (NTCM)
PJE........... Private Jet Expeditions, Inc. [ICAO designator] (FAAC)
PJL........... Printer Job Language [Computer science]
PJS .... Jet Aviation, Business Jets AG [Switzerland] [ICAO designator] (FAAC)
PK .... West Irian [Aircraft nationality and registration mark] (FAAC)
PKA .... Equator Airlines Ltd. [Kenya] [ICAO designator] (FAAC)
PKP........... Phi Kappa Phi [Honor society] (AEE)
PKS........... Polyketide Synthase [An enzyme]
PLA........... Polynesian Air-Ways [ICAO designator] (FAAC)
PLAME...... Propulsive Left Landing with Aerodynamic Maneuvering Entry (PDAA)
PLASI........ Pulsating Visual Approach Slope Indicator [Aviation] (FAAC)
PLASI........ Pulse Light Approach Slope Indicator (PDAA)
PLASMA ... Plant Services Maintenance (PDAA)
PLATS....... Precision Location and Tracking System (PDAA)
PLATT .... Page Level Availability Time Test [Computer science]
PLAY......... Providing Lifetime Activity for Youth
PLC........... Police Aviation Services [British] [ICAO designator] (FAAC)
PLC........... Preparative Layer Chromatography
PLCC .... Plastic Leaded Chip Carrier [Computer science]
PLCC .... Power Line Carrier Communication (PDAA)
PLCCE .... Program Life-Cycle Cost Estimate [Army]
PLDIS....... Public Library Development Incentive Scheme [British]
PLEM........ Pipeline End Manifold (PDAA)
PLEX........ Plant Experimentation (PDAA)
PLF........... Pohjanmaan Lento OY [Finland] [ICAO designator] (FAAC)
PLGA......... Polylacticco-Glycolic Acid [Organic chemistry]
PLI............ Empresa de Transporte Aereo del Peru [ICAO designator] (FAAC)
PLLS........ Portable Landing Light System (PDAA)
PLN .... Polnippon [Poland] [ICAO designator] (FAAC)
PLN .... Potassium Lithium Niobate (PDAA)
plnd .... Planned (DA)
PLOKTA... Press Lots of Keys to Abort [Computer term]
PLP............ Phoenix Aviation [British] [ICAO designator] (FAAC)
PLP............ Plastic-Lined Pipe
PLR............ Northwestern Air Lease Ltd. [Canada] [ICAO designator] (FAAC)
PLRA.......... Photo-Litho Reproducers' Association [British] (BI)
PLS............ Palio Air Service [Italy] [ICAO designator] (FAAC)
PLUM .... Programmes Library Update and Maintenance (PDAA)
PLUM .... Programming Language for Users of MAVIS [Microprocessor-Based Audio Visual Information System] (PDAA)
PLV............ Polaravia OY [Finland] [ICAO designator] (FAAC)
PLVL......... Present Level [Aviation] (FAAC)
PLY........... Photoluminescence Yield [Spectroscopy]
PM............ Popular Movement Against the European Community (ECON)
PMA.......... Pan Malaysian Air Transport [ICAO designator] (FAAC)
PMA.......... Pianoforte Manufacturers' Association Ltd. [British] (BI)
PMA .... Plumbers' Merchants Association [British] (BI)
PMA .... Probability of Mission Abort [Navy] (ANA)
PMA/ARR ... Probable Missed Approach per Arrival [Aviation] (PDAA)

PMAC .... Pharmaceutical Manufacturers Association of Canada
PMASA ...... Printers' Medical Aid and Sanatoria Association [*British*]   (BI)
PMATA ...... Paint Manufacture and Allied Trades' Association [*British*]   (BI)
PMC .... Performance Management Computer   (PDAA)
PMC .... Pre-Mission Calibration   (PDAA)
PMEP........ Pumping Mean Effective Pressure [*Automotive engine testing*]
PMG .... Power Metal Grid   (PDAA)
PMIF .... Powder Metal Industries Federation
PMK .... Palair Macedonian [*Yugoslavia*] [*ICAO designator*]   (FAAC)
PMMO........ Particulate Methane Monooxygenase [*Biochemistry*]
PMP .... Piecewise Markov Process   (PDAA)
PMR .... Polise-Air [*Russian Federation*] [*ICAO designator*]   (FAAC)
PMS........... P-Methylstyrene [*Plastics*]
PMS........... Planemasters Services, Inc. [*ICAO designator*]   (FAAC)
PMSP .... Plant Modelling System Program   (PDAA)
PMT .... Post-Market Trading
PMT .... Pre-Determined Motion-Time [*Management*]   (PDAA)
PMV .... Passenger Motor Vehicle
PMVI......... Periodic Motor Vehicle Inspection   (PDAA)
PMW .... Preventive Maintenance Welding   (PDAA)
PMX .... Petroleos Mexicanos [*Mexico*] [*ICAO designator*]   (FAAC)
PN .... Peroxide Number [*Hydrocarbon fuel specifications*]
PN.............. Polish Notation [*Mathematics*]
PNA .... Peptide Nucleic Acid [*Biochemistry*]
PNA .... Professional Numismatists' Association [*British*]   (BI)
PNA .... Universal Airlines, Inc. [*ICAO designator*]   (FAAC)
PNAMBIC ... Pay No Attention to the Man Behind the Curtain [*Computer
            hacker terminology*]   (NHD)
PNCE......... Private New Capital Expenditure
PND........... Pressed Notch Depth   (PDAA)
PNI .... Aerovias de Poniente SA de CV [*Mexico*] [*ICAO designator*]
            (FAAC)
PNI .... Pictorial Navigation Indicator [*Aviation*]   (DA)
PNI .... Pulsed Neutron Interrogation   (PDAA)
PNKA .... Protein Induced by Vitamin K Absence and Antagonists   (PDAA)
PNL .... Aero Personal SA de CV [*Mexico*] [*ICAO designator*]   (FAAC)
PNL .... Instrument Panel [*Automotive engineering*]
PNR .... Panair [*Spain*] [*ICAO designator*]   (FAAC)
PNS .... Pooled Normal Serum   (PDAA)
PNS .... Post Nickel Strike   (PDAA)
PNS .... Project of National Significance
PNS .... Survey Udara (Penas) PT [*Indonesia*] [*ICAO designator*]   (FAAC)
PNT .... Project Network Technique   (PDAA)
PNV .... Panavia SA [*ICAO designator*]   (FAAC)
PNX .... Imperial Airways, Inc. [*ICAO designator*]   (FAAC)
PO .... Professional Officer
POA........... Le Point Air [*France*] [*ICAO designator*]   (FAAC)
POA........... Polarized Orbital Approximation   (PDAA)
POA........... Police Officers' Association [*British*]   (BI)
POA........... Privately-Owned Open Air-Braked [*Railway wagons*]   (PDAA)
POBA .... Plain Old Balloon Angioplasty [*Cardiology*] [*Facetious*]
POC........... Pocono Airlines, Inc. [*ICAO designator*]   (FAAC)
POCE .... Pantone Open Color Environment [*Joint venture between
            Pantone, Inc. and LightSource Computer Images*] [*Computer
            science*]   (PCM)
POD........... Piece of Data [*Computer science*]   (NHD)
PODS .... Portable Data Store [*Computer science*]   (PDAA)
POE .... Point of Exposure [*Environmental Protection Agency*]   (ERG)
POET........ Portable Optic-Electronic Tracker   (PDAA)
POF .... Plastic Optical Fiber [*Automotive electronics*]
POGO........ Pre-Oxidation Gettering of the Other Side   (PDAA)
POH.......... Pilot's Operating Handbook [*Aviation*]   (DA)
POINTER ... Pre-University Orbital Information Tracker Equipment and
            Recorder   (PDAA)
POL .... Polar International Airlines, Inc. [*ICAO designator*]   (FAAC)
POL .... Polite
POL .... Practical Quantification Limit [*Metallurgy*]
POLAC...... Problem-Oriented Language for Analytical Chemistry [*Computer
            science*]   (PDAA)
POLARS .... Pathology On-Line Logging and Reporting System [*Computer
            science*]   (PDAA)
POLKA...... Periodical On-Line Keyword Access [*Computer science*]   (PDAA)
POLO .... Problem-Oriented Language Organizer [*Computer science*]
            (PDAA)
POM.......... Phase of the Moon [*Astronomy*]   (NHD)
POM.......... Polymerized and Oxidized Material [*Food science*]
POM.......... Professionals, Owners, and Managers [*A. C. Nielsen Co.*]
            [*Demographic category*]   (NTCM)
POMA .... Polyoctyl Methacrylate [*Organic chemistry*]
POMP .... Pre Coded Originating Mail Processor   (PDAA)
POMS .... Poly-Ortho-methylstyrene [*Organic chemistry*]
POMT .... Patriot Organizational Maintenance Trainer [*Army*]
PON........... Phosphorotioate Oligonucleotide [*Biochemistry*]
PON........... Portuguese Navy [*ICAO designator*]   (FAAC)
POP .... Performance-Oriented Packaging [*for hazardous materials*]
POPS......... Performance-Oriented Packing Standard
POPSI .... Postulate-Based Permuted Subject Indexing   (PDAA)
POQ.......... Period Order Quantity   (PDAA)
POQL .... Probability Outgoing Quality Limit   (PDAA)
PORTAS .... Penetration of Radiation Through Aperture Simulation   (PDAA)
PORT CEM ... Portland Cement [*Technical drawings*]   (DAC)
POS .... Aeroposta SA [*Argentina*] [*ICAO designator*]   (FAAC)
POS .... Primary Operating Stock [*DoD*]

POS .... Program of Study   (AEE)
POSER .... Process Organization to Simplify Error Recovery   (PDAA)
POSNO ...... Position Number [*Military*]   (ADDR)
POSSUM ... Pictures of Specific Syndromes and Unknown Malformations
            [*Database*]
POST......... Polar Stratospheric Telescope
POST......... Prototype Ocean Surveillance Terminal [*Navy*]   (ANA)
POW(J)...... Prisoner of War of Japan
PP .... Pocketpiece [*A. C. Nielsen Co.*] [*Rating report*]   (NTCM)
PP .... Popular Party [*European political movement*]   (ECON)
PP .... Pour Point [*Petroleum characteristic*]
PP .... Priority Message Precedence [*Telecommunications*]   (ADDR)
PP .... Proposals Paper
P-P .... Pulse to Pulse
PPA .... Parallel Processing Automata   (PDAA)
PPA .... Phosphoric Acid Anodized   (PDAA)
PPA .... Pianoforte Publicity Association [*British*]   (BI)
PPA .... Pilot Pulse Amplitude
PPA .... Pool Promoters Association [*British*]   (BI)
PPA .... Prescription Pricing Authority   (PDAA)
PPA .... Propheter Construction Co., Inc. [*ICAO designator*]   (FAAC)
PPAAR ...... Princeton University, Pennsylvania University, Army Avionics
            Research   (PDAA)
PP-AC........ Air-Conditioning Power Panel   (DAC)
PPAR .... Peroxisome Proliferator-Activated Receptor
PPARC .... Particle Physics and Astronomy Research Council [*British*]
PPBE .... Passenger Protective Breathing Equipment [*Aviation*]   (DA)
PPBH......... Pharmaceutical Partners for Better Healthcare   (ECON)
PPC.......... Predicted Propagation Correction   (PDAA)
PPC.......... Pressure Pulse Contour [*Cardiac computer*]   (PDAA)
PPD .... Personal Protective Device [*Toxicology*]
PPD .... Principal Project Designer [*Engineering project management*]
PPDD .... Pershing Physical Deception Device [*Army*]
PPE........... Polypentene [*Organic chemistry*]
PPE........... Polyphenylene Ether Plastic [*Materials science*]
PPETS....... Pretreatment Permitting and Enforcement Tracking System
            [*Environmental Protection Agency*]   (ERG)
PPF .... Power Plant Frame [*Mazda Miata*] [*Connecting engine and
            transmission to final drive*]
PPGL......... Polished Plate Glass [*Technical drawings*]   (DAC)
PPH .... Pages per Hour
PPH .... Peak-to-Peak Heights [*Spectrometry*]
PPI .... Professional Photographers of Israel   (PDAA)
PPICS........ Production Planning Inventory Control System   (PDAA)
PPIP .... Physics Post-Doctoral Information Pool [*American Institute of
            Physics*]   (PDAA)
PPIU .... Policy, Planning and Implementation Unit
PPIV .... Positive Personnel Identity Verification   (PDAA)
PPK........... Ramp 66, Inc. [*ICAO designator*]   (FAAC)
PPL........... PCBoard Programming Language [*Clark Development Co.*]
            (PCM)
PPL........... Peripheral Blood Leukocyte [*Medicine*]   (PDAA)
PPL........... Photogrammetric Programming Language [*Computer science*]
            (PDAA)
PPM .... Pictures per Minute   (NTCM)
PPM .... Post-Program Monitoring
PPMA .... Polypropyl Methacrylate [*Organic chemistry*]
PPMRD...... Pre-Positioned Material Receipt Document
PPO .... Patriot Project Office [*Army*]
PPO .... Permanent Paranormal Object
PPRC......... Physician Payment Review Commission
PPT........... Pilot's Power Tool
PPT........... Probabilistic Potential Theory   (PDAA)
PPTE......... Permanent Part-Time Employment
PPTS .... Pre-Planned Training System   (PDAA)
PQA .... Pacific Coast Airlines [*ICAO designator*]   (FAAC)
PQC.......... Chieftain Airways PLC [*British*] [*ICAO designator*]   (FAAC)
PQE.......... Post-Qualification Education   (PDAA)
PQL .... Practical Quantitation Level [*Environmental chemistry*]   (ERG)
PQL .... Practical Quantitation Limit [*Environmental chemistry*]
PQMF........ Parallel Quadrature Mirror Filter   (PDAA)
PQOS .... Pre-Qualified Offsets Supplier
PQOSS .... Pre-Qualified Offsets Supplier Status
PR .... Photo Reconnaissance [*ICAO designator*]   (FAAC)
PR .... Piezo Resistive [*Automotive electronics*]
PR .... Primary RADAR   (DA)
PR .... Print [*or Printed*]   (NTCM)
PR .... Publicity Release   (NTCM)
PRA .... Personal Rights Association [*British*]   (BI)
PRA .... Propionic Acid [*Organic chemistry*]
PRA .... Prospair Ltd. [*British*] [*ICAO designator*]   (FAAC)
PRAGMA... Processing Routines Aided by Graphics for Manipulation of
            Arrays   (PDAA)
PRAM .... Preliminary Repair Level Decision Analysis Model   (PDAA)
PRAV........ Planned Restricted Availability [*Navy*]   (ANA)
PRB........... Press-Radio Bureau   (PDAA)
PRB........... Private Radio Bureau [*FCC*]   (NTCM)
PRB........... Proteus Air Systeme [*France*] [*ICAO designator*]   (FAAC)
PRBC .... Parasitized Red Blood Cell [*Medicine*]
PRBO .... Position Relief Briefing Observed [*Aviation*]   (FAAC)
PRC........... Pacific Air Charter, Inc. [*ICAO designator*]   (FAAC)
PRC........... Polysulphide Rubber Compound   (PDAA)
PRCTN....... Precaution [*ICAO designator*]   (FAAC)

PRD .... Precompetitive Research and Development
PRDS .... Processed RADAR Display System   (PDAA)
PRE .... Precision Valley Aviation [*ICAO designator*]   (FAAC)
PREDICT... Pollution Reduction by Information and Control Technology
PRELUDE ... Pre-Optimization Linearization of Undulation and Detection of Errors   (PDAA)
PRE-OPS ... Pre-Operational Support [*Military*]
PREP .... Programmed Electronics Pattern   (PDAA)
PRES100 .... Presidential's Hundred Tab [*Military*]
PRESAGE ... Program to Realistically Evaluate Strategic Anti-Ballistic Missile Gaming Effectiveness [*Military*]   (PDAA)
PREV .... Previous Program Selection [*In-car entertainment*] [*Electronics*]
PRG .... Empresa Aero-Servicios Parrague Ltd. [*Chile*] [*ICAO designator*]   (FAAC)
PRG .... Performance-Related Gift   (ECON)
PRG .... Powerful Radio Galaxy [*Cosmology*]
PRHA .... People Refreshment House Association [*British*]   (BI)
PRI .... Princeville Airways, Inc. [*ICAO designator*]   (FAAC)
PRI .... Public Relations Institute of Ireland   (BI)
PRIMA ...... Public Radio in Mid-America   (NTCM)
PRIRA .... Primary RADAR   (FAAC)
PRISM .... Pliocene Research, Interpretations and Synoptic Mapping [*Climatology*]
PRISM .... Power Reactor Innovation Small Module [*Nuclear energy*]
PRL .... Aviaprima [*Russian Federation*] [*ICAO designator*]   (FAAC)
PRM .... Period of Reduced Melting [*Climatology*]
PRM .... Prime Air, Inc. [*ICAO designator*]   (FAAC)
PRMP......... Production Readiness Master Plan
PRN .... Princess Air [*British*] [*ICAO designator*]   (FAAC)
PRO .... Parents Reaching Out [*An association*]   (EA)
PR/O .... Pilot Repair/Overhaul [*Military*]
PRO .... Propair, Inc. [*Canada*] [*ICAO designator*]   (FAAC)
PROBE...... Profile Resolution Obtained by Excitation   (PDAA)
Proc Amp .... Processing Amplifier   (NTCM)
PROCAS ..... Process-Oriented Contract Administration Services
PROCON ... Protocol Converter   (DA)
PROCSIM ... Processor Simulation Language [*Computer science*]   (PDAA)
PRODAM ... Production Orientated Draughting and Manufacturing   (PDAA)
ProDOS ..... Professional Disk Operating System [*Computer science*]
Pro-Fax...... Production Facility   (NTCM)
PROMAST ... Production Master Scheduling System   (PDAA)
PROMATS ... Probabilistic Materials System   (PDAA)
Promo......... Promotional Announcement   (NTCM)
PROST .... Pronuclear Oocyte and Sperm Transfer [*Embryology*]
PRP............ Profit-Related Pay
PRP........... Program Random Process   (PDAA)
PRP-T........ Polyribosylribitol Phosphate Conjugated to Tetanus Toxoid [*Medicine*]
PRS .... Paint Research Station [*British*]   (BI)
PRS .... Pars Systems (CRS) [*ICAO designator*]   (FAAC)
PRS .... Program Rating Summary Report [*Television ratings*]   (NTCM)
PRT .... Air Cargo Carriers, Inc. [*ICAO designator*]   (FAAC)
PRV .... Provincial Express, Inc. [*Canada*] [*ICAO designator*]   (FAAC)
PS .... Parallel Single [*Outdoor advertising*]   (NTCM)
PS .... Porous Silicon [*Physics*]
PS .... Positive Value   (DA)
PS .... Power Spectra [*Neurophysiology*]
PS .... [*Manual*] Pull Station [*NFPA pre-fire planning symbol*]   (NFPA)
P1S .... Planed One Side [*Technical drawings*]   (DAC)
P4S .... Planed Four Sides [*Technical drawings*]   (DAC)
PSA............ Pacific Island Aviation, Inc. [*Mariana Islands*] [*ICAO designator*]   (FAAC)
PSA............ Peugot Societe Anonyme [*Peugeot Co. Ltd.*] [*French*]
PSA............ Pipe Stress Analysis   (PDAA)
PSA............ Power Saw Association [*British*]   (BI)
PSA............ Presunrise Service Authority   (NTCM)
PSA............ Public Service Act
PSB............ Plough, Sweeper, and Blower   (DA)
PSBA.......... Public School Bursars' Association [*British*]   (BI)
PSBH.......... Phonon Side-Band Hole [*Spectroscopy*]
PSC............ Propagating Space Charge   (PDAA)
PSDA.......... Paper Sack Development Association [*British*]   (BI)
PSE............ Aeroservicio Sipse SA de CV [*Mexico*] [*ICAO designator*]   (FAAC)
pse.............. Planed and Square-Edge   (DAC)
PSE............ Post-Separation Employment
P1S2E........ Planed One Side and Two Edges [*Technical drawings*]   (DAC)
PSEK........ Probability of Single Shot Engagement Kill [*Military*]
PSF .... Polysulfone [*Organic chemistry*]
PSH .... Productive Standard Hour   (PDAA)
PSHFA........ Public Servants' Housing and Finance Association [*British*]   (BI)
PSI .... Page Survival Index   (PDAA)
PSI .... Pharmaceutical Society of Ireland   (BI)
PSI .... Photographic Society of Ireland   (BI)
psj.............. Planed and Square-Jointed   (DAC)
PSL .... Polystyrene Latex   (PDAA)
PSL .... Professionnel Air Systems [*France*] [*ICAO designator*]   (FAAC)
PSM .... Physician and Sports Medicine [*A publication*]
PSMT........ Paced Sequential Memory Task   (PDAA)
PSN .... Potosina del Aire SA de CV [*Mexico*] [*ICAO designator*]   (FAAC)
PSNAL....... Personal   (FAAC)
PSO .... Protective Security Officer
PSP .... Pre-Season Predictor Model [*Television ratings*]   (NTCM)

PSP .... Primary Smog Product   (PDAA)
PSPC .... Position-Sensitive Proportional Counter [*Instrumentation*]
PSPRT....... Partial Sequential Probability Ratio Test   (PDAA)
PSPS........... Paddle Steamer Preservation Society [*British*]   (BI)
P4SR........... Predicted Four Hour Sweat Rate   (PDAA)
PSS .... Plume Suppression System [*Combustion technology*]
PSSDS....... Portable Surface Supported Diving System   (PDAA)
PSSP......... Personnel Security and Surety Program [*Military*]   (ADDR)
PST .... Airwork (New Zealand) Ltd. [*ICAO designator*]   (FAAC)
PST .... Pooled Superannuation Trust
PSV............ Polished-Stone Value   (PDAA)
PSWB .... Patented Steel Wire Bureau [*British*]   (BI)
PSWF .... Prolate Spheroidal Wave Function   (PDAA)
PSyCHES... Psychiatric Case History Event System   (PDAA)
PSZ............ Pro Air Service [*ICAO designator*]   (FAAC)
PT .... Polymeric Triglyceride [*Food science*]
PT .... Public Transport   (DA)
PTA .... Paper Towel Association [*British*]   (BI)
PTA .... Peritonsillar Abscess [*Medicine*]
PTA .... Ptarmigan Airways Ltd. [*Canada*] [*ICAO designator*]   (FAAC)
P'TACH ..... Parents for Torah for All Children [*Program for learning disabled children*]
PTCHY....... Patchy [*Meteorology*]   (DA)
PTCS .... Percutaneous Transhepatic Cholangioscopy [*Medicine*]
PTDL.......... Programmable Tapped Delay Line   (PDAA)
PTG .... Planed, Tongued, and Grooved   (DAC)
PThD .... Punch-Through Device   (PDAA)
PTI .... Previously-Taxed Income
PTIRFM...... Polarized Total Internal Reflection Fluorescence Microscopy
PTK .... Probability of Track [*Military*]
PTL .... Providence Air Charter [*ICAO designator*]   (FAAC)
PTM .... Parasite Tubing Method   (PDAA)
PTM .... Photon Tunneling Microscope
PTM .... Southeastern Airways Corp. [*ICAO designator*]   (FAAC)
PTMCA....... Pit Tub and Mine Car Manufacturers' Association [*British*]   (BI)
PTMV......... Percutaneous Transvenous Mitral Valvotomy [*Cardiology*]
PTN .... Pantanal Linhas Aereas Sul-Matogrossenses SA [*Brazil*] [*ICAO designator*]   (FAAC)
PTN .... Public Telephone Network   (DA)
PTO .... North West Geomatics Ltd. [*Canada*] [*ICAO designator*]   (FAAC)
PTO .... Part Time Operation   (DA)
PTOJ .... Passive Track-On-Jam
PTP .... Protein Tyrosine Phosphatase [*An enzyme*]
PTPR .... Production Test Program Report
PTS .... Philatelic Traders' Society Ltd. [*British*]   (BI)
PTS .... Plane Transport System   (DA)
PTS .... Points of Call Airlines Ltd. [*Canada*] [*ICAO designator*]   (FAAC)
PTS .... Polar Track Structure [*Aviation*]   (FAAC)
PTS .... Project Tracking System [*Environmental Protection Agency*]   (ERG)
PTS .... Provisional Technical Secretariat [*United Nations*]
PTSA .... Piano Teachers' Association [*British*]   (BI)
PTTL .... Photo-Transferred Thermoluminescence   (PDAA)
PTWI.......... Provisional Tolerable Weekly Intake [*Toxicology*]
PTX............ Aereo Postal de Mexico SA de CV [*ICAO designator*]   (FAAC)
PUA .... Primeras Lineas Uruguayas de Navegacion Aerea [*Uruguay*] [*ICAO designator*]   (FAAC)
Pub Hist...... [*The*] Public Historian [*A publication*]
Pub Int....... Public Interest [*A publication*]
PUBL.......... Publish   (FAAC)
PUD........... Parallel Undocumented Development   (PDAA)
PUL .... Pul. Przedsiebiorstwo Uslug Lotniczych [*Poland*] [*ICAO designator*]   (FAAC)
PULPP .... Peripheral Ultra-Low Power Processor   (PDAA)
PUR .... Spurwing Airlines (Pty) Ltd. [*South Africa*] [*ICAO designator*]   (FAAC)
PURRC...... Polyurethane Recycle and Recovery Council [*Plastics recycling research*]
PUS............ Passive Ultrasonic Sensor   (PDAA)
PUSH .... Public Use Sample Helper   (PDAA)
PUT .... Aeroput [*Yugoslavia*] [*ICAO designator*]   (FAAC)
pU/T .... Pilot Under Training [*Aviation*]   (DA)
PV .... Potential Viewer [*Television ratings*]   (NTCM)
PVA .... Aerotransportes Privados SA de CV [*Mexico*] [*ICAO designator*]   (FAAC)
PVA .... Portable Vehicle Analyzer [*Auto repair*] [*Electronics*]
PVA .... Procedure Value Analysis   (PDAA)
PVASI .... Pulsating/Steady Visual Approach Slope Indicator [*Aviation*]   (FAAC)
PVBE .... Polyvinyl Butyl Ether [*Organic chemistry*]
PVBr .... Polyvinyl Bromide   (PDAA)
PVCCF .... Polyvinyl Chloride-Coated Fabric   (PDAA)
PVCF .... Phase Variable Canonical Form   (PDAA)
PVEE .... Polyvinyl Ethyl Ether [*Organic chemistry*]
PVF............ Pension Valuation Factor
PVFS .... Pinnacle Virtual File System [*Pinnacle Micro, Inc.*] [*Computer science*]   (PCM)
PVHE .... Polyvinyl Hexyl Ether [*Organic chemistry*]
PVM .... Parallel Virtual Machine [*Software package*]
PVM .... Parasitophorous Vacuole Membrane [*Malaria*]
PVN .... Poly(vinyl Nitrate) [*Organic chemistry*]
PVO .... Bearing Supplies Ltd. [*British*] [*ICAO designator*]   (FAAC)
PVOA .... Passenger Vehicle Operation Association Ltd. [*British*]   (BI)

PVS............ Plan-View Size   (PDAA)
PVT............ Personal Verifier Terminal   (DA)
PVT............ Persons Viewing Television [*Television ratings*]   (NTCM)
PVTS .... Pressure Vessel Thermal Shock   (PDAA)
PWB .... Private Wine Buyers' Society [*British*]   (BI)
PWC .... Pratt & Whitney Canada, Inc. [*ICAO designator*]   (FAAC)
PWD .... Participative Work Design
PWD.......... People with Disabilities
PWF............ Pure Water Flux [*Engineering*]
PWI .... Alas Panamenas SA [*Panama*] [*ICAO designator*]   (FAAC)
PWK .... Prestwick BAE [*British*] [*ICAO designator*]   (FAAC)
PWL............ Powell Air Ltd. [*Canada*] [*ICAO designator*]   (FAAC)
PWMR .... Periventricular White-Matter Radiolucency [*Medicine*]
PWNDA ..... Provincial Wholesale Newspaper Distributors' Association
                 [*British*]   (BI)
PWR-FLECHT ... Pressurized Water Ractor - Full Length Emergency Cooling
                 Heat Transfer [*Nuclear energy*]   (PDAA)
PWSA........ Professional Women Singers Association   (EA)
PWSWA..... Processed Woodchip, Sawdust, and Woodflour Association
                 [*British*]   (BI)
PXH .... Pacific Express Holdings Ltd. [*New Zealand*] [*ICAO designator*]
                 (FAAC)
PYC............ Aeropycsa SA de CV [*Mexico*] [*ICAO designator*]   (FAAC)
PYR .... Pyramid Air Lines [*Egypt*] [*ICAO designator*]   (FAAC)
PYSZ .... Partially Yttria-Stabilized Zirconia [*Industrial ceramics*]
PZ .... Surinam [*Aircraft nationality and registration mark*]   (FAAC)
PZL............ Panstwowe Zaklady Lotnicze [*Poland*] [*ICAO designator*]
                 (FAAC)
PZY............ Performance Executive Airlines Ltd. [*British*] [*ICAO
                 designator*]   (FAAC)

Q

8Q .... Maldives [*Aircraft nationality and registration mark*]   (FAAC)
Q8 .... Quadraphonic Eight [*Tape cartridge format*]   (NTCM)
9Q .... Zaire [*Aircraft nationality and registration mark*]   (FAAC)
QAF .... Qatar Amiri Flight [*ICAO designator*]   (FAAC)
QAH .... Quick Airways Holland BV [*Netherlands*] [*ICAO designator*]
        (FAAC)
QAP .... Quality Assurance Package
QAS .... Quisqueya Airlines SA [*Haiti*] [*ICAO designator*]   (FAAC)
QAT .... Aero Taxi [*Canada*] [*ICAO designator*]   (FAAC)
QAT .... Quality Action Team [*Industrial engineering*]
QAW........... Quality at Work [*Quality Decision Management*] [*Computer
        science*]   (PCM)
QB .... Queensland Ballet [*Australia*]
QBS .... Qualifications-Based Selection [*Metallurgy*]
QC .... Quantum Cascade [*LASER*]   (ECON)
QCC .... Qwest Commuter Corp. [*ICAO designator*]   (FAAC)
QCM .... Quick-Connects for Bulkhead Mounting   (PDAA)
QC-PCR ..... Quantitative Competitive Polymerase Chain Reaction [*Analytical
        biochemistry*]
Q-DBS .... Quasi-Direct Broadcast Satellite
QDGS......... Quick-Draw Graphics System   (PDAA)
QEMH........ Queen Elizabeth Military Hospital [*Ministry of Defense*]
        [*British*]   (PDAA)
QENS .... Quasielastic Neutron Scattering [*Physics*]
QFA .... Qantas Airways Ltd. [*Australia*] [*ICAO designator*]   (FAAC)
QFD .... Quality Function Development [*Failure analysis*]
QHP............ Quasi-Hydrostatic Pressure [*Physics*]
QHY .... Quantized High Y [*Picture resolution*]   (NTCM)
QIAC .... Quantimet Image Analyzing Computer   (PDAA)
QIC .... Aero Quick [*Mexico*] [*ICAO designator*]   (FAAC)
QIP .... Quality Improvement Process [*Quality control*]
QK............... Quick Kinescope [*Film replay*]   (NTCM)
QKC........... Aero Taxi Aviation, Inc. [*ICAO designator*]   (FAAC)
QKL .... Aeromaritime (CAAA) [*France*] [*ICAO designator*]   (FAAC)
QL .... Quantum League [*An association*]   (EA)
QLA .... Aviation Quebec Labrador Ltd. [*Canada*] [*ICAO designator*]
        (FAAC)
QMA........... Quarterly Moving Average
QMAC........ Quarter-Orbit Magnetic Attitude Control   (PDAA)
QMB........... Qualified Medicare Beneficiary
QMC........... Quekett Microscopical Club [*British*]   (BI)
QME........... Queueing Matrix Evaluation   (PDAA)
QMOD .... Queue Modification Process
QNK........... Kabo Air Travels [*Nigeria*] [*ICAO designator*]   (FAAC)
QP .... Perceptual Quotient [*Education*]   (AEE)
Q/P .... Quartz/Phenolic
QPQ............ Quench Polish Quench   (PDAA)
QPT .... Quarterly Provisional Tax
QR .... Quarter-Round [*Technical drawings*]   (DAC)
QR .... Quota Restriction
QRD............ Quality Reliability Deployment [*Automotive engineering*]
QSC .... African Safari Airways Ltd. [*Kenya*] [*ICAO designator*]   (FAAC)
QSE .... Quantum Size Effect   (PDAA)
QUA .... Quassar de Mexico SA de CV [*ICAO designator*]   (FAAC)
Quad .... Quadrant [*A publication*]
QUAD .... Quadruplex [*Videotape recording*]   (NTCM)
QUAILLS... Quick Update and Access Interlibrary Loans System
QUAST ...... Quality Assurance Service Test   (PDAA)
QUEST....... Quantification of Uncertainty in Estimating Support Tradeoffs
        (PDAA)
QUI............ Aero Quimmco SA de CV [*Mexico*] [*ICAO designator*]   (FAAC)
QUILT........ Quantitative Intelligence Analysis Technique   (PDAA)
QWA........... Qwestair [*Australia*] [*ICAO designator*]   (FAAC)
QWSSUA... Quasi-Wide-Sense-Stationary Uncorrelated Scattering   (PDAA)
QXE .... Horizon Airlines, Inc. [*ICAO designator*]   (FAAC)
7QY............. Malawi [*Aircraft nationality and registration mark*]   (FAAC)

R

R .... Reader (NTCM)
R .... Regular Priority [*Wire service symbol*] (NTCM)
R .... Religious Program (NTCM)
R .... Renewed License [*FCC*] (NTCM)
R .... Rewind
R .... Rock [*Maps and charts*]
R .... Room (NFPA)
R .... Runway [*Aviation*] (DA)
4R .... Sri Lanka [*Aircraft nationality and registration mark*] (FAAC)
8R .... Guyana [*Aircraft nationality and registration mark*] (FAAC)
Ra .... RADAR
RA .... Recrystallization-Anneal (PDAA)
RA .... Resource Application (ERG)
RAA .... Rynes Aviation, Inc. [*ICAO designator*] (FAAC)
RAAF .... Royal Australian Air Force [*ICAO designator*] (FAAC)
RAATS ...... RCRA [*Resource Conservation and Recovery Act*]
            Administrative Action Tracking System (ERG)
RABA .... Re-Chargeable Air-Breathing Apparatus (PDAA)
RABAL .... Radiosonde Balloon Wind Data [*Meteorology*] (FAAC)
RABATS .... Rapid Analytical Block Aerial Triangulation System (PDAA)
RABDF .... Royal Association of British Dairy Farmers [*British*] (BI)
RAC .... Radio Advisory Committee [*Corporation for Public
            Broadcasting*] (NTCM)
RAC .... Refueling Area Commander [*Navy*] (ANA)
RAC .... Response Action Contractor [*Metallurgy*]
RAC .... Response Action Coordinator [*Environmental Protection
            Agency*] (ERG)
RAC .... Rhomboidal Air Controller (PDAA)
RAC .... River Assault Craft [*Navy*] (ANA)
RAC .... Rotorua Aero Club [*New Zealand*] [*ICAO designator*] (FAAC)
RAD .... RADAR Approach Aid [*Aviation*] (DA)
RAD .... Right Angle Drive (PDAA)
RADAG ...... RADAR Area Correlation Guidance System (PDAA)
RADAR ...... Radio's All-Dimension Audience Research (NTCM)
RADD .... Royal Association in Aid of the Deaf and Dumb [*British*] (BI)
RADDS ...... Raytheon Automated Digital Design System (PDAA)
RADEX .... RADAR Data Extractor (PDAA)
RADI .... Radio Area of Dominant Influence [*The Pulse, Inc.*] (NTCM)
RADI .... Retail Alarm for Display and Intruder (PDAA)
RADMAP... Radiological Monitoring Assessment Prediction System (PDAA)
RADNO...... Report Missing Account Radio Failure [*Meteorology*] (FAAC)
RADRU ...... Rapid Access Data Retrieval Unit [*Computer science*] (PDAA)
RADS......... RADAR Alphanumeric Display Sub-System (PDAA)
RAFC .... Regional Area Forecast Center [*ICAO designator*] (FAAC)
RAFM....... Repair-at-Failure Maintenance (PDAA)
RAFSA ...... Royal Air Force Sailing Association [*British*] (BI)
RAFT........ Receiving Ambient Function Test (PDAA)
RAFT .... Retail Association for the Furnishing Trade [*British*] (BI)
RAGB .... Refractories Association of Great Britain (BI)
RAGS......... Risk Assessment Guidance for Superfund [*Environmental
            science*]
RAH............ Regent Air [*Canada*] [*ICAO designator*] (FAAC)
RAI .... Royal Air Inter-Compagnie d'Exploitation de Lignes Aer
            Interieures [*Morocco*] [*ICAO designator*] (FAAC)
RAID .... Rapid Alerting and Identification Display (PDAA)
RAI/OP...... Repetitive Activity Input/Output Plan (PDAA)
RAIS.......... Rail Air International Service (PDAA)
RAJ............ Raji Airlines [*Pakistan*] [*ICAO designator*] (FAAC)
RAL .... Regional Adjunct Language [*Computer science*] (PDAA)
RAL .... Roswell Airlines, Inc. [*ICAO designator*] (FAAC)
RAM.......... Radio Audience Measurement (NTCM)
RAM .... Royal Air Maroc - Compagnie Nationale de Transports Aeriens
            [*Morocco*] [*ICAO designator*] (FAAC)
RAMB .... Rabbit Anti-Mouse Brain (PDAA)
RAMP .... Rate and Acceleration Measuring Pendulum (PDAA)
RAMPLAN ... Rock Mechanics Applied to Mine Planning (PDAA)
RAN........... Defence Products Ltd. [*British*] [*ICAO designator*] (FAAC)
RANDOLS ... Random Domain Library Screening [*Genetic laboratory
            technique*]
RANK........ Replacement Alpha Numeric Keyboard [*Computer science*]
            (DA)
RANMOG ... Reactivity-Adjusted Non-Methane Organic Gas [*Automotive
            emissions*]

RAO............ Response Amplitude Operator (PDAA)
RAOT........ Rocker Arm Oiling Time (PDAA)
RAOTA ...... Radio Amateur Old Timers' Association [*British*] (BI)
RAP .... Rapid Air [*France*] [*ICAO designator*] (FAAC)
RAPI.......... Radiosonde Report Already Sent in PIBAL [*Pilot Balloon
            Observation*] Collection [*Aviation*] (FAAC)
RAPID....... Rail Gun Armature Plasma Investigation Device (PDAA)
RAPIER ..... Rapid Analysis of Products by Integrated Engineering Routines
            [*Computer-assisted design*]
RAPPORT ... Rapid Alert Programmed, Power Management of RADAR
            Targets [*Military*] (PDAA)
RAPSAT..... Ranging and Processing Satellite (DA)
RAPT.......... Reception Automatic Picture Transmission (PDAA)
RAR .... Aviaross [*Russian Federation*] [*ICAO designator*] (FAAC)
RAR .... RADAR Arrival Route [*Aviation*] (DA)
RARA .... Rural and Remote Area
RAS............ [*Jim*] Ratliff Air Service, Inc. [*ICAO designator*] (FAAC)
RAS............ Regimental Aviation Squadron [*Army*] (ADDR)
RAS............ Relative Aerobic Strain (PDAA)
RASB......... Rapid Access to Sequential Block [*Computer science*] (PDAA)
RASCAL .... Rudimentary Adaptive System for Computer-Aided Learning
            (PDAA)
RASO .... Radio Allocations Study Organization (NTCM)
RAT .... Ratioflug Luftfahrtunternehmen GmbH [*Germany*] [*ICAO
            designator*] (FAAC)
RAT .... Routing Automation Technique (PDAA)
RATTLE .... Road Accident Tabulation Language (PDAA)
RAV .... Receipt Authority Voucher
RAV .... Recreational Active Vehicle [*Toyota*] [*Concept car*]
RAV .... Rogers Aviation Ltd. [*British*] [*ICAO designator*] (FAAC)
RAW .... Regional Air (Pty) Ltd. [*South Africa*] [*ICAO designator*]
            (FAAC)
RAW .... Revenue Anticipation Warrant
RAZ .... Rijnmond Air Services BV [*Netherlands*] [*ICAO designator*]
            (FAAC)
RB .... Right Base [*Aviation*] (FAAC)
RBA .... Risk-Based Audit
RBA .... Road Bitumen Association [*British*] (BI)
RBA .... Royal Brunei Airlines [*ICAO designator*] (FAAC)
RBAN .... Regular Best Asymptotically Normal (PDAA)
RBB .... Rabbit-Air AG, Zurich [*Switzerland*] [*ICAO designator*] (FAAC)
RBCTK....... Red Blood Cell Transketolase [*Medicine*] (PDAA)
RBD .... RNA [*Ribonucleic Acid*] Binding Domain [*Biochemistry*]
RBD .... Rubber Block Drive [*Mechanical power transmission*]
RBD .... Trans World Express, Inc. [*ICAO designator*] (FAAC)
RBE .... Arbet International Ltd. [*Hungary*] [*ICAO designator*] (FAAC)
RBE .... Remain Behind Equipment [*Navy*] (ANA)
RBGF .... Resin-Bonded Glass-Fiber (PDAA)
RBH........... Regal Bahamas International Airways Ltd. [*ICAO designator*]
            (FAAC)
RBI............. Relative Bearing Indicator [*Aviation*] (DA)
RBM .... Reasonable Benefit Multiple.
RBN .... Red Baron Aviation, Inc. [*ICAO designator*] (FAAC)
RBNA .... Royal British Nurses' Association [*British*] (BI)
RBO .... Rainbow Cargo Express [*Ghana*] [*ICAO designator*] (FAAC)
RBOC .... Report Back on Course [*Aviation*] (FAAC)
RBOF......... Report Back on Frequency [*Aviation*] (FAAC)
R-BOT........ Rotating Bomb Oxidation Test [*Lubricant testing*] [*Automotive
            engineering*]
RBT .... Robinton Aereo CA [*Dominican Republic*] [*ICAO designator*]
            (FAAC)
RBV .... Air Roberval [*Canada*] [*ICAO designator*] (FAAC)
RBW .... Rainbow Group [*European political movement*] (ECON)
RC .... Remote Control Authority [*FCC*] (NTCM)
RCA .... Richland Aviation [*ICAO designator*] (FAAC)
RCA .... Royal Choral Association [*British*] (BI)
RCCP......... Rough Cut Capacity Planning [*Manufacturing management*]
RCDS........ Reinforced Concrete Detailing System (PDAA)
RCE .... Aerocer SA [*Mexico*] [*ICAO designator*] (FAAC)
RCE .... Repetitive Counterelectrophoresis (PDAA)
RCE .... Rotary Combustion Engine (PDAA)
RCH........... Helicopter Air Service, Inc. [*ICAO designator*] (FAAC)
RCHS .... Railway and Canal Historical Society [*British*] (BI)

RCHS .... Royal Caledonian Horticultural Society [*British*]   (BI)
RCI .... Royal Channel Islands Yacht Club   (BI)
RCLL.......... Runway Center Line Lights [*ICAO designator*]   (FAAC)
RCM .... Aircam Aviation Ltd. [*British*] [*ICAO designator*]   (FAAC)
RCMA .... Research Council of Makeup Artists   (NTCM)
RCMS......... Resonator-Controlled Microwave Source   (PDAA)
RCN .... Relay-Contact Network   (PDAA)
RCO .... Aero Renta de Coahuila SA de CV [*Mexico*] [*ICAO designator*]   (FAAC)
RCO .... Recuperative Catalytic Oxidation [*Chemical engineering*]
RCOM .... Enroute Communications [*Aviation*]   (FAAC)
RCPG......... Regional Cooperative Physics Group [*Educational institutions in Ohio, Michigan, Illinois and Pennsylvania*]   (PDAA)
RCR .... Randle Cliff RADAR   (PDAA)
RCR .... Recrystallization Controlled Rolling   (PDAA)
RCR .... Route Contingency Reserve [*Aviation*]   (DA)
RCRIS .... Resource Conservation and Recovery Information System   (ERG)
R-CRS......... Report on Course [*Aviation*]   (DA)
RCS............. Rehost Computer System [*Aviation*]   (FAAC)
RCS............. Rent Control System
RCS-RF ...... Rabbit Aorta Contracting Substance-Releasing Factor [*Medicine*]   (PDAA)
RCTM .... Remote Control Tunnelling Machine
RCU .... Road Construction Unit   (PDAA)
RCUT .... Rapid Carbohydrate Utilization Test   (PDAA)
RCVNO...... Receiving Capability Out [*Aviation*]   (FAAC)
RD............... Rate Difference [*Toxicology*]
RD............... Report Departing [*Aviation*]   (DA)
RDA .... Regularize Discriminant Analysis [*Mathematics*]
RDA .... Retail Distributors Association, Inc. [*British*]   (BI)
RDA .... Royal Docks Association [*British*]   (BI)
RDA .... TK Travel Ltd. [*Gambia*] [*ICAO designator*]   (FAAC)
RDB .... Relational Data Base   (PDAA)
RDC .... Regional Dissemination Centers [*NASA*]   (PDAA)
RDCE .... Radio Distribution and Control Equipment [*Aviation*]   (DA)
RDF .... Refuse-Derived Fuel   (ERG)
RDGE .... Resorcinol Diglycidyl Ether [*Organic chemistry*]
RDH .... Reference Datum Height [*Aviation*]   (DA)
RDK .... Irish Air Tours [*ICAO designator*]   (FAAC)
RDL............ Roadair Lines IC [*Canada*] [*ICAO designator*]   (FAAC)
RDM........... Respirable Dust Monitor   (PDAA)
RDN............ Dinar SA [*Argentina*] [*ICAO designator*]   (FAAC)
RDN............ Resource Decision Network   (PDAA)
RDR .... RADAR Departure Route [*Aviation*]   (DA)
RD/RA .... Remedial Design/Remedial Action [*Environmental Protection Agency*]   (ERG)
RDS .... Radio Data System [*Driver information systems*]
RDS .... Random Digit Sample   (NTCM)
RDS .... Religious Drama Society of Great Britain   (BI)
RDS .... Rhoades Aviation, Inc. [*ICAO designator*]   (FAAC)
RDSS .... RADAR Determination Satellite System [*Aviation*]   (DA)
RDU............ Remote Data Uplink [*SmartOffice*] [*Computer science*]
RE............... Remote Pickup [*FCC*]   (NTCM)
R & E......... Restructuring and Efficiency
REA .... Aer Arann Teoranta [*Ireland*] [*ICAO designator*]   (FAAC)
REA .... Registered Environmental Assessor
REACT....... Requirements Evaluated against Cargo Transportation   (PDAA)
REAP......... Regional Enforcement Activities Plan [*Environmental Protection Agency*]   (ERG)
REAP......... Reliability Engineering Analysis and Planning   (PDAA)
REB .... Rare Earth Boride   (PDAA)
REBAT ...... Reference Breakdown Air Traffic Control Services Report   (FAAC)
REBEEL..... Realistic Battlefield Environment-Electronic [*Military*]   (PDAA)
REBLT .... Rebuilt [*Automotive advertising*]
REC .... Radio Executives Club   (NTCM)
REC .... Railway Enthusiasts' Club [*British*]   (BI)
REC .... Recorded Program   (NTCM)
REC .... Regional Express Co. [*ICAO designator*]   (FAAC)
RECA .... Repetitive Element Column Analysis   (PDAA)
RECLR .... Recleared [*Aviation*]   (FAAC)
RED .... Comite International de La Croix-Rouge [*Switzerland*] [*ICAO designator*]   (FAAC)
RED .... Repeat Expansion Detection [*Genetics*]
REDL.......... Runway Edge Light [*ICAO designator*]   (FAAC)
REDZ .... Recent Drizzle [*Meteorology*]   (DA)
REE .... Registered Export Establishment
REELS........ Reflected Electron Energy Loss Spectra
REFIL........ Recharged from Inversion Layer   (PDAA)
REFLECS ... Retrieval from the Literature on Electronics and Computer Sciences   (PDAA)
REFRA .... Recent Freezing Rain [*Meteorology*]   (DA)
REG .... Registration [*ICAO designator*]   (FAAC)
REG .... Regourd Aviation [*France*] [*ICAO designator*]   (FAAC)
REGAL....... Remote Generalized Application Language [*Computer science*]   (PDAA)
REGEXP .... Regular Expression [*Computer science*]   (NHD)
REGM .... Register Module
REGR .... Recent Hail [*Meteorology*]   (DA)
REIB .... Report Established in Block [*Aviation*]   (FAAC)
RELKIN ..... Relativistic Kinematics   (PDAA)
REM .... Rack Entry Module   (PDAA)

REM .... Registered Environmental Manager
REMAP...... Regional Environment Management Allocation Process   (PDAA)
REMCALC ... Relative Motion Collision Avoidance Calculator   (PDAA)
REML......... Risley Engineering and Materials Laboratory   (PDAA)
REMOTE... Reflective Mossbauer Technique   (PDAA)
REMP........ Rapid Eye Movement Period   (PDAA)
REMUS...... Routine for Executive Multi-Unit Simulation   (PDAA)
REN .... Aero-Rent SA de CV [*Mexico*] [*ICAO designator*]   (FAAC)
RENG .... Radio Electronic News Gathering   (NTCM)
RENL .... Runway End Light [*Aviation*]   (FAAC)
RENOT ...... Regional Office Notice [*Aviation*]   (FAAC)
REO .... Rio Airways, Inc. [*ICAO designator*]   (FAAC)
REP............ Registered Environmental Professional
REPA.......... Registered Environmental Property Assessor
REPCON.... Rain Repellant and Surface Conditioner   (PDAA)
REPEET..... Reusabler Engines, Partially Enternal Expendable Tankage   (PDAA)
REQP......... Recursive Equality Quadratic Program   (PDAA)
RERA .... Recent Rain [*Meteorology*]   (DA)
RERTE .... Reroute [*Aviation*]   (FAAC)
RES............ Restauraciones Aeronauticas SA de CV [*Mexico*] [*ICAO designator*]   (FAAC)
RESA .... Runway End Safety Area [*Aviation*]   (DA)
RESH .... Recent Shower [*Meteorology*]   (DA)
RESN......... Recent Snow [*Meteorology*]   (DA)
RET .... Rotational Energy Transfer [*Chemical physics*]
RETCON.... Retroactive Continuity [*Computer science*]   (NHD)
RETM........ Rare Earth Transition Metal [*Computer science*]
RETS .... Recent Thunderstorm   (DA)
REU .... Air Reunion [*France*] [*ICAO designator*]   (FAAC)
REU .... Rated Exposure Unit [*Advertising*]   (NTCM)
REV .... Range Extender Vehicle [*Gasoline-electric hybrid*]
REV .... Reversal Film [*Cinematography*]   (NTCM)
REV .... Revision Message [*Aviation*]   (DA)
REVERB..... Reverberation   (NTCM)
REX .... Radio Exploration Satellite   (PDAA)
REX .... Ram Air Freight, Inc. [*ICAO designator*]   (FAAC)
REXA......... Radioisotope-Excited X-Ray Analyzer   (PDAA)
REY .... Aero-Rey SA de CV [*Mexico*] [*ICAO designator*]   (FAAC)
REZ .... Airplanes, Inc. [*ICAO designator*]   (FAAC)
RF .... Rainer Foundation [*British*]   (BI)
RF .... Reported Frequency   (NTCM)
RFA .... Raleigh Flying Service, Inc. [*ICAO designator*]   (FAAC)
RFA .... Rugby Fives Association [*British*]   (BI)
RFBPA ...... Raw Fat and Bone Processors Association [*British*]   (BI)
RFBR......... Russian Foundation for Basic Research
RFCC .... Resid Fluid Catalytic Cracking [*Petroleum refining*]
RFE............ Aero Fe SA [*Mexico*] [*ICAO designator*]   (FAAC)
RFE............ Request for Enhancement [*Computer science*]   (NHD)
RFGD .... Radio-Frequency Glow Discharge [*Materials science*]
RFLG......... Refuelling   (DA)
RFMVR...... Recency-Frequency-Monetary Value Ratio   (NTCM)
RFO .... Air Royal [*France*] [*ICAO designator*]   (FAAC)
RFPI .... Request for Proposal Information [*Competitive bidding*]
RFPR......... Reversed-Field Pinch Reactor [*Plasma physics*]   (PDAA)
RFR............ Royal Air Force [*British*] [*ICAO designator*]   (FAAC)
RFS............ Rossair Pty Ltd. [*Australia*] [*ICAO designator*]   (FAAC)
RFSH......... Recombinant Follicle-Stimulating Hormone [*Endocrinology*]
RFSP......... Replacement Flight Strip Printer [*Aviation*]   (DA)
RFT............ Repeat Formation Tester [*Well drilling*]
RFTM .... Radiator Fan Timer Module [*Cooling systems*] [*Automotive engineering*]
RFX............ [*J. P.*] Hunt Inc. [*ICAO designator*]   (FAAC)
RGA........... Region Air [*Seychelles*] [*ICAO designator*]   (FAAC)
RGD........... Radiation Gasdynamics   (PDAA)
RGDATA ... Retail Grocery, Dairy, and Allied Trades Association [*British*]   (BI)
RGI .... Regional Airlines [*France*] [*ICAO designator*]   (FAAC)
RGL .... Regionair Ltd. [*British*] [*ICAO designator*]   (FAAC)
RGL .... Runway Guard Light [*Aviation*]   (DA)
RGM........... Rangemile Ltd. [*British*] [*ICAO designator*]   (FAAC)
RGO........... Argo SA [*Dominican Republic*] [*ICAO designator*]   (FAAC)
RGP .... Reliability Growth Program   (PDAA)
RGR............ Region Air, Inc. [*Canada*] [*ICAO designator*]   (FAAC)
RGRDE ..... Rotating Gold Ring-Disc Electrode   (PDAA)
RGS .... Renown Aviation, Inc. [*ICAO designator*]   (FAAC)
RGY .... Regency Airlines Ltd. [*ICAO designator*]   (FAAC)
RHA .... Rice Husk Ash   (PDAA)
RHAG........ Rotary Hydraulic Arresting Gear   (PDAA)
RHINO....... RADAR Range Height Indicator Not Operating on Scan [*Meteorology*]   (FAAC)
RHINO....... Repeating Handheld Improved Non-Rifled Ordnance   (PDAA)
RHL........... Rectangular Hysteresis Loop   (PDAA)
RHN .... Rhonavia [*France*] [*ICAO designator*]   (FAAC)
RHSA......... Radio Historical Society of America   (NTCM)
RHSP......... Registered Hazardous Substances Professional [*Environmental science*]
RI .... Ribonuclease Inhibitor
RI .... Room Index   (PDAA)
RIA .... Rich International Airways, Inc. [*ICAO designator*]   (FAAC)
RIAADA..... Research Institute of African and African Diaspora Arts   (EA)
RIB............. River Ice Breaker   (PDAA)
RIBC.......... Rigid Intermediate Bulk Container

RIC .... Reciprocal Impedance Converter (PDAA)
RIC .... Replacement Ion Chromatography [*Spectrometry*]
RIC .... Richardson's Airway, Inc. [*ICAO designator*] (FAAC)
RICS .... Rubber-Impregnated Chopped Strand (PDAA)
RIF .... Rapid Infrared Forming Technique [*Materials science*]
RIF .... Reclearance in Flight [*Aviation*] (FAAC)
RIG .... Refractive Index Gradient [*Analytical chemistry*]
RIG .... Riga Airlines [*Latvia*] [*ICAO designator*] (FAAC)
RIGS .... Radioimmunoguided Surgery [*Medicine*]
RIK .... Eurojet Compagnie [*British*] [*ICAO designator*] (FAAC)
RIKE .... Raman-Induced Kerr Effect (PDAA)
RIL .... Res Ipsa Loquitur [*The Thing Speaks for Itself*] [*Latin*]
RIM .... Rimrock Airlines, Inc. [*ICAO designator*] (FAAC)
RIME .... Ranking Index for Maintenance Expenditures (PDAA)
RIO .... Radio Information Office [*National Audience Board*] (NTCM)
RIOT .... Remote Independently-Operated Transceiver
RIP .... Remote Instrument Package (PDAA)
RIPS .... Research Institute of Pharmaceutical Sciences [*University of Mississippi*] (PDAA)
RIS .... Air Services Ltd. [*Czechoslovakia*] [*ICAO designator*] (FAAC)
RIS .... RADAR Information Service [*Aviation*] (DA)
RIS .... Railway Invigoration Society [*British*] (BI)
RIS .... Relevent Industry Sales (PDAA)
RIT .... Red Interamericana de Telecommunicaciones [*Inter-American Telecommunication Network*] (NTCM)
RITA .... Recognition for Information Technology Achievement [*An award*] (PDAA)
RITAL .... Red Internacional de American Latina [*International Telecommunication Network for Latin America*] (NTCM)
RITE .... Right [*Direction of Turn*] [*ICAO designator*] (FAAC)
RIV .... Rapid Intervention Vehicle (DA)
RJA .... Royal Jordanian [*ICAO designator*] (FAAC)
RJZ .... Royal Jordanian Air Force [*ICAO designator*] (FAAC)
RKA .... Air Afrique [*Ivory Coast*] [*ICAO designator*] (FAAC)
RKA .... Reaction Kinetic Analysis (PDAA)
RL .... Real Life (NHD)
RL .... Romeo Series L [*Alfa-Romeo*] [*Automotive model designation*]
RL .... Runway Light [*Aviation*] (DA)
RLA .... Lar-Liniile Aeriene Romance [*Romania*] [*ICAO designator*] (FAAC)
RLB .... Air Alba Ltd. [*British*] [*ICAO designator*] (FAAC)
RLC .... Avial (Russian Co. Ltd.) [*Former USSR*] [*ICAO designator*] (FAAC)
RLC .... Real-time Lens Error Correction [*Computer science*] (NTCM)
RLCE .... Request Level Change Enroute [*Aviation*] (DA)
RLD .... Rheinland Air Service [*Germany*] [*ICAO designator*] (FAAC)
RLDB .... Reference Library Data Base
RLK .... Air Nelson Ltd. [*New Zealand*] [*ICAO designator*] (FAAC)
RLLS .... Runway Lead-In Lighting System [*Aviation*] (FAAC)
RLM .... Royal American Airways, Inc. [*ICAO designator*] (FAAC)
RLN .... Romeo Series L Normale [*Alfa-Romeo*] [*Automotive model designation*]
RLNA .... Request Level Not Available [*Aviation*] (FAAC)
RLR .... Reserves to Loans Ratio
RLRD .... Register Load and Read
RLS .... Romeo Series L Sport [*Alfa-Romeo*] [*Automotive model designation*]
RLSS .... Romeo Series L Super Sport [*Alfa-Romeo*] [*Automotive model designation*]
RLST .... Read Least Significant Time [*Military*]
RLT .... Radionavigation Land Test (PDAA)
RLT .... Reliant Airlines, Inc [*ICAO designator*] (FAAC)
RLT .... Remote Line Tester
RLT .... Romeo Series L Turismo [*Alfa-Romeo*] [*Automotive model designation*]
RLTF .... Romeo Series L Targa Florio [*Alfa-Romeo*] [*Automotive model designation*]
RLV .... Range Location Velocity
RLV .... Real Aviation Ltd. [*Ghana*] [*ICAO designator*] (FAAC)
RLVL .... Report Level [*Aviation*] (FAAC)
RM .... Recordimeter (NTCM)
RM .... Remark [*Aviation*] (FAAC)
R & M .... Repairs and Maintenance
RMA .... Rail Makers' Association [*British*] (BI)
RMA .... Relaxation Map Analysis [*Coatings*]
RMA .... Rocky Mountain Airways, Inc. [*ICAO designator*] (FAAC)
RMCDE ..... RADAR Message Conversion and Distribution (DA)
RME .... Armenian International Airlines [*ICAO designator*] (FAAC)
RME .... Reasonable Maximum Exposure [*Toxicology*]
RMF .... Rotating Magnetic Field [*Spectrometry*]
RMF .... Royal Malaysian Air Force [*ICAO designator*] (FAAC)
RMIG .... Royal Masonic Institution for Girls [*British*] (BI)
RMMRA .... Rocky Mountain Midget Racing Association [*Automobile competition organizer*]
RMN .... Reuters Money Network [*Reality Technologies*] (PCM)
RMN .... RN Aviation Ltd. [*British*] [*ICAO designator*] (FAAC)
RMP .... Raw Materials Processing
RMP .... Risk Management Plan
RMPCK ...... Ramp Check [*Aviation*] (FAAC)
RMRK .... Remark (FAAC)
RMS .... Regulator of Mitotic Spindle Assembly [*Cytology*]
RMS .... Reliability, Maintainability, Supportability [*Automotive engineering*]

RMS .... TAS Aviation, Inc. [*ICAO designator*] (FAAC)
RMU.......... Romeo Series M Unificto [*Alfa-Romeo*] [*Automotive model designation*]
RMV .... Romavia [*Romania*] [*ICAO designator*] (FAAC)
RMYC .... Royal Motor Yacht Club [*British*] (BI)
RNA........... Royal Nepal Airlines Corp. [*ICAO designator*] (FAAC)
RNCF .... Reserve Naval Construction Force [*Navy*] (PDAA)
RNHU .... Royal National Homing Union [*British*] (BI)
RNLS......... Resume Normal Speed [*Aviation*] (FAAC)
RNMWS ... Royal Naval Minewatching Service [*British*] (BI)
RNO .... Air Normandie [*France*] [*ICAO designator*] (FAAC)
RNP .... Required Navigation Performance [*Aviation*] (FAAC)
RNS .... Services Aeronautiques Roannais [*France*] [*ICAO designator*] (FAAC)
RNT .... Rentavion CA [*Venezuela*] [*ICAO designator*] (FAAC)
RO .... Report Over (DA)
RO .... Reporting Officer
ROA .... Reno Air, Inc. [*ICAO designator*] (FAAC)
ROA .... Return on Assets [*Business term*]
ROA .... Roller Owners' Association [*British*] (BI)
ROAST ...... Ring Out and Stress Tester (PDAA)
ROBOT ..... Record Organization Based on Transposition (PDAA)
ROC .... Readily-Oxidizable Carbon (PDAA)
ROC .... Rocky Mountain [*Canada*] [*ICAO designator*] (FAAC)
ROCC .... Region Operations Control Center [*NORAD*] [*ICAO designator*] (FAAC)
ROCS......... Railroad Operations Control System (PDAA)
ROD........... Repair on Demand (PDAA)
ROF .... Aerofrance [*France*] [*ICAO designator*] (FAAC)
ROFA .... Radio of Free Asia (NTCM)
ROFOR ..... Route Forcast [*Aviation*] (FAAC)
ROG........... Rogel [*C.C. Sergio Gonzales*], Ing. [*Mexico*] [*ICAO designator*] (FAAC)
ROLS......... Rainbow Optical Landing System (PDAA)
ROM.......... Empresa Aeromar [*Dominican Republic*] [*ICAO designator*] (FAAC)
ROMAN..... Remotely-Operated Mobile Manipulator (PDAA)
RON .... Air Nauru [*ICAO designator*] (FAAC)
ROP .... Royal Oman Police [*ICAO designator*] (FAAC)
ROP .... Run of Publication (NTCM)
ROR........... Return on Revenue
ROS .... ATS-Servicii de Transport Aerian [*Italy*] [*ICAO designator*] (FAAC)
ROS .... Reporter on Scene (NTCM)
ROSP......... Report on Syndicated Programs (NTCM)
ROSR .... Real-Time On-Scene Report (NTCM)
ROT .... Tarom, Romanian Air Transport [*ICAO designator*] (FAAC)
ROTFL....... Rolling on the Floor Laughing [*Computer hacker terminology*] (NHD)
ROTO........ Rotogravure [*Printing process*] (NTCM)
ROV.......... Rover Airways International, Inc. [*ICAO designator*] (FAAC)
ROWS....... Register of Weather Stations [*Meteorological Office*] (PDAA)
ROY........... Conifair Aviation, Inc. [*Canada*] [*ICAO designator*] (FAAC)
RP .... [*Fire Alarm*] Reset Panel [*NFPA pre-fire planning symbol*] (NFPA)
RP .... Reverse Processing [*Chemical engineering*]
RPA .... Provence Aero Service [*France*] [*ICAO designator*] (FAAC)
RPA .... Replication Protein A [*Genetics*]
RPA .... Rubber Proofers' Association [*British*] (BI)
RPC........... Recreational Pilot Certificate [*Aviation*] (DA)
RPC........... Rotation Planar Chromatography
RPD .... Research Planning Diagram (PDAA)
RPDT........ RADAR Prediction Data Table (PDAA)
RPF .... Rigid Plastic Foam
RPF........... Rwandan Patriotic Front [*Political party*]
RPFMA ...... Rubber and Plastic Footwear Manufacturers' Association [*British*] (BI)
RPFS .... Radio Position Fixing System [*Aviation*] (DA)
RPI............ Reaction Product Imaging [*Chemistry*]
RPL........... Rotary Pellet Launcher [*Military*] (PDAA)
RPM .... Raised Pavement Marker [*Highway design*]
RPM .... Relative Plate Motion [*Geophysics*]
RPMB........ Remotely-Piloted Mini-Blimp (PDAA)
RPOADS.... Remotely-Piloted Observation Aircraft Designator System (PDAA)
RPPS .... Reactive Perfluoroalkyl Polymeric Surfactant [*Organic chemistry*]
RPS .... Randomized Pattern Search (PDAA)
RPS .... Regional Pressure Setting (DA)
RPS............ Reversed-Phase Series (PDAA)
RPSI.......... Railway Preservation Society of Ireland (BI)
RPTP......... Receptor Protein Tyrosine Phosphatase [*Biochemistry*]
RPX .... BAC Aircraft Ltd. [*British*] [*ICAO designator*] (FAAC)
RQG........... Reduced Quantity Generator (ERG)
RQM.......... Ride Quality Meter [*Automotive testing*]
RQP.......... Request Flight Plan [*Aviation*] (DA)
RQX........... Air Engiadina [*Switzerland*] [*ICAO designator*] (FAAC)
RR .... Routine Message Precedence [*Telecommunications*] (ADDR)
RRA .... RADAR Recording and Analysis Equipment (DA)
RR-BB .... Rayon-Rayon Bias-Belted (PDAA)
RRDC .... Railroad Data Center [*Association of American Railroad*] (PDAA)
R/REA....... Rural/Regional Education Association (AEE)
RREL.......... Risk Reduction Engineering Laboratory

RRI .... Rowett Research Institute [*British*]   (BI)
RRID .... Reverse Radial Immunodiffusion   (PDAA)
RRL .... Rolls Royce Ltd. [*British*] [*ICAO designator*]   (FAAC)
RRM .... Rotation Remanent Magnetization   (PDAA)
RRP .... Reader and Reader-Printer   (PDAA)
RRPM .... Reflective Raised Pavement Marker [*Highway design*]
RRR .... RAF-HQSTC (Air Transport) [*British*] [*ICAO designator*]   (FAAC)
RRR .... Resource Rent Royalty
RRS .... Bedford Rae [*British*] [*ICAO designator*]   (FAAC)
RRT .... Reflected-Reflected-Transmitted [*Wave mechanics*]
RRV .... Rhesus Rotavirus [*Medicine*]
RRZ .... RADAR Regulation Zone   (DA)
RS .... Reverse Shot [*Cinematography*]   (NTCM)
RSA .... Air Service Affaires [*France*] [*ICAO designator*]   (FAAC)
RSA .... Rated Sail Area [*IOR*] [*Yacht racing*]
RSA .... Relay Services Association of Great Britain   (BI)
RSAS .... Royal Surgical Aid Society [*British*]   (BI)
RSB .... Samaero SA [*Romania*] [*ICAO designator*]   (FAAC)
RSBT .... Recovery Storage Unit Boot Test [*Military*]
RSC .... Raytheon Service Co.
RSC .... Relaxation-Sensitive Cell   (PDAA)
RSC .... RISC Single Chip [*IBM*] [*Computer science*]
RSCD .... Runway Surface Condition [*Aviation*]   (FAAC)
RSFS .... Real Scene Focus Sensor   (PDAA)
RSI .... Air Sunshine, Inc. [*ICAO designator*]   (FAAC)
RSI .... Refractory Reusable Surface Insulation   (PDAA)
RSL .... Rio-Sul, Servicos Aereos Regionais SA [*Brazil*] [*ICAO designator*]   (FAAC)
RSN .... Royal Swazi National Airways Corp. [*Swaziland*] [*ICAO designator*]   (FAAC)
RSO .... Aero Asia [*Pakistan*] [*ICAO designator*]   (FAAC)
RSO .... Rectified Skew Orthomorphic   (PDAA)
RSO .... Relativistic and Spin-Orbit   (PDAA)
RSPT .... Report Starting Procedure Turn [*Aviation*]   (DA)
RSS .... Root Sum Square   (DA)
RSS .... Russian Spring-Summer Encephalitis [*Medicine*]   (MAH)
RST .... Regularly-Scheduled Training [*Military*]   (ADDR)
RST .... Reliability Shakedown Test   (PDAA)
RST .... Resort Airline, Inc. [*ICAO designator*]   (FAAC)
RSU .... Recovery Storage Unit [*Military*]
RSUA .... Royal Society of Ulster Architects [*British*]   (BI)
RSV .... Resupply Vehicle [*Military*]
RSVP .... Random Signal Vibration Protector   (PDAA)
RSVP .... Relational Structure Vertex Processor   (PDAA)
RSZ .... Air Service State Co. [*Hungary*] [*ICAO designator*]   (FAAC)
RT .... Radio Telephony   (NTCM)
RT .... Reverberation Time   (NTCM)
RT .... Roundtable [*Bulletin board system*] [*Computer science*]   (PCM)
RTA .... Required Time of Arrival   (DA)
RTAMA ..... Railway Tyre and Axle Manufacturers Association [*British*]   (BI)
RTAN .... Rubber-Toughened Amorphous Nylon [*Organic chemistry*]
RTC .... Radio Technical Committee for Aeronautics   (NTCM)
RTCA .... Real-Time Control Area   (NTCM)
RTCIP .... Real-Time Cell-Identification Processor   (PDAA)
RTDDAS .... Real-Time Digital Data Acquisition System   (PDAA)
RTE .... Aeronorte - Transportes Aereos Lda. [*Portugal*] [*ICAO designator*]   (FAAC)
RTE .... Reciprocal Thermal Efficiency   (PDAA)
RTEB .... Radio Trades Examination Board [*British*]   (BI)
RTFAQ .... Read the Frequently Asked Questions [*Computer hacker terminology*]   (NHD)
RTHL .... Runway Threshold Light [*Aviation*]   (FAAC)
RTI .... Return from Interrupt [*Computer science*]   (NHD)
RTL .... Rheintalflug-Rolf Seewald [*Austria*] [*ICAO designator*]   (FAAC)
RTM .... Trans Am Compania Ltda. [*Ecuador*] [*ICAO designator*]   (FAAC)
RTO .... Regenerative Thermal Oxidation [*Metallurgy*]
RTOAA ...... Rejected Takeoff Area Available [*Aviation*]   (DA)
RTP .... Restrictive Trade Practice
RTPF .... Round Tube-Plate Fin [*Heat exchanger*]
RTPMMA ... Rubber-Toughened Polymethyl Methacrylate [*Organic chemistry*]
RTPS .... Real-Time Telemetry Processing System   (PDAA)
RTPU.,........ Reinforced Thermoplastic Polyurethane [*Plastics*]
RTR .... Real-Time Record   (NTCM)
RTR .... Sociedade Brazileira de Turismo (ROTATUR) [*Brazil*] [*ICAO designator*]   (FAAC)
RTRI .... Real-Time Record Interpreter   (NTCM)
RTS .... Relief Transport Services Ltd. [*British*] [*ICAO designator*]   (FAAC)
RTT .... Radioteleprinter   (DA)
R & TWUS ... Research and Technology Work Unit Summary
RTXE .... Real-Time Executive Extended   (PDAA)
RTY .... Ross Air Training [*British*] [*ICAO designator*]   (FAAC)
RTZL .... Runway Touchdown Zone Light [*Aviation*]   (FAAC)
R/U .... Record/Update
RU .... Rutgers-[*The*] State University [*New Brunswick, NJ*]   (PDAA)
RUCAPS .... Really Universal Computer-Aided Production System   (PDAA)
RUDS .... Reflectance Units of Dirt Shade   (PDAA)
RUF .... Refractory Users Federation [*British*]   (BI)
RUMAC ..... Rubber-Modified Asphalt Concrete
RUMIC ...... Remote Underwater Mine Countermeasure   (PDAA)
RUS .... Air Russia Airlines [*Russian Federation*] [*ICAO designator*]   (FAAC)

RUSH .... Rudder Shaped Hull   (PDAA)
RV .... Riser Valve [*NFPA pre-fire planning symbol*]   (NFPA)
RVA .... RADAR Vectoring Area [*Aviation*]   (DA)
RVA .... Raven Air, Inc. [*ICAO designator*]   (FAAC)
RVC .... Richards Aviation, Inc. [*ICAO designator*]   (FAAC)
RVI .... RV-Aviation [*Finland*] [*ICAO designator*]   (FAAC)
RVL .... Airvallee SpA-Services Aeriens de Val d'Aoste [*Italy*] [*ICAO designator*]   (FAAC)
RVR .... Raven Air Ltd. [*British*] [*ICAO designator*]   (FAAC)
RVRC .... Runway Visual Range Center [*Aviation*]   (DA)
RVTV .... Rear Vision Television [*Driver safety systems*] [*Automotive engineering*]
RVV .... Reeve Aleutian Airways, Inc. [*ICAO designator*]   (FAAC)
RWA .... Aligiulia SpA [*Italy*] [*ICAO designator*]   (FAAC)
RWAS .... Royal Welsh Agricultural Society   (BI)
RWD .... Air Rwanda [*ICAO designator*]   (FAAC)
RWE .... Aero West Airlines, Inc. [*ICAO designator*]   (FAAC)
RWF .... Radio Wholesalers Federation [*British*]   (BI)
RWG .... Redwing Airways, Inc. [*ICAO designator*]   (FAAC)
R/W & L .... Random Width and Length   (DAC)
RWS .... Air Whitsunday [*Australia*] [*ICAO designator*]   (FAAC)
RXA .... Arax Airlines Ltd. [*Nigeria*] [*ICAO designator*]   (FAAC)
RXA .... Repairable Exchange Activity [*Army*]
RXD .... Research or Exploratory Development   (PDAA)
RXL .... Air Exel [*France*] [*ICAO designator*]   (FAAC)
RYA .... Royal Yachting Association [*British*]   (BI)
RYA .... Ryan Air Services, Inc. [*ICAO designator*]   (FAAC)
RYN .... Ryan Aviation Corp. [*ICAO designator*]   (FAAC)
RYR .... Ryanair [*Ireland*] [*ICAO designator*]   (FAAC)
RyRC .... Ryanodine Receptor Channel [*Biochemistry*]
RZR .... Zephyr Aviation Services, Inc. [*ICAO designator*]   (FAAC)

S

S .... Seamless (DAC)
S .... Sharing Time (NTCM)
S .... Sized (NTCM)
S .... Smoke (NFPA)
S .... Sports Program (NTCM)
S .... Supplementary Frequency (DA)
S2 .... Bangladesh [*Aircraft nationality and registration mark*] (FAAC)
S7 .... Seychelles [*Aircraft nationality and registration mark*] (FAAC)
S9 .... Sao Tome and Principe [*Aircraft nationality and registration mark*] (FAAC)
SA .... Arsine [*Medicine*] (ADDR)
SA .... Safety Altitude [*Aviation*] (DA)
SA .... Slide Agglutination (PDAA)
SA .... Spiritualist Association of Great Britain (BI)
SAA .... Screen Advertising Association Ltd. [*British*] (BI)
SAA .... South African Airways [*ICAO designator*] (FAAC)
SAAGS ..... Semi-Automated Artwork Generator System (PDAA)
SAAR........ Solar Aureole Almucantar Radiance (PDAA)
SAAT........ Society of Architects and Associated Technicians [*British*] (BI)
SAB............ SABENA [*Societe Anonyme Belge d'Exploitation de la Nav Aerienne*] [*Belgium*] [*ICAO designator*] (FAAC)
SABP .... Salicylic Acid Binding Protein [*Biochemistry*]
SABRE ...... Steerable Adaptive Broadcast Reception Equipment (PDAA)
SAC............ Sudanese Aeronautical Services Co. Ltd. [*Sudan*] [*ICAO designator*] (FAAC)
SAC............ Sudania Aviation Co. [*Sudan*] [*ICAO designator*] (FAAC)
SACCM...... Slow Access Charge-Coupled Memory [*Computer science*] (PDAA)
SACL.......... Stress and Arousal Adjective Checklist (PDAA)
SACMFCS ... Small Arms Common Module Fire Control System [*Army*]
SACT......... Special Advisory Committee on Telecommunications (NTCM)
SAD .... Servicios Aereos de La Capital [*Colombia*] [*ICAO designator*] (FAAC)
SADE........ Sensitive Acoustic Detection Equipment (PDAA)
SADF........ Statistical Analysis of Documentation Files (PDAA)
SAE........... Skyways Africa Ltd. [*Kenya*] [*ICAO designator*] (FAAC)
SAEF .... Stock Exchange Automatic Execution Facility
SAESA .... Compania de Servicios Aereos SA [*Spain*] [*ICAO designator*] (FAAC)
SAF .... Republic of Singapore Air Force [*ICAO designator*] (FAAC)
SAFE .... Source and Application Inspection Equipment
SAFE .... System for Automated Flight Efficiency (PDAA)
SAFER ...... System for Aircrew Flight Extension and Return (PDAA)
SAFI .... Semiautomatic Flight Inspection Aircraft (FAAC)
SAFO......... Self-Adhesive Foreign Object (PDAA)
SAFZ......... San Andreas Fault Zone [*Geology*]
SAG .... Sagittarius [*Constellation*]
SAG .... Self-Agglomerator
SAG .... Swedish Air Ambulance [*ICAO designator*] (FAAC)
SAG .... Syntax Analyzer Generator (PDAA)
SAGAGB.... Sand and Gravel Association of Great Britain (BI)
SAGGA ...... Scout and Guide Graduate Association [*British*] (BI)
SAGT......... Systematic Approach to Group Technology (PDAA)
SAH .... Sayakhat [*Kazakhstan*] [*ICAO designator*] (FAAC)
SAHC .... Sleep Analyzing Hybrid Computer (PDAA)
SAHP .... Solar-Assisted Heat Pump (PDAA)
SAHR .... Society of Army Historical Research [*British*] (BI)
SAI............ Shaheen Air International [*Pakistan*] [*ICAO designator*] (FAAC)
SAIC.......... Ship Acquisition and Improvement Council [*Navy*] (ANA)
SAIC-WG... Ship Acquisition and Improvement Council-Working Group [*Navy*] (ANA)
SAILA .... Simplified Aircraft Instrument Landing System (PDAA)
SAIMA .... Selected Acquisitions Information and Management System (PDAA)
SAJ .... Golden Eagle Air Services Ltd. [*Canada*] [*ICAO designator*] (FAAC)
SAK .... Red Arrows Display Squadron [*British*] [*ICAO designator*] (FAAC)
SAKI.......... Saudi Arabia - Kuwait - Iraq
SAL............ Caspair Ltd. [*Kenya*] [*ICAO designator*] (FAAC)
SAL............ Strong Acid Leach (PDAA)
SALS .... Separate Access Landing System [*Aviation*] (DA)
SALS .... Simple Approach Lighting System [*Aviation*] (FAAC)

SALS .... Single Anchor Leg Storage (PDAA)
SAM .... Six-Axis Manipulator (PDAA)
SAM .... Sociedad Aeronautica de Medellin [*Colombia*] [*ICAO designator*] (FAAC)
SAM .... Sound-Activated Mobile (PDAA)
SAM .... Station Acquisition Marketing Plan [*PBS*] (NTCM)
SAM .... Subsystem Action Message [*Military*]
SAMCAP ... Surface-to-Air Missile Capability (PDAA)
SAMECS.... Structural Analysis Method for Evaluation of Complex Structures (PDAA)
SAMHO..... Society of Administrative Mental Health Offices [*British*] (BI)
SAMI......... Speed of Approach Measurement Indicator (PDAA)
SAMIDS .... Ships Anti-Missile Integrated Defense System (PDAA)
SAMOS ..... Spot Accumulation and Melting of Snow (PDAA)
SAMP........ Salary Administration and Manpower Planning (PDAA)
SAMS........ School for Advanced Military Studies [*Army*]
SAMS........ Six Axis Motion System (PDAA)
SAMSA ..... Silica and Moulding Sands Association [*British*] (BI)
SAN .... Servicios Aereos Nacionales [*Ecuador*] [*ICAO designator*] (FAAC)
SAO .... Sahel Aviation Service [*Mali*] [*ICAO designator*] (FAAC)
SAOA .... Semi-Ascending Order Arrangement (PDAA)
SAP............ Scampton FTU [*British*] [*ICAO designator*] (FAAC)
SAP............ Start of Active Profile (PDAA)
SAP............ Strategic Audit Plan
SAP............ Substituted Accounting Period
SAP............ Superabsorbent Polymer [*Organic chemistry*]
SAPU......... South African Police Union (ECON)
SAQ .... Springbank Aviation Ltd. [*Canada*] [*ICAO designator*] (FAAC)
SAR............ Saturation Alleviation Rules
SAR............ Search and Rescue (FAAC)
SAR............ Servicios Aereos de Pilotos Ejecutivos [*Colombia*] [*ICAO designator*] (FAAC)
SARA......... Sexually-Acquired Reactive Arthritis [*Medicine*] (PDAA)
SARC......... Split Armature Receiver Capsule (PDAA)
SARCA....... Senior Army Reserve Commanders Association
SARIMS..... Swept Area Retarding Ion Mass Spectrometer (PDAA)
SAROA ...... Salvation Army Retired Officers Association
SARP......... Sophisticated Automatic RADAR Processing (PDAA)
SARS .... Semi-Active RADAR Simulator [*Military*]
SARSEP .... Salary Reduction Simplified Employee Pension
SAS............ Scandinavian Airlines System [*Sweden*] [*ICAO designator*] (FAAC)
SAS............ Secondary Alkane Sulfonate [*Surfactant*] [*Organic chemistry*]
SAS............ Senior Assistant Secretary
SAS............ Smart Armor System [*Army*]
SASCO .... Sudanese Aeronautical Services Co. Ltd. [*Sudan*] [*ICAO designator*] (FAAC)
SAS/CSS.... Stability Augmentation System with Control Stick Steering (PDAA)
SASE......... Statistical Analysis of a Series of Events (PDAA)
SASIS .... Semi-Automatic Speaker Identification System (PDAA)
SAT............ Scholastic Assessment Test [*Formerly, Scholastic Aptitude Test*]
SAT............ Servico Acoriana de Transportes Aereos [*Portugal*] [*ICAO designator*] (FAAC)
SAT............ Social Assessment of Technology (PDAA)
SAT............ Socially-Appropriate Technology (PDAA)
SATA......... Servicios Auxiliares de Transportes [*ICAO designator*] (FAAC)
SATAN....... Speed and Throttle Automatic Network (PDAA)
SATAN...... Storage Array Tester and Analyzer (PDAA)
SATCOM... Satellite Communication (NTCM)
SATF .... Strike and Terrain Following RADAR [*Military*] (PDAA)
SATI.......... Selective Access to Tactical Information (PDAA)
SATT......... Shear Area Transition Temperature (PDAA)
SAU .... United Aviation Services SA [*Spain*] [*ICAO designator*] (FAAC)
SAV .... Strike Attack Vector [*Navy*] (ANA)
SAV .... Sudania Aviation Co. [*Sudan*] [*ICAO designator*] (FAAC)
SAVI.......... Students Audio Visual Interface (PDAA)
SAW.......... Seeking, Asking, and Written [*Questionnaire*] (PDAA)
SAW.......... Sterling Airways Ltd. [*Denmark*] [*ICAO designator*] (FAAC)
SAWD .... Surface Acoustic Wave Device (PDAA)
SAWDLO... Surface Acoustic Wave Delay Line Oscillator (PDAA)
SAWES ..... Small Arms Weapons Effects Simulator [*Military*] (PDAA)

SAX............. Sabah Air [*Malaysia*] [*ICAO designator*] (FAAC)
SAY............. Suckling Airways [*British*] [*ICAO designator*] (FAAC)
SAYTA....... Say Time Able [*Aviation*] (FAAC)
SAZ............. Swiss Air-Ambulance Ltd. [*ICAO designator*] (FAAC)
SB .... Safety Bulletin
SB .... Signal Band
SB .... Single Bayonet [*Lamp base*] (NTCM)
SBA............. Sequential Boolean Analyzer (PDAA)
SBA............. STA-Mali [*ICAO designator*] (FAAC)
SBCI .... Solar Box Cookers International [*An association*] (EA)
SBCUK....... School Broadcasting Council for the United Kingdom (BI)
SBD .... Southeast Aviation Group, Inc. [*ICAO designator*] (FAAC)
SBDD .... Structure-Based Drug Design [*Organic chemistry*]
SBE............. Screen-Based Equipment
SBEA.......... Small Business Exporters Association (EA)
SBF............. Seven Bar Flying Service, Inc. [*ICAO designator*] (FAAC)
SBF............. Small Business Funding
SBG GEDD ... Schottky-Barrier Gate Gunn-Effect Digital Device
                 [*Electronics*] (PDAA)
SBGI .... Society of British Gas Industries (BI)
SBI............. Signal Band Indication
SBL............. Short Brothers PLC [*British*] [*ICAO designator*] (FAAC)
SBL............. Structure Building Language (PDAA)
SBMA......... Sand and Ballast Merchants' Alliance [*British*] (BI)
SBMA......... Stock Brick Manufacturers Association [*British*] (BI)
SBML.......... Signal Band Mainlobe
SBP............. Sugar Beet Pulp (PDAA)
SBPE.......... Standard Battle Plan Emplacement [*Military*]
SBPIM........ Society of British Printing Ink Manufacturers (BI)
SBQ .... Smithkline Beacham Clincal Labs [*ICAO designator*] (FAAC)
SBR............. Saber Aviation, Inc. [*ICAO designator*] (FAAC)
SBRS .... Side and Back Rack System (PDAA)
SBS .... Servicios Aereos Barsa SA de CV [*Mexico*] [*ICAO designator*]
                 (FAAC)
SBS .... Short Baseline SONAR (PDAA)
SBS .... Simultaneous Buying and Selling Arrangement
SBSA .... Show and Breed Secretaries' Association [*British*] (BI)
SBSC .... Schottky Barrier Solar Cell [*Electronics*] (PDAA)
SBT .... Southern Bluefin Tuna [*Fish*]
SBU .... Starwelt Airways [*Burundi*] [*ICAO designator*] (FAAC)
SBY............. BFS [*Berliner Spezial Flug*], Luftahrtunternehmen GmbH
                 [*Germany*] [*ICAO designator*] (FAAC)
SBZ............. Scibe Airlift [*Zaire*] [*ICAO designator*] (FAAC)
SBZ............. Sulfabromomethazine [*Antibacterial*] [*Veterinary medicine*]
SC .... Single Contact [*Lamp base*] (NTCM)
SCA............. Single Camshaft Type A [*Cosworth racing engines*] [*Automotive*
                 engineering]
SCA............. South Central Air, Inc. [*ICAO designator*] (FAAC)
SCA............. Spinocerebellar Ataxia [*Genetics*]
SCA............. Stamp Collectors' Association [*British*] (BI)
SCA............. Stealth Club of America (EA)
SCA............. Steel Castings Association [*British*] (BI)
SCA............. Supersonic Cruise Aircraft (PDAA)
SCAM........ SCSI [*Small Computer System Interface*] Configuration Auto
                 Magically [*Computer science*] (PCM)
SCAM........ Source-Coder's Cost Analysis Model (PDAA)
SCANS....... Spectra Calculation from Activated Nuclide Sets (PDAA)
SCANTIE... Submersible Craft Acoustic Navigation and Track Indication
                 Equipment (PDAA)
SCARE...... Sensor Control Anti-Anti-Radiation Missile RADAR
                 Evaluation (PDAA)
SCAT......... System for Computer Automated Typesetting (PDAA)
SCATMINWARIN ... Scatterable Minefield Warning [*Army*] (ADDR)
SCB........... Society of Craftsmen Bakers [*British*] (BI)
SCCM........ Short Circuit Conductance Matrix (PDAA)
SCDAuto ... Sub Carrier Demodulation, Automatic (PDAA)
SCDE......... School, College, Department of Education (AEE)
SCDWG...... System Concept Development Working Group
SCE............. Secondary Chemical Equilibria [*Chromatography*]
SCE............. Sky Care Ltd. [*New Zealand*] [*ICAO designator*] (FAAC)
SCEPTRE ... Software-Controlled Electronic-Processing Traffic-Recording
                 Equipment (PDAA)
SCF............. Skywings AB [*Sweden*] [*ICAO designator*] (FAAC)
SCFG.......... Stochastic Context-Free Grammar (PDAA)
SCG .... Sitra Cargo Systems [*Peru*] [*ICAO designator*] (FAAC)
SCH........... Schreiner Airways BV [*Netherlands*] [*ICAO designator*] (FAAC)
SCI............. Special Cargo Airlines [*Russian Federation*] [*ICAO designator*]
                 (FAAC)
SCIDS .... Small Container Intermodal Distribution System (PDAA)
SCIIA .... Sudden Changes in the Integrated Intensity of Atmospherics
                 (PDAA)
SCIM......... Silicon Coating by Inverted Meniscus (PDAA)
SCIRP........ Semiconductor Infrared Photography (PDAA)
SCIRT........ Supplier Capability Information Retrieval Technique (PDAA)
SCIU.......... SDPC [*Shuttle Data Processing Complex*] Configuration/Isolation
                 Unit [*NASA*]
SCJ .... Scanjet AB [*Sweden*] [*ICAO designator*] (FAAC)
SCK............. Air Sinclair Ltd. [*British*] [*ICAO designator*] (FAAC)
SCL............. Swiftair Cargo Ltd. [*Canada*] [*ICAO designator*] (FAAC)
SCLIGFET ... Space-Charge-Limited Insulated-Gate Field Effect Transistor
                 (PDAA)
SCM .... Aero Servicio de Carga Mexicana SA de CV [*Mexico*] [*ICAO*
                 designator] (FAAC)

SCM .... Smaller Companies Market [*Business term*]
SCMA....... Sterilised Cat Gut Manufacturers' Association [*British*] (BI)
SCMCR...... Simulated Countercurrent Moving-Bed Chromatographic Reactor
                 [*Chemical engineering*]
SCN .... South American Airlines [*Peru*] [*ICAO designator*] (FAAC)
SCO .... Euro Air Helicopter Service AB [*Sweden*] [*ICAO designator*]
                 (FAAC)
SCO .... System Check-Out Computer (PDAA)
SCOB......... Scheduled-Controlled Operant Behavior [*Environmental*
                 Protection Agency]
SCOD......... Surface Crack Opening Displacement (PDAA)
SCOLD...... Small Company Online Data [*Computer science*] (PDAA)
SCOPE...... Specifiable Coordinating Positioning Equipment (PDAA)
SCOPE...... System for Capacity and Orders Planning and Enquiries (PDAA)
SCORE...... Scenario-Oriented Recurring Evaluation (PDAA)
SCORE...... Select Concrete Objectives for Research Emphasis (PDAA)
SCORES.... Steering Column and Occupant Response Simulation
                 [*Automotive safety*] [*Computer-aided design*]
SCORPIO ... Submarine Craft for Ocean Repair, Positioning, Inspection, and
                 Observation (PDAA)
SCOT........ Semi-Automated Computer-Oriented Text (PDAA)
SCOT........ Shaken and Circulatory Oxidation Test (PDAA)
SCP........... Specialist Component Producer
SCP........... Standard Corporate Protocol [*Telecommunications*]
SCP........... Waukegan Avionics, Inc. [*ICAO designator*] (FAAC)
SCPV......... Silkworm Cytoplasmic Polyhedrosis Virus (PDAA)
SCR............. Si-Chang Flying Service Co. Ltd. [*Thailand*] [*ICAO designator*]
                 (FAAC)
SCRAP ...... South Coast Recycled Auto Project [*Air pollution controls credits*
                 from mobile sources for stationary sources]
SC-RB....... Separable Costs-Remaining Benefits (PDAA)
SCRDC....... Silicon Controlled Rectifier Regulated Direct Current (PDAA)
SCRR......... Solar Central Receiver Reformer (PDAA)
SCRV......... Spill Control Recovery Valve (PDAA)
SCS............. Speed Control System (PDAA)
SCSRMA ... Surface Coating Synthetic Resin Manufacturers Association
                 [*British*] (BI)
SCT............. Saab Aircraft AB [*Sweden*] [*ICAO designator*] (FAAC)
SCV............. Swirl Control Valve [*Automotive engine design*]
SCVT......... Suzuki Continuously-Variable Transmission [*Automotive*
                 powertrain]
SCW .... Malmo Aviation AB [*Sweden*] [*ICAO designator*] (FAAC)
SCW .... Space Charge Wave (PDAA)
SCX............. Sun Country Airlines, Inc. [*ICAO designator*] (FAAC)
SD .... Sleep Deprivation (PDAA)
SDA .... St. Andrews Ltd. [*Canada*] [*ICAO designator*] (FAAC)
SDA .... Saw Diamond Abrasive (PDAA)
SDAU .... Safety Data and Analysis Unit [*British*] (DA)
SDB .... Silver-Dye-Bleach (PDAA)
SDC .... Solenoid Detector Collaboration [*Physics*]
SDC .... Swedish Airforce [*ICAO designator*] (FAAC)
SDCF......... Software Development Computer Facility
SDD .... RIC, Inc. [*ICAO designator*] (FAAC)
SDE........... Standard-Dose Epinephrine [*Medicine*]
SDF............. Step Down Fix [*Aviation*] (DA)
SDF............. Stromal Cell-Derived Factor [*Biochemistry*]
SDF............. Sundorph Aeronautical, Corp. [*ICAO designator*] (FAAC)
SDFT .... System Demonstration Flight Test [*DoD*]
SDFU......... Sanitary Drainage Fixture Unit (DAC)
SDG .... Aerosierra de Durango [*Mexico*] [*ICAO designator*] (FAAC)
SDH........... Servicio de Helicopteros SL [*Spain*] [*ICAO designator*] (FAAC)
SDISEM.... Strategic Defense Initiative System Evaluation Model
SDK .... Sociedad Aerea del Caqueta Ltd. [*Colombia*] [*ICAO designator*]
                 (FAAC)
SDM .... Sulfadimethoxine [*Antibacterial*] [*Veterinary medicine*]
SDMA .... Surgical Dressing Manufacturers Association [*British*] (BI)
SDMA/SS-TDMA ... Space Division Multiple Access/Spacecraft Switched-
                 Time Division Multiple Access (PDAA)
SDNF......... Shortened Disjuctive Normal Form (PDAA)
SDNM........ Sampled-Data Nonlinearity Matrix (PDAA)
SDP........... Aero Sudpacifico SA [*Mexico*] [*ICAO designator*] (FAAC)
SDR .... Search, Detection and Recognition [*Military*]
SDR .... Spatial Delayed-Response [*Ophthalmology*]
SDR .... Standard Dimension Ratio (DAC)
SDR .... Syder [*Bulgaria*] [*ICAO designator*] (FAAC)
SDS............. CAA Training Standards [*British*] [*ICAO designator*] (FAAC)
SDS............. Slowing Down Spectrometer (PDAA)
SDS............. Sound-Deadened Steel (PDAA)
SDS............. Support Data Sheet [*Military*]
SD & T....... Staff Development and Training
SDT .... Terrain SDP SA [*Spain*] [*ICAO designator*] (FAAC)
SDTU .... Sign and Display Trades Union [*British*] (BI)
SDU .... Satellite Data Unit (DA)
SDU .... Westair Commuter Airlines, Inc. [*ICAO designator*] (FAAC)
SDV .... Servicios Aereos del Vaupes Ltd. [*Colombia*] [*ICAO designator*]
                 (FAAC)
SDX .... Sigma Delta Chi [*Fraternity*] (NTCM)
SDY .... Safe Air International, Inc. [*ICAO designator*] (FAAC)
SE .... Sound Effect (NTCM)
SE .... Super Einspritz [*Super, Injection*] [*Mercedes-Benz automotive*
                 model designation]
S & E.......... Surfaced One Side and Edge [*Lumber*] (DAC)
S2E .... Surfaced Two Edges [*Lumber*] (DAC)

SEA............ Shipbuilding Exports Association [*British*]   (BI)
SEA............ Small Earth-Approacher [*Asteroid*]
SEA............ Southeast Air, Inc. [*ICAO designator*]   (FAAC)
SEA............ Space Energy Association   (EA)
SEA............ Support Electronics Assembly [*Military*]
SEABIRD... Ship-Design Engineering-Aided by Interactive Remote Display (PDAA)
SEADRM ... Seadrome [*Aviation*]   (FAAC)
SEAP........ Secreted Alkaline Phosphatase [*Biochemistry*]
SEAS.......... State Estimation Algorithm for Small-Scale System   (PDAA)
SEB............ Southeastbound [*ICAO designator*]   (FAAC)
SEC............ South East College of Air Training [*British*] [*ICAO designator*] (FAAC)
SEC............ Special Event Charter Flight [*Aviation*]   (DA)
SEC............ Supr Einspritz Coupe [*Super, Fuel Injection, Coupe*] [*Mercedes-Benz automotive model designation*]
SECAL....... Separate Engineering Control Air Limits [*Environmental science*]
SECOM...... Security Committee
SECRAC .... System Engineering Cost Reduction Assistance Contractor (PDAA)
SECS......... Single-Electron Capacitance Spectroscopy
SED .... Sedona Air Center, Inc. [*ICAO designator*]   (FAAC)
SED .... Simulative Electronic Deception [*Army*]   (ADDR)
SED .... Smoke-Emitting Diode [*Computer hacker terminology*]   (NHD)
SEDI.......... Semi-Empirical Design of Impellers [*Hydraulics*] [*Computer-aided design*]
SEDS......... Systems Engineering Detailed Schedule
SEE............ Significant Emotional Events
SEE............ South East Air [*British*] [*ICAO designator*]   (FAAC)
SEEA......... Southeast European Airlines [*Greece*] [*ICAO designator*]   (FAAC)
SEEDS ...... Shipboard Equipments Environmental Design Study   (PDAA)
SEEPZ....... Santacruz Electronics Export Processing Zone
SEFIS........ Small Engine Fuel Injection System
SEG........... Skyline [*Norway*] [*ICAO designator*]   (FAAC)
SEGV........ Segmentation Violation [*Computer science*]   (NHD)
SEH........... Waglisla Air, Inc. [*Canada*] [*ICAO designator*]   (FAAC)
SEI............ Space Exploration Initiative [*NASA*]
SEI............ Sumitomo Electric Industries [*Auto inudustry supplier*]
SEJ .... Southeastern Jurisdictional Conference [*United Methodist Church*]
SEL........... Selectair Ltd. [*British*] [*ICAO designator*]   (FAAC)
SEL........... Sensitized-Erythrocyte-Lysis   (PDAA)
SELCIR...... Systems Engineering Laboratory Circuit-Drawing Program (PDAA)
SEM........... Cape Central Airways, Inc. [*ICAO designator*]   (FAAC)
SEM........... Semester
SEMA........ Spray Equipment Manufacturers' Association [*British*]   (BI)
SEMANOL ... Semantics-Oriented Language [*Computer science*]   (PDAA)
SEMBRAT ... Single Echelon Multi-Base Resource Allocation Technique (PDAA)
SEMIROX ... Semi-Recessed Oxide   (PDAA)
SEMP........ Self-Erecting Marine Platform   (PDAA)
SEMPE ...... Socio-Economic Model of the Planet Earth   (PDAA)
SEMR........ Standard Electronic Module RADAR   (PDAA)
SEMS........ Systems Engineering Master Schedule
SEN .... Sacred Earth Network [*An association*]   (EA)
SEN .... Senair Charter Ltd. [*British*] [*ICAO designator*]   (FAAC)
SENEAM ... Servicios a la Navegacion en el Espacio Aereo Mexicano [*Mexico*] [*ICAO designator*]   (FAAC)
SENS......... Sensitivity   (FAAC)
SEOP........ Segment End of Pulse
SEP........... Segment End Pulse
SEP........... Stimulated Emission Pumping [*Spectroscopy*]
SEPMAG ... Separate Magnetic   (NTCM)
SEPSIT ...... Solar Electric Propulsion Integration Technology   (PDAA)
SEQT........ System Environment Qualification Test
SER........... Aerocalifornia SA [*Mexico*] [*ICAO designator*]   (FAAC)
SERC.......... State Emergency Response Commission [*Environmental science*]
SERDES CRC ... Serializer-Deserializer Cyclic Redundancy Check   (PDAA)
SERTEL...... Servicios Telereservacios SA de CV [*ICAO designator*]   (FAAC)
SERTOG .... Space Experiment on Relativistic Theories of Gravitation (PDAA)
SERVIVENSA ... Empresa Servicicious Avensa SA [*Venezuela*] [*ICAO designator*]   (FAAC)
SES .... Systems Engineering Support
SES .... Systems Engineering Work Statement
SESA .... Single End Strip Adhesion   (PDAA)
SESC .... Special Environmental Sample Container [*NASA*]   (PDAA)
SE Sdg .... Square-Edge Siding   (DAC)
SET............ Sociedad Ecuatoriana de Transportes Aereos Ltda. [*Ecuador*] [*ICAO designator*]   (FAAC)
SET............ Society for Environmental Truth   (EA)
SET............ Stored-Energy Transmission   (PDAA)
SETAC....... Society of Environmental Toxicology and Chemistry   (EA)
SETD......... Scheduled Estimated Time of Departure [*Aviation*]   (DA)
SETWEG ... Statistical Engine Test Work Group [*Lubricants testing*] [*Automotive engineering*]
SEU .... Scottish European Airways Ltd. [*British*] [*ICAO designator*] (FAAC)
SEWMA..... Simple Exponentially-Weighted Moving-Average   (PDAA)
SEX........... Sign Extend [*Computer science*]   (NHD)
SEX........... Size Exclusion [*Analytical chemistry*]
SEX........... Software Exchange [*Computer science*]   (NHD)

SEY............ Air Seychelles [*ICAO designator*]   (FAAC)
SF.............. Soft Focus [*Cinematography*]   (NTCM)
SFA............ Aerotransportes Entre Rios SRL [*Argentina*] [*ICAO designator*] (FAAC)
SFB .... Air Sofia [*Bulgaria*] [*ICAO designator*]   (FAAC)
SFB .... Society of Furnace Builders [*British*]   (BI)
SFC............ Shuswap Flight Centre Ltd. [*Canada*] [*ICAO designator*]   (FAAC)
SFCES........ Survivable Flight Control Electronic Set [*Aviation*]   (PDAA)
SFDLR .... Stock Funding Depot - Level Repairables [*Army*]
SFF .... Solid Freeform Fabrication [*Metallurgy*]
SFG............ Sudflug Suddeutsche Fluggesellschaft MbH [*Germany*] [*ICAO designator*]   (FAAC)
SFGA .... Single Floating-Gate Amplifier [*Electronics*]   (PDAA)
SFHR......... Society for Film History Research [*British*]   (BI)
SFI .... Sky Freighters NV [*Belgium*] [*ICAO designator*]   (FAAC)
SFID .... Self-floating Integrated Deck   (PDAA)
SFL............ Southflight Aviation Ltd. [*New Zealand*] [*ICAO designator*] (FAAC)
SFLOC .... Synopic Reporting of the Location of Sources of Atmospherics [*Aviation*]   (DA)
SFMA........ School Furniture Manufacturers' Association [*British*]   (BI)
SFMS .... Shipwrecked Fishermen and Mariners Royal Benevolent Society [*British*]   (BI)
SFN............ Safiran Airlines [*Iran*] [*ICAO designator*]   (FAAC)
SFPP.......... Stored Flight Plan Program [*Aviation*]   (FAAC)
SFR .... Safair Freighters (Pty) Ltd. [*South Africa*] [*ICAO designator*] (FAAC)
SFR .... Serial Flechette Rifle   (PDAA)
SFRL.......... Spin-Flip Raman LASER   (PDAA)
SFS .... Free Software Foundation   (EA)
SFS .... Southern Frontier Air Transport Ltd. [*Canada*] [*ICAO designator*]   (FAAC)
SFT .... Skyfreight, Inc. [*ICAO designator*]   (FAAC)
SFT .... Soft Top [*Automotive advertising*]
SFT .... Sudanese Flight [*Sudan*] [*ICAO designator*]   (FAAC)
SFTA .... Society of Film and Television Arts Ltd. [*British*]   (BI)
SFUDS .... Simplified Federal Urban Driving Schedule [*Electric vehicle testing*]
SFW........... Swept Forward Wing [*Aviation*]   (PDAA)
SFY .... Gulf Flite Center, Inc. [*ICAO designator*]   (FAAC)
SG .... Stern-Gerlach [*Experiment for measuring atomic magnetism*]
S & G.......... Stud and Girt   (DAC)
SGA........... Air Saigon [*Vietnam*] [*ICAO designator*]   (FAAC)
SGBI.......... Schoolmistresses' and Governesses' Benevolent Institution [*British*]   (BI)
SGC........... Swept Gain Control   (DA)
SGH........... Servisair Ltd. [*British*] [*ICAO designator*]   (FAAC)
SGK........... Skyward Aviation Ltd. [*Canada*] [*ICAO designator*]   (FAAC)
SGL............ Senegalair [*Senegal*] [*ICAO designator*]   (FAAC)
SGL............ Slightly-Grounded Lightplane   (PDAA)
SGM .... Single Geometric Model [*Computer-assisted design*]
SGPO......... Speed-Gate-Pull-Off   (PDAA)
SGS........... Stactic Gel Strength [*Well drilling technology*]
SGS............ Stage Golfing Society [*British*]   (BI)
SGT............ Small Group Trial
SGT............ Societa' Aerotaxi SUD [*Italy*] [*ICAO designator*]   (FAAC)
SGY........... Skagway Air Service, Inc. [*ICAO designator*]   (FAAC)
SH............. Second Harmonic   (PDAA)
SH............. Single-Hung   (DAC)
SHA........... Servicio Aereo de Honduras SA [*ICAO designator*]   (FAAC)
SHA........... Software Hazard Analysis [*Military*]
SHAB .... Soft and Hard Acid and Base   (PDAA)
SHALE....... Stand-off, High Altitude, Long Endurance   (PDAA)
SHARP...... Society for the History of Authorship, Reading and Publishing (EA)
SHB .... Shabair [*Zaire*] [*ICAO designator*]   (FAAC)
SHB .... Super Highband [*Radio frequency*]   (NTCM)
SHC........... Sensitized Human Cell   (PDAA)
SHC........... Sky Harbor Air Service, Inc. [*ICAO designator*]   (FAAC)
SHC........... Synthesized Hydrocarbon   (PDAA)
SHE........... Shell Aircraft Ltd. [*British*] [*ICAO designator*]   (FAAC)
SHE........... Support, Help, and Empowerment
SHEA .... Society for Hospital Epidemiology of America
SHF............ Support Helicopter Flight NI [*British*] [*ICAO designator*] (FAAC)
SHG........... Sexual Harassment Guidelines
SHG........... Shoprite Group Ltd. [*British*] [*ICAO designator*]   (FAAC)
SHI .... Substance Hazard Index [*Environmental science*]
SHIN PADS ... Shipboard Integrated Processing Display System [*Military*]
SHJ............ Sharjah Ruler's Flight [*United Arab Emirates*] [*ICAO designator*]   (FAAC)
SHK........... Shorouk Air [*Egypt*] [*ICAO designator*]   (FAAC)
SHKDNCRU ... Shakedown Cruise [*Navy*]   (ANA)
SHL........... Samson Aviation Services [*British*] [*ICAO designator*]   (FAAC)
SHL........... Studio-to-Headend Link [*Transmitter site relay*]   (NTCM)
SHLM .... Society of Hospital Laundry Managers [*British*]   (BI)
SHN........... Shaheen Airport Services [*Pakistan*] [*ICAO designator*]   (FAAC)
SHO........... North Shore Aero Club, Inc. [*New Zealand*] [*ICAO designator*] (FAAC)
SHO........... Show [*Automotive advertising*]
SHORD...... Short-Range Air Defense
SHORN...... Short-Range Navigation System   (FAAC)

SHORSTAS ... Short-Range Surveillance and Target Acquisition System (PDAA)
SHORSTRAMPS ... Shore Requirements Strength and Manpower Planning System [*Navy*]   (ANA)
SHORT ...... Shard Hospital Online Real-Time Time-Sharing   (PDAA)
SHORTIE ... Short Range Thermal Imaging Equipment   (PDAA)
SHP .... Service Aerien Francais [*France*] [*ICAO designator*]   (FAAC)
SHR .... Shooter Air Courier Corp. [*ICAO designator*]   (FAAC)
SHS .... Sunshine Aviation SA [*Switzerland*] [*ICAO designator*]   (FAAC)
SHT .... British Airways Shuttle [*ICAO designator*]   (FAAC)
SHV .... Shavano Air, Inc. [*ICAO designator*]   (FAAC)
SHW .... Air South, Inc. [*ICAO designator*]   (FAAC)
SHWRM .... Showroom [*Automotive advertising*]
SIA .... Singapore Airlines Ltd. [*ICAO designator*]   (FAAC)
SIA .... Stereo-Image Alternator   (PDAA)
SIB .... Societa' Siba Aviation [*Italy*] [*ICAO designator*]   (FAAC)
SICDO .... Society of Industrial Civil Defence Officers [*British*]   (BI)
SICIS .... Strategic Issue Competitive Information System   (PDAA)
SICLOPS ... Simplified Interpretive COBOL Operating System   (PDAA)
SICP .... Shut-in Casing Pressure [*Well drilling technology*]
SID .... Sidfin Air Ltd. [*Zambia*] [*ICAO designator*]   (FAAC)
SID .... Structure Isolation Dynamics [*Vehicle development*] [*Automotive engineering*]
SID .... Suprathermal Ion Detector   (PDAA)
SIDD .... Standard Inside Diameter Dimension Ratio   (DAC)
SIDF .... System Independent Data Format [*Computer science*]   (PCM)
SIDS .... Screening Information Data Set [*Environmental science*]
SIE .... Sierra Express, Inc. [*ICAO designator*]   (FAAC)
SIF .... Skycy Freighters International Ltd. [*Kenya*] [*ICAO designator*]   (FAAC)
SIF .... Source Input Format [*Computer science*]
SIFEM .... Side-Impact Finite Element Model [*Automotive safety*] [*Computer-assisted design*]
SIFR .... Serious Injury Frequency Rate
SIGNET ...... Supplies Invoice Generation Network   (PDAA)
SIGWX .... Significant Weather [*Aviation*]   (FAAC)
SII .... Siimes Aviation AB [*Finland*] [*ICAO designator*]   (FAAC)
SII .... Sponsor Identification Index [*Advertising*]   (NTCM)
SIL .... Sea Island Air Ltd. [*Canada*] [*ICAO designator*]   (FAAC)
SIL .... Silent   (NTCM)
SIL .... Smart Integral Linearizer [*Instrumentation*]
SIM .... Similar   (DAC)
SIM .... Simulated Approach [*Aviation*]   (FAAC)
SIM .... Simulated Flight Training Ltd. [*British*] [*ICAO designator*]   (FAAC)
SIMAL ...... Simplified Accountancy Language   (PDAA)
SIMAL ...... Simulated All-Purpose Language   (PDAA)
SIMTOP .... Silicon Nitride-Masked Thermally-Oxidized Post-Diffused Mesa Process   (PDAA)
SIMU .... Suspended from Issue, Movement, and Use [*Army*]   (ADDR)
SIN .... Sinair [*France*] [*ICAO designator*]   (FAAC)
SINPO .... Strength, Interference, Noise, Propagation, and Overall Merit Code [*Signal reception quality rating*]   (NTCM)
SINS .... Ship's Inertial Navigation System
SIP .... Air Spirit, Inc. [*ICAO designator*]   (FAAC)
SIP .... Sea Ice Penetrometer   (PDAA)
SIP .... Silicon-on-Insulator and Polysilicon   (PDAA)
SIP .... Society of Independent Producers   (NTCM)
SIP .... Station Independence Program [*Public television project*]   (NTCM)
SIP .... Surface Impulsion Propulsion   (PDAA)
SIPS .... Side-Impact Protection System [*Automotive safety*]
SIPSF .... Space Invariant Point Spread Function   (PDAA)
SIR .... Salair, Inc. [*ICAO designator*]   (FAAC)
SIR .... Serial Infrared Communications Interface [*Hewlett Packard Co.*]   (PCM)
SIROF ...... Sputtered Iridium Oxide Film   (PDAA)
SIRS .... Systemic Inflammatory Response Syndrome [*Medicine*]
SIS .... Seychelles International Safari Air Ltd. [*ICAO designator*]   (FAAC)
SIS .... Solid-State Imaging Spectrometer
SISC .... Sentry Interceptor Subsystem Contractor [*DoD*]
SISDG .... Shipboard Information System Development Group [*Maritime Transportation ResearchBoard*]   (PDAA)
SIT .... Societe International de Telecommunications Aeronautiques [*Belgium*] [*ICAO designator*]   (FAAC)
SIT .... Sterile Insect Technology
SITEL .... Societe des Ingenieurs do Telecommunication [*Belgium*]
SITS .... Student Interactive Training System
SIXES .... Selectively-Induced X-Ray Emission Spectroscopy
SJA .... Servicios Aereos Especiales de Jalisco SA de CV [*Mexico*] [*ICAO designator*]   (FAAC)
SJC .... Southend Jet Centre Ltd. [*British*] [*ICAO designator*]   (FAAC)
SJCL .... Standardized Job Control Language   (PDAA)
SJFZ .... San Jacinto Fault Zone [*Geology*]
SJI .... Sun Jet International Airlines, Inc. [*ICAO designator*]   (FAAC)
SJM .... Southern Air Transport, Inc. [*ICAO designator*]   (FAAC)
SJMO .... Smithsonian Jazz Masterworks Orchestra
SJN .... Chartair, Inc. [*ICAO designator*]   (FAAC)
SJT .... Yorkshire European Airways Ltd. [*British*] [*ICAO designator*]   (FAAC)
SK .... Sky Condition [*Aviation*]   (FAAC)
SKA .... Skegair [*British*] [*ICAO designator*]   (FAAC)

SKB .... Skyfreighters Corp. [*ICAO designator*]   (FAAC)
SKC .... Skycare Management Services Ltd. [*British*] [*ICAO designator*]   (FAAC)
SKD .... Skyguard Ltd. [*British*] [*ICAO designator*]   (FAAC)
SKE .... Sky Tours, Inc. [*ICAO designator*]   (FAAC)
SKF .... Skycraft, Inc. [*ICAO designator*]   (FAAC)
SKF .... Svenska Kullager Frabikon [*Swedish Ball Bearing Manufacturing*]
SKG .... Skycraft Air Transport, Inc. [*Canada*] [*ICAO designator*]   (FAAC)
SKH .... Skywatch Ltd. [*British*] [*ICAO designator*]   (FAAC)
SKI .... Skylink Airlines [*Canada*] [*ICAO designator*]   (FAAC)
SKJ .... Skyjet, Inc. [*Antigua and Barbuda*] [*ICAO designator*]   (FAAC)
SKK .... Skylane Air Charter [*British*] [*ICAO designator*]   (FAAC)
SKL .... Skycharter (Malton) Ltd. [*Canada*] [*ICAO designator*]   (FAAC)
SKLT .... Station Keeping Light   (NFPA)
SKM .... Fayetteville Flying Service & Scheduled Skyways System [*ICAO designator*]   (FAAC)
SKN .... Skyline Aviation Services, Inc. [*ICAO designator*]   (FAAC)
SKO .... Scottish Airways Flyers Ltd. [*ICAO designator*]   (FAAC)
SKP .... Aero North Aviation Services [*Canada*] [*ICAO designator*]   (FAAC)
SKR .... Skyrover Ltd. [*British*] [*ICAO designator*]   (FAAC)
SKS .... Sky Service [*Belgium*] [*ICAO designator*]   (FAAC)
SKT .... Dyad Services Ltd. [*British*] [*ICAO designator*]   (FAAC)
SKW .... Sky West, Inc. [*ICAO designator*]   (FAAC)
SKX .... Skyways AB [*Sweden*] [*ICAO designator*]   (FAAC)
SKY .... Cooper Skybird Air Charters Ltd. [*Kenya*] [*ICAO designator*]   (FAAC)
S/L .... Shiplap   (DAC)
SL .... Student Load
SLA .... Sierra National Airlines [*Sierra Leone*] [*ICAO designator*]   (FAAC)
SLAMMR ... Side Looking Modular Multi-Mission RADAR   (PDAA)
S/LAP .... Shiplap   (DAC)
SLAP .... Slot Allocation Procedure [*Aviation*]   (DA)
SLAPS .... Serious Literary, Artistic, Political, or Scientific Value [*Obscenity law*]   (NTCM)
SLBI .... Sidelobe Blanking Indicator
SLC .... Stock Ledger Control
SLC .... Swiftlines Ltd. [*Kenya*] [*ICAO designator*]   (FAAC)
SLEAT .... Society of Licensed Aircraft Engineers and Technologists   (DA)
SLEKE .... Sabot-Launched Electric Gun Kinetic Energy [*DoD*]
SLEW .... Standby Local Early Warning and Control Center   (PDAA)
SLI .... Servicios Aeroes Litoral SA de CV [*Mexico*] [*ICAO designator*]   (FAAC)
SLIP .... Serial Line Internet Protocol [*Telecommunications*]   (PCM)
SLK .... Silkair (Singapore) Pte Ltd. [*ICAO designator*]   (FAAC)
SLL .... Saarland Airlines AG [*Germany*] [*ICAO designator*]   (FAAC)
SLM .... Signal Level Meter   (NTCM)
SLM .... Surinaamse Luchtvaart Maatschappij NV [*Surinam*] [*ICAO designator*]   (FAAC)
SLMG .... Self-Launching Motor Glider [*Aviation*]   (DA)
SLN .... Sloane Aviation Ltd. [*British*] [*ICAO designator*]   (FAAC)
SLO .... Edgartown Air, Inc. [*ICAO designator*]   (FAAC)
SLO .... Slow [*Aviation*]   (DA)
SLO MO ..... Slow Motion   (NTCM)
SLOP .... Small Lot Optimum Procurement   (PDAA)
SLP .... Safe Leeward Position
SLP .... Salpa Aviation Co. Ltd. [*Sudan*] [*ICAO designator*]   (FAAC)
SLP .... Speed Limiting Point [*Aviation*]   (FAAC)
SLP .... Standard Long Play [*VHS recorder playing time mode*]   (NTCM)
SLPM .... Scanned-LASER Photoluminescence Microscope   (PDAA)
SLR .... SOBELAIR [*Societe Belge de Transport Aeriens*] [*Belgium*] [*ICAO designator*]   (FAAC)
SLRP .... Survey, Liaison, and Reconnaissance Party [*Navy*]   (ANA)
SLS .... Aeroservicios Ejecutivos Sinaloenses SA [*Mexico*] [*ICAO designator*]   (FAAC)
SLS .... Society for Literature and Science
SLS .... Start Launch Sequence [*Military*]
SLS .... Stephenson Locomotive Society [*British*]   (BI)
SLT .... Saltair Ltd. [*British*] [*ICAO designator*]   (FAAC)
SLT .... Spontaneous Lymphocyte Transportation   (PDAA)
SLUMT ...... Slacked Unconstrained Minimization Technique   (PDAA)
SLVC .... Super Linear Variable Capacitor   (PDAA)
SLVR .... Silver [*Automotive advertising*]
SLY .... Sky Line for Air Services Ltd. [*Sudan*] [*ICAO designator*]   (FAAC)
SM .... Senior Manager
SM .... Spectrum Management   (NTCM)
SM .... Station Manager [*Broadcasting*]   (NTCM)
SM .... Status Monitor
SMA .... Saw Manufacturers' Association [*British*]   (BI)
SMA .... Schools Music Association [*British*]   (BI)
SMA .... Society of Make-up Artists   (NTCM)
SMA .... Solder Makers' Association [*British*]   (BI)
SMA .... Special Market Area   (NTCM)
SMA .... Superphosphate Manufacturers' Association [*British*]   (BI)
SMAC .... Sequential Multiple Analysis Plus Computer   (PDAA)
SMAI .... Solvated Metal Atom Impregnation [*Chemistry*]
SMARTIE ... Simple-Minded Artificial Intelligence   (PDAA)
SMARTIE ... Submarine Automatic Remote Television Inspection Equipment   (PDAA)
SMART-T ... Secure Mobile, Anti-Jam, Reliable Tactical Trainer [*Army*]
SMASS .... Small Main-Belt Asteroid Spectroscopic Survey

SMC .... Sabang Merauke Raya Air Charter PT [*Indonesia*] [*ICAO designator*]   (FAAC)

SMC .... Sealant Manufacturers Conference [*Federation of British Rubber and Allied Manufacturers*]   (BI)

SMC .... Spin Muon Collaboration [*Nuclear research*]

SMC .... Surface Mount Component [*Environmental science*]

SMCAA ..... Sheet Molding Compound Automotive Alliance [*An association*]

SMCT .... Soldier's Manual of Common Tasks [*A publication*]   (ADDR)

SMD .... Sauter Mean Droplet [*Diesel engine fuel injection*]

SMD .... Single Molecule Detection [*Analytical chemistry*]

SMD .... Soil Moisture Deficit   (PDAA)

SMD .... Speed Measuring Device   (PDAA)

SMD .... Spondylometaphyseal Dysplasias [*Medicine*]

SMDA .... Sewing Machine Dealers Association Ltd. [*British*]   (BI)

SMDR .... Structure Manning Decision Review

SME .... SM Exports Ltd. [*British*] [*ICAO designator*]   (FAAC)

SME........... Small-to-Medium Enterprise

SMEE.......... Society of Model and Experimental Engineers [*British*]   (BI)

SMFUA ...... Silk and Man-Made Fibre Users' Association [*British*]   (BI)

SMGPC ...... Small Molecule Gel Permeation Chromatography

SMH .... Smith Air, Inc. [*ICAO designator*]   (FAAC)

SMI............ Aero Sami SA de CV [*Mexico*] [*ICAO designator*]   (FAAC)

SMI............ Slipped Mutagenic Intermediate [*Biochemistry*]

SMIA......... Sheet Metal Industries Association [*British*]   (BI)

SMILI......... Synthetic Model Interferometric LASER Imaging   (PDAA)

SMITES ..... State-Municipal Income Tax Evaluation System   (PDAA)

SML........... Smith Air (1976) Ltd. [*Canada*] [*ICAO designator*]   (FAAC)

SMM .... Summit Airlines [*ICAO designator*]   (FAAC)

SMMCEQ ... Standard Method of Measurement for Civil Engineering Quantities   (PDAA)

SMMHC .... Smooth Muscle Myosin Heavy Chain [*Biochemistry*]

SMMIP ...... Strategic Material Management Information Program   (PDAA)

SMMO .... Soluble Methane Monooxygenase [*Biochemistry*]

SMN .... Satellite Music Network   (NTCM)

SMO .... Slowly Moving Object [*Astronomy*]

SMO .... Survivability Management Operation

SMOBC...... Solder Mask Over Bare Copper [*Electronics*]

SMOH....... Since Major Overhaul   (DA)

SMOP .... Simple [*or Small*] Matter of Programming   (NHD)

SMP .... Sempati Air Transport PT [*Indonesia*] [*ICAO designator*]   (FAAC)

SMPC .... Sum of Magnitudes of Pitch Matrix - Correlator

SMPE .... Society of Motion Picture Engineers [*Later, SMPTE*]   (NTCM)

SMPMA ..... Sausage and Meat Pie Manufacturers Association [*British*]   (BI)

SMPS .... Sum of Magnitudes of Pitch Matrix - Skin

SMPS .... Switched-Mode Power Supply   (PDAA)

SMR .... Samaritan Health Services [*ICAO designator*]   (FAAC)

SMRA........ Spare Module Replacement Analysis

SMS........... Servicios Aerolineas Mexicanas SA de CV [*Mexico*] [*ICAO designator*]   (FAAC)

SMS........... Sheet-Metal Screw   (DAC)

SMS........... Status Monitor Software

SMSC .... Sum of Magnitudes of Sum [*Channel Matrix*] Correlator

SMSLP .... Smithsonian Marine Station at Link Port

SMSS .... Sum of Magnitudes of Sum [*Channel Matrix*] Skin

SMSU........ Southwest Missouri State University   (PDAA)

SMTF .... Spectrum Management Task Force [*Electromagnetic spectrum regulation*]   (NTCM)

SMV .... Special Mobility Vehicle

SMWC....... Society for the Ministry of Women in the Church [*British*]   (BI)

SMWG .... Space Shuttle Structures and Materials Working Group [*NASA*]   (PDAA)

SMWO .... Society of Mental Welfare Officers [*British*]   (BI)

SMZ .... Sonmez Airlines [*Turkey*] [*ICAO designator*]   (FAAC)

SMZ .... Sulfamethazine [*Antibacterial*] [*Veterinary medicine*]

SNA .... Soil Nutrient Availability

SNA .... Standard National Account [*Economics*]

SNA .... Steel Nail Association [*British*]   (BI)

SNA .... Stern Air, Inc. [*ICAO designator*]   (FAAC)

SNAP........ Satellite Navigation Alert Plotter   (PDAA)

SNAP........ Significant New Alternatives Policy [*Environmental science*]

SNAP........ Stereonet Analysis Program   (PDAA)

SNAP........ Synaptosomal-Associated Protein [*Biochemistry*]

SNARC....... Short Nickel Line Accumulating Register Calculator   (PDAA)

SNase........ Staphylococcal Nuclease [*An enzyme*]

SNAU .... Society for North American Union   (EA)

SNBS .... Sodium Nitrobenzene Sulfonate [*Organic chemistry*]

SNC .... Air Cargo Carriers, Inc. [*ICAO designator*]   (FAAC)

SNCC........ Selected Non-Communist Countries

SNE .... Servicios Aereos Norte Sur SA de CV [*Mexico*] [*ICAO designator*]   (FAAC)

SNF........... Sampled N-Path Filter   (PDAA)

SNG .... Satellite News Gathering [*Trademark*]   (NTCM)

SNI .... Serial Network Interface   (PDAA)

SNI .... Societe Nigerienne de Transports Aeriens [*Niger*] [*ICAO designator*]   (FAAC)

SNIPE .... Simple Network Interacting Program Executive   (PDAA)

SNL .... Soonair Lines, Inc. [*ICAO designator*]   (FAAC)

SNM .... SNAM SpA [*Italy*] [*ICAO designator*]   (FAAC)

SNO .... Delta Air Charter Ltd. [*Canada*] [*ICAO designator*]   (FAAC)

SNOM....... Scanning Near-Field Optical Microscope   (ECON)

SNR .... Aero Sonora SA de CV [*Mexico*] [*ICAO designator*]   (FAAC)

SNR .... Subject to Nonrenewal   (NTCM)

SNS........... Slovak National Party [*Political party*]   (ECON)

SNS........... Societe Centrafricaine de Transport Aerien [*Central African Republic*] [*ICAO designator*]   (FAAC)

SNT .... Suncoast Aviation, Inc. [*ICAO designator*]   (FAAC)

SNU .... Snunit Aviation [*Israel*] [*ICAO designator*]   (FAAC)

SNV .... Aero Servicio del Norte SA de CV [*Mexico*] [*ICAO designator*]   (FAAC)

SNV .... Satellite News Vehicle   (NTCM)

SNW .... Scottsdale Charter, Inc. [*ICAO designator*]   (FAAC)

SNX .... Sun Air Aviation Services [*Canada*] [*ICAO designator*]   (FAAC)

SNY .... Air Sandy, Inc. [*Canada*] [*ICAO designator*]   (FAAC)

SO .... State Officer

SOA .... Skoda Air [*Czechoslovakia*] [*ICAO designator*]   (FAAC)

SOA .... Specially-Oriented Advertisements [*Consumer Protection Packet - US Post Office*]

SOACMS ... Special Operations Aviation Combat Mission Simulator [*Military*]

SOAP........ Silicate-Oxy-Apatite   (PDAA)

SOAR .... Special Operations Aviation Regiment [*Military*]

SOC .... Severity of Ozone Cracking   (PDAA)

SOC .... Start of Climb [*Aviation*]   (DA)

SOCC........ Sector Operations Control Center [*NORAD*]   (FAAC)

SOCC........ Self-Orthogonal Convolutional Code   (PDAA)

SOCCENT ... Special Operations Command, Central Command [*Military*]

SOCGPA.... Seed, Oil, Cake, and General Produce Association [*British*]   (BI)

SOCMA ..... Second Order Coherent Multiple Access   (PDAA)

SOCOORD ... Special Operations Coordination [*DoD*]

SODC .... Sporting Owner Drivers' Club Ltd. [*British*]   (BI)

SOE .... Specific Optimal Estimation   (PDAA)

SOEC......... Statistical Office of the European Communities   (PDAA)

SOES.......... Small Order Execution System [*Business term*]

SOFI.......... Supersearch-Online Friendly Interface [*Computer science*]

SOH.......... Southern Ohio Aviation Sales Co. [*ICAO designator*]   (FAAC)

SOI .... Start of Injection [*Fuel systems*] [*Automotive engineering*]

SOI .... Structure of Intellect [*Education*]   (AEE)

SOIS.......... Silicon on Insulating Substrate   (PDAA)

SOL .... Soliloquy [*Theater term*]

SOL .... Solomon Airlines Ltd. [*Solomon Islands*] [*ICAO designator*]   (FAAC)

Sol Is .... Solomon Islands

SOLMIS..... Supply Online Management Information System [*Computer science*]   (PDAA)

SOLO .... System for Online Optimization [*Computer science*]   (PDAA)

SOM .... Somali Airlines [*Somalia*] [*ICAO designator*]   (FAAC)

SOMM .... Stand-Off Modular Missile   (PDAA)

SOMS......... Space Operations Management System   (PDAA)

SOMSG ..... See Our Message [*Aviation*]   (FAAC)

SOMTE...... Soldier-Operator-Maintainer-Tester-Evaluator [*Military*]   (PDAA)

SON........... Linea Aerea Aerosanta [*Chile*] [*ICAO designator*]   (FAAC)

SONITA..... Societe Nigerienne de Transports Aeriens [*Niger*] [*ICAO designator*]   (FAAC)

SOOA .... Solus Outdoor Advertising Association [*British*]   (BI)

SOP .... Sales Order Processing [*Manufacturing management*]

SOP .... Selective Oxidation Process   (PDAA)

SOP .... Solution Output Processor   (PDAA)

SOR .... Air Stord AS [*Norway*] [*ICAO designator*]   (FAAC)

SORFO....... Society of Rural Financial Officers [*British*]   (BI)

SORTRAN ... Syntax-Oriented Translator   (PDAA)

SOS........... Save Our Souls

SOS........... Senior Officer Service

SOS........... Senior Officer Structure

SOS........... Sound on Sound   (NTCM)

SOSD......... System Ordnance Safing Device [*Military*]

SOT .... Southeast Correct Craft, Inc. [*ICAO designator*]   (FAAC)

SOTA .... SIGINT [*Signal Intelligence*] Operational Tasking Authority [*Military*]

SOU.......... Flight Line, Inc. [*ICAO designator*]   (FAAC)

SOVNROF ... State of Vietnam Ribbon of Friendship [*Presidential unit commendation*]

SOW .... Sowind Air Ltd. [*Canada*] [*ICAO designator*]   (FAAC)

SP............. Sailing Plan Report

SP............. Smoke Control and Pressurization Panel [*NFPA pre-fire planning symbol*]   (NFPA)

SP............. Solution Provider [*Microsoft workgroup*]   (PCM)

SP............. Staff Planner [*DoD*]

SP............. Sulfopropyl [*Organic chemistry*]

SPA .... Schedules Planning and Analysis [*Aviation*]   (DA)

SPA .... Sierra Pacific Airlines [*ICAO designator*]   (FAAC)

SPA .... State Property Agency [*Hungary*]   (ECON)

SPA .... Syndicated Program Analysis   (NTCM)

SPAN......... Solid Phase Alloy Nucleation   (PDAA)

SPANS .... Spectral Processing Analysis System   (PDAA)

SPAR......... Store Port Allocation Register   (PDAA)

SPAREM ... Spares Provisioning and Requirements Effectiveness Model   (PDAA)

SPASA........ Servicios Politecnicos Aereos SA [*Spain*] [*ICAO designator*]   (FAAC)

SPB............ ASA [*Former USSR*] [*ICAO designator*]   (FAAC)

SPC............ Skyworld Airlines, Inc. [*ICAO designator*]   (FAAC)

SPC............ Systemwide Program Committee [*Individually-guided education*]   (AEE)

SPCS.......... Ship Production Control System   (PDAA)

SPD............ Airspeed Aviation, Inc. [*Canada*] [*ICAO designator*]   (FAAC)

SPD............ Summary Plan Description
SPDA.......... Sea Photo Diffraction Analysis (PDAA)
SPE............ Sprague Electric Co. [*ICAO designator*] (FAAC)
SPECA .... Supplier Performance Evaluation and Corrective Action (PDAA)
SPECI........ Selected Special Weather Report [*Aviation*] (FAAC)
SPECI........ Special Weather Report [*Aviation*] (DA)
SPEEDS ..... System for Pinpointed, Exhaustive and Expeditious Dissemination of Subjects (PDAA)
SPF .... South Pacific Airline SA [*Chile*] [*ICAO designator*] (FAAC)
SPFD .... Solid-Particle Filter Dye [*Color film technology*]
SPG............ Signal Processor Group
SPG............ Springdale Air Services, Inc. [*ICAO designator*] (FAAC)
SPGTA .... Signal Processor Group Test Assembly
SPI............. Serial Peripheral Interface [*Electronics*]
SPI............. South Pacific Island Airways, Inc. [*ICAO designator*] (FAAC)
SPID .... Seismic Personnel Intrusion Detector (PDAA)
SPIR .... Single Pilot Instrument Rating [*Aviation*] (DA)
SPIRAS ...... Setpoint Precision Infrared Angular Scanner (PDAA)
SPIRIT ...... Systematic Productivity Improvement Review In TRADOC [*Training and Doctrine Command*] [*Army*]
SPJ .... Society of Professional Journalists [*Also, SDX*] (NTCM)
SPK .... Diamond Aviation, Inc. [*ICAO designator*] (FAAC)
SPKC .... Small Pig Keepers' Council [*British*] (BI)
SPL .... Scan-Pol Ltd. [*Poland*] [*ICAO designator*] (FAAC)
SPL .... Set Priority Level [*Computer science*] (NHD)
SPL............ Short-Pulse LASER
SPLCF .... Sustained Peak Low-Cycle Fatigue (PDAA)
SPLICE ...... Shorthand Programming Language in a COBOL Environment [*Computer science*] (PDAA)
SPLIT........ Spent Pot Lining Insolubilisation Technology [*Metallurgy*]
SPM........... Air Saint-Pierre SA [*France*] [*ICAO designator*] (FAAC)
SPM........... Statistical Parametric Mapping [*Data treatment*]
SPMA........ Sewage Plant Manufacturers' Association [*British*] (BI)
SPMA........ String Polling Multiple Access (PDAA)
SPMC........ Standard Procedure Monitor Chart (PDAA)
SPME........ Solar Proton-Monitoring Experiment (PDAA)
SPME........ Spectroscopic Phase-Modulated Ellipsometry
SPN .... Skorpion Air [*Bulgaria*] [*ICAO designator*] (FAAC)
SPNFZT...... South Pacific Nuclear Free Zone Treaty
SPNHC ...... Society for the Preservation of Natural History Collections (EA)
SPNR......... Society for the Promotion of Nature Reserves [*British*] (BI)
SPNS .... Standard Product Numbering System (PDAA)
SPO .... Aeroservicios Ejecutivos del Pacifico SA [*Mexico*] [*ICAO designator*] (FAAC)
SPOT......... Spot Wind [*Meteorology*] (DA)
SPP .... Spainair [*Spain*] [*ICAO designator*] (FAAC)
SPP .... Specific Purpose Payment
SPR .... Eastern Flying Service Ltd. [*Canada*] [*ICAO designator*] (FAAC)
SPR .... Society for Physical Research [*British*] (BI)
SPRITE ...... Sequential Polling and Review of Interacting Teams of Experts (PDAA)
SPROSS ..... Simulation Program for Sequential System (PDAA)
SPRP .... Signalling Preprocessing Program (PDAA)
SPS .... Society of Portrait Sculptors [*British*] (BI)
SPS .... SPASA Servicios Politecnicos Aereos SA [*Spain*] [*ICAO designator*] (FAAC)
SPSD .... Shipboard Passive Surveillance and Detection System (PDAA)
SPTL .... Superconducting Power Transmission Line (PDAA)
SPU........... Southeast Airmotive Corp. [*ICAO designator*] (FAAC)
SPU........... Special Power Unit (NTCM)
SPU........... System Power Up
SPUP .... School of Public and Urban Policy [*Pennsylvania University*] (PDAA)
SPURT .... Simulation Package for University Research and Teaching (PDAA)
SPV........... Space Position Value [*Outdoor advertising*] (NTCM)
SPW........... Speedwings SA [*Switzerland*] [*ICAO designator*] (FAAC)
SPX........... Stepped Piston Crossover (PDAA)
SQ .... Squawk (DA)
SqE & S...... Square-Edge and Sound (DAC)
SQK .... Squawk [*Aviation*] (FAAC)
SQL........... Servicious de Alquiler Aereo SA de CV [*Mexico*] [*ICAO designator*] (FAAC)
SQPSK .... Staggered Quadraphase Phase Shift Key Modulation [*Computer science*] (PDAA)
SQTP......... System Qualification Test Phase
SQUANK .. Simpson Quadrature Used Adaptively - Noise Killed (PDAA)
SQUIRE ..... System for Quick Ultra-Fiche-Based Information Retrieval [*Computer science*] (PDAA)
SR .... Sound Reinforcement (NTCM)
SR .... Specific Reactivity [*Exhaust emissions*] [*Automotive engineering*]
SR .... Strategic Reconnaissance [*Military*]
SRA........... Sair Aviation [*ICAO designator*] (FAAC)
SRA........... Satellite RADAR Altimetry [*Instrumentation*]
SRA........... Shift Register Available
SRA........... Standard Reference Aerosol (PDAA)
SRA........... Strategic Resource Area (PDAA)
SRB........... Suburban Air Freight, Inc. [*ICAO designator*] (FAAC)
SRC........... Selective Ride Control [*Suspension systems*] [*Automotive engineering*]
SRCG......... Safety Razor Collectors Guild (EA)
SRCMA ...... Steel Radiator and Convector Manufacturers' Association [*British*] (BI)

SRD .... Search & Rescue 22 [*British*] [*ICAO designator*] (FAAC)
SRDC......... Shopfitting Research and Development Council [*British*] (BI)
SRET......... Subroutine Recipe Entry Pointer Table
SRF............ Secondary Refrigerant Freezing (PDAA)
SRF............ Short Rotary Furnace [*Metallurgy*]
SRF............ Sliding Roof [*Automotive advertising*]
SRFO......... Society of Rural Financial Officers [*British*] (BI)
SRG .... Search & Rescue 202 [*British*] [*ICAO designator*] (FAAC)
SRGS......... Stimulated Raman Gain Spectroscopy (PDAA)
SRI............ Air Safaris & Services (NZ) Ltd. [*New Zealand*] [*ICAO designator*] (FAAC)
SRI............ Satellite RADAR Interferometry
SRI............ Sulfate Reduction Index [*Environmental chemistry*]
SRI............ System of Reinforcement-Inhibition (PDAA)
SRK........... Skywork SA [*Switzerland*] [*ICAO designator*] (FAAC)
SRL........... Varmlandsflyg AB [*Sweden*] [*ICAO designator*] (FAAC)
SRM........... Flying Swiss Ambulance Maldives (Pvt) Ltd. [*ICAO designator*] (FAAC)
SRM........... Selected-Reaction Monitoring [*Spectrometry*]
SRM .... Subsystem Response Message [*Military*]
SRMA......... Split-Channel Reservation Multiple Access (PDAA)
SRMH .... Single Role Mine-Hunter [*Military*] (PDAA)
SR-MIR...... Specific Reactivity - Maximum Incremental Reactivity [*Exhaust emissions*] [*Automotive engineering*]
SRN .... Slurry Response Number [*Well drilling technology*]
SRNA .... Shipbuilders and Repairers' National Association [*British*] (BI)
SRO .... Senior Ranking Officer [*Army*] (ADDR)
SRO .... Servicios Aereos Rutas Oriente SA de CV [*Mexico*] [*ICAO designator*] (FAAC)
SRO .... Shop Readiness Objective
SRP........... Sequential Range Policy (PDAA)
SRP........... Sink Resistant Plastic (PDAA)
SRP............ Slot Reference Point (DA)
SRP/PDS ... Stabilization Reference Package / Position Determination System [*Military*]
SRPT .... Shortest Remaining Processing Time (PDAA)
SRPT .... Small Repair Parts Transporter
SRPT .... Stress Relaxation Processability Tester (PDAA)
SRR........... Star Air IS [*Denmark*] [*ICAO designator*] (FAAC)
SRRP......... Source Reduction Review Program [*Environmental science*]
SRS .... Selkirk Remote Sensing Ltd. [*Canada*] [*ICAO designator*] (FAAC)
SR-SS .... Sunrise-Sunset (DA)
SRT........... Shift-Register Transfer [*Computer science*]
SRT........... Society of Romanian Air Transports [*ICAO designator*] (FAAC)
SRTCA ...... Senate Radio-Television Correspondents Association (NTCM)
SRTOS .... Special Real-Time Operating System (PDAA)
SRTS .... Steam Railway Traction Society [*British*] (BI)
SRU .... Student Response Unit
SRV........... Surveillance (DA)
SRVCD....... Serviced [*Automotive advertising*]
SRW .... Search & Rescue HQ [*British*] [*ICAO designator*] (FAAC)
SRY........... Secondary [*ICAO designator*] (FAAC)
SRZ........... Surveillance RADAR Zone (DA)
SS............. Sans Serif [*Typeface*] [*Printing*] (NTCM)
SS............. Sodium Sulfite [*Inorganic chemistry*]
SS............. Stock Shot (NTCM)
SS............. Survivability System [*Military*]
SSA .... Safe Sector Altitude [*Aviation*] (DA)
SSA .... Solid State Amplifier (NTCM)
SSA .... Special Service Authorization [*FCC*] (NTCM)
SSA .... Steel Sleeper Association [*British*] (BI)
SSAL.......... Sequenced Flashing Lights [*Aviation*] (DA)
SSAS......... Stable Super-Active Scavenger [*Color film technology*]
SSB .... Salvo Squeezebore (PDAA)
SSB .... Special Separation Benefit [*DoD*]
SSC .... Shape Selective Cracking (PDAA)
SSC .... Single-Site Catalyst [*Chemistry*]
SSC .... Solid State Frequency Converter (DA)
SSC .... Southern Seaplane, Inc. [*ICAO designator*] (FAAC)
SSC .... Spontaneous Synaptic Current [*Neuroscience*]
S2S & CM ... Surfaced Two Sides and Center Matched [*Lumber*] (DAC)
SSCS......... Spatial Spectrum Center Shifting (PDAA)
S4S & CS .... Surfaced Four Sides and Caulking Seam [*Lumber*] (DAC)
SSD........... Star Service International [*France*] [*ICAO designator*] (FAAC)
SSD........... Supplementary Special Deposit [*British*]
SSDA .... Stainless Steel Development Association [*British*] (BI)
SSE .... Society of Shipping Executives [*British*] (BI)
SSE .... Stockholm Stock Exchange
S1S2E .... Surfaced One Side and Two Edges [*Lumber*] (DAC)
S2S1E .... Surfaced Two Sides and One Edge [*Lumber*] (DAC)
SSEC .... Secondary School Examinations Council [*British*] (BI)
SSF .... Smallest Serving Factor (PDAA)
SSFA .... Stainless Steel Fabricators' Association of Great Britain (BI)
SSFF.......... Solid Smokeless Fuels Federation [*British*] (BI)
SSHA......... System Safety Hazard Analysis [*Military*]
SSI .... Satellite Sequential Imaging
SSI .... Solid-State Imaging [*Physics*]
SSIDA .... Steel Sheet Information and Developement Association [*British*] (BI)
SSILA........ Society for the Study of Indigenous Languages of the Americas (EA)
SSIT........... Semi-Submarine Ice-Breaking Tanker (PDAA)

SSK............ Skystar International [*ICAO designator*]   (FAAC)
SSK............ Super Sport Kurz [*Super, Sport, Short chassis*] [*Mercedes-Benz automotive model designation*]
SSKTP........ Society for Spreading the Knowledge of True Prayer [*British*] (BI)
SSM............ Aero 1 Prop-Jet, Inc. [*Canada*] [*ICAO designator*]   (FAAC)
SSM............ Semisolid Material [*Metallurgy*]
SSM............ Standard Schedule Message   (DA)
SSMT........ Stress Survival Matrix Test   (PDAA)
SSNTD...... Solid-State Nuclear Track Detection   (PDAA)
SSP............ Size-Selective Precipitation [*Physics*]
SSP............ Sole Supporting Parent
SSP............ Starspeed Ltd. [*British*] [*ICAO designator*]   (FAAC)
SSPA......... Solid State Power Amplifier   (DA)
SSPS.......... Small Solar-Power System [*Energy source*]
SSQ............ Noosa Air Sunstate Airlines [*Australia*] [*ICAO designator*] (FAAC)
SSR............ Sempati Air PT [*Indonesia*] [*ICAO designator*]   (FAAC)
SSR............ Sustained Silent Reading [*Education*]   (AEE)
SSR............ Switching Selector Repeater   (PDAA)
SSRE......... Shear-Stress Responsive Element [*Biochemistry*]
SSRI.......... Selective Serotonin Reuptake Inhibitor [*Physiology*]
SSRP......... Structure-Specific Recognition Protein [*Biochemistry*]
SSRT......... Slow Strain Rate Technique   (PDAA)
SSS............ Compania de Servicios Aereos SA [*Spain*] [*ICAO designator*] (FAAC)
SSS............ Self-Shifting Synchronizing   (PDAA)
SSS............ Serial Signalling Scheme   (PDAA)
SSS............ Sodium Styrenesulfonate [*Organic chemistry*]
SSS............ Stability and Safety Screening [*Sailing terminology*]
S2S & SL .... Surfaced Two Sides and Shiplapped [*Technical drawings*]   (DAC)
SSSP.......... Secondary School Science Project [*Princeton University*]   (AEE)
SST............ Sunwest Airlines Ltd. [*Canada*] [*ICAO designator*]   (FAAC)
SSTM........ Solid-State Target Monoscope   (PDAA)
SSTR......... Solid-State Track Recorder   (PDAA)
SSTS......... Sight Switch Technology System   (PDAA)
SSTT......... Subsea Test Tree   (PDAA)
SSU............ Sangamon State University   (PDAA)
ST .... Schmidt Telescope
ST .... Strainer   (DAC)
STA............ Special Temporary Allowance
STA............ Star Aviation [*British*] [*ICAO designator*]   (FAAC)
STA............ Straight in Approach [*Aviation*]   (DA)
STA............ Subscription Television Association   (NTCM)
STABE........ Second-Time-Around-Beacon-Echo   (PDAA)
STAC......... Submarine Tactical Acoustic Communications [*Navy*]   (ANA)
STAD......... Student Teams-Achievement Division   (AEE)
STAGING ... Sturctural Analysis via Generalized Interactive Graphics   (PDAA)
STALAPCO ... State and Local Air Pollution Control Official [*Environmental Protection Agency*]   (ERG)
STALOC .... Self-Tracking Automatic Lock-On Circuit   (PDAA)
STAM........ Sequential Thermal Anhysteric Magnetization [*Helical scan videotape duplicating system*]   (NTCM)
STAM........ Statistical Analog Monitor   (PDAA)
STANAVFORLANT ... Standing Naval Force, Atlantic   (ANA)
STAPL......... Ship Tethered Aerial Platform   (PDAA)
STAPP........ Short-Term Anxiety-Provoking Psychotherapy   (PDAA)
STAR......... Screening Tracking and Retrieval
STAR......... Society of Romanian Air Transports [*ICAO designator*]   (FAAC)
STARS....... Soot Trap and Regeneration System [*Diesel engine exhaust emission controls*]
STAT......... Photostat   (NTCM)
STAT......... Signal Transducer and Activator of Transcription [*Biochemistry*]
STB............ Snci-Tours Benin Inter Regional [*ICAO designator*]   (FAAC)
STB............ Stop Bar   (DA)
STC............ Societe de Transports et de Tourisme [*Mali*] [*ICAO designator*] (FAAC)
STC............ Society of Town Clerks [*British*]   (BI)
STC............ Solar Thermal Commission   (PDAA)
STC............ Solid Tantalum Capacitor   (PDAA)
STCA......... Short Term Conflict Alert System [*Aviation*]   (DA)
STCS......... Society of Technical Civil Servants [*British*]   (BI)
STD .... South Tibetan Detachment [*Geology*]
STD .... Stream Tree Data   (PDAA)
StdM.......... Standard Matched   (DAC)
STE............ Semitool Europe Ltd. [*British*] [*ICAO designator*]   (FAAC)
STEAM...... Schema Tuning, Evaluation, and Analytical Model   (PDAA)
STEAM...... Stochastic Evolutionary Adoption Model   (PDAA)
STEC......... Surface Treatment Enhancement Council [*Metallurgy*]
STE/ICE .... Standard Test Equipment / Internal Combustion Engine
STELLA ..... System Ten European Language Ledger Accounting   (PDAA)
STEM........ Short-Term Energy Monitoring [*Colorado State University*]
STEP .... Stand for Exchange of Product Model Data [*Computer-assisted engineering*]
STEP .... Standard for the Exchange of Product Data [*Materials science*]
STEPO .... Self-Contained, Toxic Environment, Protective Outfit [*Army*] (INF)
STEPS....... Strategy Evaluator and Planning-Production System   (PDAA)
STF .... SFT-Sudanese Flight [*ICAO designator*]   (FAAC)
STG............ Sedalia-Marshall-Booville Stage Line, Inc. [*ICAO designator*] (FAAC)
STH .... Southern Airlines Ltd. [*British*]   (FAAC)
STHE.......... Special Tools and Handling Equipment

STI.............. Shear Thinning Index   (PDAA)
STI.............. Shielding Technologies Inc.
STI.............. Straight Times Index [*Singapore Stock Exchange*]
STIA .... Satellite Television Industry Association [*Formerly, SPACE*] (NTCM)
STIF........... Search Track Intermediate Frequency [*Military*]
STI/SS........ Scientific and Technical Information System and Service   (PDAA)
STK............ Stick Shift [*Automotive advertising*]
STL............ Secondary Target Line [*Army*]
STL............ Stapleford Flight Center [*British*] [*ICAO designator*]   (FAAC)
STM........... Simply Transformed Manufacture
STM........... Streamline Aviation [*British*] [*ICAO designator*]   (FAAC)
STMS .... Short-Term Monetary Support [*Finance*]
STMV........ Stump-Tailed Macaque Virus   (PDAA)
STN .... St. Athan MU [*British*] [*ICAO designator*]   (FAAC)
STO .... Aero Santos SA de CV [*Mexico*] [*ICAO designator*]   (FAAC)
STO .... Senior Training Officer
STOC-TV ... Satellite Technical and Operational Committee - Television (NTCM)
STOM .... Shot through Obscuration MILES [*Multiple Integrated LASER Engagement System*] [*Army*]
STOPP .... Stop Planned Parenthood [*An association*]   (EA)
STP............ Holidair Airways [*Canada*] [*ICAO designator*]   (FAAC)
STP............ Separation Transfer Point [*Army*]   (ADDR)
STP............ Skills Training Program
STP............ Special Trade Passenger Ship   (PDAA)
STPG......... Sequential Test Plan Generator   (PDAA)
STR............ Short Term Reinitialization [*Army*]
STR............ Stellair [*France*] [*ICAO designator*]   (FAAC)
STR............ System Test Report [*Military*]
STRIKWARN ... Strike Warning Message [*Army*]   (ADDR)
STRIP........ Strategic Intermediate Planner   (PDAA)
STRIPE...... Stress-Induced Pseudoelasticity   (PDAA)
STRS......... Stimulated Thermal Rayleigh Scattering   (PDAA)
STRV........ Short Tons Raw Value
STS............ Servicios Auxiliares de Transportes Aereos [*Brazil*] [*ICAO designator*]   (FAAC)
STS............ Single Thread System
STS............ Status [*ICAO designator*]   (FAAC)
STSTA....... Small Aerial Surveillance and Target Acquisition   (PDAA)
STT............ Air St. Thomas [*ICAO designator*]   (FAAC)
STTE .... Society of Travel and Tourism Educators   (EA)
STU .... Transportes Aereos Fueguino [*Argentina*] [*ICAO designator*] (FAAC)
STUMP...... Submersible, Transportable Utility, Marine Pump   (PDAA)
STUTIS...... Secondary, Technical, and University Teachers' Insurance Society [*British*]   (BI)
STV........... Southern Aviation Ltd. [*Ghana*] [*ICAO designator*]   (FAAC)
STV........... Steerable Low-Light-Level Television   (PDAA)
STV........... Subscription Television Authority [*FCC*]   (NTCM)
STV........... Subscription TV, Inc.   (NTCM)
STVP .... Salinity, Temperature, Sound-Velocity and Pressure-Sensing System   (PDAA)
STW........... Short-Term Waviness [*Surface finish*]
STW........... Starways SA [*Switzerland*] [*ICAO designator*]   (FAAC)
STWL........ Stopway Light [*Aviation*]   (FAAC)
STX............ Aerocharter [*Czechoslovakia*] [*ICAO designator*]   (FAAC)
STYCAR .... Screening Tests for Young Children and Retardates   (MAH)
SUA .... Aviation Associates, Inc. [*St. Croix*] [*ICAO designator*]   (FAAC)
SUBINSURV (LANT) (PAC) ... Sub Board of Inspection and Survey of Atlantic and Pacific [*Navy*]   (ANA)
SUBJ .... Subject To [*ICAO designator*]   (FAAC)
SUD .... Sudan Airways [*ICAO designator*]   (FAAC)
SUE .... Aerolineas del Sureste SA [*Mexico*] [*ICAO designator*]   (FAAC)
SUF .... Sunflower Airlines Ltd. [*Fiji*] [*ICAO designator*]   (FAAC)
SUI .... Bundesamt fur Militarflugplatze [*Switzerland*] [*ICAO designator*]   (FAAC)
SUIS .... Ship Upkeep Information System [*Ministry of Defense*] [*British*]   (PDAA)
SUIT.......... Simple User Interface Toolkit [*University of Virginia*]
SUN .... Antillana de Nevegacion Aerea SA [*Dominican Republic*] [*ICAO designator*]   (FAAC)
SUP............ Aerosuper AS de CV [*Mexico*] [*ICAO designator*]   (FAAC)
SUPER ...... Supercalendered   (NTCM)
SUPER ...... Superimposition   (NTCM)
SURE......... Safeguards Upgrade Rule Evaluation   (PDAA)
SURF......... Synthetic Unrandomization of Randomized Fragments [*Chemistry*]
SUS............ Steel User Service [*British*]   (BI)
SUS............ Sun-Air of Scandinavia AS [*Denmark*] [*ICAO designator*] (FAAC)
SUY .... Aerial Surveys (1980) Ltd. [*New Zealand*] [*ICAO designator*] (FAAC)
SVA .... Saudi Arabian Airlines [*ICAO designator*]   (FAAC)
SVAT......... Synaptic Vesicle Amine Transporter [*Biochemistry*]
SVE........... Aero Servicios Especializados SA de CV [*Mexico*] [*ICAO designator*]   (FAAC)
SVE........... Soil Vapor Extraction [*Environmental science*]
SVG .... Serving   (FAAC)
SVGL......... Silicon Valley Group Lithography   (ECON)
SVL........... Saak [*Russian Federation*] [*ICAO designator*]   (FAAC)
SVM........... Aeroservicios Monterrey SA de CV [*Mexico*] [*ICAO designator*] (FAAC)

SVN .... Space Vehicle Number [*Aviation*]   (FAAC)
SVP............. Single-Voyage Permit
SVR............. Sverdlovsk Airline [*Russian Federation*] [*ICAO designator*]
                    (FAAC)
SVS .... Society for Visiting Scientists Ltd. [*British*]   (BI)
SVV............. Empresa Servicicious Avensa SA [*Venezuela*] [*ICAO
                    designator*]   (FAAC)
SVY............. GCA Surveys [*British*] [*ICAO designator*]   (FAAC)
SW .... Single Wheel [*Landing gear*] [*Aviation*]   (DA)
S/W............ Surface Wind [*Meteorology*]   (DA)
SWA .... Southwest Airlines Co. [*ICAO designator*]   (FAAC)
SWA .... Sports Writers' Association [*British*]   (BI)
SWAAT...... Sea-Water Acetic Acid Test   (PDAA)
SWAB........ Swap Byte [*Computer science*]   (NHD)
SWAPS ...... Standing-Wave Acoustic Parametric Source   (PDAA)
SWB........... Southwestbound [*ICAO designator*]   (FAAC)
SWB........... Sweden Airways [*ICAO designator*]   (FAAC)
SWBM........ Still-Water Bending Moment   (PDAA)
SWC .... South West Air Ltd. [*Canada*] [*ICAO designator*]   (FAAC)
SWCD .... Solar Wind Composition Detector   (PDAA)
SWCE........ Solar Wind Composition Experiment   (PDAA)
SwD........... Students with Disabilities
SWD .... Swinderby FTU [*British*] [*ICAO designator*]   (FAAC)
SWE........... Swedair AB [*Sweden*] [*ICAO designator*]   (FAAC)
SWF........... Air Swift [*British*] [*ICAO designator*]   (FAAC)
SWF........... Screw Worm Fly
SWFM....... Standing-Wave Fluorescence Microscopy
SWG .... Ground Air Transfer, Inc. [*ICAO designator*]   (FAAC)
SWI............ Sidewall Indentation [*Tire manufacturing*]
SWI............ Sunworld International Airways, Inc. [*ICAO designator*]   (FAAC)
SWING...... Sterling Warrant into Gilt-Edged Stock [*British*]
SWJ .... StatesWest Airlines, Inc. [*ICAO designator*]   (FAAC)
SWK .... General Aerospace, Inc. [*Canada*] [*ICAO designator*]   (FAAC)
SWM .... Society of Women Musicians, Inc. [*British*]   (BI)
SWMA .... Steel Wool Manufacturers' Association [*British*]   (BI)
SWMU ...... Solid Waste Management Unit [*Environmental science*]
SWOP........ Standard Web Offset Press [*Computer science*]   (PCM)
SWPA......... Steel Works Plant Association [*British*]   (BI)
SW/PM ...... System Management/Performance Monitor
SWPPP...... Storm Water Pollution Prevention Plan [*Environmental science*]
SWR .... Standing Wave Ratio   (NTCM)
SWR .... Swissair (Societe Anonyme Switzerland pour la Navigation
                    Aerienne) [*ICAO designator*]   (FAAC)
SWRA........ Stepwise Regression Analysis   (PDAA)
SWS........... Lindquist Investment Co., Inc. [*ICAO designator*]   (FAAC)
SWS........... Slow Wave Structure [*Satellite delay tube*]   (NTCM)
SWSL .... Supplemental Weather Service Location [*Aviation*]   (FAAC)
SWS/SUM PTS ... Selection Work Sheets/Summary Parts
SWT............ Swiftair SA [*Spain*] [*ICAO designator*]   (FAAC)
SWY .... Skyway Business Travel Ltd. [*British*] [*ICAO designator*]
                    (FAAC)
SXA............ Shannon Executive Aviation Ireland Ltd. [*ICAO designator*]
                    (FAAC)
SXS............ Gunes Ekspres Havacilik AS (Sunexpress) [*Turkey*] [*ICAO
                    designator*]   (FAAC)
SXX............ Satellite Aero, Inc. [*ICAO designator*]   (FAAC)
SYB............ Symbol [*Spain*] [*ICAO designator*]   (FAAC)
SYF .... Sky One Express Airlines, Inc. [*ICAO designator*]   (FAAC)
SYJ .... Slate Falls Airways Ltd. [*Canada*] [*ICAO designator*]   (FAAC)
SYMES ...... Systematic Machinery and Equipment Selection   (PDAA)
SYMPLE.... Syntax Macro Preprocessor for Language Evaluation [*Computer
                    science*]   (PDAA)
SYN .... Syncrude Canada Ltd. [*ICAO designator*]   (FAAC)
SYNC......... Synchronizing Character [*Computer science*]   (IAA)
SYNCCODE ... Synchronization Code   (IAA)
SYNCIN..... Synchronization Input [*Computer science*]   (IAA)
SYNCOM ... Synchronous Communication Satellite [*Telecommunications*]
                    (IAA)
SYNCOUT ... Synchronization Output   (IAA)
SYNCSCP ... Synchronoscope   (IAA)
SYR............ Syrian Arab Airlines [*ICAO designator*]   (FAAC)
SYS .... Shawbury FTU [*British*] [*ICAO designator*]   (FAAC)
SYSCMA ... System Core Image Library Maintenance Program [*Computer
                    science*]   (IAA)
SYSTID...... System Time-Domain Simulation Program [*Computer science*]
                    (PDAA)
SYSTIM..... Systematic Interaction Model   (PDAA)
SYSTSW .... System Software [*Computer science*]   (IAA)
SYSX .... Systems Exchange [*Computer science*]   (IAA)
SZ .... Size   (IAA)
SZA............ Aerolineas de El Salvador SA [*ICAO designator*]   (FAAC)
SZI............. Service Zone Indication [*Computer science*]   (IAA)

T

T................ Tamper (NFPA)
T................ Telemeter [*or Telemetry*] [*Telecommunications*] (IAA)
T................ Television [*FCC*] (NTCM)
T................ Terrain Clearance Altitude [*Aviation*] (DA)
T................ Testamentum [*Will*] [*Latin*]
T................ Threshold Lighting [*Aviation*] (DA)
T................ Thrust (IAA)
T................ Time Constant (IAA)
T................ Timer (IAA)
T................ Toggle [*Telecommunications*] (IAA)
T................ Tone (IAA)
T................ Transistor [*Electronics*] (IAA)
T................ Transmission [*Telecommunications*] (IAA)
T................ Transmission Stop (NTCM)
T................ Transponder (IAA)
T................ Travel News [*Wire service code*] (NTCM)
t................ Trend Landing Forecast [*Aviation*] (DA)
T................ Trigger (IAA)
T................ Trimmer (IAA)
T................ Trunk (IAA)
T................ Tube (IAA)
T................ Tubular (IAA)
T_3............ Train-the-Trainer [*Army*]
7T............ Algeria [*Aircraft nationality and registration mark*] (FAAC)
TA................ Tape (IAA)
TA................ Terminal Address (IAA)
TA................ Test Announcer (IAA)
TA................ Top Assembly
TA................ Track Address (IAA)
TA................ Trunk Amplifier (IAA)
TAA............ Aerotamatan SA de CV [*Mexico*] [*ICAO designator*] (FAAC)
TAA............ Time and Attendance (IAA)
TAA............ Total Army Authorization
TAA............ Transfer and Accountability (IAA)
TAAC......... [*The*] Association of American Cultures (EA)
TAAM......... Terminal Area Altitude Monitoring (PDAA)
TAAM......... Theoretical and Applied Mechanics (IAA)
TAAN......... Transporte Aereo Andino SA [*Venezuela*] [*ICAO designator*] (FAAC)
TAB .... Tabloid (NTCM)
TAB .... Tabulating Machine (IAA)
TAB .... Technical Advisory Board (IAA)
TAB .... Technical Assistance Bureau [*ICAO*] (DA)
TAB .... Title Abstract Bulletin (IAA)
TAB .... Tone Answer Back [*Telecommunications*] (IAA)
TAB .... Top and Bottom (IAA)
TAB .... Totalizer Agency Board (IAA)
TAB .... Towed Assault Bridge [*Army*]
TAB .... Transportes Aereos da Bacia Amazonica SA [*Brazil*] [*ICAO designator*] (FAAC)
TAB .... Transportes Aereos Bolivianos [*Bolivia*] [*ICAO designator*] (FAAC)
TAB .... Turned and Bored (IAA)
TABC......... Tabulator Character (IAA)
TABS......... Telephone Automated Briefing Service (DA)
TABSIM .... Table Simulation [*or Simulator*] (IAA)
TABSTONE ... Target and Background Signal-to-Noise Experiment (IAA)
TAC .... Tape Adapter Cabinet (IAA)
TAC .... Targeting and Control (IAA)
TAC .... Thai Airways Co. Ltd. [*ICAO designator*] (FAAC)
TAC .... Time and Charges [*Telecommunications*] (IAA)
TAC .... Tokyo Automatic Computer (IAA)
TAC .... Total Automatic Color (IAA)
TAC .... Transistorized Automatic Computer (IAA)
TAC .... Transmitter Assembler Compiler [*Telecommunications*] (IAA)
TAC .... Transportes Aereos Coyhaique [*Chile*] [*ICAO designator*] (FAAC)
TACALS..... Tactical Air Control and Landing System [*Military*] (IAA)
TACAWS ... [*The*] Army Combined Arms Weapons System
TACC......... Temporary Augmentation for Command and Control [*Navy*] (ANA)
TACDEN.... Tactical Data Entry [*Army*] (IAA)
TACE.......... Turbine Automatic Control Equipment (IAA)

TACELINT ... Tactical Electronic Intelligence [*Navy*] (ANA)
TACELRON ... Tactical Electronic Warfare Squadron [*Navy*] (ANA)
TACET....... Television Advisory Committee for Educational Television (NTCM)
TACF......... Temporary Alteration Control Form (IAA)
TACH........ Tachometer Generator (IAA)
TACI......... Tactical Initialization [*Computer software*] [*Military*]
TACL........ Tactical Loader [*Preparation software*] [*Army*]
TACMAR... Tactical Memory Address Register [*Computer science*] (IAA)
TACMEMO ... Tactical Memorandum [*Navy*] (ANA)
TACMOD ... Tactical Modular Display [*Army*] (PDAA)
TACO .... Technical Appliance Corp. (IAA)
TACOMA ... Television Advisory Committee of Mexican Americans (NTCM)
TACOPS .... Tactical Organization Paperless System [*Army*]
TACRAC .... Technical and Cost Reduction Assistance Contract
TACS......... Talker Active State [*Telecommunications*] (IAA)
TACSAT ... Tactical Satellite [*Military*] (IAA)
TACT......... Technological Aid to Creative Thought (PDAA)
TACT......... Total Audit Concept Technique (PDAA)
TACV......... Transportes Aereos de Cabo Verde [*Cape Verde*] [*ICAO designator*] (FAAC)
TACV/LIM ... Tracked Air Cushion Vehicle Powered by Linear Induction Motor (PDAA)
TAD........... Technical Acceptance Demonstration (IAA)
TAD........... Telemetry and Data [*Telecommunications*] (IAA)
TAD........... Test Acceptance Document [*Computer science*] (IAA)
TAD........... Theater Air Defense [*Military*]
TAD........... Training Aid and Device [*Military*]
TAD........... Transmission and Distribution (IAA)
TAD........... Transporte Aereo Dominicano SA [*Dominican Republic*] [*ICAO designator*] (FAAC)
TADA......... Tracking and Data Acquisition (IAA)
TADIL....... Tactical Data Information Link [*DoD*]
TADIX....... Tactical Data Information Exchange Subsystem [*Navy*] (ANA)
TADS......... Throw Away Detector (PDAA)
TADS......... Transportable Automatic Digital Switch (PDAA)
TADSS ...... Training Aid, Device, Simulation and Simulator [*Military*]
TAE .... Technician Aeronautical Engineering (IAA)
TAE .... Time and Event (IAA)
TAE .... Transportes Aereos Militares Ecatorianos CA [*Ecuador*] [*ICAO designator*] (FAAC)
TAEREC .... Time and Event Recorder (IAA)
TAES......... Techicas Aereas de Estudios y Servicios SA [*Spain*] [*ICAO designator*] (FAAC)
TAES......... Transportes Aereos de El Salvador SA de CV [*ICAO designator*] (FAAC)
TAF............ Time Air Ltd. [*Canada*] [*ICAO designator*] (FAAC)
TAF............ Transaxel Fluid (IAA)
TAG .... Orion Air, Inc. [*ICAO designator*] (FAAC)
TAG .... Technical Advisory Group (IAA)
TAG .... Tongue and Groove [*Lumber*] (IAA)
TAG .... Treatment Action Group [*for AIDS medication*] [*FDA*]
TAG .... Turmor-Associated Glycoprotein [*Biochemistry*]
TAGRET .... Thermal Advanced Gas-Cooled Reactor Exploiting Thorium [*Nuclear energy*] (IAA)
TAH........... Air Moorea [*France*] [*ICAO designator*] (FAAC)
TA/H.......... Turn Altitude/Height [*Aviation*] (DA)
TAHBSO.... Total Abdominal Hysterectomy Bilateral Salpingo-Oophorectomy [*Medicine*] (MAH)
TAI .... TACA International Airlines SA [*El Salvador*] [*ICAO designator*] (FAAC)
TAIS .... Technology Applications Information System
TAJ............ Tunisavia - Societe de Transport, Services et Travaux Aeriens [*Tunisia*] [*ICAO designator*] (FAAC)
TAK .... Transkei Airways [*South Africa*] [*ICAO designator*] (FAAC)
TAL .... Talair Pty Ltd. [*New Guinea*] [*ICAO designator*] (FAAC)
TAM .... [*The*] Access Method (IAA)
TAM .... Teleprocessing Access Method [*Telecommunications*] (IAA)
TAM .... Towed Acoustic Monitor (PDAA)
TAM .... Traction Asynchronous Motor (PDAA)
TAM .... Transportacion Aerea Mexicana [*Mexico*] [*ICAO designator*] (FAAC)

TAM.......... Transportes Aereos Regionais SA [*Brazil*] [*ICAO designator*]
　　　　　　(FAAC)
TAM.......... Tyrosine Activation Motif [*Biochemistry*]
TAMA......... Threat to Army Mission Areas
TAMI .... Television Accessory Manufacturers Institute　(NTCM)
TAMP........ Tactical Antimissile Measurement Program [*Military*]　(IAA)
TAMPA...... Tender Assist Minimum Platform Arrangement　(PDAA)
TAMPNL... Trigger and Monitor Panel　(IAA)
TAN........... Taxation Assessment Notice
TAN ALT ... Tangent Altitude [*Photography*]
TANDEL.... Temperature Autostabilizing Nonlinear Dielectric Element　(IAA)
TANSE....... Transportes Aereos Neuquinos Sociedad de Estado [*Argentina*]
　　　　　　[*ICAO designator*]　(FAAC)
TAO........... Test and Operation　(IAA)
TAO........... Transportes Aeromar [*Mexico*] [*ICAO designator*]　(FAAC)
TAP........... Target and Penetration　(IAA)
TAP........... Term Availability Plan　(IAA)
TAP........... Time-sharing Accounting Package [*Computer science*]　(IAA)
TAP........... Total Audience Plan [*Radio advertising*]　(NTCM)
TAP........... Transporter Associated with Antigen Processing [*Biochemistry*]
TAP........... Transportes Aereos Portugueses EP [*Portugal*] [*ICAO
　　　　　　designator*]　(FAAC)
TAPES ...... Total Army Personnel Evaluation System
TAPES ...... Transformer Analog Polynomial Equation Solver　(PDAA)
TAQA........ Test and Quality Assurance　(IAA)
TAR........... Temporary Accumulator　(IAA)
TAR........... Temporary Accumulator Register　(IAA)
TAR........... Test and Return　(IAA)
TAR........... Transaction Area　(IAA)
TAR........... Transmit and Receive　(IAA)
TAR........... Tunis Air-Societe Tunisienne de l'Air [*Tunisia*] [*ICAO
　　　　　　designator*]　(FAAC)
TARA........ Terrain Avoidance RADAR　(IAA)
TARAC...... Terminology, Aids, References, Applications, and Coordination
　　　　　　(IAA)
TARAD ...... Tracking Asynchronous RADAR Data　(DA)
TARBIT ..... Three-Axis Rout Byro Inertial Tracker　(IAA)
TAREF .... [*The*] Acronym Generator Reference [*RCA computer program*]
　　　　　　(IAA)
TARIT....... Telegraph Automatic Routing in the Field　(IAA)
TARPS ...... True and Relative Motion Plotting System　(IAA)
TARS......... Technical Aircraft Reliability Statistics　(IAA)
TARS......... Terrain and RADAR Simulator　(IAA)
TARS......... Tethered Aerostat RADAR System [*Aviation*]　(FAAC)
TAS........... Telegraphy with Automatic Switching [*Telecommunications*]
　　　　　　(IAA)
TAS........... Teleprogrammer Assembly System [*Computer science*]　(IAA)
TAS........... TRW Advanced Steering [*Automotive components*]
TASA........ Telecommunicacoes Aeronauticas SA [*Brazil*] [*ICAO
　　　　　　designator*]　(FAAC)
TASCS...... Tactical Air Support Control System [*Military*]　(PDAA)
TASF .... Tactical Air Support Force [*Air Force*]
TASIC .... Thermal Analysis of Substrates and Intergrated Circuits　(PDAA)
TASK........ Temporary Assembled Skeleton [*Computer science*]　(IAA)
TASK........ Training and Skills Program
TASR........ Temperature Auto Stabilizing Regime　(IAA)
TASS......... Theater Army Signal System　(IAA)
TAST......... Tracking Adjunct Systems Trainer
TAT........... European Airlines [*France*] [*ICAO designator*]　(FAAC)
TAT........... Telephone and Telegraph　(IAA)
TAT........... Tuned Aperiodic Tuned　(IAA)
TAT........... Turbine Trip and Throttle Valve [*Nuclear energy*]　(IAA)
TAU........... Tape Adapter Unit [*Computer science*]　(IAA)
TAU........... Toros Airlines [*Turkey*] [*ICAO designator*]　(FAAC)
TAV........... Compania de Servicios Aereos, TAVISA [*Spain*] [*ICAO
　　　　　　designator*]　(FAAC)
TAVG........ Temperature Average　(IAA)
TAW.......... Transway Air Services, Inc. [*Liberia*] [*ICAO designator*]　(FAAC)
TAWS........ Thomasville Aircraft and Warning Station　(IAA)
TAX........... Travelair GmbH [*Germany*] [*ICAO designator*]　(FAAC)
TAY........... Talia Airlines [*Turkey*] [*ICAO designator*]　(FAAC)
TAZ........... Transporte Aereo de la Amazonia [*Colombia*] [*ICAO
　　　　　　designator*]　(FAAC)
TB.............. Through Bolt　(DAC)
TB.............. Transmitter Buffer [*Telecommunications*]　(IAA)
TB.............. Trunk Barrier [*Telecommunications*]　(IAA)
TB.............. Turbulence [*Aviation*]　(FAAC)
TBA........... Thoroughbred Breeders' Association [*British*]　(BI)
TBA........... Transbrasil SA Linhas Aereas [*Brazil*] [*ICAO designator*]
　　　　　　(FAAC)
TBC........... Tie Line Bias Control [*Telecommunications*]　(IAA)
TBCE......... Time Buffered Coarse Fine　(IAA)
TBE........... Total Binding Energy　(IAA)
TBED......... Time Base Error Difference [*Computer science*]　(IAA)
TBFFU...... Twin-Ball Fire Fighting Unit [*Military*]　(PDAA)
TBFI .... Throttle Body Fuel Injection [*Fuel systems*] [*Automotive
　　　　　　engineering*]
TBH........... Trinity Air Bahamas [*ICAO designator*]　(FAAC)
TBHP .... Tertiary-Butylhydroperioxide [*Organic chemistry*]
TBI............ Tissue Banks International [*An association*]　(EA)
TBI............ To Be Initiated　(IAA)
TBL........... [*The*] Berline, Berlin-Brandenburgisches Luftfahrtunternehmen
　　　　　　GmbH [*Germany*] [*ICAO designator*]　(FAAC)

TBLE......... Trouble　(IAA)
TBM .... Terrestrial Biogeochemical Model [*for climate effects*]
TBM .... Trophoblastic Basement Membrane　(PDAA)
TBMU .... Transitional Butterworth Modified Ultraspherical Filter　(PDAA)
TBPA......... Torso Back Protective Armor　(PDAA)
TBPB......... Tertiary-Butyl Perbenzoate [*Organic chemistry*]
TBR .... Temporary Base Register [*Computer science*]　(IAA)
TBS........... Taut Band Suspension　(IAA)
TBS............ Tensile Bond Strength [*Materials science*]
TBS............ Terminal Business System [*Computer science*]　(IAA)
TBT........... Transitional Butterworth Thomson　(IAA)
TBTA......... Thames Boating Trades' Association [*British*]　(BI)
TBU........... Transitional Butterworth Ultraspherical Filter　(PDAA)
TBV!P........ Total Blood Volume Predicted from Body Surface [*Physiology*]
　　　　　　(MAH)
TBW .... Time Band-Width　(IAA)
TBWP........ Triple-Braid Weatherproof　(IAA)
TBX .... Tactical Range Ballistic Missile [*Military*]　(IAA)
TC.............. Tank Circuit　(IAA)
TC.............. Taxiway Centerline Lighting [*Aviation*]　(DA)
TC.............. Telecomputing Corp.　(IAA)
TC.............. Telefunken Computer AG　(IAA)
TC.............. Telephone Center　(IAA)
TC.............. Telephone Central Office　(IAA)
TC.............. Temperature in Degrees Centigrade　(IAA)
TC.............. Test Case Specification　(IAA)
TC.............. [*Inspector's*] Test Connection [*NFPA pre-fire planning symbol*]
　　　　　　(NFPA)
T & C......... Test and Crossmatch [*Medicine*]　(MAH)
TC.............. Thames Conservancy [*British*]　(BI)
TC.............. Time Code　(NTCM)
TC.............. Time Compression [*Computer science*]　(IAA)
TC.............. Time Controlled [*Computer science*]　(IAA)
TC.............. Title Card　(NTCM)
TC.............. Tone Control [*Telecommunications*]　(IAA)
TC.............. Top Cap　(IAA)
TC.............. Towed Cable [*Telecommunications*]　(IAA)
TC.............. Transcontinental　(NTCM)
TC.............. Transitional Control　(IAA)
TC.............. Transmission Control [*Telecommunications*]　(IAA)
TC.............. Transmitter Tuning Circuit [*Telecommunications*]　(IAA)
TC.............. Trip Cell　(IAA)
TC.............. Tuned Circuit [*Telecommunications*]　(IAA)
TC.............. Tungsten Carbide　(IAA)
TCA .... Tahiti Conquest Airlines [*France*] [*ICAO designator*]　(FAAC)
TCA .... Task Control Area　(IAA)
TCA .... Temperature Control Amplifier　(IAA)
TCA .... Transcontinental Control Area [*Aviation*]　(DA)
TCAC......... Tone-Count Audiometric Computer　(PDAA)
TCAD .... Traffic Alert and Collision Avoidance Device [*Aviation*]　(DA)
TCAM .... Telegraph Construction and Maintenance　(IAA)
TCARS ...... Test Call Answer Relay Set　(PDAA)
TCB........... [*The*] Computer Bulletin　(IAA)
TCB........... Tape Control Block [*Computer science*]　(IAA)
TCB........... Transporte del Caribe [*Colombia*] [*ICAO designator*]　(FAAC)
TCB........... Trouble Came Back [*Computer hacker terminology*]　(NHD)
TCC........... Telegraph Condenser Co.　(IAA)
TCC........... Total COBOL [*Common Business-Oriented Language*] Capability
　　　　　　[*Computer science*]　(IAA)
TCC........... Tractor Computing Corp.　(IAA)
TCC........... Transportable Cassette Converter　(IAA)
TCCA......... Textile and Clothing Contractors' Association [*British*]　(BI)
TCCN......... TransCanada Computer Communications Network　(IAA)
TCCO .... Temperature-Controlled Crystal Oscillator　(IAA)
TCD .... Temperature Control Device for Crystal Units　(IAA)
TCDA .... Touring Car Drivers Association [*Automobile racing*]
TCDD .... Tower Cab Digital Display　(PDAA)
TCE........... Talker Communication Error　(IAA)
TCE........... Test Connection Equipment　(IAA)
TCE........... Trans-Colorado Airlines, Inc. [*ICAO designator*]　(FAAC)
TCF!.......... Totally Chlorine-Free [*Pulp and paper processing*]
TCI............ Turbocharged Generation One [*Automotive engine identification*]
TCI............ Turks & Caicos National Airlines [*ICAO designator*]　(FAAC)
TCIV.......... Turbocharged Generation 4 [*Automotive engine identification*]
TCL........... Escape Aviation [*ICAO designator*]　(FAAC)
TCL........... Target Cleanup Level [*Environmental science*]　(ERG)
TCL........... Traction Control [*Mitsubishi*] [*Transmission systems*]
TCL........... Transmit Clock　(IAA)
TCLo......... Toxic Concentration Low　(ERG)
TCM .... Teledyne Continental Motors [*ICAO designator*]　(FAAC)
TCM .... Temperature-Compensated Mask　(IAA)
TCM .... Temperature-Compensation　(IAA)
TCM .... Time Compression Multiplex　(IAA)
TCM .... Tone Code Modulation　(IAA)
TCM .... Translator CAM [*Computer-Aided Manufacturing*] Magnet
　　　　　　(IAA)
TCMA .... Telephone Cable Makers' Association [*British*]　(BI)
TCMA .... Tufted Carpet Manufacturers' Association [*British*]　(BI)
TCMIS ...... TRADOC [*Training and Doctrine Command*] Command
　　　　　　Management Information System [*Military*]
TCML........ Target Correlation Map Locator [*Military*]　(PDAA)
TCN........... Trans Continental Airlines [*ICAO designator*]　(FAAC)
TCO........... Temperature Coefficient of Offset　(IAA)

TCO .... Transfer on Channel in Operation (IAA)
TCO .... Translational Control (IAA)
TCOCD ...... Thermocouple Open Circuit Detection (IAA)
TCP............. [The] Acronym Generator Converter Program [RCA computer program] (IAA)
TCP............ Telecommunications Processor (IAA)
TCP............ Thermoform Continuous Percolation (IAA)
TCP............ Transcorp Airways [British] [ICAO designator] (FAAC)
TCP............ Transfer of Control Point [Aviation] (FAAC)
TCPLD .... Tunable Compound Phase-Locked Demodulator (IAA)
TCR .... Laneas Aeraes Trans Costa Rica SA [ICAO designator] (FAAC)
TCR .... Tactical Control RADAR (IAA)
TCR .... Television Cathode Ray (IAA)
TCR .... Thermal Coefficient of Resistance (IAA)
TCR .... Transistorized Car Radio (IAA)
TCR .... Transportable Cassette Recorder (IAA)
TCS............. Tactical Call Sign (IAA)
TCS............. Temperature Coefficient of Sensitivity (IAA)
TCS............. Terminal Count Sequence (IAA)
TCS............. Thermal Conditioning Service (IAA)
TCS............. Tone Call Squelch [Telecommunications] (IAA)
TCS............. Transmission Control System (IAA)
TCS............. Transportes de Carga Aerea Especializada y Servicios Aeronauticos [Mexico] [ICAO designator] (FAAC)
TCS............. Trichosanthin [Botany]
TCSEV .... Twin-Cushion Surface Effect Vehicle (PDAA)
TCSL .... Transistor Current Switching Logic [Electronics] (IAA)
TCT............. Terminal Control Table [Computer science] (IAA)
TCT............. Tur Avrupa Havayollari AS [Turkey] [ICAO designator] (FAAC)
TCTS .... Tactical Combat Training System [Navy]
TCU .... Target Control Unit (IAA)
TCU .... Tight Close-Up [Cinematography] (NTCM)
TCV .... Transportes Aereos de Cabo Verde [Cape Verde] [ICAO designator] (FAAC)
TD............... Tape Distributor [Computer science] (IAA)
TD............... Telephone Depot (IAA)
TD............... Test and Diagnostics (IAA)
TD............... Threshold Decoding [Computer science] (IAA)
TD............... Toyota Diffusion/Deposition (IAA)
TD............... Transaction Driven (IAA)
TD............... Transducer [Electronics] (IAA)
TD............... Trapped Domain (IAA)
TDA .... Temporary Danger Area (DA)
TDA .... Transcarga SA [Costa Rica] [ICAO designator] (FAAC)
TDaRI........ Tropical Development and Research Institute (PDAA)
TDAS.......... Tactical Data Automation System (IAA)
TDB .... Task Database [Computer science] (PCM)
TDB .... Welch Aviation, Inc. [ICAO designator] (FAAC)
TDC .... Tadair SA [Spain] [ICAO designator] (FAAC)
TDC .... Technical Development Capital (IAA)
TDC .... Time of Day Clock (IAA)
TDC .... Tone Digital Command (IAA)
TDC .... Top Desk Computer (IAA)
TDC .... Totally Decentralized Control (IAA)
TDC .... Transistor Digital Circuit (IAA)
TDC .... Transistor Digital Control (IAA)
TDC .... Transmission Distribution Center (IAA)
TDC .... Transport Code for Computer (IAA)
TDC .... Two-Dimensional Finite Cylinder (IAA)
TDD .... Telecommunications for the Deaf and Disabled
TDD........... Timing Data Distributor (IAA)
TDDLPO.... Time-Division Data Link Print-Out [Telecommunications] (IAA)
TDDS .... Two-Dimensional Deflection System (IAA)
TDE .... Time Displacement Error (IAA)
TDF .... Transformer Differential (IAA)
TDFL .... Tunnel-Diode FET [Field-Effect Transistor] Logic (IAA)
TDI .... Tolerable Daily Intake [Toxicology]
TDIA .... Transient Data Input Area [Computer science] (IAA)
TDIPRE..... Target Data Inventory Master Tape Preparation [Military] (IAA)
TDL .... Telemetry Data Link [Telecommunications] (IAA)
TDLo .... Toxic Dose Low (ERG)
TDMA .... Time Distributed Multiple Access (IAA)
TDMS......... Telegraphic Distortion Measuring Set (IAA)
TDO........... Task Direction Order [Military]
TDO........... Technical Direction Order
TDO........... Transistor Dip Oscillator (IAA)
TDO........... Transporte Aereco Dominicano [Dominican Republic] [ICAO designator] (FAAC)
TDOA/DME ... Time Difference of Arrival / Distance Measuring Equipment (PDAA)
TDPI.......... Two-Dimensional Probabilistic Image (PDAA)
TDPM .... Time-Domain Prony Method (IAA)
TDR .... Canair Cargo [Canada] [ICAO designator] (FAAC)
TDR .... Short Tour Return Date [Military]
TDR .... Traffic Data Record (DA)
TDS .... Teleprocessing Design Center [Army] (PDAA)
TDS .... Test Data Specification (IAA)
TDS .... Tuned LASER Differential Spectrometry (IAA)
TDSSC ...... Tone Dial Switching System Control (IAA)
TDTO .... Transmission and Drive Train Oil
TDY .... Air Today, Inc. [ICAO designator] (FAAC)
TDZE.......... Touchdown Zone Elevation [Aviation] (DA)

TE .... Tape Error [Computer science] (IAA)
TE .... Taxiway Edge Lighting [Aviation] (DA)
TE .... Telemetry Event [Telecommunications] (IAA)
TE .... Telephone Equipment Room [NFPA pre-fire planning symbol] (NFPA)
TE .... Terminal [Computer science] (IAA)
TE .... Threshold Element (IAA)
TE .... Threshold Exceeded (IAA)
TE .... Time Equipment (IAA)
TE .... Transistor Equivalent [Electronics] (IAA)
TE .... Transverse Electrostatic (IAA)
TEA .... Trans European Airways [Belgium] [ICAO designator] (FAAC)
TEA .... Triethylaluminum (IAA)
TEADDA.... Teledyne Electrically-Alterable Digital Differential Analyzer (IAA)
TEAM .... Training Equipment and Maintenance [Aviation] (DA)
TEAM .... Truth, Esteem, Attitude, and Motivation [Name of actor Chuck Norris' anti-gang project]
TEARS ...... Traffic Engineering for Automatic Route Selection (PDAA)
TEAWC...... Totally-Enclosed Air Water-Cooled Reactor [Nuclear energy] (IAA)
TEB............ Tape Error Block [Computer science] (IAA)
TEB............ Tris-Ethylenediaminetetra-Acetate Borate [Organic chemistry] (MAH)
TEC............ [The] Elongated Collectors [An association] (EA)
TEC............ Tea Cyprus Ltd. [ICAO designator] (FAAC)
TEC............ Test Evaluation and Control (IAA)
TEC............ Thermoelectric Cooler (IAA)
TECCS .... Tactical Engagement Close Combat System [Army]
TECDOC.... Technical Documentation [DoD]
TECHSPECS ... Technical Specifications (IAA)
TED .... Teddy Air AS [Norway] [ICAO designator] (FAAC)
TED .... Teleprinter Error Detector (IAA)
TEE .... Tubular Extendible Element (PDAA)
TEEAR ...... Test Equipment Error Analysis Report (IAA)
TEF............ Thyrotroph Embryonic Factor [Genetics]
TEF............ Tilted Electric Field (PDAA)
TEF............ Total Effective Fare (PDAA)
TEF............ Total Energy Feasibility (IAA)
TEF............ Toxic Equivalency Factor [Environmental Protection Agency]
TEFC .... Totally-Enclosed Force-Cooled Reactor [Nuclear energy] (IAA)
TEGI.......... Train-Elevated Guideway Interaction (PDAA)
TEH........... Tempelhof Airways, Inc. [Germany] [ICAO designator] (FAAC)
TEHOS ...... Tetrakis(ethylhexoxy)silane [Organic chemistry]
TEI .... Societa' Tea Italia [Italy] [ICAO designator] (FAAC)
TEI .... Time Error Indicated (IAA)
TEISS........ [The] Enhanced Integrated Soldier System [Army]
TEJ .... Transportes Aeros Ejecutivos SA de CV [Mexico] [ICAO designator] (FAAC)
TEL............ Telegraphic (NTCM)
TEL............ Telephone Group (IAA)
TEL............ Telephone Station (IAA)
TEL............ Telephonic (NTCM)
TEL............ Telephony (NTCM)
TEL............ Teletype (NTCM)
TEL............ Television (IAA)
TEL............ Telford Aviation, Inc. [ICAO designator] (FAAC)
TEL............ Tokyo Electron Ltd. (IAA)
TEL............ Total Energy Loss (IAA)
TELATEL ... Telephone and Telegraph (IAA)
TELAU...... Teleautograph [ICAO designator] (FAAC)
TELCO ...... Telephone Communications (IAA)
TELCO .... Telephone Company [ICAO designator] (FAAC)
TELD........ Teledate Equipment [Military]
TELD........ Transferred Electron Logic Device (IAA)
TELDEC .... Telefunken-Decca [Video disk system] (IAA)
TELE .... Telephoto (NTCM)
TELECON ... Teletypewriter Conference (IAA)
TELEFAC ... Television Facsimile (NTCM)
TELENGR ... Telephone Engineer [Telecommunications] (IAA)
Telescription ... Television Transcription (NTCM)
TELEX ...... Telegraph Exchange [Telecommunications] (IAA)
TELEX ...... Teleprinter Exchange [Telecommunications] (IAA)
TELEX ...... Teleprocessing Executive [Telecommunications] (IAA)
TELL .... Teacher-Aiding Electronic Learning Link (PDAA)
TELN......... Telephone (IAA)
TELNO ...... Telephone Number (IAA)
TELOP....... Television Optical (NTCM)
TELSAT .... Television Satellite (NTCM)
TELSTATS ... Telemetry Station System [Telecommunications] (IAA)
TELTAP.... Telephone Tape (IAA)
TELTIPS.... Technical Effort Locator and Technical Interest Profile System [Army] (IAA)
TELTRAC ... Telemetry Tracking [Telecommunications] (IAA)
TEM .... TELEX Extended Memory (IAA)
TEM .... Terrestrial Ecosystem Model [for climate effects]
TEM .... Text Excursion Module (IAA)
TEM .... Transmission Engineering Memorandum (IAA)
TEM .... Transverse Electromagnetic Mode [Telecommunications] (IAA)
TEMA .... Tank Equipment Manufacturers' Association (IAA)
TEMA .... Telecommunication Engineering and Manufacturing Association [British] (IAA)
TEMA .... Test Macro [Computer science] (IAA)

TEMANS... Tactical Effectiveness of Minefields in the Antiarmor Weapons System (PDAA)
TEMMA .... Transmission Electron Microscopy and Microprobe Analysis (PDAA)
T(EMP)...... Time to Emplacement [*Military*]
TEN .... Tennessee Airways, Inc. [*ICAO designator*] (FAAC)
TEP............ Temporary Entry Permit
TEP............ Tetraethyl Pyrophosphate [*Insecticide*] [*Pharmacology*] (IAA)
TEP............ Training Equipment Plan
TEPC......... Tissue Equivalent Proportional Counter (PDAA)
TE & R........ Tactical Engagement and Range [*Army*]
TER .... Teleprinter Retransmitting [*Telecommunications*] (IAA)
TER .... Territorial Airlines, Inc. [*ICAO designator*] (FAAC)
TER .... Transmission Engineering Recommendation [*Telecommunications*] (IAA)
TERCO...... Telephone Rationalization by Computer (PDAA)
TEREC...... Tactical Electromagnetic Reconnaissance [*Air Force*] (IAA)
TERI .... Table of Equipment Ready Issue [*Navy*] (ANA)
TERN .... Terminal and Enroute Navigation (PDAA)
TERP........ Turbine Engine Reliability Program (PDAA)
TERRA...... Terrain Evaluation and Retrieval for Road Alignment (IAA)
TES.......... Transportes Aereos de El Salvador SA de CV [*ICAO designator*] (FAAC)
TESAT...... Teaching Sample Table (PDAA)
TESH........ Test Shop
TESS .... [*The*] Educational Software Selector [*Database*] (AEE)
TESS .... Total Energy Systems Service (IAA)
TESSAC..... Tactical Electromagnetic Systems Study Action Council [*Navy*] (ANA)
TESSAR..... Test Event Sequencing, Simulating, and Recording System (PDAA)
TESY .... Terminal Editing System [*Computer science*] (PDAA)
TET........... Traveling-Wave Tube (IAA)
TETRA ...... Terminal Trajectory Telescope (IAA)
TETRAC ... Tetraiodothyroacetic Acid [*Organic chemistry*] (MAH)
TETROON ... Tethered Meteorological Balloon (IAA)
TEU .... Trailing Edge Up
TEV .... T-Platform Electric Van [*Chrysler*] [*Automotive engineering*]
TEWR........ Thrust to Earth Weight Ratio (IAA)
TEX .... Catex Compagnie [*France*] [*ICAO designator*] (FAAC)
TEX .... Teleprinter Exchange Service [*Telecommunications*] (IAA)
TEX .... Temperature Excess (PDAA)
TEXTINDY ... Textile Industry (IAA)
TEY .... Total Electron Yield [*Spectroscopy*]
TF .... Talker Function [*Telecommunications*] (IAA)
TF .... Thermionic Field (IAA)
TF .... Threshold Function (IAA)
TF .... Time Frequency (IAA)
TF .... Total Float (IAA)
TF .... Transfer (IAA)
TF .... Transversal Filter (IAA)
Tf............. Trufocus [*Lamp base type*] (NTCM)
TFA.......... Technology Forecasting and Assessment (IAA)
TFA.......... TELEX File Adapter (IAA)
TFA.......... Trans-Florida Airlines, Inc. [*ICAO designator*] (FAAC)
TFAD......... Thin-Film Active Device (IAA)
TFB.......... Towed Flexible Barge (PDAA)
TFE.......... Television Film Exhibit (NTCM)
TFE.......... Thermal Field Emission (IAA)
TFET .... Thin-layer Field-Effect Transistor (IAA)
TFF .... Thermoplastic Covered Fixture Wire Flexible Stranding (IAA)
TFF .... Thin-Film FET [*Field-Effect Transistor*] (IAA)
TFF .... Toggle Flip-Flop [*Computer science*] (IAA)
TFFET....... Thin-Film Field-Effect Transistor (IAA)
TFFT .... Truly Fast Fourier Transform (PDAA)
TFG .... Thrust Floated Gyroscope (PDAA)
TFH .... Temporal Fourier Hologram (PDAA)
TFH .... Thai Flying Helicopter Service Co. Ltd. [*Thailand*] [*ICAO designator*] (FAAC)
TFHC .... Thick-Film Hybrid Circuit (IAA)
TFIC .... Thin-Film Integrated Circuit (IAA)
TFIO......... Thin Film Integrated Optics (PDAA)
TFL........... Tayflight Ltd. [*British*] [*ICAO designator*] (FAAC)
TFL........... Transformerless (IAA)
TFM .... TFTR [*Tokamak Fusion Test Reactor*] Flexibility Modification
TFM .... Time Quantized Frequency Modulation [*Telecommunications*] (IAA)
TFOF......... Taxi Fleet Operators' Federation [*British*] (BI)
TFR.......... Trans European Airways SA [*France*] [*ICAO designator*] (FAAC)
TFS-CT...... Tin-Free Steel Chromium-Type (PDAA)
TFSK .... Time Frequency Shift Keying [*Computer science*] (IAA)
TFTC .... Thin-Film Thermocouple (IAA)
TFY........... Tayside Aviation Ltd. [*British*] [*ICAO designator*] (FAAC)
TG .... Tangent [*Mathematics*] (IAA)
TG .... Tasmanian Greens [*Australia*] [*Political party*]
TG .... Timing Gage (IAA)
TG .... Torque Generator (IAA)
TG .... Transfer Gate (IAA)
TG .... Transformational Grammar
TG .... Transmission Group (IAA)
TG .... Trigger (IAA)
TG .... Trigger Generator
TGA .... Togo Airlines [*ICAO designator*] (FAAC)

TGC .... Terminator Group Controller (IAA)
TGC .... TG Aviation Ltd. [*British*] [*ICAO designator*] (FAAC)
TGC .... Time Gain Control (IAA)
TGCA .... Transportable Ground Control Approach (IAA)
TGE .... Trabajos Aereos SA [*Spain*] [*ICAO designator*] (FAAC)
TGGE .... Temperature-Gradient Gel Electrophoresis [*Analytical biochemistry*]
TGI .... Target Group Index (NTCM)
TGL .... Trans-Atlantic Airlines Ltd. [*Gambia*] [*ICAO designator*] (FAAC)
TGO .... Canada-Transport Canada [*ICAO designator*] (FAAC)
TGS.......... Transfer Generator System (IAA)
TGS........... True Ground Speed (IAA)
TGS.......... Turret Gun System [*Army*]
TGT .... Teams-Games-Tournaments [*Education*] (AEE)
TGT .... Ticket-Granting Ticket [*Computer science*]
TGT .... Transformational Grammar Tester (IAA)
TGTP......... Tuned Grid Tuned Plate [*Electronic plate*] (IAA)
TGZMP....... Temperature-Gradient Zone-Melting Process [*Chemistry*] (IAA)
TH............ Tape-Handler [*Computer science*] (IAA)
TH............ Telegraph (IAA)
TH............ Test Header (Fire Pump) [*NFPA pre-fire planning symbol*] (NFPA)
TH............ Threat
TH............ Thyssen Henschel
TH............ Tracking Head (IAA)
THA.......... Thai Airways International Ltd. [*Thailand*] [*ICAO designator*] (FAAC)
THC.......... Tar Heel Aviation, Inc. [*ICAO designator*] (FAAC)
THC.......... Third-Harmonic Distortion [*Physics*] (IAA)
THC-CRC ... Tetrahydrocannabinol Cross-Reacting-Cannabinoid [*Active principle of marijuana*] (PDAA)
THD.......... Third-Harmonic Distortion [*Physics*] (IAA)
THEUS ...... Theoretical Earth Utilization System (PDAA)
THFA........ Thermal Hartree-Fock Approximation (PDAA)
THG.......... Thurston Aviation Ltd. [*British*] [*ICAO designator*] (FAAC)
THL.......... Air Thanet [*British*] [*ICAO designator*] (FAAC)
THN .... Athens Air [*Greece*] [*ICAO designator*] (FAAC)
THO.......... Trans-Hudson Orogen [*Geology*]
THOF .... Triple Conductor, Heat, Oil, and Flame Resistant (IAA)
THOMOTROL ... Thyratron Motor Control [*Electronics*] (IAA)
THORAD... Transistorized High-Speed Operations Recorder Advanced (IAA)
THOT .... Transportation Horoscope of Trade Goods (PDAA)
THP .... Thousands Position (IAA)
THPI .... Tetrahydrophthalimide [*Organic chemistry*]
Thr .... Threshold Lights [*Aviation*] (DA)
THR.......... Total Heat Rejection (IAA)
THRES...... Threshold (IAA)
THROE....... Tessaral Harmonic Resonance of Orbital Elements (PDAA)
THS.......... Transports Aeros Hispanos SA [*Spain*] [*ICAO designator*] (FAAC)
THT .... Token-Holding Time [*Computer science*]
THT .... Turk Hava Tasimaciligi [*Turkish Air Transport*] [*ICAO designator*] (FAAC)
THTRA ...... Thorium High Temperature Reactor Association (IAA)
THU .... Truck Hub Unit [*Suspension*] [*Automotive engineering*]
THY.......... Thyratron [*Electronics*] (IAA)
THY........... Turk Hava Yollari [*Turkish Airlines*] [*ICAO designator*] (FAAC)
TI .... Tape Indicator [*Computer science*] (IAA)
TI .... Technoogy Innovation (IAA)
TI .... Television Intercity [*FCC*] (NTCM)
TI .... Terminator Interrupt [*Computer science*] (IAA)
TI .... Tourismo Internationale [*International Touring*] [*Italian*]
T and I....... Trade and Industrial Education (AEE)
TI .... Tuning Inductance (IAA)
TI .... Turismo Internazionale [*Automobile model designation*]
TIA .... Temporary Incapacity Allowance
TIA .... Trans International Airlines [*ICAO designator*] (FAAC)
TIAA-CREF ... Teachers Insurance and Annuity Association-College Retirement Equities Fund (AEE)
TIAM .... Terminal Interactive Access Method [*Computer science*] (IAA)
TIB............. Technical Intelligence Branch [*National Coal Board*] (PDAA)
TIB............. Twin I-Beam [*Ford Motor Co.*] [*Truck front suspension*]
TIBA......... Traffic Information Broadcast by Aircraft (DA)
TIC........... Tantalum Integrated Circuit [*Electronics*] (PDAA)
TIC........... Thermal Image Camera (PDAA)
TICA......... Thermal Insulation Contractors' Association [*British*] (BI)
TICS .... Timing and Injection Rate Control System [*Diesel engines*]
TID .... Tax Installment Deduction
TID .... Thermal Identification Device
TID .... Touch Input Device [*Computer science*] (IAA)
TIDE......... Transponder Interrogation and Decoding Equipment [*Telecommunications*] (IAA)
TIDG .... TAPER Isolated Dynamic Gain (IAA)
TIDS.......... Talker Idle State [*Telecommunications*] (IAA)
TIFET........ Thin-Layer Field Effect Transistor (IAA)
TIGFFO...... Teenage, Infants, and Girls' Fashion Fair Organisation [*British*] (BI)
TIGOR ...... Time Interval Gage of Relays [*Telecommunications*] (IAA)
TIGR......... [*The*] Institute of Genomic Research
TIHBSS...... [*The*] I Hate Barney Secret Society (EA)
TII............. Tourismo Internationale Injection [*International Touring-fuel Injection*] [*Italian*]

TILCAR ..... Tactical Infantry Load Carrier Amphibious Remote [*Military*] (PDAA)
TILT .... Texas Instruments Language Translator [*Computer science*] (IAA)
TIM .... Temperature Independent Material   (IAA)
TIM .... Terminal Interface Monitor   (IAA)
TIM .... Time Indicator   (IAA)
TIM .... Trends in Microbiology [*A publication*]
TIMADS .... Timber Management Decision System   (PDAA)
TIMARC.... Time Multiplexed Analogue Radio Control   (PDAA)
TIMIX .... Texas Instruments Minicomputer Information Exchange   (IAA)
TIMNET .... Time Share International Data Communications Network [*Telecommunications*]   (IAA)
TIMS .... Technical Information Management System
TIMS .... Telecommunications Instruction Module System   (IAA)
TIMS .... Transmission Impairment Measuring System   (IAA)
TIN .... Taino Tours [*Dominican Republic*] [*ICAO designator*]   (FAAC)
TINA .... Truth in Negotiations Act
TINS .... Trains Inertial Navigation System   (IAA)
TINT.......... Teletype Interpreter   (PDAA)
TIO .... Technology Innovation Office [*Environmental Protection Agency*]
TIO .... Transistorized Image Orthicon Camera   (IAA)
TIOL.......... Texas Instruments Cassette Operating Language   (IAA)
TIP............ C & M Aviation, Inc. [*ICAO designator*]   (FAAC)
TIP............ Technology in Production   (IAA)
TIP............ Traveling in Core Probe   (IAA)
TIPISPO .... Tactical Intelligence Processing and Interpretation System Program Office [*Air Force*]   (PDAA)
TIR............ Test Incident Report   (IAA)
TIR............ Thermal Infrared   (PDAA)
TIR.......... True Indicated Radius   (IAA)
TIRES......... Transient Infrared Emission Spectroscopy
TIRFM ...... Total Internal Reflectional Fluorescence Microscopy
TIRIS......... Texas Instruments Registration and Identification System [*Auto theft deterrent*]
TIROS-N.... Television Infrared-Observation Satellite NOAA [*National Oceanographic and Atmospheric Administration*] [*Navy*]   (ANA)
TIS............ Technical Information Series   (IAA)
TIS............ Tesis [*Russian Federation*] [*ICAO designator*]   (FAAC)
TIS............ Transit Injection Station   (IAA)
TISAB .... Total Ionic Strength Adjustment Buffer   (PDAA)
TISE .... Technical Information Service   (IAA)
TIT............ Ternary Digit   (IAA)
TIT............ Trouble Indicator Trunk [*Telecommunications*]   (IAA)
TITAN....... Teamster's International Terminal and Accounting Network (IAA)
TITF .... Test Item Transmittal Form   (IAA)
TITTI .... Texas Instruments Transistor Transistor Logic   (IAA)
TIV .... Total Indicator Variation   (IAA)
TIVICON ... Texas Instruments Vidicon   (IAA)
TIWP......... Toxicology Information Working Party   (PDAA)
TIX............ Transfer on Index [*Telecommunications*]   (IAA)
TIX............ Triax Airlines Ltd. [*Nigeria*] [*ICAO designator*]   (FAAC)
TIZ............ Traffic Information Zone   (DA)
TJ.............. Cameroon [*Aircraft nationality and registration mark*]   (FAAC)
TJ.............. Trunk Junctor [*Telecommunications*]   (IAA)
TJF .... Test Jack Field [*Telecommunications*]   (IAA)
TJK .... Tajikair [*Tajikistan*] [*ICAO designator*]   (FAAC)
TJT .... Tri-Junction Transistor   (IAA)
TK .... Trunk   (IAA)
TKA .... Air Troika [*Russian Federation*] [*ICAO designator*]   (FAAC)
TKE .... Trek Airways [*South Africa*] [*ICAO designator*]   (FAAC)
TKH .... Thick [*Aviation*]   (DA)
TKR .... Canadian Interagency Forest Fire Centre [*ICAO designator*] (FAAC)
TL .... Terminology Library [*Computer science*]   (IAA)
TL .... Trailer Length [*Specifications*] [*Automotive engineering*]
TL .... Transformation Line [*Telecommunications*]   (IAA)
TL .... Transistor Logic   (IAA)
TL .... Transition Level   (DA)
TL .... Transmission Line [*Telecommunications*]   (IAA)
TL .... Transmission Loss [*Telecommunications*]   (IAA)
TL .... Trunk Load [*Telecommunications*]   (IAA)
TLA .... TELEX Line Adapter   (IAA)
TLA .... Thin-Layer Activation [*Engine wear testing*]
TLA .... Three-Letter Acronym [*Computer hacker terminology*]   (NHD)
TLA .... Translift Airways Ltd. [*British*] [*ICAO designator*]   (FAAC)
TLAM/C .... Tomahawk Land Attack Missile/Conventional [*Navy*]   (ANA)
TLC............ Caribbean Express, Inc. [*ICAO designator*]   (FAAC)
TLC............ Teachable Language Comprehender   (PDAA)
TLC............ Temperature Level Control   (IAA)
TLC............ Texaco Lubricants Co. [*Automotive industry supplier*]
TLC............ Thermochromic Liquid Crystal
TLC............ Total Library Computerization
TLC............ Traditional Life Cycle   (PDAA)
TLC............ Transmit Level Control   (PDAA)
TLCC .... Training Launch Control Center   (IAA)
TLD .... Telephone Line Doubler   (IAA)
TLE .... Air Toulouse [*France*] [*ICAO designator*]   (FAAC)
TLE .... Test Laboratory Engineer   (IAA)
TLET .... Transitional Low-Emission Truck
TLG .... Telegram   (IAA)

TLG .... Timing Level Generator   (IAA)
TLIR .... Time-Limited Impulse Response [*Telecommunications*]   (IAA)
TLJP.......... Thermal Liquid Junction Potential   (PDAA)
TLLE .... Twin Linear Loop Exciter   (IAA)
TLM .... Transformer Load Management   (IAA)
TLMCTLPNL ... Telemetry Control Panel   (IAA)
TLP............ Term Lease Plan   (IAA)
TLP............ Tulip Air [*Netherlands*] [*ICAO designator*]   (FAAC)
TLR........... Northern Airlines [*British*] [*ICAO designator*]   (FAAC)
TLRP .... Trace Last Reference Position   (IAA)
TLRS .... Tramway and Light Railway Society [*British*]   (BI)
TLS .... Target Level of Safety   (DA)
TLS .... Test Line Signal   (IAA)
TLS .... TLC Air, Inc. [*ICAO designator*]   (FAAC)
TLS .... Translocated in Liposarcoma [*Genetics*]
TLSER....... Theoretical Linear Solvation Energy Relationship [*Physical chemistry*]
TLT........... Telecommunications Translator   (IAA)
TLT........... Terminal List Table   (IAA)
TLT........... Turtle Airways Ltd. [*Fiji*] [*ICAO designator*]   (FAAC)
TLTP .... Teletype   (IAA)
TLU .... Teaching-Learning Unit   (AEE)
TLV........... Television   (IAA)
TLV-C........ Threshold Limit Value - Ceiling [*Industrial hygiene*]   (PDAA)
TLV-STEL ... Threshold Limit Value - Short Term Exposure Limit [*Industrial hygiene*]   (PDAA)
TLV-TWA ... Threshold Limit Value - Time-Weighted Average [*Industrial hygiene*]   (PDAA)
tlymn.......... Tallyman
TM............ Task Memory [*Computer science*]   (IAA)
TM............ Team Manager
TM............ Terminal Multiplexer [*Computer science*]   (IAA)
TM............ Time   (FAAC)
TM............ Transaction Manager [*Computer science*]
TM............ Transaction Mode   (IAA)
TM............ Translator Code Magnet   (IAA)
TM............ Trunk Mark [*Telecommunications*]   (IAA)
TMA .... Telemetry Manufacturers' Association   (IAA)
TMA .... Total Market Coverage [*Advertising*]   (NTCM)
TMA .... Trans Mediterranean Airlines [*Lebanon*] [*ICAO designator*] (FAAC)
TMA .... Travelling and Meal Allowance
TMA .... Truck Master Association [*Auto enthusiast organization*]
TM/ACS .... True-Motion, Anti-Collision System   (PDAA)
TMAMA .... Textile Machinery and Accessory Manufacturers Association [*British*]   (BI)
TM/BAC .... True-Motion, Basic Collision Avoidance   (PDAA)
TMC.......... Tarmac Plc [*British*] [*ICAO designator*]   (FAAC)
TMC.......... Telephone Manufacturing Company   (IAA)
TMC.......... Terminal Control   (DA)
TMC.......... Test Monitoring Center [*ASTM*] [*Engineering standards*]
TMC.......... Traffic Management Channel [*Navigation and driver information systems*]
TMCF......... Toastmasters and Masters of Ceremonies Federation [*British*] (BI)
TMCP......... Technical Manual Control Panel   (IAA)
TMCP......... Thermal Mechanical Controlled Processing   (PDAA)
TMD.......... Total Mean Downtime [*Computer science*]   (IAA)
TMD.......... Transmed Airlines [*Egypt*] [*ICAO designator*]   (FAAC)
TMDI .... Theoretical Maximum Daily Intake [*Toxicology*]
TME .... Temperature Measuring Equipment   (IAA)
TMF .... Third Moment of Frequency   (PDAA)
TMF .... Time Multiplication Factor [*Offshore racing*]
TMG .... Thermometeroid Garnet   (IAA)
TmG.......... [*Maximal*] Tubular Reabsorption Rate of Glucose [*Physiology*] (MAH)
TMHF .... Transit Missile Hold Facility [*Military*]   (IAA)
TMHR........ Tandem Mirror Hybrid Reactor   (PDAA)
TMI .... Telemeter Magnetics, Inc.   (IAA)
TMI .... Texas Microelectronics, Inc.   (IAA)
TMI .... Tuning Meter Indicator   (IAA)
TMIC......... Test Management Information System
TMIS......... Television Management Information System   (IAA)
TMIS......... Transmission Impairment Measuring Set [*Telecommunications*]   (IAA)
TMK.......... Tomahawk Airways, Inc. [*ICAO designator*]   (FAAC)
TML .... Two Mixed Layer   (IAA)
TMM......... TELEX Main Memories [*Telecommunications*]   (IAA)
TMME .... Toyota Motor Marketing and Engineering [*Automotive industry, corporate subsidiary*]
TMN.......... Tjumenaviatrans [*Russian Federation*] [*ICAO designator*] (FAAC)
TMOF........ Trypsin-Modulating Oostatic Factor [*Biochemistry*]
TMOPS...... TRADOC [*Training and Doctrine Command*] Mobilization and Operations Planning System [*Military*]
TMP .... Test Market Plan [*Advertising*]   (NTCM)
TMP .... Test Market Profile [*Advertising*]   (NTCM)
TMP .... Tetramesitylporphyrin [*Organic chemistry*]
TMP .... Top Management Program
TMPA........ Traffic Management Program Alert [*Aviation*]   (FAAC)
TMQ.......... Thames Air Services & Charter Ltd. [*Nigeria*] [*ICAO designator*]   (FAAC)
TMR .... Teledyne Materials Research   (IAA)

TMR..........	True Motion RADAR (IAA)
TMS...........	[*The*] Metallurgy Society [*Formerly, MS*] (IAA)
TMS...........	Tape Management Software [*Computer science*] (IAA)
TMS...........	Telegraphy with Manual Switching [*Telecommunications*] (IAA)
TMS...........	Telemeter Transmitter (IAA)
TMS...........	Temsco Helicopters, Inc. [*ICAO designator*] (FAAC)
TMS...........	Track Monitor Supervisor (IAA)
TMT...........	Trans Midwest Airlines, Inc. [*ICAO designator*] (FAAC)
TMU..........	Time-Multiplexer Unit [*Telecommunications*] (IAA)
TMU..........	Twin and Multiply (IAA)
TMV..........	Triplicated Majority Voting (IAA)
TMX..........	Tactical Missile Experimental (IAA)
TMX..........	Transportacion Aerea Mexicana [*Mexico*] [*ICAO designator*] (FAAC)
TN.............	Task Number [*Computer science*] (IAA)
TN.............	Thanks (IAA)
TN.............	Tuning (IAA)
TNA...........	Tanavco Airways Ltd. [*Tanzania*] [*ICAO designator*] (FAAC)
TNA...........	Transistor Noise Analyzer (IAA)
TNA...........	Turn Altitude [*Aviation*] (FAAC)
TNB...........	Turnbull Associates [*British*] [*ICAO designator*] (FAAC)
TNC...........	National Aviation Consultants Ltd. [*Canada*] [*ICAO designator*] (FAAC)
TNC...........	Threaded Nut Connector (IAA)
TNC...........	Total Numerical Control (IAA)
TNC...........	Track Number Conversion (IAA)
TNC...........	Twisted Nematic Liquid [*Telecommunications*] (IAA)
TND...........	Tim Donut Ltd. [*Canada*] [*ICAO designator*] (FAAC)
TNE...........	Taxis Aereos del Noroeste SA de CV [*Mexico*] [*ICAO designator*] (FAAC)
TNEL.......	Total Noise Exposure Level (DA)
TNFE.......	Twisted Nemetic Field Effect [*Telecommunications*] (IAA)
TNG...........	G & B Aviation Ltd. [*British*] [*ICAO designator*] (FAAC)
TNGS.......	Theory of Neuronal Group Selection [*Neurology*]
TNH...........	Turn Height [*Aviation*] (FAAC)
TNLCD......	Twisted Nematic Liquid Crystal Display [*Telecommunications*] (IAA)
TNM..........	Twisted Nematic Mode [*Telecommunications*] (IAA)
TNR...........	Tanana Air Service [*ICAO designator*] (FAAC)
TNR...........	Total Network Recall [*Systems Enhancement Corp.*] [*Computer science*] (PCM)
TNR...........	Trinucleotide Repeat Sequence [*Genetics*]
TNS...........	Servicios Aereos do Vale Amazonico SA [*Brazil*] [*ICAO designator*] (FAAC)
TNS...........	Tumor Necrosis Serum (PDAA)
TNT...........	Target Network Television [*Cable television network*] (NTCM)
TNT...........	Theater Network Television (IAA)
TNT...........	Trans North Turbo Air Ltd. [*Canada*] [*ICAO designator*] (FAAC)
TNT...........	Tuned-Not-Tuned (IAA)
TNV...........	Tecnavia [*France*] [*ICAO designator*] (FAAC)
TNZ...........	Rex Aviation (New Zealand) Ltd. [*ICAO designator*] (FAAC)
TNZ...........	Transfer on No Zero (IAA)
TO.............	Take-Off (IAA)
TO.............	Telemetry Oscillator (IAA)
TO.............	Terminal Office [*Computer science*] (IAA)
TO.............	Time Over (IAA)
TO.............	Tool Offset (IAA)
TO.............	Tracking Officer (IAA)
TO.............	Turnover (NTCM)
TOA...........	Transferred on Assembly (IAA)
TOB...........	Tender Option Bond
TOCR........	Turn-Off Controlled Rectifier (PDAA)
TOCS........	Technological Aides to Creative Thoughts (IAA)
TOD...........	Transfer on Death [*Finance*]
TODC........	Triple Overriding Dual Control (IAA)
TOE...........	Tape Overlap Emulator [*Computer science*] (IAA)
TOF...........	Topcliffe FTU [*British*] [*ICAO designator*] (FAAC)
TOI............	Tactical Operations Initiation
TOJ...........	Time on Jamming (IAA)
TOJV.........	Track-on-Jam Valid [*Military*]
TOL...........	Tol-Air Services, Inc. [*ICAO designator*] (FAAC)
TOLCCS....	Trends in Online Computer Control Systems (PDAA)
TOLO........	Type of Legal Organization
TOM..........	Teleprinter on Multiplex [*Telecommunications*] (IAA)
TOM..........	Test Set, Overall Missile (IAA)
TOM..........	Toolmanager [*Computer science*] (IAA)
TOM..........	Transistor Oscillator Multiplier (IAA)
TOM..........	Transmitted Optical Microscopy
TOM..........	Transparent Office Manager [*Computer science*] (IAA)
TOMCIS....	Test of Multiple Corridor Identification System (IAA)
TOMHS....	Treatment of Mild Hypertension Study
TON..........	Aero Tonala [*Mexico*] [*ICAO designator*] (FAAC)
TON..........	Talk Only (IAA)
TONC........	Transient On-State Characteristics (PDAA)
TOOS........	Transaction-Oriented Operating System (IAA)
TOP...........	Aero Top SRL Societa [*Italy*] [*ICAO designator*] (FAAC)
TOP...........	Tool Package (IAA)
TOP...........	Top of Potentiometer [*Electronics*] (IAA)
TOP...........	Training for Opportunities in Programming (IAA)
TOP...........	Two-Axis Optical Pickoff (IAA)
TOPAZ.......	Technique for the Optimum Placement of Activities in Zones (PDAA)
TOPI..........	Tons of Paper In [*Computer science*] (IAA)

TOPIC.......	Teletext Output of Price Information by Computer [*London Stock Exchange*]
TOPL.........	Terminal-Operated Production Language (IAA)
TOPM........	Takeoff Performance Monitor [*Aviation*] (DA)
TOPO........	Tons of Paper Out [*Computer science*] (IAA)
TOPP.........	Training Outside Public Practice (PDAA)
TOPR........	Thermoplastic Optical Phase Recorder (IAA)
TOPSY.......	Time-Sharing Operation of Product Structure Directory System (PDAA)
TOR...........	Technical Oversight Representative
TOR...........	Teletype on Radio [*Telecommunications*] (IAA)
TOR...........	Thermal Overload Relay (IAA)
TOR...........	Toronto Airways Ltd. [*Canada*] [*ICAO designator*] (FAAC)
TOR...........	Track-on-Repeater [*Military*]
TORA.........	TRADOC [*Training and Doctrine Command*] Operations Research Activity [*Military*]
TORTOS....	Terminal Oriental Real-Time Operating System [*Computer science*] (IAA)
TOS	Time-Sharing Operating System [*Computer science*] (IAA)
TOS	Traffic Orientation Scheme (DA)
TOS	Tropical Air Services [*Belize*] [*ICAO designator*] (FAAC)
TOSA........	Takeoff Space Available [*Aviation*] (DA)
TOSAR......	Topological Representation of Synthetic and Analytical Relations of Concepts (PDAA)
TOST.........	Turbine Oil Stability Test [*Lubricant testing*] [*Automotive engineering*]
TOT...........	Total Outage Time (IAA)
TOT...........	Trioctyltin [*Organic chemistry*]
TOURS......	Tourist Observation and Underwater Research Submarine (PDAA)
TOV...........	Transfer on Overflow (IAA)
TOW..........	Tower Air, Inc. [*ICAO designator*] (FAAC)
TOWT........	Take Off Weight (IAA)
TOY...........	Toyota Canada, Inc. [*ICAO designator*] (FAAC)
TP.............	Television Pickup [*FCC*] (NTCM)
TP.............	Test Process
TP.............	Tire Pressure [*Automotive engineering*]
TP.............	Train Printer [*Computer science*] (IAA)
TP.............	Trigger Pulse [*Telecommunications*] (IAA)
TPA	Technical Performance Audit
TPA	Test Point Access (IAA)
TPA	Transportes Aereos Mercantiles Panamericanos [*Colombia*] [*ICAO designator*] (FAAC)
TPA	Two-Photon Absorption (PDAA)
TPAD	Teleprocessing Analysis and Design Program [*Computer science*] (IAA)
TPB............	Triphenylbenzene [*Organic chemistry*]
TPBV.........	Two-Point Boundary Value (PDAA)
TPC............	Air Caledonie [*France*] [*ICAO designator*] (FAAC)
TPC............	Telecommunications Program and Control (IAA)
TPC............	Total Print Control [*Computer science*] (IAA)
TPCOMP ...	Tape Compare [*Computer science*] (IAA)
TPCU........	Test Power Control Unit (IAA)
TPD	Total Program Diagnostic [*Computer science*] (IAA)
TPD	Trivial Problem Discriminator [*Computer science*] (IAA)
TPDC........	Test Point Data Chart [*Military*]
TPDT........	True Position Dimensioning and Tolerancing (PDAA)
TPDUP......	Tape Duplicate [*Computer science*] (IAA)
TPE...........	Total Publishing Environment [*Computer science*] (IAA)
TPE...........	Transmission Parity Error [*Computer science*] (IAA)
TPEM........	Tactical Peripherals Equipment Monitor [*Military*]
TPEO........	Trunk Piston Engine Oil [*Automotive lubricants*]
TPF...........	Toilet Preparations Federation [*British*] (BI)
TPF-A........	Total Package Fielding - Activation [*Military*]
TPG	Transmission Project Group (IAA)
TPG	Transportes Aereos Pegaso SA de CV [*Mexico*] [*ICAO designator*] (FAAC)
TPGID.......	Tank Precision Gunnery in Bore Device [*Army*]
TPH	Through Plated Hole [*Printed circuit board feature*] (IAA)
TPI............	Topair Ltd. [*Czechoslovakia*] [*ICAO designator*] (FAAC)
TPIB	Technical Panel for International Broadcast (NTCM)
TPIC	Thermophysical Properties Information Center [*Purdue University*] (IAA)
TPINIT......	Tape Initializer [*Computer science*] (IAA)
TPL...........	Teacher Programming Language [*Computer science*] (PDAA)
TPL...........	Telecommunications Programming Language (IAA)
TPL...........	Terminal Programming Language [*Computer science*] (IAA)
TPL...........	Total Peak Loss (IAA)
TPL...........	Turbopool Ltd. [*British*] [*ICAO designator*] (FAAC)
TPM	Total Preventative Maintenance [*Manufacturing*]
TPO	Threshold Planning Quantity (ERG)
TPO	Transmitter Power Output (NTCM)
T-POS.......	Target Position
TPP...........	Test Point Prelaunch Automatic Checkout Equipment [*NASA*] (IAA)
TPPD........	Technical Program Planning Document [*Air Force*] (IAA)
TPPR........	Tape-to-Printer [*Computer science*] (IAA)
TPR...........	Air Transport Pyrenees [*France*] [*ICAO designator*] (FAAC)
TPR...........	T-Pulse Response [*Telecommunications*] (IAA)
TPRA........	Tape-to-Random Access [*Computer science*] (IAA)
TPROC......	Test Procedure Specification [*NASA*] (IAA)
TPS...........	Teleprocessing System [*Computer science*] (IAA)
TPS...........	Television Program Standard

TPS............ Thyristor Power Supply [*Electronics*] (IAA)
TPS............ Tracking Antenna Pedestal System (IAA)
TPS............ Training Package System Planning (IAA)
TPSFG....... Two-Post Signal Flow Graph (PDAA)
TPSRS....... Terminal Primary and Secondary RADAR System (DA)
TPTC........ Temperature Pressure Test Chamber (IAA)
TPTP......... Tape-to-Tape [*Computer science*] (IAA)
TPU........... Terminal Processing Unit [*Computer science*] (IAA)
TPU........... Time Processing Unit [*Automotive engineering*] [*Electronics*]
TPU........... Transverse Propulsion Unit (PDAA)
TPY........... Trans-Provincial Airlines Ltd. [*Canada*] [*ICAO designator*] (FAAC)
TPZ........... Transportes La Paz SA de CV [*Mexico*] [*ICAO designator*] (FAAC)
TQF .... [*The*] Queen's Flight [*British*] [*ICAO designator*] (FAAC)
TQL .... Total Quality Leadership
TQP .... Total Quality and Productivity
TQS .... Total Quality Service
TQTMT...... TACJAM [*Tactical Communications Jamming System*] Quickfix, Trail Blazer Maintenance Trainer [*Army*]
TR .... Tactical RADAR [*Military*] (IAA)
TR .... Telegraph Repeater [*Telecommunications*] (IAA)
TR .... Testa Rossa [*Red engine cylinder head*] [*Ferrari automotive model designation*] [*Italian*]
TR .... Tetrode [*Electronics*] (IAA)
TR .... Thermal Resistance (IAA)
TR .... Time Delay Relay [*Computer science*] (IAA)
TR .... Time Routine [*Computer science*] (IAA)
TR .... Torque Receiver (IAA)
TR .... Torque Repeater (IAA)
TR .... Total Reaction (DA)
TR .... Transistor (IAA)
TR .... Translation (IAA)
TR .... Transmitter Receiver (IAA)
TR .... Transponder RADAR (IAA)
TRA .... [*The*] Razorback Award (IAA)
TRA .... Temporary Rental Allowance
TRA .... Temporary Reserved Airspace [*ICAO designator*] (FAAC)
TRA .... Transavia Holland BV [*Netherlands*] [*ICAO designator*] (FAAC)
TRAC........ Tracking and Communications [*Aviation*] (IAA)
TRAC........ Train Regulation Advisory Control (PDAA)
TRAC........ Trials Recording and Analysis Console (PDAA)
TRACAL.... Traffic Control and Landing [*Aviation*] (IAA)
TRACALS .. Traffic Control and Landing System [*Aviation*] (IAA)
TRACE....... Tape-Controlled Reckoning and Checkout Equipment [*Component of automatic pilot*] [*Aviation*] (IAA)
TRACE....... Time Repetitive Analog Contour Equipment (PDAA)
TRACE....... Transaction, Accounting, Control, and Endorsing (PDAA)
TRACE....... Transaction Control and Encoding (IAA)
TRACON ... Terminal RADAR Control (IAA)
TRACS ...... Traffic Reporting and Control System (IAA)
TRAD .... Traductrice (IAA)
TRAD .... Training Requirements Analysis Directorate [*Army*]
TRAD .... Training Research and Development (IAA)
TRADEX.... Tracking RADAR Experiment (IAA)
TRADIC.... Transistorized Digital Computer [*Air Force*] (IAA)
TRADO ...... Transporte Aereo Dominicano [*Dominican Republic*] [*ICAO designator*] (FAAC)
TRAFO...... Transformer (IAA)
TRAMEA... TRADOC [*Training and Doctrine Command*] Management Engineering Activity [*Military*]
TRAMMS ... Transportation Automated Material Movements System [*Army*] (PDAA)
TRAMP...... Target Radiation Measurement Program (IAA)
TRAMPS ... Text Information Retrieval and Management Program System [*Computer science*] (IAA)
TRAN .... Tax Revenue Anticipation Note [*Finance*]
TRANEX.... Transaction Executive (IAA)
TRANSAIEE ... Transactions of the American Association of Electrical Engineers (IAA)
TRANSALT ... Transition Altitude [*Aviation*] (DA)
TRANSC.... Transcribe (IAA)
TRANSC.... Transcription (IAA)
TRANSFDESENGR ... Transformer Design Engineer (IAA)
TRANSLEV ... Transition Level (DA)
TRANSRA ... Transistorized RADAR (IAA)
TRAPATT ... Trapped Plasma Avalanche Transit Time [*Bell Laboratories*] (IAA)
TRASER..... Transformer LASER (IAA)
TRAV .... Television, Radio, and Audio-Visuals of the Presbyterian Church in the United States (NTCM)
TRAX........ Three-Axis (IAA)
TRB .... Trans Air Bretagne [*France*] [*ICAO designator*] (FAAC)
TRC .... Technical Review Criteria (ERG)
TRC .... Time Ratio Control (IAA)
TRC .... Tobacco Research Council [*British*] (BI)
TRC .... Traffic Count and Listing [*Aviation*] (DA)
TRC .... Trans Air Charter, Inc. [*ICAO designator*] (FAAC)
TRC .... Transmitter Circuit (IAA)
TRC .... Transportation Research Command [*Army*] (IAA)
TRCF .... Transcription-Repair Coupling Factor [*Genetics*]
TRCHII...... Tanned Red Cell Hemagglutination Inhibition Immunoasay [*Immunology*] (PDAA)

TRCV......... Tri-color Visual Approach Slope Indicator [*Aviation*] (FAAC)
TRCVR....... Transceiver Transmitter Receiver (IAA)
TRD .... Technical Requirements Document
TRD .... Thermo-Reactive Deposition [*Metal treating*]
TRD .... Trans Island Air [*Barbados*] [*ICAO designator*] (FAAC)
TRDET....... Trouble Detection (IAA)
TRE .... Tax-Response Element [*Genetics*]
TRE .... Trans-Eastern Airlines Ltd. [*Kenya*] [*ICAO designator*] (FAAC)
TRE .... Type Rating Examiner [*Aviation*] (DA)
TREAS DEPT ... Department of the Treasury
TRF........... Air Transafrik Ltd. [*Ghana*] [*ICAO designator*] (FAAC)
TRG .... Atlantic Island Air [*Iceland*] [*ICAO designator*] (FAAC)
TRG .... Technical Review Group
TRGB........ Tail Rotor Gearbox [*Aviation*] (DA)
TRH........... Airmark Aviation, Inc. [*ICAO designator*] (FAAC)
TRI............ Transmission Interface Converter (IAA)
TRI............ Triclinic [*Crystallography*] (IAA)
TRIA.......... Tracking Range Instrumented Aircraft (PDAA)
TRIAC........ Triode Alternating Current (IAA)
TRIASS...... Triumph Adler Assembler (IAA)
TRIC.......... Tri-Camera (IAA)
Tric........... Tricycle [*A publication*]
TRICE .... Transistorized Real-Time Incremental Computer Expandable (IAA)
TRICO....... Tri- [*or Triple*] Coincidence Navigation (IAA)
TRIM.......... Task Related Instructional Methodology (PDAA)
TRIM.......... Tri-Mask Process (IAA)
TRIP .... Total Replenishment Inventory Program (PDAA)
TRIP .... Trajectory Integration Program (PDAA)
TRIP .... Truck Routing Improvement Program (IAA)
TRIPOD..... Tactical Reconstruction Information Pod [*Navy*] (ANA)
TRITET...... Triode-Tetrode (IAA)
TRIXIE...... Transistor and Nixie Tube (IAA)
TRJ .... AJT Air International [*Russian Federation*] [*ICAO designator*] (FAAC)
TRK .... Air Truck [*Spain*] [*ICAO designator*] (FAAC)
TRLVL ...... Transition Level [*Aviation*] (FAAC)
TrM .... Track Magnetic [*Aviation*] (DA)
TRM .... Transports Aeriens Mediterraneens [*France*] [*ICAO designator*] (FAAC)
TRMC .... Tetramethylrhodamino-Isothiocyanate [*Organic chemistry*] (MAH)
TRMPS ..... Temperature Regualtor and Missile Power Supply (IAA)
TRN........... Theron Airways [*South Africa*] [*ICAO designator*] (FAAC)
TRN........... Track Reference Number (IAA)
TRN........... Translation (IAA)
TRO........... Air Molokai-Tropic Airlines [*ICAO designator*] (FAAC)
Trop F H .... Tropical Fish Hobbyist [*A publication*]
TROS......... Time-Sharing Real-Time Operating System (IAA)
TROS......... Transducer Read Only Storage (IAA)
TROV .... Telepresence-Controlled Remotely-Operated Vehicle [*NASA*]
TRP........... Technology Reinvestment Project [*for converting military to civilian applications*]
TRP........... Time-Resolved Phosphorimetry [*Analytical chemistry*]
TRPCD....... Tropical Continental [*Meteorology*] (FAAC)
TRPSK ...... Transmitted Reference Phase Shift Keying [*Computer science*] (IAA)
TRR .... Take Real Result [*Computer science*] (IAA)
TRR .... Technical Risk Reduction [*Military*]
TRR .... Tramson Ltd. [*Sudan*] [*ICAO designator*] (FAAC)
TRR .... Transmitted-Reflected-Reflected [*Wave mechanics*]
TRR .... Trouble Recorder (IAA)
TRRA H & TS ... Terminal Railroad Association Historical and Technical Society (EA)
TRS............ Telephone Repeater Station (IAA)
TRS............ Track and Store [*Computer science*] (IAA)
TRS............ Transmit-Receive Switch (IAA)
TRS............ Transmitter (IAA)
TRS............ Transport International Aerien [*Belgium*] [*ICAO designator*] (FAAC)
TRSSM....... Tactical Range Ship-to-Shore Missile (IAA)
TrT............. Track True [*Aviation*] (DA)
TRT .... Trans Arabian Air Transport [*Sudan*] [*ICAO designator*] (FAAC)
TRT .... Translate and Test (IAA)
TRT .... Tropical Radio Telegraph [*Telecommunications*] (IAA)
TRUMF..... Total Package Unit Material Fielding [*Army*]
TRUS......... Transrectal Ultrasonography [*Medicine*]
TRUST....... Tamper-Resistant Unattended Safeguard Technique (PDAA)
TRUST....... Total Reevaluation Under SPRINT Thrust [*Army*]
TRV .... Transavia (Pty) Ltd. [*South Africa*] [*ICAO designator*] (FAAC)
TRW .... Trans Western Airlines of Utah [*ICAO designator*] (FAAC)
TRX .... Air Terrex [*Czechoslovakia*] [*ICAO designator*] (FAAC)
TRZON ..... Three Ton Range and Azimuth Only (IAA)
TS .... Tamper Switch [*NFPA pre-fire planning symbol*] (NFPA)
TS .... Telephone Set (IAA)
TS .... Television Studio-Transmitter-Link [*FCC*] (NTCM)
TS .... Terminal Series (IAA)
TS .... Terminal Station (IAA)
TS .... Terminating System (IAA)
TS .... Test and Set [*Computer science*] (IAA)
TS .... Three-State [*Computer science*] (IAA)
TS .... Time Service (IAA)
TS .... Torque Synchro Transmitter (IAA)

TS .... Torque Transmitter (IAA)
TS .... Track Store Unit (IAA)
TS .... Translation Service
TS .... Transmit [*or Transmitter*] (IAA)
TS .... Transversale Spyder [*Ferrari automotive model designation*]
TS .... Transverse Staggering (IAA)
TS .... Tristate [*Electronics*] (IAA)
TS .... Turbosynchro Transmitter (IAA)
TS .... Turn per Second (IAA)
TS .... Type of Shift (IAA)
TSA............. Target Service Agents [*Computer science*] (PCM)
TSA............. Theater Storage Area [*Military*]
TSA............. Total System Analyzer (IAA)
TSA............. Transair France [*ICAO designator*] (FAAC)
TSA............. Tree Structured Attribute (IAA)
TSAF .... Todos Santos Ambulance Fund [*An association*] (EA)
TSAR.......... Time-Sharing Activity Report System [*Computer science*] (IAA)
TSATLC..... Trans-Atlantic [*Aviation*] (FAAC)
TSAZ......... Target Selector Azimuth (IAA)
TSB............. Transports Aeriens du Benin [*ICAO designator*] (FAAC)
TSBP.......... Time-Sharing Business Package [*Computer science*] (IAA)
TSC............. Air Transat [*Canada*] [*ICAO designator*] (FAAC)
TSC............. Telecommunications Systems Corp. (IAA)
TSC............. Test Score Category [*DoD*]
TSC............. Transmitting Switch Control (IAA)
TSC............. Treatment Services Control
TSC............. Tristate Control [*Electronics*] (IAA)
TSC............. Troop Support Center [*Army*]
TSC............. Two Subcarrier (IAA)
TSD .... Time-Span-of-Discretion (PDAA)
TSD .... Time-Speed-Distance [*Vehicle testing*]
TSDA........ Television Service Dealers' Association (IAA)
TSDA........ Thermal Single-Determinant Approximation (PDAA)
TSE............. Telecommunications Systems Engineering (IAA)
TSE............. Telemetry Support Equipment (IAA)
TSE............. Total Shielding Effectiveness (IAA)
TSEB .... Twin Sideband (IAA)
TSEC .... Terminal Secondary RADAR Beacon [*Aviation*] (FAAC)
TSEL .... Tentative Safe Exposure Level [*Toxicology*]
TSEM........ Transmission Secondary Electron Multiplication [*Physics*] (IAA)
TSET .... Transmitter Signal Element Timing (IAA)
TSEXEC..... Time-Shared Executive [*Computer science*] (IAA)
TSF .... Through Supergroup Filter (IAA)
TSG............. Technical Service Group (IAA)
TSG............. Triggered Spark Gap (IAA)
TSI .... Technical Systems, Inc. (IAA)
TSI .... Tensile Safety Index [*Engineering design*]
TSI .... Time Slot Input [*Telecommunications*] (IAA)
TSI .... Transistor Specialities, Inc. (IAA)
TSI .... True Speed Indicator (IAA)
TSIC .... Time Slot Interchange Circuit [*Telecommunications*] (IAA)
TSIP .... Tank [*Missile*] Sight Improvement Program [*Army*]
TSL............. Thermally-Stimulated Luminescence (PDAA)
TSL............. Three-State Logic [*Computer science*] (IAA)
TSL............. Total Signal Lines (IAA)
TSL............. Translator (IAA)
TSL............. Tree Searching Language [*Computer science*] (PDAA)
TSM............ Time-Sharing Multiplex [*Telecommunications*] (IAA)
TSM............ Time, Space, and Matter [*Princeton University course title*] (AEE)
TSM............ Transair Mali SA [*ICAO designator*] (FAAC)
TSM............ Trouble Shooting Manual (IAA)
TSMA........ Tinplate Stockholders' and Merchants' Association [*British*] (BI)
TSMTR ...... Transmitter (DA)
TSMU .... Time-Sharing Multiplex Unit [*Telecommunications*] (IAA)
TSN .... Task Sequence Number (IAA)
TSN .... Trans-Air Services Ltd. [*Nigeria*] [*ICAO designator*] (FAAC)
TSNC.......... Time-Sharing and Multiplexing Numerical Control [*Telecommunications*] (IAA)
TSO .... Technical Service Order [*Aviation*] (DA)
TSO .... Time Slot Zero [*Telecommunications*] (IAA)
TSO .... Transaero Airlines [*Former USSR*] [*ICAO designator*] (FAAC)
TSOC.......... Tape System Output Converter [*Computer science*] (IAA)
TSOC.......... Time-Sharing Operating Control System [*Computer science*] (IAA)
TSP............. Terminal Support Processor [*Computer science*] (PDAA)
TSP............. Time-Share Peripherals [*Computer science*] (IAA)
TSPRT....... Truncated Sequential Probability Ratio Test (PDAA)
TSPRTR..... Truncated Sequential Probability Ratio Test for Reliability (PDAA)
TSR............. Test Summary Report (IAA)
TSR............. Training Support Requirements [*Military*]
TSR............. Trans Service Airlift [*Zaire*] [*ICAO designator*] (FAAC)
TSRC.......... Transmitter-Receiver (IAA)
TSS............. Tape Storage System
TSS............. Technical Staff Surveillance [*Military*] (IAA)
TSS............. Time-Shared Supervisory System (IAA)
TSS............. Track Store Switch (IAA)
TSS............. Train Supervisory System (IAA)
TSS............. Treatment System Support
TSS............. Tropical Sea Airlines [*Thailand*] [*ICAO designator*] (FAAC)
TSS............. Turbine Supersonic Speed (ERG)
TSSAM ...... Tri-Service Standoff Attack Missile

TSSCC....... Toy Stores Steiff Collectors Club (EA)
TSSD........ Typesetting System for Scientific Document [*Computer science*] (PDAA)
TS/SPAR ... Time Sharing System Performance Activity Recorder (PDAA)
TSSS .... Trainer Software Support System [*Military*]
TST............ Time-Shared Terminal [*Computer science*] (IAA)
TST............ Truncated Sequential Test (PDAA)
TST............ Tuberculin Skin Test [*Medicine*] (PDAA)
TSTICT..... Test Incoming Trunk [*Telecommunications*] (IAA)
TSTS .... Tracking System Test Stand (IAA)
TSU .... Technical Support Unit (IAA)
TSUP......... Trunk Supervisor [*Telecommunications*] (IAA)
TSV............ Thermal Sensitive Vote [*Automotive interior comfort survey*]
TSV............ Tropair Airservices [*British*] [*ICAO designator*] (FAAC)
TSW............ Trans European Airways [*Switzerland*] [*ICAO designator*] (FAAC)
TSX............ Time-Sharing Execution [*Computer science*] (IAA)
TSX............ Time-Sharing Executive System [*Computer science*] (IAA)
TT .... Test Terminator (IAA)
TT .... Test [*or Testing*] Time (IAA)
TT .... Test Tube (IAA)
TT .... Thermally Tuned (IAA)
TT .... Thermomagnetic Treatment (IAA)
TT .... Thermostat Switch (IAA)
TT .... Top-to-Top (IAA)
TT .... Touch-Tone [*Telecommunications*] (IAA)
TT .... Transfer Trip [*Telecommunications*] (IAA)
TT .... Transmitting Typewriter [*Telecommunications*] (IAA)
TT .... Trunk Test [*Telecommunications*] (IAA)
TTA .... Telecommunication Traffic Association [*British*] (BI)
TTA .... Television Technicians' Association
TTA .... Theatrical Traders Association Ltd. [*British*] (BI)
TTA .... Transporte e Trabalho Aero [*Mozambique*] [*ICAO designator*] (FAAC)
TTAC......... Tracking, Telemetry, and Command [*AEC*] (IAA)
TTB............ Test Two Bits (IAA)
TTB............ Twin Traction-Beam [*Ford Motor Co.*] [*Truck four-wheel drive front suspension*]
TTBS .... Timber Trades' Benevolent Society [*British*] (BI)
TTC............ Tactical Telephone Central [*Telecommunications*] (IAA)
TTC............ Tape Transport Cassette
TTC............ Telephone Toll Call (IAA)
TTC............ Teletype Center [*Telecommunications*] (IAA)
TTC............ Teletype Message Converter [*Telecommunications*] (IAA)
TTC............ Translunar Trajectory Characteristics [*AEC*] (IAA)
TTCP .... Transmitting Typewriter with Card Punch (IAA)
TTCS .... Tank Turret Camouflage System [*Army*]
TTE............ Thermal Transfer Equipment (IAA)
TTG .... Tactical Transport Group [*Military*]
TTGR......... Time-to-Go Rating [*Air Force*] (IAA)
TTHFA....... Twisted-Pair, Telephone, Heat and Flame Resistant, Armored [*Wire technology*] (IAA)
TTI .... Teletype Input (IAA)
TTI .... Thoracic Trauma Index [*Automotive safety research*]
TTM .... Total Time Management [*Industrial engineering*]
TTML......... Transistor-Transistor Micrologic (IAA)
TTN .... Highland Express [*British*] [*ICAO designator*] (FAAC)
TTO .... Tactical Training Officer [*Army*]
TTO .... Teletype Output [*Telecommunications*] (IAA)
TTO .... Trailing-Throttle Oversteer [*Automobile driving*]
TTP............ Tabular [*or Tabulator*] Tape Processor [*Computer science*] (IAA)
TTR............ Tape Reading Typing Relay (IAA)
TTR............ Tatra Air [*Slovakia*] [*ICAO designator*] (FAAC)
TTR............ Teletype Translator [*Telecommunications*] (IAA)
TTR............ Terminal Radiation Airborne Program Translator [*Air Force*] (IAA)
TTR............ Touch-Tone Receiver [*Telecommunications*] (IAA)
TTR............ Transistor Telegraph Relay [*Telecommunications*] (IAA)
TTS............ TASD (Transporti Aerei Speciali) [*Italy*] [*ICAO designator*] (FAAC)
TTS............ Text-to-Speech [*Computer science*]
TTS............ Three-State Transceiver [*Computer science*] (IAA)
TTS............ Time to Station (DA)
TTS............ Triple Transit Suppression (IAA)
TTSA .... Tank Turret Safety Adapter [*Army*]
TTT............ Template Tracing Technique (DA)
TTTA .... Tobacco Trade Travellers' Association [*British*] (BI)
TTTN .... Tandem Tie Trunk Network (PDAA)
TTTP .... Transmitting Typewriter with Tape Punch (IAA)
TTU .... Texas Technological University (PDAA)
TTU .... Tracer Test Unit (IAA)
TTX .... Den Sivile Flyskole [*Norway*] [*ICAO designator*] (FAAC)
TTY .... Teletypewriter Equipment (IAA)
TU .... Take-Up (IAA)
TU .... Tulsa University [*Oklahoma*] (PDAA)
TU .... Tuning Unit [*JETDS nomenclature*] [*Military*] (IAA)
TUA .... Turkmenistan [*ICAO designator*] (FAAC)
TUD.......... Total Underground Distribution (IAA)
TUDAT ..... Tunnel-Diode Arithmetic Tester (IAA)
TUG........... Transistorized Automatic Computer Users' Group (IAA)
TUI .... Text User Interface [*Computer science*]
TUI .... Tuninter [*Tunisia*] [*ICAO designator*] (FAAC)
TUIP.......... Transurethral Incision of the Prostate [*Medicine*]

TUK............ TEA (UK) Ltd. [*British*] [*ICAO designator*]   (FAAC)
TULIP........ Transurethral Ultrasound - Guided LASER-Induced
            Prostatectomy [*Medicine*]
TULIPS...... Telemetered Ultrasonic Liquid Interface Plotting System   (PDAA)
TUN............ Air Tungaru [*British*] [*ICAO designator*]   (FAAC)
TUNNET ... Tunnel Transit Time   (IAA)
TUR............ Aerotur SA [*Mexico*] [*ICAO designator*]   (FAAC)
TUR............ Toxic Use Reduction [*Manufacturing*]
TURBT....... Transurethral Resection of Bladder Tumor [*Medicine*]   (MAH)
TUT .... GB Air Academy Ltd. [*British*] [*ICAO designator*]   (FAAC)
TUU............ Compania Aerea de Servicios Tur Air [*Spain*] [*ICAO
            designator*]   (FAAC)
TUU............ Transitional Ultraspherical-Ultraspherical Filter   (PDAA)
TUV............ Turavia [*Poland*] [*ICAO designator*]   (FAAC)
TUY............ Empresa Aerotuy [*Venezuela*] [*ICAO designator*]   (FAAC)
TV .... Test Voltage   (IAA)
TV .... Thyroid Vein [*Medicine*]   (PDAA)
TV .... Tube Voltmeter   (IAA)
TVA .... Target Value Analysis [*Army*]   (ADDR)
TVA .... Time Variant Automation   (IAA)
TVA .... Trans America Airlines, Inc. [*ICAO designator*]   (FAAC)
TVE .... Total Vertical Error [*Aviation*]   (DA)
TVE .... Township and Village Enterprise [*People's Republic of China*]
            (ECON)
TVF............ Taylor Vortex Flow [*Fluid mechanics*]
TVG .... Television Video Generator
TVHH .... Television Household [*Ratings*]   (NTCM)
TVIS .... Television Information Storage   (IAA)
TVL............ Time Variation of Loss   (IAA)
TVL............ Transmit [*or Transmitting*] Variolosser   (IAA)
TVMAP...... Track-via-Missile Analog Processor [*Military*]
TVN............ Transcolombiana de Aviacion SA [*Colombia*] [*ICAO
            designator*]   (FAAC)
TVO............ Ditta Transavio di I. Ballerio [*Italy*] [*ICAO designator*]   (FAAC)
TVO............ Throttle Valve Opening [*Automotive engineering*]
TVOM .... Transistorized Volt Ohm Milliammeter   (IAA)
TVOR .... Terminal Very High Frequency Omnirange   (IAA)
TVP............ Time Variable Parameter   (IAA)
TVRE.......... Transportable Vehicle Refuelling Equipment   (PDAA)
TVSM........ Time-Varying Signal Measurement   (IAA)
TVSS .... Tactile Vision Substitution System   (PDAA)
TVSS .... Transient Voltage Surge Suppression
TVSYS....... Television System   (IAA)
TW .... Twin   (IAA)
TW .... Twisted   (IAA)
TWA .... Trans World Airlines, Inc. [*ICAO designator*]   (FAAC)
TWA .... Two-Way Alternate   (IAA)
TWAC .... Time-Weighted Average Concentration [*Toxicology*]
TWAE .... Time-Weighted Average Exposure [*Toxicology*]
TWC .... Express Airlines II, Inc. [*ICAO designator*]   (FAAC)
TWC .... Teletype Service Without Voice Communication
            [*Telecommunications*]   (IAA)
TWC .... Total Wear Coefficient [*Materials science*]
TWD.......... Touch Wire Display   (PDAA)
TWE .... Transwede [*Sweden*] [*ICAO designator*]   (FAAC)
TWG.......... Television Writer's Guild   (NTCM)
TWG.......... Trans Wings AS [*Norway*] [*ICAO designator*]   (FAAC)
TWG.......... Transition Work Group
TWIN .... Test Ware Instrument   (PDAA)
TWL.......... Tradewinds Aviation Ltd. [*Canada*] [*ICAO designator*]   (FAAC)
TWLC........ Two Way Logic Circuit   (PDAA)
TWM........ Traveling-Wave Magnetron   (IAA)
TWNA....... Truck Writers of North America [*An association*]   (EA)
TWNS .... Trans World News Service   (NTCM)
TWO.......... Travelling-Wave Oscillator   (IAA)
TWP .... Tactical Work Program
TWPL........ Total Weighted Pollutant Load   (ERG)
TWS........... Trans West African Airlines Ltd. [*Gambia*] [*ICAO designator*]
            (FAAC)
TWS........... Translator Writing System [*Computer science*]   (IAA)
TWS........... Two-Way Simultaneous   (IAA)
TWT .... Time Wire Transmission   (IAA)
TWTT........ Two-Way Travel Time [*Seismology*]
TWU.......... Trace Watch Unit   (IAA)
TWUD....... Tactical Weapons Unit Diagnostics
TWV .... Three-Way Valve [*Hydraulics*]
TXA .... Task Extension Area [*Computer science*]   (IAA)
TXA .... Texair Charter, Inc. [*ICAO designator*]   (FAAC)
TXC .... Transaviaexport [*Belarus*] [*ICAO designator*]   (FAAC)
TXI............ Aereotaxis SA de CV [*Mexico*] [*ICAO designator*]   (FAAC)
TXL............ Aereo Taxi de Leon SA de CV [*Mexico*] [*ICAO designator*]
            (FAAC)
TXL............ Transfer on Index Low   (IAA)
TXM .... Taxi Aereo de Mexico [*ICAO designator*]   (FAAC)
TXN .... Texas National Airlines [*ICAO designator*]   (FAAC)
TXP............ Linea Aerea Taxpa Ltda. [*Chile*] [*ICAO designator*]   (FAAC)
TXR .... Taxirey SA de CV [*Mexico*] [*ICAO designator*]   (FAAC)
TXS........... Texas Airlines, Inc. [*ICAO designator*]   (FAAC)
TXV .... Throttling Expansion Valve [*Automotive air conditioning*]
TY .... Benin [*Aircraft nationality and registration mark*]   (FAAC)
TY .... Target Year
TY .... Teletypewriter [*Telecommunications*]   (IAA)
TYE .... Tyee Airways Ltd. [*Canada*] [*ICAO designator*]   (FAAC)

TYJ............. Tyrolean Jet Service [*Austria*] [*ICAO designator*]   (FAAC)
TYM .... Tyumen Airlines [*Russian Federation*] [*ICAO designator*]
            (FAAC)
TYPO .... Typographical Error   (NTCM)
TYR .... Tyrolean Airways [*Austria*] [*ICAO designator*]   (FAAC)
TZ .... Tubolare Zagato [*Automotive model designation*] [*Alfa-Romeo*]
TZK .... Tajikistan [*ICAO designator*]   (FAAC)
TZS............ Technologie Zentrum Steyr [*Steyr Technology Center*] [*German*]

U

U .... Undefined (IAA)
U .... Unified Atomic Mass Unit [*Nuclear energy*] (IAA)
U .... Unit of Measure (IAA)
U .... Unlicensed (DA)
U .... Unnumbered Acknowledge [*or Acknowledgement*]
.... [*Telecommunications*] (IAA)
u .... Unpaved Surface [*Aviation*] (DA)
U .... Until (DA)
9U .... Burundi [*Aircraft nationality and registration mark*] (FAAC)
UA .... Unassigned [*Telecommunications*] (IAA)
UA .... United Society of Artists [*British*] (BI)
UA .... University of Akron [*Ohio*] (PDAA)
UA .... Until Advised (DA)
UA .... Urban Area (NTCM)
UA .... User Agency
UAA .... Uas-One [*British*] [*ICAO designator*] (FAAC)
UAA .... Upper Advisory Area [*Aviation*] (DA)
UAC .... United Air Charters [*Zimbabwe*] [*ICAO designator*] (FAAC)
UAC .... Upper Air Control (IAA)
UA/C .... Uric Acid-Creatinine Ratio [*Physiology*] (MAH)
UAC .... Utility Assemble Communication Pool (IAA)
UAD .... Univex SRL [*Italy*] [*ICAO designator*] (FAAC)
UAD .... Upper Advisory Route [*Aviation*] (DA)
UAD .... User Attribute Definition [*Computer science*] (IAA)
UAE .... United Arab Emirates [*ICAO designator*] (FAAC)
UAEM .... University Association for Emergency Medicine
UAF .... United Arab Emirates Air Force [*ICAO designator*] (FAAC)
UAF .... Universal Active Filter (IAA)
UAG .... Uas-Two [*British*] [*ICAO designator*] (FAAC)
UAG .... User Advisory Group (RDA)
UAI .... Uni Air SA [*France*] [*ICAO designator*] (FAAC)
UAJ .... Uas-Three [*British*] [*ICAO designator*] (FAAC)
UAL .... United Air Lines, Inc. [*ICAO designator*] (FAAC)
UAL .... Universal Assembly Language (IAA)
UAMC .... Utility Assemble Master Communication (IAA)
UAP .... Unite Australia Party [*Political party*]
UAP .... Upper Atmosphere Phenomena (IAA)
UAPRE .... University Association for Professional Radio Education
.... [*Broadcast Education Association*] (NTCM)
UAR .... Uni Air [*France*] [*ICAO designator*] (FAAC)
UARBC ...... United Arab Republic Broadcasting Corp. (IAA)
UARDS ...... Unexplained Acute Respiratory Distress Syndrome
UARP .... Upper Atmospheric Research Program [*NASA*] (PDAA)
UARZ .... University of Arizona (PDAA)
UAS .... Uas-Four [*British*] [*ICAO designator*] (FAAC)
UAT .... Uniform Asymptotic Theory (IAA)
UAU .... Underwater-to-Air-to-Underwater (IAA)
UAV .... United Aviation Ltd. [*New Zealand*] [*ICAO designator*] (FAAC)
UAV-CR ..... Unmanned Aerial Vehicle-Close Range [*Military*]
UAZ-EES .... University of Arizona-Engineering Experiment Station (PDAA)
UBA .... Myanmar Airways [*ICAO designator*] (FAAC)
UBA .... Universal Ballet Academy [*Washington, DC*]
UBD .... User Brain Damage [*Computer hacker terminology*] (NHD)
UBF .... Underground Baggage Facility [*Aviation*] (DA)
UBI .... Unibus Interface (IAA)
UBL .... Unit Basic Load [*Army*]
UBVR .... Ultraviolet-Blue-Visible-Red [*Photometry*]
UC .... University of Chicago [*Illinois*] (PDAA)
UC .... Unloader Coil (IAA)
UC .... Upper Characters (IAA)
UC .... Upper Control (IAA)
UCA .... Champlain Enterprises, Inc. [*ICAO designator*] (FAAC)
UCA .... United Chemists' Association Ltd. [*British*] (BI)
UCAL .... Universal Cable Adapter (IAA)
UCC .... Ultra Clean Coal (ERG)
UCCIS .... USAREUR [*United States Army, Europe*] Command and Control
.... Information System
UCDP .... Uncorrelated Data Processor (IAA)
UCE .... Union Carbide Electronics (IAA)
UCE .... Unit Control Error (IAA)
UCG .... Ultrasound Cardiogram (IAA)
UCHCIS ..... Urban Comprehensive Health Care Information System (PDAA)
UCID .... User Control Interface Device [*Army*]

UCL .... Unclamp (IAA)
UCM .... User Communications Manager [*Audio-video*] (NTCM)
UCP .... Uncoupling Protein [*Biochemistry*]
UCP .... Unit Construction Practice (IAA)
UCP .... Unit Construction Principle (IAA)
UCRB .... Upper Circulating Reflux Bottom Section [*Chemical engineering*]
UCRT .... Upper Circulating Reflux Top Section [*Chemical engineering*]
UCS .... United Carriers Systems, Inc. [*ICAO designator*] (FAAC)
UCS .... University College School [*British*] (BI)
UCSMP ...... University of Chicago School Mathematics Project (AEE)
UCTA .... United Commercial Travellers Association of Great Britain and
.... Ireland, Inc. (BI)
UDA .... Pusdiklat Perhubungan Udara/PLP [*Indonesia*] [*ICAO
.... designator*] (FAAC)
UDA .... United Democratic Alliance [*European political movement*]
.... (ECON)
UDACS ...... Underwater Detection and Classification System (IAA)
UDAS .... Unified Direct Access Standards (IAA)
UDB .... Universal Data Base (IAA)
UDC .... Unidirectional Current (IAA)
UDC .... Universal Decimal Code (IAA)
UDCA .... US Deaf Cycling Association (EA)
UDCD .... Unit Data and Control Diagram (IAA)
UDI .... Universal Digital Instrument (IAA)
UDICON .... Universal Digital Communications Network [*Computer
.... science*] (IAA)
UDIL .... University Directors of Industrial Liaison (PDAA)
UDOFTT .... Universal Digital Operational Flight Trainer Tool [*Navy*] (IAA)
UDPgal ...... Uridine Diphosphate Galactose [*Biochemistry*] (MAH)
UDRC .... Utility Data Reduction Control (IAA)
UDRO .... Utility Data Reduction Output (IAA)
UDS .... Ultronic Data Systems (IAA)
UDT .... Unidirectional Transducer (IAA)
U/E .... Unedged (DAC)
UECL .... Ultra Electronics Components Ltd. (IAA)
UED .... Air LA, Inc. [*ICAO designator*] (FAAC)
UED .... Ultrasonic Echo Detection (PDAA)
UED .... United Electro Dynamics (IAA)
UEGO .... Universal Exhaust Gas Oxygen Sensor [*Fuel systems*]
.... [*Automotive engineering*]
UEL .... Ultra Electronics Ltd. (IAA)
UEL .... Upper Earnings Limit (PDAA)
UEPG .... United European Power Grid (IAA)
UERN .... Utilities Emergency Radio Network (IAA)
UES .... United Engineering Societies (IAA)
UET .... Underground Explosion Test (IAA)
UEW .... United Electrical, Radio, and Machine Workers of America [*Also,
.... UERMWA*] (NTCM)
UF .... Uncertainty Factor [*Toxicology*]
UF .... Uplink Frequency
UFD .... Unit Functional Diagram (IAA)
UFET .... Unipolar Field-Effect Transistor (IAA)
UFO .... Users Files on Line (IAA)
UFR .... United Africa Airline (Liberia), Inc. [*ICAO designator*] (FAAC)
UFS .... UFS, Inc. [*ICAO designator*] (FAAC)
UFS .... United Feeder Service [*ICAO designator*] (FAAC)
UG .... Union Guide
UGA .... Uganda Airlines Corp. [*ICAO designator*] (FAAC)
UGA .... University of Georgia (PDAA)
UGB .... Upper Guard Band
UGG .... Ugland Air AS [*Norway*] [*ICAO designator*] (FAAC)
UGL .... Inter-Island Air, Inc. [*ICAO designator*] (FAAC)
UGSS .... Union of Girls' Schools for Social Service [*British*] (BI)
UHA .... Unable Higher Altitude [*Aviation*] (FAAC)
UHB .... Ultra High Bypass [*Aviation*] (DA)
UHDODT ... Unable Higher Due Opposite Direction Traffic [*Aviation*]
.... (FAAC)
UHDSDT ... Unable Higher Due Same Direction Traffic [*Aviation*] (FAAC)
UHDT .... Unable Higher Due Traffic [*Aviation*] (FAAC)
UHP .... Ultra-High Porosity [*Materials science*]
UHP .... Ultra-High Pressure [*Water cutting tools*]
UHP .... United Air Service [*Nigeria*] [*ICAO designator*] (FAAC)
UHT .... Umbilical Handling Technician [*Computer science*] (IAA)

111

UHVI......... Ultra High Viscosity Index
UI.............. Unique Indentifier [*Computer science*]
UI.............. Unnumbered Information   (IAA)
UIB .... United Independent Broadcasters   (NTCM)
UIC .... United Insulator Co.   (IAA)
UID........... Universal Identifier   (IAA)
UIE .... Union Internationale des Editeurs [*International Union of Publishers*]   (NTCM)
UIR .... Union Internationale de Radiodiffusion [*International Broadcasting Union*] [*Also, IBU*]   (NTCM)
UIRV .... Universal Infrared Viewer   (PDAA)
UIS .... United Inventors and Scientists   (IAA)
UIS .... Upper Information Service   (DA)
UJTO .... Unijunction Transistor Oscillator   (IAA)
UKA.......... Air UK Ltd. [*British*] [*ICAO designator*]   (FAAC)
UKAACREG ... United Kingdom Airways and Communication Region   (IAA)
UKBG .... United Kingdom Bartenders' Guild   (BI)
UKCA .... United Kingdom Coffee Association Ltd.   (BI)
UKCSMA... United Kingdom Cutlery and Silverware Manufacturers Association   (BI)
UKDRC ..... United Kingdom Dutch Rabbit Club   (BI)
UKFA .... United Kingdom Fellmongers Association   (BI)
UKGPA ...... United Kingdom Glycerine Producers' Association   (BI)
UKJGA .... United Kingdom Jute Goods Association Ltd.   (BI)
UKMANZRA ... United Kingdom Manufacturers and New Zealand Representatives Association   (BI)
UKOBA ...... United Kingdom Outboard Boating Association   (BI)
UKP........... UK Home Office [*British*] [*ICAO designator*]   (FAAC)
UKR........... Air Ukraine [*ICAO designator*]   (FAAC)
UKR........... United Kingdom Atomic Energy Authority Office at Risley   (IAA)
UKSMA ...... United Kingdom Sugar Merchants' Association   (BI)
UKY........... University of Kentucky   (PDAA)
UL.............. Unit Load
ULA .... Universal Logic Array [*Computer science*]   (IAA)
ULA .... Zuliana de Aviacion [*Venezuela*] [*ICAO designator*]   (FAAC)
ULC .... Ultra-Low Carbon [*Metallurgical engineering*]
ULCANS... Ultralightweight Camouflage Net System [*Army*]
ULCS .... Uniform Lightness and Chromaticity Scale   (PDAA)
ULD........... Universal Language Description [*Computer science*]   (IAA)
ULDT .... Unable Lower Due Traffic [*Aviation*]   (FAAC)
ULE .... Leisure International Airways Ltd. [*British*] [*ICAO designator*]   (FAAC)
ULEB......... Ultra-Low Emissions Bus [*Automotive engineering*]
ULEE......... Ultra-Low Emissions Engine [*Automotive engineering*]
ULET......... Ultra-Low Emissions Truck [*Automotive engineering*]
ULEV .... Ultra-Low-Emission Vehicle [*Military*]
ULI .... Ultra-Low Interstitial   (PDAA)
ULICP .... Universal Log Interpretation Computer Program   (PDAA)
ULLNG ...... Ultra-Large Liquified Natural Gas Carrier   (PDAA)
ULMA .... Upper Level Management Advisor   (IAA)
ULN........... Unlaunchable   (IAA)
ULOR .... Upward Light Output Ratio   (PDAA)
ULP .... Ultra-Lightweight Panel   (PDAA)
ULP .... Universal Logic Primitive   (PDAA)
ULR .... Ultra Long Range   (DA)
ULRGW ..... Ultra-Long Range Guided Weapon   (IAA)
ULS........... Carroll Air Service, Inc. [*ICAO designator*]   (FAAC)
ULT .... UltrAir, Inc. [*ICAO designator*]   (FAAC)
Umax .... Urinary Osmolality Maximum [*Physiology*]   (MAH)
UMER .... Ultrasonically-Modulated Electron Resonance   (PDAA)
UMF .... Users Master File   (IAA)
UMMIS...... Uniform Material Movement and Issue Priority System [*Navy*]   (ANA)
UMO .... Unit Movement Officer [*Army*]   (INF)
UMOST ..... U-Groove Power Metal-Oxide Semiconductor Field Effect Transistor   (IAA)
UMR.......... Unit Manning Report [*Army*]   (ADDR)
UMVS .... United Methodist Voluntary Services
UMVUE ..... Uniformly Minimum Variance Unbiased Estimator   (PDAA)
UNA .... Unable [*ICAO designator*]   (FAAC)
UNA .... Universair [*Spain*] [*ICAO designator*]   (FAAC)
UNAP........ Unable to Approve [*ICAO designator*]   (FAAC)
UNATNDD ... Unattended [*Aviation*]   (FAAC)
UNC........... Unconditional   (IAA)
UNC........... Undercurrent   (IAA)
UNC........... Unified National Coarse Thread   (IAA)
UNC........... Universal Naming Convention [*Computer science*]   (PCM)
UNCDRP ... Universal Card Read-In Program   (IAA)
UNCIRC..... Uncircumcising Information Resources Center [*National Support Group*]
UNCITRAL ... United Nations Commission on International Trade Law   (PDAA)
UNCL......... Unified Numerical Control Language   (IAA)
UNCOL..... Universal Computer-Oriented Language   (IAA)
UNCTLD ... Uncontrolled   (DA)
Underw Nat ... Underwater Naturalist [*A publication*]
UNEF .... Unified National Extra Fine Thread   (IAA)
UNEO........ United Nations Emergency Operation   (PDAA)
UNF........... Unified National Fine   (IAA)
UNF........... Union Flight [*ICAO designator*]   (FAAC)
UNH.......... University of New Hampshire   (PDAA)
UNIBI........ Unipolar Bipolar   (IAA)

UNIBORS ... UNIVAC [*Universal Automatic Computer*] Bill of Material Processor Random System [*Computer science*]   (IAA)
UNIBOSS ... UNIVAC [*Universal Automatic Computer*] Bill of Material Processor Sequential System [*Computer science*]   (IAA)
UNICLO .... United Nations Information Center and Liaison Office   (PDAA)
UNICOH... Unidensity Coherent Light Recording   (IAA)
UNICOL... Universal Computer-Oriented Language   (IAA)
UNICRIM ... Uniform Crime Reporting System   (PDAA)
UNIHEDD ... Universal Head-Down Display [*Computer science*]   (PDAA)
UNL........... Unlisten   (IAA)
UNLD .... Unload   (IAA)
UNM .... University of New Mexico   (PDAA)
UNPKD...... Unpacked   (IAA)
UNRAU...... Unified Numeric Representation Arithmetic Unit   (PDAA)
UNRELBL ... Unreliable   (FAAC)
UNSERV.... Unserviceable   (IAA)
UOC........... Uranium Ore Concentrate
UOO........... Unavailable, On Order [*Business term*]   (NTCM)
UORC......... Used Oil Recycling Coalition [*Automotive lubricants*]
UORS......... Unusual Occurence Report   (IAA)
UP.............. Units Position   (IAA)
UPA .... Air Foyle Ltd. [*British*] [*ICAO designator*]   (FAAC)
UPA .... United Power Association   (IAA)
UPAPH ...... United Patients Association for Pulmonary Hypertension   (EA)
UPC........... Uniform Plumbing Code   (DAC)
UPC........... Universal Postal Congress   (IAA)
UPCS......... United Pastrycooks' and Confectioners' Society [*British*]   (BI)
UPD........... Universally Programmable Digitizer Update   (IAA)
UPDT .... Update [*National Weather Service*]   (FAAC)
UPF .... Ultrapherical Polynomial Filter   (IAA)
UPIA .... United Press International Audio   (NTCM)
UPIN .... United Press International News-Features   (NTCM)
UPIRN ...... United Press International Radio Network   (NTCM)
UPITN....... United Press International Television News   (NTCM)
UPLM .... Uplink Logic Module
UPP .... Universal Procedure Pointer [*Computer science*]
UPR .... Unearned Premiums Reserve [*Finance*]
UPS........... Uninterruptible AC [*Alternating Current*] Electric Power System   (IAA)
UPS........... United Parcel Service Co. [*ICAO designator*]   (FAAC)
UPSTRM ... Upstream [*Meteorology*]   (FAAC)
UPTE......... Ultra-Precision Test Equipment   (PDAA)
UPTS......... Undergraduate Pilot Training System   (IAA)
UPWP .... Unified Planning Work Program
UR.............. Ultrared   (IAA)
UR.............. Unit Real   (IAA)
URA .... Uralinteravia [*Russian Federation*] [*ICAO designator*]   (FAAC)
Urb For ...... Urban Forests [*A publication*]
URC........... Uniform Resistance Capacitance [*Electronics*]   (IAA)
URC........... United Ratepayers' Campaign [*British*]   (BI)
URD........... Underground Rural Distribution   (IAA)
URD........... Unit Reference Designation [*Army*]
URDS .... Unknown Respiratory Stress Syndrome [*Medicine*]
URI .... Unintentional RADAR Interference   (IAA)
URI .... Universite Radiophonique Internationale [*International University of the Air*]   (NTCM)
URI .... Utility Read-In Program   (IAA)
URL........... Uralavialy [*Russian Federation*] [*ICAO designator*]   (FAAC)
URM .... Uniform Reflectivity Mirror   (PDAA)
URMS .... Universal Reproducing Matrix System   (PDAA)
URR........... Unconstrained Requirements Report [*Army*]
URS .... Uniformly Reflexive Structure   (IAA)
URSIES...... Ultravariable Resolution Single Interferometer Echelle Scanner   (PDAA)
US.............. Unconditional Stop   (IAA)
US.............. Underwater-to-Surface   (IAA)
US.............. Undistorted Signal   (IAA)
US.............. United States Reports [*A publication*]   (NTCM)
US.............. Upstream   (NTCM)
US.............. Utility Satellite   (IAA)
USA .... United Savers Association   (EA)
USA .... US Air [*ICAO designator*]   (FAAC)
USAABNAELCTBD ... United States Army Airborne and Electronics Board   (IAA)
USAACS .... United States Army Armor Center and School
USAARDEC ... United States Army Armament Research Development and Engineering Center
USAAS....... United States Army Armor Signals   (IAA)
USAB........ United States Activities Board   (IAA)
USABD....... United States Army Air Defense Artillery Board
USAC .... United States Activities Committee   (IAA)
USACERCOM ... United States Army Communications and Electronics Material and Readiness Command
USACORADCOM ... United States Army Communications Research and Development Command
USAEC ...... United States Army Environmental Center   (RDA)
USAEL....... United States Army Electronics Laboratories   (IAA)
USAELCTPG ... United States Army Electronic Proving Ground   (IAA)
USAERDL ... United States Army Engineer Research and Development Laboratories   (IAA)
USAFACS ... United States Army Field Artillery Center and School
USAFCED ... United States Air Force Communications Electronics Doctrine   (IAA)

USAHI .... United States Army History Institute (PDAA)
USAIC........ United States Army Intelligence Center (IAA)
USAID/W ... United States Agency for International Development, Washington (PDAA)
USAJPG..... United States Army Jefferson Proving Ground (PDAA)
USALOGCTR ... United States Army Logistics Center
USAM........ Uniformly-Sampled-Autoregressive Moving Average (PDAA)
USAOTEA ... United States Army Operational Test and Evaluation Agency
USAPPA .... United States Army Publications and Printing Agency
USAQMCS ... United States Army Quartermaster Center and School
USARNG ... United States Army National Guard
USARP....... United States Army Research Program (IAA)
USARSPACE ... United States Army Space Command
USASAM .... United State Army School of Aviation Medicine (PDAA)
USASCA .... United States Army Satellite Communications Agency (IAA)
USASCS..... United States Army Signal Corps School (IAA)
USASCSOCR ... United States of America Standard Character Set for Optical Characters (IAA)
USASEL..... United States Army Signal Engineering Laboratory (IAA)
USASIGENGLAB ... United States Army Signal Engineering Laboratory (IAA)
USASIGRSCHUNIT ... United States Army Signal Research Unit (IAA)
USASIGTC ... United States Army Signal Training Center (IAA)
USASII....... United States of America Standard Code for Information Interchange (IAA)
USASMSA ... United States Army Signal Missile Support Agency (IAA)
USASSDC ... United States Army Space and Strategic Defense Command
USASTCEN ... United States Army Signal Training Center (IAA)
USATCS .... United States Army Transportation Center and School
USBC.......... Universal Standard Book Code (PDAA)
USBCODE ... Unipolar Straight Binary Code (IAA)
USBT.......... Upper Surface Blowing Technique [*Aviation*] (DA)
USBUC....... Upper Sideband Upconverter (IAA)
USC .... United States Components (IAA)
USC .... US Check Airlines [*ICAO designator*] (FAAC)
USCAGS ... United States Coast and Geodetic Survey (IAA)
USCC......... United States Capacitor Corp. (IAA)
USCCAN.... United States Code Congressional and Administrative News [*A publication*]
USCIGW.... Union of Salt, Chemical, and Industrial General Workers [*British*] (BI)
USDA-APHIS-PP/Q ... United States Department of Agriculture, Animal and Plant Health Inspection Service, Plant Protection and Quarantine Programs (PDAA)
USDA-FS ... United States Department of Agriculture - Forest Service (PDAA)
USDA-REA ... United States Department of Agriculture - Rural Electrification Administration (PDAA)
USE .... Universal Automatic Computer Scientific Exchange (IAA)
USEJ .... United States Society for Esperantists Youth (EA)
USG .... United States Gallon (IAA)
USGAL....... United States Gallon (IAA)
USGSG....... United States Government Standard Gage (IAA)
USI .... United States Industry
USIBA .... United States International Book Association (NTCM)
USITE .... United States International Transportation Exposition (PDAA)
USJ............ Uniformed Services Journal [*A publication*]
USJ............ US Jet, Inc. [*ICAO designator*] (FAAC)
USJCB....... Unites States Joint Communication Board (IAA)
USL............ Upper Square Law Limit (IAA)
USLI.......... Ultra Large Scale Integration (NTCM)
USLMRA ... United States Lawn Mower Racing Association
USMA .... Underfeed Stoker Makers' Association [*British*] (BI)
USMP .... United States Microgravity Payload [*NASA*]
USNBS....... United States National Bureau of Standards (IAA)
USNRC ...... United States National Research Council [*Toxicology*]
USNS......... United States National Committee on Standardization
USNS......... United States NOTAM [*Notice to Airmen*] System [*Aviation*] (FAAC)
USNUSL.... United States Navy Undersea Laboratory (IAA)
USOO........ United States Oceanographic Office (PDAA)
USP............ Unsuppressed Selling Price
USPC......... United States Pharmacopoeial Convention
USR .... Universal Series Regulator (IAA)
USS............ Shuttle, Inc. [*ICAO designator*] (FAAC)
USS............ Universal Scheduling System (IAA)
USS............ Unsmoked Sheets (PDAA)
USSA......... United States Space Administration (IAA)
USSP......... Unsuppressed Selling Price
USTAG....... United States Technical Advisory Group (IAA)
USU .... Utah State University (PDAA)
USVRU ...... Ultra-Stable Voltage Reference Unit (PDAA)
USWP........ Ultrashort Wave Propagation Panel (IAA)
USX .... US Express [*ICAO designator*] (FAAC)
UT............. Unitech (IAA)
UT............. Units Tens (IAA)
UT............. Universal Tube (IAA)
UTA .... Union des Transports Aeriens [*France*] [*ICAO designator*] (FAAC)
UTA .... Upper Testing Area (IAA)
UTC .... United Technology Center (IAA)
UTC .... United Telephone Cables (IAA)
UTC .... United Transformer Corp. (IAA)
UTD........... Uniform Theory of Diffraction (IAA)

UTD........... United Air [*South Africa*] [*ICAO designator*] (FAAC)
UTEA .... Unit Training Effectiveness Analysis [*Army*]
UTI .... Undistributed Taxable Income
UTPE......... United Trekkers of Planet Earth [*An association*] (EA)
UTRIP....... Universal Triangulation Program (IAA)
UTSL......... Use the Source, Luke [*Computer hacker terminology, used to parody commands to Luke Skywalker in the movie "Star Wars"*] (NHD)
UUA .... Universal Automatic Computer Users' Association (IAA)
UUMP........ Unification of Units of Measurement Panel [*ICAO*] (DA)
UUUU .... Unidentified [*Marketing surveys*] (NTCM)
UVA........... Universal Airways, Inc. [*ICAO designator*] (FAAC)
UVAS .... Ultraviolet Astronomical Satellite (PDAA)
UVDIAL.... Ultraviolet Differential Absorption LIDAR [*Light Detection and Ranging*] (PDAA)
UVEROM ... Ultraviolet Eraseable Read Only Memory (PDAA)
UVM.......... University of Vermont (PDAA)
UVROM..... Ultraviolet Read Only Memory (IAA)
UVRR........ Ultraviolet Resonance Raman [*Spectroscopy*]
UVS........... Uninterruptable Voltage Source [*Electric power supply*]
UVS........... Universal Versaplot Software (IAA)
UW .... Unique Word (IAA)
UW .... Upwind [*Aviation*] (FAAC)
UWIS......... University of Wisconsin (PDAA)
UWNDS..... Upper Winds [*Meteorology*] (FAAC)
UWY.......... Upper Airway [*Aviation*] (DA)
UYA........... Yute Air Alaska, Inc. [*ICAO designator*] (FAAC)
UYC........... Cameroon Airlines [*ICAO designator*] (FAAC)
UZB .... Uzbekistan Havo Jullary [*Uzbekistan Airways*] [*ICAO designator*] (FAAC)
UZM.......... Unsaturated Zone Monitoring [*Environmental Protection Agency*] (ERG)

V

V .... Vacuum Tube (IAA)
V4 .... St. Kitts and Nevis [*Aircraft nationality and registration mark*]
              (FAAC)
6V .... Senegal [*Aircraft nationality and registration mark*] (FAAC)
V8 .... Brunei Darussalam [*Aircraft nationality and registration mark*]
              (FAAC)
9V .... Singapore [*Aircraft nationality and registration mark*] (FAAC)
VA .... Variometer (IAA)
VA .... Velocity Aid
VA .... Vertical Amplifier (IAA)
VA .... Victor Airways [*Aviation*] (FAAC)
VA .... Voltage Amplifier (IAA)
VA .... Voltammeter (IAA)
VAA .... Variable Attenuator Amplified
VAA .... Venda Airways [*South Africa*] [*ICAO designator*] (FAAC)
VAAC .... Vectored Thrust Aircraft [*Aviation*] (DA)
VAAM .... Voice Actuated Address Mechanism (PDAA)
VAAT .... Vibration and Acoustic Testing (IAA)
VAC .... Vacationair, Inc. [*Canada*] [*ICAO designator*] (FAAC)
VAC .... Verified Audit Circulation Corp. (NTCM)
VAC .... Visual Approach Chart [*Aviation*] (FAAC)
VAEC .... Variety and Allied Entertainments Council [*British*] (BI)
VAF .... Variety Artistes' Federation [*British*] (BI)
VAFC .... VESA [*Video Electronics Standards Association*] Advanced
              Feature Connector
VAI .... Vocational Awards International [*British*]
VAKUME ... Visual Audio Kinetic Unit Multiples and Environments (PDAA)
VAL .... Value-Oriented Algorithmic Language [*Computer science*]
              (PDAA)
VAL .... Voyageur Airways Ltd. [*Canada*] [*ICAO designator*] (FAAC)
VALOR ...... Veterans Affairs Learning Opportunities Residency Program
VAM .... Value Added Manufacture [*Program*]
VAMAS ..... Versailles Project on Advanced Materials and Standards
VAMC .... Visual Approach Monitor Chart (PDAA)
VAMP .... Vesicle-Associated Membrane Protein [*Biochemistry*]
VAMP .... Volume, Area, and Mass Properties (PDAA)
VAP .... Versatile Automatic Test Equipment Assembly Program
              [*Computer science*]
VAPOX ...... Vapor Deposit Oxide (IAA)
VAPPRF..... Vapor Proof (IAA)
VAR........... Valley Air Services, Inc. [*ICAO designator*] (FAAC)
VAR........... Varistor [*Telecommunications*] (IAA)
VAR........... Varying (IAA)
VAR........... Voltage Ampere Reactance [*AC electric motors*]
VARACTOR ... Variable Reactor (IAA)
VARCAP.... Variable Capacitor (IAA)
VARH........ Volt-Ampere Reactive Hour (IAA)
VARIAC .... Variable Capacitor (IAA)
VARIMU.... Variable Mu Tube [*Electronics*] (IAA)
VAS .... Aviatrans [*Former USSR*] [*ICAO designator*] (FAAC)
VAS .... Virtual Acoustic Synthesis [*Electronics*] (PS)
VASCA....... Electronic Valve and Semiconductor Manufacturers'
              Association (IAA)
VASCO....... Value-Added Supply Chain Optimization [*Automotive industry
              cost management*]
VAST......... Vehicle Activity Status Transmission (PDAA)
VAST......... Vehicle Automatic State Transmitter (PDAA)
VAST......... Versatile Avionics Ship Test (IAA)
VAT .... Variable Autotransformer (IAA)
VAT .... Vernier Auto Track (IAA)
VAT .... Visibility, Amount, Height of Cloud Top, Base [*Weather*] [*DoD*]
VATOL....... Verical Altitude and Take-Off and Landing (PDAA)
VAX .... Vesta Airex [*Czechoslovakia*] [*ICAO designator*] (FAAC)
VB .... Vacancy Bit (IAA)
VB .... Vibrator (IAA)
VB .... Voltage Board (IAA)
VBA .... Variable Body Armor (INF)
VBA .... Very Big Accelerator (PDAA)
VBC .... Velocity Bin Commanded
VBE/AI ...... VESA [*Video Electronics Standards Association*] BIOS [*Basic
              Input-Output System*] Extension/Audio Interface (PCM)
VBO .... Voltage Breakover (IAA)
VBW .... Air Burkina [*Burkina Faso*] [*ICAO designator*] (FAAC)

VC .... Validity Check [*Data entry test program*] [*Computer science*]
              (IAA)
VC .... Vanadium Carbide (PDAA)
VC .... Vertical Circle (IAA)
VC .... Vertical Spacing (IAA)
VC .... Voice Coil of Speaker [*Computer hardware*] (IAA)
VC .... Voltage Changer (IAA)
VCA .... Vegetarian Catering Association [*British*] (BI)
VCA .... Voltage-Controlled Amplifier (NTCM)
VCA .... Voltage-Current Adapter (IAA)
VCC .... Variable Cycle Controller (IAA)
VCC .... Veteran Car Club of Great Britain (BI)
VCC .... Voice-Controlled Carrier [*Telecommunications*] (IAA)
VCC .... Voltage-Controlled Clock (IAA)
VCCO .... Voltage-Controlled Crystal Oscillator (IAA)
VCE .... Virtual Coulomb Excitation (PDAA)
VCF .... Victor Fly [*Italy*] [*ICAO designator*] (FAAC)
VCG .... Vertical Line Through Center of Gravity (IAA)
VCNC .... Voltage-Controlled Negative Capacitance (IAA)
VCNR .... Voltage-Controlled Negative Resistance (IAA)
VCO .... Aviacion Colombiana Ltd. [*Colombia*] [*ICAO designator*]
              (FAAC)
VCO .... Variable Crystal Oscillator (IAA)
VCO .... Voice Coder [*Telecommunications*] (IAA)
VCP .... Vacuum Condensing Point (IAA)
VCP .... Vector Collecting Program [*Electronics design*] (IAA)
VCP .... Virtual Communication Path [*Computer science*] (IAA)
VCP .... Virtual Control Processor [*Computer science*] (IAA)
VCP .... Visual Comfort Probability (IAA)
VCP .... Voice Communication Panel
VCR .... Video Cartridge Recorder (IAA)
VCR .... Voltage Control Resistor (IAA)
VCS........... Vacuum Actuated Control Switch (IAA)
VCS........... Victorian Cinema Society (IAA)
VCT .... Video Contrast Tracker (PDAA)
VCT .... Viscount Air Services, Inc. [*ICAO designator*] (FAAC)
VCT .... Voltage Clock Trigger (IAA)
VCT .... Voltage-Controlled Transfer (IAA)
VCU.......... Variable Correction Unit (IAA)
VCU.......... Very Close-Up [*Cinematography*] (NTCM)
VCU.......... Video Combiner Unit (IAA)
VCY.......... Vicinity [*Aviation*] (FAAC)
VD............. Vacuum Distillation (PDAA)
VD............. Video Display (IAA)
VDA.......... Vision Distribution Amplifier (IAA)
VDA.......... Volga-Dnepr [*Former USSR*] [*ICAO designator*] (FAAC)
VDAC .... Video Display Controller (IAA)
VDANL ...... Vehicle Dynamics Analysis [*Computer simulation*] [*Automotive
              engineering*]
VDD........... Virtual Display Driver [*Computer science*]
VDES......... Voice Data Encoding System [*Telecommunications*] (IAA)
VDGS......... Visual Docking Guidance System [*Aviation*] (DA)
VDH .... Vickers Diamond Hardness (IAA)
VDI .... Variable Duration Impulse (IAA)
VDI .... Visual Doppler Indicator (IAA)
VDIFF .... Visual Difference [*Computer science*] (NHD)
VDNCS...... Vapor-Deposited Noncrystalline Solid (PDAA)
VDR........... Videotape Recorder (IAA)
VDSQ .... Video Data Sequence (NTCM)
VDT........... Variable Data Table
VDT........... Vayudoot [*India*] [*ICAO designator*] (FAAC)
VDT........... Vertical Deflection Terminal (IAA)
VDT........... Visual Display Terminal (IAA)
VDU.......... Variable Delay Unit (IAA)
VDU.......... Video Distribution Unit
VDWE .... Van der Waals Epitaxy [*Physics*]
VE .... Voltage (IAA)
VEC .... Valence Electron Concentration (PDAA)
VEC .... Venezolana Servicios Expresos de Carga Internacional CA
              [*Venezuela*] [*ICAO designator*] (FAAC)
VEDILIS .... Vehicle Discharge Lighting System
VEFV......... Voice-Excited Formant Vocoder (PDAA)

115

VEG .... Vega Aircompany [*Russian Federation*] [*ICAO designator*] (FAAC)
VEGAS .... Virtual-Egress Analysis and Simulation (ECON)
VEGF .... Vascular Endothelial Growth Factor [*Biochemistry*]
VEHDYN ... Vehicle Dynamics
VEJ .... Aero Ejecutivos CA [*Venezuela*] [*ICAO designator*] (FAAC)
VEL .... Verified Encoded Logging (NTCM)
VEM .... Vector Element by Element Multiply (IAA)
VEMS .... Versatile Exercise Mine System [*Military*] (PDAA)
VEN .... Capital Aviation Services Ltd. [*Canada*] [*ICAO designator*] (FAAC)
VENUS ...... Variable and Efficient Network Utility Service (IAA)
VENUS ...... Vertical Alignment Design by the Nodal-Tangent and Undulation System (PDAA)
VERA .... Voluntary Early Retirement Authority [*DoD*]
VERB .... Visual Electronic Remote Blackboard (PDAA)
VERDAN ... Vertical Digital Analyzer (IAA)
VEREAD .... Value Engineering Retrieval of Esoteric Administrative Data (PDAA)
VERRP .... Voluntary Early Release and Retirement Program [*Army*]
VERVIS ..... Vertical Visibility [*Aviation*] (DA)
VES .... Vector Element by Element Sum (IAA)
VES .... Vieques Air Link, Inc. [*ICAO designator*] (FAAC)
VESCAD .... Vehicle Electrical System Computer-Aided Design
VESID .... Vocational and Educational Services for Individuals with Disabilities
VESMC ...... Vinyl Ester Sheet Molding Compound [*Plastics*]
VETFR .... Veterans Transition Franchise Initiative Program
VETY .... Vocabulary Etymology
VF .... Viscosity Factor (IAA)
VFC .... Variable Frequency Clock (IAA)
VFC .... Variable Frequency Crystal (IAA)
VFD .... Voltage Fault Detector [*Electronics*] (IAA)
VFEA .... Vacuum Freezing Ejector Absorption (PDAA)
VFEQT .... Voice Frequency Equipment [*Telecommunications*] (IAA)
VFET .... Vertical Field Effect Transistor (IAA)
VFOAR ...... Vandenberg Field Office of Aerospace Research [*Air Force*] (PDAA)
VFSS .... Variable Frequency Selection System [*Aviation*] (DA)
VFX .... Variable Frequency Mixer (IAA)
VFX .... Vector Float-to-Fix (IAA)
VGCC .... Voltage-Gated Calcium Channel [*Neurophysiology*]
VGE .... Air Service Vosges [*France*] [*ICAO designator*] (FAAC)
VGG .... Video Graphics Generator
VGH .... Verlagsgruppe Georg von Holtzbrinck [*Commercial firm*] [*Germany*]
VGI .... Veiling Glare Index [*Vision research*]
VGM .... Variable Grating Mode (PDAA)
VGR .... Variable Gear Ratio [*Automotive steering systems*]
VGS .... Vings [*Bulgaria*] [*ICAO designator*] (FAAC)
VH .... Vertical Hook (IAA)
VH .... Very Hard (IAA)
VHAD .... Vehicle Headlight Aiming Device [*Automotive engineering*]
VHD .... Viral Haemorrhagic Disease
VHES .... Vitro Hanford Engineering Service (IAA)
VHFRT .... Very-High Frequency Radio Telephony (PDAA)
VHI .... Vapro Hazard Index [*Environmental science*]
VHI .... Vehicle Heading Indicator
VHIC .... Vermont Health Care Information, Consortium
VHM .... Vibrating Head Magnetometer (IAA)
VHMWPE ... Very-High Molecular Weight Polyethylene (PDAA)
VHPIC .... Very-High Performance Integrated Circuit [*Electronics*] (PDAA)
VHV .... Very-High Voltage (IAA)
VHVI .... Very High Viscosity Index [*Petroleum oils*]
VI .... Variable Intensity Light [*Aviation*] (DA)
VI .... Variable Intensity (IAA)
VI .... Vertical Incidence (IAA)
VI .... Virgin Islands (IAA)
VI .... Visual Interface [*Computer science*] (NHD)
VIA .... Versatile Interface Adapter [*Telecommunications*] (IAA)
VIA .... VIASA, Venezolana International de Aviacion SA [*Venezuela*] [*ICAO designator*] (FAAC)
VIATLS ...... Visual Airborne Target Locator System [*Military*] (PDAA)
VIB .... Vibrator (IAA)
VIBAC .... Vehicle Ice-Breaking Air Cushion (PDAA)
VIBT .... Vibrator (IAA)
VIC .... Video Image Correlation
VICC .... Visual Information Control Console [*Telecommunications*] (IAA)
VICCI .... Voice-Initiated Cockpit Control and Integration [*Aviation*] (PDAA)
VICES .... Voice Internal Communications Equipment for Submarines (PDAA)
VICS .... Vehicle Information and Control System [*Highway traffic management*]
VID .... Variable Intermittent Duty (IAA)
VIDOC .... Video Documentary (NTCM)
VIDOC .... Visual Information Documentation [*Military*]
VID-R .... Visual Information Display and Retrieval System [*Computer science*] (PDAA)
VIDS .... Vehicle Integrated Defense System [*Military*]
VIDSEC ..... Video Systems Exposition and Conference (PDAA)
VIDT .... Variable Inductance Displacement Transducer (PDAA)
VIE .... Vacuum Insulated Evaporator (PDAA)

VIE .... Virtual Information Environment [*Computer science*] (PCM)
VIE .... Visual Indicating Equipment [*Telecommunications*] (IAA)
VIF .... Voice Interface Frame [*Telecommunications*] (IAA)
VIK .... Viking International Airlines [*ICAO designator*] (FAAC)
VIM .... Air-Via [*Bulgaria*] [*ICAO designator*] (FAAC)
VIMCOS .... Vehicle for the Investigation of Maintenance Control System (PDAA)
VIMS .... Versatile Interior Multiplex System (PDAA)
VIMS .... Visible-Infrared Mapping Spectrometer [*Instrumentation*]
VIN .... Vinair-Helicopteros Ltda. [*Portugal*] [*ICAO designator*] (FAAC)
VIP .... V-Isolation with Polysilicon Backfill
VIP .... V-Shaped Isolation Regions Filled with Polycrystalline Silicon (IAA)
VIP .... Vector Inner Product (IAA)
VIP .... Verifying Interpreting Punch (IAA)
VIP .... Virtual Instruction Package (IAA)
VIP .... Visual Image Processor (IAA)
VIP .... Visual Indicator Panel (IAA)
VIP .... Visual Interactive Programming [*Computer science*]
ViP .... Visual Programmer [*Computer science*] (PCM)
VIP .... Voltage Impulse Protection (IAA)
VIR .... Virgin Atlantic [*British*] [*ICAO designator*] (FAAC)
VIRS .... Vertical Interval Reference Signal [*Automatic color adjustment*] [*Television*] (IAA)
VIS .... Jet Servisx SA de CV [*Mexico*] [*ICAO designator*] (FAAC)
VIS .... Voltage Inverter Switch (IAA)
VISAM ...... Virtual Index Sequential Access Method (IAA)
VisiCalc ..... Visible Calculation [*Electronic spreadsheet program brand*]
VISQI .... Visual Image Quality Indicator (PDAA)
VISTA .... Visual Talking [*Telecommunications*] (IAA)
VIT .... Variable Injection Timing [*Diesel engines*]
VIT .... Vertical Interval Test [*Automatic color adjustment*] [*Television*] (IAA)
VIT .... Very Intelligent Terminal (IAA)
VITA .... Volunteers for International Technical Assistance (IAA)
VITC .... Vertical Interval Time Code (NTCM)
VITEAC ..... Video Transmission Engineering Advisory Committee [*Army*] (PDAA)
VITROLAIN ... Vitreous Enamel Porcelain (IAA)
VIV .... Viajes Internacionales de Vacaciones SA [*Spain*] [*ICAO designator*] (FAAC)
VIVA .... Viajes Internacionales de Vacaciones SA [*Spain*] [*ICAO designator*] (FAAC)
VIZ .... Vizmo [*Projection device*] (NTCM)
VJA .... ValuJet Airlines, Inc. [*ICAO designator*] (FAAC)
VKG .... Scanair Ltd. [*Denmark*] [*ICAO designator*] (FAAC)
VKL .... Aerovekel SA [*Mexico*] [*ICAO designator*] (FAAC)
VKR .... Video Kinescope Recording (PDAA)
VL .... Voltage-Logic [*Electronics*] (IAA)
VLA .... Very Large Airplane (PDAA)
VLA .... Very Large Antenna [*Telecommunications*] (IAA)
VLBC .... Very Large Bulk-Cargo Carrier (PDAA)
VLC .... Vehicle Launch Center [*Automotive industry project management*]
VLCD .... Very-Low-Cost Display (IAA)
VLDS .... Variable Length Distinguishing Sequence (IAA)
VLE .... Voice Line Expansion [*Telecommunications*] (IAA)
VLEA .... Very Long Endurance Aircraft (PDAA)
VLFD .... Very-Low-Frequency Direct [*Electronics*] (IAA)
VLFD .... Via Low Frequency Direct [*Aviation*] (FAAC)
VLG .... Trans Air Valtologia [*Moldova*] [*ICAO designator*] (FAAC)
VLI .... Very-Low Impedance (IAA)
VLL .... Valley SAR Training Unit [*British*] [*ICAO designator*] (FAAC)
VLM .... Vlaamse Luchttransportmaatschappij NV [*Belgium*] [*ICAO designator*] (FAAC)
VLN .... Variable Length (IAA)
VLOOC ...... Very Large Ore-Oil Carrier (PDAA)
VLP .... Volunteer Lawyers for the Poor [*An association*]
VLR .... Volare [*Russian Federation*] [*ICAO designator*] (FAAC)
VLY .... Volley (IAA)
VM .... Virtual Multi-Access [*Computer science*] (IAA)
VM .... Viscosity Modifier [*Lubricants*]
VMA .... Monmouth Airlines, Inc. [*ICAO designator*] (FAAC)
VMAI .... Veterinary Medical Association of Ireland (BI)
VMC .... Vector Move Convert (IAA)
VMC .... Vitramon Microwave Corp. (IAA)
VMD .... Vertical Main Distribution (IAA)
VME .... Volvo Mechanical Equipment [*Auto industry supplier*]
VMH .... Visual Maneuvering Height [*Aviation*] (DA)
VMOS .... Vertical Metal-Oxide Semiconductor (IAA)
VMOS .... Virtual Memory Operating System (IAA)
VMS .... Valve Monitoring System (IAA)
VMS .... Variable Magnetic Shunt [*Electronics*] (IAA)
VMS .... Variable Memory System [*Computer science*] (IAA)
VMS .... Voice Mail System [*Telecommunications*] (IAA)
VM/SP .... Virtual Machine/System Product [*Operating system for large IBM mainframe computers*]
VMU .... Variable Match Unit (IAA)
VMU .... Vehicle Management Unit [*Powertrain*] [*Automotive engineering*]
VMU .... Voice Management Unit (DA)
VNA .... Very Narrow Aisle Truck (PDAA)
VNA .... Warbelow's Air Ventures, Inc. [*ICAO designator*] (FAAC)
VNCM .... Vietnam Campaign Medal [*Military decoration*]

VNR........... Viennair Luftfahrt GmbH [*Austria*] [*ICAO designator*] (FAAC)
VNRC........ Vegetarian Nutritional Research Center (PDAA)
VNS .... Vehicular Navigation System [*Military*]
VNS .... Venus Air Services Ltd. [*Ghana*] [*ICAO designator*] (FAAC)
VNS .... Vicarious Nucleophilic Substitution [*Organic chemistry*]
VNX........... Venexcargo (Transporte Aereo de Carga SA) [*Venezuela*] [*ICAO designator*] (FAAC)
VO.............. Vacuum-Tube Oscillator (IAA)
VO.............. Vertical Output (IAA)
VO.............. Video Operator (NTCM)
VOC........... Voice of the Customer [*Business term*]
VOC........... Voice-Operated Control [*Telecommunications*] (IAA)
VOC........... Voice-Operated Relay Circuit (IAA)
VOCSU ...... Voice-Operated Carrier Switching Unit (IAA)
VOF........... Volatile Organic Fraction [*Automotive exhaust emission testing*]
VOICES ..... Voice-Operated Identification Computer Entry System (PDAA)
VOL........... Volume Label (IAA)
VOL........... Volvo AB [*Sweden*] [*ICAO designator*] (FAAC)
VOLCAT.... Volume Catalog (IAA)
VOLLIM.... Voltage Limiter (IAA)
VOLVAR.... Volume-Variety (PDAA)
VOLWARE ... Volume-Weighted Averages of Realized Prices
VOM........... Volt-Ohm-Milliampere Meter [*Electronics*] (IAA)
VOM........... Volt Ohmmeter [*Electronics*] (IAA)
VOMA........ Volt-Ohm-Milliampere [*Electronics*] (IAA)
VOP........... Value Option Package [*Automotive marketing*]
VOP........... Value of Production
VOQ .... Vehicle Owner's Questionnaire [*Auto safety research*]
VOR........... Sunna Air Ltd. [*Iceland*] [*ICAO designator*] (FAAC)
VORDAC ... VHF [*Very-High-Frequency*] Omnidirectional Range and Distance Measuring Equipment for Average Coverage (IAA)
VORTAC.... VHF [*Very-High-Frequency*] Omnidirectional Range Collocated with TACAN [*Tactical Air Navigation System*] (IAA)
VORTAC.... VHF [*Very-High-Frequency*] Omnidirectional Range Tactical Air Navigation (IAA)
VORTAL.... Vertical Ommi-Range, Take-Off, Approach, and Landing System (PDAA)
VORTEX.... Varian Omnitaste Real Time Executive [*Computer science*] (IAA)
VOS .... Vacuum Oven Sublimation [*Automotive exhaust emission testing*]
VOS .... Vertical Obstacle SONAR (IAA)
VOS .... Vision on Sound (IAA)
VOSE......... Vacuum Operation of Spacecraft Equipment (IAA)
VO/SOT..... Voiceover/Sound on Tape [*Television*] (NTCM)
VOT........... Visual Omnirange Test [*Aviation*] (IAA)
VOTEM ..... Voice-Operated Typewriter Employing Morse [*Telecommunications*] (IAA)
VOY........... Voice-Operated Relay (IAA)
VP.............. Validation Parameter (DA)
VP.............. Velocity of Propagation (IAA)
VP.............. Virtual Machine Control Program [*Computer science*] (IAA)
VPA........... Village Produce Association [*British*] (BI)
VPB........... Virtually-Pivoted Beam LASER (IAA)
VPC .... Vertical Path Computer (PDAA)
VPC .... Virginia Panel Corp. (IAA)
VPCF......... Vapor Pressure Correction Factor [*Nuclear energy*] (IAA)
VPCIS........ Voice-Operated Computerized Identification System (PDAA)
VPD .... Vapor Phase Deposition [*Coating technology*]
VPD .... Visual Pattern Discrimination (PDAA)
VPE........... Vapor Growth Epitaxy [*Materials processing*] (IAA)
VPE........... Visual Programming Environment
VPE........... Vulcanized Polyethylene (IAA)
VPH........... Vickers Pyramid Hardness Number (PDAA)
VPH........... Viewers-per-Household [*Television ratings*] (NTCM)
VPI............ Vehicle Personality Module [*Automotive engineering*]
VPM........... Volts per Mile (IAA)
VPOC .... Variable Performance Optimizing Controller (IAA)
VPR .... Vacuum Pipette Rig (PDAA)
VPR .... Variable Parameter Record [*Statistics*] (IAA)
VPR .... Voice Position Report (DA)
VPRESSVB ... Vice-Presidential Service Badge [*Military decoration*]
VPS........... Vapor Phase Soldering (PDAA)
VPVH .... Viewers-per-Viewing Household [*Television ratings*] (NTCM)
VR.............. Variable Resistance [*or Resistor*] (IAA)
VR.............. Vertical Redundancy [*Telecommunications*] (IAA)
VR.............. Virtual Equals Real [*Computer science*] (IAA)
VR.............. Visual Route (DA)
VRB .... Valve-Regulated Battery [*Energy source*]
VRB .... VHF [*Very-High-Frequency*] Recovery Beacon (IAA)
VRC .... Taxi Aereo de Veracruz [*Mexico*] [*ICAO designator*] (FAAC)
VRC .... Vehicle Reference Controller [*Military*]
VRC .... Visible Record Computer (IAA)
VRCM .... Variable Relay Control Module [*Cooling systems*] [*Automotive engineering*]
VRCR........ Vertical Redundancy Check Register [*Telecommunications*] (IAA)
VRD........... Variable Ratio Divider (IAA)
VRDO........ Variable Rate Demand Obligation
VRDU........ Variable Range Delay Unit (PDAA)
V-RG......... Vaccinia-Rabies Glycoprotein [*Medicine*]
VRG........... Vertical Reference Gyro (DA)

VRG .... Viacao Aerea Rio-Grandense SA [*Brazil*] [*ICAO designator*] (FAAC)
VRM .... Virtual Resource Manager [*Computer science*] (IAA)
VRO........... Aerovitro SA de CV [*Mexico*] [*ICAO designator*] (FAAC)
VRP........... Visual Reporting Point (DA)
VRS........... Virtual Reality and Simulation
VRU........... Vehicle Reference Unit
VRU........... Voice Read Out Unit [*Telecommunications*] (IAA)
VRY .... Very [*Automotive advertising*]
VRZ .... Aero Veracruz SA de CV [*Mexico*] [*ICAO designator*] (FAAC)
VS .... Vector Scan [*Digital imaging*] (IAA)
VS .... Very Soft (IAA)
VS .... Video and Synchronization [*Telecommunications*] (IAA)
VS .... Voice Switching [*Telecommunications*] (IAA)
VS .... Voltage Switching (IAA)
V1S .... Vee One Side (DAC)
VSA .... Variable Speed Assembly [*Mechanical powertrain*]
VSAM........ Variable, Spanned, and Undefined Mode (IAA)
VSB........... Vickers Ltd. [*British*] [*ICAO designator*] (FAAC)
VSBS .... Voluntary Standards Bodies (IAA)
VSC........... Aerovias Especiales de Carga Ltda. [*Colombia*] [*ICAO designator*] (FAAC)
VSD .... Voter-Switch-Disagreement Detector (PDAA)
VSE........... Vuelos Asesorias y Representaciones SA de CV [*Mexico*] [*ICAO designator*] (FAAC)
VSF........... VETRONICS [*Vehicle Electronics*] Simulation Facility [*Army*] (RDA)
VSFS.......... Voice Store and Forward Messaging System [*Telecommunications*] (IAA)
VSG .... Video Symbology Generator
VSI............ Variable Separation Incentive [*DoD*]
VSI............ Vertical Sideband [*Radio frequency*] [*Telecommunications*] (IAA)
VSI............ Voluntary Separation Incentive [*DoD*]
VSIP .... Voluntary Separation Incentive Program [*DoD*]
VSN .... Vision Airways Corp. [*Canada*] [*ICAO designator*] (FAAC)
VSN .... Volume Serial Number [*Computer science*] (IAA)
VSO........... Voltage-Sensitive Oscillator (IAA)
VSP........... Viacao Aerea Sao Paulo SA [*Brazil*] [*ICAO designator*] (FAAC)
VSP........... Voltage-Stabilized Polyethylene (IAA)
VSPI.......... Visual Glide Path Indicator [*Aviation*] (FAAC)
VSQG .... Very Small Quantity Generator [*Environmental science*]
VSR........... Variable Length Shift Register [*Computer science*] (IAA)
VSS........... Vapor Suppression System [*Nuclear energy*] (IAA)
VSS........... Vented Suppressive Shielding
VSS........... Virgin Islands Seaplane Shuttle, Inc. [*ICAO designator*] (FAAC)
VST........... Visible Speech Translator (IAA)
VSYNCH ... Vertical Synchronization [*Computer science*] (IAA)
VT .... Vacuum Telegraphy [*Telecommunications*] (IAA)
VT .... Variable Threshold (IAA)
VT .... Voltage Transformer (IAA)
VTA .... Air Tahiti [*France*] [*ICAO designator*] (FAAC)
VTAM .... Varian Telecommunication Access Method (IAA)
VTC .... Vacuum Thermal Chamber (IAA)
VTC .... Variable Timing Control [*Intake subsystem*] [*Automotive engineering*]
VTC .... Viscosity Temperature Coefficient (IAA)
VTC .... Volvo Truck Corp.
VTCT........ Vocational Training Charitable Trust [*British*]
VTD .... Vacuum-Tube Detector (IAA)
VTD .... Vertical Tape Display (IAA)
VTO........... Vacuum-Tube Oscillator (IAA)
VTOF......... Voltage-to-Frequency (IAA)
VTR........... Vitkovice Air [*Czech Republic*] [*ICAO designator*] (FAAC)
VTRAM...... Variable Topology Random Access Memory [*Computer science*] (PDAA)
VTS........... Virtual Terminal System [*Computer science*] (IAA)
VTSU......... Virtual Terminal Support [*Computer science*] (IAA)
VTU........... Vibrating Tie Under-Cutter (PDAA)
VTZ .... Vitjaz [*Russian Federation*] [*ICAO designator*] (FAAC)
VUE........... Visual User Environment [*Military*]
VUEC .... Variable Underwater Experimental Community (PDAA)
VUN........... Air Ivoire Societe [*Ivory Coast*] [*ICAO designator*] (FAAC)
VUVM .... Voluntary Universal Marking Program (IAA)
VV .... Valve Voltmeter (IAA)
VV .... Vertical Visibility (DA)
VV .... Volume (NTCM)
VVC .... Variable Voltage Capacitor (IAA)
V/VH .... Viewers-per-Viewing Household [*Television ratings*] (NTCM)
VVM.......... Valve Voltmeter (IAA)
VVV........... Intercontinental Airlines Ltd. [*Nigeria*] [*ICAO designator*] (FAAC)
VWA.......... Volkswagen of America (ECON)
VWAM....... Very Wide Area Mine (RDA)
VWS .... Vortex Wake System [*Aviation*] (DA)
VYC .... Yvic Airlines [*Nigeria*] [*ICAO designator*] (FAAC)
VYT .... Valley FTU [*British*] [*ICAO designator*] (FAAC)

W

W .... Microwatt (IAA)
W .... [*Domestic*] Water Shutoff [*NFPA pre-fire planning symbol*] (NFPA)
W .... Watt Meter (IAA)
W .... Wireless [*Communication*] (IAA)
4W .... Yemen Arab Republic [*Aircraft nationality and registration mark*] (FAAC)
5W .... Samoa Islands [*Aircraft nationality and registration mark*] (FAAC)
6W .... Senegal [*Aircraft nationality and registration mark*] (FAAC)
WA .... Wave Analyzer (IAA)
WA .... Wideband Amplifier
WA .... Wing Attack [*Netball*]
WAA .... Worked All America [*Amateur radio*] [*Contacted at least one station in all counties*] (IAA)
WAAC .... Working Ampere Alternating Current (IAA)
WAACS ...... Western Airways and Air Communications Service (IAA)
WAB .... Aero Industries, Inc. [*ICAO designator*] (FAAC)
WAC .... Wagner Computer (IAA)
WAC .... Weak Affinity Chromatography [*Analytical chemistry*]
WAC .... Worked All Countries [*Contacted at least one station in all countries*] [*Amateur radio*] (IAA)
WAC .... World Air Network Co. Ltd. [*Japan*] [*ICAO designator*] (FAAC)
WACB .... World Association for Christian Broadcasting (IAA)
WACK .... Wait and Acknowledge (IAA)
WACS .... Wide Angle Collimated Display System [*Aviation*] (DA)
WAD .... Weapons Alert Designator [*Army*] (ADDR)
WAD .... Work Adjustment Program [*Education*]
WADR .... Waste Acid Detoxification and Reclamation [*Environmental science*]
WADSEP ... Walking and Dredging Self-Elevating Platform (PDAA)
WAE .... Worked All Europe [*Contacted at least one station in all European countries*] [*Amateur radio*] (IAA)
WAF .... Flamenco Airways, Inc. [*ICAO designator*] (FAAC)
WAF .... Wrap-Around-Fin (PDAA)
WAFC .... World Area Forecast Center [*Aviation*] (FAAC)
WAFV .... Wheeled Armoured Fighting Vehicle [*Military*]
WAG .... Worked All Goose (IAA)
WAG .... World Airline (Gambia) Ltd. [*ICAO designator*] (FAAC)
WAGBI ...... Wildfowlers' Association of Great Britain and Ireland (BI)
WAH .... Wage and Hour Division [*Department of Labor*] (IAA)
WAI .... Worked All Italy [*Amateur radio*] (IAA)
WAIM .... Wide-Angle Impedance Matching (PDAA)
WAIP .... Worked All Italian Provinces [*Amateur radio*] (IAA)
WAIS .... Wide Area Information Server [*Computer science*]
WAK .... Alaska Juneau Aeronautics, Inc. [*ICAO designator*] (FAAC)
WAL .... Western Artic Air Ltd. [*Canada*] [*ICAO designator*] (FAAC)
WAMCE ..... Western Association of Minority Consulting Engineers (IAA)
WAMI .... Wide-Angle Michelson Interferometer (PDAA)
WAMI .... World Association for Medical Informatics (IAA)
WAMP .... Wire Antenna Modeling Program (PDAA)
WAND .... Westinghouse Alphanumeric Display (IAA)
WAO .... Wet-Air Oxidation (PDAA)
WAPDA ..... Water and Power Development Authority (IAA)
WAR .... NZ Warbirds Association, Inc. [*New Zealand*] [*ICAO designator*] (FAAC)
WARC .... World Administrative Radio Conference [*International Telecommunication Union*] (NTCM)
WARC-BS ... World Administrative Radio Conference for Broadcast Satellite Service [*International Telecommunication Union*] (NTCM)
WARM .... Wartime Reserve Mode [*Military*]
WARR .... Waste Acid Release Reduction [*Environmental science*]
WARSIM ... Warfighters' Simulation [*DoD*]
WAS .... Walsten Air Services [*Canada*] [*ICAO designator*] (FAAC)
WAS .... Wide Area Surveillance [*Military*]
WASA .... Wax Anti-Settling Additive [*Diesel fuel*]
WASPM ..... Wide Area Side Penetrator Mine [*Army*] (ADDR)
WAST .... Western Alaska Standard Time
WASTN ...... Wireless Auxiliary Station [*Telecommunications*] (IAA)
WAT .... Wings Air Transport Co. [*Sudan*] [*ICAO designator*] (FAAC)
WATC .... Wide-Area Traffic Control (PDAA)
WATG .... Wave-Activated Turbine Generator (PDAA)
WATS .... Wide-Area Telephone Service [*Telecommunications*] (IAA)

WAV .... West-Avin Oy [*Finland*] [*ICAO designator*] (FAAC)
WAVE .... Westinghouse Audio Visual Electronics (IAA)
WAVEGD ... Waveguide Standards (IAA)
WAW .... Wings Airways [*ICAO designator*] (FAAC)
WAW .... Write-After-Write [*Computer science*]
WAY .... Worked All Yokosuka [*Amateur radio*] (IAA)
WAZ .... Worked All Zones [*Contacted at least one station in all zones*] [*Amateur radio*] (IAA)
WB .... [*Sprinkler System*] Water Flow Bell [*NFPA pre-fire planning symbol*] (NFPA)
WB .... Welded Base (DAC)
WB .... White Bag Propellant [*Army*] (ADDR)
WB .... White Balance [*Television*] (NTCM)
WBA .... West Coast Air [*Gambia*] [*ICAO designator*] (FAAC)
WBIC .... Weather and Battle-Induced Contaminant (PDAA)
WBPA .... Western Book Publishers Association (NTCM)
WBPB .... Wideband Patch Bay [*Telecommunications*] (IAA)
WBPT .... Wet-Bulb Potential Temperature (PDAA)
WBS .... Wide Body STOL [*Short Takeoff and Landing*] [*Aviation*] (IAA)
WBS .... World Broadcasting System (NTCM)
WBSM .... Weber per Square Meter (IAA)
WBWP .... Warner Brothers Worldwide Publishing [*Commercial firm*]
WC .... Weather Center [*Meteorology*] (DA)
WC .... Western Civilization
WC .... Wet Chemical System [*NFPA pre-fire planning symbol*] (NFPA)
WC .... Wireless Communication (IAA)
WC .... Working Current (IAA)
WCA .... Warm Cranking Amperes [*Battery*] [*Automotive engineering*]
WCA .... Wholesale Confectioners Alliance Ltd. [*British*] (BI)
WCA .... Wind Correction Angle [*Aviation*] (DA)
WCARU ...... Western Carolina University (PDAA)
WCB .... West Africa Airlines Ltd. [*Ghana*] [*ICAO designator*] (FAAC)
WCC .... Sports Air Travel, Inc. [*ICAO designator*] (FAAC)
WCC .... Write Control Character [*Computer science*] (IAA)
WCCDBP ... Weapon Control Computer Debug Program [*Military*]
WCCE .... World Conference on Computers in Education
WCD .... Weather Card Data (IAA)
WCD .... Worse Case Difference (IAA)
WCDPC ...... War Control Data Processing Center (IAA)
WCF .... Workers' Christian Fellowship [*British*] (BI)
WCG .... West Coast Airlines Ltd. [*Ghana*] [*ICAO designator*] (FAAC)
WCM .... World-Class Manufacturing [*Management technique*]
WCMF .... World Congress on Metal Finishing (PDAA)
WCMR .... World Conference on Missionary Radio [*Later, ICB*] (NTCM)
WCNDT ...... World Conference on Non-Destructive Testing (PDAA)
WCO .... Columbia Helicopters, Inc. [*ICAO designator*] (FAAC)
WCQL .... Worst Cycle Quantity Level (PDAA)
WCS .... Watercolor Spectrometer (PDAA)
WCS .... Work Control Status
WCT .... Water-Cooled Tube [*Nuclear energy*] (IAA)
WCY .... Viking Express, Inc. [*ICAO designator*] (FAAC)
WD .... Waveform Digitizer [*Telecommunications*] (IAA)
WD .... Waveform Distortion [*Telecommunications*] (IAA)
WD .... Williams Domain [*Computer science*] (IAA)
WD .... Wing Defence [*Netball*]
WD .... Wiring Diagram (IAA)
WDA .... Wardair Canada Ltd. [*ICAO designator*] (FAAC)
WDA .... World Dance Alliance
WDAG .... Word Driver and Gate [*Computer science*] (IAA)
WDF .... Wave Digital Filter (PDAA)
WDFM .... Wright Dust Feed Mechanism (PDAA)
WDG .... Ministry of Agriculture Fisheries and Food [*British*] [*ICAO designator*] (FAAC)
WDM .... Weapon Delivery Model (PDAA)
WDMCC .... Walt Disney Memorial Cancer Institute
WDR .... Winged Russia [*Russian Federation*] [*ICAO designator*] (FAAC)
WDS .... Four Winds Aviation Ltd. [*ICAO designator*] (FAAC)
WDT .... Weight Data Transmitter (IAA)
WDTRS ...... Westinghouse Development Test Requirement Specification (IAA)
WDY .... Phoenix Airline Services, Inc. [*ICAO designator*] (FAAC)
WEAC .... West European Advisory Committee [*Radio Free Europe*] (NTCM)

WEC .... Universal Airlines, Inc. [*ICAO designator*]   (FAAC)
WED .... World Environment Day
WEDA .... Wholesale Egg Distributors' Association [*British*]   (BI)
WEERC ...... Western Electric Engineering Research Center   (IAA)
WEF .... Waste Environmental Federation
WEF .... Women's Employment Federation [*British*]   (BI)
WEFC .... Weather Facsimile [*Environmental Science Services Administration*]   (IAA)
WEICO ...... Westinghouse Electric International Co.   (IAA)
WEJ .... West Air Sweden AB [*ICAO designator*]   (FAAC)
WEMA .... Winding Engine Manufacturers' Association [*British*]   (BI)
WEN .... Write Enable [*Computer science*]   (IAA)
WEPU .... Weighted Elementary Pupil Unit [*Education*]   (AEE)
WES .... Women's Engineering Society   (IAA)
WESC .... Wire-Explosion-Spray Coating   (PDAA)
WESCARS ... West Coast Amateur Radio Service   (PDAA)
WESDEX ... Western Design Engineering Exposition   (PDAA)
WET .... Weighted Effective Temperature   (IAA)
WET .... Western European Time   (IAA)
WEW .... West Wind Aviation, Inc. [*Canada*] [*ICAO designator*]   (FAAC)
WEX .... Wings Express, Inc. [*ICAO designator*]   (FAAC)
WEZ .... Weapon Engagement Zone [*Army*]   (ADDR)
WF .... Wave Frequency [*Telecommunications*]   (IAA)
WF .... Waveform [*Telecommunications*]   (IAA)
WF .... Wide Flange   (DAC)
WF .... Wind Finding RADAR   (IAA)
WFD .... Woodford BAE [*British*] [*ICAO designator*]   (FAAC)
WFD .... Work Function Difference [*Physics*]   (IAA)
WFDA .... Wholesale Floorcovering Distributors' Association [*British*]   (BI)
WFDA .... Wholesale Footwear Distributors' Association [*British*]   (BI)
WFES .... Windshield Flight Environment Simulator   (PDAA)
WFF .... Wavy Vortex Flow [*Fluid mechanics*]
WFGA .... Women's Farm and Garden Association [*British*]   (BI)
WFIV .... White Light Fringe Image Velocimeter   (PDAA)
WFO .... Wilbur's, Inc. [*ICAO designator*]   (FAAC)
WFP .... Water for People [*An association*]   (EA)
WGF .... Women's Gas Federation [*British*]   (BI)
WGK .... Wasser Gefahrdungsklasse [*Water hazard classification*] [*Germany*]
WGN .... White Gaussian Noise [*Random interference caused by movement of electricity in line*] [*Telecommunications*]   (IAA)
WGP .... William Grand Prix Racing Ltd. [*Cayman Islands*] [*ICAO designator*]   (FAAC)
WGT .... Wet Globe Temperature   (PDAA)
WH .... Wall Hydrant [*NFPA pre-fire planning symbol*]   (NFPA)
WHE .... Westland Helicopters Ltd. [*British*] [*ICAO designator*]   (FAAC)
WHI .... Women's Health Initiative [*National Institutes of Health*]
WHIMS ..... Wet High Intensity Magnetic Separation   (PDAA)
WHLS .... Wheels [*Automotive advertising*]
WHRA .... Welwyn Hall Research Association   (PDAA)
WHRM ...... Watt-Hour Meter   (IAA)
WHY .... Air Sorel Ltd. [*Canada*] [*ICAO designator*]   (FAAC)
WI .... Water Inlet   (DAC)
WI .... Wilderness Inquiry [*An association*]   (EA)
WIA .... Windward Islands Airways International NV [*Netherlands*] [*ICAO designator*]   (FAAC)
WIAA .... Women's International Association of Aeronautics   (IAA)
WIBNI .... Wouldn't It Be Nice If [*Computer hacker terminology*]   (NHD)
WICE .... World Industry Council for the Environment
WICHE ...... Western Interstate Commission for Higher Education   (AEE)
WIF .... Wideroe's Flyveselskap AS [*Norway*] [*ICAO designator*]   (FAAC)
WIG .... Wiggins Airways [*ICAO designator*]   (FAAC)
WIGE .... Wing-in-Ground Effect   (PDAA)
WIK .... Waikato Aero Club, Inc. [*New Zealand*] [*ICAO designator*]   (FAAC)
WIN .... Winlink (St. Lucia) Ltd. [*ICAO designator*]   (FAAC)
WINTEM... [*Upper*] Wind and Temperature Forecast [*Meteorology*]   (DA)
WISE .... Wheaton Information System for Education   (IAA)
WISHA ...... Washington Industrial Safety and Health Act   (IAA)
WISL .... Westinghouse Information Systems Laboratory   (IAA)
WIT .... Wier-in-Tube Sensor   (PDAA)
WIT .... Wittering FTU [*British*] [*ICAO designator*]   (FAAC)
WIT .... Workflow Innovation Toolkit   (PCM)
WIT .... Worst Injection Timing   (PDAA)
WIUAB ..... Women's Inter-University Athletic Board [*British*]   (BI)
WIZ .... Merlin Executive Aviation Group Ltd. [*British*] [*ICAO designator*]   (FAAC)
WJD .... Water Jet Drilling   (PDAA)
WKC .... Western Kenya Aircharters Co. Ltd. [*ICAO designator*]   (FAAC)
WKGV ...... Working Voltage   (IAA)
WL .... Width-to-Length [*Ratio*]   (IAA)
WL .... Word Length   (IAA)
WLA .... West London Aero Services Ltd. [*British*] [*ICAO designator*]   (FAAC)
WLD .... Warning Light Driver   (IAA)
WLD .... Wilderness Airline (1975) Ltd. [*Canada*] [*ICAO designator*]   (FAAC)
WLDA .... Wholesale Leather Distributors Association [*British*]   (BI)
WLDG .... Welding   (IAA)
WLHN....... Wideband-Limiter-Heterodyne-Narrowband   (PDAA)
WLO .... Willowair Ltd. [*British*] [*ICAO designator*]   (FAAC)
WLR .... Wallisair Compagnie [*France*] [*ICAO designator*]   (FAAC)
WLS .... Williams Air, Inc. [*ICAO designator*]   (FAAC)

WM .... Western Microwave, Inc.   (IAA)
WMB .... West Merchant Bank   (ECON)
WMIN .... Words per Minute   (IAA)
WMNC....... Whole Mononuclear Cell [*Biochemistry*]
WMOA....... Waste Minimization Opportunity Assessment [*Environmental science*]
WMS .... WMS Airways BV [*Netherlands*] [*ICAO designator*]   (FAAC)
WMSS....... Westinghouse Microscan System   (IAA)
WNAB .... Weekly Newspaper Advertising Bureau [*British*]   (BI)
WNC .... Wenic Air Services [*Singapore*] [*ICAO designator*]   (FAAC)
WNG .... Wing Airways (Pty) Ltd. [*South Africa*] [*ICAO designator*]   (FAAC)
WNG .... Wiring   (IAA)
WNW........ Wingwork Aviation [*British*] [*ICAO designator*]   (FAAC)
WOA......... World Airways, Inc. [*ICAO designator*]   (FAAC)
WOAH ...... World Organization of Automotive Hobbyists
WOD .... Woodgate Air Services [*British*] [*ICAO designator*]   (FAAC)
WOK .... Kovar Air [*Czechoslovakia*] [*ICAO designator*]   (FAAC)
WOM .... Write Circuit for Queuing Messages [*Computer science*]   (IAA)
Woman's J ... Woman's Journal [*A publication*]
WOMBAT ... Waste of Money, Brains, and Time   (NHD)
WOMJEP ... [*A*] Woman in Jeopardy [*Screenwriter's lexicon*]
WON .... Juan Air (1979) Ltd. [*Canada*] [*ICAO designator*]   (FAAC)
WOOM ...... Wives of Older Men [*An association*]   (EA)
WOPAG..... Wireless Operator and Air Gunner [*British military*]   (IAA)
WOPR .... Woody's Office Power Pack [*Pinecliffe International*] [*Computer science*]   (PCM)
WOPTR..... Wireless Operator [*British military*]   (IAA)
WOSAPCON ... World Safety and Accident Prevention Congress   (PDAA)
WOW .... Without Whiskers   (IAA)
WOWM..... Write Once, Write Mostly [*Computer science*]   (IAA)
WP .... Water-Dispersible Powder [*Pesticide formulation*]
WP .... Workprint [*Cinematography*]   (NTCM)
WP .... Workspace Register Pointer [*Computer science*]   (IAA)
WP .... Worst Pattern   (IAA)
WPA .... Western Pacific Airservice [*Solomon Islands*] [*ICAO designator*]   (FAAC)
WPA .... Wire Products Association [*British*]   (BI)
WPA .... Women's Press Association   (NTCM)
WPC .... Watt-per-Channel   (IAA)
WPCP........ Water Polution Control Plant [*Environmental science*]
WPFA........ Wholesale Photo Finishers' Association [*British*]   (BI)
WPIS .... Wafer Parameter Identification System   (IAA)
WPK .... Air-Lift Associates, Inc. [*ICAO designator*]   (FAAC)
WPL .... Aeronaves del Peru SA [*ICAO designator*]   (FAAC)
WPL .... Windows Personal Librarian [*Computer software*]
WPMA .... Wall Paper Merchants' Association of Great Britain   (BI)
WPO .... Women's Project Officer
WPRA .... Waste Paper Recovery Association Ltd. [*British*]   (BI)
WPRO .... Wartime Personnel Replacement Operation [*Military*]
WPS .... Word Processing Society
WPT .... Wapiti Aviation Ltd. [*Canada*] [*ICAO designator*]   (FAAC)
WPU .... Wet Pick Up   (IAA)
WPWP....... Western Pacific Warm Pool [*Oceanography*]
WPX .... Worked All Prefixes [*Amateur radio*]   (IAA)
WQB .... Water Quality Based [*Environmental science*]
WR .... Workshop Reporting   (IAA)
WRA .... White River Air Services Ltd. [*Canada*] [*ICAO designator*]   (FAAC)
WRA .... Wrinkle Recovery Angle   (IAA)
WRAPS...... Workload and Repair Activity Process Simulator   (PDAA)
WRCHK.... Write Check [*Computer science*]   (IAA)
WRIA .... Worked Republic of India Award [*Amateur radio*]   (IAA)
WRLS .... Wireless [*Telecommunications*]   (IAA)
WRN.......... Wrangler Aviation, Inc. [*ICAO designator*]   (FAAC)
WRR.......... WRA, Inc. [*ICAO designator*]   (FAAC)
WRT .... With Regard To   (NHD)
WRT .... Wright Air Lines, Inc. [*ICAO designator*]   (FAAC)
WRV .... Winged Reentry Vehicle   (IAA)
WS .... Waveform Synthesizer   (IAA)
WS .... Wind Shear [*Aviation*]   (FAAC)
WS .... Winding Specification   (IAA)
WS .... Wireless Station   (IAA)
WS .... Workshop Control   (IAA)
WSA .... Westates Airlines [*ICAO designator*]   (FAAC)
WSA .... Workers Solidarity Alliance   (EA)
WSAS........ Weather Service Airport   (DA)
WSD .... Water Supply and Destination
WSEV........ Winged Surface Effect Vehicle   (PDAA)
WSFC........ Wallops Space Flight Center [*NASA*]   (IAA)
WSG .... Wasaya Airways Ltd. [*Canada*] [*ICAO designator*]   (FAAC)
WSG .... Weapons Spectrum Generator   (PDAA)
WSHT .... Wave Superheater Hypersonic Tunnel   (IAA)
WSM .... Wisman Aviation [*ICAO designator*]   (FAAC)
W/SNWS ... With Snow Tires [*Automotive advertising*]
WSP.......... Wheel Slide Protection   (PDAA)
WSPME ..... Weavelength-Scanning Polarization-Modulation Ellipsometry   (PDAA)
WSR .... Canadian Helicopters [*ICAO designator*]   (FAAC)
WSRA........ Women's Squash Rackets Association [*British*]   (BI)
WSRN .... Western Satellite Research Network   (PDAA)
WSS........... Wide Sense Stationary [*Telecommunications*]   (IAA)

WSSUS ...... Wide Sense Stationary Uncorrelated Scattering
            [*Telecommunications*]   (IAA)
WST........... West Aviation AS [*Norway*] [*ICAO designator*]   (FAAC)
WST........... World Satellite Terminal [*Telecommunications*]   (IAA)
WST........... World System Teletext   (NTCM)
WSU .... Wichita State University [*Kansas*]   (PDAA)
WSV .... Wooly-Monkey Sarcoma Virus [*Medicine*]   (PDAA)
WSX .... Wessex Air Services Ltd. [*British*] [*ICAO designator*]   (FAAC)
WSY .... MAM Aviation Ltd. [*British*] [*ICAO designator*]   (FAAC)
WT .... Watt   (IAA)
WT .... Wealth Tax   (PDAA)
WT .... World Trade   (IAA)
WTA .... Women's Tricycle Association [*British*]   (BI)
WTB .... Write Tape Binary [*Computer science*]   (IAA)
WTBA .... Water-Tube Boilermakers Association [*British*]   (BI)
WTC........... Whole Tree Chips   (PDAA)
WTC........... Woodford Flight Test Center [*British*] [*ICAO designator*]
            (FAAC)
WTCA .... Whole-Time Consultants' Association [*British*]   (BI)
WTD.......... Write Tape Decimal   (IAA)
WTDF........ Wireless Telegraph Direction Finder   (IAA)
WTDR .... Wireless Telegraphy Direction   (IAA)
WTE .... International Symposium on Wave and Tidal Energy   (PDAA)
WTH........... What the Heck [*Computer hacker terminology*] [*Bowdlerized
            version*]   (NHD)
WTM.......... Waitemata Aero Club, Inc. [*New Zealand*] [*ICAO designator*]
            (FAAC)
WTMGE .... Wireless Telegraphy Message   (IAA)
WTN .... Warton BAE [*British*] [*ICAO designator*]   (FAAC)
WTO........... Worked Three Oceans [*Amateur radio*]   (IAA)
WTPFT ...... Weight per Foot   (IAA)
WTS........... Wireless Telegraphy Station [*Telecommunications*]   (IAA)
WTS........... World Terminal Synchronous   (IAA)
WTTA .... Wholesale Tobacco Trade Association of Great Britain and
            Northern Ireland   (BI)
WTTELE.... World Trade Telegraph   (IAA)
WTV .... Fowler [*Rick*] [*ICAO designator*]   (FAAC)
WU .... Washington University   (PDAA)
WUCU .... Western Union Computer Utilities   (IAA)
WUF .... Where Used File [*Computer science*]   (IAA)
WUI........... Workers' Union of Ireland   (BI)
WUPS........ Westinghouse Uninterruptible Power System   (IAA)
WVA .... H & D Aviation [*ICAO designator*]   (FAAC)
WVL .... Wavelength [*Electronics*]   (IAA)
WVL .... Woodvale Aviation Co. Ltd. [*British*] [*ICAO designator*]   (FAAC)
WVSA........ Water-Vapor-Saturated Air   (PDAA)
WVSOM .... West Virginia School of Osteopathic Medicine
WW............ Severe Weather Forecast [*National Weather Service*]   (FAAC)
WW............ Warm White   (DAC)
WW............ Working Women   (NTCM)
WWA.......... Worldwide Aviation Services Ltd. [*Venezuela*] [*ICAO
            designator*]   (FAAC)
WWC......... Wastewater Coalition [*Environmental science*]
WWC......... Worldways Canada Ltd. [*ICAO designator*]   (FAAC)
WWNSS..... Worldwide Network of Standard Seismograph Stations   (PDAA)
WWP .... World Weather Program   (PDAA)
WW/RGS... Wind Shear Warning / Recovery Guidance System   (DA)
WWS .... Wasawings AB [*Finland*] [*ICAO designator*]   (FAAC)
WWTA ...... Woollen and Worsted Trades Association [*British*]   (BI)
WWU......... Water/Wastewater Utilities [*Environmental science*]
WWWW..... Women Who Want to be Women [*An association*]   (NTCM)
WWX.......... Warm White Deluxe   (DAC)
WX............. Simplex Working [*Telecommunications*]   (ADDR)
WX............. Weather at Altitude [*Aviation*]   (FAAC)
WXCON..... Weather Reconnaissance Flight Pilot Report [*Aviation*]   (FAAC)
WYC.......... Wycombe Air Centre [*British*] [*ICAO designator*]   (FAAC)
WYG.......... Wyoming Airlines Ltd. [*ICAO designator*]   (FAAC)
WYSBYGI ... What You See Before You Get It [*Computer science*]
WYT .... Wyton FTU [*British*] [*ICAO designator*]   (FAAC)

X-Y-Z

X .... Ecstasy [*Synthetic stimulant*]
X .... Hexadecimal [*Computer science*]   (IAA)
X .... Xenon [*Chemical element*]   (IAA)
3X .... Guinea [*Aircraft nationality and registration mark*]   (FAAC)
4X .... Israel [*Aircraft nationality and registration mark*]   (FAAC)
XAA .... Aeronautical Radio, Inc. [*ICAO designator*]   (FAAC)
XAC .... Air Charter World [*ICAO designator*]   (FAAC)
XAD .... Certified Aircraft Dispatch, Inc. [*ICAO designator*]   (FAAC)
XAF .... Executive Air Fleet [*ICAO designator*]   (FAAC)
XAL .... Aerovias Xalitic SA de CV [*Mexico*] [*ICAO designator*]   (FAAC)
XAM .... AMR Combs, Inc. [*AMR Services, Inc.*] [*ICAO designator*]
    (FAAC)
XAO .... Airline Operations Services, Inc. [*ICAO designator*]   (FAAC)
XAP .... Direct Air Inc. [*ICAO designator*]   (FAAC)
XAS .... PHH Aviation Systems, Inc. [*ICAO designator*]   (FAAC)
XAT .... AT & T Aviation Group [*ICAO designator*]   (FAAC)
XBO .... Baseops International, Inc. [*ICAO designator*]   (FAAC)
XCL .... Contel ASC [*ICAO designator*]   (FAAC)
XCO .... Compuflight Operation Service, Inc. [*ICAO designator*]   (FAAC)
XCS .... CompuServe, Inc. [*ICAO designator*]   (FAAC)
XCT .... Execute   (IAA)
XCU .... Extreme Close-Up [*Also, VCU*] [*Cinematography*]   (NTCM)
XCX .... Citibank NA [*ICAO designator*]   (FAAC)
XDA .... Bureau Veritas SA [*France*] [*ICAO designator*]   (FAAC)
XDD .... Lockheed Duats [*ICAO designator*]   (FAAC)
XDS .... Dispatch Services, Inc. [*ICAO designator*]   (FAAC)
XDT .... Data Transformation Corp. [*ICAO designator*]   (FAAC)
XDY .... DynAir Services, Inc. [*ICAO designator*]   (FAAC)
XEL .... Helicopteros Xel-Ha SA de CV [*Mexico*] [*ICAO designator*]
    (FAAC)
XFS .... American Flight Service Systems, Inc. [*ICAO designator*]
    (FAAC)
XFSS .... Auxiliary Flight Service Station [*Aviation*]   (FAAC)
XFX .... Airways Corp. of New Zealand Ltd. [*ICAO designator*]   (FAAC)
XGA .... General Aviation Terminal, Inc. [*Canada*] [*ICAO designator*]
    (FAAC)
XGG .... IMP Group Ltd. Aviation Services [*Canada*] [*ICAO designator*]
    (FAAC)
XGS .... Global Systems, Inc. [*ICAO designator*]   (FAAC)
XGW .... Global Weather Dynamics, Inc. [*ICAO designator*]   (FAAC)
XIA .... Irving Oil Ltd. [*Canada*] [*ICAO designator*]   (FAAC)
XK .... Experimental-Eleventh Generation [*Jaguar*] [*Automotive
    engineering*]
XKA .... Kavouras, Inc. [*ICAO designator*]   (FAAC)
XL .... Existing Light [*Photography*]   (NTCM)
XLD .... Jepenssen Data Plan, Inc. [*ICAO designator*]   (FAAC)
XLG .... Lockheed Air Terminal, Inc. [*Guam*] [*ICAO designator*]   (FAAC)
XLL .... Extra Lightly Loaded   (IAA)
XLT .... Telecomunicacoes Aeronauticas SA [*Brazil*] [*ICAO designator*]
    (FAAC)
XMA .... Martin Aviation Services [*ICAO designator*]   (FAAC)
XMAS .... Expandable Machine Accounting System   (IAA)
XMIM .... Transmitter Interface Module [*Army*]
XMITR .... Transmitter   (ADDR)
XMITTER ... Transmitter   (NTCM)
XMX .... Servicios a la Navegacion en el Espacio Aereo Mexicano [*Mexico*]
    [*ICAO designator*]   (FAAC)
XNG .... Crossing [*Aviation*]   (FAAC)
XNS .... Navtech Systems Support, Inc. [*Canada*] [*ICAO designator*]
    (FAAC)
XNT .... NOTAMS International, Inc. [*ICAO designator*]   (FAAC)
XNV .... TIGIN Ltd. [*ICAO designator*]   (FAAC)
XPL .... Explain [*or Explanation*]   (IAA)
XPS .... Expert System [*Computer science*]   (IAA)
XPS .... XP International BV [*Netherlands*] [*ICAO designator*]   (FAAC)
XPX .... Phoenix Flight Operations Ltd. [*Canada*] [*ICAO designator*]
    (FAAC)
XR .... Extension Register
9XR .... Rwanda [*Aircraft nationality and registration mark*]   (FAAC)
XRB .... X-Ray Background [*Cosmology*]
XRM .... External ROM [*Read Only Memory*] Mode [*Computer science*]
    (IAA)
X/S .... Over the Shoulder Shot [*Also, OS*] [*Cinematography*]   (NTCM)

XSA .... Spectrum Air Service, Inc. [*ICAO designator*]   (FAAC)
XSAM .... Experimental Surface-to-Air Missile [*Military*]   (IAA)
XSCID .... X-Linked Server Combined Immunodeficiency [*"Bubble Boy"
    disease*] [*Medicine*]
XSN .... Stepheville Aviation Services [*Canada*] [*ICAO designator*]
    (FAAC)
XSSM .... Experimental Surface-to-Surface Missile [*Military*]   (IAA)
XT .... Extended
XTC .... Excess Three Code   (IAA)
XTJ .... Advance Aviation Services, Inc. [*ICAO designator*]   (FAAC)
XTM .... X-Ray Tomographic Microscope
XTR .... Sector Airlines [*Canada*] [*ICAO designator*]   (FAAC)
XTRAN .... Experimental Translation Language   (IAA)
XUT .... Aerorepresentaciones Tupac Amaru [*Peru*] [*ICAO designator*]
    (FAAC)
XW .... Crosswind [*Aviation*]   (FAAC)
XWS .... WSI Corp. [*ICAO designator*]   (FAAC)
XWW .... World Weatherwatch [*Canada*] [*ICAO designator*]   (FAAC)
XXH .... Double Extra Heavy   (DAC)
XXS .... Skyplan Services Ltd. [*Canada*] [*ICAO designator*]   (FAAC)
XXV .... Administracion de Aeropuertos [*Bolivia*] [*ICAO designator*]
    (FAAC)
XY .... Myanmar [*Aircraft nationality and registration mark*]   (FAAC)
XYC .... Aero Chasqui SA [*Peru*] [*ICAO designator*]   (FAAC)
XYZ .... Island Airlines [*ICAO designator*]   (FAAC)
XZ .... Myanmar [*Aircraft nationality and registration mark*]   (FAAC)
Y .... Y-Punch   (IAA)
6Y .... Jamaica [*Aircraft nationality and registration mark*]   (FAAC)
9Y .... Trinidad and Tobago [*Aircraft nationality and registration
    mark*]   (FAAC)
YA .... Yet Another [*Computer hacker terminology*]   (NHD)
YABA .... Yet Another Bloody Acronym [*Computer hacker terminology*]
    (NHD)
YAIG .... Yttrium Aluminnum Iron Garnet [*LASER technology*]   (IAA)
YARDS .... Yard Activity Reporting and Decision System   (PDAA)
YASGB ...... Youth Association of Synagogues in Great Britain   (BI)
YAUN .... Yet Another Unix Nerd [*Computer hacker terminology*]   (NHD)
YBE .... Stewart Aviation Services, Inc. [*ICAO designator*]   (FAAC)
YCA .... Youth Camping Association [*British*]   (BI)
YCND .... Youth Campaign for Nuclear Disarmament [*British*]   (BI)
YCPO .... Young Children: Priority One [*Kiwanis Club*]
YD .... Younger Dryas [*Geoscience*]
YFS .... Young Flying Service [*ICAO designator*]   (FAAC)
YJ .... Vanuatu [*Aircraft nationality and registration mark*]   (FAAC)
YL .... Yellow Lamp   (IAA)
YLCC .... Yellow Lamp Century Certificate   (IAA)
YLM .... Young Launderers' Movement [*British*]   (BI)
YMBA .... Yacht and Motor Boat Association [*British*]   (BI)
YMSG .... Your Message [*Aviation*]   (FAAC)
YMSGD ..... Your Message Date [*Aviation*]   (FAAC)
YNA .... Young Newspapermen's Association [*British*]   (BI)
YOG .... Central Aviation, Inc. [*ICAO designator*]   (FAAC)
YRG .... Air Yugoslavia [*ICAO designator*]   (FAAC)
YRGB .... Yellow Red Green Blue   (IAA)
YRR .... Scenic Airlines, Inc. [*ICAO designator*]   (FAAC)
YST .... Yukon Standard Time   (IAA)
YV .... Yield Value   (IAA)
Z .... Zimbabwe [*Aircraft nationality and registration mark*]   (FAAC)
Z .... Zone Code   (IAA)
ZAC .... Zambia Airways [*ICAO designator*]   (FAAC)
ZAC .... Zinc Aluminium Coater [*Metallurgy*]
ZADCA .... Zinc Alloy Die Casters' Association [*British*]   (BI)
ZAI .... Zaire Aero Service [*ICAO designator*]   (FAAC)
ZAM .... Zinc, Aluminium, Magnesium   (PDAA)
ZAN .... Zantop International Airlines, Inc. [*ICAO designator*]   (FAAC)
ZAR .... Zairean Airlines [*Zaire*] [*ICAO designator*]   (FAAC)
ZAS .... Zaire Aero Service [*ICAO designator*]   (FAAC)
ZB .... Zero-Based
ZBA .... [*Z.*] Boskovic Air Charters Ltd. [*Kenya*] [*ICAO designator*]
    (FAAC)
ZBB .... Zero Base Budgeting [*Environmental Protection Agency*]   (ERG)
ZBR .... Zone Bit Recording [*Computer science*]
ZCAV .... Zone Constant Angular Velocity [*Computer science*]

ZCCFAR .... Zero Crossing Constant False Alarm Rate   (IAA)
ZCD .... Zone Controlled Deposition   (IAA)
ZCR .... Zone of Correct Reading   (IAA)
ZCT .... Zero Count Table   (IAA)
ZE .... Zeros Extended   (IAA)
ZEB............ Zero-Emissions Bus
ZET............ Zero-Emissions Truck
ZFMA........ Zip Fastener Manufacturers Association [*British*]   (BI)
ZFS .... Zone Field Selection [*Physics*]   (IAA)
Z/G .... Zoster Immune Globulin [*Immunology*]   (MAH)
ZHE............ Zero Headspace Extractor [*Environmental Protection Agency*]
                     (ERG)
ZII-ZD........ Zero Intersymbol Interference - Zero Derivative   (PDAA)
ZMAR .... Zeus Malfunction Array RADAR [*Missile defense*]   (IAA)
ZMAR .... Zeus Multiple Array RADAR [*Missile defense*]   (IAA)
ZMC .... Zero-Magnetostrictive Composition   (PDAA)
ZNL .... Zero Memory Non-Linear   (IAA)
ZNR........... Zinc Oxide Non-Linear Resistance   (IAA)
ZO.............. Zone   (IAA)
ZOC........... Zone of Convergence [*Aviation*]   (DA)
ZOG........... Zeatin-O-Glucoside [*Biochemistry*]
ZOI .... Zero Order Interpolar   (IAA)
ZOI .... Zone of Incorporation [*Environmental Protection Agency*]
                     (ERG)
ZP .... Zone Punch [*Computer science*]   (IAA)
ZPC............ Zero Print Control   (IAA)
ZPDA .... Zinc Pigment Development Association [*British*]   (BI)
ZPH............ Zero-Phonon Hole [*Spectroscopy*]
ZPI............. Zone Position Indicator   (IAA)
ZPO .... Zone Project Officer
ZRBSC .... Zirconium Boride Silicon Carbide   (PDAA)
ZS .... Zero State   (IAA)
ZSF .... Zero Skip Frequency   (IAA)
ZSUP......... Zero Suppress   (IAA)
ZV .... [*Sprinkler*] Zone Valve [*NFPA pre-fire planning symbol*]   (NFPA)
ZZM .... Agence Nationale des Aerodromes et de la Meteorologie [*Ivory
                     Coast*] [*ICAO designator*]   (FAAC)

New Acronyms, Initialisms & Abbreviations

By Meaning

A

A-Beta-Lipoproteinemia [*Medicine*] (MAH) .... ABL
Aalborg Airtaxi [*Denmark*] [*ICAO designator*] (FAAC) .... DAX
Ab Urbe Condite [*From the Year of the Founding*] [*Latin*] .... AUC
Abandoned (ABBR) .... ABDND
Abandoner (ABBR) .... ABDNR
Abandonment (ABBR) .... ABANDMT
Abandonment (ABBR) .... ABDMT
Abandonment (ABBR) .... ABDNNT
Abandonment (ABBR) .... ABNDMNT
Abasement (ABBR) .... ABASNT
Abasement (ABBR) .... ABAST
Abasing (ABBR) .... ABASG
Abatable (ABBR) .... ABATB
Abatement (ABBR) .... ABATMT
Abatement (ABBR) .... ABATNT
Abating (ABBR) .... ABATG
Abbas Air Ltd. [*British*] [*ICAO designator*] (FAAC) .... ABA
Aberrant (ABBR) .... ABER
Abbotsford Air Services [*Canada*] [*ICAO designator*] (FAAC) .... ABE
Abbreviated (ABBR) .... ABBRD
Abbreviated Precision Approach Path Indicator [*Aviation*] (DA) ..... APAPI
Abbreviated Visual Approach Slope Indicator System [*Aviation*] (DA) ...... AV
Abbreviating (ABBR) .... ABBRG
Abbreviation (ABBR) .... ABBRN
Abbreviator (ABBR) .... ABBRR
Abbreviomania (ABBR) .... ABBREVIO
ABC [*Air Business Contact*] [*France*] [*ICAO designator*] (FAAC) .... ACB
ABC World Airways Guide [*ICAO designator*] (FAAC) .... ABC
Abdicate (ABBR) .... ABDI
Abdicated (ABBR) .... ABDID
Abdication (ABBR) .... ABDIN
Abdomen (ABBR) .... ABDM
Abdominal (ABBR) .... ABDML
Abdominally (ABBR) .... ABDMLY
Abdominally (ABBR) .... ABDMY
Abducted (ABBR) .... ABDCD
Abducting (ABBR) .... ABDCG
Abduction (ABBR) .... ABDCN
Abductor (ABBR) .... ABDCR
Abelag Aviation [*Belgium*] [*ICAO designator*] (FAAC) .... AAB
Aberdeen Airways [*British*] [*ICAO designator*] (FAAC) .... AAW
Aberrance (ABBR) .... ABRN
Aberrancy (ABBR) .... ABRNC
Aberrant (ABBR) .... ABRNT
Aberrantly (ABBR) .... ABRNTY
Aberration (ABBR) .... ABERN
Aberration (ABBR) .... ABRAN
Aberrational (ABBR) .... ABERNL
Aberrational (ABBR) .... ABRANL
Abetment (ABBR) .... ABETMT
Abetment (ABBR) .... ABETNT
Abetted (ABBR) .... ABETD
Abetting (ABBR) .... ABETG
Abettor (ABBR) .... ABETR
Abeyance (ABBR) .... ABYNC
Abeyant (ABBR) .... ABYNT
Abhorred (ABBR) .... ABHRD
Abhorrence (ABBR) .... ABHRNC
Abhorrent (ABBR) .... ABHRNT
Abhorrent (ABBR) .... ABHRT
Abhorrently (ABBR) .... ABHRTY
Abhorrently (ABBR) .... ABHRTY
Abhorrer (ABBR) .... ABHRR
Abhorring (ABBR) .... ABHRG
Abidance (ABBR) .... ABIDNC
Abiding (ABBR) .... ABIDG
Abidingly (ABBR) .... ABIDGY
Ability (ABBR) .... ABIL
Ability (ABBR) .... ABLT
Abject (ABBR) .... ABJT
Abjection (ABBR) .... ABJTN
Abjectly (ABBR) .... ABJTY
Abjectness (ABBR) .... ABJTNS

Abjuration (ABBR) .... ABJRN
Abjure (ABBR) .... ABJR
Abjured (ABBR) .... ABJRD
Abjurer (ABBR) .... ABJRR
Abjuring (ABBR) .... ABJRG
Ablative (ABBR) .... ABLTV
Ablaze (ABBR) .... ABLZ
Able (ABBR) .... ABL
Abler (ABBR) .... ABLR
Ablest (ABBR) .... ABLT
Abloom (ABBR) .... ABLM
Ablution (ABBR) .... ABLUN
Ablutionary (ABBR) .... ABLUNRY
Ablutionary (ABBR) .... ABLUNY
Abnegate (ABBR) .... ABNG
Abnegate (ABBR) .... ABNGA
Abnegated (ABBR) .... ABNGAD
Abnegated (ABBR) .... ABNGD
Abnegates (ABBR) .... ABNGS
Abnegating (ABBR) .... ABNGAG
Abnegating (ABBR) .... ABNGG
Abnegation (ABBR) .... ABNGN
Abnegator (ABBR) .... ABNGR
Abnormality (ABBR) .... ABNMT
Abnormally (ABBR) .... ABNMY
Aboard (ABBR) .... ABRD
Abode (ABBR) .... ABOD
Aboitiz Air Transport Corp. [*Philippines*] [*ICAO designator*] (FAAC) .... BOI
Abolish (ABBR) .... ABLH
Abolishable (ABBR) .... ABLHB
Abolished (ABBR) .... ABOLD
Abolisher (ABBR) .... ABLHR
Abolishing (ABBR) .... ABOLG
Abolishment (ABBR) .... ABLHNT
Abolishment (ABBR) .... ABOLT
Abolition (ABBR) .... ABOLN
Abolitionism (ABBR) .... ABOLNM
Abolitionist (ABBR) .... ABOLNST
Abolitionist (ABBR) .... ABOLNT
Abominable (ABBR) .... ABMNB
Abominable (ABBR) .... ABOML
Abominably (ABBR) .... ABMNBY
Abominate (ABBR) .... ABMNA
Abominate (ABBR) .... ABOM
Abominated (ABBR) .... ABOMD
Abominating (ABBR) .... ABMNAG
Abominating (ABBR) .... ABOMG
Abomination (ABBR) .... ABMNAN
Abomination (ABBR) .... ABOMN
Abonminated (ABBR) .... ABMNAD
Aboriginal (ABBR) .... ABO
Aboriginal (ABBR) .... ABORL
Aboriginal (ABBR) .... ABRGNL
Aboriginally (ABBR) .... ABORLY
Aborigine (ABBR) .... ABO
Aborigine (ABBR) .... ABRGN
Aborted (ABBR) .... ABRTD
Aborting (ABBR) .... ABRTG
Abortion (ABBR) .... ABRTN
Abortionist (ABBR) .... ABRTNST
Abortionist (ABBR) .... ABRTNT
Abortive (ABBR) .... ABRTV
Abortively (ABBR) .... ABRTVY
Abortiveness (ABBR) .... ABRTVNS
Abound (ABBR) .... ABND
About-Face (ABBR) .... ABT-FC
Above-Board (ABBR) .... ABV-BRD
Above Grade (DAC) .... AG
Above Ordnance Datum [*Military*] (DA) .... AOD
Abrade (ABBR) .... ABRAD
Abrade (ABBR) .... ABRD
Abraded (ABBR) .... ABRADD
Abraded (ABBR) .... ABRDD

Abrading	(ABBR)	ABRDG
Abraham	(ABBR)	ABR
Abraham	(ABBR)	ABRA
Abraham	(ABBR)	ABRAM
Abrasion	(ABBR)	ABRAN
Abrasion	(ABBR)	ABRAS
Abrasion	(ABBR)	ABRSN
Abrasive	(ABBR)	ABR
Abrasive	(ABBR)	ABRAV
Abrasive Flow Machining [*Mechanical engineering*]		AFM
Abreast	(ABBR)	ABRST
Abridge	(ABBR)	ABRG
Abridgeable	(ABBR)	ABRGB
Abridged	(ABBR)	ABRGD
Abridged	(ABBR)	ABRID
Abridger	(ABBR)	ABRGR
Abridging	(ABBR)	ABRGG
Abridgment	(ABBR)	ABRGNT
Abridgment	(ABBR)	ABRGT
Abroad	(ABBR)	ABRD
Abroad	(ABBR)	ABROD
Abrogate	(ABBR)	ABRGA
Abrogate	(ABBR)	ABROG
Abrogated	(ABBR)	ABRGAD
Abrogated	(ABBR)	ABROGD
Abrogating	(ABBR)	ABROGAG
Abrogating	(ABBR)	ABROGG
Abrogation	(ABBR)	ABRGAN
Abrogation	(ABBR)	ABROGN
Abrupt	(ABBR)	ABRP
Abruptness	(ABBR)	ABRPNS
Abscess	(ABBR)	AB
Abscess	(ABBR)	ABCS
Abscessed	(ABBR)	ABCSD
Abscesses	(ABBR)	ABS
Abscessing	(ABBR)	ABCSG
Abscond	(ABBR)	ABSC
Abscond	(ABBR)	ABSCD
Absence	(ABBR)	ABSC
Absence	(ABBR)	ABSNC
Absent	(ABBR)	ABSNT
Absented	(ABBR)	ABSD
Absentee	(ABBR)	ABSNTE
Absentee	(ABBR)	ABST
Absenteeism	(ABBR)	ABSNTEM
Absenteeism	(ABBR)	ABSTM
Absenting	(ABBR)	ABSG
Absently	(ABBR)	ABSY
Absolute	(ABBR)	ABSLT
Absolute Plate Motion [*Geophysics*]		APM
Absolutely	(ABBR)	ABSLTY
Absolutely	(ABBR)	ABSOLY
Absoluteness	(ABBR)	ABSOLNS
Absolution	(ABBR)	ABSLTN
Absolution	(ABBR)	ABSOLN
Absolutism	(ABBR)	ABSLTM
Absolutist	(ABBR)	ABSLTST
Absolvable	(ABBR)	ABSLVB
Absolve	(ABBR)	ABSLV
Absolved	(ABBR)	ABSLVD
Absolver	(ABBR)	ABSLVR
Absolving	(ABBR)	ABSLVG
Absonant	(ABBR)	ABS
Absorb	(ABBR)	ABSB
Absorbability	(ABBR)	ABSBBT
Absorbable	(ABBR)	ABSBB
Absorbance	(ABBR)	ABSBNC
Absorbed	(ABBR)	ABSBD
Absorbency	(ABBR)	ABSBCY
Absorbency	(ABBR)	ABSBNC
Absorbent	(ABBR)	ABSBT
Absorber	(ABBR)	ABSBR
Absorbing	(ABBR)	ABSBG
Absorption	(ABBR)	ABSBN
Absorption	(ABBR)	ABSPN
Absorptive	(ABBR)	ABSPV
Absorptivity	(ABBR)	ABSPT
Abstain	(ABBR)	ABSTA
Abstained	(ABBR)	ABSTAD
Abstaining	(ABBR)	ABSTAG
Abstemious	(ABBR)	ABSTMS
Abstemiously	(ABBR)	ABSTMSY
Abstemiousness	(ABBR)	ABSTMSNS
Abstention	(ABBR)	ABSTN
Abstinence	(ABBR)	ABSTNC
Abstinent	(ABBR)	ABSTNT
Abstracted	(ABBR)	ABSTRD
Abstracter	(ABBR)	ABSTRR
Abstraction	(ABBR)	ABSTRN
Abstractly	(ABBR)	ABSTRY
Abstractness	(ABBR)	ABSTRNS
Abstrene	(ABBR)	ABS
Abstruse	(ABBR)	ABSTRS
Abstruse	(ABBR)	ABSTRU
Abstrusely	(ABBR)	ABSTRUY
Abstruseness	(ABBR)	ABSTRUNS
Absurd	(ABBR)	ABSRD
Absurdity	(ABBR)	ABSDT
Absurdity	(ABBR)	ABSRDT
Absurdly	(ABBR)	ABSRDY
Absurdness	(ABBR)	ABSRDNS
Abulia	(ABBR)	ABUL
Abuliomania	(ABBR)	ABUL
Abundance	(ABBR)	ABNDNC
Abundance	(ABBR)	ABUNDNC
Abundant	(ABBR)	ABNDNT
Abundant	(ABBR)	ABT
Abundant	(ABBR)	ABUNDT
Abundantly	(ABBR)	ABNDNTY
Abundantly	(ABBR)	ABUNDTY
Abuse	(ABBR)	ABS
Abuse	(ABBR)	ABUS
Abused	(ABBR)	ABSD
Abused	(ABBR)	ABUSD
Abuser	(ABBR)	ABSR
Abuser	(ABBR)	ABUSR
Abusing	(ABBR)	ABSG
Abusing	(ABBR)	ABUSG
Abusive	(ABBR)	ABSV
Abusive	(ABBR)	ABUSV
Abusively	(ABBR)	ABSVY
Abusively	(ABBR)	ABUSVY
Abusiveness	(ABBR)	ABUSVNS
Abutment	(ABBR)	ABTNT
Abutment	(ABBR)	ABUT
Abutment	(ABBR)	ABUTMT
Abutted	(ABBR)	ABTD
Abutted	(ABBR)	ABUTD
Abutting	(ABBR)	ABTG
Abutting	(ABBR)	ABUTG
Abysmal	(ABBR)	ABSML
Abysmal	(ABBR)	ABYSM
Abyss	(ABBR)	ABYS
Academe	(ABBR)	ACDM
Academic	(ABBR)	ACAD
Academic	(ABBR)	ACADC
Academic	(ABBR)	ACDMK
Academical	(ABBR)	ACADL
Academical	(ABBR)	ACDMKL
Academically	(ABBR)	ACADCLY
Academically	(ABBR)	ACDMKY
Academician	(ABBR)	ACADCN
Academician	(ABBR)	ACDMN
Academy	(ABBR)	ACDMY
Acadia	(ABBR)	ACAD
Acapulco [*Mexico*]	(ABBR)	ACAP
Accede	(ABBR)	ACD
Accede	(ABBR)	ACED
Acceded	(ABBR)	ACDD
Accedence	(ABBR)	ACDNC
Acceder	(ABBR)	ACDR
Acceding	(ABBR)	ACDG
Accelerate	(ABBR)	ACEL
Accelerate	(ABBR)	ACLRA
Accelerated	(ABBR)	ACELD
Accelerated	(ABBR)	ACLRAD
Accelerated Claimant Match		ACM
Accelerates	(ABBR)	ACELS
Accelerating	(ABBR)	ACELG
Accelerating	(ABBR)	ACLRAG
Acceleration	(ABBR)	ACELN
Acceleration	(ABBR)	ACLRAN
Acceleration Enrichment [*Automotive fuel systems*]		AE
Accelerative	(ABBR)	ACELV
Accelerative	(ABBR)	ACLRAV
Accelerator	(ABBR)	ACELR
Accelerator	(ABBR)	ACLRTR
Accent	(NTCM)	A
Accent	(ABBR)	ACNT
Accented	(ABBR)	ACNTD
Accenting	(ABBR)	ACNTG
Accentual	(ABBR)	ACNTL
Accentuate	(ABBR)	ACNTU
Accentuated	(ABBR)	ACNTUD
Accentuating	(ABBR)	ACNTUG
Accentuation	(ABBR)	ACNTUN
Accept	(ABBR)	ACCPT
Acceptability	(ABBR)	ACPTBT
Acceptability	(ABBR)	ACPTBY
Acceptable	(ABBR)	ACPTB
Acceptable Means of Compliance	(DA)	AMC
Acceptable Use Policy		AUP
Acceptableness	(ABBR)	ACPTNS
Acceptably	(ABBR)	ACPTY
Acceptance	(ABBR)	ACPTNC
Accepted	(ABBR)	ACPTD

Accepting (ABBR)	ACPTG
Access Control Committee	ACC
[*The*] Access Method (IAA)	TAM
Accessibility (ABBR)	ACSBT
Accessible (ABBR)	ACSB
Accessibleness (ABBR)	ACSBNS
Accessibly (ABBR)	ACSBY
Accession (ABBR)	ACSN
Accessional (ABBR)	ACSNL
Accessioned (ABBR)	ACSND
Accessioning (ABBR)	ACSNG
Accessory (ABBR)	ACSRY
Accessory Manufacturers Racing Association [*British*] (BI)	AMRA
Accident Documentation System [*Safety research*] [*Automotive engineering*]	ADS
Accident Offices Association [*British*] (BI)	AOA
Accidental (ABBR)	ACDNTL
Accidental (ABBR)	ACDTL
Accidentally (ABBR)	ACDNTLY
Acclaim (ABBR)	ACLM
Acclamation (ABBR)	ACLMAN
Acclamation (ABBR)	ACLMN
Acclamatory (ABBR)	ACLMY
Acclimate (ABBR)	ACLIM
Acclimate (ABBR)	ACLMA
Acclimated (ABBR)	ACLIMD
Acclimated (ABBR)	ACLMAD
Acclimating (ABBR)	ACLIMG
Acclimating (ABBR)	ACLMAG
Acclimation (ABBR)	ACLIMN
Acclimatization (ABBR)	ACLIMZN
Acclimatization (ABBR)	ACLMATZN
Acclimatize (ABBR)	ACLIMZ
Acclimatize (ABBR)	ACLMATZ
Acclimatized (ABBR)	ACLIMZD
Acclimatized (ABBR)	ACLMATZD
Acclimatizing (ABBR)	ACLIMZG
Acclimatizing (ABBR)	ACLMATZG
Accolade (ABBR)	ACLD
Accommodate (ABBR)	ACMD
Accommodated (ABBR)	ACMDD
Accommodating (ABBR)	ACMDG
Accommodation (ABBR)	ACMDN
Accommodative (ABBR)	ACMDV
Accompanied (ABBR)	ACMPD
Accompanied (ABBR)	ACMPYD
Accompaniment (ABBR)	ACMPNT
Accompaniment (ABBR)	ACMPT
Accompaniment (ABBR)	ACOMP
Accompanist (ABBR)	ACMPST
Accompany (ABBR)	ACMPY
Accompany (ABBR)	ACOMP
Accompanying (ABBR)	ACMPG
Accomplice (ABBR)	ACMPL
Accomplice (ABBR)	ACMPLS
Accomplish (ABBR)	ACMPLH
Accomplish (ABBR)	ACOMP
Accomplishable (ABBR)	ACMPLHB
Accomplishable (ABBR)	ACOMPB
Accomplished (ABBR)	ACMPLHD
Accomplished (ABBR)	ACOMPD
Accomplisher (ABBR)	ACOMPR
Accomplishing (ABBR)	ACOMPG
Accomplishment (ABBR)	ACMPLHNT
Accomplishment (ABBR)	ACOMPT
Accord (ABBR)	ACD
Accord (ABBR)	ACRD
Accordance (ABBR)	ACRDNC
Accordant (ABBR)	ACRDT
Accorded (ABBR)	ACRDD
According (ABBR)	ACRDG
Accordingly (ABBR)	ACRDGY
Accost (ABBR)	ACOS
Accost (ABBR)	ACST
Accosted (ABBR)	ACOSD
Accosting (ABBR)	ACOSG
Account (ABBR)	ACONT
Accountability (ABBR)	ACONTBT
Accountable (ABBR)	ACCTB
Accountable (ABBR)	ACONTB
Accountableness (ABBR)	ACCTBNS
Accountably (ABBR)	ACCTBY
Accountably (ABBR)	ACONTBLY
Accountancy (ABBR)	ACCTY
Accountancy (ABBR)	ACONTNC
Accountant (ABBR)	ACCT
Accountant (ABBR)	ACCTNT
Accountant (ABBR)	ACTT
Accounted (ABBR)	ACCTD
Accounting (ABBR)	ACONTG
Accredit (ABBR)	ACRD
Accredit (ABBR)	ACRT
Accreditation	acred
Accredited (ABBR)	ACRTD
Accredited Quality Assurance	AQA
Accrediting (ABBR)	ACRTG
Accrete (ABBR)	ACCR
Accreted (ABBR)	ACCRD
Accreting (ABBR)	ACCRG
Accretion (ABBR)	ACCRN
Accretion (ABBR)	ACRN
Accretion-Induced Collapse [*Astronomy*]	AIC
Accretive (ABBR)	ACCRV
Accretive (ABBR)	ACRV
Accrue (ABBR)	ACRU
Accrued (ABBR)	ACRD
Accrued (ABBR)	ACRUD
Accruement (ABBR)	ACRUT
Accruing (ABBR)	ACRUG
Accumulable (ABBR)	ACUMB
Accumulate (ABBR)	ACMLA
Accumulate (ABBR)	ACUM
Accumulated (ABBR)	ACMLAD
Accumulated (ABBR)	ACUMD
Accumulating (ABBR)	ACMLAG
Accumulating (ABBR)	ACUMG
Accumulation (ABBR)	ACMLAN
Accumulation (ABBR)	ACUMN
Accumulative (ABBR)	ACMLAV
Accumulative (ABBR)	ACUMV
Accumulator (ABBR)	ACMLATR
Accumulator (ABBR)	ACUMR
Accumulator Makers' Association [*British*] (BI)	AMA
Accuracy (ABBR)	ACRCY
Accuracy (ABBR)	ACURC
Accurate (ABBR)	ACRA
Accurate (ABBR)	ACUR
Accurately (ABBR)	ACRAY
Accurately (ABBR)	ACURY
Accurateness (ABBR)	ACRANS
Accurateness (ABBR)	ACURNS
Accursed (ABBR)	ACRSD
Accursedly (ABBR)	ACRSDY
Accursedness (ABBR)	ACRSDNS
Accurst (ABBR)	ACRST
Accusation (ABBR)	ACUSN
Accusative (ABBR)	ACSTV
Accusative (ABBR)	ACUSV
Accusatorial (ABBR)	ACUSTL
Accusatory (ABBR)	ACUSTRY
Accusatory (ABBR)	ACUSTY
Accuse (ABBR)	ACUS
Accused (ABBR)	ACUSD
Accuser (ABBR)	ACUSR
Accusing (ABBR)	ACUSG
Accusingly (ABBR)	ACUSGY
Accustom (ABBR)	ACSTM
Accustomed (ABBR)	ACSTMD
Accustoming (ABBR)	ACSTMG
Ace Air Cargo Express, Inc. [*ICAO designator*] (FAAC)	AER
Acellular Vaccine [*Medicine*]	ACV
Acerbity (ABBR)	ACRBT
Acetate (ABBR)	ACTA
Acetic (ABBR)	ACE
Acetone (ABBR)	ACTNE
Acetylene (ABBR)	ACETL
Acetylene (ABBR)	ACTYLN
Ached (ABBR)	ACHD
Aches (ABBR)	ACHS
Achievable (ABBR)	ACHVB
Achieve (ABBR)	ACHV
Achieve (ABBR)	ACHVE
Achieved (ABBR)	ACHVD
Achievement (ABBR)	ACHIEV
Achievement (ABBR)	ACHVNT
Achievement (ABBR)	ACHVT
Achiever (ABBR)	ACHVR
Achieving (ABBR)	ACHVG
Achilles Tendon Reflex Test [*Medicine*] (MAH)	ART
Aching (ABBR)	ACHG
Achromatic (ABBR)	ACHR
Achromatic (ABBR)	ACHRMTK
Achromatically (ABBR)	ACHRY
Achromaticity (ABBR)	ACHRT
Achromatism (ABBR)	ACHRM
Achromatism (ABBR)	ACHROM
Acicular (ABBR)	ACIC
Acid Mine Drainage [*Mining technology*]	AMD
Acid Rock Draining [*Mining technology*]	ARD
Acknowledge (ABBR)	ACNWLG
Acknowledgeable (ABBR)	ACKB
Acknowledgeable (ABBR)	ACNWLGB
Acknowledged (ABBR)	ACNWLGD
Acknowledger (ABBR)	ACNWLGR
Acknowledging (ABBR)	ACKG
Acknowledging (ABBR)	ACNWLGG

Acknowledgment (ABBR) ... ACKT
Acknowledgment (ABBR) ... ACNWLGNT
Acme [*Spain*] [*ICAO designator*] (FAAC) ... AKM
Acme Aviation Ltd. [*British*] [*ICAO designator*] (FAAC) ... ADP
Acolyte (ABBR) ... ACLYT
Acoustic (ABBR) ... ACOUST
Acoustic Thermometry of Ocean Climate [*International oceanographic project*] ... ATOC
Acoustical (ABBR) ... ACSTL
Acoustically (ABBR) ... ACSTLY
Acousto-Optic Tunable Filter [*Instrumentation*] ... AOTF
Acousto-Optic Tunable Scanning [*Instrumentation*] ... AOTS
Acquaint (ABBR) ... ACQNT
Acquaintance (ABBR) ... ACQNTNC
Acquaintanceship (ABBR) ... ACQNTNCSP
Acquainted (ABBR) ... ACQNTD
Acquainting (ABBR) ... ACQNTG
Acquiesce (ABBR) ... ACQS
Acquiesced (ABBR) ... ACQSD
Acquiescence (ABBR) ... ACQSNC
Acquiescent (ABBR) ... ACQSNT
Acquiescently (ABBR) ... ACQSNTY
Acquiescing (ABBR) ... ACQSG
Acquirable (ABBR) ... ACQRB
Acquire (ABBR) ... ACQR
Acquired (ABBR) ... ACQRD
Acquirement (ABBR) ... ACQRNT
Acquirement (ABBR) ... ACQRT
Acquirer (ABBR) ... ACQRR
Acquiring (ABBR) ... ACQRG
Acquisition (ABBR) ... ACQIS
Acquisition (ABBR) ... ACQSN
Acquit (ABBR) ... ACQT
Acquittal (ABBR) ... ACQTL
Acquittance (ABBR) ... ACQTNC
Acquitted (ABBR) ... ACQTD
Acquitting (ABBR) ... ACQTG
Acre Foot (ABBR) ... AC FT
Acreage (ABBR) ... ACRG
Acrid (ABBR) ... ACRI
Acridity (ABBR) ... ACRDT
Acridity (ABBR) ... ACRIT
Acrimonious (ABBR) ... ACRMNIS
Acrimonious (ABBR) ... ACRMS
Acrimony (ABBR) ... ACRM
Acrimony (ABBR) ... ACRMNY
Acrobatic (ABBR) ... ACRBTC
Acrobatically (ABBR) ... ACRBTCY
Acrolect (ABBR) ... ACROL
Acronym (ABBR) ... ACRNM
[*The*] **Acronym Generator Converter Program** [*RCA computer program*] (IAA) ... TCP
[*The*] **Acronym Generator Reference** [*RCA computer program*] (IAA) ... TAREF
Acrophobe [*or Acrophobia*] (ABBR) ... ACRO
Acrophobia (ABBR) ... ACPHOB
Acrostic (ABBR) ... ACROS
Acrylonitrile-Butadiene-Styrene and Styrene-Acrylonitrile [*Organic chemistry*] (ERG) ... ABS/SAN
Acrylonitrile Styrene Acrylate [*Plastics*] [*Organic chemistry*] ... ASA
Acted (ABBR) ... ACTD
Actionable (ABBR) ... ACTNB
Activate (ABBR) ... ACTVA
Activated (ABBR) ... ACTVAD
Activated (ABBR) ... ACTVTD
Activating (ABBR) ... ACTVAG
Activating (ABBR) ... ACTVTG
Activation (ABBR) ... ACTVAN
Activation (ABBR) ... ACTVTN
Activator (ABBR) ... ACTVOR
Active (FAAC) ... ACTV
Active Beacon Collision Avoidance System [*Aviation*] (DA) ... A-BCAS
Active Employment Strategy ... AES
Active Employment Training Organization ... AETO
Active Lane Control [*Image control and lane positioning*] [*Automotive engineering*] ... ALC
Active Roll Stabilization [*Automotive suspension*] ... ARS
Active Valve Train [*Automotive engineering*] ... AVT
Actively (ABBR) ... ACTVY
Activeness (ABBR) ... ACTVNS
Activity (ABBR) ... ACTIV
Activity Test ... AT
Actress (ABBR) ... ACTRE
Actress (ABBR) ... ACTRS
Actuality (ABBR) ... ACTLT
Actualization (ABBR) ... ACTLZAN
Actualization (ABBR) ... ACTLZN
Actualize (ABBR) ... ACTLZ
Actualized (ABBR) ... ACTLZD
Actualizing (ABBR) ... ACTLZG
Actually (ABBR) ... ACTLY
Actuary (ABBR) ... ACTRY
Actuary (ABBR) ... ACTUR
Actuate (ABBR) ... ACTU
Actuated (ABBR) ... ACTAD
Actuated (ABBR) ... ACTUD
Actuating (ABBR) ... ACTAG
Actuating (ABBR) ... ACTUG
Actuation (ABBR) ... ACTAN
Actuation (ABBR) ... ACTUN
Actuator (ABBR) ... ACTAR
Acumen (ABBR) ... ACMN
Acupuncture (ABBR) ... ACUP
Acute-Phase Response Factor [*Biochemistry*] ... APRF
Acute Physiology and Chronic Health Evaluation ... APACHE
Acutely (ABBR) ... ACTY
Acuteness (ABBR) ... ACTNS
Acuteness (ABBR) ... ACUTNS
Ad Hoc Schedule Message (DA) ... ASM
Ad-Page Exposure (NTCM) ... APX
Adage (ABBR) ... ADG
Adamant (ABBR) ... ADAMT
Adamant (ABBR) ... ADMNT
Adamantine (ABBR) ... ADAM
Adamantly (ABBR) ... ADAMTY
Adamantly (ABBR) ... ADMNTY
Adaptability (ABBR) ... ADPBT
Adaptable (ABBR) ... ADAPB
Adaptable (ABBR) ... ADPB
Adaptably (ABBR) ... ADAPY
Adaptation (ABBR) ... ADAPN
Adaptation (ABBR) ... ADAPTTN
Adapted (ABBR) ... ADAPD
Adapter (ABBR) ... ADAPR
Adapting (ABBR) ... ADAPG
Adaption (ABBR) ... ADAPN
Adaptive (ABBR) ... ADAPTV
Adaptive (ABBR) ... ADAPV
Adaptive Differential Pulse Code Modulation [*Computer science*] ... ADCPM
Adaptive Learn Processor [*Fuel systems*] [*Automotive engineering*] ... ADP
Adastra Aviation Ltd. [*Canada*] [*ICAO designator*] (FAAC) ... ADD
Adbuct (ABBR) ... ABDC
Addend (ABBR) ... ADND
Addenda (ABBR) ... ADNDA
Addendum (ABBR) ... ADDNDM
Addendum (ABBR) ... ADNDM
Addict (ABBR) ... ADDC
Addicted (ABBR) ... ADDCD
Addicting (ABBR) ... ADDCG
Addiction (ABBR) ... ADDCN
Adding (ABBR) ... ADDG
Addition (ABBR) ... ADTN
Additional (DA) ... ADNI
Additional (ABBR) ... ADTNL
Additional Information Form ... AIF
Additional Traffic [*Air Traffic Control*] (FAAC) ... ADNL TFC
Additionally (ABBR) ... ADDNLY
Additionally (ABBR) ... ADTNLY
Additive (ABBR) ... ADDV
Additive (ABBR) ... ADTV
Addressed (ABBR) ... ADDRD
Addressed (ABBR) ... ADDSD
Addressee (ABBR) ... ADDRE
Addressee (ABBR) ... ADRSE
Addressing (ABBR) ... ADDRG
Adducable (ABBR) ... ADUCB
Adduce (ABBR) ... ADC
Adduce (ABBR) ... ADUC
Adduced (ABBR) ... ADUCD
Adducing (ABBR) ... ADUCG
Adduct (ABBR) ... ADCT
Adducted (ABBR) ... ADUCTD
Adducting (ABBR) ... ADUCTG
Adduction (ABBR) ... ADCTN
Adduction (ABBR) ... ADUCTN
Adductive (ABBR) ... ADCTV
Adductive (ABBR) ... ADUCTV
Adenosine Deceminase Binding Protein [*Biochemistry*] ... ADABP
Adept (ABBR) ... ADPT
Adeptly (ABBR) ... ADPY
Adeptness (ABBR) ... ADEPNS
Adeptness (ABBR) ... ADPNS
Adequacy (ABBR) ... ADQC
Adequacy (ABBR) ... ADQCY
Adequate (ABBR) ... ADQA
Adequately (ABBR) ... ADQAY
Adequately (ABBR) ... ADQTY
Adequateness (ABBR) ... ADQTNS
Adhere (ABBR) ... ADHR
Adhered (ABBR) ... ADHRD
Adherence (ABBR) ... ADHRNC
Adherens Junction [*Cytology*] ... AJ
Adherent (ABBR) ... ADHRNT
Adherent (ABBR) ... ADHRT
Adherently (ABBR) ... ADHRTY
Adhering (ABBR) ... ADHRG

By Meaning

Adhesion (ABBR)	ADHN
Adhesive (ABBR)	ADHSV
Adhesive (ABBR)	ADNV
Adhesive Active [*Tire manufacturing*]	AA
Adhesively (ABBR)	ADHSVY
Adhesiveness (ABBR)	ADHSVNS
Adhesiveness (ABBR)	ADHVNS
Adjacency (ABBR)	ADJC
Adjacency (ABBR)	ADJCNC
Adjacent (ABBR)	ADJA
Adjacent (ABBR)	ADJCNT
Adjacently (ABBR)	ADJAY
Adjacently (ABBR)	ADJCNTY
Adjectival (ABBR)	ADJVL
Adjective (ABBR)	ADJV
Adjoin (ABBR)	ADJN
Adjoining (ABBR)	ADJNG
Adjoint (ABBR)	ADJ
Adjourn (ABBR)	ADJRN
Adjourned (ABBR)	ADJRND
Adjourning (ABBR)	ADJRNG
Adjournment (ABBR)	ADJRNNT
Adjournment (ABBR)	ADJRNT
Adjudge (ABBR)	ADJDG
Adjudged (ABBR)	ADJDGD
Adjudging (ABBR)	ADJDGG
Adjudicate (ABBR)	ADJDCA
Adjudicate (ABBR)	ADJUD
Adjudicated (ABBR)	ADJDCAD
Adjudicated (ABBR)	ADJUDD
Adjudicating (ABBR)	ADJDCAG
Adjudicating (ABBR)	ADJUDG
Adjudication (ABBR)	ADJDCAN
Adjudication (ABBR)	ADJUDN
Adjudicator (ABBR)	ADJDCR
Adjudicator (ABBR)	ADJUDR
Adjudicatory (ABBR)	ADJUDRY
Adjunct (ABBR)	ADJNC
Adjunctive (ABBR)	ADJNCV
Adjuration (ABBR)	ADJRAN
Adjuratory (ABBR)	ADJRAY
Adjure (ABBR)	ADJR
Adjured (ABBR)	ADJRD
Adjurer (ABBR)	ADJRR
Adjuring (ABBR)	ADJRG
Adjust (ABBR)	ADJS
Adjustable (ABBR)	ADJSB
Adjustable Rear Plate [*Air conditioning systems*] [*Automotive engineering*]	ARP
Adjustably (ABBR)	ADJSBY
Adjusted (ABBR)	ADJSD
Adjuster (ABBR)	ADJSR
Adjuster (ABBR)	ADJSTR
Adjusting (ABBR)	ADJSG
Adjustment (ABBR)	ADJSNT
Adjustment (ABBR)	ADJST
Adjutancy (ABBR)	ADJTNC
Adjutant (ABBR)	ADJT
Adjutants (ABBR)	ADJTS
Adlerian Society of Great Britain (BI)	ASGB
Administer (ABBR)	ADMN
Administer (ABBR)	ADMSTR
Administered (ABBR)	ADMND
Administering (ABBR)	ADMNG
Administracion de Aeropuertos [*Bolivia*] [*ICAO designator*] (FAAC)	XXV
Administrate (ABBR)	ADMNT
Administrate (ABBR)	ADMSTRA
Administrated (ABBR)	ADMNTD
Administrates (ABBR)	ADMNTS
Administrating (ABBR)	ADMNTG
Administration (ABBR)	ADMNTN
Administration (ABBR)	ADMSTRAN
Administrative (ABBR)	ADMNTV
Administrative (ABBR)	ADMSTRAV
Administrative Order on Consent [*Environmental Protection Agency*] (ERG)	AOC
Administrative Reform Unit	ARU
Administrative Service Officer Class	ASOC
Administrative Service Officer Structure	ASOS
Administrative Service Test	AST
Administratively (ABBR)	ADMNTVY
Administrator (ABBR)	ADMNTR
Administrator (ABBR)	ADMSTRATR
Administratrix (ABBR)	ADMNTX
Administratrix (ABBR)	ADMRX
Admirable (ABBR)	ADMRB
Admirably (ABBR)	ADMRY
Admiralty (ABBR)	ADMLT
Admiralty (ABBR)	ADMRLT
Admiralty (ABBR)	ADMTY
Admiration (ABBR)	ADMRAN
Admiration (ABBR)	ADMRN
Admire (ABBR)	ADMR
Admired (ABBR)	ADMRD
Admirer (ABBR)	ADMRR
Admiring (ABBR)	ADMRG
Admiringly (ABBR)	ADMRGY
Admissibility (ABBR)	ADMSBLT
Admissibility (ABBR)	ADMSBT
Admissible (ABBR)	ADMSB
Admissive (ABBR)	ADMSV
Admit (ABBR)	ADMT
Admittance (ABBR)	ADMTNC
Admitted (ABBR)	ADMTD
Admittedly (ABBR)	ADMTDY
Admitting (ABBR)	ADMTG
Admixture (ABBR)	ADMXR
Admonish (ABBR)	ADMNH
Admonish (ABBR)	ADMON
Admonished (ABBR)	ADMOND
Admonisher (ABBR)	ADMNHR
Admonisher (ABBR)	ADMONR
Admonishing (ABBR)	ADMONG
Admonishingly (ABBR)	ADMONGY
Admonishment (ABBR)	ADMONT
Admonition (ABBR)	ADMNN
Admonition (ABBR)	ADMONTN
Admonitions (ABBR)	ADMNTNS
Adolescence (ABBR)	ADLSNC
Adolescent (ABBR)	ADLSNT
Adolescent (ABBR)	ADLST
Adoptable (ABBR)	ADOPB
Adopted (ABBR)	ADOPD
Adoptee-Birthparent Center [*An association*] (EA)	ABC
Adopter (ABBR)	ADOPR
Adopting (ABBR)	ADOPG
Adoption (ABBR)	ADOP
Adoption (ABBR)	ADOPN
Adoptive (ABBR)	ADOPV
Adorability (ABBR)	ADORBT
Adorable (ABBR)	ADORB
Adorableness (ABBR)	ADORBNS
Adorably (ABBR)	ADORBL
Adorably (ABBR)	ADORBY
Adoration (ABBR)	ADORAN
Adoration (ABBR)	ADORTN
Adored (ABBR)	ADORD
Adoring (ABBR)	ADORG
Adoringly (ABBR)	ADORGY
Adornment (ABBR)	ADORNT
Adornment (ABBR)	ADRNT
Adrenal [*Gland*] (ABBR)	ADREN
Adrenaline (ABBR)	ADRN
Adria Airways [*Yugoslavia*] [*ICAO designator*] (FAAC)	ADR
Adriatic (ABBR)	ADR
Adroit (ABBR)	ADRT
Adroitly (ABBR)	ADRTY
Adroitness (ABBR)	ADRTNS
Adsorb (ABBR)	ADSB
Adsorbent (ABBR)	ADSBNT
Adsorbent (ABBR)	ADSBT
Adsorption (ABBR)	ADSPN
ADT Aviation Ltd. [*British*] [*ICAO designator*] (FAAC)	AUC
Adulate (ABBR)	ADLA
Adulate (ABBR)	ADUL
Adulated (ABBR)	ADLAD
Adulated (ABBR)	ADULD
Adulating (ABBR)	ADLAG
Adulating (ABBR)	ADULG
Adulation (ABBR)	ADLAN
Adulation (ABBR)	ADULN
Adulator (ABBR)	ADLAR
Adulator (ABBR)	ADULR
Adulatory (ABBR)	ADLARY
Adulatory (ABBR)	ADULY
Adult (ABBR)	ADLT
Adulterant (ABBR)	ADLTNT
Adulterant (ABBR)	ADLTRNT
Adulterant (ABBR)	ADULT
Adulterate (ABBR)	ADLTA
Adulterate (ABBR)	ADLTRA
Adulterate (ABBR)	ADULT
Adulterated (ABBR)	ADLTAD
Adulterated (ABBR)	ADLTRAD
Adulterating (ABBR)	ADLTAG
Adulterating (ABBR)	ADLTRAG
Adulteration (ABBR)	ADLTRAN
Adulteration (ABBR)	ADULT
Adulteration (ABBR)	ADLTR
Adulterer (ABBR)	ADLTR
Adulterer (ABBR)	ADLTRR
Adulteress (ABBR)	ADLTRES
Adulteress (ABBR)	ADLTRS
Adulterous (ABBR)	ADLTRU
Adulterous (ABBR)	ADLTUS
Adulterously (ABBR)	ADLTUSY
Adultery (ABBR)	ADLTRY

Adulthood (ABBR) ... ADLTHD
Adumbrate (ABBR) ... ADMB
Adumbrate (ABBR) ... ADMBRA
Adumbrated (ABBR) ... ADMBD
Adumbrated (ABBR) ... ADMBRAD
Adumbrating (ABBR) ... ADMBG
Adumbrating (ABBR) ... ADMBRAG
Advance [*Wire service code*] (NTCM) ... A
Advance (ABBR) ... ADVNC
Advance Air Charters [*Canada*] [*ICAO designator*] (FAAC) ... ADV
Advance Australia Party [*Political party*] ... AAP
Advance Aviation Services, Inc. [*ICAO designator*] (FAAC) ... XTJ
Advance Boundary Information (DA) ... ABI
Advance Electronic Diagnostics [*Automotive industry supplier*] ... AED
Advance Prediction Computer Program ... APCP
Advance Purchase Excursion Fare [*Aviation*] (DA) ... APEX
Advanced (ABBR) ... ADVNCD
Advanced Combustion Engineering ... ACE
Advanced Communication and Timekeeping Technology [*Seiko Telecommunications Systems*] [*FM data receiver chip set*] (PCM) ... ACTT
Advanced Computer Program Multiple Array Processor System ... ACMAPS
Advanced Education Institution ... AEI
Advanced Engine Development [*Automotive industry supplier*] ... AED
Advanced Experimental Vehicle - 5th Generation [*Toyota*] ... AXV-V
Advanced Firefighter [*Military*] ... AFF
Advanced Flight Management System (DA) ... AFMS
Advanced Instruction Technique (DA) ... AIT
Advanced Logistics Support Base [*Navy*] ... ALSB
Advanced Oxidation Process [*Chemistry*] ... AOP
Advanced Public Transportation Systems ... APTS
Advanced Quickfix [*Military*] ... AQF
Advanced RISC [*Reduced Instruction-Set Computerizing*] **Machine** (ECON) ... ARM
Advanced Road Profile Measurement Vehicle [*Suspension design and testing*] [*Automotive engineering*] ... ARPMV
Advanced Robotics Research ... ARR
Advanced Safety Vehicle [*Automotive engineering*] ... ASV
Advanced Satellite for Cosmology and Astrophysics [*Japanese spacecraft*] ... ASCA
Advanced Shipment Notification [*Inventory control*] [*Automotive manufacturing*] ... ASN
Advanced Technology Park ... ATP
Advanced Television Services [*FCC*] (NTCM) ... ATS
Advanced Television Systems Committee [*FCC*] (NTCM) ... ATSC
Advanced Traffic Information Supply System [*Highway traffic management*] ... ATISS
Advanced Travel Information Systems [*Formerly, ADI*] [*Highway safety research*] ... ATIS
Advanced Turbo Systems [*Automotive industry supplier*] ... ATS
Advanced Vehicle Identification ... AVI
Advancement (ABBR) ... ADVNCNT
Advancement (ABBR) ... ADVNCT
Advancing (ABBR) ... ADVNCG
Advancing the Consumer Interest [*A publication*] ... ACI
Advantage (ABBR) ... ADVATG
Advantage (ABBR) ... ADVNTG
Advantage (ABBR) ... ADVTG
Advantaged (ABBR) ... ADVNTGD
Advantageous (ABBR) ... ADVATGUS
Advantageous (ABBR) ... ADVNTGU
Advantageously (ABBR) ... ADVATGUSY
Advantageously (ABBR) ... ADVNTGUY
Advantaging (ABBR) ... ADVNTGG
Advection (ABBR) ... ADVEC
Advection (ABBR) ... ADVECT
Advent (ABBR) ... ADVNT
Adventist World Radio (NTCM) ... AWR
Adventure (ABBR) ... ADVNTR
Adventured (ABBR) ... ADVNTRD
Adventurer (ABBR) ... ADVNTRR
Adventuresome (ABBR) ... ADVNTRSM
Adventuress (ABBR) ... ADVNTRES
Adventuring (ABBR) ... ADVNTRG
Adventurous (ABBR) ... ADVNTRU
Adventurous (ABBR) ... ADVNTRUS
Adventurously (ABBR) ... ADVNTRUSY
Adverbial (ABBR) ... ADVBL
Adverbial (ABBR) ... ADVL
Adversary (ABBR) ... ADVRSRY
Adversary (ABBR) ... ADVSY
Adversative (ABBR) ... ADVERSAT
Adverse (ABBR) ... ADVRS
Adverse Reactions Reporting System [*FDA*] ... ARRS
Adversely (ABBR) ... ADVRSY
Adverseness (ABBR) ... ADVRSNS
Adversity (ABBR) ... ADVRST
Advertence (ABBR) ... ADVERTNC
Advertent (ABBR) ... ADVRTNT
Advertised (ABBR) ... ADVTD
Advertisement (ABBR) ... ADVRTZNT
Advertisement (ABBR) ... ADVTMT
Advertisement Contractors' Association [*British*] (BI) ... ACA
Advertiser (ABBR) ... ADVRTZR
Advertiser (ABBR) ... ADVTR
Advertiser Syndicated Television Association (NTCM) ... ASTA
Advertising (ABBR) ... ADVRTZG
Advertising (ABBR) ... ADVTG
Advertising Agency (NTCM) ... AA
Advertising Council of America, Inc. (NTCM) ... ACA
[*The*] **Advertising Council, Inc.** (NTCM) ... ACI
Advertising Film Producers Association [*British*] (BI) ... AFPA
Advertising-Press Club [*Republic of Ireland*] (BI) ... APC
Advisability (ABBR) ... ADVSBT
Advisable (ABBR) ... ADVSB
Advisably (ABBR) ... ADVSBY
Advise at What Time Able [*Aviation*] (FAAC) ... AAWTA
Advised (ABBR) ... ADVSD
Advisedly (ABBR) ... ADVSDY
Advisement (ABBR) ... ADVSNT
Advisement (ABBR) ... ADVST
Advising (ABBR) ... ADVSG
Advisory (ABBR) ... ADVSRY
Advisory Committee on Advanced Television Service [*FCC high-definition television*] (NTCM) ... ACATS
Advisory Committee for Land-Mobile Radio Services (NTCM) ... ACLMRS
Advisory Committee on Toxic Substances [*British*] ... ACTS
Advisory Council for the Elimination of Tuberculosis ... ACET
Advisory Council of National Organizations [*Corporation for Public Broadcasting*] (NTCM) ... ACNO
Advisory Rule (DA) ... ADR
Advocacy (ABBR) ... ADVCY
Advocate (ABBR) ... ADVCA
Advocate (ABBR) ... ADVO
Advocated (ABBR) ... ADVCAD
Advocated (ABBR) ... ADVOD
Advocates (ABBR) ... ADVOS
Advocating (ABBR) ... ADVCAG
Advocating (ABBR) ... ADVOG
Advocation (ABBR) ... ADVCAN
Advocation (ABBR) ... ADVON
Advocator (ABBR) ... ADVOR
Aegean Aviation [*Greece*] [*ICAO designator*] (FAAC) ... AEE
Aer Arann Teoranta [*Ireland*] [*ICAO designator*] (FAAC) ... REA
Aer Lingus Teoranta [*Ireland*] [*ICAO designator*] (FAAC) ... EIN
Aer Turas Teoranta [*Republic of Ireland*] [*ICAO designator*] (FAAC) ... ATT
Aeration (ABBR) ... AERA
Aereo Postal de Mexico SA de CV [*ICAO designator*] (FAAC) ... PTX
Aereo Taxi de Leon SA de CV [*Mexico*] [*ICAO designator*] (FAAC) ... TXL
Aereotaxis SA de CV [*Mexico*] [*ICAO designator*] (FAAC) ... TXI
Aerial Enterprises Ltd. [*British*] [*ICAO designator*] (FAAC) ... AEG
Aerial Ropeways Association [*British*] (BI) ... ARA
Aerial Surveys (1980) Ltd. [*New Zealand*] [*ICAO designator*] (FAAC) ... SUY
Aerial Transit Co. [*ICAO designator*] (FAAC) ... AEZ
Aerialist (ABBR) ... AERLT
Aero 1 Prop-Jet, Inc. [*Canada*] [*ICAO designator*] (FAAC) ... SSM
Aero Albatros [*Mexico*] [*ICAO designator*] (FAAC) ... ALB
Aero-Alentejo, Servicos Aereos Lda. [*Portugal*] [*ICAO designator*] (FAAC) ... ANJ
Aero Asia [*Pakistan*] [*ICAO designator*] (FAAC) ... RSO
Aero Astra [*Mexico*] [*ICAO designator*] (FAAC) ... OSA
Aero Aviation Centre Ltd. [*Canada*] [*ICAO designator*] (FAAC) ... AAD
Aero Barloz SA de CV [*Mexico*] [*ICAO designator*] (FAAC) ... BLZ
Aero Campeche SA de CV [*Mexico*] [*ICAO designator*] (FAAC) ... CPC
Aero Chasqui SA [*Peru*] [*ICAO designator*] (FAAC) ... XYC
Aero Chombo SA [*Mexico*] [*ICAO designator*] (FAAC) ... CHM
Aero Coach Aviation International, Inc. [*ICAO designator*] (FAAC) ... DFA
Aero Continente [*Peru*] [*ICAO designator*] (FAAC) ... ACQ
Aero Contractors Company of Nigeria Ltd. [*ICAO designator*] (FAAC) ... NIG
Aero Control Air Ltd. [*Canada*] [*ICAO designator*] (FAAC) ... LFC
Aero Costa Rica [*ICAO designator*] (FAAC) ... AEK
Aero Ejecutiva SA [*Mexico*] [*ICAO designator*] (FAAC) ... EJT
Aero Ejecutivo de Baja California SA de CV [*Mexico*] [*ICAO designator*] (FAAC) ... EBC
Aero Ejecutivo SA de CV [*Mexico*] [*ICAO designator*] (FAAC) ... AJO
Aero Ejecutivos CA [*Venezuela*] [*ICAO designator*] (FAAC) ... VEJ
Aero Empresa Mexicana SA [*Mexico*] [*ICAO designator*] (FAAC) ... AFO
Aero Fe SA [*Mexico*] [*ICAO designator*] (FAAC) ... RFE
Aero Filipanas Ltd. [*Philippines*] [*ICAO designator*] (FAAC) ... AFI
Aero Industries, Inc. [*ICAO designator*] (FAAC) ... WAB
Aero Jalisco SA de CV [*Mexico*] [*ICAO designator*] (FAAC) ... AJL
Aero-Jet SA [*Switzerland*] [*ICAO designator*] (FAAC) ... AOJ
Aero Leasing Italiana SpA [*Italy*] [*ICAO designator*] (FAAC) ... ALJ
Aero Lider SA de CV [*Mexico*] [*ICAO designator*] (FAAC) ... LDR
Aero Lloyd Flugreisen GmbH [*Germany*] [*ICAO designator*] (FAAC) ... AEF
Aero Madrid [*Spain*] [*ICAO designator*] (FAAC) ... AEM
Aero North Aviation Services [*Canada*] [*ICAO designator*] (FAAC) ... SKP
Aero North Icelandic, Inc. [*ICAO designator*] (FAAC) ... ANF
Aero-Palma SA [*Spain*] [*ICAO designator*] (FAAC) ... AET
Aero Personal SA de CV [*Mexico*] [*ICAO designator*] (FAAC) ... PNL
Aero Quick [*Mexico*] [*ICAO designator*] (FAAC) ... QIC
Aero Quimmco SA de CV [*Mexico*] [*ICAO designator*] (FAAC) ... QUI
Aero-Rent SA de CV [*Mexico*] [*ICAO designator*] (FAAC) ... REN

Aero Renta de Coahuila SA de CV [*Mexico*] [*ICAO designator*] (FAAC) ... RCO
Aero-Rey SA de CV [*Mexico*] [*ICAO designator*] (FAAC) ... REY
Aero Sami SA de CV [*Mexico*] [*ICAO designator*] (FAAC) ... SMI
Aero Santos SA de CV [*Mexico*] [*ICAO designator*] (FAAC) ... STO
Aero Service Bolivia [*ICAO designator*] (FAAC) ... GHM
Aero Services [*Barbados*] [*ICAO designator*] (FAAC) ... BAS
Aero Services Executive [*France*] [*ICAO designator*] (FAAC) ... BES
Aero Servicio de Carga Mexicana SA de CV [*Mexico*] [*ICAO designator*] (FAAC) ... SCM
Aero Servicio del Norte SA de CV [*Mexico*] [*ICAO designator*] (FAAC) ... SNV
Aero Servicios Especializados SA de CV [*Mexico*] [*ICAO designator*] (FAAC) ... SVE
Aero Sierra Eco SA de CV [*Mexico*] [*ICAO designator*] (FAAC) ... ACO
Aero Sonora SA de CV [*Mexico*] [*ICAO designator*] (FAAC) ... SNR
Aero Sudpacifico SA [*Mexico*] [*ICAO designator*] (FAAC) ... SDP
Aero Taxi [*Canada*] [*ICAO designator*] (FAAC) ... QAT
Aero Taxi Aviation, Inc. [*ICAO designator*] (FAAC) ... QKC
Aero Tonala [*Mexico*] [*ICAO designator*] (FAAC) ... TON
Aero Top SRL Societa [*Italy*] [*ICAO designator*] (FAAC) ... TOP
Aero Trade International [*Romania*] [*ICAO designator*] (FAAC) ... AON
Aero Trades (Western) Ltd. [*Canada*] [*ICAO designator*] (FAAC) ... ATW
Aero Transporte SA [*Peru*] [*ICAO designator*] (FAAC) ... AMP
Aero Transporti Italiani SpA [*Italy*] [*ICAO designator*] (FAAC) ... ATI
Aero Veracruz SA de CV [*Mexico*] [*ICAO designator*] (FAAC) ... VRZ
Aero Vics SA de CV [*Mexico*] [*ICAO designator*] (FAAC) ... ARI
Aero West Airlines, Inc. [*ICAO designator*] (FAAC) ... RWE
Aeroamistad SA de CV [*Mexico*] [*ICAO designator*] (FAAC) ... MST
Aerobeira, Sociedade de Transporties Aeros [*Portugal*] [*ICAO designator*] (FAAC) ... ARA
Aerocalifornia SA [*Mexico*] [*ICAO designator*] (FAAC) ... SER
Aerocancun [*Mexico*] [*ICAO designator*] (FAAC) ... ACU
Aerocer SA [*Mexico*] [*ICAO designator*] (FAAC) ... RCE
Aerocesar, Aerovias del Cesar [*Colombia*] [*ICAO designator*] (FAAC) ... AEC
Aerochago [*Dominican Republic*] [*ICAO designator*] (FAAC) ... AHG
Aerocharter [*Czechoslovakia*] [*ICAO designator*] (FAAC) ... STX
Aerocharter GmbH [*Austria*] [*ICAO designator*] (FAAC) ... MOZ
Aerocharter, Inc. [*Canada*] [*ICAO designator*] (FAAC) ... MRM
Aerocharter Midlands Ltd. [*British*] [*ICAO designator*] (FAAC) ... ACC
Aerochiapas SA de CV [*Mexico*] [*ICAO designator*] (FAAC) ... AHP
Aerocombi SA [*Spain*] [*ICAO designator*] (FAAC) ... HSW
Aerocozumel SA [*Mexico*] [*ICAO designator*] (FAAC) ... AZM
Aerodespachos de El Salvador [*ICAO designator*] (FAAC) ... DNA
Aerodienst GmbH [*Germany*] [*ICAO designator*] (FAAC) ... ADN
Aerodin SA de CV [*Mexico*] [*ICAO designator*] (FAAC) ... DIN
Aerodrome Beacon (DA) ... ABE
Aerodrome Damage Repair [*NATO*] ... ADR
Aerodrome Emergency Service (DA) ... AES
Aerodrome Flight Information Service (Officer) (DA) ... AFIS(O)
Aerodrome Operation (DA) ... AOP
Aerodrome Owners Association [*British*] (BI) ... AOA
Aerodrome Reference Code Panel [*ICAO*] (DA) ... ARCP
Aerodrome Report [*Aviation*] (DA) ... Ae
Aerodrome Warning (DA) ... AW
Aerodromes, Air Routes, and Ground Aid (DA) ... AGA
Aerodynamic (ABBR) ... AERDYN
Aerodynamic Mean Chord (DA) ... AMC
Aerodynamics-Thermodynamics-Acoustic Wind Tunnel [*Automotive research*] ... ATAWT
Aerodyne Charter [*ICAO designator*] (FAAC) ... AQZ
Aerodyne Executive Aviation Services [*ICAO designator*] (FAAC) ... ADY
Aeroejecutivos, Aeroservicios Ejecutivos [*Colombia*] [*ICAO designator*] (FAAC) ... AJS
Aeroexpreso Bogota [*Colombia*] [*ICAO designator*] (FAAC) ... ABO
Aeroexpreso Interamerican [*Colombia*] [*ICAO designator*] (FAAC) ... AEI
Aerofer, SL [*Spain*] [*ICAO designator*] (FAAC) ... ARF
Aeroflot - Russian International Airlines [*Russian Federation*] [*ICAO designator*] (FAAC) ... AFL
Aerofrance [*France*] [*ICAO designator*] (FAAC) ... ROF
Aerofrisco [*Mexico*] [*ICAO designator*] (FAAC) ... FCO
Aeroguayacan [*Chile*] [*ICAO designator*] (FAAC) ... AGY
Aerojet de Costa Rica SA [*ICAO designator*] (FAAC) ... ARJ
Aerojobeni SA de CV [*Mexico*] [*ICAO designator*] (FAAC) ... JOB
Aeroleasing SA [*Switzerland*] [*ICAO designator*] (FAAC) ... FPG
Aerolift Philippines Corp. [*ICAO designator*] (FAAC) ... LFT
Aerolinas Nacionales del Ecuador SA [*ICAO designator*] (FAAC) ... EDA
Aerolinas Uruguayas SA [*Uruguay*] [*ICAO designator*] (FAAC) ... AUY
Aerolinea Muri [*Mexico*] [*ICAO designator*] (FAAC) ... MUR
Aerolineas Argentinas [*Argentina*] [*ICAO designator*] (FAAC) ... ARG
Aerolineas Centrales de Colombia [*ICAO designator*] (FAAC) ... AES
Aerolineas Centroamericanas SA [*Central American Airlines*] [*Nicaragua*] [*ICAO designator*] (FAAC) ... ACN
Aerolineas Coco Club Hoteles de Mexico SA de CV [*ICAO designator*] (FAAC) ... CCO
Aerolineas Cordillera Ltda. [*Chile*] [*ICAO designator*] (FAAC) ... AEROCOR
Aerolineas Cordillera Ltda. [*Chile*] [*ICAO designator*] (FAAC) ... CRD
Aerolineas Dominicanas SA [*Dominican Republic*] [*ICAO designator*] (FAAC) ... ADM
Aerolineas Ejecutivas SA [*Mexico*] [*ICAO designator*] (FAAC) ... LET
Aerolineas Ejecutivas de San Luis Potosi SA de CV [*Mexico*] [*ICAO designator*] (FAAC) ... ELP
Aerolineas de El Salvador SA [*ICAO designator*] (FAAC) ... SZA
Aerolineas Especiales de Colombia [*ICAO designator*] (FAAC) ... ALE
Aerolineas Latinas CA [*Venezuela*] [*ICAO designator*] (FAAC) ... LTN
Aerolineas Marcos SA de CV [*Mexico*] [*ICAO designator*] (FAAC) ... MCO
Aerolineas Medellin [*Colombia*] [*ICAO designator*] (FAAC) ... AMD
Aerolineas Mexicanas JS SA de CV [*Mexico*] [*ICAO designator*] (FAAC) ... LMX
Aerolineas de Michoacan [*Mexico*] [*ICAO designator*] (FAAC) ... MIC
Aerolineas del Oeste SA de CV [*Mexico*] [*ICAO designator*] (FAAC) ... AST
Aerolineas Pacifico Atlantico SA [*Spain*] [*ICAO designator*] (FAAC) ... APP
Aerolineas del Sureste SA [*Mexico*] [*ICAO designator*] (FAAC) ... SUE
Aeromak [*Yugoslavia*] [*ICAO designator*] (FAAC) ... AMK
Aeromaritime (CAAA) [*France*] [*ICAO designator*] (FAAC) ... QKL
Aeromarket Express [*Spain*] [*ICAO designator*] (FAAC) ... ARM
Aeromedicare Ltd. [*British*] [*ICAO designator*] (FAAC) ... AMQ
Aeromega Ltd. [*British*] [*ICAO designator*] (FAAC) ... OMG
Aeromonterrey SA [*Mexico*] [*ICAO designator*] (FAAC) ... MOT
Aeromorelos SA de CV [*Mexico*] [*ICAO designator*] (FAAC) ... MRL
Aeromyl SA de CV [*Mexico*] [*ICAO designator*] (FAAC) ... MYL
Aeron International Airlines, Inc. [*ICAO designator*] (FAAC) ... AXI
Aeronardi SpA [*Italy*] [*ICAO designator*] (FAAC) ... NRD
Aeronaut (ABBR) ... AERN
Aeronautica Interespacial SA de CV [*Mexico*] [*ICAO designator*] (FAAC) ... ITS
Aeronautica Venezolana CA [*Venezuela*] [*ICAO designator*] (FAAC) ... AEROVENCA
Aeronautica Venezolana, CA [*Venezuela*] [*ICAO designator*] (FAAC) ... AVC
Aeronautical (ABBR) ... AE
Aeronautical (ABBR) ... AERNL
Aeronautical Chart Automation Project [*Military*] (DA) ... ACAP
Aeronautical Data Communication Network (DA) ... ADCN
Aeronautical Digital Information Display System (DA) ... ADIDS
Aeronautical Earth Station (DA) ... AES
Aeronautical Enroute Information Service (DA) ... AEIS
Aeronautical Fixed Systems Planning for Data Interchange Panel [*ICAO*] (DA) ... ASPP
Aeronautical Frequency Management Committee [*British*] (DA) ... AFMLC
Aeronautical Information Service Automation Group [*ICAO*] (DA) ... AAG
Aeronautical Information Service Automation Group [*ICAO*] (DA) ... AISAG
Aeronautical Information Service Automation Specialist Panel [*ICAO*] (DA) ... AISAP
Aeronautical Mobile Satellite Service [*ICAO designator*] (FAAC) ... AMSS
Aeronautical Mobile Satellite Service Panel [*ICAO*] (DA) ... AMSSP
Aeronautical Public Correspondence (DA) ... APC
Aeronautical Radio, Inc. [*ICAO designator*] (FAAC) ... XAA
Aeronautical Satellite (DA) ... AEROSAT
Aeronautical Satellite Communications Processor (DA) ... ASCAP
Aeronautical Society of Great Britain (BI) ... ASGB
Aeronautically (ABBR) ... AERNLY
Aeronautics (ABBR) ... AERNC
Aeronaves del Centro [*Venezuela*] [*ICAO designator*] (FAAC) ... AGA
Aeronaves del Peru SA [*ICAO designator*] (FAAC) ... WPL
Aeronavs La Dprada SA [*Spain*] [*ICAO designator*] (FAAC) ... ALD
Aeronorte SA [*Colombia*] [*ICAO designator*] (FAAC) ... ANR
Aeronorte - Transportes Aereos Lda. [*Portugal*] [*ICAO designator*] (FAAC) ... RTE
Aeropelican Air Services Pty Ltd. [*Australia*] [*ICAO designator*] (FAAC) ... PEL
Aeropetrel [*Chile*] [*ICAO designator*] (FAAC) ... PET
Aeropiloto-Sociedade Exploradora de Servicos Aereos Lda. [*Portugal*] [*ICAO designator*] (FAAC) ... AOP
Aeroposta SA [*Argentina*] [*ICAO designator*] (FAAC) ... POS
Aeropro [*Canada*] [*ICAO designator*] (FAAC) ... APO
Aeropuma SA [*El Salvador*] [*ICAO designator*] (FAAC) ... APU
Aeroput [*Yugoslavia*] [*ICAO designator*] (FAAC) ... PUT
Aeropycsa SA de CV [*Mexico*] [*ICAO designator*] (FAAC) ... PYC
Aerora SA [*Mexico*] [*ICAO designator*] (FAAC) ... ARR
Aerorepresentaciones Tupac Amaru [*Peru*] [*ICAO designator*] (FAAC) ... XUT
Aeroservicio Sipse SA de CV [*Mexico*] [*ICAO designator*] (FAAC) ... PSE
Aeroservicios Carabobo CA [*Venezuela*] [*ICAO designator*] (FAAC) ... ASERCA
Aeroservicios Carabobo CA (ASERCA) [*Venzuela*] [*ICAO designator*] (FAAC) ... OCA
Aeroservicios Ejecutivos del Occidente SA de CV [*Mexico*] [*ICAO designator*] (FAAC) ... AEO
Aeroservicios Ejecutivos del Pacifico SA [*Mexico*] [*ICAO designator*] (FAAC) ... SPO
Aeroservicios Ejecutivos Sinaloenses SA [*Mexico*] [*ICAO designator*] (FAAC) ... SLS
Aeroservicios Monterrey SA de CV [*Mexico*] [*ICAO designator*] (FAAC) ... SVM
Aerosevicios Ecuatorianos CA [*Ecuador*] [*ICAO designator*] (FAAC) ... EAE
Aerosi SA de CV [*Mexico*] [*ICAO designator*] (FAAC) ... OSI
Aerosierra de Durango [*Mexico*] [*ICAO designator*] (FAAC) ... SDG
Aerosol (ABBR) ... AERSL
Aerospace (ABBR) ... AERSPC
Aerostar Airlines, Inc. [*ICAO designator*] (FAAC) ... FNT
Aerosucre SA [*Colombia*] [*ICAO designator*] (FAAC) ... HRE
AeroSun International, Inc. [*ICAO designator*] (FAAC) ... ASI
Aerosuper AS de CV [*Mexico*] [*ICAO designator*] (FAAC) ... SUP

Aerotal Aerolineas Territoriales de Colombia Ltd. [ICAO designator] (FAAC) ... ART
Aerotamatan SA de CV [Mexico] [ICAO designator] (FAAC) ... TAA
Aerotaxi Casanare Ltda. [Colombia] [ICAO designator] (FAAC) ... ATK
Aerotaxi del Valle [Colombia] [ICAO designator] (FAAC) ... AOX
Aerotaxis de Aguascalientes SA de CV [Mexico] [ICAO designator] (FAAC) ... GUA
Aerotaxis Calzada SA de CV [Mexico] [ICAO designator] (FAAC) ... CLZ
Aerotaxis del Centro SA [Mexico] [ICAO designator] (FAAC) ... CTO
Aerotaxis Corporativo SA de CV [Mexico] [ICAO designator] (FAAC) ... CRP
Aerotaxis Latinoamericanos SA de CV [Mexico] [ICAO designator] (FAAC) ... LTI
Aerotaxis Pegaso SA de CV [Mexico] [ICAO designator] (FAAC) ... APG
Aerotours Dominican, C por A [Dominican Republic] [ICAO designator] (FAAC) ... ATD
Aerotransporte Peruanos Internacionales SA [Peru] [ICAO designator] (FAAC) ... APS
Aerotransportes Barlovento SA de CV [Mexico] [ICAO designator] (FAAC) ... BLO
Aerotransportes Entre Rios SRL [Argentina] [ICAO designator] (FAAC) ... SFA
Aerotransportes Especiales Ltda. [Colombia] [ICAO designator] (FAAC) ... ATP
Aerotransportes Mas de Carga SA de CV [Mexico] [ICAO designator] (FAAC) ... MAA
Aerotransportes Privados SA de CV [Mexico] [ICAO designator] (FAAC) ... PVA
Aerotur SA [Mexico] [ICAO designator] (FAAC) ... TUR
Aerovekel SA [Mexico] [ICAO designator] (FAAC) ... VKL
Aeroventas SA [Mexico] [ICAO designator] (FAAC) ... AEV
Aerovia del Altiplano SA de CV [Mexico] [ICAO designator] (FAAC) ... APN
Aeroviajes Ejecuitvos SA de CV [Mexico] [ICAO designator] (FAAC) ... AVJ
Aerovial [Chile] [ICAO designator] (FAAC) ... AVL
Aerovias del Atlantico Ltd. [Colombia] [ICAO designator] (FAAC) ... AOK
Aerovias Bueno Ltd. [Colombia] [ICAO designator] (FAAC) ... ABU
Aerovias Caribe SA [Mexico] [ICAO designator] (FAAC) ... CBE
Aerovias Castillo SA [Mexico] [ICAO designator] (FAAC) ... CLL
Aerovias Dap [Chile] [ICAO designator] (FAAC) ... DAP
Aerovias Especiales de Carga Ltda. [Colombia] [ICAO designator] (FAAC) ... AVESCA
Aerovias Especiales de Carga Ltda. [Colombia] [ICAO designator] (FAAC) ... VSC
Aerovias de Lagos SA de CV [Mexico] [ICAO designator] (FAAC) ... LAG
Aerovias de Mexico SA de CV [ICAO designator] (FAAC) ... AMX
Aerovias Oaxaquenas SA [Mexico] [ICAO designator] (FAAC) ... AVO
Aerovias de Poniente SA de CV [Mexico] [ICAO designator] (FAAC) ... PNI
Aerovias Xalitic SA de CV [Mexico] [ICAO designator] (FAAC) ... XAL
Aerovitro SA de CV [Mexico] [ICAO designator] (FAAC) ... VRO
Aesthete (ABBR) ... AESTH
Aesthetically (ABBR) ... AESTHY
Affability (ABBR) ... AFBT
Affable (ABBR) ... AFB
Affably (ABBR) ... AFBY
Affectation (ABBR) ... AFCTAN
Affected (ABBR) ... AFCTD
Affectedly (ABBR) ... AFCTDY
Affecting (ABBR) ... AFCTG
Affectingly (ABBR) ... AFCTGY
Affection (ABBR) ... AFCTN
Affectionate (ABBR) ... AFCTNA
Affectionate (ABBR) ... AFCTNT
Affectionately (ABBR) ... AFCTNAY
Affectionately (ABBR) ... AFCTNTY
Affirmative [ICAO designator] (FAAC) ... AFM
Affretair [Zimbabwe] [ICAO designator] (FAAC) ... AFM
Africa Air Links [Sierra Leone] [ICAO designator] (FAAC) ... AFK
Africa Report [A publication] ... Afr Rpt
Africair Service [Senegal] [ICAO designator] (FAAC) ... FFB
African Airlines International Ltd. [Kenya] [ICAO designator] (FAAC) ... AIK
African Cultural Foundation (EA) ... ACF
African Export Import Bank ... AFREXIMBANK
African International Airlines [Lesotho] [ICAO designator] (FAAC) ... AFN
African International Airways [Swaziland] [ICAO designator] (FAAC) ... AIN
African Region Traffic Analysis Forecasting Group [ICAO] (DA) ... ATAFG
African Safari Airways Ltd. [Kenya] [ICAO designator] (FAAC) ... QSC
African West Air [Senegal] [ICAO designator] (FAAC) ... AFC
African West Air [Senegal] [ICAO designator] (FAAC) ... AWA
Afro Unity Airways [Benin] [ICAO designator] (FAAC) ... AFU
After Dinner Opera Co. ... ADOCo
Agderfly AS [Norway] [ICAO designator] (FAAC) ... AGD
Agence Nationale des Aerodromes et de la Meteorologie [Ivory Coast] [ICAO designator] (FAAC) ... ZZM
Agency for Instructional Television (NTCM) ... AIT
Aggregate Base Course (DAC) ... ABC
Aggregate Estimated Net Pool Return [Business term] ... AENPR
Agile Intelligent Manufacturing [Computer-assisted manufacturing] ... AIM
Aging Aircraft Program [FAA] (DA) ... AAP
Agnostics' Adoption Society [British] (BI) ... AAS
Agrar-Aviacion SA [Spain] [ICAO designator] (FAAC) ... AGI
Agricultural Advisory Council for England and Wales (BI) ... AAC
Agricultural Central Cooperative Association Ltd. [British] (BI) ... ACCA
Agricultural Credit Corp. Ltd. [British] (BI) ... ACC
Agricultural Land Commission [British] (BI) ... ALC
Agricultural Program (NTCM) ... A
Agricultural Research Services, Animal Health Division [Department of Agriculture] [ICAO designator] (FAAC) ... AGR
Agricultural Show Exhibitors' Association [British] (BI) ... ASEA
AIDS Education/Services for the Deaf [An association] ... AESD
AIDS Society for Asia and the Pacific ... ASFAP
Aigle Azur [France] [ICAO designator] (FAAC) ... AAF
Air 2000 Airlines Ltd. [Canada] [ICAO designator] (FAAC) ... CMM
Air 2000, Ltd, [British] [ICAO designator] (FAAC) ... AMM
Air 500 Ltd. [Canada] [ICAO designator] (FAAC) ... BRM
Air Affaires EJA France [ICAO designator] (FAAC) ... AEJ
Air Afrique [Ivory Coast] [ICAO designator] (FAAC) ... RKA
Air-to-Air Refuelling Area (DA) ... AARA
Air Alba Ltd. [British] [ICAO designator] (FAAC) ... RLB
Air Algerie [Algeria] [ICAO designator] (FAAC) ... DAH
Air Alliance, Inc. [Canada] [ICAO designator] (FAAC) ... AAQ
Air Alma, Inc. [Canada] [ICAO designator] (FAAC) ... AAJ
Air Alpha, AS [Denmark] [ICAO designator] (FAAC) ... AHA
Air Alpha, Inc. [ICAO designator] (FAAC) ... DBA
Air Alsie, AS [Denmark] [ICAO designator] (FAAC) ... ALS
Air Angouleme [France] [ICAO designator] (FAAC) ... AGL
Air Antares Ltd. [Romania] [ICAO designator] (FAAC) ... AAY
Air Aquitaine [France] [ICAO designator] (FAAC) ... AQE
Air Aruba [ICAO designator] (FAAC) ... ARU
Air Assault Task Force [Army] (ADDR) ... AATF
Air Atlantic [Canada] [ICAO designator] (FAAC) ... ATL
Air Atlantic Uruguay [ICAO designator] (FAAC) ... AUM
Air Atlantique [British] [ICAO designator] (FAAC) ... AAG
Air Atlantique Air Publicite [France] [ICAO designator] (FAAC) ... APB
Air Atonabee Ltd. [Canada] [ICAO designator] (FAAC) ... OUL
Air Aurora, Inc. [ICAO designator] (FAAC) ... AAI
Air BC Ltd. [Canada] [ICAO designator] (FAAC) ... ABL
Air Belgium [ICAO designator] (FAAC) ... ABB
Air Berlin, USA [Germany] [ICAO designator] (FAAC) ... BER
Air Botswana (Pty) Ltd. [ICAO designator] (FAAC) ... BOT
Air Bras d'Or [Canada] [ICAO designator] (FAAC) ... BRL
Air Bravo [Uganda] [ICAO designator] (FAAC) ... BRF
Air Brousse, Inc. [Canada] [ICAO designator] (FAAC) ... ABT
Air Budapest Club Ltd. [Hungary] [ICAO designator] (FAAC) ... BUD
Air Burkina [Burkina Faso] [ICAO designator] (FAAC) ... VBW
Air-Burundi [ICAO designator] (FAAC) ... PBU
Air Business Contact [France] [ICAO designator] (FAAC) ... ABC
Air Bypass Valve [Automotive engineering] ... ABV
Air Cadets School [RAF] [British] [ICAO designator] (FAAC) ... ACW
Air Caledonia, Inc. [Canada] [ICAO designator] (FAAC) ... ACM
Air Caledonie [France] [ICAO designator] (FAAC) ... TPC
Air Caledonie International [France] [ICAO designator] (FAAC) ... ACI
Air Canada [ICAO designator] (FAAC) ... ACA
Air Canarias S. Coop Ltd. [Spain] [ICAO designator] (FAAC) ... CAN
Air Cape [ICAO designator] (FAAC) ... ACK
Air Cape [South Africa] [ICAO designator] (FAAC) ... ACP
Air Capitol [Italy] [ICAO designator] (FAAC) ... ACL
Air Cargo America, Inc. [ICAO designator] (FAAC) ... MVM
Air Cargo Carriers, Inc. [ICAO designator] (FAAC) ... PRT
Air Cargo Carriers, Inc. [ICAO designator] (FAAC) ... SNC
Air Cargo Fast Flow (DA) ... ACFF
Air Charter [France] [ICAO designator] (FAAC) ... ACF
Air Charter Express [France] [ICAO designator] (FAAC) ... CHX
Air Charter Express AS [Norway] [ICAO designator] (FAAC) ... ECR
Air Charter Services [Zaire] [ICAO designator] (FAAC) ... CHR
Air Charter Services (Pty) Ltd. South Africa [ICAO designator] (FAAC) ... IPL
Air Charter World [ICAO designator] (FAAC) ... XAC
Air Charters, Inc. [Canada] [ICAO designator] (FAAC) ... ACX
Air China [ICAO designator] (FAAC) ... CCA
Air City SA [Switzerland] [ICAO designator] (FAAC) ... ACY
Air Colombia [ICAO designator] (FAAC) ... ACO
Air Columbus SA [Portugal] [ICAO designator] (FAAC) ... CNB
Air Commerce [Yugoslavia] [ICAO designator] (FAAC) ... ACS
Air Condal SA [Spain] [ICAO designator] (FAAC) ... JID
Air Condition [Technical drawings] (DAC) ... AIR COND
Air Conditioning Equipment Room [NFPA pre-fire planning symbol] (NFPA) ... AC
Air-Conditioning Power Panel (DAC) ... PP-AC
Air Continental, Inc. [ICAO designator] (FAAC) ... NAR
Air Corse [France] [ICAO designator] (FAAC) ... ARK
Air Cote d'Opale [France] [ICAO designator] (FAAC) ... OPL
Air Creebec [Canada] [ICAO designator] (FAAC) ... CRQ
Air-Dale Ltd. [Canada] [ICAO designator] (FAAC) ... ADL
Air Data Inertial Reference System (DA) ... ADIRS
Air Data Screening System [Environmental Protection Agency] (ERG) ... ADSS
Air Defense Control Facility (FAAC) ... ADCF
Air Defense Operations Area [Army] (ADDR) ... ADDA
Air Device Systems [Honda Motor Co.] [Automotive air conditioning] ... ADSYS
Air Direct Ltd. [British] [ICAO designator] (FAAC) ... DFT
Air Djibouti [ICAO designator] (FAAC) ... DJB
Air Dolomiti [Italy] [ICAO designator] (FAAC) ... DLA
Air Dorval Ltd. [Canada] [ICAO designator] (FAAC) ... ADT

Air Education Recreation Organization [*British*] (DA) ... AERO
Air Engiadina [*Switzerland*] [*ICAO designator*] (FAAC) ... RQX
Air Enterprise [*France*] [*ICAO designator*] (FAAC) ... AEN
Air Europa [*Spain*] [*ICAO designator*] (FAAC) ... AEA
Air Europe SpA [*Italy*] [*ICAO designator*] (FAAC) ... AEL
Air Evasion [*France*] [*ICAO designator*] (FAAC) ... IVS
Air Evex GmbH [*Germany*] [*ICAO designator*] (FAAC) ... EVE
Air Exchange, Inc. [*ICAO designator*] (FAAC) ... EXG
Air Exel [*France*] [*ICAO designator*] (FAAC) ... RXL
Air Exel Belgique [*Belgium*] [*ICAO designator*] (FAAC) ... BXL
Air Exel Executive [*France*] [*ICAO designator*] (FAAC) ... AOL
Air Exel Netherlands BV [*ICAO designator*] (FAAC) ... AXL
Air Experienc Flight [*British*] [*ICAO designator*] (FAAC) ... AED
Air Express AS [*Norway*] [*ICAO designator*] (FAAC) ... AXP
Air Express, Inc. [*ICAO designator*] (FAAC) ... ARX
Air Express in Norrkoping AB [*Sweden*] [*ICAO designator*] (FAAC) ... GOT
Air Fecteau Ltd. [*Canada*] [*ICAO designator*] (FAAC) ... AFH
Air Florida [*ICAO designator*] (FAAC) ... FLA
Air Force Coronary Atherosclerosis Prevention Study ... AFCAPS
Air Force Route (DA) ... AFR
Air Foyle (Executive) Ltd. [*British*] [*ICAO designator*] (FAAC) ... AFY
Air Foyle Ltd. [*British*] [*ICAO designator*] (FAAC) ... UPA
Air France [*ICAO designator*] (FAAC) ... AFR
Air Freight Express, Inc. [*ICAO designator*] (FAAC) ... AFX
Air Gambia [*ICAO designator*] (FAAC) ... AGS
Air GEFCO [*France*] [*ICAO designator*] (FAAC) ... GEF
Air Glaciers SA [*Switzerland*] [*ICAO designator*] (FAAC) ... AGV
Air Guam [*ICAO designator*] (FAAC) ... AGM
Air Guinea [*Guinea*] [*ICAO designator*] (FAAC) ... GIB
Air Guyane [*France*] [*ICAO designator*] (FAAC) ... GUY
Air Hainaut [*France*] [*ICAO designator*] (FAAC) ... AHN
Air Haiti [*ICAO designator*] (FAAC) ... HJA
Air Hanson Ltd. [*British*] [*ICAO designator*] (FAAC) ... AHL
Air Holland Regional (AHR) [*ICAO designator*] (FAAC) ... AHR
Air Hong Kong Ltd. [*ICAO designator*] (FAAC) ... AHK
Air Ile de France [*ICAO designator*] (FAAC) ... AIF
Air Iliria [*Yugoslovia*] [*ICAO designator*] (FAAC) ... ILR
Air Illinois, Inc. [*ICAO designator*] (FAAC) ... AIL
Air India [*ICAO designator*] (FAAC) ... AIC
Air Integra, Inc. [*Canada*] [*ICAO designator*] (FAAC) ... AII
Air Inter Gabon [*ICAO designator*] (FAAC) ... AIG
Air Inter, Societe [*France*] [*ICAO designator*] (FAAC) ... ITF
Air International [*British*] [*ICAO designator*] (FAAC) ... AIX
Air International (Holdings) PLC [*British*] [*ICAO designator*] (FAAC) ... JPR
Air Inuit Ltd. [*Canada*] [*ICAO designator*] (FAAC) ... AIE
Air Ivoire Societe [*Ivory Coast*] [*ICAO designator*] (FAAC) ... VUN
Air Jamaica [*ICAO designator*] (FAAC) ... AJM
Air Jet [*ICAO designator*] (FAAC) ... AIJ
Air Kilroe Ltd. [*British*] [*ICAO designator*] (FAAC) ... AKL
Air Korea Co. Ltd. [*South Korea*] [*ICAO designator*] (FAAC) ... AKA
Air Koryo [*North Korea*] [*ICAO designator*] (FAAC) ... KOR
Air LA, Inc. [*ICAO designator*] (FAAC) ... UED
Air Lanka [*Sri Lanka*] [*ICAO designator*] (FAAC) ... ALK
Air Liberia [*ICAO designator*] (FAAC) ... ALI
Air Liberte [*France*] [*ICAO designator*] (FAAC) ... LIB
Air Liberte Tunisie [*Tunisia*] [*ICAO designator*] (FAAC) ... LBT
Air Lietuva [*Lithuania*] [*ICAO designator*] (FAAC) ... KLA
Air-Lift Associates, Inc. [*ICAO designator*] (FAAC) ... WPK
Air Limousin TA [*France*] [*ICAO designator*] (FAAC) ... LMT
Air Lincoln, Inc. [*ICAO designator*] (FAAC) ... ALN
Air Littoral [*France*] [*ICAO designator*] (FAAC) ... LIT
Air London [*British*] [*ICAO designator*] (FAAC) ... ACG
Air Madagascar, Societe Nationale Malgache de Transports Aeriens [*ICAO designator*] (FAAC) ... MDG
Air Malawi [*ICAO designator*] (FAAC) ... AML
Air Maldives [*ICAO designator*] (FAAC) ... AMI
Air Malta Co. Ltd. [*ICAO designator*] (FAAC) ... AMC
Air Margarita [*Venezuela*] [*ICAO designator*] (FAAC) ... MAG
Air Material AG [*Switzerland*] [*ICAO designator*] (FAAC) ... AMG
Air Mauritanie [*Mauritania*] [*ICAO designator*] (FAAC) ... MRT
Air Mauritius Ltd. [*ICAO designator*] (FAAC) ... MAU
Air Med Jetoperations [*Austria*] [*ICAO designator*] (FAAC) ... JDE
Air Medical Ltd. [*British*] [*ICAO designator*] (FAAC) ... MCD
Air Mercury International [*Belgium*] [*ICAO designator*] (FAAC) ... AMI
Air Meuse - Dat Wallonie [*Belgium*] [*ICAO designator*] (FAAC) ... AMZ
Air Midwest, Inc. [*ICAO designator*] (FAAC) ... AMW
Air Mobility Command [*Aviation*] (FAAC) ... AMC
Air Moldova [*ICAO designator*] (FAAC) ... MLD
Air Molokai-Tropic Airlines [*ICAO designator*] (FAAC) ... TRO
Air Montenegro [*Yugoslavia*] [*ICAO designator*] (FAAC) ... AMN
Air Montreal, Inc. [*Canada*] [*ICAO designator*] (FAAC) ... AMO
Air Moorea [*France*] [*ICAO designator*] (FAAC) ... TAH
Air Moravia [*Czechoslovakia*] [*ICAO designator*] (FAAC) ... MAI
Air-Moving Device [*Technical drawings*] (DAC) ... AMD
Air Muskoka [*Canada*] [*ICAO designator*] (FAAC) ... AMS
Air Nauru [*ICAO designator*] (FAAC) ... RON
Air Navigation (General) Regulation [*British*] (DA) ... ANGR
Air Navigation Plan (DA) ... ANP
Air Navigation & Trading Co. Ltd. [*British*] [*ICAO designator*] (FAAC) ... ANB
Air Nelson Ltd. [*New Zealand*] [*ICAO designator*] (FAAC) ... RLK
Air Nevada Airlines, Inc. [*ICAO designator*] (FAAC) ... ANV
Air New Zealand Ltd. [*ICAO designator*] (FAAC) ... ANZ
Air Newark, Inc. [*ICAO designator*] (FAAC) ... NER
Air Niagara Express, Inc. [*Canada*] [*ICAO designator*] (FAAC) ... DBD
Air Niger [*ICAO designator*] (FAAC) ... AWN
Air Nippon Co. Ltd. [*Japan*] [*ICAO designator*] (FAAC) ... ANK
Air Niugini [*Papua New Guinea*] [*ICAO designator*] (FAAC) ... ANG
Air Nordic in Vasteras AB [*Sweden*] [*ICAO designator*] (FAAC) ... NOX
Air Normandie [*France*] [*ICAO designator*] (FAAC) ... RNO
Air North Charter [*Canada*] [*ICAO designator*] (FAAC) ... ANT
Air North Ltd. [*Australia*] [*ICAO designator*] (FAAC) ... ANO
Air Nova [*British*] [*ICAO designator*] (FAAC) ... HMT
Air Nova, Inc. [*Canada*] [*ICAO designator*] (FAAC) ... ARN
Air Ontario Ltd. [*Canada*] [*ICAO designator*] (FAAC) ... ONT
Air Orkney [*British*] [*ICAO designator*] (FAAC) ... ORK
Air Pacific Airlines [*ICAO designator*] (FAAC) ... APM
Air Pacific Crake [*Philippines*] [*ICAO designator*] (FAAC) ... CRK
Air Pacific Ltd. [*Fiji*] [*ICAO designator*] (FAAC) ... FJI
Air Panama Internacional [*ICAO designator*] (FAAC) ... API
Air Parcel Express [*ICAO designator*] (FAAC) ... APE
Air Park Aviation Ltd. [*Canada*] [*ICAO designator*] (FAAC) ... APA
Air Philippines Corporation, Inc. [*ICAO designator*] (FAAC) ... APQ
Air Power History [*A publication*] ... APH
Air Public Relations Association [*British*] (BI) ... APRA
Air Quality Improvement Research Program [*Automotive industry, research consortium*] ... AQIRP
Air Queensland [*Australia*] [*ICAO designator*] (FAAC) ... AQN
Air Report [*Aviation*] [*ICAO designator*] (FAAC) ... AIREP
Air Resorts [*ICAO designator*] (FAAC) ... ARZ
Air Reunion [*France*] [*ICAO designator*] (FAAC) ... REU
Air Roberval [*Canada*] [*ICAO designator*] (FAAC) ... RBV
Air Routing International Corp. [*ICAO designator*] (FAAC) ... ARC
Air Royal [*France*] [*ICAO designator*] (FAAC) ... RFO
Air Russia Airlines [*Russian Federation*] [*ICAO designator*] (FAAC) ... RUS
Air Rwanda [*ICAO designator*] (FAAC) ... RWD
Air Safaris & Services (NZ) Ltd. [*New Zealand*] [*ICAO designator*] (FAAC) ... SRI
Air Saigon [*Vietnam*] [*ICAO designator*] (FAAC) ... SGA
Air Saint-Pierre SA [*France*] [*ICAO designator*] (FAAC) ... SPM
Air St. Thomas [*ICAO designator*] (FAAC) ... STT
Air Sandy, Inc. [*Canada*] [*ICAO designator*] (FAAC) ... SNY
Air Sardinia International [*ICAO designator*] (FAAC) ... ARS
Air Sardinia SpA [*Italy*] [*ICAO designator*] (FAAC) ... ASZ
Air Sarthe Organisation - Societe [*France*] [*ICAO designator*] (FAAC) ... ASO
Air Satellite, Inc. [*Canada*] [*ICAO designator*] (FAAC) ... ASJ
Air Savoie [*France*] [*ICAO designator*] (FAAC) ... ASV
Air Schefferville, Inc. [*Canada*] [*ICAO designator*] (FAAC) ... ASF
Air Senegal, Societe Nationatial de Transport Aerien [*ICAO designator*] (FAAC) ... DSB
Air Service [*Poland*] [*ICAO designator*] (FAAC) ... ASQ
Air Service [*Mali*] [*ICAO designator*] (FAAC) ... ODB
Air Service Affaires [*France*] [*ICAO designator*] (FAAC) ... RSA
Air-Service-Gabon [*ICAO designator*] (FAAC) ... AGB
Air Service State Co. [*Hungary*] [*ICAO designator*] (FAAC) ... RSZ
Air Service Training Ltd. [*British*] [*ICAO designator*] (FAAC) ... ATZ
Air Service Vosges [*France*] [*ICAO designator*] (FAAC) ... VGE
Air Services Agreement (DA) ... ASA
Air Services Ltd. [*Czechoslovakia*] [*ICAO designator*] (FAAC) ... RIS
Air Services Nantes [*France*] [*ICAO designator*] (FAAC) ... ASN
Air Seychelles [*ICAO designator*] (FAAC) ... SEY
Air Sinai [*Egypt*] [*ICAO designator*] (FAAC) ... ASD
Air Sinclair Ltd. [*British*] [*ICAO designator*] (FAAC) ... SCK
Air Sofia [*Bulgaria*] [*ICAO designator*] (FAAC) ... SFB
Air Sorel Ltd. [*Canada*] [*ICAO designator*] (FAAC) ... WHY
Air South, Inc. [*ICAO designator*] (FAAC) ... SHW
Air Southwest [*Canada*] [*ICAO designator*] (FAAC) ... ASW
Air Special [*Czechoslovakia*] [*ICAO designator*] (FAAC) ... ASX
Air Specialties Corp. [*ICAO designator*] (FAAC) ... AMR
Air Spirit, Inc. [*ICAO designator*] (FAAC) ... SIP
Air-Spray 1967 Ltd. [*Canada*] [*ICAO designator*] (FAAC) ... ASB
Air Star Corp. [*Canada*] [*ICAO designator*] (FAAC) ... ASC
Air Star Zanzibar [*Tanzania*] [*ICAO designator*] (FAAC) ... AZU
Air Starline AG [*Switzerland*] [*ICAO designator*] (FAAC) ... ASA
Air Stord AS [*Norway*] [*ICAO designator*] (FAAC) ... SOR
Air Sunshine, Inc. [*ICAO designator*] (FAAC) ... RSI
Air Sur [*Spain*] [*ICAO designator*] (FAAC) ... NCR
Air Swazi Cargo (Pty) Ltd. [*Swaziland*] [*ICAO designator*] (FAAC) ... CWS
Air Swift [*British*] [*ICAO designator*] (FAAC) ... SWF
Air Tahiti [*France*] [*ICAO designator*] (FAAC) ... VTA
Air Tanzania [*ICAO designator*] (FAAC) ... ATC
Air Tara Ltd. [*Republic of Ireland*] [*ICAO designator*] (FAAC) ... AGP
Air Tchad, Societe de Transport Aeriens [*Chad*] [*ICAO designator*] (FAAC) ... HTT
Air Tenglong [*China*] [*ICAO designator*] (FAAC) ... CTE
Air Terrex [*Czechoslovakia*] [*ICAO designator*] (FAAC) ... TRX
Air Thanet [*British*] [*ICAO designator*] (FAAC) ... THL
Air Today, Inc. [*ICAO designator*] (FAAC) ... TDY
Air Tonga [*ICAO designator*] (FAAC) ... ATO
Air Toronto, Inc. [*Canada*] [*ICAO designator*] (FAAC) ... CNE
Air Toulon [*France*] [*ICAO designator*] (FAAC) ... ATU
Air Toulouse [*France*] [*ICAO designator*] (FAAC) ... TLE
Air Traffic Control Advises (FAAC) ... ATCA
Air Traffic Control Assistant (DA) ... ATCA

Air Traffic Control Clears   (FAAC) .... ATCC
Air Traffic Control and Landing System [*DoD*] .... ATCALS
Air Traffic Control Project for Satellite   (DA) .... ATCPROSAT
Air Traffic Control Request   (FAAC) .... ATCR
Air Traffic Division [*Air Traffic Control*]   (FAAC) .... ATD
Air Traffic Engineer [*British*]   (DA) .... ATE
Air Traffic Flow Management [*ICAO designator*]   (FAAC) ..... ATEM
Air Traffic Flow Management   (DA) .... ATFM
Air Traffic Flow Management Unit   (DA) .... ATFMU
Air Traffic GmbH [*Germany*] [*ICAO designator*]   (FAAC) ..... ATJ
Air Traffic Information Service   (DA) .... ATIS
Air Traffic Services Outside Regulated Airspace [*British*]   (DA) .... ATSORA
Air Traffic Services Planning Manual   (DA) .... ATSPM
Air Training Association [*British*]   (DA) .... ATA
Air Tranport School [*Former USSR*] [*ICAO designator*]   (FAAC) .... AIS
Air Transafrik Ltd. [*Ghana*] [*ICAO designator*]   (FAAC) ...... TRF
Air Transat [*Canada*] [*ICAO designator*]   (FAAC) .... TSC
Air Transport Auxiliary Association   (DA) .... ATAA
Air Transport (Chatham Island) Ltd. [*New Zealand*] [*ICAO
    designator*]   (FAAC) .... CVA
Air Transport Industry Training Association   (DA) .... ATITA
Air Transport International [*ICAO designator*]   (FAAC) .... ATN
Air Transport Ltd. [*Slovakia*] [*ICAO designator*]   (FAAC) ..... EAT
Air Transport Pyrenees [*France*] [*ICAO designator*]   (FAAC) ... TPR
Air Transport Regulation Panel [*ICAO*]   (DA) .... ATRP
Air Transport Schiphol [*Netherlands*] [*ICAO designator*]   (FAAC) ..... ATQ
Air Transport Service [*Zaire*] [*ICAO designator*]   (FAAC) ...... ATS
Air Transport Users' Association [*British*]   (DA) .... ATUA
Air Transportable Telecommunications Unit .... ATTU
Air Travel Corp. [*ICAO designator*]   (FAAC) .... ATH
Air Troika [*Russian Federation*] [*ICAO designator*]   (FAAC) ..... TKA
Air Truck [*Spain*] [*ICAO designator*]   (FAAC) .... TRK
Air Tungaru [*British*] [*ICAO designator*]   (FAAC) .... TUN
Air UK (Leisure) Ltd. [*British*] [*ICAO designator*]   (FAAC) ..... LEI
Air UK Ltd. [*British*] [*ICAO designator*]   (FAAC) .... UKA
Air Ukraine [*ICAO designator*]   (FAAC) .... UKR
Air Ukraine International [*ICAO designator*]   (FAAC) .... AUI
Air Vanuatu [*ICAO designator*]   (FAAC) .... AVN
Air Varna Co. [*Bulgaria*] [*ICAO designator*]   (FAAC) .... BAV
Air Vendee [*France*] [*ICAO designator*]   (FAAC) .... AVD
Air-Via [*Bulgaria*] [*ICAO designator*]   (FAAC) .... VIM
Air West [*Canada*] [*ICAO designator*]   (FAAC) .... AWT
Air West Airlines, Inc. [*ICAO designator*]   (FAAC) .... LEP
Air Whitsunday [*Australia*] [*ICAO designator*]   (FAAC) ...... RWS
Air Wisconsin [*ICAO designator*]   (FAAC) .... AWI
Air Yugoslavia [*ICAO designator*]   (FAAC) .... YRG
Air Zaire, Societe [*ICAO designator*]   (FAAC) .... AZR
Air Zanzibar [*Tanzania*] [*ICAO designator*]   (FAAC) .... AZL
Air Zimbabwe [*ICAO designator*]   (FAAC) .... AZW
Airavia [*France*] [*ICAO designator*]   (FAAC) .... IAV
Airbag Central Sensor [*Automotive safety*] .... ACS
Airborne [*ICAO designator*]   (FAAC) .... AB
Airborne Express, Inc. [*ICAO designator*]   (FAAC) .... ABX
Airborne Proximity Warning Indicator   (DA) .... APWI
Airborne RADAR Unit [*Aviation*]   (FAAC) .... ARU
Airborne of Sweden AB [*ICAO designator*]   (FAAC) .... MIW
Airborne Synthetic Aperture RADAR [*Instrumentation*] .... AIRSAR
Airbus Industrie [*France*] [*ICAO designator*]   (FAAC) .... AIB
Aircam Aviation Ltd. [*British*] [*ICAO designator*]   (FAAC) ... RCM
Aircarrier   (DA) .... AC
Aircorp Airlines, Inc. [*Canada*] [*ICAO designator*]   (FAAC) .... BBJ
Aircraft Accident Investigation System .... AAIS
Aircraft and Adventure Factory [*Mallard*] .... AAF
Aircraft Airworthiness Certification Authority   (DA) .... AACA
Aircraft Carrier   (ABBR) .... ACFTC
Aircraft Classification Number [*Aviation*]   (FAAC) .... ACN
Aircraft Classification Number/Pavement Classification Number
    (DA) .... ACN/PCN
Aircraft Earth Station [*ICAO designator*]   (FAAC) .... AES
Aircraft Installation Delay   (DA) .... AID
Aircraft Maintenance Co. [*Egypt*] [*ICAO designator*]   (FAAC) ... AMV
Aircraft Operator   (DA) .... AO
Aircraft Precision Position Location Equipment   (DA) .... APPL
Aircraft Proximity Hazard   (DA) .... APHAZ
Aircraft Rescue and Fire Fighting [*Air Traffic Control*]   (FAAC) ...... ARFF
Aircraft Servicing Platform   (DA) .... ASP
Aires, Aerovias de Integracion Regional SA [*Colombia*] [*ICAO
    designator*]   (FAAC) .... ARE
Airfast Service Indonesia PT [*ICAO designator*]   (FAAC) ..... AFE
Airlec [*France*] [*ICAO designator*]   (FAAC) .... ARL
Airlen [*Russian Federation*] [*ICAO designator*]   (FAAC) ...... LNA
Airlift International, Inc. [*ICAO designator*]   (FAAC) .... AIR
Airline Administrative Message   (DA) .... AAM
Airline of Adriatic [*Croatia*] [*ICAO designator*]   (FAAC) ..... ADC
Airline Aviation Academy, Inc. [*ICAO designator*]   (FAAC) ... ACD
Airline of the Marshall Islands [*ICAO designator*]   (FAAC) .... MRS
Airline Operations Services, Inc. [*ICAO designator*]   (FAAC) ... XAO
Airline Request Communication System   (DA) .... ARCS
Airline Revenue   (DA) .... ARE
Airline Tariff Analysis   (DA) .... ATA
Airlines of Hainan Province [*China*] [*ICAO designator*]   (FAAC) ... CHH
Airlines of Tasmania [*Australia*] [*ICAO designator*]   (FAAC) .... ATM
Airlink Airlines (Pty) Ltd. [*South Africa*] [*ICAO designator*]   (FAAC) .... LNK

Airlink Luftverkehrsgesellschaft GmbH [*Austria*] [*ICAO designator*]
    (FAAC) .... JAR
Airlis SA [*Spain*] [*ICAO designator*]   (FAAC) .... LIS
Airluxor Ltda. [*Portugal*] [*ICAO designator*]   (FAAC) .... LXR
Airmark Aviation, Inc. [*ICAO designator*]   (FAAC) .... TRH
Airpac Airlines, Inc. [*ICAO designator*]   (FAAC) .... APC
Airplane   (ABBR) .... A
Airplanes, Inc. [*ICAO designator*]   (FAAC) .... REZ
Airport Acceptance Rate [*Aviation*]   (FAAC) .... AARTE
Airport Data Information System   (DA) .... ADIS
Airport of Entry   (DA) .... AOE
Airport Fire Officer   (DA) .... AFO
Airport Management and Information Display System   (DA) ...... AMIDS
Airport Movement RADAR   (DA) .... AMR
Airport Operation Area   (DA) .... AOA
Airport in Sight   (FAAC) .... AIS
Airport Surface Surveillance RADAR   (DA) .... ASSR
Airports Authority Group [*Transport Canada*]   (DA) .... AAG
Airports Economic Panel [*ICAO*]   (DA) .... AEP
Airspace Management   (DA) .... ASM
Airspace Management   (DA) .... ASMT
Airspace Reservation Unit [*Canada*]   (FAAC) .... ARU
Airspace and Traffic Management [*ICAO*]   (DA) .... ATM
Airspace and Traffic Management Center   (DA) .... ATMC
Airspeed Aviation, Inc. [*Canada*] [*ICAO designator*]   (FAAC) ... SPD
Airtaxi Bedarfsluftverkehrsges GmbH [*Austria*] [*ICAO designator*]
    (FAAC) .... JOK
Airtaxi Wings AG [*Switzerland*] [*ICAO designator*]   (FAAC) .... AWG
Airtours International Airways Ltd. [*British*] [*ICAO designator*]
    (FAAC) .... AIH
Airvallee SpA-Services Aeriens de Val d'Aoste [*Italy*] [*ICAO
    designator*]   (FAAC) .... RVL
AirVantage, Inc. [*ICAO designator*]   (FAAC) .... AVV
Airwave Transport, Inc. [*Canada*] [*ICAO designator*]   (FAAC) ... AWV
Airways Corp. of New Zealand Ltd. [*ICAO designator*]   (FAAC) .... XFX
Airways International, Inc. [*ICAO designator*]   (FAAC) .... AWB
Airwork Ltd. [*British*] [*ICAO designator*]   (FAAC) .... HRN
Airwork (New Zealand) Ltd. [*ICAO designator*]   (FAAC) ...... PST
Airwork Service Training [*British*] [*ICAO designator*]   (FAAC) .... AWK
Airworthiness Circular   (DA) .... AC
AJ Services Ltd. [*British*] [*ICAO designator*]   (FAAC) .... AJA
AJT Air International [*Russian Federation*] [*ICAO designator*]
    (FAAC) .... TRJ
Ajustable   (ABBR) .... ADJSTB
Akhal [*Turkmenistan*] [*ICAO designator*]   (FAAC) .... AKH
Aklak Air Ltd. [*Canada*] [*ICAO designator*]   (FAAC) .... AKK
Aktiv Hinten Kinematik [*Active Rear-Axle Movement*] [*German*] ..... AHK
Alak [*Former USSR*] [*ICAO designator*]   (FAAC) .... LSV
Alarm System [*Automotive advertising*] .... ALRM
Alarm Valve   (DAC) .... ALV
Alas Nacionales SA [*Dominican Republic*] [*ICAO designator*]
    (FAAC) .... ALW
Alas Panamenas SA [*Panama*] [*ICAO designator*]   (FAAC) ... ALPANSA
Alas Panamenas SA [*Panama*] [*ICAO designator*]   (FAAC) ... PWI
Alaska Airlines, Inc. [*ICAO designator*]   (FAAC) .... ASA
Alaska Island Air, Inc. [*ICAO designator*]   (FAAC) .... AAK
Alaska Juneau Aeronautics, Inc. [*ICAO designator*]   (FAAC) .... WAK
Albanian Airline Co. [*ICAO designator*]   (FAAC) .... LBC
Albanian Airways [*ICAO designator*]   (FAAC) .... ABW
Albatros Airline, Inc. [*Turkey*] [*ICAO designator*]   (FAAC) .... ABK
Albatrosz Ltd. [*Hungary*] [*ICAO designator*]   (FAAC) .... ALT
Alberni Airway [*Canada*] [*ICAO designator*]   (FAAC) .... BNI
Alberta Government [*Canada*] [*ICAO designator*]   (FAAC) .... GOA
Albumin-Globulin Ratio [*Physiology*]   (MAH) .... ALB/GLOB
Alcove   (ABBR) .... A
Alert Weather Watch [*Meteorology*]   (DA) .... AWW
Alexandair, Inc. [*Canada*] [*ICAO designator*]   (FAAC) .... JMR
Alfa Air [*Czechoslovakia*] [*ICAO designator*]   (FAAC) .... AFA
Alfa Jet [*Spain*] [*ICAO designator*]   (FAAC) .... AJE
Algarvilara Transportes Aereos Algarvios SA [*Portugal*] [*ICAO
    designator*]   (FAAC) .... ALR
Algeria [*Aircraft nationality and registration mark*]   (FAAC) 7T
Algerian-Franc   (ABBR) .... A-FR
Algoma Airways, Inc. [*Canada*] [*ICAO designator*]   (FAAC) ... AGG
Alianza Federal des Pueblos Libres [*An association*]   (NTCM) ..... AFPL
Aliblu Airways SpA [*Italy*] [*ICAO designator*]   (FAAC) ...... KRO
Alidaunia SRL [*Italy*] [*ICAO designator*]   (FAAC) .... LID
Aligiulia SpA [*Italy*] [*ICAO designator*]   (FAAC) .... RWA
Alinord [*Italy*] [*ICAO designator*]   (FAAC) .... DNO
Aliserio [*Italy*] [*ICAO designator*]   (FAAC) .... ALL
Alitalia-Linee Aeree Italiane SpA [*Italy*] [*ICAO designator*]   (FAAC) ... AZA
Alitaxi SRL [*Italy*] [*ICAO designator*]   (FAAC) .... ALX
Alkair Flight Operations APS [*Denmark*] [*ICAO designator*]
    (FAAC) .... LKA
Alkan Air Ltd. [*Canada*] [*ICAO designator*]   (FAAC) .... AKN
Alkenyl Succinic Anhydride [*Organic chemistry*] .... ASA
Alkyl Ketene Dimer [*Organic chemistry*] .... AKA
All After [*Aviation*]   (DA) .... AA
All-Channel Television Society [*UHF interest group*]   (NTCM) ..... ACTS
All Charter Ltd. [*British*] [*ICAO designator*]   (FAAC) .... BLA
All-India Institute of Medial Sciences .... AIMS
All-Industry Radio Music Licensing Committee   (NTCM) .... AIRMLC
All Nippon Airways Co. Ltd. [*Japan*] [*ICAO designator*]   (FAAC) ... ANA

By Meaning

All Purpose Structure Eurocontrol RADAR Information Exchange
(DA) .... ASTERIX
All-Radio Methodology Study [Audience ratings] (NTCM) .... ARMS
All-Source Production [Army] (ADDR) .... ASP
All-Source Production Section [Army] (ADDR) .... ASPS
All Star Airlines, Inc. [ICAO designator] (FAAC) .... ASR
All Taxa Biodiversity Inventory [Proposed] [National Science
Foundation] .... ATBI
All Wales Ladies Lacrosse Association (BI) .... AWLLA
All Weather Operations (DA) .... AWO
All-Wheel Control [Mitsubishi] [Transmisssion systems] .... AWC
All Wood Screw (DAC) .... AWS
Allcanada Express Ltd. [Canada] [ICAO designator] (FAAC).... CNX
Allen Vision Test (MAH) .... AVT
Alliance for Environmental Technology .... AET
Alliance of Individual Grocers [British] (BI) .... AIG
Alliance for a Paving Moratorium (EA) .... APM
Allied Command Europe [ICAO designator] (FAAC) ...... ALF
Allied Electrical Publication [Military] .... AELP
Alloy Phase Diagram .... APD
Allyl Methacrylate [Organic chemistry] .... ALMA
Aloha Airlines [ICAO designator] (FAAC) .... AAH
Alpenair GmbH & Co. KG [Austria] [ICAO designator] (FAAC)... LPN
Alpha Aviation, Inc. [ICAO designator] (FAAC) .... ALH
Alpha Aviation, Inc. [ICAO designator] (FAAC) .... APH
Alpha Delta Sigma [Fraternity] (NTCM) .... ADS
Alpha Epsilon Rho [Also, AERho] [Fraternity] (NTCM) .... AER
Alpha-Hydroxy Acid [Organic chemistry] .... AHA
Alpha-Hydroxybutyric Dehydrogenase [An enzyme] (MAH) .... AHB
Alpi Eagles SpA [Italy] [ICAO designator] (FAAC) ...... ELG
Alpine Aviation Inc. [ICAO designator] (FAAC) .... AIP
Alpine Luft-Transport AB [Switzerland] [ICAO designator] (FAAC).... ALU
Alpliner AG [Switzerland] [ICAO designator] (FAAC) .... ALP
Already Been Chewed [Gum] .... ABC
Alsair Societe [France] [ICAO designator] (FAAC) ...... LSR
Alsavia, Societe [France] [ICAO designator] (FAAC) .... ALV
Alta Flights Ltd. [Canada] [ICAO designator] (FAAC) .... ALZ
Altair Aviation Ltd. [Canada] [ICAO designator] (FAAC).... ALQ
Alteration [Technical drawings] (DAC) .... ALTN
Alternate Departure Route [Air Traffic Control] (FAAC) .... ADRT
Alternate Training Assemby [Army] (ADDR) .... ATA
Alternating Current Plasma Detector [Spectrometry] .... ACPD
Alternative Control Technology [Environmental science] .... ACT
Alternative Fuel Electronics [Fuel systems] [Automotive engineering] .... AFE
Alternative Fuel Vehicle .... AFV
Altimetry System Error [Aviation] (DA) .... ASE
Altitude Indicator [Aviation] (DA) .... AI
Altitude Instrument Flying (DA) .... AIF
Altitude Reporting (DA) .... A/R
Altus Airlines [ICAO designator] (FAAC) .... AXS
Aluminum Extruders Association (DAC) .... AEA
Aly Aviation [British] [ICAO designator] (FAAC).... AAV
Alyemda-Democratic Yemen Airlines [ICAO designator] (FAAC) .... DYA
Alyeska Air Service [ICAO designator] (FAAC) .... ALY
Alzheimer's Disease Assessment Scale .... ADAS
Amadeus Global Travel Distrution SA [Spain] [ICAO designator]
(FAAC) .... AGT
Amadeusair GmbH [Austria] [ICAO designator] (FAAC)........ AMU
Amalgamated Slaters, Tilers and Roofing Operatives Society
[British] (BI) .... ASTRO
Amalgamated Society of Woodcutting Machinists [British] (BI)........ ASWM
Amalgamated Society of Woodworkers [British] (BI) .... ASW
Amateur All-Star Baseball [An association] (EA) .... AABI
Amateur Basketball Association [British] (BI) .... ABBA
Amateur Basketball Association of Scotland (BI) .... ABAS
Amateur Drama League [Republic of Ireland] (BI) .... ADL
Amateur Football Alliance [British] (BI) .... AFA
Amateur Volleyball Association [British] (BI) .... AVA
Ambassador Airways Ltd. [British] [ICAO designator] (FAAC) .... AMY
Amber Airways Ltd. [British] [ICAO designator] (FAAC) .... ABM
Ambient Air Quality Standard (ERG) .... AAQS
Ambulancias Insulares SA [Spain] [ICAO designator] (FAAC) .... AIM
America West Airlines [ICAO designator] (FAAC) .... AWE
Americam Philatelist [A publication] .... Am Phil
American Academy of Dramatic Arts (NTCM) .... AADA
American Academy of Pain Medicine (EA) .... AAPM
American Air Services, Inc. [ICAO designator] (FAAC) .... EJM
American Airlines, Inc. [ICAO designator] (FAAC) .... AAL
American Association of Independent Publishers (NTCM) .... AAIP
American Association of Psychiatric Technicians .... AAPT
American Board of Criminalistics (EA) .... ABC
American Broadcasting Co. Television Satellite (NTCM)........ ABSAT
American Broadcasting-Paramount Theatres, Inc. (NTCM) .... AB-PT
American Cable Network, Inc. .... ACN
American Citizens [Military] (ADDR) .... AMCITS
American Citizens for Justice [An association] (EA)............ ACJ
American Council on Rural Special Education .... ACRES
American Executives for Management Excellence [An association]
(EA) .... AEME
American Fish Decoy Association (EA) .... AFDA
American Flight Service Systems, Inc. [ICAO designator] (FAAC) .... XFS
American Humane Education Society .... AHES
American Indian Arts Council (EA) .... AIAC

American Indian Institute (EA) .... AII
American Institute of Electrical and Electronics Engineers [Also,
IEEE] (NTCM) .... AIEEE
American Institute of Public Opinion [Also, ARI] (NTCM) .... AIPO
American International Airways, Inc. [ICAO designator] (FAAC) .... AIT
American Journal of Clinical Hypnosis [A publication]......... AJCH
American Lithotripsy Society (EA) .... ALS
American Methanol Institute .... AMI
American Music [A publication] .... Am M
American Oceans Campaign [An association] (EA) .... AOC
American Scouting Traders Association (EA) .... ASTA
American Society of Advertising and Promotion, Inc. (NTCM)..... ASAP
American Society of Electrical Engineers (NTCM) .... ASEE
American Society of Wedding Professionals (EA) .... ASWP
American Television Society (NTCM) .... ATS
American Trans Air, Inc. [ICAO designator] (FAAC) .... AMT
American-Turkish Friendship Council (EA)..................... ATFC
American Visions [A publication] .... Am Vis
American Woman above Ground [Lifestyle classification] .... AWAG
American Wood Window Institute (DAC) .... AWWI
Americans with Disabilities Act [An association] (EA) .... ADA
Ameriflight, Inc. [ICAO designator] (FAAC) .... AMF
Amerijet International [ICAO designator] (FAAC)........ AJT
AMI (Air Mercury International) [Belgium] [ICAO designator]
(FAAC) .... MIA
Aminoethylhomocysteine [Biochemistry] .... AEHC
Amiri Flight-Bahrain [ICAO designator] (FAAC) .... BAH
Ammonium Dinitramide [Potential rocket fuel component]
[Inorganic chemistry] .... ADN
Amnesty International Medical Group .... AIMG
Amnesty International Parliamentary Group..................... AIPG
Amorphous Polyamide [Organic chemistry] .... APA
Amperes per Square Inch [Electrochemistry] .... ASI
Amphibious Infantry Combat Vehicle [Army] (ADDR) .... AICV
Amplification Controlling Element [Genetics]..................... ACE
Amplitude-Companded Single Sideband (DA) .... ACSSB
AMR American Eagle, Inc. [ICAO designator] (FAAC) .... EGF
AMR Combs, Inc. [AMR Services, Inc.] [ICAO designator] (FAAC)........ XAM
Amusement Caterers' Association [British] (BI) .... ACA
Amusement Trades Association [British] (BI) .... ATA
Anaesthetic .... An
Anair - Anich Airways [Croatia] [ICAO designator] (FAAC).... ANH
Anax Aviation [France] [ICAO designator] (FAAC)........ ANX
Anchor Block Foundation (EA)..................... ABF
Ancient Conserved Region [Genetics] .... ACR
Ancillary Education Establishment .... AEE
Andrea Airlines SA [Peru] [ICAO designator] (FAAC) .... NDR
Androgenic Anabolic Agent [Biochemistry] (MAH)..................... AAA
Angle Shot [Cinematography] (NTCM) .... AS
Angled (NTCM) .... A
Angled End [Outdoor advertising] (NTCM)..................... AE
Angled Single [Outdoor advertising] (NTCM)..................... AS
Anglia and Prefect Owners' Club [British] (BI) .... APOC
Anglo-American Families Association [British] (BI) .... AAFA
Anglo Cargo Ltd. [British] [ICAO designator] (FAAC) .... ANC
Anglo-Israel Association [British] (BI) .... AIA
Angola [Aircraft nationality and registration mark] (FAAC).... D2
Angola Air Charter Ltd. [ICAO designator] (FAAC) .... AAC
Angola Air Charter Ltd. [ICAO designator] (FAAC) .... AGO
Angus Aviation Ltd. [Canada] [ICAO designator] (FAAC) .... AAZ
Animal Health Trust [British] (BI) .... AHT
Animal and Plant Health Inspection Service..................... APHI
Anisidine Value [Food science] .... AnV
Anisotropic Magnetoresistance .... AMR
Annapolis Lymphoblast Globulin [Biochemistry] (MAH)..................... ALG
Annealing (ABBR) .... A
Announce Booth [Soundproof room] [Television studio] (NTCM) .... AB
Announcer (NTCM) .... ANN
Annual Course Contribution .... ACC
Annual License Fee [FCC] (NTCM) .... ALF
Annual Work Schedule .... AWS
Annular Pressure Loss [Well drilling technology]..................... APL
Annunciator (NFPA) .... A
[Fire Alarm] Annunciator Panel [NFPA pre-fire planning symbol]
(NFPA) .... AP
Anode Current Efficiency [Environmental science]..................... ACE
Anomalous Cosmic Ray .... ACR
Ansett Airlines of Australia [ICAO designator] (FAAC) .... AAA
Ansett Airlines of New South Wales [Australia] [ICAO designator]
(FAAC) .... NSW
Answer Print (NTCM) .... AP
Antarctic Medal .... AntM
Antenatal Diagnosis .... AND
Anterior Interpositus Nucleus [Anatomy]..................... AIN
Anthracite (ABBR) .... A
Anthropometric Test Device [Automotive safety] .... ATD
Anti-Common Market League [British] (BI) .... ACML
Anti-Friction [Lubricants] .... AF
Anti-Icing Fluid [Aviation] (DA) .... AAF
Anti-Saccade Oculomotor Delayed Response [Neurobiology]..................... AS-OUR
Antigenreceptor Homology [Immunochemistry] .... ARH
Antigua and Barbuda Airways International Ltd. [ICAO designator]
(FAAC) .... ABI

Antillana de Nevegacion Aerea SA [*Dominican Republic*] [*ICAO designator*]　(FAAC)............ SUN
Antilliaanse Luchtvaart Maatschappij [*Netherlands*] [*ICAO designator*]　(FAAC)............ ALM
Antineutrophil Cytoplasmic Antibody [*Immunology*]............ ANCA
Antipersonnel Improved Conventional Munitions [*Army*]　(ADDR)....... APICM
Antique Automobile Coalition [*Legislative lobbying group*]............ AAC
Antique Bowie Knife Association　(EA)............ ABKA
Antiskywave Antenna　(NTCM)............ ASWA
Antiterrorism [*Measure*] [*DoD*]............ AT
Antonov Design Bureau [*Former USSR*] [*ICAO designator*]　(FAAC)......... ADB
APA Internacional [*Dominican Republic*] [*ICAO designator*]　(FAAC)............ APY
Apex Air Cargo [*ICAO designator*]　(FAAC)............ APX
Appalachian Flying Service, Inc. [*ICAO designator*]　(FAAC)............ APL
Apparel and Fashion Industry's Association [*British*]　(BI)............ AFIA
Apple [*Computer*] Infected Disk Syndrome　(NHD)............ AIDS
Apple Open Collaboration Environment [*Computer science*]　(PCM)....... AOCE
Apple-Talk Update-Based Routing Protocol [*Computer science*]............ AURP
Applicable Approved Accounting Standard............ AAAS
Application Specific Coding Flag　(NTCM)............ ASCF
Applications of Space Technology Panel to Requirements of Civil Aviation [*ICAO*]　(DA)............ ASTRA
Approach Control RADAR　(DA)............ APP-R
Approach Lighting [*Aviation*]　(DA)............ A
Approach Path Alignment Panel [*Aviation*]　(FAAC)............ APAP
Approved Force Inventory Objective [*Military*]............ AFIC
Approved Quality Assurance............ AQA
Approved Research Institute............ ARI
Approved Test Officer............ ATO
Aquadag [*Graphite coating*]　(NTCM)............ DAG
Aquair Luftfahrt GmbH [*Germany*] [*ICAO designator*]　(FAAC)............ AQU
Aquarius [*Constellation*]............ AQU
Aquila Air, Inc. [*ICAO designator*]　(FAAC)............ PCY
Aquila Air Ltd. [*Canada*] [*ICAO designator*]　(FAAC)............ AQL
Arab Agricultural Aviation [*Egypt*] [*ICAO designator*]　(FAAC)............ AGC
Arab Air Cargo [*Jordan*] [*ICAO designator*]　(FAAC)............ AWF
Arab Wings Co. [*Jordan*] [*ICAO designator*]　(FAAC)............ AWS
Aravco Ltd. [*British*] [*ICAO designator*]　(FAAC)............ ARV
Arax Airlines Ltd. [*Nigeria*] [*ICAO designator*]　(FAAC)............ RXA
Arbet International Ltd. [*Hungary*] [*ICAO designator*]　(FAAC)............ RBE
Arbitron's Information on Demand [*Arbitron Co.*] [*Information service or system*]　(NTCM)............ AID
Arc　(ABBR)............ A
Arca Aerovias Colombians Ltda. [*Colombia*] [*ICAO designator*]　(FAAC)............ AKC
Archdiocesan　(ABBR)............ ADIOCN
Archdiocese　(ABBR)............ ADIOC
Archenemy　(ABBR)............ AENM
Architects' Benevolent Society [*British*]　(BI)............ ABS
Architects Council of Europe　(DAC)............ ACE
Architectural Aluminum Association　(DAC)............ AAA
Architectural and Industrial Maintenance [*Coatings*]............ AIM
Architectural Metal Craftsmen's Association [*British*]　(BI)............ AMCA
Architectural Terra-Cotta [*Technical drawings*]　(DAC)............ ATC
Architecture Bulletin [*A publication*]............ AB
Architecture New York [*A publication*]............ ANY
Arctic [*Iceland*] [*ICAO designator*]　(FAAC)............ AEB
Arctic Circle Service, Inc. [*ICAO designator*]　(FAAC)............ CIR
Arctic Control Area [*Aviation*]　(FAAC)............ ACA
Arctic Research Consortium of the United States............ ARCUS
Arcus-Air-Logistic GmbH [*Germany*] [*ICAO designator*]　(FAAC)............ AZE
Arduously　(ABBR)............ ADUY
Area Control Center　(DA)............ ACC
Area Control-RADAR　(DA)............ ACC-R
Area Data Distribution System [*Army*]　(ADDR)............ ADDS
Area Forecast　(DA)............ ARFOR
Area Fuel Consumption Allocation [*Environmental Protection Agency*]　(ERG)............ AFCA
Area of Intense Air Activity　(DA)............ AIAA
Area Minimum Altitude [*Aviation*]　(FAAC)............ AMA
Argo SA [*Dominican Republic*] [*ICAO designator*]　(FAAC)............ RGO
Argosy Airways [*Canada*] [*ICAO designator*]　(FAAC)............ ARY
Ariana Afghan Airlines [*Afganistan*] [*ICAO designator*]　(FAAC)............ AFG
Arizona Air [*Aviation Services West, Inc.*] [*ICAO designator*]　(FAAC)............ AAE
Arizona Airways, Inc. [*ICAO designator*]　(FAAC)............ AZY
Arizona Pacific Airways [*Arizona Flight School, Inc.*] [*ICAO designator*]　(FAAC)............ AZP
Arkia Israel Inland Airlines [*ICAO designator*]　(FAAC)............ AIZ
Armani Exchange　(ECON)............ A/X
Armed Forces Television Service　(NTCM)............ AFTS
Armenian International Airlines [*ICAO designator*]　(FAAC)............ RME
Armstrong Air, Inc. [*Canada*] [*ICAO designator*]　(FAAC)............ ARQ
Army Air Corps [*British*] [*ICAO designator*]　(FAAC)............ AAC
Army Airspace Command and Control　(ADDR)............ A2C2
Army Aviation Centre [*British*]　(BI)............ AAvnC
[*The*] Army Combined Arms Weapons System............ TACAWS
Army Environmental Center [*Aberdeen Proving Ground, MD*]　(RDA)............ AEC
Army Good Conduct Medal............ AGCM
Army Master Data File Retrieval Microform System............ ARMS
Army Physical Fitness Training　(ADDR)............ APFT

Army Reserve Association............ AResA
Army Reserve Officers Training Corps　(AEE)............ AROTC
Army School of Education and Depot [*British*]　(BI)............ ASED
Arrest　(FAAC)............ ARST
Arrival Aircraft Interval [*Aviation*]　(FAAC)............ AAITVL
Arrival and Assembly Operations Element [*Navy*]　(ANA)............ AAOE
Arrival and Assembly Operations Group [*Navy*]　(ANA)............ AAOG
Arrival and Assembly Support Party [*Navy*]　(ANA)............ AASP
Arrival Delay [*Air Traffic Control*]　(FAAC)............ ADLY
Arrival Time Distribution [*Instrumentation*]............ ATD
Arrow Airways, Inc. [*ICAO designator*]　(FAAC)............ APW
Arrow Aviation Ltd. [*Canada*] [*ICAO designator*]　(FAAC)............ ARO
Arrowhead Airways [*ICAO designator*]　(FAAC)............ ARH
Arrows Ltd. [*British*] [*ICAO designator*]　(FAAC)............ ARW
Arsine [*Medicine*]　(ADDR)............ SA
Art Libraries Society [*British*]　(BI)............ ARLIS
Art and Mechanical [*Graphics*]　(NTCM)............ A & M
Arthur Adaptation of the Leiter International Performance Scale [*Education*]............ AALIPS
Artibus Asiae [*A publication*]............ Art Asiae
Artificial Flower Manufacturers' Association of Great Britain　(BI)........ AFMA
Artificial Intelligence Research Support [*Program*] [*Computer science*]............ AIRS
Artillery Counterfire Information [*Army*]　(ADDR)............ ACIF
Artillery Meteorological Team [*Army*]　(ADDR)............ ARTYMET
Artists' Service Bureau　(NTCM)............ ASB
Aruba [*Aircraft nationality and registration mark*]　(FAAC)............ P4
Arubair [*Aruba*] [*ICAO designator*]　(FAAC)............ ARB
As Low as Reasonably Practicable [*Radiation exposure*] [*Nuclear Regulatory Commission*]............ ALARP
AS Lufttransport [*Norway*] [*ICAO designator*]　(FAAC)............ LTR
AS Morefly [*Norway*] [*ICAO designator*]　(FAAC)............ MOR
AS Norving [*Norway*] [*ICAO designator*]　(FAAC)............ NOR
As Quoted [*Business term*]............ AQ
As Rolled [*Technical drawings*]　(DAC)............ AR
ASA [*Former USSR*] [*ICAO designator*]　(FAAC)............ SPB
ASA, Air Starline, AG [*Switzerland*] [*ICAO designator*]　(FAAC)............ ACR
Asahi New Cast [*Metal fabrication*]............ ANC
Asbestos Cement Manufacturers Association [*British*]　(BI)............ ACMA
Asbestos-Containing Building Material　(ERG)............ ACBM
Asbestos Contractor Tracking System [*Environmental Protection Agency*]　(ERG)............ ACTS
Ascor Flyservice AS [*Norway*] [*ICAO designator*]　(FAAC)............ NOC
Asea Brown Boveri [*Swedish-Swiss manufacturing company*]　(ECON)....... ABB
Asia Aero Survey & Consulting Engineers, Inc. [*Korea*] [*ICAO designator*]　(FAAC)............ KAA
Asia Education Foundation............ AEF
Asia-Oceania Clinical Oncology Association............ AsOCOA
Asia-Oceania Federation of Nuclear Medicine............ AsOFNM
Asia Pacific Air Cargo PTE Ltd. [*Singapore*] [*ICAO designator*]　(FAAC)............ APK
Asia-Pacific Aviation Medicine Association............ AsPAvMA
Asia Pacific Distribution [*Australia*] [*ICAO designator*]　(FAAC)............ APD
Asia Pacific Economic Group............ APEG
Asia-Pacific Fellowship............ APF
Asia-Pacific Society for Impotence Research............ AsPSIR
Asialoglycoprotein Receptor [*Biochemistry*]............ ASGPR
Asian Broadcasting Conference　(NTCM)............ ABC
Asian-Pacific Association of LASER Medical Surgery............ AsPALMS
Asian-Pacific Association for the Study of the Liver............ AsPASL
Asian-Pacific Society of Cardiology............ AsPSC
Asian-Pacific Society for Digestive Endoscopy............ AsPCDE
Asian-Pacific Society of Nephrology............ AsPSN
Asian-Pacific Society of Paediatric Gastroenterology and Nutrition............ AsPSPGN
Asiana Airlines [*South Korea*] [*ICAO designator*]　(FAAC)............ AAR
Asking [*Automotive advertising*]............ ASKNG
Aspen Institute Program on Communications and Society　(NTCM)........ AIPCS
Asphalt　(DA)............ ASPH
Asphalt Roads Association [*British*]　(BI)............ ARA
Asphalt Surface Course　(DAC)............ ASC
Aspiryl Chloride [*Organic chemistry*]　(MAH)............ ACI
Assigned Altitude Deviation [*Aviation*]　(DA)............ AAD
Assignment [*FCC*]　(NTCM)............ A
Assignment of (Construction) Permit [*FCC*]　(NTCM)............ AP
Assignment of (Construction) Permit and License [*FCC*]　(NTCM)............ APL
Assignment of License [*FCC*]　(NTCM)............ AL
Assistant Customs Officer............ ACO
Assistant Flying Instructor　(DA)............ AFI
Assistant Sector Controller [*Aviation*]　(DA)............ ASC
Assisted Resonance　(NTCM)............ AR
Associate Computer Professional............ ACP
Associate Enforcement Counsel　(ERG)............ AEC
Associated Board of the Royal Schools of Music [*British*]　(BI)............ ABRSM
Associated Business Papers　(NTCM)............ ABP
Associated Music Publishers　(NTCM)............ AMP
Associated Press Radio Network　(NTCM)............ APRN
[*The*] Association of American Cultures　(EA)............ TAAC
Association for Armenian Information Professionals　(EA)............ AAIP
Association of Assistant Mistresses in Secondary Schools [*British*]　(BI)............ AAM
Association of Autoelectrical Technicians Ltd. [*British*]　(BI)............ AET
Association of Blind Piano Tuners [*British*]　(BI)............ ABPT

Association of Boiler Setters, Chimney and Furnace Constructors [*British*]   (BI) .... ABSC
Association of British Aero Clubs   (BI) .... ABAC
Association of British Aviation Consultants   (DA) .... ABAC
Association of British Conference Organisers   (BI) .... ABCO
Association of British Foam Laminators   (BI) .... ABFL
Association of British Manufacturers of Agricultural Chemicals (BI) .... ABMAC
Association of British Organic and Compound Fertilisers Ltd.   (BI) ...... ABOCF
Association of British Packing Contractors   (BI) .... ABPC
Association of British Plywood and Veneer Manufacturers   (BI) .... ABPVM
Association of British Reclaimed Rubber Manufacturers   (BI) .... ABRRM
Association of British Riding Schools   (BI) .... ABRS
Association of British Roofing Felt Manufacturers Ltd.   (BI) .... ABRFM
Association of British Yacht Agents   (BI) .... ABYA
Association of British Zoologists   (BI) .... ABZ
Association of Bronze and Brass Founders [*British*]   (BI) .... ABBF
Association of Building Centres [*British*]   (BI) .... ABC
Association of Casing Importers Ltd. [*British*]   (BI) .... ASCIM
Association of Chief Education Officers [*British*]   (BI) .... ACEO
Association of Circus Proprietors of Great Britain   (BI) .... ACP
Association of College and University Broadcasting Stations (NTCM) .... ACUBS
Association of Commonwealth Students [*British*]   (BI) .... ACS
Association of Conference and Events Directors-International (EA) .... ACED-I
Association of Contact Lens Practitioners [*British*]   (BI) .... ACLP
Association of Corrugated Papermakers [*British*]   (BI) .... ACPM
Association of Crane Makers [*British*]   (BI) .... ACM
Association of Dental Hospitals of Great Britain and Northern Ireland   (BI) .... ADH
Association for Educational Communications and Technology (NTCM) .... ACET
Association of Embroiderers and Pleaters [*British*]   (BI) .... AEP
Association of Engineering Distributors [*British*]   (BI) .... AED
Association of European Express Carriers   (DA) .... AEEC
Association of Family Case-Workers [*British*]   (BI) ...... AFCW
Association of Fatty Acid Distillers [*British*]   (BI) ...... AFAD
Association of Flooring Contractors [*British*]   (BI) ...... AFC
Association of Folding Furniture Manufacturers [*British*]   (BI) .... AFFM
Association of Gaugers and Appraisers Ltd. [*British*]   (BI) .... AGA
Association of Good Motorists [*British*]   (BI) .... AGM
Association of Green Crop Driers [*British*]   (BI) .... AGCD
Association of Gut Processors [*British*]   (BI) .... AGP
Association of Headmistresses [*British*]   (BI) .... AHM
Association of Headmistresses of Preparatory Schools [*British*]   (BI) .... AHPS
Association for High Speed Photography [*British*]   (BI) .... AHSP
Association of Hospital and Welfare Administrators [*British*]   (BI) .... AHWA
Association of Hotel Booking Agents [*British*]   (BI) ...... AHBA
Association for Improving Moral Standards [*British*]   (BI) .... AIMS
Association of Independent Commercial Editors   (NTCM) .... AICE
Association of Independent Hospitals and Kindred Organisations [*British*]   (BI) .... AIH
Association of Independent Metropolitan Stations   (NTCM) .... AIMS
Association of Independent Television Stations, Inc.   (NTCM) .... AITS
Association of Industrial Medical Officers [*British*]   (BI) .... AIMO
Association of Industrialized Building Component Manufacturers Ltd. [*British*]   (BI) .... AIBCM
Association of Insurance Brokers Ltd. [*British*]   (BI) .... AIB
Association of Insurance Managers in Industry and Commerce [*British*]   (BI) .... AIMC
Association of International Education Administrators   (EA) .... AIEA
Association of Investment Trusts [*British*]   (BI) .... AIT
Association of Light Alloy Refiners and Smelters Ltd. [*British*]   (BI) .... ALAR
Association of Local Air Pollution Control Officers [*Environmental Protection Agency*]   (ERG) .... ALAPO
Association of London Borough Engineers and Surveyors [*British*] (BI) .... ALBES
Association of Malt Products Manufacturers [*British*]   (BI) .... AMPM
Association of Managerial Electrical Executives [*British*]   (BI) .... AMEE
Association of Manipulative Medicine [*British*]   (BI) .... AMM
Association of Manufacturers and Exporters of Concentrated and Unconcentrated Soft Drinks [*British*]   (BI) .... AMECUSD
Association of Marine Traders [*British*]   (BI) .... AMT
Association of Master Lightermen and Barge Owners [*British*]   (BI) .... AML
Association of Master Upholsterers [*British*]   (BI) .... AMU
Association of Media Sales Executives [*British*]   (BI) .... AMSE
Association of Medical Record Officers [*British*]   (BI) .... AMRO
Association of Medical Secretaries [*British*]   (BI) .... AMS
Association of Memoirists and Family Historians   (EA) .... AMFH
Association for Moral and Social Hygiene [*British*]   (BI) .... AMSH
Association of Musical Instrument Industries [*British*]   (BI) .... AMII
Association of Occupational Therapists [*British*]   (BI) .... AOT
Association of Optical Practitioners [*British*]   (BI) ...... AOP
Association for Parents of Addicts [*British*]   (BI) .... APA
Association of Parents Paying Child Support   (EA) .... APPCS
Association of Piano Class Teachers [*British*]   (BI) ...... APCT
Association of Plastic Cable Makers [*British*]   (BI) ...... APCM
Association of Playing Fields' Officers [*British*]   (BI) .... APFO
Association of Pleasure Craft Operators [*British*]   (BI) .... APCO
Association for the Preservation of Rural Life [*British*]   (BI) ...... APRL
Association for the Preservation of Rural Scotland   (BI) .... APRS
Association of Private Traders [*British*]   (BI) .... APT

Association of Professional Recording Studios Ltd. [*British*]   (BI) .... APRS
Association for Promoting Retreats [*British*]   (BI) .... APR
Association of Psychiatric Social Workers [*British*]   (BI) .... APSW
Association of Public Address Engineers [*British*]   (BI) .... APAE
Association of Public Lighting Engineers [*British*]   (BI) .... APLE
Association pour le Rayonnement de l'Opera de Paris [*France*] .... AROP
Association de Recherche et d'Exploitation de Diamant et de l'Or [*Guinea*] [*ICAO designator*]   (FAAC) .... GIN
Association of Registered Driving Instructors [*British*]   (BI) .... ARDI
Association for Relatives of the Mentally, Emotionally, and Nervously Disturbed [*British*]   (BI) .... AMEND
Association of Resort Publicity Officers [*British*]   (BI) .... ARPO
Association of River Authorities [*British*]   (BI) .... ARA
Association of Road Surface Dressing Contractors [*British*]   (BI) .... ARSD
Association of Rural District Council Surveyors [*British*]   (BI) .... ARDCS
Association of Scottish Climbing Clubs   (BI) .... ASCC
Association of Secondary Teachers, Ireland   (BI) .... ASTI
Association of Ships' Compositions Manufacturers [*British*]   (BI) .... ASCM
Association of Shopfront Section Manufacturers [*British*]   (BI) .... ASSM
Association of Short-Circuit Testing Authorities, Inc. [*British*]   (BI) .... ASTA
Association of Social Workers [*British*]   (BI) .... ASW
Association of Solid Woven Belting Manufacturers [*British*]   (BI) .... ASWB
Association for Special Education [*British*]   (BI) .... ASE
Association of Specialised Film Producers [*British*]   (BI) .... ASFP
Association of Steel Drum Manufacturers [*British*]   (BI) .... ASDM
Association of Street Lighting Erection Contractors [*British*]   (BI) .... ASLEC
Association of String Class Teachers [*British*]   (BI) ...... ASCT
Association of Surgeons of Great Britain and Ireland   (BI) .... AS
Association of Swimming Pool Contractors [*British*]   (BI) .... ASPC
Association of Teachers of Domestic Science [*British*]   (BI) .... ATDS
Association for Technical Education in Schools [*British*]   (BI) .... ATES
Association of Toilet Paper Manufacturers [*British*]   (BI) .... ATPM
Association of Touring and Production Managers [*British*]   (BI) .... ATPM
Association of Toy and Fancy Goods Factors [*British*]   (BI) .... ATFGF
Association of Ukrainians in Great Britain Ltd.   (BI) ...... AUGB
Association of Unit Trust Managers [*British*]   (BI) .... AUTM
Association of Used Tyre Merchants [*British*]   (BI) .... AUTM
Association of Vermiculite Exfoliators Ltd. [*British*]   (BI) .... AVE
Association of Veterinary Students of Great Britain and Ireland   (BI) .... AVS
Association of Voluntary Groups [*Republic of Ireland*]   (BI) .... AVG
Association of Waterworks Officers [*British*]   (BI) .... AWO
Association of the Wholesale Licensed Trade of Northern Ireland (BI) .... AWLTNI
Association of Wholesale Woollen Merchants Ltd. [*British*]   (BI) .... AWWM
Association of Women Launderers [*British*]   (BI) .... AWL
Association of Women Surgeons   (EA) .... AWS
Astro Air International, Inc. [*Philippines*] [*ICAO designator*]   (FAAC) .... AAP
Astronomical Information Processing System [*Computer program*] .... AIPS
At Home .... AH
At and Maintain [*Aviation*]   (FAAC) .... ATAM
AT & T Aviation Group [*ICAO designator*]   (FAAC) .... XAT
Ata-Aerocondor Transportes Aereos Ltda. [*Portugal*] [*ICAO designator*]   (FAAC) .... ARD
Athabaska Airways Ltd. [*Canada*] [*ICAO designator*]   (FAAC) .... ABS
Athens Air [*Greece*] [*ICAO designator*]   (FAAC) .... THN
Athletic Clothing Manufacturers' Association [*British*]   (BI) .... ACMA
Atlanta [*Iceland*] [*ICAO designator*]   (FAAC) .... ABD
Atlantair Ltd. [*Canada*] [*ICAO designator*]   (FAAC) .... ATB
Atlantic [*Ocean*]   (ABBR) .... A
Atlantic Aero, Inc. [*ICAO designator*]   (FAAC) .... MDC
Atlantic Air BVI Ltd. [*British*] [*ICAO designator*]   (FAAC) .... BLB
Atlantic Airways, PF (Faroe Islands) [*Denmark*] [*ICAO designator*] (FAAC) .... FLI
Atlantic Coast Airlines [*Westair Airlines, Inc.*] [*ICAO designator*] (FAAC) .... BLR
Atlantic Gulf Airlines, Inc. [*ICAO designator*]   (FAAC) .... AGF
Atlantic Island Air [*Iceland*] [*ICAO designator*]   (FAAC) .... TRG
Atlantic Richfield Co. [*ICAO designator*]   (FAAC) .... NRS
Atlantic Route [*Aviation*]   (FAAC) .... AR
Atlantic Southeast Airlines, Inc. [*ICAO designator*]   (FAAC) .... ASE
Atlantic Stratocumulus Transition Experiment [*Meteorology*] .... ASTEX
Atlantic World Airways, Inc. [*ICAO designator*]   (FAAC) .... BJK
Atlantis Airlines [*ICAO designator*]   (FAAC) .... AAO
Atlantis Transportation Services Ltd. [*Canada*] [*ICAO designator*] (FAAC) .... ATE
Atlas Air, Inc. [*ICAO designator*]   (FAAC) .... GTI
Atlas Airlines [*ICAO designator*]   (FAAC) .... ATR
Atlas of Australian Resources [*A publication*] .... AAR
Atmosphere   (ABBR) .... A
ATS Aircharter Ltd. [*British*] [*ICAO designator*]   (FAAC) .... AVT
ATS-Servicii de Transport Aerian [*Italy*] [*ICAO designator*]   (FAAC) .... ROS
Attached Pressurized Module [*European Space Agency*] .... APM
Attack Helicopter Battalion [*Army*]   (ADDR) .... ATKHB
Attendant Care Evaluation .... ACE
Attention [*Electronics*] .... AT
Auction Transfer Authority .... ATA
Audeli Air Express [*Spain*] [*ICAO designator*]   (FAAC) .... ADI
Audi Air, Inc. [*ICAO designator*]   (FAAC) .... AUD
Audi Space Frame [*Concept car*] [*Automotive engineering*] .... ASF
Audience Measurement by Market for Outdoor   (NTCM) .... AMMO
Audience Research   (NTCM) .... AR
Audience Research Institute [*Also, AIPO*]   (NTCM) ...... ARI
Audimeter/Diary System [*A. C. Nielson Co.*]   (NTCM) .... A/D

Audio Data Sequence [*Telecommunications*] (NTCM) ... ADSQ
Audio Fidelity (NTCM) ... AF
Audio Follow Video [*Tape editing*] (NTCM) ... AFV
Audio Integrating System (DA) ... AIS
Audio Operator (NTCM) ... AO
Audio Receive Only (NTCM) ... ARO
Auditorium (DAC) ... AUD
Auditory (ABBR) ... A
Auditory Brainstem Implant [*Hearing technology*] ... ABI
Aurigny Air Services Ltd. [*British*] [*ICAO designator*] (FAAC) ... AUR
Aus-Air [*Australia*] [*ICAO designator*] (FAAC) ... AUZ
Ausfrech-Melcher-Grossapach [*Mercedes-Benz cars*] [*High-performance parts supplier*] ... AMG
Austral Lineas Aereas [*Argentina*] [*ICAO designator*] (FAAC) ... AUT
Australia Antigen [*Medicine*] (MAH) ... Au(l)
Australia Asia Airlines Ltd. [*ICAO designator*] (FAAC) ... AAU
Australia First [*Political party*] ... AF
Australia-France Technological Exchange Scheme ... AFTEX
Australia-Indonesia Youth Exchange Program ... AIYEP
Australia Television International ... ATVI
Australian Air International ... AAI
Australian Airlines ... AA
Australian Airlines [*ICAO designator*] (FAAC) ... AUS
Australian Armed Forces Radio ... AAFR
Australian Casemix Bulletin [*A publication*] ... ACB
Australian Civil Aviation Authority, Flying Unit [*ICAO designator*] (FAAC) ... ADA
Australian Dance Theatre [*Adelaide*] ... ADT
Australian Disabilities Review [*A publication*] ... ADR
Australian Energy Management News [*A publication*] ... AEMN
Australian Film Corp. ... AFC
Australian Film Finance Corp. ... AFFC
Australian Inventory of Chemical Substances ... AICS
Australian Journal of Experimental Agriculture [*A publication*] ... AJEA
Australian Literary Awards and Fellowships [*A publication*] ... ALAF
Australia's Indigenous Peoples Party [*Political party*] ... AIP
Austrian Air Ambulance [*ICAO designator*] (FAAC) ... OAF
Austrian Air Services [*ICAO designator*] (FAAC) ... AAS
Austrian Airlines [*ICAO designator*] (FAAC) ... AUA
Austrian Airtransport [*ICAO designator*] (FAAC) ... AAT
Authorized Medical Examiner (DA) ... AME
Authorized Review Officer ... ARO
Authorized Terminal Strength ... ATS
Autism Network International (EA) ... ANI
Auto Camping Club Ltd. [*British*] (BI) ... ACC
Auto Headway Control [*Mitsubishi*] [*Automotive engineering*] ... AHC
Auto Read Reallocation [*Computer science*] ... ARRE
Automated Flight Information Service [*ICAO designator*] (FAAC) ... FISA
Automated Manifest System (DA) ... AMS
Automated Mapping/Facility Management [*Computer science*] ... AMFM
Automated Multiphasic Screening [*Medicine*] (MAH) ... AMS
Automated Percutaneous Discectomy [*Spinal surgery*] ... APD
Automated Screen Trading [*Business term*] ... AST
Automated Surface Observing System [*Meteorology*] (FAAC) ... ASOS
Automated Telecommunications System [*Army*] (ADDR) ... ATS
Automatic Assemble Editing (NTCM) ... AAE
Automatic Closing Device (DAC) ... ACD
Automatic Clutch System [*Powertrain*] [*Automotive engineering*] ... ACS
Automatic Clutch and Throttle System [*Automotive powertrain*] ... ACTS
Automatic Damping Control [*Automotive suspensions*] ... ADC
Automatic Dependent Surveillance Unit [*ICAO designator*] (FAAC) ... ADSU
Automatic Drivetrain Management [*Automotive engineering*] ... ADM
Automatic Flight Control and Augmentation System (DA) ... AFCAS
Automatic Flight Inspection (DA) ... AFIS
Automatic Leveling Seat [*Automotive engineering*] ... ALS
Automatic Mapping and Planning System [*Environmental Protection Agency*] (ERG) ... AMPS
Automatic Power Control (NTCM) ... APC
Automatic Procurement Capability System ... AUTOPROC
Automatic Remote Cassette Handler (NTCM) ... ARCH
Automatic Retransmission Request for Correction [*Computer science*] (NTCM) ... ARQ
Automatic Scan Tracking [*Videotape head*] (NTCM) ... AST
Automatic Sequence Register (NTCM) ... ASR
Automatic Threat Detection System [*Aviation*] (DA) ... ATD
Automatic Timing Device [*Diesel engines*] ... ATD
Automatic Transmission System [*Telecommunications*] (NTCM) ... ATS
Automatic Vehicle Location System (DA) ... AVLS
Automatic Vending Machine Association [*British*] (BI) ... AVMA
Automatic Voice Alerting Device (DA) ... AVAD
Automatic Weather Broadcast (DA) ... AB
Automatically Deployable Emergency Locator Transmitter [*Aviation*] (DA) ... ADELT
Automation on Air Traffic Flow Management (DA) ... AUT-ATFM
Automobilvertriebs Aktiengesellschaft [*Austria*] [*ICAO designator*] (FAAC) ... MBA
Automotive Climate Control ... ACC
Automotive Consortium on Recycling and Disposal [*Industry research group*] ... ACORD
Automotive Information Network Service ... AINS
Automotive, Metal, and Engineering Union ... AMEU
Automotive Recyclers Association [*Salvage yards*] ... ARA
Automotors Salta SACYF [*Argentina*] [*ICAO designator*] (FAAC) ... LES
Autonomous Intelligent Cruise Control [*Automotive engineering*] ... AICC
Auxiliary Emission Control Device (ERG) ... AECD
Auxiliary Flight Service Station [*Aviation*] (FAAC) ... XFSS
Avair, Inc. [*ICAO designator*] (FAAC) ... FVA
Avanti Air [*Austria*] [*ICAO designator*] (FAAC) ... ATV
Avcon AG [*Switzerland*] [*ICAO designator*] (FAAC) ... AVX
Avensa Aerovias Venezolanas SA [*Venezuela*] [*ICAO designator*] (FAAC) ... AVE
Average Annual Performance Rate ... AAPR
Average Female Weekly Earnings ... AFWE
Average Male Weekly Earnings ... AMWE
Avesen SA de CV [*Mexico*] [*ICAO designator*] (FAAC) ... ESE
Avia Express Ltd. [*Hungary*] [*ICAO designator*] (FAAC) ... AEH
Avia Filipines International, Inc. [*Philippines*] [*ICAO designator*] (FAAC) ... FIL
Avia Sud [*France*] [*ICAO designator*] (FAAC) ... AVU
Aviacion de Chiapas [*Mexico*] [*ICAO designator*] (FAAC) ... CHP
Aviacion Colombiana Ltd. [*Colombia*] [*ICAO designator*] (FAAC) ... VCO
Aviacion y Comercio SA [*Spain*] [*ICAO designator*] (FAAC) ... AYC
Aviacion Ejecutiva Mexicana SA [*Mexico*] [*ICAO designator*] (FAAC) ... AVM
Aviacion Ejecutiva del Noroeste SA de CV [*Mexico*] [*ICAO designator*] (FAAC) ... NST
Aviacion del Noroeste SA de CV [*Mexico*] [*ICAO designator*] (FAAC) ... ANW
Aviair Aviation Ltd. [*Canada*] [*ICAO designator*] (FAAC) ... AVF
Avial (Russian Co. Ltd.) [*Former USSR*] [*ICAO designator*] (FAAC) ... RLC
Avialgarve, Taxis Aereos do Algarve Ltd. [*Portugal*] [*ICAO designator*] (FAAC) ... AVG
Avianca, Aerovias Nacionales de Colombia SA [*ICAO designator*] (FAAC) ... AVA
Avianova SpA [*Italy*] [*ICAO designator*] (FAAC) ... NOV
Aviaprima [*Russian Federation*] [*ICAO designator*] (FAAC) ... PRL
Aviaross [*Russian Federation*] [*ICAO designator*] (FAAC) ... RAR
Aviation [*FCC*] (NTCM) ... A
Aviation Administrative Communication (DA) ... AAC
Aviation Amos [*M et J*], **Inc.** [*Canada*] [*ICAO designator*] (FAAC) ... AMJ
Aviation Associates, Inc. [*St. Croix*] [*ICAO designator*] (FAAC) ... SUA
Aviation Beauport Ltd. [*British*] [*ICAO designator*] (FAAC) ... AVB
Aviation Charter & Management [*British*] [*ICAO designator*] (FAAC) ... FTN
Aviation Development Co. Nigeria Ltd. [*ICAO designator*] (FAAC) ... ADK
Aviation Enterprises [*Denmark*] [*ICAO designator*] (FAAC) ... AVP
Aviation Industries of China (ECON) ... AVIC
Aviation Insurance Officers Association (DA) ... AIOA
Aviation Legere de l'Armee de Terre [*France*] [*ICAO designator*] (FAAC) ... LAT
Aviation Management Corp. [*ICAO designator*] (FAAC) ... AAM
Aviation Quebec Labrador Ltd. [*Canada*] [*ICAO designator*] (FAAC) ... QLA
Aviation Security Panel [*ICAO*] (DA) ... AVSEC
Aviation Services, Inc. [*ICAO designator*] (FAAC) ... AVQ
Aviation Services Ltd. [*Guam*] [*ICAO designator*] (FAAC) ... FRE
Aviation Seychelles Ltd. [*ICAO designator*] (FAAC) ... AVS
Aviation Standards National Field Office [*ICAO designator*] (FAAC) ... FLC
Aviation Transport Services [*Italy*] [*ICAO designator*] (FAAC) ... ATS
Aviation Weather Processor [*ICAO designator*] (FAAC) ... AWP
Aviator SA [*Greece*] [*ICAO designator*] (FAAC) ... AVW
Aviatrans [*Former USSR*] [*ICAO designator*] (FAAC) ... VAS
Avijet SA de CV [*Mexico*] [*ICAO designator*] (FAAC) ... IJE
Aviogenex [*Yugoslavia*] [*ICAO designator*] (FAAC) ... AGX
Avioimpex [*Yugloslavia*] [*ICAO designator*] (FAAC) ... AXX
Avion Taxi Canada, Inc. [*ICAO designator*] (FAAC) ... ADQ
Avionair, Inc. [*Canada*] [*ICAO designator*] (FAAC) ... ANU
Aviones y Servicios del Golfo SA de CV [*Mexico*] [*ICAO designator*] (FAAC) ... ADG
Aviones de Sonora SA [*Mexico*] [*ICAO designator*] (FAAC) ... ADS
Aviones Unidos SA de CV [*Mexico*] [*ICAO designator*] (FAAC) ... AUN
Avionics Standard Communications Bus (DA) ... ASCB
Avior Pty Ltd. [*Australia*] [*ICAO designator*] (FAAC) ... AVR
Aviorrenta SA [*Mexico*] [*ICAO designator*] (FAAC) ... AVI
Aviser SA [*Spain*] [*ICAO designator*] (FAAC) ... AVH
Avistar (Cyprus) Ltd. [*ICAO designator*] (FAAC) ... KJA
Avitat [*British*] [*ICAO designator*] (FAAC) ... ESO
Avoirdupois Ounce ... advp oz
Away from Home ... AFH
Away from Keyboard [*Computer hacker terminology*] (NHD) ... AFK
Awood Air Ltd. [*Canada*] [*ICAO designator*] (FAAC) ... AWO
Axel Rent SA [*Mexico*] [*ICAO designator*] (FAAC) ... AXR
Axial Summit Caldera [*Volcanology*] ... ASC
Axis (ABBR) ... A
Azalavia-Azerbaijan Hava Yollari [*ICAO designator*] (FAAC) ... AHY
Azamat [*Kazakhstan*] [*ICAO designator*] (FAAC) ... AZB
Azauridine [*Organic chemistry*] (MAH) ... AZUR
Azimut SA [*Spain*] [*ICAO designator*] (FAAC) ... AZT
Azure (ABBR) ... A

B

BAC Aircraft Ltd. [*British*] [*ICAO designator*] (FAAC) ... RPX
Bachelor of Arts (AEE) ... AB
Bachelor of Business - Health Administration ... BBusHA
Bachelor of Human Biology ... BHB
Bachelor of Medicine, Bachelor of Surgery ... BMBCh
Bachelor of Medicine, Master of Surgery ... MBMS
Bachelor of Music (Performance) ... BMusPerf
Bachelor of Physical Education ... BPhysEd
Bachelor of Science (Mechanical Engineering) ... BSc(MechEng)
Bachelor of Science (Oenology) ... BSc(Oen)
Bachelor of Science (Surgery) ... BSc(Surg)
Bachelor of Technical Science ... BTechSc
Bacillary Angiomatosis-Bacillary Peliosis ... BAP
Back to the Bible Broadcast (NTCM) ... BBB
Back Taxiing [*Aviation*] (FAAC) ... BT
Background (NTCM) ... BKG
Background Luminance Monitor [*Aviation*] (DA) ... BLM
Background Natural Organic Matter [*Environmental chemistry*] ... BNOM
Background Paper ... BP
Bacterial Sulfate Reduction ... BSR
Bahama Route [*Aviation*] (FAAC) ... BR
Bahamas [*Aircraft nationality and registration mark*] (FAAC) ... C6
Bahamasair Holdings Ltd. [*Bahamas*] [*ICAO designator*] (FAAC) ... BHS
Bahrain [*Aircraft nationality and registration mark*] (FAAC) ... A9C
Baikal [*Russian Federation*] [*ICAO designator*] (FAAC) ... BKL
Baker Aviation, Inc. [*ICAO designator*] (FAAC) ... BAJ
Bakers' and Allied Traders' Golfing Society [*British*] (BI) ... BATS
Bakery and Allied Trades Association Ltd. [*British*] (BI) ... BATA
Bakery Students Association of Scotland (BI) ... BSAS
Balair AG [*Switzerland*] [*ICAO designator*] (FAAC) ... BBB
Balance of Commitments ... BCOM
Bali International Air Service [*Indonesia*] [*ICAO designator*] (FAAC) ... BLN
Balkan-Bulgarian Airlines [*ICAO designator*] (FAAC) ... LAZ
Ballets de San Juan [*Puerto Rico*] ... BST
Ballistic Missile Defense Organization ... BMDO
Baltia Air Lines, Inc. [*ICAO designator*] (FAAC) ... BTL
Baltic Airlines Ltd. [*ICAO designator*] (FAAC) ... HOT
Baltic Aviation, Inc. [*ICAO designator*] (FAAC) ... BLT
Baltic International Airlines [*Latvia*] [*ICAO designator*] (FAAC) ... BIA
[*J. C.*] **Bamford (Excavators) Ltd.** [*British*] [*ICAO designator*] (FAAC) ... JCB
Banco de Mexico [*ICAO designator*] (FAAC) ... BMX
Banco di Napoli [*Italy*] ... BDN
Banded Two Sides and One End [*Lumber*] (DAC) ... B2S1E
Bangkok Airways [*Thailand*] [*ICAO designator*] (FAAC) ... BKP
Bangladesh [*Aircraft nationality and registration mark*] (FAAC) ... S2
Bangladesh Biman [*ICAO designator*] (FAAC) ... BBC
Bank Education Service [*British*] (BI) ... BES
Bankair, Inc. [*ICAO designator*] (FAAC) ... BKA
Bankruptcy Official Receivers' Information System ... BORIS
Bantam (ABBR) ... BTM
Bantamweight (ABBR) ... BTMWT
Baptist Women's Missionary Auxilliary [*British*] (BI) ... BWMA
Bar Harbor Airlines [*ICAO designator*] (FAAC) ... AJC
Bar Journal [*A publication*] ... BJ
Barair SA [*Spain*] [*ICAO designator*] (FAAC) ... BAI
Barbados [*Aircraft nationality and registration mark*] (FAAC) ... 8P
Barcklay Flying Service [*ICAO designator*] (FAAC) ... ACH
Bardsey Bird and Field Observatory [*British*] (BI) ... BBFO
Barken International, Inc. [*ICAO designator*] (FAAC) ... BKJ
Barns Olson Aeroleasing Ltd. [*British*] [*ICAO designator*] (FAAC) ... CLN
Baron Aviation Services, Inc. [*ICAO designator*] (FAAC) ... BVN
Barrier-Equivalent Velocity [*Automotive safety*] ... BEV
Barrister (ABBR) ... BRSTR
Bartender (ABBR) ... BRTNDR
Barter (ABBR) ... BRTR
Barth's Aviation [*France*] [*ICAO designator*] (FAAC) ... BTH
Basair AB [*Sweden*] [*ICAO designator*] (FAAC) ... BSR
Base-Catalyzed Destination [*Environmental science*] ... BCD
Baseball (ABBR) ... BSBL
Baseboard (ABBR) ... BSBD
Based (ABBR) ... BSD
Baseless (ABBR) ... BSLS
Baseops International, Inc. [*ICAO designator*] (FAAC) ... XBO
Bashful (ABBR) ... BSHFL
Bashfully (ABBR) ... BSHFLY
Bashfulness (ABBR) ... BSHFLNS
Basic and Applied Myology [*A publication*] ... BAM
Basic Area of Interest [*Army*] (ADDR) ... BAI
Basic Decision Height [*Aviation*] (DA) ... BCH
Basic Minimum Descent Height [*Aviation*] (DA) ... BMDH
Basic Operational Requirements and Planning Criteria Group [*ICAO*] (DA) ... BORG
Basically (ABBR) ... BSCY
Basing (ABBR) ... BSG
Basked (ABBR) ... BSKD
Basketball (ABBR) ... BSKBL
Basketry (ABBR) ... BSKTY
Basking (ABBR) ... BSKG
Basler Flight Service, Inc. [*ICAO designator*] (FAAC) ... BFC
Basque (ABBR) ... BSQ
Bastard (ABBR) ... BSTRD
Bastardize (ABBR) ... BSTRDZ
Bastardized (ABBR) ... BSTRDZD
Bastardizing (ABBR) ... BSTRDZG
Bastardly (ABBR) ... BSTRDY
Baste (ABBR) ... BST
Basted (ABBR) ... BSTD
Basting (ABBR) ... BSTG
Batched (ABBR) ... BTCHD
Batching (ABBR) ... BTCHG
Bateria Artifical Chromosome [*Genetics*] ... BAC
Bathroom [*Classified advertising*] ... BA
Bathtub (ABBR) ... BT
Batik (ABBR) ... BTK
Battalion (ABBR) ... BTLN
Battle (ABBR) ... BTL
Battled (ABBR) ... BTLD
Battlefield (ABBR) ... BTLFLD
Battlefield Combat Identification [*Army*] (RDA) ... BCID
Battlement (ABBR) ... BTLMT
Battleship (ABBR) ... BTLSP
Battling (ABBR) ... BTLG
Bay Air Aviation [*New Zealand*] [*ICAO designator*] (FAAC) ... BAY
Bayonet Base [*Lens mount*] (NTCM) ... BB
Bayonet Naval Connector [*Electronics*] (NTCM) ... BNC
Bayu Indonesia Air PT [*ICAO designator*] (FAAC) ... BYU
BCA Charter [*British*] [*ICAO designator*] (FAAC) ... BRC
Be Back Later [*Computer hacker terminology*] (NHD) ... BBL
Be Right Back [*Computer hacker terminology*] (NHD) ... BRB
Beacon Collision Avoidance System [*Aviation*] (DA) ... BACS
Beacon Data [*Aviation*] (FAAC) ... BDAT
Beam Spacer (DAC) ... BS
Beam Steering Unit (DA) ... BSU
Bearing Pile [*Technical drawings*] (DAC) ... BP
Bearing Supplies Ltd. [*British*] [*ICAO designator*] (FAAC) ... PVO
Bearskin Lake Air Service Ltd. [*Canada*] [*ICAO designator*] (FAAC) ... BLS
Beautician (ABBR) ... BTCN
Beautification (ABBR) ... BTFCN
Beautiful (ABBR) ... BTFL
Beautiful Music (NTCM) ... BM
Beautifully (ABBR) ... BTFLY
Beautifulness (ABBR) ... BTFLNS
Beautify (ABBR) ... BTFY
Beautifying (ABBR) ... BTFYG
Become (DA) ... BC
Bedarfsflugunternehmen Dr. L. Polsterer [*Austria*] [*ICAO designator*] (FAAC) ... OPV
Bedford Rae [*British*] [*ICAO designator*] (FAAC) ... RRS
Beech Aircraft Corp. [*ICAO designator*] (FAAC) ... BEC
Beef Recording Association [*British*] (BI) ... BRA
Beeswax (ABBR) ... BSWX
Beet Invert Syrup [*Food sweetener*] ... BIS
Beet Medium Invert Syrup [*Food sweetener*] ... BMIS
Beginning of Business ... BOB

Beginning of Year Significant Non-Complier [*Environmental Protection Agency*] (ERG) ... BOYSNC
Behavioral Risk Factor Surveillance System ... BRESS
Behind the Lens (NTCM) ... BTL
Belair [*Belarus*] [*ICAO designator*] (FAAC) ... BLI
Belavia [*Belarus*] [*ICAO designator*] (FAAC) ... BRU
Belgavia (Societe de Handling) [*Belgium*] [*ICAO designator*] (FAAC) ... BLG
Belgian Flight Centre [*ICAO designator*] (FAAC) ... ABF
Belgian Fourragere [*Military decoration*] ... BEFOURRA
Belgian International Air Carriers [*ICAO designator*] (FAAC) ... BIC
Belize Trans Air [*ICAO designator*] (FAAC) ... JGR
Belize Transair [*ICAO designator*] (FAAC) ... BTR
Bell (NFPA) ... B
Bell-Air Executive Air Travel Ltd. [*New Zealand*] [*ICAO designator*] (FAAC) ... BEL
Bell-View Airlines Ltd. [*Nigeria*] [*ICAO designator*] (FAAC) ... BLV
Belt Driven Retrofit [*Cosworth racing engines*] [*Automotive engineering*] ... BDR
Belt Driven Turbocharged [*Cosworth racing engines*] [*Automotive engineering*] ... BDT
Belt Driven Type A [*Cosworth racing engines*] [*Automotive engineering*] ... BDA
Bemidji Aviation Services, Inc. [*ICAO designator*] (FAAC) ... BMJ
Benair [*Italy*] [*ICAO designator*] (FAAC) ... BEI
Benday [*Engraving*] (NTCM) ... DAY
Bendix Atlantic Inflator Co. [*Automotive industry supplier*] ... BAICO
Benefits Control System [*Insurance*] ... BCS
Benelux Falcon Service [*Belgium*] [*ICAO designator*] (FAAC) ... BFS
Benin [*Aircraft nationality and registration mark*] (FAAC) ... TY
Benin Air Express [*ICAO designator*] (FAAC) ... BEX
Bennington Aviation, Inc. [*ICAO designator*] (FAAC) ... BEN
Benzaldehyde [*Organic chemistry*] ... BAL
Benzothiopyranoindazole [*Organic chemistry*] ... BTPI
Bereave (ABBR) ... BRVE
Bereaved (ABBR) ... BRVED
Bering Air, Inc. [*ICAO designator*] (FAAC) ... BRG
Berkeley Association (EA) ... BA
Berlin European [*ICAO designator*] (FAAC) ... ECJ
[*The*] **Berline, Berlin-Brandenburgisches Luftfahrtunternehmen GmbH** [*Germany*] [*ICAO designator*] (FAAC) ... TBL
Berry (ABBR) ... BRY
Berry Aviation, Inc. [*ICAO designator*] (FAAC) ... AHS
Berrying (ABBR) ... BRYG
Berserk (ABBR) ... BSRK
Beseech (ABBR) ... BSCH
Beseech (ABBR) ... BSECH
Beseeched (ABBR) ... BSCHD
Beseeched (ABBR) ... BSECHD
Beseeching (ABBR) ... BSCHG
Beside (ABBR) ... BSD
Beside (ABBR) ... BSID
Besiege (ABBR) ... BSEG
Besiege (ABBR) ... BSG
Besieged (ABBR) ... BSEGD
Besieged (ABBR) ... BSGD
Besieging (ABBR) ... BSEGG
Besieging (ABBR) ... BSGG
Besmear (ABBR) ... BSMER
Besmear (ABBR) ... BSMR
Besmeared (ABBR) ... BSMRD
Besmearing (ABBR) ... BSMRG
Besmirch (ABBR) ... BSMRCH
Best of Both Worlds [*Apple Computer's Macintosh Due System's nickname*] [*Pronounced as a proper name: Bob W.*] ... Bob W
Best Control Technology [*Environmental Protection Agency*] (ERG) ... BCT
Best Expert Judgment [*Environmental Protection Agency*] (ERG) ... BEJ
Best Practicable Control Technology Currently Available [*Clean Water Act*] (ERG) ... BPTCA
Bestial (ABBR) ... BSTL
Bestiality (ABBR) ... BSTLT
Bestially (ABBR) ... BSTLY
Bestow (ABBR) ... BSTO
Bestow (ABBR) ... BSTW
Bestowable (ABBR) ... BSTWB
Bestowal (ABBR) ... BSTWL
Bestowed (ABBR) ... BSTWD
Bestowing (ABBR) ... BSTWG
Bestowment (ABBR) ... BSTWT
Beta, Atla, and Themis [*Regions on planet Venus*] ... BAT
Betoken (ABBR) ... BTKN
Betsy-Tacy Society (EA) ... BTS
Beveled on Four Edges [*Lumber*] (DAC) ... B4E
Beveled Plate Glass (DAC) ... BPG
Beveled on Three Edges [*Lumber*] (DAC) ... B3E
Bezene, Toluene, Ethylbenzene, and Xylene [*Organic mixture*] ... BTEX
BFS [*Berliner Spezial Flug*], **Luftahrtunternehmen GmbH** [*Germany*] [*ICAO designator*] (FAAC) ... SBY
Bhoja Airlines [*Pakistan*] [*ICAO designator*] (FAAC) ... BHO
Bhutan [*Aircraft nationality and registration mark*] (FAAC) ... A5
Bible Lands' Missions Aid Society [*British*] (BI) ... BLMAS
Biennial Flight Review [*Aviation*] (DA) ... BFR
Big Island Air, Inc. [*ICAO designator*] (FAAC) ... BIG
Big Red Switch [*Computer science*] (NHD) ... BRS
Big Sky Airline [*ICAO designator*] (FAAC) ... BSY
Biggin Executive Aviation Ltd. [*British*] [*ICAO designator*] (FAAC) ... BHE
Bighorn Airways, Inc. [*ICAO designator*] (FAAC) ... BHR
Bilateral Quarantine Agreement ... BQA
Bilingual Information Instructor ... BII
Bilingual Information Officer ... BIO
Billiards Association [*British*] (BI) ... BA
Billiards Trade Association [*British*] (BI) ... BTA
Billings Ovulation Method Association of the United States (EA) ... BOM
Binary Compatibility Specification [*Computer science*] (PCM) ... BCS
Binaural Analysis System [*Noise testing*] [*Automotive engineering*] ... BAS
Binter Canarais [*Spain*] [*ICAO designator*] (FAAC) ... IBB
Binter-Mediterraneo [*Spain*] [*ICAO designator*] (FAAC) ... BIM
Biological Effect Monitoring [*Toxicology*] ... BEM
Bipolar Affective Disorder [*Genetics*] ... BPAD
Bipost [*Lamp base*] (NTCM) ... Bp
Bird Leasing, Inc. [*ICAO designator*] (FAAC) ... BIR
Bird Sweep Completed [*Aviation*] (FAAC) ... BSC
Birgenair [*Turkey*] [*ICAO designator*] (FAAC) ... BHY
Birmingham Aviation Ltd. [*British*] [*ICAO designator*] (FAAC) ... ATX
Birth Control Advisory Bureau [*British*] (BI) ... BCAB
Birthday (ABBR) ... BRTDY
Birthday (ABBR) ... BRTHDY
Birthmark (ABBR) ... BRTHMK
Birthmark (ABBR) ... BRTMK
Birthplace (ABBR) ... BRTHPL
Birthplace (ABBR) ... BRTPLC
Birthright (ABBR) ... BRTHRGT
Birthright (ABBR) ... BRTRT
Birthstone (ABBR) ... BRTHSTN
Birthstone (ABBR) ... BRTST
Biscuit (ABBR) ... BSCUT
Bismuth Sulfite [*Agar*] [*Bacteriology*] ... BS
Bison (ABBR) ... BSN
Biting (ABBR) ... BTG
Bituminous Treated Base (DAC) ... BTB
Black Audio Network, Inc. (NTCM) ... BAN
Black Box Under Glass Variable Angle Controllled Temperature [*Automotive paint duability testing*] ... BBUGVACT
Black Elderly Twin Study [*National Institute on Aging*] ... BETS
Black Human Resources Network [*An association*] (EA) ... BHRN
Black Magic Project Ltd. [*British*] [*ICAO designator*] (FAAC) ... BLM
Black Mental Health Alliance (EA) ... BMHA
Black Panel Temperature [*Automotive paint durability testing*] ... BPT
Blackhawk Airways, Inc. [*ICAO designator*] (FAAC) ... BAK
Blade Integrity Monitor [*Aviation*] (DA) ... BIM
Bleached Eucalypt Kraft ... BEK
Blimped Noiseless Reflex Camera (NTCM) ... BNC
Blind Transmission Broadcast [*Army*] (ADDR) ... BTB
Blit [*Computer science*] (NHD) ... BLT
Block in the Anterosuperior Division of the Left Branch [*Medicine*] (MAH) ... BSDLB
Block Grant Authority ... BGA
Block Order Exposure System [*Business term*] ... BLOX
Blowing Snow [*Meteorology*] (DA) ... BLSN
Blue Airlines [*Zaire*] [*ICAO designator*] (FAAC) ... BUL
Blue Horizon Travel Club [*ICAO designator*] (FAAC) ... BLH
Blue Sky Carrier Co. Ltd. [*Poland*] [*ICAO designator*] (FAAC) ... BSC
Bluestone (ABBR) ... BS
Board of Architectural Education [*British*] (BI) ... BAE
Body Armor System Individual Countermine Armor [*Army*] (INF) ... BASIC
Body in White [*Automotive manufacturing*] ... BIW
Boeing Commericial Airplane Group [*ICAO designator*] (FAAC) ... BOE
Boeing Dehavilland Canada [*ICAO designator*] (FAAC) ... DHC
Bogazici Hava Tasimacilik AS [*Turkey*] [*ICAO designator*] (FAAC) ... BHT
Boilermaker/Welder ... BMW
Boisterous (ABBR) ... BSTRU
Boisterous (ABBR) ... BSTRUS
Boisterously (ABBR) ... BSTRUSY
Boisterousness (ABBR) ... BSTRUSNS
Bollard [*Shipping*] [*British*] ... Bol
Bolshoi Ballet Academy [*Former USSR*] ... BA
Bolt (ABBR) ... BT
Bon Accord Airways [*British*] [*ICAO designator*] (FAAC) ... BON
Bonair Aviation Ltd. [*Canada*] [*ICAO designator*] (FAAC) ... BNR
Bond Air Services Ltd. [*Uganda*] [*ICAO designator*] (FAAC) ... BOD
Bond Helicopters Ltd. [*British*] [*ICAO designator*] (FAAC) ... BND
Bond Investors Guaranty Insurance ... BIGI
Bone Marrow Stem Cell [*Hematology*] ... BMSC
Book Publisher's Association (NTCM) ... BPA
Book Publishers Representatives' Association [*British*] (BI) ... BPRA
Book Shelf [*Technical drawings*] (DAC) ... BK SH
Booking Agents Association of Great Britain Ltd. (BI) ... BAA
Bookmakers' Protection Association Ltd. (BI) ... BPA
Boot and Shoe Manufacturers' Association and Leather Trades Protection Society [*British*] (BI) ... BASMA
Bop Air (Pty) Ltd. [*South Africa*] [*ICAO designator*] (FAAC) ... BOP
Bordaire Ltd. [*Canada*] [*ICAO designator*] (FAAC) ... BOF
Bordeaux Agents Association [*British*] (BI) ... BAA
Border Airways [*South Africa*] [*ICAO designator*] (FAAC) ... BDA
Borrowed Light (DAC) ... Bit
Borrower's Option for Notes and Underwritten Standby [*Finance*] ... BONUS

Bosal International Management NV [*Belgium*] [*ICAO designator*] (FAAC) ... BOS
Boscombe Down MOD/PE [*British*] [*ICAO designator*] (FAAC) ... BDN
[*Z.*] **Boskovic Air Charters Ltd.** [*Kenya*] [*ICAO designator*] (FAAC) ... ZBA
Bosnaair [*Yugoslavia*] [*ICAO designator*] (FAAC) ... BAA
Bosphorus Hava Yollari Turizm Ve Ticaret AS [*Turkey*] [*ICAO designator*] (FAAC) ... BSP
Boston Women's Health Book Collective ... BWHBC
Bother (ABBR) ... BTHR
Bothered (ABBR) ... BTHRD
Bothering (ABBR) ... BTHRG
Bothersome (ABBR) ... BTHRSM
Botswana [*Aircraft nationality and registration mark*] (FAAC) ... A2
Bottled (ABBR) ... BTLD
Bottling (ABBR) ... BTLG
Bottom Hole Assembly [*Well drilling technology*] ... BHA
Bottomed (ABBR) ... BTMD
Bottoming (ABBR) ... BTMG
Bottomless (ABBR) ... BTMLS
Botulism [*Medicine*] (ABBR) ... BTLM
Boundary Layer Control Outlet [*Mitsubishi*] [*Aerodynamics*] [*Automotive engineering*] ... BLCO
Boundary Lights [*Aviation*] (DA) ... BO
Bouraq Indonesia Airlines PT [*ICAO designator*] (FAAC) ... BOU
Bowman Aviation, Inc. [*ICAO designator*] (FAAC) ... BMN
BP Flight Operations Ltd. [*British*] [*ICAO designator*] (FAAC) ... BPO
Braathens Helicopter AS [*Norway*] [*ICAO designator*] (FAAC) ... BRH
Braathens South American & Far East Airtransport AS [*Norway*] [*ICAO designator*] (FAAC) ... BRA
Bracing (DAC) ... Brcg
Bradley Air (Charter) Services Ltd. [*Canada*] [*ICAO designator*] (FAAC) ... BAR
Brainstorm (ABBR) ... BRSTRM
Brainstorming (ABBR) ... BRSTRMG
Brake Specific Oxides of Nitrogen [*Exhaust emissions*] [*Automotive engineering*] ... BSNO
Braking [*Aviation*] (FAAC) ... BRKG
Branch if Less Than [*Computer science*] (NHD) ... BLT
Branch Processing Unit [*Computer science*] ... BPO
Branched Ribonucleic Acid [*Genetics*] ... bRNA
Branded Furniture Society [*British*] (BI) ... BFS
Branded Knitting-Wool Association Ltd. [*British*] (BI) ... BKWA
Brasil-Central Linhas Areas Regional SA [*Brazil*] [*ICAO designator*] (FAAC) ... BLC
Brassiere (ABBR) ... BRSSIR
Brassiness (ABBR) ... BRSNS
Brassy (ABBR) ... BRSSY
Brassy (ABBR) ... BRSY
Bravado (ABBR) ... BRVDO
Brave (ABBR) ... BRV
Braved (ABBR) ... BRVD
Bravely (ABBR) ... BRVY
Braveness (ABBR) ... BRVNS
Braving (ABBR) ... BRVG
Brawled (ABBR) ... BRWLD
Brawling (ABBR) ... BRWLG
Brazed (ABBR) ... BRZD
Brazen (ABBR) ... BRZN
Brazened (ABBR) ... BRZND
Brazening (ABBR) ... BRZNG
Brazier (ABBR) ... BRZIR
Brazilian Air Force [*ICAO designator*] (FAAC) ... BRS
Brazing (ABBR) ... BRZG
Break-Lock ECM [*Electronic Countermeasures*] **Training** [*Navy*] (ANA) ... BKLKTNG
Breast (ABBR) ... BRST
Breastbone (ABBR) ... BRSTBN
Breastplate (ABBR) ... BRSTPLT
Breathe (ABBR) ... BRTH
Breathe (ABBR) ... BRTHE
Breathed (ABBR) ... BRTHD
Breathing (ABBR) ... BRTHG
Breathtaking (ABBR) ... BRTHTKG
Breeze (ABBR) ... BRZ
Breezeway (ABBR) ... BRZWY
Breezier (ABBR) ... BRZIR
Breeziest (ABBR) ... BRZST
Breeziness (ABBR) ... BRZNS
Breezy (ABBR) ... BRZY
Brenair Ltd. [*British*] [*ICAO designator*] (FAAC) ... BNX
Brencham Air Charter Ltd. [*British*] [*ICAO designator*] (FAAC) ... BRE
Brethren (ABBR) ... BRTHRN
Brevity (ABBR) ... BRVT
Brewer (ABBR) ... BRWR
Bright Annealed (DAC) ... BA
Bright Two Sides [*Lumber*] (DAC) ... B2S
Brilliant Buff Finishing [*Metal finishing*] ... BBF
Brisbane [*Australia*] ... Bris
Brisket (ABBR) ... BRSKT
Briskly (ABBR) ... BRSKY
Bristle (ABBR) ... BRSL
Bristled (ABBR) ... BRSLD
Bristling (ABBR) ... BRSLG
Bristol BAE [*British*] [*ICAO designator*] (FAAC) ... GEM
Bristol Flying Centre Ltd. [*British*] [*ICAO designator*] (FAAC) ... CLF
Bristol & Wessex Aeroplane Club Ltd. [*British*] [*ICAO designator*] (FAAC) ... FLP
Bristow Helicopters Group Ltd. [*British*] [*ICAO designator*] (FAAC) ... BHL
Bristow Masayu Helicopter PT [*Indonesia*] [*ICAO designator*] (FAAC) ... BMH
Britain-China Friendship Association (BI) ... BCFA
Britair SA [*France*] [*ICAO designator*] (FAAC) ... BZH
Britannia Airways Ltd. [*British*] [*ICAO designator*] (FAAC) ... BAL
British Acetylene Association (BI) ... BAA
British Aeromedical Practitioners Association (DA) ... BAPA
British Aerospace Air Combat Maneuvering Instrumentation Range (DA) ... BAACMIR
British Aerospace Flying College Ltd. [*ICAO designator*] (FAAC) ... AYR
British Aerospace PLC [*ICAO designator*] (FAAC) ... BAE
British Air Ferries Ltd. [*ICAO designator*] (FAAC) ... BAF
British Air Mail Society (BI) ... BAMS
British Air Transport Association (DA) ... BATA
British Airways [*ICAO designator*] (FAAC) ... BAW
British Airways Shuttle [*ICAO designator*] (FAAC) ... SHT
British Alsatian Association (BI) ... BAA
British Aluminium Building Service (BI) ... BABS
British Aluminium Foil Rollers Association (BI) ... BAFRA
British Amateur Press Association (BI) ... BAPA
British Amateur Radio Teleprinter Group (BI) ... BARTG
British Amateur Wrestling Association (BI) ... BAWA
British Architectural Students' Association (BI) ... BASA
British Aromatic Compounds Manufacturers' Association (BI) ... BACMA
British Artists' Colour Manufacturers' Association (BI) ... BACMA
British Association of Accountants and Auditors (BI) ... BAA
British Association for the Advancement of Science (BI) ... BA
British Association of Airport Equipment Manufacturers and Services (DA) ... BAAEMS
British Association of Consultants in Agriculture and Horticulture (BI) ... BACAH
British Association of Machine Tool Merchants, Inc. (BI) ... BAMTM
British Association of Meat Wholesalers Ltd. (BI) ... BAMW
British Association for Open Learning ... Baol
British Association of Overseas Furniture Removers (BI) ... BAOFR
British Association of Palestine-Israel Philatelists (BI) ... BAPIP
British Association of Physical Medicine (BI) ... BAPM
British Association of Pig Producers (BI) ... BAPP
British Association of Residential Settlements (BI) ... BARS
British Association Sovereign and Military Order of Malta (BI) ... BASMON
British Association of Sports Ground and Landscape Contractors Ltd. (BI) ... BASLC
British Association of Young Scientists (BI) ... BAYS
British Baby Carriage Manufacturers' Association (BI) ... BBCMA
British Bacon Curers' Federation (BI) ... BBCF
British Bath Manufacturers' Association Ltd. (BI) ... BBMA
British Battery Makers' Society (BI) ... BBMS
British Bee Keepers Association (BI) ... BBKA
British Bird Breeders' Association (BI) ... BBBA
British Board of Film Censors (BI) ... BBFC
British Boot, Shoe and Allied Trades Research Association (BI) ... BBSATRA
British Broiler Growers' Association (BI) ... BBGA
British Bureau of Non-Ferrous Metal Statistics (BI) ... BNFMS
British Button Manufacturers Association (BI) ... BBMA
British Camp Fire Girls (BI) ... BCFG
British-Canadian Holstein-Friesian Association (BI) ... BCHFA
British Canadian Trade Association (BI) ... BCTA
British Car Rental Association (BI) ... BCRA
British Caribbean Airways Ltd. [*ICAO designator*] (FAAC) ... BCL
British Carton Association (BI) ... BCA
British Ceramic Tile Council Ltd. (BI) ... BCTC
British Charter [*ICAO designator*] (FAAC) ... BCR
British Chemical and Dyestuffs Traders' Association (BI) ... BCDTA
British Chemical Plant Manufacturers' Association (BI) ... BCPMA
British Chess Federation (BI) ... BCF
British Chicken Association Ltd. (BI) ... BCA
British Chip Board Manufacturers' Association (BI) ... BCMA
British Circus Ring (BI) ... BCR
British Columbia Government [*Canada*] [*ICAO designator*] (FAAC) ... BCG
British Columbia Lumber Manufacturers' Association [*Canada*] (BI) ... BCLMA
British Columbia Power and Hydro Authority [*Canada*] [*ICAO designator*] (FAAC) ... BCH
British Columbia Telephone Ltd. [*Canada*] [*ICAO designator*] (FAAC) ... BCT
British Confectioners' Association (BI) ... BCA
British Cooking Industry Association (BI) ... BCIA
British Correspondence Chess Association (BI) ... BCCA
British Cotton Growing Association (BI) ... BCGA
British Council for the Promotion of International Trade (BI) ... BCPIT
British Council for Rehabilitation of the Disabled (BI) ... BCRD
British Deaf and Dumb Association (BI) ... BDDA
British Dental Students' Association (BI) ... BDSA
British Disinfectant Manufacturers' Association (BI) ... BDMA
British Display Society (BI) ... BDS
British Drag Racing Association (BI) ... BDRA
British Driving Society (BI) ... BDS

British Eastern Merchant Shippers' Association (BI)........ BEMSA
British Egg Association (BI)........ BEA
British Electro-Ceramic Manufacturers' Association (BI)........ BECMA
British Emergency Air Medical Service (DA)........ BEAMS
British Esperanto Association, Inc. (BI)........ BEA
British Essence Manufacturers' Association (BI)........ BEMA
British Exhibitors' Association (BI)........ BEA
British Farm Produce Council (BI)........ BFPC
British Federation of Aesthetics and Cosmetology (BI)........ BFAC
British Federation of Iron and Steel Stockholders (BI)........ BFISS
British Friction Materials Council (BI)........ BFMC
British Fuchsia Society (BI)........ BFS
British Furniture Manufacturers' Federated Associations (BI)........ BFM
British Gladiolus Society (BI)........ BGS
British Golf Greenkeepers' Association (BI)........ BGGA
British Guild of Flight Operations Officers (DA)........ BritGFO
British Hardware Promotion Council Ltd. (BI)........ BHPC
British Heavy Steel Association (BI)........ BHSA
British Herdsmen's Club (BI)........ BHC
British Holiday Fellowship Ltd. (BI)........ BHF
British Hotels and Restaurants Association (BI)........ BHRA
British Independent Airways [*ICAO designator*] (FAAC)........ BXH
British Institute of Dealers in Securities [*Defunct*]........ BIDS
British Institute of Hardwood Flooring Specialists (BI)........ BIHFS
British Institute of Jazz Studies (BI)........ BIJS
British Institute of Practical Psychology Ltd. (BI)........ BIPP
British International Helicopters Ltd. [*ICAO designator*] (FAAC)........ BIH
British Iron, Steel and Kindred Trades Association (BI)........ BISAKTA
British Ironfounders Association (BI)........ BIA
British Junior Chambers of Commerce (BI)........ BJCC
British Laboratory Ware Association Ltd. (BI)........ BLWA
British Lamp Blown Scientific Glassware Manufacturers' Association Ltd. (BI)........ BLSGMA
British Landrace Pig Society (BI)........ BLPS
British Leather Federation (BI)........ BLF
British Leprosy Relief Association (BI)........ BLRA
British Maize Starch and Glucose Manufacturers Association (BI)........ BMSGMA
British Malleable Tube Fittings Association (BI)........ BMTFA
British Man-Made Fibres Federation (BI)........ BMFF
British Mantle Manufacturers' Association (BI)........ BMMA
British Manufacturers' Association Ltd. (BI)........ BMA
British Mat and Matting Manufacturers Association (BI)........ BMMMA
British Medical Charter [*ICAO designator*] (FAAC)........ BMD
British Medical Representatives Association (BI)........ BMRA
British Medical Students Association (BI)........ BMSA
British Menswear Guild Ltd. (BI)........ BMG
British Midland Airways Ltd. [*ICAO designator*] (FAAC)........ BMA
British Moth Boat Association (BI)........ BMBA
British Motor Trade Association (BI)........ BMTA
British Music Hall Society (BI)........ BMHS
British Musicians' Pensions Society (BI)........ BMPS
British National Carnation Society (BI)........ BNCS
British National Committee on Surface Active Agents (BI)........ BNCSAA
British Non-Ferrous Metals Federation (BI)........ BNFMF
British Nursery Goods Association (BI)........ BNGA
British Nursing Association (BI)........ BNA
British Oil Burner Manufacturers' Association (BI)........ BOBMA
British Onion Growers' Association (BI)........ BOGA
British Overseas Mining Association (BI)........ BOMA
British Percheron Horse Society (BI)........ BPHS
British Pharmaceutical Code........ BPC
British Pharmaceutical Students' Association (BI)........ BPSA
British Philatelic Association Ltd. (BI)........ BPA
British Ploughing Association (BI)........ BPA
British Polled Hereford Society Ltd. (BI)........ BPHS
British Postal Chess Federation (BI)........ BPCF
British Precision Pilots Association (DA)........ BPPA
British Pressure Gauge Manufacturers Association (BI)........ BPGMA
British Pyrotechnists' Association (BI)........ BPA
British Rabbit Council (BI)........ BRC
British Racing Tobaggan Association (BI)........ BRTA
British Radiesthesia Association (BI)........ BRA
British Railwaymen's Touring Club (BI)........ BRTC
British Rainwear Manufacturers Federation (BI)........ BRMF
British Ready Mixed Concrete Association (BI)........ BRMCA
British Regional Television Association (BI)........ BRTA
British Rheumatism and Arthritis Association (BI)........ BRA
British Rivet Export Group (BI)........ BREG
British Road Federation Ltd. (BI)........ BRF
British Road Tar Association (BI)........ BRTA
British Roller Canary Association (BI)........ BRCA
British Roller Canary Club (BI)........ BRCC
British Rubber and Resin Adhesive Manufacturers' Association (BI)........ BRRAMA
British Sailors Society (BI)........ BSS
British Samoyed Club (BI)........ BSC
British Sanitary Fireclay Association (BI)........ BSFA
British Shipbreakers' Association (BI)........ BSA
British Shipbuilding Exports (BI)........ BSE
British Skate Makers' Association (BI)........ BSMA
British Societies Institute (BI)........ BSI
British Society of Commerce (BI)........ BSC
British Society for International Understanding (BI)........ BSIU
British Society of Master Glass Painters (BI)........ BSMGP
British Society for Research in Agricultural Engineering (BI)........ BSRAE
British Society of Stamp Journalists (BI)........ BSSJ
British Society for the Study of Orthodontics (BI)........ BSSO
British Sound Recording Association (BI)........ BSRA
British Soviet Friendship Society (BI)........ BSFS
British Speedway Promoters Association (BI)........ BSPA
British Speleological Association (BI)........ BSA
British Stationery and Office Equipment Association (BI)........ BSOEA
British Steel Export Association (BI)........ BSEA
British Stone Federation (BI)........ BSF
British Student Tuberculosis Foundation (BI)........ BSTF
British Sub-Aqua Club (BI)........ BSAC
British Sulphate of Ammonia Federation Ltd. (BI)........ BSAF
British Sulphate of Copper Association (Export) Ltd. (BI)........ BSCA
British Surgical Support Suppliers Association (BI)........ BSSSA
British Surgical Trades Association (BI)........ BSTA
British Tanning Extract Manufacturers' Association (BI)........ BTEMA
British Tarpaviors Federation Ltd. (BI)........ BTF
British Temperance Society (BI)........ BTS
British Theatre Museum (BI)........ BTM
British Tire & Rubber Co........ BTR
British Toymakers' Guild (BI)........ BTG
British Transport Staff College (BI)........ BTSC
British Travel Association (BI)........ BTA
British Tugowners Association (BI)........ BTA
British Turkey Federation Ltd. (BI)........ BTF
British Twinning and Bilingual Association (BI)........ BTBA
British Veterinary Code........ BVC
British Vigilance Association (BI)........ BVA
British Waste Paper Utilisation Council (BI)........ BWPUC
British Water Colour Society (BI)........ BWS
British Waterfowl Association (BI)........ BWA
British Weed Control Council (BI)........ BWCC
British Whiting Federation (BI)........ BWF
British Wire Rod Rollers' Association (BI)........ BWRRA
British Women's Temperance Association (BI)........ BWTA
British Woodwork Manufacturers' Association (BI)........ BWMA
British Workmen's Institute (BI)........ BWI
British Young Naturalists Association (BI)........ BYNA
Britt Airways, Inc. [*ICAO designator*] (FAAC)........ BTA
Brittle (ABBR)........ BRTL
Broad Audit Guidelines........ BAG
Broad Economic Category........ BEC
Broad Emission Line [*Spectra*]........ BEL
Broad-Line Radio Galaxy [*Astrophysics*]........ BLRG
Broad-Line Region [*Spectra*]........ BLR
Broadcast [*FCC*] (NTCM)........ B
Broadcast Advertising Producers Society of America (NTCM)........ BAPSA
Broadcast Bureau of Measurement [*FCC*] (NTCM)........ BBM
Broadcast Capital Fund, Inc. (NTCM)........ BROADCAP
Broadcast Institute of North America (NTCM)........ BINA
Broadcast Measurement Bureau (NTCM)........ BMB
Broadcast News Ltd. (NTCM)........ BNL
Broadcast News Service (NTCM)........ BNS
Broadcast Officer........ BOR
Broadcast Pioneers Educational Fund, Inc. (NTCM)........ BPEF
Broadcast Pioneer's Library (NTCM)........ BPL
Broadcast Production Officer........ BPO
Broadcast-Television Recording Engineers [*An association*] (NTCM)........ BTRE
Broadcast Television Systems Committee Recommendation [*FCC*] (NTCM)........ BTSC
Broadcaster's Foundation, Inc. (NTCM)........ BFI
Broadcasting Co. of America (NTCM)........ BCA
Broadcasting and Film Commission/National Council of the Churches of Christ in the USA (NTCM)........ BFC/NCC
Broadcasting Maintenance District........ BMD
Broadcasting Operations Recording and Information System........ BORIS
Brock Air Services Ltd. [*Canada*] [*ICAO designator*] (FAAC)........ BRD
Broken Clouds or Better [*Meteorology*] (DA)........ BCOP
Broken Cubic Meter (DAC)........ BCM
Broken Cubic Yard (DAC)........ BCY
Broken as Designed [*Computer hacker terminology*] (NHD)........ BAD
Bromma Flygskola/Cabair [*Sweden*] [*ICAO designator*] (FAAC)........ CVN
Bronchoalveolar Lavage Fluid [*Medicine*]........ BALF
Brothel (ABBR)........ BRTHL
Brotherly (ABBR)........ BRY
Brothers-in-Law (ABBR)........ BRSNLW
Browbeat (ABBR)........ BRWBT
Browbeaten (ABBR)........ BRWBTN
Browbeating (ABBR)........ BRWBTG
Brown Brothers Harriman (ECON)........ BBH
Browse (ABBR)........ BRWS
Browsed (ABBR)........ BRWSD
Browsing (ABBR)........ BRWSG
Bruise (ABBR)........ BRUS
Bruised (ABBR)........ BRUSD
Bruiser (ABBR)........ BRUSR
Bruising (ABBR)........ BRUSG
Brunei Darussalam [*Aircraft nationality and registration mark*] (FAAC)........ V8
Brunet (ABBR)........ BRUT

Brusque (ABBR) .... BRSQ
Brusquely (ABBR) .... BRSQY
Brusqueness (ABBR) .... BRSQNS
Brutal (ABBR) .... BRTL
Brutality (ABBR) .... BRTLT
Brutalize (ABBR) .... BRTLZ
Brutalized (ABBR) .... BRTLZD
Brutalizing (ABBR) .... BRTLZG
Brutally (ABBR) .... BRTLY
Brute (ABBR) .... BRT
Brutish (ABBR) .... BRTSH
Brutish (ABBR) .... BRUTH
Brutishly (ABBR) .... BRTSHY
Brutishness (ABBR) .... BRTSHNS
Bruton's Tyrosine Kinase [An enzyme] .... Btk
Brymon European Airway [British] [ICAO designator]   (FAAC) .... BRY
Budget-Funded Agency .... BFA
Budget Management System .... BMS
Budget System .... BUSY
Buffalo Airways [ICAO designator]   (FAAC) .... BVA
Buffalo Airways Ltd. [Canada] [ICAO designator]   (FAAC) .... BFL
Buffalo Express Airlines, Inc. [ICAO designator]   (FAAC) .... BRX
Build Absolutely Nothing Anywhere Near Anything [Facetious
    successor to NIMBY] .... BANANA
Builders' Benevolent Institution [British]   (BI) .... BBI
Building Advisory Service [British]   (BI) .... BAS
Building Code (DAC) .... BC
Building and Service Industry .... B & SI
Building Space Requirement (DAC) .... BSR
Built (DAC) .... Bit
Bulgarian Air Cargo [ICAO designator]   (FAAC) .... BCA
Bulgarian Lucky Flight [ICAO designator]   (FAAC) .... BLF
Bulleid Pacific Preservation Society [British]   (BI) .... BPPS
Bulletin (NTCM) .... BUN
Bulletin Board for Libraries [British] .... BUBL
Bundesamt fuer Militarflugplatze [Switzerland] [ICAO designator]
    (FAAC) .... BAMF
Bundesamt fur Militarflugplatze [Switzerland] [ICAO designator]
    (FAAC) .... SUI
Bundesaufsichtsamt fur das Kreditwesen [Federal Supervisory Office
    for Credit] [Germany] .... BAK
Bundesgrenzschutz [Germany] [ICAO designator]   (FAAC) .... BGS
Bureau of Advertising [American Newspaper Publishers Association]
    (NTCM) .... B of A
Bureau of Broadcast Measurement [Canada]   (NTCM) .... BBM
Bureau Veritas SA [France] [ICAO designator]   (FAAC) .... XDA
Bursar (ABBR) .... BRSR
Bursary (ABBR) .... BRSRY
Bursitis (ABBR) .... BRSTS
Bursting (ABBR) .... BRSTG
Burundi [Aircraft nationality and registration mark]   (FAAC) 9U
Burying (ABBR) .... BRYG
Busboy (ABBR) .... BSBY
Bushed (ABBR) .... BSHD
Bushel (ABBR) .... BSHL
Bushier (ABBR) .... BSHR
Bushiest (ABBR) .... BSHST
Bushiness (ABBR) .... BSHNS
Bushwhack (ABBR) .... BSHWHK
Bushwhacker (ABBR) .... BSHWHKR
Busily (ABBR) .... BSLY
Business (ABBR) .... BSNS
Business Air AG [Switzerland] [ICAO designator]   (FAAC) .... BUR
Business Air Ltd. [British] [ICAO designator]   (FAAC) .... GNT
Business Air Services (Toronto) Ltd. [Canada] [ICAO designator]
    (FAAC) .... BAM
Business Air Taxi [Switzerland] [ICAO designator]   (FAAC) .... BUT
Business Aviation AS [Denmark] [ICAO designator]   (FAAC) .... BUA
Business Development Group .... BDG
Business Expenditure Research and Development .... BERD
Business Express [ICAO designator]   (FAAC) .... GAA
Business Express Delivery Ltd. [Canada] [ICAO designator]   (FAAC) .... EXP
Business Flight Service [Denmark] [ICAO designator]   (FAAC) .... BSF
Business Flights Ltd. [Canada] [ICAO designator]   (FAAC) .... BFA
Business Plan System .... BPS
Business Process Re-Engineering (ECON) .... BPR
Business Start-Up Scheme [British] .... BSS
Businesslike (ABBR) .... BSNSLK
Businessman (ABBR) .... BSNSMN
Businesswoman (ABBR) .... BSNSWMN
Businesswomen (ABBR) .... BSNSWMEN
Buskin (ABBR) .... BSKN
Bustle (ABBR) .... BSTL
Bustled (ABBR) .... BSTLD
Bustling (ABBR) .... BSTLG
Busy Bee of Norway AS [ICAO designator]   (FAAC) .... BEE
Busybody (ABBR) .... BSYBDY
Busying (ABBR) .... BSYG
Butane Buzzard Aviation Corp. [British] [ICAO designator]   (FAAC) .... BZZ
Butcher (ABBR) .... BTCHR
Butchery (ABBR) .... BTCHRY
Butler (ABBR) .... BTLR
Butterfly Valve (DAC) .... BV

Buzz Word Quotient [Computer science]   (NHD) .... BWQ
Buzzworm's Earth Journal [A publication] .... Buzz E J
BW Air Services Ltd. [British] [ICAO designator]   (FAAC) .... BWO

C

C & M Aviation, Inc. [*ICAO designator*]   (FAAC) .... TIP
CAA Calibration Flight [*British*] [*ICAO designator*]   (FAAC).................... CLB
CAA Flight Examiners [*British*] [*ICAO designator*]   (FAAC)...................... EXM
CAA Flying Unit [*British*] [*ICAO designator*]   (FAAC) .... CFU
CAA Training Standards [*British*] [*ICAO designator*]   (FAAC) .... SDS
CAAA Air Martinique [*France*] [*ICAO designator*]   (FAAC) .... MTQ
Cabinet [*Technical drawings*]   (NFPA).. C
Cable Arts Foundation, Inc.   (NTCM) .... CAF
Cable FM [*Radio*]   (NTCM)... CAFM
Cable Households Using Television [*Cable television ratings*]
    (NTCM).. CHUT
Cable Makers' Association [*British*]   (BI) .... CMA
Cable/Show Cause [*FCC*]   (NTCM) .... CSC
Cable/Special Relief [*FCC*]   (NTCM) .... CSR
Cable/Special Temporary Authority [*FCC*]   (NTCM) .... CSTA
Cable Television Relay   (NTCM).. CAR
Cable Television Technical Advisory Committee [*FCC*]   (NTCM)............. CTAC
Cadaveric Donor Renal Transplantation [*Medicine*] .... CDRTx
Cadkey Object Developer [*Computer science*]............................... COD
CAI [*Compagnia Aeronautica Italiana SpA*] [*Italy*] [*ICAO
    designator*]   (FAAC).. KVY
Cairo Air Transport Co. [*Egypt*] [*ICAO designator*]   (FAAC)...................... CCE
Cal Aviation SA [*Greece*] [*ICAO designator*]   (FAAC)........................... CLV
Calcium Influx Factor [*Neurobiology*].. CIF
Calculated Estimated Time of Departure [*Aviation*]   (DA)..................... CETD
Calculated Estimated Time of Overflight [*Aviation*]   (DA) .... CETO
Calculated Time of Arrival   (DA) .... CTA
Caledonian Airways Ltd. [*British*] [*ICAO designator*]   (FAAC)................. CKT
Calf Pulmonary Artery Endthelial [*Cell line*]............................... CPAE
Calfskin [*Book cover material*]   (NTCM)...................................... CALF
California Low-Emission Vehicle [*Automotive industry*]..................... CALEV
California Ultra-Low-Emission Vehicle [*Automotive industry*]......... CALULEV
Caliop [*France*] [*ICAO designator*]   (FAAC)................................ IOP
Call for Action [*An association*]   (NTCM).................................... CFA
Calm Air [*Canada*] [*ICAO designator*]   (FAAC)............................. CAV
Cam Air Management Ltd. [*British*] [*ICAO designator*]   (FAAC) .... CMR
Cam Profile Switching [*Automotive engine design*]............................ CPS
Camargue Air Transport [*France*] [*ICAO designator*]   (FAAC)................. CMG
Camera   (ABBR)... CMRA
Cameroon [*Aircraft nationality and registration mark*]   (FAAC)................ TJ
Cameroon Airlines [*ICAO designator*]   (FAAC)............................. UYC
Camp   (ABBR) .... CMP
Camp Fire, Inc.   (AEE) .... CFI
Camping Trade Association of Great Britain Ltd.   (BI) .... CTA
Campus   (ABBR) .... CMPS
Campus-Wide Information Systems [*Internet*] .... CWIS
Canada-Transport Canada [*ICAO designator*]   (FAAC)...................... TGO
Canada West Air Ltd. [*ICAO designator*]   (FAAC) .... CWA
Canadian Airlines International Ltd. [*ICAO designator*]   (FAAC)............. CDN
Canadian Airspace Reservation Unit [*Aviation*]   (FAAC).................... CARU
Canadian Armed Forces [*ICAO designator*]   (FAAC)....................... CFC
Canadian Association of Advertising Agencies   (NTCM) .... CAAA
Canadian Association of Metal Finishers .... CAMF
Canadian Association of Poison Control Centres .... CAPCC
Canadian Coast Guard [*ICAO designator*]   (FAAC)........................ CTG
Canadian Defense Preparedness Association .... CDPA
Canadian Eagle Aviation Ltd. [*ICAO designator*]   (FAAC)................... HIA
Canadian Flight Experiment [*NASA*] .... CANEX
Canadian Forces Air Defense Command [*ICAO designator*]
    (FAAC)... CFADC
Canadian Helicopters [*ICAO designator*]   (FAAC)........................ WSR
Canadian Interagency Forest Fire Centre [*ICAO designator*]   (FAAC)........ TKR
Canadian Lumber Size   (DAC) .... CLS
Canadian NORAD Region [*Aviation*]   (FAAC) .... CANR
Canadian Radio Technical Planning Board   (NTCM)...................... CRTPB
Canadian Warplane Heritage Museum [*ICAO designator*]   (FAAC)...... CWH
Canair Cargo [*Canada*] [*ICAO designator*]   (FAAC)...................... TDR
Canal Transport Marketing Board [*British*]   (BI) .... CTMB
Canari Airlines [*Israel*] [*ICAO designator*]   (FAAC)...................... CRI
Canavaninosuccinic Acid [*Organic chemistry*]   (MAH) .... CSA
Cancelable   (ABBR).. CNCLB
Canceled   (ABBR) .... CNCLD
Canceler   (ABBR) .... CNCLR

Canceling   (ABBR)... CNCLG
Cancellation   (ABBR) .... CNCLAN
Cancellation   (ABBR) .... CNCLN
Cancer [*Constellation*] .... CAN
Cancer   (ABBR) .... CNCR
Cancer Detection Centre [*British*]... CDC
Cancer Fund of America .... CFA
Cancun Avioturismo SA [*Mexico*] [*ICAO designator*]   (FAAC)............. CAU
Cane Invert Syrup [*Food sweetener*] .... CIS
Cane Medium Invert Syrup [*Food sweetener*] .... CMIS
Canifair Aviation, Inc. [*Canada*] [*ICAO designator*]   (FAAC)............... CNF
Canoe-Camping Club [*British*]   (BI).. CCC
Canonical Correlation Analysis [*Mathematics*].............................. CCA
Canpax-Air AG [*Switzerland*] [*ICAO designator*]   (FAAC)................. CAX
Canvas   (DAC)... Can
CAP PA Gutierrez [*Hernando R.*] Ordonez [*Mexico*] [*ICAO
    designator*]   (FAAC)... ORD
Cape Central Airways, Inc. [*ICAO designator*]   (FAAC) .... SEM
Cape Smyth Air [*ICAO designator*]   (FAAC).............................. CMY
Cape Verde [*Aircraft nationality and registration mark*]   (FAAC)............ D4
Capital Air Service, Inc. [*ICAO designator*]   (FAAC)....................... CPX
Capital Airlines, Inc. [*ICAO designator*]   (FAAC)......................... CAP
Capital Aviation Services Ltd. [*Canada*] [*ICAO designator*]   (FAAC)......... VEN
Capital Guaranty Insurance .... CGI
Capital Investment Analysis [*Business term*] .... CIA
Capital Trading Aviation Ltd. [*British*] [*ICAO designator*]   (FAAC)........... EGL
Capitol Air Express [*ICAO designator*]   (FAAC)........................... CEX
Capsular Polysaccharide Complex [*Biochemistry*].......................... CPC
Capsule/Tablet [*Medicine*] .... Caplet
Capture/Compare [*Electronics*] [*Automotive engineering*] .... CAPCOM
Car and Motorcycle Drivers Association Ltd. [*British*]   (BI) .... CAMDA
Carbide-Forming Element [*Metal treating*] .... CFE
Carbon Adsorption/Absorption [*for vapor recovery*] .... CAA
Carbon-Free Medium [*Cytology*] .... CFM
Carbon Molecular Sieve [*Adsorption technology*] .... CMS
Carbonyl Value [*Food science*] CV
Carboxyamidoimidazole [*Organic chemistry*]............................... CAI
(Carboxyphenyl)benzoyl-Aminopenicillanic Acid [*Biochemistry*].............. CBAP
Card Information Structure [*Computer science*]............................. CIS
Career Development Scheme .... CDS
Career Woman [*A publication*] .... Car Wom
Careers and the Disabled [*A publication*] .... Car Dis Ab
Careers on the Move for Engineers of Tomorrow [*An association*] .... COMET
Carga Aerea Dominicana [*Dominican Republic*] [*ICAO designator*]
    (FAAC) .... CDM
Carga Aerea Venezolana Caraven SA [*Venezuela*] [*ICAO designator*]
    (FAAC) .... CCR
Cargo Agents Reservation Airwaybill Insurance and Tracking System
    (DA) .... CARAT
Cargo Dor Ltd. [*Ghana*] [*ICAO designator*]   (FAAC)..................... CDO
Cargo Information System [*Aviation*] .... CIS
Cargo & Passenger Air Services Ltd. [*Switzerland*] [*ICAO
    designator*]   (FAAC) .... CPS
Cargo & Passenger Air Services Ltd. [*Switzerland*] [*ICAO
    designator*]   (FAAC) .... CPZ
Cargolux Airline International [*Luxembourg*] [*ICAO designator*]
    (FAAC).. CLX
Cargoman [*Oman*] [*ICAO designator*]   (FAAC) .... CGM
Cargosur [*Spain*] [*ICAO designator*]   (FAAC) .... OWS
Caribbean Air Cargo [*Barbados*] [*ICAO designator*]   (FAAC)............... DCC
Caribbean Air Transport Co., Inc. [*Netherlands*] [*ICAO designator*]
    (FAAC).. CLT
Caribbean Airways [*Barbados*] [*ICAO designator*]   (FAAC) .... IQQ
Caribbean Express, Inc. [*ICAO designator*]   (FAAC)....................... TLC
Caribbean Press Association   (NTCM)...................................... CPA
Caribintair SA [*Haiti*] [*ICAO designator*]   (FAAC) .... CRT
Caribjet, Inc. [*Antigua and Barbuda*] [*ICAO designator*]   (FAAC) .... CBJ
Carlos Cervantes del Rio [*Mexico*] [*ICAO designator*]   (FAAC)............. CCD
Carlsberg Automated Meridian Circle [*Astronomy*]....................... CAMC
Carnival Air [*ICAO designator*]   (FAAC)................................. CAA
Carolina Air Transit, Inc. [*ICAO designator*]   (FAAC)..................... CTX
Carrier and Sideband   (DA).. CSB
Carroll Air Service, Inc. [*ICAO designator*]   (FAAC) .... ULS

Carroll Aircraft Corp. PLC [*British*] [*ICAO designator*] (FAAC) ... FBO
Carryover from Previous Log [*Aviation*] (FAAC) ... CFPL
Cartridge Tape (NTCM) ... CT
Cascade [*Meteorology*] (FAAC) ... CASCD
Casein Glue Manufacturers Association [*British*] (BI) ... CGMA
Casement Aviation [*ICAO designator*] (FAAC) ... CMT
Cash Flow Return on Investment ... CFROI
Caspair Ltd. [*Kenya*] [*ICAO designator*] (FAAC) ... SAL
Casper Air Service, Inc. [*ICAO designator*] (FAAC) ... CSP
Cassovia Air [*Slovakia*] [*ICAO designator*] (FAAC) ... CVI
Castle Aviation, Inc. [*ICAO designator*] (FAAC) ... CSJ
Casualty Assistance Officer [*Army*] (ADDR) ... CAO
Cat Aviation, AG [*Switzerland*] [*ICAO designator*] (FAAC) ... CAZ
Cata SACIFI [*Argentina*] [*ICAO designator*] (FAAC) ... CTZ
Catalytic Extraction Processing [*Recycling*] ... CEP
Catering Equipment Manufacturers' Association [*British*] (BI) ... CEMA
Catering Managers Association of Great Britain and Northern Ireland (BI) ... CMA
Caterpillar Micro Oxidation Test [*Automotive lubricant*] ... CMOT
Catex Compagnie [*France*] [*ICAO designator*] (FAAC) ... TEX
Cathay Pacific Airways Ltd. [*British*] [*ICAO designator*] (FAAC) ... CPA
Cathode Current Efficiency [*Electrochemistry*] ... CCE
Cathode Electrodeposited Paint [*Environmental science*] ... CEP
Catholic Apostolate of Radio, Television, and Advertising (NTCM) ... CARTA
Catholic Communications Foundation (NTCM) ... CCF
Catholic Truth Society [*British*] (BI) ... CTS
Catholic Young Men's Society [*Ireland*] (BI) ... CYMS
Catwalk [*Technical drawings*] (DAC) ... CATW
Caulking Seam (DAC) ... CS
Causeway Section, Nonpowered [*Navy*] (ANA) ... CSNP
Cave Research Group of Great Britain (BI) ... CRG
Cavei Avir Lemitanim [*Israel*] [*ICAO designator*] (FAAC) ... ICL
Cayman Airways Ltd. [*British*] [*ICAO designator*] (FAAC) ... CAY
CB Exective Helicopters [*British*] [*ICAO designator*] (FAAC) ... CBH
CCAir, Inc. [*ICAO designator*] (FAAC) ... CDL
Cecil Aviation Ltd. [*ICAO designator*] (FAAC) ... CIL
Ceeta-Kel Air [*France*] [*ICAO designator*] (FAAC) ... CET
Cefi Aviation SRL [*Italy*] [*ICAO designator*] (FAAC) ... IFC
Cega Aviation Ltd. [*British*] [*ICAO designator*] (FAAC) ... CEG
Ceiling (DA) ... CIG
Ceiling Grille [*Technical drawings*] (DAC) ... CG
Celiac Disease Foundation (EA) ... CDF
Celmar Servicios Aereos SA de CV [*Mexico*] [*ICAO designator*] (FAAC) ... CER
Celtic Inernational Ltd. [*British*] [*ICAO designator*] (FAAC) ... CIC
Cement-Asbestos Board (DAC) ... CAB
Cement-Asbestos Board (DAC) ... Cem Ab
Cement Finish (DAC) ... Cem Fin
Cement Floor [*Technical drawings*] (DAC) ... Cem Fl
Cement Mortar [*Technical drawings*] (DAC) ... Cem Mort
Cement Plaster [*Technical drawings*] (DAC) ... Cem Plas
Cemetery (ABBR) ... CMTRY
Ceneast Airlines Ltd. [*Kenya*] [*ICAO designator*] (FAAC) ... CEL
Census of Graduate Medical Trainees ... CGMT
Centennial [*Spain*] [*ICAO designator*] (FAAC) ... CNA
Centennial Airlines, Inc. [*ICAO designator*] (FAAC) ... CNL
Centennial Flight Centre [*Canada*] [*ICAO designator*] (FAAC) ... CNS
Center for Advanced Heart Research ... CAHR
Center for Advanced Television Studies [*British*] (NTCM) ... CATS
Center Beam One Side [*Lumber*] (DAC) ... CB1S
Center Beam Two Sides [*Lumber*] (DAC) ... CB2S
Center for Devices and Radiological Health [*FDA*] ... CDRH
Center of Effort [*Sailing*] ... CE
Center Groove Two Edges [*Lumber*] (DAC) ... CG2E
Center for International Forestry Research ... CIFOR
Center Light [*Aviation*] (DA) ... C/L
Center for Living Democracy (EA) ... CLD
Center for Produce Quality ... CPQ
Center for Public Integrity ... CPI
Center for the Study of Beadwork [*An association*] (EA) ... CSB
Center Vee One Side [*Lumber*] (DAC) ... CV1S
Center Vee Two Sides [*Lumber*] (DAC) ... CV2S
Centerline Light [*Aviation*] (DA) ... CL
Centerline Lighting Will be Provided [*Aviation*] (DA) ... CLL
Centers for Education and Research in Therapeutics [*FDA*] ... CERT
Centigray (ADDR) ... CGY
Central Airlines, Inc. [*ICAO designator*] (FAAC) ... CTL
Central Airways Corp. [*Canada*] [*ICAO designator*] (FAAC) ... CEN
Central Association of Irish Schoolmistresses (BI) ... CAISM
Central Aviation, Inc. [*ICAO designator*] (FAAC) ... YOG
Central Control Function [*Aviation*] (DA) ... CCF
Central Council for British Naturism (BI) ... CCBN
Central Database System (DA) ... CDBS
Central Development Unit ... CDU
Central and Eastern Europe ... CEE
Central Economic Zone ... CEZ
Central European Airlines [*Czechoslovakia*] [*ICAO designator*] (FAAC) ... CMA
Central Executive Unit (DA) ... CEU
Central Forecast Office (DA) ... CFO
Central Instrument Warning System [*Aviation*] (DA) ... CIWS
Central Mountain Air Ltd. [*Canada*] [*ICAO designator*] (FAAC) ... GLR
Central North Pacific [*Aviation*] (FAAC) ... CENPAC
Central Provident Fund [*Singapore*] (ECON) ... CPF
Central Purchasing Organization ... CPO
Central Skyport, Inc. [*ICAO designator*] (FAAC) ... CSI
Centrale de Livraison de Valeurs Mobilieres ... CEDEL
Centralized or Distributed Integrated Access Control [*Computer science*] ... CODIAC
Centralized Flow Management Unit (DA) ... CFMU
Centralized Lighting System [*Automotive engineering*] ... CLS
Centralized Lubrication [*Automotive engineering*] ... CL
Centre Airlines, Inc. [*ICAO designator*] (FAAC) ... DTV
Centre d'Essaies Vehicule Automobile [*Motor Vehicle Test Center*] [*French*] ... CEVA
Centre d'Essais en Vol [*France*] [*ICAO designator*] (FAAC) ... CEV
Centre d'Etude du Polymorphisme Humain [*Medicine*] (ECON) ... CEPH
Centre International d'Enseignement Superieur de Journalisme [*UNESCO*] (NTCM) ... CIESJ
Centre National d'Etudes des Telecommunications [*France*] [*ICAO designator*] (FAAC) ... CNET
Centre National d'Etudes des Telecommunications [*France*] [*ICAO designator*] (FAAC) ... CNT
Centreboard Factor [*IOR*] ... CBF
Centro Gerontologico Latino [*An association*] (EA) ... CGL
Ceramic Matrix Composite [*Materials science*] ... CMC
Certificate of Compliance [*FCC*] (NTCM) ... COC
Certificate of Exemption ... C of E
Certificate of Experience (DA) ... C of E
Certificate of General Education ... CGE
Certificate of Occupancy (DAC) ... CO
Certificate of Participation ... COP
Certification Short Test [*Exhaust emissions testing*] [*Automotive engineering*] ... CST
Certified Aircraft Dispatch, Inc. [*ICAO designator*] (FAAC) ... XAD
Certified Engineering Geologist [*Environmental science*] ... CEG
Certified Engineering Technologist [*Environmental science*] ... CET
Certified Environmental Auditor [*Environmental science*] ... CEA
Certified Environmental Professional [*Environmental science*] ... CEP
Certified Environmental Trainer ... CET
Certified Hazardous Materials Manager [*Environmental science*] ... CHMM
Certified Legal Assistant ... CLA
Certified Professional Geologist ... CPG
Certified Professional Soil Scientist [*Environmental science*] ... CPSS
Certified Radio Marketing Consultant (NTCM) ... CRMC
Certified Registered Nurse of Infusion ... CRNI
Certified Security and Safety Professional [*Environmental science*] ... CSSP
Ceskoslovenske Aerolinie [*Czechoslovakia*] [*ICAO designator*] (FAAC) ... CSA
Cetfa SA [*Spain*] [*ICAO designator*] (FAAC) ... CTF
Chaillotine Air Service [*France*] [*ICAO designator*] (FAAC) ... CIS
Chain of Custody ... COC
Chain Testers Association of Great Britain (BI) ... CTA
Chair Frame Manufacturers' Association [*British*] (BI) ... CFMA
Chalk Quarrying Association [*British*] (BI) ... CQA
Challenge Air Cargo, Inc. [*ICAO designator*] (FAAC) ... CWC
Challenge Air Transport, Inc. [*ICAO designator*] (FAAC) ... OFF
Challenge Aviation Pty Ltd. [*Australia*] [*ICAO designator*] (FAAC) ... CHS
Challenge Handshake Authentication Protocol [*Telecommunications*] (PCM) ... CHAP
Chambre de Compensation des Instruments Financiers de Paris ... CCIFP
Champagne-Mumm Admiral's Cup [*Yacht racing*] ... C-MAC
Championship Drivers Licensing Group [*Automobile racing*] ... CDLG
Champlain Enterprises, Inc. [*ICAO designator*] (FAAC) ... UCA
CHAMPUS [*Civilian Health and Medical of the Uniformed Services*] **Regional Review System** ... CRRS
Changchu International Symposium on Analytical Chemistry [*1990*] ... CISAC
Changeover [*Aviation*] (FAAC) ... CHOV
Channel Aviation Ltd. [*British*] [*ICAO designator*] (FAAC) ... GID
Channel Express (Air Services) Ltd. [*British*] [*ICAO designator*] (FAAC) ... EXS
Channel Handicap System [*Yacht racing*] ... CHS
Channel Island Aviation [*ICAO designator*] (FAAC) ... CHN
Chaparral Airlines [*ICAO designator*] (FAAC) ... CPL
Character-to-Date [*Microsoft Corp. FoxPro function*] (PCM) ... CTOD
Charcoal [*Automotive advertising*] ... CH
Chartair, Inc. [*ICAO designator*] (FAAC) ... SJN
Chartered Auctioneers' and Estate Agents' Institute [*British*] (BI) ... CAEAI
Chartered Institute of Loss Adjusters [*British*] (BI) ... CILA
Chartered Institute of Patent Agents [*British*] (BI) ... CIPA
Chartered Institute of Secretaries [*British*] (BI) ... CIS
Chauffair Ltd. [*British*] [*ICAO designator*] (FAAC) ... CFR
Chautauqua Airlines [*ICAO designator*] (FAAC) ... CHQ
Checkwriting Redemptions [*Business term*] ... CWR
Chemical (NFPA) ... C
Chemical Biological Defense Agency [*Army*] ... CBDA
Chemical Collection/Request Tracking System [*Environmental Protection Agency*] (ERG) ... CC/RTS
Chemical Education Material Study [*American Chemical Society*] (AEE) ... CHEMS
Chemical Hazards Response Information System/Hazard Assessment Computer System [*Coast Guard*] (ERG) ... CHRIS/HACS
Chemical List Index and Processing System [*Environmental Protection Agency*] (ERG) ... CLIPS

Chemical Network [*Chemical Transportation Emergency Center*] (ERG) .... CHEMNET
Chemical Neutron Activation Analysis .... CNAA
Chemical Reaction Interface Mass Spectrometry .... CRIMS
Chemists' Defence Association [*British*] (BI) .... CDA
Chemonucleolysis [*Surgery*] .... CNL
Cherokee Leasing, Inc. [*ICAO designator*] (FAAC) .... CBM
Chesapeake Air Services [*ICAO designator*] (FAAC) .... CAB
Cheshire Air Training School [*British*] [*ICAO designator*] (FAAC) .... CHZ
Chess Life [*A publication*] .... Chess L
Chest and Heart Association [*British*] (BI) .... CHA
Cheyenne Airways, Inc. [*ICAO designator*] (FAAC) .... CYA
Chicago Air, Inc. [*ICAO designator*] (FAAC) .... CGO
Chief State School Officer (AEE) .... CSSO
Chieftain Airways PLC [*British*] [*ICAO designator*] (FAAC) .... PQC
Chieftain Aviation PC [*South Africa*] [*ICAO designator*] (FAAC) .... LNP
Chilchota Taxi Aereo SA de CV [*Mexico*] [*ICAO designator*] (FAAC) .... CCH
Chilcotin Caribou Aviation [*Canada*] [*ICAO designator*] (FAAC) .... DES
Child Care Assistance .... CCA
Child Health Assessment Program .... CHAP
Child Poverty Action Group [*British*] (BI) .... CPAG
Child Restraint and Air Bag Information [*Automotive safety*] .... CRABI
Child Safety Seat Questionnaire [*Auto safety research*] .... CSSQ
Child Service Demonstration Center [*Department of Education*] .... CSDC
Children's Alliance for Protection of the Environment (EA) .... CAPE
Childrens Fashion Group [*British*] (BI) .... CFG
Children's Film Foundation Ltd. [*British*] (BI) .... CFF
Children's Heart Fund (EA) .... CHF
Children's Medical Research .... CMR
Children's Miracle Network [*Medicine*] .... CMN
Children's Miracle Network Television .... CMNT
Children's Play Activities Ltd. [*British*] (BI) .... CPA
Children's Radio Network (NTCM) .... CRN
Children's Relief International [*British*] (BI) .... CRI
Chilliwack Aviation Ltd. [*Canada*] [*ICAO designator*] (FAAC) .... CAD
Chiltern Airways [*British*] [*ICAO designator*] (FAAC) .... CHA
Chimney [*Technical drawings*] (DAC) .... Chim
China Air Cargo [*ICAO designator*] (FAAC) .... CHY
China Airlines [*Taiwan*] [*ICAO designator*] (FAAC) .... CAL
China Eastern Airlines [*ICAO designator*] (FAAC) .... CES
China General Aviation Corp. [*ICAO designator*] (FAAC) .... CGAC
China General Aviation Corp. [*ICAO designator*] (FAAC) .... CTH
China Northwest Airlines [*ICAO designator*] (FAAC) .... CNW
China Ocean Helicopter Corp. [*ICAO designator*] (FAAC) .... CHC
China Ocean Helicopter Corp. [*ICAO designator*] (FAAC) .... COHC
China Review International .... Ch Rev Int
China Southwest Airlines [*ICAO designator*] (FAAC) .... CXN
China Today [*A publication*] .... China T
China Travel Service (ECON) .... CTS
China United Airlines [*ICAO designator*] (FAAC) .... CUA
Chinchilla Fur Breeders' Association [*British*] (BI) .... CFBA
Chinchilla Pelt Marketing Association Ltd. [*British*] (BI) .... CPMA
Chinese American Arts Council (EA) .... CAAC
Chippewa Air Commuter, Inc. [*ICAO designator*] (FAAC) .... CPW
Chivenor FTU [*British*] [*ICAO designator*] (FAAC) .... CHV
Chloraromatic Compound [*Organic chemistry*] .... CAP
Chlorinated Aromatic Compound [*Organic chemistry*] .... CAC
Cholesterol Esters [*Organic chemistry*] (MAH) .... CHOL E
Chorus Object-Oriented Layer [*Computer science*] .... COOL
Christadelphian Auxiliary Lecturing Society [*British*] (BI) .... CALS
Christian Alliance of Women and Girls [*British*] (BI) .... CAWG
Christian Book Distributors [*An association*] .... CBD
Christian Democrats [*European political movement*] (ECON) .... CD
Christian Film Distributors Association (NTCM) .... CFDA
Christian Friends of Israel [*British*] .... CFI
Christian Leaders for Responsible Television (NTCM) .... CLeaR-TV
Christian League for the Handicapped (EA) .... CLH
Christian-Muslim Dialogue Committee (EA) .... CMDC
Christian Road Safety League [*British*] (BI) .... CRSL
Christman Air System [*ICAO designator*] (FAAC) .... CAS
Christmas Island Services Corp. .... CISC
Chroma-Time Compressed Multiplex (NTCM) .... CTCM
Chromaffin Granule Amine Transporter [*Biochemistry*] .... CGAT
Chrysler Collision Detection [*Automotive safety and electronics*] C2D
CHS Aviation Ltd. [*Kenya*] [*ICAO designator*] (FAAC) .... HSA
Church Aircraft Ltd. [*ICAO designator*] (FAAC) .... CHU
Church of England Youth Council (BI) .... CEYC
Church Literature Association [*British*] (BI) .... CLA
Church Music Trust [*British*] (BI) .... CMT
Church Schools Company Ltd. [*British*] (BI) .... CSC
Ciga Hotels Aviation SpA [*Italy*] [*ICAO designator*] (FAAC) .... CHO
Ciguatoxin [*Agent in fish poisoning*] .... CTX
Cimber Air, Sonderjyllands Flyveselskab [*Denmark*] [*ICAO designator*] (FAAC) .... DQI
Cimex [*Genus of microorganisms*] (MAH) C
Cinema (NTCM) .... CINE
Circling Guidance Light [*Aviation*] (FAAC) .... CGL
Circuit Breaker (NTCM) .... BKR
Circuit Breaker [*Technical drawings*] (DAC) .... CIR BKR
Circular Mail .... CM
Circulation (NTCM) .... CIR
Cirrus Air, Inc. [*ICAO designator*] (FAAC) .... NTS

Cis-Air [*Czechoslovakia*] [*ICAO designator*] (FAAC) .... CSR
Ciskei International Airways Corp. [*South Africa*] [*ICAO designator*] (FAAC) .... COK
Citibank NA [*ICAO designator*] (FAAC) XCX
Citizens Against Rationing Health [*An association*] .... CARH
Citizens for Cable Awareness (NTCM) .... CCA
Citizens Communication Center (NTCM) CCC
Citizens Democracy Corps [*An association*] (EA) .... CDC
Citty Taxi Aereo Nacional SA de CV [*Mexico*] [*ICAO designator*] (FAAC) .... CCT
City Air Ltd. [*British*] [*ICAO designator*] (FAAC) .... ISY
City-Jet Luftverklerhsges, GmbH [*Austria*] [*ICAO designator*] (FAAC) .... CIT
City-Link Airlines Ltd. [*Nigeria*] [*ICAO designator*] (FAAC) .... CRG
Cityflyer Express [*British*] [*ICAO designator*] (FAAC) .... CFE
Civic Catering Association [*British*] (BI) .... CCA
Civic Entertainment Officers' Association [*British*] (BI) .... CEOA
Civil Aircraft Inspection Procedure (DA) .... CAIP
Civil Aviation Authority of New Zealand [*ICAO designator*] (FAAC) CIV
Civil Aviation Inspectorate of the Czech Republic [*ICAO designator*] (FAAC) .... CBA
Civil Aviation Order .... CAO
Civil Aviation Packet Switching Integrated Network (DA) .... CAPSIN
Civil Aviation Purchasing Service [*ICAO*] (DA) .... CAPS
Civil Disobedience .... CD
Civil Mediator Organisation [*British*] (DA) .... CASOR
Civil Service Motoring Association [*British*] (BI) .... CSMA
Civil Tilt Rotor [*Aviation*] (DA) .... CTR
Clapham Notre Dame Association [*British*] (BI) .... CNDA
Clark Aviation Corp. [*ICAO designator*] (FAAC) .... CLK
Class A Airspace [*Aviation*] (FAAC) .... CAAS
Class B Airspace [*Aviation*] (FAAC) .... CBAS
Class B Surface Area [*Aviation*] (FAAC) .... CBSA
Class C Airspace [*Aviation*] (FAAC) .... CCAS
Class C Surface Area [*Aviation*] (FAAC) .... CCSA
Class D Airspace [*Aviation*] (FAAC) .... CDAS
Class D Surface Area [*Aviation*] (FAAC) .... CDSA
Class E Airspace [*Aviation*] (FAAC) .... CEAS
Class E Surface Area [*Aviation*] (FAAC) .... CESA
Class G Airspace [*Aviation*] (FAAC) .... CGAS
Classic Air AG [*Switzerland*] [*ICAO designator*] (FAAC) CLC
Classical Swine Fever Virus .... CSFV
Classification and Classified List of Occupations .... CCLO
Classification, Hazard Information and Packaging [*British*] .... CHIP
Classification, Packaging and Labelling [*Toxicology*] .... CPL
Clean Shelter Area [*Army*] (ADDR) .... CSA
Cleansing Officers' Guild [*British*] (BI) .... COG
Clear Ice [*Aviation*] (DA) .... CLA
Clearance Void if Not Off [*Aviation*] (FAAC) .... CVINO
Clerical Administration .... CLAD
Clerk of the Works (DAC) .... C/W
Cleveland Graphite [*American Cleveland Graphite Corp.*] [*Automotive parts supplier*] .... CLEVITE
Client Liaison Officer .... CLO
Climate Control International [*Auto industry supplier*] CCI
Climb [*or Climbing*] [*Aviation*] (FAAC) .... CMB
Climb at Pilot's Discretion [*Aviation*] (FAAC) .... CAPD
Clinical Gene Therapy Branch .... CGTB
Clinical Global Impression of Change .... CGIC
Closed Circuit Radio Transmitter (NTCM) .... CCRT
Cloud Point [*Petroleum characteristic*] .... CP
Club Air Europe Ltd. [*British*] [*ICAO designator*] (FAAC) .... CLU
Club Cricket Conference [*British*] (BI) CCC
Club & Institute Union Ltd. [*British*] (BI) .... CIU
Clyde Surveys Ltd. [*British*] [*ICAO designator*] (FAAC) .... CLY
Cneius (ABBR) .... CN
Co-Channel Interference (NTCM) CCI
Coal Development Establishment [*British*] (BI) .... CDE
Coal Industry Society [*British*] (BI) .... CIS
Coal Tar Research Association [*British*] (BI) .... CTRA
Coalition for Auto Repair Equality [*Automotive aftermarket parts lobbying group*] .... CARE
Coalition for Consumer Health and Safety (EA) .... CCHS
Coalition for Harmony of Races in the US (EA) .... CHORUS
Coalition for Life for All Mollusks .... CLAM
Coalition of Minority Policy Professionals (EA) .... CoMPP
Coarse Grain (DAC) .... CG
Coast Air KS [*Norway*] [*ICAO designator*] (FAAC) .... CST
Coast Air Ltd. [*Kenya*] [*ICAO designator*] (FAAC) .... CQA
Coast Guard Assistance Instruction Data .... COGAID
Coast Guard Combat Veterans Association (EA) .... CGCVA
Coastair [*Denmark*] [*ICAO designator*] (FAAC) .... CSX
Coastal Air Transport [*St. Croix*] [*ICAO designator*] (FAAC) .... CXT
Coastal Airways [*ICAO designator*] (FAAC) .... CNG
Coastal Confluence Zone [*Aviation*] (DA) .... CCZ
Coated Abrasive Manufacturers' Association [*British*] (BI) .... CAMA
Coating Ageing-Resistant Aluminum Technology [*Materials science*] .... CARAT
Coaxial Cable Information System (NTCM) .... CCIS
Cocesna [*ICAO designator*] (FAAC) .... COC
Cochleare Amplum [*Heaping spoonful*] [*Pharmacy*] (MAH) .... COCHL AMP
Code Fragment Manager [*Computer science*] .... CFM
Coefficient of Friction .... COF

Coefficient of Induced Drag [*Aviation*] (DA) ... C!Di
Coefficient of Linear Thermal Expansion ... CLTE
Coefficient of Profile Drag [*Aviation*] (DA) ... C!Dp
Coefficient Z-Axis [*Downforce on a racing car*] [*Aerodynamics*] ... CZ
Cohlmia Aviation [*ICAO designator*] (FAAC) ... CHL
Coin World [*A publication*] ... Coin W
Coke Oven Managers' Association [*British*] (BI) ... COMA
Cold-Shock Domain [*Genetics*] ... CSD
Cold Temperature Carbon Monoxide Test Procedure [*Exhaust emissions testing*] [*Automotive engineering*] ... CTCOTP
[*Charles J.*] **Colgan & Associates, Inc.** [*ICAO designator*] (FAAC) ... CJC
Collagen-Induced Arthritis [*Medicine*] ... CIA
Collapsible Tube Manufacturers' Association [*British*] (BI) ... CTMA
Collector of Public Moneys ... CPM
College of Estate Management [*British*] (BI) ... CEM
College of General Practitioners [*British*] (BI) ... CGP
Collegium International Neuro-Psychopharmacologicum ... CINP
Collingwood Air Services Ltd. [*Canada*] [*ICAO designator*] (FAAC) ... BLE
Collins Motor Corp. [*Alternative engine technology*] ... CMC
Collision Risk Model [*Aviation*] (DA) ... CRM
Colloidal Array Filters [*for LASER applications*] ... CAF
Colo-Rectal Surgical Society ... CRSS
Colonial, Fish-Eating Water Bird ... CFEWB
Color Pigments Manufacturing Association ... CPMA
Color Reversal Intermediate [*Photography*] (NTCM) ... CRI
Color Temperature (NTCM) ... CT
Colour Users' Association [*British*] (BI) ... CUA
Coloured Workers' Welfare Association [*British*] (BI) ... CWWA
Colt Car Co. [*British*] [*ICAO designator*] (FAAC) ... CEA
Columbia [*Italy*] [*ICAO designator*] (FAAC) ... CLA
Columbia Airlines Ltd. [*Canada*] [*ICAO designator*] (FAAC) ... COL
Columbia Helicopters, Inc. [*ICAO designator*] (FAAC) ... WCO
Columbus Air Transport, Inc. [*ICAO designator*] (FAAC) ... KLR
Colvin Aviation, Inc. [*ICAO designator*] (FAAC) ... NVE
Comair, Inc. [*ICAO designator*] (FAAC) ... COM
Combat Stress Reaction [*Army*] (ADDR) ... CSR
Combat Systems Mobile Training Team [*Navy*] (ANA) ... CSMTT
Combat Systems Post-Overhaul Examination [*Navy*] (ANA) ... CSPOE
Combat Visual Information Support Center [*DoD*] ... CVISC
Combatant Command [*Military*] ... COCOM
Combination and Dissemination of Experiment Data System [*Army*] (RDA) ... CADEX
Combined Training Exercise [*Military*] (ADDR) ... CTX
Combustion Control by Vortex Stratification [*Automotive engine design*] ... CCVS
Comercial Aerea SA de CV [*Mexico*] [*ICAO designator*] (FAAC) ... CRS
Comic Book Retailers International [*An association*] (EA) ... CBRI
Comite International de La Croix-Rouge [*Switzerland*] [*ICAO designator*] (FAAC) ... RED
Command Airways [*South Africa*] [*ICAO designator*] (FAAC) ... CAH
Command, Control, Communications and Intelligence Acquisition Center [*Army*] (RDA) ... C3IAC
Command Inspection Program [*Army*] (INF) ... CIP
Command Power Cruise Control [*Diesel engines*] [*Automotive engineering*] ... CPCC
Commandement du Transport Aerien Militaire Francais [*France*] [*ICAO designator*] (FAAC) ... CTM
Commander Air Carter Ltd. [*Canada*] [*ICAO designator*] (FAAC) ... CML
Commander, Allied Forces Southern Norway [*Navy*] (ANA) ... COMSONOR
Commander, Maritime Prepositioned Force [*Navy*] (ANA) ... CMPF
Commander Mexicana SA de CV [*Mexico*] [*ICAO designator*] (FAAC) ... CRM
Commander, Special Operating Forces Central Command [*Navy*] (ANA) ... COMSOCCENT
Commander, US Naval Forces Central Command (ANA) ... COMUSNAVCENT
Commander's Critical Information Requirement [*Army*] (INF) ... CCIR
Commanders' Target Criteria [*Army*] (ADDR) ... CTC
Commerce (ABBR) ... CMRC
Commercial [*FCC*] (NTCM) ... C
Commercial (ABBR) ... CMRCL
Commercial Air Transport (DA) ... CAT
Commercial Announcement (NTCM) ... CA
Commercial Continuity [*Broadcasting*] (NTCM) ... CC
Commercial Rabbit Association [*British*] (BI) ... CRA
Commercial Sex Worker [*Social science terminology for a prostitute*] ... CSW
Commercial Television [*FCC*] (NTCM) ... CT
Commercial Vehicle Operations [*Highway safety*] ... CVO
Commercial Vehicle and Road Transport Club [*British*] (BI) ... CVRTC
Commercialism (ABBR) ... CMRCLSM
Commercialist (ABBR) ... CMRCLST
Commercialistic (ABBR) ... CMRCLSTC
Commercialize (ABBR) ... CMRCLZ
Commercialized (ABBR) ... CMRCLZD
Commercializing (ABBR) ... CMRCLZG
Commericial Air Services (Pty) Ltd. [*South Africa*] [*ICAO designator*] (FAAC) ... CAW
Commiserate (ABBR) ... CMSRA
Commiserated (ABBR) ... CMSRAD
Commiserating (ABBR) ... CMSRAG
Commiseration (ABBR) ... CMSRAN
Commiserative (ABBR) ... CMSRAV
Commiseratively (ABBR) ... CMSRAVY
Commiserator (ABBR) ... CMSRAR
Commissar (ABBR) ... CMSAR
Commissar (ABBR) ... CMSR
Commissary (ABBR) ... CMSARY
Commissary (ABBR) ... CMSRY
Commission (ABBR) ... CMSSN
Commission for Historical Architectural Preservation ... CHAP
Commission des Operations de Bourse ... COB
Commissional (ABBR) ... CMSNL
Commissionary (ABBR) ... CMSNY
Commissione Nazionale per le Societa e la Borsa ... CONSOB
Commissioned (DA) ... COMSND
Commissioner (ABBR) ... CMSSNR
Commissioning (ABBR) ... CMSNG
Commited (ABBR) ... CMTD
Commiting (ABBR) ... CMTG
Commitment (ABBR) ... CMTMT
Committee for Action for Rural Indians (EA) ... CARI
Committee on Aircraft Engine Emissions [*ICAO*] (DA) ... CAEE
Committee on Aircraft Noise [*ICAO*] (DA) ... CAN
Committee on Carcinogenicity [*British*] ... COC
Committee on Children's Television, Inc. (NTCM) ... CCTI
Committee for Competitive Television (NTCM) ... CCT
Committee for Crescent Observation International (EA) ... CCOI
Committee to End the Marion Lockdown (EA) ... CEML
Committee on Local Radio Audience Measurement [*National Association of Broadcasters*] (NTCM) ... COLRAM
Committee on Local Television Audience Measurement [*National Association of Broadcasters*] (NTCM) ... COLTAM
Committee on Mutagenicity [*British*] ... COM
Committee for the National Institute for the Environment [*Lobby group*] ... CNIE
Committee on Nationwide Television Audience Measurement (NTCM) ... CONTAM
Committee for an Open Archives (EA) ... COA
Committee on the Peaceful Uses of Outer Space [*United Nations*] (NTCM) ... CUPUOS
Committee of the Regions [*Belgium*] (ECON) ... COR
Committee on Women in Public Relations (NTCM) ... CWPR
Commodore Aviation [*Australia*] [*ICAO designator*] (FAAC) ... GAR
Commodore Training [*Computer science*] ... COMTRAIN
Common Carrier [*FCC*] (NTCM) ... C
Common Chassis Advanced Technology Transition Demonstrator ... CCATTD
Common-Midpoint ... CMP
Common Object Model [*Microsoft*] ... COM
Common Task Training [*Military*] (ADDR) ... CTT
Commonwealth Advisory Aeronautical Research Council (BI) ... CAARC
Commonwealth Air Transport Council (BI) ... CATC
Commonwealth Broadcasting Network [*British*] (NTCM) ... CBN
Commonwealth Bureau of Helminthology (BI) ... CBH
Commonwealth Correspondents' Association (BI) ... CCA
Commonwealth Jet Services, Inc. [*ICAO designator*] (FAAC) ... CJS
Commonwealth Writers of Britain (BI) ... CWB
Commune (ABBR) ... CMUN
Communed (ABBR) ... CMUND
Communicability (ABBR) ... CMUNCBT
Communicable (ABBR) ... CMUNCB
Communicableness (ABBR) ... CMUNCBNS
Communicably (ABBR) ... CMUNCBY
Communicant (ABBR) ... CMUNCNT
Communicate (ABBR) ... CMUNC
Communicated (ABBR) ... CMUNCD
Communicating (ABBR) ... CMUNCG
Communication (ABBR) ... CMUNCN
Communication Navigation (NFPA) ... CNI
[*Fire Alarm Voice*] **Communication Panel** [*NFPA pre-fire planning symbol*] (NFPA) ... CP
Communications and Data Processing Exposition ... COMDEX
Communications and Information Services - Communications ... CIS-COMMS
Communications Port [*Computer science*] ... COM
Communicative (ABBR) ... CMUNCV
Communicatively (ABBR) ... CMUNCVY
Communicatory (ABBR) ... CMUNCY
Communing (ABBR) ... CMUNG
Communion (ABBR) ... CMUNN
Communique (ABBR) ... CMUNG
Communism (ABBR) ... CMUNSM
Communist (ABBR) ... CMUNST
Communistic (ABBR) ... CMUNSTC
Community (ABBR) ... CMUNT
Community Aerodrome Radio Station (DA) ... CARS
Community Development Bank ... CDB
Community Legal Aid ... CLA
Community Program for Clinical Research on AIDS [*FDA*] ... CPCRA
Community Research Bureau ... CRB
Community Service Obligation ... CSO
Communization (ABBR) ... CMUNZN
Communize (ABBR) ... CMUNZ
Communized (ABBR) ... CMUNZD
Communizing (ABBR) ... CMUNZG
Commutability (ABBR) ... CMUTABT
Commutable (ABBR) ... CMUTAB
Commutate (ABBR) ... CMUTA

Commutated (ABBR) ... CMUTAD
Commutating (ABBR) ... CMUTAG
Commutative (ABBR) ... CMUTAV
Commutator (ABBR) ... CMUTAR
Commute (ABBR) ... CMUT
Commuted (ABBR) ... CMUTD
Commuter (ABBR) ... CMUTR
Commuting (ABBR) ... CMUTG
Compact Disc and Cathode Ray Tube Applied Format [Automotive navigation systems] ... CDCRAFT
Compact Disc File Manager [Computer science] (NTCM) ... CD-FM
Compact Fluorescent Light ... CFL
Compact Helicopter Approach Path Indicator (DA) ... CHAPI
Compagnia Aeronautica Italiana SPA [Italy] [ICAO designator] (FAAC) ... CAI
Compagnie Aerienne du Languedoc [France] [ICAO designator] (FAAC) ... LGD
Compagnie Aeronautique Europeene [France] [ICAO designator] (FAAC) ... FEU
Compagnie des Agents de Change ... CAC
Compagnie Air Mediterrannee [France] [ICAO designator] (FAAC) ... MDT
Compagnie de Bauxites de Guinee [Guinea] [ICAO designator] (FAAC) ... GIC
Compagnie Francaise pour l'Assurance du Commerce Exterieur ... COFACE
Compagnie Nationale Air Gabon [ICAO designator] (FAAC) ... AGN
Compagnie Nationale Naganagani [Burkina Faso] [ICAO designator] (FAAC) ... BFN
Compagnie de Transport Aerien [Switzerland] [ICAO designator] (FAAC) ... CTA
Compania Aerea de Servicios Tur Air [Spain] [ICAO designator] (FAAC) ... TUU
Compania Aerea del Sur SA [Uruguay] [ICAO designator] (FAAC) ... ASU
Compania Aero Transportes Panamenos SA [Panama] [ICAO designator] (FAAC) ... AEP
Compania Aerotecnicas Fotograficas [Spain] [ICAO designator] (FAAC) ... ATF
Compania de Aviacion Faucett SA [Peru] [ICAO designator] (FAAC) ... CFP
Compania Dominicana de Aviacion SA [Dominican Republic] [ICAO designator] (FAAC) ... DOA
Compania Helicopteros del Sureste SA [Spain] [ICAO designator] (FAAC) ... HSE
Compania Helicopteros de Transporte SA [Spain] [ICAO designator] (FAAC) ... HSO
Compania Hispano Irlandesa de Aviacion [Spain] [ICAO designator] (FAAC) ... FUA
Compania Internadia de Aviacion [Colombia] [ICAO designator] (FAAC) ... IAN
Compania Mexicana de Aeroplanos SA [Mexico] [ICAO designator] (FAAC) ... MDR
Compania Mexicana de Aviacion SA [Mexico] [ICAO designator] (FAAC) ... MXA
Compania Mexicana de Taxis Aereos SA [Mexico] [ICAO designator] (FAAC) ... CMX
Compania Panamena de Aviacion SA [Panama] [ICAO designator] (FAAC) ... CMP
Compania de Servicios Aereos SA [Spain] [ICAO designator] (FAAC) ... SAESA
Compania de Servicios Aereos SA [Spain] [ICAO designator] (FAAC) ... SSS
Compania de Servicios Aereos, TAVISA [Spain] [ICAO designator] (FAAC) ... TAV
Compania Spantax [Spain] [ICAO designator] (FAAC) ... BXS
Company Average VOC [Volatile Organic Compound] Emission [Environmental Protection Agency] ... CAVE
Company Export Planning ... CEP
Company Owned (NTCM) ... C-O
Compartmental (ABBR) ... CMPRTL
Compartmentalize (ABBR) ... CMPRTLZ
Compartmentalized (ABBR) ... CMPRTLZD
Compartmentalizing (ABBR) ... CMPRTLZG
Compass Airlines of Australia [ICAO designator] (FAAC) ... CYM
Compass Aviation [British] [ICAO designator] (FAAC) ... CPS
Compass Locator [Aviation] (DA) ... COMO
Competitive Inhibition Enzyme Immunoassay [Analytical biochemistry] ... CIEIA
Complement of Latitude ... Co-Lat
Complement Mediated Cell Lysis [Immunology] ... CML
Complete Drawing [Animation] (NTCM) ... CD
Complete Service Supplier [Vendor operations] ... CSS
Completion Guarantor [Motion picture financing] (NTCM) ... CG
Complex Assessment Officer ... CAO
Complex Layered Oxide [Physical chemistry] ... CLO
Component Analog Video (NTCM) ... CAV
Component Intergration Laboratories ... CIL
Composite (ABBR) ... CMPSIT
Composite Double-Base [Propellant] ... CDB
Composite-Modified Double-Base [Propellant] ... CMDB
Composition and Make-Up ... CAM
Compost (ABBR) ... CMPS
Compost (ABBR) ... CMPST
Composted (ABBR) ... CMPSTD
Composting (ABBR) ... CMPSTG
Composure (ABBR) ... CMPSU
Compound Animal Feeding Stuffs Manufacturers National Association [British] (BI) ... CAFSMNA
Compound Annual Growth Rate [Business term] ... CAGR
Comprehensive (Ground Water) Monitoring Evaluation [Environmental Protection Agency] (ERG) ... CME
Comprehensive (Ground Water) Monitoring Evaluation Log [Environmental Protection Agency] (ERG) ... CMEL
Comprehensive State Ground Water Protection Program [Environmental science] ... CSGWPP
Compress (ABBR) ... CMPRS
Compressed (ABBR) ... CMPRSD
Compressed Mosiacked Image Data Record [Geology] ... CMIDR
Compressibility (ABBR) ... CMPRSBT
Compressible (ABBR) ... CMPRSB
Compressibleness (ABBR) ... CMPRSBNS
Compressing (ABBR) ... CMPRSG
Compression (ABBR) ... CMPRSN
Compressive (ABBR) ... CMPRSV
Compressive Safety Index [Engineering design] ... CSI
Compressively (ABBR) ... CMPRSVY
Compressor (ABBR) ... CMPRSR
Compressor (ABBR) ... CMPSR
Comptroller (ABBR) ... CMPTR
Comptroller (ABBR) ... CMTRLR
Compuflight Operation Service, Inc. [ICAO designator] (FAAC) ... XCO
Compulsion (ABBR) ... CMPUL
Compulsive (ABBR) ... CMPULV
Compulsorily (ABBR) ... CMPULRY
Compulsorily Preserved Superannuation Benefit ... CPSB
Compulsory (ABBR) ... CMPULR
Compunction (ABBR) ... CMPUN
Compunctiously (ABBR) ... CMPUNSY
Compurgation (ABBR) ... CMPUR
CompuServe, Inc. [ICAO designator] (FAAC) ... XCS
CompuServe Navigator [CompuServe, Inc.] [Telecommunications] (PCM) ... CSNav
Computation (ABBR) ... CMPUTAN
Computation (ABBR) ... CMPUTN
Computational Fluid Dynamics [Chemical engineering] ... CFD
Compute (ABBR) ... CMPU
Computed (ABBR) ... CMPUTD
Computer (ABBR) ... CMPUTR
Computer-Aided Lighting [Automotive engineering] ... CAL
Computer-Aided Pulse Plating [Electrochemistry] ... CAPP
Computer-Aided Rapid Prototyping ... CARP
Computer-Assisted Molecular Modeling [Chemistry] ... CAMM
Computer-Assisted Training ... CAT
[The] Computer Bulletin (IAA) ... TCB
Computer-Controlled Test Management System [Environmental science] ... CTMS
Computer-Controlled Vehicle [Public transit systems] ... CCV
Computer Education Group [British] (BI) ... CEG
Computer Mediated Communication ... CMC
Computer-Oriented Metering Planning and Advisory System [Aviation] (DA) ... COMPAS
Computer Output to LASER Disk (PCM) ... COLD
Computer Readable System ... CRS
Computer Security Technical Vulnerability Reporting Program [Army] (ADDR) ... CSTVRP
Computerize (ABBR) ... CMPUTRZ
Computerized (ABBR) ... CMPUTRZD
Computerized Patient Record ... CPR
Computerized Tomography (ECON) ... CT
Computerizing (ABBR) ... CMPUTRZG
Computing (ABBR) ... CMPUG
Computing (ABBR) ... CMPUTG
Computing System for Air Cargo (DA) ... COSAC
Comrade (ABBR) ... CMRD
Comradeship (ABBR) ... CMRDSP
Conair AS [Denmark] [ICAO designator] (FAAC) ... OYC
Conair Aviation Ltd. [Canada] [ICAO designator] (FAAC) ... CRC
Conceal (ABBR) ... CNCEL
Concealable (ABBR) ... CNCELB
Concealed (ABBR) ... CNCELD
Concealer (ABBR) ... CNCELR
Concealing (ABBR) ... CNCELG
Concealment (ABBR) ... CNCELT
Concede (ABBR) ... CNCED
Conceded (ABBR) ... CNCEDD
Concededly (ABBR) ... CNCEDDY
Conceder (ABBR) ... CNCEDR
Conceding (ABBR) ... CNCEDG
Conceit (ABBR) ... CNCET
Conceited (ABBR) ... CNCETD
Conceitedly (ABBR) ... CNCETDY
Conceiting (ABBR) ... CNCETG
Conceivability (ABBR) ... CNCEVBT
Conceivable (ABBR) ... CNCEVB
Conceivably (ABBR) ... CNCEVBY
Conceive (ABBR) ... CNCEV
Conceived (ABBR) ... CNCEVD
Conceiver (ABBR) ... CNCEVR
Conceiving (ABBR) ... CNCEVG

Concentrate (ABBR) ... CNCEN
Concentrate (ABBR) ... CNCNTRA
Concentrated (ABBR) ... CNCED
Concentrating (ABBR) ... CNCEG
Concentrating (ABBR) ... CNCNTRAG
Concentration (ABBR) ... CNCENN
Concentration (ABBR) ... CNCNTRN
Concentration-Based Exemption Criteria [*Environmental science*] ... CBEC
Concentrative (ABBR) ... CNCENV
Concentratively (ABBR) ... CNCENVY
Concentrator (ABBR) ... CNCENR
Concentric (ABBR) ... CNCENC
Concentric (ABBR) ... CNCNTRC
Concentrically (ABBR) ... CNCENCY
Concentricity (ABBR) ... CNCENCT
Concept (ABBR) ... CNCPT
Conception (ABBR) ... CNCPN
Conceptive (ABBR) ... CNCPTV
Conceptual (ABBR) ... CNCPTL
Conceptualism (ABBR) ... CNCPTSM
Conceptualist (ABBR) ... CNCPTST
Conceptualize (ABBR) ... CNCPTLZ
Conceptualized (ABBR) ... CNCPTLZD
Conceptualizing (ABBR) ... CNCPTLZG
Conceptually (ABBR) ... CNCPTLY
Concern (ABBR) ... CNCR
Concern (ABBR) ... CNCRN
Concerned (ABBR) ... CNCRND
Concerning (ABBR) ... CNCRG
Concerning (ABBR) ... CNCRNG
Concerns of Police Survivors [*An association*] ... COPS
Concert Artists Association [*British*] (BI) ... CAA
Conciliable (ABBR) ... CNCLAB
Conciliate (ABBR) ... CNCLA
Conciliated (ABBR) ... CNCLAD
Conciliating (ABBR) ... CNCLAG
Conciliation (ABBR) ... CNCLAN
Conciliator (ABBR) ... CNCLAR
Conciliatory (ABBR) ... CNCLARTRY
Conciliatory (ABBR) ... CNCLARY
Concise (ABBR) ... CNCIS
Concisely (ABBR) ... CNCISY
Concision (ABBR) ... CNCISN
Conclave (ABBR) ... CNCLAV
Conclave (ABBR) ... CNCLV
Conclude (ABBR) ... CNCLD
Conclude (ABBR) ... CNCLU
Concluded (ABBR) ... CNCLUD
Concluder (ABBR) ... CNCLUR
Concluding (ABBR) ... CNCDG
Concluding (ABBR) ... CNCLUG
Conclusion (ABBR) ... CNCLSN
Conclusion (ABBR) ... CNCLUN
Conclusive (ABBR) ... CNCLSV
Conclusive (ABBR) ... CNCLUV
Conclusively (ABBR) ... CNCLUVY
Concoct (ABBR) ... CNCOC
Concocted (ABBR) ... CNCOCD
Concocting (ABBR) ... CNCOCG
Concoction (ABBR) ... CNCOCN
Concoctive (ABBR) ... CNCOCV
Concoctor (ABBR) ... CNCOCR
Concomitance (ABBR) ... CNCOM
Concomitant (ABBR) ... CNCMTNT
Concomitant (ABBR) ... CNCOMT
Concord (ABBR) ... CNCRD
Concord Airlines Nigeria Ltd. [*ICAO designator*] (FAAC) ... CND
Concordance (ABBR) ... CNCRDNC
Concordant (ABBR) ... CNCRDT
Concordantly (ABBR) ... CNCRDTY
Concourse (ABBR) ... CNCOR
Concrete Mixer Manufacturers' Association [*British*] (BI) ... CMMA
Concurring (ABBR) ... CNCRG
Condensation Figure [*Surface physical chemistry*] ... CF
Condition [*Automotive advertising*] ... CD
Conditional Authorization [*Environmental science*] ... CA
Conditional Exemption [*Environmental science*] ... CE
Conditionally Exempt Specified Wastestream [*Environmental science*] ... CESW
Condor Aero Services, Inc. [*ICAO designator*] (FAAC) ... CNR
Condor Flugdienst GmbH [*Germany*] [*ICAO designator*] (FAAC) ... CFG
Confectioners Benevolent Fund [*British*] (BI) ... CBF
Confectionery and Allied Trades Sports Association [*British*] (BI) ... CATSA
Confederate National Congress (EA) ... CNC
Conference of the Electronics Industry [*British*] (BI) ... CEI
Confidence-Building Measure ... CBM
Confortair, Inc. [*Canada*] [*ICAO designator*] (FAAC) ... COF
Congregational Church in England and Wales (BI) ... CCEW
Congressional Air Ltd. [*ICAO designator*] (FAAC) ... CGA
Congressional Border Caucus [*An association*] (EA) ... CBC
Conifair Aviation, Inc. [*Canada*] [*ICAO designator*] (FAAC) ... ROY
Coningsby FTU [*British*] [*ICAO designator*] (FAAC) ... CBY
Conjugate Gradient Optimization Algorithm Program [*Lighting system design*] ... CGOAP
Conjugation Factor [*Plant genetics*] ... CF
Connectair Charters Ltd. [*Canada*] [*ICAO designator*] (FAAC) ... BSN
Connection (NFPA) ... C
Conquest Airlines Corp. [*ICAO designator*] (FAAC) ... CAC
Conroe Aviation Services, Inc. [*ICAO designator*] (FAAC) ... CXO
Conscience [*A publication*] ... Cons
Consecutive Weeks Discount (NTCM) ... CWD
Conservation and Environment Library Information System ... CELIS
Conservative Party of Australia [*Political party*] ... CVP
Consolidated Revenue ... CR
Consort Aviation [*British*] [*ICAO designator*] (FAAC) ... CFL
Consortium on Advanced Biosensors (EA) ... CAB
Constant Optimum Separation Lane [*Aviation*] (DA) ... COS
Constant Power (DA) ... CP
Construction of Embedded Dedicated Real-Time System [*Computer science*] ... CEDAR
Construction Quality Assurance [*Environmental science*] ... CQA
Construction Quality Control [*Environmental science*] ... CQC
Construction Specification (DAC) ... Con Spec
Consumer Electronics Group [*Education Industries Association*] (NTCM) ... CEG
Consumer Savings Alliance (EA) ... CSA
Contact Approach [*Aviation*] (DA) ... CAP
Contactair Flugdienst & Co. [*Germany*] [*ICAO designator*] (FAAC) ... KIS
Container, Weapon, Individual Equipment [*Army*] (ADDR) ... CWIE
Contamination Control Area [*Army*] (ADDR) ... CCA
Contel ASC [*ICAO designator*] (FAAC) ... XCL
Contemporary Acapella Society of America (EA) ... CASA
Contents of Decrement Part of Register [*Computer science*] (NHD) ... CDR
Conti-Flug Koln/Bonn [*Germany*] [*ICAO designator*] (FAAC) ... EPC
Continental Airlines, Inc. [*ICAO designator*] (FAAC) ... COA
Continental Association of Funeral and Memorial Societies ... CAFMS
Continental Aviation Ltd. [*Ghana*] [*ICAO designator*] (FAAC) ... CCL
Continental Micronesia, Inc. [*Guam*] [*ICAO designator*] (FAAC) ... CMI
Continental NORAD Region [*Aviation*] (FAAC) ... CONR
Continental Oil Co. [*ICAO designator*] (FAAC) ... CON
Continental Tropical Air [*Meteorology*] (DA) ... CT
Continuing Airworthiness Panel [*ICAO*] (DA) ... CAP
Continuous Ideally Stirred Tank Reactor [*Chemical engineering*] ... CISTR
Continuous Process Improvement [*Chemical engineering*] ... CPI
Continuous Segregated Stirred Tank Reactor [*Chemical engineering*] ... CSSTR
Continuously Varying Cell Constant [*Electrochemical instrumentation*] ... CVCC
Contract Amendment Proposal ... CAP
Contractor Evidence Audit Team [*Environmental Protection Agency*] (ERG) ... CEAT
Contractors' Mechanical Plant Engineers [*British*] (BI) ... CMPE
Contrast Spatial Frequency [*Vision research*] ... CSF
Control Board Operator [*Lighting*] (NTCM) ... CBO
Control Key [*Electronics*] ... CNTRL
Control of Pesticides Regulations [*British*] ... COPR
Control System Program [*Manufacturing engineering*] [*Computer science*] ... CSP
Controlled Airspace [*ICAO designator*] (FAAC) ... CTAS
Controlled Circulation [*Newspaper and magazine distribution*] (NTCM) ... CC
Controlled Firing Area [*Aviation*] (FAAC) ... CFA
Controlled Swirl Scavenging [*Automotive engine design*] ... CSS
Convector (DAC) ... Conv
Convenor ... Cvnr
Convent of the Holy Rood [*British*] (BI) ... CHR
Conventional Vehicle [*Environmental science*] ... CV
Conventional Weapons Loading Exercise [*Navy*] (ANA) ... CONVWEPS LOADEX
Conversion for Reclaiming Earth in the Americas [*An association*] ... CREA
Cook Inlet Aviation, Inc. [*ICAO designator*] (FAAC) ... CKA
Cook Islands International [*New Zealand*] [*ICAO designator*] (FAAC) ... CII
Cookery and Food Association [*British*] (BI) ... CFA
Cool White (DAC) ... CW
Cool White Deluxe (DAC) ... CWX
Cooper Skybird Air Charters Ltd. [*Kenya*] [*ICAO designator*] (FAAC) ... SKY
Cooperating Administrator [*Education*] (AEE) ... CA
Cooperative Independent Surveillance (DA) ... CIS
Cooperative Operating System Environment [*Computer science*] ... COSE
Coordination [*ICAO designator*] (FAAC) ... CDN
Coordination Number Invariance [*Chemistry*] ... CNI
Copenhagen Airtaxi [*Denmark*] [*ICAO designator*] (FAAC) ... CAT
Copper Cylinder and Boiler Manufacturers' Association [*British*] (BI) ... CCBM
Copy to Go (NTCM) ... CTG
Corair [*France*] [*ICAO designator*] (FAAC) ... COZ
Coreceptor Skewed [*Immunology*] ... CRS
Corn Items Collectors Association (EA) ... CIC
Cornell Reconstruction of Accident Speeds on the Highway ... CRASH
Corner Bead [*Technical drawings*] (DAC) ... COR BD
Cornice (DAC) ... Corn
Coronado Aerolineas Ltda. [*Colombia*] [*ICAO designator*] (FAAC) ... CRA
Coronae Borealis [*Astronomy*] ... CrB
Corporacion Aereo Cencor SA de CV [*Mexico*] [*ICAO designator*] (FAAC) ... CNC

Corporacion Aereo Internacional SA de CV [*Mexico*] [*ICAO designator*] (FAAC) .... CAI
Corporacion Area Ejecutiva SA de CV [*Mexico*] [*ICAO designator*] (FAAC) .... CEJ
Corporate Affairs Processing System .... CAPS
Corporate Air [*ICAO designator*] (FAAC) .... CPT
Corporate Air, Inc. [*ICAO designator*] (FAAC) .... CPR
Corporate Aircraft Co. [*ICAO designator*] (FAAC) .... CPO
Corporate Aviation Services, Inc. [*ICAO designator*] (FAAC) .... CKE
Corporate Customer Satisfaction Monitor .... CCSM
Corporate Information Technology .... CIT
Corporate Information Technology Plan .... CITP
Corporate Information Technology Strategy .... CITS
Corporate Library Update [*A publication*] .... CLU
Corporate and Staff Development .... C & SD
Correct, Pause, Recovery [*Automobile driving*] .... CPR
Corrective Action Management Unit [*Environmental science*] .... CAMU
Corrective Action Order [*Environmental Protection Agency*] (ERG) .... CAO
Corrective Measure Study [*Environmental science*] .... CMS
Corridor (DA) .... CORR
Corse Aero Service [*France*] [*ICAO designator*] (FAAC) .... CSS
Corse Air International [*France*] [*ICAO designator*] (FAAC) .... CRL
Corse-Mediterranee Compagnie [*France*] [*ICAO designator*] (FAAC) .... CCM
Corynebacterium [*Genus of microorganisms*] (MAH) C
Cosmic Microwave Background Radiation .... CMBR
Cost Allocation Review .... CAR
Cost per Gross Rating Point [*Advertising*] (NTCM) .... CPGRP
Cotswold Executive Aviation [*British*] [*ICAO designator*] (FAAC) .... CWD
Cottesmore TTTE [*British*] [*ICAO designator*] (FAAC) .... COT
Cotton Canvas Manufacturers Association [*British*] (BI) .... CCMA
Cotton and Rayon Merchants Association [*British*] (BI) .... CRMA
Cougar Air, Inc. [*Canada*] [*ICAO designator*] (FAAC) .... CAJ
Cougar Helicopter, Inc. [*Canada*] [*ICAO designator*] (FAAC) .... CHI
Council for Accreditation of Counseling and Related Educational Programs (AEE) .... CACREP
Council on Aging .... COA
Council on Broadcast Education [*Later, CEEM*] (NTCM) .... COBE
Council on Children, Media, and Merchandising (NTCM) .... CCMM
Council for Democratic Government [*Japan*] (ECON) .... CDG
Council for Education on Electronic Media (NTCM) .... CEEM
Council on Graduate Medical Education [*Department of Health and Human Services*] .... COGME
Council of Iron Producers [*British*] (BI) .... CIP
Council for Learning Resources in Colleges [*British*] .... COLRIC
Council of Lebanese American Organizations (EA) .... CLAO
Council on Superconductivity for American Competitiveness .... CSAC
Councilor (ABBR) .... CNCLR
Countercurrent Decantation [*Engineering*] .... CCD
Country Bound Connection [*An association*] (EA) .... CBC
Country Wool Merchants Association [*British*] (BI) .... CWMA
County Air Services Ltd. [*British*] [*ICAO designator*] (FAAC) .... CAK
County Architects Society [*British*] (BI) .... CAS
County Councils Association [*British*] (BI) .... CCA
County/Coverage Service [*ISI audience data*] (NTCM) .... C/CS
Courier-Mail (Brisbane) [*A publication*] .... BCM
Courier Services, Inc. [*ICAO designator*] (FAAC) .... CSD
Court Reporting Typist .... CRT
Courtesy Announcement (NTCM) .... CA
Coval Air Ltd. [*Canada*] [*ICAO designator*] (FAAC) CVL
Covered Conductors Association [*British*] (BI) .... CCA
Cow Observers Worldwide [*An association*] (EA) .... COW
CPA Cesar Augusto de la Cruze Lepe [*Mexico*] [*ICAO designator*] (FAAC) .... AUG
Crainfield Institute of Technology [*British*] [*ICAO designator*] (FAAC) .... CFD
Crankcase Depression Regulator Valve [*Emissions*] [*Automotive engineering*] .... CDRV
Cranking Amperes [*Battery*] [*Automotive engineering*] .... CA
Cranwell FTU [*British*] [*ICAO designator*] (FAAC) .... CWL
Crash Impact Absorbing Structure [*Automotive safety*] .... CIAS
Creative Tourist Agents' Conference [*British*] (BI) .... CTAC
Credit Lyonnais Bank Nederland [*Credit Lyonnais' Dutch subsidiary*] (ECON) .... CLBN
Credit Union Share Draft .... CUSD
Cree Airways Corp. [*Canada*] [*ICAO designator*] (FAAC) .... CRE
Cretan Airlines SA [*Greece*] [*ICAO designator*] (FAAC) .... KRT
Criminal Records Directorate [*Army*] (ADDR) .... CRD
Cripples' Help Society [*British*] (BI) .... CHS
Criterion Action Element [*Army*] (ADDR) .... CAE
Critical Flow Venture-Constant Volume Sampler (ERG) .... CFV-CVS
Critical Friendly Zone [*Army*] (ADDR) .... CFZ
Critical Height (DA) .... CH
Critical Height [*Aviation*] (DA) .... HC
Critical Outcome Data Evaluation System [*Auto safety research*] .... CODES
Critical Reflection Activation Analysis .... CRAA
Croatia Airlines [*ICAO designator*] (FAAC) .... CTN
Cross (DAC) .... Cr
Cross Air AG [*Switzerland*] [*ICAO designator*] (FAAC) .... CRX
Cross Cultural Medicine .... CCM
Cross Industry Standard .... CIS
Crossing [*Aviation*] (FAAC) .... XNG
Crosswind [*Aviation*] (FAAC) .... XW
Crown Air Systems [*ICAO designator*] (FAAC) .... CKR

Crown Airways, Inc. [*ICAO designator*] (FAAC) .... CRO
Crown Cork Manufacturers' Technical Council [*British*] (BI) .... CCMTS
Crownair [*Canada*] [*ICAO designator*] (FAAC) .... CRW
Crucible and Tool Steel Association [*British*] (BI) .... CTSA
Crude Palm Kernel Oil .... CPKO
Crude Sulfate Turpentine .... CST
Cruise [*Automotive advertising*] .... CRUZ
Cruisermen's Association (EA) .... CA
Cryderman Air Service [*ICAO designator*] (FAAC) .... CTY
Cryogenic Transmission Electron Microscopy .... CTEM
Cryptologic Van Junction Box [*Navy*] (ANA) .... CVJB
Crystal Shamrock [*ICAO designator*] (FAAC) .... CYT
CSA Air, Inc. [*ICAO designator*] (FAAC) .... IRO
[*C.C. Enrique*] Cuahonte Delgado [*Mexico*] [*ICAO designator*] (FAAC) .... CUO
Cubic Yard Bank Measurement (DAC) .... Cybm
Cubic Yard Compacted Measurement (DAC) .... CYCM
Culex [*Genus of microorganisms*] (MAH) C
Cultural Awareness Program .... CAP
Culture Supernatant [*Microbiology*] .... CS
Cumulate (ABBR) .... CMULA
Cumulated (ABBR) .... CMULAD
Cumulating (ABBR) .... CMULAG
Cumulation (ABBR) .... CMULAN
Cumulative (ABBR) .... CMULAV
Cumulative Radio Audience Method (NTCM) .... CRAM
Cumulative Working Level Months [*Radon exposure measure*] (ERG) .... CWLM
Cumulatively (ABBR) .... CMULAVY
Cumulonimbus (ABBR) .... CMULNBMS
Cumulus (ABBR) .... CMUL
Cumulus (ABBR) .... CMULS
Cumulus (ABBR) .... CMULU
Curriculum Assessment and Teacher/Trainer Training .... CATTT
Cushion Control Point [*Navy*] (ANA) .... CCP
Cushion Landing Zone [*Navy*] (ANA) .... CLZ
Custodial Parent .... CP
Custom Asynchronous Receiver/Transmitter [*Automotive engineering*] .... CART
Custom Electronic Design Installation Association (EA) .... CEDIA
Customer Access Network .... CAN
Customized Health Information Project [*Computer science*] .... CHIP
Customs Available [*Aviation*] (DA) .... CUS
Cut Down, Annoyed, Guilty, Eye-Opener [*Clinical questions asked to detect alcoholism*] .... CAGE
Cutting Disposal System [*Oil well drilling*] .... CDS
Cyanohydroxybutene [*Organic chemistry*] .... CHB
Cyclic Adenosine Diphosphoribose [*Biochemistry*] .... CADPR
Cyclic-Adenosine Monophosphate-Responsive Element Modulator [*Genetics*] .... CREM
Cyclic Instrumental Neutron Activation Analysis .... CINAA
Cyclic Nucleotide-Gated [*Neurobiology*] .... CNG
Cyclic Voltametric Stripping [*Electrochemistry*] .... CVS
Cyclin-Dependent Kinase [*Biochemistry*] .... CDK
Cyclooxygenase [*An enzyme*] .... COX
Cyclopentyltheophylline [*Organic chemistry*] .... CPT
Cypair Tours Ltd. [*Cyprus*] [*ICAO designator*] (FAAC) .... CYC
Cyprus Airways Ltd. [*ICAO designator*] (FAAC) .... CYP
Cytochrome Oxidase I [*An enzyme*] .... COI
Cytoskeleton [*Cytology*] .... CSK
Czech Air Force [*ICAO designator*] (FAAC) .... CEF
Czech Air Handling [*Czechoslovakia*] [*ICAO designator*] (FAAC) .... AHD
Czech Government Flying Service [*ICAO designator*] (FAAC) .... CGF

D

Daily Average Occupied Beds [*Medicine*] .... DAOB
Daily Call-In .... DCI
Daily Effective Circulation (NTCM) .... DEC
Daily Mirror [*A publication*] .... DM
Dairo Air Services Ltd. [*Uganda*] [*ICAO designator*] (FAAC) .... DSR
Dairy Appliance Manufacturers' and Distributors' Association Ltd. (BI) .... DAMDA
Dairy Engineers' Association [*British*] (BI) .... DEA
Daka [*Kazakhstan*] [*ICAO designator*] (FAAC) .... DKA
Dakair [*France*] [*ICAO designator*] (FAAC) .... DAK
Dakomat [*Poland*] [*ICAO designator*] (FAAC) .... DKM
Dales Pony Society [*British*] (BI) .... DPS
Dampproof Membrane (DAC) .... Dpm
Danair AS [*Denmark*] [*ICAO designator*] (FAAC) .... DAN
Danbury Airways, Inc. [*ICAO designator*] (FAAC) .... DSA
Danger Area (DA) .... DA
Dangerous Goods Panel [*ICAO*] (DA) .... DGP
Danish Air Force [*ICAO designator*] (FAAC) .... DAE
Danish Air Transport [*ICAO designator*] (FAAC) .... DTR
Danish Army [*ICAO designator*] (FAAC) .... DAR
Danish Navy [*ICAO designator*] (FAAC) .... DNY
Danube-Air Ltd. [*Hungary*] [*ICAO designator*] (FAAC) .... DBE
[*E. H.*] **Darby Aviation** [*ICAO designator*] (FAAC) .... EHD
Darta [*France*] [*ICAO designator*] (FAAC) .... DRT
Data Base Administrator/Manager [*Army*] .... DBA/M
Data-Cache Unit [*Computer science*] .... DCU
Data Communication Terminal System [*Computer science*] (DA) .... DCTS
Data Exchange Test Facility (DA) .... DETF
Data Link Controller-Processor [*Automotive engineering*] [*Electronics*] .... DLCP
Data Link Processor Unit (DA) .... DLPU
Data Link Splitter (DA) .... DLS
Data Link and Transponder Analysis System (DA) .... DATAS
Data-Matching Agency .... DMA
Data Transformation Corp. [*ICAO designator*] (FAAC) .... XDT
Date of Commencement .... DOC
Date of Departure [*Army*] .... DOPRT
Date of Introduction (ADDR) .... DOI
Dawn Air, Inc. [*ICAO designator*] (FAAC) .... DWN
Day Press Rate [*Telegraph rate*] (NTCM) .... DPR
Daylight (NTCM) .... DAY
Daylight Factor (DAC) .... DF
Daytime (NTCM) .... D
Dead White Male .... DWM
Deadly Serious Party of Australia [*Political party*] .... DSA
Deaf and Hard of Hearing Entrepreneurs Council (EA) .... DHHEC
Deafen (ABBR) .... DEFN
Deafened (ABBR) .... DEFND
Deafening (ABBR) .... DEFNG
Deafeningly (ABBR) .... DEFNGY
Deafer (ABBR) .... DEFR
Deafest (ABBR) .... DEFST
Deafly (ABBR) .... DEFY
Deafmute (ABBR) .... DEFMT
Deafness (ABBR) .... DEFNS
Dealer (ABBR) .... DELR
Dealer [*Automotive sales*] .... DR
Dealing (ABBR) .... DELG
Deanship (ABBR) .... DENSP
Dearness (ABBR) .... DERNS
Debita Spissitudo [*Proper Consistency*] [*Pharmacy*] (MAH) .... DEB SPIS
Decatur Aviation, Inc. [*ICAO designator*] (FAAC) .... DAA
Deceleration Enleanment [*Automotive fuel systems*] .... DE
Decency in Broadcasting (NTCM) .... DIB
Deception Battalion [*Army*] (ADDR) .... BAT-D
Decision Altitude [*Aviation*] (DA) .... DA
Decking (DAC) .... Dkg
Declared Management Zone .... DMZ
Deed of Grant in Trust .... DOGIT
Deere & Co. [*ICAO designator*] (FAAC) .... JDC
Deere Funk [*Automotive industry supplier*] .... DF
Deescalate (ABBR) .... DEESC
Deescalated (ABBR) .... DEESCD
Deescalating (ABBR) .... DEESCG
Deescalation (ABBR) .... DEESCN
Defection [*or Defector*] (ABBR) .... DEF
Defence and Ex-Services Party of Australia [*Political party*] .... DEP
Defence Information Bulletin [*A publication*] .... DIB
Defence Products Ltd. [*British*] [*ICAO designator*] (FAAC) .... RAN
Defendant .... D
Defense Modeling and Simulation Office [*Military*] .... DMSO
Defense Retiree and Annuitant Pay System [*DoD*] .... DRAS
Defense Security Officer [*Military*] .... DSO
Defense Simulation Internet [*Army*] (RDA) .... DSI
Defense Systems Acquisition Management [*DoD*] .... DSAM
Defense Visual Flight Rule [*Military*] (DA) .... DFVR
Defensive Counterair [*Army*] (ADDR) .... DCA
Deficiency (ABBR) .... DEFI
Deflagrate (ABBR) .... DEF
Deflate (ABBR) .... DEFL
Deflect (ABBR) .... DEF
Deflection (DAC) .... Dflct
Defloration (ABBR) .... DEFLOR
Deftness (ABBR) .... DEFTNS
Degradable (ABBR) .... DEGRAD
Degree of Disorder [*Coatings*] .... DOD
Deification (ABBR) .... DEIFCN
Deified (ABBR) .... DEIFD
Deifier (ABBR) .... DEIFR
Deifying (ABBR) .... DEIFG
Delay Indefinite (DA) .... DLI
Delay Time [*Aviation*] (FAAC) .... DLAT
Delete (ABBR) .... DELE
Deliberate (ABBR) .... DEL
Delinquency (ABBR) .... DELCY
Delinquency (ABBR) .... DELIN
Delta Aerotaxi [*Italy*] [*ICAO designator*] (FAAC) .... DEA
Delta Air Charter Ltd. [*Canada*] [*ICAO designator*] (FAAC) .... SNO
Delta Air Lines, Inc. [*ICAO designator*] (FAAC) .... DAL
Delta Air Transport [*Belgium*] [*ICAO designator*] (FAAC) .... DAT
Delta Aviation SA [*Spain*] [*ICAO designator*] (FAAC) .... DET
Delta Jet SA [*Spain*] [*ICAO designator*] (FAAC) .... DEJ
Delta Pi Epsilon [*Fraternity*] (AEE) .... DPE
Deltex [*Slovakia*] [*ICAO designator*] (FAAC) .... DTX
Deluge Valve (DAC) .... DEL V
Delusion (ABBR) .... DELU
Demand (ABBR) .... DEM
Demobilized (ABBR) .... DEMOBED
Democracy (ABBR) .... DEMOC
Democratic People's Republic of Korea [*Aircraft nationality and registration mark*] (FAAC) .... P
Demographic Adjustment Factor (NTCM) .... DAF
Demonologic (ABBR) .... DEMONOL
Demonology (ABBR) .... DEMON
Demur (ABBR) .... DEM
Den Sivile Flyskole [*Norway*] [*ICAO designator*] (FAAC) .... TTX
Dendrology (ABBR) .... DEND
Dendrology (ABBR) .... DENDROL
Dendrometer (ABBR) .... DENDRO
Denotation (ABBR) .... DENOT
Dental Aptitude Test [*Education*] (AEE) .... DAT
Dental Explanation of Benefits [*Army*] .... DEOB
Dentatorubral Pallidoluysian Atrophy [*Medicine*] .... DRPLA
Denture (ABBR) .... DENT
Denver Express, Inc. [*ICAO designator*] (FAAC) .... FEC
Denver International Airport [*Facetious translation: Delay It Again*] (ECON) .... DIA
Denver Jet, Inc. [*ICAO designator*] (FAAC) .... DJT
Deodorant (ABBR) .... DEOD
Deodorization (ABBR) .... DEODZN
Deodorize (ABBR) .... DEODZ
Deodorized (ABBR) .... DEODZD
Deodorizer (ABBR) .... DEODZR
Deodorizing (ABBR) .... DEODZG
Deoxyerythronolide B Synthase [*An enzyme*] .... DEBS
Depart (DA) .... DP

Departamento de Agricultura de la Generalitat de Cataluna [*Spain*] [*ICAO designator*] (FAAC) .... FGC
Departed (ABBR) .... DEPD
Departing (ABBR) .... DEPG
Department of Defense Consolidated List of Principal Military Items .... DODCLIPMI
Department of Transport [*British*] (DA) .... DOTp
Department of the Treasury .... TREAS DEPT
Departmental (ABBR) .... DEPTL
Departmental Personnel Instruction .... DPI
Departmentally-Initiated Review .... DIR
Departure (ABBR) .... DEPT
Departure (ABBR) .... DEPU
Departure Airfield Group [*Army*] (ADDR) .... DACO
Departure Control (DA) .... DPC
Departure End of Runway [*Aviation*] (DA) .... DER
Dependency (ABBR) .... DEPEND
Dependents' Dental Plan [*DoD*] .... DDP
Deperming [*Navy*] (ANA) .... DEPERM
Depilate (ABBR) .... DEP
Depilation (ABBR) .... DEPL
Depilatory (ABBR) .... DEP
Deployment Exercise [*Military*] (ADDR) .... DEPEX
Deployment Readiness Review [*Aviation*] (FAAC) .... DRR
Deponent (ABBR) .... DEPON
Deposit Byte [*Computer science*] (NHD) .... DPB
Deposition Form [*Army*] (ADDR) .... DF
Deposition Rate [*Electrochemistry*] .... DR
Depository Institutions Deregulation and Monetary Decontrol Act [*1980*] .... DIDMCA
Depth-Selective Conversion Electron Mossbauer Spectroscopy .... DSCEMS
Deputation (ABBR) .... DEPUTN
Deputy Chief of Staff for Operations and Intelligence [*Army*] .... DCSOT
Deputy Managing Director .... DMD
Deraya Air Taxi PT [*Indonesia*] [*ICAO designator*] (FAAC) .... DRY
Derivable (ABBR) .... DERIVB
Derivation (ABBR) .... DERIVN
Derivative (ABBR) .... DERIVV
Derived (ABBR) .... DERIVD
Deriving (ABBR) .... DERIVG
Dermatology (ABBR) .... DERMAT
Dermatophyte (ABBR) .... DERM
Desalinization (ABBR) .... DESAL
Descend at Pilot's Discretion [*Aviation*] (FAAC) .... DAPD
Descendants of Mexican War Veterans [*An association*] (EA) .... DMWV
Description (ABBR) .... DESCRPN
Desert Camouflage Uniform [*Military*] .... DCU
Desiderata (ABBR) .... DESID
Desiderative (ABBR) .... DESIDER
Design Change .... DC
Design Failure-Mode Effects Analysis [*Automotive engineering*] .... DFMEA
Designated Operational Coverage (DA) .... DOC
Designated Security-Assessed Position .... DSAP
Designated Work Group .... DWG
Designed Agency Safety and Health Official (ERG) .... DASHO
Designer (ABBR) .... DESIG
Designers and Art Directors Association [*British*] (BI) .... DADA
Desired (ABBR) .... DESID
DeskTop Conferencing [*Fujitsu Networks Industry, Inc.*] [*Computer science*] (PCM) .... DTC
Desktop Marketing System [*CD-ROM*] [*Computer science*] .... DTMS
Desoxycorticosterone Acetate [*Endocrinology*] (MAH) .... DCA
Detailed Functional Specification (DA) .... DFS
Detector (NFPA) .... D
Detector (NFPA) .... DE
Detergent Inhibitor [*Lubricants*] .... DI
Detroit Diesel Corp. [*Automotive industry supplier*] .... DDC
Deutsche Ba Luftfahrtgesellschaft MBH [*Germany*] [*ICAO designator*] (FAAC) .... BAG
Deutsche Forschungs-and Versuchsanstalt fur Luft EV [*Germany*] [*ICAO designator*] (FAAC) .... AOT
Deutsche Lufthansa, AG [*Germany*] [*ICAO designator*] (FAAC) .... DLH
Deutsche Rettungsflugwacht EV [*Germany*] [*ICAO designator*] (FAAC) .... AMB
Deutsche Tourenwagen Meisterschaft [*German Touring Car Championship*] .... DTM
Deutz Magnetic Valve System [*Diesel engines*] .... DMVS
Developing Country .... DC
Development Needs Analysis .... DNS
Development Training Group .... DTG
Deviation Approved as Requested [*Aviation*] (FAAC) .... DAAR
Deviation Report .... DR
Device Communications [*Computer science*] .... DEVCOM
Di-Tertiary-Butylbiphenyl [*Organic chemistry*] .... DTBB
Diagnostic Development Branch [*National Institutes of Health*] .... DDB
Diagnostic Energy Reserve Module [*Airbags and safety systems*] .... DERM
Dialkylglycine Decarboxylase [*An enzyme*] .... DGD
Diallyl Sulfide .... DAS
Dialogue (NTCM) .... DIA
Diametral Tensile Strength [*Material science*] .... DTS
Diamond Aviation, Inc. [*ICAO designator*] (FAAC) .... SPK
Diaphosgene [*A choking agent*] (ADDR) .... DP
Diaphragm (NTCM) .... DIA
Diary Publishers' Association [*British*] (BI) .... DPA
Dibutylmalonic Acid [*Organic chemistry*] .... DBMA
Dibutyltin [*Organic chemistry*] .... DBT
Did Not Respond .... DNR
Diesel (ABBR) .... DESL
Diesel Engine Oil .... DEO
Diesel Particulate Filter [*Automotive emissions*] .... DPF
Differential Cross Section [*Chemistry*] .... DCS
Differential Survey Treatment (NTCM) .... DST
Differentiated Staffing [*Education*] (AEE) .... DS
Difficulty Index (AEE) .... DI
Diffuse Leiomyomatosis [*Medicine*] .... DL
Digest .... D
Digital Audio Stationary Head [*Recording*] (NTCM) .... DASH
Digital-to-Binary (NTCM) .... D/B
Digital Equipment Corp. [*ICAO designator*] (FAAC) .... DGT
Digital Satellite System .... DSS
Digital Signature Algorithm [*Telecommunications*] .... DSA
Digital Synchronizing Load Sensing Control [*Electronic controls*] [*Diesel engines*] .... DSLC
Digital Video Compression .... DVC
Digital Video Recording (NTCM) .... DVR
Dihydrocodeine [*An analgesic*] [*Pharmacology*] .... DHC
Dilutin Attenuation Factor [*Metallurgy*] .... DAF
Dimensional Fund Advisors [*Fund-management firm*] (ECON) .... DFA
Dimensionally-Stable Polyester [*Tire manufacturing*] .... DSP
Dimethoxyethyl Amphetamine [*A hallucinogenic drug, more commonly known as STP*] (MAH) .... DOET
Di(N-carbazoly)hexadiyne [*Organic chemistry*] .... DCHD
Dinar SA [*Argentina*] [*ICAO designator*] (FAAC) .... RDN
Dining Room (DAC) .... DR
Dioctyltin [*Organic chemistry*] .... DOT
Diploma in Agricultural Economics .... DipAgE
Diploma in Anatomy .... DipAnat
Diploma in Applied Kinesiology .... DipAK
Diploma in Applied Statistics .... DipAppSt
Diploma in Cardiovascular Disease .... DipCVD
Diploma in Chest Diseases .... DipChD
Diploma in Child Psychiatry .... DipCPsy
Diploma in Clinical Epidemiology .... DipCEpi
Diploma in Clinical Hypnosis .... DipClinHyp
Diploma in Clinical Nutrition .... DipClinNut
Diploma in Clinical Pharmacology .... DipClinPharm
Diploma in Commerce (Accounting) .... DipComm(Acc)
Diploma in Community Medicine .... DipCM
Diploma in Dermatology .... DipDermat
Diploma in Drug Development and Clinical Pharmacology .... DipDDCP
Diploma in Environmental Health .... DipEnvHlth
Diploma in Epidemiology .... DipEpid
Diploma in Family Medicine .... DipFamMed
Diploma in Family Planning .... DipFP
Diploma in Family Therapy .... DipFamT
Diploma in Financial Management .... DipFinMan
Diploma in Genito-Urinary Medicine .... DipGUM
Diploma in Health Education .... DipHlthE
Diploma in Human Biology .... DipHumBiol
Diploma in Human Nutrition .... DipHumNut
Diploma in Hypnosis .... DipHyp
Diploma in Internal Medicine .... DipIntMed
Diploma in Labor Law and Industrial Relations .... DipLLIRel
Diploma in Mechanical and Electrical Engineering .... DipMEE
Diploma in Medical Acupuncture .... DipMedAc
Diploma in Medical Hypnosis .... DipMedHyp
Diploma in Medical Jurisprudence (Clinical) .... DipMJ(Clin)
Diploma in Medical Laboratory Technology .... DipMLT
Diploma in Medical Rehabilitation .... DMR
Diploma in Medicine .... DipMed
Diploma in Medicine, Surgery, Obstetrics and Gynecology .... DMSOG
Diploma in Microbiology .... DipMic
Diploma in Midwifery .... DipMid
Diploma in Museum Studies .... DipMS
Diploma in Nursing Administration .... DipNA
Diploma in Nursing Education .... DipNE
Diploma in Occupational Hazard Management .... DipOccHazMan
Diploma in Occupational Health .... DipOccHlth
Diploma in Occupational Health and Safety .... DipOHS
Diploma in Occupational Medicine .... DipOccMed
Diploma in Oral Surgery .... DipOS
Diploma in Orthopedics .... DOrth
Diploma in Otorhinolaryngology .... DORL
Diploma in Palliative Care .... DipPall
Diploma in Parent Education and Counselling .... DPEC
Diploma in Pediatrics .... DP
Diploma in Philosophy of Medicine .... DipPhilMed
Diploma in Physical Anthropology .... DipPhysAnth
Diploma in Physiology .... DPhysiol
Diploma in Practical Dermatology .... DipPrDerm
Diploma in Professional Management .... DipPM
Diploma in Psychiatric Medicine and Neurology .... DPsyMedNeuro
Diploma in Psychiatry .... DipPsy
Diploma in Psychotherapy .... DipPsy
Diploma in Shared Obstetric Care .... DipSObC
Diploma in Sports Medicine .... DipSM

Diploma in Sports Science ... DipSpSci
Diploma in Surgery Medicine ... DpSM
Diploma in Theological Studies ... DTS
Diploma in Therapeutic Radiology and Electrology ... DTRE
Diploma in Traditional Chinese Medicine ... DipTChM
Diploma in Tropical Health ... DTH
Diploma in Tuberculosis and Chest Diseases ... DipTCD
Diploma in Women's Health ... DWH
Dirac Aviation [*France*] [*ICAO designator*] (FAAC) ... DAV
Direccion General de la Inteligencia [*Intelligence agency*] [*Cuba*] ... DGI
Direct Aid Program ... DAP
Direct Air [*British*] [*ICAO designator*] (FAAC) ... DAJ
Direct Air, Inc. [*Germany*] [*ICAO designator*] (FAAC) ... DIA
Direct Air Inc. [*ICAO designator*] (FAAC) ... XAP
Direct Cylinder Injection [*Engine design*] ... DCI
Direct Flight Ltd. [*British*] [*ICAO designator*] (FAAC) ... DCT
Direct Operating Cost (DA) ... DC
Direct Overwrite [*Computer science*] ... DOW
Direct Reading Thinking Activity [*Education*] (AEE) ... DRTA
Direct Support Battery [*Army*] (ADDR) ... DSB
Direct User Access Terminal (DA) ... DUAT
Direct User Access Terminal System [*Aviation*] (FAAC) ... DUATS
Direct Voice (NTCM) ... DV
Direct Voice Input (DA) ... DVI
Directed Metalation Group [*Organic chemistry*] ... DMG
Direction Light [*Navigation*] ... DirLt
Directly-Observed Therapy ... DOT
Director, Navy Configuration Survival and Safety ... DNCSS
Director, Submarine Policy and Warfare [*Military*] ... DSMPW
Directorate of Naval Command, Control and Communications ... DNCCC
Directorate of Naval Communications Engineering ... DNCE
Directorate of Naval Survival and Safety ... DONSS
Directorate of Operational Support Services - Air Force ... DOSS-AF
Directorate of Project Management B - Air Force ... DPMB-AF
Directorate of Weapons and Vehicle Procurement - Army ... DWVP-A
Directorate of Weapons and Vehicle Procurement - Army - Vehicles ... DWVP-A-VEH
Dirgantara Air Service PT [*Indonesia*] [*ICAO designator*] (FAAC) ... DIR
Disability Officer ... DO
Disabled Businesspersons Association (EA) ... DBA
Disadvantaged Person ... DP
Disaster Recovery (DA) ... DR
Disaster Services Liaison Officer ... DSLO
Disc Jockey Association (NTCM) ... DJA
Disconnect (NTCM) ... DC
Discovery Airways [*ICAO designator*] (FAAC) ... DVA
Discriminant Analysis with Shrunken Coveriances [*Mathematics*] ... DASCO
Discriminating Stimulus [*Psychology*] (AEE) ... DS
Disease Intervention Specialist [*Medicine*] ... DIS
Dismounted Battlespace Battle Lab [*Army*] (INF) ... DBBL
Dispatch Services, Inc. [*ICAO designator*] (FAAC) ... XDS
Dispensing Opticians Manufacturing Organisation [*British*] (BI) ... DOMO
Display Control Program (NTCM) ... DCP
Display of Extracted RADAR Data (DA) ... DERD
Disposal Unit (DAC) ... DU
Disseminated Nontuberculous Mycobacterial Infection ... DNTM
Dissolve (NTCM) ... D
Dissolve (NTCM) ... DIZ
Distance from Touchdown Indicator [*Aviation*] (DA) ... DFTI
Distinguished Visitor Program [*Army*] ... DVP
Distributed Active Archive Center [*NASA*] ... DAAC
Distributed Application [*Automotive engineering*] ... DA
Distributed Foundation Wireless Media Access Control [*Computer science*] ... DFWMAC
Distributed Operator Console [*Environmental science*] ... DOC
Distributed Virtual Memory [*Computer science*] ... DVM
Distribution Disk Builder [*Computer science*] ... DDB
Distributive Trades' Alliance [*British*] (BI) ... DTA
District ... D
Ditta Transavio di I. Ballerio [*Italy*] [*ICAO designator*] (FAAC) ... TVO
Diversified Pharmaceutical Services (ECON) ... DPS
Djibouti [*Aircraft nationality and registration mark*] (FAAC) ... J2
DNA [*Deoxyribonucleic Acid*] Unwinding Element [*Genetics*] ... DUE
Do It Now Foundation [*An association*] ... DIN
Do Not Pass to Air Defense RADAR [*Air Traffic Control*] (FAAC) ... NOPAR
Do What I Mean, Correctly [*Computer hacker terminology*] (NHD) ... DWIMC
Do What I Say [*Computer science*] ... DWIS
Dobrolet Airlines [*Russian Federation*] [*ICAO designator*] (FAAC) ... DOB
Docosahexaenoic Acid [*Organic chemistry*] ... DHA
Doctor Martens [*Footwear*] ... DM
Doctor of Technology ... DT
Doctors to the World [*An association*] (EA) ... DTTW
Dollar Air Services Ltd. [*British*] [*ICAO designator*] (FAAC) ... DAS
Dolly Out [*Cinematography*] (NTCM) ... DO
Dolly Shot [*Cinematography*] (NTCM) ... DS
Dolphin [*Mooring post*] [*British*] ... Dn
Domain Name System [*Computer science*] ... DNS
Domain-Referenced Test [*Education*] (AEE) ... DRT
Dome Petroleum Ltd. [*Canada*] [*ICAO designator*] (FAAC) ... DPL
Domestic Refrigeration Development Committee [*British*] (BI) ... DORDEC
Domestic Substances List [*Canada*] ... DSL
Domestic Textiles Federation [*British*] (BI) ... DTF
Dominica [*Aircraft nationality and registration mark*] (FAAC) ... J7
Donair Flying Club Ltd. [*British*] [*ICAO designator*] (FAAC) ... DON
Donauflug Bedarfsfluggesellschaft GmbH [*Austria*] [*ICAO designator*] (FAAC) ... DFL
Don't Get Sucked In ... DGSI
Doppler Acoustic Vortex Sensing Equipment [*Meteorology*] (DA) ... DAVSS
Dorado Air [*Dominican Republic*] [*ICAO designator*] (FAAC) ... DAD
Dornier Reparaturwerft GmbH [*Germany*] [*ICAO designator*] (FAAC) ... DOR
Dos Mundos [*Dominican Republic*] [*ICAO designator*] (FAAC) ... DOM
Double Column [*Publishing*] (NTCM) ... DC
Double Contact [*Lamp base type*] (NTCM) ... DC
Double Dual Tandem [*Aviation*] (DA) ... DDT
Double End Trimmed (DAC) ... DET
Double Extra Heavy (DAC) ... XXH
Double Four Valve [*Cosworth racing engines*] ... DFV
Double Four-Valve Long Distance [*Cosworth racing engines*] ... DFL
Double-Headed Ceiling (DAC) ... DB Clg
Double Tongue and Groove (DAC) ... DT & G
Double Valve [*Stutz car model designation*] ... DV
Downdraft (DA) ... DFT
Downdraft (DA) ... DWN
Downstream Venous Pressure [*Physiology*] (MAH) ... DSVP
Downwind [*Aviation*] (FAAC) ... DNWND
Draft Legislation ... DL
Drafting Site [*NFPA pre-fire planning symbol*] (NFPA) ... DS
Dramatic and Lyric Theatres Association [*British*] (BI) ... DALTA
Dravidian Air Services Ltd. [*British*] [*ICAO designator*] (FAAC) ... DRA
Drawing Office Material Manufacturers' and Dealers' Association [*British*] (BI) ... DOMMDA
Drenair [*Spain*] [*ICAO designator*] (FAAC) ... DRS
Dressed and Center Matched [*Lumber*] (DAC) ... D & CM
Dressed Four Sides [*Lumber*] (DAC) ... D4S
Dressed and Matched Beaded [*Lumber*] (DAC) ... C & MB
Dressed One Side [*Lumber*] (DAC) ... D1S
Dressed and Standard Matched [*Lumber*] (DAC) ... D & SM
Dressed Two Sides [*Lumber*] (DAC) ... D2S
Dressed Two Sides and Center Matched [*Lumber*] (DAC) ... D2S & CM
Dressed Two Sides and Matched [*Lumber*] (DAC) ... D2S & M
Dressed Two Sides and Standard Matched [*Lumber*] (DAC) ... D2S & SM
Dressing Room (DAC) ... DR
Dried Tree Fruit ... DTF
Dried Vine Fruit ... DVF
Dries [*Maps and charts*] [*British*] ... Dr
Drill and Ceremony [*Military*] (ADDR) ... D & C
Drive Parameter Tracking [*Computer science*] (PCM) ... DPT
Dropout Compensator (NTCM) ... DOC
Drug Detector Dog Unit ... DDDU
Drug Rehabilitation ... DR
Druk Air [*Bhutan*] [*ICAO designator*] (FAAC) ... DRK
Drum Trap (DAC) ... DT
Dry (NFPA) ... D
Dry Cell Mass ... DCM
Dry Chemical System [*NFPA pre-fire planning symbol*] (NFPA) ... DC
Dry Cubic Feet (ERG) ... DCF
Dry Wall (DAC) ... Drwl
Dual Progress Plan [*Education*] (AEE) ... DPP
Dual Tandem [*Aviation*] (DA) ... DT
Dubai Airwing [*United Arab Emirates*] [*ICAO designator*] (FAAC) ... DUB
Duchess of Brittany (Jersey) Ltd. [*British*] [*ICAO designator*] (FAAC) ... DBJ
Duct (NFPA) ... D
Duct Detector [*NFPA pre-fire planning symbol*] (NFPA) ... DD
Duncan Aviation, Inc. [*ICAO designator*] (FAAC) ... PHD
Dunford BAE [*British*] [*ICAO designator*] (FAAC) ... DUN
During Climb [*Aviation*] (FAAC) ... DURC
During Descent [*Aviation*] (FAAC) ... DURD
Duty Air Traffic Control Officer (DA) ... DATCO
Duty-Free Into-Store Cost ... DFIST
Dwyer Aircraft Sales, Inc. [*ICAO designator*] (FAAC) ... DFS
Dyad Services Ltd. [*British*] [*ICAO designator*] (FAAC) ... SKT
Dyers' and Cleaners' Research Association (BI) ... DCRA
Dyers of Man-Made Fibre Fabrics Federation [*British*] (BI) ... DMF
Dylan Flight Service SA [*Switzerland*] [*ICAO designator*] (FAAC) ... DFX
DynAir Services, Inc. [*ICAO designator*] (FAAC) ... XDY
Dynamair Aviation, Inc. [*Canada*] [*ICAO designator*] (FAAC) ... DNR
Dynamic Air [*Netherlands*] [*ICAO designator*] (FAAC) ... DYE
Dynamic Mid-Ride Controls [*Truck seating*] ... DMRC
Dynamic Ocean Track System (DA) ... DOTS
Dynamic Simulation Language [*Computer science*] ... DSL
Dynamic Ventures, Inc. [*ICAO designator*] (FAAC) ... DYN
Dynamically-Correlated Domain [*Physics*] ... DCD
Dystrophin-Associated Protein [*Biochemistry*] ... DAP
Dystrophin-Related Protein [*Biochemistry*] ... DRP

E

Eagle Aero, Inc. [*ICAO designator*] (FAAC) ... ICR
Eagle Air Ltd. [*Switzerland*] [*ICAO designator*] (FAAC) ... EAB
Eagle Air Ltd. [*Iceland*] [*ICAO designator*] (FAAC) ... ISL
Eagle Airways Ltd. [*British*] [*ICAO designator*] (FAAC) ... EGT
Eagle Flying Services Ltd. [*British*] [*ICAO designator*] (FAAC) ... EAG
Early Assistance Unit ... EAU
Early Childhood Health ... ECH
Early Emissions Reduction [*Environmental science*] ... EER
Earnings Before Interest, Taxes, Depreciation and Amortization [*Business term*] ... EBITDA
Earth Environment University Roundtable [*of America*] ... EEUR
Earth Pressure Balance [*Civil engineering*] ... EPB
Earth Systems Model [*Climatology*] ... ESM
Eased Edge (DAC) ... EE
East Coast Airlines [*Australia*] [*ICAO designator*] (FAAC) ... ECO
East Coast Airlines Ltd. [*Kenya*] [*ICAO designator*] (FAAC) ... ECK
East Hampton Aire [*ICAO designator*] (FAAC) ... EHA
East Kansas City Aviation, Inc. [*ICAO designator*] (FAAC) ... EKC
East-West Airlines Ltd. [*Australia*] [*ICAO designator*] (FAAC) ... EWA
East West European [*Bulgaria*] [*ICAO designator*] (FAAC) ... EWE
Eastern Air Executive Ltd. [*British*] [*ICAO designator*] (FAAC) ... EAX
Eastern California Shear Zone [*Geology*] ... ECSZ
Eastern Carolina Aviation, Inc. [*ICAO designator*] (FAAC) ... ECI
Eastern Federation of Building Trades' Employers [*British*] (BI) ... EFBTE
Eastern Flying Service Ltd. [*Canada*] [*ICAO designator*] (FAAC) ... SPR
Eastern Pacific Aviation Ltd. [*Canada*] [*ICAO designator*] (FAAC) ... EPB
Eastern Public Radio Network (NTCM) ... EPRN
Eastland Air [*Australia*] [*ICAO designator*] (FAAC) ... ELA
Easy Listening [*Radio*] (NTCM) ... EZ
Ebsco, Inc. [*ICAO designator*] (FAAC) ... DOL
Eccentricity (ABBR) ... ECTCT
Ecclesiastical (ABBR) ... ECLSTCL
Eclecticism (ABBR) ... ECLTM
Eclipse (ABBR) ... ECLPS
Eclipse Airlines, Inc. [*ICAO designator*] (FAAC) ... BRN
Eclipsed (ABBR) ... ECLPSD
Eclipsing (ABBR) ... ECLPSG
Ecoforestry Institute - United States (EA) ... EI
Ecogeographer (ABBR) ... ECOGEO
Ecogeographer (ABBR) ... ECOGEOR
Ecogeographic (ABBR) ... ECOGEOC
Ecole d'Aviation Civile [*Belgium*] [*ICAO designator*] (FAAC) ... BSA
Ecologic (ABBR) ... ECOLC
Ecological (ABBR) ... ECOLCL
Ecologically (ABBR) ... ECOLCLY
Ecologist (ABBR) ... ECOLST
Econometric (ABBR) ... ECONOMET
Economic (ABBR) ... ECO
Economic (ABBR) ... ECONC
Economic and Employment Development Officer ... EEDO
Economic Rate of Return ... ERR
Economic Transactions Framework ... ETF
Economical (ABBR) ... ECONCL
Economical (ABBR) ... ECONL
Economically (ABBR) ... ECONCLY
Economics (ABBR) ... ECS
Economist (ABBR) ... ECONST
Economists Allied for Arms Reduction [*An association*] (EA) ... ECAAR
Economize (ABBR) ... ECONZ
Economized (ABBR) ... ECONZD
Economizer (ABBR) ... ECONZR
Economizing (ABBR) ... ECONZG
Economy (ABBR) ... ECONY
Ecophysiologic (ABBR) ... ECOPHYS
Ecosystem (ABBR) ... ECOSYS
Ecosystem (ABBR) ... ECSYT
Ecstasy (ABBR) ... ECST
Ecstasy [*Synthetic stimulant*] ... X
Ecstatic (ABBR) ... ECSTC
Ecstatically (ABBR) ... ECSTCY
Ectohormone (ABBR) ... ECTOHORM
Ecuato Guineana de Aviacion [*Equatorial Guinea*] [*ICAO designator*] (FAAC) ... EGA
Ecumania (ABBR) ... ECU
Ecumenic (ABBR) ... ECUM
Ecumenic (ABBR) ... ECUMN
Ecumenical (ABBR) ... ECUMEN
Ecumenical (ABBR) ... ECUML
Ecumenical (ABBR) ... ECUMNL
Ecumenicalism (ABBR) ... ECUMLSM
Ecumenically (ABBR) ... ECUMLY
Ecumenically (ABBR) ... ECUMNLY
Ecumenism (ABBR) ... ECUMNM
Ecurie Ecosse Association Ltd. [*British*] (BI) ... EEA
Eczema (ABBR) ... ECZM
Eddied (ABBR) ... EDD
Eddy-Current Killed Oscillator [*Engineering instrumentation*] ... ECKO
Eddying (ABBR) ... EDYG
Edentate (ABBR) ... EDENT
Edgartown Air, Inc. [*ICAO designator*] (FAAC) ... SLO
Edge Bead One Side [*Lumber*] (DAC) ... EB1S
Edge Enhancement Technology [*Tandy*] ... EET
Edge Number [*Film stock identification number*] (NTCM) ... EN
Edge Vee One Side [*Lumber*] (DAC) ... EV1S
Edged (ABBR) ... EDGD
Edgewise (ABBR) ... EDGWS
Edgier (ABBR) ... EDGR
Edgier (ABBR) ... EDGYR
Edgiest (ABBR) ... EDGST
Edgiest (ABBR) ... EDGYST
Edginess (ABBR) ... EDGNS
Edging (ABBR) ... EDGG
Edible (ABBR) ... EDB
Edict (ABBR) ... EDT
Edification (ABBR) ... EDFCN
Edifice (ABBR) ... EDFC
Edified (ABBR) ... EDFD
Edified (ABBR) ... EDFYD
Edifying (ABBR) ... EDFG
Edifying (ABBR) ... EDFYG
Edit (ABBR) ... EDT
Edit-Level Video (NTCM) ... ELV
Edit Sync Guide (NTCM) ... ESG
Edited (ABBR) ... EDTD
Editing (ABBR) ... EDTG
Editing Macros [*Computer science*] (NHD) ... EMACS
Edition (ABBR) ... EDTN
Editor (ABBR) ... EDTR
Editorial (ABBR) ... EDTL
Editorial Support Group ... ESG
Editorialize (ABBR) ... EDTLZ
Editorialized (ABBR) ... EDTLZD
Editorializing (ABBR) ... EDTLZG
Editorship (ABBR) ... EDTRSP
Editorship (ABBR) ... EDTSP
Edmonton [*Canada*] (ABBR) ... EDMN
Educable (ABBR) ... EDCAB
Educable (ABBR) ... EDCBL
Educable (ABBR) ... EDUCB
Educate (ABBR) ... EDCA
Educated (ABBR) ... EDCAD
Educated (ABBR) ... EDUCD
Educating (ABBR) ... EDCAG
Educating (ABBR) ... EDCG
Educating (ABBR) ... EDUCG
Education (ABBR) ... EDCAN
Education of Girls in Mathematics and Science ... EGMS
Education and Information Dissemination ... E & ID
Education Student Assistance System ... ESAS
Educational [*FCC*] (NTCM) ... ED
Educational (ABBR) ... EDCANL
[*The*] **Educational Broadcasting Institute** [*National Association of Educational Broadcasters*] (NTCM) ... EBI
Educational Cable Television (NTCM) ... ECATV
Educational Exhibitors' Association [*British*] (BI) ... EEA
Educational FM Station (NTCM) ... EDFM

Educational Group of the Music Industries Association [*British*] (BI) .... EGMIA
Educational Institution Program (NTCM) .... ED
Educational Puppetry Association [*British*] (BI) .... EPA
[*The*] **Educational Software Selector** [*Database*] (AEE) .... TESS
Educational Television [*FCC*] (NTCM) .... ET
Educational Television by Satellite (NTCM) .... ETVS
Educationalist (ABBR) .... EDUCNLST
Educative (ABBR) .... EDCAV
Educative (ABBR) .... EDUCV
Educator (ABBR) .... EDCATR
Educator (ABBR) .... EDUCR
Eerie (ABBR) .... EER
Eerier (ABBR) .... EERR
Eeriest (ABBR) .... EERST
Eerily (ABBR) .... EERY
Eeriness (ABBR) .... EERNS
Eesti Lennukompani [*Estonia*] [*ICAO designator*] (FAAC) .... ELK
Efface (ABBR) .... EFC
Effaceable (ABBR) .... EFACB
Effaced (ABBR) .... EFACD
Effaced (ABBR) .... EFCD
Effacement (ABBR) .... EFACT
Effacement (ABBR) .... EFCNT
Effacer (ABBR) .... EFACR
Effacer (ABBR) .... EFCR
Effacing (ABBR) .... EFACG
Effacing (ABBR) .... EFCG
Effect (ABBR) .... EFCT
Effected (ABBR) .... EFCTD
Effectible (ABBR) .... EFCTB
Effecting (ABBR) .... EFCTG
Effecting (ABBR) .... EFTAG
Effective (ABBR) .... EF
Effective (ABBR) .... EFCTV
Effective (ABBR) .... EFFECT
Effective Sample Base (NTCM) .... ESB
Effectively (ABBR) .... EFCTVY
Effectively (ABBR) .... EFTVY
Effectiveness (ABBR) .... EFCTVNS
Effectiveness (ABBR) .... EFTVNS
Effectivity (ABBR) .... EFFECT
Effector (ABBR) .... EFCTR
Effects [*Automotive advertising*] .... EFFCTS
Effectual (ABBR) .... EFCTL
Effectual (ABBR) .... EFTL
Effectuality (ABBR) .... EFCTLT
Effectually (ABBR) .... EFCTLY
Effectualness (ABBR) .... EFCTLNS
Effectuate (ABBR) .... EFCTA
Effectuate (ABBR) .... EFTA
Effectuated (ABBR) .... EFCTAD
Effectuated (ABBR) .... EFTAD
Effectuating (ABBR) .... EFCTAG
Effeminacy (ABBR) .... EFEMC
Effeminate (ABBR) .... EFEM
Effeminately (ABBR) .... EFEMAY
Effeminately (ABBR) .... EFEMY
Effeminateness (ABBR) .... EFEMNS
Efferent (ABBR) .... EFFER
Effervesce (ABBR) .... EFERVS
Effervesce (ABBR) .... EFRVS
Effervesced (ABBR) .... EFERVSD
Effervesced (ABBR) .... EFRVSD
Effervescence (ABBR) .... EFERVSNC
Effervescence (ABBR) .... EFRVSNC
Effervescent (ABBR) .... EFERVST
Effervescent (ABBR) .... EFRVST
Effervescing (ABBR) .... EFERVSG
Effervescing (ABBR) .... EFRVSG
Effete (ABBR) .... EFFT
Efficacious (ABBR) .... EFICU
Efficacy (ABBR) .... EFIC
Efficiency (ABBR) .... EFICNC
Efficiency (ABBR) .... EFICNY
Efficient (ABBR) .... EFICNT
Efficiently (ABBR) .... EFICNTY
Efficiently (ABBR) .... EFICY
Effigy (ABBR) .... EFGY
Effloresce (ABBR) .... EFLOR
Effloresced (ABBR) .... EFLORD
Efflorescence (ABBR) .... EFLORNC
Efflorescent (ABBR) .... EFFL
Efflorescent (ABBR) .... EFLORT
Efflorescing (ABBR) .... EFLORG
Effluence (ABBR) .... EFLUNC
Effluent (ABBR) .... EFLU
Effluvia (ABBR) .... EFLUVA
Effluvial (ABBR) .... EFLUVL
Effluvium (ABBR) .... EFLUVM
Effort (ABBR) .... EFRT
Effortless (ABBR) .... EFRTLS
Effortlessly (ABBR) .... EFRTLSY
Effortlessness (ABBR) .... EFRTLSNS
Effrontery (ABBR) .... EFRNT
Effulgence (ABBR) .... EFULGNC
Effulgent (ABBR) .... EFULG
Effuse (ABBR) .... EFUS
Effused (ABBR) .... EFUSD
Effusing (ABBR) .... EFUSG
Effusion (ABBR) .... EFUSN
Effusive (ABBR) .... EFUSV
Effusively (ABBR) .... EFUSVY
Effusiveness (ABBR) .... EFUSVNS
Efs-Flugservice GmbH [*Germany*] [*ICAO designator*] (FAAC) .... FSD
Egalitarian (ABBR) .... EGALTR
Egalitarianism (ABBR) .... EGALSM
Egalitarianism (ABBR) .... EGALTRM
Egypt Air [*ICAO designator*] (FAAC) .... MSR
Egyptian Aviation Co. [*ICAO designator*] (FAAC) .... EMA
EI Air Exports Ltd. [*Ireland*] [*ICAO designator*] (FAAC) .... EIX
Eighteenth Century Scottish Studies Society (EA) .... ECSSS
Eightfold (ABBR) .... EGHTFD
Eightieth (ABBR) .... EGHTH
El Al-Israel Airlines Ltd. [*ICAO designator*] (FAAC) .... ELY
El Sal Air [*El Salvador*] [*ICAO designator*] (FAAC) .... ELS
Elaborately-Transformed Manufacture .... ETM
Elastic Active Aerodynamics [*Mitsubishi*] [*Automotive engineering*] .... EAA
Elbow (DAC) .... E
Eldinder Aviation [*Sudan*] [*ICAO designator*] (FAAC) .... DND
Electonic Remote Control [*Automotive electronic systems*] .... ERC
Electric Cable Makers' Confederation [*British*] (BI) .... ECMC
Electric-Field-Induced Second-Harmonic Generation .... EFISHG
Electric Lamp Industry Council [*British*] (BI) .... ELIC
Electric Lamp Manufacturers' Association of Great Britain Ltd. (BI) .... ELMA
Electric Light Fittings Association [*British*] (BI) .... ELFA
Electric Shutoff [*NFPA pre-fire planning symbol*] (NFPA) .... E
Electric Vehicle Association of Great Britain Ltd. (BI) .... EVA
Electric Vehicle Capsulated Contact [*Automotive electrical systems*] .... EVCC
Electrical Cell-Substrate Impedance Sensing [*for cell-culture study*] .... ECIS
Electrical Contractors' Association [*British*] (BI) .... ECA
Electrical Floor Warming Association [*British*] (BI) .... EFA
Electrical Industries Benevolent Association [*British*] (BI) .... EIBA
Electrical Industries Federation of Ireland (BI) .... EIFI
Electrical Metallic Conduit (DAC) .... EMC
Electrical Trades' Commercial Travellers' Association [*British*] (BI) .... ETCTA
Electrical/Transformer Room [*NFPA pre-fire planning symbol*] (NFPA) .... ET
Electrical Wholesalers Federation [*British*] (BI) .... EWF
Electricity (NTCM) .... E
Electricity Board for Northern Ireland (BI) .... EBNI
Electricity Supply Board [*Republic of Ireland*] (BI) .... ESB
Electro-Magnetic Pulse .... EMP
Electro-Magnetically Controlled Differential [*Powertrain*] [*Automotive engineering*] .... EMCD
Electro-Medical Trade Association [*British*] (BI) .... EMTA
Electrochemical Deposition [*Metallurgy*] .... ECD
Electrochemichromic [*Optoelectronics*] .... ECC
Electron-Capture Negative Chemical Ionization [*Spectrometry*] .... EC-NCI
Electron Transparent Zone [*Biochemistry*] .... ETZ
Electronic Acquisition Systems Instrumentation [*Vehicle testing*] [*Automotive engineering*] .... EASI
Electronic Air Suspension [*Automotive engineering*] .... EAS
Electronic Automatic Transaxle [*Automotive engineering*] .... EATX
Electronic Brake-Force Distribution [*Anti-lock brake systems*] [*Automotive engineering*] .... EBD
Electronic Compass Logic Module [*Automotive navigation systems*] .... ECLM
Electronic Counter Services .... ECS
Electronic Data Interchange/Electronic Commerce [*Computer science*] [*Army*] (RDA) .... EDI/EC
Electronic Diesel Control [*Automotive engineering*] .... EDC
Electronic Document Collection .... EDC
Electronic Engine Control - 5th Generation [*Automotive engineering*] .... EEC-V
Electronic Forms Designer [*Microsoft Corp.*] (PCM) .... EFD
Electronic Governor System [*Heavy-duty automotive engines*] .... EGS
Electronic Mock-Up [*Computer-aided design*] .... EMU
Electronic Modular Control Panel [*Motor-generator set design*] .... EMCP
Electronic Postproduction (NTCM) .... EPP
Electronic Price Information Computer .... EPIC
Electronic Reference Document .... ERD
Electronic Rentals Association [*British*] (BI) .... ERA
Electronic Target Generator [*Military*] (DA) .... ETG
Electronic Technical Support Center [*DiagSoft*] .... ETSC
Electronic Valve and Semiconductor Manufacturers' Association (IAA) .... VASCA
Electronic Valve Timing [*Automobile engine design*] .... EVT
Electronic Video Recording [*or Recorder*] (NTCM) .... EVR
Electrooptical Intelligence [*DoD*] .... ELECTRO-OPTINT
Electrophysiological Study Versus Electrocardiographic Monitoring [*Medical study*] .... ESVEM
Electrostatic Energy Analyzer [*Instrumentation*] .... EEA
Electrotypers' and Stereotypers' Managers and Overseers Association [*British*] (BI) .... ESMOA

Elevated Temperature Polyethylene ... ETPE
Elevator [*Technical drawings*] (NFPA) ... E
Elevator Code (NFPA) ... EIC
Elevator Equipment Room [*NFPA pre-fire planning symbol*] (NFPA) ... EE
Eley-Rideal Mechanism [*Chemistry*] ... ER
Elf Air Ltd. [*Russian Federation*] [*ICAO designator*] (FAAC) ... EFR
Elgaz [*Poland*] [*ICAO designator*] (FAAC) ... LGA
Eli-Fly SpA [*Italy*] [*ICAO designator*] (FAAC) ... EBS
Eliadamello SPA [*Italy*] [*ICAO designator*] (FAAC) ... LLO
Eligible Layout ... EL
Eligible Liability [*British*] ... EL
Elitos SpA [*Italy*] [*ICAO designator*] (FAAC) ... EHS
Elizabethan Railway Society [*British*] (BI) ... ERS
Elliott Beechcraft of Omaha, Inc. [*ICAO designator*] (FAAC) ... ELT
[*The*] **Elongated Collectors** [*An association*] (EA) ... TEC
Elrom Aviation & Investments [*Israel*] [*ICAO designator*] (FAAC) ... ELR
Embarked Personnel Material Report [*Navy*] (ANA) ... EPMR
Emergency Call Announcer [*Hearing technology*] ... ECA
Emergency Condition [*Navy*] (ANA) ... EMERGCON
Emergency Controlling Authority (DA) ... ECA
Emergency Distance [*Aviation*] (DA) ... ED
Emergency Generator Room [*NFPA pre-fire planning symbol*] (NFPA) ... EG
Emergency Relief ... ER
Emergency Remote Tracking Station [*Navy*] (ANA) ... ERTS
Emergency Response Planning Guideline [*Environmental science*] ... ERPG
Emery Worldwide Airlines, Inc. [*ICAO designator*] (FAAC) ... EWW
Emission Data Vehicle [*Exhaust emissions testing*] [*Automotive engineering*] ... EDV
Empire Air Service, Inc. [*ICAO designator*] (FAAC) ... EMP
Empire Airlines, Inc. [*ICAO designator*] (FAAC) ... CFS
Empire Cotton Growing Corp. [*British*] (BI) ... ECGC
Empire Test Pilots School [*British*] [*ICAO designator*] (FAAC) ... ETP
Employee Skills Upgrade ... ESU
Employer-Paid Advertising ... EPA
Employer Relations Officer ... ERO
Employers Mutual Indemnity Ltd. ... EMI
Employment Agents' Federation of Great Britain (BI) ... EAF
Employment Incentive Scheme ... EIS
Employment Officer ... EO
Employment Schedule [*Navy*] (ANA) ... EMPSKD
Empresa Aero-Servicios Parrague Ltd. [*Chile*] [*ICAO designator*] (FAAC) ... PRG
Empresa Aero Uruguay SA [*ICAO designator*] (FAAC) ... AUO
Empresa Aerocaribbean SA [*Cuba*] [*ICAO designator*] (FAAC) ... CRN
Empresa Aeromar [*Dominican Republic*] [*ICAO designator*] (FAAC) ... ROM
Empresa Aerotuy [*Venezuela*] [*ICAO designator*] (FAAC) ... TUY
Empresa Brasileira de Aeronautica SA [*Brazil*] [*ICAO designator*] (FAAC) ... EMB
Empresa Cubana de Aviacion [*Cuba*] [*ICAO designator*] (FAAC) ... CUB
Empresa Ecuatoriana de Aviacion [*Ecuador*] [*ICAO designator*] (FAAC) ... EEA
Empresa Guatemalteca de Aviacion [*Guatemala*] [*ICAO designator*] (FAAC) ... GUG
Empresa Servicicious Avensa SA [*Venezuela*] [*ICAO designator*] (FAAC) ... SERVIVENSA
Empresa Servicicious Avensa SA [*Venezuela*] [*ICAO designator*] (FAAC) ... SVV
Empresa de Transporte Aereo del Peru [*ICAO designator*] (FAAC) ... PLI
Enabled Artists United [*An association*] (EA) ... EAU
Encyclopedia ... encycl
End of Arm Tooling [*Robotics*] ... EAOT
End of Line [*Computer science*] ... EOLN
End of User [*Computer hacker terminology*] (NHD) ... EOU
End of Year Financial Statement ... EOYFS
Endangerment Information Report [*Environmental Protection Agency*] (ERG) ... EIR
Endless Vacation [*A publication*] ... Endl Vac
Endowment (ABBR) ... EDWNT
Endue (ABBR) ... EDU
Energetic Heavy Ion Composition Experiment [*NASA*] ... EHIC
Energy (ABBR) ... NRG
Energy of Crush Factor [*Automotive safety*] ... ECF
Energy Expenditure ... EE
Enforcement Decision Document [*Environmental Protection Agency*] (ERG) ... EDD
Engagement Zone [*Army*] (ADDR) ... EZ
Engine Angular Speed Variation [*Automotive engineering*] ... EASV
Engine Fuel Economy Control System [*Automotive engineering*] ... EFECS
Engine Monitoring Unit [*Automotive electronics*] ... EMU
Engine Oil Filterability Test ... EOFT
Engine Oil Licensing and Certification System [*American Petroleum Institute*] ... EOLCS
Engine and Propeller Factor [*IOR*] [*Yacht racing*] ... EPF
Engineer/Architect (DAC) ... E/A
Engineered Polypropylene [*Plastics*] [*Automotive engineering*] ... EPP
Engineering Analysis Services [*Auto industry supplier*] ... EAS
Engineering Casualty Control Evaluation Team [*Navy*] (ANA) ... ECCET
Engineering Concern Action Report [*Industrial engineering*] ... ECAR
Engineering Equipment Users' Association [*British*] (BI) ... EEUA
Engineering and Physical Sciences Research Council [*British*] ... EPSRC
Engineering Quality Improvement ... EQUIP
Engineers' and Allied Hand Tool Makers' Association [*British*] (BI) ... EAHTMA
English Bridge Union (BI) ... EBU
English Country Cheese Council (BI) ... ECCC
English Cross Country Union (BI) ... ECCU
English Golf Union (BI) ... EGU
English Lacrosse Union (BI) ... ELU
English New Education Fellowship (BI) ... ENEF
English Orienteering Association (BI) ... EOA
English Schools' Athletic Association (BI) ... ESAA
English Schools Cricket Association (BI) ... ESCA
English Schools' Rugby Union (BI) ... ESRU
English Schools' Swimming Association (BI) ... ESSA
English-Speaking Country ... ESC
English-Speaking Tape Respondents Association [*British*] (BI) ... ESTRA
English Timber Merchants' Association (BI) ... ETMA
Enhanced [*ICAO designator*] (FAAC) ... ENHNCD
Enhanced Airline Communications and Reporting System (DA) ... E-CARS
Enhanced Drive Parameter Table [*Computer science*] ... EDPT
[*The*] **Enhanced Integrated Soldier System** [*Army*] ... TEISS
Enhanced Telephone ... ET
Enhanced Thematic Mapper [*Geoscience*] ... ETM
Enhancement [*ICAO designator*] (FAAC) ... ENHNCMNT
Enroute Communications [*Aviation*] (FAAC) ... RCOM
Enroute Control Center [*Aviation*] (DA) ... ERCC
Enroute Metering [*Aviation*] (FAAC) ... ERMG
Enroute RADAR [*Aviation*] (FAAC) ... ERAD
Enroute Spacing Program [*Aviation*] (FAAC) ... ERSP
Enroute Tracking Automatic RADAR Service [*Aviation*] (FAAC) ... ETARS
Ensor Air [*Czechoslovakia*] [*ICAO designator*] (FAAC) ... ENR
Enter Controlled Airspace [*Air Traffic Control*] (FAAC) ... ECAS
Entergy Services, Inc. [*ICAO designator*] (FAAC) ... ENS
Enterprise Network Services [*Banyan*] [*Computer science*] ... ENS
Enterprise Support Service ... ESS
Enterprise Support Unit ... ESU
Enterprise Workshops Ltd. ... EWL
Entertainment [*Wire service code*] (NTCM) ... E
Environment Lapse Rate (DA) ... ELR
Environment Management Industry ... EMI
Environment and Resource Management Division [*World Wildlife Fund-United States*] ... ERMD
Environmental Action Plan [*Environmental Protection Agency*] (ERG) ... EAP
Environmental Business Council ... EBC
Environmental Cleanup and Responsibility Act [*1983*] (ERG) ... ECRA
Environmental Exposure Level [*Toxicology*] ... EEL
Environmental Impact Research Program [*Army*] (RDA) ... EIRP
Environmental Load Unit [*Recycling, emissions*] [*Automotive engineering*] ... ELU
Environmental Management Plan ... EMP
Environmental Priorities Strategies [*Volvo*] [*Automotive engineering*] ... EPS
Environmental Requirement ... ER
Environmental Resources Information Network [*Australia*] ... ERIN
Environmental Restoration [*Metallurgy*] ... ER
Environmental Science Research [*Concept car*] [*Automotive engineering*] ... ESR
Environmental Security Technology Certification Program [*Army*] (RDA) ... ESTCP
Environmental Self-Assessment Program ... ESAP
Environmental Sustainment Laboratory (RDA) ... ESL
Environmental Technician ... ET
Environmental Training Project [*World Wildlife Fund-United States*] ... ETP
EPAG - Group Air France [*ICAO designator*] (FAAC) ... IAF
Epps Air Service, Inc. [*ICAO designator*] (FAAC) ... EPS
Equal Opportunity [*A publication*] ... Equal Opp
Equator Airlines Ltd. [*Kenya*] [*ICAO designator*] (FAAC) ... PKA
Equatorial Airlines of Sao Tome and Principe [*ICAO designator*] (FAAC) ... EQL
Equatorial Guinea [*Aircraft nationality and registration mark*] (FAAC) ... 3C
Equipment (NFPA) ... E
Equivalent Circulating Density [*Well drilling*] ... ECD
Equivalent Fuel Efficiency Improvement ... EFEI
Equivalent Full-Time Student Unit ... EFTSU
Equivalent Mud Weight [*Well drilling technology*] ... EMW
ERA Helicopters, Inc. [*ICAO designator*] (FAAC) ... ERH
Erase, Record, and Playback (NTCM) ... ERP
Ergonomics Research Society [*British*] (BI) ... ERS
ERIC [*Educational Resources Information Center*] **Document Reproduction Service** [*Stanford University*] (NTCM) ... EDRS
Erie Airways, Inc. [*ICAO designator*] (FAAC) ... ERE
Escape Aviation [*ICAO designator*] (FAAC) ... TCL
Escrowed to Maturity ... ETM
Espana, Direccion General de Aviacion Civil [*Spain*] [*ICAO designator*] (FAAC) ... ENA
Essence Export Group [*British*] (BI) ... EEG
Essential Pharmacy Allowance ... EPA
Esso Rosources Canada Ltd. [*ICAO designator*] (FAAC) ... ERC
Estate Agents' Council [*British*] (BI) ... EAC
Estimated Daily Intake [*Toxicology*] ... EDI
Estimated Exposure Concentration [*Toxicology*] ... EEC
Estimated Exposure Dose [*Toxicology*] ... EED
Estimated Maximum Daily Intake [*Toxicology*] ... EMDI
Estimated Off-Block Time [*ICAO designator*] (FAAC) ... EOBT

Estonian Air [ICAO designator] (FAAC) ... ELL
Estrellas del Aire SA de CV [Mexico] [ICAO designator] (FAAC) ... ETA
Ethambutol Hydrochloride [Pharmacology] ... EMB
Ethanolamine Ammonia Lyase [An enzyme] ... EAL
Ethical, Legal and Social Implications [Genetic research] ... ELSI
Ethiopian Airlines Corp. [ICAO designator] (FAAC) ... ETH
Ethoxylated Bisphenol A Dimethacrylate [Organic chemistry] ... EBPAD
Ethyldichloroarsine [Medicine] (ADDR) ... ED
Ethylene Vinyl Alcohol [Plastics] ... EVOH
Euralair [France] [ICAO designator] (FAAC) ... ERL
Euralair International [France] [ICAO designator] (FAAC) ... EUL
Eurasian Ice Sheet [Climatology] ... EIS
Euravia [Spain] [ICAO designator] (FAAC) ... EUI
Euro Air Helicopter Service AB [Sweden] [ICAO designator] (FAAC) ... SCO
Euroair Transport Ltd. [British] [ICAO designator] (FAAC) ... EUZ
Euroberlin [France] [ICAO designator] (FAAC) ... EEB
Eurocommander SA [Spain] [ICAO designator] (FAAC) ... ERA
Eurocontrol [Belgium] [ICAO designator] (FAAC) ... EUC
Eurocopter [France] [ICAO designator] (FAAC) ... ECF
Eurocypria Airlines Ltd. [Cyprus] [ICAO designator] (FAAC) ... ECA
Euroflight Sweden, AB [ICAO designator] (FAAC) ... EUW
Eurofly [Italy] [ICAO designator] (FAAC) ... EEU
Eurofly SPA [Italy] [ICAO designator] (FAAC) ... EEZ
Eurojet Aviation Ltd. [British] [ICAO designator] (FAAC) ... GOJ
Eurojet Compagnie [British] [ICAO designator] (FAAC) ... RIK
Eurojet Italia [Italy] [ICAO designator] (FAAC) ... ERJ
Eurojet SA [Spain] [ICAO designator] (FAAC) ... EUR
Europe Aero Service [France] [ICAO designator] (FAAC) ... EYT
Europe Air [France] [ICAO designator] (FAAC) ... EUA
Europe Falcon Service [France] [ICAO designator] (FAAC) ... EFS
Europeaero Service National [France] [ICAO designator] (FAAC) ... EXN
European Academy of Science and Technology ... EAST
European Air Navigation Plan [ICAO] (DA) ... EUR ANP
European Air Traffic Control Harmonization and Integration Program [Eurocontrol] ... EATCHIP
European Air Transport [ICAO designator] (FAAC) ... BCS
European Airlines [France] [ICAO designator] (FAAC) ... TAT
European Aviation Services Ltd. [British] [ICAO designator] (FAAC) ... CCC
European Bioinformatics Institute ... EBI
European Democratic Alliance [Political movement] (ECON) ... EDA
European Expidite [Belgium] [ICAO designator] (FAAC) ... EUX
European Federation of Chemical Engineering ... EFChE
European Frequency Coordinating Body [ICAO] (DA) ... EUR FCB
European Geotraverse [A collaborative lithosphere study] ... EGT
European Jet Ltd. [British] [ICAO designator] (FAAC) ... JET
European League of Institutes of the Arts [British] ... ELIA
European Lubricant Testing Committee ... ELTC
European Lubricating Grease Institute [An association] ... ELGI
European Medicines Evaluation Agency (ECON) ... EMEA
European Monetary Co-Operation Fund ... EMCOF
European Right [Political movement] (ECON) ... ER
European Symposium on Computer Aided Process Engineering ... ESCAPE
European Union [Formerly, European Community] ... EU
European Urban Driving Cycle [Automotive emissions] ... EUDC
European Volcanological Project ... EVOP
European Wings [Czechoslovakia] [ICAO designator] (FAAC) ... EWS
European Year of Older People and Solidarity Between Generations ... EYOP
Eurowings (NFD & RFG Luftverhehrs AG) [Germany] [ICAO designator] (FAAC) ... NFD
Eutectic Mixture of Local Anesthetics [Topical anesthetic cream] ... EMLA
Evangelical Alliance [British] (BI) ... EA
[The] Evangelical Alliance Mission [An association] (NTCM) ... EAM
Evangelical Radio Alliance [British] (BI) ... ERA
Evergreen International Airlines [ICAO designator] (FAAC) ... EIA
Everton's Genealogical Helper [A publication] ... EGH
Every Other Week Till Forbid (NTCM) ... EOWTF
Evolutionary Factor Analysis [Statistics] ... EFA
Excalibur Aviation [British] [ICAO designator] (FAAC) ... EXC
Excelsior Airlines Ltd. [Ghana] [ICAO designator] (FAAC) ... ESR
Exceptional Children [A publication] ... Ex Child
Excess Emission Report [Environmental Protection Agency] (ERG) ... EER
Excess Fare Allowance ... EFA
Excess Three Code (IAA) ... XTC
Excess Travelling Time ... ETT
Excess Weight Loss [Morbid obesity surgical treatment] ... EWL
Excluded Goods Schedule ... EGS
Excutive Aerospace (Pty) Ltd. [South Africa] [ICAO designator] (FAAC) ... EAS
Exec Express II, Inc. [ICAO designator] (FAAC) ... LSS
Execaire Aviation Ltd. [Canada] [ICAO designator] (FAAC) ... EXA
Execujet [British] [ICAO designator] (FAAC) ... EXQ
Execute (IAA) ... XCT
Executive Air [Zimbabwe] [ICAO designator] (FAAC) ... AXE
Executive Air Charter [ICAO designator] (FAAC) ... EAC
Executive Air Fleet [ICAO designator] (FAAC) ... XAF
Executive Air Transport Ltd. [Switzerland] [ICAO designator] (FAAC) ... EXV
Executive Aviation Services Ltd. [Nigeria] [ICAO designator] (FAAC) ... ESY
Executive Flight, Inc. [ICAO designator] (FAAC) ... EXE
Executive Jet Aviation, Inc. [ICAO designator] (FAAC) ... EJA
Executive Jet Italiana SRL [Italy] [ICAO designator] (FAAC) ... EXJ
Executive Transports [France] [ICAO designator] (FAAC) ... EXU
Exhibitor (NTCM) ... EXHIB
Exin [Poland] [ICAO designator] (FAAC) ... EXN
Existing Lapse Rate (DA) ... ELR
Existing Light [Photography] (NTCM) ... XL
Expandable Machine Accounting System (IAA) ... XMAS
Expanded Characteristics Option [Metallurgy] ... ECHO
Expanded Polystyrene Product Manufacturers' Association [British] (BI) ... EPPMA
Expanded Quota Flow [Aviation] (FAAC) ... EXOF
Expanded Sample Frame (NTCM) ... ESF
Expansion Bolt [Technical drawings] (DAC) ... EXP BT
Exparc [Russian Federation] [ICAO designator] (FAAC) ... EPA
Expect (DA) ... EX
Expected Date of Confinement ... EDOC
Expected Time of Arrival ... ETA
Experience de Recherche d'Objects Sombres [Astronomy] ... EROS
Experimental Building Station ... EBS
Experimental-Eleventh Generation [Jaguar] [Automotive engineering] ... XK
Experimental Flight Management System [Aviation] (DA) ... EFMS
Experimental Mobile Satellite System (DA) ... EMSS
Experimental Surface-to-Air Missile [Military] (IAA) ... XSAM
Experimental Surface-to-Surface Missile [Military] (IAA) ... XSSM
Experimental Translation Language (IAA) ... XTRAN
Expert System [Computer science] (IAA) ... XPS
Explain [or Explanation] (IAA) ... XPL
Explanatory Memorandum ... EM
Explosive Vapor Detector (DA) ... EVD
Explosively-Formed Penetrator [Army] (RDA) ... EFP
Export Air del Peru SA Cargo Air Lines [ICAO designator] (FAAC) ... EXD
Export Clearance Number ... ECN
Export Credit Enhanced Leverage ... EXCEL
Export Finance and Insurance Fund ... EFIF
Export Integrated System ... EXIT
Export Meat Order ... EMO
Export Propensity ... EP
Exposure Monitoring Test Site [Environmental Protection Agency] (ERG) ... EMTS
Expreso Aereo [Peru] [ICAO designator] (FAAC) ... EPR
Express Air, Inc. [ICAO designator] (FAAC) ... FXA
Express Airlines I, Inc. [ICAO designator] (FAAC) ... FLG
Express Airlines II, Inc. [ICAO designator] (FAAC) ... TWC
Express Airways Nigeria Ltd. [ICAO designator] (FAAC) ... EAN
Express One International, Inc. [ICAO designator] (FAAC) ... LHN
Exprisoner ... EP
Extended [Automotive advertising] ... EXTEN
Extended ... XT
Extended Air Defense Simulation [Army] (RDA) ... EADSIM
Extended Communications Search [DoD] ... EXCOM
Extended Eligibility Temporary Entry Permit ... EETEP
Extended Exercise [Navy] (ANA) ... EXTENDEX
Extended Glaciological Timescale [Climatology] ... EGT
Extended Length Message (DA) ... ELM
Extended Parliamentary Network ... EPN
Extended Range Cap [Navy] (ANA) ... ERC
Extended Range Twin Operation [Aviation] (DA) ... ETOPS
Extending Concepts through Language Activities [Education] (AEE) ... ECOLA
Extensible Object Orientation ... EOO
Extension Register ... XR
External Architectural Students Association [British] (BI) ... EASA
External Germinal Layer [Cytology] ... EGL
External Mold Release [Plastic fabrications] ... EMR
External ROM [Read Only Memory] Mode [Computer science] (IAA) ... XRM
Extra Executive Transport [Germany] [ICAO designator] (FAAC) ... EXT
Extra Lightly Loaded (IAA) ... XLL
Extra Long Range [ICAO designator] (FAAC) ... ELR
Extracorporeal Liver-Assist Device [Medicine] (ECON) ... ELAD
Extraneous Residue Limit [Toxicology] ... ERL
Extreme Close-Up [Also, VCU] [Cinematography] (NTCM) ... XCU
Extreme Close-Up Indeed [Photography] [British] (NTCM) ... ECUI
Extreme Disablement Adjustment ... EDA
Extremely Hazardous Air Pollutant [Environmental science] ... EHAP
Extremity (MAH) ... extr
Extropy Institute (EA) ... ExI

F

Ferrichrome Recording Tape (NTCM) .... FeCr
Ferrule Contact [*Lamp base type*] (NTCM) .... F
Feuerstein's Instrumental Enrichment [*Education*] (AEE) .... FIE
Feynman-Kak Formula [*Particle physics*] .... F-K
FFS [*Flight Service Station*] **Guarding Service B** [*Aviation*] (FAAC) .... FGSB
Fiber-Optic Gyroscope [*Automotive navigation systems*] .... FOG
Fibre Building Board Development Organisation Ltd. [*British*] (BI) .... FIDOR
Fibre Trade Federation [*British*] (BI) .... FTF
Fibreboard Packing Case Employers' Association [*British*] (BI) .... FPCEA
Fibreboard Packing Case Manufacturers' Association [*British*] (BI) .... FPCMA
Field Aircraft Services Ltd. [*British*] [*ICAO designator*] (FAAC) .... FAS
Field Aviation GmbH & Co. [*Germany*] [*ICAO designator*] (FAAC) .... FIE
Field Condition Report [*Aviation*] (FAAC) .... FCRP
Field Engineering Bureau [*FCC*] (NTCM) .... FEB
Field Engineering Instruction [*British*] (DA) .... FEI
Field Entry Standard [*Military*] (ADDR) .... FES
Field Impact Insulation Class (DAC) .... FIIC
Field Information Report [*CIA*] .... FIR
Field Investigation Team [*Environmental Protection Agency*] (ERG) .... FIT
Field Maintenance Request .... FMR
Field Operations Bureau [*FCC*] (NTCM) .... FOB
Field Sound Transmission Class (DAC) .... FSTC
Fieldair Freight Ltd. [*New Zealand*] [*ICAO designator*] (FAAC) .... FLD
Fiji [*Aircraft nationality and registration mark*] (FAAC) .... DQ
Fiji Air Services Ltd. [*ICAO designator*] (FAAC) .... FAJ
Filamentous Hemagglutinin [*Medicine*] .... FHA
File-Set Description [*Computer science*] .... FSD
File Structure Volume Descriptor Record (NTCM) .... FSVDR
File Trade Association [*British*] (BI) .... FTA
File Transfer Protocol .... ftp
Filed Flight Plan (DA) .... FPL
Filipinas Orient Airways, Inc. [*Philippines*] [*ICAO designator*] (FAAC) .... FOA
Fillip (ABBR) .... FLP
Film Laboratory Association Ltd. [*British*] (BI) .... FLA
Film Production Association of Great Britain (BI) .... FPA
Filmier (ABBR) .... FLMR
Filmiest (ABBR) .... FLMST
Filminess (ABBR) .... FLMNS
Filmy (ABBR) .... FLMY
Filthier (ABBR) .... FLTHR
Filthiest (ABBR) .... FLTHST
Filthiness (ABBR) .... FLTHNS
Filthy (ABBR) .... FLTHY
Final Approach Course [*Aviation*] (DA) .... FAC
Final Approach Fix [*Aviation*] (DA) .... FAF
Final Approach Track [*Aviation*] (DA) .... FAT
Financial Accounting System .... FAS
Financial AirExpress [*ICAO designator*] (FAAC) .... FAK
Financial Information and Accounting System .... FIAS
Financial Management and Information System .... FINMIS
Financial Sector Adjustment Program [*West Africa*] .... FINSAP
Financial Security Assurance .... FSA
Financial Services Volunteer Corps [*An association*] (EA) .... FSVC
Fine Airlines, Inc. [*ICAO designator*] (FAAC) .... FBF
Fine Gardening [*A publication*] .... Fine Gard
Fine Scale Modeler [*A publication*] .... FSM
Finger of Death [*Fantasy gaming*] (NHD) .... FOD
Finished Goods Store .... FGS
Finist' Air [*France*] [*ICAO designator*] (FAAC) .... FTR
Finite Difference [*Metallurgy*] .... FD
Finite Volume [*Metallurgy*] .... FV
Finnair OY [*Finland*] [*ICAO designator*] (FAAC) .... FIN
Finnaviation OY [*Finland*] [*ICAO designator*] (FAAC) .... FAV
Finningley FTU [*British*] [*ICAO designator*] (FAAC) .... FYY
Finnish Air Force Headquarters [*ICAO designator*] (FAAC) .... FNF
FINSAP Implementation Secretariat [*West Africa*] .... FIS
Fire Coordination Exercise [*Military*] (ADDR) .... FCX
Fire Department Access Point [*NFPA planning symbol*] (NFPA) .... FD
Fire Escape (DAC) .... FE
Fire Extinguisher Trades Association [*British*] (BI) .... FETA
Fire Pump Room [*NFPA pre-fire planning symbol*] (NFPA) .... FP
Firearms Acquisition Certificate [*Canada*] .... FAC
Fireclay Grate Back Association [*British*] (BI) .... FGBA
First Air [*British*] [*ICAO designator*] (FAAC) .... HLE
First Air (Bradley Schedules) Ltd. [*Canada*] [*ICAO designator*] (FAAC) .... FAB
First Air Courier, Inc. [*ICAO designator*] (FAAC) .... FAC
First Edition Club (NTCM) .... FEC
First European Airways Ltd. [*British*] [*ICAO designator*] (FAAC) .... FEL
First Generation Non-English-Speaking Background NESB1
Fish Exports Inspector .... FEI
Fish and Shellfish Immunology [*A publication*] .... FSI
Fishing Boat Builders Association [*British*] (BI) .... FBBA
Fishing Vessel .... FV
Fitting-Out of Leased Premises .... FOLP
Flagship Express Services, Inc. [*ICAO designator*] (FAAC) .... FSX
Flamboyance (ABBR) .... FLMNC
Flamboyant (ABBR) .... FLMNT
Flamboyantly (ABBR) .... FLMNTY
Flame Infrared Emission .... FIRE
Flamenco Airways, Inc. [*ICAO designator*] (FAAC) .... WAF
Flamingly (ABBR) .... FLMNGY
Flanders Airlines [*Belgium*] [*ICAO designator*] (FAAC) .... FLN
Flandre Air International [*France*] [*ICAO designator*] (FAAC) .... FRI
Flandre Air Service [*France*] [*ICAO designator*] (FAAC) .... FRS
Flanged Connection [*Piping*] .... FC
Flank (ABBR) .... FLNK
Flanked (ABBR) .... FLNKD
Flanker (ABBR) .... FLNKR
Flanking (ABBR) .... FLNKG
Flapped (ABBR) .... FLPD
Flapping (ABBR) .... FLPG
Flash (ABBR) .... FLSH
Flash Advisory [*Meteorology*] (FAAC) .... FL
Flash Airline Ltd. [*Nigeria*] [*ICAO designator*] (FAAC) .... FSH
Flash-Back (ABBR) .... FLSH-BK
Flashed (ABBR) .... FLSHD
Flashehood (ABBR) .... FLSHD
Flasher (ABBR) .... FLSHR
Flashier (ABBR) .... FLSHR
Flashier (ABBR) .... FLSHYR
Flashiest (ABBR) .... FLSHYST
Flashily (ABBR) .... FLSHLY
Flashily (ABBR) .... FLSHYY
Flashiness (ABBR) .... FLSHNS
Flashiness (ABBR) .... FLSHYNS
Flashing (DAC) .... FL
Flashing (ABBR) .... FLSHG
Flashlight (ABBR) .... FLSHLT
Flashy (ABBR) .... FLSHY
Flat-Car (ABBR) .... FLT-CR
Flat-Foot (ABBR) .... FLT-FT
Flatly (ABBR) .... FLTY
Flatness (ABBR) .... FLTNES
Flatness (ABBR) .... FLTNS
Flatted (ABBR) .... FLTD
Flatten (ABBR) .... FLTN
Flattened (ABBR) .... FLTND
Flattener (ABBR) .... FLTRNR
Flattening (ABBR) .... FLTNG
Flatter (ABBR) .... FLTR
Flattered (ABBR) .... FLTRD
Flattered (ABBR) .... FLTRR
Flattering (ABBR) .... FLTRG
Flatteringly (ABBR) .... FLTRGY
Flattery (ABBR) .... FLTRY
Flattest (ABBR) .... FLTST
Flatting (ABBR) .... FLTG
Flatware (ABBR) .... FLTWR
Flauntiest (ABBR) .... FLNTEST
Flautist (ABBR) .... FLST
Flautist (ABBR) .... FLTST
Flavor (ABBR) .... FLVR
Flavored (ABBR) .... FLVRD
Flavorer (ABBR) .... FLVRR
Flavorful (ABBR) .... FLVRFL
Flavorfully (ABBR) .... FLVRFLY
Flavoring (ABBR) .... FLVRG
Flavorless (ABBR) .... FLVRLS
Flavorous (ABBR) .... FLVRUS
Flavorsome (ABBR) .... FLVRSM
Fleet Imagery Satellite Terminal [*Navy*] (ANA) .... FIST
Fleet Requirement Air Direction Unit [*British*] [*ICAO designator*] (FAAC) .... BWY
Fleeting (ABBR) .... FLTG
Fleetingly (ABBR) .... FLTGY
Fleetingness (ABBR) .... FLTGNS
Fleetly (ABBR) .... FLTY
Fleetness (ABBR) .... FLTNS
Fleshiest (ABBR) .... FLSHST
Fleshly (ABBR) .... FLSHY
Fleshpots (ABBR) .... FLSH-PTS
Flexair BV [*Netherlands*] [*ICAO designator*] (FAAC) .... FXY
Flexair Ltd. [*British*] [*ICAO designator*] (FAAC) .... CFX
Flexible-Fuel Engine [*Automotive engineering*] .... FFE
Flexible-Fueled [*Automotive engineering*] .... FF
Flexible Manufacturing Cell [*Industrial engineering*] .... FMC
Flexible Numerical Control [*Manufacturing engineering*] [*Computer science*] .... FNC
Flexible Track System [*Aviation*] (DA) .... FTS
Flight Calibration Procedure [*Aviation*] (DA) .... FLTCAL
Flight Centre Victoria [*Canada*] [*ICAO designator*] (FAAC) .... FCV
Flight-Chernobyl Association [*Russian Federation*] [*ICAO designator*] (FAAC) .... FCH
Flight Corp. [*New Zealand*] [*ICAO designator*] (FAAC) .... FCP
Flight Data and Flow Management Group [*ICAO*] (DA) .... FDFM
Flight Data Input/Output [*Aviation*] (FAAC) .... FDIO
Flight Data Input/Output Repeater [*Aviation*] (FAAC) .... FDIOR
Flight Data Processing System (DA) .... FDPS
Flight Express, Inc. [*ICAO designator*] (FAAC) .... EXR
Flight Ferry [*Navy*] (ANA) .... FF
Flight Information Billing System (DA) .... FIBS
Flight Input Workstation (DA) .... FIW

Flight Line, Inc. [*ICAO designator*] (FAAC) ... ACT
Flight Line, Inc. [*ICAO designator*] (FAAC) ... SOU
Flight Management and Guidance System (DA) ... FMGS
Flight Plan Area [*Aviation*] (FAAC) ... FPA
Flight Preparation Ltd. [*British*] [*ICAO designator*] (FAAC) ... FPP
Flight Radio Telephony Operator (DA) ... FRTO
Flight Safety Ltd. [*British*] [*ICAO designator*] (FAAC) ... FSL
Flight Surgeon Badge [*Military decoration*] [*Army*] ... FLTSURBAD
Flight Technical Error [*Aviation*] (DA) ... FTE
Flight Technical Tolerance [*Aviation*] (DA) ... FIT
Flight Time Limitation [*Aviation*] (DA) ... FTL
Flight Training Device [*Aviation*] (DA) ... FTD
Flight West Airlines [*Australia*] [*ICAO designator*] (FAAC) ... FWQ
Flightcrew Licensing (DA) ... FCL
Flightcrew Record System (DA) ... FCRS
Flightexec Ltd. [*Canada*] [*ICAO designator*] (FAAC) ... FEX
Flightline [*British*] [*ICAO designator*] (FAAC) ... FLT
Flimsier (ABBR) ... FLMSR
Flimsiest (ABBR) ... FLMSST
Flimsily (ABBR) ... FLMSY
Flimsiness (ABBR) ... FLMSNS
Flimsy (ABBR) ... FLMSY
Flinch (ABBR) ... FLNH
Flincher (ABBR) ... FLNHR
Flinchingly (ABBR) ... FLNHGY
Flinging (ABBR) ... FLNGG
Flint (ABBR) ... FLNT
Flintier (ABBR) ... FLNTR
Flintiest (ABBR) ... FLNTST
Flintily (ABBR) ... FLNTYY
Flintiness (ABBR) ... FLNTNS
Flintiness (ABBR) ... FLNTYNS
Flinty (ABBR) ... FLNTY
Flippancy (ABBR) ... FLPNC
Flippant (ABBR) ... FLPNT
Flippantly (ABBR) ... FLPNTY
Flirtation (ABBR) ... FLRTN
Flirtatious (ABBR) ... FLRTU
Float (ABBR) ... FLOT
Floatable (ABBR) ... FLTB
Floatage (ABBR) ... FLOTGE
Floatation (ABBR) ... FLTN
Floated (ABBR) ... FLOTD
Floater (ABBR) ... FLOTR
Floater (ABBR) ... FLTR
Floating (ABBR) ... FLOTG
Floating Point Operation [*Computer science*] ... FLOP
Floating Point Register [*Computer science*] ... FBR
Floccule (ABBR) ... FLOC
Flocculent (ABBR) ... FLOC
Floccus (ABBR) ... FLOC
Flood (ABBR) ... FLOD
Flooded (ABBR) ... FLODD
Flooding (ABBR) ... FLODG
Floodlight (DA) ... Flo
Floor Covering Contractors' Association [*British*] (BI) ... FCCA
Floor Proximity Emergency Escape Path Marking [*Aviation*] (DA) ... FPEEPM
Floor Rug Manufacturers' Association [*British*] (BI) ... FRMA
Floored (ABBR) ... FLRD
Flooring (ABBR) ... FLORG
Flooring (ABBR) ... FLRG
Floorwalker (ABBR) ... FLOR-WKR
Flopped (ABBR) ... FLOPD
Flopper (ABBR) ... FLOPR
Floppier (ABBR) ... FLOPR
Floppier (ABBR) ... FLOPYR
Floppiest (ABBR) ... FLOPST
Floppiest (ABBR) ... FLOPYST
Floppily (ABBR) ... FLOPLY
Floppiness (ABBR) ... FLOPNS
Flopping (ABBR) ... FLOPG
Floppy (ABBR) ... FLOPY
Flora (ABBR) ... FLRA
Floral (ABBR) ... FLRAL
Floret (ABBR) ... FLRT
Floricultural (ABBR) ... FLRCLTRL
Floriculturalist (ABBR) ... FLRCLTRST
Floriculture (ABBR) ... FLRCLTR
Florid (ABBR) ... FLRID
Florida Air, Inc. [*ICAO designator*] (FAAC) ... OJY
Florida Express, Inc. [*ICAO designator*] (FAAC) ... FLX
Florida West Airlines [*ICAO designator*] (FAAC) ... FWL
Floridity (ABBR) ... FLRIDT
Floridly (ABBR) ... FLRIDY
Floridness (ABBR) ... FLRIDNS
Florist (ABBR) ... FLRST
Flossier (ABBR) ... FLSR
Flossiest (ABBR) ... FLSST
Flossy (ABBR) ... FLSY
Flotation (ABBR) ... FLOTN
Flotation (ABBR) ... FLTAN
Flotilla (ABBR) ... FLOTL
Flotilla (ABBR) ... FLTLA
Flotsam (ABBR) ... FLOT
Flotsam (ABBR) ... FLOTM
Flotsam (ABBR) ... FLTSM
Flounced (ABBR) ... FLNCD
Flouncing (ABBR) ... FLNCG
Flounder (ABBR) ... FLNDR
Floundered (ABBR) ... FLNDRD
Floundering (ABBR) ... FLNDRG
Flourescence (ABBR) ... FLRSNC
Flourescent (ABBR) ... FLRSNT
Flouridate (ABBR) ... FLRDA
Flouridated (ABBR) ... FLRDAD
Flouridating (ABBR) ... FLRDAG
Flouridation (ABBR) ... FLRDN
Flourier (ABBR) ... FLORR
Flouriest (ABBR) ... FLORST
Flourish (ABBR) ... FLRH
Flourishing (ABBR) ... FLRHG
Flouroscope (ABBR) ... FLSCP
Floury (ABBR) ... FLORY
Flouter (ABBR) ... FLUTR
Flow (NFPA) ... F
Flow Control Decision Message (DA) ... FCDM
Flow Control Execution Message (DA) ... FCEM
Flow Management Position [*ICAO*] (DA) ... FMP
Flow Management Unit [*Aviation*] (FAAC) ... FMU
Flowers Publicity Council Ltd. [*British*] (BI) ... FPC
Fluctuant (ABBR) ... FLUCNT
Fluctuated (ABBR) ... FLUCD
Fluctuating (ABBR) ... FLUCG
Fluctuation (ABBR) ... FLUCN
Flue-Gas-through-the-Tubes [*Incinerator*] ... FGTT
Fluency (ABBR) ... FLUNC
Fluent (ABBR) ... FLUNT
Fluently (ABBR) ... FLUNTY
Fluffed (ABBR) ... FLUFD
Fluffier (ABBR) ... FLUFYR
Fluffiest (ABBR) ... FLUFYST
Fluffily (ABBR) ... FLUFYY
Fluffiness (ABBR) ... FLUFYNS
Fluffing (ABBR) ... FLUFG
Fluffy (ABBR) ... FLUFY
Flugdienst Fehlhaber GmbH [*Germany*] [*ICAO designator*] (FAAC) ... FFG
Flugfelag Austerlands Ltd. Egilsstadir [*Iceland*] [*ICAO designator*] (FAAC) ... EST
Flugfelag Nordurlands [*Iceland*] [*ICAO designator*] (FAAC) ... FNA
Fluid Dynamics Analysis Package [*Computer-assisted engineering*] ... FIDAP
Fluid Power Take-Off [*Hydraulic transmissions*] ... FPTO
Fluidity (ABBR) ... FLT
Fluidness (ABBR) ... FLNS
Fluke (ABBR) ... FLUK
Flummery (ABBR) ... FLMRY
Flunky (ABBR) ... FLNKY
Fluorescence Line-Narrowing Spectroscopy ... FLNS
Fluorescence Pattern Photobleaching Recovery [*for study of surfaces*] ... FPPR
Fluorescent (ABBR) ... FLUORES
Fluorescent Treponemal Antibody-Absorption Syphilis Test [*Medicine*] (MAH) ... FTA-AB
Fluoriodocarbon [*Fire extinguishing compound*] ... FIC
Fluorocarbon (ERG) ... FC
Flurried (ABBR) ... FLRD
Flurrying (ABBR) ... FLRG
Flushing Cistern Makers' Association [*British*] (BI) ... FCMA
Flushing, NY (ABBR) ... FLS
Fluster (ABBR) ... FLSTR
Flute (ABBR) ... FLUT
Fluted (ABBR) ... FLUTD
Fluting (ABBR) ... FLUTG
Flutist (ABBR) ... FLST
Flutist (ABBR) ... FLUTST
Flutter (ABBR) ... FLTR
Flutter (ABBR) ... FLUTR
Fluttered (ABBR) ... FLUTRD
Flutterer (ABBR) ... FLUTRR
Flutterier (ABBR) ... FLTRIR
Flutteriest (ABBR) ... FLTRIST
Fluttering (ABBR) ... FLTRG
Fluttering (ABBR) ... FLUTRG
Flutteringly (ABBR) ... FLTRGY
Fluttery (ABBR) ... FLTRY
Fluttery (ABBR) ... FLUTRY
Flux (ABBR) ... FLUX
Fluxed (ABBR) ... FLUXD
Fluxing (ABBR) ... FLUXG
Fluxion (ABBR) ... FLUXN
Fly-In Echelon [*Navy*] (ANA) ... FIE
Flying Boat, Inc. [*ICAO designator*] (FAAC) ... CHK
Flying Cargo Private Ltd. [*Maldives*] [*ICAO designator*] (FAAC) ... FCM
Flying Dutchman [*Racing dinghy*] ... FD
Flying Duty Period (DA) ... FDP
Flying Instructor Course (DA) ... FIC

Flying Swiss Ambulance Maldives (Pvt) Ltd. [*ICAO designator*]
(FAAC) .... SRM
FM Broadcast Translator [*FCC*]   (NTCM) .... FT
Foam System [*NFPA pre-fire planning symbol*]   (NFPA) .... FO
Focus, Aperture, Shutter, Tachometer [*Cinematography*]   (NTCM) .... FAST
Fokker Flight Operations [*Netherlands*] [*ICAO designator*]   (FAAC) .... FOP
Folkestone-Boulogne Ferries [*English Channel ferry-boat service*]
[*British*]   (ECON) .... FBF
Follow Shot [*Photography*]   (NTCM) .... FS
Fonds European d'Orientation et de Garantie Agriculturel [*European
Agricultural Guidance and Guarantee Fund*] .... FEOGA
Fonnafly AS [*Norway*] [*ICAO designator*]   (FAAC).......... NOF
Food Brokers Ltd. [*Canada*] [*ICAO designator*]   (FAAC) ...... FBL
Food, Drug, and Cosmetic Act .... FD & C
Food Machinery Association [*British*]   (BI) .... FMA
Food Trades Protection Society Ltd. [*British*]   (BI) .... FTPS
Foodland Associates Ltd. .... FAL
Foolscap   (NTCM) .... FC
Foolscap   (ABBR) .... FLS-CP
Foolscap   (NTCM) .... FSC
Footwear Components Association Ltd. [*British*]   (BI).......... FCA
Footwear Distributors Federation [*British*]   (BI) .... FDF
For [*Telecommunications*]   (ADDR) .... FR
For Further Headings   (DA) .... FFH
For Your Amusement [*Computer hacker terminology*]   (NHD)........ FYA
Force Aerienne Belge [*Belgium*] [*ICAO designator*]   (FAAC)....... AFB
Force Movement Control Center [*Marines*]   (ANA) .... FMCC
Force Over-the-Horizon Targeting Coordinator [*Navy*]   (ANA) .... FOTC
Forces Aeriennes Francaises [*France*] [*ICAO designator*]   (FAAC)........... FAF
Forces Help Society [*British*]   (BI)................................. FHS
Ford of Britain [*Corporate subsidiary*] .... FOB
Ford Motor Co. [*ICAO designator*]   (FAAC).................... FRD
Ford Motor Co. Ltd. [*ICAO designator*]   (FAAC) .... FOB
Foreign Bases Project   (EA) .... FBP
Foreign Bird League [*British*]   (BI) .... FBL
Foreign Correspondents Club of Japan   (NTCM) .... FCC
Foreign Editor   (NTCM) .... FE
Foreign Exchange Gains and Losses .... FXGL
Foreign Fishing Vessel .... FFV
Foreign Investment Fund .... FIF
Foreign Investment Law .... FIL
Foreign Military Intelligence Collection Activities [*Navy*]
(ANA) .... FORMICA
Foreign-Owned or Affiliated [*Business term*] .... FOA
Foreign Program [*FCC*]   (NTCM) .... FP
Foreign Tax Credit System .... FTCS
Foremost Aviation Ltd. [*Nigeria*] [*ICAO designator*]   (FAAC) .... FMA
Forest Airline South Africa [*ICAO designator*]   (FAAC)....... FOL
Forging Ingot Makers' Association [*British*]   (BI) .... FIMA
Formed-in-Place Plastic Gasket [*Automotive engineering*] ...... FIPG
Forming Limit Curve [*Steel sheet fabrication*] .... FLC
Fortified [*Nutrition*] .... fort
Fortune SRL [*Italy*] [*ICAO designator*]   (FAAC) .... FOR
Forty-Mile Air [*ICAO designator*]   (FAAC) .... MLA
Forward Air Control Party Training [*Navy*]   (ANA) .... FACPTNG
Forward Area Air Defense Command and Control [*Military*] .... FAAD C2
Forward Logistics Site [*Navy*] .... FLS
Forward Visibility More than ____ Miles [*Aviation*]   (FAAC) .... MFV
Foster Aviation [*ICAO designator*]   (FAAC) .... FSA
Foster Yeoman Ltd. [*British*] [*ICAO designator*]   (FAAC) .... JFY
Fotografia F3 SA [*Spain*] [*ICAO designator*]   (FAAC)....... FTE
Foundation of Automation and Employment Ltd. [*British*]   (BI) .... FAE
Foundation to Improve Television   (EA) .... FIT
Foundation for Moral Restoration   (EA) .... FMR
Foundry Industry Training Committee [*British*]   (BI) ...... FITC
Four Island Air Ltd. [*Antigua and Barbuda*] [*ICAO designator*]
(FAAC) .... FIA
Four Star Aviation, Inc. [*Virgin Islands*] [*ICAO designator*]   (FAAC).......... FSC
Four Valve Type A [*Cosworth racing engines*]................. FVA
Four Winds Aviation Ltd. [*ICAO designator*]   (FAAC) ...... WDS
Fourier Transform Inductively-Coupled Plasma [*Spectrometry*]........ FT-ICP
Fourier Transform Ion Cyclotron Resonance Mass Spectrometry .... FT-ICRMS
Fowler [*Rick*] [*ICAO designator*]   (FAAC)..................... WTV
Foxair Ltd. [*British*] [*ICAO designator*]   (FAAC)......... FXR
FR Aviation Ltd. [*British*] [*ICAO designator*]   (FAAC)......... FRA
Fracture Gradient .... FG
Frames per Second   (NTCM) .... F/S
France Europe Avia Jet [*ICAO designator*]   (FAAC)......... FEJ
France Marine Nationale [*ICAO designator*]   (FAAC)....... FMN
Francis Drake Fellowship [*British*]   (BI) .... FDF
Fraud Control Plan .... FCP
Free Erythrocyte Protoporphyrin [*Hematoloy*]   (MAH)........ FEPP
Free Estimated Time of Overflight [*Aviation*]   (DA) .... FETO
Free-Form Fabrication   (ECON) .... FFF
Free of Heart Center   (DAC) .... FOHC
Free Software Foundation   (EA) .... SFS
Freedom Airlines, Inc. [*ICAO designator*]   (FAAC).......... FDM
Freeway Air BV [*Netherlands*] [*ICAO designator*]   (FAAC)........ FWC
Freeway Iberica SA [*Spain*] [*ICAO designator*]   (FAAC)......... FIB
Freezing Rain Endurance Test [*Aviation*]   (DA) .... FRET
Freight Runners Express, Inc. [*ICAO designator*]   (FAAC) .... FRG
French Fourragere [*Military decoration*] .... FRFOURRA

Frequence Optimum de Travail [*Optimum Working Frequency*]
(NTCM)... FOT
Frequency Change Approved [*Aviation*]   (FAAC) .... FCA
Frequency Management [*Aviation*]   (DA)........................ FM
Frequent Asked Question List [*Computer science*]   (NHD)........ FAQL
Frevag Airlines [*Belgium*] [*ICAO designator*]   (FAAC)....... FVG
Friction Pendulum System [*for earthquake protection*]............... FPS
Frictional Force   (DA) .... F!r
Friends of International Education [*An association*]   (EA) .... FIE
Friends of the Jessup [*An association*]   (EA) .... FOJ
Friends' Work Camp Committee [*British*]   (BI)............... FWCC
Friendship Air Alaska [*ICAO designator*]   (FAAC)........... FAL
Frifly SpA [*Italy*] [*ICAO designator*]   (FAAC)................. FIF
Frigate LAMPS [*Light Airborne Multipurpose System*] Integrated
Team Training [*Navy*]   (ANA) .... FLITT
Fringe Festival of Independent Dance Artists [*Canada*] .... fFIDA
Frobisher NV (European Airlines) [*Belgium*] [*ICAO designator*]
(FAAC) .... FRO
Front of House Spot [*Theatrical lighting*]   (NTCM)........... FOH
Front Projection   (NTCM) .... FP
Frontier Flying Service, Inc. [*ICAO designator*]   (FAAC)......... FTA
Frontispiece   (NTCM) .... Fp
Frost [*Meteorology*]   (DA).. FRST
FSS [*Flight Service Station*] Assumes Flight-Plan Area [*Aviation*]
(FAAC) .... FAFAB
FSS [*Flight Service Station*] Returns Flight-Plan Area and Service B
[*Aviation*]   (FAAC) .... FRFAB
FSS [*Flight Service Station*] Returns Service B [*Aviation*]   (FAAC) .... FRSB
Fuel Injection Equipment [*Diesel engines*] .... FIE
Fuel Injection System [*Automotive engineering*] .... FIS
Fuel-Jet   (DA) .... FJ
Fuel and Oil Metering Pump [*Engine design*] .... FOMP
Fuel (Petroleum)   (DA) .... FP
Fuel Supply Unknown [*Aviation*]   (FAAC) .... FENKN
Fuerza Aerea Argentina [*ICAO designator*]   (FAAC) ...... FAG
Fuerza Aerea del Peru [*ICAO designator*]   (FAAC) .... FPR
Fuerzas Aereas Espanolas [*Spain*] [*ICAO designator*]   (FAAC) .... AME
Fujairah Aviation Centre [*United Arab Emirates*] [*ICAO designator*]
(FAAC) .... FUJ
Fuji International Speedway Co. [*Automobile racing*] ...... FISCO
Full Aperture [*Photography*]   (NTCM)........................... FA
Full Performance Level [*Aviation*]   (FAAC) .... FPL
Full Shot [*Photography*]   (NTCM)................................... FS
Full-State Assumption [*Education*]   (AEE) .... FSA
Fullscale   (ABBR) .... FLSCL
Fully Distributed Cost .... FDC
Fulminating   (ABBR) .... FLMNAG
Fulmination   (ABBR) .... FLMNAN
Fulsome   (ABBR) .... FLSM
Fulsomely   (ABBR) .... FLSMY
Fulsomeness   (ABBR) .... FLSMNS
Fumigacion Aerea Andalusa SA [*Spain*] [*ICAO designator*]   (FAAC)......... FAM
Functionally Gradient Material [*Materials science*] .... FGM
Fundamentals of Engineering [*Exam*] .... FE
Funds Allocation Control System .... FACS
Funtshi Aviation Service [*Zaire*] [*ICAO designator*]   (FAAC)...... FUN
Furnishing Springmakers Federation [*British*]   (BI) ...... FSMF
Furniture and Bedding Publicity Association Ltd. [*British*]   (BI).......... FABPA
Furniture Development Council [*British*]   (BI) .... FDC
Furniture and Timber Industry Training Board [*British*]   (BI) .... FTITB
Furniture Trades Benevolent Association [*British*]   (BI) .... FTBA
Furthest-On Circle [*Navy*]   (ANA) .... FOC
Fusible   (DAC) .... Fus
Future Concept Vehicle .... FCV
Future Sports-Sedan Experimental [*Concept car*] .... FS-X

G

G & B Aviation Ltd. [*British*] [*ICAO designator*]   (FAAC)...................... TNG
G-Myeloma Protein [*Biochemistry*]   (MAH).............................. G-MP
Gabon-Air-Transport [*ICAO designator*]   (FAAC)........................ GRT
Gaily   (ABBR)... GY
Galaxy Airways Ltd. [*Nigeria*] [*ICAO designator*]   (FAAC)................ GXY
Galena Air Services, Inc. [*ICAO designator*]   (FAAC)..................... GAS
Gallic Aviation [*France*] [*ICAO designator*]   (FAAC).................... GLI
Galvanised Tank Manufacturers' Association [*British*]   (BI) .... GTMA
Gama Aviation Ltd. [*British*] [*ICAO designator*]   (FAAC) .... GMA
Gamair Ltd. [*Gambia*] [*ICAO designator*]   (FAAC)...................... KBS
Gambcrest Enterprises Ltd. [*Gambia*] [*ICAO designator*]   (FAAC)......... GEL
Gambia [*Aircraft nationality and registration mark*]   (FAAC) C5
Gambia .... GAM
Gambia Air Shuttle Ltd. [*ICAO designator*]   (FAAC)..................... GSH
Gambia Airways [*ICAO designator*]   (FAAC)............................. GAW
Gambling and Betting Addiction... GABA
Gamekeepers' Association of the United Kingdom   (BI) .... GAUK
Gaming Entertainment Television [*Interactive-gambling TV station*]
    (ECON) .... GET
Gander Automated Message Processing System [*ICAO*]   (DA) .... GAMPS
Gander Aviation Ltd. [*Canada*] [*ICAO designator*]   (FAAC) .... GAN
Gap Media Project [*An association*]   (EA) .... GMP
Garaged [*Automotive advertising*].. GARGD
Garden State Airlines, Inc. [*ICAO designator*]   (FAAC)................... GSA
Garrison Aviation Ltd. [*Canada*] [*ICAO designator*]   (FAAC)......... AHM
Garuda Indonesia PT [*ICAO designator*]   (FAAC)........................ GIA
Gas Cleaning System [*Combustion technology*]................................ GCS
Gas Discharge Lamp .... GDL
Gas Injection Molding [*Plastic fabrications*]................................. GIM
Gas-Scintillation Imaging Spectrometer .... GIS
Gas Shutoff [*NFPA pre-fire planning symbol*]   (NFPA)..................... G
Gasoline-Fueled [*Automotive engineering*].................................... GF
Gastric Reservoir Reduction [*Morbid obesity surgical treatment*] .... GRR
Gastric Wrap [*Morbid obesity surgical treatment*]............................ GW
Gastrointestinal System [*Medicine*]   (MAH)............................... GIS
Gatari Hutama Air Services PT [*Indonesia*] [*ICAO designator*]
    (FAAC).. GHS
Gate Operating System [*Aviation*]   (DA) .... GOS
Gate Valve   (DAC)... GV
Gatwick Handling Ltd. [*British*] [*ICAO designator*]   (FAAC)........... GHL
Gays and Lesbians Opposing Violence [*An association*]..................... GLOV
GB Air Academy Ltd. [*British*] [*ICAO designator*]   (FAAC)............ TUT
GB Airways Ltd. [*British*] [*ICAO designator*]   (FAAC)................. GBL
GCA Surveys [*British*] [*ICAO designator*]   (FAAC).................... SVY
Geeseair [*Canada*] [*ICAO designator*]   (FAAC)......................... GEE
Geevax Ltd. [*British*] [*ICAO designator*]   (FAAC)..................... GVX
Gelatine and Glue Research Association [*British*]   (BI) .... GGRA
Gemial [*Slovakia*] [*ICAO designator*]   (FAAC)......................... GML
Gemini Airlines Ltd. [*Ghana*] [*ICAO designator*]   (FAAC)............. GAL
Gemmological Association of Great Britain   (BI) .... GAGB
Genavco Air Ltd. [*British*] [*ICAO designator*]   (FAAC)................ GEN
Genavia SRL [*Italy*] [*ICAO designator*]   (FAAC)....................... JVA
Gendall Air Ltd. [*Canada*] [*ICAO designator*]   (FAAC)................ GAB
Gendarmerie Nationale [*France*] [*ICAO designator*]   (FAAC)........... FGN
Gender Equality in Mathematics and Science.................................. GEMS
General Aerospace, Inc. [*Canada*] [*ICAO designator*]   (FAAC)......... SWK
General Air Cargo [*Venezuela*] [*ICAO designator*]   (FAAC)............ GAC
General Air Services Ltd. [*Nigeria*] [*ICAO designator*]   (FAAC)........ NGS
General Association of Ladies Hairdressers [*British*]   (BI)............... GALH
General Audit Manual .... GAM
General Aviation Manufacturers' and Traders' Association [*British*]
    (DA) .... GAMTA
General Aviation Terminal, Inc. [*Canada*] [*ICAO designator*]
    (FAAC).. XGA
General Cognitive Index... GCI
General Conditions of Contract... GCOC
General Corporation for Light Air Transport & Technical Sevices
    [*Libya*] [*ICAO designator*]   (FAAC).................................. GLT
General Disposal Authority.. GDA
General Electric Comprehensive Operating System [*Computer
    science*]   (NHD) .... GECOS
General Enrollment Manual .... GEM
General Entry Permit .... GEP

General Knowledge Test .... GKT
General Lighting System [*Incadescent lighting*] .... GLS
General Medical Services Council [*British*]   (BI) .... GMSC
General Motors Corp. [*ICAO designator*]   (FAAC)....................... GMC
General Payments System .... GPAY
General Public License   (NHD) .... GPL
General Public Virus [*Computer science*]   (NHD)......................... GPV
General Recurrent Grant... GRG
General Stores Officer.. GSO
General System Mobile [*Telephone*]... GSM
General Training Program .... GTP
General Transcription Factor [*Genetics*]..................................... GTF
Generalist Intelligence Officer .... GIO
Generally Accepted Accounting Principles [*Environmental
    Protection Agency*]   (ERG)... GAAP
Generated Symbol [*Computer science*]   (NHD).......................... GENSYM
Generic Run-Time [*Computer science*]....................................... GRI
Generic Security Service Application Program Interface...................... GSSAPI
Generous Tit for Tat [*Game strategy*].. GTFT
Geographic Air Surveys Ltd. [*Canada*] [*ICAO designator*]   (FAAC) .... GSL
Geological Survey of Great Britain and Museum of Practical Geology
    (BI) .... GSM
Georgia Air [*Czechoslovakia*] [*ICAO designator*]   (FAAC)............ GEA
Georgian Bay Airways [*Canada*] [*ICAO designator*]   (FAAC)......... GBA
Geostationary Launch Vehicle [*Indian Space Research Organization*]........ GSLV
German Air Force [*ICAO designator*]   (FAAC)............................ GAF
German Army [*ICAO designator*]   (FAAC)............................... GAM
German Cargo Services [*ICAO designator*]   (FAAC)...................... GEC
German Navy [*ICAO designator*]   (FAAC)................................ GNY
German-Texan Heritage Society   (EA) .... GTHS
Germania Fluggesellschaft Koln [*Germany*] [*ICAO designator*]
    (FAAC).. GMI
Gesellschaft fur Flugzieldarstellung GmbH [*Germany*] [*ICAO
    designator*]   (FAAC).. GFD
Gestair Executive Jet [*Spain*] [*ICAO designator*]   (FAAC) .... GES
Geuserland Airways Ltd. [*New Zealand*] [*ICAO designator*]   (FAAC)......... GEY
Geyser   (ABBR)... GYSR
Ghana [*Aircraft nationality and registration mark*]   (FAAC) 9G
Ghana Airways Corp. [*ICAO designator*]   (FAAC)....................... GHA
Giant Magnetoresistance [*Materials science*]................................. GMR
Gibson Aviation [*ICAO designator*]   (FAAC)............................. NTC
Giga-Instructions per Second [*Computer science*]   (NHD)................. GIPS
Gill Aviation Ltd. [*British*] [*ICAO designator*]   (FAAC)............... GIL
Girls Brigade [*British*]   (BI).. GB
Girls and Mathematics and Science Teaching .... GAMAST
Girls' School Company Ltd. [*British*]   (BI)............................... GSC
Girls' Schools Lawn Tennis Association [*British*]   (BI)................... GSLTA
Girls' Venture Corps [*British*]   (BI)....................................... GVC
Gitanair [*Italy*] [*ICAO designator*]   (FAAC) .... GTA
Give   (ABBR) .... GV
Giveaway   (ABBR).. GVAWY
Given   (ABBR)... GVN
Glacial Acrylic Acid [*Organic chemistry*] .... GAA
Glass Block   (DAC).. GB
Glazed Cement Manufacturers Association Ltd. [*British*]   (BI)........... GCMA
Global Air [*Bulgaria*] [*ICAO designator*]   (FAAC).................... GLB
Global Air Link [*Nigeria*] [*ICAO designator*]   (FAAC) .... GNB
Global Directory Agent .... GDA
Global Directory Service .... GDS
Global Environmental Management Initiative [*Environmental
    science*].. GEMI
Global Getra Ltd. [*Bulgaria*] [*ICAO designator*]   (FAAC)............ GLJ
Global International Ltd. [*Bulgaria*] [*ICAO designator*]   (FAAC)...... GLS
Global Learning and Observations to Benefit the Environment
    [*NASA*].. GLOBE
Global Maritime Distress and Safety System   (DA) .... GMDSS
Global Radio Navigation System [*Aviation*]   (DA) .... GRANAS
Global Space Station [*Proposed by NASA and ESA*] .... GSS
Global Systems, Inc. [*ICAO designator*]   (FAAC)........................ XGS
Global University Funding... GUF
Global Utilization of Streptokinase and TPA [*Tissue Plasminogen
    Activator*] for Occluded Arteries [*Comparative study*].................... GUSTO
Global Warming International Center [*An association*]   (EA)................. GWIC

Global Weather Dynamics, Inc. [*ICAO designator*] (FAAC) ... XGW

Globe Air Cargo [*Antigua and Barbuda*] [*ICAO designator*] (FAAC) ... GBC

Glove Collector Club (EA) ... GCC

Glyceraldehyde Phosphate Dehydrogenase [*Organic chemistry*] (MAH) ... GAPD

Glycidydiisopropylidenexylitol [*Organic chemistry*] ... GDX

Glycidyldiisopropylidenearabitol [*Organic chemistry*] ... GDA

Glycidylisopropylideneglycerol [*Organic chemistry*] ... GIG

Goal Attack [*Netball*] ... GA

Goal Defence [*Netball*] ... GD

Goal-Free Evaluation [*Education*] (AEE) ... GFE

Goal Keeper [*Netball*] ... GK

Goal Shooter [*Netball*] ... GS

Gold Belt Air Transport, Inc. [*Canada*] [*ICAO designator*] (FAAC) ... GBT

Golden Air Commuter AB [*Sweden*] [*ICAO designator*] (FAAC) ... GAO

Golden CommPass [*Front-end computer processor*] (PCM) ... GCP

Golden Eagle Air Services Ltd. [*Canada*] [*ICAO designator*] (FAAC) ... SAJ

Golden Star Air Cargo Co. Ltd. [*Sudan*] [*ICAO designator*] (FAAC) ... GLD

Goldfields Air Services [*Australia*] [*ICAO designator*] (FAAC) ... GOS

Golf Ball Manufacturers' Conference [*British*] (BI) ... GBMC

Golfe Air Quebec Ltd. [*Canada*] [*ICAO designator*] (FAAC) ... GAQ

Gonni Air Services Ltd. [*Suriname*] [*ICAO designator*] (FAAC) ... GON

[*Maria Elisa*] **Gonzales Farelas** [*Mexico*] [*ICAO designator*] (FAAC) ... FRL

Good Agricultural Practice [*Toxicology*] ... GAP

Good Practice ... GP

Governing Council of the Cat Fancy [*British*] (BI) ... GCCF

Government Procurement Service ... GPS

Government Purpose Classification ... GPC

Government Technology Productivity ... GTP

Gowned (ABBR) ... GWND

GP Express Airlines, Inc. [*ICAO designator*] (FAAC) ... GPE

Grade C and Better (DAC) ... C & Btr

Graduate Diploma ... GD

Graduate Diploma in Administration ... GDA

Graduate Diploma in Arts (Counselling) ... GDipA(Couns)

Graduate Diploma in Business Administration ... GDBusAd

Graduate Diploma in Child Development ... GDipCD

Graduate Diploma in Chiropractic ... GDipCh

Graduate Diploma in Clinical Science ... GDipClinSc

Graduate Diploma in Community Health ... GDCH

Graduate Diploma in Computer Studies ... GDipCompSt

Graduate Diploma in Economics ... GDipEc

Graduate Diploma in Ergonomics ... GDipErg

Graduate Diploma in Exercise and Sport Science ... GDipExerSpSc

Graduate Diploma in Health Administration ... GDipHA

Graduate Diploma in Health Counselling ... GDipHC

Graduate Diploma in Health Services Management ... GDipHSM

Graduate Diploma in Human Nutrition ... GDipHumNut

Graduate Diploma in Legal Studies ... GDipLS

Graduate Diploma in Management ... GDipM

Graduate Diploma in Manipulative Therapy ... GDManTher

Graduate Diploma in Medical Laboratory Science ... GDipMLS

Graduate Diploma in Occupational Health ... GDOccHlth

Graduate Diploma in Parent Education and Counselling ... GDipPEC

Graduate Diploma in Primary Health ... GDipPHC

Graduate Diploma in Professional Management ... GDipPrfMgt

Graduate Diploma in Public Law ... GDipPubL

Graduate Diploma in Safety and Health ... GDSafH

Graduate Diploma in Safety Science ... GDSafS

Graduate Diploma in Sport Science ... GDSSc

Grafted Rubber Concentrate [*Organic chemistry*] ... GRC

Gramophone Record Retailers Association [*British*] (BI) ... GRRA

Grampian Helicopter Charter Ltd. [*British*] [*ICAO designator*] (FAAC) ... GMR

Gran Turismo Cabriolet [*Automobile model designation*] ... GTC

Granada Aviacion [*Spain*] [*ICAO designator*] (FAAC) ... GAV

Grand Airways, Inc. [*ICAO designator*] (FAAC) ... GNV

Grand Order of Water Rats [*British*] (BI) ... GOWR

Grandfather-Father-Son [*Computer science*] (PCM) ... GFS

Grant of Resident Status ... GORS

Grants Operations Balance [*Environmental Protection Agency*] (ERG) ... GOB

Graphic Engine Monitor (DA) ... GEM

Graphical User Interface for Blind People ... GUIB

Gravel (DA) ... GRVL

Great American Airways [*ICAO designator*] (FAAC) ... GRA

Great China Airlines [*Taiwan*] [*ICAO designator*] (FAAC) ... GCA

Great Lakes Aviation Ltd. [*ICAO designator*] (FAAC) ... GLA

Great Lakes Booksellers Association (EA) ... GLBA

Great Wall Airlines [*China*] [*ICAO designator*] (FAAC) ... CGW

Great Wall Airlines [*China*] [*ICAO designator*] (FAAC) ... GWA

Greatest (ABBR) ... GTST

Greatly (ABBR) ... GTY

Green Fluorescent Protein [*Biochemistry*] ... GFP

Green Forest Lumber Ltd. [*Canada*] [*ICAO designator*] (FAAC) ... GFL

[*The*] **Green Party South Australia** [*Political party*] ... GSA

Green Tobacco Sickness [*Illness resulting from exposure to dissolved nicotine*] ... GTS

Greenair Hava Tasimaciligi AS [*Turkey*] [*ICAO designator*] (FAAC) ... GRN

Greenclose Aviation Services Ltd. [*British*] [*ICAO designator*] (FAAC) ... GCL

Greenlandair Charter AS [*Denmark*] [*ICAO designator*] (FAAC) ... GRC

[*The*] **Greens** [*Australia*] [*Political party*] ... GRE

[*The*] **Greens (Western Australia) Inc.** ... GWA

Grenada [*Aircraft nationality and registration mark*] (FAAC) ... J3

Grid North [*Army*] (ADDR) ... GN

Grille Opening Reinforcement [*Automotive engineering*] ... GOR

Grim File Reaper [*Computer hacker terminology*] (NHD) ... GFR

Gronlandsfly Ltd. [*Denmark*] [*ICAO designator*] (FAAC) ... GRL

Grooved Roofing [*Lumber*] (DAC) ... G/Rfg

Gross Fixed Capital Expenditure ... GFCE

Gross Impression [*Television ratings*] (NTCM) ... GI

Gross Operating Surplus [*Economics*] ... GOS

Gross Value of Production ... GVP

Grosser Touren Kombiwagen [*Grand Touring Station Wagon*] [*German*] ... GTK

Grosvenor Aviation Services [*British*] [*ICAO designator*] (FAAC) ... GRV

Ground Air Transfer, Inc. [*ICAO designator*] (FAAC) ... SWG

Ground Based Common Sensor-Light/Heavy [*Military*] ... GBCS-L/H

Ground-Based Traffic Information System [*Aviation*] (DA) ... GTIS

Ground Control [*Aviation*] (DA) ... G

Ground-Control Intercept Training [*Navy*] (ANA) ... GCITING

Ground Network Management System [*Aviation*] (DA) ... GNMS

Ground Run-Up Enclosure [*Aviation*] (DA) ... GRE

Ground Wind Vortex Sensing System [*Aviation*] (DA) ... GWVSS

Groundwater Modeling Program [*US Army Engineer Waterways Experiment Station*] (RDA) ... GMP

Group Training Company ... GTC

Guangzhou Regional Administration of CAA of China [*ICAO designator*] (FAAC) ... CSN

Guanylate Binding Protein [*Biochemistry*] ... GBP

Guarantee (ABBR) ... GUARTE

Guarantee (ABBR) ... GURNT

Guaranteed (ABBR) ... GUARTED

Guaranteed (ABBR) ... GURNTD

Guaranteeing (ABBR) ... GUARTEG

Guaranteeing (ABBR) ... GURTG

Guarantor (ABBR) ... GUARTR

Guarantor (ABBR) ... GURNTR

Guaranty (ABBR) ... GUART

Guaranty (ABBR) ... GURNTY

Guarantying (ABBR) ... GURNTG

Gubernatorial (ABBR) ... GUBER

Guerilla (ABBR) ... GUERL

Guernsey Airlines Ltd. [*British*] [*ICAO designator*] (FAAC) ... GER

Guidance (ABBR) ... GUDNC

Guide (ABBR) ... GUD

Guidebook (ABBR) ... GUDBK

Guided (ABBR) ... GUDD

Guided Acoustic Wave Brillouin Scattering [*Physics*] ... GAWBS

Guidepost (ABBR) ... GUDPST

Guiding (ABBR) ... GUDG

Guild of Architectural Ironmongers [*British*] (BI) ... GAI

Guild of Aviation Artists (DA) ... GAvA

Guild of Bricklayers [*British*] (BI) ... GB

Guild of British Dispensing Opticians (BI) ... GBDO

Guild of British Newspapers Editors (BI) ... GBNE

Guild of Drama Adjudicators [*British*] (BI) ... GODA

Guild of Dyers and Cleaners [*British*] (BI) ... GDC

Guild of Insurance Officials [*British*] (BI) ... GIO

Guild of Lady Drivers [*British*] (BI) ... GOLD

Guild of Memorial Craftsmen [*British*] (BI) ... GMC

Guild of Professional Launderers and Cleaners [*British*] (BI) ... GPLC

Guild of Public Pharmacists [*British*] (BI) ... GPP

Guild of Teachers of Backward Children [*British*] (BI) ... GTBC

Guilder (ABBR) ... GUIL

Guildhall (ABBR) ... GUILDHL

Guileful (ABBR) ... GUILFL

Guilefully (ABBR) ... GUILFY

Guileless (ABBR) ... GUILS

Guilelessly (ABBR) ... GUILSY

Guillotine (ABBR) ... GULTN

Guillotined (ABBR) ... GULTND

Guillotining (ABBR) ... GULTNG

Guinea [*Aircraft nationality and registration mark*] (FAAC) ... 3X

Guinee Air Lines SA [*Guinea*] [*ICAO designator*] (FAAC) ... GIF

Guinee Air Service [*Guinea*] [*ICAO designator*] (FAAC) ... GIS

Guinee Inter Air [*Guinea*] [*ICAO designator*] (FAAC) ... GIE

Gulf Air [*United Arab Emirates*] [*ICAO designator*] (FAAC) ... GFA

Gulf Air, Inc. [*ICAO designator*] (FAAC) ... GAT

Gulf Central Airlines, Inc. [*ICAO designator*] (FAAC) ... GCN

Gulf Flite Center, Inc. [*ICAO designator*] (FAAC) ... SFY

Gulfstream Aerospace Corp. [*ICAO designator*] (FAAC) ... GLF

Gulfstream Airlines, Inc. [*ICAO designator*] (FAAC) ... GFS

Gulfstream International Airlines, Inc. [*ICAO designator*] (FAAC) ... GFT

Gull Air [*ICAO designator*] (FAAC) ... GUL

Gullet (ABBR) ... GULT

Gullibility (ABBR) ... GULBT

Gullible (ABBR) ... GULB

Gullibly (ABBR) ... GULBLY

Gully (ABBR) ... GUL

Gullying (ABBR) ... GULYG

Gumminess (ABBR) ... GUMNS

Gun Trade Association Ltd. [*British*] (BI) ... GTA

Gunboat (ABBR) ... GUNBT

Guncotton (ABBR) ... GUN

Guncrete   (ABBR).. GUN
Gunes Ekspres Havacilik AS (Sunexpress) [*Turkey*] [*ICAO*
   designator]   (FAAC)... SXS
Gunfight   (ABBR)... GUNFIT
Gunfighter   (ABBR)... GUNFITR
Gunfire   (ABBR)... GUNFR
Gunman   (ABBR)... GUNMA
Gunned   (ABBR)... GUND
Gunner   (ABBR)... GUNR
Gunnery   (ABBR)... GUNRY
Gunnery   (ABBR).. GY
Gunning   (ABBR)... GUNG
Gunny   (ABBR).. GUN
Gunnybag   (ABBR).. GUNYBG
Gunpowder   (ABBR).. GUN
Gunpowder   (ABBR).. GUNPWDR
Gunshot   (ABBR)... GUNSH
Gunsmith   (ABBR).. GUNSM
Gunstock   (ABBR)... GUNST
Gunwhale   (ABBR)... GUNWHL
Guppy   (ABBR)... GUP
Gurgled   (ABBR)... GURGLD
Gurgling   (ABBR).. GURGLG
Gurgu   (ABBR).. GUR
Gushier   (ABBR)... GUSHR
Gushiest   (ABBR).. GUSHST
Gushiness   (ABBR)... GUSHNS
Gushing   (ABBR)... GUSHG
Gusset   (ABBR)... GUST
Gustier   (ABBR).. GUSTR
Gustiest   (ABBR)... GUSTST
Gustily   (ABBR).. GUSTY
Gustiness   (ABBR).. GUSTNS
Gutted   (ABBR).. GUTD
Gutter   (ABBR).. GUTR
Gutteral   (ABBR)... GUTRL
Gutterally   (ABBR).. GUTRY
Gutting   (ABBR).. GUTG
Guyana [*Aircraft nationality and registration mark*]   (FAAC)...................... 8R
Guyana Airways Corp. [*ICAO designator*]   (FAAC)............................... GYA
Guyana Republican Party [*Political party*]   (EA)............................... GRP
Guzzle   (ABBR)... GUZL
Guzzle   (ABBR).. GZL
Guzzled   (ABBR)... GUZLD
Guzzled   (ABBR)... GZLD
Guzzler   (ABBR)... GUZLR
Guzzler   (ABBR)... GZLR
Guzzling   (ABBR).. GUZLG
Guzzling   (ABBR)... GZLG
Gymnasium   (ABBR)... GYMN
Gymnast   (ABBR)... GYMNST
Gymnast   (ABBR)... GYMST
Gymnastic   (ABBR)... GYMSTC
Gymnastic Equipment Manufacturers' Association [*British*]   (BI)........... GEMA
Gymnastically   (ABBR)... GYMSTCY
Gynecologic   (ABBR).. GYNC
Gynecological   (ABBR)... GYNCL
Gynecologist   (ABBR).. GYNST
Gypped   (ABBR)... GYPD
Gypping   (ABBR)... GYPG
Gypsiologic   (ABBR).. GYPSIOL
Gypsum Plasterboard Development Association [*British*]   (BI)................ GPDA
Gypsy   (ABBR)... GYP
Gyrafrance [*France*] [*ICAO designator*]   (FAAC)...................................... GYR
Gyrate   (ABBR)... GYRA
Gyrated   (ABBR)... GYRAD
Gyrated   (ABBR)... GYRTD
Gyrating   (ABBR).. GYRAG
Gyration   (ABBR).. GYR
Gyration   (ABBR).. GYRAN
Gyrator   (ABBR)... GYRAR
Gyratory   (ABBR).. GYRARY
Gyro   (ABBR)... GY
Gyrocar   (ABBR)... GY
Gyrocompass   (ABBR)... GY
Gyrocompass   (ABBR)... GYRCMPS
Gyrocompass   (ABBR)... GYRO
Gyrocopter   (ABBR)... GYROCOP
Gyrodynamic   (ABBR)... GYRODYN
Gyrodyne   (ABBR).. GY
Gyrometer   (ABBR)... GYRMTR
Gyroplane   (ABBR).. GYRO
Gyroplane   (ABBR)... GYRPLN
Gyroscope   (ABBR)... GYRSCP
Gyrostabilizer   (ABBR).. GYRSTBR
Gyrus   (ABBR)... GYR

H

171

Helicopteros Xel-Ha SA de CV [*Mexico*] [*ICAO designator*] (FAAC) .... XEL
Heliflyg AG [*Sweden*] [*ICAO designator*] (FAAC) .... HFL
Helijet [*Spain*] [*ICAO designator*] (FAAC) .... HJS
Helijet Airways [*Canada*] [*ICAO designator*] (FAAC) .... JBA
Helikopter Service AS [*Norway*] [*ICAO designator*] (FAAC) .... HKS
Helikoptertransport AB [*Sweden*] [*ICAO designator*] (FAAC) .... KTR
Heliport [*ICAO designator*] (FAAC) .... HELI
Heliportugal-Trabalhos e Transporte Aereo, Representacoes, Importacao e Exportacao Lda. [*Portugal*] [*ICAO designator*] (FAAC) .... HPL
Heliserv SA de CV [*Mexico*] [*ICAO designator*] (FAAC) .... HLV
Heliservicio Campeche SA de CV [*Mexico*] [*ICAO designator*] (FAAC) .... HEC
Heliservico-Sociedade Portuguesa de Exploracao de Meios Aeros Lda. [*Portugal*] [*ICAO designator*] (FAAC) .... HSV
Helitrans Air Service, Inc. [*ICAO designator*] (FAAC) .... HTS
Hella Electronics Corp. [*Automotive industry supplier*] .... HEC
Hellenic Air Force [*Greece*] [*ICAO designator*] (FAAC) .... HAF
Hellenic Air SA [*Greece*] [*ICAO designator*] (FAAC) .... HLN
Hemmeter Aviation, Inc. [*ICAO designator*] (FAAC) .... HEM
Hemoglobin M [*Biochemistry*] (MAH) .... HbM
Hemus Air [*Bulgaria*] [*ICAO designator*] (FAAC) .... HMS
Henebury Aviation Co. [*Australia*] [*ICAO designator*] (FAAC) .... HAC
Heparan Sulfate Proteoglycan [*Biochemistry*] .... HSPG
Her Majesty's Customs and Excise [*British*] (BI) .... HMC
Her Majesty's Nautical Almanac Office [*British*] (PDAA) .... NAO
Herbig-Haro [*Astronomy*] .... HH
Hereditary Neuropathy with Liability to Pressure Palsies .... HNPP
Hermens/Markair Express [*ICAO designator*] (FAAC) .... MRX
Heussler Air Service Corp. [*ICAO designator*] (FAAC) .... HUS
Hexadecimal [*Computer science*] (IAA) X
Hexadecimal Digit [*Computer science*] (NHD) .... HEXIT
Hexadecyltrichlorosilane [*Organic chemistry*] .... HDTCS
Hex'air [*France*] [*ICAO designator*] (FAAC) .... HER
Hibiscus Air Services Ltd. [*New Zealand*] [*ICAO designator*] (FAAC) .... HIB
Hierarchical Database Management System .... HDBMS
High Altitude/High Opening [*Army*] (ADDR) .... HAHO
High-Altitude Solar Energy (PS) .... HALSOL
High Blood Cholesterol .... HBC
High Definition Electronic Production (NTCM) .... HDEP
High Impact Incarceration Program [*60-day paramilitary regimen for prisoners*] .... HIIP
High Interest Unit [*Navy*] (ANA) .... HIU
High-Line Airways, Inc. [*Canada*] [*ICAO designator*] (FAAC) .... HLB
High Melt Strength [*Plastic moldings*] .... HMS
High Osmolar Contrast Agent [*Medicine*] .... HOCA
High Resilience [*Plastics*] .... HR
High-Resolution Capacitive Imaging Sensor [*Instrumentation*] .... HIRCIS
High School Magazine [*A publication*] .... H Sch M
High-Speed Direct Injection [*Diesel engines*] .... HSDI
High Speed Generation [*Hybrid vehicles*] [*Automotive engineering*] .... HSG
High Speed Steel Association [*British*] (BI) .... HSSA
High Speed Taxi-Way Turn Off [*Aviation*] (DA) .... HST
High-Speed Video [*Instrumentation*] .... HSV
High-Sulfur Diesel Fuel [*Petroleum marketing*] .... HSD
Higher Education Act Amendment [*1992*] .... HEAA
Highest Astronomical Tide .... HAT
Highland Express [*British*] [*ICAO designator*] (FAAC) .... TTN
Highly-Indebted Middle-Income Country .... HIMIC
Highly Polarized Quasar [*Galactic science*] .... HPQ
Highway Vehicle Object Simulation Model [*Computer-aided design*] [*Automotive engineering*] .... HVOSM
Hilar High-Frequency Stimulation [*Neurophysiology*] .... HHFS
Hill Start Assist [*Transmission and braking systems*] [*Automotive engineering*] .... HSA
Hindu (ABBR) .... H
Hino Fuel Economy Clean Air High-Durability [*Hino diesel engines*] .... HFCD
Hino Micro Mixing System [*Diesel engines*] .... HMMS
Hino Super Flow Turbine [*Diesel engine*] .... HSET
Hire Purchase Trade Association [*British*] (BI) .... HPTA
Hispania Lineas Aereas SL [*Spain*] [*ICAO designator*] (FAAC) .... HSL
Hispanic Bar Association (EA) .... HBA
Hispaniola Airways [*Dominican Republic*] [*ICAO designator*] (FAAC) .... HIS
Historic Aircraft Preservation Society Ltd. [*British*] (BI) .... HAPS
Historic Churches Preservation Trust [*British*] (BI) .... HCPT
Historical Model Railway Society [*British*] (BI) .... HMRS
Hogan Air [*ICAO designator*] (FAAC) .... HGA
Hold in Abeyance [*Military*] .... HIA
Holders of Public Office .... HOPO
Holidair Airways [*Canada*] [*ICAO designator*] (FAAC) .... STP
Holiday Airlines, Inc. [*ICAO designator*] (FAAC) .... HOL
Holiday Happenings Ornament Collectors Club (EA) .... HHOCC
Hollow-Fiber Bioreactor [*Chemical engineering*] .... HFBR
Hollow-Metal Door (DAC) .... HMD
Hollowback (DAC) .... HB
Hollyfordair Travel Ltd. [*New Zealand*] [*ICAO designator*] (FAAC) .... HFT
Holmstrom Flyg AB [*Sweden*] [*ICAO designator*] (FAAC) .... ENT
Holstenair Lubeck, Luftverkehrsservice GmbH [*Germany*] [*ICAO designator*] (FAAC) .... HTR
Home-Based Maintenance Allowance .... HBMA
Home Consumption Price .... HCP
Home Drug Infusion Therapy [*Medicine*] .... HDIT
Home Equity Conversion .... HEC
Home Finance Contract .... HFC
Home Grown Timber Marketing Corp. Ltd. [*British*] (BI) .... HGTMC
Home Satellite Dish (NTCM) .... HSD
Home Testing Institute, Inc. (NTCM) .... HTI
Home Timber Merchants' Association of England and Wales (BI) .... HTMAEW
Home Uterine Activity Monitoring .... HUAM
Home Video Recorder (NTCM) .... HVR
Home Wine and Beer Trade Association (EA) .... HWBTA
Homeobox [*Genetics*] .... HOX
Homer (DA) .... Hmr
Homes Using Radio [*Ratings*] (NTCM) .... HUR
HomeVideo [*Videocassette tape*] (NTCM) .... HV
Hominid Corridor Research Project [*Palaeontology*] .... HCRP
Homosexual Law Reform Society [*British*] (BI) .... HLRS
Hong Kong Association of Banks (ECON) .... HKAB
Hong Kong Dragon Airlines Ltd. [*ICAO designator*] (FAAC) .... HDA
Hong Kong University of Science and Technology (ECON) .... HKUST
Honington FTU [*British*] [*ICAO designator*] (FAAC) .... HON
Honorary Member, American Institute of Architects (DAC) .... HAIA
Hop Merchants Association [*British*] (BI) .... HMA
Hops Warehousing Association [*British*] (BI) .... HWA
Horizon (ABBR) .... H
Horizon Air-Taxi Ltd. [*Switzerland*] [*ICAO designator*] (FAAC) .... HOR
Horizon Airlines, Inc. [*ICAO designator*] (FAAC) .... QXE
Horizon Cargo Transport, Inc. [*ICAO designator*] (FAAC) .... KOK
Hormonal Growth Promotant .... HGP
Horticultural Advisory Council for England and Wales (BI) .... HAC
Horticultural Marketing Council [*British*] (BI) .... HMC
Horticultural Trades Association [*British*] (BI) .... HTA
Hose (NFPA) .... H
Hose Cabinet [*or Connection*] [*NFPA pre-fire planning symbol*] (NFPA) .... HC
Hosiery and Allied Trades Research Association [*British*] (BI) .... HATRA
Hospital Aircraft [*ICAO designator*] (FAAC) .... HOSP
Hospital Patient Transport Vehicle .... HTV
Hospital Saving Association [*British*] (BI) .... HSA
Host Nation Support Agreement [*Navy*] (ANA) .... HNSA
Hosted Bus Controller Chip [*Electronics*] .... HBCC
Hostel Care .... HC
Hot-Air Solder Leveling [*Materials science*] .... HASL
Hot Cranking Amperes [*Battery*] [*Automotive engineering*] .... HCA
Hot Dip Galvanizers Association [*British*] (BI) .... HDGA
Hot Finished [*Drawing*] (DAC) .... HF
Hot-Water Recirculation (DAC) .... HWRC
Hotel and Catering Industry Training Board [*British*] (BI) .... HCITB
Hotel and Catering Institute [*British*] (BI) .... HCI
Hotel and Catering Trades Benevolent Association [*British*] (BI) .... HCTBA
Hotel Properties Ltd. [*Singapore*] (ECON) .... HPL
Hoteles Dinamicos SA de CV [*Mexico*] [*ICAO designator*] (FAAC) .... HDI
Household Textiles Association [*British*] (BI) .... HTA
Household Tracking Report [*Television ratings*] (NTCM) .... HTR
Housing Corp. [*British*] (BI) .... HC
Housing Developers Association Ltd. [*British*] (BI) .... HDA
Housing Development Program .... HDP
Houston Helicopters, Inc. [*ICAO designator*] (FAAC) .... HHO
HR Magazine [*A publication*] .... HR Mag
Hsinchu Science-Based Industrial Park [*Taiwan*] (ECON) .... HSIP
Hughes Aircraft Co. (Aeronautical Operations) [*ICAO designator*] (FAAC) .... GMH
Hugo Rizzuto [*ICAO designator*] (FAAC) .... KHX
Human Beta-Globin [*Genetics*] .... HBB
Human-Computer Interaction Laboratory [*University of Maryland*] (PCM) .... HCIL
Human Fertilization and Embryology Authority [*British*] .... HFEA
Human Gene-Mapping .... HGM
Human Resources Training .... HRT
Human Rights Committee .... HRC
Human Science Research [*Concept car*] [*Automotive engineering*] .... HSR
Humber Aviation Ltd. [*British*] [*ICAO designator*] (FAAC) .... HUA
Hummingbird Helicopters Maldives (Pvt) Ltd. [*ICAO designator*] (FAAC) .... HUM
Hungarian-Ukranian Heavy Lift Ltd. [*Hungary*] [*ICAO designator*] (FAAC) .... HUK
Hunger Relief and Development [*An association*] (EA) .... HRAD
[*J. P.*] **Hunt Inc.** [*ICAO designator*] (FAAC) .... RFX
Hunters' Improvement Society [*British*] (BI) .... HIS
Hunting Aviation Services Ltd. [*British*] [*ICAO designator*] (FAAC) .... NVL
Hunting Business Aviation [*British*] [*ICAO designator*] (FAAC) .... HUN
Hunting Cargo Airlines Ltd. [*British*] [*ICAO designator*] (FAAC) .... ABR
Hyack Air Ltd. [*Canada*] [*ICAO designator*] (FAAC) .... HYA
Hyannis Air Service, Inc. [*ICAO designator*] (FAAC) .... KAP
Hybrid-Electric Vehicle .... HEV
Hydraulic Association of Great Britain (BI) .... HA
Hydraulic Brake Hose [*Automotive engineering*] .... HBH
Hydraulic Electronic Unit Injector [*Fuel system*] [*Automotive engineering*] .... HEUI
Hydraulic End Design System [*Computer-aided design*] .... HEDS
Hydraulic Horse Power .... HHP
Hydraulic Lash Adjuster [*Automotive engine design*] .... HLA
Hydraulic Oil .... HYDO
Hydraulic Overspeed Control [*Mechanical power transmission*] .... HOC

Hydraulic Variable-Valve Train [*Automotive engine design*] .... HVT
Hydrobromofluorocarbons [*Organic chemistry*] .... HBCF
Hydrofluorocarbon .... FC
Hydrogen Diffusion Anode [*Electrochemistry*] .... HDA
Hydroxy-Terminated Polybutadiene [*Organic chemistry*] .... HTPB
Hydroxypropyl Starch [*Organic chemistry*] .... HPS
Hyeres Aero Service [*France*] [*ICAO designator*]   (FAAC) .... HYE
Hyper Immunoglobulin Syndrome [*Medicine*] .... HIM
Hyper-Rayleigh Scattering [*Physics*] .... HRS
Hyundai California Design [*Concept car*] .... HCD

I

Injection of Fuel Containing Dissolved Gas [*Diesel engines*] — IFCDG
Injury Severity Score [*Auto safety research*] — ISS
Inland Fisheries Trust, Inc. [*Republic of Ireland*] (BI) — IFT
Innotech Aviation Ltd. [*Canada*] [*ICAO designator*] (FAAC) — IVA
Innovation and Entrepreneurship — I & E
Innovative Project — IP
Innovative Rural Education and Training Program — IRETP
Innovative Software Design [*South Africa*] [*ICAO designator*] (FAAC) — ISD
Innovative Training Project — ITP
Innovative Training Projects - National Skills Shortage — ITP-NSS
Innovative Vehicle Electronic Control System [*Motor vehicles*] — INVECS
Inorganic Chemical [*Environmental science*] — IOC
Inquiry/Response [*Automotive engineering*] [*Electronics*] — I/R
Insert Shot [*Film production*] (NTCM) — INS
Inside Face (DAC) — IF
Inside Front Cover [*Publishing*] (NTCM) — IFC
Inside Pipe Size (DAC) — IPS
Inside Trim (DAC) — IST
Inspection and Maintenance (ERG) — I/M
Instalbud [*Poland*] [*ICAO designator*] (FAAC) — INB
Installable Compression, Manager [*Computer science*] — ICM
Institute of Advertising Practitioners in Ireland (BI) — IAPI
Institute of Amateur Cinematographers [*British*] (BI) — IAC
Institute of Automobile Assessors [*British*] (BI) — IAA
Institute of Baths Management [*British*] (BI) — IBM
Institute of British Bakers (BI) — IBB
Institute of British Carriage and Automobile Manufacturers (BI) — IBCAM
Institute of British Geographers (BI) — IBG
Institute of British Surgical Technicians (BI) — IBST
Institute of Broadcast Engineers [*Later, SBE*] (NTCM) — IBE
Institute of Building Estimators Ltd. [*British*] (BI) — IBE
Institute of Building Site Management [*British*] (BI) — IBSM
Institute of Certified Ambulance Personnel [*British*] (BI) — ICAP
Institute of Chartered Accountants in England and Wales (BI) — ICA
Institute of Chemistry of Ireland (BI) — ICI
Institute of Chocolate and Confectionery Distributors [*British*] (BI) — ICCD
Institute of Clay Workers [*British*] (BI) — ICW
Institute of Commercial and Technical Representatives Ltd. [*British*] (BI) — ICTR
Institute for the Comparative Study of History, Philosophy, and the Sciences Ltd. [*British*] (BI) — ICS
Institute of Corn and Agricultural Merchants Ltd. [*British*] (BI) — ICAM
Institute of Cost and Works Accountants [*British*] (BI) — ICWA
Institute for Education by Radio [*Defunct*] (NTCM) — IER
Institute for Education by Radio-Television (NTCM) — IERT
Institute of Fuel [*British*] (BI) — IOF
[*The*] **Institute of Genomic Research** — TIGR
Institute for Global Communications (EA) — IGC
Institute of Hospital Administrators [*British*] (BI) — IHA
Institute of Housing Managers [*British*] (BI) — IHM
Institute of Incorporated Practitioners in Advertising [*British*] (BI) — IIPA
Institute of Inventors [*British*] (BI) — II
Institute of Islamic and Arabic Sciences in America (EA) — IIASA
Institute of Journalists [*British*] (NTCM) — IJ
Institute of Linguists [*British*] (BI) — IL
Institute of Machine Woodworking Technology [*British*] (BI) — IMWoodT
Institute of Marketing and Sales Management [*British*] (BI) — IMSM
Institute of Master Tutors of Driving [*British*] (BI) — IMTD
Institute of Materials Handling [*British*] (BI) — IMH
Institute of Medical Social Workers [*British*] (BI) — IMSW
Institute for Mental Health Initiatives (EA) — IMHI
Institute of the Motor Industry, Inc. [*British*] (BI) — IMI
Institute of Municipal Maintenance Engineers [*British*] (BI) — IMME
Institute of Musical Instrument Technology [*British*] (BI) — IMIT
Institute of Office Management [*British*] (BI) — IOM
Institute of Packaging [*British*] (BI) — IOP
Institute of Park and Recreation Administration [*British*] (BI) — IPRA
Institute of Petroleum [*British*] (BI) — IOP
Institute for Puerto Rican Policy (EA) — IPRP
Institute of Qualified Private Secretaries Ltd. [*British*] (BI) — IQPS
Institute of Rural Life at Home and Overseas [*British*] (BI) — IRL
Institute of Shops Acts Administration [*British*] (BI) — ISAA
Institute of Social Welfare [*British*] (BI) — ISW
Institute and Society of Practictioners in Electrolysis Ltd. [*British*] (BI) — ISPE
Institute of Technical Publicity and Publications [*British*] (BI) — ITPP
Institute of Travel Agents [*British*] (BI) — ITA
Institute of Wood Science [*British*] (BI) — IWS
Institute of Work Study Practitioners [*British*] (BI) — IWSP
Institution of Body Engineers [*British*] (BI) — IBE
Institution of Civil Engineering Surveyors (DAC) — InstCES
Institution of Civil Engineers of Ireland (BI) — ICEI
Institution of Engineering Designers [*British*] (BI) — IED
Institution of Engineering Inspection [*British*] (BI) — IEI
Institution of Engineers-in-Charge [*British*] (BI) — IEIC
Institution of Professional Civil Servants [*British*] (BI) — IPCS
Institution of Sales Engineers [*British*] (BI) — ISE
Institution of Water Engineers [*British*] (BI) — IWE
Instituto Cartografico de Cataluna [*Spain*] [*ICAO designator*] (FAAC) — ICC
Instruction Cache Unit [*Computer science*] — ICU
Instruction and Research [*Individually-guided education*] (AEE) — I & R
Instruction-Set Translator [*IBM Corp.*] — IST
Instructional Improvement Committee [*Individually-guided education*] (AEE) — IIC
Instructional Program (NTCM) — I
Instructional Programming Model [*Individually-guided education*] (AEE) — IPM
Instructional Television, Fixed [*FCC*] (NTCM) — IF
Instructional Television Funding Cooperative (NTCM) — ITBC
Instrument Guidance System [*Aviation*] (DA) — IGS
Instrument Panel [*Automotive engineering*] — PNL
Instrument Rating Examiner [*Aviation*] (DA) — IRE
Instrument Restricted Controlled Airspace (DA) — IR
Instrument/Visual Controlled Airspace (DA) — I/V
Instrumental [*Grammar*] — instr
Instrumented Runway Visual Range [*Aviation*] (DA) — IRVR
Insufficient Scheduled Time Available [*Aviation*] (FAAC) — INSUF
Insulation, Building, and Hard Board Association [*British*] (BI) — IBHA
Insulin Convulsive Therapy [*Medicine*] (MAH) — ICT
Insulin Receptor Substrate [*Biochemistry*] — IRS
Intair, Inc. [*Canada*] [*ICAO designator*] (FAAC) — INT
Integrated Action Plan — IAP
Integrated Air/Fuel System [*Automotive engine design*] — IAFS
Integrated Clinical Encounters — ICE
Integrated Compatible Use Zone [*Army*] (RDA) — ICUZ
Integrated Data for Enforcement Analysis System [*Environmental science*] — IDEA
Integrated Departmental Instructions Manual — IDIM
Integrated Flight Prediction System [*Aviation*] (DA) — IFLIPS
Integrated Initial Flight Plan Processing System [*Aviation*] (DA) — IFPS
Integrated Pollution Prevention and Control [*Environmental science*] — IPPC
Integrated Review Model — IRM
Integrated Structural Seat [*Automotive engineering*] — ISS
Integrated Tourism Resort — ITR
Intelligence Electronic Warfare Support Element (ADDR) — IEWSE
Intelligence Property Book [*Army*] (ADDR) — IPB
Intelligent Computer-Aided Design — ICAD
Intelligent Dummy Data Acquisition System [*Crash testing*] [*Automotive engineering*] — IDDAS
Intelligent Forms Language [*Delrina Corp.*] [*Computer science*] (PCM) — IFL
Intelligent Image Caching Software [*Courtland Group, Inc.*] (PCM) — IICS
Intensive Military Training Area (DA) — IMTA
Intensive Training Program — ITP
Inter Air AB [*Sweden*] [*ICAO designator*] (FAAC) — INR
Inter-Air, Inc. [*ICAO designator*] (FAAC) — ITA
Inter-American Defense Board Medal [*Military decoration*] — IADB-MED
Inter-Byte Separation [*Automotive engineering*] [*Electronics*] — IBS
Inter-Canadian [*ICAO designator*] (FAAC) — ICN
Inter-Image Amplifying Chemistry [*Color film technology*] — IIAC
Inter-Island Air, Inc. [*ICAO designator*] (FAAC) — UGL
Inter-Island Air Services Ltd. [*Grenada*] [*ICAO designator*] (FAAC) — IES
Inter-Mountain Airways [*ICAO designator*] (FAAC) — IMA
Inter RCA [*Central African Republic*] [*ICAO designator*] (FAAC) — CAR
Inter-School Christian Fellowship [*British*] (BI) — ISCF
Inter-Varsity Fellowship of Evangelical Unions [*British*] (BI) — IVF
Interactive Brain Wave Analyzer [*IBVA Technology*] [*Computer science*] (PCM) — IBVA
Interactive Photorealistic Rendering [*Computer-assisted design*] — IPR
Interactive Video Enterprises [*US West, Inc.*] (PCM) — IVE
Interair Aviation Ltd. [*British*] [*ICAO designator*] (FAAC) — INA
Interamericana de Aviacion Ltda. [*Colombia*] [*ICAO designator*] (FAAC) — IIA
Intercity Relay [*Broadcasting*] (NTCM) — ICR
Intercontinental Airlines Ltd. [*Nigeria*] [*ICAO designator*] (FAAC) — VVV
Intercontinental de Aviacion Ltd. [*Colombia*] [*ICAO designator*] (FAAC) — ICT
Interdepartment Council on Radio Propagation and Standards (NTCM) — ICAS
Interdepartment Courier Service — IDCS
Interest Coverage Ratio — ICR
Interestatal de Aviacion SA de CV [*Mexico*] [*ICAO designator*] (FAAC) — ITE
Interested Parties List — IPL
Intereuropean Airways Ltd. [*British*] [*ICAO designator*] (FAAC) — IEA
Interface Definition Language [*Computer science*] — IDL
Interface Group, Inc. [*ICAO designator*] (FAAC) — FIV
Interflight [*British*] [*ICAO designator*] (FAAC) — IFT
Interflight, Inc. [*ICAO designator*] (FAAC) — DEX
Interflight (Learjet) Ltd. [*British*] [*ICAO designator*] (FAAC) — IJT
Interfreight Forwarding Ltd. [*Sudan*] [*ICAO designator*] (FAAC) — IFF
Interfunk & Co. [*Yugoslavia*] [*ICAO designator*] (FAAC) — IFK
Intergovernmental Advisory Council on Education (AEE) — IACE
Intergrated Avionics Computer (DA) — IAC
Interim [*FCC*] (NTCM) — I
Interleukin-Converting Enzyme [*Biochemistry*] — ICE
Intermediate Gearbox (DA) — IGB
Intermediate School District (AEE) — ISD
Intermembrane Space [*Biochemistry*] — IMS
Intermodulation Distortion (NTCM) — IM
Internal Granule Layer [*Cytology*] — IGL
International Advertising Executives' Association (NTCM) — IAEA
International Aeradio PLC [*British*] [*ICAO designator*] (FAAC) — IAL
International Air Cargo Corp. [*Egypt*] [*ICAO designator*] (FAAC) — IACC
International Air Cargo Corp. [*Egypt*] [*ICAO designator*] (FAAC) — IAK

International Air Carrier Association [*ICAO designator*] (FAAC)................ ITC
International Air Service Co. [*ICAO designator*] (FAAC) .... IAS
International Air Transport Association [*ICAO designator*] (FAAC) .... IAT
International Airports Authority of India [*ICAO designator*] (FAAC)....... ATY
International Alliance of Theatrical Stage Employees (NTCM)................. IA
International Association of Broadcasting (NTCM)................ IAB
International Association of Latin American Air Carriers [*ICAO
    designator*] (FAAC)................ ALA
International Association of Silver Art Collectors (EA)................ IASAC
International Association of Women in Radio and Television
    (NTCM)................ IAWRT
International Bone Marrow Transplant Registry................ IBMTR
International Broadcasting and Television Organization (NTCM)............. IBTO
International Broadcasting Union [*Defunct*] (NTCM)................ IBU
International Business Air [*Sweden*] [*ICAO designator*] (FAAC)................ IBZ
International Business Aircraft Association (DA)................ IBAA
International Cartridge Recycling Association (EA)................ ICRA
International Charter Xpress Limited Liability Co. [*ICAO
    designator*] (FAAC)................ ICX
International Christian Accrediting Association (EA)................ ICAA
International Civil Aviation Organization [*ICAO designator*] (FAAC)........ ICO
International Conference on the Applications of the Mossbauer
    Effect................ ICAME
International Control Mechanism................ ICM
International Council of Health Fitness and Sports Therapists
    [*British*]................ ICHFST
International Council of Holistic Therapists [*British*]................ ICHT
International Cultural Exchange [*An association*] (EA)................ ICE
International Data Exchange for Aviation Safety [*ICAO*] (DA)............. IDEAS
International Deep Profiling of Tibet and the Himalaya [*Geology*]
    [*China*]................ INDEPTH
International Diabetic Athletes Association (EA)................ IDAA
International Education Information Program................ IEIP
International Federation of Health and Beauty Therapists................ IFHBT
International Federation of Newspaper Publishers (NTCM)................ IFNP
International Flying Services SRL [*Italy*] [*ICAO designator*] (FAAC)........ IFS
International Freeze-Dry Floral Association (EA)................ IFDFA
International Graduate School of Management................ IGSM
International Health and Beauty Council [*British*]................ IHBC
International Industrial Television Association (NTCM)................ ITVA
International Institute for Applied Systems Analysis................ IIASA
International Institute of Genetics and Biophysics [*Italy*]................ IIGB
International Institute of Health and Holistic Therapies [*British*]............. IIHHT
International Institute of Sports Therapy [*British*]................ IIST
International Inter-Visitation Program in Educational Administration
    [*UniverstiyCouncil for Educational Administration*] (AEE)................ IIP
International Journal of Leprosy [*A publication*]................ IJL
International Journal of Osteoarchaeology [*A publication*]................ IJO
International Legal Services Advisory Committee................ ILSAC
International Lubricant Standardization and Approval Committee
    [*Automotive engine oils*]................ ILSAC
International Morse Code (ADDR)................ IMC
International Motor Sports Hall of Fame [*Automotive racing
    history*]................ IMHOF
International Muslim Students Union (EA)................ IMSU
International Organization for Plant Information................ IOPI
International Pharmaceutical Excipients Council (EA)................ IPEC
International Plant Genetic Resources Institute [*Italy*]................ IPGRI
International Productions and Safety Research [*Auto accident
    reconstruction*]................ INTERSEARCH
International Public Television [*An association*] (NTCM)................ INPUT
International Radio Carrier (NTCM)................ IRC
International Radio and Television Foundation, Inc. [*International
    Radio and Television Society*] (NTCM)................ IRTF
International Scale of Nuclear Events................ ISNE
International Scientific Collectors Association (EA)................ ISCA
International Seminars Support Scheme................ ISSS
International Society for AIDS Education (EA)................ ISAE
International Society of Offshore and Polar Engineers................ ISOPE
International Space Exploration and Colonization Company [*An
    association*] (EA)................ ISECCo
International Superconductivity Industry Summit [*Conference*]................ ISIS
International Swizzle Stick Collectors Association (EA)................ ISSCA
International Symposium on the Industrial Applications of the
    Mossbauer Effect................ ISIAME
International Symposium on Laboratory Automation and Robotics........... ISLAR
International Symposium on Microchemistry................ ISM
International Symposium on Wave and Tidal Energy (PDAA)................ WTE
International Test Pilot School [*British*] [*ICAO designator*] (FAAC)........... ITP
International Toll Free [*Telecommunications*]................ ITF
International Toxicity Equivalency Factor [*Toxicology*]................ I-TEF
International Trade Enhancement Program................ ITEP
International Training Institute................ ITI
International Transplant Nurses Society (EA)................ ITNS
International Trauma Anesthesia and Critical Care Society (EA)................ ITACCS
International Truck of the Year................ ITOY
International Union for Toxicology................ IUTOX
International Willow Collectors [*An association*] (EA)................ IWC
International Year of the Child [*United Nations*] (AEE)................ IYC
International Year of the Family................ IYF
Internationalization [*The 18 replaces the eighteen letters between I
    and N*] [*C omputer hacker terminology*] (NHD)................ I18N
Internegative [*Photography*] (NTCM)................ ITN

Interoperability [*The 14 replaces the fourteen letters between I and
    Y*] [*Computer hacker terminology*] (NHD)................ I14Y
Interot Air Service [*Germany*] [*ICAO designator*] (FAAC)................ IRT
Interphone (Service F) Resumed Operation [*Aviation*] (FAAC)................ IFORO
Interport Corp. [*ICAO designator*] (FAAC)................ IPT
Interprofessional Fostering of Ophthalmic Care for Underserved
    Sectors [*An association*] (EA)................ IFOCUS
Interrupted Feedback [*Wireless earphone*] (NTCM)................ IFB
Interspike Interval Histogram [*Neurophysiology*]................ ISIH
Interstate Airlines Ltd. [*Nigeria*] [*ICAO designator*] (FAAC)................ IAE
Interstitial-Free [*Metallurgical engineering*]................ IF
Intervalence Charge-Transfer [*Phyical chemistry*]................ IVCT
Intervuelo SA [*Mexico*] [*ICAO designator*] (FAAC)................ ITV
Intra-Industry Trade................ IIT
Intron Binding Site [*Genetics*]................ IBS
Introversion/Extroversion [*Psychology*] (AEE)................ I/E
Inverse Polymerase Chain Reaction [*Genetics*]................ IPCR
Inverse Synthetic Aperture RADAR [*Navy*] (ANA)................ ISAR
Inversia [*Latvia*] [*ICAO designator*] (FAAC)................ INV
Investment Promotion Program................ IPP
Invisible Panel Warming Association [*British*] (BI)................ IPWA
Invitation to Register Interest................ ITRI
Ion Beam Analysis................ IBA
Ion Dip Spectroscopy................ IDS
Ion Microprobe Analysis................ IMPA
Iona National Airways Ltd. [*Republic of Ireland*] [*ICAO designator*]
    (FAAC)................ IND
Iowa Airways, Inc. [*ICAO designator*] (FAAC)................ IOA
Ipec Aviation Pty Ltd. [*Australia*] [*ICAO designator*] (FAAC)................ IPA
Iran Asseman Airline [*ICAO designator*] (FAAC)................ IRC
Iran National Airlines Corp. [*ICAO designator*] (FAAC)................ IRA
Iranair Tours Co. [*Iran*] [*ICAO designator*] (FAAC)................ IRB
Iraqi Airways [*ICAO designator*] (FAAC)................ IAW
Irish Academy of Letters (BI)................ IAL
Irish Agricultural Officers Organisation (BI)................ IAOO
Irish Agricultural Organisation Society Ltd. (BI)................ IAOS
Irish Agricultural Wholesale Society Ltd. (BI)................ IAWS
Irish Air Corps [*ICAO designator*] (FAAC)................ IRL
Irish Air Tours [*ICAO designator*] (FAAC)................ RDK
Irish Amateur Boxing Association (BI)................ IABA
Irish Association for the Blind (BI)................ IAB
Irish Association of Master Bakers (BI)................ IAMB
Irish Central Library for Students (BI)................ ICL
Irish Computer Society................ ICS
Irish Countrywomen's Association (BI)................ ICA
Irish Creamery Milk Suppliers' Association (BI)................ ICMSA
Irish Dental Association (BI)................ IDA
Irish Dinghy Racing Association (BI)................ IDRA
Irish Drug Association (BI)................ IDA
Irish Flour Millers Association (BI)................ IFMA
Irish Football Association (BI)................ IFA
Irish Gas Association (BI)................ IGA
Irish Genealogical Research Society (BI)................ IGRS
Irish Graphical Society (BI)................ IGS
Irish Hotel and Restaurant Managers' Association (BI)................ IHRMA
Irish Institute of Secretaries Ltd. (BI)................ IIS
Irish National Productivity Committee (BI)................ INPC
Irish National Union of Woodworkers (BI)................ INUW
Irish Nurses Organisation (BI)................ INO
Irish Paper Box Association (BI)................ IPBA
Irish Printing Federation (BI)................ IPF
Irish Research Scientists Association................ IRSA
Irish Tourist Office (BI)................ ITO
Irish Union of Distributive Workers and Clerks (BI)................ IUDWC
Irish Wholesale Ryegrass Machiners Association (BI)................ IWRMA
Irish Work Study Institute Ltd. (BI)................ IWSI
Iron Dragon-Fly Ltd. [*Russian Federation*] [*ICAO designator*]
    (FAAC)................ IDF
Iron and Steel Industry Training Board [*British*] (BI)................ ISITB
Iron and Steel Trades Employers' Association [*British*] (BI)................ ISTEA
Ironfounders' National Confederation [*British*] (BI)................ INC
Irregular Outer Edge [*Army*] (ADDR)................ IOE
Irving Oil Ltd. [*Canada*] [*ICAO designator*] (FAAC)................ XIA
Isla Grande Flying School [*Puerto Rico*] [*ICAO designator*] (FAAC)......... IGS
Islamic Research Foundation (EA)................ IRF
Island (DA)................ IS
Island Air Charters, Inc. [*ICAO designator*] (FAAC)................ ISC
Island Air Ltd. [*Fiji*] [*ICAO designator*] (FAAC)................ IML
Island Airlines [*ICAO designator*] (FAAC)................ XYZ
Island Airlines, Inc. [*ICAO designator*] (FAAC)................ ISA
Island Aviation & Travel Ltd. [*British*] [*ICAO designator*] (FAAC)......... IOM
Island Helicopters, Inc. [*ICAO designator*] (FAAC)................ MTP
Islena de Inversiones SA [*Honduras*] [*ICAO designator*] (FAAC)................ ISV
Isles of Scilly Skybus Ltd. [*British*] [*ICAO designator*] (FAAC)................ IOS
Isolated Camera (NTCM)................ ISO
Isotope Dilution Thermal Ionization Mass Spectrometry................ IDTIMS
Israel [*Aircraft nationality and registration mark*] (FAAC)................ 4X
Israel Aircraft Industries Ltd. [*ICAO designator*] (FAAC)................ IAI
Israeli Air-Force [*ICAO designator*] (FAAC)................ IAF
Issue Authority Voucher................ IAV
Istanbul Airlines [*Turkey*] [*ICAO designator*] (FAAC)................ IST
Istra Air [*Slovakia*] [*ICAO designator*] (FAAC)................ ISR
It Would Be Nice If [*Computer hacker terminology*] (NHD)................ IWBNI

ITA [*Itapemirim Transportes Aereos SA*] [*Brazil*] [*ICAO designator*]
    (FAAC) .... ITM
Itapemirim Transportes Aereos SA [*Brazil*] [*ICAO designator*]
    (FAAC) .... ITA

J

J & J Air Charters Ltd. [British] [ICAO designator] (FAAC) .... JAY	Jenney Beechcraft, Inc. [ICAO designator] (FAAC) .... JNY
Jack Daniels [A brand name of whiskey] .... JD	Jeopardize (ABBR) .... JEOPZ
Jackal (ABBR) .... JKL	Jeopardize (ABBR) .... JPRDZ
Jackass (ABBR) .... JKAS	Jeopardized (ABBR) .... JEOPZD
Jackboot (ABBR) .... JKBT	Jeopardizing (ABBR) .... JEOPZG
Jacked (ABBR) .... JKD	Jeopardizing (ABBR) .... JPRDZG
Jacket (ABBR) .... JKET	Jeopardy (ABBR) .... JEOP
Jacketed (ABBR) .... JKTD	Jeopardy (ABBR) .... JPRDY
Jacketing (ABBR) .... JKTG	Jepenssen Data Plan, Inc. [ICAO designator] (FAAC) .... XLD
Jacketted (ABBR) .... JKETD	Jerked (ABBR) .... JRKD
Jackhammer (ABBR) .... JKMR	Jerker (ABBR) .... JRKR
Jacking (ABBR) .... JKG	Jerkier (ABBR) .... JRKIR
Jackknife (ABBR) .... JKNIF	Jerkiest (ABBR) .... JRKST
Jackpot (ABBR) .... JKPT	Jerkily (ABBR) .... JRKLY
Jacks (ABBR) .... JKS	Jerkin (ABBR) .... JRKN
Jackson Air Services Ltd. [Canada] [ICAO designator] (FAAC) .... JCK	Jerkiness (ABBR) .... JRKNS
Jailbird (ABBR) .... JLBD	Jerking (ABBR) .... JRKG
Jailbreak (ABBR) .... JLBRK	Jerrybuild (ABBR) .... JRYBLD
Jailer (ABBR) .... JLR	Jerrybuilder (ABBR) .... JRYBLDR
Jakarta [Indonesia] (ABBR) .... JKA	Jerrybuilding (ABBR) .... JRYBLDG
Jamahiriya Airways [Libya] [ICAO designator] (FAAC) .... JAW	Jerrybuilt (ABBR) .... JRYBLT
Jamahiriya Libyan Arab Airlines [ICAO designator] (FAAC) .... LAA	Jersey (ABBR) .... JRSY
Jamaica [Aircraft nationality and registration mark] (FAAC) 6Y	Jersey European Airways [British] [ICAO designator] (FAAC) .... JEA
Jamb (ABBR) .... JMB	Jerusalem (ABBR) .... JLEM
Jamboree (ABBR) .... JMBRE	Jes Air [Bulgaria] [ICAO designator] (FAAC) .... JES
James Brake [Aviation] (DA) .... JBD	Jet-Air Bedarfsflugunternehmen [Austria] [ICAO designator] (FAAC) .... JTR
JanAir, Inc. [ICAO designator] (FAAC) .... JAX	Jet Air Internacional Charters CA [Venezuela] [ICAO designator]
Janes Aviation 748 Ltd. [British] [ICAO designator] (FAAC) .... JAN	(FAAC) .... INC
Janes Aviation Ltd. [British] [ICAO designator] (FAAC) .... JAV	Jet Alsace [France] [ICAO designator] (FAAC) .... JLS
Janitor (ABBR) .... JNTR	Jet Aviation, Business Jets AG [Switzerland] [ICAO designator]
Janitorial (ABBR) .... JTRL	(FAAC) .... PJS
January (ABBR) .... JNY	Jet Business Airlines [Belgium] [ICAO designator] (FAAC) .... JAB
Japan Air Charter Co. Ltd. [ICAO designator] (FAAC) .... JAZ	Jet Cargo-Liberia [ICAO designator] (FAAC) .... JCL
Japan Air Commuter Co. Ltd. [ICAO designator] (FAAC) .... JAC	Jet Center Flight Training SA [Spain] [ICAO designator] (FAAC) .... JCF
Japan Air Lines Ltd. [ICAO designator] (FAAC) .... JAL	Jet East, Inc. [ICAO designator] (FAAC) .... JED
Japan Air System Co. Ltd. [ICAO designator] (FAAC) .... JAS	Jet Express, Inc. [ICAO designator] (FAAC) .... JEX
Japan Asia Airways Co. Ltd. [ICAO designator] (FAAC) .... JAA	Jet Freighters, Inc. [ICAO designator] (FAAC) .... CFT
Japan Asian Dance Event .... JADE	Jet Fret [France] [ICAO designator] (FAAC) .... JFT
Japan Australia Venture Capital Fund .... JAVCF	Jet Heritage Ltd. [British] [ICAO designator] (FAAC) .... JHL
Japan Transocean Air Co. Ltd. [ICAO designator] (FAAC) .... JTA	Jet Rent SA [Mexico] [ICAO designator] (FAAC) .... JRN
Japan Universal System Transport Co. Ltd. [ICAO designator]	Jet Servisx SA de CV [Mexico] [ICAO designator] (FAAC) .... VIS
(FAAC) .... JST	Jet Way, Inc. [ICAO designator] (FAAC) .... JWY
Japanese Government Bond (ECON) .... JGB	Jetag AB [Switzerland] [ICAO designator] (FAAC) .... JAG
Japanese Plating Supplier's Association [Environmetal science] .... JPSA	Jetair APS [Denmark] [ICAO designator] (FAAC) .... FOX
Japanese Standards Association (NTCM) .... JSA	Jetall Holdings, Corp. [Canada] [ICAO designator] (FAAC) .... JTL
Jarful (ABBR) .... JRFL	Jetcom SA [Switzerland] [ICAO designator] (FAAC) .... JCA
Jargon (ABBR) .... JRGN	Jetcopter [Denmark] [ICAO designator] (FAAC) .... JCP
Jaro International SA [Romania] [ICAO designator] (FAAC) .... MDJ	Jetflite OY [Finland] [ICAO designator] (FAAC) .... JEF
Jarred (ABBR) .... JRD	Jetliner (ABBR) .... JETLNR
Jarring (ABBR) .... JRG	Jets Corporativos SA de CV [Mexico] [ICAO designator] (FAAC) .... JTC
Jasmine (ABBR) .... JSMIN	Jets Ejecutivos SA [Mexico] [ICAO designator] (FAAC) .... JEJ
Jaunt (ABBR) .... JNT	Jetsam (ABBR) .... JET
Jauntier (ABBR) .... JNTIR	Jetstream International Airlines [ICAO designator] (FAAC) .... JIA
Jauntiest (ABBR) .... JNTST	Jetstream Ltd. [Hungary] [ICAO designator] (FAAC) .... JSH
Jauntily (ABBR) .... JNTLY	Jetted (ABBR) .... JETD
Jauntiness (ABBR) .... JNTINS	Jetting (ABBR) .... JETG
Jaunty (ABBR) .... JNTY	Jetworld Airways Ltd. [Antigua and Barbuda] [ICAO designator]
Jealous (ABBR) .... JELOS	(FAAC) .... JWA
Jealous (ABBR) .... JLUS	Jeweler (ABBR) .... JLR
Jealously (ABBR) .... JLUSLY	Jewish Autonomous Region [Siberia] .... JAR
Jealousness (ABBR) .... JLUSNS	JIB, Inc. [ICAO designator] (FAAC) .... AXQ
Jealousy (ABBR) .... JELOSY	Jibing (ABBR) .... JIBG
Jealousy (ABBR) .... JLUSY	Jiffy (ABBR) .... JFY
Jehovah (ABBR) .... JHVH	Jigger (ABBR) .... JIGR
Jehovah's Witnesses for Animal Rights [An association] (EA) ..... JWAR	Jiggle (ABBR) .... JIGL
Jejunectomy (ABBR) .... JEJUN	Jiggled (ABBR) .... JIGLD
Jejunitis (ABBR) .... JEJUN	Jiggling (ABBR) .... JIGLG
Jellied (ABBR) .... JLYD	Jiggly (ABBR) .... JIGLY
Jelly (ABBR) .... JLY	Jigsaw (ABBR) .... JGSW
Jellybean (ABBR) .... JLYBN	Jilter (ABBR) .... JLTR
Jellyfish (ABBR) .... JLYFSH	Jimmy (ABBR) .... JMY
Jellylike (ABBR) .... JLYLK	Jimmying (ABBR) .... JMYG
Jenair Ltd. [Cyprus] [ICAO designator] (FAAC) .... JEN	Jingled (ABBR) .... JINGLD

Jingling   (ABBR) .... JINGLG
Jitter   (ABBR)... JITR
Jitterbug   (ABBR)... JITRBG
Jittery   (ABBR).. JITRY
Job Center... JC
Job Club.. JC
Job Redesign Working Group.. JRWG
Job Search Training Program.. JSTP
Job Skills Training.. JST
Job Skills Training Course .... JSTC
Jobbed   (ABBR).. JOBD
Jobber   (ABBR).. JOBR
Jobbing   (ABBR).. JOBG
Jobholder   (ABBR)... JOBHLDR
Jobs Illustrated [CD-ROM] .... JILL
Jockey   (ABBR)... JOCK
Jockstrap   (ABBR).. JOCK
Jocular   (ABBR)... JOC
Jogged   (ABBR).. JOGD
Jogger   (ABBR)... JOGR
Jogging   (ABBR)... JOGG
Joggle   (ABBR)... JOGL
Joggled   (ABBR).. JOGLD
Joggling   (ABBR).. JOGLG
Johannesburg [South Africa]   (ABBR)................................. JHB
[James M.] Johnson [ICAO designator]   (FAAC) .... JMJ
Johnson Air, Inc. [ICAO designator]   (FAAC).................... JHN
Joinable   (ABBR)... JNB
Joinder   (ABBR)... JNDR
Joined   (ABBR).. JND
Joiner   (ABBR).. JNR
Joiner   (ABBR).. JONR
Joinery Managers' Association [British]   (BI)...................... JMA
Joinery and Woodwork Employers' Federation [British]   (BI)..... JWEF
Joint Agency Training.. JAT
Joint Airmiss Section [Aviation]   (DA)................................ JAS
Joint Defense Space Communications Station .... JDSCS
Joint Development Program .... JDP
Joint Engineers [Army]   (RDA) .... JE
Joint Engineers Management Panel [Army]   (RDA)............ JEMP
Joint Selection Committee .... JSC
Joint Staffing Review .... JSR
Joint Tactical Exploitation of National Systems [Army]   (ADDR).......... J-TENS
Joint Target Acquistion Ground Station [Military] .... JTAGS
Joint Task Force... JTF
Joint Venture Scheme .... JVS
Joint Working Group .... JWG
Joint Working Paper .... JWP
Jointed   (ABBR)... JNTD
Jointer   (ABBR)... JNTR
Jointly   (ABBR).. JNTLY
Jointly   (ABBR)... JNTY
Jointure   (ABBR).. JNTUR
Jointured   (ABBR)... JNTURD
Jointuring   (ABBR).. JNTURG
Jokester   (ABBR).. JOKSTR
Joking   (ABBR)... JOKG
Jokingly   (ABBR).. JOKGLY
Jokingly   (ABBR)... JOKGY
Jollied   (ABBR)... JOLD
Joltingly   (ABBR)... JOLTGLY
Jonquil   (ABBR)... JNGL
[H.] Jonsson Air Taxi [Iceland] [ICAO designator]   (FAAC)...................... ODI
Jordan   (ABBR)... JORD
Joseph Malins Crusade of Youth [British]   (BI)................. JMCY
Jotted   (ABBR)... JOTD
Jotting   (ABBR).. JOTG
Journal   (ABBR)... JOUR
Journal of the Australian Natural Therapists Association [A
    publication].. JANTA
Journal of Military History [A publication] .... J Mil H
Journal of Third World Studies [A publication]................... JTWS
Journal of Workforce Diversity [A publication] .... JWD
Journalism   (ABBR).. JRNLM
Journalism   (ABBR)... JRNLSM
Journalist   (ABBR)... JRNLST
Journalist   (ABBR).. JRNLT
Journalistic   (ABBR)... JRNLSTC
Journalistic   (ABBR).. JRNLTC
Journalistically   (ABBR)... JRNLTCY
Journalists, Authors and Poets on Stamps Study Unit   (EA) .... JAPOS
Journalize   (ABBR)... JRNLZ
Journalized   (ABBR)... JRNLZD
Journalizer   (ABBR).. JRNLZR
Journalizing   (ABBR).. JRNLZG
Journey   (ABBR)... JOURN
Journey   (ABBR)... JRNY
Journeyed   (ABBR).. JRNYD
Journeying   (ABBR)... JRNYG
Journeyman   (ABBR).. JRNYMAN
Journeyman Bakers' and Confectioners Pension Society [British]
    (BI).. JBCPS
Joy [Poland] [ICAO designator]   (FAAC)............................ JOY

Juan Air (1979) Ltd. [Canada] [ICAO designator]   (FAAC)...................... WON
Juanda Flying School [Indonesia] [ICAO designator]   (FAAC)..... JFS
Jubilee Airways Ltd. [British] [ICAO designator]   (FAAC)........... DKE
Judge... J
Jugoslovenski Aerotransport [Yugoslavia] [ICAO designator]   (FAAC) .... JAT
Jukebox   (ABBR).. JKBX
Julep   (ABBR)... JLEP
Julienne   (ABBR).. JLEN
Jumble   (ABBR)... JMBL
Jumbled   (ABBR)... JMBLD
Jumbling   (ABBR).. JMBLG
Jump if Flag Set and Then Clear the Flag [Computer science]
    (NHD)... JFCL
Jumped   (ABBR).. JMPD
Jumpiness   (ABBR).. JMPNS
Jumping   (ABBR).. JMPG
Jumpmaster Personnel Inspection [Army]   (ADDR)........ JMPI
Jumpoff   (ABBR).. JMPOF
Junction   (ABBR).. JNCN
Junction   (ABBR)... JNT
Juncture   (ABBR)... JNCUR
Juncture   (ABBR).. JNT
June   (ABBR)... JNE
Jungle   (ABBR).. JNGL
Junior American Citizens [An association]   (EA) .... JAC
Junior Bird League [British]   (BI)..................................... JBL
Junior Offshore Group [Racing] [British].......................... JOG
Junior Philatelic Society [British]   (BI)............................. JPS
Juniper   (ABBR).. JNPR
Junked   (ABBR)... JNKD
Junket   (ABBR)... JNKT
Junketed   (ABBR)... JNKTD
Junketer   (ABBR)... JNKTR
Junketing   (ABBR)... JNKTG
Junkie   (ABBR)... JNKI
Junking   (ABBR).. JNKG
Junkman   (ABBR).. JNKMA
Jurisdictional   (ABBR)... JRSDCNL
Jurisprudence   (ABBR).. JRSPDNC
Jurisprudent   (ABBR).. JRSPDN
Jurisprudential   (ABBR)... JRSPDTL
Jurist   (ABBR).. JRST
Juror   (ABBR)... JRR
Jury   (ABBR)... JRY
Juryman   (ABBR).. JRYMA
Just a Minute [Computer hacker terminology]   (NHD)........... JAM
Just for Openers [An association]   (EA) .... JFO
Juvenile Missionary Association [British]   (BI) .... JMA
JV Avcom [Russian Federation] [ICAO designator]   (FAAC)................ AOC

K

K2 Del Aire SA de CV [*Mexico*] [*ICAO designator*]   (FAAC) .... KDS
Kabo Air Travels [*Nigeria*] [*ICAO designator*]   (FAAC) .... QNK
Kafue International Air Services Ltd. [*Zambia*] [*ICAO designator*]
   (FAAC) .... KAF
Kaiser   (ABBR) .... KSR
Kaleidoscope   (ABBR) .... KLDSOP
Kaleidoscopic   (ABBR) .... KLDSOPC
[*Connie*] Kalitta Services, Inc. [*ICAO designator*]   (FAAC) .... CKS
Kanaf-Arkia Airlines Ltd. [*Israel*] [*ICAO designator*]   (FAAC) ... KIZ
Kangaroo   (ABBR) .... KNGR
Kano Transport International Ltd. KATI Air [*Nigeria*] [*ICAO*
   designator]   (FAAC) .... KTI
Kapok   (ABBR) .... KPK
Kappa Delta Pi [*Honor society*]   (AEE) .... KDP
Kar-Air OY [*Finland*] [*ICAO designator*]   (FAAC) .... KAR
Karat   (ABBR) .... KR
Karate   (ABBR) .... KRTE
Karatin   (ABBR) .... KRTN
Karma   (ABBR) .... KRM
Karmic   (ABBR) .... KRMC
Karpatair [*Hungary*] [*ICAO designator*]   (FAAC) .... KPT
Kattegat Air, AS [*Denmark*] [*ICAO designator*]   (FAAC) ...... KAT
Katydid   (ABBR) .... KTYD
Kavouras, Inc. [*ICAO designator*]   (FAAC) .... XKA
Kayak   (ABBR) .... KYK
Kazakhstan Airlines [*ICAO designator*]   (FAAC) .... KAZAIR
Kazakhstan Airlines [*ICAO designator*]   (FAAC) .... KZA
KD Air Corp. [*ICAO designator*]   (FAAC) .... KDC
Keeper   (ABBR) .... KPR
Keepsake   (ABBR) .... KPSK
Kellogg National Fellowship Program .... KNFP
Kelowna Flightcraft Air Charter Ltd. [*Canada*] [*ICAO designator*]
   (FAAC) .... KFA
Kendall Airlines [*Australia*] [*ICAO designator*]   (FAAC) ...... KDA
Kenn Borek Air Ltd. [*Canada*] [*ICAO designator*]   (FAAC) ... KBA
Kennel   (ABBR) .... KNL
Kenneled   (ABBR) .... KNLD
Kenneling   (ABBR) .... KNLG
Kensington Palace Gardens [*British interrogation center*] .... KPM
Kent Aviation Ltd. [*Canada*] [*ICAO designator*]   (FAAC) ...... KAH
Kent Executive Aviation Ltd. [*British*] [*ICAO designator*]   (FAAC) .... KEA
Kentair (International) Ltd. [*British*] [*ICAO designator*]   (FAAC)............. INK
Kenuz Airlines Ltd. [*Nigeria*] [*ICAO designator*]   (FAAC)...................... KNS
Kenya Airways Ltd. [*ICAO designator*]   (FAAC) .... KQA
Kenya Flamingo Airways Ltd. [*ICAO designator*]   (FAAC) ...... KFL
Kerchief   (ABBR) .... KRCHF
Kernel   (ABBR) .... KNRL
Kernel   (ABBR) .... KRNL
Kernel Programming Interface [*Computer science*] .... KPI
Kerosene   (ABBR) .... KRSEN
Kestrel   (ABBR) .... KSTRL
Ketchup   (ABBR) .... KTCHP
Ketone [*Organic chemistry*]   (ABBR) .... KTON
Kettle   (ABBR) .... KTL
Kettledrum   (ABBR) .... KTLDR
[*Fire Department*] Key Box [*NFPA pre-fire planning symbol*]   (NFPA) .... K
Key Result Area .... KRA
Keyboard Display Station [*Computer science*]   (DA) .... KDS
Keyfile Open Access Layer [*Workflow automation software*]
   (PCM) .... KOALA
Keyhole   (ABBR) .... KYHL
Keynote   (ABBR) .... KYNT
Keynoting   (ABBR) .... KYNTG
Keystone   (ABBR) .... KYSTN
Keystone Air Services Ltd. [*Canada*] [*ICAO designator*]   (FAAC) ... KEE
Khan   (ABBR) .... KN
Khazar [*Turkmenistan*] [*ICAO designator*]   (FAAC) .... KHR
Khranit' Vechno [*To be Kept in Perpetuity*] [*KGB file status*] .... KhV
Kidney, Ureter, and Spleen [*Anatomy*]   (MAH) .... KUS
Kids for Saving Earth [*An association*]   (EA) .... KSE
Killdeer   (ABBR) .... KLDR
Killing   (ABBR) .... KLG
Killjoy   (ABBR) .... KLJY

Kilocycle   (ABBR) .... KLCCL
Kilogram   (ABBR) .... KLGM
Kilohertz .... kH
Kilohm   (ABBR) .... KO
Kilometer   (ABBR) .... KLMTR
Kiloton   (ABBR) .... KLTN
Kilourane   (ABBR) .... KU
Kilowatt   (ABBR) .... KLWT
Kilowatthour   (ABBR) .... KWHR
Kilter   (ABBR) .... KLTR
Kimono   (ABBR) .... KMNO
Kinder   (ABBR) .... KNDR
Kindergarten   (ABBR) .... KNDGTN
Kindergarten   (ABBR) .... KNDRG
Kindergartener   (ABBR) .... KNDRGR
Kindest   (ABBR) .... KNDST
Kindhearted   (ABBR) .... KNDHTD
Kindheartedness   (ABBR) .... KNDHTDNS
Kindle   (ABBR) .... KNDL
Kindled   (ABBR) .... KNDLD
Kindless   (ABBR) .... KNDLES
Kindlier   (ABBR) .... KNDLIR
Kindliest   (ABBR) .... KNDLST
Kindliness   (ABBR) .... KNDLNS
Kindling   (ABBR) .... KNDLG
Kindly   (ABBR) .... KNDLY
Kindly   (ABBR) .... KNDY
Kindness   (ABBR) .... KNDNS
Kindred   (ABBR) .... KNDRD
Kinescope   (ABBR) .... KNSCP
Kinetic   (ABBR) .... KNTC
Kinfolk   (ABBR) .... KNFLK
King Aviation [*British*] [*ICAO designator*]   (FAAC) .... KNG
Kingdom   (ABBR) .... KNGDM
Kingfish   (ABBR) .... KNGFSH
Kingfisher   (ABBR) .... KNGFSHR
Kinglier   (ABBR) .... KNGLR
Kingliest   (ABBR) .... KNGLST
Kingliness   (ABBR) .... KNGLNS
Kingly   (ABBR) .... KNGLY
Kingly   (ABBR) .... KNGY
Kingman Aviation, Inc. [*ICAO designator*]   (FAAC) .... GPA
Kingpin   (ABBR) .... KNGPN
Kingsize   (ABBR) .... KNGSZ
Kingston Air Services [*Canada*] [*ICAO designator*]   (FAAC) ...... KAS
Kinkier   (ABBR) .... KNKR
Kinkiest   (ABBR) .... KNKST
Kinship   (ABBR) .... KNSHP
Kinsman   (ABBR) .... KNSMN
Kinswoman   (ABBR) .... KNSWMN
Kiosk   (ABBR) .... KSK
Kisbee Air Ltd. [*New Zealand*] [*ICAO designator*]   (FAAC) ...... KSE
Kish Air [*Iran*] [*ICAO designator*]   (FAAC) .... IRK
Kismet   (ABBR) .... KSMT
Kissable   (ABBR) .... KSSB
Kisser   (ABBR) .... KSSR
Kitchen   (ABBR) .... KTCN
Kitchennette   (ABBR) .... KTCNET
Kitchenware   (ABBR) .... KTCNWR
Kiting   (ABBR) .... KITG
Kitsch   (ABBR) .... KTSC
Kitten   (ABBR) .... KITN
Kitten   (ABBR) .... KTN
Kittenish   (ABBR) .... KTNH
Kitty   (ABBR) .... KTY
Kitty-Corner   (ABBR) .... KTYCR
Kitty Hawk Aircargo, Inc. [*ICAO designator*]   (FAAC) .... PAI
Kitty Hawk Airways, Inc. [*ICAO designator*]   (FAAC) .... KHA
KIWI International Air Lines, Inc. [*ICAO designator*]   (FAAC) ...... KIA
Klebsiella [*Genus of microorganisms*]   (MAH) .... Kleb
Klenow Fragment [*Genetics*] .... KF
Kleptomania   (ABBR) .... KLEPTO
Kleptomania   (ABBR) .... KLPTMN

Kleptomaniac   (ABBR) .... KLPTMNC
KLM Cityhopper BV [*Netherlands*] [*ICAO designator*]   (FAAC) .... KLC
KLM Helicopters NV [*Netherlands*] [*ICAO designator*]   (FAAC) .... KLH
KLM Royal Dutch Airlines [*Netherlands*] [*ICAO designator*]
    (FAAC) .... KLM
Knapsack   (ABBR) .... KNPSK
Knave   (ABBR) .... KNV
Knavery   (ABBR) .... KNVRY
Knavish   (ABBR) .... KNVH
Knavishly   (ABBR) .... KNVHLY
Kneecap   (ABBR) .... KNECP
Kneedeep   (ABBR) .... KNEDP
Kneeling   (ABBR) .... KNELG
Kneller   (ABBR) .... KNELR
Knickers   (ABBR) .... KNKRS
Knife   (ABBR) .... KNF
Knifed   (ABBR) .... KNFD
Knifelike   (ABBR) .... KNFLK
Knifing   (ABBR) .... KNFG
Knight   (ABBR) .... KN
Knight   (ABBR) .... KNGT
Knight   (ABBR) .... KNHT
Knight Air Ltd. [*Canada*] [*ICAO designator*]   (FAAC) .... KNA
Knight-Errant   (ABBR) .... KNGT-RNT
Knighthawk Air Express Ltd. [*Canada*] [*ICAO designator*]   (FAAC) ... KNX
Knighthood   (ABBR) .... KNGTHD
Knightly   (ABBR) .... KNGTLY
Knightway Air Charter Ltd. [*British*] [*ICAO designator*]   (FAAC) .... KNT
Knitter   (ABBR) .... KNITR
Knitting   (ABBR) .... KNITG
Knobbier   (ABBR) .... KNBR
Knobbiest   (ABBR) .... KNBST
Knobby   (ABBR) .... KNBY
Knock-knee   (ABBR) .... KNCKKN
Knockabout   (ABBR) .... KNCKBT
Knockdown   (ABBR) .... KNCKDN
Knocker   (ABBR) .... KNCKR
Knockout   (ABBR) .... KNCKOT
Knoll   (ABBR) .... KNL
Knothole   (ABBR) .... KNTHL
Knotless   (ABBR) .... KNTLS
Knotlike   (ABBR) .... KNTLK
Knotted   (ABBR) .... KNTD
Knotting   (ABBR) .... KNTG
Knotty   (ABBR) .... KNTY
Know-How   (ABBR) .... KNWHW
Know-Nothing   (ABBR) .... KNWNTHG
Knowable   (ABBR) .... KNWB
Knower   (ABBR) .... KNWR
Knowing   (ABBR) .... KNWG
Knowingly   (ABBR) .... KNWGY
Knowingness   (ABBR) .... KNWGNS
Knowledge   (ABBR) .... KNWL
Knowledge   (ABBR) .... KNWLDG
Knowledge, Absent Without Leave [*Army*]   (ADDR) .... KAWOL
Knowledge-Based Engineering [*Expert systems*] [*Computer-aided
    design*] .... KBE
Knowledgeable   (ABBR) .... KNWLB
Knowledgeable   (ABBR) .... KNWLDGB
Knoxville [*Tennessee*]   (ABBR) .... KNXV
Knuckle   (ABBR) .... KNKL
Knuckled   (ABBR) .... KNKLD
Knuckling   (ABBR) .... KNKLG
Kob Air Ltd. [*Uganda*] [*ICAO designator*]   (FAAC) .... KOB
Kone Air Ltd. [*Finland*] [*ICAO designator*]   (FAAC) .... KOA
Kookier   (ABBR) .... KOOKR
Kookiest   (ABBR) .... KOOKST
Kopeck   (ABBR) .... KPCK
Korea Institute for Industrial Economics and Trade   (ECON) .... KIET
Korean Air Lines Co. Ltd. [*ICAO designator*]   (FAAC) .... KAL
Korsar [*Russian Federation*] [*ICAO designator*]   (FAAC) .... KRS
Kosher   (ABBR) .... KSHR
Kosovaair [*Yugoslavia*] [*ICAO designator*]   (FAAC) .... KOS
Kovar Air [*Czechoslovakia*] [*ICAO designator*]   (FAAC) .... WOK
Kraiaero [*Russian Federation*] [*ICAO designator*]   (FAAC) .... KIO
Kraken   (ABBR) .... KRKN
Krone   (ABBR) .... KN
Kronen   (ABBR) .... KN
Krypton   (ABBR) .... KRYPN
KS Nordic Air, Denmark [*ICAO designator*]   (FAAC) .... NDI
Kuder-Richardson Formula [*Education*]   (AEE) .... K-R
Kumquat   (ABBR) .... KMQUT
Kustbevakningen [*Sweden*] [*ICAO designator*]   (FAAC) .... KBV
Kuwait   (ABBR) .... KUW
Kuwait Airways Corp. [*ICAO designator*]   (FAAC) .... KAC
Kymograph   (ABBR) .... KYMO
Kyrghyzstan Airlines [*ICAO designator*]   (FAAC) .... KGA
Kyrnair [*France*] [*ICAO designator*]   (FAAC) .... KYN

L

LA Helicopter, Inc. [*ICAO designator*]   (FAAC) .... LAH
Labor of Genetic Disease Research [*National Institutes of Health*] .... LGDR
Labrador Airways Ltd. [*Canada*] [*ICAO designator*]   (FAAC) .... LAL
Labrador Retriever [*Dog breed*] .... LAB
Labyrinth Air Induction System [*Automotive engineering*] .... LAIS
Ladies' Home Mission Union [*British*]   (BI) .... LHMU
Ladies Kennel Association [*British*]   (BI) .... LKA
Lager   (ABBR) .... LGR
Laggard   (ABBR) .... LGRD
Lagged Reserve Requirement [*Finance*] .... LRR
Lagniappe   (ABBR) .... LGNAP
Lagoon   (ABBR) .... LGON
Lake Air Helicopters Ltd. [*British*] [*ICAO designator*]   (FAAC) .... LKR
Lake Havasu Air Service [*ICAO designator*]   (FAAC) .... HCA
Lakeland Aviation [*ICAO designator*]   (FAAC) .... LKL
Laker Airways (Bahamas) Ltd. [*ICAO designator*]   (FAAC) .... LBH
Lakeside Aviation Ltd. [*British*] [*ICAO designator*]   (FAAC) .... LKS
Lambair Ltd. [*Canada*] [*ICAO designator*]   (FAAC) .... LWL
Lamda Airlines [*Greece*] [*ICAO designator*]   (FAAC) .... LMD
Laminated Plastics Fabricators Association [*British*]   (BI) .... LPFA
Lamphole   (ABBR) .... LH
Land-Grant College of Agriculture .... LGCA
Land-Grant University .... LGU
Land Mobile Service   (DA) .... LMS
Land-Ocean Interaction in the Costal Zone [*International Geosphere
    Biosphere Programme*] .... LOICZ
Land Transportation [*FCC*]   (NTCM) L
Landed Duty Free .... LDF
Landed Estate Companies Association [*British*]   (BI) .... LECA
Landing Force Support Party [*Navy*]   (ANA) .... LFSP
Landing Traffic [*Aviation*]   (FAAC) .... LTFC
Landline Telephony [*Aviation*]   (DA) .... LTF
Laneas Aereas Trans Costa Rica SA [*ICAO designator*]   (FAAC) .... TCR
Langor   (ABBR) .... LGOR
Langorous   (ABBR) .... LGORU
Langorously   (ABBR) .... LGORUY
Lanthanide Ion Probe Spectroscopy .... LIPS
Lao Aviaton [*Laos*] [*ICAO designator*]   (FAAC) .... LAO
Laparoscopically-Assisted Vaginal Hysterectomy [*Medicine*] .... LAVH
LapLink Remote Access [*Traveling Software, Inc.*] [*Computer
    science*]   (PCM) .... LLRA
Lar-Liniile Aeriene Romance [*Romania*] [*ICAO designator*]   (FAAC) ..... RLA
LAR Transregional, Linhas Aereas Regionais SA [*Portugal*] [*ICAO
    designator*]   (FAAC) .... PDF
Laredo Air, Inc. [*ICAO designator*]   (FAAC) .... LRD
Large Binocular Telescope .... LBT
Large Millimeter Telescope [*US-Mexico project*] [*Proposed, 1994*] ..... LMT
Large Scale   (ABBR) .... LGSC
Large Virus-Like Particle .... LVLP
Largely   (ABBR) .... LGY
Largeness   (ABBR) .... LGNS
Largest   (ABBR) .... LGT
Larghetto   (ABBR) .... LGHET
Largo   (ABBR) .... LGO
LASER Discectomy [*Spinal surgery*] .... LD
LASER Feedback Microscope .... LFM
LASER Initiated Transfer Energy Subsystem [*Detonator, developed
    by US Navy*] .... LITES
LASER without Inversion .... LWI
Last Day of Attendance .... LDA
Last Interglacial Period [*Climatology*] .... LIG
Last Telecast   (NTCM) .... LT
Lastp-Linhas Aereas de Sao Tome e Principe [*ICAO designator*]
    (FAAC) .... OTN
Latch and Lock   (DAC) .... L & L
Latch, Lock, and Bolt   (DAC) .... LL & B
Latch and Plaster   (DAC) .... L & P
Late Change Message [*Aviation*]   (DA) .... LCM
Latin America Antiquity [*A publication*] .... L A Ant
Latitudinal Species-Diversity Gradient [*Biodiversity*] .... LSDG
Lattice-Preferred Orientation [*Geophysics*] .... LPO
Latvian Airlines [*ICAO designator*]   (FAAC) .... LTL
Lauda Air [*Austria*] [*ICAO designator*]   (FAAC) .... LDA

Lauda Air [*Italy*] [*ICAO designator*]   (FAAC) .... LDI
Laugh   (ABBR) .... LGH
Laughable   (ABBR) .... LGHB
Laughably   (ABBR) .... LGHBY
Laughed   (ABBR) .... LGHD
Laugher   (ABBR) .... LGHR
Laughing   (ABBR) .... LGHG
Laughingly   (ABBR) .... LGHGY
Laughter   (ABBR) .... LGHTR
Laurentide Ice Sheet [*Climatology*] .... LIS
Lavaliere [*Lapel microphone*]   (NTCM) .... LAV
Law Enforcement Security Access Position .... LESAP
Law-Related Education   (AEE) .... LRE
Lawn Tennis Ball Convention [*British*]   (BI) .... LTBC
Lawn Tennis Registered Coaches Association [*British*]   (BI) .... LTRCA
Lawrence Aviation, Inc. [*ICAO designator*]   (FAAC) .... LAR
Layer Cloud [*Meteorology*]   (DA) .... LYR
Layered Metal Phosphates [*Physical chemistry*] .... LMP
Le Point Air [*France*] [*ICAO designator*]   (FAAC) .... POA
Lead .... Pb
Lead Air Jet Service [*France*] [*ICAO designator*]   (FAAC) .... LEA
Lead Design Supervisor [*Engineering*] .... LDS
Lead Piping Engineer .... LPE
Lead Technical Information Bureau [*British*]   (BI) .... LTIB
Leadership Education and Development USA   (EA) .... LEAD USA
Leafage   (ABBR) .... LFAG
Leafier   (ABBR) .... LFR
Leafiest   (ABBR) .... LFT
Leafiness   (ABBR) .... LFNS
Leafless   (ABBR) .... LFLS
Leafstalk   (ABBR) .... LFSTK
Leafy   (ABBR) .... LFY
League   (ABBR) .... LGU
League for Programming Freedom   (EA) .... LPF
League of Safe Drivers [*British*]   (BI) .... LSD
Leagued   (ABBR) .... LGUD
Leaguing   (ABBR) .... LGUG
Leak-Off Test .... LOT
Lean Misfire Limit [*Automotive engine testing*] .... LML
Learning Activity Packet   (AEE) .... LAP
Lease-A-Plane International [*ICAO designator*]   (FAAC) .... LPL
Leather [*Automotive advertising*] .... LTH
Leather Producers' Association for England, Scotland, and Wales
    (BI) .... LPA
Lebanese Air Transport [*ICAO designator*]   (FAAC) .... LAQ
Lebanon Airport Development Corp. [*ICAO designator*]   (FAAC) .... LAD
Lebap [*Turkmenistan*] [*ICAO designator*]   (FAAC) .... LEB
Lec Refrigeration Ltd. [*British*] [*ICAO designator*]   (FAAC) ..... LEC
LeConte Airlines [*ICAO designator*]   (FAAC) .... LCA
Lectura y Vida [*A publication*] .... Lect y V
Leeward Islands Air Transport (1974) Ltd. [*Antigua and Barbuda*]
    [*ICAO designator*]   (FAAC) .... LIA
Left   (ABBR) .... LFT
Left Base [*Aviation*]   (FAAC) .... LB
Left plus Right [*Stereo signals*]   (NTCM) .... L + R
Left minus Right [*Stereo signals*]   (NTCM) .... L - R
Left Unity Group [*European political movement*]   (ECON) .... LU
Lefthanded   (ABBR) .... LFTHDD
Lefthandedly   (ABBR) .... LFTHDY
Leftist   (ABBR) .... LFTT
Leftover   (ABBR) .... LFTOV
Leftwing   (ABBR) .... LFTWG
Leftwinger   (ABBR) .... LFTWR
Legacy   (ABBR) .... LGCY
Legal   (ABBR) .... LGL
Legal Environmental Assistance Foundation   (EA) .... LEAF
Legal Office Information System .... LOIS
Legal Services Group .... LSG
Legalism   (ABBR) .... LGLM
Legalist   (ABBR) .... LGLST
Legalistic   (ABBR) .... LGLSTC
Legalistic   (ABBR) .... LGLTC
Legalistically   (ABBR) .... LGLSTCY

183

Legality (ABBR) ... LGLT
Legalization (ABBR) ... LGLZN
Legalize (ABBR) ... LGLZ
Legalized (ABBR) ... LGLZD
Legalizing (ABBR) ... LGLZG
Legally (ABBR) ... LGLY
Legate (ABBR) ... LGT
Legatee (ABBR) ... LGTE
Legation (ABBR) ... LGTN
Legato (ABBR) ... LGTO
Legend (ABBR) ... LGND
Legendary (ABBR) ... LGNDY
Legerdemain (ABBR) ... LGDMN
Legging (ABBR) ... LGG
Leggy (ABBR) ... LGY
Leghorn (ABBR) ... LGHN
Legibility (ABBR) ... LGBT
Legible (ABBR) ... LGB
Legibly (ABBR) ... LGBY
Legion (ABBR) ... LGN
Legionaire (ABBR) ... LGNAR
Legionary (ABBR) ... LGNY
Legislate (ABBR) ... LGLA
Legislated (ABBR) ... LGLAD
Legislating (ABBR) ... LGLAG
Legislation (ABBR) ... LGLAN
Legislative (ABBR) ... LGLAY
Legislator (ABBR) ... LGLAR
Legislature (ABBR) ... LGLAR
Legitimate (ABBR) ... LGITMA
Legitimated (ABBR) ... LGITMAD
Legitimately (ABBR) ... LGITMY
Legitimating (ABBR) ... LGITMAG
Legitimist (ABBR) ... LGITIT
Legitimize (ABBR) ... LGITIZ
Legitimized (ABBR) ... LGITIZD
Legitimizing (ABBR) ... LGITIZG
Legitmacy (ABBR) ... LGITMC
Legume (ABBR) ... LGU
Leguminous (ABBR) ... LGUNU
Leisure International Airways Ltd. [*British*] [*ICAO designator*] (FAAC) ... ULE
Lenex [*Poland*] [*ICAO designator*] (FAAC) ... LNX
Lengthen (ABBR) ... LGTHN
Lengthened (ABBR) ... LGTHND
Lengthening (ABBR) ... LGTHNG
Lengthier (ABBR) ... LGTHR
Lengthiest (ABBR) ... LGTHT
Lengthily (ABBR) ... LGTHIY
Lengthiness (ABBR) ... LGTHNS
Lengthwise (ABBR) ... LGTHWS
Lengthy (ABBR) ... LGTHY
[*Michael A.*] **Lenihan & Associates Ltd.** [*British*] [*ICAO designator*] (FAAC) ... LCL
Lennox Airways [*Kenya*] [*ICAO designator*] (FAAC) ... LAK
Lennox Airways, Gambia Ltd. [*ICAO designator*] (FAAC) ... GLN
Lentini Aviation, Inc. [*ICAO designator*] (FAAC) ... LEN
Leo Taxi Aereo SA de CV [*Mexico*] [*ICAO designator*] (FAAC) ... LTX
Leonhartsberger Flugunternchmen GmbH [*Austria*] [*ICAO designator*] (FAAC) ... LFU
Leopair SA [*Switzerland*] [*ICAO designator*] (FAAC) ... LEO
Lesotho [*Aircraft nationality and registration mark*] (FAAC) ... 7P
Lesotho Airways Corp. [*ICAO designator*] (FAAC) ... LAI
Letaba Airways [*South Africa*] [*ICAO designator*] (FAAC) ... LKZ
Lethal (ABBR) ... LHAL
Lethal Concentration Low (ERG) ... LCLo
Lethal Dose Low (ERG) ... LDLo
Leucine-Rich Repeat [*Biochemistry*] ... LRR
Leukemia Inhibitory Factor Receptor [*Biochemistry*] ... LIFR
Level of Concern [*Environmental Protection Agency*] (ERG) ... LOC
Lexical (ABBR) ... LEXI
Lexicographer (ABBR) ... LEX
Lexicographer (ABBR) ... LEXICO
Lexicographer (ABBR) ... LEXPHR
Lexicography (ABBR) ... LEXPHY
Lexicological (ABBR) ... LEXOGL
Lexicologist (ABBR) ... LEXOGT
Lexicology (ABBR) ... LEXOG
Lexicon (ABBR) ... LEXN
L'Express, Inc. [*ICAO designator*] (FAAC) ... LEX
Liability (ABBR) ... LIABT
Liability (ABBR) ... LIBT
Liable (ABBR) ... LIBL
Liberal, Democratic, and Reformist Group [*European political movement*] (ECON) ... LDR
Liberalize (ABBR) ... LIBRLZ
Liberalizing (ABBR) ... LIBLZG
Liberated (ABBR) ... LIBERD
Liberating (ABBR) ... LIBERG
Liberation (ABBR) ... LIBERN
Liberator (ABBR) ... LIBERR
Liberia (ABBR) ... LI
Liberian World Airlines, Inc. [*ICAO designator*] (FAAC) ... LWA
Libertarian Education Institute (EA) ... LEI
Liberty (ABBR) ... LIBT
Library (ABBR) ... LIBRY
Library Association Publishing Ltd. [*British*] ... LAPL
Library Materials Management System ... LMMS
Library Resources Exhibition [*British*] ... LRE
Libyan Arab Company for Air Cargo [*ICAO designator*] (FAAC) ... LCR
Licensable (ABBR) ... LICB
Licensed Animal Slaughterers and Salvage Association [*British*] (BI) ... LASSA
Licensed Victuallers' Defence League of England and Wales (BI) ... LVDL
Licensing (ABBR) ... LICG
Liechtenstein (ABBR) ... LIECH
Lief (ABBR) ... LIF
Liege (ABBR) ... LIG
Lieutenancy (ABBR) ... LIEUTC
Lieutenancy (ABBR) ... LIEUTE
Life (ABBR) ... LF
Life Assurance Premium Relief [*Business term*] ... LAPR
Lifeblood (ABBR) ... LFBD
Lifeboat (ABBR) ... LFBT
Lifeboat Station [*Coast Guard*] ... LB
Lifeguard (ABBR) ... LFGRD
Lifelessly (ABBR) ... LFLSY
Lifelike (ABBR) ... LFLK
Lifeline (ABBR) ... LFLN
Lifer (ABBR) ... LFR
Lifesaver (ABBR) ... LFSV
Lifesize (ABBR) ... LFSZ
Lifestyle [*Wire service code*] (NTCM) ... L
Lifestyle (ABBR) ... LFST
Lifetime (ABBR) ... LFTM
Lifework (ABBR) ... LFWK
Lifting (ABBR) ... LIFTG
Lifting Equipment Manufacturers Association [*British*] (BI) ... LEMA
Liftoff (ABBR) ... LFTF
Ligament (ABBR) ... LGMN
Ligation-Mediated Polymerase Chain Reaction [*Genetics*] ... LMPCR
Ligature (ABBR) ... LGTR
Ligatured (ABBR) ... LGTRD
Ligaturing (ABBR) ... LGTRG
Light (ABBR) ... LHT
Light Atomic Gas Oil [*Petroleum product*] ... LAGO
Light Compact Performance [*Filtration systems*] [*Automotive engineering*] ... LCP
Light-Duty Diesel Truck [*Automotive emissions*] ... LDDT
Light Edge Tool and Allied Trades Association [*British*] (BI) ... LETATA
Light-Emitting Resistor [*Computer hacker terminology*] (NHD) ... LER
Light-Expanded Clay Aggregate (DAC) ... LECA
Light Reflective Capacitor [*Electronics*] (DA) ... LRC
Light-Vehicle Animation Simulation [*Accident reconstruction*] [*Automotive engineering*] ... LVAS
Light-Vehicle Dynamics Simulation [*Accident reconstruction*] [*Automotive engineering*] ... LVDS
Lighted (ABBR) ... LHTD
Lighten (ABBR) ... LGTN
Lighten (ABBR) ... LHTEN
Lightened (ABBR) ... LHTEND
Lightener (ABBR) ... LGTR
Lightening (ABBR) ... LHTENG
Lighter (ABBR) ... LHTR
Lightest (ABBR) ... LHTST
Lightfingered (ABBR) ... LGTFGR
Lightfooted (ABBR) ... LGTFTD
Lightfootedly (ABBR) ... LGTFTY
Lightheaded (ABBR) ... LGTHD
Lightheadedly (ABBR) ... LGTHDY
Lighthearted (ABBR) ... LGTHRTD
Lightheartedly (ABBR) ... LGTHRTY
Lightheartedness (ABBR) ... LGTHRTNS
Lighthouse (ABBR) ... LGTHS
Lighting (ABBR) ... LGTG
Lighting (ABBR) ... LHTG
Lighting (ABBR) ... LIGHT
Lighting Designer (NTCM) ... LD
Lighting Director (NTCM) ... LD
Lighting Director Engineer (NTCM) ... LDE
Lighting Equipment Manufacturers' Association (DAC) ... LEMA
Lightly (ABBR) ... LGTY
Lightly (ABBR) ... LHTY
Lightminded (ABBR) ... LGTMDD
Lightmindedly (ABBR) ... LGTMDY
Lightning (ABBR) ... LGTNG
Lightning (ABBR) ... LHTNG
Lightning (ABBR) ... LIGHT
Lightweight (ABBR) ... LGTWT
Lightweight Leader Computer [*Army*] (INF) ... LLC
Lightweight Sports [*Concept car*] [*Automotive engineering*] ... LWS
Lightyear (ABBR) ... LGTYR
Lignes Aerienne Seychelles [*ICAO designator*] (FAAC) ... LAS
Lignes Nationales Aeriennes - Linacongo [*Congo*] [*ICAO designator*] (FAAC) ... GCB
Likely Operational Range [*Navy*] (ANA) ... LOR

Lilliputian (ABBR) ... LIL
Limas Bulgarian Airlines [*ICAO designator*] (FAAC) ... LBA
Lime and Cement Mortar (DAC) ... L & CM
Lime Mortar (DAC) ... LM
Limited Range Intercept [*Telecommunications*] [*Navy*] (ANA) ... LRI
Limiting Dome Height [*Automotive metal stamping*] ... LDH
Lincoln Airlines, Inc. [*ICAO designator*] (FAAC) ... LUX
Lincoln Highway Association [*Motoring history organization*] ... LHA
Linda Gray's Official Fan Club (EA) ... LGOFC
Lindquist Investment Co., Inc. [*ICAO designator*] (FAAC) ... SWS
Lindsay Aviation, Inc. [*ICAO designator*] (FAAC) ... LSY
Line of Arrested Growth [*Biology*] ... LAG
Line of Departure/Line of Contact [*Army*] (ADDR) ... LD/LC
Line (of Print) [*Publishing*] (NTCM) ... L
Linea Aerea Aerosanta [*Chile*] [*ICAO designator*] (FAAC) ... SON
Linea Aerea del Cobre Ltda. [*Chile*] [*ICAO designator*] (FAAC) ... LCO
Linea Aerea Nacional de Chile [*ICAO designator*] (FAAC) ... LAN
Linea Aerea Nacional (Lansa) [*Dominican Republic*] [*ICAO designator*] (FAAC) ... LSA
Linea Aerea Privadas Argentina [*ICAO designator*] (FAAC) ... LPR
Linea Aerea Tama [*Chile*] [*ICAO designator*] (FAAC) ... LTA
Linea Aerea Taxpa Ltda. [*Chile*] [*ICAO designator*] (FAAC) ... TXP
Linea Aeropostal Venezolana [*Venezuela*] [*ICAO designator*] (FAAC) ... LAV
Linea Federal Argentina SEM [*ICAO designator*] (FAAC) ... FED
Linear Friction Welding [*Environmental science*] ... LFW
Linear Interpolation [*Computer science*] (NHD) ... LERP
Linear Rotary Differential Capacitance Transducer [*Instrumentation*] ... LRDCT
Linear Solvation Energy Relationship [*Physical chemistry*] ... LSER
Linearized Augmented Plane Wave [*Physical chemistry*] ... LAPW
Lineas Aereas Allegro SA de CV [*Mexico*] [*ICAO designator*] (FAAC) ... GRO
Lineas Aereas Canarias SA [*Spain*] [*ICAO designator*] (FAAC) ... LCN
Lineas Aereas del Caribe [*Colombia*] [*ICAO designator*] (FAAC) ... LIC
Lineas Aereas Colombianas Ltd. [*Colombia*] [*ICAO designator*] (FAAC) ... LAE
Lineas Aereas Costarricenses SA [*Costa Rica*] [*ICAO designator*] (FAAC) ... LACAS
Lineas Aereas Costarricenses SA [*Costa Rica*] [*ICAO designator*] (FAAC) ... LRC
Lineas Aereas Eldorado Ltd. [*Colombia*] [*ICAO designator*] (FAAC) ... EDR
Lineas Aereas del Estado [*Argentina*] [*ICAO designator*] (FAAC) ... LDE
Lineas Aereas de Ixtlan SA de CV [*Mexico*] [*ICAO designator*] (FAAC) ... IXT
Lineas Aereas Latur SA de CV [*Mexico*] [*ICAO designator*] (FAAC) ... LUR
Lineas Aereas Paraguayas [*Paraguay*] [*ICAO designator*] (FAAC) ... LAP
Lineas Aereas Petroleras [*Colombia*] [*ICAO designator*] (FAAC) ... APT
Lineas Aereas Suramericanas Ltd. [*Colombia*] [*ICAO designator*] (FAAC) ... LAU
Linen Industry Research Association [*British*] (BI) ... LIRA
Linhas Aereas de Mocambique [*Mozambique*] [*ICAO designator*] (FAAC) ... LAM
Linhas Aereas Regionais SA [*Portugal*] [*ICAO designator*] (FAAC) ... LAR
Link Airways of Australia [*Australia*] [*ICAO designator*] (FAAC) ... LAW
Linton-on-Ouse FTU [*British*] [*ICAO designator*] (FAAC) ... LOP
Lionair SA [*Luxembourg*] [*ICAO designator*] (FAAC) ... LIR
Liquid Propane-Gas Shutoff [*NFPA pre-fire planning symbol*] (NFPA) ... LPG
Liquid Volume Charge Density [*Automotive fuel systems*] ... LVCD
Literacy and Learning Program ... LLP
Lithium Ion Storage Battery (PCM) ... LISB
Lithuanian Airlines [*ICAO designator*] (FAAC) ... LIL
Little (ABBR) ... LIL
Little Red Air Service [*Canada*] [*ICAO designator*] (FAAC) ... LRA
[*Arthur D.*] **Little Research Institute** [*British*] (BI) ... ADLRI
Live Action (NTCM) ... LA
Live Environment Training [*Military*] (ADDR) ... LET
Living Allowance ... LA
Living Related Renal Transplantation [*Medicine*] ... LRTx
Living Unrelated Renal Transplantation [*Medicine*] ... LURTx
Lloyd Aereo Boliviano SA [*Bolivia*] [*ICAO designator*] (FAAC) ... LLB
Load Classification Group (DA) ... LCG
Load Sheet Fuel [*Aviation*] (DA) ... LSF
Load Threshold Value (DA) ... LTV
Local [*Broadcasting program*] (NTCM) ... L
Local Airport Advisory [*Aviation*] (FAAC) ... LAA
Local Density of States [*Solid state physics*] ... LDOS
Local Dental Officer ... LDO
Local Enterprise Program ... LEP
Local Flying Area [*Aviation*] (DA) ... LFA
Local Interstellar Cloud [*Astronomy*] ... LIC
Local Management Committee ... LMC
Local Public Transportation ... LPT
Local Qualitative Radio [*Ratings*] (NTCM) ... LQR
Locally-Originated Program [*Broadcasting*] (NTCM) ... LOP
Locator [*Compass*] (DA) ... Latr
Locator Back Marker [*Aviation*] (DA) ... LBM
Locator Inner Marker [*Aviation*] (DA) ... LIM
Locavia 49 [*France*] [*ICAO designator*] (FAAC) ... LOC
Lockheed Air Terminal, Inc. [*Guam*] [*ICAO designator*] (FAAC) ... XLG
Lockheed Aircraft Corp. [*ICAO designator*] (FAAC) ... LAC
Lockheed Duats [*ICAO designator*] (FAAC) ... XDD
Locking [*Lamp base type*] (NTCM) ... L
Locomotive and Allied Manufacturers' Association [*British*] (BI) ... LAMA
Locomotive and Carriage Institution of Great Britain and Eire (BI) ... LCIGB
Locomotive Club of Great Britain (BI) ... LCGB
Loeser, Luftfarhtgesellschaft GmbH [*Germany*] [*ICAO designator*] (FAAC) ... LOE
Loftier (ABBR) ... LFTIR
Loftiest (ABBR) ... LFTIT
Loftiness (ABBR) ... LFTINS
Lofty (ABBR) ... LFTY
Loganair Ltd. [*British*] [*ICAO designator*] (FAAC) ... LOG
Loganberry (ABBR) ... LGBR
Loganberry (ABBR) ... LGNBRY
Logger (ABBR) ... LGGR
Loggerhead (ABBR) ... LGGRHD
Logical (ABBR) ... LGCL
Logical Acknowledgement Message [*Aviation*] (DA) ... LAM
Logicality (ABBR) ... LGCLT
Logically (ABBR) ... LGCLY
Logician (ABBR) ... LGCN
Logistic (ABBR) ... LGSTC
Logistic (ABBR) ... LGTIC
Logistic Movement Coordination Center [*Navy*] (ANA) ... LMCC
Logistical (ABBR) ... LGSTCL
Logistical (ABBR) ... LGTICL
Logistician (ABBR) ... LGSTCN
Lomas Helicopters Ltd. [*British*] [*ICAO designator*] (FAAC) ... LMS
London Airtours Ltd. [*British*] [*ICAO designator*] (FAAC) ... LAJ
London Business Aviation [*British*] [*ICAO designator*] (FAAC) ... LBS
London European Airways PLC [*British*] [*ICAO designator*] (FAAC) ... LON
London Flight Centre (Stansted) Ltd. [*British*] [*ICAO designator*] (FAAC) ... LOV
London Flights (Biggin Hill) Ltd. [*British*] [*ICAO designator*] (FAAC) ... LNF
London Interbank Bid Rate [*Finance*] [*British*] ... LIBID
Long Play [*VHS recorder mode*] (NTCM) ... LP
Long Range Communications (NTCM) ... LRC
Long-Term Unemployed ... LTU
Long-Term Waviness [*Surface finish*] ... LTW
Longest Perpendicular [*IOR*] [*Yacht racing*] ... LP
Longitude (ABBR) ... LGTUD
Longitudinal (ABBR) ... LGTUDL
Longitudinal Stability Augmentation System [*Aviation*] (DA) ... LSAS
Longitudinal Time Code (NTCM) ... LTC
Longitudinally (ABBR) ... LGTUDY
Loose Cubic Meter (DAC) ... LCM
Loose Cubic Yard (DAC) ... LCY
Lorry-Mounted Crane Association [*British*] (BI) ... LMCA
Loss of Imprinting [*Genetics*] ... LOI
Lossiemouth FTU [*British*] [*ICAO designator*] (FAAC) ... LOS
Lothario (ABBR) ... LHAR
Low [*Automotive advertising*] ... LW
Low Altitude Air Defense Battalion [*Navy*] (ANA) ... LAADBN
Low-Density Reinforced Reaction Injection Molding [*Plastics*] ... LDRRIM
Low-Density Structural Reaction Injection Molding [*Plastics*] ... LD-SRIM
Low-Emissions Bus ... LEB
Low-Emissions Truck ... LET
Low Intensity Two-Color Approach Slope Indicator [*Aviation*] (DA) ... LITAS
Low Level Language [*Computer programming*] (NTCM) ... LLL
Low Osmolar Contrast Agent [*Medicine*] ... LOCA
Low Power Distress Transmitter [*Aviation*] (DA) ... LPDT
Low-Pressure Molding Compound [*Environmental science*] ... LPMC
Low heat Release [*Adiabatic engines*] [*Automotive engineering*] ... LHR
Low Rigging Penalty [*IOR*] [*Yacht racing*] ... LRP
Low-Sulfur Diesel Fuel [*Petroleum marketing*] ... LSD
Low Velocity Air Drop [*Military vehicle specifications*] ... LVAD
Lowband Color [*Broadcasting*] (NTCM) ... LBC
Lowband Monochrome [*Broadcasting*] (NTCM) ... LBM
Lower Airspace RADAR Advisory Service [*British*] (DA) ... LARS
Lower Middle Income Country ... LMIC
Lowest Observed Effect Level [*Toxicology*] ... LOEL
Lowest Safe Altitude [*Aviation*] (DA) ... LSALT
Loyal Order of Ancient Shepherds [*British*] (BI) ... LOAS
LTU [*Lufttransport Unternehmen Sud*] **GmbH** [*Germany*] [*ICAO designator*] (FAAC) ... LTS
LTV Jet Fleet Corp. [*ICAO designator*] (FAAC) ... JFC
Lubricant Test Monitoring System [*Automotive engineering*] ... LTMS
Lucas-Sumitomo Brakes [*Auto industry supplier*] ... LSB
Luftfahrzeug Service - Aircraft Service [*Austria*] [*ICAO designator*] (FAAC) ... LFS
Lufthansa (ABBR) ... LH
Lufthansa Cityline [*Germany*] [*ICAO designator*] (FAAC) ... CLH
Lufttarhtgesellschaft Walter GmbH [*Germany*] [*ICAO designator*] (FAAC) ... LGW
Lufttransport Unternehmen GmbH [*Germany*] [*ICAO designator*] (FAAC) ... LTU
Luftwaffe (ABBR) ... LFTWF
Luggage (ABBR) ... LGAG
Lugsail (ABBR) ... LGSL
Lugubrious (ABBR) ... LGBRU
Lugubriously (ABBR) ... LGBRUY
Lupenga Air Charters [*Zambia*] [*ICAO designator*] (FAAC) ... LUP

Lusiana [*Czechoslovakia*] [*ICAO designator*]　(FAAC)............................... LUB
Lusitanair-Transportes Aereos Comercials SA [*Portugal*] [*ICAO designator*]　(FAAC)... LUS
Lux [*Unit of Illumination*]　(NTCM).. Lx
Luxair-Societe Luxembourgeoise de Navigation Aerienne SA [*Germany*] [*ICAO designator*]　(FAAC)................................ LGL
Luxembourg Stock Exchange .... LSE
Lymph Node T Cells [*Immunology*] .... LNTC
Lymphoid Tissue Mononuclear Cell [*Physiology*]..................... LTMC
Lynch Flying Service, Inc. [*ICAO designator*]　(FAAC)............... LCH
Lynton Aviation [*British*] [*ICAO designator*]　(FAAC)................ LYN
Lyon Air [*France*] [*ICAO designator*]　(FAAC)............................ LYA

M

M & M Aviation, Inc. [*ICAO designator*] (FAAC) ..... GSP
MAC Aviation SL [*Spain*] [*ICAO designator*] (FAAC) ..... MAO
Mac Dan Aviation Corp. [*ICAO designator*] (FAAC) ..... MCN
[*N. B.*] **MacDonald Service Ltd.** [*New Zealand*] [*ICAO designator*] (FAAC) ..... DBK
Macedonia AS [*Yugoslavia*] [*ICAO designator*] (FAAC) ..... MDO
Machine-Aided Translation Editing (PDAA) ..... MATE
Machine Analyzer Package (PDAA) ..... MAP
Machine Automated Speech Transcription (PDAA) ..... MAST
Machine Examination Teaching, Evaluation, and Re-education (PDAA) ..... METER
Machine-Gun Artillery Division [*Former USSR*] ..... MGAD
Machine-Readable Passport (DA) ..... MRP
Machine User Symbiotic Environment (PDAA) ..... MUSE
Machine Utilization Reporting System (PDAA) ..... MURS
Machinery of Government ..... MOG
Machinery and Occupational Safety Act [*Environmental science*] ..... MOS
Machinery Users' Association [*British*] (BI) ..... MUA
Macknight Airlines [*Australia*] [*ICAO designator*] (FAAC) ..... MTD
Macro-Associative Processor Programming Language [*Computer science*] (PDAA) ..... MAPPLE
Macrophage Growth Factor (PDAA) ..... MGF
Maersk Air IS [*Denmark*] [*ICAO designator*] (FAAC) ..... DMA
Maersk Commuter IS [*Netherlands*] [*ICAO designator*] (FAAC) ..... MAE
Magadan Airlines [*Russian Federation*] [*ICAO designator*] (FAAC) ..... MVL
Magazine (ABBR) ..... MGN
Magazine of History [*A publication*] ..... M of Hist
Magazine Publisher's Association (NTCM) ..... MPA
Magec Aviation Ltd. [*British*] [*ICAO designator*] (FAAC) ..... MGC
Maggot (ABBR) ..... MGOT
Magic (ABBR) ..... MGC
Magical (ABBR) ..... MGCL
Magical Blend [*A publication*] ..... Mag Bl
Magically (ABBR) ..... MGCLY
Magician (ABBR) ..... MGCN
Magisterial (ABBR) ..... MGSTL
Magistrate (ABBR) ..... MGSTRA
Magma (ABBR) ..... MGMA
Magnanimity (ABBR) ..... MGNMT
Magnanimous (ABBR) ..... MGNMU
Magnate (ABBR) ..... MGNT
Magnesia-Buffered Zinc Oxide (PDAA) ..... MBZ
Magnesium Industry Council [*British*] (BI) ..... MIC
Magnet (ABBR) ..... MGNT
Magnetic (ABBR) ..... MGNETC
Magnetic Anti-Intrusion Detector (PDAA) ..... MAID
Magnetic Character Typewriter (PDAA) ..... MCT
Magnetic Disc Recorder (NTCM) ..... MDR
Magnetic Electron Multiplier (PDAA) ..... MEM
Magnetic Field Integral Equation (PDAA) ..... MFIE
Magnetic Intrusion Line Sensor (PDAA) ..... MILES
Magnetic Metal-Oxide-Semiconductor Field-Effect Transistor (PDAA) ..... MAGFET
Magnetic Reaction Analyzer (PDAA) ..... MRA
Magnetic Shield Simulator (PDAA) ..... MAGSIM
Magnetic Spark Spectrometer (PDAA) ..... MSS
Magnetic Speed Variable Assist [*General Motors*] [*Power steering*] ..... MSVA
Magnetic Tape Loader ..... MTL
Magnetically (ABBR) ..... MGNETCY
Magnetism (ABBR) ..... MGNETSM
Magnetization (ABBR) ..... MGNETZ
Magnetize [*or Magnetized*] (ABBR) ..... MGNETZ
Magneto-Elastic Resonance (PDAA) ..... MER
Magneto-Electronic (PDAA) ..... ME
Magneto-Optic Rotary Dispersion (PDAA) ..... MORD
Magnetohydrodynamic Generator (PDAA) ..... MHDG
Magnetohydrodynamic LASER (PDAA) ..... MHDL
Magnetometer (ABBR) ..... MGNETMTR
Magnifiable (ABBR) ..... MGNFIB
Magnification (NTCM) ..... M
Magnification (ABBR) ..... MGNFIN
Magnificence (ABBR) ..... MGNFNC
Magnificent (ABBR) ..... MGNFNT
Magnificently (ABBR) ..... MGNFTY
Magnified (ABBR) ..... MGNFID
Magnifier (ABBR) ..... MGNFIR
Magnify (ABBR) ..... MGNFI
Magnifying (ABBR) ..... MGNFIG
Magnitude (ABBR) ..... MGNTUD
Magnitude Square of the Complex Coherence (PDAA) ..... MSC
Mail Chute (DAC) ..... MC
Mail Order Publisher Authority (PDAA) ..... MOPA
Mailing Label and Directory Lookup Package (PDAA) ..... MLDLP
Main Array Signal Band ..... MASB
Main Battle Air Vehicle [*Military*] (PDAA) ..... MBAV
Main Fixed Earth Station [*NASA*] (PDAA) ..... MFES
Main Himalayan Thrust [*Geology*] ..... MHT
Main Lobe ..... ML
Main Timing Register ..... MTR
Main Turbine / Gearing Unit (PDAA) ..... MTGU
Maine Aviation Corp. [*ICAO designator*] (FAAC) ..... MAT
Mainsail Hoist Lenght [*IOR*] ..... P
Maintained [*Automotive advertising*] ..... MNT
Maintenance [*Automotive advertising*] ..... MAINTN
Maintenance Action Request ..... MAR
Maintenance Aided Computer-HAWK- [*Homing All The Way Killer*]- **Intelligence/Institutional/Instructor** [*Military*] ..... MACH III
Maintenance Assembly and Check-Out Model (PDAA) ..... MACOM
Maintenance Data Bank ..... MDB
Maintenance Demonstration [*DoD*] ..... M-DEMO
Maintenance Design Disclosure ..... MDD
Maintenance-Free Lifetime (PDAA) ..... MFL
Maintenance Management System ..... MMS
Maintenance of Property ..... MOP
Maintenance and Reliability Simulation Model (PDAA) ..... MRSM
Maintenance Schedule (DA) ..... MS
Maintenance Schedule Code (PDAA) ..... MASCO
Maintenance Support Base [*Military*] ..... MSB
Maintenance Support Test Package [*Military*] ..... MSTP
Maize Oil (PDAA) ..... MO
Majestic Airlines, Inc. [*ICAO designator*] (FAAC) ..... MAJ
Major Air Disaster (PDAA) ..... MAD
Major Business Development Initiative ..... MBDI
Major Command Worldwide Ammunition Reporting System [*Army*] ..... MWARS
Major End Item ..... MEI
Major Incidents Computer Application (PDAA) ..... MICA
Major Project Funding ..... MPF
Make-Up Gas [*Chemical engineering*] ..... MUG
Makung Airlines [*Taiwan*] [*ICAO designator*] (FAAC) ..... MKO
Malawi [*Aircraft nationality and registration mark*] (FAAC) 7QY
Malawi Rural Finance Co. Ltd. ..... MRFC
Malaysia [*Aircraft nationality and registration mark*] (FAAC) 9M
Malaysian Airline System [*ICAO designator*] (FAAC) ..... MAS
Maldives [*Aircraft nationality and registration mark*] (FAAC) 8Q
Male Bonding Alert [*Screenwriter's lexicon*] ..... MBA
Male or Female (NHD) ..... MORF
Male Specific Antigen (PDAA) ..... MSA
Malev-Hungarian Airlines [*ICAO designator*] (FAAC) ..... MAH
Malfunction Detector Analyzer (PDAA) ..... MDA
Malfunctioning Display (DA) ..... MFD
Mali-Tinbouctou Air Service [*ICAO designator*] (FAAC) ..... HBM
Maliair Ltd. [*British*] [*ICAO designator*] (FAAC) ..... MAK
Mall Airways, Inc. [*ICAO designator*] (FAAC) ..... MLS
Malmo Aviation AB [*Sweden*] [*ICAO designator*] (FAAC) ..... SCW
Malta [*Aircraft nationality and registration mark*] (FAAC) 9H
Malta Air Charter Co. Ltd. [*ICAO designator*] (FAAC) ..... MAC
MAM Aviation Ltd. [*British*] [*ICAO designator*] (FAAC) ..... WSY
Man Communication and Display for an Automatic Computer (PDAA) ..... MACDAC
Man-in-the-Loop Simulator [*Military*] ..... MITLS
Man/Machine ..... M/M
Man-Machine Interactive Processing System (PDAA) ..... MMIPS
Man Machine System for the Optimum Design and Construction of Buildings (PDAA) ..... MODCON

Man-Made Fibres Producing Industry Training Board [*British*] (BI) ... MMFITB
Man-Made Soling Association Ltd. [*British*] (BI) ... MANSA
Man Station [*Military*] ... MS
Manage (ABBR) ... MGE
Manageability (ABBR) ... MGBT
Manageability (ABBR) ... MGEBT
Manageable (ABBR) ... MGB
Manageable (ABBR) ... MGEB
Manageably (ABBR) ... MGBY
Manageably (ABBR) ... MGEBY
Managed (ABBR) ... MGED
Management (ABBR) ... MGENT
Management Administration Control System ... MACS
Management Advisory System using Computerized Optimization Techniques (PDAA) ... MASCOT
Management Audit Information System ... MAIS
Management Control Unit (PDAA) ... MCU
Management of Expenditure and Resident-Linked Information Network [*Computer science*] ... MERLIN
Management Farm Information Service (PDAA) ... MAFIS
Management Improvement and Evaluation ... MIE
Management Information Format File [*Computer science*] ... MIFF
Management Information Planning and Accountancy Service (PDAA) ... MIPAS
Management Information Strategy ... MIS
Management Information System for Expenditure Reporting (PDAA) ... MISER
Management Job Description (PDAA) ... MJD
Management of Repair Parts Expenditure [*Army*] (PDAA) ... MARPEX
Management Skills - Knowledge Profile [*Business term*] ... MSKP
Management Systems Concept (PDAA) ... MASC
Management by Talking Around [*Business term*] ... MTA
Management by Walking Around ... MWA
Manager (ABBR) ... MGER
Managerial (ABBR) ... MGERL
Managerial (ABBR) ... MGRL
Managing (ABBR) ... MGEG
Managing (ABBR) ... MGG
Managing Your Money [*MECA Software, Inc.*] (PCM) ... MYM
Mandala Airlines PT [*Indonesia*] [*ICAO designator*] (FAAC) ... MDL
Mandarian Airlines [*ICAO designator*] (FAAC) ... MDA
Mandatory Broadcast Zone [*Telecommunications*] (DA) ... MBZ
Mandatory Frequency (DA) ... MF
Mandatory Modification and Inspection Summary [*Aviation*] (DA) ... MAMIS
Maneuver Control System / Common Hardware System [*Computer science*] ... MCS/CHS
Maneuver Force Air Defense ... MFAD
Maneuver Right Area [*Army*] ... MRA
Maneuverability Augmentation System for Tactical Air Combat Simulation (PDAA) ... MASTACS
Manifestable (ABBR) ... MFSTB
Manifestation (ABBR) ... MFSTN
Manifested (ABBR) ... MFSTD
Manifesting (ABBR) ... MFSTG
Manifesto (ABBR) ... MFSTO
Manipulative Communications Cover [*Military*] (ADDR) ... MCC
Manipulator Language [*Computer science*] ... ML
Manitoulin Air Services Ltd. [*Canada*] [*ICAO designator*] (FAAC) ... MTO
Mankato Industrial Corp. [*Automotive industry supplier*] ... MICO
[*Alan*] **Mann Helicopters Ltd.** [*British*] [*ICAO designator*] (FAAC) ... AMH
Manned Attack Torpedo Carrying Helicopter (PDAA) ... MATCH
Manned Lunar Roving Vehicle [*NASA*] (PDAA) ... MLRV
Mannion Air Charter, Inc. [*ICAO designator*] (FAAC) ... MAN
Manpower Consultative Service [*Canada*] (PDAA) ... MCS
Manpower Needs [*Military*] ... MPNE
Manpower Planning Quota (PDAA) ... MPQ
Manpower Requirements Analysis Report [*Military*] ... MRAR
Man's Environments - Display Implication and Applications (PDAA) ... MEDIA
Mansion House Association on Transport, Inc. [*British*] (BI) ... MHA
Mantle Bouguer Anomaly [*Geology*] ... MBA
Mantrust Asahi Airways PT [*Indonesia*] [*ICAO designator*] (FAAC) ... MTS
Manual Abell-Kendall [*Clinical chemistry*] ... MAK
Manual Adaptive TMA [*Target Motion Analysis*] **Estimator** [*Navy*] (ANA) ... MATE
Manual Assisted Gaming of Integrated Combat (PDAA) ... MAGIC
Manufactory (ABBR) ... MFRY
Manufactory (ABBR) ... MFY
Manufactured (ABBR) ... MFRD
Manufacturer (ABBR) ... MFRR
Manufacturers' Agents Association of Great Britain and Ireland (BI) ... MAA
Manufacturer's Weight Empty (DA) ... MWE
Manufacturing Confectioners' Commercial Travellers Association [*British*] (BI) ... MCCTA
Manufacturing Management (PDAA) ... MANMAM
Manufacturing Management Accounting System (PDAA) ... MMAS
Manufacturing Operations Development and Integration Laboratory ... MODIL
Manufacturing Outreach Center ... MOC
Manufacturing Planning and Control System (PDAA) ... MANUPACS
Manufacturing in Space ... MS
Manufacturing Technology Center ... MTC
Manufaturing Execution System [*Engineering*] ... MES
Manx Airlines (Europe) Ltd. [*British*] [*ICAO designator*] (FAAC) ... MXE
Manx Airlines Ltd. [*British*] [*ICAO designator*] (FAAC) ... MNX
Many-Body Alloy [*Metallurgy*] ... MBA
Maple (DAC) ... mpl
Maple Air Services Ltd. [*Canada*] [*ICAO designator*] (FAAC) ... MAD
Mapper Application Interface [*Computer science*] ... MAI
Marble and Granite Association [*British*] (BI) ... MGA
MARC [*Machine-Readable Cataloging*] **Automated Serials System** (PDAA) ... MASS
Marcaptan Terminated Polybutadiene (PDAA) ... MTB
March Helicopters Ltd. [*British*] [*ICAO designator*] (FAAC) ... MAR
March Order [*Military*] ... MO
Marche International des Programmes de Television International [*International Marketplace for Buyers and Sellers of Television Programs*] (NTCM) ... MIP
Marche a Terme des Instruments Financiers [*French Financial Futures Market*] ... MATIF
Margaret Morris Movement [*British*] (BI) ... MMM
Margate Air Services [*South Africa*] [*ICAO designator*] (FAAC) ... MGT
Margin of Exposure [*Toxicology*] ... MOE
Marginal Producers Cost [*Engineering economics*] ... MPC
Marginalia (ABBR) ... MGNIA
Marginality (ABBR) ... MGNLT
Marginally (ABBR) ... MGNLY
Margination (ABBR) ... MGNAN
Marine [*FCC*] (NTCM) ... M
Marine-Aided Inertial Navigation System (PDAA) ... MAINS
Marine & Aviation Management International [*British*] [*ICAO designator*] (FAAC) ... MMM
Marine Centralized Automatic Control System (PDAA) ... MCACS
Marine Computer System (PDAA) ... MARCS
Marine Corps Mustang Association (EA) ... MCMA
Marine Corrosion Research Laboratory [*Navy*] (PDAA) ... MCRL
Marine Cranking Amperes [*Battery*] [*Automotive engineering*] ... MCA
Marine Electric Power Plant (PDAA) ... MEPP
Marine Engine Condition Monitor (PDAA) ... MECOM
Marine-Estuarine-Environmental Sciences (PDAA) ... MEES
Marine and Estuarine Protected Area ... MEPA
Marine Fire Detection Control Center ... MFDCC
Marine Power Plant (PDAA) ... MPP
Marine RADAR Interrogator-Transponder (PDAA) ... MRIT
Marine Search and Attack System (PDAA) ... MARSAS
Marine Vapor Control System ... MVCS
Marine Wing Support Squadron [*Navy*] (ANA) ... MWSS
Maritime Prepositioned Equipment and Supplies [*Navy*] (ANA) ... MPE/S
Markair, Inc. [*ICAO designator*] (FAAC) ... MRK
Marked Temperature Inversion [*Aviation*] (DA) ... MTI
Market Odd-Lot Execution (PDAA) ... MOLE
Marketing and Product Line Evaluation (PDAA) ... MAPLE
Mars Roving Vehicle [*NASA*] (PDAA) ... MRV
Marshall of Cambridge (Engineering) Ltd. [*British*] [*ICAO designator*] (FAAC) ... MCE
Marshall [*Space Flight Center*] **Information Retrieval and Display System** [*NASA*] (PDAA) ... MIRADS
Martin Aviation Services [*ICAO designator*] (FAAC) ... XMA
Martin-Baker Ltd. [*British*] [*ICAO designator*] (FAAC) ... MBE
Martin Marietta Missile Electronics Division [*Military*] ... MMME
Martin Marietta Missile System [*Military*] ... MMMS
Martinair Holland NV [*Netherlands*] [*ICAO designator*] (FAAC) ... MPH
Martinaire [*ICAO designator*] (FAAC) ... MRA
Martinique ... Mart
Marvin Ltd. [*British*] [*ICAO designator*] (FAAC) ... MVN
Maryland Automotive Reclamation Corp. [*Automotive materials recycling project*] ... MARC
Masked Terrain Map [*Military*] ... MTM
Masked Terrain Trainer [*Military*] ... MTT
Mass Communication (NTCM) ... MC
Mass Flow of Air [*Aviation*] (DA) ... M!a
Mass Flow of Fuel [*Aviation*] (DA) ... M!f
Mass Fraction Burn [*Automotive engine combustion analysis*] ... MFB
Mass Target Sensor ... MTS
Mass Transfer Limiting Current (PDAA) ... MTLC
Massachusetts Institute of Technology [*ICAO designator*] (FAAC) ... MTH
Massey University School of Aviation [*New Zealand*] [*ICAO designator*] (FAAC) ... MSY
Massive Compact Halo Objects [*Astronomy*] ... MACHO
Mast Check System ... MCS
Master Acoustical Console [*Army*] ... MAC
Master of Applied Statistics ... MAStat
Master of Bioethics ... MBioEth
Master of Biotechnology ... MBiotech
Master Builders Federation [*British*] (BI) ... MBF
Master of Clinical Biochemistry ... MClBiochem
Master of Clinical Nutrition ... MCN
Master Communications (PDAA) ... MASCOM
Master Cross-Reference List ... MRCL
Master of Development Management ... MDM
Master Digital Data Tape (PDAA) ... MDDT
Master of Environmental Planning ... MEnvPlan
Master Force List [*DoD*] ... MFL
Master Frequency Record [*FCC list*] (NTCM) ... MFR

Master in International Economics and Management (ECON) MIEM
Master Locksmiths Association [*British*] (BI) MLA
Master of Medical Education MMedEd
Master of Medicine (Anaesthesia) MMedAnaes
Master of Medicine (Cardiology) MMedCardiol
Master of Medicine (Community Medicine) MMed(CM)
Master of Medicine (Diagnostic Radiology) MMedRadD
Master of Medicine (Paediatrics) MMedPaed
Master of Medicine (Pathology) MMedPath
Master of Medicine (Venereology) MMedVen
Master Minimum Equipment List (DA) MMEL
Master of Paediatrics MPaed
Master Photographers Association of Great Britain (BI) MPA
Master Planner, Inc. [*ICAO designator*] (FAAC) MPL
Master of Psychotherapy MPsychTh
Master Real-Time Circulation Controller (PDAA) MARCCO
Master Reference Gyro (PDAA) MRG
Master of Safety Science MSafSc
Master Scene [*Major script sequence*] (NTCM) MS
Master of Science (Aeromedicine) MSc(AeroMed)
Master of Science (Biochemistry) MSc(Biochem)
Master of Science (Community Medicine) MSc(CommMed)
Master of Science (Epidemiology) MSc(Epid)
Master of Science (Neurochemistry) MSc(NeuChem)
Master of Science (Nutrition) MSc(Nut)
Master of Science (Occupational Medicine) MSc(OccMed)
Master of Science (Ophthalmology) MSc(Ophth)
Master of Science (Rehabilitation Medicine) MSc(Rehab)
Master Shot [*Film production*] (NTCM) MS
Master Sign Makers' Association [*British*] (BI) MSMAN
Master and Slave Oscillator Array (PDAA) MASOA
Master of Surgery (Orthopedic) MS(Orth)
Master Training Plan [*Navy*] (ANA) MTP
Master of Tropical Health MTH
Master of Tropical Medicine MTM
Master Vision Screener (PDAA) MAVIS
Masters of Foxhounds Association [*British*] (BI) MFHA
Mastic Asphalt Advisory Council [*British*] (BI) MAAC
Mastic Asphalt Employers' Federation [*British*] (BI) MAEF
Matair Ltd. [*British*] [*ICAO designator*] (FAAC) MAO
Matched Sale-Purchase Agreement [*Business term*] MSP
Material Management Center Theater Supply [*Army*] MMCTS
Material Planning System [*Manufacturing management*] MPS
Material Professional [*Army*] MP
Materials Engineering Code MEC
Materials Evaluation (PDAA) ME
Materials Flow Management [*Manufacturing*] MFM
Materials-Process-Product Model (PDAA) MPPM
Materials Requirement Analysis (PDAA) MRA
Materiel Change [*Military*] MC
Materiel Deployment Schedule MDS
Materiel Developer's Test Program [*Military*] MDTP
Mathematical Association [*British*] (BI) MA
Mathematical Foundation of Computer Science (PDAA) MFCS
Mathematical Programming Language [*Computer science*] (PDAA) MPL
Mathematical Sciences Research Institute [*University of California, Berkeley*] (PDAA) MSRI
Mathematical Sciences Research Institute [*University of Minnesota*] (PDAA) MSRI
Matrix-Addressed Liquid Crystal Display MALCD
Matrix-Assisted LASER Desorption/Ionization [*Spectrometry*] MALDI
Matrix Generating and Reporting System [*Computer science*] (PDAA) MAGEN
Matrix Reducibility Algorithm (PDAA) MRA
Matrix Scheme for Algorithms (PDAA) MSA
Matrix Solid-Phase Dispersion [*Analytical chemistry*] MSPD
Matter-Anti-Matter (PDAA) MAM
Mature Students' Association [*British*] (BI) MSA
Maui Airlines, Inc. [*ICAO designator*] (FAAC) OWL
Mauritius [*Aircraft nationality and registration mark*] (FAAC) 3B
Max-Aviation [*Canada*] [*ICAO designator*] (FAAC) MAV
Max Sea Food SA de CV [*El Salvador*] [*ICAO designator*] (FAAC) MSF
Maximal Acceptable Load (PDAA) MAL
Maximal Compatible Set (PDAA) MCS
Maximal Temperature of the Synthesis Reaction [*Chemical engineering*] MTSR
Maximized Relative Likelihood (PDAA) MRL
Maximum Allowable Concentration [*Toxicology*] MAC
Maximum Allowable Emission Rate [*Environmental Protection Agency*] (ERG) MAER
Maximum Allowable Percent Defective (PDAA) MAPD
Maximum Allowable Working Pressure (PDAA) MAWP
Maximum Beam [*IOR*] BMAX
Maximum Economic Potential MEP
Maximum Entropy Principle (PDAA) MEP
Maximum Incremental Reactivity [*Exhaust emissions*] [*Automotive engineering*] MIR
Maximum Landing Weight [*Aviation*] (DA) Mlnd
Maximum Landing Weight Authorized [*Aviation*] (DA) MLWA
Maximum Lateral Damage (PDAA) MLD
Maximum Operating Mach Number [*Aviation*] (DA) M!mo
Maximum Operational Capacity [*Chemical engineering*] MOC
Maximum Output Entropy (PDAA) MOE
Maximum Overall Length (DAC) MOL
Maximum Ozone Reactivity [*Exhaust emissions*] [*Automotive engineering*] MOR
Maximum Permissible Dose Equivalent (ERG) MPDE
Maximum Precipitation Intensity [*Meteorology*] (PDAA) MPI
Maximum Probability Ratio Sequential Test (PDAA) MPRST
Maximum Repair Time (PDAA) MRT
Maximum Residue Limit (PDAA) MRL
Maximum Tolerable Concentration [*Toxicology*] MTC
Maximum Tolerable Exposure Level [*Toxicology*] MTEL
May Air Xpress, Inc. [*ICAO designator*] (FAAC) MXP
Maya Airways Ltd. [*Belize*] [*ICAO designator*] (FAAC) MAY
Maya Carga Internacional SA de CV [*Mexico*] [*ICAO designator*] (FAAC) MCI
Mayo Clinic Health Letter [*A publication*] MCHL
Mazda Research of Europe [*Automobile manufacturer operations*] MRE
[*Alfred*] McAlpine Aviation Ltd. [*British*] [*ICAO designator*] (FAAC) AMA
McAlpine Aviation Ltd. [*British*] [*ICAO designator*] (FAAC) MAL
McAlpine Helicopters Ltd. [*British*] [*ICAO designator*] (FAAC) MCH
McDonnell Douglas Corp. [*ICAO designator*] (FAAC) DAC
Mean Effective Injection Pressure [*Diesel engines*] MEIP
Mean Equivalent Wind [*Meteorology*] (DA) MEW
Mean Fibre Extent (PDAA) MFE
Mean Forced Outage Time (PDAA) MFOT
Mean Hook Extent (PDAA) MHE
Mean Integral Square Error (PDAA) MISER
Mean Lower Low Water Line [*Tides and currents*] (PDAA) MLLWL
Mean Square Error of Prediction [*Statistics*] (PDAA) MSEP
Mean Squared Distance Between Pairs [*Statistics*] (PDAA) MSDBP
Mean Time between Confirmed Defects [*Quality control*] (PDAA) MTBCD
Mean Time between Defects [*Quality control*] (PDAA) MTBD
Mean Time between Depot Repair [*Quality control*] (PDAA) MTBDR
Mean Time between Failures, Critical [*Military*] MTBFC
Mean Time to First System Failure [*Quality control*] (PDAA) MTTFSF
Mean Time to First System Repair [*Quality control*] (PDAA) MTTFSR
Mean Time to System Failure [*Quality control*] (PDAA) MTSF
Mean Time to System Failure [*Quality control*] (PDAA) MTTSF
Mean Time between Unscheduled Maintenance [*Quality control*] (PDAA) MTBUM
Mean Time between Unscheduled Maintenance Actions MBUMA
Mean Time to Unscheduled Replacement [*Quality control*] (PDAA) MTUR
Mean Transverse Emmission Energy (PDAA) MTEE
Mean Tryptic Activity (PDAA) MTA
Mean Wildlife Index Value [*Statistics*] (PDAA) MWIV
Meaning (ABBR) MENG
Meaningful (ABBR) MENGF
Meaningfully (ABBR) MENGFY
Meaningless (ABBR) MENGLS
Meaninglessly (ABBR) MENGLSY
Meanness (ABBR) MENNS
Measure of Training Effectiveness [*Military*] MOTE
Measured Rate of Time (PDAA) MRT
Measured Rating [*IOR*] [*Yacht racing*] MR
Measurement Compensation Factor (PDAA) MCF
Mechanical Auxiliary Ventricle (PDAA) MAV
Mechanical Diode [*Mechanical power transmission*] MD
Mechanical Equipment Room (DAC) MER
Mechanical Handling Engineers' Association [*British*] (BI) MHEA
Mechanical/Hydraulic MECH/HYD
Mechanism Integration Design and Analysis System [*Computer-assisted engineering*] MIDAS
Mechanization of Algebraic Operations (PDAA) MAO
Med-Trans of Florida, Inc. [*ICAO designator*] (FAAC) MEK
Media Account Control System (PDAA) MACS
Media Law Reporter [*A publication*] (NTCM) Med L Rptr
Media Liaison Officer MLO
[*The*] Media Report [*A publication*] (NTCM) MR
Median Sample Number (PDAA) MSN
Medical Audit Statistics (PDAA) MAS
Medical Aviation Services Ltd. [*British*] [*ICAO designator*] (FAAC) MCL
Medical Bioengineering Research and Development Command [*Army*] (PDAA) MBRDC
Medical Campaign against Nuclear Weapons (PDAA) MCANW
Medical Commission on Accident Prevention (PDAA) MCAP
Medical Data Acquisition System MDAC
Medical Defence Union Ltd. [*British*] (BI) MDU
Medical Education Research and Information Database MERI
Medical Education for South African Blacks [*An association*] (EA) MESAB
Medical Equipment Test and Evaluation [*Army Medical Material Agency*] (PDAA) MET & E
Medical Function Control System (PDAA) MFCS
Medical Instrument Calibration System (PDAA) MICS
Medical Oncology Group MOG
Medical Research Committee MRC
Medical Research Endowment Fund MREF
Medical Research Ethics Committee MREC
Medicare Advocacy Project MAP
Medicine Cabinet [*Technical drawings*] (NFPA) MC
Medieval Latin [*Language*] Med Lat

Mediterranean Airlines SA [*Greece*] [*ICAO designator*] (FAAC) ... MAX
Medium Aperture Optical Telescope (PDAA) ... MAOT
Medium Intensity Approach Light System [*Aviation*] (DA) ... MIALS
Medium Range Surveillance Aircraft [*Military*] (PDAA) ... MRSA
Medium Range Truck [*Military*] ... MRT
Medium Side Prong [*Lamp base type*] (NTCM) ... MSP
Medium-Term Financial Assistance ... MTFA
Medium Viscosity Index (PDAA) ... MVI
Medium Viscosity Index-Naphthenic (PDAA) ... MVIN
Medium Viscosity Index-Paraffinic (PDAA) ... MVIP
Medjet International, Inc. [*ICAO designator*] (FAAC) ... MEJ
Mega-Floating Point Operation ... MFLOP
Megacycle (NTCM) ... MEG
Megacycle (ABBR) ... MGCYL
Megalomania (ABBR) ... MGLMNA
Megalomaniac (ABBR) ... MGLMNAC
Megalopolis (ABBR) ... MGLPS
Megaphone (ABBR) ... MGPHN
Melamine Paper Laminate (PDAA) ... MPLAW
Melcom Optical Software Applications for Integrated Commercial Systems (PDAA) ... MOSAICS
Member of the Appropriate Sex (NHD) ... MOTAS
Member of the Opposite Sex (NHD) ... MOTOS
Member of the Same Sex (NHD) ... MOTSS
Members of Anything Bill [*Clinton*] **Was Ever Part Of** [*Pronounced "Mo-ab-wee-po"*] ... MOABWEPO
Membrane Fecal Coliform (PDAA) ... MFC
Membrane Light Modulator (PDAA) ... MLM
Memorandum Opinion and Order (NTCM) ... MO & O
Memorialization (ABBR) ... MEMLZN
Memorialize (ABBR) ... MEMLZ
Memorialized (ABBR) ... MEMLZD
Memorializer (ABBR) ... MEMLZR
Memorializing (ABBR) ... MEMLZG
Memory-Assisted Terminal Equipment (PDAA) ... MATE
Memory Bank ... MB
Memory Raster Colour Display (PDAA) ... MRCD
Memrykord Ltd. [*British*] [*ICAO designator*] (FAAC) ... JPN
Mendial Geniculate Nucleus (PDAA) ... MGN
Mennonite (ABBR) ... MEN
Mennonite (ABBR) ... MENNON
Menopausal (ABBR) ... MENPL
Menopause (ABBR) ... MENP
Menorrhoea (ABBR) ... MENO
Mense [*or Menses*] (ABBR) ... MEN
Menstrual (ABBR) ... MENSTL
Menstruated (ABBR) ... MENSTD
Menstruating (ABBR) ... MENSTG
Menstruation (ABBR) ... MEN
Menstruation (ABBR) ... MENSTN
Mensuration (ABBR) ... MEN
Mental Retardation Research Center ... MMRC
Mentalis (ABBR) ... MENT
Mentality (ABBR) ... MENTT
Mentally (ABBR) ... MENTY
Menthyldiphenyphosphine [*Organic chemistry*] ... MDP
Mentionable (ABBR) ... MENTNB
Mentioned (ABBR) ... MENTND
Mentioner (ABBR) ... MENTNR
Mentioning (ABBR) ... MENTNG
[*E. C.*] **Menzies Aviation Ltd.** [*New Zealand*] [*ICAO designator*] (FAAC) ... MEN
Mercantilism (ABBR) ... MERCM
Mercantilist (ABBR) ... MERCT
Merchandise Information System (PDAA) ... MIS
Merchant Airship Cargo Satellite (PDAA) ... MACS
Merchant Express Aviation [*Nigeria*] [*ICAO designator*] (FAAC) ... MXX
Merchant Jewellers' Association Ltd. [*British*] (BI) ... MJA
Merchant Ship Search and Rescue (PDAA) ... MERSAR
Mercurial (ABBR) ... MERC
Mercury Aircourier Service [*ICAO designator*] (FAAC) ... MEC
Mercury Substitution and Nucleonic Detection (PDAA) ... MSND
Mercury, Venus, Earth, Mars, Jupiter (PDAA) ... MeVEMsJ
Meridian (ABBR) ... MERID
Meridian Air Cargo, Inc. [*ICAO designator*] (FAAC) ... MRD
Meridiana SpA [*Italy*] [*ICAO designator*] (FAAC) ... ISS
Meritocracy (ABBR) ... MERITOC
Meritocrat (ABBR) ... MERITOC
Merlin Executive Aviation Group Ltd. [*British*] [*ICAO designator*] (FAAC) ... WIZ
Merpati Nusantara Airlines PT [*Indonesia*] [*ICAO designator*] (FAAC) ... MNA
Merrix Air Ltd. [*British*] [*ICAO designator*] (FAAC) ... MXR
Mesa Airlines, Inc. [*ICAO designator*] (FAAC) ... ASH
Mesaba Aviation [*ICAO designator*] (FAAC) ... MES
Message (ABBR) ... MESGE
Message Act Concellation (DA) ... MAC
Message Center [*Aviation*] (FAAC) ... MSGCTR
Message Header Generator (PDAA) ... MHG
Message Processor ... MP
Message Transport Agent [*Telecommunications*] (PCM) ... MTA
Messenger (ABBR) ... MESGER
Mestizo (ABBR) ... MEST
Meta Aviotransport-Macedonia [*Yugoslavia*] [*ICAO designator*] (FAAC) ... MAM
Metabolic (ABBR) ... METABC
Metabolic Fecal Nitrogen (PDAA) ... MFN
Metabolize (ABBR) ... METABZ
Metabolized (ABBR) ... METABZD
Metabolizing (ABBR) ... METABZG
Metal-Dielectric Semiconductor [*Electronics*] (PDAA) ... MDS
Metal-Dielectric-Semiconductor Integrated Circuit [*Electronics*] (PDAA) ... MDSIC
Metal-Finishing Industy ... MFI
Metal-Glass-Oxide-Silicon (PDAA) ... MGOS
Metal Injection Molding [*Metal fabrication*] ... MIM
Metal-Liquid-Insulator Semiconductor [*Electronics*] (PDAA) ... MLIS
Metal Oxide Semiconductor Analogue Shift Register [*Electronics*] (PDAA) ... MOSASR
Metal Oxide Substrate Field Effect Transistor ... MOSFETS
Metal-Skinned, Paper-Honeycomb Cored (PDAA) ... MPHC
Metal-Working Machine and Robot ... MWM & R
Metal-Working Machine Tool ... MWMT
Metallic [*Automotive advertising*] ... MET
[*The*] **Metallurgy Society** [*Formerly, MS*] (IAA) ... TMS
Metals-Based Engineering ... MBE
Metals-Based Engineering Program ... MBEP
Metalworking under Pressure (PDAA) ... MUP
Metaphyseal Chondrodysplasia [*Medicine*] ... MCD
Metaphysic (ABBR) ... METAPHYS
Metaphysician (ABBR) ... METAPH
Meteor Scatter (PDAA) ... MS
Meteorological Acquisition and Display System (PDAA) ... METADS
Meteorological Advisory Group [*ICAO*] (DA) ... METAG
Meteorological Analog Test and Evaluation (PDAA) ... MATE
Meteorological Applied Problem Solving ... MAPS
Meteorological Office Weather Observing System (PDAA) ... MOWOS
Meteorological Optical Range (PDAA) ... MOR
Meteorological Research Flight [*British*] [*ICAO designator*] (FAAC) ... MET
Meteorology (ABBR) ... METEOROLO
Meteosat Ground Computer System [*Aviation*] (DA) ... MGCS
Meter Fix Time [*Aviation*] (FAAC) ... MFXT
Metered Market Service [*A. C. Nielsen Co.*] (NTCM) ... MM
Metering and Traffic Recording with Offline Processing (PDAA) ... METRO
Methadone (ABBR) ... METH
Methamphetamine (ABBR) ... METH
Methane Monooxygenase [*An enzyme*] ... MMO
Method for Analysis of Fleet Tactical Effectiveness Performance [*Navy*] (PDAA) ... MAFTEP
Method for Asynchronous Graphics Integral Control [*Computer science*] (PDAA) ... MAGIC
Method of Designing Instructional Alternatives (PDAA) ... MODIA
Method of Implicit Nonstationary Iteration (PDAA) ... MINI
Method of Mixed Ranges (PDAA) ... MMR
Method of Scenic Alternative Impacts by Computer (PDAA) ... MOSAIC
Methodic (ABBR) ... METHC
Methodist Association of Youth Clubs [*British*] (BI) ... MAYC
Methodist Homes for the Aged [*British*] (BI) ... MHA
Methodize (ABBR) ... METHZ
Methodized (ABBR) ... METHZD
Methodological (ABBR) ... METHOGL
Methodology (ABBR) ... METHO
Methodology (ABBR) ... METHOG
Methodology for Assessing Radiological Consequences (PDAA) ... MARC
Methods Time Measurement and General Purpose Data (PDAA) ... MTM-GPD
Methow Aviation, Inc. [*ICAO designator*] (FAAC) ... MER
Methoxy-Hydroxyphenylethanol [*Organic chemistry*] (MAH) ... MHPE
Methyl Alcohol ... MEOH
Methyl Amyl Ketone [*Organic chemistry*] ... MAK
Methylacridone [*Organic chemistry*] ... MAD
Methylcyclohexanol [*Organic chemistry*] ... MCH
Methylene Bisacrylamide (PDAA) ... MBAA
Methylmeth (ABBR) ... METH
Methyprylon (ABBR) ... METH
Meticulous (ABBR) ... METIC
Metric Color Tag [*Computer science*] (PCM) ... MCT
Metro Express II, Inc. [*ICAO designator*] (FAAC) ... MEX
Metro Express, Inc. [*ICAO designator*] (FAAC) ... EME
Metro Manila Airways International, Inc. [*Philippines*] [*ICAO designator*] (FAAC) ... MMA
Metro Rating Area [*Arbitron television ratings*] (NTCM) ... MRA
Metroflight, Inc. [*ICAO designator*] (FAAC) ... MTR
Metropolis [*or Metropolitan*] (ABBR) ... METROPOL
Metropolitan Area Digital Network (NTCM) ... MADN
Metropolitan Dairymen's Society [*British*] (BI) ... MDS
Metropolitan Entertainers' Association [*British*] (BI) ... MEA
Metropolitan Public Gardens Association [*British*] (BI) ... MPGA
Metropolitan School Study Council [*Columbia University*] (AEE) ... MSSC
Mexair SA [*Switzerland*] [*ICAO designator*] (FAAC) ... MXC
Mezzanine (ABBR) ... MEZN
Mezzosoprano (ABBR) ... MEZZO
Mezzotint [*Printing*] (ABBR) ... MEZT
Mezzotint [*Printing*] (ABBR) ... MEZZ
MGM Grand Air, Inc. [*ICAO designator*] (FAAC) ... MGM
Mi-Avia [*Russian Federation*] [*ICAO designator*] (FAAC) ... MIV

Miami Air Charter [*ICAO designator*] (FAAC) .... HUR
Miami Air International, Inc. [*ICAO designator*] (FAAC) .... BSK
Michelson Interferometer (PDAA) .... MI
Michigan Airways, Inc. [*ICAO designator*] (FAAC) .... DRE
Michigan-Dartmouth-Massachusetts Institute of Technology [*Observatory*] .... MDM
Micro-Alloyed Steel [*Metallurgical engineering*] .... MAS
Micro-Analytic Simulation of Households (PDAA) .... MASH
Micro-Graphic Reporting (PDAA) .... MGR
Micro Interactive Retrieval System (PDAA) .... MIRS
Micro Power Light [*Automotive lighting*] .... MPL
Microbeam [*Physics*] .... MB
Microbial Check Valve (PDAA) .... MCV
Microbial Evaluation Analysis Device (PDAA) .... MEAD
Microcircuit Module, Driver/Receiver .... MMDR
Microclimatic Conditioning .... MCC
Microcomputer Advice and Selection Expert System (PDAA) .... MASES
Microcone Networking Protocol .... MNP
Microelectronics Center .... MEC
Microfiche File Update System [*Computer science*] (PDAA) .... MFUSYS
Microfilm Advisory Service of the Public Archives of Canada (PDAA) .... MASPAC
Microfilm Enhanced Data System (PDAA) .... MEDAS
Microfilm Information Master Image Converter (PDAA) .... MIMIC
Microfilmed Reports and Accounts (PDAA) .... MIRAC
Micrograin (ABBR) .... MGN
Micromodule Microprogrammed Computer System (PDAA) .... MIMICS
Microprocessor Arithmetic Model .... MARM
Microprocessor-Based Audio Visual Information System (PDAA) .... MAVIS
Microprogramable Arithmetic Processor System (PDAA) .... MAPS
Microprogrammed Experimental Machine with a Basic Executive for Real-Time Systems (PDAA) .... MEMBERS
Microscopic Image Digital Acquisition System (PDAA) .... MIDAS
Microwatt (IAA) .... W
Microwave Accurate Surface Antenna Reflector (PDAA) .... MASAR
Microwave Atmosphere Sounding Radiometer (PDAA) .... MASR
Microwave Circuit Analysis Package (PDAA) .... MCAP
Microwave Multi-Application Payload [*NASA*] (PDAA) .... MMAP
Microwave Optical Double Resonance (PDAA) .... MODR
Microwave Oven (PDAA) .... MO
Microwave Radiation System (PDAA) .... MICRADS
Microwave Repeater Test Set (DA) .... MRTS
Microwave Stripline-Circuit (PDAA) .... MSC
Mid-Function Integral Control Alarm Module [*Electronics systems*] [*Automotive engineering*] .... MICAM
Mid-Ocean Ridge Peridotite [*Geology*] .... MORP
Mid Pacific Air Corp. [*ICAO designator*] (FAAC) .... MPA
Mid-Term Review .... MTR
Midas Commuter Airlines CA [*Venezuela*] [*ICAO designator*] (FAAC) .... MIO
Midcontinent Airlines, Inc. [*ICAO designator*] (FAAC) .... MCA
Midcourse Airborne Target Signature [*Military*] (PDAA) .... MATS
Middle Air Space (PDAA) .... MAS
Middle Airspace RADAR Advisory Service [*Military*] (DA) .... MARAS
Middle East Airlines - Airliban [*Liberia*] [*ICAO designator*] (FAAC) .... MEA
Middle Management Development .... MMD
Middle Management Development Program .... MMDP
Middle Manager .... MM
Midstate Airlines, Inc. [*ICAO designator*] (FAAC) .... MIS
Midtfly Aps [*Denmark*] [*ICAO designator*] (FAAC) .... MDF
Midway Aviation, Inc. [*ICAO designator*] (FAAC) .... MDW
Midwest Air Freighters, Inc. [*ICAO designator*] (FAAC) .... FAX
Midwest Aviation [*Southwest Aviation, Inc.*] [*ICAO designator*] (FAAC) .... MWT
Midwest Aviation Corp. [*ICAO designator*] (FAAC) .... NIT
Midwest Express Airlines, Inc. [*ICAO designator*] (FAAC) .... MEP
Mightier (ABBR) .... MGTIR
Mightiest (ABBR) .... MGTIST
Mightiness (ABBR) .... MGTNS
Mighty (ABBR) .... MGTY
Migrant (ABBR) .... MGRT
Migrant Advisory Committee .... MACS
Migrant with English Language Difficulty .... MD
Migrate (ABBR) .... MGRA
Migrated (ABBR) .... MGRAD
Migrating (ABBR) .... MGRAG
Migration (ABBR) .... MGRAN
Migration (ABBR) .... MGRN
Migrational (ABBR) .... MGRNL
Migrator (ABBR) .... MGRATR
Migratory (ABBR) .... MGRATRY
Migratory (ABBR) .... MGRTY
Migratory Animal Pathological Survey (PDAA) .... MAPS
Mikromatika Air Cargo Ltd. [*Hungary*] [*ICAO designator*] (FAAC) .... MMH
MILES [*Multiple Integrated LASER Engagement System*] **Action Item Log** [*Army*] .... MAIL
Milford Docks Air Services Ltd. [*British*] [*ICAO designator*] (FAAC) .... MDS
Militarischer Abschirmdienst [*Military counterintelligence*] [*Germany*] .... MAD
Military Aeronautical Research and Development (PDAA) .... MARD
Military Assistance Program Address File .... MAPAF
Military/Commercial Transport Aircraft Simulation (PDAA) .... MCTAS
Military Construction, Army / Five Year Plan .... MCA/FYP
Military District Commander .... MDC
Military Emergency Diversion Aerodrome (DA) .... MEDA
Military Engineering Applications of Commercial Explosives [*Army*] (PDAA) .... MEACE
Military Health Service System .... MHSS
Military Introductory Letter .... MIC
Military Maintenance Technician .... MMT
Military Oceanography (PDAA) .... MILOC
Military Photo-Reconnaissance (PDAA) .... MPR
Military RADAR Unit [*Aviation*] (FAAC) .... MRU
Military Training Area (DA) .... MTA
Military Upper Traffic Control Area (DA) .... MUTA
Military Utility Tactical Transport .... MUTT
Milk Bars Association of Great Britain and Ireland Ltd. (BI) .... MBA
Milk Ring Test (PDAA) .... MRT
Millardair Ltd. [*Canada*] [*ICAO designator*] (FAAC) .... MAB
Miller Air Transporters [*ICAO designator*] (FAAC) .... MIT
Miller-Dieker Lissencephaly Syndrome [*Medicine*] .... MDS
Miller Flying Services, Inc. [*ICAO designator*] (FAAC) .... MFS
Millhouse Developments Ltd. [*British*] [*ICAO designator*] (FAAC) .... MHO
Milli-Second Delay Detonator [*Military*] (PDAA) .... MSDD
Milligals (ABBR) .... MGALS
Milligauss (ABBR) .... MG
Millimeter Insular Line Integrated Circuit (PDAA) .... MILIC
Millimeter Wave Large Antenna Experiment [*NASA*] (PDAA) .... MWLAE
Millinery Distributors Association [*British*] (BI) .... MDA
Millinery Institute of Great Britain (BI) .... MIGB
Million Adds per Second .... MAPS
Million Air, Inc. [*ICAO designator*] (FAAC) .... OXO
Million European Units of Account (PDAA) .... MEUA
Million Monetary Units (PDAA) .... MMU
Million Theoretical Operations per Second [*Computer science*] .... MTOPS
Millions of Floating Point Operations per Second (PDAA) .... MEGAFLOPS
Millions of Particles per Cubic Foot (PDAA) .... MPCF
Mimimum Off-Route Altitude [*Aviation*] (DA) .... MORA
Mine Clearing Line Charge [*Army*] .... MCLC
Mine Counter-Measures Hovercraft [*Military*] (PDAA) .... MCMH
Mine Countermeasure Support Ship [*Military*] (PDAA) .... MCSS
Mine Identification and Neutralization (PDAA) .... MIN
Mine Operating System (PDAA) .... MINOS
Mine Radiographic Outfit [*Military*] (PDAA) .... MRO
Mine Ventilation System [*Engineering*] .... MVS
Minehunter Ocean [*Navy*] (ANA) .... MHO
Minehunter Sweeper Ocean [*Navy*] (ANA) .... MHSO
Mineral Resource Simulation Model (PDAA) .... MIRSIM
Miners' Lamp Manufacturers' Association [*British*] (BI) .... MLMA
Mines Air Service Zambia Ltd. [*ICAO designator*] (FAAC) .... MAZ
Mingle (ABBR) .... MGL
Mingled (ABBR) .... MGLD
Mingling (ABBR) .... MGLG
Mini Conference System (PDAA) .... MCS
Mini-Manned Aircraft System (PDAA) .... MMAS
Mini-Module Drive (PDAA) .... MMD
Mini-Remotely Piloted Vehicle (PDAA) .... MRPV
Miniature Excitatory Synaptic Current [*Neurophysiology*] .... MESC
Miniature, Indicating and Sampling Electronic Respirometer (PDAA) .... MISER
Miniature Information Storage and Retrieval (PDAA) .... MISAR
Miniature Insulated Contact Range (PDAA) .... MICRA
Miniature Screw [*Lamp base*] (NTCM) .... MS
Miniature Synaptic Calcium Transient [*Neurophysiology*] .... MSCT
Miniature Tube (NTCM) .... MT
Miniliner SRL [*Italy*] [*ICAO designator*] (FAAC) .... MNL
Minimization of Earthworks for Vertical Alignment (PDAA) .... MINERVA
Minimum (DA) .... MIM
Minimum Air Low Noise (PDAA) .... MALN
Minimum Descent Height [*Aviation*] (FAAC) .... MDH
Minimum Electrical Resistance Condition (PDAA) .... MERC
Minimum Eye Height over Threshold [*Aviation*] (FAAC) .... MEHT
Minimum Final Prediction Error (PDAA) .... MFPE
Minimum Flight Altitude [*Aviation*] (DA) .... MFA
Minimum List Heading [*Standard Industrial Classification*] (PDAA) .... MLH
Minimum Mean Square (PDAA) .... MMS
Minimum Navigation Performance Specification [*Aviation*] (FAAC) .... MNPS
Minimum Navigation Performance Specification Airspace [*Aviation*] (FAAC) .... MNPSA
Minimum Norm Quadratic Unbiased Estimation [*Statistics*] (PDAA) .... MINQUE
Minimum Obstacle Clearance [*Aviation*] (FAAC) .... MOC
Minimum Operational Performance Standard [*Aviation*] (DA) .... MOPS
Minimum Performance Specification (DA) .... MPS
Minimum Processing Requirement .... MPR
Minimum Remaining Slack Time (PDAA) .... MRST
Minimum Reporting Standard [*Broadcasting*] (NTCM) .... MRS
Minimum Resolvable Temperature Difference (PDAA) .... MRTD
Minimum Triggering Level [*Aviation*] (DA) .... MTL
Minimum-Variance Reduced-Order [*Statistics*] (PDAA) .... MVRO
Minimum-Weighted-Absolute Error [*Statistics*] (PDAA) .... MWAE
Mining, Construction, and Agricultural Equipment .... MCAE
Mining Qualifications Board [*British*] (BI) .... MQB
Ministic Air [*Canada*] [*ICAO designator*] (FAAC) .... MNS

Ministry of Agriculture Fisheries and Food [*British*] [*ICAO designator*] (FAAC) .... WDG
Ministry of Geology and Mineral Resources [*China*] ...... MGMR
Ministry of Posts and Telecommunications [*People's Republic of China*] (ECON) .... MPT
Minnesota School Mathematics and Science Teaching Project [*University of Minnesota*] (AEE) .... MINNEMAST
Minor Atomic Prolonged Life Equipment (PDAA) .... MAPLE
Minson Aviation, Inc. [*ICAO designator*] (FAAC)........ CSL
Minute of Program [*Broadcasting*] (NTCM) ...... MOP
Minuteman Defense Study [*DoD*] .... MDS
Miramichi Air Services Ltd. [*Canada*] [*ICAO designator*] (FAAC)........ MIR
Miriadair [*France*] [*ICAO designator*] (FAAC) ...... MYR
Mirror Electron Microscope (PDAA) ...... MEM
Misr Iran Development Bank .... MIDB
MISR Overseas Airways [*Egypt*] [*ICAO designator*] (FAAC) ...... MOS
Miss Distance Optical Recorder [*Military*] (PDAA) ...... MIDOR
Missed Approach Point [*Aviation*] (FAAC) ...... MAPT
Missile Acquisition and Track ...... MAT
Missile Attack Warning and Assessment [*Military*] (PDAA) ...... MAWA
Missile Electric System Test Set [*Military*] (PDAA) ...... MESTS
Missile Electronics and Computer Assembly [*Military*] (PDAA) ...... MECA
Missile Element Need Statement ...... MENS
Missile Lethality [*Military*] ...... ML
Missile Logistics Center [*Army*] ...... MLC
Missile Piercing Discarding Sabot (PDAA) ...... MPDS
Missile Range Calibration Satellite ...... MRCS
Missile Recertification Equipment ...... MRE
Missile Research Corp. ...... MRC
Missile Response Simulation Software ...... MRSS
Missile Restraint Release ...... MRR
Missile Round Test Equipment ...... MRTE
Missile Round Test Set ...... MRTS
Missile X/Minuteman Missile ...... MX/MM
Mission Aviation Fellowship [*Indonesia*] [*ICAO designator*] (FAAC) ...... MAF
Mission-Critical Function (PDAA) ...... MCF
Mission Defendent Experiment ...... MDE
Mission Essential Subsystem Matrix [*Navy*] (ANA) ...... MESM
Mission to Planet Earth [*Proposed NASA satellite*] ...... MTPE
Missionary Internship [*An association*] (EA) ...... MI
Missionary Union of the Clergy [*British*] (BI) ...... MUC
Missions Gouvernementales Francaises [*France*] [*ICAO designator*] (FAAC) ...... MRN
Mississippi State University (PDAA) ...... MSSU
Mississippi Valley Airlines, Inc. [*ICAO designator*] (FAAC) ...... MVA
Mistral Air SRL [*Italy*] [*ICAO designator*] (FAAC) ...... MSA
MIT Airlines Ltd. [*ICAO designator*] (FAAC) ...... MNC
Mitchell Aero, Inc. [*ICAO designator*] (FAAC) ...... MTA
Mitsubishi Multi-Communication System [*Driver information system*] ...... MMCS
Mitsubishi Variable Intake System [*Automotive engine design*] ...... MVIC
Mixed Integer and Linear Programming Open Deck (PDAA) ...... MILPOD
Mixed Integer Operational Scheduling (PDAA) ...... MINOS
Mixed Language System (PDAA) ...... MLS
Mixed Potential System (PDAA) ...... MPS
MK Aircargo [*British*] [*ICAO designator*] (FAAC) ...... MKA
MK Burundi Air Cargo [*ICAO designator*] (FAAC) ...... BUC
Mobil Oil Ltd. [*Canada*] [*ICAO designator*] (FAAC) ...... MBO
Mobile Air Research Laboratory (PDAA) ...... MARLAB
Mobile Ammunition and Reconditioning Unit [*Military*] ...... MAER
Mobile Automated Microwave Test Facility (PDAA) ...... MAMTF
Mobile Automatic X-Ray (PDAA) ...... MAX
Mobile-Base Simulator (PDAA) ...... MBS
Mobile Computer System ...... MCS
Mobile Data Service (DA) ...... MDS
Mobile Earth Station (DA) ...... MES
Mobile Electrical Network Testing, Observation, and Recording (PDAA) ...... MENTOR
Mobile Eletromagnetic Incompatibility (PDAA) ...... MEMIC
Mobile Emergency Response Support ...... MERS
Mobile Lunar Excursion Module [*NASA*] (PDAA) ...... MOLEM
Mobile Ocean Basing System (PDAA) ...... MOBS
Mobile Production Unit [*On-site television recording*] (NTCM) ...... MPU
Mobile Radio Service (DA) ...... MRS
Mobile Satellite System (DA) ...... MSS
Mobile Tactical Computer (PDAA) ...... MTC
Mobile Terminal (DA) ...... MT
Mobile and Three-Dimensional Air Defense Operations RADAR [*Military*] (PDAA) ...... MATADOR
Mobile Transponder Performance Analyzer [*Aviation*] (DA) ...... MTPA
Mobile Treatment Unit (ERG) ...... MTU
Mobile Universal Test Equipment (PDAA) ...... MUTE
Mock-Up Spallation Target Assembly (PDAA) ...... MUSTA
Mode Annunciator and Logic Unit (PDAA) ...... MALU
Model-Based System Analysis (PDAA) ...... MBSA
Model Engineering Trade Association [*British*] (BI) ...... META
Model of International Relations in Agriculture (PDAA) ...... MOIRA
Model Office Project ...... MOP
Model Railroader [*A publication*] ...... Model R
Model Reference Adaptive System (PDAA) ...... MRAS
Model to Understand Simple English (PDAA) ...... MUSE
Modern Greek [*Language*] ...... ModGr
Modern Language Aptitude Test-Elementary [*Education*] (AEE) ...... EMLAT

Modern Latin [*Language*] ...... ModL
Modernized National Military Intelligence Center ...... MNMIC
Modification [*FCC*] (NTCM) ...... M
Modification of Special Service Authorization [*FCC*] (NTCM) ...... MSSA
Modified Anarchy Flood Routing (PDAA) ...... MAFR
Modified Anglia Engine [*Cosworth racing engines*] ...... MAE
Modified Boiling Test (PDAA) ...... MBT
Modified Construction Permit [*FCC*] (NTCM) ...... MP
Modified Construction Permit and License [*FCC*] (NTCM) ...... MP/L
Modified Construction Permit and Modified License [*FCC*] (NTCM) ...... MP/ML
Modified Diffusion Approximation (PDAA) ...... MDA
Modified Diode Transistor Logic [*Electronics*] (PDAA) ...... MDTL
Modified Effective-Range Theory (PDAA) ...... MERT
Modified Fluid in Cell [*Automotive engine combustion analysis*] ...... MFLIC
Modified Lensless Fourier Transform (PDAA) ...... MLLFT
Modified License [*FCC*] (NTCM) ...... ML
Modified New Least Square (PDAA) ...... MNLS
Modified Programmers Language [*Computer science*] (PDAA) ...... MPLAW
Modified Service Contract and Procedures [*DoD*] ...... MOSCAP
Modifying Factor [*Toxicology*] ...... MF
Modo Praescripto [*In the Manner Prescribed*] [*Latin*] [*Pharmacy*] (MAH) ...... MOD PRAESC
Modular Allocation Technique (PDAA) ...... MAT
Modular Application Executive for Computer Networks (PDAA) ...... MAXNET
Modular Audio Visual Unit (PDAA) ...... MAVU
Modular Automated Integrated Systems / Interoperability Test and Evaluation (PDAA) ...... MAINSITE
Modular Automated System to Identify Friend from Foe [*Military*] (PDAA) ...... MASTIFF
Modular Banking System (PDAA) ...... MBS
Modular Chaff/Flare Dispenser (PDAA) ...... MCFD
Modular Concept Unit (DA) ...... MCU
Modular Electronic Digital Instrumentation Assemblies (PDAA) ...... MEDIA
Modular Flare Chaff Dispenser [*Military*] (PDAA) ...... MFCD
Modular Midcourse Package [*DoD*] ...... MMP
Modular Organization Charting (PDAA) ...... MOC
Modular Rigid Frame (PDAA) ...... MRF
Modulated Frequency Radio Telephone (PDAA) ...... MFRT
Modulated Noise Generator (PDAA) ...... MNG
Modulated Wavy Vortex [*Fluid mechanics*] ...... MWV
Modulated Zone Plate (PDAA) ...... MZP
Module Rack Assembly ...... MRA
Mogul End Prong [*Lamp base*] (NTCM) ...... MEP
Mohawk Airlines [*ICAO designator*] (FAAC) ...... MOW
Mohawk Synchronous Communication Data Recorder [*Military*] (PDAA) ...... MSCDR
Moire Fringe Effect (PDAA) ...... MFE
Moisture Evaluation Analysis (PDAA) ...... MEA
Moisture Volume Fraction (PDAA) ...... MVF
Molecular Marine Biology and Biotechnology [*A publication*] ...... MMBB
Molecular Neutron Activation Analysis ...... MNAA
Molecular Orbital Self-Consistent Energy System (PDAA) ...... MOSES
Molecular Sieve Oxygen Generating (PDAA) ...... MSOG
Molecular Weight Cut-Off [*Metallurgy*] ...... MWCU
Moment Estimator (PDAA) ...... ME
Monacair-Agusta [*Monaco*] [*ICAO designator*] (FAAC) ...... MCR
Monair SA [*Switzerland*] [*ICAO designator*] (FAAC) ...... MNR
Monarch Airlines [*ICAO designator*] (FAAC) ...... MNH
Monarch Airlines Ltd. [*British*] [*ICAO designator*] (FAAC) ...... MON
Monaural Detection with Contralateral Cue (PDAA) ...... MDCC
Moncton Flying Club [*Canada*] [*ICAO designator*] (FAAC) ...... MFC
Mongolian Airlines [*ICAO designator*] (FAAC) ...... MGL
Mongrel (ABBR) ...... MGL
Monitoring and Risk Assessment Centre [*British*] ...... MARC
Monky Aerotaxis SA [*Mexico*] [*ICAO designator*] (FAAC) ...... MKY
Monmouth Airlines, Inc. [*ICAO designator*] (FAAC) ...... VMA
Mono-Stereo Compatible (PDAA) ...... MSC
Monoamine Oxidase A [*An enzyme*] ...... MAOA
Monoamine Transporter [*Biochemistry*] ...... MAT
Monoclonal Antibody (ERG) ...... MAB
Monograph ...... M
Monoisopropylbiphenyl (PDAA) ...... MIPB
Monolithic Focal Plane Array (PDAA) ...... MFPA
Monolithic Memory Unit ...... MMU
Monolithic Memory Unit Diagnostic ...... MMUD
Monolithic Mirror Telescope ...... MMT
Monomer Reactivity Ratio (PDAA) ...... MRR
Monopropellant Gas Generator (PDAA) ...... MGG
Monopulse Secondary Surveillance RADAR (DA) ...... MSSR
Monostatic Infrared Intrusion Detector (PDAA) ...... MIRID
Montauk Caribbean Airways, Inc. [*ICAO designator*] (FAAC) ...... ORA
Montlucon Air Service [*France*] [*ICAO designator*] (FAAC) ...... MLU
Montserrat Airways Ltd. [*Antigua and Barbuda*] [*ICAO designator*] (FAAC) ...... MNT
Moonroof [*Automotive advertising*] ...... MNRF
Mooring Leg Deployment Device (PDAA) ...... MLDD
Mooring Salvage and Boom Vessel (PDAA) ...... MSBV
Morale Tendency Score (AEE) ...... MTS
More Heart More Edge [*Screenwriter's lexicon*] ...... MHME
Morgan Aviation Services Ltd. [*Nigeria*] [*ICAO designator*] (FAAC) ...... MGN
Morphological Dictionary Adaptor Program (PDAA) ...... MDAP

Morris Air Service [*ICAO designator*]   (FAAC) .... MSS
Morrison Commemorative Stamp Committee   (EA) .... MCC
Morrison Flying Service, Inc. [*ICAO designator*]   (FAAC) .... MRO
Morse Mission Trainer .... MMT
Mortar [*Technical drawings*]   (DAC) .... MRTR
Mortar/Artillery Locating RADAR   (PDAA) .... MALR
MOS [*Military Occupation Specialty*] Training Plan .... MTP
Moscow Airways [*Russian Federation*] [*ICAO designator*]   (FAAC) .... MSC
Mother Guardian Allowance .... MGA
Mother-of-Pearl Clouds [*Meteorology*]   (PDAA) .... MPC
Mothers of Super Twins [*Military*] .... MOST
Motion Picture   (NTCM) .... MP
Motion Picture Machine Operator [*A union*]   (NTCM) .... MPMO
Motion Picture Museum Association [*British*]   (BI) .... MPMA
Motor Cab Owner Drivers' Association [*British*]   (BI) .... MCODA
Motor Factors Association [*British*]   (BI) .... MFA
Motor Glider Instructor Rating [*Aviation*]   (DA) .... MGIR
Motor Schools' Association of Great Britain   (BI) .... MSA
Motor Vehicle Allowance .... MVA
Motor Vehicle Plan Administration .... MVPA
Motor Vehicle Post Crash Communications System   (PDAA) .... MVPCCS
Motor Vehicles Dismantlers Association [*British*]   (BI) .... MVDA
Motorola Interconnect [*Electronics*] .... MI
Moulded Fiber Technology .... MTF
Mount Cook Airlines [*New Zealand*] [*ICAO designator*]   (FAAC) .... NZM
Mount Sinai School of Medicine [*New York*]   (PDAA) .... MSSM
Mountain Air Cargo, Inc. [*ICAO designator*]   (FAAC) .... MTN
Mountain Air Service, Inc. [*ICAO designator*]   (FAAC) .... BRR
Mountain High Aviation [*ICAO designator*]   (FAAC) .... MHA
Mountain Pacific Air Ltd. [*Canada*] [*ICAO designator*]   (FAAC) .... MPC
Mountain Valley Air Service, Inc. [*ICAO designator*]   (FAAC) .... MTV
Mountaineering Association [*British*]   (BI) .... MA
Mounting Tray .... MT
Movable Appendage Factor [*IOR*] [*Yacht racing*] .... MAF
Movement After-Effect   (PDAA) .... MAE
Moving Part Logic   (PDAA) .... MPLAW
Mozambique [*Aircraft nationality and registration mark*]   (FAAC) C9
Mud Weight [*Well drilling technology*] .... MW
Muffin   (ABBR) .... MFN
Muffler [*Automotive advertising*] .... MFFLR
Mug   (ABBR) .... MG
Mugged   (ABBR) .... MGD
Mugger   (ABBR) .... MGR
Mugginess   (ABBR) .... MGINS
Mugging   (ABBR) .... MGG
Muggy   (ABBR) .... MGY
Muk Air Taxi [*Denmark*] [*ICAO designator*]   (FAAC) .... MUK
Mullard Space Science Laboratory [*University of London*]   (PDAA) .... MSSL
Multi-Access Systems Control Terminal   (PDAA) .... MASEC
Multi-Adaptive Linear Neuron   (PDAA) .... MADALINE
Multi-Anode Microchannel Array   (PDAA) .... MAMA
Multi-Automatic System for Simulation and Operational Planning   (PDAA) .... MASSOP
Multi-Band Portable Signal Generator   (PDAA) .... MPSG
Multi-Barrel Smoke Discharger [*Military*]   (PDAA) .... MBSD
Multi-Carrier Station Radio [*or Remote*] Control Equipment   (PDAA) .... MSR
Multi-Channel Automatic Remote Recording .... MARRC
Multi-Channel In-Band Airborne Relay   (PDAA) .... MIBAR
Multi-Dimensional Random Sea Facility [*Hydraulics Research Station*]   (PDAA) .... MDRSF
Multi-Disciplinary Counter Intelligence .... MDIC
Multi-Effect Multistage Distillation   (PDAA) .... MMD
Multi-Frequency Code [*Telecommunications*]   (DA) .... MFC
Multi-Frequency / Local Battery [*Telecommunications*]   (DA) .... MFC/LB
Multi-Function, Multi-Band Airborne Radio System   (PDAA) .... MFMBARS
Multi-Hundred-Watt Radioisotope Thermoelectric Generator   (PDAA) .... MHW-RTG
Multi-Impact Signature Register   (PDAA) .... MISR
Multi-Industry Interest .... MI
Multi-Input-Safety-Shutdown   (PDAA) .... MISS
Multi-Layer Steel [*Engine gaskets*] [*Automotive engineering*] .... MLS
Multi-Layered Packaging   (PDAA) .... MLP
Multi-Microprocessor Flight Control System   (PDAA) .... M²FCS
Multi-Missile Fire Control System [*Military*] .... MMFCS
Multi-Mission Redeye Air-Launched Missile [*Military*]   (PDAA) .... MRAM
Multi-Object Phase-Tracking and Ranging System [*FAA*]   (PDAA) .... MOPTARS
Multi-Option Fuze, Artillery .... MOFA
Multi-Phase and Amplitude-Shift-Keying [*Computer science*]   (PDAA) .... MPASK
Multi-point Fuel Injection .... MFI
Multi-Programming Operating System [*Computer science*]   (PDAA) .... MOPSY
Multi-Purpose Display System   (DA) .... MPDS
Multi-Purpose Electric Furnace   (PDAA) .... MEF
Multi-purpose Infrared Sight   (PDAA) .... MIRS
Multi-Purpose Lithium Grease .... MPLG
Multi-Purpose Molybdenum Grease .... MPMG
Multi-RADAR Track Reconstitution [*Aviation*]   (DA) .... MURATREC
Multi-Rail Rocket System   (PDAA) .... MRRS
Multi-Reflecton [*Lighting*] .... MR
Multi-Spectral Thermal Imager Spacecraft [*Department of Energy*] .... MTI

Multi Station Boundary Layer Model System   (PDAA) .... MSBLMS
Multi-Year Development Plan [*Environmental Protection Agency*]   (ERG) .... MYDP
Multiantimicrobial Resistant Hemophilus Influenza B .... MRHIB
Multibus Accounting Package   (PDAA) .... MAP
Multichannel Acoustic Relay [*Navy*]   (ANA) .... MCAR
Multichip Integration [*Computer science*]   (PDAA) .... MCI
Multicultural Information Strategy .... MIS
Multidirectional Harassment   (PDAA) .... MDH
Multielectron Photoactive Center [*Physical chemistry*] .... MPC
Multiformat Electroluminescent Display   (PDAA) .... MED
Multilayer Ceramic Substrates [*Electronic circuit boards*] .... MLCS
Multilayer Side-Cladded Ridge Waveguide   (PDAA) .... MSCR
Multimedia Video Processor [*Texas Instruments*]   (PS) .... MVP
Multimode Airborne Solid-State Array RADAR System [*Military*]   (PDAA) .... MASAR
Multinational Company [*Business term*] .... MNC
Multipath Intersymbol Interference   (PDAA) .... MISI
Multiple Acceleration Sensor Unit   (PDAA) .... MASU
Multiple Aerial Refueling System   (PDAA) .... MARS
Multiple Agency Processing System .... MAPS
Multiple Aim Point System / Alternate Launch Point System   (PDAA) .... MAPS/ALPS
Multiple Aircraft Identification Display   (PDAA) .... MAID
Multiple-Aircraft Simulation Terminal   (DA) .... MAST
Multiple Anodic Stripping Analyzer   (PDAA) .... MASA
Multiple Answering Teaching Aid   (PDAA) .... MATA
Multiple Choice Objective Question   (DA) .... MCOQ
Multiple Conductor Transmission Line   (PDAA) .... MTL
Multiple Critical Root Maximally Flat   (PDAA) .... MUCROMAF
Multiple Engagement Test Environment [*Military*]   (PDAA) .... METE
Multiple Event Record and Playback System   (NTCM) .... MERPS
Multiple-Event Time Recording Apparatus   (PDAA) .... METRA
Multiple Goal Water Quality Model   (PDAA) .... MULQUAL
Multiple Independently-Guided Re-entry Vehicle [*NASA*]   (PDAA) .... MIRV
Multiple Input Describing Function   (PDAA) .... MIDF
Multiple-Input Phase-Variable Canonical Form   (PDAA) .... MIPVCE
Multiple-Integrated LASER Engagement Simulation / Air Ground Engagement Simulator .... MILES/AGES
Multiple Launch Rocket System Extended Range Rocket [*Military*] .... MLRS ER
Multiple Mode Integrated Propulsion System   (PDAA) .... MMIPS
Multiple Number of Faults per Pass   (PDAA) .... MNFP
Multiple Object Spectroscopy   (PDAA) .... MOS
Multiple Objective Linear Programming [*Computer science*]   (PDAA) .... MOLP
Multiple-Pass Heuristic Procedure   (PDAA) .... MPHP
Multiple Pool Processor and Computer   (PDAA) .... MULTIPAC
Multiple Position Letter Sorting Machine   (PDAA) .... MPLSM
Multiple Product Announcement   (NTCM) .... MPA
Multiple RADAR-Integrated Tracking [*Military*]   (PDAA) .... MERIT
Multiple Rapid Automatic Test of Monolithic Integrated Circuits   (PDAA) .... MR ATOMIC
Multiple RPV [*Remotely Piloted Vehicle*] Control System   (PDAA) .... MRCS
Multiple Shoe Retailers' Association [*British*]   (BI) .... MSRA
Multiple-Sine-Slit Microdensitometer   (PDAA) .... MSSM
Multiple Station Analytical Triangulation   (PDAA) .... MUSAT
Multiple Tailors Association [*British*]   (BI) .... MTA
Multiple Test Acceptance Code [*Lubricants testing*] [*Automotive engineering*] .... MTAC
Multiple Test Acceptance Criteria .... MTAC
Multiple Time Around Clutter .... MTAC
Multiple Wine Merchants Association [*British*]   (BI) .... MWMA
Multiplex .... MVX
Multiplex Information Transfer System   (PDAA) .... MITS
Multiplex Transmitter Input Signals   (PDAA) .... MTIS
Multiprogramming Control Program for Microcomputers .... MP/M
Multiprogramming with a Finite Amount of Trouble [*Computer science*] .... MFT
Multipulse Linear Productive Coding   (PDAA) .... MPLPC
Multipulse Scaling-Law Code using Data Base Interpolation   (PDAA) .... MPLAW
Multipurpose Program that Learns [*Computer science*]   (PDAA) .... MULTIPLE
Multipurpose, Tracer, Self-Destruct [*Army*] .... MPT-SD
Multiservicios Aeronauticos SA de CV [*Mexico*] [*ICAO designator*]   (FAAC) .... MUT
Multisource Unified Data Distribution   (PDAA) .... MUDD
Multistage Flash Distillation   (PDAA) .... MFD
Multivariate, Univariate, and Discriminant Analysis of Irregular Data   (PDAA) .... MUDAID
Municipal and Industry Strategy for Abatement .... MISA
Municipal Passenger Transport Association, Inc. [*British*]   (BI) .... MPTA
Munition Data Requirement .... MDR
Murray Aviation, Inc. [*ICAO designator*]   (FAAC) .... MUA
Mushroom Body [*Nerve center in insects*] .... MB
Music Director   (NTCM) .... MD
Music Industries Golfing Society [*British*]   (BI) .... MIGS
Music Information System for Theorists   (PDAA) .... MIST
Music Teachers' Association [*British*]   (BI) .... MTA
Music Trades' Association [*British*]   (BI) .... MTA
Musical Performing Arts Association   (NTCM) .... MPAA
Musicassette Quality Committee   (NTCM) .... MCQC

Musicians Benevolent Fund [*British*]   (BI) .... MBF
Mustique Airways [*Barbados*] [*ICAO designator*]   (FAAC) .... MAW
Mutliple Access Remote Computing   (PDAA).. MARC
Mutual Age... MA
Mutual Black Network   (NTCM).. MBN
Mutual Households Associations Ltd. [*British*]   (BI)................................ MHA
Mutual Recognition... MR
Muzzle Loaders Association of Great Britain   (BI).............................. MLAGB
My Favorite Toy Language [*Computer hacker terminology*]   (NHD) .... MFTL
Myanmar [*Aircraft nationality and registration mark*]   (FAAC)................... XY
Myanmar [*Aircraft nationality and registration mark*]   (FAAC)................... XZ
Myanmar Airways [*ICAO designator*]   (FAAC)...................................... UBA
Myflug HF [*Iceland*] [*ICAO designator*]   (FAAC)................................. MYA
Myopic Keratomileusis   (PDAA) .... MKM
Myxoid Liposarcoma [*Genetics*] .... MLPS

N

N-Glycidylpyrrolidone [*Organic chemistry*] .... NGP
N-Methyl-D-Aspartic Acid Receptor [*Neurochemistry*] .... NMDAR
N-Phenylglycine [*Organic chemistry*] .... NPG
N-Vinylpyrrolidone [*Organic chemistry*] .... NVP
Nadym Airlines [*Russian Federation*] [*ICAO designator*]   (FAAC)............ NDM
Nahanni Air Services Ltd. [*Canada*] [*ICAO designator*]   (FAAC) .... NAH
Namakwaland Lugdiens (EDMS) BPK [*South Africa*] [*ICAO
    designator*]   (FAAC).. NLD
Names   (ABBR)... NN
Namesake   (ABBR). [*Namibia*] [*ICAO designator*]   (FAAC)................ NMSK
Namib Air (Pty) Ltd. [*Namibia*] [*ICAO designator*]   (FAAC)................... NMB
Nancy Aviation [*France*] [*ICAO designator*]   (FAAC)........................... NCY
Nanofiltration .... NF
Naphthalene Dicarboxylate [*Organic chemistry*] .... NDC
Napier Air Service, Inc. [*ICAO designator*]   (FAAC)........................... NAP
Napped   (ABBR)... NPD
Napper   (ABBR)... NPR
Napping   (ABBR)... NPG
Narcisism   (ABBR)... NRCSM
Narcisist   (ABBR)... NRCST
Narcisistic   (ABBR).. NRSTK
Narcotic   (ABBR)... NRCTK
Narcotics Intelligence [*Military*]   (ADDR)........................... NARCINT
Narrated   (ABBR)... NRRAD
Narrating   (ABBR).. NRRAG
Narration   (ABBR).. NRRAN
Narrative   (ABBR).. NRRAV
Narrator   (ABBR)... NRRAR
Narrow Band Gaussian Random Noise   (PDAA) .... NBGRN
Narrow-Band Optimiziation of the Alignment of Highways   (PDAA)....... NOAH
Narrow-Band Voice Modulation   (PDAA).................................... NBVM
Narrow-Minded   (ABBR)... NRWMDD
Narrow-Mindedness   (ABBR).. NRWMDDNS
Narrow Resonance Infinite Absorber   (PDAA)............................. NRIA
Narrowed   (ABBR).. NRWD
Narrowing   (ABBR)... NRWG
Nasal   (ABBR)... NSL
Nasally   (ABBR)... NSLY
Nascence   (ABBR).. NSCNC
Nascent   (ABBR).. NSCNT
Nastlly   (ABBR).. NSTY
Nastiness   (ABBR).. NSTNS
Nasty   (ABBR).. NST
National Academy of Cable Programming   (NTCM)................... NACP
National Academy of Sciences Board on Ocean Science Affairs
    (PDAA)... NASBOSA
National Academy of Sciences Committee on Motor Vehicle
    Emissions   (PDAA) .... NASCMVE
National Advisory Committee on the Handicapped .... NACH
National Aero Research Laboratory [*Canada*]   (PDAA)................... NARL
National Aerospace and Defense Contractors Accreditation Program
    [*DoD*] .... NADCAP
National Agricultural and Industrial Development Association
    [*Republic of Ireland*]   (BI).. NAIDA
National AIDS Research Institute [*India*] .... NARI
National Air Charter PT [*Indonesia*] [*ICAO designator*]   (FAAC) .... NSR
National Air Monitoring Station [*Environmental Protection Agency*]
    (ERG).. NAMS
National Air Photo Library [*Canada*]   (PDAA)............................. NAPL
National Airlines, Inc. [*ICAO designator*]   (FAAC)....................... NAN
National Airspace Performance Reporting System [*Aviation*]
    (FAAC)... NAPRS
National Airspace System Interfacility Communications System
    (FAAC).. NICS
National Airways Corp. (Pty) Ltd. [*South Africa*] [*ICAO designator*]
    (FAAC)... NTN
National Alliance for the Advancement of Nodnarbian Philosophy
    (EA)... NAANP
National Alliance of Black School Superintendents   (AEE)............ NABSS
National Allotments and Gardens Society Ltd. [*British*]   (BI) .... NAGS
National Amalgamated Stevedores and Dockers Union [*British*]
    (BI).. NASDU
National Amateur Body Building Association [*British*]   (BI)............. NABBA

National Amateur Tobacco Growers' Association [*British*]   (BI)............ NATGA
National Anti-Vaccination League [*British*]   (BI)............................ NAVL
National Archives for Electrical Science and Technology   (PDAA).......... NAEST
National Arrangements for Incidents Involving Radioactivity
    (PDAA)... NAIR
National Assocation of Radio Broadcasters   (NTCM)..................... NARB
National Association of Agricultural Contractors [*British*]   (BI) .... NAAC
National Association of Bingo Clubs [*British*]   (BI)....................... NABC
National Association of Black Television and Film Producers
    (NTCM).. NABTFP
National Association of Bookmakers Ltd. [*British*]   (BI)................... NAB
National Association for Cave Diving   (EA).............................. NACD
National Association of Choirs [*British*]   (BI).......................... NAC
National Association of Church Furnishers [*British*]   (BI)................. NACF
National Association of Cider Makers [*British*]   (BI)..................... NACM
National Association of Counselors   (EA).............................. NAC
National Association of Craftsman Tailors [*British*]   (BI) .... NACT
National Association of Crankshaft and Cylinder Grinders [*British*]
    (BI).. NACCG
National Association of Cycle Traders [*British*]   (BI) .... NACT
National Association for Educational Television   (NTCM).................. NAET
National Association of Engravers and Die-Stampers [*British*]
    (BI).. NAEDS
National Association of Exhibition Contractors [*British*]   (BI)............. NAEC
National Association of Farm Directors   (NTCM) .... NAFD
National Association of Flower Arrangement Societies of Great
    Britain   (BI)... NAFAS
National Association of Funeral Directors [*British*]   (BI).................. NAFD
National Association of Hospital Supplies Officers [*British*]   (BI)......... NAHSO
National Association for Information Services   (EA)...................... NAIS
National Association of Inland Water Carriers [*British*]   (BI)............. NAIWC
National Association of Inspectors of Schools and Educational
    Organisers [*British*]   (BI)... NAIEO
National Association of Labor-Management Committees   (EA)........... NALMC
National Association of Labour Student Organisations [*British*]
    (BI).. NALSO
National Association of Launderette Owners Ltd. [*British*]   (BI) .... NALO
National Association of Lift Makers [*British*]   (BI)....................... NALM
National Association of Malleable Ironfounders [*British*]   (BI)............. NAMI
National Association of Manufacturers   (NTCM)......................... NAM
National Association of Marine Enginebuilders [*British*]   (BI)............. NAME
National Association for Mediation in Education   (EA).................... NAME
National Association of Medical Minority Educators   (EA)............... NAMME
National Association of Multiple Grocers [*British*]   (BI)................. NAMG
National Association of Nephrology Technologists   (EA)................. NANT
National Association of Parish Councils [*British*]   (BI).................. NAPC
National Association of Park Administrators [*British*]   (BI)............... NAPA
National Association of Pharmaceutical Distributors [*British*]   (BI)......... NAPD
National Association of Poultry Packers Ltd. [*British*]   (BI)............... NAPP
National Association of Presbyterian Scouters   (EA) .... NAPS
National Association of Prison Visitors [*British*]   (BI).................... NAPV
National Association of Private Secretaries [*British*]   (BI)................ NAPS
National Association of Public Golf Courses [*British*]   (BI)............... NAPGC
National Association of Railroad and Utility Commissioners
    (NTCM)... NARCU
National Association of Sack Merchants and Reclaimers [*British*]
    (BI).. NASMAR
National Association for School Magazines [*British*]   (BI)................ NASM
National Association of Scottish Woollen Manufacturers [*British*]
    (BI).. NASWM
National Association of Seed Potato Merchants [*British*]   (BI)............ NASPM
National Association of Shopfitters [*British*]   (BI)....................... NAS
National Association of Software and Service Companies .... NASSCOM
National Association of State Enrolled Nurses [*British*]   (BI) .... NASEN
National Association of Television Program Executives   (NTCM).......... NATPE
National Association of Television and Radio Announcers
    (NTCM)... NATRA
National Association of Tenants and Residents [*British*]   (BI)............. NATR
National Association of Theatre Nurses [*British*]   (BI)................... NATN
National Association of Tool Dealers [*British*]   (BI) .... NATD
National Association of Toy Retailers [*British*]   (BI) .... NATR
National Association of Training Corps for Girls [*British*]   (BI)............ NATCG

National Association of Wholesale Paint Merchants [*British*] (BI) .... NAWPM
National Association of Window Blind Manufacturers [*British*] (BI) .... NAWBM
National Audience Board [*An association*] (NTCM) .... NAB
National Audience Composition [*Nielsen Television Index*] (NTCM) .... NAC
National Audience Demographics Report [*Nielsen Television Index*] (NTCM) .... NAD
National Automotive and Truck Model and Toy Museum of the United States .... NATMATMUS
National Average Weekly Male Earning .... NAWME
National Aviation Co. [*Egypt*] [*ICAO designator*] (FAAC) .... GTY
National Aviation Consultants Ltd. [*Canada*] [*ICAO designator*] (FAAC) .... TNC
National Bakery School [*British*] (BI) .... NBS
National Benzole and Allied Products Association [*British*] (BI) .... NBA
National Biological Survey [*Department of the Interior*] .... NBS
National Black Business Alliance (EA) .... NBBA
National Board for Bakery Education [*British*] (BI) .... NBBE
National Book Week (NTCM) .... NBW
National Brassfoundry Association [*British*] (BI) .... NBA
National British Softbill Society (BI) .... NBSS
National Broadcasters' Club (NTCM) .... NBC
National Bureau for Co-Operation in Child Care [*British*] (BI) .... NBCCC
National Cable Antenna Television Association of Canada (NTCM) .... NCATA
National Cactus and Succulent Society [*British*] (BI) .... NCSS
National Caravan Council Ltd. [*British*] (BI) .... NCC
National Catholic Welfare Conference News Service (NTCM) .... NCWC
National Catholic Youth Association [*British*] (BI) .... NCYA
National Center for American Indian and Alaska Native Mental Health Research (EA) .... NCAIANMHR
National Center for Excellence in Metalworking Technology [*Navy*] .... NCEMT
National Center for Human Genome Research .... NCHGR
National Center for Research Resources [*National Institutes of Health*] .... NCRR
National Certification Skills Test [*Psychiatry*] .... NCST
National Chamber of Trade [*British*] (BI) .... NCT
National Championship Stock Car Racing [*Later, NASCAR*] .... NCSCC
National Check Traders Federation [*British*] (BI) .... NCTF
National Citizens' Advice Bureaux Committee [*British*] (BI) .... NCABC
National Civil Aviation Council [*British*] (BI) .... NCAC
National Club Cricket Association [*British*] (BI) .... NCCA
National Coalition of Concerned Legal Professionals (EA) .... CCLP
National College of Rubber Technology (PDAA) .... NCRT
National College for the Training of Youth Leaders [*British*] (BI) .... NCTYL
National Commercial Temperance League [*British*] (BI) .... NCTL
National Commission on Air Quality [*Environmental Protection Agency*] (ERG) .... NCAO
National Committee for the Full Development of Instructional Television Fixed Services [*ITFS regulation*] (NTCM) .... NCFDITFS
National Communications Working Party [*Australia*] [*Political party*] .... NCWP
National Commuter Airways [*British*] [*ICAO designator*] (FAAC) .... NCL
National Computer Users Forum [*National Computing Center*] (PDAA) .... NCUF
National Corporation for the Care of Old People [*British*] (BI) .... NCCOP
National Council of Churches Broadcasting Network (NTCM) .... NCCBN
National Council of Churches of Christ in the USA (NTCM) .... NCC/USA
National Council for Civic Theatres Ltd. [*British*] (BI) .... NCCT
National Council for the Conservation of Plants and Gardens (PDAA) .... NCCPG
National Council for Diplomats in Art and Design [*British*] (BI) .... NCDAD
National Council of Educational Opportunity Associations (EA) .... NCEOA
National Council for Quality and Reliabiltiy [*British*] (BI) .... NCQR
National Council for the Single Woman and Her Dependants Ltd. [*British*] (BI) .... NCSW
National Council of Women of Great Britain (BI) .... NCW
National Dairymen's Association, Inc. [*British*] (BI) .... NDA
National Dairymen's Benevolent Institution, Inc. [*British*] (BI) .... NDBI
National Deaf Children's Society [*British*] (BI) .... NDCS
National Defense Center for Environmental Excellence [*DoD*] (RDA) .... NDCEE
National Defense Manufacturing Technology Plan .... NDMTP
National Display Equipment Association [*British*] (BI) .... NDEA
National Dog Owners' Association [*British*] (BI) .... NDOA
National Drama Festivals Association [*British*] (BI) .... NDFA
National Educational Radio Network [*Defunct*] (NTCM) .... NERN
National Egg Packers' Association Ltd. [*British*] (BI) .... NEPAL
National Electrical Safety Code [*Also, NEC*] (NTCM) .... NESC
National Electromagnetic Compatibility Analysis Facility [*Department of Commerce*] (PDAA) .... NECAF
National Electronic Reliability Council (NTCM) .... NERC
National Employers Association of Rayon Yarn Producers [*British*] (BI) .... NEARYP
National Engineering and Electrical Trade Union [*Republic of Ireland*] (BI) .... NEETU
National Engineers Commission on Air Resources (PDAA) .... NECAR
National English Rabbit Club [*British*] (BI) .... NERC
National Estate .... NE
National Examination Board in Occupational Safety and Health (PDAA) .... NEBOSH
National Farmers' Association [*Republic of Ireland*] (BI) .... NFA
National Federation of Anglers [*British*] (BI) .... NFA
National Federation of Bakery Students' Societies [*British*] (BI) .... NFBSS
National Federation of Builders' and Plumbers' Merchants [*British*] (BI) .... NFBPM
National Federation of Clay Industries [*British*] (BI) .... NFCI
National Federation of Clubs for Divorced and Separated [*British*] (BI) .... NFCDS
National Federation of Cold Storage and Ice Trades [*British*] (BI) .... NFCSIT
National Federation of Construction Supervisors [*British*] (BI) .... NFCS
National Federation of Constructional Glass Associations [*British*] (BI) .... NFCGA
National Federation of Corn Trade Associations [*British*] (BI) .... NFCTA
National Federation of Drapers and Allied Traders Ltd. [*Republic of Ireland*] (BI) .... NFD
National Federation of Engineering and General Ironfounders [*British*] (BI) .... NEGI
National Federation of Fish Friers [*British*] (BI) .... NFFF
National Federation of Freestone Quarry Owners [*British*] (BI) .... NFFQO
National Federation of Fruit and Potato Trades [*British*] (BI) .... NFFPT
National Federation of Furniture Trade Unions [*British*] (BI) .... NFFTU
National Federation of Iron and Steel Merchants [*British*] (BI) .... NFISM
National Federation of Ironmongers' and Builders' Merchants' Staff Associations [*British*] (BI) .... FIBMA
National Federation of Master Painters and Decorators of England and Wales (BI) .... NFMP
National Federation of Meat Traders [*British*] (BI) .... NFMT
National Federation of Off-Licence Holders Associations of England and Wales (BI) .... NFOHA
National Federation of Old Age Pensioners' Associations [*British*] (BI) .... NFOAPA
National Federation of Permanent Holiday Camps Ltd. [*British*] (BI) .... NFPHC
National Federation of Plastering Contractors [*British*] (BI) .... NFPC
National Federation of Plumbers and Domestic Heating Engineers [*British*] (BI) .... NFPDHE
National Federation of Property Owners [*British*] (BI) .... NFPO
National Federation of Terrazzo-Mosaic Specialists [*British*] (BI) .... NFTMS
National Federation of Vehicle Trades [*British*] (BI) .... NFVT
National Federation of Wholesale Grocers and Provision Merchants [*British*] (BI) .... NFWG
National Fenton Glass Society (EA) .... NFGS
National Film Finance Corp. [*British*] (BI) .... NFFC
National Fire Loss Data System [*Military*] (PDAA) .... NFLDS
National Fireplace Makers Association [*British*] (BI) .... NFMA
National Flight Data Processing System [*ICAO*] (DA) .... NFDPS
National Froebel Foundation [*British*] (BI) .... NFF
National Fund for Research into Poliomyelitis and Other Crippling Diseases [*British*] (BI) .... NFPR
National Grid Co. [*British*] [*ICAO designator*] (FAAC) .... GRD
National Guild of Telephonists [*British*] (BI) .... NGT
National Hairdressers' Association [*British*] (BI) .... NHA
National Hairdressers' Federation [*British*] (BI) .... NHF
National Highway .... NH
National Highway System [*Federal transportation planning*] .... NHS
National Hunter and Jumper Association (EA) .... NHJA
National Imagery Exploitation Tasking Study .... NIETS
National Impact Model [*Environmental Protection Agency*] (ERG) .... NIM
National Industrial Basic Language (PDAA) .... NIBL
National Industrial Safety Conference (PDAA) .... NISCON
National Industrial Salvage and Recovery Association [*British*] (BI) .... NISRA
National Institute of Hardware [*British*] (BI) .... NIH
National Institute of Housecraft [*British*] (BI) .... NIH
National Institute of Industrial Psychology (PDAA) .... NIIP
National Institute for Medical Research Online Database (PDAA) .... NIMROD
National Institute Northern Accelerator (PDAA) .... NINA
National Institute of Poultry Husbandry [*British*] (BI) .... NIPH
National Instructional Television Association (NTCM) .... NITA
National Instructional Television Center (NTCM) .... NITC
National Interest .... NI
National Ironfounding Employers Association [*British*] (BI) .... NIEF
National Jet Service, Inc. [*ICAO designator*] (FAAC) .... AND
National Jewellers' Association [*British*] (BI) .... NJA
National Land Use Classification (PDAA) .... NLUC
National Latino Media Coalition [*Citizen's group*] (NTCM) .... NLMC
National League for Social Understanding (EA) .... NLSU
National Learning Disabilities Assistance Project .... NaLDAP
National Light Castings Ironfounders' Federation [*British*] (BI) .... NLCIF
National Map Accuracy Standards (PDAA) .... NMAS
National Marble Club of America (EA) .... NMCA
National Means Test Proposal .... NMTP
National Media Liaison Officer .... NMLO
National Milk Publicity Council [*British*] (BI) .... NMPC
National Milk Record [*British*] (BI) .... NMR
National Mouse Club [*British*] (BI) .... NMC
National Music and Disability Information Service [*British*] .... NMDIS
National Music Theater Network (EA) .... NMTN
National Nature Reserve (PDAA) .... NNR
National Nosocomial Infections Surveillance [*Medicine*] .... NNIS
National Ocean Survey Analytical Plotter [*NOAA*] (PDAA) .... NOSAP

National Oceanic and Atmospheric Administration [*ICAO designator*] (FAAC)............ MAP
National Oceanic and Atmospheric Administration [*Department of Commerce*] [*ICAO designator*] (FAAC)............ NAA
National Oceanic and Atmospheric Administration Technical Report-National Marine Fisheries Service-Circular [*A publication*] (PDAA)............ NOAA-TR-NMFS-Circ
National Oceanic and Atmospheric Administration-Technical Report-National Marine Fisheries Service-Special Scientific Report Fisheries (PDAA)............ NOAA-TR-NMFS-SSRF
National Oil and Hazardous Substances Contingency Plan [*Environmental Protection Agency*] (ERG)............ NOHSCP
National Organization to Halt the Abuse and Routine Mutilation of Males (EA)............ NOHARMM
National Organization of Miniaturists and Dollers (EA)............ NOMAD
National Overseas Airline Co. [*Egypt*] [*ICAO designator*] (FAAC)............ NOL
National Performance Review [*A publication*]............ NPR
National Pharmaceutical Union (PDAA)............ NPU
National Pig Breeders' Association [*British*] (BI)............ NPBA
National Pig Carvers Association (EA)............ NPCA
National Pizza and Pasta Association (EA)............ NPPA
National Point of Contact (PDAA)............ NPOC
National Pollutant Discharge Elimination System [*Environmental Protection Agency*] (ERG)............ NPDS
National Press Women's Club (NTCM)............ NPWC
National Pretreatment Program [*Metal finishing technology*]............ NPP
National Prices Network............ NPN
National Priorities List............ NPL
National Private Circuit Digital Network (PDAA)............ NPCDN
National Program Director............ NPD
National Program Production and Aquisition Grant [*Corporation for Public Broadcasting*] [*Radio*] (NTCM)............ NPPAG
National Project in Agricultural Communication (PDAA)............ NPAC
National Radio Conference [*Broadcast regulations*] (NTCM)............ NRC
National Registry of Environmental Professionals (EA)............ NREP
National Research Institute [*Audience research organization*] (NTCM)............ NRI
National Residue Database............ NRDB
National Respiratory and Enteric Virus Surveillance System............ NREVSS
National Roller Canary Society [*British*] (BI)............ NRCS
National Roller Hockey Association of Great Britain (BI)............ NRHA
National Rounders Association [*British*] (BI)............ NRA
National Sample Survey (PDAA)............ NSS
National Savings Bank [*British*]............ NSB
National Sawmilling Association [*British*] (BI)............ NSA
National School Development Council (AEE)............ NSCD
National Science Technology Council............ NSTC
National Scouting Collectors Society (EA)............ NSCS
National Search and Rescue Secretariat [*Canada*] (DA)............ NSS
National Service Center............ NSC
National Sheep Breeders' Association [*British*] (BI)............ NSBA
National Society for the Abolition of Cruel Sports [*British*] (BI)............ NSACS
National Society of Electrotypers and Stereotypers [*British*] (BI)............ NSES
National Society of Environmental Consultants (EA)............ NSEC
National Society of Master Patternmakers [*British*] (BI)............ NSMP
National Society for Mentally Handicapped Children [*British*] (BI)............ NSMHC
National Society of TV Producers (NTCM)............ NSTP
National Space Development Agency [*Japan*]............ NASDA
National Sweet Pea Society [*British*] (BI)............ NSPS
National Taxi and Car Hire Association [*British*] (BI)............ NTCHA
National Teachers Association (AEE)............ NTA
National Technology Transfer Center............ NTTS
National Telefilm Associates, Inc. (NTCM)............ NTA
National Tissue Typing Reference Laboratory (PDAA)............ NTTRL
National Track Analysis Program [*Aviation*] (FAAC)............ NTAP
National Type Approval (PDAA)............ NTA
National Union of Funeral and Cemetery Workers [*British*] (BI)............ NUFCW
National Union of Rate-Payers' Associations [*British*] (BI)............ NURA
National Union of Retail Confectioners [*British*] (BI)............ NURC
National Union of Retail Tobacconists [*British*] (BI)............ NURT
National United States-Arab Chamber of Commerce (EA)............ NUSACC
National Villa Association [*British*] (BI)............ NVA
National Weather Service-Central Region (PDAA)............ NWS-CR
National Weather Service-Eastern Region (PDAA)............ NWS-ER
National Weather Service-Southern Region (PDAA)............ NWS-SR
National Weather Service-Western Region (PDAA)............ NWS-WR
National Wool Textile Export Corp. [*British*] (BI)............ NWTEC
National Yacht Harbour Association [*British*] (BI)............ NYHA
Nationally-Certified Psychiatric Technician............ NCPT
Native Forest Council (EA)............ NFC
NATO Command and Control Systems Management Agency (PDAA)............ NACCSMA
NATO Electronic Technical Recommendation (PDAA)............ NETR
NATO Multi-Role Combat Aircraft Management Organization (PDAA)............ NAMMO
NATO Tactical Fighter Weapons Training Center............ NTFWTC
Natty (ABBR)............ NT
Natural Axial Resonant Frequency (PDAA)............ NARF
Natural Gas Shutoff [*NFPA pre-fire planning symbol*] (NFPA)............ NG
Natural Image Computer (PDAA)............ NIC
Natural Language Processing System for Queuing Problems [*Computer science*] (PDAA)............ NLPQ
Natural Law Party [*Australia*] [*Political party*]............ NLP
Natural Organic Carbon............ NOC
Natural Organic Matter............ NOM
Natural Resource-Based Product............ NRBP
Natural Resource Damage [*Environmental science*]............ NRD
Natural Rubber Producers' Research Association [*British*] (BI)............ NRPRA
Naturally-Occurring Radioactive Material............ NORM
Nauru [*Aircraft nationality and registration mark*] (FAAC)............ C2
Naval Air Effect Model (PDAA)............ NAEM
Naval Armaments Stores System (PDAA)............ NASS
Naval Autonomous Intelligent Console (PDAA)............ NAUTIC
Naval Basic Instrument Trainer (PDAA)............ NAVBIT
Naval Compass Stabilizer (PDAA)............ NCS
Naval Emergency Monitoring Teams (PDAA)............ NEMT
Naval Engineering Test Establishment [*Canadian Armed Forces*] (PDAA)............ NETE
Naval Facilities Engineering Command (PDAA)............ NAVFECO
Naval In-Shore Warfare (PDAA)............ NISW
Naval Medical Command (ANA)............ NAVMEDCOM
Naval Military Personnel Command (ANA)............ NMPC
Naval Oceanographic Processing Facility (ANA)............ NOPF
Naval Ordnance Inspection Establishment [*Ministry of Defence*] [*British*] (PDAA)............ NOIE
Naval Radiological Protection Service (PDAA)............ NRPS
Naval Reserve Cargo-Handling Battalion............ NRCHB
Naval Reserve Cargo-Handling Training Battalion............ NRCHTB
Naval Supplies............ NAVSUP
Naval Surface Weapons Center (PDAA)............ NAVSURFWPNCEN
Naval Tactical Command and Control System (PDAA)............ NTCCS
Naval Undersea Warfare Museum Foundation (PDAA)............ NUWMF
Naval War College Review [*A publication*]............ NWCR
Naval Weapons Engineering Support Activity (PDAA)............ NAWESA
NAVDAC [*Naval Data Automation Command*] **Assembly, Monitor, Executive System** (PDAA)............ NAMES
Navegacion y Servicios Aereos Canarios SA [*Spain*] [*ICAO designator*] (FAAC)............ NAY
Navigation/Attack Systems Trainer (PDAA)............ NAST
Navigation Display Unit [*Military*]............ NDU
Navigation Flight Test [*Aviation*] (DA)............ NFT
Navigation Heading and Altitude Reference System [*Aviation*] (PDAA)............ NAVHARS
Navigation Management System (PDAA)............ NMS
Navigation Satellite System (PDAA)............ NASS
Navigation Technology Satellite (PDAA)............ NTS
Navigation/Weapon Delivery Computer (PDAA)............ NWDC
Navigational Warning East Atlantic and Mediterranean [*Navy*] (PDAA)............ NAVEAMS
Navtech Systems Support, Inc. [*Canada*] [*ICAO designator*] (FAAC)............ XNS
Navy Advanced SATCOM [*Satellite Communications*] **Program** (ANA)............ NASP
Navy Department Fuel and Lubricants Advisory Committee [*Ministry of Defense*] [*British*] (PDAA)............ NAFLAC
Navy Exchange Service Command............ NEXCOM
Navy Extended Electrode Technique (PDAA)............ NEET
Navy Management Systems Center (PDAA)............ NMSC
Navy Material Command Support Activity (PDAA)............ NMSCA
Navy Quality Management............ NQM
Navy Resale System Office (PDAA)............ NAVRESO
Navy Resale System Office (PDAA)............ NSRO
Nawa Air Transport [*Hungary*] [*ICAO designator*] (FAAC)............ NWH
Near-Field Calibration Array (PDAA)............ NFCA
Near-Object Detection Sensor [*Automotive electronics*]............ NODS
Near-Sighted (ABBR)............ NRSITD
Near-Sightedness (ABBR)............ NRSITNS
Near-Term Hybrid Vehicle (PDAA)............ NTHV
Near-Term Scout Helicopter [*Army*]............ NTSH
Nearest Grid Point (PDAA)............ NGP
Nearfield Bearing and Range Accuracy Calibration System (PDAA)............ NEFBRACS
Nearly (ABBR)............ NRY
Nearly Airborne Truck (PDAA)............ NAT
Nearness (ABBR)............ NRNS
Necrofile [*A publication*]............ Necro
Needle Makers Association [*British*] (BI)............ NMA
Needs [*Automotive advertising*]............ NDS
Nefteyugansk Aviation Division [*Russian Federation*] [*ICAO designator*] (FAAC)............ NFT
Negative Equity Baby Boomer [*Home buyers in debt*]............ NEBBY
Negative Immittance Inverter (PDAA)............ NII
Negative Resistance Amplifier (PDAA)............ NRA
Negative Resistor (PDAA)............ NEGISTOR
Negotiated Consent Order [*Environmental Protection Agency*] (ERG)............ NCO
Negotiation Information System............ NIS
Neighborhoods, Voluntary Associations and Consumer Protection [*Environmental Protection Agency*] (ERG)............ NVACP
Neiltown Air Ltd. [*Canada*] [*ICAO designator*] (FAAC)............ NLA
Nelson Aviation College [*New Zealand*] [*ICAO designator*] (FAAC)............ CGE
Nemesis (ABBR)............ NMSS
Neomenthyldiphenylphosphine [*Organic chemistry*]............ NMDP
Neon Discharge Lighting [*Automotive lighting*]............ NDL
Nepal [*Aircraft nationality and registration mark*] (FAAC)............ 9N
Nepotism (ABBR)............ NPTSM

Nepotist (ABBR) ... NPTST
Nerve (ABBR) ... NRV
Nerve Agent Immobilised Enzyme Alarm and Detector (PDAA) ... NAIAD
Nerve-Wracking (ABBR) ... NRVWRKG
Nerved (ABBR) ... NRVD
Nerveless (ABBR) ... NRVLS
Nerving (ABBR) ... NRVG
Nervous (ABBR) ... NRVU
Nervous (ABBR) ... NRVUS
Nervously (ABBR) ... NRVUSY
Nervously (ABBR) ... NRVUY
Nervousness (ABBR) ... NRVUNS
Nervousness (ABBR) ... NRVUSNS
Nervy (ABBR) ... NRVI
Nest (ABBR) ... NST
Nesting (ABBR) ... NSTG
Nestled (ABBR) ... NSTL
Nestling (ABBR) ... NSTLG
Net Advertising Circulation [*Outdoor advertising*] (NTCM) ... NAC
Net Annual Gain [*Business term*] (PDAA) ... NAG
Net Borrowing Requirement (PDAA) ... NBR
Net Calorific Value (PDAA) ... NCV
Net Domestic Product [*Business term*] (PDAA) ... NDP
Net Ecosystem Exchange [*Biology*] ... NEE
Net Ecosystem Production [*Biology*] ... NEP
Net Financing Requirement ... NFR
Net Liquidity Ratio (PDAA) ... NLR
Net Positive Suction Head Available [*Pumps*] (PDAA) ... NPSHA
Net Present Value at the Horizon (PDAA) ... NPVH
Net Rating Points [*Media ratings*] (NTCM) ... NRP
Net Registered Tonnage ... NRT
Net Requirementes Estimation Model (PDAA) ... NETREM
Net Section Fracture Strength (PDAA) ... NSFS
Net-of-Tax Rate (ECON) ... NTR
Network [*FCC program source designation*] (NTCM) ... N
Network Analysis (PDAA) ... NETANAL
Network Analytical Simulator (PDAA) ... NEASIM
Network-Based Project Management (PDAA) ... NBPM
Network Channel [*Broadcasting*] (NTCM) ... NC
Network Definition Language [*Computer science*] (PDAA) ... NEDELA
Network of European CNS [*Central Nervous System*] **Transplantation and Restoration** ... NECTAR
Network Identification [*Broadcasting*] (NTCM) ... NI
Network Independent File Transfer Protocol (PDAA) ... NIFTP
Network Information Retrieval ... NIR
Network Information Service ... NIS
Network Management System (DA) ... NMS
Network-Oriented Project Management System (PDAA) ... NOPMS
Network Reliability Assessment Model (PDAA) ... NERAM
Network-Terminating Equipment (PDAA) ... NTE
Network Transmission Committee [*Video Transmission Engineering Committee*] (NTCM) ... NTC
Neural Pulse Frequency Modulation (PDAA) ... NPFM
Neurotoxin [*Biochemistry*] ... NT
Neutral Speed Stability (PDAA) ... NSS
Neutralization Index (PDAA) ... NI
Neutralization Self-Solidification Process (PDAA) ... NSSP
Neutraminidase Inhibition (PDAA) ... NI
Neutron Instruments for Nuclear Analysis (PDAA) ... NINA
Neutron Intermediate Standard Uranium Source (PDAA) ... NISUS
New Air Ltd. [*British*] [*ICAO designator*] (FAAC) ... FLS
New Caledonia ... N Cal
New Chemical Compound [*Food science*] ... NCC
New Democracy [*European political movement*] (ECON) ... ND
New Electroactive Organic Materials for Electronics [*Esprit*] ... NEOME
New Electronic Media (NTCM) ... NEM
New England Air Express, Inc. [*ICAO designator*] (FAAC) ... NEW
New England Airlines, Inc. [*ICAO designator*] (FAAC) ... NEA
New England Center for Organizational Effectiveness (EA) ... NECOE
New Head [*Also, NL*] [*News stories*] (NTCM) ... NH
New and Improved Materials and Processes (PDAA) ... NIMP
New Lead [*Also, NH*] [*News stories*] (NTCM) ... NL
New Least Square (PDAA) ... NLS
New Organization Training ... NOT
New Position ... NP
New and Renewable Energy (PDAA) ... NRE
New Vehicle Satisfaction with Dealer Service [*Quality research*] ... NVSDS
New World Services, Inc. ... NWSI
New York Helicopter Corp. [*ICAO designator*] (FAAC) ... NYH
New Zealand Air Services Ltd. [*ICAO designator*] (FAAC) ... ENZ
Newair [*Denmark*] [*ICAO designator*] (FAAC) ... NAW
Newair, Inc. [*ICAO designator*] (FAAC) ... HVA
Newark (ABBR) ... NRK
Newfoundland Labrador Air Transport Ltd. [*Canada*] [*ICAO designator*] (FAAC) ... NLT
Newly-Industrialized Economy ... NIE
News Director (NTCM) ... ND
News Program (NTCM) ... N
Newspaper Composition (PDAA) ... NEWSCOMP
Newspaper in Education Program ... NIE
Newspaper and Printing Industries Pension Fund [*British*] (BI) ... NPIPF
Newspapers Mutual Insurance Society Ltd. [*British*] (BI) ... NMIS
Newton Tool Kit [*Computer science*] ... NTK
Next to Reading Matter [*Also, NRM*] [*Advertising*] (NTCM) ... NR
Nicaraguense de Aviacion SA [*Nicaragua*] [*ICAO designator*] (FAAC) ... NICA
Nicaraguense de Aviacion SA [*Nicaragua*] [*ICAO designator*] (FAAC) ... NIS
Nichols Air Service, Inc. [*ICAO designator*] (FAAC) ... CBL
Nickel-Metal Hydride [*Organic chemistry*] (PS) ... NiMH
Nickel Producers Environmental Research Association ... NIPERA
Nickel-Silver ... NI-SIL
Nicotine Chewing Gum (PDAA) ... NCG
Nielsen Broadcast Index [*A. C. Nielsen Co.*] (NTCM) ... NBI
[*A. C.*] **Nielsen Co.** (NTCM) ... ACN
Nielsen Engineering & Research, Inc. ... NEAR
Nielsen Home Video Index [*A. C. Nielsen Co.*] (NTCM) ... NHI
Nigerian International Air Services Ltd. [*ICAO designator*] (FAAC) ... HMZ
Night Vision Pilotage System [*Military*] ... NVPS
Nightcap (ABBR) ... NTCP
Nighttime (NTCM) ... N
Nile Safaris Aviation [*Sudan*] [*ICAO designator*] (FAAC) ... NSA
Nile Valley Aviation Co. [*Egypt*] [*ICAO designator*] (FAAC) ... NVA
Nimbus Aviation [*British*] [*ICAO designator*] (FAAC) ... NBS
Nine Inch Nails [*Rock music group*] ... NIN
Nineteen-Hundred [*Computer*] **Management and Recovery of Documentation** (PDAA) ... NIMROD
Ninhydrine [*Chemical agent used in espionage*] ... NIN
Nippon Cargo Airlines Co. Ltd. [*Japan*] [*ICAO designator*] (FAAC) ... NCA
Nippon Hoso Kyokai [*Japanese national broadcasting system*] (NTCM) ... NHK
Nissan Safety Device Advisor [*Driver information system*] ... NSDA
Niton (ABBR) ... NT
Nitrate Ester Plasticized Polyethylene (PDAA) ... NEPE
Nitric Acid Dihydrate [*Inorganic chemistry*] ... NAD
Nitride Forming Element [*Metal treating*] ... NFE
Nitro-(amino)butyric Acid ... NABA
No-Adjust Car Building Process [*Ford Motor Co.*] [*Automotive engineering*] ... NACBP
No Arrival Report [*Aviation*] (FAAC) ... NORIV
No-Dig International [*A publication*] ... NDI
No Field Lubrication (PDAA) ... NFL
No Frills Fund ... NFF
No Operating Zone (DA) ... NOZ
No Pay Due [*Military*] (ADDR) ... NPD
No Pilot Balloon Observation Due to Snow [*Meteorology*] (FAAC) ... PISO
No Printer Listed (NTCM) ... NP
No Publisher Listed (NTCM) ... NP
No Reply Heard [*ICAO designator*] (FAAC) ... NRH
No Significant Cloud [*Meteorology*] (FAAC) ... NSC
No Sound [*Script notation*] (NTCM) ... NS
No Traffic Reported [*Air Traffic Control*] (FAAC) ... NTC
Noah (ABBR) ... NO
Nobelair [*Turkey*] [*ICAO designator*] (FAAC) ... NAD
Nobility (ABBR) ... NOB
Nobility (ABBR) ... NOBT
Noble (ABBR) ... NOB
Nobleman (ABBR) ... NOBMN
Nobler (ABBR) ... NOBR
Noblest (ABBR) ... NOBST
Noblewomen (ABBR) ... NOBWN
Nobly (ABBR) ... NOBY
Node Location Code (PDAA) ... NLC
Noise (ABBR) ... NSE
Noise Amplitude Distribution Measuring Equipment (PDAA) ... NADME
Noise Diotic, Signal Monaural (PDAA) ... NOSM
Noise-Equivalent Charge (PDAA) ... NEC
Noise-Equivalent Temperature Difference [*Thermography*] ... NETD
Noise Exposure Computer Integrator (PDAA) ... NECI
Noise-Induced Permanent Hearing Loss (PDAA) ... NIPHL
Noise Isolation Class (PDAA) ... NIC
Noise Nuisance Index (PDAA) ... NNI
Noise and Number Exposure (PDAA) ... NNE
Noise Power Spectra [*Spectrometry*] ... NPS
Noise Preferential Route [*Aviation*] (DA) ... NPR
Noise, Shock, and Vibration (PDAA) ... NSV
Noise, Spikes, and Transients (PDAA) ... NST
Noise Supressor [*Radio*] (NTCM) ... NS
Noiseless (ABBR) ... NSELS
Noiseless Camera (NTCM) ... NC
Noisily (ABBR) ... NSLY
Noisiness (ABBR) ... NSENS
Noisy (ABBR) ... NSY
Nolisair International, Inc. [*Canada*] [*ICAO designator*] (FAAC) ... NXA
Nomenclature for Imports and Exports [*European Community*] (PDAA) ... NIMEX
Nominal Stress Approach (PDAA) ... NSA
Nominalism (ABBR) ... NOMLM
Nominalist (ABBR) ... NOMLT
Nominally (ABBR) ... NOMLY
Nominated (ABBR) ... NOMD
Nominated Air Traffic Service Unit (DA) ... NATSU
Nominating (ABBR) ... NOMG
Nominative (ABBR) ... NOMV
Nominator (ABBR) ... NOMR
Nominee (ABBR) ... NOMEE
Non-Adherent Peritoneal Cell (PDAA) ... NAPC

Non-Ammonia-Nitrogen (PDAA) .... NAN
Non-Asbestos Organic [*Friction materials*] .... NAO
Non-Attached [*European political movement*] (ECON) .... NA
Non-Collimated Source (PDAA) .... NCS
Non-Custodial Parent .... NCP
Non-Destructive Assay Technique [*Military*] (PDAA) .... NDAT
Non-Destructive Testing Information Center [*Army Materials and Mechanics Research Center*] (PDAA) .... NDTIAC
Non-Deterministic Incomplete Sequential Machine (PDAA) .... NISM
Non-Directional Mud-and-Snow (PDAA) .... NDMS
Non Domestic Substances List [*Canada*] .... NDSL
Non-Electronic Part Data Collection (PDAA) .... NEDCO
Non-English-Speaking Country .... NESC
Non-Erasing Deterministic Stack Automation (PDAA) .... NEDSA
Non-Essential Amino Acid N [*Biochemistry*] (PDAA) .... NEAAN
Non-Extraction Steam Rate (PDAA) .... NXSR
Non-Firing Test [*Military*] .... NFT
Non-Government Non-Catholic [*School*] .... NGNC
Non-Injurious Free-on-Board .... NIFOB
Non-Instrument Runway [*Aviation*] (DA) .... NINST
Non-Linear Analysis Program (PDAA) .... NOLAP
Non-Linear Charge Storage Element (PDAA) .... NLCSE
Non-Linear Ferromagnetic Resonance (PDAA) .... NFMR
Non-Linear Material Effect (PDAA) .... NLME
Non-Metric Multidimensional Scaling (PDAA) .... NMS
Non-Noise Certificated Aircraft (DA) .... NNC
Non-Nuclear Lance Missile .... NNL
Non-Nuclear Munitions Safety Board .... NMMSB
Non-Nucleoside Reverse Transcriptase Inhibitor [*Biochemistry*] .... NNRTI
Non-Precision Approach Runway [*Aviation*] (DA) .... NONP
Non-Pressure Thermit Welding (PDAA) .... NTW
Non-Productive Standard Minute (PDAA) .... NPSM
Non-Profit Distributing Organization (PDAA) .... NPDO
Non-Reciprocal Impedance Converter (PDAA) .... NRIC
Non-Reciprocal Junction (PDAA) .... NRJ
Non-Redundant Pinhole Array (PDAA) .... NRPA
Non-Resetting Data Reconstruction (PDAA) .... NRDR
Non-Resetting Data Reconstruction with Continuous Feedback (PDAA) .... NRDR-CF
Non-Resetting Data Reconstruction with Discrete Feedback (PDAA) .... NRDR-DF
Non-Selective Catalyst Reduction [*Diesel engine emissions*] .... NCR
Non-Standard FORTRAN [*Computer science*] (PDAA) .... NSFORT
Non-Statutory Body .... NSB
Non-Sterling Area (PDAA) .... NSA
Non-Syncytium-Inducing [*Medicine*] .... NSI
Non-Tactical Peripheral Equipment [*Military*] .... NTPE
Non-Tactical Tape [*Military*] .... NTT
Non-Tactical Training Equipment [*Military*] .... NTTE
Non-Transposed Loop Sensor (PDAA) .... NTLS
Non-urea Adducting Fatty Acid [*Food science*] .... NAF
Non-Vacuum Electron Beam Welding (PDAA) .... NVEBW
Noncommercial Education [*FCC*] (NTCM) .... NCE
Noncommercial Spot Announcement [*Public service announcement*] (NTCM) .... NCSA
Noncumulative (ABBR) .... NON-CM
Nondeterministic Time-Variant Automation (PDAA) .... NTVA
Nondirectional Beacon .... NBD
Nonentity (ABBR) .... NONTT
Nonfiction (NTCM) .... NF
Nonlinear Quantization [*Telecommunications*] (NTCM) .... NLQ
Nonlinear Transient Fuel Film Compsensation [*Automotive fuel system*] .... NTFC
Nonmetallic (ABBR) .... NMTLK
Nonparticipating (ABBR) .... NONPAR
Nonpartisan (ABBR) .... NPRTSN
Nonpartisanship (ABBR) .... NPRTSNSP
Nonperforated (ABBR) .... NONPERF
Nonphased Color [*Television signals*] (NTCM) .... NPC
Nonplus (ABBR) .... NPLS
Nonplused (ABBR) .... NPLSD
Nonprofit (ABBR) .... NPRFT
Nonprofit International Consortium for Eiffel (EA) .... NICE
Nonprogrammer Language [*Computer science*] (PDAA) .... NL
Nonresidence (ABBR) .... NRSDNC
Nonresident (ABBR) .... NRSDNT
Nonrestrictive (ABBR) .... NRSTCTV
Nonscheduled (ABBR) .... NONSKED
Nonsectarian (ABBR) .... NSCTRN
Nonsense (ABBR) .... NSNS
Nonsensical (ABBR) .... NSNCL
Nonsensically (ABBR) .... NSNSCLY
Nonslip (ABBR) .... NS
Nonstandard Part Approval Request .... NSPR
Nonsupport (ABBR) .... NSPRT
Nontactical [*Military*] .... N
Nonvolatile Charge-Addressed Memory [*Computer science*] (PDAA) .... NOVCAM
Nonvolatile Semiconductor Memory Device (PDAA) .... NVSMD
Nonwireline Multiple-Access Communications Exchange System (PDAA) .... NMAX
Noosa Air Sunstate Airlines [*Australia*] [*ICAO designator*] (FAAC) .... SSQ
Nora-2000 [*Bulgaria*] [*ICAO designator*] (FAAC) .... ANE

Norcanair [*Canada*] [*ICAO designator*] (FAAC) .... NKA
Nord-Sud [*Benin*] [*ICAO designator*] (FAAC) .... NSB
Nordeste, Linhas Aereas Regionais SA [*Brazil*] [*ICAO designator*] (FAAC) .... NES
Nordic East International Aircraft, AB [*Sweden*] [*ICAO designator*] (FAAC) .... ELN
Norfolk Island Airlines [*Australia*] [*ICAO designator*] (FAAC) .... NIA
Norlink Air Ltd. [*British*] [*ICAO designator*] (FAAC) .... NLK
Normal Administrative Practice .... NAP
Normal Coordinate Analysis .... NCA
Normal Frequency [*Telecommunications*] (NTCM) .... NF
Normal Incidence Pyrheliometer (PDAA) .... NIP
Normal Incidence Spectrometer (PDAA) .... NIS
Normal Light Perception [*Physiology*] (MAH) .... NLP
Normalcy (ABBR) .... NRMLC
Normality (ABBR) .... NRMLT
Normalization (ABBR) .... NRMLZN
Normalize (ABBR) .... NRMLZ
Normalized (ABBR) .... NRMLZD
Normalized Variance (PDAA) .... NVAR
Normalizer (ABBR) .... NRMLZR
Normalizing (ABBR) .... NRMLZG
Normally (ABBR) .... NRMLY
Normative (ABBR) .... NRMV
Normatively (ABBR) .... NRMVY
Norontair [*Canada*] [*ICAO designator*] (FAAC) .... NOA
Norsk Luftambulanse AS [*Norway*] [*ICAO designator*] (FAAC) .... DOC
Norskair [*Norway*] [*ICAO designator*] (FAAC) .... NIR
Nort Jet [*Spain*] [*ICAO designator*] (FAAC) .... ENJ
North (ABBR) .... NRTH
North American Airlines, Inc. [*ICAO designator*] (FAAC) .... NAO
North American Airlines, Inc. [*Canada*] [*ICAO designator*] (FAAC) .... NTM
North American Broadcast Teletext Standard (NTCM) .... NABTS
North American Commission on the Environment .... NACE
North American Council for Muslim Women (EA) .... NACMW
North American Deep Drawing Research Group [*Automotive metal stampings*] .... NADDRG
North American Defense Industrial Base Organization .... NADIBO
North American English Ford Registry (EA) .... NAEFR
North American Lighting [*Automotive industry supplier*] .... NAL
North American Research Group on Management (PDAA) .... NARGOM
North American Trap Collector Association (EA) .... NATCA
North Atlantic Air, Inc. [*ICAO designator*] (FAAC) .... NAT
North Atlantic Cooperation Council .... NACC
North Atlantic Deepwater Oil Terminal (PDAA) .... NADOT
North Atlantic Fisheries Research Center (PDAA) .... NAFRC
North Atlantic Treaty Organization Airborne Early Warning Program .... NATO AEW
North Atlantic Treaty Organization Military Committee .... NATO MC
North British Airlines Ltd. [*ICAO designator*] (FAAC) .... NBN
North Caribou Flying Service Ltd. [*Canada*] [*ICAO designator*] (FAAC) .... NCB
North Coast Air Services Ltd. [*Canada*] [*ICAO designator*] (FAAC) .... NCC
North Coast Aviation [*ICAO designator*] (FAAC) .... AOH
North East Bolivian Airways [*ICAO designator*] (FAAC) .... NBA
North East Bolivian Airways [*ICAO designator*] (FAAC) .... NEBA
North-East Cargo Airlines [*Russian Federation*] [*ICAO designator*] .... MGD
North-Eastbound [*Aviation*] (FAAC) .... NEB
North Flying AS [*Denmark*] [*ICAO designator*] (FAAC) .... NFA
North Pacific [*Aviation*] (FAAC) .... NOPAC
North Shore Aero Club, Inc. [*New Zealand*] [*ICAO designator*] (FAAC) .... SHO
North-South Station-Keeping (PDAA) .... NSSK
North West Airline [*Australia*] [*ICAO designator*] (FAAC) .... NWW
North West Geomatics Ltd. [*Canada*] [*ICAO designator*] (FAAC) .... PTO
Northair Aviation Ltd. [*British*] [*ICAO designator*] (FAAC) .... NTL
Northaire Freight Lines Ltd. [*ICAO designator*] (FAAC) .... NFL
Northcoast Executive Airlines [*ICAO designator*] (FAAC) .... NCE
Northeast Aviation Services Ltd. [*British*] [*ICAO designator*] (FAAC) .... NAS
Northeast Express Regional Airlines, Inc. [*ICAO designator*] (FAAC) .... NEE
Northeast Management, Inc. [*ICAO designator*] (FAAC) .... DSH
Northeastern Spoon Collectors Guild (EA) .... NSCG
Northerly (ABBR) .... NORTH
Northern (ABBR) .... NO
Northern (ABBR) .... NORTH
Northern Air Cargo, Inc. [*ICAO designator*] (FAAC) .... NAC
Northern Air Service, Inc. [*ICAO designator*] (FAAC) .... NTX
Northern Airlines [*British*] [*ICAO designator*] (FAAC) .... TLR
Northern Airways, Inc. [*ICAO designator*] (FAAC) .... NDA
Northern Commuter Airlines [*New Zealand*] [*ICAO designator*] (FAAC) .... NLE
Northern Executive Aviation Ltd. [*British*] [*ICAO designator*] (FAAC) .... NEX
Northern Extratropical Land [*Geography*] .... NEL
Northern Great Plains Resource Program [*Dept. of the Interior, Dept. of Agriculture and Environmental Protection Agency*] (PDAA) .... NGPRP
Northern Illinois Commuter [*ICAO designator*] (FAAC) .... NIC
Northern Thunderbird Air Ltd. [*Canada*] [*ICAO designator*] (FAAC) .... NTA
Northland Aviation, Inc. [*ICAO designator*] (FAAC) .... KOE
Northside Aviation Ltd. [*British*] [*ICAO designator*] (FAAC) .... NSD
Northstar Aviation, Inc. [*ICAO designator*] (FAAC) .... NSS

Northumberland (ABBR) .... NORTHM
Northward (ABBR) .... NOWD
Northway Aviation Ltd. [*Canada*] [*ICAO designator*] (FAAC) .... NAL
Northwest Air Services Ltd. [*Nigeria*] [*ICAO designator*] (FAAC) .... NWD
Northwest Airlines, Inc. [*ICAO designator*] (FAAC) .... NWA
Northwest Region Spinners Association (EA) .... NwRSA
Northwest Territorial Airways [*Canada*] [*ICAO designator*] (FAAC) .... NWT
Northwestbound [*ICAO designator*] (FAAC) .... NWB
Northwestern Air Lease Ltd. [*Canada*] [*ICAO designator*] (FAAC) .... PLR
Northwinds Northern Ltd. [*Canada*] [*ICAO designator*] (FAAC) .... NWN
Nortland Air Manitoba [*Canada*] [*ICAO designator*] (FAAC) .... NAM
Norway Airlines [*ICAO designator*] (FAAC) .... NOS
Norwegian (ABBR) .... NRW
Nosed (ABBR) .... NOSD
Nosed One Edge [*Lumber*] (DAC) N1E
Nosed Two Edges [*Lumber*] (DAC) N2E
Nosier (ABBR) .... NSIR
Nosiness (ABBR) .... NOSINS
Nosing (ABBR) .... NOS
Nosing (ABBR) .... NOSG
Nostalgia (ABBR) .... NSTLG
Nostalgic (ABBR) .... NSTLGC
Not an A-List Writer [*Screenwriter's lexicon*] .... NALW
Not Allowed .... NA
Not Before [*ICAO designator*] (FAAC) .... NBFR
Not Emanating Main Office [*Remote broadcast*] (NTCM) .... NEMO
Not Employed .... NE
Not Engaged .... NE
Not Entailing Excessive Cost [*Environmental technology*] .... NEEC
Not Greater Than .... NGT
Not Releasable to Foreign Nationals .... NORFORM
Not Suitable .... NS
Not Under the Act .... NUA
Not Used .... NU
Not Yet Operating (DA) .... NYO
Not Yet Specified .... NYS
Notable (ABBR) .... NTAB
Notable (ABBR) .... NTB
Notably (ABBR) .... NTABY
Notably (ABBR) .... NTBY
NOTAMS International, Inc. [*ICAO designator*] (FAAC) .... XNT
Notary (ABBR) .... NTARY
Notation (ABBR) .... NTATN
Notational (ABBR) .... NTATNL
Notch-Bend (PDAA) .... NB
Notebook (ABBR) .... NTBK
Notice of Proposed Amendment (DA) .... NPA
Noticeable (ABBR) .... NTCB
Noticeably (ABBR) .... NTCBY
Noticed (ABBR) .... NTCD
Notices to Airmen Publication [*A publication*] (FAAC) .... NTAP
Noticing (ABBR) .... NTCG
Notion (ABBR) .... NOTN
Nourish (ABBR) .... NOUR
Nourish (ABBR) .... NRSH
Nourished (ABBR) .... NOURD
Nourished (ABBR) .... NRSHD
Nourishing (ABBR) .... NOURG
Nourishing (ABBR) .... NRSHG
Nourishment (ABBR) .... NOURT
Nourishment (ABBR) .... NRSHNT
Novair-Aviacao Geral SA [*Portugal*] [*ICAO designator*] (FAAC) .... NOP
Novelist (ABBR) .... NOV
Novelist (ABBR) .... NOVST
Novelty (ABBR) .... NOVT
Novice (ABBR) .... NOVC
Novye Torit [*Newly Flattened*] [*KGB term for newly recruited agent
   abroad*] .... NOVATOR
Noxious (ABBR) .... NOX
Noxiously (ABBR) .... NOXY
Nuance (ABBR) .... NNC
Nuclear Activation Analysis (PDAA) .... NAA
Nuclear Age Resource Center (EA) .... NARC
Nuclear Electric Resonance (PDAA) .... NER
Nuclear Energy Information Service [*An association*] (EA) .... NEIS
Nuclear Fuel Cost (PDAA) .... NUFUCO
Nuclear Magnetic Imaging .... NMI
Nuclear Magnetic Relaxation Dispension [*Physics*] .... NMRD
Nuclear Magnetism Log (PDAA) .... NML
Nuclear Materials Accounting and Control .... NMAC
Nuclear Orbit Transfer Stage (PDAA) .... NOTS
Nuclear Power Advisory Board (PDAA) .... NPAB
Nuclear Power Plant Training Simulator (PDAA) .... NPPTS
Nuclear-Powered Container Ship (PDAA) .... NCS
Nuclear-Powered Merchant Ship (PDAA) .... NMS
Nuclear Safety Standard (PDAA) .... NUSS
Nuclear Science Symposium (PDAA) .... NSS
Nuclear Sediment Density Meter (PDAA) .... NSDM
Nuclear Submarine Control Trainer (PDAA) .... NUSCOT
Nuclear Submarine Maneuvering Room Training Simulator
   (PDAA) .... NSMRTS
Nuclear Suppliers' Group [*Australia*] (ECON) .... NSG
Nuclear Warning Message [*Military*] (ADDR) .... NUCWARN

Nuclear Weapons Control .... NWC
Nuclear Weapons Emergency Destruct System [*Navy*] (ANA) .... NUWEDS
Nuclease-Hypersensitive Element [*Biochemistry*] .... NHE
Nucleotide-Excision Repair .... NER
Nuisance (ABBR) .... NSNCE
Null Filter Mobile RADAR (PDAA) .... NFMRAD
Nulla per Os Hora Somni [*Nothing by Mouth at Bedtime*] [*Latin*]
   [*Pharmacy*] (MAH) .... NPO/HS
Number Allocation and Inspection Module (PDAA) .... NAIM
Number of Elements Loaded [*Army*] .... NELTS
Number of Engine Revolutions per Minute per Vehicle Miles per
   Hour [*Automotive engineering*] .... N/V
Number of Remaining Words .... NRW
Number of Simultaneous Engagements [*Military*] .... NSE
Number of Video Samples .... NVS
Numeric Meta Language Processing System (PDAA) .... NUMEPS
Numerical Control Language [*Computer science*] (PDAA) .... NUCOL
Numerical Oceanographic Prediction (PDAA) .... NOP
Numerical Surveying Technique (PDAA) .... NST
Numerical and Textile Information System (PDAA) .... NUTIS
Numismatic (ABBR) .... NMSMK
Numismaticist (ABBR) .... NMSMTST
Nuna Air AS [*Denmark*] [*ICAO designator*] (FAAC) .... NUA
Nunasi-Central Airlines Ltd. [*Canada*] [*ICAO designator*] (FAAC) .... NUN
Nunnery (ABBR) .... NNRY
Nuptial (ABBR) .... NPTL
[*John*] Nurminen OY [*Finland*] [*ICAO designator*] (FAAC) .... JNA
Nurse (ABBR) .... NRS
Nurse (ABBR) .... NRSE
Nurse Practitioner .... NP
Nursed (ABBR) .... NRSD
Nursed (ABBR) .... NRSED
Nursemaid (ABBR) .... NRSEMD
Nursing (ABBR) .... NRSEG
Nursing the Environment .... NTE
Nurture (ABBR) .... NRTR
Nurture-Outreach-Witness [*Religion*] .... NOW
Nurtured (ABBR) .... NRTRD
Nurturing (ABBR) .... NRTRG
Nutcracker (ABBR) .... NTCKR
Nutrient Data Table .... NUTTAB
Nutrition Labeling Education Act .... NLEA
NV Luchtvaartmaatschappij Twente [*Netherlands*] [*ICAO
   designator*] (FAAC) .... LTW
Nyge Aero AB [*Sweden*] [*ICAO designator*] (FAAC) .... NYG
NZ Warbirds Association, Inc. [*New Zealand*] [*ICAO designator*]
   (FAAC) .... WAR

O

Oak Ridge Data Evaluation and Analysis Language [*Department of Energy*] (PDAA) .... ORDEAL
Oasis International Airlines [*Spain*] [*ICAO designator*] (FAAC) .... AAN
Obidiah [*Old Testament*] .... OB
Object Identifier [*Computer science*] .... OID
Oblate Radial (PDAA) .... OBRAD
Oblate Spheroid (PDAA) .... OSPRDS
Obscene [*Legal term*] .... Obs
Obscurant .... OBS
Observation/Losing [*Army*] (ADDR) .... O/L
Observed Effect Concentration [*Environmental science*] (ERG) .... OEC
Observer's Thermal Imaging System (PDAA) .... OTIS
Obstacle Assessment Surface [*Aviation*] (DA) .... OAS
Obstacle Breaching Vehicle [*Military*] .... OBV
Obstacle Clearance (PDAA) .... OC
Obstacle Clearance Altitude [*Aviation*] (DA) .... OCA
Obstacle Clearance Height [*Aviation*] (FAAC) .... OCH
Obstacle Identification Surface [*Aviation*] (DA) .... OIS
Obstacle Light [*Aviation*] (DA) .... Obs
Occasional Paper .... OP
Occlude (DA) .... OCI
Occluded Corrosion Cell (PDAA) .... OCC
Occupational Back Pain .... OBP
Occupational Health Hazard Assessment .... OHHA
Occupational Health Monitoring and Evaluation System (PDAA) .... OHMES
Occupational Health and Safety .... OHAS
Occupational Health and Safety Technologist .... OHST
Occupational Psychologist .... OP
Occupational Superannuation Standard .... OSS
Ocean Color Scanner (PDAA) .... OCS
Ocean Sampling and Environmental Analysis System (PDAA) .... OSEAS
Ocean and Science Engineering Inc. .... OSE
Oceanair-Transportes Aeroes Regional SA [*Portugal*] [*ICAO designator*] (FAAC) .... OCN
Oceanic Boundary Layer .... OBL
Oceanic Control Area [*Aviation*] (DA) .... OCTA
Oceanic Navigation Research Society (EA) .... ONRS
Oceanic Navigational Error Report [*Aviation*] (FAAC) .... ONER
Octadecyltrichlorosilane [*Organic chemistry*] .... OTS
Octahedral Molecular Sieve [*Inorganic chemistry*] .... OMS
Octane Blending Value (PDAA) .... OBV
Octanol [*Organic chemistry*] .... OCT
Ocurrence of Reinforcing Information (PDAA) .... ORI
Odiham FTU [*British*] [*ICAO designator*] (FAAC) .... ODM
Odor Detection Threshold (PDAA) .... ODT
Odyssey International [*Canada*] [*ICAO designator*] (FAAC) .... ODY
Oerlikon-Buehrle [*Switzerland*] .... O-B
Off-Load Control Officer [*Navy*] (ANA) .... OCO
Off-Load Preparation Party [*Navy*] (ANA) .... OPP
Off Load Route [*Aviation*] (DA) .... OLR
Off-Site Surveillance Data [*Military*] .... OSSD
Offensive Counterair [*Army*] (ADDR) .... OCA
Office of Air, Noise, and Radiation [*Environmental Protection Agency*] (ERG) .... OANR
Office of Alcoholism and Drug Abuse Prevention [*Department of Health and Human Services*] .... OADAP
Office of the Assistant Secretary of Defense (Public Affairs) (NTCM) .... OASD(PA)
Office of Cable Signal Theft [*National Cable Television Association*] (NTCM) .... OCST
Office of Combat Indentification Technology [*Army*] .... OCRIT
Office of the Deputy Under Secretary of Defense (Environmental Security) [*DoD*] (RDA) .... ODUSD(ES)
Office of the Director, Telecommunications, and Command and Control Systems [*DoD*] (PDAA) .... ODTACCS
Office of Emergency Communications [*FCC*] (NTCM) .... OEC
Office Federal de l'Aviation Civile [*Sweden*] [*ICAO designator*] (FAAC) .... FOC
Office of Legal Aid Administration .... OLAA
Office of Legal Aid and Family Services .... OLAFS
Office of National Assessments [*Australia*] .... ONA
Office of Producer Affairs [*Federal Telecommunications Commission*] .... OPA
Office de Radiodiffusion-Television Francaise [*National Broadcasting Organization*] [*France*] (NTCM) .... ORTF
Office of the Registrar of Restrictive Trading Agreements (PDAA) .... ORRTA
Office of the Secretary of Defense Productivity Investment Funding .... OS-PIF
Office of the Under Secretary of Defense for Acquisition .... OUSDA
Office of Water Enforcement [*Environmental Protection Agency*] (ERG) .... OWE
Office of Water and Waste Management (ERG) .... OWWM
Officer in Tactical Command Information Exchange Subsystem [*Navy*] (ANA) .... OTCIXS
Official Airline Guide, Inc. [*ICAO designator*] (FAAC) .... OAG
Official Board of Ballroom Dancing [*British*] (BI) .... OB
Official Development Finance .... ODF
Official Languages Act [*Canada*] .... OLA
Officine Meccaniche [*Italian auto manufacturer*] .... OM
Offline Orthophoto Printer [*Computer science*] (PDAA) .... OOP
Offshore Buoy-Observing Equipment (PDAA) .... OBOE
Offshore Drilling and Production Exhibition (PDAA) .... ODPEX
Offshore Logistics, Inc. [*ICAO designator*] (FAAC) .... ALG
Offshore Mechanics and Polar Engineering Council .... OMPEC
Offshore Racing Council .... ORC
Offshore Survival Craft Emergency Radiotelephone [*Telecommunications*] (PDAA) .... OSCER
Ogooue Air Cargo [*Gabon*] [*ICAO designator*] (FAAC) .... GBO
OH Aviationa [*France*] [*ICAO designator*] (FAAC) .... OHA
Oh, By the Way [*Computer hacker terminology*] (NHD) .... OBTW
Ohio Academy of Science (PDAA) .... OAS
Ohio Aerospace Institute .... OAI
Oil Appliance Manufacturers' Association [*British*] (BI) .... OAMA
Oil Companies' Materials Association [*British*] (BI) .... OCMA
Oil Extended Styrene Butadiene Rubber (PDAA) .... OESBR
Oil Extended Synthetic Rubber (PDAA) .... OESR
Oil Spillage Analytical and Identification Service [*Laboratory of the Government Chemist*] (PDAA) .... OSAIS
Oilskin Manufacturers' Association of Great Britain Ltd. (BI) .... OMA
Okada Airlines Ltd. [*Nigeria*] [*ICAO designator*] (FAAC) .... OKJ
Oklahoma University Health Sciences Center .... OUHSC
Old Lesbians Organizing for Change [*An association*] (EA) .... OLOC
Old Style [*Printing*] (NTCM) .... OS
Oldtime Radio Collectors and Traders Society (EA) .... ORCATS
Olive Green [*Army*] (ADDR) .... OG
[*Fred*] **Olsen Flyselskap AS** [*Norway*] [*ICAO designator*] (FAAC) .... FOF
Olympic Airways SA [*Greece*] [*ICAO designator*] (FAAC) .... OAL
Olympic Aviation SA [*Greece*] [*ICAO designator*] (FAAC) .... OLY
Olympic Job Opportunities Program .... OJOP
Olympic Project for Human Rights .... OPHR
Oman [*Aircraft nationality and registration mark*] (FAAC) A40
Oman Aviation Services Co. [*ICAO designator*] (FAAC) .... OAS
Oman Royal Flight [*ICAO designator*] (FAAC) .... ORF
Omega Navigation (PDAA) .... ON
Omni-Aviacao e Tecnologia Lda. [*Portugal*] [*ICAO designator*] (FAAC) .... OAV
Omnidirectional Point Source (PDAA) .... OPS
Omniflys SA de CV [*Mexico*] [*ICAO designator*] (FAAC) .... OMF
On Air Ltd. [*Canada*] [*ICAO designator*] (FAAC) .... ORL
On Air Test (NTCM) .... OAT
On-Axis Pointing (PDAA) .... OAP
On-Board Gunnery Simulator (PDAA) .... OBGS
On Grade (DAC) .... OG
On the Job Training .... OTJT
On-Line Benefits Processing .... OBP
On the Shoulders of Giants [*Literature*] .... OTSOG
On-Site Inspection Agency [*DoD*] [*ICAO designator*] (FAAC) .... OPS
On-Time Marker [*Computer science*] .... OTM
Once-Run Distillate (PDAA) .... ORD
Oncostatin [*Antibiotic*] .... OSM
One-Man Atmospheric Submersible (PDAA) .... OMAS
One Player Median Competitive (PDAA) .... OPMC
One-Time Carbon [*Paper*] (PDAA) .... OTC
Online Data Compression System (PDAA) .... ODCS
Online Data Interchange (DA) .... OLDI
Online Data Processor (PDAA) .... OLDAP
Online Enquiry [*System*] .... OLE

Online Filing [*Computer science*] (PDAA) ... OLF
Online Information ... OLI
Online Instrumentation via Energetic Radioisotopes [*Computer science*] (PDAA) ... OLIVER
Online Manufacturing and Control System [*Computer science*] (PDAA) ... OMACS
Online Object Patching System [*Computer science*] (PDAA) ... OOPS
Online Patient Billing and Accounts Receivable System [*Computer science*] (PDAA) ... OL/PBAR
Online Search Information Retrieval Information Storage [*Computer science*] (PDAA) ... OSIRIS
Online System Availability and Service Simulation [*Computer science*] (PDAA) ... OLSASS
Online Test Executive Program [*Computer science*] (PDAA) ... OLTE
Online Version Storage [*Computer science*] (PDAA) ... OVS
Online X-ray Evaluation over Video-Display Including Documentation (PDAA) ... ORVID
Ontario Express Ltd. [*Canada*] [*ICAO designator*] (FAAC) ... OEL
Ontario Hydroelectric [*Canada*] ... OH
Onur Hava Tasimacilik AWMS [*Turkey*] [*ICAO designator*] (FAAC) ... OHY
Opal Air Pty Ltd. [*Australia*] [*ICAO designator*] (FAAC) ... OPA
Open Circuit Potential (PDAA) ... OCP
Open Computing Facility ... OCF
Open-Cycle Gas Turbine (PDAA) ... OCGT
Open Database Server [*Computer science*] ... ODS
Open Government Document (PDAA) ... OGD
Open-Loop Feedback Optimal (PDAA) ... OLFO
Open Network Computing Plus [*Computer science*] (PCM) ... ONC+
Open Promoter Complex [*Genetics*] ... OPC
Open Reciprocating Brayton Engine (PDAA) ... ORBE
Operating Level Days ... OLD
Operating and Support Cost Reduction [*Army*] ... OSCR
Operation Hours (DA) ... Op Hrs
Operation Planning and Execution System for Railway Unified Network (PDAA) ... OPERUN
Operational Analysis Code Package (PDAA) ... OACP
Operational Assignment (DA) ... OPAS
Operational Aviation Services - Australia [*ICAO designator*] (FAAC) ... OAX
Operational Documentation [*Military*] ... OPDOC
Operational Flight Information Service [*ICAO*] (DA) ... OFIS
Operational Hydromet Data Management System (PDAA) ... OHDMS
Operational Linescan System [*Navy*] (ANA) ... OLS
Operational Mission Summary [*Army*] ... OMS
Operational Nuclear Planning Group [*Military*] ... ONPG
Operational Performance Standard [*Aviation*] (DA) ... OPS
Operational Planning Identification File [*Military*] ... OPDIF
Operational Preference (DA) ... OPR
Operational Readiness-Oriented Supply System [*Army*] (PDAA) ... OROSS
Operational Readiness Platform [*Aviation*] (DA) ... ORP
Operational Research in Electrical Power Systems (PDAA) ... OREPS
Operational Research and Systems Analysis (PDAA) ... ORASA
Operational Search Lower Bound [*RADAR*] ... OSLB
Operations Fixed Service [*Microwave service*] (NTCM) ... OFS
Operations for Military Assistance to the Community (PDAA) ... OPMAC
Operations in a Nuclear Environment [*DoD*] ... OPINE
Operations Panel [*ICAO*] (DA) ... OPSP
Operations Request [*Military*] ... OR
Operations Research and Development Management (PDAA) ... OPRAD
Operations Research Technical Assistance Group [*Army*] (PDAA) ... ORTAG
Operator System Program [*Manufacturing engineering*] [*Computer science*] ... OPS
Oppose Sortie [*Navy*] (ANA) ... OPOSTOR
Opposed Zone Reheating Furnace (PDAA) ... OZRF
Opposing Forces Vehicle [*Military*] ... OFV
Oppositely-Directed Travelling Wave (PDAA) ... ODTW
Optical Activity Detection ... OAD
Optical Character Recognition Engine (PDAA) ... OCHRE
Optical Coincidence Coordinate Indexing (PDAA) ... OCCI
Optical Electron Microscope (PDAA) ... OEM
Optical Grating Reflectance Evaluator (PDAA) ... OGRE
Optical Gravitational Lens Experiment [*Astronomy*] ... OGLE
Optical Gun Fire Director [*Military*] (PDAA) ... OFD
Optical Heterodyne Detection ... OHD
Optical Kerr Effect [*Birefringence induced in an electrical field*] ... OKE
Optical Klystron (PDAA) ... OK
Optical Link in the Atmosphere (PDAA) ... OLA
Optical Night Landing Approach System [*Aviation*] (PDAA) ... ONLAS
Optical-Optical Double Resonance Multiphonton Ionization [*Spectrocopy*] ... OODR-MPI
Optical Particle Counter (PDAA) ... OPC
Optical Path-Length Variation (PDAA) ... OPV
Optical Phase Distortion (PDAA) ... OPD
Optical Power Spectrum (PDAA) ... OPS
Optical Property of Orbiting Satellite [*NASA*] (PDAA) ... OPOS
Optical Quantum Amplifier (PDAA) ... OQA
Optical Readout Cherenkov Imaging Detector [*Computer science*] (PDAA) ... ORCID
Optical Satellite Communications ... OPSTACOM
Optical Storage Access Method [*Computer science*] (PDAA) ... OPSAM
Optical Telescope Technology Workshop [*NASA*] (PDAA) ... OTTW
Optical Tracking and Ranging Kit (PDAA) ... OPTRAK
Optically-Detected Nuclear Magnetic Resonance [*Spectroscopy*] ... ODNMR
Optically-Thin Thermal Bremsstrahlung [*Astrophysics*] ... OTTB
Optico-Electronic Device for Registering Coincidences (PDAA) ... OEDRC
Optimal Financial Decision Strategy (PDAA) ... OFDS
Optimal Pneumatic Systems Analysis (PDAA) ... OPSA
Optimal Terminal Descent (PDAA) ... OTD
Optimization of Systems for Data Processing and Transmission (PDAA) ... OSDPT
Optimized Test-Oriented Language [*Computer science*] (PDAA) ... OPTOL
Optimum Life Cycle Costing (PDAA) ... OLCC
Optimum Private Trunk Network Embodying Tandems (PDAA) ... OPTNET
Optimum Report Level Analysis [*Military*] ... ORLA
Optimum Resource Extraction (PDAA) ... ORE
Optimum Vehicle for Effective Reconnaissance [*Air Force*] (PDAA) ... OVER
Optional Character Reader [*Computer science*] (DA) ... OCR
Optioned [*Automotive advertising*] ... OPT'D
Orbi [*Former USSR*] [*ICAO designator*] (FAAC) ... DVU
Orbit Analysis ... OA
Orbital Antenna Farm (PDAA) ... OAF
Orbital Combustion Process (PDAA) ... OCP
Orbiter Data Reduction Center [*NASA*] ... ORDC
Orbiter Logistics Support Plan [*NASA*] ... OLSA
Orbiter (Operational) Downlink [*NASA*] ... OD
Orbiting Astronomical Explorer (PDAA) ... OAE
Orbiting Far and Extreme Ultraviolet Spectrometer [*Telescope*] ... ORFEUS
Orbiting Radio Beacon Ionosphere Satellite for Calibration [*NASA*] (PDAA) ... ORBIS CAL
Orbitor Avionics Simulator [*NASA*] ... OAS
Orchestral Employers' Association [*British*] (BI) ... OEA
Order Billing Inventory Technique (PDAA) ... ORBIT
Order of Engineers of Quebec [*Canada*] (PDAA) ... OEQ
Ordering as Required (PDAA) ... OAR
Ordnance Missile and Munitions Center and School [*Army*] ... OMMCS
Ordnance Shock Test [*Military*] ... OST
Organic Chemical, Plastic, and Synthetic Fiber ... OCPSF
Organic Rankine Cycle [*for power generation*] (PDAA) ... ORC
Organisation Value Analysis Chart (PDAA) ... OVAC
Organization Iberoamericaine de Television (NTCM) ... OIT
Organizational Analysis ... OA
Organizational and Operational Plan [*Army*] ... O & OP
Organizational Role Analysis (PDAA) ... ORA
Organizational Support Equipment [*Army*] ... OSE
Organized Organic Monolayer [*Organic chemistry*] ... OOM
Organo-Transition-Metal (PDAA) ... OTM
Organotin Compound [*Organic chemistry*] ... OTC
Orient Air Ltd. [*British*] [*ICAO designator*] (FAAC) ... ORI
Orient Airways [*Pakistan*] [*ICAO designator*] (FAAC) ... ORN
Oriental Airlines (Gambia) Ltd. [*ICAO designator*] (FAAC) ... ORG
Oriental Airlines Ltd. [*Nigeria*] [*ICAO designator*] (FAAC) ... OAC
Oriental Pearl Airways Ltd. [*British*] [*ICAO designator*] (FAAC) ... OJA
Original Action Record ... OAR
Original Online Module [*Computer science*] (PDAA) ... OOM
Original Paper Doll Artists Guild (EA) ... OPDAG
Oriol Avia [*Russian Federation*] [*ICAO designator*] (FAAC) ... OAU
Orion Air [*Bulgaria*] [*ICAO designator*] (FAAC) ... BOR
Orion Air, Inc. [*ICAO designator*] (FAAC) ... TAG
Orion SpA [*Italy*] [*ICAO designator*] (FAAC) ... MTT
Ormetoprim [*Potentiator for antibacterials*] [*Veterinary medicine*] ... OMP
Ortho Tolidine (PDAA) ... OT
Orthodox Job Enrichment (PDAA) ... OJE
Orwex [*Poland*] [*ICAO designator*] (FAAC) ... ORW
Oryx Aviation [*South Africa*] [*ICAO designator*] (FAAC) ... ORX
Oscillating-Analyzer Ellipsometer (PDAA) ... OAE
Oscillating-Compensator Oscillating-Analyzer Polarimeter (PDAA) ... OCOAP
Oscillator Single Gain Region (PDAA) ... OSGR
Oscillogram Scan and Recorder System (PDAA) ... OSCAR
OSHA [*Occupational Safety and Health Administration*] **Computerized Information System** [*Environmental science*] ... OCIS
Oshkosh Truck Corp. ... OTC
Osteogenesis Imperfecta [*Brittle bone disease*] ... OA
Osterogenic Protein ... OP
Osteryoung Square Wave Voltammogram [*Electrochemistry*] ... OSWV
Ostfriesische Lufttransport GmbH [*Germany*] [*ICAO designator*] (FAAC) ... OLT
Other Program (NTCM) ... O
Our Bodies Ourselves [*A publication*] ... OBOS
Our Message [*Aviation*] (FAAC) ... OMSG
Out of Controlled Airspace [*Aviation*] (FAAC) ... OCAS
Out for Maintenance [*Aviation*] (FAAC) ... OFM
Out of School Hours ... OOSH
Out of Stock (NTCM) ... OS
Outbound [*ICAO designator*] (FAAC) ... OUBD
Outdoor Advertising Total System (PDAA) ... OATS
Outer Air Battle [*Navy*] (ANA) ... OAB
Outer Fix Time [*Aviation*] (FAAC) ... OFXT
Outpatient Nonavailability Statement [*DoD*] ... ONAS
Output Status Register ... OSR
Outside Front Cover [*Publishing*] (NTCM) ... OFC
Outside School Hours Care ... OSHC
Oval-Headed Screw (DAC) ... OHS
Over-All Sound Pressure (PDAA) ... OASP
Over-Night Cargo Ltd. [*Nigeria*] [*ICAO designator*] (FAAC) ... OCL

Over-the-Nose Vision Line (PDAA) .... ONVL
Over-the-Shoulder Cinematography (NTCM).................................... OS
Over the Shoulder Shot [*Also, OS*] [*Cinematography*] (NTCM)................. X/S
Over-Voltage Factor (PDAA) .... OVF
Overall Manufacturers' Association of Great Britain (BI) .... OMA
Overall Power Watt Level (PDAA) .... OAPWL
Overall Systems Combat Operability Test [*Navy*] (ANA) .... OSCOT
Overburden Drill (PDAA) .... OD
Overhead Trickle Purification (PDAA) .... OTP
Overheating Temperature (PDAA) .... OHT
Overrun Standard Approach Lighting System [*Aviation*] (DA)............. OVRN
Overrunning (DA)... OVRNG
Overseas [*Aviation*] (FAAC)... OVSEA
Overseas Custody (Child Removal) .... OCCR
Overseas Deployment Data [*Military*] .... ODD
Overseas Economic Intelligence Committee [*Military*] .... OEIC
Overseas Media Visitor.. OMV
Overseas National Airways [*Belgium*] [*ICAO designator*] (FAAC)............ ONA
Overseas Student Health Coverage .... OSHC
Oversight of Resources and Capability for Logistics Effectiveness
    (PDAA)... ORACLE
Overtaken by Events [*Military*] .... OTBE
Ovonic Memory Switch (PDAA) .... OMS
Owens Group Ltd. [*New Zealand*] [*ICAO designator*] (FAAC)................ OWN
Own-the-Night [*Technology*] [*Army*] (INF)...................................... OTN
Owners Abroad Aviation Ltd. [*British*] [*ICAO designator*] (FAAC) .... OAB
Ownership Accountability of Selected Secondary Items Stocked .... OASIS
Oxidant [*Photochemical*] (ERG) .... OX
Oxidation-Induced Stacking Fault (PDAA)... OSF
Oxidative Pentose Phosphate (PDAA) .... OPP
Oxide-Aligned Transistor [*Electronics*] (PDAA) .... OAT
Oxley Aviation [*Australia*] [*ICAO designator*] (FAAC).......................... OAA
Oxygen Adsorption, Out-gassing, and Chemical Reduction (PDAA)....... OAOR
Oxygen-Dope Polysilicon (PDAA) .... O-POS
Oxygen Evolution Reaction (PDAA)... OER
Oxygen-Evolving Complex [*Photosynthesis*]...................................... OEC
Oxyhaemoglobin Dissociation Curve (PDAA)...................................... ODC
Ozone-Forming Potential-Maximum Incremental Reactivity [*Exhaust
    emissions*] [*Automotive engineering*]... OFP-MIR
Ozone Transport Commission [*State environmental agencies*]...................... OTC

P

P-Methylstyrene [*Plastics*] ... PMS
Paced Sequential Memory Task (PDAA) ... PSMT
Pacific Air Boats Ltd. [*Canada*] [*ICAO designator*] (FAAC) ... PAB
Pacific Air Charter, Inc. [*ICAO designator*] (FAAC) ... PRC
Pacific Air Express [*ICAO designator*] (FAAC) ... PCF
Pacific Airlines Holding Co. [*Vietnam*] [*ICAO designator*] (FAAC) ... PIC
Pacific Alaska Airlines [*ICAO designator*] (FAAC) ... PAK
Pacific-Antarctic Ridge [*Geology*] ... PAR
Pacific Coast Airlines [*ICAO designator*] (FAAC) ... PQA
Pacific Coastal Airline [*Canada*] [*ICAO designator*] (FAAC) ... PCO
Pacific East Asia Cargo Airline, Inc. [*Philippines*] [*ICAO designator*] (FAAC) ... PEC
Pacific Express Holdings Ltd. [*New Zealand*] [*ICAO designator*] (FAAC) ... PXH
Pacific Island Aviation, Inc. [*Mariana Islands*] [*ICAO designator*] (FAAC) ... PSA
Package for Architectural Computer Evaluation (PDAA) ... PACE
Package Operating System (PDAA) ... PACOS
Pad Automatic Data Equipment (PDAA) ... PADE
Paddle Steamer Preservation Society [*British*] (BI) ... PSPS
Page Generation [*or Generator*] (PDAA) ... PAGE
Page Level Availability Time Test [*Computer science*] ... PLATT
Page Survival Index (PDAA) ... PSI
Pages per Hour ... PPH
Paint Manufacture and Allied Trades' Association [*British*] (BI) ... PMATA
Paint Research Station [*British*] (BI) ... PRS
Paisajes Espanoles SA [*Spain*] [*ICAO designator*] (FAAC) ... PAE
Pakistan International Airlines Corp. [*ICAO designator*] (FAAC) ... PIA
PAL Aerolineas SA de CV [*Mexico*] [*ICAO designator*] (FAAC) ... LPA
Palair Macedonian [*Yugoslavia*] [*ICAO designator*] (FAAC) ... PMK
Palestine Economic Council for Development and Reconstruction (ECON) ... PECDAR
Palio Air Service [*Italy*] [*ICAO designator*] (FAAC) ... PLS
Palleted Automated Transport (PDAA) ... PAT
Pan Air, Inc. [*ICAO designator*] (FAAC) ... PAX
Pan Europeenne Air Service [*France*] [*ICAO designator*] (FAAC) ... PEA
Pan Malaysian Air Transport [*ICAO designator*] (FAAC) ... PMA
Panaf Airways Ltd. [*Gambia*] [*ICAO designator*] (FAAC) ... PAF
Panair [*Spain*] [*ICAO designator*] (FAAC) ... PNR
Panair International SRL [*Italy*] [*ICAO designator*] (FAAC) ... PIT
Panavia SA [*ICAO designator*] (FAAC) ... PNV
Panel (NFPA) ... P
Panorama Air Tour, Inc. [*ICAO designator*] (FAAC) ... PAH
Panorama Flight Service [*ICAO designator*] (FAAC) ... AFD
Panstwowe Zaklady Lotnicze [*Poland*] [*ICAO designator*] (FAAC) ... PZL
Pantanal Linhas Aereas Sul-Matogrossenses SA [*Brazil*] [*ICAO designator*] (FAAC) ... PTN
Pantone Open Color Environment [*Joint venture between Pantone, Inc. and LightSource Computer Images*] [*Computer science*] (PCM) ... POCE
Papair Terminal SA [*Haiti*] [*ICAO designator*] (FAAC) ... HMP
Paper-Core Quad Trunk (PDAA) ... PCQT
Paper Sack Development Association [*British*] (BI) ... PSDA
Paper Towel Association [*British*] (BI) ... PTA
Papua New Guinea [*Aircraft nationality and registration mark*] (FAAC) ... P2
Paradise Island Airlines, Inc. [*ICAO designator*] (FAAC) ... PDI
Parallax Aircraft Parking Aid (PDAA) ... PAPA
Parallax Second [*Unit of interstellar-space measure*] ... PC
Parallel Access Multiple Distribution (PDAA) ... PAMD
Parallel-Flow Condenser [*Air conditioning systems*] ... PFC
Parallel Processing Automata (PDAA) ... PPA
Parallel Quadrature Mirror Filter (PDAA) ... PQMF
Parallel Single [*Outdoor advertising*] (NTCM) ... PS
Parallel Undocumented Development (PDAA) ... PUD
Parallel Virtual Machine [*Software package*] ... PVM
Parametric Array Doppler SONAR (PDAA) ... PADS
Parasite-Induced Erythrocyte Surface Antigen [*Immunology*] ... PIESA
Parasite Tubing Method (PDAA) ... PTM
Parasitized Red Blood Cell [*Medicine*] ... PRBC
Parasitophorous Vacuole Membrane [*Malaria*] ... PVM
Parent Advisory Committee [*Migrant education*] (AEE) ... PAC
Parent Country National (PDAA) ... PCN
Parentheses (NTCM) ... PARENS
Parents Active for Vision Education [*An association*] (EA) ... PAVE
Parents of Adult Jewish Singles ... PAJES
Parents' Choice [*A publication*] ... Par Ch
Parents, Educators and Environmentalists to Save Anchoives [*An association*] ... PEETSA
Parents Reaching Out [*An association*] (EA) ... PRO
Parents for Torah for All Children [*Program for learning disabled children*] ... P'TACH
Parked Aircraft Intrusion Detector (PDAA) ... PAID
Parked Aircraft Security System (PDAA) ... PASS
Pars Systems (CRS) [*ICAO designator*] (FAAC) ... PRS
Parsons Airways Northern Ltd. [*Canada*] [*ICAO designator*] (FAAC) ... FAP
Part Time Operation (DA) ... PTO
Parti Bersatu Sabah [*Malaysia*] [*Political party*] (ECON) ... PBS
Partial Sequential Probability Ratio Test (PDAA) ... PSPRT
Partially-Balanced Incomplete Block (PDAA) ... PBIB
Partially-Hydrolyzed Polyacrylamide [*Well drilling technology*] ... PHPA
Partially Yttria-Stabilized Zirconia [*Industrial ceramics*] ... PYSZ
Participation-Achievement-Reward (PDAA) ... PAR
Participation in Architectural Layout (PDAA) ... PARTIAL
Participative Work Design ... PWD
Particle Doppler Shift Spectrometer (PDAA) ... PDSS
Particle Physics and Astronomy Research Council [*British*] ... PPARC
Particle Size Analogue Computer (PDAA) ... PARSAC
Particulate Instrumentation by LASER Light Scattering (PDAA) ... PILLS
Particulate Methane Monooxygenase [*Biochemistry*] ... PMMO
Partitive Analytical Forecasting (PDAA) ... PAF
Passenger Address System [*Aviation*] (DA) ... PA
Passenger Car Motor Oil ... PCMO
Passenger Motor Vehicle ... PMV
Passenger Protective Breathing Equipment [*Aviation*] (DA) ... PPBE
Passenger Vehicle Operation Association Ltd. [*British*] (BI) ... PVOA
Passive Driving Periscope [*Military*] (PDAA) ... PDP
Passive Immune Hemolysis (PDAA) ... PIH
Passive Microwave Radiometer Satellite (PDAA) ... PAMIRASAT
Passive Track-On-Jam ... PTOJ
Passive Ultrasonic Sensor (PDAA) ... PUS
Patchy [*Meteorology*] (DA) ... PTCHY
Patent Cooperation Treaty [*World Intellectual Property Organization*] ... PCT
Patented Steel Wire Bureau [*British*] (BI) ... PSWB
Pathology On-Line Logging and Reporting System [*Computer science*] (PDAA) ... POLARS
Patient as Customer Evaluation Survey ... PACES
Patriot Air Defense Information Language [*Army*] ... PADIL
Patriot Airlines, Inc. [*ICAO designator*] (FAAC) ... PAA
Patriot Antimissile Capability [*Army*] ... PAC
Patriot Field Report [*Army*] ... PFR
Patriot Integration and Test System [*Army*] ... PITS
Patriot Organizational Maintenance Trainer [*Army*] ... POMT
Patriot Project Office [*Army*] ... PPO
Pattern Card Makers' Society [*British*] (BI) ... PCMS
Pattern Delayed-Response [*Ophthalmology*] ... PDR
Patterson Aviation Co. [*ICAO designator*] (FAAC) ... ETL
Paved Surface [*Aviation*] (DA) ... P
Pavement Classification Number [*Aviation*] (DA) ... PCN
Pavement Condition Index [*Aviation*] (DA) ... PCI
Pawan Hans Ltd. [*India*] [*ICAO designator*] (FAAC) ... PHE
Pay No Attention to the Man Behind the Curtain [*Computer hacker terminology*] (NHD) ... PNAMBIC
PCBoard Programming Language [*Clark Development Co.*] (PCM) ... PPL
PDQ Air Service, Inc. [*ICAO designator*] (FAAC) ... PDQ
Pea Growing Research Organisation Ltd. [*British*] (BI) ... PGRO
Peace Air Togo [*ICAO designator*] (FAAC) ... PCT
Peacetime Contingency Operation [*Army*] (ADDR) ... PCO
[*H. E.*] Peacock & Son (Thorney) Ltd. [*British*] [*ICAO designator*] (FAAC) ... PCK
Peak Area Ratio [*Chromatographic analysis*] ... PAR
Peak Design Heat Loss (PDAA) ... PDHL
Peak Instantaneous Airborne Count (DA) ... PIAC
Peak-to-Peak Heights [*Spectrometry*] ... PPH
Peanut Butter and Jelly ... PBJ
Pearl Air Services (U) Ltd. [*Uganda*] [*ICAO designator*] (FAAC) ... PBY

Pearl Airways Compagne Haitienne [*Haiti*] [*ICAO designator*] (FAAC) .... HPA
Pearson Aviation Corp. [*ICAO designator*] (FAAC) .... PCR
Pegasus Hava Tasimaciligi AS [*Turkey*] [*ICAO designator*] (FAAC) .... PGT
Pelita Air Service PT [*Indonesia*] [*ICAO designator*] (FAAC) .... PAS
PEM-AIR Ltd. [*Canada*] [*ICAO designator*] (FAAC) .... PEM
Pen Input to Computer and Scanned Screen Output [*Computer science*] (PDAA) .... PICASSO
Penetration Diameter [*Military*] .... P/D
Penetration of Radiation Through Aperture Simulation (PDAA) .... PORTAS
Peninsula Airways, Inc. [*ICAO designator*] (FAAC) .... PEN
Penning Ionization Spectroscopy (PDAA) .... PIS
Pennsylvania Commuter Airlines, Inc. [*ICAO designator*] (FAAC) .... ALO
Pension Valuation Factor .... PVF
Pentafluorophenylhydrazine [*Organic chemistry*] .... PFPH
People with Arthritis Can Exercise [*Medical program*] .... PACE
People with Disabilities .... PWD
People Refreshment House Association [*British*] (BI) .... PRHA
People's Institute for Survival and Beyond (EA) .... PISB
Peptide Nucleic Acid [*Biochemistry*] .... PNA
Per Employee per Annum .... PEPA
Perceptual Quotient [*Education*] (AEE) .... QP
Percutaneous Cholecystostomy [*Medicine*] .... PC
Percutaneous Transhepatic Cholangioscopy [*Medicine*] .... PTCS
Percutaneous Transvenous Mitral Valvotomy [*Cardiology*] .... PTMV
Performance (DA) .... PER
Performance Accountability and Improvement Report .... PAIR
Performance Analysis and Prediction Study (PDAA) .... PAPS
Performance-Based Pay .... PBP
Performance and Demand Analyser (PDAA) .... PANDA
Performance Executive Airlines Ltd. [*British*] [*ICAO designator*] (FAAC) .... PZY
Performance Management Computer (PDAA) .... PMC
Performance-Oriented Packaging [*for hazardous materials*] .... POP
Performance-Oriented Packing Standard .... POPS
Performance-Related Gift (ECON) .... PRG
Performing and Captive Animals Defence League [*British*] (BI) .... PADL
Perimeter Array Antenna (PDAA) .... PARAN
Perimeter Aviation Ltd. [*Canada*] [*ICAO designator*] (FAAC) .... PAG
Period Order Quantity (PDAA) .... POQ
Period of Reduced Melting [*Climatology*] .... PRM
Periodic Motor Vehicle Inspection (PDAA) .... PMVI
Periodical On-Line Keyword Access [*Computer science*] (PDAA) .... POLKA
Peripheral Blood Leukocyte [*Medicine*] (PDAA) .... PPL
Peripheral Interface and Program Interrupt Translator (PDAA) .... PIPIT
Peripheral Ultra-Low Power Processor (PDAA) .... PULPP
Peritonsillar Abscess [*Medicine*] .... PTA
Periventricular White-Matter Radiolucency [*Medicine*] .... PWMR
Permanent Entry Permit After Entry .... PEPAE
Permanent Entry Visa .... PEV
Permanent Paranormal Object .... PPO
Permanent Part-Time Employment .... PPTE
Permitted Flying Route [*Aviation*] (DA) .... PFR
Peroxide Number [*Hydrocarbon fuel specifications*] .... PN
Peroxisome Proliferator-Activated Receptor .... PPAR
Perpendicular Diffraction Delay Line (PDAA) .... PDDL
Pershing Audio Reproduction System (PDAA) .... PARS
Pershing Physical Deception Device [*Army*] .... PPDD
Personal (DA) .... P
Personal (FAAC) .... PSNAL
Personal Arms and Equipment [*Army*] (ADDR) .... PAE
Personal Care .... PC
Personal Dust Exposure Monitor (PDAA) .... PDEM
Personal-E Mailbox [*Computer software*] (PCM) .... PEM
Personal Financial Specialist .... PFS
Personal Protective Device [*Toxicology*] .... PPD
Personal Rights Association [*British*] (BI) .... PRA
Personal Verifier Terminal (DA) .... PVT
Personnel Availability Model (PDAA) .... PAM
Personnel Casualty Report [*Navy*] (ANA) .... PERS CASREP
Personnel Development .... PD
Personnel and Equipment Working [*Aviation*] (FAAC) .... PAEW
Personnel Security and Surety Program [*Military*] (ADDR) .... PSSP
Persons Viewing Television [*Television ratings*] (NTCM) .... PVT
Pest Infestation Laboratory [*Agricultural Research Council*] (PDAA) .... PIL
Pesticide Data Program [*Environmental Protection Agency*] .... PDP
Petroleos Mexicanos [*Mexico*] [*ICAO designator*] (FAAC) .... PMX
Petroleum Ether Insoluble Oxidized Fatty Acid [*Food science*] .... PIOFA
Petroleum Helicopters de Colombia SA [*ICAO designator*] (FAAC) .... PHC
Petroleum Helicopters, Inc. [*ICAO designator*] (FAAC) .... PHM
Petroleum Industry Local Authority Reporting (PDAA) .... PILAR
Peugot Societe Anonyme [*Peugeot Co. Ltd.*] [*French*] .... PSA
Phagocyte Glycoprotein [*Biochemistry*] .... PGP
Pharmaceutical Manufacturers Association of Canada .... PMAC
Pharmaceutical Partners for Better Healthcare (ECON) .... PPBH
Pharmaceutical Society of Ireland (BI) .... PSI
Phase Amplitude Monopulse (PDAA) .... PHAM
Phase-Change [*Physics*] .... PC
Phase of the Moon [*Astronomy*] (NHD) .... POM
Phase Variable Canonical Form (PDAA) .... PVCF
Phased Array RADAR Detection System (PDAA) .... PARDS
Phased Array RADAR and Divers Integrated Semiconductor Elements (PDAA) .... PARADISE
Phased Control Technique (PDAA) .... PACT
Phenyl-Dichlorophosphine (PDAA) .... PDP
(Phenylethyl)Phenyltetrahydropyridine [*Organic chemistry*] .... PEPTP
PHH Aviation Systems, Inc. [*ICAO designator*] (FAAC) .... XAS
Phi Kappa Phi [*Honor society*] (AEE) .... PKP
Philatelic Literature Review [*A publication*] .... Phil Lit R
Philatelic Traders' Society Ltd. [*British*] (BI) .... PTS
Philippine Air Lines, Inc. [*ICAO designator*] (FAAC) .... PAL
Philips Aviation Services [*Netherlands*] [*ICAO designator*] (FAAC) .... PHI
Phillips Head (DAC) .... PH
Phillips Michigan City Flying Service, Inc. [*ICAO designator*] (FAAC) .... PHL
Phoenix 2000 Airtaxi Ltd. [*Hungary*] [*ICAO designator*] (FAAC) .... PHX
Phoenix Air Service GmbH [*Germany*] [*ICAO designator*] (FAAC) .... PAM
Phoenix Airline Services, Inc. [*ICAO designator*] (FAAC) .... WDY
Phoenix Aviation [*British*] [*ICAO designator*] (FAAC) .... PLP
Phoenix Flight Operations Ltd. [*Canada*] [*ICAO designator*] (FAAC) .... XPX
Phonon Side-Band Hole [*Spectroscopy*] .... PSBH
Phosphate Ester Base (PDAA) .... PEB
Phosphatidylinositol Transfer Protein [*Biochemistry*] .... PITP
Phosphogluconate Dehydrogenase [*Organic chemistry*] (MAH) .... PDG
Phosphoric Acid Anodized (PDAA) .... PPA
Phosphorotioate Oligonucleotide [*Biochemistry*] .... PON
Photo-Anodic Engraving (PDAA) .... PAE
Photo-Electric Portable Probe Reader (PDAA) .... PEPPER
Photo-Electron Spectroscopy of Inner-Shell (PDAA) .... PESIS
Photo-Electron Spectroscopy of Outer-Shell (PDAA) .... PESOS
Photo-Litho Reproducers' Association [*British*] (BI) .... PLRA
Photo Optical Cable Controlled Submersible (PDAA) .... PHOCAS
Photo Reconnaissance [*ICAO designator*] (FAAC) .... PR
Photo-Transferred Thermoluminescence (PDAA) .... PTTL
Photodissociation Mass Spectrometry .... PDMS
Photodissociation [*or Photodominated*] **Region** [*Galactic science*] .... PDR
Photoelectric Transducer (PDAA) .... PET
Photogrammetric Circulatory Survey (PDAA) .... PHOCIS
Photogrammetric Programming Language [*Computer science*] (PDAA) .... PPL
Photographic Dealers' Association [*British*] (BI) .... PDA
Photographic Importers Association [*British*] (BI) .... PIA
Photographic Society of Ireland (BI) .... PSI
Photoluminescence Yield [*Spectroscopy*] .... PLY
Photon Adjoint with Neutron (PDAA) .... PAWN
Photon Tunneling Microscope .... PTM
Photonburst Mass Spectrometry .... PBMS
Photostat (NTCM) .... STAT
Phototype Environment Buoy (PDAA) .... PEB
Physician Payment Review Commission .... PPRC
Physician and Sports Medicine [*A publication*] .... PSM
Physics Online Information System [*Computer science*] (PDAA) .... PHYLIS
Physics Post-Doctoral Information Pool [*American Institute of Physics*] (PDAA) .... PPIP
Piano Trade Suppliers' Association [*British*] (BI) .... PTSA
Pianoforte Manufacturers' Association Ltd. [*British*] (BI) .... PMA
Pianoforte Publicity Association [*British*] (BI) .... PPA
Picnic Basket Porphyrin [*Organic chemistry*] .... PBP
Pictorial Navigation Indicator [*Aviation*] (DA) .... PNI
Picture Description Test (PDAA) .... PDT
Picture Element (NTCM) .... PEL
Picture Element (NTCM) .... Pixel
Pictures per Minute (NTCM) .... PPM
Pictures of Specific Syndromes and Unknown Malformations [*Database*] .... POSSUM
Piece of Data [*Computer science*] (NHD) .... POD
Piece-Wise Application of Radiation through the Electromagnetic-Pulse Simulator (PDAA) .... PARTES
Piecewise Markov Process (PDAA) .... PMP
Piedmont Airlines, Inc. [*ICAO designator*] (FAAC) .... PDT
Piezo Resistive [*Automotive electronics*] .... PR
Piezoelectric Field-Effect Transistor (PDAA) .... PI-FET
Pig Industry Development Authority [*British*] (BI) .... PIDA
Pilatus Britten-Norman Ltd. [*British*] [*ICAO designator*] (FAAC) .... PBN
Pilot Aerial Survival System (PDAA) .... PASS
Pilot Controller Glossary [*Aviation*] (FAAC) .... P/CG
Pilot Decision Making [*Aviation*] (DA) .... PDM
Pilot Pulse Amplitude .... PPA
Pilot Repair/Overhaul [*Military*] .... PR/O
Pilot Under Training [*Aviation*] (DA) .... pU/T
Pilot's Operating Handbook [*Aviation*] (DA) .... POH
Pilot's Power Tool .... PPT
Ping Intercept Passive Ranging SONAR [*Military*] .... PIPRS
Pinnacle Virtual File System [*Pinnacle Micro, Inc.*] [*Computer science*] (PCM) .... PVFS
Pioneer Airlines, Inc. [*ICAO designator*] (FAAC) .... PIO
Pipe Flow (PDAA) .... PIFL
Pipe Stress Analysis (PDAA) .... PSA
Pipeline End Manifold (PDAA) .... PLEM
[*K. C.*] **Piper Sales, Inc.** [*ICAO designator*] (FAAC) .... KCE
Pit Tub and Mine Car Manufacturers' Association [*British*] (BI) .... PTMCA
Pitch Augmentation Control System (PDAA) .... PACS
Pitch Fibre Pipe Association of Great Britain (BI) .... PEPA
Pitch-Synchronous Digital Feature Extraction System (PDAA) .... PDFES
Pitting Corrosion (PDAA) .... PC
Pituitary Adenylyl Cyclase-Activating Polypeptide [*Endocrinology*] .... PACAP

Plain End [*Lumber*] (DAC) ... PE
Plain Old Balloon Angioplasty [*Cardiology*] [*Facetious*] ... POBA
Plaintiff ... P
Plaited Cordage Manufacturers Association [*British*] (BI) ... PCMA
Plan Handling and RADAR Operating System [*Aviation*] (DA) ... PHAROS
Plan-View Size (PDAA) ... PVS
Planar Distributed Function Generator (PDAA) ... PDFG
Plane Transport System (DA) ... PTS
Planed All Round (DAC) ... PAR
Planed Four Sides [*Technical drawings*] (DAC) ... P4S
Planed One Edge [*Technical drawings*] (DAC) ... P1E
Planed One Side [*Technical drawings*] (DAC) ... P1S
Planed One Side and Two Edges [*Technical drawings*] (DAC) ... P1S2E
Planed and Square-Edge (DAC) ... pse
Planed and Square-Jointed (DAC) ... psj
Planed, Tongued, and Grooved (DAC) ... PTG
Planemasters Services, Inc. [*ICAO designator*] (FAAC) ... PMS
Planetary Entry Radiation Facility [*Langley Research Center*] [*NASA*] (PDAA) ... PERF
Planned (DA) ... plnd
Planned Availability Concept (PDAA) ... PAC
Planned Flight Data [*Aviation*] (DA) ... PFD
Planned Program Product Improvement [*Army*] ... P_3I
Planned Restricted Availability [*Navy*] (ANA) ... PRAV
Planning and Control Made Easy (PDAA) ... PACE
Plant Experimentation (PDAA) ... PLEX
Plant Genetic Materials ... PGM
Plant Modelling System Program (PDAA) ... PMSP
Plant Services Maintenance (PDAA) ... PLASMA
Plaque-Forming Factor (PDAA) ... PFF
Plasma Electron Beam (PDAA) ... PEB
Plastic Leaded Chip Carrier [*Computer science*] ... PLCC
Plastic-Lined Pipe ... PLP
Plastic Optical Fiber [*Automotive electronics*] ... POF
Plate Glass Association [*British*] (BI) ... PGA
Platinum Compensating Lead Wire (PDAA) ... PCLW
Pliocene Research, Interpretations and Synoptic Mapping [*Climatology*] ... PRISM
Plough, Sweeper, and Blower (DA) ... PSB
Plumbers' Merchants Association [*British*] (BI) ... PMA
Plume Suppression System [*Combustion technology*] ... PSS
[*Horace*] **Plunkett Foundation for Co-Operative Studies** [*British*] (BI) ... HPF
Pluto-Charon System [*Planetary science*] ... PCS
PM Air, Inc. [*ICAO designator*] (FAAC) ... PAZ
Pocketpiece [*A. C. Nielsen Co.*] [*Rating report*] (NTCM) ... PP
Pocono Airlines, Inc. [*ICAO designator*] (FAAC) ... POC
Pogo Fan Club and Walt Kelly Society (EA) ... PFCWTS
Pohjanmaan Lento OY [*Finland*] [*ICAO designator*] (FAAC) ... PLF
Point Air Defense System ... PADS
Point of Exposure [*Environmental Protection Agency*] (ERG) ... POE
Points of Call Airlines Ltd. [*Canada*] [*ICAO designator*] (FAAC) ... PTS
Pol-Fly [*Poland*] [*ICAO designator*] (FAAC) ... PFL
Polar Air Co. [*Russian Federation*] [*ICAO designator*] (FAAC) ... JPC
Polar Component [*Food science*] ... PC
Polar International Airlines, Inc. [*ICAO designator*] (FAAC) ... POL
Polar Stratospheric Telescope ... POST
Polar Track Structure [*Aviation*] (FAAC) ... PTS
Polaravia OY [*Finland*] [*ICAO designator*] (FAAC) ... PLV
Polarized Orbital Approximation (PDAA) ... POA
Polarized Total Internal Reflection Fluorescence Microscopy ... PTIRFM
Polarizer-Compensator-Analyzer (PDAA) ... PCA
Police Attendance Line ... PAL
Police Aviation Services [*British*] [*ICAO designator*] (FAAC) ... PLC
Police Officers' Association [*British*] (BI) ... POA
Policy, Planning and Implementation Unit ... PPIU
Polise-Air [*Russian Federation*] [*ICAO designator*] (FAAC) ... PMR
Polish Notation [*Mathematics*] ... PN
Polished Plate Glass [*Technical drawings*] (DAC) ... PPGL
Polished-Stone Value (PDAA) ... PSV
Polite ... POL
Political Action Committee for Cable Television (NTCM) ... PACCT
Pollution Control Revenue ... PCR
Pollution Generation Multiplier from Output Table (PDAA) ... PGMOT
Pollution Prevention Information Exchange System [*Environmental science*] ... PIES
Pollution Reduction by Information and Control Technology ... PREDICT
Polnippon [*Poland*] [*ICAO designator*] (FAAC) ... PLN
Polskie Linie Lotnicze [*Poland*] [*ICAO designator*] (FAAC) ... LOT
Poly-Ortho-methylstyrene [*Organic chemistry*] ... POMS
Polyaluminum Chloride [*Inorganic chemistry*] ... PAC
Polyaspartic Ester [*Organic chemistry*] ... PAE
Polybromostyrene [*Organic chemistry*] ... PBRS
Polybutene [*Organic chemistry*] ... PBE
Polybutyl Acrylate [*Organic chemistry*] ... PBA
Polybutyl Methacrylate [*Organic chemistry*] ... PBMA
Polychlorinated Diaromatic Hydrocarbon [*Organic chemistry*] ... PCDH
Polychlorstyrene [*Organic chemistry*] ... PCLST
Polycrystalline Diamond Compact [*Well drilling technology*] ... PDC
Polydimethyl Phenylene Oxide [*Organic chemistry*] ... PDMPO
Polyestercarbonate [*Organic chemistry*] ... PEC
Polyethyl Methacrylate [*Organic chemistry*] ... PEMA
Polyethylene Isopthalate [*Organic chemistry*] ... PEIS
Polyglycidal Methacrylate-Ethyl Acrylate [*Organic chemistry*] (PDAA) ... PGMA-EA
Polyhexyl Methacrylate [*Organic chemistry*] ... PHMA
Polyketide Synthase [*An enzyme*] ... PKS
Polylacticco-Glycolic Acid [*Organic chemistry*] ... PLGA
Polymeric Fatty Acid [*Food science*] ... PFA
Polymeric Triglyceride [*Food science*] ... PT
Polymerised Cashew Nut Shell Liquid (PDAA) ... PCNSL
Polymerized and Oxidized Material [*Food science*] ... POM
Polynesian Air-Ways [*ICAO designator*] (FAAC) ... PLA
Polynesian Airline Operations Ltd. [*Western Samoa*] [*ICAO designator*] (FAAC) ... PAO
Polynomial Discriminant Method (PDAA) ... PDM
Polyoctyl Methacrylate [*Organic chemistry*] ... POMA
Poly(p-phenylene Benzobisoxazole) (RDA) ... PBO
Polypentene [*Organic chemistry*] ... PPE
Polyphenylene Ether Plastic [*Materials science*] ... PPE
Polypropyl Methacrylate [*Organic chemistry*] ... PPMA
Polyribosylribitol Phosphate Conjugated to Tetanus Toxoid [*Medicine*] ... PRP-T
Polystyrene Latex (PDAA) ... PSL
Polysulfone [*Organic chemistry*] ... PSF
Polysulphide Rubber Compound (PDAA) ... PRC
Polyurethane Recycle and Recovery Council [*Plastics recycling research*] ... PURRC
Polyvinyl Bromide (PDAA) ... PVBr
Polyvinyl Butyl Ether [*Organic chemistry*] ... PVBE
Polyvinyl Chloride-Coated Fabric (PDAA) ... PVCCF
Polyvinyl Ethyl Ether [*Organic chemistry*] ... PVEE
Polyvinyl Hexyl Ether [*Organic chemistry*] ... PVHE
Poly(vinyl Nitrate) [*Organic chemistry*] ... PVN
Pool Promoters Association [*British*] (BI) ... PPA
Pooled Analytical Stereoplotter System (PDAA) ... PASS
Pooled Normal Serum (PDAA) ... PNS
Pooled Superannuation Trust ... PST
Poor Clergy Relief Corp. [*British*] (BI) ... PCRC
Popular Movement Against the European Community (ECON) ... PM
Popular Party [*European political movement*] (ECON) ... PP
Porous Silicon [*Physics*] ... PS
Portable Data Store [*Computer science*] (PDAA) ... PODS
Portable Distributed Objects [*Next*] ... PDO
Portable Electric Tool Manufacturers' Association [*British*] (BI) ... PETMA
Portable Electronic Runway Lighting (PDAA) ... PERL
Portable Interactive Computing Object ... PiCO
Portable Landing Light System (PDAA) ... PLLS
Portable Optic-Electronic Tracker (PDAA) ... POET
Portable Surface Supported Diving System (PDAA) ... PSSDS
Portable Vehicle Analyzer [*Auto repair*] [*Electronics*] ... PVA
Portland Cement [*Technical drawings*] (DAC) ... PORT CEM
Portugalia, Companhia Portuguesa de Transportes Aeros SA [*Portugal*] [*ICAO designator*] (FAAC) ... PGA
Portugese Air Force [*ICAO designator*] (FAAC) ... AFP
Portuguese Navy [*ICAO designator*] (FAAC) ... PON
Position Error Correction (DA) ... PEC
Position Number [*Military*] (ADDR) ... POSNO
Position Relief Briefing Observed [*Aviation*] (FAAC) ... PRBO
Position-Sensitive Proportional Counter [*Instrumentation*] ... PSPC
Positioning and Locating System [*Aviation*] (PDAA) ... PALS
Positive Chemical Ionization Mass Spectroscopy ... PCIMS
Positive Definitive Successive Over-Relaxation (PDAA) ... PDSOR
Positive Displacement Pump-Constant Volume Sampler (ERG) ... PDP-CVS
Positive Immittance Converter (PDAA) ... PIC
Positive Personnel Identity Verification (PDAA) ... PPIV
Positive Value (DA) ... PS
Post-Consumer Resin [*Plastic recycling*] ... PCR
Post and Girder [*Lumber*] (DAC) ... P & G
Post-Market Trading ... PMT
Post Nickel Strike (PDAA) ... PNS
Post-Program Monitoring ... PPM
Post-Qualification Education (PDAA) ... PQE
Post-Separation Employment ... PSE
Postal Address Reader Indexer System (PDAA) ... PARIS
Postconviction Remedy ... PCR
Postulate-Based Permuted Subject Indexing (PDAA) ... POPSI
Potassium Hydroxide [*Electric vehicle batteries*] ... KOH
Potassium Lithium Niobate (PDAA) ... PLN
Potential Icing Category [*Meteorology*] (DA) ... PIC
Potential Viewer [*Television ratings*] (NTCM) ... PV
Potosina del Aire SA de CV [*Mexico*] [*ICAO designator*] (FAAC) ... PSN
Poultry Education Association [*British*] (BI) ... PEA
Pour Point [*Petroleum characteristic*] ... PP
Powder Injection Molding [*Metallurgy*] ... PIM
Powder Metal Industries Federation ... PMIF
Powell Air Ltd. [*Canada*] [*ICAO designator*] (FAAC) ... PWL
Power-Assist System [*Motorcycle steering*] ... PAS
Power Diffraction Search and Match System (PDAA) ... PDSMS
Power Flying Control Unit [*Aviation*] (DA) ... PFCU
Power-Generating Fusion Reaction ... PGFR
Power Line Carrier Communication (PDAA) ... PLCC
Power Metal Grid (PDAA) ... PMG
Power Plant Frame [*Mazda Miata*] [*Connecting engine and transmission to final drive*] ... PPF
Power Reactor Innovation Small Module [*Nuclear energy*] ... PRISM

Power Saw Association [*British*] (BI) ... PSA
Power Spectra [*Neurophysiology*] ... PS
Powered Air Purifying Respirator (ERG) ... PAPR
Powerful Radio Galaxy [*Cosmology*] ... PRG
Powszechny Bank Gospodarczy [*Poland*] ... PBG
Practical Absolute Cavity Radiometer (PDAA) ... PACRAD
Practical Quantification Limit [*Metallurgy*] ... POL
Practical Quantitation Level [*Environmental chemistry*] (ERG) ... PQL
Practical Quantitation Limit [*Environmental chemistry*] ... PQL
Practice Extraction and Report Language [*Facetious translation: Pathologically Eclectic Rubbish Lister*] [*Computer science*] (NHD) ... PERL
Prairie Flying Service (1976) Ltd. [*Canada*] [*ICAO designator*] (FAAC) ... PFS
Pratt & Whitney Canada, Inc. [*ICAO designator*] (FAAC) ... PWC
Pre Coded Originating Mail Processor (PDAA) ... POMP
Pre-Conditioned Air System [*Aviation*] (DA) ... PCA
Pre-Determined Motion-Time [*Management*] (PDAA) ... PMT
Pre-Determined Route [*Aviation*] (DA) ... PDR
Pre-Flight Information Bulletin [*Aviation*] (DA) ... PIB
Pre-Mission Calibration (PDAA) ... PMC
Pre-Operational Support [*Military*] ... PRE-OPS
Pre-Optimization Linearization of Undulation and Detection of Errors (PDAA) ... PRELUDE
Pre-Oxidation Gettering of the Other Side (PDAA) ... POGO
Pre-Planned Training System (PDAA) ... PPTS
Pre-Positioned Material Receipt Document ... PPMRD
Pre-Qualified Offsets Supplier ... PQOS
Pre-Qualified Offsets Supplier Status ... PQOSS
Pre-Season Predictor Model [*Television ratings*] (NTCM) ... PSP
Pre-University Orbital Information Tracker Equipment and Recorder (PDAA) ... POINTER
Precaution [*ICAO designator*] (FAAC) ... PRCTN
Precise and Accurate Time and Time Interval [*An experiment aboard the Spacelab*] [*NASA*] (PDAA) ... PATTI
Precise Automated Tracking System (PDAA) ... PATS
Precision Aerobatics Model Pilots Association (EA) ... PAMPA
Precision Anti-Radiation Missile [*Military*] (PDAA) ... PARM
Precision Approach Lighting System [*Aviation*] (FAAC) ... PALS
Precision Doppler VHF Omni-Range (PDAA) ... PDVOR
Precision Guided Maneuvering Re-Entry Vehicle (PDAA) ... PGMARV
Precision Hover Sensor (PDAA) ... PHS
Precision Location and Tracking System (PDAA) ... PLATS
Precision Valley Aviation [*ICAO designator*] (FAAC) ... PRE
Precompetitive Research and Development ... PRD
Precracked Charpy V-Notch (PDAA) ... PCVN
Predicted Fire Weapon System [*Army*] ... PFWS
Predicted Four Hour Sweat Rate (PDAA) ... P4SR
Predicted Propagation Correction (PDAA) ... PPC
Prediction Error Transform (PDAA) ... PET
Predictive Analysis and Crash Testing [*Automotive safety research*] ... PACT
Predominant [*National Weather Service*] (FAAC) ... PDMT
Preferential Arrival Route [*Aviation*] (DA) ... PAR
Preferential Departure [*Aviation*] (DA) ... PDAR
Preferred Flights, Inc. [*Canada*] [*ICAO designator*] (FAAC) ... EMS
Prefetch [*Computer science*] ... PF
Preinitiation Complex [*Genetics*] ... PIC
Preliminary Assessment (ERG) ... PA
Preliminary Guaranteed Minimum Price ... PGMP
Preliminary Repair Level Decision Analysis Model (PDAA) ... PRAM
Premenstrual Dysphoric Disorder [*Proposed psychiatric diagnosis*] ... PDD
Preparative Layer Chromatography ... PLC
Preparatory Academy for the Royal Academy of Dramatic Art [*British*] (BI) ... PARADA
Preparing for AIDS/HIV Vaccine Evaluation [*National Institutes of Health project*] ... PAVE
Presbyterian Church House [*British*] (BI) ... PCH
Prescribed Goods (General) Order ... PGGO
Prescription Pricing Authority (PDAA) ... PPA
Present Level [*Aviation*] (FAAC) ... PLVL
Presidential's Hundred Tab [*Military*] ... PRES100
Press-Button Signalling (PDAA) ... PBS
Press Club (NTCM) ... PC
Press Independence and Critical Ability (NTCM) ... PICA
Press Lots of Keys to Abort [*Computer term*] ... PLOKTA
Press-Radio Bureau (NTCM) ... PRB
Pressed Brick Makers' Association Ltd. [*British*] (BI) ... PBMA
Pressed Felt Manufacturers' Association [*British*] (BI) ... PFMA
Pressed Notch Depth (PDAA) ... PND
Pressure Anomaly Difference (PDAA) ... PAD
Pressure Compensator Over-Ride (PDAA) ... PCOR
Pressure Pulse Contour [*Cardiac computer*] (PDAA) ... PPC
Pressure Vessel Thermal Shock (PDAA) ... PVTS
Pressurized Water Ractor - Full Length Emergency Cooling Heat Transfer [*Nuclear energy*] (PDAA) ... PWR-FLECHT
Prestwick BAE [*British*] [*ICAO designator*] (FAAC) ... PWK
Presunrise Service Authority (NTCM) ... PSA
Pretreatment Permitting and Enforcement Tracking System [*Environmental Protection Agency*] (ERG) ... PPETS
Preventive Maintenance Welding (PDAA) ... PMW
Previous Program Selection [*In-car entertainment*] [*Electronics*] ... PREV
Previously-Taxed Income ... PTI
Price Adjusted Single Sampling (PDAA) ... PASS
Price Adjusting Sampling Plan (PDAA) ... PASP
Prim-Air Aps [*Denmark*] [*ICAO designator*] (FAAC) ... PIR
Primary Afferent Depolarization (PDAA) ... PAMIRASAT
Primary Data User Station [*Computer science*] (PDAA) ... PDUS
Primary Demographic Report [*A. C. Nielsen Co.*] (NTCM) ... PDR
Primary Industry and Energy ... PIE
Primary Operating Stock [*DoD*] ... POS
Primary RADAR (DA) ... PR
Primary RADAR (FAAC) ... PRIRA
Primary Smog Product (PDAA) ... PSP
Prime Air, Inc. [*ICAO designator*] (FAAC) ... PRM
Prime Compatible Set (PDAA) ... PCS
Prime Disjunctive Normal Form (PDAA) ... PDNF
Primeras Lineas Uruguayas de Navegacion Aerea [*Uruguay*] [*ICAO designator*] (FAAC) ... PUA
Primordial Hot Mantle Plume (PDAA) ... PHMP
Prince Edward Air Ltd. [*Canada*] [*ICAO designator*] (FAAC) ... CME
Princess Air [*British*] [*ICAO designator*] (FAAC) ... PRN
Princeton Aviation Corp. [*ICAO designator*] (FAAC) ... PCN
Princeton University, Pennsylvania University, Army Avionics Research (PDAA) ... PPAAR
Princeville Airways, Inc. [*ICAO designator*] (FAAC) ... PRI
Principal Project Designer [*Engineering project management*] ... PPD
Print [*or Printed*] (NTCM) ... PR
Printer Job Language [*Computer science*] ... PJL
Printers' Costing Association [*British*] (BI) ... PCA
Printers' Medical Aid and Sanatoria Association [*British*] (BI) ... PMASA
Printing, Bookbinding, and Kindred Trades' Overseers Association [*British*] (BI) ... PBKTOA
Priority Air Transport [*Army*] (FAAC) ... PAT
Priority Aviation Co., Inc. [*ICAO designator*] (FAAC) ... BCK
Priority Message Precedence [*Telecommunications*] (ADDR) ... PP
PRISM [*Personnel Record Information System for Management*] **Information RetrievalLanguage** [*Computer science*] (PDAA) ... PIRL
Prisoner-Initiated Review ... PIR
Prisoner of War of Japan ... POW(J)
Privacy Commission ... PC
Privacy-Enhanced Mail [*Software package*] ... PEM
Private Aircraft Inspection Reporting System (PDAA) ... PAIRS
Private Aircraft Reporting System [*FAA*] (PDAA) ... PARS
Private Automatic Telegraph Exchange (PDAA) ... PATX
Private Grocers' Merchandising Association [*British*] (BI) ... PGMA
Private Jet Expeditions, Inc. [*ICAO designator*] (FAAC) ... PJE
Private New Capital Expenditure ... PNCE
Private Radio Bureau [*FCC*] (NTCM) ... PRB
Private Wine Buyers' Society [*British*] (BI) ... PWB
Privately-Owned Open Air-Braked [*Railway wagons*] (PDAA) ... POA
Pro Air Service [*ICAO designator*] (FAAC) ... PSZ
Probabilistic Materials System (PDAA) ... PROMATS
Probabilistic Potential Theory (PDAA) ... PPT
Probability of False Alarm [*DoD*] ... PFA
Probability of Mission Abort [*Navy*] (ANA) ... PMA
Probability Outgoing Quality Limit (PDAA) ... POQL
Probability of Single Shot Engagement Kill [*Military*] ... PSEK
Probability of Track [*Military*] ... PTK
Probable Missed Approach per Arrival [*Aviation*] (PDAA) ... PMA/ARR
Problem-Oriented Language for Analytical Chemistry [*Computer science*] (PDAA) ... POLAC
Problem-Oriented Language Organizer [*Computer science*] (PDAA) ... POLO
Procedure Value Analysis (PDAA) ... PVA
Proceed [*ICAO designator*] (FAAC) ... PCD
Proceed Directly on Course [*Aviation*] (FAAC) ... PDDC
Process Engineering Evaluation Techniques Package (PDAA) ... PEETPACK
Process Hazard Analysis [*Environmental science*] ... PHA
Process Hazardous Review [*Environmental science*] ... PHR
Process Organization to Simplify Error Recovery (PDAA) ... POSER
Process-Oriented Contract Administration Services ... PROCAS
Processed RADAR Display System (PDAA) ... PRDS
Processed Woodchip, Sawdust, and Woodflour Association [*British*] (BI) ... PWSWA
Processing Amplifier (NTCM) ... Proc Amp
Processing Routines Aided by Graphics for Manipulation of Arrays (PDAA) ... PRAGMA
Processor Simulation Language [*Computer science*] (PDAA) ... PROCSIM
Procurement Information Notice [*Environmental Protection Agency*] (ERG) ... PIN
Product Data Exchange using STEP [*Sequentially Timed Events Plotting*] ... PDES
Product Development Team [*Automotive project management*] ... PDT
Product of Incomplete Combustion [*Environmental Protection Agency*] (ERG) ... PIC
Product Innovation and Design ... PID
Product Inventory Electronically Recorded (PDAA) ... PIER
Product Inventory Level Estimator (PDAA) ... PILE
Production Director (NTCM) ... PD
Production Facility (NTCM) ... Pro-Fax
Production Flow Analysis (PDAA) ... PFA
Production Master Scheduling System (PDAA) ... PROMAST
Production Orientated Draughting and Manufacturing (PDAA) ... PRODAM
Production Planning Inventory Control System (PDAA) ... PPICS
Production Readiness Master Plan ... PRMP
Production Test Program Report ... PTPR

Productive Standard Hour (PDAA) .... PSH
Professional Association of Christian Educators (EA) .... PACE
Professional Digital [*Recording*] (NTCM) .... PD
Professional Diploma [*Education*] (AEE) .... PD
Professional Disk Operating System [*Computer science*] .... ProDOS
Professional Educational Development Corp. [*An association*] (EA) .... PEDC
Professional Emphasis Group [*National Audience Board*] (NTCM) .... PEG
Professional Express Courier Service, Inc. [*ICAO designator*] (FAAC) .... PAD
Professional Footballers' Association [*British*] (BI) .... PFA
Professional Geologist .... PG
Professional Hydrologist .... PH
Professional Numismatists' Association [*British*] (BI) .... PNA
Professional Officer .... PO
Professional Photographers of Israel (PDAA) .... PPI
Professional and Technical Workers Aliyah [*British*] (BI) .... PATWA
Professional Women Singers Association (EA) .... PWSA
Professionals, Owners, and Managers [*A. C. Nielsen Co.*] [*Demographic category*] (NTCM) .... POM
Professionnel Air Systems [*France*] [*ICAO designator*] (FAAC) .... PSL
Profile Analysis and Recording Control (PDAA) .... PARC
Profile Resolution Obtained by Excitation (PDAA) .... PROBE
Profit-Related Pay .... PRP
Program to Analyse the Block System [*Computer science*] (PDAA) .... PABLOS
Program Analysis System (PDAA) .... PANSY
Program Device Librarian [*Computer science*] .... PDL
Program Idea Quotient [*Home testing measurement*] (NTCM) .... PIQ
Program for Interactive Multiple Process Simulation (PDAA) .... PIMP
Program Life-Cycle Cost Estimate [*Army*] .... PLCCE
Program Random Process (PDAA) .... PRP
Program Rating Summary Report [*Television ratings*] (NTCM) .... PRS
Program to Realistically Evaluate Strategic Anti-Ballistic Missile Gaming Effectiveness [*Military*] (PDAA) .... PRESAGE
Program of Study (AEE) .... POS
Programmable Analogue Matched Filter (PDAA) .... PAMF
Programmable Automatic Transistor Tester (PDAA) .... PATT
Programmable Digital Controller (PDAA) .... PDC
Programmable Guidance Controller [*Military*] .... PGC
Programmable Tapped Delay Line (PDAA) .... PTDL
Programmed Appropriation Commitments - Fixed Asset Control System (PDAA) .... PAC-FACS
Programmed Cell Death [*Biology*] .... PCD
Programmed Electronics Pattern (PDAA) .... PREP
Programmed Inert Gas Multi-Electrode (PDAA) .... PIGME
Programmed Inquiry, Learning or Teaching [*Computer science*] .... PILOT
Programmer Brain Damage [*Computer hacker terminology*] (NHD) .... PBD
Programmes Library Update and Maintenance (PDAA) .... PLUM
Programming Language for Users of MAVIS [*Microprocessor-Based Audio Visual Information System*] (PDAA) .... PLUM
Project Activities Relationship Diagram (PDAA) .... PARD
Project Breed Rescue Efforts and Education [*An association*] (EA) .... BREED
Project Evaluation and Review Technique (DAC) .... PERT
Project of National Significance .... PNS
Project Network Technique (PDAA) .... PNT
Project Tracking System [*Environmental Protection Agency*] (ERG) .... PTS
Projected Charge Density (PDAA) .... PCD
Prolate Spheroidal Wave Function (PDAA) .... PSWF
Promotional Announcement (NTCM) .... Promo
Prompt Action to Telephone Inquiries (PDAA) .... PATTI
Pronuclear Oocyte and Sperm Transfer [*Embryology*] .... PROST
Propagating Space Charge (PDAA) .... PSC
Propair, Inc. [*Canada*] [*ICAO designator*] (FAAC) .... PRO
Propeller-Excited Vibration (PDAA) .... PEV
Propheter Construction Co., Inc. [*ICAO designator*] (FAAC) .... PPA
Propionic Acid [*Organic chemistry*] .... PRA
Proposals Paper .... PP
Proprietary Articles Trade Association [*British*] (BI) .... PATA
Propulsion Alarm and Monitoring System (PDAA) .... PALMS
Propulsion Arming and Firing Unit [*Military*] .... PAFU
Propulsive Left Landing with Aerodynamic Maneuvering Entry (PDAA) .... PLAME
Prospair Ltd. [*British*] [*ICAO designator*] (FAAC) .... PRA
Prostaglandin Hydrogen Synthase [*An enzyme*] .... PGHS
Protective Action for Children's Television (NTCM) .... PACT
Protective Security Officer .... PSO
Protein Induced by Vitamin K Absence and Antagonists (PDAA) .... PNKA
Protein Tyrosine Phosphatase [*An enzyme*] .... PTP
Proteoglycans/Glyosaminoglyans .... PG/GAG
Proteus Air Systeme [*France*] [*ICAO designator*] (FAAC) .... PRB
Prothrombin Consumption Index (PDAA) .... PCI
Protocol for Automotive Local Area Network .... PALMNET
Protocol Converter (DA) .... PROCON
Protocol Implementation Review Committee [*National Institutes of Health*] .... PIRC
Proton Exchange Membrane .... PEM
Proton Flare Project (PDAA) .... PFP
Prototype Ocean Surveillance Terminal [*Navy*] (ANA) .... POST
Provence Aero Service [*France*] [*ICAO designator*] (FAAC) .... RPA
Providence Air Charter [*ICAO designator*] (FAAC) .... PTL
Providing Lifetime Activity for Youth .... PLAY
Provincial Express, Inc. [*Canada*] [*ICAO designator*] (FAAC) .... PRV
Provincial Wholesale Newspaper Distributors' Association [*British*] (BI) .... PWNDA
Provisional Cut [*Television*] (NTCM) .... PC
Provisional Technical Secretariat [*United Nations*] .... PTS
Provisional Tolerable Weekly Intake [*Toxicology*] .... PTWI
Proximity Automatic Vehicle Monitoring (PDAA) .... PAVM
Psychiatric Case History Event System (PDAA) .... PSyCHES
Psycho-Acoustical Measuring System (PDAA) .... PACMS
Ptarmigan Airways Ltd. [*Canada*] [*ICAO designator*] (FAAC) .... PTA
Public Access by New Technology to Highly Elaborate Online Networks [*Computer science*] (PDAA) .... PANTHEON
Public Awareness Program .... PAP
Public Broadcasting Laboratory (NTCM) .... PBL
Public Dividend Capital (PDAA) .... PDC
Public, Educational, Government [*Cable television access channels*] (NTCM) .... PEG
Public Health Inspectors' Registration Board [*British*] (BI) .... PHIRB
[*The*] **Public Historian** [*A publication*] .... Pub Hist
Public Holiday (DA) .... PH
Public Information Assist Team [*Environmental Protection Agency*] (ERG) .... PIAT
Public Information in Rural Areas Technology Experiment [*British Library*] (PDAA) .... PIRATE
Public Interest [*A publication*] .... Pub Int
Public Interest Immunity Certificate [*British*] (ECON) .... PIIC
Public Library Development Incentive Scheme [*British*] .... PLDIS
Public Radio in Mid-America (NTCM) .... PRIMA
Public Relations Institute of Ireland (BI) .... PRI
Public Safety [*FCC*] (NTCM) .... P
Public School Bursars' Association [*British*] (BI) .... PSBA
Public Servants' Housing and Finance Association [*British*] (BI) .... PSHFA
Public Service Act .... PSA
Public Telephone Network (DA) .... PTN
Public Transport (DA) .... PT
Public Use Sample Helper (PDAA) .... PUSH
Publicity Release (NTCM) .... PR
Publish (FAAC) .... PUBL
Publishers' Accounts Clearing House [*British*] (BI) .... PACH
Pul. Przedsiebiorstwo Uslug Lotniczych [*Poland*] [*ICAO designator*] (FAAC) .... PUL
Pull (NFPA) .... P
Pull Back (NTCM) .... PB
Pull Chain [*Technical drawings*] (DAC) .... PC
[*Manual*] **Pull Station** [*NFPA pre-fire planning symbol*] (NFPA) .... PS
Pulsating/Steady Visual Approach Slope Indicator [*Aviation*] (FAAC) .... PVASI
Pulsating Visual Approach Slope Indicator [*Aviation*] (FAAC) .... PLASI
Pulse Amplitude and Phase Modulation (PDAA) .... PAPM
Pulse-Amplitude Transmission System (PDAA) .... PATSY
Pulse Burst Period (PDAA) .... PBP
Pulse-Coded Optical Landing Aid [*Aviation*] (PDAA) .... PCOLA
Pulse-Doppler Elevation Scan (PDAA) .... PDES
Pulse-Doppler Non-Elevation Scan (PDAA) .... PDNES
Pulse Light Approach Slope Indicator (PDAA) .... PLASI
Pulse to Pulse .... P-P
Pulsed Acoustic Doppler Wind Shear Sensing System (PDAA) .... PADWSS
Pulsed Appendage Large Mobile Electromagnetic-Pulse Simulator (PDAA) .... PALMES
Pulsed Neutron Interrogation (PDAA) .... PNI
Pump Control Valve [*Hydraulics*] .... PCV
Pumping Mean Effective Pressure [*Automotive engine testing*] .... PMEP
Punch-Through Device (PDAA) .... PThD
Purchased Input Concept Optimization with Suppliers [*Auto industry quality and cost management program*] .... PICOS
Pure Water Flux [*Engineering*] .... PWF
Purkinje Cell Layer [*Cytology*] .... PCL
Pusdiklat Perhubungan Udara/PLP [*Indonesia*] [*ICAO designator*] (FAAC) .... UDA
Pyramid Air Lines [*Egypt*] [*ICAO designator*] (FAAC) .... PYR
Pyroelectric Vidicon (PDAA) .... PEV
Pyrotechnic Development Vehicle (PDAA) .... PDV

Q

Qantas Airways Ltd. [*Australia*] [*ICAO designator*]   (FAAC)...................... QFA
Qatar Amiri Flight [*ICAO designator*]   (FAAC) .... QAF
Quadrant [*A publication*]... Quad
Quadraphonic Eight [*Tape cartridge format*]   (NTCM)................................... Q8
Quadruplex [*Videotape recording*]   (NTCM) .... QUAD
Qualifications-Based Selection [*Metallurgy*] .... QBS
Qualified Medicare Beneficiary .... QMB
Quality Action Team [*Industrial engineering*] .... QAT
Quality Assurance Package .... QAP
Quality Assurance Service Test   (PDAA) .... QUAST
Quality Function Development [*Failure analysis*] .... QFD
Quality Improvement Process [*Quality control*] .... QIP
Quality Reliability Deployment [*Automotive engineering*]........................... QRD
Quality at Work [*Quality Decision Management*] [*Computer
    science*]   (PCM)... QAW
Quantification of Uncertainty in Estimating Support Tradeoffs
    (PDAA)... QUEST
Quantimet Image Analyzing Computer   (PDAA) .... QIAC
Quantitative Competitive Polymerase Chain Reaction [*Analytical
    biochemistry*]... QC-PCR
Quantitative Intelligence Analysis Technique   (PDAA)........................... QUILT
Quantized High Y [*Picture resolution*]   (NTCM).. QHY
Quantum Cascade [*LASER*]   (ECON) .... QC
Quantum League [*An association*]   (EA).. QL
Quantum Size Effect   (PDAA).. QSE
Quarter-Orbit Magnetic Attitude Control   (PDAA) .... QMAC
Quarter-Round [*Technical drawings*]   (DAC) .... QR
Quarterly Moving Average .... QMA
Quarterly Provisional Tax .... QPT
Quartz/Phenolic .... Q/P
Quasi-Direct Broadcast Satellite .... Q-DBS
Quasi-Hydrostatic Pressure [*Physics*]... QHP
Quasi-Wide-Sense-Stationary Uncorrelated Scattering   (PDAA) .... QWSSUA
Quasielastic Neutron Scattering [*Physics*] .... QENS
Quassar de Mexico SA de CV [*ICAO designator*]   (FAAC)......................... QUA
Queen Elizabeth Military Hospital [*Ministry of Defense*] [*British*]
    (PDAA)... QEMH
[*The*] Queen's Flight [*British*] [*ICAO designator*]   (FAAC) .... TQF
Queensland Ballet [*Australia*]... QB
Quekett Microscopical Club [*British*]   (BI).. QMC
Quench Polish Quench   (PDAA)... QPQ
Queue Modification Process .... QMOD
Queueing Matrix Evaluation   (PDAA)... QME
Quick Airways Holland BV [*Netherlands*] [*ICAO designator*]
    (FAAC)... QAH
Quick-Connects for Bulkhead Mounting   (PDAA)...................................... QCM
Quick-Draw Graphics System   (PDAA) .... QDGS
Quick Kinescope [*Film replay*]   (NTCM) .... QK
Quick Update and Access Interlibrary Loans System........................... QUAILLS
Quisqueya Airlines SA [*Haiti*] [*ICAO designator*]   (FAAC)......................... QAS
Quota Restriction .... QR
Qwest Commuter Corp. [*ICAO designator*]   (FAAC).................................... QCC
Qwestair [*Australia*] [*ICAO designator*]   (FAAC).. QWA

R

Rabbit-Air AG, Zurich [*Switzerland*] [*ICAO designator*] (FAAC) .... RBB
Rabbit Anti-Mouse Brain (PDAA) .... RAMB
Rabbit Aorta Contracting Substance-Releasing Factor [*Medicine*] (PDAA) .... RCS-RF
Race Cargo Airlines [*Ghana*] [*ICAO designator*] (FAAC) .... ACE
Rack Entry Module (PDAA) .... REM
RADAR .... Ra
RADAR Alphanumeric Display Sub-System (PDAA) .... RADS
RADAR Approach Aid [*Aviation*] (DA) .... RAD
RADAR Area Correlation Guidance System (PDAA) .... RADAG
RADAR Arrival Route [*Aviation*] (DA) .... RAR
RADAR Data Extractor (PDAA) .... RADEX
RADAR Departure Route [*Aviation*] (DA) .... RDR
RADAR Determination Satellite System [*Aviation*] (DA) .... RDSS
RADAR Information Service [*Aviation*] (DA) .... RIS
RADAR Message Conversion and Distribution (DA) .... RMCDE
RADAR Prediction Data Table (PDAA) .... RPDT
RADAR Range Height Indicator Not Operating on Scan [*Meteorology*] (FAAC) .... RHINO
RADAR Recording and Analysis Equipment (DA) .... RRA
RADAR Regulation Zone (DA) .... RRZ
RADAR Vectoring Area [*Aviation*] (DA) .... RVA
Rader Aviation, Inc. [*ICAO designator*] (FAAC) .... GBR
Radiation Gasdynamics (PDAA) .... RGD
Radiator Fan Timer Module [*Cooling systems*] [*Automotive engineering*] .... RFTM
Radio Advisory Committee [*Corporation for Public Broadcasting*] (NTCM) .... RAC
Radio Allocations Study Organization (NTCM) .... RASO
Radio Amateur Old Timers' Association [*British*] (BI) .... RAOTA
Radio Area of Dominant Influence [*The Pulse, Inc.*] (NTCM) .... RADI
Radio Audience Measurement (NTCM) .... RAM
Radio Data System [*Driver information systems*] .... RDS
Radio Distribution and Control Equipment [*Aviation*] (DA) .... RDCE
Radio Electronic News Gathering (NTCM) .... RENG
Radio Executives Club (NTCM) .... REC
Radio Exploration Satellite (PDAA) .... REX
Radio of Free Asia (NTCM) .... ROFA
Radio-Frequency Glow Discharge [*Materials science*] .... RFGD
Radio Historical Society of America (NTCM) .... RHSA
Radio Information Office [*National Audience Board*] (NTCM) .... RIO
Radio Position Fixing System [*Aviation*] (DA) .... RPFS
Radio Technical Committee for Aeronautics (NTCM) .... RTC
Radio Telephony (NTCM) .... RT
Radio Trades Examination Board [*British*] (BI) .... RTEB
Radio Wholesalers Federation [*British*] (BI) .... RWF
Radioimmunoguided Surgery [*Medicine*] .... RIGS
Radioisotope-Excited X-Ray Analyzer (PDAA) .... REXA
Radiological Monitoring Assessment Prediction System (PDAA) .... RADMAP
Radionavigation Land Test (PDAA) .... RLT
Radio's All-Dimension Audience Research (NTCM) .... RADAR
Radiosonde Balloon Wind Data [*Meteorology*] (FAAC) .... RABAL
Radiosonde Report Already Sent in PIBAL [*Pilot Balloon Observation*] Collection [*Aviation*] (FAAC) .... RAPI
Radioteleprinter (DA) .... RTT
Raf-Avia [*Latvia*] [*ICAO designator*] (FAAC) .... MTL
RAF-HQSTC (Air Transport) [*British*] [*ICAO designator*] (FAAC) .... RRR
Rail Air International Service (PDAA) .... RAIS
Rail Gun Armature Plasma Investigation Device (PDAA) .... RAPID
Rail Makers' Association [*British*] (BI) .... RMA
Railroad Data Center [*Association of American Railroad*] (PDAA) .... RRDC
Railroad Operations Control System (PDAA) .... ROCS
Railway and Canal Historical Society [*British*] (BI) .... RCHS
Railway Enthusiasts' Club [*British*] (BI) .... REC
Railway Invigoration Society [*British*] (BI) .... RIS
Railway Preservation Society of Ireland (BI) .... RPSI
Railway Tyre and Axle Manufacturers Association [*British*] (BI) .... RTAMA
Rain Repellant and Surface Conditioner (PDAA) .... REPCON
Rainbow Cargo Express [*Ghana*] [*ICAO designator*] (FAAC) .... RBO
Rainbow Group [*European political movement*] (ECON) .... RBW
Rainbow Optical Landing System (PDAA) .... ROLS
Rainer Foundation [*British*] (BI) .... RF
Raised Pavement Marker [*Highway design*] .... RPM
Raji Airlines [*Pakistan*] [*ICAO designator*] (FAAC) .... RAJ
Raleigh Flying Service, Inc. [*ICAO designator*] (FAAC) .... RFA
Ram Air Freight, Inc. [*ICAO designator*] (FAAC) .... REX
Raman-Induced Kerr Effect (PDAA) .... RIKE
Ramp 66, Inc. [*ICAO designator*] (FAAC) .... PPK
Ramp Check [*Aviation*] (FAAC) .... RMPCK
Randle Cliff RADAR (PDAA) .... RCR
Random Digit Sample (NTCM) .... RDS
Random Domain Library Screening [*Genetic laboratory technique*] .... RANDOLS
Random Signal Vibration Protector (PDAA) .... RSVP
Random Width and Length (DAC) .... R/W & L
Randomized Pattern Search (PDAA) .... RPS
Range Extender Vehicle [*Gasoline-electric hybrid*] .... REV
Range Location Velocity .... RLV
Rangemile Ltd. [*British*] [*ICAO designator*] (FAAC) .... RGM
Ranging and Processing Satellite (DA) .... RAPSAT
Ranking Index for Maintenance Expenditures (PDAA) .... RIME
Rapid Access Data Retrieval Unit [*Computer science*] (PDAA) .... RADRU
Rapid Access to Sequential Block [*Computer science*] (PDAA) .... RASB
Rapid Air [*France*] [*ICAO designator*] (FAAC) .... RAP
Rapid Alert Programmed, Power Management of RADAR Targets [*Military*] (PDAA) .... RAPPORT
Rapid Alerting and Identification Display (PDAA) .... RAID
Rapid Analysis of Products by Integrated Engineering Routines [*Computer-assisted design*] .... RAPIER
Rapid Analytical Block Aerial Triangulation System (PDAA) .... RABATS
Rapid Carbohydrate Utilization Test (PDAA) .... RCUT
Rapid Eye Movement Period (PDAA) .... REMP
Rapid Infrared Forming Technique [*Materials science*] .... RIF
Rapid Intervention Vehicle (DA) .... RIV
Rare Earth Boride (PDAA) .... REB
Rare Earth Transition Metal [*Computer science*] .... RETM
Rate and Acceleration Measuring Pendulum (PDAA) .... RAMP
Rate Difference [*Toxicology*] .... RD
Rated Exposure Unit [*Advertising*] (NTCM) .... REU
Rated Sail Area [*IOR*] [*Yacht racing*] .... RSA
Ratioflug Luftfahrtunternehmen GmbH [*Germany*] [*ICAO designator*] (FAAC) .... RAT
[*Jim*] Ratliff Air Service, Inc. [*ICAO designator*] (FAAC) .... RAS
Raven Air, Inc. [*ICAO designator*] (FAAC) .... RVA
Raven Air Ltd. [*British*] [*ICAO designator*] (FAAC) .... RVR
Raw Fat and Bone Processors Association [*British*] (BI) .... RFBPA
Raw Materials Processing .... RMP
Rayon-Rayon Bias-Belted (PDAA) .... RR-BB
Raytheon Automated Digital Design System (PDAA) .... RADDS
Raytheon Service Co .... RSC
[*The*] Razorback Award (IAA) .... TRA
RCRA [*Resource Conservation and Recovery Act*] Administrative Action Tracking System (ERG) .... RAATS
Re-Chargeable Air-Breathing Apparatus (PDAA) .... RABA
Reaction Kinetic Analysis (PDAA) .... RKA
Reaction Product Imaging [*Chemistry*] .... RPI
Reactive Perfluoroalkyl Polymeric Surfactant [*Organic chemistry*] .... RPPS
Reactivity-Adjusted Non-Methane Organic Gas [*Automotive emissions*] .... RANMOG
Read the Frequently Asked Questions [*Computer hacker terminology*] (NHD) .... RTFAQ
Read Least Significant Time [*Military*] .... RLST
Reader (NTCM) .... R
Reader and Reader-Printer (PDAA) .... RRP
Readily-Oxidizable Carbon (PDAA) .... ROC
Real Aviation Ltd. [*Ghana*] [*ICAO designator*] (FAAC) .... RLV
Real Life (NHD) .... RL
Real Scene Focus Sensor (PDAA) .... RSFS
Real-Time Cell-Identification Processor (PDAA) .... RTCIP
Real-Time Control Area (NTCM) .... RTCA
Real-Time Digital Data Acquisition System (PDAA) .... RTDDAS
Real-Time Executive Extended (PDAA) .... RTXE
Real-time Lens Error Correction [*Computer science*] (NTCM) .... RLC
Real-Time On-Scene Report (NTCM) .... ROSR
Real-Time Record (NTCM) .... RTR

Real-Time Record Interpreter   (NTCM) .... RTRI
Real-Time Telemetry Processing System   (PDAA) .... RTPS
Realistic Battlefield Environment-Electronic [Military]   (PDAA) .... REBEEL
Really Universal Computer-Aided Production System   (PDAA) .... RUCAPS
Rear Vision Television [Driver safety systems] [Automotive
    engineering] .... RVTV
Reasonable Benefit Multiple .... RBM
Reasonable Maximum Exposure [Toxicology] .... RME
Rebuilt [Automotive advertising] .... REBLT
Receipt Authority Voucher .... RAV
Receiving Ambient Function Test   (PDAA) .... RAFT
Receiving Capability Out [Aviation]   (FAAC) .... RCVNO
Recency-Frequency-Monetary Value Ratio   (NTCM) .... RFMVR
Recent Drizzle [Meteorology]   (DA) .... REDZ
Recent Freezing Rain [Meteorology]   (DA) .... REFRA
Recent Hail [Meteorology]   (DA) .... REGR
Recent Rain [Meteorology]   (DA) .... RERA
Recent Shower [Meteorology]   (DA) .... RESH
Recent Snow [Meteorology]   (DA) .... RESN
Recent Thunderstorm   (DA) .... RETS
Reception Automatic Picture Transmission   (PDAA) .... RAPT
Receptor Protein Tyrosine Phosphatase [Biochemistry] .... RPTP
Recharged from Inversion Layer   (PDAA) .... REFIL
Reciprocal Impedance Converter   (PDAA) .... RIC
Reciprocal Thermal Efficiency   (PDAA) .... RTE
Reclearance in Flight [Aviation]   (FAAC) .... RIF
Recleared [Aviation]   (FAAC) .... RECLR
Recognition for Information Technology Achievement [An award]
    (PDAA) .... RITA
Recombinant Follicle-Stimulating Hormone [Endocrinology] .... RFSH
Record Organization Based on Transposition   (PDAA) .... ROBOT
Record/Update .... R/U
Recorded Program   (NTCM) .... REC
Recordimeter   (NTCM) .... RM
Recovery Storage Unit [Military] .... RSU
Recovery Storage Unit Boot Test [Military] .... RSBT
Recreational Active Vehicle [Toyota] [Concept car] .... RAV
Recreational Pilot Certificate [Aviation]   (DA) .... RPC
Recrystallization-Anneal   (PDAA) .... RA
Recrystallization Controlled Rolling   (PDAA) .... RCR
Rectangular Hysteresis Loop   (PDAA) .... RHL
Rectified Skew Orthomorphic   (PDAA) .... RSO
Recuperative Catalytic Oxidation [Chemical engineering] .... RCO
Recursive Equality Quadratic Program   (PDAA) .... REQP
Red Arrows Display Squadron [British] [ICAO designator]   (FAAC) ... SAK
Red Baron Aviation, Inc. [ICAO designator]   (FAAC) .... RBN
Red Blood Cell Transketolase [Medicine]   (PDAA) .... RBCTK
Red Devils Parachute Display Team [British] [ICAO designator]
    (FAAC) .... DEV
Red Interamericana de Telecommunicaciones [Inter-American
    Telecommunication Network]   (NTCM) .... RIT
Red Internacional de American Latina [International
    Telecommunication Network for Latin America]   (NTCM) ...... RITAL
Reduced Quantity Generator   (ERG) .... RQG
Redwing Airways, Inc. [ICAO designator]   (FAAC) .... RWG
Reeve Aleutian Airways, Inc. [ICAO designator]   (FAAC) .... RVV
Reference Breakdown Air Traffic Control Services Report   (FAAC) ...... REBAT
Reference Datum Height [Aviation]   (DA) .... RDH
Reference Library Data Base .... RLDB
Reflectance Units of Dirt Shade   (PDAA) .... RUDS
Reflected Electron Energy Loss Spectra .... REELS
Reflected-Reflected-Transmitted [Wave mechanics] .... RRT
Reflective Mossbauer Technique   (PDAA) .... REMOTE
Reflective Raised Pavement Marker [Highway design] .... RRPM
Refractive Index Gradient [Analytical chemistry] .... RIG
Refractories Association of Great Britain   (BI) .... RAGB
Refractory Reusable Surface Insulation   (PDAA) .... RSI
Refractory Users Federation [British]   (BI) .... RUF
Refueling Area Commander [Navy]   (ANA) .... RAC
Refuelling   (DA) .... RFLG
Refuse-Derived Fuel   (ERG) .... RDF
Regal Bahamas International Airways Ltd. [ICAO designator]
    (FAAC) .... RBH
Regency Airlines Ltd. [ICAO designator]   (FAAC) .... RGY
Regenerative Thermal Oxidation [Metallurgy] .... RTO
Regent Air [Canada] [ICAO designator]   (FAAC) .... RAH
Regimental Aviation Squadron [Army]   (ADDR) .... RAS
Region Air [Seychelles] [ICAO designator]   (FAAC) .... RGA
Region Air, Inc. [Canada] [ICAO designator]   (FAAC) .... RGR
Region Operations Control Center [NORAD] [ICAO designator]
    (FAAC) .... ROCC
Regionair Ltd. [British] [ICAO designator]   (FAAC) .... RGL
Regional Adjunct Language [Computer science]   (PDAA) .... RAL
Regional Air (Pty) Ltd. [South Africa] [ICAO designator]   (FAAC) ...... RAW
Regional Airlines [France] [ICAO designator]   (FAAC) .... RGI
Regional Area Forecast Center [ICAO designator]   (FAAC) .... RAFC
Regional Cooperative Physics Group [Educational institutions in
    Ohio, Michigan, Illinois and Pennsylvania]   (PDAA) .... RCPG
Regional Dissemination Centers [NASA]   (PDAA) .... RDC
Regional Enforcement Activities Plan [Environmental Protection
    Agency]   (ERG) .... REAP
Regional Environment Management Allocation Process   (PDAA) ...... REMAP
Regional Express Co. [ICAO designator]   (FAAC) .... REC

Regional Office Notice [Aviation]   (FAAC) .... RENO
Regional Pressure Setting   (DA) .... RPS
Regionnair, Inc. [Canada] [ICAO designator]   (FAAC) .... GIO
Register Load and Read .... RLRI
Register Module .... REGM
Register of Weather Stations [Meteorological Office]   (PDAA) .... ROWS
Registered Environmental Assessor .... REA
Registered Environmental Manager .... REM
Registered Environmental Professional .... REP
Registered Environmental Property Assessor .... REPA
Registered Export Establishment .... REE
Registered Hazardous Substances Professional [Environmental
    science] .... RHSP
Registration [ICAO designator]   (FAAC) .... REG
Regourd Aviation [France] [ICAO designator]   (FAAC) .... REG
Regular Best Asymptotically Normal   (PDAA) .... RBAN
Regular Expression [Computer science]   (NHD) .... REGEXP
Regular Priority [Wire service symbol]   (NTCM) .... R
Regularize Discriminant Analysis [Mathematics] .... RDA
Regularly-Scheduled Training [Military]   (ADDR) .... RST
Regulator of Mitotic Spindle Assembly [Cytology] .... RMS
Rehost Computer System [Aviation]   (FAAC) .... RCS
Reinforced Concrete Detailing System   (PDAA) .... RCDS
Reinforced Thermoplastic Polyurethane [Plastics] .... RTPU
Rejected Takeoff Area Available [Aviation]   (DA) .... RTOAA
Relational Data Base   (PDAA) .... RDB
Relational Structure Vertex Processor   (PDAA) .... RSVP
Relative Aerobic Strain   (PDAA) .... RAS
Relative Bearing Indicator [Aviation]   (DA) .... RBI
Relative Motion Collision Avoidance Calculator   (PDAA) .... REMCALC
Relative Plate Motion [Geophysics] .... RPM
Relativistic Kinematics   (PDAA) .... RELKIN
Relativistic and Spin-Orbit   (PDAA) .... RSO
Relaxation Map Analysis [Coatings] .... RMA
Relaxation-Sensitive Cell   (PDAA) .... RSC
Relay-Contact Network   (PDAA) .... RCN
Relay Services Association of Great Britain   (BI) .... RSA
Relevent Industry Sales   (PDAA) .... RIS
Reliability Engineering Analysis and Planning   (PDAA) .... REAP
Reliability Growth Program   (PDAA) .... RGP
Reliability, Maintainability, Supportability [Automotive engineering] .... RMS
Reliability Shakedown Test   (PDAA) .... RST
Reliant Airlines, Inc [ICAO designator]   (FAAC) .... RLT
Relief Transport Services Ltd. [British] [ICAO designator]   (FAAC) ...... RTS
Religious Drama Society of Great Britain   (BI) .... RDS
Religious Program   (NTCM) .... R
Remain Behind Equipment [Navy]   (ANA) .... RBE
Remark [Aviation]   (FAAC) .... RM
Remark   (FAAC) .... RMRK
Remedial Design/Remedial Action [Environmental Protection
    Agency]   (ERG) .... RD/RA
Remote Control Authority [FCC]   (NTCM) .... RC
Remote Control Tunnelling Machine .... RCTM
Remote Data Uplink [SmartOffice] [Computer science] .... RDU
Remote Generalized Application Language [Computer science]
    (PDAA) .... REGAL
Remote Independently-Operated Transceiver .... RIOT
Remote Instrument Package   (PDAA) .... RIP
Remote Line Tester   (PDAA) .... RLT
Remote Pickup [FCC]   (NTCM) .... RE
Remote Underwater Mine Countermeasure   (PDAA) .... RUMIC
Remotely-Operated Mobile Manipulator   (PDAA) .... ROMAN
Remotely-Piloted Mini-Blimp   (PDAA) .... RPMB
Remotely-Piloted Observation Aircraft Designator System
    (PDAA) .... RPOADS
Renewed License [FCC]   (NTCM) .... R
Reno Air, Inc. [ICAO designator]   (FAAC) .... ROA
Renown Aviation, Inc. [ICAO designator]   (FAAC) .... RGS
Rent Control System .... RCS
Rentavion CA [Venezuela] [ICAO designator]   (FAAC) .... RNT
Repair on Demand   (DA) .... ROD
Repair-at-Failure Maintenance   (PDAA) .... RAFM
Repairable Exchange Activity [Army] .... RXA
Repairs and Maintenance .... R & M
Repeat Expansion Detection [Genetics] .... RED
Repeat Formation Tester [Well drilling] .... RFT
Repeating Handheld Improved Non-Rifled Ordnance   (PDAA) ...... RHINO
Repetitive Activity Input/Output Plan   (PDAA) .... RAI/OP
Repetitive Counterelectrophoresis   (PDAA) .... RCE
Repetitive Element Column Analysis   (PDAA) .... RECA
Replacement Alpha Numeric Keyboard [Computer science]   (DA) ...... RANK
Replacement Flight Strip Printer [Aviation]   (DA) .... RFSP
Replacement Ion Chromatography [Spectrometry] .... RIC
Replication Protein A [Genetics] .... RPA
Report Back on Course [Aviation]   (FAAC) .... RBOC
Report Back on Frequency [Aviation]   (FAAC) .... RBOF
Report on Course [Aviation]   (DA) .... R-CRS
Report Departing [Aviation]   (DA) .... RD
Report Established in Block [Aviation]   (FAAC) .... REIB
Report Level [Aviation]   (FAAC) .... RLVL
Report Missing Account Radio Failure [Meteorology]   (FAAC) ...... RADNO
Report Over   (DA) .... RO
Report Starting Procedure Turn [Aviation]   (DA) .... RSPT

Report on Syndicated Programs (NTCM) ROSP
Reported Frequency (NTCM) RF
Reporter on Scene (NTCM) ROS
Reporting Officer RO
Republic of Singapore Air Force [*ICAO designator*] (FAAC) SAF
Request for Enhancement [*Computer science*] (NHD) RFE
Request Flight Plan [*Aviation*] (DA) RQP
Request Level Change Enroute [*Aviation*] (DA) RLCE
Request Level Not Available [*Aviation*] (FAAC) RLNA
Request for Proposal Information [*Competitive bidding*] RFPI
Required Navigation Performance [*Aviation*] (FAAC) RNP
Required Time of Arrival (DA) RTA
Requirements Evaluated against Cargo Transportation (PDAA) REACT
Reroute [*Aviation*] (FAAC) RERTE
Res Ipsa Loquitur [*The Thing Speaks for Itself*] [*Latin*] RIL
Research Council of Makeup Artists (NTCM) RCMA
Research or Exploratory Development (PDAA) RXD
Research Institute of African and African Diaspora Arts (EA) RIAADA
Research Institute of Pharmaceutical Sciences [*University of Mississippi*] (PDAA) RIPS
Research Planning Diagram (PDAA) RPD
Research and Technology Work Unit Summary R & TWUS
Reserve Naval Construction Force [*Navy*] (PDAA) RNCF
Reserves to Loans Ratio RLR
[*Fire Alarm*] **Reset Panel** [*NFPA pre-fire planning symbol*] (NFPA) RP
Resid Fluid Catalytic Cracking [*Petroleum refining*] RFCC
Resin-Bonded Glass-Fiber (PDAA) RBGF
Resonator-Controlled Microwave Source (PDAA) RCMS
Resorcinol Diglycidyl Ether [*Organic chemistry*] RDGE
Resort Airline, Inc. [*ICAO designator*] (FAAC) RST
Resource Application (ERG) RA
Resource Conservation and Recovery Information System (ERG) RCRIS
Resource Decision Network (PDAA) RDN
Resource Rent Royalty RRR
Respirable Dust Monitor (PDAA) RDM
Response Action Contractor [*Metallurgy*] RAC
Response Action Coordinator [*Environmental Protection Agency*] (ERG) RAC
Response Amplitude Operator (PDAA) RAO
Restauraciones Aeronauticas SA de CV [*Mexico*] [*ICAO designator*] (FAAC) RES
Restrictive Trade Practice RTP
Restructuring and Efficiency R & E
Resume Normal Speed [*Aviation*] (FAAC) RNLS
Resupply Vehicle [*Military*] RSV
Retail Alarm for Display and Intruder (PDAA) RADI
Retail Association for the Furnishing Trade [*British*] (BI) RAFT
Retail Distributors Association, Inc. [*British*] (BI) RDA
Retail Grocery, Dairy, and Allied Trades Association [*British*] (BI) RGDATA
Retrieval from the Literature on Electronics and Computer Sciences (PDAA) REFLECS
Retroactive Continuity [*Computer science*] (NHD) RETCON
Return on Assets [*Business term*] ROA
Return from Interrupt [*Computer science*] (NHD) RTI
Return on Revenue ROR
Reusable Engines, Partially External Expendable Tankage (PDAA) REPEET
Reuters Money Network [*Reality Technologies*] (PCM) RMN
Revenue Anticipation Warrant RAW
Reverberation (NTCM) REVERB
Reverberation Time (NTCM) RT
Reversal Film [*Cinematography*] (NTCM) REV
Reverse Processing [*Chemical engineering*] RP
Reverse Radial Immunodiffusion (PDAA) RRID
Reverse Shot [*Cinematography*] (NTCM) RS
Reversed-Field Pinch Reactor [*Plasma physics*] (PDAA) RFPR
Reversed-Phase Series (PDAA) RPS
Revision Message [*Aviation*] (DA) REV
Rewind R
Rex Aviation (New Zealand) Ltd. [*ICAO designator*] (FAAC) TNZ
Rheinland Air Service [*Germany*] [*ICAO designator*] (FAAC) RLD
Rheintalflug-Rolf Seewald [*Austria*] [*ICAO designator*] (FAAC) RTL
Rhesus Rotavirus [*Medicine*] RRV
Rhoades Aviation, Inc. [*ICAO designator*] (FAAC) RDS
Rhomboidal Air Controller (PDAA) RAC
Rhonavia [*France*] [*ICAO designator*] (FAAC) RHN
Ribonuclease Inhibitor RI
RIC, Inc. [*ICAO designator*] (FAAC) SDD
Rice Husk Ash (PDAA) RHA
Rich International Airways, Inc. [*ICAO designator*] (FAAC) RIA
Richards Aviation, Inc. [*ICAO designator*] (FAAC) RVC
Richardson's Airway, Inc. [*ICAO designator*] (FAAC) RIC
Richland Aviation [*ICAO designator*] (FAAC) RCA
Ride Quality Meter [*Automotive testing*] RQM
Riga Airlines [*Latvia*] [*ICAO designator*] (FAAC) RIG
Right [*Direction of Turn*] [*ICAO designator*] (FAAC) RITE
Right Angle Drive (PDAA) RAD
Right Base [*Aviation*] (FAAC) RB
Rigid Intermediate Bulk Container RIBC
Rigid Plastic Foam RPF
Rijnmond Air Services BV [*Netherlands*] [*ICAO designator*] (FAAC) RAZ
Rimrock Airlines, Inc. [*ICAO designator*] (FAAC) RIM
Ring Out and Stress Tester (PDAA) ROAST
Rio Airways, Inc. [*ICAO designator*] (FAAC) REO
Rio-Sul, Servicos Aereos Regionais SA [*Brazil*] [*ICAO designator*] (FAAC) RSL
RISC Single Chip [*IBM*] [*Computer science*] RSC
Riser Valve [*NFPA pre-fire planning symbol*] (NFPA) RV
Risk Assessment Guidance for Superfund [*Environmental science*] RAGS
Risk-Based Audit RBA
Risk Management Plan RMP
Risk Reduction Engineering Laboratory RREL
Risley Engineering and Materials Laboratory (PDAA) REML
River Assault Craft [*Navy*] (ANA) RAC
River Ice Breaker (PDAA) RIB
RN Aviation Ltd. [*British*] [*ICAO designator*] (FAAC) RMN
RNA [*Ribonucleic Acid*] **Binding Domain** [*Biochemistry*] RBD
Road Accident Tabulation Language (PDAA) RATTLE
Road Bitumen Association [*British*] (BI) RBA
Road Construction Unit (PDAA) RCU
Roadair Lines IC [*Canada*] [*ICAO designator*] (FAAC) RDL
Robinton Aereo CA [*Dominican Republic*] [*ICAO designator*] (FAAC) RBT
Rock [*Maps and charts*] R
Rock Mechanics Applied to Mine Planning (PDAA) RAMPLAN
Rocker Arm Oiling Time (PDAA) RAOT
Rocky Mountain [*Canada*] [*ICAO designator*] (FAAC) ROC
Rocky Mountain Airways, Inc. [*ICAO designator*] (FAAC) RMA
Rocky Mountain Midget Racing Association [*Automobile competition organizer*] RMMRA
Rog-Air Ltd. [*Canada*] [*ICAO designator*] (FAAC) FAD
Rogel [*C.C. Sergio Gonzales*], **Ing.** [*Mexico*] [*ICAO designator*] (FAAC) ROG
Rogers Aviation Ltd. [*British*] [*ICAO designator*] (FAAC) RAV
Roller Owners' Association [*British*] (BI) ROA
Rolling on the Floor Laughing [*Computer hacker terminology*] (NHD) ROTFL
Rolls Royce Ltd. [*British*] [*ICAO designator*] (FAAC) RRL
Rolls Royce Ltd. (Bristol Engine Division) [*British*] [*ICAO designator*] (FAAC) BTU
Romavia [*Romania*] [*ICAO designator*] (FAAC) RMV
Romeo Series L [*Alfa-Romeo*] [*Automotive model designation*] RL
Romeo Series L Normale [*Alfa-Romeo*] [*Automotive model designation*] RLN
Romeo Series L Sport [*Alfa-Romeo*] [*Automotive model designation*] RLS
Romeo Series L Super Sport [*Alfa-Romeo*] [*Automotive model designation*] RLSS
Romeo Series L Targa Florio [*Alfa-Romeo*] [*Automotive model designation*] RLTF
Romeo Series L Turismo [*Alfa-Romeo*] [*Automotive model designation*] RLT
Romeo Series M Unificto [*Alfa-Romeo*] [*Automotive model designation*] RMU
Room (NFPA) R
Room Index (PDAA) RI
Root Sum Square (DA) RSS
Ross Air Training [*British*] [*ICAO designator*] (FAAC) RTY
Ross Aviation, Inc. [*ICAO designator*] (FAAC) NRG
Rossair Pty Ltd. [*Australia*] [*ICAO designator*] (FAAC) RFS
Roswell Airlines, Inc. [*ICAO designator*] (FAAC) RAL
Rotary Combustion Engine (PDAA) RCE
Rotary Hydraulic Arresting Gear (PDAA) RHAG
Rotary Pellet Launcher [*Military*] (PDAA) RPL
Rotating Bomb Oxidation Test [*Lubricant testing*] [*Automotive engineering*] R-BOT
Rotating Gold Ring-Disc Electrode (PDAA) RGRDE
Rotating Magnetic Field [*Spectrometry*] RMF
Rotation Planar Chromatography RPC
Rotation Remanent Magnetization (PDAA) RRM
Rotational Energy Transfer [*Chemical physics*] RET
Rotogravure [*Printing process*] (NTCM) ROTO
Rotorua Aero Club [*New Zealand*] [*ICAO designator*] (FAAC) RAC
Rough Cut Capacity Planning [*Manufacturing management*] RCCP
Round Tube-Plate Fin [*Heat exchanger*] RTPF
Roundtable [*Bulletin board system*] [*Computer science*] (PCM) RT
Route Contingency Reserve [*Aviation*] (DA) RCR
Route Forcast [*Aviation*] (FAAC) ROFOR
Routine for Executive Multi-Unit Simulation (PDAA) REMUS
Routine Message Precedence [*Telecommunications*] (ADDR) RR
Routing Automation Technique (PDAA) RAT
Rover Airways International, Inc. [*ICAO designator*] (FAAC) ROV
Rowett Research Institute [*British*] (BI) RRI
Royal Air Force [*British*] [*ICAO designator*] (FAAC) RFR
Royal Air Force of Oman (Air Transport) [*ICAO designator*] (FAAC) MJN
Royal Air Force Sailing Association [*British*] (BI) RAFSA
Royal Air Inter-Compagnie d'Exploitation de Lignes Aer Interieures [*Morocco*] [*ICAO designator*] (FAAC) RAI
Royal Air Maroc - Compagnie Nationale de Transports Aeriens [*Morocco*] [*ICAO designator*] (FAAC) RAM
Royal American Airways, Inc. [*ICAO designator*] (FAAC) RLM
Royal Association in Aid of the Deaf and Dumb [*British*] (BI) RADD
Royal Association of British Dairy Farmers [*British*] (BI) RABDF
Royal Australian Air Force [*ICAO designator*] (FAAC) ASY
Royal Australian Air Force [*ICAO designator*] (FAAC) RAAF
Royal British Nurses' Association [*British*] (BI) RBNA

Royal Brunei Airlines [*ICAO designator*]   (FAAC)... RBA
Royal Caledonian Horticultural Society [*British*]   (BI) .... RCHS
Royal Channel Islands Yacht Club   (BI)... RCI
Royal Choral Association [*British*]   (BI).. RCA
Royal Docks Association [*British*]   (BI)... RDA
Royal Jordanian [*ICAO designator*]   (FAAC) .... RJA
Royal Jordanian Air Force [*ICAO designator*]   (FAAC)............................ RJZ
Royal Malaysian Air Force [*ICAO designator*]   (FAAC)........................... RMF
Royal Masonic Institution for Girls [*British*]   (BI) .... RMIG
Royal Motor Yacht Club [*British*]   (BI) .... RMYC
Royal National Homing Union [*British*]   (BI)... RNHU
Royal Naval Minewatching Service [*British*]   (BI) .... RNMWS
Royal Navy [*British*] [*ICAO designator*]   (FAAC) .... NVY
Royal Nepal Airlines Corp. [*ICAO designator*]   (FAAC)........................... RNA
Royal Netherlands Air Force [*ICAO designator*]   (FAAC) .... NAF
Royal Netherlands Navy [*ICAO designator*]   (FAAC)................................ NRN
Royal New Zealand Ballet... NZB
Royal Norwegian Air Force [*ICAO designator*]   (FAAC)........................... NOW
Royal Oman Police [*ICAO designator*]   (FAAC)... ROP
Royal Phoenix Airlines [*Nigeria*] [*ICAO designator*]   (FAAC) .... DBO
Royal Society of Ulster Architects [*British*]   (BI) .... RSUA
Royal Surgical Aid Society [*British*]   (BI)... RSAS
Royal Swazi National Airways Corp. [*Swaziland*] [*ICAO designator*]
    (FAAC) .... RSN
Royal Tongan Airlines [*Tonga*] [*ICAO designator*]   (FAAC) .... HRH
Royal Welsh Agricultural Society   (BI)... RWAS
Royal Yachting Association [*British*]   (BI) .... RYA
RST Aviation, NV [*Belgium*] [*ICAO designator*]   (FAAC)......................... DMD
Rubber Block Drive [*Mechanical power transmission*] .... RBD
Rubber-Impregnated Chopped Strand   (PDAA).. RICS
Rubber-Modified Asphalt Concrete.. RUMAC
Rubber and Plastic Footwear Manufacturers' Association [*British*]
    (BI)... RPFMA
Rubber Proofers' Association [*British*]   (BI)... RPA
Rubber-Toughened Amorphous Nylon [*Organic chemistry*] .... RTAN
Rubber-Toughened Polymethyl Methacrylate [*Organic chemistry*] ....
                                                                                                                    RTPMMA
Rudder Shaped Hull   (PDAA)... RUSH
Rudimentary Adaptive System for Computer-Aided Learning
    (PDAA).. RASCAL
Rugby Fives Association [*British*]   (BI)... RFA
Run of Publication   (NTCM) .... ROP
Runway [*Aviation*]   (DA) .... R
Runway Center Line Lights [*ICAO designator*]   (FAAC) .... RCLL
Runway Edge Light [*ICAO designator*]   (FAAC)... REDL
Runway End Light [*Aviation*]   (FAAC) .... RENL
Runway End Safety Area [*Aviation*]   (DA)... RESA
Runway Guard Light [*Aviation*]   (DA) .... RGL
Runway Lead-In Lighting System [*Aviation*]   (FAAC)................................ RLLS
Runway Light [*Aviation*]   (DA).. RL
Runway Surface Condition [*Aviation*]   (FAAC).. RSCD
Runway Threshold Light [*Aviation*]   (FAAC).. RTHL
Runway Touchdown Zone Light [*Aviation*]   (FAAC).................................. RTZL
Runway Visual Range Center [*Aviation*]   (DA).. RVRC
Rural/Regional Education Association   (AEE).. R/REA
Rural and Remote Area .... RARA
Russian Foundation for Basic Research .... RFBR
Russian Spring-Summer Encephalitis [*Medicine*]   (MAH)........................... RSS
Rutgers- [*The*] State University [*New Brunswick, NJ*]   (PDAA) .... RU
RV-Aviation [*Finland*] [*ICAO designator*]   (FAAC).................................. RVI
Rwanda [*Aircraft nationality and registration mark*]   (FAAC) 9XR
Rwandan Patriotic Front [*Political party*] .... RPF
Ryan Air Services, Inc. [*ICAO designator*]   (FAAC).................................... RYA
Ryan Aviation Corp. [*ICAO designator*]   (FAAC)....................................... RYN
Ryanair [*Ireland*] [*ICAO designator*]   (FAAC)... RYR
Ryanodine Receptor Channel [*Biochemistry*] .... RyRC
Rynes Aviation, Inc. [*ICAO designator*]   (FAAC) .... RAA

S

217

Seamless (DAC) ... S
Search, Detection and Recognition [*Military*] ... SDR
Search and Rescue (FAAC) ... SAR
Search & Rescue 22 [*British*] [*ICAO designator*] (FAAC) ... SRD
Search & Rescue 202 [*British*] [*ICAO designator*] (FAAC) ... SRG
Search & Rescue HQ [*British*] [*ICAO designator*] (FAAC) ... SRW
Search Track Intermediate Frequency [*Military*] ... STIF
Second Generation Non-English-Speaking Background ... NESB2
Second Harmonic (PDAA) ... SH
Second Order Coherent Multiple Access (PDAA) ... SOCMA
Second-Time-Around-Beacon-Echo (PDAA) ... STABE
Secondary [*ICAO designator*] (FAAC) ... SRY
Secondary Alkane Sulfonate [*Surfactant*] [*Organic chemistry*] ... SAS
Secondary Chemical Equilibria [*Chromatography*] ... SCE
Secondary Refrigerant Freezing (PDAA) ... SRF
Secondary School Examinations Council [*British*] (BI) ... SSEC
Secondary School Science Project [*Princeton University*] (AEE) ... SSSP
Secondary Target Line [*Army*] ... STL
Secondary, Technical, and University Teachers' Insurance Society [*British*] (BI) ... STUTIS
Secreted Alkaline Phosphatase [*Biochemistry*] ... SEAP
Sector Airlines [*Canada*] [*ICAO designator*] (FAAC) ... XTR
Sector Operations Control Center [*NORAD*] (FAAC) ... SOCC
Secure Mobile, Anti-Jam, Reliable Tactical Trainer [*Army*] ... SMART-T
Security Committee ... SECOM
Sedalia-Marshall-Booville Stage Line, Inc. [*ICAO designator*] (FAAC) ... STG
Sedona Air Center, Inc. [*ICAO designator*] (FAAC) ... SED
See Our Message [*Aviation*] (FAAC) ... SOMSG
SEEA-Southeast European Airlines [*Greece*] [*ICAO designator*] (FAAC) ... GRE
Seed, Oil, Cake, and General Produce Association [*British*] (BI) ... SOCGPA
Seeking, Asking, and Written [*Questionnaire*] (PDAA) ... SAW
Segment End of Pulse ... SEOP
Segment End Pulse ... SEP
Segmentation Violation [*Computer science*] (NHD) ... SEGV
Seismic Personnel Intrusion Detector (PDAA) ... SPID
Select Concrete Objectives for Research Emphasis (PDAA) ... SCORE
Selectair Ltd. [*British*] [*ICAO designator*] (FAAC) ... SEL
Selected Acquisitions Information and Management System (PDAA) ... SAIMA
Selected Non-Communist Countries ... SNCC
Selected-Reaction Monitoring [*Spectrometry*] ... SRM
Selected Special Weather Report [*Aviation*] (FAAC) ... SPECI
Selection Work Sheets/Summary Parts ... SWS/SUM PTS
Selective Access to Tactical Information (PDAA) ... SATI
Selective Oxidation Process (PDAA) ... SOP
Selective Ride Control [*Suspension systems*] [*Automotive engineering*] ... SRC
Selective Serotonin Reuptake Inhibitor [*Physiology*] ... SSRI
Selectively-Induced X-Ray Emission Spectroscopy ... SIXES
Self-Adhesive Foreign Object (PDAA) ... SAFO
Self-Agglomerator (PDAA) ... SAG
Self-Contained, Toxic Environment, Protective Outfit [*Army*] (INF) ... STEPO
Self-Erecting Marine Platform (PDAA) ... SEMP
Self-floating Integrated Deck (PDAA) ... SFID
Self-Launching Motor Glider [*Aviation*] (DA) ... SLMG
Self-Orthogonal Convolutional Code (PDAA) ... SOCC
Self-Shifting Synchronizing (PDAA) ... SSS
Self-Tracking Automatic Lock-On Circuit (PDAA) ... STALOC
Selkirk Remote Sensing Ltd. [*Canada*] [*ICAO designator*] (FAAC) ... SRS
Semantics-Oriented Language [*Computer science*] (PDAA) ... SEMANOL
Semester ... SEM
Semi-Active RADAR Simulator [*Military*] ... SARS
Semi-Ascending Order Arrangement (PDAA) ... SAOA
Semi-Automated Artwork Generator System (PDAA) ... SAAGS
Semi-Automated Computer-Oriented Text (PDAA) ... SCOT
Semi-Automatic Speaker Identification System (PDAA) ... SASIS
Semi-Empirical Design of Impellers [*Hydraulics*] [*Computer-aided design*] ... SEDI
Semi-Recessed Oxide (PDAA) ... SEMIROX
Semi-Submarine Ice-Breaking Tanker (PDAA) ... SSIT
Semiautomatic Flight Inspection Aircraft (FAAC) ... SAFI
Semiconductor Infrared Photography (PDAA) ... SCIRP
Semisolid Material [*Metallurgy*] ... SSM
Semitool Europe Ltd. [*British*] [*ICAO designator*] (FAAC) ... STE
Sempati Air PT [*Indonesia*] [*ICAO designator*] (FAAC) ... SSR
Sempati Air Transport PT [*Indonesia*] [*ICAO designator*] (FAAC) ... SMP
Senair Charter Ltd. [*British*] [*ICAO designator*] (FAAC) ... SEN
Senate Radio-Television Correspondents Association (NTCM) ... SRTCA
Senegal [*Aircraft nationality and registration mark*] (FAAC) ... 6V
Senegal [*Aircraft nationality and registration mark*] (FAAC) ... 6W
Senegalair [*Senegal*] [*ICAO designator*] (FAAC) ... SGL
Senior Army Reserve Commanders Association ... SARCA
Senior Assistant Secretary ... SAS
Senior Manager ... SM
Senior Officer Service ... SOS
Senior Officer Structure ... SOS
Senior Ranking Officer [*Army*] (ADDR) ... SRO
Senior Training Officer ... STO
Sensitive Acoustic Detection Equipment (PDAA) ... SADE
Sensitivity (FAAC) ... SENS
Sensitized-Erythrocyte-Lysis (PDAA) ... SEL
Sensitized Human Cell (PDAA) ... SHC
Sensor Control Anti-Anti-Radiation Missile RADAR Evaluation (PDAA) ... SCARE
Sentry Interceptor Subsystem Contractor [*DoD*] ... SISC
Separable Costs-Remaining Benefits (PDAA) ... SC-RB
Separate Access Landing System [*Aviation*] (DA) ... SALS
Separate Engineering Control Air Limits [*Environmental science*] ... SECAL
Separate Magnetic (NTCM) ... SEPMAG
Separation Transfer Point [*Army*] (ADDR) ... STP
Sequenced Flashing Lights [*Aviation*] (DA) ... SSAL
Sequential Boolean Analyzer (PDAA) ... SBA
Sequential Multiple Analysis Plus Computer (PDAA) ... SMAC
Sequential Polling and Review of Interacting Teams of Experts (PDAA) ... SPRITE
Sequential Range Policy (PDAA) ... SRP
Sequential Test Plan Generator (PDAA) ... STPG
Sequential Thermal Anhysteric Magnetization [*Helical scan videotape duplicating system*] (NTCM) ... STAM
Serial Flechette Rifle (PDAA) ... SFR
Serial Infrared Communications Interface [*Hewlett Packard Co.*] (PCM) ... SIR
Serial Line Internet Protocol [*Telecommunications*] (PCM) ... SLIP
Serial Network Interface (PDAA) ... SNI
Serial Peripheral Interface [*Electronics*] ... SPI
Serial Signalling Scheme (PDAA) ... SSS
Serializer-Deserializer Cyclic Redundancy Check (PDAA) ... SERDES CRC
Serib Wings [*Italy*] [*ICAO designator*] (FAAC) ... ISW
Serious Injury Frequency Rate ... SIFR
Serious Literary, Artistic, Political, or Scientific Value [*Obscenity law*] (NTCM) ... SLAPS
SERTEL [*Servicios Telereservacios SA de CV*] [*ICAO designator*] (FAAC) ... LOM
Service Aerien Francais [*France*] [*ICAO designator*] (FAAC) ... SHP
Service Aerien Gouvernmental Ministere des Transports Gouvernment du Quebec [*Canada*] [*ICAO designator*] (FAAC) ... BOM
Service Zone Indication [*Computer science*] (IAA) ... SZI
Serviced [*Automotive advertising*] ... SRVCD
Services Aeronautiques Roannais [*France*] [*ICAO designator*] (FAAC) ... RNS
Servicio Aereo de Honduras SA [*ICAO designator*] (FAAC) ... SHA
Servicio de Helicopteros SL [*Spain*] [*ICAO designator*] (FAAC) ... SDH
Servicio Leo Lopez SA de CV [*Mexico*] [*ICAO designator*] (FAAC) ... LLA
Servicio de Vigilancia Aerea del Ministerio de Seguridad Publica [*Costa Rica*] [*ICAO designator*] (FAAC) ... MSP
Servicios Aereolineas Mexicanas SA de CV [*Mexico*] [*ICAO designator*] (FAAC) ... SMS
Servicios Aereos Barsa SA de CV [*Mexico*] [*ICAO designator*] (FAAC) ... SBS
Servicios Aereos Cruzeiro do Sul SA [*Brazil*] [*ICAO designator*] (FAAC) ... CRZ
Servicios Aereos Especiales de Jalisco SA de CV [*Mexico*] [*ICAO designator*] (FAAC) ... SJA
Servicios Aereos Especializados en Transportes Petroleros [*Colombia*] [*ICAO designator*] (FAAC) ... KSP
Servicios Aereos Gadel SA de CV [*Mexico*] [*ICAO designator*] (FAAC) ... GDE
Servicios Aereos de La Capital [*Colombia*] [*ICAO designator*] (FAAC) ... SAD
Servicios Aereos de Los Angeles SA de CV [*Mexico*] [*ICAO designator*] (FAAC) ... AGE
Servicios Aereos Nacionales [*Ecuador*] [*ICAO designator*] (FAAC) ... SAN
Servicios Aereos del Nazas SA de CV [*Mexico*] [*ICAO designator*] (FAAC) ... NAZ
Servicios Aereos Norte Sur SA de CV [*Mexico*] [*ICAO designator*] (FAAC) ... SNE
Servicios Aereos de Pilotos Ejecutivos [*Colombia*] [*ICAO designator*] (FAAC) ... SAR
Servicios Aereos Rutas Oriente SA de CV [*Mexico*] [*ICAO designator*] (FAAC) ... SRO
Servicios Aereos del Sol SA de CV [*Mexico*] [*ICAO designator*] (FAAC) ... AOS
Servicios Aereos do Vale Amazonico SA [*Brazil*] [*ICAO designator*] (FAAC) ... TNS
Servicios Aereos del Vaupes Ltd. [*Colombia*] [*ICAO designator*] (FAAC) ... SDV
Servicios Aeroes Litoral SA de CV [*Mexico*] [*ICAO designator*] (FAAC) ... SLI
Servicios Aeros de Chihuahua Aerochisa SA de CV [*Mexico*] [*ICAO designator*] (FAAC) ... AHI
Servicios Auxiliares de Transportes [*ICAO designator*] (FAAC) ... SATA
Servicios Auxiliares de Transportes Aereos [*Brazil*] [*ICAO designator*] (FAAC) ... STS
Servicios a la Navegacion en el Espacio Aereo Mexicano [*Mexico*] [*ICAO designator*] (FAAC) ... SENEAM
Servicios a la Navegacion en el Espacio Aereo Mexicano [*Mexico*] [*ICAO designator*] (FAAC) ... XMX
Servicios Politecnicos Aereos SA [*Spain*] [*ICAO designator*] (FAAC) ... SPASA
Servicios Telereservacios SA de CV [*ICAO designator*] (FAAC) ... SERTEL
Servicious de Alquiler Aereo SA de CV [*Mexico*] [*ICAO designator*] (FAAC) ... SQL
Servico Acoriana de Transportes Aereos [*Portugal*] [*ICAO designator*] (FAAC) ... SAT

Serving (FAAC) .... SVG
Servisair Ltd. [*British*] [*ICAO designator*] (FAAC) .... SGH
Set Priority Level [*Computer science*] (NHD) .... SPL
Setpoint Precision Infrared Angular Scanner (PDAA) .... SPIRAS
Seven Bar Flying Service, Inc. [*ICAO designator*] (FAAC) .... SBF
Severe Weather Forecast [*National Weather Service*] (FAAC) .... WW
Severity of Ozone Cracking (PDAA) .... SOC
Sewage Plant Manufacturers' Association [*British*] (BI) .... SPMA
Sewing Machine Dealers Association Ltd. [*British*] (BI) .... SMDA
Sexual Harassment Guidelines .... SHG
Sexually-Acquired Reactive Arthritis [*Medicine*] (PDAA) .... SARA
Seychelles [*Aircraft nationality and registration mark*] (FAAC) S7
Seychelles International Safari Air Ltd. [*ICAO designator*] (FAAC) .... SIS
SFT-Sudanese Flight [*ICAO designator*] (FAAC) .... STF
Shabair [*Zaire*] [*ICAO designator*] (FAAC) .... SHB
Shaheen Air International [*Pakistan*] [*ICAO designator*] (FAAC) .... SAI
Shaheen Airport Services [*Pakistan*] [*ICAO designator*] (FAAC) .... SHN
Shakedown Cruise [*Navy*] (ANA) .... SHKDNCRU
Shaken and Circulatory Oxidation Test (PDAA) .... SCOT
Shanghai Airlines [*China*] [*ICAO designator*] (FAAC) .... CSH
Shannon Executive Aviation Ireland Ltd. [*ICAO designator*] (FAAC) .... SXA
Shape Selective Cracking (PDAA) .... SSC
Shard Hospital Online Real-Time Time-Sharing (PDAA) .... SHORT
Sharing Time (NTCM) .... S
Sharjah Ruler's Flight [*United Arab Emirates*] [*ICAO designator*] (FAAC) .... SHJ
Shavano Air, Inc. [*ICAO designator*] (FAAC) .... SHV
Shawbury FTU [*British*] [*ICAO designator*] (FAAC) .... SYS
Shear Area Transition Temperature (PDAA) .... SATT
Shear-Stress Responsive Element [*Biochemistry*] .... SSRE
Shear Thinning Index (PDAA) .... STI
Sheet Metal Industries Association [*British*] (BI) .... SMIA
Sheet-Metal Screw (DAC) .... SMS
Sheet Molding Compound Automotive Alliance [*An association*] .... SMCAA
Shell Aircraft Ltd. [*British*] [*ICAO designator*] (FAAC) .... SHE
Shenyang Regional Administration of CAA of China [*ICAO designator*] (FAAC) .... CBF
Shielding Technologies Inc. .... STI
Shift Register Available .... SRA
Shift-Register Transfer [*Computer science*] .... SRT
Ship Acquisition and Improvement Council [*Navy*] (ANA) .... SAIC
Ship Acquisition and Improvement Council-Working Group [*Navy*] (ANA) .... SAIC-WG
Ship-Design Engineering-Aided by Interactive Remote Display (PDAA) .... SEABIRD
Ship Production Control System (PDAA) .... SPCS
Ship Tethered Aerial Platform (PDAA) .... STAPL
Ship Upkeep Information System [*Ministry of Defense*] [*British*] (PDAA) .... SUIS
Shipboard Equipments Environmental Design Study (PDAA) .... SEEDS
Shipboard Information System Development Group [*Maritime Transportation ResearchBoard*] (PDAA) .... SISDG
Shipboard Integrated Processing Display System [*Military*] .... SHIN PADS
Shipboard Passive Surveillance and Detection System (PDAA) .... SPSD
Shipbuilders and Repairers' National Association [*British*] (BI) .... SRNA
Shipbuilding Exports Association [*British*] (BI) .... SEA
Shiplap (DAC) .... S/L
Shiplap (DAC) .... S/LAP
Ships Anti-Missile Integrated Defense System (PDAA) .... SAMIDS
Ship's Inertial Navigation System .... SINS
Shipwrecked Fishermen and Mariners Royal Benevolent Society [*British*] (BI) .... SFMS
Shooter Air Courier Corp. [*Canada*] [*ICAO designator*] (FAAC) .... SHR
Shop Readiness Objective .... SRO
Shopfitting Research and Development Council [*British*] (BI) .... SRDC
Shoprite Group Ltd. [*British*] [*ICAO designator*] (FAAC) .... SHG
Shore Requirements Strength and Manpower Planning System [*Navy*] (ANA) .... SHORSTRAMPS
Shorouk Air [*Egypt*] [*ICAO designator*] (FAAC) .... SHK
Short Baseline SONAR (PDAA) .... SBS
Short Brothers PLC [*British*] [*ICAO designator*] (FAAC) .... SBL
Short Circuit Conductance Matrix (PDAA) .... SCCM
Short Nickel Line Accumulating Register Calculator (PDAA) .... SNARC
Short-Pulse LASER .... SPL
Short-Range Air Defense .... SHORD
Short-Range Navigation System (FAAC) .... SHORN
Short-Range Surveillance and Target Acquisition System (PDAA) .... SHORSTAS
Short Range Thermal Imaging Equipment (PDAA) .... SHORTIE
Short Rotary Furnace [*Metallurgy*] .... SRF
Short-Term Anxiety-Provoking Psychotherapy (PDAA) .... STAPP
Short Term Conflict Alert System [*Aviation*] (DA) .... STCA
Short-Term Energy Monitoring [*Colorado State University*] .... STEM
Short-Term Monetary Support [*Finance*] .... STMS
Short Term Reinitialization [*Army*] .... STR
Short-Term Waviness [*Surface finish*] .... STW
Short Tons Raw Value .... STRV
Short Tour Return Date [*Military*] .... TDR
Shortened Disjunctive Normal Form (PDAA) .... SDNF
Shortest Remaining Processing Time (PDAA) .... SRPT
Shorthand Programming Language in a COBOL Environment [*Computer science*] (PDAA) .... SPLICE

Shot through Obscuration MILES [*Multiple Integrated LASER Engagement System*] [*Army*] .... STOM
Show [*Automotive advertising*] .... SHO
Show and Breed Secretaries' Association [*British*] (BI) .... SBSA
Showroom [*Automotive advertising*] .... SHWRM
Shuswap Flight Centre Ltd. [*Canada*] [*ICAO designator*] (FAAC) .... SFC
Shut-in Casing Pressure [*Well drilling technology*] .... SICP
Shuttle, Inc. [*ICAO designator*] (FAAC) .... USS
Si-Chang Flying Service Co. Ltd. [*Thailand*] [*ICAO designator*] (FAAC) .... SCR
Sichuan Airlines [*China*] [*ICAO designator*] (FAAC) .... CSC
Side and Back Rack System (PDAA) .... SBRS
Side-Impact Finite Element Model [*Automotive safety*] [*Computer-assisted design*] .... SIFEM
Side-Impact Protection System [*Automotive safety*] .... SIPS
Side Looking Modular Multi-Mission RADAR (PDAA) .... SLAMMR
Sidelobe Blanking Indicator .... SLBI
Sidewall Indentation [*Tire manufacturing*] .... SWI
Sidfin Air Ltd. [*Zambia*] [*ICAO designator*] (FAAC) .... SID
Sierra Express, Inc. [*ICAO designator*] (FAAC) .... SIE
Sierra Leone [*Aircraft nationality and registration mark*] (FAAC) 9L
Sierra National Airlines [*Sierra Leone*] [*ICAO designator*] (FAAC) .... SLA
Sierra Pacific Airlines [*ICAO designator*] (FAAC) .... SPA
Sight Switch Technology System (PDAA) .... SSTS
Sigi Air [*Bulgaria*] [*ICAO designator*] (FAAC) .... BGR
SIGINT [*Signal Intelligence*] Operational Tasking Authority [*Military*] .... SOTA
Sigma Delta Chi [*Fraternity*] (NTCM) .... SDX
Sign and Display Trades Union [*British*] (BI) .... SDTU
Sign Extend [*Computer science*] (NHD) .... SEX
Signal Band .... SB
Signal Band Indication .... SBI
Signal Band Mainlobe .... SBML
Signal Level Meter (NTCM) .... SLM
Signal Processor Group .... SPG
Signal Processor Group Test Assembly .... SPGTA
Signal Transducer and Activator of Transcription [*Biochemistry*] .... STAT
Signalling Preprocessing Program (PDAA) .... SPRP
Significant Emotional Events .... SEE
Significant New Alternatives Policy [*Environmental science*] .... SNAP
Significant Weather [*Aviation*] (FAAC) .... SIGWX
Siimes Aviation AB [*Finland*] [*ICAO designator*] (FAAC) .... SII
Silent (NTCM) .... SIL
Silica and Moulding Sands Association [*British*] (BI) .... SAMSA
Silicate-Oxy-Apatite (PDAA) .... SOAP
Silicon Coating by Inverted Meniscus (PDAA) .... SCIM
Silicon Controlled Rectifier Regulated Direct Current (PDAA) .... SCRDC
Silicon on Insulating Substrate (PDAA) .... SOIS
Silicon-on-Insulator and Polysilicon (PDAA) .... SIP
Silicon Nitride-Masked Thermally-Oxidized Post-Diffused Mesa Process (PDAA) .... SIMTOP
Silicon Valley Group Lithography (ECON) .... SVGL
Silk and Man-Made Fibre Users' Association [*British*] (BI) .... SMFUA
Silkair (Singapore) Pte Ltd. [*ICAO designator*] (FAAC) .... SLK
Silkworm Cytoplasmic Polyhedrosis Virus (PDAA) .... SCPV
Silvair, Inc. [*ICAO designator*] (FAAC) .... IJS
Silver [*Automotive advertising*] .... SLVR
Silver-Dye-Bleach (PDAA) .... SDB
Similar (DAC) .... SIM
Simple Approach Lighting System [*Aviation*] (FAAC) .... SALS
Simple Exponentially-Weighted Moving-Average (PDAA) .... SEWMA
Simple [*or Small*] Matter of Programming (NHD) .... SMOP
Simple-Minded Artificial Intelligence (PDAA) .... SMARTIE
Simple Network Interacting Program Executive (PDAA) .... SNIPE
Simple User Interface Toolkit [*University of Virginia*] .... SUIT
Simplex Working [*Telecommunications*] (ADDR) .... WX
Simplified Accountancy Language (PDAA) .... SIMAL
Simplified Aircraft Instrument Landing System (PDAA) .... SAILA
Simplified Federal Urban Driving Schedule [*Electric vehicle testing*] .... SFUDS
Simplified Interpretive COBOL Operating System (PDAA) .... SICLOPS
Simply Transformed Manufacture .... STM
Simpson Air Ltd. [*Canada*] [*ICAO designator*] (FAAC) .... NCS
Simpson Quadrature Used Adaptively - Noise Killed (PDAA) .... SQUANK
Simulated All-Purpose Language (PDAA) .... SIMAL
Simulated Approach [*Aviation*] .... SIM
Simulated Countercurrent Moving-Bed Chromatographic Reactor [*Chemical engineering*] .... SCMCR
Simulated Flight Training Ltd. [*British*] [*ICAO designator*] (FAAC) .... SIM
Simulation Package for University Research and Teaching (PDAA) .... SPURT
Simulation Program for Sequential System (PDAA) .... SPROSS
Simulative Electronic Deception [*Army*] (ADDR) .... SED
Simultaneous Buying and Selling Arrangement .... SBS
Sinair [*France*] [*ICAO designator*] (FAAC) .... SIN
Since Major Overhaul (DA) .... SMOH
Singapore [*Aircraft nationality and registration mark*] (FAAC) 9V
Singapore Airlines Ltd. [*ICAO designator*] (FAAC) .... SIA
Single Anchor Leg Storage (PDAA) .... SALS
Single Bayonet [*Lamp base*] .... SB
Single Camshaft Type A [*Cosworth racing engines*] [*Automotive engineering*] .... SCA
Single Contact [*Lamp base*] (NTCM) .... SC

Single Echelon Multi-Base Resource Allocation Technique (PDAA) ... SEMBRAT
Single-Electron Capacitance Spectroscopy ... SECS
Single End Strip Adhesion (PDAA) ... SESA
Single Floating-Gate Amplifier [*Electronics*] (PDAA) ... SFGA
Single Geometric Model [*Computer-assisted design*] ... SGM
Single-Hung (DAC) ... SH
Single Molecule Detection [*Analytical chemistry*] ... SMD
Single Pilot Instrument Rating [*Aviation*] (DA) ... SPIR
Single Role Mine-Hunter [*Military*] (PDAA) ... SRMH
Single-Site Catalyst [*Chemistry*] ... SSC
Single Thread System ... STS
Single-Voyage Permit ... SVP
Single Wheel [*Landing gear*] [*Aviation*] (DA) ... SW
Singly-Occupied Molecular Orbital [*Physical chemistry*] ... OMO
Sink Resistant Plastic (PDAA) ... SRP
Sitra Cargo Systems [*Peru*] [*ICAO designator*] (FAAC) ... SCG
Six-Axis Manipulator (PDAA) ... SAM
Six Axis Motion System (PDAA) ... SAMS
Size (IAA) ... SZ
Size Exclusion [*Analytical chemistry*] ... SEX
Size-Selective Precipitation [*Physics*] ... SSP
Sized (NTCM) ... S
Skagway Air Service, Inc. [*ICAO designator*] (FAAC) ... SGY
Skegair [*British*] [*ICAO designator*] (FAAC) ... SKA
Skills Training Program ... STP
Skoda Air [*Czechoslovakia*] [*ICAO designator*] (FAAC) ... SOA
Skorpion Air [*Bulgaria*] [*ICAO designator*] (FAAC) ... SPN
Sky Air Cargo Services (UK) Ltd. [*British*] [*ICAO designator*] (FAAC) ... NJA
Sky Care Ltd. [*New Zealand*] [*ICAO designator*] (FAAC) ... SCE
Sky Condition [*Aviation*] (FAAC) ... SK
Sky Freighters NV [*Belgium*] [*ICAO designator*] (FAAC) ... SFI
Sky Harbor Air Service, Inc. [*ICAO designator*] (FAAC) ... SHC
Sky Line for Air Services Ltd. [*Sudan*] [*ICAO designator*] (FAAC) ... SLY
Sky Liners Air Services Ltd. [*Suriname*] [*ICAO designator*] (FAAC) ... LNR
Sky One Express Airlines, Inc. [*ICAO designator*] (FAAC) ... SYF
Sky Service [*Belgium*] [*ICAO designator*] (FAAC) ... SKS
Sky Tours, Inc. [*ICAO designator*] (FAAC) ... SKE
Sky West, Inc. [*ICAO designator*] (FAAC) ... SKW
Skybus, Inc. [*ICAO designator*] (FAAC) ... FLH
Skycare Management Services Ltd. [*British*] [*ICAO designator*] (FAAC) ... SKC
Skycharter (Malton) Ltd. [*Canada*] [*ICAO designator*] (FAAC) ... SKL
Skycraft Air Transport, Inc. [*Canada*] [*ICAO designator*] (FAAC) ... SKG
Skycraft, Inc. [*ICAO designator*] (FAAC) ... SKF
Skycy Freighters International Ltd. [*Kenya*] [*ICAO designator*] (FAAC) ... SIF
Skyfreight, Inc. [*ICAO designator*] (FAAC) ... SFT
Skyfreighters Corp. [*ICAO designator*] (FAAC) ... SKB
Skyguard Ltd. [*British*] [*ICAO designator*] (FAAC) ... SKD
Skyjet, Inc. [*Antigua and Barbuda*] [*ICAO designator*] (FAAC) ... SKJ
Skylane Air Charter [*British*] [*ICAO designator*] (FAAC) ... SKK
Skyline [*Norway*] [*ICAO designator*] (FAAC) ... SEG
Skyline Aviation Services, Inc. [*ICAO designator*] (FAAC) ... SKN
Skylink Airlines [*Canada*] [*ICAO designator*] (FAAC) ... SKI
Skyplan Services Ltd. [*Canada*] [*ICAO designator*] (FAAC) ... XXS
Skyrover Ltd. [*British*] [*ICAO designator*] (FAAC) ... SKR
Skystar International [*ICAO designator*] (FAAC) ... SSK
Skyward Aviation Ltd. [*Canada*] [*ICAO designator*] (FAAC) ... SGK
Skywatch Ltd. [*British*] [*ICAO designator*] (FAAC) ... SKH
Skyway Business Travel Ltd. [*British*] [*ICAO designator*] (FAAC) ... SWY
Skyways AB [*Sweden*] [*ICAO designator*] (FAAC) ... SKX
Skyways Africa Ltd. [*Kenya*] [*ICAO designator*] (FAAC) ... SAE
Skywings AB [*Sweden*] [*ICAO designator*] (FAAC) ... SCF
Skywork SA [*Switzerland*] [*ICAO designator*] (FAAC) ... SRK
Skyworld Airlines, Inc. [*ICAO designator*] (FAAC) ... SPC
Slacked Unconstrained Minimization Technique (PDAA) ... SLUMT
Slate Falls Airways Ltd. [*Canada*] [*ICAO designator*] (FAAC) ... SYJ
Sleep Analyzing Hybrid Computer (PDAA) ... SAHC
Sleep Deprivation (PDAA) ... SD
Slide Agglutination (PDAA) ... SA
Sliding Roof [*Automotive advertising*] ... SRF
Slightly-Grounded Lightplane (PDAA) ... SGL
Slipped Mutagenic Intermediate [*Biochemistry*] ... SMI
Sloane Aviation Ltd. [*British*] [*ICAO designator*] (FAAC) ... SLN
Slot Allocation Procedure [*Aviation*] (DA) ... SLAP
Slot Reference Foint (DA) ... SRP
Slov-Air [*Slovakia*] [*ICAO designator*] (FAAC) ... OIR
Slovak National Party [*Political party*] (ECON) ... SNS
Slow [*Aviation*] (DA) ... SLO
Slow Access Charge-Coupled Memory [*Computer science*] (PDAA) ... SACCM
Slow Motion (NTCM) ... SLO MO
Slow Strain Rate Technique (PDAA) ... SSRT
Slow Wave Structure [*Satellite delay tube*] (NTCM) ... SWS
Slowing Down Spectrometer (PDAA) ... SDS
Slowly Moving Object [*Astronomy*] ... SMO
Slurry Response Number [*Well drilling technology*] ... SRN
SM Exports Ltd. [*British*] [*ICAO designator*] (FAAC) ... SME
Small Aerial Surveillance and Target Acquisition (PDAA) ... STSTA
Small Arms Common Module Fire Control System [*Army*] ... SACMFCS
Small Arms Weapons Effects Simulator [*Military*] (PDAA) ... SAWES
Small Business Exporters Association (EA) ... SBEA
Small Business Funding ... SBF
Small Company Online Data [*Computer science*] (PDAA) ... SCOLD
Small Container Intermodal Distribution System (PDAA) ... SCIDS
Small Earth-Approacher [*Asteroid*] ... SEA
Small Engine Fuel Injection System ... SEFIS
Small Group Trial ... SGT
Small Lot Optimum Procurement (PDAA) ... SLOP
Small Main-Belt Asteroid Spectroscopic Survey ... SMASS
Small-to-Medium Enterprise ... SME
Small Molecule Gel Permeation Chromatography ... SMGPC
Small Order Execution System [*Business term*] ... SOES
Small Pig Keepers' Council [*British*] (BI) ... SPKC
Small Repair Parts Transporter ... SRPT
Small Seismic Intrusion Detector (PDAA) ... MICROSID
Small Solar-Power System [*Energy source*] ... SSPS
Smaller Companies Market [*Business term*] ... SCM
Smallest Serving Factor (PDAA) ... SSF
Smart Armor System [*Army*] ... SAS
Smart Integral Linearizer [*Instrumentation*] ... SIL
Smith Air (1976) Ltd. [*Canada*] [*ICAO designator*] (FAAC) ... SML
Smith Air, Inc. [*ICAO designator*] (FAAC) ... SMH
Smithkline Beacham Clincal Labs [*ICAO designator*] (FAAC) ... SBQ
Smithosonian Jazz Masterworks Orchestra ... SJMO
Smithsonian Marine Station at Link Port ... SMSLP
Smoke (NFPA) ... S
Smoke Control and Pressurization Panel [*NFPA pre-fire planning symbol*] (NFPA) ... SP
Smoke-Emitting Diode [*Computer hacker terminology*] (NHD) ... SED
Smoke Layer Aloft [*Meteorology*] (FAAC) ... KLYR
Smoke Layer Estimated (Feet) Deep [*Meteorology*] (FAAC) ... KDEP
Smooth Muscle Myosin Heavy Chain [*Biochemistry*] ... SMMHC
SNAM SpA [*Italy*] [*ICAO designator*] (FAAC) ... SNM
Snci-Tours Benin Inter Regional [*ICAO designator*] (FAAC) ... STB
Snunit Aviation [*Israel*] [*ICAO designator*] (FAAC) ... SNU
SOBELAIR [*Societe Belge de Transport Aeriens*] [*Belgium*] [*ICAO designator*] (FAAC) ... SLR
Social Assessment of Technology (PDAA) ... SAT
Socially-Appropriate Technology (PDAA) ... SAT
Sociedad Aerea del Caqueta Ltd. [*Colombia*] [*ICAO designator*] (FAAC) ... SDK
Sociedad Aeronautica de Medellin [*Colombia*] [*ICAO designator*] (FAAC) ... SAM
Sociedad Ecuatoriana de Transportes Aereos Ltda. [*Ecuador*] [*ICAO designator*] (FAAC) ... SET
Sociedade Brazileira de Turismo (ROTATUR) [*Brazil*] [*ICAO designator*] (FAAC) ... RTR
Societa' Adriatica [*Italy*] [*ICAO designator*] (FAAC) ... ADH
Societa' Aerotaxi SUD [*Italy*] [*ICAO designator*] (FAAC) ... SGT
Societa' Italjet [*Italy*] [*ICAO designator*] (FAAC) ... ITJ
Societa' Siba Aviation [*Italy*] [*ICAO designator*] (FAAC) ... SIB
Societa' Tea Italia [*Italy*] [*ICAO designator*] (FAAC) ... TEI
Societe 3S Aviation (Aerope) [*France*] [*ICAO designator*] (FAAC) ... OPE
Societe Air Bretagne Service [*France*] [*ICAO designator*] (FAAC) ... ABH
Societe Anonyme de Transports Aeriens Air-Guadeloupe [*France*] [*ICAO designator*] (FAAC) ... AGU
Societe Centrafricaine de Transport Aerien [*Central African Republic*] [*ICAO designator*] (FAAC) ... SNS
Societe Chaleng Air [*France*] [*ICAO designator*] (FAAC) ... CLG
Societe d'Exploitation Aeropostale [*France*] [*ICAO designator*] (FAAC) ... ARP
Societe Helitrans France [*ICAO designator*] (FAAC) ... HTF
Societe des Ingenieurs do Telecommunication [*Belgium*] ... SITEL
Societe International de Telecommunications Aeronautiques [*Belgium*] [*ICAO designator*] (FAAC) ... SIT
Societe Nigerienne de Transports Aeriens [*Niger*] [*ICAO designator*] (FAAC) ... SNI
Societe Nigerienne de Transports Aeriens [*Niger*] [*ICAO designator*] (FAAC) ... SONITA
Societe Nouvelle d'Exploitation Air Provence [*France*] [*ICAO designator*] (FAAC) ... APR
Societe Novajet [*France*] [*ICAO designator*] (FAAC) ... NJT
Societe Seca [*France*] [*ICAO designator*] (FAAC) ... CEK
Societe de Transports et de Tourisme [*Mali*] [*ICAO designator*] (FAAC) ... STC
Society of Administrative Mental Health Offices [*British*] (BI) ... SAMHO
Society of Architects and Associated Technicians [*British*] (BI) ... SAAT
Society of Army Historical Research [*British*] (BI) ... SAHR
Society of British Gas Industries (BI) ... SBGI
Society of British Printing Ink Manufacturers (BI) ... SBPIM
Society of Craftsmen Bakers [*British*] (BI) ... SCB
Society of Environmental Toxicology and Chemistry (EA) ... SETAC
Society for Environmental Truth (EA) ... SET
Society for Film History Research [*British*] (BI) ... SFHR
Society of Film and Television Arts Ltd. [*British*] (BI) ... SFTA
Society of Furnace Builders [*British*] (BI) ... SFB
Society for the History of Authorship, Reading and Publishing (EA) ... SHARP
Society for Hospital Epidemiology of America ... SHEA
Society of Hospital Laundry Managers [*British*] (BI) ... SHLM
Society of Independent Producers (NTCM) ... SIP
Society of Industrial Civil Defence Officers [*British*] (BI) ... SICDO
Society of Licensed Aircraft Engineers and Technologists (DA) ... SLEAT

Society for Literature and Science .... SLS
Society of Make-up Artists (NTCM) .... SMA
Society of Mental Welfare Officers [*British*] (BI) .... SMWO
Society for the Ministry of Women in the Church [*British*] (BI) .... SMWC
Society of Model and Experimental Engineers [*British*] (BI) .... SMEE
Society of Motion Picture Engineers [*Later, SMPTE*] (NTCM) .... SMPE
Society for North American Union (EA) .... SNAU
Society for Physical Research [*British*] (BI) .... SPR
Society of Portrait Sculptors [*British*] (BI) .... SPS
Society for the Preservation of Natural History Collections (EA) .... SPNHC
Society of Professional Journalists [*Also, SDX*] (NTCM) .... SPJ
Society for the Promotion of Nature Reserves [*British*] (BI) .... SPNR
Society of Romanian Air Transports [*ICAO designator*] (FAAC) .... SRT
Society of Romanian Air Transports [*ICAO designator*] (FAAC) .... STAR
Society of Rural Financial Officers [*British*] (BI) .... SORFO
Society of Rural Financial Officers [*British*] (BI) .... SRFO
Society of Shipping Executives [*British*] (BI) .... SSE
Society for Spreading the Knowledge of True Prayer [*British*] (BI) .... SSKTP
Society for the Study of Indigenous Languages of the Americas (EA) .... SSILA
Society of Technical Civil Servants [*British*] (BI) .... STCS
Society of Town Clerks [*British*] (BI) .... STC
Society of Travel and Tourism Educators (EA) .... STTE
Society for Visiting Scientists Ltd. [*British*] (BI) .... SVS
Society of Women Musicians, Inc. [*British*] (BI) .... SWM
Socio-Economic Model of the Planet Earth (PDAA) .... SEMPE
Sodium Nitrobenzene Sulfonate [*Organic chemistry*] .... SNBS
Sodium Styrenesulfonate [*Organic chemistry*] .... SSS
Sodium Sulfite [*Inorganic chemistry*] .... SS
Soft Focus [*Cinematography*] (NTCM) .... SF
Soft and Hard Acid and Base (PDAA) .... SHAB
Soft Top [*Automotive advertising*] .... SFT
Software-Controlled Electronic-Processing Traffic-Recording Equipment (PDAA) .... SCEPTRE
Software Development Computer Facility .... SDCF
Software Exchange [*Computer science*] (NHD) .... SEX
Software Hazard Analysis [*Military*] .... SHA
Sogervair/Transoceanic Aviation [*France*] [*ICAO designator*] (FAAC) .... OAT
Soil Moisture Deficit (PDAA) .... SMD
Soil Nutrient Availability .... SNA
Soil Vapor Extraction [*Environmental science*] .... SVE
Solar-Assisted Heat Pump (PDAA) .... SAHP
Solar Aureole Almucantar Radiance (PDAA) .... SAAR
Solar Box Cookers International [*An association*] (EA) .... SBCI
Solar Central Receiver Reformer (PDAA) .... SCRR
Solar Electric Propulsion Integration Technology (PDAA) .... SEPSIT
Solar Proton-Monitoring Experiment (PDAA) .... SPME
Solar Thermal Commission (PDAA) .... STC
Solar Wind Composition Detector (PDAA) .... SWCD
Solar Wind Composition Experiment (PDAA) .... SWCE
Solder Makers' Association [*British*] (BI) .... SMA
Solder Mask Over Bare Copper [*Electronics*] .... SMOBC
Soldier-Operator-Maintainer-Tester-Evaluator [*Military*] (PDAA) .... SOMTE
Soldier's Manual of Common Tasks [*A publication*] (ADDR) .... SMCT
Sole Supporting Parent .... SSP
Solenoid Detector Collaboration [*Physics*] .... SDC
Solid Freeform Fabrication [*Metallurgy*] .... SFF
Solid-Particle Filter Dye [*Color film technology*] .... SPFD
Solid Phase Alloy Nucleation (PDAA) .... SPAN
Solid Smokeless Fuels Federation [*British*] (BI) .... SSFF
Solid State Amplifier (NTCM) .... SSA
Solid State Frequency Converter (DA) .... SSC
Solid-State Imaging [*Physics*] .... SSI
Solid-State Imaging Spectrometer .... SIS
Solid-State Nuclear Track Detection (PDAA) .... SSNTD
Solid State Power Amplifier (DA) .... SSPA
Solid-State Target Monoscope (PDAA) .... SSTM
Solid-State Track Recorder (PDAA) .... SSTR
Solid Tantalum Capacitor (PDAA) .... STC
Solid Waste Management Unit [*Environmental science*] .... SWMU
Soliloquy [*Theater term*] .... SOL
Solomon Airlines Ltd. [*Solomon Islands*] [*ICAO designator*] (FAAC) .... SOL
Solomon Islands [*Aircraft nationality and registration mark*] (FAAC) H4
Solomon Islands .... Sol Is
Soluble Methane Monooxygenase [*Biochemistry*] .... SMMO
Solus Outdoor Advertising Association [*British*] (BI) .... SOOA
Solution Output Processor (PDAA) .... SOP
Solution Provider [*Microsoft workgroup*] (PCM) .... SP
Solvated Metal Atom Impregnation [*Chemistry*] .... SMAI
Somali Airlines [*Somalia*] [*ICAO designator*] (FAAC) .... SOM
Somalia [*Aircraft nationality and registration mark*] (FAAC) 6O
Sonmez Airlines [*Turkey*] [*ICAO designator*] (FAAC) .... SMZ
Soonair Lines, Inc. [*ICAO designator*] (FAAC) .... SNL
Soot Trap and Regeneration System [*Diesel engine exhaust emission controls*] .... STARS
Sophisticated Automatic RADAR Processing (PDAA) .... SARP
Sound-Activated Mobile (PDAA) .... SAM
Sound-Deadened Steel (PDAA) .... SDS
Sound Effect (NTCM) .... SE
Sound Reinforcement (NTCM) .... SR
Sound on Sound (NTCM) .... SOS
Source and Application Inspection Equipment .... SAFE
Source-Coder's Cost Analysis Model (PDAA) .... SCAM
Source Input Format [*Computer science*] .... SIF
Source Reduction Review Program [*Environmental science*] .... SRRP
South African Airways [*ICAO designator*] (FAAC) .... SAA
South African Police Union (ECON) .... SAPU
South American Airlines [*Peru*] [*ICAO designator*] (FAAC) .... SCN
South Central Air, Inc. [*ICAO designator*] (FAAC) .... SCA
South Coast Recycled Auto Project [*Air pollution controls credits from mobile sources for stationary sources*] .... SCRAP
South East Air [*British*] [*ICAO designator*] (FAAC) .... SEE
South East College of Air Training [*British*] [*ICAO designator*] (FAAC) .... SEC
South Pacific Airline SA [*Chile*] [*ICAO designator*] (FAAC) .... SPF
South Pacific Island Airways, Inc. [*ICAO designator*] (FAAC) .... SPI
South Pacific Nuclear Free Zone Treaty .... SPNFZT
South Tibetan Detachment [*Geology*] .... STD
South West Air Ltd. [*Canada*] [*ICAO designator*] (FAAC) .... SWC
Southeast Air, Inc. [*ICAO designator*] (FAAC) .... SEA
Southeast Airmotive Corp. [*ICAO designator*] (FAAC) .... SPU
Southeast Aviation Group, Inc. [*ICAO designator*] (FAAC) .... SBD
Southeast Correct Craft, Inc. [*ICAO designator*] (FAAC) .... SOT
Southeast European Airlines [*Greece*] [*ICAO designator*] (FAAC) .... SEEA
Southeastbound [*ICAO designator*] (FAAC) .... SEB
Southeastern Airways Corp. [*ICAO designator*] (FAAC) .... PTM
Southeastern Jurisdictional Conference [*United Methodist Church*] .... SEJ
Southend Jet Centre Ltd. [*British*] [*ICAO designator*] (FAAC) .... SJC
Southern Air Ltd. [*British*] [*ICAO designator*] (FAAC) .... HSN
Southern Air Transport, Inc. [*ICAO designator*] (FAAC) .... SJM
Southern Airlines Ltd. [*British*] [*ICAO designator*] (FAAC) .... STH
Southern Aviation Ltd. [*Ghana*] [*ICAO designator*] (FAAC) .... STV
Southern Bluefin Tuna [*Fish*] .... SBT
Southern Frontier Air Transport Ltd. [*Canada*] [*ICAO designator*] (FAAC) .... SFS
Southern Jersey Airways, Inc. [*ICAO designator*] (FAAC) .... ALC
Southern Ohio Aviation Sales Co. [*ICAO designator*] (FAAC) .... SOH
Southern Seaplane, Inc. [*ICAO designator*] (FAAC) .... SSC
Southflight Aviation Ltd. [*New Zealand*] [*ICAO designator*] (FAAC) .... SFL
Southwest Airlines Co. [*ICAO designator*] (FAAC) .... SWA
Southwest Missouri State University (PDAA) .... SMSU
Southwestbound [*ICAO designator*] (FAAC) .... SWB
Sowind Air Ltd. [*Canada*] [*ICAO designator*] (FAAC) .... SOW
Space-Charge-Limited Insulated-Gate Field Effect Transistor (PDAA) .... SCLIGFET
Space Charge Wave (PDAA) .... SCW
Space Division Multiple Access/Spacecraft Switched-Time Division Multiple Access (PDAA) .... SDMA/SS-TDMA
Space Energy Association (EA) .... SEA
Space Experiment on Relativistic Theories of Gravitation (PDAA) .... SERTOG
Space Exploration Initiative [*NASA*] .... SEI
Space Invariant Point Spread Function (PDAA) .... SIPSF
Space Operations Management System (PDAA) .... SOMS
Space Position Value [*Outdoor advertising*] (NTCM) .... SPV
Space Shuttle Structures and Materials Working Group [*NASA*] (PDAA) .... SMWG
Space Vehicle Number [*Aviation*] (FAAC) .... SVN
Spainair [*Spain*] [*ICAO designator*] (FAAC) .... SPP
Spair [*Russian Federation*] [*ICAO designator*] (FAAC) .... PAR
Spare Module Replacement Analysis .... SMRA
Spares Provisioning and Requirements Effectiveness Model (PDAA) .... SPAREM
SPASA Servicios Politecnicos Aereos SA [*Spain*] [*ICAO designator*] (FAAC) .... SPS
Spatial Delayed-Response [*Ophthalmology*] .... SDR
Spatial Spectrum Center Shifting (PDAA) .... SSCS
Special Advisory Committee on Telecommunications (NTCM) .... SACT
Special Cargo Airlines [*Russian Federation*] [*ICAO designator*] (FAAC) .... SCI
Special Effects (NTCM) .... EFX
Special Environmental Sample Container [*NASA*] (PDAA) .... SESC
Special Event Charter Flight [*Aviation*] (DA) .... SEC
Special Market Area (NTCM) .... SMA
Special Mobility Vehicle .... SMV
Special Operations Aviation Combat Mission Simulator [*Military*] .... SOACMS
Special Operations Aviation Regiment [*Military*] .... SOAR
Special Operations Command, Central Command [*Military*] .... SOCCENT
Special Operations Coordination [*DoD*] .... SOCOORD
Special Power Unit (NTCM) .... SPU
Special Real-Time Operating System (PDAA) .... SRTOS
Special Separation Benefit [*DoD*] .... SSB
Special Service Authorization [*FCC*] (NTCM) .... SSA
Special Temporary Allowance .... STA
Special Tools and Handling Equipment .... STHE
Special Trade Passenger Ship (PDAA) .... STP
Special Weather Report [*Aviation*] (DA) .... SPECI
Specialist Component Producer .... SCP
Specially-Oriented Advertisements [*Consumer Protection Packet - US Post Office*] .... SOA
Specifiable Coordinating Positioning Equipment (PDAA) .... SCOPE
Specific Optimal Estimation (PDAA) .... SOE
Specific Purpose Payment .... SPP
Specific Reactivity [*Exhaust emissions*] [*Automotive engineering*] .... SR

Specific Reactivity - Maximum Incremental Reactivity [*Exhaust emissions*] [*Automotive engineering*]....................................... SR-MIR
Spectra Calculation from Activated Nuclide Sets   (PDAA)..... SCANS
Spectral Processing Analysis System   (PDAA)................... SPANS
Spectroscopic Phase-Modulated Ellipsometry.......................... SPME
Spectrum Air Service, Inc. [*ICAO designator*]   (FAAC) .... XSA
Spectrum Management   (NTCM) .... SM
Spectrum Management Task Force [*Electromagnetic spectrum regulation*]   (NTCM)... SMTF
Speed of Approach Measurement Indicator   (PDAA)......... SAMI
Speed Control System   (PDAA) .... SCS
Speed-Gate-Pull-Off   (PDAA) .... SGPO
Speed Limiting Point [*Aviation*]   (FAAC)........................ SLP
Speed Measuring Device   (PDAA).. SMD
Speed and Throtte Automatic Network   (PDAA) .... SATAN
Speedwings SA [*Switzerland*] [*ICAO designator*]   (FAAC) ..... SPW
Spent Pot Lining Insolubilisation Technology [*Metallurgy*]...... SPLIT
Spill Control Recovery Valve   (PDAA) .... SCRV
Spin-Flip Raman LASER   (PDAA) .... SFRL
Spin Muon Collaboration [*Nuclear research*]......................... SMC
Spinocerebellar Ataxia [*Genetics*]....................................... SCA
Spiritualist Association of Great Britain   (BI) .... SA
Split Armature Receiver Capsule   (PDAA) .... SARC
Split-Channel Reservation Multiple Access   (PDAA) .... SRMA
Spondylometaphyseal Dysplasias [*Medicine*] .... SMD
Sponsor Identification Index [*Advertising*]   (NTCM) .... SII
Spontaneous Lymphocyte Transportation   (PDAA) .... SLT
Spontaneous Synaptic Current [*Neuroscience*]....................... SSC
Sporting Owner Drivers' Club Ltd. [*British*]   (BI)............ SODC
Sports Air Travel, Inc. [*ICAO designator*]   (FAAC) .... WCC
Sports Program   (NTCM) .... S
Sports Writers' Association [*British*]   (BI) .... SWA
Spot Accumulation and Melting of Snow   (PDAA) .... SAMOS
Spot Wind [*Meteorology*]   (DA)...................................... SPOT
Sprague Electric Co. [*ICAO designator*]   (FAAC)............. SPE
Spray Equipment Manufacturers' Association [*British*]   (BI)..... SEMA
Springbank Aviation Ltd. [*Canada*] [*ICAO designator*]   (FAAC) .... SAQ
Springdale Air Services, Inc. [*ICAO designator*]   (FAAC)....... SPG
Spurling Aviation [*ICAO designator*]   (FAAC) .... ASL
Spurwing Airlines (Pty) Ltd. [*South Africa*] [*ICAO designator*]   (FAAC)... PUR
Sputtered Iridium Oxide Film   (PDAA) .... SIROF
Square-Edge Siding   (DAC) .... SE Sdg
Square-Edge and Sound   (DAC) .... SqE & S
Squawk   (DA).. SQ
Squawk [*Aviation*]   (FAAC)...................................... SQK
Sri Lanka [*Aircraft nationality and registration mark*]   (FAAC)..... 4R
STA-Mali [*ICAO designator*]   (FAAC) .... SBA
Stability Augmentation System with Control Stick Steering   (PDAA)... SAS/CSS
Stability and Safety Screening [*Sailing terminology*] .... SSS
Stabilization Reference Package / Position Determination System [*Military*]... SRP/PDS
Stable Super-Active Scavenger [*Color film technology*]............ SSAS
Stactic Gel Strength [*Well drilling technology*] .... SGS
Staff Development and Training.. SD & T
Staff Planner [*DoD*] .... SP
Stage Golfing Society [*British*]   (BI)........................... SGS
Staggered Quadraphase Phase Shift Key Modulation [*Computer science*]   (PDAA)... SQPSK
Stainless Steel Development Association [*British*]   (BI) ...... SSDA
Stainless Steel Fabricators' Association of Great Britain   (BI) ..... SSFA
Stamp Collectors' Association [*British*]   (BI)................... SCA
Stand for Exchange of Product Model Data [*Computer-assisted engineering*]... STEP
Stand-off, High Altitude, Long Endurance   (PDAA).......... SHALE
Stand-Off Modular Missile   (PDAA) .... SOMM
Standard Battle Plan Emplacement [*Military*]........................ SBPE
Standard Corporate Protocol [*Telecommunications*]................. SCP
Standard Dimension Ratio   (DAC) .... SDR
Standard-Dose Epinephrine [*Medicine*]................................. SDE
Standard Electronic Module RADAR   (PDAA) .... SEMR
Standard for the Exchange of Product Data [*Materials science*] ..... STEP
Standard Inside Diameter Dimension Ratio   (DAC)............ SIDD
Standard Long Play [*VHS recorder playing time mode*]   (NTCM)..... SLP
Standard Matched   (DAC) .... StdM
Standard Method of Measurement for Civil Engineering Quantities   (PDAA)... SMMCEQ
Standard National Account [*Economics*]................................ SNA
Standard Procedure Monitor Chart   (PDAA)..................... SPMC
Standard Product Numbering System   (PDAA) .... SPNS
Standard Reference Aerosol   (PDAA)................................. SRA
Standard Schedule Message   (DA).................................... SSM
Standard Test Equipment / Internal Combustion Engine.......... STE/ICE
Standard Web Offset Press [*Computer science*]   (PCM)....... SWOP
Standardized Job Control Language   (PDAA)...................... SJCL
Standby Local Early Warning and Control Center   (PDAA) .... SLEW
Standing Naval Force, Atlantic   (ANA)............. STANAVFORLANT
Standing-Wave Acoustic Parametric Source   (PDAA) .... SWAPS
Standing-Wave Fluorescence Microscopy.............................. SWFM
Standing Wave Ratio   (NTCM)...................................... SWR
Staphylococcal Nuclease [*An enzyme*].................................. SNase
Stapleford Flight Center [*British*] [*ICAO designator*]   (FAAC)..... STL

Star Air IS [*Denmark*] [*ICAO designator*]   (FAAC)............. SRI
Star Aviation [*British*] [*ICAO designator*]   (FAAC)............ STA
Star Service International [*France*] [*ICAO designator*]   (FAAC)...... SSI
Starspeed Ltd. [*British*] [*ICAO designator*]   (FAAC)......... SSI
Start of Active Profile   (PDAA) .... SAP
Start of Climb [*Aviation*]   (DA) .... SOC
Start of Injection [*Fuel systems*] [*Automotive engineering*]........ SOI
Start Launch Sequence [*Military*].. SLS
Starways SA [*Switzerland*] [*ICAO designator*]   (FAAC)........ STW
Starwelt Airways [*Burundi*] [*ICAO designator*]   (FAAC)........ SBU
State Emergency Response Commission [*Environmental science*]..... SERC
State Estimation Algorithm for Small-Scale System   (PDAA)..... SEAS
State and Local Air Pollution Control Official [*Environmental Protection Agency*]   (ERG)................................. STALAPCO
State-Municipal Income Tax Evaluation System   (PDAA)..... SMITES
State Officer .... SO
State Property Agency [*Hungary*]   (ECON) .... SPA
State of Vietnam Ribbon of Friendship [*Presidential unit commendation*] .... SOVNROF
Statens Trafikkflygerskole [*Norway*] [*ICAO designator*]   (FAAC) ..... FBD
StatesWest Airlines, Inc. [*ICAO designator*]   (FAAC) ...... SWJ
Station Acquisition Marketing Plan [*PBS*]   (NTCM)......... SAM
Station Independence Program [*Public television project*]   (NTCM)..... SIP
Station Keeping Light   (NFPA) .... SKLT
Station Manager [*Broadcasting*]   (NTCM)...................... SM
Statistical Analog Monitor   (PDAA) .... STAM
Statistical Analysis of Documentation Files   (PDAA)......... SADF
Statistical Analysis of a Series of Events   (PDAA)............. SASE
Statistical Engine Test Work Group [*Lubricants testing*] [*Automotive engineering*] .... SETWEG
Statistical Office of the European Communities   (PDAA)...... SOEC
Statistical Parametric Mapping [*Data treatment*]................... SPM
Status [*ICAO designator*]   (FAAC)................................. STS
Status Monitor .... SM
Status Monitor Software .... SMS
Stealth Club of America   (EA).. SCA
Steam Railway Traction Society [*British*]   (BI) .... SRTS
Steel Castings Association [*British*]   (BI) .... SCA
Steel Nail Association [*British*]   (BI) .... SNA
Steel Radiator and Convector Manufacturers' Association [*British*]   (BI)... SRCMA
Steel Sheet Information and Developement Association [*British*]   (BI)... SSIDA
Steel Sleeper Association [*British*]   (BI) .... SSA
Steel User Service [*British*]   (BI).................................. SUS
Steel Wool Manufacturers' Association [*British*]   (BI)........ SWMA
Steel Works Plant Association [*British*]   (BI)................... SWPA
Steerable Adaptive Broadcast Reception Equipment   (PDAA)..... SABRE
Steerable Low-Light-Level Television   (PDAA).................. STV
Steering Column and Occupant Response Simulation [*Automotive safety*] [*Computer-aided design*] .... SCORES
Stellair [*France*] [*ICAO designator*]   (FAAC)................. STR
Step Down Fix [*Aviation*]   (DA)................................... SDF
Stephenson Locomotive Society [*British*]   (BI) .... SLS
Stepheville Aviation Services [*Canada*] [*ICAO designator*]   (FAAC)..... XSN
Stepped Piston Crossover   (PDAA)................................... SPX
Stepwise Regression Analysis   (PDAA) .... SWRA
Stereo-Image Alternator   (PDAA).................................... SIA
Stereonet Analysis Program   (PDAA)............................. SNAP
Sterile Insect Technology .... SIT
Sterilised Cat Gut Manufacturers' Association [*British*]   (BI)..... SCMA
Sterling Airways Ltd. [*Denmark*] [*ICAO designator*]   (FAAC)..... SAW
Sterling Warrant into Gilt-Edged Stock [*British*] .... SWING
Stern Air, Inc. [*ICAO designator*]   (FAAC) .... SNA
Stern-Gerlach [*Experiment for measuring atomic magnetism*] .... SG
Stewart Aviation Services, Inc. [*ICAO designator*]   (FAAC) ..... YBE
Stick Shift [*Automotive advertising*] .... STK
Still-Water Bending Moment   (PDAA).............................. SWBM
Stimulated Emission Pumping [*Spectroscopy*] .... SEP
Stimulated Raman Gain Spectroscopy   (PDAA)................. SRGS
Stimulated Thermal Rayleigh Scattering   (PDAA)............. STRS
Stochastic Context-Free Grammar   (PDAA) .... SCFG
Stochastic Evolutionary Adoption Model   (PDAA)............ STEAM
Stock Brick Manufacturers Association [*British*]   (BI)........ SBMA
Stock Exchange Automatic Execution Facility .... SAEF
Stock Funding Depot - Level Repairables [*Army*] .... SFDLR
Stock Ledger Control .... SLC
Stock Shot   (NTCM) .... SS
Stockholm Stock Exchange.. SSE
Stop Bar   (DA) .... STB
Stop Planned Parenthood [*An association*]   (EA)............. STOPP
Stopway Light [*Aviation*]   (FAAC)............................... STWL
Storage Array Tester and Analyzer   (PDAA) .... SATAN
Store Port Allocation Register   (PDAA) .... SPAR
Stored-Energy Transmission   (PDAA) .... SET
Stored Flight Plan Program [*Aviation*]   (FAAC) .... SFPP
Storm Water Pollution Prevention Plan [*Environmental science*]...... SWPPP
Straight in Approach [*Aviation*]   (DA) .... STA
Straight Times Index [*Singapore Stock Exchange*] .... STI
Strainer   (DAC) .... ST
Strategic Audit Plan... SAP
Strategic Defense Initiative System Evaluation Model............... SDISEM
Strategic Intermediate Planner   (PDAA) .... STRIP

Strategic Issue Competitive Information System (PDAA) .... SICIS
Strategic Material Management Information Program (PDAA) .... SMMIP
Strategic Reconnaissance [*Military*] .... SR
Strategic Resource Area (PDAA) .... SRA
Strategy Evaluator and Planning-Production System (PDAA) .... STEPS
Stratford Airways Ltd. [*Canada*] [*ICAO designator*] (FAAC) .... FCA
Stream Tree Data (PDAA) .... STD
Streamline Aviation [*British*] [*ICAO designator*] (FAAC) .... STM
Strength, Interference, Noise, Propagation, and Overall Merit Code [*Signal reception quality rating*] (NTCM) .... SINPO
Stress and Arousal Adjective Checklist (PDAA) .... SACL
Stress-Induced Pseudoelasticity (PDAA) .... STRIPE
Stress Relaxation Processability Tester (PDAA) .... SRPT
Stress Survival Matrix Test (PDAA) .... SSMT
Strike Attack Vector [*Navy*] (ANA) .... SAV
Strike and Terrain Following RADAR [*Military*] (PDAA) .... SATF
Strike Warning Message [*Army*] (ADDR) .... STRIKWARN
String Polling Multiple Access (PDAA) .... SPMA
Stromal Cell-Derived Factor [*Biochemistry*] .... SDF
Strong Acid Leach (PDAA) .... SAL
Structural Analysis Method for Evaluation of Complex Structures (PDAA) .... SAMECS
Structure-Based Drug Design [*Organic chemistry*] .... SBDD
Structure Building Language (PDAA) .... SBL
Structure of Intellect [*Education*] (AEE) .... SOI
Structure Isolation Dynamics [*Vehicle development*] [*Automotive engineering*] .... SID
Structure Manning Decision Review .... SMDR
Structure-Specific Recognition Protein [*Biochemistry*] .... SSRP
Stud and Girt (DAC) .... S & G
Student Interactive Training System .... SITS
Student Load .... SL
Student Response Unit .... SRU
Student Teams-Achievement Division (AEE) .... STAD
Students Audio Visual Interface (PDAA) .... SAVI
Students with Disabilities .... SwD
Studio-to-Headend Link [*Transmitter site relay*] (NTCM) .... SHL
Stump-Tailed Macaque Virus (PDAA) .... STMV
Sturctural Analysis via Generalized Interactive Graphics (PDAA) .... STAGING
Sub Board of Inspection and Survey of Atlantic and Pacific [*Navy*] (ANA) .... SUBINSURV (LANT) (PAC)
Sub Carrier Demodulation, Automatic (PDAA) .... SCDAuto
Subject to Nonrenewal (NTCM) .... SNR
Subject To [*ICAO designator*] (FAAC) .... SUBJ
Submarine Automatic Remote Television Inspection Equipment (PDAA) .... SMARTIE
Submarine Craft for Ocean Repair, Positioning, Inspection, and Observation (PDAA) .... SCORPIO
Submarine Tactical Acoustic Communications [*Navy*] (ANA) .... STAC
Submersible Craft Acoustic Navigation and Track Indication Equipment (PDAA) .... SCANTIE
Submersible, Transportable Utility, Marine Pump (PDAA) .... STUMP
Subroutine Recipe Entry Pointer Table .... SRET
Subscription Television Association (NTCM) .... STA
Subscription Television Authority [*FCC*] (NTCM) .... STV
Subscription TV, Inc. (NTCM) .... STV
Subsea Test Tree (PDAA) .... SSTT
Substance Hazard Index [*Environmental science*] .... SHI
Substituted Accounting Period .... SAP
Subsystem Action Message [*Military*] .... SAM
Subsystem Response Message [*Military*] .... SRM
Suburban Air Freight, Inc. [*ICAO designator*] (FAAC) .... SRB
Suckling Airways [*British*] [*ICAO designator*] (FAAC) .... SAY
Sud Air Transport SA [*Guinea*] [*ICAO designator*] (FAAC) .... GID
Sudan Airways [*ICAO designator*] (FAAC) .... SUD
Sudanese Aeronautical Services Co. Ltd. [*Sudan*] [*ICAO designator*] (FAAC) .... SAC
Sudanese Aeronautical Services Co. Ltd. [*Sudan*] [*ICAO designator*] (FAAC) .... SASCO
Sudanese Flight [*Sudan*] [*ICAO designator*] (FAAC) .... SFT
Sudania Aviation Co. [*Sudan*] [*ICAO designator*] (FAAC) .... ASK
Sudania Aviation Co. [*Sudan*] [*ICAO designator*] (FAAC) .... SAC
Sudania Aviation Co. [*Sudan*] [*ICAO designator*] (FAAC) .... SAV
Sudden Changes in the Integrated Intensity of Atmospherics (PDAA) .... SCIIA
Sudflug Suddeutsche Fluggesellschaft MbH [*Germany*] [*ICAO designator*] (FAAC) .... SFG
Sugar Beet Pulp (PDAA) .... SBP
Sulfabromomethazine [*Antibacterial*] [*Veterinary medicine*] .... SBZ
Sulfadimethoxine [*Antibacterial*] [*Veterinary medicine*] .... SDM
Sulfamethazine [*Antibacterial*] [*Veterinary medicine*] .... SMZ
Sulfate Reduction Index [*Environmental chemistry*] .... SRI
Sulfopropyl [*Organic chemistry*] .... SP
Sum of Magnitudes of Pitch Matrix - Correlator .... SMPC
Sum of Magnitudes of Pitch Matrix - Skin .... SMPS
Sum of Magnitudes of Sum [*Channel Matrix*] **Correlator** .... SMSC
Sum of Magnitudes of Sum [*Channel Matrix*] **Skin** .... SMSS
Sumitomo Electric Industries [*Auto inudustry supplier*] .... SEI
Summary Plan Description .... SPD
Summit Airlines [*ICAO designator*] (FAAC) .... SMM
Sun Air Aviation Services [*Canada*] [*ICAO designator*] (FAAC) .... SNX
Sun-Air of Scandinavia AS [*Denmark*] [*ICAO designator*] (FAAC) .... SUS
Sun Country Airlines, Inc. [*ICAO designator*] (FAAC) .... SCX
Sun Jet International Airlines, Inc. [*ICAO designator*] (FAAC) .... SJI
Suncoast Aviation, Inc. [*ICAO designator*] (FAAC) .... SNT
Sundor International Air Services Ltd. [*Israel*] [*ICAO designator*] (FAAC) .... ERO
Sundorph Aeronautical, Corp. [*ICAO designator*] (FAAC) .... SDF
Sunflower Airlines Ltd. [*Fiji*] [*ICAO designator*] (FAAC) .... SUF
Sunna Air Ltd. [*Iceland*] [*ICAO designator*] (FAAC) .... VOR
Sunrise-Sunset (DA) .... SR-SS
Sunshine Aviation SA [*Switzerland*] [*ICAO designator*] (FAAC) .... SHS
Sunwest Airlines Ltd. [*Canada*] [*ICAO designator*] (FAAC) .... SST
Sunworld International Airways, Inc. [*ICAO designator*] (FAAC) .... SWI
Super Einspritz [*Super, Injection*] [*Mercedes-Benz automotive model designation*] .... SE
Super Highband [*Radio frequency*] (NTCM) .... SHB
Super Linear Variable Capacitor (PDAA) .... SLVC
Super Sport Kurz [*Super, Sport, Short chassis*] [*Mercedes-Benz automotive model designation*] .... SSK
Superabsorbent Polymer [*Organic chemistry*] .... SAP
Supercalendered (NTCM) .... SUPER
Superconducting Power Transmission Line (PDAA) .... SPTL
Superimposition (NTCM) .... SUPER
Superior Aviation, Inc. [*ICAO designator*] (FAAC) .... HKA
Superphosphate Manufacturers' Association [*British*] (BI) .... SMA
Supersearch-Online Friendly Interface [*Computer science*] .... SOFI
Supersonic Cruise Aircraft (PDAA) .... SCA
Supplemental Weather Service Location [*Aviation*] (FAAC) .... SWSL
Supplementary Frequency (DA) .... S
Supplementary Special Deposit [*British*] .... SSD
Supplier Capability Information Retrieval Technique (PDAA) .... SCIRT
Supplier Performance Evaluation and Corrective Action (PDAA) .... SPECA
Supplies Invoice Generation Network (PDAA) .... SIGNET
Supply Online Management Information System [*Computer science*] (PDAA) .... SOLMIS
Support Data Sheet [*Military*] .... SDS
Support Electronics Assembly [*Military*] .... SEA
Support Helicopter Flight NI [*British*] [*ICAO designator*] (FAAC) .... SHF
Support, Help, and Empowerment .... SHE
Supr Einspritz Coupe [*Super, Fuel Injection, Coupe*] [*Mercedes-Benz automotive model designation*] .... SEC
Suprathermal Ion Detector (PDAA) .... SID
Supreme Court Reports, Lawyer's Edition [*A publication*] (NTCM) .... L Ed US
Surface Acoustic Wave Delay Line Oscillator (PDAA) .... SAWDLO
Surface Acoustic Wave Device (PDAA) .... SAWD
Surface-to-Air Missile Capability (PDAA) .... SAMCAP
Surface Coating Synthetic Resin Manufacturers Association [*British*] (BI) .... SCSRMA
Surface Crack Opening Displacement (PDAA) .... SCOD
Surface Impulsion Propulsion (PDAA) .... SIP
Surface Mount Component [*Environmental science*] .... SMC
Surface Treatment Enhancement Council [*Metallurgy*] .... STEC
Surface Wind [*Meteorology*] (DA) .... S/W
Surfaced Four Sides and Caulking Seam [*Lumber*] (DAC) .... S4S & CS
Surfaced One Side and Edge [*Lumber*] (DAC) .... S & E
Surfaced One Side and Two Edges [*Lumber*] (DAC) S1S2E
Surfaced Two Edges [*Lumber*] (DAC) S2E
Surfaced Two Sides and Center Matched [*Lumber*] (DAC) .... S2S & CM
Surfaced Two Sides and One Edge [*Lumber*] (DAC) S2S1E
Surfaced Two Sides and Shiplapped [*Technical drawings*] (DAC) .... S2S & SL
Surgical Dressing Manufacturers Association [*British*] (BI) .... SDMA
Surinaamse Luchtvaart Maatschappij NV [*Surinam*] [*ICAO designator*] (FAAC) .... SLM
Surinam [*Aircraft nationality and registration mark*] (FAAC) .... PZ
Surveillance (DA) .... SRV
Surveillance RADAR Zone (DA) .... SRZ
Survey, Liaison, and Reconnaissance Party [*Navy*] (ANA) .... SLRP
Survey Udara (Penas) PT [*Indonesia*] [*ICAO designator*] (FAAC) .... PNS
Survivability Management Operation .... SMO
Survivability System [*Military*] .... SS
Survivable Flight Control Electronic Set [*Aviation*] (PDAA) .... SFCES
Suspended from Issue, Movement, and Use [*Army*] (ADDR) .... SIMU
Sustained Peak Low-Cycle Fatigue (PDAA) .... SPLCF
Sustained Silent Reading [*Education*] (AEE) .... SSR
Suzuki Continuously-Variable Transmission [*Automotive powertrain*] .... SCVT
Svenska Kullager Frabikon [*Swedish Ball Bearing Manufacturing*] .... SKF
Sverdlovsk Airline [*Russian Federation*] [*ICAO designator*] (FAAC) .... SVR
SW Electricity Board [*British*] [*ICAO designator*] (FAAC) .... ELE
Swap Byte [*Computer science*] (NHD) .... SWAB
Swazi Air Charter (Pty) Ltd. [*Swaziland*] [*ICAO designator*] (FAAC) .... HWK
Swaziland [*Aircraft nationality and registration mark*] (FAAC) 3D
Swedair AB [*Sweden*] [*ICAO designator*] (FAAC) .... SWE
Sweden Airways [*ICAO designator*] (FAAC) .... SWB
Swedish Air Ambulance [*ICAO designator*] (FAAC) .... SAG
Swedish Airforce [*ICAO designator*] (FAAC) .... SDC
Swept Angle Retarding Ion Mass Spectrometer (PDAA) .... SARIMS
Swept Forward Wing [*Aviation*] (PDAA) .... SFW
Swept Gain Control (DA) .... SGC
Swiftair Cargo Ltd. [*Canada*] [*ICAO designator*] (FAAC) .... SCL
Swiftair SA [*Spain*] [*ICAO designator*] (FAAC) .... SWT
Swiftlines Ltd. [*Kenya*] [*ICAO designator*] (FAAC) .... SLC

Swinderby FTU [*British*] [*ICAO designator*]   (FAAC) .... SWD
Swirl Control Valve [*Automotive engine design*].. SCV
Swiss Air-Ambulance Ltd. [*ICAO designator*]   (FAAC) .... SAZ
Swissair (Societe Anonyme Switzerland pour la Navigation Aerienne)
    [*ICAO designator*]   (FAAC)... SWR
Switched-Mode Power Supply   (PDAA) .... SMPS
Switching Selector Repeater   (PDAA)... SSR
Syder [*Bulgaria*] [*ICAO designator*]   (FAAC) .... SDR
Symbol [*Spain*] [*ICAO designator*]   (FAAC)... SYB
Synaptic Vesicle Amine Transporter [*Biochemistry*] .... SVAT
Synaptosomal-Associated Protein [*Biochemistry*]...................................... SNAP
Synchronization Code   (IAA).. SYNCCODE
Synchronization Input [*Computer science*]   (IAA) .... SYNCIN
Synchronization Output   (IAA).. SYNCOUT
Synchronizing Character [*Computer science*]   (IAA).............................. SYNC
Synchronoscope   (IAA) .... SYNCSCP
Synchronous Communication Satellite [*Telecommunications*]
    (IAA).. SYNCOM
Syncrude Canada Ltd. [*ICAO designator*]   (FAAC)...................................... SYN
Syndicated Program Analysis   (NTCM) .... SPA
Synopic Reporting of the Location of Sources of Atmospherics
    [*Aviation*]   (DA).. SFLOC
Syntax Analyzer Generator   (PDAA).. SAG
Syntax Macro Preprocessor for Language Evaluation [*Computer
    science*]   (PDAA).. SYMPLE
Syntax-Oriented Translator   (PDAA).. SORTRAN
Synthesized Hydrocarbon   (PDAA) .... SHC
Synthetic Model Interferometric LASER Imaging   (PDAA) .... SMILI
Synthetic Unrandomization of Randomized Fragments [*Chemistry*]........... SURF
Syrian Arab Airlines [*ICAO designator*]   (FAAC) .... SYR
System for Aircrew Flight Extension and Return   (PDAA)...................... SAFER
System for Automated Flight Efficiency   (PDAA)..................................... SAFE
System for Capacity and Orders Planning and Enquiries   (PDAA)........... SCOPE
System Check-Out Computer   (PDAA) .... SCO
System for Computer Automated Typesetting   (PDAA)............................. SCAT
System Concept Development Working Group .... SCDWG
System Core Image Library Maintenance Program [*Computer
    science*]   (IAA) .... SYSCMA
System Demonstration Flight Test [*DoD*] .... SDFT
System Engineering Cost Reduction Assistance Contractor
    (PDAA)... SECRAC
System Environment Qualification Test.. SEQT
System Independent Data Format [*Computer science*]   (PCM) .... SIDF
System Management/Performance Monitor... SW/PM
System for Online Optimization [*Computer science*]   (PDAA) .... SOLO
System Ordnance Safing Device [*Military*].. SOSD
**System for Pinpointed, Exhaustive and Expeditious Dissemination of
    Subjects**   (PDAA) .... SPEEDS
System Power Up .... SPU
System Qualification Test Phase .... SQTP
System for Quick Ultra-Fiche-Based Information Retrieval
    [*Computer science*]   (PDAA) .... SQUIRE
System of Reinforcement-Inhibition   (PDAA)... SRI
System Safety Hazard Analysis [*Military*] .... SSHA
System Software [*Computer science*]   (IAA)....................................... SYSTSW
System Ten European Language Ledger Accounting   (PDAA)............... STELLA
System Test Report [*Military*]... STR
System Time-Domain Simulation Program [*Computer science*]
    (PDAA).. SYSTID
Systematic Approach to Group Technology   (PDAA) .... SAGT
Systematic Interaction Model   (PDAA).. SYSTIM
Systematic Machinery and Equipment Selection   (PDAA)....................... SYMES
Systemic Inflammatory Response Syndrome [*Medicine*]............................. SIRS
Systems Engineering Detailed Schedule .... SEDS
Systems Engineering Laboratory Circuit-Drawing Program
    (PDAA).. SELCIR
Systems Engineering Master Schedule .... SEMS
Systems Engineering Support.. SES
Systems Engineering Work Statement .... SES
Systems Exchange [*Computer science*]   (IAA) .... SYSX
Systemwide Program Committee [*Individually-guided education*]
    (AEE).. SPC
Systmatic Productivity Improvement Review In TRADOC [*Training
    and Doctrine Command*] [*Army*] .... SPIRIT

T

T-Platform Electric Van [*Chrysler*] [*Automotive engineering*]...................... TEV
T-Pulse Response [*Telecommunications*] (IAA)...................... TPR
TAAG, Linhas Aereas de Angola [*ICAO designator*] (FAAC) .... DTA
Table of Equipment Ready Issue [*Navy*] (ANA)...................... TERI
Table Simulation [*or Simulator*] (IAA)...................... TABSIM
Tabloid (NTCM)...................... TAB
Tabular [*or Tabulator*] Tape Processor [*Computer science*] (IAA)............ TTP
Tabulating Machine (IAA) .... TAB
Tabulator Character (IAA) .... TABC
TACA International Airlines SA [*El Salvador*] [*ICAO designator*]
    (FAAC)...................... TAI
Tachometer Generator (IAA)...................... TACH
TACJAM [*Tactical Communications Jamming System*] Quickfix,
    Trail Blazer Maintenance Trainer [*Army*] .... TQTMT
Tactical Air Control and Landing System [*Military*] (IAA)................... TACALS
Tactical Air Support Control System [*Military*] (PDAA) .... TASCS
Tactical Air Support Force [*Air Force*] .... TASF
Tactical Antimissile Measurement Program [*Military*] (IAA)................. TAMP
Tactical Call Sign (IAA) .... TCS
Tactical Combat Training System [*Navy*]...................... TCTS
Tactical Control RADAR (IAA) .... TCR
Tactical Data Automation System (IAA) .... TDAS
Tactical Data Entry [*Army*] (IAA)...................... TACDEN
Tactical Data Information Exchange Subsystem [*Navy*] (ANA) .... TADIX
Tactical Data Information Link [*DoD*] .... TADIL
Tactical Effectiveness of Minefields in the Antiarmor Weapons
    System (PDAA) .... TEMANS
Tactical Electromagnetic Reconnaissance [*Air Force*] (IAA) .... TEREC
Tactical Electromagnetic Systems Study Action Council [*Navy*]
    (ANA)...................... TESSAC
Tactical Electronic Intelligence [*Navy*] (ANA)...................... TACELINT
Tactical Electronic Warfare Squadron [*Navy*] (ANA)................... TACELRON
Tactical Engagement Close Combat System [*Army*] .... TECCS
Tactical Engagement and Range [*Army*] .... TE & R
Tactical Infantry Load Carrier Amphibious Remote [*Military*]
    (PDAA)...................... TILCAR
Tactical Initialization [*Computer software*] [*Military*]...................... TACI
Tactical Intelligence Processing and Interpretation System Program
    Office [*Air Force*] (PDAA)...................... TIPISPO
Tactical Loader [*Preparation software*] [*Army*]...................... TACL
Tactical Memorandum [*Navy*] (ANA) .... TACMEMO
Tactical Memory Address Register [*Computer science*] (IAA)........... TACMAR
Tactical Missile Experimental (IAA)...................... TMX
Tactical Modular Display [*Army*] (PDAA)...................... TACMOD
Tactical Operations Initiation...................... TOI
Tactical Organization Paperless System [*Army*]...................... TACOPS
Tactical Peripherals Equipment Monitor [*Military*]...................... TPEM
Tactical RADAR [*Military*] (IAA) .... TR
Tactical Range Ballistic Missile [*Military*] (IAA) .... TBX
Tactical Range Ship-to-Shore Missile (IAA) .... TRSSM
Tactical Reconstruction Information Pod [*Navy*] (ANA) .... TRIPOD
Tactical Satellite [*Military*] (IAA) .... TACSAT
Tactical Telephone Central [*Telecommunications*] (IAA)...................... TTC
Tactical Training Officer [*Army*]...................... TTO
Tactical Transport Group [*Military*]...................... TTG
Tactical Weapons Unit Diagnostics...................... TWUD
Tactical Work Program...................... TWP
Tactile Vision Substitution System (PDAA)...................... TVSS
Tadair SA [*Spain*] [*ICAO designator*] (FAAC)...................... TDC
TAES [*Tecnicas Aereas de Estudios y Servicios SA*] [*Spain*] [*ICAO
    designator*] (FAAC)...................... ESS
TAF Helicopters SA [*Spain*] [*ICAO designator*] (FAAC) .... HET
Tahiti Conquest Airlines [*France*] [*ICAO designator*] (FAAC) .... TCA
Tail Rotor Gearbox [*Aviation*] (DA)...................... TRGB
Taino Tours [*Dominican Republic*] [*ICAO designator*] (FAAC)............ TIN
Tajikair [*Tajikistan*] [*ICAO designator*] (FAAC)...................... TJK
Tajikistan [*ICAO designator*] (FAAC)...................... TZK
Take-Off (IAA)...................... TO
Take Off Weight (IAA)...................... TOWT
Take Real Result [*Computer science*] (IAA)...................... TRR
Take-Up (IAA)...................... TU
Takeoff Performance Monitor [*Aviation*] (DA)...................... TOPM
Takeoff Space Available [*Aviation*] (DA)...................... TOSA

Talair Pty Ltd. [*New Guinea*] [*ICAO designator*] (FAAC)...................... TAL
Talia Airlines [*Turkey*] [*ICAO designator*] (FAAC)...................... TAY
Talk Only (IAA)...................... TON
Talker Active State [*Telecommunications*] (IAA)...................... TACS
Talker Communication Error (IAA)...................... TCE
Talker Function [*Telecommunications*] (IAA)...................... TF
Talker Idle State [*Telecommunications*] (IAA)...................... TIDS
Tallyman...................... tlymn
Tamas Darida Enterprise [*Hungary*] [*ICAO designator*] (FAAC)........... DTE
Tamper (NFPA)...................... T
Tamper-Resistant Unattended Safeguard Technique (PDAA) .... TRUST
Tamper Switch [*NFPA pre-fire planning symbol*] (NFPA)...................... TS
Tanana Air Service [*ICAO designator*] (FAAC)...................... TNR
Tanavco Airways Ltd. [*Tanzania*] [*ICAO designator*] (FAAC) .... TNA
Tandem Mirror Hybrid Reactor (PDAA) .... TMHR
Tandem Tie Trunk Network (PDAA) .... TTTN
Tangent [*Mathematics*] (IAA) .... TG
Tangent Altitude [*Photography*]...................... TAN ALT
Tank Circuit (IAA)...................... TC
Tank Equipment Manufacturers' Association (IAA) .... TEMA
Tank Precision Gunnery in Bore Device [*Army*]...................... TPGID
Tank [*Missile*] Sight Improvement Program [*Army*] .... TSIP
Tank Turret Camouflage System [*Army*]...................... TTCS
Tank Turret Safety Adapter [*Army*] .... TTSA
Tanned Red Cell Hemagglutination Inhibition Immunoasay
    [*Immunology*] (PDAA)...................... TRCHII
Tantalum Integrated Circuit [*Electronics*] (PDAA)...................... TIC
Tape (IAA)...................... TA
Tape Adapter Cabinet (IAA)...................... TAC
Tape Adapter Unit [*Computer science*] (IAA)...................... TAU
Tape Compare [*Computer science*] (IAA) .... TPCOMP
Tape Control Block [*Computer science*] (IAA)...................... TCB
Tape-Controlled Reckoning and Checkout Equipment [*Component of
    automatic pilot*] [*Aviation*] (IAA)...................... TRACE
Tape Distributor [*Computer science*] (IAA) .... TD
Tape Duplicate [*Computer science*] (IAA)...................... TPDUP
Tape Error [*Computer science*] (IAA)...................... TE
Tape Error Block [*Computer science*] (IAA)...................... TEB
Tape-Handler [*Computer science*] (IAA)...................... TH
Tape Indicator [*Computer science*] (IAA)...................... TI
Tape Initializer [*Computer science*] (IAA)...................... TPINIT
Tape Management Software [*Computer science*] (IAA)...................... TMS
Tape Overlap Emulator [*Computer science*] (IAA)...................... TOE
Tape-to-Printer [*Computer science*] (IAA)...................... TPPR
Tape-to-Random Access [*Computer science*] (IAA)...................... TPRA
Tape Reading Typing Relay (IAA) .... TTR
Tape Storage System...................... TSS
Tape System Output Converter [*Computer science*] (IAA)...................... TSOC
Tape-to-Tape [*Computer science*] (IAA)...................... TPTP
Tape Transport Cassette...................... TTC
TAPER Isolated Dynamic Gain (IAA)...................... TIDG
Tar Heel Aviation, Inc. [*ICAO designator*] (FAAC)...................... THC
Target and Background Signal-to-Noise Experiment (IAA)............ TABSTONE
Target Cleanup Level [*Environmental science*] (ERG) .... TCL
Target Control Unit (IAA)...................... TCU
Target Coordinate Map Locator [*Military*] (PDAA)...................... TCML
Target Data Inventory Master Tape Preparation [*Military*] (IAA)....... TDIPRE
Target Group Index (NTCM)...................... TGI
Target Level of Safety (DA)...................... TLS
Target Network Television [*Cable television network*] (NTCM)...................... TNT
Target and Penetration (IAA)...................... TP
Target Position...................... T-POS
Target Radiation Measurement Program (IAA) .... TRAMP
Target Selector Azimuth (IAA)...................... TSAZ
Target Service Agents [*Computer science*] (PCM) .... TSA
Target Value Analysis [*Army*] (ADDR)...................... TVA
Target Year...................... TY
Targeting and Control (IAA)...................... TAC
Tarmac Plc [*British*] [*ICAO designator*] (FAAC)...................... TMC
Tarom, Romanian Air Transport [*ICAO designator*] (FAAC)...................... ROT
TAS Aviation, Inc. [*ICAO designator*] (FAAC)...................... RMS
TASD (Transporti Aerei Speciali) [*Italy*] [*ICAO designator*] (FAAC) .... TTS
Task Control Area (IAA) .... TCA

Task Database [Computer science]   (PCM)................ TDB
Task Direction Order [Military]................................. TDO
Task Extension Area [Computer science]   (IAA)....... TXA
Task Memory [Computer science]   (IAA)................... TM
Task Number [Computer science]   (IAA)................... TN
Task Related Instructional Methodology   (PDAA)..... TRIM
Task Sequence Number   (IAA)................................. TSN
Tasmanian Greens [Australia] [Political party]............ TG
Tatra Air [Slovakia] [ICAO designator]   (FAAC)...... TTR
Tauern Air Gesellschaft GmbH [Austria] [ICAO designator]   (FAAC)........ FAN
Tauranga Aero Club, Inc. [New Zealand] [ICAO designator]   (FAAC)..... PGS
Taut Band Suspension   (IAA)................................... TBS
Tax Installment Deduction   .... TID
Tax-Response Element [Genetics]   .... TRE
Tax Revenue Anticipation Note [Finance]   .... TRAN
Taxation Assessment Notice   .... TAN
Taxi Aereo de Jimulco SA de CV [Mexico] [ICAO designator]
   (FAAC)... JML
Taxi Aereo de Mexico [ICAO designator]   (FAAC)... TXM
Taxi Aereo de Veracruz [Mexico] [ICAO designator]   (FAAC).......... VRC
Taxi Fleet Operators' Federation [British]   (BI)........ TFOF
Taxirey SA de CV [Mexico] [ICAO designator]   (FAAC)... TXR
Taxis Aereos del Noroeste SA de CV [Mexico] [ICAO designator]
   (FAAC)... TNE
Taxiway Centerline Lighting [Aviation]   (DA)........... TC
Taxiway Edge Lighting [Aviation]   (DA)................... TE
Tayflight Ltd. [British] [ICAO designator]   (FAAC).. TFL
Taylor Vortex Flow [Fluid mechanics]   .... TVF
Tayside Aviation Ltd. [British] [ICAO designator]   (FAAC)...... TFY
Tea Cyprus Ltd. [ICAO designator]   (FAAC)............ TEC
TEA (UK) Ltd. [British] [ICAO designator]   (FAAC)... TUK
Teachable Language Comprehender   (PDAA)............ TLC
Teacher-Aiding Electronic Learning Link   (PDAA).... TELL
Teacher Programming Language [Computer science]   (PDAA)............ TPL
Teachers Insurance and Annuity Association-College Retirement
   Equities Fund   (AEE)..................................... TIAA-CREF
Teaching-Learning Unit   (AEE)............................... TLU
Teaching Sample Table   (PDAA)............................. TESAT
Team Manager   .... TM
Teams-Games-Tournaments [Education]   (AEE)....... TGT
Teamster's International Terminal and Accounting Network   (IAA)....... TITAN
Techicas Aereas de Estudios y Servicios SA [Spain] [ICAO
   designator]   (FAAC)...................................... TAES
Technical Acceptance Demonstration   (IAA)............ TAD
Technical Advisory Board   (IAA)............................. TAB
Technical Advisory Group   (IAA)............................ TAG
Technical Aircraft Reliability Statistics   (IAA).......... TARS
Technical Appliance Corp.   (IAA)............................ TACO
Technical Assistance Bureau [ICAO]   (DA).............. TAB
Technical and Cost Reduction Assistance Contract   ... TACRAC
Technical Development Capital   (IAA)...................... TDC
Technical Direction Order   .... TDO
Technical Documentation [DoD]   .... TECDOC
Technical Effort Locator and Technical Interest Profile System
   [Army]   (PDAA)... TELTIPS
Technical Information Management System   .... TIMS
Technical Information Series   (IAA)......................... TIS
Technical Information Service   (IAA)....................... TISE
Technical Intelligence Branch [National Coal Board]   (PDAA)......... TIB
Technical Manual Control Panel   (IAA).................... TMCP
Technical Oversight Representative   .... TOR
Technical Panel for International Broadcast   (NTCM)... TPIB
Technical Performance Audit   .... TPA
Technical Program Planning Document [Air Force]   (IAA)............. TPPD
Technical Requirements Document   .... TRD
Technical Review Criteria   (ERG)............................ TRC
Technical Review Group   .... TRG
Technical Risk Reduction [Military]   .... TRR
Technical Service Group   (IAA)............................... TSG
Technical Service Order [Aviation]   (DA)................. TSO
Technical Specifications   (IAA)................................ TECHSPECS
Technical Staff Surveillance [Military]   (IAA)........... TSS
Technical Support Unit   (IAA).................................. TSU
Technical Systems, Inc.   (IAA)................................. TSI
Technician Aeronautical Engineering   (IAA)............. TAE
Technique for the Optimum Placement of Activities in Zones
   (PDAA).. TOPAZ
Technological Aid to Creative Thought   (PDAA)....... TACT
Technological Aides to Creative Thoughts   (IAA)...... TOCS
Technologie Zentrum Steyr [Steyr Technology Center] [German]................. TZS
Technology Applications Information System   .... TAIS
Technology Forecasting and Assessment   (IAA)........ TFA
Technology Innovation Office [Environmental Protection Agency]............... TIO
Technology in Production   (IAA).............................. TIP
Technology Reinvestment Project [for converting military to civilian
   applications]   .... TRP
Technoogy Innovation   (IAA).................................. TI
Tecnavia [France] [ICAO designator]   (FAAC)......... TNV
Teddy Air AS [Norway] [ICAO designator]   (FAAC).. TED
Teenage, Infants, and Girls' Fashion Fair Organisation [British]
   (BI).. TIGFFO
Teleautograph [ICAO designator]   (FAAC)............... TELAU

Telecommunicacoes Aeronauticas SA [Brazil] [ICAO designator]
   (FAAC)... TASA
Telecommunication Engineering and Manufacturing Association
   [British]   (IAA)... TEMA
Telecommunication Traffic Association [British]   (BI).... TTA
Telecommunications for the Deaf and Disabled   .... TDD
Telecommunications Instruction Module System   (IAA)... TIMS
Telecommunications Processor   (IAA)...................... TCP
Telecommunications Program and Control   (IAA)..... TPC
Telecommunications Programming Language   (IAA).. TPL
Telecommunications Systems Corp.   (IAA)............... TSC
Telecommunications Systems Engineering   (IAA)..... TSE
Telecommunications Translator   (IAA)..................... TLT
Telecomputing Corp.   (IAA)................................... TC
Telecomunicacoes Aeronauticas SA [Brazil] [ICAO designator]
   (FAAC)... XLT
Teledate Equipment [Military]   .... TELD
Teledyne Continental Motors [ICAO designator]   (FAAC)........... TCM
Teledyne Electrically-Alterable Digital Differential Analyzer
   (IAA).. TEADDA
Teledyne Materials Research   (IAA)........................ TMR
Telefunken Computer AG   (IAA)............................. TC
Telefunken-Decca [Video disk system]   (IAA).......... TELDEC
Telegram   (IAA).. TLG
Telegraph   (IAA)... TH
Telegraph Automatic Routing in the Field   (IAA)...... TARIT
Telegraph Condenser Co.   (IAA)............................. TCC
Telegraph Construction and Maintenance   (IAA)....... TCAM
Telegraph Exchange [Telecommunications]   (IAA)... TELEX
Telegraph Repeater [Telecommunications]   (IAA)..... TR
Telegraphic   (NTCM).. TEL
Telegraphic Distortion Measuring Set   (IAA)............ TDMS
Telegraphy with Automatic Switching [Telecommunications]   (IAA)........... TAS
Telegraphy with Manual Switching [Telecommunications]   (IAA)............. TMS
Telemeter [or Telemetry] [Telecommunications]   (IAA)............. T
Telemeter Magnetics, Inc.   (IAA)............................. TMI
Telemeter Transmitter   (IAA).................................. TMS
Telemetered Ultrasonic Liquid Interface Plotting System   (PDAA)........ TULIPS
Telemetry Control Panel   (IAA).............................. TLMCTLPNL
Telemetry and Data [Telecommunications]   (IAA).... TAD
Telemetry Data Link [Telecommunications]   (IAA)... TDL
Telemetry Event [Telecommunications]   (IAA).......... TE
Telemetry Manufacturers' Association   (IAA)............ TMA
Telemetry Oscillator   (IAA).................................... TO
Telemetry Station System [Telecommunications]   (IAA)................ TELSTATS
Telemetry Support Equipment   (IAA)....................... TSE
Telemetry Tracking [Telecommunications]   (IAA)..... TELTRAC
Telephone   (NTCM)... PHONE
Telephone   (IAA)... TELN
Telephone Automated Briefing Service   (DA)............ TABS
Telephone Cable Makers' Association [British]   (BI)... TCMA
Telephone Center   (IAA).. TC
Telephone Central Office   (IAA)............................. TC
Telephone Communications   (IAA).......................... TELCO
Telephone Company [ICAO designator]   (FAAC)...... TELCO
Telephone Depot   (IAA)... TD
Telephone Engineer [Telecommunications]   (IAA).... TELENGR
Telephone Equipment Room [NFPA pre-fire planning symbol]   (NFPA)....... TE
Telephone Group   (IAA)... TEL
Telephone Line Doubler   (IAA)............................... TLD
Telephone Manufacturing Company   (IAA)............... TMC
Telephone Number   (IAA)....................................... TELNO
Telephone Rationalization by Computer   (PDAA)...... TERCO
Telephone Repeater Station   (IAA).......................... TRS
Telephone Set   (IAA)... TS
Telephone Station   (IAA)....................................... TEL
Telephone Tape   (IAA)... TELTAP
Telephone and Telegraph   (IAA)............................. TAT
Telephone and Telegraph   (IAA)............................. TELATEL
Telephone Toll Call   (IAA)..................................... TTC
Telephonic   (NTCM).. TEL
Telephony   (NTCM).. TEL
Telephoto   (NTCM).. TELE
Telepresence-Controlled Remotely-Operated Vehicle [NASA]..................... TROV
Teleprinter Error Detector   (IAA)............................ TED
Teleprinter Exchange [Telecommunications]   (IAA)... TELEX
Teleprinter Exchange Service [Telecommunications]   (IAA)............ TEX
Teleprinter on Multiplex [Telecommunications]   (IAA)............. TOM
Teleprinter Retransmitting [Telecommunications]   (IAA)........... TER
Teleprocessing Access Method [Telecommunications]   (IAA)............ TAM
Teleprocessing Analysis and Design Program [Computer science]
   (IAA).. TPAD
Teleprocessing Design Center [Army]   (PDAA)......... TDS
Teleprocessing Executive [Telecommunications]   (IAA)............. TELEX
Teleprocessing System [Computer science]   (IAA).... TPS
Teleprogrammer Assembly System [Computer science]   (IAA)............ TAS
Teletext Output of Price Information by Computer [London Stock
   Exchange].. TOPIC
Teletype   (NTCM)... TEL
Teletype   (IAA).. TLTP
Teletype Center [Telecommunications]   (IAA).......... TTC
Teletype Input   (IAA).. TTI
Teletype Interpreter   (PDAA).................................. TINT

Teletype Message Converter [*Telecommunications*] (IAA) TTC
Teletype Output [*Telecommunications*] (IAA) TTO
Teletype on Radio [*Telecommunications*] (IAA) TOR
Teletype Service Without Voice Communication [*Telecommunications*] (IAA) TWC
Teletype Translator [*Telecommunications*] (IAA) TTR
Teletypewriter [*Telecommunications*] (IAA) TY
Teletypewriter Conference (IAA) TELECON
Teletypewriter Equipment (IAA) TTY
Television [*FCC*] (NTCM) T
Television (IAA) TEL
Television (IAA) TLV
Television Accessory Manufacturers Institute (NTCM) TAMI
Television Advisory Committee for Educational Television (NTCM) TACET
Television Advisory Committee of Mexican Americans (NTCM) TACOMA
Television Cathode Ray (IAA) TCR
Television Facsimile (NTCM) TELEFAC
Television Film Exhibit (NTCM) TFE
Television Household [*Ratings*] (NTCM) TVHH
Television Information Storage (IAA) TVIS
Television Infrared-Observation Satellite NOAA [*National Oceanographic and Atmospheric Administration*] [*Navy*] (ANA) TIROS-N
Television Intercity [*FCC*] (NTCM) TI
Television Management Information System (IAA) TMIS
Television Optical (NTCM) TELOP
Television Pickup [*FCC*] (NTCM) TP
Television Program Standard TPS
Television, Radio, and Audio-Visuals of the Presbyterian Church in the United States (NTCM) TRAV
Television Satellite (NTCM) TELSAT
Television Service Dealers' Association (IAA) TSDA
Television Studio-Transmitter-Link [*FCC*] (NTCM) TS
Television System (IAA) TVSYS
Television Technicians' Association (IAA) TTA
Television Transcription (NTCM) Telescription
Television Video Generator TVG
Television Writer's Guild (NTCM) TWG
TELEX Extended Memory (IAA) TEM
TELEX File Adapter (IAA) TFA
TELEX Line Adapter (IAA) TLA
TELEX Main Memories [*Telecommunications*] (IAA) TMM
Telford Aviation, Inc. [*ICAO designator*] (FAAC) TEL
TEM Enterprises [*ICAO designator*] (FAAC) CXP
Tempelhof Airways, Inc. [*Germany*] [*ICAO designator*] (FAAC) TEH
Temperature Auto Stabilizing Regime (IAA) TASR
Temperature Autostabilizing Nonlinear Dielectric Element (IAA) TANDEL
Temperature Average (IAA) TAVG
Temperature Coefficient of Offset (IAA) TCO
Temperature Coefficient of Sensitivity (IAA) TCS
Temperature-Compensated Mask (IAA) TCM
Temperature-Compensation (IAA) TCM
Temperature Control Amplifier (IAA) TCA
Temperature Control Device for Crystal Units (IAA) TCD
Temperature-Controlled Crystal Oscillator (IAA) TCCO
Temperature in Degrees Centigrade (IAA) TC
Temperature Excess (PDAA) TEX
Temperature-Gradient Gel Electrophoresis [*Analytical biochemistry*] TGGE
Temperature-Gradient Zone-Melting Process [*Chemistry*] (IAA) TGZMP
Temperature Independent Material (IAA) TIM
Temperature Level Control (IAA) TLC
Temperature Measuring Equipment (IAA) TME
Temperature Pressure Test Chamber (IAA) TPTC
Temperature Regualtor and Missile Power Supply (IAA) TRMPS
Template Tracing Technique (DA) TTT
Temporal Fourier Hologram (PDAA) TFH
Temporary Accumulator (IAA) TAR
Temporary Accumulator Register (IAA) TAR
Temporary Alteration Control Form (IAA) TACF
Temporary Assembled Skeleton [*Computer science*] (IAA) TASK
Temporary Augmentation for Command and Control [*Navy*] (ANA) TACC
Temporary Base Register [*Computer science*] (IAA) TBR
Temporary Danger Area (DA) TDA
Temporary Entry Permit TEP
Temporary Incapacity Allowance TIA
Temporary Rental Allowance TRA
Temporary Reserved Airspace [*ICAO designator*] (FAAC) TRA
Temsco Helicopters, Inc. [*ICAO designator*] (FAAC) TMS
Tender Assist Minimum Platform Arrangement (PDAA) TAMPA
Tender Option Bond TOB
Tennessee Airways, Inc. [*ICAO designator*] (FAAC) TEN
Tensile Bond Strength [*Materials science*] TBS
Tensile Safety Index [*Engineering design*] TSI
Tentative Safe Exposure Level [*Toxicology*] TSEL
Term Availability Plan (IAA) TAP
Term Lease Plan (IAA) TLP
Terminal [*Computer science*] (IAA) TE
Terminal Address (IAA) TA
Terminal Area Altitude Monitoring (PDAA) TAAM
Terminal Business System [*Computer science*] (IAA) TBS
Terminal Control (DA) TMC
Terminal Control Table [*Computer science*] (IAA) TCT
Terminal Count Sequence (IAA) TCS
Terminal Editing System [*Computer science*] (PDAA) TESY
Terminal and Enroute Navigation (PDAA) TERN
Terminal Interactive Access Method [*Computer science*] (IAA) TIAM
Terminal Interface Monitor (IAA) TIM
Terminal List Table (IAA) TLT
Terminal Multiplexer [*Computer science*] (IAA) TM
Terminal Office [*Computer science*] (IAA) TO
Terminal-Operated Production Language (IAA) TOPL
Terminal Oriental Real-Time Operating System [*Computer science*] (IAA) TORTOS
Terminal Primary and Secondary RADAR System (DA) TPSRS
Terminal Processing Unit [*Computer science*] (IAA) TPU
Terminal Programming Language [*Computer science*] (IAA) TPL
Terminal RADAR Control (IAA) TRACON
Terminal Radiation Airborne Program Translator [*Air Force*] (IAA) TTR
Terminal Railroad Association Historical and Technical Society (EA) TRRA H & TS
Terminal Secondary RADAR Beacon [*Aviation*] (FAAC) TSEC
Terminal Series (IAA) TS
Terminal Station (IAA) TS
Terminal Support Processor [*Computer science*] (PDAA) TSP
Terminal Trajectory Telescope (IAA) TETRA
Terminal Very High Frequency Omnirange (IAA) TVOR
Terminating System (IAA) TS
Terminator Group Controller (IAA) TGC
Terminator Interrupt [*Computer science*] (IAA) TI
Terminology, Aids, References, Applications, and Coordination (IAA) TARAC
Terminology Library [*Computer science*] (IAA) TL
Ternary Digit (IAA) TIT
Terrain Avoidance RADAR (IAA) TARA
Terrain Clearance Altitude [*Aviation*] (DA) T
Terrain Evaluation and Retrieval for Road Alignment (IAA) TERRA
Terrain and RADAR Simulator (IAA) TARS
Terrain SDP SA [*Spain*] [*ICAO designator*] (FAAC) SDT
Terrestrial Biogeochemical Model [*for climate effects*] TBM
Terrestrial Ecosystem Model [*for climate effects*] TEM
Territorial Airlines, Inc. [*ICAO designator*] (FAAC) TER
Tertiary-Butyl Perbenzoate [*Organic chemistry*] TBPB
Tertiary-Butylhydroperioxide [*Organic chemistry*] TBHP
Tesis [*Russian Federation*] [*ICAO designator*] (FAAC) TIS
Tessaral Harmonic Resonance of Orbital Elements (PDAA) THROE
Test Acceptance Document [*Computer science*] (IAA) TAD
Test Announcer (IAA) TA
Test Call Answer Relay Set (PDAA) TCARS
Test Case Specification (IAA) TC
[*Inspector's*] **Test Connection** [*NFPA pre-fire planning symbol*] (NFPA) TC
Test Connection Equipment (IAA) TCE
Test and Crossmatch [*Medicine*] (MAH) T & C
Test Data Specification (IAA) TDS
Test and Diagnostics (IAA) TD
Test Equipment Error Analysis Report (IAA) TEEAR
Test Evaluation and Control (IAA) TEC
Test Event Sequencing, Simulating, and Recording System (PDAA) TESSAR
Test Header (Fire Pump) [*NFPA pre-fire planning symbol*] (NFPA) TH
Test Incident Report (IAA) TIR
Test Incoming Trunk [*Telecommunications*] (IAA) TSTICT
Test Item Transmittal Form (IAA) TITF
Test Jack Field [*Telecommunications*] (IAA) TJF
Test Laboratory Engineer (IAA) TLE
Test Line Signal (IAA) TLS
Test Macro [*Computer science*] (IAA) TEMA
Test Management Information System TMIC
Test Market Plan [*Advertising*] (NTCM) TMP
Test Market Profile [*Advertising*] (NTCM) TMP
Test Monitoring Center [*ASTM*] [*Engineering standards*] TMC
Test of Multiple Corridor Identification System (IAA) TOMCIS
Test and Operation (IAA) TAO
Test Point Access (IAA) TPA
Test Point Data Chart [*Military*] TPDC
Test Point Prelaunch Automatic Checkout Equipment [*NASA*] (IAA) TPP
Test Power Control Unit (IAA) TPCU
Test Procedure Specification [*NASA*] (IAA) TPROC
Test Process TP
Test and Quality Assurance (IAA) TAQA
Test and Return (IAA) TAR
Test Score Category [*DoD*] TSC
Test and Set [*Computer science*] (IAA) TS
Test Set, Overall Missile (IAA) TOM
Test Shop TESH
Test Summary Report (IAA) TSR
Test Terminator (IAA) TT
Test [*or Testing*] **Time** (IAA) TT
Test Tube (IAA) TT
Test Two Bits (IAA) TTB
Test Voltage (IAA) TV
Test Ware Instrument (PDAA) TWIN
Testa Rossa [*Red engine cylinder head*] [*Ferrari automotive model designation*] [*Italian*] TR

Testamentum [*Will*] [*Latin*] ... T
Tethered Aerostat RADAR System [*Aviation*] (FAAC) ... TARS
Tethered Meteorological Balloon (IAA) ... TETROON
Tetraethyl Pyrophosphate [*Insecticide*] [*Pharmacology*] (IAA) ... TEP
Tetrahydrocannabinol Cross-Reacting-Cannabinoid [*Active principle of marijuana*] (PDAA) ... THC-CRC
Tetrahydrophthalimide [*Organic chemistry*] ... THPI
Tetraiodothyroacetic Acid [*Organic chemistry*] (MAH) ... TETRAC
Tetrakis(ethylhexoxy)silane [*Organic chemistry*] ... TEHOS
Tetramesitylporphyrin [*Organic chemistry*] ... TMP
Tetramethylrhodamino-Isothiocyanate [*Organic chemistry*] (MAH) ... TRMC
Tetrode [*Electronics*] (IAA) ... TR
Texaco Lubricants Co. [*Automotive industry supplier*] ... TLC
Texair Charter, Inc. [*ICAO designator*] (FAAC) ... TXA
Texas Airlines, Inc. [*ICAO designator*] (FAAC) ... TXS
Texas Instruments Cassette Operating Language (IAA) ... TIOL
Texas Instruments Language Translator [*Computer science*] (IAA) ... TILT
Texas Instruments Minicomputer Information Exchange (IAA) ... TIMIX
Texas Instruments Registration and Identification System [*Auto theft deterrent*] ... TIRIS
Texas Instruments Transistor Transistor Logic (IAA) ... TITTI
Texas Instruments Vidicon (IAA) ... TIVICON
Texas Microelectronics, Inc. (IAA) ... TMI
Texas National Airlines [*ICAO designator*] (FAAC) ... TXN
Texas Technological University (PDAA) ... TTU
Text Excursion Module (IAA) ... TEM
Text Information Retrieval and Management Program System [*Computer science*] (IAA) ... TRAMPS
Text-to-Speech [*Computer science*] ... TTS
Text User Interface [*Computer science*] ... TUI
Textile and Clothing Contractors' Association [*British*] (BI) ... TCCA
Textile Industry (IAA) ... TEXTINDY
Textile Machinery and Accessory Manufacturers Association [*British*] (BI) ... TMAMA
TFTR [*Tokamak Fusion Test Reactor*] **Flexibility Modification** ... TFM
TG Aviation Ltd. [*British*] [*ICAO designator*] (FAAC) ... TGC
Thai Airways Co. Ltd. [*ICAO designator*] (FAAC) ... TAC
Thai Airways International Ltd. [*Thailand*] [*ICAO designator*] (FAAC) ... THA
Thai Flying Helicopter Service Co. Ltd. [*Thailand*] [*ICAO designator*] (FAAC) ... TFH
Thames Air Services & Charter Ltd. [*Nigeria*] [*ICAO designator*] (FAAC) ... TMQ
Thames Boating Trades' Association [*British*] (BI) ... TBTA
Thames Conservancy [*British*] (BI) ... TC
Thanks (IAA) ... TN
Theater Air Defense [*Military*] ... TAD
Theater Army Signal System (IAA) ... TASS
Theater Network Television (IAA) ... TNT
Theater Storage Area [*Military*] ... TSA
Theatrical Traders Association Ltd. [*British*] (BI) ... TTA
Theoretical and Applied Mechanics (IAA) ... TAAM
Theoretical Earth Utilization System (PDAA) ... THEUS
Theoretical Linear Solvation Energy Relationship [*Physical chemistry*] ... TLSER
Theoretical Maximum Daily Intake [*Toxicology*] ... TMDI
Theory of Neuronal Group Selection [*Neurology*] ... TNGS
Thermal Advanced Gas-Cooled Reactor Exploiting Thorium [*Nuclear energy*] (IAA) ... TAGRET
Thermal Analysis of Substrates and Intergrated Circuits (PDAA) ... TASIC
Thermal Coefficient of Resistance (IAA) ... TCR
Thermal Conditioning Service (IAA) ... TCS
Thermal Field Emission (IAA) ... TFE
Thermal Hartree-Fock Approximation (PDAA) ... THFA
Thermal Identification Device ... TID
Thermal Image Camera (PDAA) ... TIC
Thermal Infrared (PDAA) ... TIR
Thermal Insulation Contractors' Association [*British*] (BI) ... TICA
Thermal Liquid Junction Potential (PDAA) ... TLJP
Thermal Mechanical Controlled Processing (PDAA) ... TMCP
Thermal Overload Relay (IAA) ... TOR
Thermal Resistance (IAA) ... TR
Thermal Sensitive Vote [*Automotive interior comfort survey*] ... TSV
Thermal Single-Determinant Approximation (PDAA) ... TSDA
Thermal Transfer Equipment (IAA) ... TTE
Thermally-Stimulated Luminescence (PDAA) ... TSL
Thermally Tuned (IAA) ... TT
Thermionic Field (IAA) ... TF
Thermo-Reactive Deposition [*Metal treating*] ... TRD
Thermochromic Liquid Crystal ... TLC
Thermocouple Open Circuit Detection (IAA) ... TCOCD
Thermoelectric Cooler (IAA) ... TEC
Thermoform Continuous Percolation (IAA) ... TCP
Thermomagnetic Treatment (IAA) ... TT
Thermometeroid Garnet (IAA) ... TMG
Thermophysical Properties Information Center [*Purdue University*] (PDAA) ... TPIC
Thermoplastic Covered Fixture Wire Flexible Stranding (IAA) ... TFF
Thermoplastic Optical Phase Recorder (IAA) ... TOPR
Thermostat Switch (IAA) ... TT
Theron Airways [*South Africa*] [*ICAO designator*] (FAAC) ... TRN
Thick [*Aviation*] (DA) ... TKH
Thick-Film Hybrid Circuit (IAA) ... TFHC
Thin-Film Active Device (IAA) ... TFAD
Thin-Film FET [*Field-Effect Transistor*] (IAA) ... TFF
Thin-Film Field-Effect Transistor (IAA) ... TFFET
Thin-Film Integrated Circuit (IAA) ... TFIC
Thin Film Integrated Optics (PDAA) ... TFIO
Thin-Film Thermocouple (IAA) ... TFTC
Thin-Layer Activation [*Engine wear testing*] ... TLA
Thin-layer Field-Effect Transistor (IAA) ... TFET
Thin-Layer Field Effect Transistor (IAA) ... TIFET
Third-Harmonic Distortion [*Physics*] (IAA) ... THC
Third-Harmonic Distortion [*Physics*] (IAA) ... THD
Third Moment of Frequency (PDAA) ... TMF
Thomasville Aircraft and Warning Station (IAA) ... TAWS
Thoracic Trauma Index [*Automotive safety research*] ... TTI
Thorium High Temperature Reactor Association (IAA) ... THTRA
Thoroughbred Breeders' Association [*British*] (BI) ... TBA
Thousands Position (IAA) ... THP
Threaded Nut Connector (IAA) ... TNC
Threat ... TH
Threat to Army Mission Areas ... TAMA
Three-Axis (IAA) ... TRAX
Three-Axis Rout Byro Inertial Tracker (IAA) ... TARBIT
Three-Letter Acronym [*Computer hacker terminology*] (NHD) ... TLA
Three-State [*Computer science*] (IAA) ... TS
Three-State Logic [*Computer science*] (IAA) ... TSL
Three-State Transceiver [*Computer science*] (IAA) ... TTS
Three Ton Range and Azimuth Only (IAA) ... TRZON
Three-Way Valve [*Hydraulics*] ... TWV
Threshold (IAA) ... THRES
Threshold Decoding [*Computer science*] (IAA) ... TD
Threshold Element (IAA) ... TE
Threshold Exceeded ... TE
Threshold Function (IAA) ... TF
Threshold Lighting [*Aviation*] (DA) ... T
Threshold Lights [*Aviation*] (DA) ... Thr
Threshold Limit Value - Ceiling [*Industrial hygiene*] (PDAA) ... TLV-C
Threshold Limit Value - Short Term Exposure Limit [*Industrial hygiene*] (PDAA) ... TLV-STEL
Threshold Limit Value - Time-Weighted Average [*Industrial hygiene*] (PDAA) ... TLV-TWA
Threshold Planning Quantity (ERG) ... TPO
Throttle Body Fuel Injection [*Fuel systems*] [*Automotive engineering*] ... TBFI
Throttle Valve Opening [*Automotive engineering*] ... TVO
Throttling Expansion Valve [*Automotive air conditioning*] ... TXV
Through Bolt (DAC) ... TB
Through Plated Hole [*Printed circuit board feature*] (IAA) ... TPH
Through Supergroup Filter (IAA) ... TSF
Throw Away Detector (PDAA) ... TADS
Thrust (IAA) ... T
Thrust to Earth Weight Ratio (IAA) ... TEWR
Thrust Floated Gyroscope (PDAA) ... TFG
Thurston Aviation Ltd. [*British*] [*ICAO designator*] (FAAC) ... THG
Thyratron [*Electronics*] (IAA) ... THY
Thyratron Motor Control [*Electronics*] (IAA) ... THOMOTROL
Thyristor Power Supply [*Electronics*] (IAA) ... TPS
Thyroid Vein [*Medicine*] (PDAA) ... TV
Thyrotroph Embryonic Factor [*Genetics*] ... TEF
Thyssen Henschel ... TH
Ticket-Granting Ticket [*Computer science*] ... TGT
Tie Line Bias Control [*Telecommunications*] (IAA) ... TBC
Tigerfly [*British*] [*ICAO designator*] (FAAC) ... MOH
Tight Close-Up [*Cinematography*] (NTCM) ... TCU
TIGIN Ltd. [*ICAO designator*] (FAAC) ... XNV
Tilted Electric Field (PDAA) ... TEF
Tim Donut Ltd. [*Canada*] [*ICAO designator*] (FAAC) ... TND
Timber Management Decision System (PDAA) ... TIMADS
Timber Trades' Benevolent Society [*British*] (BI) ... TTBS
Time (FAAC) ... TM
Time Air Ltd. [*Canada*] [*ICAO designator*] (FAAC) ... TAF
Time and Attendance (IAA) ... TAA
Time Band-Width (IAA) ... TBW
Time Base Error Difference [*Computer science*] (IAA) ... TBED
Time Buffered Coarse Fine (IAA) ... TBCE
Time and Charges [*Telecommunications*] (IAA) ... TAC
Time Code (NTCM) ... TC
Time Compression [*Computer science*] (IAA) ... TC
Time Compression Multiplex (IAA) ... TCM
Time Constant (IAA) ... T
Time Controlled [*Computer science*] (IAA) ... TC
Time of Day Clock (IAA) ... TDC
Time Delay Relay [*Computer science*] (IAA) ... TR
Time Difference of Arrival / Distance Measuring Equipment (PDAA) ... TDOA/DME
Time Displacement Error (IAA) ... TDE
Time Distributed Multiple Access (IAA) ... TDMA
Time-Division Data Link Print-Out [*Telecommunications*] (IAA) ... TDDLPO
Time-Domain Prony Method (IAA) ... TDPM
Time to Emplacement [*Military*] ... T(EMP)
Time Equipment (IAA) ... TE
Time Error Indicated ... TEI
Time and Event (IAA) ... TAE
Time and Event Recorder (IAA) ... TAEREC

Time Frequency (IAA) ..... TF
Time Frequency Shift Keying [*Computer science*] (IAA) ..... TFSK
Time Gain Control (IAA) ..... TGC
Time-to-Go Rating [*Air Force*] (IAA) ..... TTGR
Time Indicator (IAA) ..... TIM
Time Interval Gage of Relays [*Telecommunications*] (IAA) ..... TIGOR
Time on Jamming (IAA) ..... TOJ
Time-Limited Impulse Response [*Telecommunications*] (IAA) ..... TLIR
Time Multiplexed Analogue Radio Control (PDAA) ..... TIMARC
Time-Multiplexer Unit [*Telecommunications*] (IAA) ..... TMU
Time Multiplication Factor [*Offshore racing*] ..... TMF
Time Over (IAA) ..... TO
Time Processing Unit [*Automotive engineering*] [*Electronics*] ..... TPU
Time Quantized Frequency Modulation [*Telecommunications*] (IAA) ..... TFM
Time Ratio Control (IAA) ..... TRC
Time Repetitive Analog Contour Equipment (PDAA) ..... TRACE
Time-Resolved Phosphorimetry [*Analytical chemistry*] ..... TRP
Time Routine [*Computer science*] (IAA) ..... TR
Time Service (IAA) ..... TS
Time Share International Data Communications Network [*Telecommunications*] (IAA) ..... TIMNET
Time-Share Peripherals [*Computer science*] (IAA) ..... TSP
Time-Shared Executive [*Computer science*] (IAA) ..... TSEXEC
Time-Shared Supervisory System (IAA) ..... TSS
Time-Shared Terminal [*Computer science*] (IAA) ..... TST
Time-sharing Accounting Package [*Computer science*] (IAA) ..... TAP
Time-Sharing Activity Report System [*Computer science*] (IAA) ..... TSAR
Time-Sharing Business Package [*Computer science*] (IAA) ..... TSBP
Time-Sharing Execution [*Computer science*] (IAA) ..... TSX
Time-Sharing Executive System [*Computer science*] (IAA) ..... TSX
Time-Sharing Multiplex [*Telecommunications*] (IAA) ..... TSM
Time-Sharing Multiplex Unit [*Telecommunications*] (IAA) ..... TSMU
Time-Sharing and Multiplexing Numerical Control [*Telecommunications*] (IAA) ..... TSNC
Time-Sharing Operating Control System [*Computer science*] (IAA) ..... TSOC
Time-Sharing Operating System [*Computer science*] (IAA) ..... TOS
Time-Sharing Operation of Product Structure Directory System (PDAA) ..... TOPSY
Time-Sharing Real-Time Operating System (IAA) ..... TROS
Time Sharing System Performance Activity Recorder (PDAA) ..... TS/SPAR
Time Slot Input [*Telecommunications*] (IAA) ..... TSI
Time Slot Interchange Circuit [*Telecommunications*] (IAA) ..... TSIC
Time Slot Zero [*Telecommunications*] (IAA) ..... TSO
Time, Space, and Matter [*Princeton University course title*] (AEE) ..... TSM
Time-Span-of-Discretion (PDAA) ..... TSD
Time-Speed-Distance [*Vehicle testing*] ..... TSD
Time to Station (DA) ..... TTS
Time Variable Parameter (IAA) ..... TVP
Time Variant Automation (IAA) ..... TVA
Time Variation of Loss (IAA) ..... TVL
Time-Varying Signal Measurement (IAA) ..... TVSM
Time-Weighted Average Concentration [*Toxicology*] ..... TWAC
Time-Weighted Average Exposure [*Toxicology*] ..... TWAE
Time Wire Transmission (IAA) ..... TWT
Timer (IAA) ..... T
Timing Data Distributor (IAA) ..... TDD
Timing Gage (IAA) ..... TG
Timing and Injection Rate Control System [*Diesel engines*] ..... TICS
Timing Level Generator (IAA) ..... TLG
Tin-Free Steel Chromium-Type (PDAA) ..... TFS-CT
Tinplate Stockholders' and Merchants' Association [*British*] (BI) ..... TSMA
Tiphook PCL [*British*] [*ICAO designator*] (FAAC) ..... BOX
Tire Pressure [*Automotive engineering*] ..... TP
Tissue Banks International [*An association*] (EA) ..... TBI
Tissue Equivalent Proportional Counter (PDAA) ..... TEPC
Titan Airways Ltd. [*British*] [*ICAO designator*] (FAAC) ..... AWC
Title Abstract Bulletin (IAA) ..... TAB
Title Card (NTCM) ..... TC
Tjumenaviatrans [*Russian Federation*] [*ICAO designator*] (FAAC) ..... TMN
TK Travel Ltd. [*Gambia*] [*ICAO designator*] (FAAC) ..... RDA
TLC Air, Inc. [*ICAO designator*] (FAAC) ..... TLS
To Be Initiated (IAA) ..... TBI
Toastmasters and Masters of Ceremonies Federation [*British*] (BI) ..... TMCF
Tobacco Research Council [*British*] (BI) ..... TRC
Tobacco Trade Travellers' Association [*British*] (BI) ..... TTTA
Todos Santos Ambulance Fund [*An association*] (EA) ..... TSAF
Toggle [*Telecommunications*] (IAA) ..... T
Toggle Flip-Flop [*Computer science*] (IAA) ..... TFF
Togo Airlines [*ICAO designator*] (FAAC) ..... TGA
Toilet Preparations Federation [*British*] (BI) ..... TPF
Token-Holding Time [*Computer science*] ..... THT
Tokyo Automatic Computer (IAA) ..... TAC
Tokyo Electron Ltd. (IAA) ..... TEL
Tol-Air Services, Inc. [*ICAO designator*] (FAAC) ..... TOL
Tolerable Daily Intake [*Toxicology*] ..... TDI
Tomahawk Airways, Inc. [*ICAO designator*] (FAAC) ..... TMK
Tomahawk Land Attack Missile/Conventional [*Navy*] (ANA) ..... TLAM/C
Tone (IAA) ..... T
Tone Answer Back [*Telecommunications*] (IAA) ..... TAB
Tone Call Squelch [*Telecommunications*] (IAA) ..... TCS
Tone Code Modulation (IAA) ..... TCM
Tone Control [*Telecommunications*] (IAA) ..... TC
Tone-Count Audiometric Computer (PDAA) ..... TCAC
Tone Dial Switching System Control (IAA) ..... TDSSC
Tone Digital Command (IAA) ..... TDC
Tonga [*Aircraft nationality and registration mark*] (FAAC) A3
Tongue and Groove [*Lumber*] (IAA) ..... TAG
Tons of Paper In [*Computer science*] (IAA) ..... TOPI
Tons of Paper Out [*Computer science*] (IAA) ..... TOPO
Tool Offset (IAA) ..... TO
Tool Package (IAA) ..... TOP
Toolmanager [*Computer science*] (IAA) ..... TOM
Top Assembly ..... TA
Top and Bottom (IAA) ..... TAB
Top Cap (IAA) ..... TC
Top Desk Computer (IAA) ..... TDC
Top Flight Air Service, Inc. [*ICAO designator*] (FAAC) ..... CHE
Top Management Program ..... TMP
Top of Potentiometer [*Electronics*] (IAA) ..... TOP
Top-to-Top (IAA) ..... TT
Topair Ltd. [*Czechoslovakia*] [*ICAO designator*] (FAAC) ..... TPI
Topcliffe FTU [*British*] [*ICAO designator*] (FAAC) ..... TOF
Topological Representation of Synthetic and Analytical Relations of Concepts (PDAA) ..... TOSAR
Toronto Airways Ltd. [*Canada*] [*ICAO designator*] (FAAC) ..... TOR
Toros Airlines [*Turkey*] [*ICAO designator*] (FAAC) ..... TAU
Torque Generator (IAA) ..... TG
Torque Receiver (IAA) ..... TR
Torque Repeater (IAA) ..... TR
Torque Synchro Transmitter (IAA) ..... TS
Torque Transmitter (IAA) ..... TS
Torso Back Protective Armor (PDAA) ..... TBPA
Total Abdominal Hysterectomy Bilateral Salpingo-Oophorectomy [*Medicine*] (MAH) ..... TAHBSO
Total Army Authorization ..... TAA
Total Army Personnel Evaluation System ..... TAPES
Total Audience Plan [*Radio advertising*] (NTCM) ..... TAP
Total Audit Concept Technique (PDAA) ..... TACT
Total Automatic Color (IAA) ..... TAC
Total Binding Energy (IAA) ..... TBE
Total Blood Volume Predicted from Body Surface [*Physiology*] (MAH) ..... TBV!P
Total COBOL [*Common Business-Oriented Language*] **Capability** [*Computer science*] (IAA) ..... TCC
Total Effective Fare (PDAA) ..... TEF
Total Electron Yield [*Spectroscopy*] ..... TEY
Total Energy Feasibility (IAA) ..... TEF
Total Energy Loss (IAA) ..... TEL
Total Energy Systems Service (IAA) ..... TESS
Total Float (IAA) ..... TF
Total Heat Rejection (IAA) ..... THR
Total Indicator Variation (IAA) ..... TIV
Total Internal Reflectiona Fluorescence Microscopy ..... TIRFM
Total Ionic Strength Adjustment Buffer (PDAA) ..... TISAB
Total Library Computerization ..... TLC
Total Market Coverage [*Advertising*] (NTCM) ..... TMA
Total Mean Downtime [*Computer science*] (IAA) ..... TMD
Total Network Recall [*Systems Enhancement Corp.*] [*Computer science*] (PCM) ..... TNR
Total Noise Exposure Level (DA) ..... TNEL
Total Numerical Control (IAA) ..... TNC
Total Outage Time (IAA) ..... TOT
Total Package Fielding - Activation [*Military*] ..... TPF-A
Total Package Unit Material Fielding [*Army*] ..... TRUMF
Total Peak Loss (IAA) ..... TPL
Total Preventative Maintenance [*Manufacturing*] ..... TPM
Total Print Control [*Computer science*] (IAA) ..... TPC
Total Program Diagnostic [*Computer science*] (IAA) ..... TPD
Total Publishing Environment [*Computer science*] (IAA) ..... TPE
Total Quality Leadership ..... TQL
Total Quality and Productivity ..... TQP
Total Quality Service ..... TQS
Total Reaction (DA) ..... TR
Total Reevaluation Under SPRINT Thrust [*Army*] ..... TRUST
Total Replenishment Inventory Program (PDAA) ..... TRIP
Total Shielding Effectiveness (IAA) ..... TSE
Total Signal Lines (IAA) ..... TSL
Total System Analyzer (IAA) ..... TSA
Total Time Management [*Industrial engineering*] ..... TTM
Total Underground Distribution (IAA) ..... TUD
Total Vertical Error [*Aviation*] (DA) ..... TVE
Total Wear Coefficient [*Materials science*] ..... TWC
Total Weighted Pollutant Load (ERG) ..... TWPL
Totalizer Agency Board (IAA) ..... TAB
Totally Chlorine-Free [*Pulp and paper processing*] ..... TCF
Totally Decentralized Control (IAA) ..... TDC
Totally-Enclosed Air Water-Cooled Reactor [*Nuclear energy*] (IAA) ..... TEAWC
Totally-Enclosed Force-Cooled Reactor [*Nuclear energy*] (IAA) ..... TEFC
Touch Input Device [*Computer science*] (IAA) ..... TID
Touch-Tone [*Telecommunications*] (IAA) ..... TT
Touch-Tone Receiver [*Telecommunications*] (IAA) ..... TTR
Touch Wire Display (PDAA) ..... TWD
Touchdown Zone Elevation [*Aviation*] (DA) ..... TDZE
Touring Car Drivers Association [*Automobile racing*] ..... TCDA

Tourismo Internationale [*International Touring*] [*Italian*] .... TI
Tourismo Internationale Injection [*International Touring-fuel Injection*] [*Italian*] .... TII
Tourist Observation and Underwater Research Submarine (PDAA) .... TOURS
Towed Acoustic Monitor (PDAA) .... TAM
Towed Assault Bridge [*Army*] .... TAB
Towed Cable [*Telecommunications*] (IAA) .... TC
Towed Flexible Barge (PDAA) .... TFB
Tower Air, Inc. [*ICAO designator*] (FAAC) .... TOW
Tower Cab Digital Display (PDAA) .... TCDD
Township and Village Enterprise [*People's Republic of China*] (ECON) .... TVE
Toxic Concentration Low (ERG) .... TCLo
Toxic Dose Low (ERG) .... TDLo
Toxic Equivalency Factor [*Environmental Protection Agency*] .... TEF
Toxic Use Reduction [*Manufacturing*] .... TUR
Toxicology Information Working Party (PDAA) .... TIWP
Toy Stores Steiff Collectors Club (EA) .... TSSCC
Toyota Canada, Inc. [*ICAO designator*] (FAAC) .... TOY
Toyota Diffusion/Deposition .... TD
Toyota Motor Marketing and Engineering [*Automotive industry, corporate subsidiary*] .... TMME
Trabajos Aereos SA [*Spain*] [*ICAO designator*] (FAAC) .... TGE
Trace Last Reference Position (IAA) .... TLRP
Trace Watch Unit (IAA) .... TWU
Tracer Test Unit (IAA) .... TTU
Track Address (IAA) .... TA
Track-on-Jam Valid [*Military*] .... TOJV
Track Magnetic [*Aviation*] (DA) .... TrM
Track-via-Missile Analog Processor [*Military*] .... TVMAP
Track Monitor Supervisor (IAA) .... TMS
Track Number Conversion (IAA) .... TNC
Track Reference Number (IAA) .... TRN
Track-on-Repeater [*Military*] .... TOR
Track and Store [*Computer science*] (IAA) .... TRS
Track Store Switch (IAA) .... TSS
Track Store Unit (IAA) .... TS
Track True [*Aviation*] (DA) .... TrT
Tracked Air Cushion Vehicle Powered by Linear Induction Motor (PDAA) .... TACV/LIM
Tracking Adjunct Systems Trainer .... TAST
Tracking Antenna Pedestal System (IAA) .... TPS
Tracking Asynchronous RADAR Data (DA) .... TARAD
Tracking and Communications [*Aviation*] (IAA) .... TRAC
Tracking and Data Acquisition (IAA) .... TADA
Tracking Head (IAA) .... TH
Tracking Officer (IAA) .... TO
Tracking RADAR Experiment (IAA) .... TRADEX
Tracking Range Instrumented Aircraft (PDAA) .... TRIA
Tracking System Test Stand (IAA) .... TSTS
Tracking, Telemetry, and Command [*AEC*] (IAA) .... TTAC
Traction Asynchronous Motor (PDAA) .... TAM
Traction Control [*Mitsubishi*] [*Transmission systems*] .... TCL
Tractor Computing Corp. (IAA) .... TCC
Trade and Industrial Education (AEE) .... T and I
Tradewinds Aviation Ltd. [*Canada*] [*ICAO designator*] (FAAC) .... TWL
Traditional Life Cycle (PDAA) .... TLC
TRADOC [*Training and Doctrine Command*] **Command Management Information System** [*Military*] .... TCMIS
TRADOC [*Training and Doctrine Command*] **Management Engineering Activity** [*Military*] .... TRAMEA
TRADOC [*Training and Doctrine Command*] **Mobilization and Operations Planning System** [*Military*] .... TMOPS
TRADOC [*Training and Doctrine Command*] **Operations Research Activity** [*Military*] .... TORA
Traductrice (IAA) .... TRAD
Traffic Alert and Collision Avoidance Device [*Aviation*] (DA) .... TCAD
Traffic Control and Landing [*Aviation*] (IAA) .... TRACAL
Traffic Control and Landing System [*Aviation*] (IAA) .... TRACALS
Traffic Count and Listing [*Aviation*] (DA) .... TRC
Traffic Data Record (DA) .... TDR
Traffic Engineering for Automatic Route Selection (PDAA) .... TEARS
Traffic Information Broadcast by Aircraft (DA) .... TIBA
Traffic Information Zone (DA) .... TIZ
Traffic Management Channel [*Navigation and driver information systems*] .... TMC
Traffic Management Program Alert [*Aviation*] (FAAC) .... TMPA
Traffic Orientation Scheme (DA) .... TOS
Traffic Reporting and Control System (IAA) .... TRACS
Trail Lake Flying Service, Inc. [*ICAO designator*] (FAAC) .... HBA
Trailer Length [*Specifications*] [*Automotive engineering*] .... TL
Trailing Edge Up .... TEU
Trailing-Throttle Oversteer [*Automobile driving*] .... TTO
Train-Elevated Guideway Interaction (PDAA) .... TEGI
Train Printer [*Computer science*] (IAA) .... TP
Train Regulation Advisory Control (PDAA) .... TRAC
Train Supervisory System (IAA) .... TSS
Train-the-Trainer [*Army*] .... T_3
Trainer Software Support System [*Military*] .... TSSS
Training Aid and Device [*Military*] .... TAD
Training Aid, Device, Simulation and Simulator [*Military*] .... TADSS
Training Equipment and Maintenance [*Aviation*] (DA) .... TEAM
Training Equipment Plan .... TEP
Training Launch Control Center (IAA) .... TLCC
Training for Opportunities in Programming (IAA) .... TOP
Training Outside Public Practice (PDAA) .... TOPP
Training Package System Planning (IAA) .... TPS
Training Requirements Analysis Directorate [*Army*] .... TRAD
Training Research and Development (IAA) .... TRAD
Training and Skills Program .... TASK
Training Support Requirements [*Military*] .... TSR
Trains Inertial Navigation System (IAA) .... TINS
Trajectory Integration Program (PDAA) .... TRIP
Tramson Ltd. [*Sudan*] [*ICAO designator*] (FAAC) .... TRR
Tramway and Light Railway Society [*British*] (BI) .... TLRS
Trans Air Bretagne [*France*] [*ICAO designator*] (FAAC) .... TRB
Trans Air Charter, Inc. [*ICAO designator*] (FAAC) .... TRC
Trans-Air Link Corp. [*ICAO designator*] (FAAC) .... GJB
Trans-Air Services Ltd. [*Nigeria*] [*ICAO designator*] (FAAC) .... TSN
Trans Air Valtologia [*Moldova*] [*ICAO designator*] (FAAC) .... VLG
Trans Am Compania Ltda. [*Ecuador*] [*ICAO designator*] (FAAC) .... RTM
Trans America Airlines, Inc. [*ICAO designator*] (FAAC) .... TVA
Trans American Airways, Inc. [*ICAO designator*] (FAAC) .... CLR
Trans Arabian Air Transport [*Sudan*] [*ICAO designator*] (FAAC) .... TRT
Trans-Atlantic [*Aviation*] (FAAC) .... TSATLC
Trans-Atlantic Airlines Ltd. [*Gambia*] [*ICAO designator*] (FAAC) .... TGL
Trans-Colorado Airlines, Inc. [*ICAO designator*] (FAAC) .... TCE
Trans Continental Airlines [*ICAO designator*] (FAAC) .... TCN
Trans-Eastern Airlines Ltd. [*Kenya*] [*ICAO designator*] (FAAC) .... TRE
Trans European Airways [*Belgium*] [*ICAO designator*] (FAAC) .... TEA
Trans European Airways [*Switzerland*] [*ICAO designator*] (FAAC) .... TSW
Trans European Airways SA [*France*] [*ICAO designator*] (FAAC) .... TFR
Trans-Florida Airlines, Inc. [*ICAO designator*] (FAAC) .... TFA
Trans-Hudson Orogen [*Geology*] .... THO
Trans International Airlines [*ICAO designator*] (FAAC) .... TIA
Trans Island Air [*Barbados*] [*ICAO designator*] (FAAC) .... TRD
Trans Jamaican Airlines Ltd. [*ICAO designator*] (FAAC) .... JQA
Trans Mediterranean Airlines [*Lebanon*] [*ICAO designator*] (FAAC) .... TMA
Trans Midwest Airlines, Inc. [*ICAO designator*] (FAAC) .... TMT
Trans North Turbo Air Ltd. [*Canada*] [*ICAO designator*] (FAAC) .... TNT
Trans-Provincial Airlines Ltd. [*Canada*] [*ICAO designator*] (FAAC) .... TPY
Trans Service Airlift [*Zaire*] [*ICAO designator*] (FAAC) .... TSR
Trans States Airlines, Inc. [*ICAO designator*] (FAAC) .... LOF
Trans West African Airlines Ltd. [*Gambia*] [*ICAO designator*] (FAAC) .... TWS
Trans Western Airlines of Utah [*ICAO designator*] (FAAC) .... TRW
Trans Wings AS [*Norway*] [*ICAO designator*] (FAAC) .... TWG
Trans World Airlines, Inc. [*ICAO designator*] (FAAC) .... TWA
Trans World Express, Inc. [*ICAO designator*] (FAAC) .... RBD
Trans World News Service (NTCM) .... TWNS
Transaction, Accounting, Control, and Endorsing (PDAA) .... TRACE
Transaction Area (IAA) .... TAR
Transaction Control and Encoding (IAA) .... TRACE
Transaction Driven (IAA) .... TD
Transaction Executive (IAA) .... TRANEX
Transaction Manager [*Computer science*] .... TM
Transaction Mode (IAA) .... TM
Transaction-Oriented Operating System (IAA) .... TOOS
Transactions of the American Association of Electrical Engineers (IAA) .... TRANSAIEE
Transaero Airlines [*Former USSR*] [*ICAO designator*] (FAAC) .... TSO
Transair France [*ICAO designator*] (FAAC) .... TSA
Transair Mali SA [*ICAO designator*] (FAAC) .... TSM
Transavia Holland BV [*Netherlands*] [*ICAO designator*] (FAAC) .... TRA
Transavia (Pty) Ltd. [*South Africa*] [*ICAO designator*] (FAAC) .... TRV
Transaviaexport [*Belarus*] [*ICAO designator*] (FAAC) .... TXC
Transaxel Fluid (IAA) .... TAF
Transbrasil SA Linhas Aereas [*Brazil*] [*ICAO designator*] (FAAC) .... TBA
TransCanada Computer Communications Network (IAA) .... TCCN
Transcarga SA [*Costa Rica*] [*ICAO designator*] (FAAC) .... TDA
Transceiver Transmitter Receiver (IAA) .... TRCVR
Transcolombiana de Aviacion SA [*Colombia*] [*ICAO designator*] (FAAC) .... TVN
Transcontinental (NTCM) .... TC
Transcontinental Control Area [*Aviation*] (DA) .... TCA
Transcorp Airways [*British*] [*ICAO designator*] (FAAC) .... TCP
Transcribe (IAA) .... TRANSC
Transcription (IAA) .... TRANSC
Transcription-Repair Coupling Factor [*Genetics*] .... TRCF
Transducer [*Electronics*] (IAA) .... TD
Transducer Read Only Storage (IAA) .... TROS
Transfer (IAA) .... TF
Transfer and Accountability (IAA) .... TAA
Transfer on Channel in Operation (IAA) .... TCO
Transfer of Control Point [*Aviation*] (FAAC) .... TCP
Transfer on Death [*Finance*] .... TOD
Transfer Gate (IAA) .... TG
Transfer Generator System (IAA) .... TGS
Transfer on Index [*Telecommunications*] (IAA) .... TIX
Transfer on Index Low (IAA) .... TXL
Transfer on No Zero (IAA) .... TNZ
Transfer on Overflow (IAA) .... TOV
Transfer Trip [*Telecommunications*] (IAA) .... TT
Transferred on Assembly (IAA) .... TOA
Transferred Electron Logic Device (IAA) .... TELD

By Meaning

Transformation Line [*Telecommunications*] (IAA)	TL
Transformational Grammar	TG
Transformational Grammar Tester (IAA)	TGT
Transformer (IAA)	TRAFO
Transformer Analog Polynomial Equation Solver (PDAA)	TAPES
Transformer Design Engineer (IAA)	TRANSFDESENGR
Transformer Differential (IAA)	TDF
Transformer LASER (IAA)	TRASER
Transformer Load Management (IAA)	TLM
Transformerless (IAA)	TFL
Transient Data Input Area [*Computer science*] (IAA)	TDIA
Transient Infrared Emission Spectroscopy	TIRES
Transient On-State Characteristics (PDAA)	TONC
Transient Voltage Surge Suppression	TVSS
Transistor [*Electronics*] (IAA)	T
Transistor (IAA)	TR
Transistor Current Switching Logic [*Electronics*] (IAA)	TCSL
Transistor Digital Circuit (IAA)	TDC
Transistor Digital Control (IAA)	TDC
Transistor Dip Oscillator (IAA)	TDO
Transistor Equivalent [*Electronics*] (IAA)	TE
Transistor Logic (IAA)	TL
Transistor and Nixie Tube (IAA)	TRIXIE
Transistor Noise Analyzer (IAA)	TNA
Transistor Oscillator Multiplier (IAA)	TOM
Transistor Specialities, Inc. (IAA)	TSI
Transistor Telegraph Relay [*Telecommunications*] (IAA)	TTR
Transistor-Transistor Micrologic (IAA)	TTML
Transistorized Automatic Computer (IAA)	TAC
Transistorized Automatic Computer Users' Group (IAA)	TUG
Transistorized Car Radio (IAA)	TCR
Transistorized Digital Computer [*Air Force*] (IAA)	TRADIC
Transistorized High-Speed Operations Recorder Advanced (IAA)	THORAD
Transistorized Image Orthicon Camera (IAA)	TIO
Transistorized RADAR (IAA)	TRANSRA
Transistorized Real-Time Incremental Computer Expandable (IAA)	TRICE
Transistorized Volt Ohm Milliammeter (IAA)	TVOM
Transit Injection Station (IAA)	TIS
Transit Missile Hold Facility [*Military*] (IAA)	TMHF
Transition Altitude [*Aviation*] (DA)	TRANSALT
Transition Level (DA)	TL
Transition Level (IAA)	TRANSLEV
Transition Level [*Aviation*] (FAAC)	TRLVL
Transition Work Group	TWG
Transitional Butterworth Modified Ultraspherical Filter (PDAA)	TBMU
Transitional Butterworth Thomson (IAA)	TBT
Transitional Butterworth Ultraspherical Filter (PDAA)	TBU
Transitional Control (IAA)	TC
Transitional Low-Emission Truck	TLET
Transitional Ultraspherical-Ultraspherical Filter (PDAA)	TUU
Transkei Airways [*South Africa*] [*ICAO designator*] (FAAC)	TAK
Translate and Test (IAA)	TRT
Translation (IAA)	TR
Translation (IAA)	TRN
Translation Service	TS
Translational Control (IAA)	TCO
Translator (IAA)	TSL
Translator CAM [*Computer-Aided Manufacturing*] Magnet (IAA)	TCM
Translator Code Magnet (IAA)	TM
Translator Writing System [*Computer science*] (IAA)	TWS
Translift Airways Ltd. [*British*] [*ICAO designator*] (FAAC)	TLA
Translocated in Liposarcoma [*Genetics*]	TLS
Translunar Trajectory Characteristics [*AEC*] (IAA)	TTC
Transmed Airlines [*Egypt*] [*ICAO designator*] (FAAC)	TMD
Transmission [*Telecommunications*] (IAA)	T
Transmission Control [*Telecommunications*] (IAA)	TC
Transmission Control System (IAA)	TCS
Transmission and Distribution (IAA)	TAD
Transmission Distribution Center (IAA)	TDC
Transmission and Drive Train Oil	TDTO
Transmission Electron Microscopy and Microprobe Analysis (PDAA)	TEMMA
Transmission Engineering Memorandum (IAA)	TEM
Transmission Engineering Recommendation [*Telecommunications*] (IAA)	TER
Transmission Group (IAA)	TG
Transmission Impairment Measuring Set [*Telecommunications*] (IAA)	TMIS
Transmission Impairment Measuring System (IAA)	TIMS
Transmission Interface Converter (IAA)	TRI
Transmission Line [*Telecommunications*] (IAA)	TL
Transmission Loss [*Telecommunications*] (IAA)	TL
Transmission Parity Error [*Computer science*] (IAA)	TPE
Transmission Project Group (IAA)	TPG
Transmission Secondary Electron Multiplication [*Physics*] (IAA)	TSEM
Transmission Stop (NTCM)	T
Transmit [*or Transmitter*] (IAA)	TS
Transmit Clock (IAA)	TCL
Transmit Level Control (PDAA)	TLC
Transmit and Receive (IAA)	TAR
Transmit-Receive Switch (IAA)	TRS

Transmit [*or Transmitting*] Variolosser (IAA)	TVL
Transmitted Optical Microscopy	TOM
Transmitted Reference Phase Shift Keying [*Computer science*] (IAA)	TRPSK
Transmitted-Reflected-Reflected [*Wave mechanics*]	TRR
Transmitter (IAA)	TRS
Transmitter (DA)	TSMTR
Transmitter (ADDR)	XMITR
Transmitter (NTCM)	XMITTER
Transmitter Assembler Compiler [*Telecommunications*] (IAA)	TAC
Transmitter Buffer [*Telecommunications*] (IAA)	TB
Transmitter Circuit (IAA)	TRC
Transmitter Interface Module [*Army*]	XMIM
Transmitter Power Output (NTCM)	TPO
Transmitter Receiver (IAA)	TR
Transmitter-Receiver (IAA)	TSRC
Transmitter Signal Element Timing (IAA)	TSET
Transmitter Tuning Circuit [*Telecommunications*] (IAA)	TC
Transmitting Switch Control (IAA)	TSC
Transmitting Typewriter [*Telecommunications*] (IAA)	TT
Transmitting Typewriter with Card Punch (IAA)	TTCP
Transmitting Typewriter with Tape Punch (IAA)	TTTP
Transparent Office Manager [*Computer science*] (IAA)	TOM
Transponder (IAA)	T
Transponder Interrogation and Decoding Equipment [*Telecommunications*] (IAA)	TIDE
Transponder RADAR (IAA)	TR
Transport Air Centre [*France*] [*ICAO designator*] (FAAC)	CTR
Transport Code for Computer (IAA)	TDC
Transport International Aerien [*Belgium*] [*ICAO designator*] (FAAC)	TRS
Transportable Automatic Digital Switch (PDAA)	TADS
Transportable Cassette Converter (IAA)	TCC
Transportable Cassette Recorder (IAA)	TCR
Transportable Ground Control Approach (IAA)	TGCA
Transportable Vehicle Refuelling Equipment (PDAA)	TVRE
Transportacion Aerea Mexicana [*Mexico*] [*ICAO designator*] (FAAC)	TAM
Transportacion Aerea Mexicana [*Mexico*] [*ICAO designator*] (FAAC)	TMX
Transportation America Corp. [*ICAO designator*] (FAAC)	DEE
Transportation Automated Material Movements System [*Army*] (PDAA)	TRAMMS
Transportation Horoscope of Trade Goods (PDAA)	THOT
Transportation Research Command [*Army*] (IAA)	TRC
Transporte Aereco Dominicano [*Dominican Republic*] [*ICAO designator*] (FAAC)	TDO
Transporte Aereo de la Amazonia [*Colombia*] [*ICAO designator*] (FAAC)	TAZ
Transporte Aereo Andino SA [*Venezuela*] [*ICAO designator*] (FAAC)	EAA
Transporte Aereo Andino SA [*Venezuela*] [*ICAO designator*] (FAAC)	TAAN
Transporte Aereo Dominicano [*Dominican Republic*] [*ICAO designator*] (FAAC)	TRADO
Transporte Aereo Dominicano SA [*Dominican Republic*] [*ICAO designator*] (FAAC)	TAD
Transporte Aereo Rioplatense [*Argentina*] [*ICAO designator*] (FAAC)	HRT
Transporte de Carga Aeropacifico SA de CV [*Mexico*] [*ICAO designator*] (FAAC)	APF
Transporte del Caribe [*Colombia*] [*ICAO designator*] (FAAC)	TCB
Transporte e Trabalho Aero [*Mozambique*] [*ICAO designator*] (FAAC)	TTA
Transporter Associated with Antigen Processing [*Biochemistry*]	TAP
Transportes Aereos da Bacia Amazonica SA [*Brazil*] [*ICAO designator*] (FAAC)	TAB
Transportes Aereos Bolivians [*Bolivia*] [*ICAO designator*] (FAAC)	TAB
Transportes Aereos de Cabo Verde [*Cape Verde*] [*ICAO designator*] (FAAC)	TACV
Transportes Aereos de Cabo Verde [*Cape Verde*] [*ICAO designator*] (FAAC)	TCV
Transportes Aereos Coyhaique [*Chile*] [*ICAO designator*] (FAAC)	COY
Transportes Aereos Coyhaique [*Chile*] [*ICAO designator*] (FAAC)	TAC
Transportes Aereos de El Salvador SA de CV [*ICAO designator*] (FAAC)	TAES
Transportes Aereos de El Salvador SA de CV [*ICAO designator*] (FAAC)	TES
Transportes Aereos Fueguino [*Argentina*] [*ICAO designator*] (FAAC)	STU
Transportes Aereos Mercantiles Panamericanos [*Colombia*] [*ICAO designator*] (FAAC)	TPA
Transportes Aereos Militares Ecatorianos CA [*Ecuador*] [*ICAO designator*] (FAAC)	TAE
Transportes Aereos Neuquen [*Argentina*] [*ICAO designator*] (FAAC)	NQN
Transportes Aereos Neuquinos Sociedad de Estado [*Argentina*] [*ICAO designator*] (FAAC)	NEU
Transportes Aereos Neuquinos Sociedad de Estado [*Argentina*] [*ICAO designator*] (FAAC)	TANSE
Transportes Aereos Norte-Sur Ltda. [*Chile*] [*ICAO designator*] (FAAC)	ANS
Transportes Aereos Pegaso SA de CV [*Mexico*] [*ICAO designator*] (FAAC)	TPG
Transportes Aereos Portugueses EP [*Portugal*] [*ICAO designator*] (FAAC)	TAP

Transportes Aereos Regionais SA [*Brazil*] [*ICAO designator*] (FAAC) ... TAM
Transportes Aeromar [*Mexico*] [*ICAO designator*] (FAAC) ... TAO
Transportes Aeros Bolivianos [*Bolivia*] [*ICAO designator*] (FAAC) ... BOL
Transportes Aeros Ejecutivos SA de CV [*Mexico*] [*ICAO designator*] (FAAC) ... TEJ
Transportes de Carga Aerea Especializada y Servicios Aeronauticos [*Mexico*] [*ICAO designator*] (FAAC) ... TCS
Transportes La Paz SA de CV [*Mexico*] [*ICAO designator*] (FAAC) ... TPZ
Transports Aeriens du Benin [*ICAO designator*] (FAAC) ... TSB
Transports Aeriens de la Guinee-Bissau [*Guinea-Bissau*] [*ICAO designator*] (FAAC) ... GBU
Transports Aeriens Mediterraneens [*France*] [*ICAO designator*] (FAAC) ... TRM
Transports Aeros Hispanos SA [*Spain*] [*ICAO designator*] (FAAC) ... THS
Transrectal Ultrasonography [*Medicine*] ... TRUS
Transurethral Incision of the Prostate [*Medicine*] ... TUIP
Transurethral Resection of Bladder Tumor [*Medicine*] (MAH) ... TURBT
Transurethral Ultrasound - Guided LASER-Induced Prostatectomy [*Medicine*] ... TULIP
Transversal Filter (IAA) ... TF
Transversale Spyder [*Ferrari automotive model designation*] ... TS
Transverse Electromagnetic Mode [*Telecommunications*] (IAA) ... TEM
Transverse Electrostatic (IAA) ... TE
Transverse Propulsion Unit (PDAA) ... TPU
Transverse Staggering (IAA) ... TS
Transway Air Services, Inc. [*Liberia*] [*ICAO designator*] (FAAC) ... TAW
Transwede [*Sweden*] [*ICAO designator*] (FAAC) ... TWE
Trapped Domain (IAA) ... TD
Trapped Plasma Avalanche Transit Time [*Bell Laboratories*] (IAA) ... TRAPATT
Travel News [*Wire service code*] (NTCM) ... T
Travelair GmbH [*Germany*] [*ICAO designator*] (FAAC) ... TAX
Traveling in Core Probe (IAA) ... TIP
Traveling-Wave Magnetron (IAA) ... TWM
Traveling-Wave Tube (IAA) ... TET
Travelling and Meal Allowance ... TMA
Travelling-Wave Oscillator (IAA) ... TWO
Treatment Action Group [*for AIDS medication*] [*FDA*] ... TAG
Treatment of Mild Hypertension Study ... TOMHS
Treatment Services Control ... TSC
Treatment System Support ... TSS
Tree Searching Language [*Computer science*] (PDAA) ... TSL
Tree Structured Attribute (IAA) ... TSA
Trek Airways [*South Africa*] [*ICAO designator*] (FAAC) ... TKE
Trend Landing Forecast [*Aviation*] (DA) ... t
Trends in Microbiology [*A publication*] ... TIM
Trends in Online Computer Control Systems (PDAA) ... TOLCCS
Tri-Camera (IAA) ... TRIC
Tri- [*or Triple*] **Coincidence Navigation** (IAA) ... TRICO
Tri-color Visual Approach Slope Indicator [*Aviation*] (FAAC) ... TRCV
Tri-Junction Transistor (IAA) ... TJT
Tri-Mask Process (IAA) ... TRIM
Tri-Service Standoff Attack Missile ... TSSAM
Trials Recording and Analysis Console (PDAA) ... TRAC
Triax Airlines Ltd. [*Nigeria*] [*ICAO designator*] (FAAC) ... TIX
Trichosanthin [*Botany*] ... TCS
Triclinic [*Crystallography*] (IAA) ... TRI
Tricycle [*A publication*] ... Tric
Triethylaluminum (IAA) ... TEA
Trigger (IAA) ... T
Trigger (IAA) ... TG
Trigger Generator ... TG
Trigger and Monitor Panel (IAA) ... TAMPNL
Trigger Pulse [*Telecommunications*] (IAA) ... TP
Triggered Spark Gap (IAA) ... TSG
Trimmer (IAA) ... T
Trinidad and Tobago [*Aircraft nationality and registration mark*] (FAAC) ... 9Y
Trinidad and Tobago Airways Corp. [*ICAO designator*] (FAAC) ... BWA
Trinity Air Bahamas [*ICAO designator*] (FAAC) ... TBH
Trinucleotide Repeat Sequence [*Genetics*] ... TNR
Trioctyltin [*Organic chemistry*] ... TOT
Triode Alternating Current (IAA) ... TRIAC
Triode-Tetrode (IAA) ... TRITET
Trip Cell (IAA) ... TC
Triphenylbenzene [*Organic chemistry*] ... TPB
Triple-Braid Weatherproof (IAA) ... TBWP
Triple Conductor, Heat, Oil, and Flame Resistant (IAA) ... THOF
Triple Overriding Dual Control (IAA) ... TODC
Triple Transit Suppression (IAA) ... TTS
Triplicated Majority Voting (IAA) ... TMV
Tris-Ethylenediaminetetra-Acetate Borate [*Organic chemistry*] (MAH) ... TEB
Tristate [*Electronics*] (IAA) ... TS
Tristate Control [*Electronics*] (IAA) ... TSC
Triton Airlines, Inc. [*Canada*] [*ICAO designator*] (FAAC) ... DRC
Triumph Adler Assembler (IAA) ... TRIASS
Trivial Problem Discriminator [*Computer science*] (IAA) ... TPD
Troop Support Center [*Army*] ... TSC
Tropair Airservices [*British*] [*ICAO designator*] (FAAC) ... TSV
Trophoblastic Basement Membrane (PDAA) ... TBM
Tropical Air Services [*Belize*] [*ICAO designator*] (FAAC) ... TOS
Tropical Continental [*Meteorology*] (FAAC) ... TRPCD
Tropical Development and Research Institute (PDAA) ... TDaRI
Tropical Fish Hobbyist [*A publication*] ... Trop F H
Tropical Radio Telegraph [*Telecommunications*] (IAA) ... TRT
Tropical Sea Airlines [*Thailand*] [*ICAO designator*] (FAAC) ... TSS
Trouble (IAA) ... TBLE
Trouble Came Back [*Computer hacker terminology*] (NHD) ... TCB
Trouble Detection (IAA) ... TRDET
Trouble Indicator Trunk [*Telecommunications*] (IAA) ... TIT
Trouble Recorder (IAA) ... TRR
Trouble Shooting Manual (IAA) ... TSM
Truck Hub Unit [*Suspension*] [*Automotive engineering*] ... THU
Truck Master Association [*Auto enthusiast organization*] ... TMA
Truck Routing Improvement Program (IAA) ... TRIP
Truck Writers of North America [*An association*] (EA) ... TWNA
True Ground Speed (IAA) ... TGS
True Indicated Radius (IAA) ... TIR
True-Motion, Anti-Collision System (PDAA) ... TM/ACS
True-Motion, Basic Collision Avoidance (PDAA) ... TM/BAC
True Motion RADAR (IAA) ... TMR
True Position Dimensioning and Tolerancing (PDAA) ... TPDT
True and Relative Motion Plotting System (IAA) ... TARPS
True Speed Indicator (IAA) ... TSI
Trufocus [*Lamp base type*] (NTCM) ... Tf
Truly Fast Fourier Transform (PDAA) ... TFFT
Truncated Sequential Probability Ratio Test (PDAA) ... TSPRT
Truncated Sequential Probability Ratio Test for Reliability (PDAA) ... TSPRTR
Truncated Sequential Test (PDAA) ... TST
Trunk (IAA) ... T
Trunk (IAA) ... TK
Trunk Amplifier (IAA) ... TA
Trunk Barrier [*Telecommunications*] (IAA) ... TB
Trunk Junctor [*Telecommunications*] (IAA) ... TJ
Trunk Load [*Telecommunications*] (IAA) ... TL
Trunk Mark [*Telecommunications*] (IAA) ... TM
Trunk Piston Engine Oil [*Automotive lubricants*] ... TPEO
Trunk Supervisor [*Telecommunications*] (IAA) ... TSUP
Trunk Test [*Telecommunications*] (IAA) ... TT
Truth, Esteem, Attitude, and Motivation [*Name of actor Chuck Norris' anti-gang project*] ... TEAM
Truth in Negotiations Act ... TINA
TRW Advanced Steering [*Automotive components*] ... TAS
Trypsin-Modulating Oostatic Factor [*Biochemistry*] ... TMOF
Tube (IAA) ... T
Tube Voltmeter (IAA) ... TV
Tuberculin Skin Test [*Medicine*] (PDAA) ... TST
Tubolare Zagato [*Automotive model designation*] [*Alfa-Romeo*] ... TZ
Tubular (IAA) ... T
Tubular Extendible Element (PDAA) ... TEE
[*Maximal*] **Tubular Reabsorption Rate of Glucose** [*Physiology*] (MAH) ... TmG
Tufted Carpet Manufacturers' Association [*British*] (BI) ... TCMA
Tulip Air [*Netherlands*] [*ICAO designator*] (FAAC) ... TLP
Tulsa University [*Oklahoma*] (PDAA) ... TU
Tumor Necrosis Serum (PDAA) ... TNS
Tunable Compound Phase-Locked Demodulator (IAA) ... TCPLD
Tuned Aperiodic Tuned (IAA) ... TAT
Tuned Circuit [*Telecommunications*] (IAA) ... TC
Tuned Grid Tuned Plate [*Electronic plate*] (IAA) ... TGTP
Tuned LASER Differential Spectrometry (IAA) ... TDS
Tuned-Not-Tuned (IAA) ... TNT
Tungsten Carbide (IAA) ... TC
Tuning (IAA) ... TN
Tuning Inductance (IAA) ... TI
Tuning Meter Indicator (IAA) ... TMI
Tuning Unit [*JETDS nomenclature*] [*Military*] (IAA) ... TU
Tuninter [*Tunisia*] [*ICAO designator*] (FAAC) ... TUI
Tunis Air-Societe Tunisienne de l'Air [*Tunisia*] [*ICAO designator*] (FAAC) ... TAR
Tunisavia - Societe de Transport, Services et Travaux Aeriens [*Tunisia*] [*ICAO designator*] (FAAC) ... TAJ
Tunnel-Diode Arithmetic Tester (IAA) ... TUDAT
Tunnel-Diode FET [*Field-Effect Transistor*] **Logic** (IAA) ... TDFL
Tunnel Transit Time (IAA) ... TUNNET
Tur Avrupa Havayollari AS [*Turkey*] [*ICAO designator*] (FAAC) ... TCT
Turavia [*Poland*] [*ICAO designator*] (FAAC) ... TUV
Turbine Automatic Control Equipment (IAA) ... TACE
Turbine Engine Reliability Program (PDAA) ... TERP
Turbine Oil Stability Test [*Lubricant testing*] [*Automotive engineering*] ... TOST
Turbine Supersonic Speed (ERG) ... TSS
Turbine Trip and Throttle Valve [*Nuclear energy*] (IAA) ... TAT
Turbocharged Generation 4 [*Automotive engine identification*] ... TCIV
Turbocharged Generation One [*Automotive engine identification*] ... TCI
Turbopool Ltd. [*British*] [*ICAO designator*] (FAAC) ... TPL
Turbosynchro Transmitter (IAA) ... TS
Turbulence [*Aviation*] (FAAC) ... TB
Turismo Internationale [*Automobile model designation*] ... TI
Turk Hava Tasimaciligi [*Turkish Air Transport*] [*ICAO designator*] (FAAC) ... THT
Turk Hava Yollari [*Turkish Airlines*] [*ICAO designator*] (FAAC) ... THY
Turkmenistan [*ICAO designator*] (FAAC) ... TUA

Turks & Caicos National Airlines [*ICAO designator*]   (FAAC)...................... TCI
Turmor-Associated Glycoprotein [*Biochemistry*]... TAG
Turn Altitude [*Aviation*]   (FAAC) .... TNA
Turn Altitude/Height [*Aviation*]   (DA)... TA/H
Turn Height [*Aviation*]   (FAAC) .... TNH
Turn Left after Takeoff [*Aviation*]   (FAAC)... LT
Turn-Off Controlled Rectifier   (PDAA) .... TOCR
Turn per Second   (IAA).. TS
Turnbull Associates [*British*] [*ICAO designator*]   (FAAC)........................... TNB
Turned and Bored   (IAA).. TAB
Turnover   (NTCM).. TO
Turret Gun System [*Army*].. TGS
Turtle Airways Ltd. [*Fiji*] [*ICAO designator*]   (FAAC)................................ TLT
Twin   (IAA).. TW
Twin-Ball Fire Fighting Unit [*Military*]   (PDAA) .... TBFFU
Twin-Cushion Surface Effect Vehicle   (PDAA)....................................... TCSEV
Twin I-Beam [*Ford Motor Co.*] [*Truck front suspension*]............................... TIB
Twin Linear Loop Exciter   (IAA)... TLLE
Twin and Multiply   (IAA) .... TMU
Twin Sideband   (IAA) .... TSEB
Twin Traction-Beam [*Ford Motor Co.*] [*Truck four-wheel drive front
    suspension*] .... TTB
Twisted   (IAA).. TW
Twisted Nematic Liquid [*Telecommunications*]   (IAA) .... TNC
Twisted Nematic Liquid Crystal Display [*Telecommunications*]
    (IAA)... TNLCD
Twisted Nematic Mode [*Telecommunications*]   (IAA) .... TNM
Twisted Nemetic Field Effect [*Telecommunications*]   (IAA)...................... TNFE
Twisted-Pair, Telephone, Heat and Flame Resistant, Armored [*Wire
    technology*]   (IAA).. TTHFA
Two-Axis Optical Pickoff   (PDAA).. TOP
Two-Dimensional Deflection System   (IAA)... TDDS
Two-Dimensional Finite Cylinder   (IAA)... TDC
Two-Dimensional Probabilistic Image   (PDAA) .... TDPI
Two Mixed Layer   (IAA).. TML
Two-Photon Absorption   (PDAA) .... TPA
Two-Point Boundary Value   (PDAA).. TPBV
Two-Post Signal Flow Graph   (PDAA)... TPSFG
Two Subcarrier   (IAA).. TSC
Two-Way Alternate   (IAA).. TWA
Two Way Logic Circuit   (PDAA)... TWLC
Two-Way Simultaneous   (IAA).. TWS
Two-Way Travel Time [*Seismology*].. TWTT
Tyee Airways Ltd. [*Canada*] [*ICAO designator*]   (FAAC) .... TYE
Type of Legal Organization... TOLO
Type Rating Examiner [*Aviation*]   (DA) .... TRE
Type of Shift   (IAA).. TS
Typesetting System for Scientific Document [*Computer science*]
    (PDAA).. TSSD
Typographical Error   (NTCM)... TYPO
Tyrolean Airways [*Austria*] [*ICAO designator*]   (FAAC) .... TYR
Tyrolean Jet Service [*Austria*] [*ICAO designator*]   (FAAC)......................... TYJ
Tyrosine Activation Motif [*Biochemistry*].. TAM
Tyumen Airlines [*Russian Federation*] [*ICAO designator*]   (FAAC).......... TYM

U

U-Groove Power Metal-Oxide Semiconductor Field Effect Transistor
(IAA) .... UMOST
Uas-Four [*British*] [*ICAO designator*]   (FAAC)................. UAS
Uas-One [*British*] [*ICAO designator*]   (FAAC)................. UAA
Uas-Three [*British*] [*ICAO designator*]   (FAAC)................ UAJ
Uas-Two [*British*] [*ICAO designator*]   (FAAC)................. UAG
UFS, Inc. [*ICAO designator*]   (FAAC) .... UFS
Uganda Airlines Corp. [*ICAO designator*]   (FAAC) .... UGA
Ugland Air AS [*Norway*] [*ICAO designator*]   (FAAC)........... UGG
UK Home Office [*British*] [*ICAO designator*]   (FAAC).......... UKP
Ultra Clean Coal   (ERG)............................... UCC
Ultra Electronics Components Ltd.   (IAA)................ UECL
Ultra Electronics Ltd.   (IAA)........................ UEL
Ultra High Bypass [*Aviation*]   (DA)..................... UHB
Ultra-High Porosity [*Materials science*] .... UHP
Ultra-High Pressure [*Water cutting tools*]............... UHP
Ultra High Viscosity Index .... UHVI
Ultra-Large Liquified Natural Gas Carrier   (PDAA)......... ULLNG
Ultra Large Scale Integration   (NTCM) .... USLI
Ultra-Lightweight Panel   (PDAA) .... ULP
Ultra Long Range   (DA)............................... ULR
Ultra-Long Range Guided Weapon   (IAA)............... ULRGW
Ultra-Low Carbon [*Metallurgical engineering*].............. ULC
Ultra-Low-Emission Vehicle [*Military*].................... ULEV
Ultra-Low Emissions Bus [*Automotive engineering*]........... ULEB
Ultra-Low Emissions Engine [*Automotive engineering*]........ ULEE
Ultra-Low Emissions Truck [*Automotive engineering*]........ ULET
Ultra-Low Interstitial   (PDAA) .... ULI
Ultra-Precision Test Equipment   (PDAA) .... UPTE
Ultra-Stable Voltage Reference Unit   (PDAA) .... USVRU
UltrAir, Inc. [*ICAO designator*]   (FAAC)................ ULT
Ultralightweight Camouflage Net System [*Army*]........... ULCANS
Ultrapherical Polynomial Filter   (IAA) .... UPF
Ultrared   (IAA)..................................... UR
Ultrashort Wave Propagation Panel   (IAA)............... USWP
Ultrasonic Echo Detection   (PDAA) .... UED
Ultrasonically-Modulated Electron Resonance   (PDAA)........ UMER
Ultrasound Cardiogram   (IAA)........................ UCG
Ultravariable Resolution Single Interferometer Echelle Scanner
(PDAA).. URSIES
Ultraviolet Astronomical Satellite   (PDAA) .... UVAS
Ultraviolet-Blue-Visible-Red [*Photometry*]............... UBVR
Ultraviolet Differential Absorption LIDAR [*Light Detection and
Ranging*]   (PDAA).................................. UVDIAL
Ultraviolet Eraseable Read Only Memory   (PDAA) .... UVEROM
Ultraviolet Read Only Memory   (IAA)................... UVROM
Ultraviolet Resonance Raman [*Spectroscopy*] .... UVRR
Ultronic Data Systems   (IAA)........................ UDS
Umbilical Handling Technician [*Computer science*]   (IAA)....... UHT
Unable [*ICAO designator*]   (FAAC) .... UNA
Unable to Approve [*ICAO designator*]   (FAAC) .... UNAP
Unable Higher Altitude [*Aviation*]   (FAAC) .... UHA
Unable Higher Due Opposite Direction Traffic [*Aviation*]
(FAAC).. UHDODT
Unable Higher Due Same Direction Traffic [*Aviation*]   (FAAC)........ UHDSDT
Unable Higher Due Traffic [*Aviation*]   (FAAC) .... UHDT
Unable Lower Due Traffic [*Aviation*]   (FAAC)........... ULDT
Unassigned [*Telecommunications*]   (IAA) .... UNA
Unattended [*Aviation*]   (FAAC) .... UNATNDD
Unavailable, On Order [*Business term*]   (NTCM) .... UOO
Uncertainty Factor [*Toxicology*] .... UF
Uncircumcising Information Resources Center [*National Support
Group*].. UNCIRC
Unclamp   (IAA)..................................... UCL
Unconditional   (IAA)................................ UNC
Unconditional Stop   (IAA)............................ US
Unconstrained Requirements Report [*Army*]................ URR
Uncontrolled   (DA) .... UNCTLD
Uncorrelated Data Processor   (IAA)................... UCDP
Uncoupling Protein [*Biochemistry*]..................... UCP
Undefined   (IAA).................................... U
Undercurrent   (IAA)................................. UNC
Underfeed Stoker Makers' Association [*British*]   (BI)......... USMA

Undergraduate Pilot Training System   (IAA) .... UPTS
Underground Baggage Facility [*Aviation*]   (DA)........... UBF
Underground Explosion Test   (IAA)..................... UET
Underground Rural Distribution   (IAA).................. URD
Underwater-to-Air-to-Underwater   (IAA)................ UAU
Underwater Detection and Classification System   (IAA)........ UDACS
Underwater Naturalist [*A publication*] .... Underw Nat
Underwater-to-Surface   (IAA)......................... US
Undistorted Signal   (IAA)............................ US
Undistributed Taxable Income .... UTI
Unearned Premiums Reserve [*Finance*]................... UPR
Unedged   (DAC)..................................... U/E
Unexplained Acute Respiratory Distress Syndrome .... UARDS
Uni Air [*France*] [*ICAO designator*]   (FAAC)............. UAR
Uni Air SA [*France*] [*ICAO designator*]   (FAAC)........... UAI
Unibus Interface   (IAA).............................. UBI
Unidensity Coherent Light Recording   (IAA).............. UNICOH
Unidentified [*Marketing surveys*]   (NTCM)............... UUUU
Unidirectional Current   (IAA)......................... UDC
Unidirectional Transducer   (IAA)...................... UDT
Unification of Units of Measurement Panel [*ICAO*]   (DA) ...... UUMP
Unified Atomic Mass Unit [*Nuclear energy*]   (IAA)........... U
Unified Direct Access Standards   (IAA).................. UDAS
Unified National Coarse Thread   (IAA).................. UNC
Unified National Extra Fine Thread   (IAA)................ UNEF
Unified National Fine   (IAA).......................... UNF
Unified Numeric Representation Arithmetic Unit   (PDAA) .... UNRAU
Unified Numerical Control Language   (IAA) .... UNCL
Unified Planning Work Program .... UPWP
Unifly [*Italy*] [*ICAO designator*]   (FAAC)............... BJA
Uniform Asymptotic Theory   (IAA)..................... UAT
Uniform Crime Reporting System   (PDAA)................ UNICRIM
Uniform Lightness and Chromaticity Scale   (PDAA).......... ULCS
Uniform Material Movement and Issue Priority System [*Navy*]
(ANA)... UMMIS
Uniform Plumbing Code   (DAC)........................ UPC
Uniform Reflectivity Mirror   (PDAA).................... URM
Uniform Resistance Capacitance [*Electronics*]   (IAA)......... URC
Uniform Theory of Diffraction   (IAA) .... UTD
Uniformed Services Journal [*A publication*] .... USJ
Uniformly Minimum Variance Unbiased Estimator   (PDAA) ...... UMVUE
Uniformly Reflexive Structure   (IAA)................... URS
Uniformly-Sampled-Autoregressive Moving Average   (PDAA)....... USAM
Unijunction Transistor Oscillator   (IAA)................ UJTO
Unintentional RADAR Interference   (IAA) .... URI
Uninterruptable Voltage Source [*Electric power supply*]........ UVS
Uninterruptible AC [*Alternating Current*] Electric Power System
(IAA).. UPS
Union Carbide Electronics   (IAA)...................... UCE
Union Flight [*ICAO designator*]   (FAAC) .... UNF
Union of Girls' Schools for Social Service [*British*]   (BI) ...... UGSS
Union Guide   (IAA).................................. UG
Union Guineene de Transports [*Guinea*] [*ICAO designator*]   (FAAC) .... GIU
Union Internationale des Editeurs [*International Union of
Publishers*]   (NTCM) .... UIE
Union Internationale de Radiodiffusion [*International Broadcasting
Union*] [*Also, IBU*]   (NTCM)......................... UIR
Union of Salt, Chemical, and Industrial General Workers [*British*]
(BI).. USCIGW
Union des Transports Aeriens [*France*] [*ICAO designator*]   (FAAC) .... UTA
Unipolar Bipolar   (IAA).............................. UNIBI
Unipolar Field-Effect Transistor   (IAA)................. UFET
Unipolar Straight Binary Code   (IAA).................. USBCODE
Unique Indentifier [*Computer science*].................. UI
Unique Word   (IAA)................................. UW
Unit Basic Load [*Army*]............................... UBL
Unit Construction Practice   (IAA)..................... UCP
Unit Construction Principle   (IAA).................... UCP
Unit Control Error   (IAA)............................ UCE
Unit Data and Control Diagram   (IAA) .... UDCD
Unit Functional Diagram   (IAA)....................... UFD
Unit Load .... UL
Unit Manning Report [*Army*]   (ADDR)................. UMR

Unit of Measure (IAA) ... U
Unit Movement Officer [*Army*] (INF) ... UMO
Unit Real (IAA) ... UR
Unit Reference Designation [*Army*] ... URD
Unit Training Effectiveness Analysis [*Army*] ... UTEA
Unite Australia Party [*Political party*] ... UAP
Unitech (IAA) ... UT
United Africa Airline (Liberia), Inc. [*ICAO designator*] (FAAC) ... UFR
United Air [*South Africa*] [*ICAO designator*] (FAAC) ... UTD
United Air Charters [*Zimbabwe*] [*ICAO designator*] (FAAC) ... UAC
United Air Lines, Inc. [*ICAO designator*] (FAAC) ... UAL
United Air Service [*Nigeria*] [*ICAO designator*] (FAAC) ... UHP
United Arab Emirates [*Aircraft nationality and registration mark*] (FAAC) ... A6
United Arab Emirates [*ICAO designator*] (FAAC) ... UAE
United Arab Emirates Air Force [*ICAO designator*] (FAAC) ... UAF
United Arab Republic Broadcasting Corp. (IAA) ... UARBC
United Aviation Ltd. [*New Zealand*] [*ICAO designator*] (FAAC) ... UAV
United Aviation Services SA [*Spain*] [*ICAO designator*] (FAAC) ... SAU
United Carriers Systems, Inc. [*ICAO designator*] (FAAC) ... UCS
United Chemists' Association Ltd. [*British*] (BI) ... UCA
United Commercial Travellers Association of Great Britain and Ireland, Inc. (BI) ... UCTA
United Democratic Alliance [*European political movement*] (ECON) ... UDA
United Electrical, Radio, and Machine Workers of America [*Also, UERMWA*] (NTCM) ... UEW
United Electro Dynamics (IAA) ... UED
United Engineering Societies (IAA) ... UES
United European Power Grid (IAA) ... UEPG
United Feeder Service [*ICAO designator*] (FAAC) ... UFS
United Independent Broadcasters (NTCM) ... UIB
United Insulator Co. (IAA) ... UIC
United Inventors and Scientists (IAA) ... UIS
United Kingdom Airways and Communication Region (IAA) ... UKAACREG
United Kingdom Atomic Energy Authority Office at Risley (IAA) ... UKR
United Kingdom Bartenders' Guild (BI) ... UKBG
United Kingdom Coffee Association Ltd. (BI) ... UKCA
United Kingdom Cutlery and Silverware Manufacturers Association (BI) ... UKCSMA
United Kingdom Dutch Rabbit Club (BI) ... UKDRC
United Kingdom Fellmongers Association (BI) ... UKFA
United Kingdom Glycerine Producers' Association (BI) ... UKGPA
United Kingdom Jute Goods Association Ltd. (BI) ... UKJGA
United Kingdom Manufacturers and New Zealand Representatives Association (BI) ... UKMANZRA
United Kingdom Outboard Boating Association (BI) ... UKOBA
United Kingdom Sugar Merchants' Association (BI) ... UKSMA
United Methodist Voluntary Services ... UMVS
United Nations Commission on International Trade Law (PDAA) ... UNCITRAL
United Nations Emergency Operation (PDAA) ... UNEO
United Nations Information Center and Liaison Office (PDAA) ... UNICLO
United Parcel Service Co. [*ICAO designator*] (FAAC) ... UPS
United Pastrycooks' and Confectioners' Society [*British*] (BI) ... UPCS
United Patients Association for Pulmonary Hypertension (EA) ... UPAPH
United Power Association (IAA) ... UPA
United Press International Audio (NTCM) ... UPIA
United Press International News-Features (NTCM) ... UPIN
United Press International Radio Network (NTCM) ... UPIRN
United Press International Television News (NTCM) ... UPITN
United Ratepayers' Campaign [*British*] (BI) ... URC
United Savers Association (EA) ... USA
United Society of Artists [*British*] (BI) ... UA
United State Army School of Aviation Medicine (PDAA) ... USASAM
United States Activities Board (IAA) ... USAB
United States Activities Committee (IAA) ... USAC
United States Agency for International Development, Washington (PDAA) ... USAID/W
United States Air Force Communications Electronics Doctrine (IAA) ... USAFCED
United States of America Standard Character Set for Optical Characters (IAA) ... USASCSOCR
United States of America Standard Code for Information Interchange (IAA) ... USASII
United States Army Air Defense Artillery Board ... USABD
United States Army Airborne and Electronics Board (IAA) ... USAABNAELCTBD
United States Army Armament Research Development and Engineering Center ... USAARDEC
United States Army Armor Center and School ... USAACS
United States Army Armor Signals (IAA) ... USAAS
United States Army Communications and Electronics Material and Readiness Command ... USACERCOM
United States Army Communications Research and Development Command ... USACORADCOM
United States Army Electronic Proving Ground (IAA) ... USAELCTPG
United States Army Electronics Laboratories (IAA) ... USAEL
United States Army Engineer Research and Development Laboratories (IAA) ... USAERDL
United States Army Environmental Center (RDA) ... USAEC
United States Army Field Artillery Center and School ... USAFACS
United States Army History Institute (PDAA) ... USAHI
United States Army Intelligence Center (IAA) ... USAIC
United States Army Jefferson Proving Ground (PDAA) ... USAJPG
United States Army Logistics Center ... USALOGCTR
United States Army National Guard ... USARNG
United States Army Operational Test and Evaluation Agency ... USAOTEA
United States Army Publications and Printing Agency ... USAPPA
United States Army Quartermaster Center and School ... USAQMCS
United States Army Research Program (IAA) ... USARP
United States Army Satellite Communications Agency (IAA) ... USASCA
United States Army Signal Corps School (IAA) ... USASCS
United States Army Signal Engineering Laboratory (IAA) ... USASEL
United States Army Signal Engineering Laboratory (IAA) ... USASIGENGLAB
United States Army Signal Missile Support Agency (IAA) ... USASMSA
United States Army Signal Research Unit (IAA) ... USASIGRSCHUNIT
United States Army Signal Training Center (IAA) ... USASIGTC
United States Army Signal Training Center (IAA) ... USASTCEN
United States Army Space Command ... USARSPACE
United States Army Space and Strategic Defense Command ... USASSDC
United States Army Transportation Center and School ... USATCS
United States Capacitor Corp. (IAA) ... USCC
United States Coast and Geodetic Survey (IAA) ... USCAGS
United States Code Congressional and Administrative News [*A publication*] ... USCCAN
United States Components (IAA) ... USC
United States Department of Agriculture, Animal and Plant Health Inspection Service, Plant Protection and Quarantine Programs (PDAA) ... USDA-APHIS-PP/Q
United States Department of Agriculture - Forest Service (PDAA) ... USDA-FS
United States Department of Agriculture - Rural Electrification Administration (PDAA) ... USDA-REA
United States Gallon (IAA) ... USG
United States Gallon (IAA) ... USGAL
United States Government Standard Gage (IAA) ... USGSG
United States Industry ... USI
United States International Book Association (NTCM) ... USIBA
United States International Transportation Exposition (PDAA) ... USITE
United States Law Week [*A publication*] (NTCM) ... LW
United States Lawn Mower Racing Association ... USLMRA
United States Microgravity Payload [*NASA*] ... USMP
United States National Bureau of Standards (IAA) ... USNBS
United States National Committee on Standardization ... USNS
United States National Research Council [*Toxicology*] ... USNRC
United States Navy Undersea Laboratory (IAA) ... USNUSL
United States NOTAM [*Notice to Airmen*] **System** [*Aviation*] (FAAC) ... USNS
United States Oceanographic Office (PDAA) ... USOO
United States Pharmacopoeial Convention ... USPC
United States Reports [*A publication*] (NTCM) ... US
United States Society for Esperantists Youth (EA) ... USEJ
United States Space Administration (IAA) ... USSA
United States Technical Advisory Group (IAA) ... USTAG
United Technology Center (IAA) ... UTC
United Telephone Cables (IAA) ... UTC
United Transformer Corp. (IAA) ... UTC
United Trekkers of Planet Earth [*An association*] (EA) ... UTPE
Unites States Joint Communication Board (IAA) ... USJCB
Units Position (IAA) ... UP
Units Tens (IAA) ... UT
UNIVAC [*Universal Automatic Computer*] **Bill of Material Processor Random System** [*Computer science*] (IAA) ... UNIBORS
UNIVAC [*Universal Automatic Computer*] **Bill of Material Processor Sequential System** [*Computer science*] (IAA) ... UNIBOSS
Universair [*Spain*] [*ICAO designator*] (FAAC) ... MDN
Universair [*Spain*] [*ICAO designator*] (FAAC) ... UNA
Universal Active Filter (IAA) ... UAF
Universal Airlines, Inc. [*ICAO designator*] (FAAC) ... PNA
Universal Airlines, Inc. [*ICAO designator*] (FAAC) ... WEC
Universal Airways, Inc. [*ICAO designator*] (FAAC) ... UVA
Universal Assembly Language (IAA) ... UAL
Universal Automatic Computer Scientific Exchange (IAA) ... USE
Universal Automatic Computer Users' Association (IAA) ... UUA
Universal Ballet Academy [*Washington, DC*] ... UBA
Universal Cable Adapter (IAA) ... UCAL
Universal Card Read-In Program (IAA) ... UNCDRP
Universal Computer-Oriented Language (IAA) ... UNCOL
Universal Computer-Oriented Language (IAA) ... UNICOL
Universal Data Base (IAA) ... UDB
Universal Decimal Code (IAA) ... UDC
Universal Digital Communications Network [*Computer science*] (PDAA) ... UDICON
Universal Digital Instrument (IAA) ... UDI
Universal Digital Operational Flight Trainer Tool [*Navy*] (IAA) ... UDOFTT
Universal Exhaust Gas Oxygen Sensor [*Fuel systems*] [*Automotive engineering*] ... UEGO
Universal Head-Down Display [*Computer science*] (PDAA) ... UNIHEDD
Universal Identifier (IAA) ... UID
Universal Infrared Viewer (PDAA) ... UIRV
Universal Language Description [*Computer science*] (IAA) ... ULD
Universal Log Interpretation Computer Program (PDAA) ... ULICP
Universal Logic Array [*Computer science*] (IAA) ... ULA
Universal Logic Primitive (PDAA) ... ULP
Universal Naming Convention [*Computer science*] (PCM) ... UNC

Universal Postal Congress (IAA) .... UPC
Universal Procedure Pointer [Computer science] .... UPP
Universal Reproducing Matrix System (PDAA) .... URMS
Universal Scheduling System (IAA) .... USS
Universal Series Regulator (IAA) .... USR
Universal Standard Book Code (PDAA) .... USBC
Universal Triangulation Program (IAA) .... UTRIP
Universal Tube (IAA) .... UT
Universal Versaplot Software (IAA) .... UVS
Universally Programmable Digitizer Update (IAA) .... UPD
Universite Radiophonique Internationale [International University of the Air] (NTCM) .... URI
University of Akron [Ohio] (PDAA) .... UA
University of Arizona (PDAA) .... UARZ
University of Arizona-Engineering Experiment Station (PDAA) .... UAZ-EES
University Association for Emergency Medicine .... UAEM
University Association for Professional Radio Education [Broadcast Education Association] (NTCM) .... UAPRE
University of Chicago [Illinois] (PDAA) .... UC
University of Chicago School Mathematics Project (AEE) .... UCSMP
University College School [British] (BI) .... UCS
University Directors of Industrial Liaison (PDAA) .... UDIL
University of Georgia (PDAA) .... UGA
University of Kentucky (PDAA) .... UKY
University of New Hampshire (PDAA) .... UNH
University of New Mexico (PDAA) .... UNM
University of Vermont (PDAA) .... UVM
University of Wisconsin (PDAA) .... UWIS
Univex SRL [Italy] [ICAO designator] (FAAC) .... UAD
Unknown Respiratory Stress Syndrome [Medicine] .... URDS
Unlaunchable (IAA) .... ULN
Unlicensed (DA) .... U
Unlisten (IAA) .... UNL
Unload (IAA) .... UNLD
Unloader Coil (IAA) .... UC
Unmanned Aerial Vehicle-Close Range [Military] .... UAV-CR
Unnumbered Acknowledge [or Acknowledgement] [Telecommunications] (IAA) .... U
Unnumbered Information (IAA) .... UI
Unpacked (IAA) .... UNPKD
Unpaved Surface [Aviation] (DA) .... u
Unreliable (FAAC) .... UNRELBL
Unsaturated Zone Monitoring [Environmental Protection Agency] (ERG) .... UZM
Unserviceable (IAA) .... UNSERV
Unsmoked Sheets (PDAA) .... USS
Unsuppressed Selling Price .... USP
Unsuppressed Selling Price .... USSP
Until (DA) .... U
Until Advised (DA) .... UA
Unusual Occurence Report (IAA) .... UORS
Update [National Weather Service] (FAAC) .... UPDT
Uplink Frequency .... UF
Uplink Logic Module .... UPLM
Upper Advisory Area [Aviation] (DA) .... UAA
Upper Advisory Route [Aviation] (DA) .... UAD
Upper Air Control (IAA) .... UAC
Upper Airway [Aviation] (DA) .... UWY
Upper Atmosphere Phenomena (IAA) .... UAP
Upper Atmospheric Research Program [NASA] (PDAA) .... UARP
Upper Characters (IAA) .... UC
Upper Circulating Reflux Bottom Section [Chemical engineering] .... UCRB
Upper Circulating Reflux Top Section [Chemical engineering] .... UCRT
Upper Control (IAA) .... UC
Upper Earnings Limit (PDAA) .... UEL
Upper Guard Band .... UGB
Upper Information Service (DA) .... UIS
Upper Level Management Advisor (IAA) .... ULMA
Upper Sideband Upconverter (IAA) .... USBUC
Upper Square Law Limit (IAA) .... USL
Upper Surface Blowing Technique [Aviation] (DA) .... USBT
Upper Testing Area (IAA) .... UTA
Upper Winds [Meteorology] (FAAC) .... UWNDS
Upstream [Meteorology] (FAAC) .... UPSTRM
Upstream (NTCM) .... US
Upward Light Output Ratio (PDAA) .... ULOR
Upwind [Aviation] (FAAC) .... UW
Uralavialy [Russian Federation] [ICAO designator] (FAAC) .... URL
Uralinteravia [Russian Federation] [ICAO designator] (FAAC) .... URA
Uranium Ore Concentrate .... UOC
Urban Area (NTCM) .... UA
Urban Comprehensive Health Care Information System (PDAA) .... UCHCIS
Urban Forests [A publication] .... Urb For
Uric Acid-Creatinine Ratio [Physiology] (MAH) .... UA/C
Uridine Diphosphate Galactose [Biochemistry] (MAH) .... UDPgal
Urinary Osmolality Maximum [Physiology] (MAH) .... Umax
US Air [ICAO designator] (FAAC) .... USA
US Army Aeronautical Services [ICAO designator] (FAAC) .... GKA
US Check Airlines [ICAO designator] (FAAC) .... USC
US Deaf Cycling Association (EA) .... UDCA
US Department of Justice [ICAO designator] (FAAC) .... JUD
US Express [ICAO designator] (FAAC) .... USX
US Jet, Inc. [ICAO designator] (FAAC) .... USJ

US Marshal Service [Department of Justice] [ICAO designator] (FAAC) .... MSH
USAREUR [United States Army, Europe] Command and Control Information System .... UCCIS
Use the Source, Luke [Computer hacker terminology, used to parody commands to Luke Skywalker in the movie "Star Wars"] (NHD) .... UTSL
Used Oil Recycling Coalition [Automotive lubricants] .... UORC
User Advisory Group (RDA) .... UAG
User Agency .... UA
User Attribute Definition [Computer science] (IAA) .... UAD
User Brain Damage [Computer hacker terminology] (NHD) .... UBD
User Communications Manager [Audio-video] (NTCM) .... UCM
User Control Interface Device [Army] .... UCID
Users Files on Line (IAA) .... UFO
Users Master File (IAA) .... UMF
Utah State University (PDAA) .... USU
Utilities Emergency Radio Network (IAA) .... UERN
Utility Assemble Communication Pool (IAA) .... UAC
Utility Assemble Master Communication (IAA) .... UAMC
Utility Data Reduction Control (IAA) .... UDRC
Utility Data Reduction Output (IAA) .... UDRO
Utility Read-In Program (IAA) .... URI
Utility Satellite (IAA) .... US
Uzbekistan Havo Jullary [Uzbekistan Airways] [ICAO designator] (FAAC) .... UZB

V

Veiling Glare Index [*Vision research*] ... VGI
Velocity Aid ... VA
Velocity Bin Commanded ... VBC
Velocity of Propagation (IAA) ... VP
Venda Airways [*South Africa*] [*ICAO designator*] (FAAC) ... VAA
Venexcargo (Transporte Aereo de Carga SA) [*Venezuela*] [*ICAO designator*] (FAAC) ... VNX
Venezolana Servicios Expresos de Carga Internacional CA [*Venezuela*] [*ICAO designator*] (FAAC) ... VEC
Vented Suppressive Shielding ... VSS
Venus Air Services Ltd. [*Ghana*] [*ICAO designator*] (FAAC) ... VNS
Verical Altitude and Take-Off and Landing (PDAA) ... VATOL
Verified Audit Circulation Corp. (NTCM) ... VAC
Verified Encoded Logging (NTCM) ... VEL
Verifying Interpreting Punch (IAA) ... VIP
Verlagsgruppe Georg von Holtzbrinck [*Commercial firm*] [*Germany*] ... VGH
Vermont Health Care Information, Consortium ... VHIC
Vernier Auto Track (IAA) ... VAT
Versailles Project on Advanced Materials and Standards ... VAMAS
Versatile Automatic Test Equipment Assembly Program [*Computer science*] (IAA) ... VAP
Versatile Avionics Ship Test (IAA) ... VAST
Versatile Exercise Mine System [*Military*] (PDAA) ... VEMS
Versatile Interface Adapter [*Telecommunications*] (IAA) ... VIA
Versatile Interior Multiplex System (PDAA) ... VIMS
Vertical Alignment Design by the Nodal-Tangent and Undulation System (PDAA) ... VENUS
Vertical Amplifier (IAA) ... VA
Vertical Circle (IAA) ... VC
Vertical Deflection Terminal (IAA) ... VDT
Vertical Digital Analyzer (IAA) ... VERDAN
Vertical Field Effect Transistor (IAA) ... VFET
Vertical Hook (IAA) ... VH
Vertical Incidence (IAA) ... VI
Vertical Interval Reference Signal [*Automatic color adjustment*] [*Television*] (IAA) ... VIRS
Vertical Interval Test [*Automatic color adjustment*] [*Television*] (IAA) ... VIT
Vertical Interval Time Code (NTCM) ... VITC
Vertical Line Through Center of Gravity (IAA) ... VCG
Vertical Main Distribution (IAA) ... VMD
Vertical Metal-Oxide Semiconductor (IAA) ... VMOS
Vertical Obstacle SONAR (IAA) ... VOS
Vertical Ommi-Range, Take-Off, Approach, and Landing System (PDAA) ... VORTAL
Vertical Output (IAA) ... VO
Vertical Path Computer (PDAA) ... VPC
Vertical Redundancy [*Telecommunications*] (IAA) ... VR
Vertical Redundancy Check Register [*Telecommunications*] (IAA) ... VRCR
Vertical Reference Gyro (DA) ... VRG
Vertical Sideband [*Radio frequency*] [*Telecommunications*] (IAA) ... VSI
Vertical Spacing (IAA) ... VC
Vertical Synchronization [*Computer science*] (IAA) ... VSYNCH
Vertical Tape Display (IAA) ... VTD
Vertical Visibility [*Aviation*] (DA) ... VERVIS
Vertical Visibility (DA) ... VV
Very [*Automotive advertising*] ... VRY
Very Big Accelerator (PDAA) ... VBA
Very Close-Up [*Cinematography*] (NTCM) ... VCU
Very Hard (IAA) ... VH
Very-High Frequency Radio Telephony (PDAA) ... VHFRT
Very-High Molecular Weight Polyethylene (PDAA) ... VHMWPE
Very-High Performance Integrated Circuit [*Electronics*] (PDAA) ... VHPIC
Very High Viscosity Index [*Petroleum oils*] ... VHVI
Very-High Voltage (IAA) ... VHV
Very Intelligent Terminal (IAA) ... VIT
Very Large Airplane (PDAA) ... VLA
Very Large Antenna [*Telecommunications*] (IAA) ... VLA
Very Large Bulk-Cargo Carrier (PDAA) ... VLBC
Very Large Ore-Oil Carrier (PDAA) ... VLOOC
Very Long Endurance Aircraft (PDAA) ... VLEA
Very-Low-Cost Display (IAA) ... VLCD
Very-Low-Frequency Direct [*Electronics*] (IAA) ... VLFD
Very-Low Impedance (IAA) ... VLI
Very Narrow Aisle Truck (PDAA) ... VNA
Very Small Quantity Generator [*Environmental science*] ... VSQG
Very Soft (IAA) ... VS
Very Wide Area Mine (RDA) ... VWAM
VESA [*Video Electronics Standards Association*] **Advanced Feature Connector** ... VAFC
VESA [*Video Electronics Standards Association*] **BIOS** [*Basic Input-Output System*] **Extension/Audio Interface** (PCM) ... VBE/AI
Vesicle-Associated Membrane Protein [*Biochemistry*] ... VAMP
Vesta Airex [*Czechoslovakia*] [*ICAO designator*] (FAAC) ... VAX
Veteran Car Club of Great Britain (BI) ... VCC
Veterans Affairs Learning Opportunities Residency Program ... VALOR
Veterans Transition Franchise Initiative Program ... VETFR
Veterinary Medical Association of Ireland (BI) ... VMAI
VETRONICS [*Vehicle Electronics*] **Simulation Facility** [*Army*] (RDA) ... VSF
VHF [*Very-High-Frequency*] **Omnidirectional Range Collocated with TACAN** [*Tactical Air Navigation System*] (IAA) ... VORTAC
VHF [*Very-High-Frequency*] **Omnidirectional Range and Distance Measuring Equipmentfor Average Coverage** (IAA) ... VORDAC
VHF [*Very-High-Frequency*] **Omnidirectional Range Tactical Air Navigation** (IAA) ... VORTAC
VHF [*Very-High-Frequency*] **Recovery Beacon** (IAA) ... VRB
Via Low Frequency Direct [*Aviation*] (FAAC) ... VLFD
Viacao Aerea Rio-Grandense SA [*Brazil*] [*ICAO designator*] (FAAC) ... VRG
Viacao Aerea Sao Paulo SA [*Brazil*] [*ICAO designator*] (FAAC) ... VSP
Viajes Internacionales de Vacaciones SA [*Spain*] [*ICAO designator*] (FAAC) ... VIV
Viajes Internacionales de Vacaciones SA [*Spain*] [*ICAO designator*] (FAAC) ... VIVA
VIASA, Venezolana International de Aviacion SA [*Venezuela*] [*ICAO designator*] (FAAC) ... VIA
Vibrating Head Magnetometer (IAA) ... VHM
Vibrating Tie Under-Cutter (PDAA) ... VTU
Vibration and Acoustic Testing (IAA) ... VAAT
Vibrator (IAA) ... VB
Vibrator (IAA) ... VIB
Vibrator (IAA) ... VIBT
Vicarious Nucleophilic Substitution [*Organic chemistry*] ... VNS
Vice-Presidential Service Badge [*Military decoration*] ... VPRESSVB
Vicinity [*Aviation*] (FAAC) ... VCY
Vickers Diamond Hardness (IAA) ... VDH
Vickers Ltd. [*British*] [*ICAO designator*] (FAAC) ... VSB
Vickers Pyramid Hardness Number (PDAA) ... VPH
Victor Airways [*Aviation*] (FAAC) ... VA
Victor Fly [*Italy*] [*ICAO designator*] (FAAC) ... VCF
Victorian Computer Society (IAA) ... VCS
Video Cartridge Recorder (IAA) ... VCR
Video Combiner Unit (IAA) ... VCU
Video Contrast Tracker (PDAA) ... VCT
Video Data Sequence (NTCM) ... VDSQ
Video Display (IAA) ... VD
Video Display Controller (IAA) ... VDAC
Video Distribution Unit ... VDU
Video Documentary (NTCM) ... VIDOC
Video Graphics Generator ... VGG
Video Image Correlation ... VIC
Video Kinescope Recording (PDAA) ... VKR
Video Operator (NTCM) ... VO
Video Symbology Generator ... VSG
Video and Synchronization [*Telecommunications*] (IAA) ... VS
Video Systems Exposition and Conference (PDAA) ... VIDSEC
Video Transmission Engineering Advisory Committee [*Army*] (PDAA) ... VITEAC
Videotape Recorder (IAA) ... VDR
Viennair Luftfahrt GmbH [*Austria*] [*ICAO designator*] (FAAC) ... VNR
Vieques Air Link, Inc. [*ICAO designator*] (FAAC) ... VES
Vietnam Campaign Medal [*Military decoration*] ... VNCM
Viewers-per-Household [*Television ratings*] (NTCM) ... VPH
Viewers-per-Viewing Household [*Television ratings*] (NTCM) ... VPVH
Viewers-per-Viewing Household [*Television ratings*] (NTCM) ... V/VH
Viking Express, Inc. [*ICAO designator*] (FAAC) ... WCY
Viking International Airlines [*ICAO designator*] (FAAC) ... VIK
Village Aviation, Inc. [*ICAO designator*] (FAAC) ... CAM
Village Produce Association [*British*] (BI) ... VPA
Vinair-Helicopteros Ltda. [*Portugal*] [*ICAO designator*] (FAAC) ... VIN
Vings [*Bulgaria*] [*ICAO designator*] (FAAC) ... VGS
Vinyl Ester Sheet Molding Compound [*Plastics*] ... VESMC
Viral Haemorrhagic Disease ... VHD
Virgin Atlantic [*British*] [*ICAO designator*] (FAAC) ... VIR
Virgin Islands (IAA) ... VI
Virgin Islands Seaplane Shuttle, Inc. [*ICAO designator*] (FAAC) ... VSS
Virginia Panel Corp. (IAA) ... VPC
Virtual Acoustic Synthesis [*Electronics*] (PS) ... VAS
Virtual Communication Path [*Computer science*] (IAA) ... VCP
Virtual Control Processor [*Computer science*] (IAA) ... VCP
Virtual Coulomb Excitation (PDAA) ... VCE
Virtual Display Driver [*Computer science*] ... VDD
Virtual-Egress Analysis and Simulation (ECON) ... VEGAS
Virtual Equals Real [*Computer science*] (IAA) ... VR
Virtual Index Sequential Access Method (IAA) ... VISAM
Virtual Information Environment [*Computer science*] (PCM) ... VIE
Virtual Instruction Package (IAA) ... VIP
Virtual Machine Control Program [*Computer science*] (IAA) ... VP
Virtual Machine/System Product [*Operating system for large IBM mainframe computers*] ... VM/SP
Virtual Memory Operating System (IAA) ... VMOS
Virtual Multi-Access [*Computer science*] (IAA) ... VM
Virtual Reality and Simulation ... VRS
Virtual Resource Manager [*Computer science*] (IAA) ... VRM
Virtual Terminal Support [*Computer science*] (IAA) ... VTSU
Virtual Terminal System [*Computer science*] (IAA) ... VTS
Virtually-Pivoted Beam LASER (IAA) ... VPB
Viscosity Factor (IAA) ... VF
Viscosity Modifier [*Lubricants*] ... VM
Viscosity Temperature Coefficient (IAA) ... VTC
Viscount Air Services, Inc. [*ICAO designator*] (FAAC) ... VCT
Visibility, Amount, Height of Cloud Top, Base [*Weather*] [*DoD*] ... VAT
Visible Calculation [*Electronic spreadsheet program brand*] ... VisiCalc
Visible-Infrared Mapping Spectrometer [*Instrumentation*] ... VIMS
Visible Record Computer (IAA) ... VRC

Visible Speech Translator   (IAA) .... VST
Vision Airways Corp. [*Canada*] [*ICAO designator*]   (FAAC) .... VSN
Vision Distribution Amplifier   (IAA) .... VDA
Vision on Sound   (IAA) .... VOS
Visual Airborne Target Locator System [*Military*]   (PDAA) .... VIATLS
Visual Approach Chart [*Aviation*]   (FAAC) .... VAC
Visual Approach Monitor Chart   (PDAA) .... VAMC
Visual Audio Kinetic Unit Multiples and Environments   (PDAA) .... VAKUME
Visual Comfort Probability   (IAA) .... VCP
Visual Difference [*Computer science*]   (NHD) .... VDIFF
Visual Display Terminal   (IAA) .... VDT
Visual Docking Guidance System [*Aviation*]   (DA) .... VDGS
Visual Doppler Indicator   (IAA) .... VDI
Visual Electronic Remote Blackboard   (PDAA) .... VERB
Visual Glide Path Indicator [*Aviation*]   (FAAC) .... VSPI
Visual Image Processor   (IAA) .... VIP
Visual Image Quality Indicator   (PDAA) .... VISQI
Visual Indicating Equipment [*Telecommunications*]   (IAA) .... VIE
Visual Indicator Panel   (IAA) .... VIP
Visual Information Control Console [*Telecommunications*]   (IAA) VICC
Visual Information Display and Retrieval System [*Computer science*]
   (PDAA) .... VID-R
Visual Information Documentation [*Military*] .... VIDOC
Visual Interactive Programming [*Computer science*] .... VIP
Visual Interface [*Computer science*]   (NHD) VI
Visual Maneuvering Height [*Aviation*]   (DA) .... VMH
Visual Omnirange Test [*Aviation*]   (IAA) .... VOT
Visual Pattern Discrimination   (PDAA) .... VPD
Visual Programmer [*Computer science*]   (PCM) .... ViP
Visual Programming Environment .... VPE
Visual Reporting Point   (DA) .... VRP
Visual Route   (DA) .... VR
Visual Talking [*Telecommunications*]   (IAA) .... VISTA
Visual User Environment [*Military*] .... VUE
Vitjaz [*Russian Federation*] [*ICAO designator*]   (FAAC) .... VTZ
Vitkovice Air [*Czech Republic*] [*ICAO designator*]   (FAAC) .... VTR
Vitramon Microwave Corp.   (IAA) .... VMC
Vitreous Enamel Porcelain   (IAA) .... VITROLAIN
Vitro Hanford Engineering Service   (IAA) .... VHES
Vizmo [*Projection device*]   (NTCM) .... VIZ
Vlaamse Luchtransportmaatschappij NV [*Belgium*] [*ICAO
   designator*]   (FAAC) .... VLM
Vocabulary Etymology .... VETY
Vocational Awards International [*British*] .... VAI
Vocational and Educational Services for Individuals with Disabilities .... VESID
Vocational Training Charitable Trust [*British*] .... VTCT
Voice Actuated Address Mechanism   (PDAA) .... VAAM
Voice Coder [*Telecommunications*]   (IAA) .... VCO
Voice Coil of Speaker [*Computer hardware*]   (IAA) VC
Voice Communication Panel .... VCP
Voice-Controlled Carrier [*Telecommunications*]   (IAA) VCC
Voice of the Customer [*Business term*] .... VOC
Voice Data Encoding System [*Telecommunications*]   (IAA) .... VDES
Voice-Excitated Formant Vocoder   (PDAA) .... VEFV
Voice Frequency Equipment [*Telecommunications*]   (IAA) .... VFEQT
Voice-Initiated Cockpit Control and Integration [*Aviation*]   (PDAA) VICCI
Voice Interface Frame [*Telecommunications*]   (IAA) .... VIF
Voice Internal Communications Equipment for Submarines   (PDAA) .... VICES
Voice Line Expansion [*Telecommunications*]   (IAA) .... VLE
Voice Mail System [*Telecommunications*]   (IAA) .... VMS
Voice Management Unit   (DA) .... VMU
Voice-Operated Carrier Switching Unit   (IAA) .... VOCSU
Voice-Operated Computerized Identification System   (PDAA) .... VPCIS
Voice-Operated Control [*Telecommunications*]   (IAA) .... VOC
Voice-Operated Identification Computer Entry System   (PDAA) .... VOICES
Voice-Operated Relay   (IAA) .... VOY
Voice-Operated Relay Circuit   (IAA) .... VOC
Voice-Operated Typewriter Employing Morse [*Telecommunications*]
   (IAA) .... VOTEM
Voice Position Report   (DA) .... VPR
Voice Read Out Unit [*Telecommunications*]   (IAA) .... VRU
Voice Store and Forward Messaging System [*Telecommunications*]
   (IAA) .... VSFS
Voice Switching [*Telecommunications*]   (IAA) .... VS
Voiceover/Sound on Tape [*Television*]   (NTCM) .... VO/SOT
Volare [*Russian Federation*] [*ICAO designator*]   (FAAC) .... VLR
Volatile Organic Fraction [*Automotive exhaust emission testing*] .... VOF
Volga-Dnepr [*Former USSR*] [*ICAO designator*]   (FAAC) .... VDA
Volkswagen of America   (ECON) .... VWA
Volley   (DA) .... VLY
Volt-Ampere Reactive Hour   (IAA) .... VARH
Volt-Ohm-Milliampere [*Electronics*]   (IAA) .... VOMA
Volt-Ohm-Milliampere Meter [*Electronics*]   (IAA) .... VOM
Volt Ohmmeter [*Electronics*]   (IAA) .... VOM
Voltage   (IAA) .... VE
Voltage Ampere Reactance [*AC electric motors*] .... VAR
Voltage Amplifier   (IAA) .... VA
Voltage Board   (IAA) .... VB
Voltage Breakover   (IAA) .... VBO
Voltage Changer   (IAA) VC
Voltage Clock Trigger   (IAA) .... VCT
Voltage Control Resistor   (IAA) .... VCR
Voltage-Controlled Amplifier   (NTCM) .... VCA

Voltage-Controlled Clock   (IAA) VCC
Voltage-Controlled Crystal Oscillator   (IAA) .... VCCO
Voltage-Controlled Negative Capacitance   (IAA) .... VCNC
Voltage-Controlled Negative Resistance   (IAA) .... VCNR
Voltage-Controlled Transfer   (IAA) .... VCT
Voltage-Current Adapter   (IAA) .... VCA
Voltage Fault Detector [*Electronics*]   (IAA) .... VFD
Voltage-to-Frequency   (IAA) .... VTOF
Voltage-Gated Calcium Channel [*Neurophysiology*] .... VGCC
Voltage Impulse Protection   (IAA) .... VIP
Voltage Inverter Switch   (IAA) .... VIS
Voltage Limiter   (IAA) .... VOLLIM
Voltage-Logic [*Electronics*] VL
Voltage-Sensitive Oscillator   (IAA) .... VSO
Voltage-Stabilized Polyethylene   (IAA) .... VSP
Voltage Switching   (IAA) .... VS
Voltage Transformer   (IAA) .... VT
Voltammeter   (IAA) .... VA
Volts per Mile   (IAA) .... VPM
Volume   (NTCM) VV
Volume, Area, and Mass Properties   (PDAA) .... VAMP
Volume Catalog   (IAA) .... VOLCAT
Volume Label   (IAA) .... VOL
Volume Serial Number [*Computer science*]   (IAA) .... VSN
Volume-Variety   (PDAA) .... VOLVAR
Volume-Weighted Averages of Realized Prices .... VOLWARE
Voluntary Early Release and Retirement Program [*Army*] .... VERRP
Voluntary Early Retirement Authority [*DoD*] .... VERA
Voluntary Separation Incentive [*DoD*] .... VSI
Voluntary Separation Incentive Program [*DoD*] .... VSIP
Voluntary Standards Bodies   (IAA) .... VSBS
Voluntary Universal Marking Program   (IAA) .... VUVM
Volunteer Lawyers for the Poor [*An association*] .... VLP
Volunteers for International Technical Assistance   (IAA) .... VITA
Volvo AB [*Sweden*] [*ICAO designator*]   (FAAC) .... VOL
Volvo Mechanical Equipment [*Auto industry supplier*] .... VME
Volvo Truck Corp.   (IAA) .... VTC
Vortex Wake System [*Aviation*]   (DA) .... VWS
Voter-Switch-Disagreement Detector   (PDAA) .... VSD
Voyageur Airways Ltd. [*Canada*] [*ICAO designator*]   (FAAC) .... VAL
Vuelos Asesorias y Representaciones SA de CV [*Mexico*] [*ICAO
   designator*]   (FAAC) .... VSE
Vulcanized Polyethylene   (IAA) .... VPE

W

WAAC (Nigeria) Ltd. Nigeria Airways [*ICAO designator*]   (FAAC)........... NGA
Wafer Parameter Identification System   (IAA)..................................... WPIS
Wage and Hour Division [*Department of Labor*]   (IAA)............................ WAH
Waglisla Air, Inc. [*Canada*] [*ICAO designator*]   (FAAC)........................ SEH
Wagner Computer   (IAA) .... WAC
Waikato Aero Club, Inc. [*New Zealand*] [*ICAO designator*]   (FAAC)........... WIK
Wait and Acknowledge   (IAA) .... WACK
Waitemata Aero Club, Inc. [*New Zealand*] [*ICAO designator*]
    (FAAC)... WTM
Walking and Dredging Self-Elevating Platform   (PDAA).................... WADSEP
Wall Hydrant [*NFPA pre-fire planning symbol*]   (NFPA) .... WH
Wall Paper Merchants' Association of Great Britain   (BI) .... WPMA
Wallisair Compagnie [*France*] [*ICAO designator*]   (FAAC)................... WLR
Wallops Space Flight Center [*NASA*]   (IAA) .... WSFC
Walsten Air Services [*Canada*] [*ICAO designator*]   (FAAC)................. WAS
Walt Disney Memorial Cancer Institute .... WDMCC
Wapiti Aviation Ltd. [*Canada*] [*ICAO designator*]   (FAAC) .... WPT
War Control Data Processing Center   (IAA)............................... WCDPC
Warbelow's Air Ventures, Inc. [*ICAO designator*]   (FAAC).................. VNA
Wardair Canada Ltd. [*ICAO designator*]   (FAAC) .... WDA
Warfighters' Simulation [*DoD*].. WARSIM
Warm Cranking Amperes [*Battery*] [*Automotive engineering*]............ WCA
Warm White   (DAC) .... WW
Warm White Deluxe   (DAC).. WWX
Warner Brothers Worldwide Publishing [*Commercial firm*]............. WBWP
Warning Light Driver   (IAA) .... WLD
Wartime Personnel Replacement Operation [*Military*]................... WPRO
Wartime Reserve Mode [*Military*] .... WARM
Warton BAE [*British*] [*ICAO designator*]   (FAAC)........................... WTN
Wasawings AB [*Finland*] [*ICAO designator*]   (FAAC)....................... WWS
Wasaya Airways Ltd. [*Canada*] [*ICAO designator*]   (FAAC)................. WSG
Washington Industrial Safety and Health Act   (IAA) .... WISHA
Washington University   (PDAA) .... WU
Wasser Gefahrdungsklasse [*Water hazard classification*] [*Germany*] .... WGK
Waste Acid Detoxification and Reclamation [*Environmental
    science*] .... WADR
Waste Acid Release Reduction [*Environmental science*] .... WARR
Waste Environmental Federation .... WEF
Waste Minimization Opportunity Assessment [*Environmental
    science*].. WMOA
Waste of Money, Brains, and Time   (NHD)............................. WOMBAT
Waste Paper Recovery Association Ltd. [*British*]   (BI)................... WPRA
Wastewater Coalition [*Environmental science*]............................ WWC
Water-Cooled Tube [*Nuclear energy*]   (IAA) .... WCT
Water-Dispersible Powder [*Pesticide formulation*]......................... WP
[*Sprinkler System*] Water Flow Bell [*NFPA pre-fire planning
    symbol*]   (NFPA)... WB
Water Inlet   (DAC) .... WI
Water Jet Drilling   (PDAA) .... WJD
Water for People [*An association*]   (EA) .... WFP
Water Pollution Control Plant [*Environmental science*].................. WPCP
Water and Power Development Authority   (IAA) .... WAPDA
Water Quality Based [*Environmental science*]............................. WQB
[*Domestic*] Water Shutoff [*NFPA pre-fire planning symbol*]   (NFPA)........... W
Water Supply and Destination .... WSD
Water-Tube Boilermakers Association [*British*]   (BI).................... WTBA
Water-Vapor-Saturated Air   (PDAA) .... WVSA
Water/Wastewater Utilities [*Environmental science*]..................... WWU
Watercolor Spectrometer   (PDAA) .... WCS
Watt   (IAA) .... WT
Watt-per-Channel   (IAA).. WPC
Watt-Hour Meter   (IAA) .... WHRM
Watt Meter   (IAA).. W
Waukegan Avionics, Inc. [*ICAO designator*]   (FAAC)....................... SCP
Wave-Activated Turbine Generator   (PDAA) .... WATG
Wave Analyzer   (IAA) .... WA
Wave Digital Filter   (PDAA) .... WDF
Wave Frequency [*Telecommunications*]   (IAA)............................. WF
Wave Superheater Hypersonic Tunnel   (IAA) .... WSHT
Waveform [*Telecommunications*]   (IAA) .... WF
Waveform Digitizer [*Telecommunications*]   (IAA) .... WD
Waveform Distortion [*Telecommunications*]   (IAA).......................... WD
Waveform Synthesizer   (IAA).. WS

Waveguide Standards   (IAA).. WAVEGD
Wavelength [*Electronics*]   (IAA) .... WVL
Wavy Vortex Flow [*Fluid mechanics*]...................................... WFF
Wax Anti-Settling Additive [*Diesel fuel*]................................. WASA
Weak Affinity Chromatography [*Analytical chemistry*].................... WAC
Wealth Tax   (PDAA)... WT
Weapon Control Computer Debug Program [*Military*] .... WCCDBP
Weapon Delivery Model   (PDAA)... WDM
Weapon Engagement Zone [*Army*]   (ADDR)............................ WEZ
Weapons Alert Designator [*Army*]   (ADDR)............................ WAD
Weapons Spectrum Generator   (PDAA)................................. WSG
Weather at Altitude [*Aviation*]   (FAAC)................................ WX
Weather and Battle-Induced Contaminant   (PDAA)................... WBIC
Weather Card Data   (IAA).. WCD
Weather Center [*Meteorology*]   (DA) .... WC
Weather Facsimile [*Environmental Science Services Administration*]
    (IAA).. WEFC
Weather Reconnaissance Flight Pilot Report [*Aviation*]   (FAAC)........ WXCON
Weather Service Airport   (DA)... WSAS
Weavelength-Scanning Polarization-Modulation Ellipsometry
    (PDAA).. WSPME
Weber per Square Meter   (IAA) .... WBSM
Weekly Newspaper Advertising Bureau [*British*]   (BI) .... WNAB
Weight Data Transmitter   (IAA)... WDT
Weight per Foot   (IAA) .... WTPFT
Weighted Effective Temperature   (IAA).................................. WET
Weighted Elementary Pupil Unit [*Education*]   (AEE) .... WEPU
Welch Aviation, Inc. [*ICAO designator*]   (FAAC)........................ TDB
Welded Base   (DAC) .... WB
Welding   (IAA)... WLDG
Welwyn Hall Research Association   (PDAA)........................... WHRA
Wenic Air Services [*Singapore*] [*ICAO designator*]   (FAAC) .... WNC
Wessex Air Services Ltd. [*British*] [*ICAO designator*]   (FAAC) ...... WSX
West Africa Airlines Ltd. [*Ghana*] [*ICAO designator*]   (FAAC) ...... WCB
West Air Sweden AB [*ICAO designator*]   (FAAC)........................ WEJ
West Aviation AS [*Norway*] [*ICAO designator*]   (FAAC).............. WST
West-Avin Oy [*Finland*] [*ICAO designator*]   (FAAC)................... WAV
West Coast Air [*Gambia*] [*ICAO designator*]   (FAAC)................. WBA
West Coast Airlines Ltd. [*Ghana*] [*ICAO designator*]   (FAAC) ...... WCG
West Coast Amateur Radio Service   (PDAA) .... WESCARS
West European Advisory Committee [*Radio Free Europe*]   (NTCM) .... WEAC
West Irian [*Aircraft nationality and registration mark*]   (FAAC)............... PK
West London Aero Services Ltd. [*British*] [*ICAO designator*]
    (FAAC)... WLA
West Merchant Bank   (ECON).. WMB
West Virginia School of Osteopathic Medicine .... WVSOM
West Wind Aviation, Inc. [*Canada*] [*ICAO designator*]   (FAAC)....... WEW
Westair Aviation, Inc. [*Canada*] [*ICAO designator*]   (FAAC) .... NLF
Westair Aviation Ltd. [*Ireland*] [*ICAO designator*]   (FAAC) .... EFF
Westair Commuter Airlines, Inc. [*ICAO designator*]   (FAAC) .... SDU
WestAir Industries, Inc. [*ICAO designator*]   (FAAC)................... PCM
Westates Airlines [*ICAO designator*]   (FAAC) .... WSA
Western Airways and Air Communications Service   (IAA) .... WAACS
Western Alaska Standard Time   (IAA) .... WAST
Western Artic Air Ltd. [*Canada*] [*ICAO designator*]   (FAAC).......... WAL
Western Association of Minority Consulting Engineers   (IAA) .... WAMCE
Western Book Publishers Association   (NTCM)....................... WBPA
Western Carolina University   (PDAA) .... WCARU
Western Civilization.. WC
Western Design Engineering Exposition   (PDAA).................... WESDEX
Western Electric Engineering Research Center   (IAA)............... WEERC
Western European Time   (IAA) .... WET
Western Interstate Commission for Higher Education   (AEE) .... WICHE
Western Kenya Aircharters Co. Ltd. [*ICAO designator*]   (FAAC) ...... WKC
Western Microwave, Inc.   (IAA).. WM
Western Pacific Airservice [*Solomon Islands*] [*ICAO designator*]
    (FAAC)... WPA
Western Pacific Warm Pool [*Oceanography*] .... WPWP
Western Satellite Research Network   (PDAA) .... WSRN
Western Union Computer Utilities   (IAA)............................. WUCU
Westinghouse Alphanumeric Display   (IAA) .... WAND
Westinghouse Audio Visual Electronics   (IAA) .... WAVE

243

Westinghouse Development Test Requirement Specification (IAA) .... WDTRS
Westinghouse Electric International Co. (IAA) .... WEICO
Westinghouse Information Systems Laboratory (IAA) .... WISL
Westinghouse Microscan System (IAA) .... WMSS
Westinghouse Uninterruptible Power System (IAA) .... WUPS
Westland Helicopters Ltd. [*British*] [*ICAO designator*] (FAAC) .... WHE
Wet-Air Oxidation (PDAA) .... WAO
Wet-Bulb Potential Temperature (PDAA) .... WBPT
Wet Chemical System [*NFPA pre-fire planning symbol*] (NFPA) .... WC
Wet Globe Temperature (PDAA) .... WGT
Wet High Intensity Magnetic Separation (PDAA) .... WHIMS
Wet Pick Up (IAA) .... WPU
What the Heck [*Computer hacker terminology*] [*Bowdlerized version*] (NHD) .... WTH
What You See Before You Get It [*Computer science*] .... WYSBYGI
Wheaton Information System for Education (IAA) .... WISE
Wheel Slide Protection (PDAA) .... WSP
Wheeled Armoured Fighting Vehicle [*Military*] .... WAFV
Wheels [*Automotive advertising*] .... WHLS
Where Used File [*Computer science*] (IAA) .... WUF
White Bag Propellant [*Army*] (ADDR) .... WB
White Balance [*Television*] (NTCM) .... WB
White Gaussian Noise [*Random interference caused by movement of electricity in line*] [*Telecommunications*] (IAA) .... WGN
White Light Fringe Image Velocimeter (PDAA) .... WFIV
White River Air Services Ltd. [*Canada*] [*ICAO designator*] (FAAC) .... WRA
Whole Mononuclear Cell [*Biochemistry*] .... WMNC
Whole-Time Consultants' Association [*British*] (BI) .... WTCA
Whole Tree Chips (PDAA) .... WTC
Wholesale Confectioners Alliance Ltd. [*British*] (BI) .... WCA
Wholesale Egg Distributors' Association [*British*] (BI) .... WEDA
Wholesale Floorcovering Distributors' Association [*British*] (BI) .... WFDA
Wholesale Footwear Distributors' Association [*British*] (BI) .... WFDA
Wholesale Leather Distributors Association [*British*] (BI) .... WLDA
Wholesale Photo Finishers' Association [*British*] (BI) .... WPFA
Wholesale Tobacco Trade Association of Great Britain and Northern Ireland (BI) .... WTTA
Wichita State University [*Kansas*] (PDAA) .... WSU
Wide Angle Collimated Display System [*Aviation*] (DA) .... WACS
Wide-Angle Impedance Matching (PDAA) .... WAIM
Wide-Angle Michelson Interferometer (PDAA) .... WAMI
Wide Area Information Server [*Computer science*] .... WAIS
Wide Area Side Penetrator Mine [*Army*] (ADDR) .... WASPM
Wide Area Surveillance [*Military*] .... WAS
Wide-Area Telephone Service [*Telecommunications*] (IAA) .... WATS
Wide-Area Traffic Control (PDAA) .... WATC
Wide Body STOL [*Short Takeoff and Landing*] [*Aviation*] (IAA) .... WBS
Wide Flange (DAC) .... WF
Wide Sense Stationary [*Telecommunications*] (IAA) .... WSS
Wide Sense Stationary Uncorrelated Scattering [*Telecommunications*] (IAA) .... WSSUS
Wideband Amplifier .... WA
Wideband-Limiter-Heterodyne-Narrowband (PDAA) .... WLHN
Wideband Patch Bay [*Telecommunications*] (IAA) .... WBPB
Wideroe's Flyveselskap AS [*Norway*] [*ICAO designator*] (FAAC) .... WIF
Width-to-Length [*Ratio*] (IAA) .... WL
Wier-in-Tube Sensor (PDAA) .... WIT
Wiggins Airways [*ICAO designator*] (FAAC) .... WIG
Wilbur's, Inc. [*ICAO designator*] (FAAC) .... WFO
Wilderness Airline (1975) Ltd. [*Canada*] [*ICAO designator*] (FAAC) .... WLD
Wilderness Inquiry [*An association*] (EA) .... WI
Wildfowlers' Association of Great Britain and Ireland (BI) .... WAGBI
William Grand Prix Racing Ltd. [*Cayman Islands*] [*ICAO designator*] (FAAC) .... WGP
Williams Air, Inc. [*ICAO designator*] (FAAC) .... WLS
Williams Domain [*Computer science*] (IAA) .... WD
[*Barry*] **Williams Ltd.** [*British*] [*ICAO designator*] (FAAC) .... BWC
Willowair Ltd. [*British*] [*ICAO designator*] (FAAC) .... WLO
Wind Correction Angle [*Aviation*] (DA) .... WCA
Wind Finding RADAR (IAA) .... WF
Wind Shear [*Aviation*] (FAAC) .... WS
Wind Shear Warning / Recovery Guidance System (DA) .... WW/RGS
[*Upper*] **Wind and Temperature Forecast** [*Meteorology*] (DA) .... WINTEM
Winding Engine Manufacturers' Association [*British*] (BI) .... WEMA
Winding Specification (IAA) .... WS
Windows Personal Librarian [*Computer software*] .... WPL
Windshield Flight Environment Simulator (PDAA) .... WFES
Windward Islands Airways International NV [*Netherlands*] [*ICAO designator*] (FAAC) .... WIA
Wing Airways (Pty) Ltd. [*South Africa*] [*ICAO designator*] (FAAC) .... WNG
Wing Attack [*Netball*] .... WA
Wing Defence [*Netball*] .... WD
Wing-in-Ground Effect (PDAA) .... WIGE
Winged Reentry Vehicle (IAA) .... WRV
Winged Russia [*Russian Federation*] [*ICAO designator*] (FAAC) .... WDR
Winged Surface Effect Vehicle (PDAA) .... WSEV
Wings Air Transport Co. [*Sudan*] [*ICAO designator*] (FAAC) .... WAT
Wings Airways [*ICAO designator*] (FAAC) .... WAW
Wings Express, Inc. [*ICAO designator*] (FAAC) .... WEX
Wingwork Aviation [*British*] [*ICAO designator*] (FAAC) .... WNW
Winlink (St. Lucia) Ltd. [*ICAO designator*] (FAAC) .... WIN
Wire Antenna Modeling Program (PDAA) .... WAMP
Wire-Explosion-Spray Coating (PDAA) .... WESC
Wire Products Association [*British*] (BI) .... WPA
Wireless [*Communication*] (IAA) .... W
Wireless [*Telecommunications*] (IAA) .... WRLS
Wireless Auxiliary Station [*Telecommunications*] (IAA) .... WASTN
Wireless Communication (IAA) .... WC
Wireless Operator [*British military*] (IAA) .... WOPTR
Wireless Operator and Air Gunner [*British military*] (IAA) .... WOPAG
Wireless Station (IAA) .... WS
Wireless Telegraph Direction Finder (IAA) .... WTDF
Wireless Telegraphy Direction (IAA) .... WTDR
Wireless Telegraphy Message (IAA) .... WTMGE
Wireless Telegraphy Station [*Telecommunications*] (IAA) .... WTS
Wiring (IAA) .... WNG
Wiring Diagram (IAA) .... WD
Wisman Aviation [*ICAO designator*] (FAAC) .... WSM
With Regard To (NHD) .... WRT
With Snow Tires [*Automotive advertising*] .... W/SNWS
Without Whiskers (IAA) .... WOW
Wittering FTU [*British*] [*ICAO designator*] (FAAC) .... WIT
Wives of Older Men [*An association*] (EA) .... WOOM
WMS Airways BV [*Netherlands*] [*ICAO designator*] (FAAC) .... WMS
[*A*] **Woman in Jeopardy** [*Screenwriter's lexicon*] .... WOMJEP
Woman's Journal [*A publication*] .... Woman's J
Women Who Want to be Women [*An association*] (NTCM) .... WWWW
Women's Employment Federation [*British*] (BI) .... WEF
Women's Engineering Society (IAA) .... WES
Women's Farm and Garden Association [*British*] (BI) .... WFGA
Women's Gas Federation [*British*] (BI) .... WGF
Women's Health Initiative [*National Institutes of Health*] .... WHI
Women's Inter-University Athletic Board [*British*] (BI) .... WIUAB
Women's International Association of Aeronautics (IAA) .... WIAA
Women's Press Association (NTCM) .... WPA
Women's Project Officer .... WPO
Women's Squash Rackets Association [*British*] (BI) .... WSRA
Women's Tricycle Association [*British*] (BI) .... WTA
Woodford BAE [*British*] [*ICAO designator*] (FAAC) .... WFD
Woodford Flight Test Center [*British*] [*ICAO designator*] (FAAC) .... WTC
Woodgate Air Services [*British*] [*ICAO designator*] (FAAC) .... WOD
Woodvale Aviation Co. Ltd. [*British*] [*ICAO designator*] (FAAC) .... WVL
Woody's Office Power Pack [*Pinecliffe International*] [*Computer science*] (PCM) .... WOPR
Woollen and Worsted Trades Association [*British*] (BI) .... WWTA
Wooly-Monkey Sarcoma Virus [*Medicine*] (PDAA) .... WSV
Word Driver and Gate [*Computer science*] (IAA) .... WDAG
Word Length (IAA) .... WL
Word Processing Society .... WPS
Words per Minute (IAA) .... WMIN
Work Adjustment Program [*Education*] .... WAD
Work Control Status .... WCS
Work Function Difference [*Physics*] (IAA) .... WFD
Worked All America [*Amateur radio*] [*Contacted at least one station in all counties*] (IAA) .... WAA
Worked All Countries [*Contacted at least one station in all countries*] [*Amateur radio*] (IAA) .... WAC
Worked All Europe [*Contacted at least one station in all European countries*] [*Amateur radio*] (IAA) .... WAE
Worked All Goose (IAA) .... WAG
Worked All Italian Provinces [*Amateur radio*] (IAA) .... WAIP
Worked All Italy [*Amateur radio*] (IAA) .... WAI
Worked All Prefixes [*Amateur radio*] (IAA) .... WPX
Worked All Yokosuka [*Amateur radio*] (IAA) .... WAY
Worked All Zones [*Contacted at least one station in all zones*] [*Amateur radio*] (IAA) .... WAZ
Worked Republic of India Award [*Amateur radio*] (IAA) .... WRIA
Worked Three Oceans [*Amateur radio*] (IAA) .... WTO
Workers' Christian Fellowship [*British*] (BI) .... WCF
Workers Solidarity Alliance (EA) .... WSA
Workers' Union of Ireland (BI) .... WUI
Workflow Innovation Toolkit (PCM) .... WIT
Working Ampere Alternating Current (IAA) .... WAAC
Working Current (IAA) .... WC
Working Voltage (IAA) .... WKGV
Working Women (NTCM) .... WW
Workload and Repair Activity Process Simulator (PDAA) .... WRAPS
Workprint [*Cinematography*] (NTCM) .... WP
Workshop Control (IAA) .... WS
Workshop Reporting (IAA) .... WR
Workspace Register Pointer [*Computer science*] (IAA) .... WP
World Administrative Radio Conference [*International Telecommunication Union*] (NTCM) .... WARC
World Administrative Radio Conference for Broadcast Satellite Service [*International Telecommunication Union*] (NTCM) .... WARC-BS
World Air Network Co. Ltd. [*Japan*] [*ICAO designator*] (FAAC) .... WAC
World Aircraft Flight Operation, Inc. [*ICAO designator*] (FAAC) .... PEX
World Airline (Gambia) Ltd. [*ICAO designator*] (FAAC) .... WAG
World Airways, Inc. [*ICAO designator*] (FAAC) .... WOA
World Area Forecast Center [*Aviation*] (FAAC) .... WAFC
World Association for Christian Broadcasting (IAA) .... WACB
World Association for Medical Informatics (IAA) .... WAMI
World Broadcasting System (NTCM) .... WBS
World-Class Manufacturing [*Management technique*] .... WCM

World Conference on Computers in Education............................ WCCE
World Conference on Missionary Radio [*Later, ICB*]   (NTCM).............. WCMR
World Conference on Non-Destructive Testing   (PDAA)...................... WCNDT
World Congress on Metal Finishing   (PDAA).. WCMF
World Dance Alliance .... WDA
World Environment Day .... WED
World Industry Council for the Environment .... WICE
World Organization of Automotive Hobbyists .... WOAH
World Safety and Accident Prevention Congress   (PDAA)............. WOSAPCON
World Satellite Terminal [*Telecommunications*]   (IAA) .... WST
World System Teletext   (NTCM)... WST
World Terminal Synchronous   (IAA) .... WTS
World Trade   (IAA).. WT
World Trade Telegraph   (IAA) .... WTTELE
World Weather Program   (PDAA)... WWP
World Weatherwatch [*Canada*] [*ICAO designator*]   (FAAC)..................... XWW
Worldways Canada Ltd. [*ICAO designator*]   (FAAC)............................. WWC
Worldwide Air Charter Systems [*Canada*] [*ICAO designator*]
   (FAAC).. CSW
Worldwide Airline Services, Inc. [*ICAO designator*]   (FAAC) .... LWD
Worldwide Aviation Services Ltd. [*Venezuela*] [*ICAO designator*]
   (FAAC).. WWA
Worldwide Network of Standard Seismograph Stations   (PDAA)......... WWNSS
Worse Case Difference   (IAA) .... WCD
Worst Cycle Quantity Level   (PDAA)... WCQL
Worst Injection Timing   (PDAA) .... WIT
Worst Pattern   (IAA)... WP
Wouldn't It Be Nice If [*Computer hacker terminology*]   (NHD).............. WIBNI
WRA, Inc. [*ICAO designator*]   (FAAC)... WRR
Wrangler Aviation, Inc. [*ICAO designator*]   (FAAC)............................. WRN
Wrap-Around-Fin   (PDAA)... WAF
Wright Air Lines, Inc. [*ICAO designator*]   (FAAC) .... WRT
Wright Dust Feed Mechanism   (PDAA).. WDFM
Wright International Express, Inc. [*ICAO designator*]   (FAAC)................ DWW
Wrinkle Recovery Angle   (IAA) .... WRA
Write-After-Write [*Computer science*]... WAW
Write Check [*Computer science*]   (IAA) .... WRCHK
Write Circuit for Queuing Messages [*Computer science*]   (IAA).............. WOM
Write Control Character [*Computer science*]   (IAA)................................ WCC
Write Enable [*Computer science*]   (IAA) .... WEN
Write Once, Write Mostly [*Computer science*]   (IAA)........................... WOWM
Write Tape Binary [*Computer science*]   (IAA) .... WTB
Write Tape Decimal   (IAA).. WTD
WSI Corp. [*ICAO designator*]   (FAAC)... XWS
Wuhan Airlines [*China*] [*ICAO designator*]   (FAAC)................................ CWU
Wycombe Air Centre [*British*] [*ICAO designator*]   (FAAC) .... WYC
Wyoming Airlines Ltd. [*ICAO designator*]   (FAAC)................................ WYG
Wyton FTU [*British*] [*ICAO designator*]   (FAAC)..................................... WYT

X-Y-Z

X-Linked Server Combined Immunodeficiency [*"Bubble Boy"* disease*] [Medicine*].. XSCID
X-Ray Background [*Cosmology*] .... XRB
X-Ray Tomographic Microscope .... XTM
Xenon [*Chemical element*]   (IAA) X
Xiamen Airlines [*China*] [*ICAO designator*]   (FAAC)............................ CXA
XP International BV [*Netherlands*] [*ICAO designator*]   (FAAC)................. XPS
Y-Punch   (IAA)... Y
Yacht and Motor Boat Association [*British*]   (BI) .... YMBA
Yana Air Cargo (Kenya) Ltd. [*ICAO designator*]   (FAAC).......................... KYA
Yard Activity Reporting and Decision System   (PDAA)................... YARDS
Yellow Lamp   (IAA)... YL
Yellow Lamp Century Certificate   (IAA) .... YLCC
Yellow Red Green Blue   (IAA).. YRGB
Yemen Arab Republic [*Aircraft nationality and registration mark*]
    (FAAC)... 4W
Yemenia, Yemen Airways [*ICAO designator*]   (FAAC) .... IYE
Yet Another [*Computer hacker terminology*]   (NHD)........................... YA
Yet Another Bloody Acronym [*Computer hacker terminology*]
    (NHD)... YABA
Yet Another Unix Nerd [*Computer hacker terminology*]   (NHD) .... YAUN
Yield Value   (IAA)... YV
Yorkshire European Airways Ltd. [*British*] [*ICAO designator*]
    (FAAC)... JOR
Yorkshire European Airways Ltd. [*British*] [*ICAO designator*]   (FAAC)....... SJT
Young Children: Priority One [*Kiwanis Club*]................................... YCPO
Young Flying Service [*ICAO designator*]   (FAAC)............................... YFS
Young Launderers' Movement [*British*]   (BI) .... YLM
Young Newspapermen's Association [*British*]   (BI) .... YNA
Younger Dryas [*Geoscience*] .... YD
Your Message [*Aviation*]   (FAAC) .... YMSG
Your Message Date [*Aviation*]   (FAAC) .... YMSGD
Youth Association of Synagogues in Great Britain   (BI)....................... YASGB
Youth Campaign for Nuclear Disarmament [*British*]   (BI) .... YCND
Youth Camping Association [*British*]   (BI) .... YCA
Yttrium Alumnium Iron Garnet [*LASER technology*]   (IAA)................... YAIG
Yukon Standard Time   (IAA).. YST
Yunnan Airlines [*China*] [*ICAO designator*]   (FAAC)......................... CYH
Yute Air Alaska, Inc. [*ICAO designator*]   (FAAC)............................. UYA
Yvlc Airlines [*Nigeria*] [*ICAO designator*]   (FAAC)........................... VYC
Zaire [*Aircraft nationality and registration mark*]   (FAAC) 9Q
Zaire Aero Service [*ICAO designator*]   (FAAC)................................ ZAI
Zaire Aero Service [*ICAO designator*]   (FAAC)................................ ZAS
Zairean Airlines [*Zaire*] [*ICAO designator*]   (FAAC)......................... ZAR
Zambia [*Aircraft nationality and registration mark*]   (FAAC).................. 9J
Zambia Airways [*ICAO designator*]   (FAAC).................................. ZAC
Zantop International Airlines, Inc. [*ICAO designator*]   (FAAC).................. ZAN
Zeatin-O-Glucoside [*Biochemistry*].. ZOG
Zephyr Aviation Services, Inc. [*ICAO designator*]   (FAAC)..................... RZR
Zero Base Budgeting [*Environmental Protection Agency*]   (ERG).............. ZBB
Zero-Based   (IAA)... ZB
Zero Count Table   (IAA) .... ZCT
Zero Crossing Constant False Alarm Rate   (IAA)............................ ZCCFAR
Zero-Emissions Bus .... ZEB
Zero-Emissions Truck.. ZET
Zero Headspace Extractor [*Environmental Protection Agency*]
    (ERG)... ZHE
Zero Intersymbol Interference - Zero Derivative   (PDAA)...................... ZII-ZD
Zero-Magnetostrictive Composition   (PDAA) .... ZMC
Zero Memory Non-Linear   (IAA) .... ZNL
Zero Order Interpolar   (IAA) .... ZOI
Zero-Phonon Hole [*Spectroscopy*] .... ZPH
Zero Print Control   (IAA)... ZPC
Zero Skip Frequency   (IAA) .... ZSF
Zero State   (IAA)... ZS
Zero Suppress   (IAA)... ZSUP
Zeros Extended   (IAA).. ZE
Zeus Malfunction Array RADAR [*Missile defense*]   (IAA) .... ZMAR
Zeus Multiple Array RADAR [*Missile defense*]   (IAA) .... ZMAR
Zhejiang Airlines [*China*] [*ICAO designator*]   (FAAC)........................ CJG
Zhongyuan Aviation Co. [*China*] [*ICAO designator*]   (FAAC)................... CYN
Zimbabwe [*Aircraft nationality and registration mark*]   (FAAC) .... Z
Zimex Aviation Ltd. [*Switzerland*] [*ICAO designator*]   (FAAC) .... IMX

Zinc Alloy Die Casters' Association [*British*]   (BI) .... ZADCA
Zinc Aluminium Coater [*Metallurgy*] .... ZAC
Zinc, Aluminium, Magnesium   (PDAA) .... ZAM
Zinc Oxide Non-Linear Resistance   (IAA).................................... ZNR
Zinc Pigment Development Association [*British*]   (BI) .... ZPDA
Zip Fastener Manufacturers Association [*British*]   (BI) .... ZFMA
Zirconium Boride Silicon Carbide   (PDAA).................................... ZRBSC
Zodiac Air [*Bulgaria*] [*ICAO designator*]   (FAAC) .... AZV
Zone   (IAA).. ZO
Zone Bit Recording [*Computer science*]....................................... ZBR
Zone Code   (IAA)... Z
Zone Constant Angular Velocity [*Computer science*].......................... ZCAV
Zone Controlled Deposition   (IAA)... ZCD
Zone of Convergence [*Aviation*]   (DA)...................................... ZOC
Zone of Correct Reading   (IAA).. ZCR
Zone Field Selection [*Physics*]   (IAA)....................................... ZFS
Zone of Incorporation [*Environmental Protection Agency*]   (ERG) .... ZOI
Zone Position Indicator   (IAA) .... ZPI
Zone Project Officer .... ZPO
Zone Punch [*Computer science*]   (IAA)..................................... ZP
[*Sprinkler*] Zone Valve [*NFPA pre-fire planning symbol*]   (NFPA)............... ZV
Zoster Immune Globulin [*Immunology*]   (MAH) .... Z/G
Zuliana de Aviacion [*Venezuela*] [*ICAO designator*]   (FAAC)................... ULA

247